# The
# MACMILLAN
# DICTIONARY
## of
# CONTEMPORARY
# PHRASE & FABLE

# The
# MACMILLAN DICTIONARY
## of
# CONTEMPORARY PHRASE & FABLE

MACMILLAN

First published 2002 by Macmillan
an imprint of Pan Macmillan Ltd
Pan Macmillan, 20 New Wharf Road, London N1 9RR
Basingstoke and Oxford
Associated companies throughout the world
www.panmacmillan.com

ISBN 0 333 90636 5  Hardback
ISBN 0 333 90637 3  Paperback

9 8 7 6 5 4 3 2 1

A CIP catalogue record for this book is available from
the British Library.

Typeset by Market House Books Limited
Printed and bound in Great Britain by Mackays of Chatham plc,
Chatham, Kent

# Contents

*The Macmillan Dictionary of Contemporary Phrase & Fable* is derived in part from *Brewer's 20th-Century Phrase & Fable* (published by Cassell, 1991; revised 1993 and 1996), which was also compiled by Market House Books Ltd. For this new Macmillan version the organization of the book has been completely altered, the older entries have been substantially revised, and much entirely new material has been added.

Entries are arranged in strict alphabetical order with the exception of some entries that take the form of a sentence or longer phrase. To make the book more user-friendly, these are alphabetized by key word (usually the first main noun or verb). For instance, the catchphrase **as the actress said to the bishop** will be found at the dummy headword **actress** and the quotation **We shall never surrender** at **surrender**.

An original feature of this edition is the Name Index that follows the Dictionary. In this index the names of people (alive and dead) who receive prominent mention in the book are listed alphabetically and referred to the entries in which they appear.

Cross references in the text are indicated by a change of typeface to a sans serif face.

# Editors

(Market House Books Ltd.)

Jonathan Law
Alan Isaacs

# Contributors

Anna Berry
Callum Brines
John Daintith
Rosalind Fergusson
Robert Hine
Amanda Isaacs
Heather Jargus
Elizabeth Kirkpatrick

Elizabeth Martin
David Pickering
Joshua Raymond
Kate Reddick
Mark Salad
Kathy Seed
Anne Stibbs
John Wright

# Preface

*by*

## Philip Howard

They said that this was the last generation of printed reference books. All the information anybody needed was available on the Internet, or soon would be. In cyberspace there'd be no algebra, no learning dates and names, but only playing on golden keyboards, and reading Henry James (on screen). A researcher would no longer have to trawl through dusty libraries and plod through a labyrinth of old files.

Well, they were wrong, as usual, weren't they? The Internet is indeed a wonderful invention, certainly one of the master/mistress influences of the new century. Much of the information in the world is already on it. It is a huge democratic advance, putting the knowledge of the world at the fingertips of Everyman and Everywoman. But it has also demonstrated that, even if you put a million monkeys in a stadium with a million keyboards, they will never write the works of Shakespeare.

The sheer volume of the Internet is paradoxically its Catch-22. As the journalist said: "How do I know what I think until I read what I have written?" So the trawler through the Internet says: "How do I know what I want until I call it up by accident, and the system crashes?" And how does he know that it is accurate? There is no quality control on the Internet, as there is with an academic publisher. If a book is in a university library, it has been considered worth buying by librarians and academics. It may even contain true and interesting facts, phrases, and fables. It should not contain many direct lies. But if you call up Libya on the Internet, you will find a number of impressive official websites. They are full of beautifully presented statistics, tables, and historical summaries. The trouble is that they are built on a foundation of painted smoke. For the websites are produced by Colonel Gadaffi's spin laboratory. So they are indeed strong on fable.

I have never yet found anything on the Internet that I could not have found faster and more reliably in a book. And I am perfectly competent on the Internet, though not an infotech anorak. My requirements as a journalist are peculiar. And I have access to the best libraries. But the book is still a marvellous high-tech piece of equipment. It is portable. It is carefully edited, at least when it comes from respectable academic publishers.

Many books can be put in your pocket or read in the bath. If you know the right book, it will give you the right answers.

As a daily journalist, I need the right answers to a bewildering and unpredictable variety of questions fast. Any serious reader or writer needs within easy reach the biggest dictionary that he or she can afford. And the biggest atlas. And access to the serious encyclopedias. A journalist needs a dictionary of quotations, so that he can verify his references, before swanking: "As every schoolchild knows...". Because they are my particular interest, I have on my desk a dictionary of slang (Partridge, of course) and a classical dictionary. I have a style guide and a dictionary of etymology.

The *Macmillan Dictionary of Contemporary Phrase and Fable* will have a parking slot on my not particularly capacious desk. It answers (reliably and with citations) the questions that I did not know existed until the editor shouts "Change leaders!"

For English is the richest mine of phrase and fable in the world, for several reasons. It is becoming the world language. It already is the world language in such fields as medicine, computers, aeronautics, and navigation. It is the second language of half the world. English newspapers and other media are the nosiest and noisiest in the world. America is a melting-pot of every culture under the sun, and the United Kingdom is an ancient stewpot. Because of our extraordinary history, the sun never does set on the rich culture and languages that make up English phrase and fable. An Englishman was mocking Scottish Gaelic for being a jejune and dying tongue. 'What's the Gaelic for spaghetti?' The man from Lewis replied: 'What's the English for spaghetti?' The Angles sailed west as the first illegal immigrants. The obtuse Angles turned left and became Englishmen. But the acute Angles sailed on to Edinburgh and became the Lowland Scots. One of them was called Macmillan.

Even the most conscientious journalist with the most capacious memory cannot carry in his/her head all the phrases, facts, and fables that have left their footprints in the sand of the last century. He can bellow down the news room: 'Who wrote Catch-22?' Or he can give up, and write his way around the problem. In the hurly-burly of daily journalism, under the lash, up to the wire, towards deadline, that is what journalists call research. And now we have another weapon in our armoury in our daily struggle to find facts and phrases in a hurry; to appear knowledgeable and widely read; to disguise our ignorance. For our general knowledge is wide but shallow. We have a good working knowledge of news, and phrase, and fable. But we cannot carry it all in our busy little heads.

What song the Syrens sang, or what name Achilles assumed when he hid himself among women, though puzzling questions, are not beyond all conjecture. And you can find those conjectures in older reference books. But who wore **siren suits** and what were the **acid bath murders** are the contemporary puzzling questions. Such modern general knowledge is found aggregated only in this reference book. It is particularly strong on gruesome murders, from the **Boston Strangler** to the **Shipman mur-**

**ders**. It (rightly) gives most space to the latest, and therefore least recorded, facts and fables. Suppose that you wish/need to refresh your memory about James Bond. Here you will find entries and citations under **Bond**, **Goldfinger**, **Oddjob**, **Q.**, and **Martini, shaken, not stirred**. So the hack in a hurry can put up a convincing show of being an expert on the thud and blunder of Bondage.

Catchphrases, slang, interesting acronyms, film stars, heroes, villains, historical events, and other trivial pursuits are explained and cited. **George Smiley** meets **Miss Marple** and **the Falcon**, and they share a quip with Groucho and the **Marx Brothers**. Why is £2,000 known in the City as an **Archer**? How many **fractals** make **4711**? Name the **Teletubbies** and identify them by their colours. If you had a **close encounter** with the **Roswell incident**, would you be (a) pleased; (b) alarmed; (c) incredulous? Would you (1) wear; (2) eat; (3) dance a **zouk**?

I know where I would start to look for the answers to most of these puzzling questions. Most (all?) of them can be found on the World Wide Web. But if seven maids with seven laptops surfed the Internet for half a year, do you suppose, the Walrus said, that they could get it clear? I doubt it, said the Carpenter, and shed a bitter tear.

So move over *Oxford English Dictionary*. I shall make room on my desktop for *The Macmillan Dictionary of Contemporary Phrase and Fable*. It answers the puzzling questions that other reference books cannot reach.

This is a sufficient reason for having the book on my desk. But, of course, the necessary reason for having it at bedside or in bathroom is that it is the best browsers' pasture published.

P.H., 2002

**A**

• **A ►** A former category of film classification used by the British Board of Film Censors. When classification was introduced in the UK in 1913 A (standing for 'adult') denoted that children under the age of 16 should only be admitted if accompanied by an adult. In 1970 a new system was introduced in which A (now standing for 'advisory') meant that the film contained scenes that parents might not wish their children to see: unaccompanied children could, however, now be admitted to A films. The category was abolished in 1982.

• **AA ►** 1. A former category of film classification indicating that in the opinion of the British Board of Film Censors a film was not suitable for children under 14 years of age (whether accompanied or not). The classification was introduced in 1970 and dropped in 1982. 2. *See*: Alcoholics Anonymous.

• **Abadan Crisis ►** A political dispute between the UK and Iran following the nationalization of the Iranian oil industry in 1951. This threatened the interests of the Anglo-Iranian Oil Company (later British Petroleum), which operated the large refinery at Abadan. The UK retaliated with a blockade of Iran, thereby damaging the Iranian economy. The crisis was resolved by the formation in 1954 of an international consortium of oil companies (including Anglo-Iranian) to run the Iranian oilfields.

• **Abbey Theatre ►** A Dublin theatre, opened in 1904, renowned for staging works by contemporary Irish playwrights, including Yeats, Synge, O'Casey, and George Russell (known as AE). The Abbey Theatre was built at the instigation of Annie Horniman (1860–1937), a wealthy English patron, to provide a home for the Irish National Dramatic Society of Yeats and Lady Gregory. In 1924 it became the first state-subsidized theatre in the English-speaking world. A fire destroyed the original building in 1951 but a new playhouse was subsequently built, opening in 1966.

• **Abdication Crisis ►** The constitutional dispute between the uncrowned King Edward VIII and the British Establishment; it was caused by the king's intention to marry the twice-divorced American Mrs Wallis Simpson. Edward had been an intimate friend of Mrs Simpson for some years before acceding to the throne on 20 January 1936. In the ensuing months he continued to escort Mrs Simpson while she awaited her divorce from her second husband, Ernest Simpson. This was granted in October, and the couple hoped the final hurdle to their marriage had been cleared.

However, they reckoned without the Establishment. Prime Minister Baldwin, prodded and supported by various prominent figures alarmed by the constitutional implications, informed the king that marriage to Mrs Simpson was unacceptable while he remained on the throne. Reaction among the British public was mixed. The king had been a popular figure noted for his concern for the unemployed during the 1930s. But opposition to divorce was still widespread, a moral position staunchly upheld by the Church of England, of which Edward was the titular head.

With no hint of compromise from his prime minister, the king relinquished the throne on 11 December, to be succeeded by his brother, George VI. In a radio broadcast to the Commonwealth on the night of his abdication, the ex-king spoke movingly of his dilemma: '...I have found it impossible to carry the heavy burden of responsibility and to discharge my duties as king as I would wish to do without the help and support of the woman I love.'

Edward was created Duke of Windsor and given the title Royal Highness, although this was refused his wife after their marriage on 3 June 1937 in Paris. The Abdication, a mountain in Britain's moral landscape, retains its fascination for successive generations; at its heart it contains the dilemma of an individual torn between love and the highest office in the land.

Well, Mr Baldwin! *This* is a pretty kettle of fish!
– QUEEN MARY, speaking to the prime minister.

• **Aberfan disaster ►** A tragedy that befell the mining village of Aberfan in south Wales, near Merthyr Tydfil, on 21 October 1966. A vast tip of colliery waste slid downhill engulfing part of the village, including the school. 116 of the 144 lives lost were children. The disaster prompted an urgent review of the siting and maintenance of similar tips.

• **Abgrenzung** ▸ (German, demarcation) The former policy of separation of the German Democratic Republic and the Federal Republic of Germany following the creation of two German states after World War II. Deeply resented by many Germans in both countries, it was finally and comprehensively dropped as official policy in 1990, when the two states reunited.

• **able and willing to pull his weight** ▸ President Theodore Roosevelt's characterization of the ideal American in a widely reported speech of 1902:

> The first requisite of a good citizen in this Republic of ours is that he shall be able and willing to pull his weight.

• **ableism** ▸ Discrimination on the grounds of able-bodiedness. Employers are accused of ableism when they discriminate in favour of hiring an able-bodied person for a job rather than a person with a physical or mental handicap who could have done the job equally well. The word is formed on the same basis as racism and sexism.

• **ABM** ▸ Anti-ballistic missile. A weapon designed to shoot down an incoming enemy missile. ABMs were developed and deployed by America and the Soviet Union in the 1960s and early 1970s, ostensibly as a defensive precaution. However, the weapons soon came to be seen as a serious threat to world peace, because their existence undermined the dreadful logic of mutually assured destruction (*see*: MAD). A country with a large arsenal of ABMs might become more likely to launch a nuclear first strike, because it believed that it could survive the inevitable retaliation. The menace from ABMs was effectively neutralized by the SALT I accord (*see*: SALT) in 1972. However, in 2001 America under George W. Bush announced that it would no longer be held by this treaty.

• **A-bomb** ▸ *See*: atom bomb; nuclear weapon.

• **Abominable Snowman** ▸ A name, popularized by Eric Shipton's Everest Expedition of 1951, for the yeti, a large bearlike animal supposed by some to inhabit the high Himalayas. Although there have been no authenticated sightings, Sir Edmund Hillary found the alleged footprints of a yeti in 1960 and explained its elusiveness thus: 'There is precious little in civilization to appeal to a yeti.' *See also*: Bigfoot.

• **above-the-line** ▸ Advertising expenditure on which a commission is payable to an advertising agency. This includes all mass-media advertising. **Below-the-line** advertising, on which no commission is payable, includes direct mail, free samples, and point-of-sale material. The distinction is arbitrary but reflects the way in which company profit and loss accounts are prepared, with a horizontal line separating entries that show how the profit or loss is calculated (above the line) from those that show how it has been used or distributed (below the line).

• **abstract expressionism** ▸ *See*: action painting.

• **Absurd, Theatre of the** ▸ *See*: Theatre of the Absurd.

• **abuse** ▸ A well-established word that took on a new lease of life in the later 20th century. It has now acquired a sinister relevance in such combinations as **alcohol abuse**, **drug abuse**, **solvent abuse** (*see*: glue sniffing), sexual abuse, and child abuse. Until quite recently, to describe someone as abusive meant that they were rude; it is now more likely to imply that they are violent and sexually perverted.

The use of the term **self-abuse** to mean masturbation is now regarded as somewhat quaint. The US psychiatrist Thomas Szasz has described masturbation as 'the primary sexual activity of mankind...', concluding that 'in the nineteenth century it was a disease; in the twentieth it's a cure.'

• **Abwehr** ▸ The German military intelligence service. It was led from 1935 by Admiral Wilhelm Canaris, who saw its authority increasingly curtailed before and during World War II. Hitler favoured the rival intelligence organizations, the SD (*Sicherheits-dienst*) and the SS (*Schutzstaffel*). As a consequence, the Abwehr became a focus of opposition to Hitler. Several of its leaders, including Canaris, were implicated in the 1944 plot to overthrow the Führer, (*see*: Stauffenberg Plot) and Hitler ordered that it be merged with the SD in February 1944.

• **ACAB** ▸ All coppers are bastards. An abbreviation much used in the 1960s and 1970s in graffiti and in slogans on clothing, as well as in chants at football matches.

• **Acapulco Gold** ▸ A type of marijuana with golden leaves grown in the region around Acapulco, Mexico, and much prized for its potency. It was imported into America, particularly California, from the late 1960s.

• **ACAS** ▸ Advisory Conciliation and Arbitration Service. In the UK, a government quango set up in the 1970s to attempt to resolve industrial disputes before major damage could be done to the economic interests of the country.

• **AC/DC** ▸ Bisexual. The expression originated in America by analogy with electrical devices adaptable for either alternating or direct current. It became popular in the UK during the 1960s and 1970s. The sexual imagery of electricity is further elaborated in the tradition of 'male' and 'female' connectors in wiring etc.

• **ace** ▶ The number one on playing cards or dice, from *as*, the Latin unit of weight. In World War I the French word, *as*, was applied to an airman who had brought down ten enemy aeroplanes; it was imported in its English equivalent, ace, and later extended to any especially expert flier, golfer, etc. Anything excellent or outstanding can now be referred to as 'ace'.

> Liverpool...the city of the Beatles, *Brookside* and an ace football team is poised to storm back into fashion. – *The Independent*, 16 March 1991.

• **ace in the hole** ▶ US expression from the card game stud poker, meaning that an ace is held in the unexposed cards (the hole). More generally, the phrase is used to mean a hidden advantage or strength that is held in reserve until needed, as in 'his friendship with the chairman is his ace in the hole'. It became popular in the 1920s. A similar expression is 'ace up one's sleeve'.

• **acid** ▶ A slang name for LSD (lysergic acid diethylamide).

• **acid bath murders** ▶ The gruesome series of murders committed by John George Haigh in the 1940s. Haigh was arrested in 1949 for the murder of an elderly widow, Mrs Durand-Deacon, whom he had killed and whose body he dissolved in a bath of sulphuric acid. Haigh confessed to the crime, and to the murder of seven other people, two of which were fictitious. He claimed to have drained the blood from his victims prior to dissolving them, and to have drunk a cupful of blood from each. His plea of insanity was dismissed and he was hanged. The bath he used is preserved in Scotland Yard's Black Museum.

• **acid head** ▶ A person who frequently takes, and whose mental faculties have been affected by, LSD.

• **acid house** or **house** ▶ A style of synthesized dance music with a repetitive hypnotic beat, associated with the taking of hallucinogenic drugs, especially Ecstasy. The name 'house' came from the Warehouse Club in Chicago, where the style originated. As its popularity spread in the UK during the late 1980s, thousands of young people (many wearing 'A-c-e-e-e-d' T-shirts) congregated in deserted warehouses and club venues for all-night acid-house parties. These were frequently raided by the police in search of drugs, although party organizers always denied any drug connection. *See also*: orbital; rave; warehouse party.

• **acid rain** ▶ Originally a term used to describe the heavily polluted rainfall in the Manchester area in the 19th century. Then, as now, it refers to rain containing sulphuric and nitric acids formed from sulphur dioxide and nitrogen oxides present in the atmosphere as a result of burning fossil fuels on an industrial scale. The combustion of petrol and oil in vehicles without catalytic exhaust systems also contributes these acid-forming oxides to the environment. It is believed that acid rain can destroy crops, trees, and fish as well as causing damage to buildings. In 1985, 17 countries agreed to reduce their emissions of sulphur dioxide by 30% by 1993. In fact, the 17 signatories to the protocol exceeded this reduction, while non-signatories reduced their sulphur emissions by less than 10%.

• **acid rock** ▶ A type of rock music popular in the late 1960s involving weird electronic effects and psychedelic lightshows to suggest the effects of LSD ('acid') or other hallucinatory drugs.

• **ack-ack** ▶ Slang from World Wars I and II meaning anti-aircraft guns (from signalling code for AA).

• **ack emma** ▶ *See*: pip emma.

• **Acol system** ▶ Widely used bidding and play conventions in the game of bridge, devised in the 1930s by the London bridge theorist Jack Marx (1904–87) and his partner in international competitions, the Conservative politician Iain Macleod (1913–70). They were then members of the Acol Bridge Club in Acol Road, West Hampstead in London, which gave the system its name.

• **ACORN** ▶ A Classification of Residential Neighbourhoods, a directory of 39 different neighbourhoods in the UK, used by companies selling goods or services on the assumption that the inhabitants of particular neighbourhoods are likely to have similar interests and disposable incomes. It is much used by door-to-door and telephone salespeople offering swimming pools, double glazing, insurance, finance, etc. It also provides information on which areas to omit in a sales drive.

• **acqua alta** ▶ (Italian, high water) Italian term used of the water that periodically floods central Venice. The city was badly damaged in such floods in November 1966. In the late 1960s, in an attempt to prevent further inundations (and to halt the city's rapid deterioration from air pollution), UNESCO launched a programme of scientific and technical research. A series of flood barriers is also planned. The Venice in Peril campaign aims to promote the city's protection.

• **action painting**▸ A term coined by the US art critic Harold Rosenberg in 1952 to describe certain works produced by the New York **abstract expressionists**, the best known of whom were Jackson Pollock and Willem de Kooning. The style is characterized by dynamic spontaneous gestures, in which paint is spilt, spattered, and dripped onto canvas laid on the floor. The finished work is intended to reflect a creative expressive interplay between the artist and his materials, free from the constraints of preconceived form or subject matter.

> On the floor I am more at ease, I feel nearer, more a part of the painting, since this way I can walk around it, work from the four sides and literally be 'in' the painting. – JACKSON POLLOCK, in 1947, quoted in Tomassoni's *Pollock* (1968).

> Abstract Expressionism was invented by New York drunks. – JONI MITCHELL, interview on BBC television, 1985.

• **action replay**▸ The repetition of part of a TV broadcast, usually in slow motion, to analyse a key moment in a sports event such as a goal, winning putt, etc.

• **Actors' Studio** ▸ The New York-based workshop for professional actors founded in 1947 by Elia Kazan, Robert Lewis, and Cheryl Crawford. Under the artistic direction of Lee Strasberg (from 1948), the Studio became known as the US home of the acting technique known as the Method and nurtured many leading theatre and film stars, including Marlon Brando. The Studio is primarily a forum for exploration and experimentation, away from the pressures of commercial production. The costs are met by voluntary subscription, and membership is by invitation following audition.

• **actress**▸
 **as the actress said to the bishop** An expression added to what seems a perfectly straightforward innocent remark to create a sexual double entendre. Typical examples might include 'I never knew I had it in me' or 'I'd bend over backwards to please you'. The phrase was popular in the RAF in the 1940s, although its origin is said to be Edwardian. An alternative form of this expression is **as the art mistress said to the gardener**, which was popularized by the British actress Beryl Reid when playing the part of Monica in the BBC radio series *Educating Archie* (broadcast in the 1950s).

• **acupuncture** ▸ An ancient Chinese system of healing and pain relief in which thin needles are inserted and rotated into precisely defined points of the body. Dating back to at least 2500 BC, the system is based on achieving a balance between the opposing life forces *yin* and *yang*. In modern times it has been used widely in alternative medicine, both to treat a variety of conditions and as an anaesthetic procedure. The system appears to be effective in some cases and is even practised by some qualified doctors, although there is no accepted explanation for the way in which it works. One modern theory is that the needles stimulate subcutaneous nerves in some way that makes them release painkilling endorphins.

• **AD** ▸ Drug addict. An abbreviation used mostly in America by both drug addicts and the police. It is formed by taking the first two letters of addict, or by reversing the initial letters of the two words, thereby distinguishing it from DA for District Attorney.

• **Ada** ▸ A computer-programming language developed for the US Department of Defense. It was named after Augusta Ada Lovelace (1815–51), daughter of Lord Byron, wife of the Earl of Lovelace, and co-worker of Charles Babbage (1792–1871), the British mathematician. Babbage is given credit for the invention of computers as he built a calculating machine regarded as the forerunner of the electronic computer. The machine is preserved, unfinished, in the Science Museum in London.

• **adam** ▸ *See*: eve.

• **ADAPTS** ▸ Air Deliverable Antipollution Transfer System. A system of dealing with oil pollution employed by the US coastguard. The system relies upon entrapping the oil with inflatable nylon bags and then pumping it off the water.

• **admass** ▸ A word coined by J. B. Priestley in *Journey Down a Rainbow* (1955) to describe the mid-20th-century proliferation of commercial advertising and high-pressure salesmanship, especially in America. The word has now come to mean the vast mass of the general public to whom advertisers address their publicity.

• **admiral** ▸
 **The Admiral of the Atlantic salutes the Admiral of the Pacific** A telegram from the German emperor Wilhelm II to Tsar Nicholas II in 1905. Sent during a naval exercise, it reflected Germany's determination to assert itself as a world power, a desire that contributed to the outbreak of World War I.

• **Admiral's Cup** ▸ The trophy presented by the Admiral of the Royal Ocean Racing Club to the winners of the biennial series of races for yachts in the 29–60 foot class. The three-boat teams compete in five races along the English Channel, including the famous Fastnet Race. The competition was inaugurated in 1957.

• **advertorial** ▶ An article in a newspaper or magazine that appears to be editorial matter but is actually intended to promote a particular product or service. *See also*: plugumentary.

• **AE** ▶ The pseudonym of the Irish poet and playwright George William Russell (1867–1935). It was derived as a contraction of 'aeon', a word to which Russell ascribed great mystical significance. AE's considerable and varied output includes several volumes of poetry and the play *Deirdre* (1902). He also helped found Dublin's Abbey Theatre.

• **A-effect** ▶ (German, *V-Effekt, Verfremdungseffekt*) Alienation effect. The term coined by the playwright Bertolt Brecht (1898–1956) for his technique of deliberately limiting the degree to which both actors and audience identify with the drama. Brecht's intention was to jolt the sensibilities of all participants in order to sharpen their objectivity and political awareness. Devices used to achieve this A-effect included third person or past-tense narrative, spoken stage directions, unusual or subversive stage design, as well as the use of songs, placards, masks, etc.

• **aerial ping-pong** ▶ A facetious name for Australian Rules Football, in which much of the game is played in the air because of the high jumps and kicks involved in the style of play.

• **aerobics** ▶ (Greek, *aer* air; *bios* life) Programmes of exercise designed to improve the body's uptake of oxygen and thus benefit general health. Such exercises became popular in America in the 1980s and soon won converts throughout the Western world; proponents of the system included the film actress Jane Fonda.

• **aerosol** ▶ A type of pressurized spray can much used in perfumery, polishes, paints, etc. The use of chlorofluorocarbons (*see*: CFC) as propellants in aerosols caused concern when it was alleged that the proliferation of such substances in the atmosphere was damaging the ozone layer. In the 1980s several international agreements were signed limiting such emissions and new nonaerosols were developed.

• **affinity card** ▶ In the UK, a credit card that automatically donates a small percentage of each transaction to a specified charity or similar organization (such as a university). In America, a credit card issued through a non-profit-making organization (such as a union, club, etc.) that entitles the holder to various benefits.

• **affirmative action** ▶ *See*: quota system.

• **Affluent Society** ▶ A phrase, popular from the later 1950s, reflecting the overall growth in material prosperity of Western societies at this time. It referred primarily to the increasingly widespread ownership of cars, television sets, washing machines, refrigerators, etc., in a society further cushioned by its 'free' social services. J. K. Galbraith's *The Affluent Society* (*see*: Galbraithian) was published in 1958.

• **affluenza** ▶ A late 20th-century coinage for the condition of those who have so much money and so many possessions that their psychological well-being suffers. In the UK the term has been applied to the deleterious effects of winning large sums on the National Lottery. It is a combination of 'affluence' and 'influenza'.

• **Afghanistanism** ▶ Journalists' slang for a sudden and usually shortlived interest in events in remote parts of the world. The term was first used in the 1950s but acquired new relevance when Soviet troops invaded Afghanistan in 1980 and when US and British forces attacked the same country in 2001 (*see*: war on terrorism).

• **African National Congress** ▶ *See*: ANC.

• **Afrikaans** ▶ A language of South Africa that has evolved from the Dutch originally spoken by 17th-century settlers and their descendants, the Afrikaaners. It had become distinct as a spoken language by 1800, and in 1925 was made an official South African language (with English).

• **Afrika Korps** ▶ The combined force of two armoured divisions and one infantry division that was led by Erwin Rommel (*see*: Desert Fox) as part of the German offensive in North Africa during World War II. Formed in Feburary 1941, the Korps enjoyed a string of military successes until halted and ultimately repulsed at Alamein. The Korps finally surrendered in May 1943, although Rommel had been ordered home by Hitler in March.

• **Afro** ▶ A hairstyle consisting of a large almost spherical mass of tight curls; it became popular with Black people in the late 1960s, and early 1970s, when it was often associated with support for the Black Power movement.

• **After you, Claude – No, after you, Cecil** ▶ The catchphrase of the broker's men Cecil and Claude in the BBC radio comedy ITMA.

• **Agadir Crisis** ▶ The dispute between France and Germany triggered by the despatch of the German warship *Panther* to the Moroccan port of Agadir in July 1911. Germany held that this was a necessary response to the arrival of French troops in Morocco. The affair raised tensions throughout Europe but was settled by an agreement signed between France and Germany on 4 November. However, hostility between the two nations remained, while the crisis served to strengthen Franco-British relations. *See also*: Algeciras Conference.

• **Aga lout** ► An arrogant and prosperous town-bred person who has joined a rural community; especially one who is a vociferous Nimby. The phrase, coined by analogy with lager lout, refers to the Aga, one of several types of wood, coal, or oil-burning all-purpose stoves, much favoured by such people for their rustic image.

> ...a Liberal Democrat councillor in West Dorset blames incoming 'townies' for the gentrification of villages [and]...will be casting a baleful eye over the wrought-iron handiwork and ruthlessly trimmed verges of rural England's new 'Aga louts'. – *The Independent*, 1 June 1993.

• **Aga saga** ► A style of novel dealing with middle-class family life in rural England, where the warm heart of domesticity is symbolized by the ever-burning kitchen stove, or Aga. The term was coined in the 1990s to describe the works of Joanna Trollope, author of *A Village Affair* (1989), *The Rector's Wife*, (1991) and *The Best of Friends* (1995). In these and other books Trollope examines the stresses placed on families in tight-knit communities when faced with personal and professional crises, especially marital infidelity. The term quickly became a perjorative label for similar novels by less talented writers hoping to mine this new seam in popular fiction.

• **ageism** ► Discrimination on the grounds of age, usually against the older members of the community. Coined by Dr Robert Butler, director of the US Institute of Aging, by analogy to racism, the term is most commonly applied in the field of employment.

• **Agent Orange** ► A defoliant used in jungle war, especially by US forces in the Vietnam War, during which it gained its name as its containers had orange rings painted round them. It is highly toxic to humans. Chemically it consists of 2,4,5-trichlorophenoxyethanoic acid. Less toxic versions were **Agent Blue, Agent Purple,** and **Agent White**.

• **aggiornamento** ► (Italian, bringing up to date) The liberalization of the Roman Catholic Church in the 1960s. It was the main feature of the Second Vatican Council of 1962–65 and the result of pressure by Pope John XXIII and Pope Paul VI to reform the Church in line with developments in the modern world. It included reform of the liturgy and promotion of the ecumenical movement.

• **aggro** ► Aggressive trouble-making. In the 1960s and 1970s aggro was associated with thuggish behaviour, football hooliganism, etc., but in later usage it was employed in the less threatening sense of mild irritation, as in 'I don't need this kind of aggro'. *See also*: bovver.

• **agitpop** ► The use of pop music to put across a political message. The British singer Billy Bragg, for example, has used his music to espouse many left-wing causes. The word derives from agitprop.

• **agitprop** ► (Russian *agitatsiya propaganda*, agitation propaganda) A term coined by the Marxist thinker Georgy Plekhanov, elaborated by his disciple Lenin in *What Is To Be Done* (1902), and later applied to the massive campaign of political propaganda undertaken by Russia's new rulers in the wake of the 1917 Bolshevik Revolution. 'Agitation' implied the use of political slogans and half-truths to exploit mass grievances and mould public opinion, while 'propaganda' meant the use of rational, scientific, and historical arguments to enlighten the educated and indoctrinate Communist Party members. In 1920 the Department of Agitation and Propaganda was established by the Central Committee of the CPSU; in its various forms it controlled internal and external Communist party propaganda in the former Soviet Union.

The term is also used more loosely to refer to any dramatic, literary, or artistic work, intended to promote Communist or leftist ideology.

• **agony aunt** ► A woman who conducts an advice column in a newspaper or magazine, or its equivalent on the broadcast media, answering correspondents who seek help with their problems. Most of the letters are from girls and women concerned with family relationships, marital problems, sex, and boyfriends. The term **agony uncle** is now sometimes used for a male columnist who writes a similar column for men.

• **agony column** ► Originally, a column in a newspaper containing advertisements for missing relatives and friends (*see*: come home all is forgiven). Now commonly applied to the columns in which an agony aunt offers advice.

• **agronomics** ► The branch of economics that is concerned with agriculture and the distribution and management of agricultural land. The related discipline of **agronomy** is concerned with crop production in relation to soil management and the cultivation of land. The commercial aspects of farming are sometimes summarized as **agribusiness**.

• **AGS** ▸ Abort Guidance System. A fail-safe mechanism that comes into operation when the primary guidance system of a spacecraft fails.

• **AI** ▸ **1.** Artificial insemination. This involves semen from a male being injected into a female to cause pregnancy. The technique was developed by Soviet livestock breeders in the early 20th century and is now widely used in the agricultural industry, especially for breeding cattle, as it enables rapid improvements in the genetic quality of a herd and better control of sexually transmitted disease. With the development of research to solve the problems of human infertility, the practice of AI was extended to humans (*see*: AIH; DI; IVF; sperm bank; surrogate motherhood). **2.** *See*: artificial intelligence. **3.** *See*: Amnesty International.

• **AID** ▸ *See*: DI.

• **Aids** ▸ Acquired immune deficiency syndrome, a condition resulting from infection by the human immunodeficiency virus (HIV), first identified in 1983. The virus creates a deficiency of the white blood cells that combat infection and so renders the body vulnerable to a wide range of infections and other disorders, such as pneumonia and cancer, which are then frequently fatal. The virus is transmitted by blood, semen, or vaginal fluids. In the Western world Aids occurs most frequently in homosexual or bisexual men and intravenous drug-users who share needles; however, the virus can be transmitted by normal heterosexual intercourse, in transfusions of contaminated blood, and to the unborn babies of infected mothers. The advent of Aids has resulted in the advocacy of condoms to promote safer sex and campaigns to reduce promiscuity and drug abuse. Perhaps owing in part to such measures, the virus has not spread through the heterosexual population of Western countries to the extent predicted by many early forecasts. However, in large parts of sub-Saharan Africa, where heterosexual intercourse is the main form of transmission, it is estimated that about one in five of the adult population is now an HIV carrier; the effect on family, social, and economic life has been devastating. By the end of 2000 some 18.8 million people had died of Aids worldwide.

• **Aids terrorists** ▸ People who know that they are infected with HIV but deliberately have unprotected sex with unsuspecting partners. The intention of the Aids terrorist is to take revenge on the rest of humankind for being infected by the virus.

• **AIH** ▸ Artificial insemination by husband. This is used in cases in which a couple are unable to have children because the male, while fertile, is incapable of normal sexual intercourse: semen from the husband (or male partner) is injected into the woman. *Compare*: DI.

• **aikido** ▸ (Japanese) A Japanese martial art that became popular in the Western world in the late 20th century. An ancient form of self-defence in Japan, it involves using the momentum of an attacker to bring him to the ground without injury; it demands great mental concentration and physical control.

• **AIM** ▸ American Indian Movement. A US pressure group founded by American Indians in 1968 in an attempt to defend their civil rights. The organization seeks to redress wrongs done to Native Americans by the state in the 19th and 20th centuries.

• **AI radar** ▸ Aircraft interceptor radar. A British radar system developed during World War II to enable fighter pilots to intercept enemy aircraft at night. Ground control used high-power radar installations to direct fighters to positions close to the enemy craft, where the pilot could pick up the enemy plane on his own low-power cockpit radar. The first victim of the system was a German Ju-88, shot down in July 1940. To conceal the development of this powerful aid from the Germans, the rumour that British pilots were fed large quantities of carrots to aid their night vision was widely spread.

• **aircraft** ▸ By the end of the 19th century two things had happened to bring man close to his dream of creating a heavier-than-air machine. The first was a sufficient grasp of aerodynamics to understand that emulating the wing-flapping of birds was not the way to do it; the second was the advent of Otto's internal-combustion engine to provide the power required. It was the Wright brothers who made use of Otto Lilienthal's gliding experience and Otto's engine to introduce the powered flight that revolutionized not only travel and warfare in the 20th century, but also international relations and the world economy; indeed, it has had repercussions since in almost every field of human activity. Despite rapid developments in the early years of the 20th century – only six years separate the Wright Brothers' first twelve-second trip in 1903 and Blériot's cross-channel flight in 1909 – until World War I a 'flying machine' was still regarded as something of a circus attraction; few would have predicted the major role aircraft play in modern life. The war, in which aircraft were used initially for reconnaissance and then as bombers and then as fighters to destroy the bombers, was a great stimulus to technical innovation, forcing governments to take the potential of aviation seriously (*see*: Fokker; Handley Page bomber; Sopwith Camel). Public fascination with flying remained strong in the inter-war era, owing largely to a succession of record-breaking flights, such as those by Lindbergh (*see*: Spirit of St Louis) and Amy Johnson (*see*: Queen of the Air). The 1920s and 1930s also saw the development of commercial civil aviation, although the first transatlantic service was not introduced until 1939. In World War II heavy bombers inflicted unprecedented levels of devastation on civilian populations, but airpower did not play the decisive role that many had predicted. The main post-war development has been the advent of the jet engine and the virtual disappearance of the propeller from modern commercial aeroplanes. Jets have enabled very large aircraft (*see*: Jumbo jet) to fly faster, more economically, and high enough to be above the weather. Concorde, the first supersonic commercial plane (introduced in 1976), flew from London to New York in three hours – a trip that took 2–3 weeks by sailing ship. The shrinking of the world into a global village has enabled the average UK family to spend their annual holiday in the Mediterranean, Africa, or America, which would have been undreamt of only 70 years ago. *See also*: Alcock and Brown; Hurricane; Mach number; Spitfire.

• **air cushion vehicle** ► *See*: hovercraft.

• **airhead** ► A silly or ignorant person. The term, which came to prominence in the 1980s implies that the person so described has air where his brain should be.

• **airmiss** ► A near collision by two or more aircraft flying at less than a prescribed distance apart. Airmisses tend to occur in the vicinity of airports, especially extremely busy international airports, such as London's Heathrow.

• **aisle sitters** ► US slang for theatre critics. The phrase reflects the idea that someone sitting in or near the aisle can escape from a boring play before the end or leave to send copy to his newspaper without disturbing other theatregoers.

• **aka** ► Also known *as*. An abbreviation used (originally in America but increasingly in the UK) to preface an assumed name.

• **Akela** ► The adult leader of a Cub Scout troop, taken from the name of the leader of a wolf pack in Kipling's *The Jungle Book*. Cub Scouts greet their leader with the shout 'Akela we will do our best'. *See*: Boy Scouts.

• **Alain-Fournier** ► Pseudonym of Henri-Alban-Fournier (1886–1914), French writer whose only completed novel *Le Grand Meaulnes* (1913; *The Lost Domain*, 1959) is a classic evocation of the yearning to recapture the cherished landscape of childhood.

The novel is an entrancing blend of nostalgia and realism, set in rural France in the 1890s, in which the hero spends his life searching for a house and a beautiful girl, encountered as an adolescent running away from home. The heroine is modelled on a girl, Yvonne, whom the novelist met briefly in 1905. Fournier was killed in the first Battle of the Marne and his body was never recovered. *Le Grand Meaulnes* created a literary sensation when 'rediscovered' in the 1980s.

> I like the marvellous only when it is strictly enveloped in reality; not when it upsets or exceeds it. – ALAIN-FOURNIER, in a letter of 1911.

• **Alamein, Battles of El-** ► Two battles fought during World War II near El-Alamein, some 60 miles W of Alexandria in Egypt. The first Battle of El-Alamein took place during July 1942, when Britain's Eighth Army (*see*: Desert Rats) finally succeeded in halting the eastward advance of Rommel's Afrika Korps. Rommel's forces were weary and in need of re-supply after their rapid advance, while the British, under Claude Auchinleck, had the benefit of fresh troops and equipment.

In August of that year, General Bernard Law Montgomery replaced Auchinleck as British commander, and during September and October British and other Allied forces were greatly reinforced. The second Battle of El-Alamein started on 23 October 1942 with the launch of the British offensive. Rommel, returning from convalescence in Austria, reached the front on 25 October and directed a skilful defence, inflicting heavy casualties on the British. However, the numerical superiority of the British tanks and their secure supply lines eventually told, and Rommel began his retreat from El-Alamein on 4 November. Soon, as a famous communiqué of the time put it, Rommel was 'motoring westwards in top gear'. El-Alamein proved to be a decisive turning-point in the Allies' North African campaign.

> Before Alamein we never had a victory. After Alamein we never had a defeat. – WINSTON CHURCHILL, *The Hinge of Fate*.

• **Alamogordo** ► The US air base in New Mexico at which the first atomic bomb was detonated on 16 July 1945. *See*: Manhattan Project.

• **alas, my poor brother** ► A catchphrase borrowed from a Bovril advertisement in the 1920s. The exclamation, with its echoes of Hamlet's 'Alas, poor Yorick', is uttered by a bovine lamenting the transformation of an erstwhile sibling into a tin of the beefy beverage.

• **Alaska highway** ► A scenic route running 2451 km (1523 mi) through the Yukon between

Dawson Creek, British Columbia, and Fairbanks, Alaska. The highway was built in 1942 by US Army engineers as an overland military supply route to Alaska.

• **Alcatraz**▶ A small island in San Francisco Bay, the site of an infamous top-security prison. The island became a US possession in 1851 and was shortly after made the home for a military correction centre. The military prison erected in 1909 was transferred to the federal prison authorities in 1933. Until its closure in 1963, Alcatraz held some of America's most notorious criminals, including Al Capone (see: Scarface) and Machine-Gun Kelly. The regime was harsh: inmates were kept in solitary confinement in cells measuring 2.7 m by 1.5 m (9 ft by 5 ft). Escape was made virtually impossible by the dangerous currents surrounding the island. One inmate, the murderer Robert Strand, studied birds during his incarceration and was the subject of the 1961 film, *The Birdman of Alcatraz*.

• **Alcock and Brown**▶ The pioneering aviation partnership consisting of Captain John Alcock (1892–1919) and Lieutenant Arthur Whitten Brown (1886–1948), who in 1919 achieved the first air crossing of the Atlantic. The challenge was set by a *Daily Mail* offer of £10,000; Alcock and Brown, both heroes of World War I, were recruited by Vickers to fly a converted Vimy bomber from Newfoundland to Ireland. After months of preparation they set off (accompanied by Brown's toy cat Twinkletoes). During the next 16 hours 27 minutes they were beset by thick fog, lost all radio contact, survived an engine fire, were caught in a storm, were forced to climb out on the wing to free the air intakes of snow, and finally crash-landed in a peat bog, which they mistook for a field. Both fliers were knighted within the week and hailed as national heroes. Sadly, Alcock died in an air accident six months later; Brown was shattered by the news and never flew again.

• **Alcoholics Anonymous** ▶ An organization founded in 1935 by two Americans to help alcoholics control their addiction. The stockbroker William Griffith Wilson ('Bill W') and the surgeon Robert Holbrook Smith ('Dr Bob S') originated a programme of self-help based on small groups of sufferers sharing their experiences and giving mutual support. Members are known only by their first names and the initial of their surnames. The British branch of AA was founded in 1947.

• **alcopops**▶ Alcoholic beverages designed to taste like soft drinks and packaged and promoted accordingly. In the mid-1990s such concoctions as Alcola, an alcoholic cola drink, and Hooch, an alcoholic lemonade, became highly popular amongst young people. This led to concern amongst groups dealing with alcohol abuse, who accused the manufacturers of targeting these products at younger teenagers. In 1996 the Portman Group, the UK drinks industry watchdog, admitted that its code of practice on promoting alcohol to under-18s was being widely breached. Later that year the Group ordered Carling-Tetley to repackage its drink Thickhead, an 'alcoholic carbonated gel' described as having the taste of wine gums and the texture of vomit.

• **Aldeburgh** ▶ A small coastal town in Suffolk that hosts an annual music festival established by Benjamin Britten, Peter Pears, and their friends in 1948. The festival developed out of Britten's association with the English Opera Group, a small troupe of singers and musicians for whom many of his works were written. Aldeburgh and the nearby Maltings at Snape became an important venue for introducing Britten's new operas to the public. Despite the death of Britten in 1976 and of Pears in 1986, the festival continues.

• **Aldermaston Marches** ▶ A series of Easter protest marches (1958–63) sponsored by CND close to the site of the Atomic Weapons Research Establishment at Aldermaston, Berkshire. At their peak they attracted up to 150,000 supporters.

• **Aldwych farces**▶ A series of plays written by Ben Travers (1886–1980) and staged at the Aldwych Theatre, London, between 1925 and 1933. The series began with *A Cuckoo in the Nest* and featured a regular cast headed by Robertson Hare, Mary Brough, Tom Walls, and Ralph Lynn. Other well-known plays in the series are *Rookery Nook* (1926) and *Thark* (1927).

• **A-level**▶ In England and Wales, the public examination usually taken at the age of 17–18 that provides the main passport for university entrance. It was first introduced in 1951 (see: GCE). A-levels came under increasing criticism from reformers in the 1980s and 1990s as being too narrow and specialized but the examinations were defended by government ministers as the 'gold standard' of the British secondary education system. However, to broaden the curriculum of sixth formers, in 1989 the one-year AS-level (advanced supplementary level) was also introduced. Since 2000, A-levels have been taken in two stages, the AS-level (now meaning advanced subsidiary level) after one year and the A2-level after two years. In recent decades the steady year-on-year improvement in A-level grades has led to accusations that the exam has become too easy (see: dumbing down).

• **Alexandra Day**▶ A day in June when rose emblems are sold for the hospital fund inaugurated in 1912 by Queen Alexandra (1844–1925), Danish consort of Edward VII, to celebrate the fiftieth year of her residence in England.

• **Alexbow** ► A form of ship's bow that was designed in 1968 to facilitate a vessel's progress through ice by lifting the ice upwards. It was named after its Canadian inventor, Scott Alexander.

• **'alf a mo, Kaiser** ► A catchphrase from a British recruiting poster of World War I, depicting a British soldier pausing for a cigarette before resuming the fight. See: Kaiser Bill.

• **al-Fatah** ► (Arabic, the victory) One of the most powerful factions of the PLO. Under its leader Yassir Arafat (1929–    ) it organized a guerrilla campaign against Israel from the early 1960s onwards. However, it split into factions after Arafat signed a peace agreement with Israel in 1993.

• **Alf Garnett** ► See Garnett, Alf.

• **Algeciras Conference** ► A conference of European powers held in the Spanish port of Algeciras in 1906 to settle the issue of Moroccan sovereignty. France wanted to establish a protectorate over Morocco, a move strongly opposed by Germany. Tension had been increased in 1905 by a visit to Morocco by Kaiser Wilhelm II. The Conference ended in March, guaranteeing Moroccan independence and ensuring free access for all nations but giving a special role to France and Spain in policing. However, the issue flared up again in the Agadir Crisis.

• **Algérie française** ► (French, Algeria is French) The rallying cry of the colonial French in Algeria who opposed moves to Algerian independence during the 1950s and early 1960s. See also: OAS.

• **Algonquin Round Table** ► A group of noted US wits who met regularly to dine and exchange epigrams at New York's Algonquin Hotel in the interwar years. They included Dorothy Parker, James Thurber, Alexander Woollcott, George Kaufman, and Robert Benchley. On one occasion Dorothy Parker left her place at the Round Table saying 'Excuse me, I have to go to the bathroom.' After a pause, she added 'I really have to telephone, but I'm too embarrassed to say so.'

• **Alice blue** ► A shade of pale blue named after Alice Roosevelt Longworth (daughter of Theodore Roosevelt), who was particularly fond of it. Joseph McCarthy wrote a song called 'Alice Blue Gown'.

> In my sweet little Alice blue gown
> When I first wandered out in the town...

• **alien abduction** ► See: flying saucers.

• **A-Line** ► See: Dior.

• **aliyah** ► (Hebrew, ascent) The mass immigration of Jews from all over the world to Israel after the new state won independence in 1948. See: olim.

• **all because the lady loves Milk Tray** ► A highly successful trade slogan used in advertising campaigns for Cadbury's Milk Tray chocolates in the 1970s and 1980s. Television adverts for the product, featuring a black-clad stuntman who performed various daring feats to deliver a box of chocolates to the lady in question, were much parodied but remained substantially unchanged for 20 years.

• **All Blacks** ► The New Zealand International Rugby Union Football team (so-called from their all-black strip), which first played in England in 1905.

• **alley cat** ► A pejorative term for a person of either sex who favours a wild and promiscuous street life, used often in the phrase 'to have the morals of an alley cat'. It was originally a pre-World War II US expression, but has been heard in the UK and Australia since the 1960s.

• **Allies** ► 1. Those countries allied against Germany and the other Central Powers in World War I, notably the UK, France, Italy, Russia, and America. 2. In World War II those 49 nations allied against the Axis states, including the UK and the Commonwealth countries, America, the Soviet Union, China, and France.

• **alligator** ► In Black US jazz slang, a White musician, dancer, or fan of jazz music (first heard in the 1930s). See: See you later, alligator.

• **All Souls' Parish Magazine** ► The Times was so nicknamed during the editorship (1923–41) of G. G. Dawson, fellow of All Souls College, Oxford. He and some of his associates, who were also fellows of the college, frequently met there for discussions.

• **all systems go** ► A catchphrase of the 1960s and 1970s, meaning that everything is ready for imminent action. It derived from its use during the launch of US space missions to indicate that all the craft's components were working normally. As interest in space flight waned by the end of the 1970s, so did the use of such phrases.

• **all-terrain vehicle** ► (ATV) A motor-vehicle that is specially designed for rapid transport over rough ground. ATVs include such vehicles as **dune buggies**, intended chiefly for recreation; others include **snowcats** and various **moon buggies**.

• **all the president's men** ► A phrase embodying the notion of unquestioning loyalty to the US president, originally coined by the politician and diplomat Henry Kissinger (1923– ) in a discussion of US policy on Cambodia in 1970. It was subsequently used, with a distinct note of irony, as the title of Bob Woodward and Carl Bernstein's book about their role in exposing the Watergate scandal. A film with the same name was released in 1976, starring Dustin Hoffman and Robert Redford.

• **Ally Pally** ▸ A familiar and affectionate name for the Alexandra Palace in north London, which became the site of the world's first television transmitter when it was acquired by the BBC in 1936. It opened in 1863 as a rival to the Crystal Palace but burnt down after only 16 days and did not reopen until 1873; in World War I it was used as a barracks. In 1955 it witnessed the first experiments with colour television. It was devastated by another disastrous fire in July 1980, but much of it has been rebuilt and it now contains a skating rink and a winter garden.

• **alone** ▸

**I want to be alone** Catchphrase associated with the Swedish-born US film actress Greta Garbo (Greta Gustafson; 1905–90). She spoke the words in *Grand Hotel* (1932) and, in conjunction with her aloof beauty and long reclusive retirement (from 1941), they established one of the greatest of all cinema legends.

> Garbo's temperament reflected the rain and gloom of the long dark Swedish winters. – LIL-LIAN GISH.

• **alone** ▸

**You're never alone with a Strand** A trade slogan associated with a much-acclaimed but commercially disastrous advertising campaign of 1960. The aim of the campaign, commissioned for the launch of the cheap new Strand cigarette, was to identify the product with contemporary disaffected youth. Cinema adverts showed a fashionably dressed young man (actor Terence Brook) looking pensive as he drew on his cigarette in a downbeat urban setting. Although widely admired, this melancholy imagery failed entirely to sell the cigarette.

• **al-Qaida** ▸ (Arabic, the base) The international terrorist organization created by Osama Bin Laden (1957– ) that is presumed to have been responsible for the extraordinary and atrocious attack on America on September 11 2001. Bin Laden, a Saudi-born multimillionaire, became involved in militant Islamic politics in the late 1970s; in 1979 he travelled to Afghanistan, where he helped to finance and organize the mujaheddin resistance that eventually

drove out the Soviet invaders – a role that established him as a hero to many Muslims. In 1990–91 Bin Laden was outraged by the decision to station US troops on the sacred soil of Saudi Arabia; it is apparently this 'violation', rather than the Palestine situation or US policy in the Gulf, that has chiefly fuelled his anti-Americanism since that time. The al-Qaida organization dates from around 1991, when Bin Laden settled in Sudan and began training terrorists for his holy war against America. His trainees were responsible for bomb attacks on US servicemen in Yemen (1992), Somalia (1993), and Saudi Arabia (1995). In 1998, on the eighth anniversary of US troops landing in Saudi Arabia, the US embassies in Kenya and Tanzania were blown up, killing 700 people.

Having been expelled from Sudan in 1996, Bin Laden transferred his operations to Afghanistan, where he forged close links with the Taliban regime. By this time he had effectively transformed al-Qaida into a multinational terror business, in which the various cells operate rather like franchisees of the parent organization. There appear to be several distinct tiers of operative, with Bin Laden himself exercising an aloof form of leadership from the centre of the web. His precise role in conceiving and directing the events of September 11 is therefore hard to pin down. Although the US-led war on terrorism has destroyed al-Qaida's Afghan Command centre, it is too soon to say that its threat has been neutralized; cells with al-Qaida links are currently thought to be active in around 40 countries and some experts believe that its international support network remains largely intact.

• **alternative** ▸ A word used since the late 1960s to describe anything that offers an alternative to the usual or conventional form of that thing. **Alternative comedy**, alternative energy, **alternative lifestyle**, and alternative medicine are examples of this usage.

• **alternative energy** ▸ Energy derived from renewable energy sources rather than conventional finite mineral resources. Alternative energy sources include hydroelectric power, solar power, wind power, tidal power, wave power, geothermal energy, and biomass energy. Their attraction is that they conserve resources of fossil fuels, do not involve the dangers of nuclear power, and cause no pollution. Various estimates have been given for the time required before alternative energy could provide 10% or 20% of the UK's electricity requirements, many of them hopelessly unrealistic. In 1996 alternative sources, including hydroelectricity, provided only 0.2% of the UK's energy requirements.

• **alternative medicine** or **complementary medicine** ► A treatment for physical or mental illness that exists outside orthodox medical practice. It is usually sought by patients suffering from cancer, back pain, migraine, allergies, etc., when conventional treatments have failed to produce a cure or to alleviate symptoms.

Its methods include acupuncture, aromatherapy, faith healing, herbalism, homeopathy, hypnosis, naturopathy, osteopathy, chiropractic, and reflexology. The effectiveness of such therapies, which is largely unamenable to scientific assessment, remains controversial. However, growing public interest in alternative medicine, together with a growing acceptance in parts of the medical establishment that some of these practices appear to benefit some patients, has meant that many hospitals and surgeries now make such treatments available to those who request them. Alternative medicine is often known as **fringe** or **unorthodox medicine**. *See also*: holistic medicine.

• **Alternative Service Book** ► (ASB) A book, published in 1980, containing modern-language forms of service for Anglican worship. From the 1960s onwards the 17th-century *Book of Common Prayer* had been increasingly displaced by alternative forms of service commonly known as Series 1, Series 2, and Series 3. The *Alternative Service Book* formalized this situation by including three forms of Communion Service; namely, revised versions of Series 1 and 2 (largely based on the *Book of Common Prayer*) and the more controversial Series 3 (Revised) in modern English. However, the other services (including those for baptisms, weddings, and funerals) were all in the Series 3 idiom, and the Bible readings were all from modern translations rather than the Authorized Version. Many traditionalists disliked the new services intensely, arguing that their language was banal and lacking in poetry. They also resented the fact that, in practice, the ASB became a replacement service book rather than a mere alternative, as was supposedly the intention. The ASB was withdrawn in 2001, when it was replaced by *Common Worship*, a book that includes both modern-language and traditional services.

• **alternative society** ► Any society based on a set of values that do not conform with those of conventional society. The phrase gained currency during the hippie era of the 1960s and 1970s.

• **Althorp House** ► The ancestral home of the Spencer family since 1508. The medieval house was altered in 1787 to the present neoclassical style by Henry Holland. It is now mainly known as the resting place of Diana, Princess of Wales (*see*: People's Princess), who is buried on Round Oval Island in the ornamental lake in Althorp Park. A museum commemorating her life was opened in the Park in 1998.

• **Altmark** ► In the Royal Navy an opprobious name for a ship or an establishment with a reputation for very strict discipline. It derives from a famous naval exploit of February 1940 when Captain Philip Vian, commanding the destroyer HMS *Cossack*, entered Norwegian territorial waters to effect the release of 299 British prisoners of war from the German auxiliary-cum-prison ship *Altmark*, which had taken refuge in Josing Fjord. The boarding party was led by Lieutenant Bradwell Turner whose cry 'The Navy's here!' was widely imitated for years afterwards as a reassurance to anyone in trouble.

• **Alzheimer's disease** ► A degenerative disease of the brain first described by the German neurologist Alois Alzheimer (1864–1915) in 1906. It causes loss of short-term memory and symptoms of senility (though it may occur in middle age), and ultimately a total collapse of mental activity of any kind. Its cause is uncertain, but some forms are inherited. No cure is known, although drugs that slow the progress of the disease are now available.

• **AM** ► Amplitude modulation. *See*: FM.

• **Amadeus String Quartet** ► A British string quartet with a worldwide reputation for its ensemble playing. Although it was named in recognition of Wolfgang Amadeus Mozart, the Quartet's repertoire covered the whole range of chamber music. It was formed by three young Jewish violinists, refugees from Vienna, who met when they were interned on the Isle of Man in the early years of World War II: Norbert Brianin (who became the leader), Sigmund Nissel (second violin), and Peter Schidlof (who gave up the violin in favour of the viola). The quartet was completed in 1947 by the English cellist Martin Lovett. Having delighted audiences all over the world for 40 years, the Amadeus disbanded in 1987 on the sudden death of Schidlof. The name of the quartet sometimes caused puzzlement: its leader once received a letter addressed to Mr Amadeus String.

• **Amami** ►
   **Friday night is Amami night** A trade slogan of the 1920s. Advertising hair products, it capitalized upon the practice (common at the time) of washing one's hair on Friday night ready for the weekend.

• **amateur night** ► A poor or half-hearted effort (often with reference to athletic performance or sexual skills). The term originated in US theatres and cabaret establishments that featured amateurs, usually in a talent-spotting competition once a week. The Apollo in Harlem still holds such contests; former winners include jazz singers Ella Fitzgerald and Sarah Vaughan.

• **amber gambler ►** A driver of a motor vehicle who habitually fails to heed the amber traffic light (meaning caution, coming after green for 'go' and before red for 'stop') and speeds through as the lights change to red. The dangers of 'amber gambling' have been the subject of periodic public information campaigns in the press and on television.

• **amber nectar ►** An Australian euphemism for beer or lager. It was first popularized in the UK by the cartoon series *Barry McKenzie*, which appeared in the magazine *Private Eye* in the 1970s. However, it became much more widely used in the 1980s after its use in a TV advertisement for an Australian lager that featured the macho Australian actor Paul Hogan.

• **Ambridge ►** The fictional village whose inhabitants' lives are chronicled in the BBC radio serial *The Archers* (*see*: Archers, The). The village was based on a composite of real-life Inkberrow, Hanbury, and other villages in E Worcestershire, not far from where the programme is recorded in Birmingham. Coach tours now offer excursions round the 'actual' locations of events portrayed in the programme.

• **ambulance chaser ►** A lawyer who rushes to the scene of an accident in the hope that he will be able to retain the victim as a client in the event of any claim for compensation.

• **ambulance stocks ►** Stocks or shares that a broker recommends to a client in the hope that they will restore the client's confidence in him. If a portfolio has been performing below expectations, the broker may suggest purchasing ambulance stocks, which can be relied on to enliven his client's holdings – at least in the short term.

• **Amerasian ►** A person of mixed US and Asian parentage. First coined in the mid-1960s, the term was later used specifically of someone conceived during the Vietnam War by a Vietnamese mother with a US serviceman as the father. A resettlement programme instituted in 1982 led to many Amerasians moving to America.

• **American Caesar ►** The nickname acquired by General Douglas MacArthur (1880–1964). First bestowed in the 19th century upon Ulysses S. Grant, it was given to MacArthur as his reputation as a determined and controversial commander grew in World War II. During the Korean War he clashed with President Truman and was dismissed (1951).

• **American Dictator ►** *See*: Boss, the.

• **American Dream ►** The democratic ideals and aspirations on which America was founded: the American way of life at its best.

> It [the American dream] has been a dream of being able to grow to fullest development as man and woman, unhampered by the barriers which had slowly been erected in older civilizations, unrepressed by social orders which had developed for the benefit of classes rather than for the simple human being of any and every class. – J. T. ADAMS: *The Epic of America*, Epilogue (1931).

The phrase is often now used ironically or disparagingly:

> The Bush government thought people bought bullshit, this ridiculous American Dream that has nothing to do with our reality... – JODIE FOSTER, *Elle*, April 1993.

• **American Legion ►** The US armed forces veterans' organization. It was established in 1919 to serve the interests of US servicemen returning from the war in Europe and now includes veterans of World War II, the Korean War, and the Vietnam War. The Legion administers programmes of rehabilitation and welfare for veterans and their families, as well as promoting the rights of veterans and campaigning on defence and security issues.

• **America's Boy Friend ►** The nickname of the US matinee idol Charles 'Buddy' Rogers (1904–99). His films included *Wings* (1927), *This Reckless Age* (1932), and *Once in a Million* (1936); he was married to Mary Pickford, known as **America's Sweetheart** or the World's Sweetheart.

• **Amethyst, HMS ►** The British frigate that made a daring escape along the Yangtze River in July 1949 to evade Chinese Communist forces. The acting commander, Lieutenant-Commander J. S. Kerans, navigated the damaged *Amethyst* in a 140-mile sprint for safety, under cover of darkness and running the gauntlet of hostile shells, to rejoin the British Fleet south of Woosung.

• **Amnesty International ►** (AI) An international organization founded in 1961 and devoted to publicizing violations of human rights and campaigning for the release of political prisoners. From its London headquarters AI maintains contact with human rights activists all over the world, and through regular newsletters, annual reports, travelling exhibitions, newspaper and television campaigns, etc., encourages public scrutiny and condemnation of regimes guilty of torture and political oppression. Particularly effective is the process for supporting 'prisoners of conscience' by 'adoption groups' who send Christmas cards and correspondence to individual prisoners and also bombard guilty governments with letters of protest until the victims are released. AI's logo is a candle wrapped in barbed wire. The organization was awarded the Nobel Peace Prize in 1977.

• **amniocentesis**► The extraction of a sample of the amniotic fluid surrounding a foetus for diagnostic purposes. With the aid of an ultrasound scan, a hollow needle is inserted through the abdominal and uterine walls and a sample of the fluid, which contains foetal cells, is taken. The chromosomes from the cell nuclei can then be tested for various congenital abnormalities, such as Down's syndrome and spina bifida. Because of the chance of miscarriage (one in 100 women) the test is only carried out on women who have been proved, by means of other tests, to be at risk of carrying a fetus with a congenital abnormality.

• **Amos 'n' Andy**► The most successful US radio programme of all time, a 1930s comedy series about the tribulations of two Black characters, who were actually played by White actors – Freeman Gosden as Amos and Charles Correll as Andy. The popularity of the 15-minute programmes each weekday forced department stores to broadcast them and cinemas to switch off projectors and switch on radios. Television's commercial debut at the 1939 World's Fair in New York was an Amos 'n' Andy test programme using actors with blacked faces. With Black actors, it became a hit on early 1950s television but was cancelled after protests that its portrayal of Blacks was unrepresentative.

• **Amritsar Massacre** ► A bloody incident in which 379 Indian demonstrators were shot dead by British troops commanded by General Reginald Dyer in the city of Amritsar, Punjab. On 13 April 1919 an estimated 10,000 people packed into the walled square of Jallianwala Bagh to protest at the extension of emergency powers by the British colonial government. Dyer ordered his men to fire on the unarmed crowd, making the square a death trap. Apart from the dead, an estimated 1200 were injured. Dyer was castigated by a commission of inquiry but his action was supported by the British House of Lords. The incident prompted Mahâtma Gandhi to institute a campaign of civil disobedience against the British.

In 1984 another 1000 people died in Amritsar when Sikh extremists seized and held the Sikh shrine, the Golden Temple, until it was stormed by the Indian army. As a reprisal, Sikh members of the prime minister's bodyguard murdered Indira Gandhi later that year.

• **Amundsen Sea** ► Part of the South Pacific Ocean bordering Byrd Island in Antarctica; it is named after the Norwegian explorer Roald Amundsen (1872–1928), who in 1911 became the first man to reach the South Pole, having beaten the doomed British expedition under Captain Robert Scott (*see*: Scott of the Antarctic) by a mere 34 days.

• **anabolic steroid** ► A steroid compound that promotes the growth of tissue. Anabolic steroids, which include nandrolone and stanozol, are synthetic forms of naturally occurring male sex hormones (androgens). They are used in medicine to treat certain diseases. Anabolic steroids are also used to enhance performance in athletics and horseracing, although these uses are now banned by the relevant authorities as they can cause liver damage. Many bodies, including the International Olympic Committee, require samples of athletes' urine to prove them free of anabolic steroids.

• **Anastasia** ► Anastasiya Nikolayevna (1901–18), Grand Duchess of Russia and youngest daughter of Tsar Nicholas II. Anastasia was almost certainly executed by the Bolsheviks in a cellar in Ekaterinburg with the rest of her family. However, several women have since insisted that they were the Tsar's daughter and have claimed the Romanov fortune, deposited in Swiss banks. The suit of the most renowned of these claimants, Anna Anderson (1902–84), was rejected by the West German Federal Supreme Court in 1970 and the remaining Romanov fortune was awarded to the Duchess of Mecklenberg. In the film *Anastasia* (1956) Ingrid Bergman won an Academy Award in the title role. In 1993 DNA testing established beyond reasonable doubt that bones found near Ekaterinburg in 1991 were those of the Tsar, his wife, and three of their children (the remains of Anastasia and Tsarevich Alexei have yet to be found). After similar tests on samples of Anna Anderson's hair etc., scientists concluded that she could not have been Anastasia.

• **ANC** ► African National Congress. A Black nationalist organization in South Africa, which led the struggle against apartheid. Declared illegal in 1960, it subsequently adopted a strategy of sabotage and guerrilla activity; it finally won recognition from the South African government in 1990. Its symbolic head, Nelson Mandela (1918–   ), was imprisoned from 1964 to 1990; he became ANC president after his release. In 1994 the ANC won South Africa's first multiracial elections and Mandela became president of the republic (1994–99) and a greatly respected world statesman. He was succeeded as president of the ANC (1998– ) and president of South Africa (1999– ) by Thabo Mbeki (1942– ).

• **anchor man** ▸ A presenter of a television news programme, who coordinates film footage, live interviews, and reports both inside and outside the studio. In America the increasing tendency is for the anchor man or woman to be chosen for their appearance, while in the UK they are usually journalists by training.

• **Anderson shelter** ▸ An air-raid shelter provided for the protection of British civilians during the Blitz. It was named after its designer, Dr David A. Anderson, but the name is associated by many with the then home secretary, Sir John Anderson, who ordered their construction and distribution in 1938. They consisted of 14 corrugated iron sheets and when erected measured 6 feet high by 4 feet by 6 feet. The shelter was buried 4 feet deep, and the top was covered by soil. Sheltering inside was like 'being entombed in a small dark bicycle shed, smelling of earth and damp', according to the historian Norman Longmate. *See also*: Morrison shelter.

• **Andromeda strain** ▸ In the best-selling novel of this name (1969; filmed 1971) by US author Michael Crichton, a dangerous microorganism, hitherto unidentified by scientists, brought to earth by a returning space probe. The name is sometimes applied to any mysterious deadly bug.

• **Andy Capp** ▸ A cartoon character (created by Reg Smythe) that first appeared in the *Daily Mirror* in 1958. Capp is a determinedly lazy working-class Geordie, apparently permanently attached to his flat cap. He became something of a national institution in the 1960s and 1970s.

• **angel dust** ▸ A powdered form of the drug PCP (phencyclohexylpiperidine, or phencyclidine), which is used in veterinary medicine as an anaesthetic (*see*: hog). The powder, often homemade, can be sniffed or smoked to produce extreme psychological and physical effects, ranging from hallucinations to uncontrolled violence. As it was so easy to produce it became a serious problem in America in the late 1970s, especially among poor teenagers. Angel dust has now been largely superseded by crack.

• **Angel of Death** ▸ Name by which the German medical scientist Josef Mengele (1894–c.1979) became known for the atrocities committed under his orders at Auschwitz concentration camp, where he was camp doctor from 1943 to 1945. His barbarous medical experiments on live camp inmates accounted for many of the 400,000 deaths (mostly

of Jews) for which he was subsequently held responsible. He vanished after the defeat of Nazi Germany and was rumoured to be living in South America: it is thought he died from drowning in Brazil in 1979. A body was identified as that of Mengele in 1985. Acquaintances of his in South America said he refused to accept any guilt for the crimes he had committed.

• **Angel of the North** ▸ An enormous metal sculpture, the largest in the UK, depicting a standing figure with outspread wings (span 53 m). Created by Anthony Gormley (1950– ), it was erected on a hill outside Gateshead, NE England, in 1998. Its main purpose is to celebrate the steel industry in and around Gateshead. As it is clearly visible to drivers on the A1(M), the sculpture has already become a celebrated landmark.

The unofficial title **Angel of the South** has been given to a large wickerwork figure (height 12 m) that stands beside the M5 near Bridgwater, Somerset. This sculpture, the work of Serena de la Hey (1968– ) was erected in 2000 to honour the local willow-growing industry. It was virtually destroyed by arson in May 2001, allegedly by local witches celebrating a fertility rite; but the artist plans to restore it.

• **Angels of Mons** ▸ Supernatural reinforcements popularly supposed to have intervened on the British side during the Battle of Mons in World War I. The 3rd and 4th Divisions of the Old Contemptibles, under the command of General Dorrien-Smith, were sorely pressed in the retreat from Mons (26–27 August 1914). Their losses were heavy and that they survived at all was by some attributed to divine intervention. In a short story contributed to the *Evening News* (Sept 1914) Arthur Machen, a writer best known for his occult fantasies, described with great verisimilitude how St George and the Angels, clad in white and with flaming swords, held back the might of the German First Army. Although Machen insisted that the story was pure fiction, many soldiers later gave 'eyewitness' accounts of an army of angels at Mons.

• **angels on horseback** ▸ A savoury dish first created in the early 20th century; it consists of oysters rolled in bacon and served on toast, either as the culminating delicacy of a dinner menu or as a supper dish. The name – a translation of the French *anges à cheval* – contrasts the celestial flavour of the oyster with the more mundane saddle of the bacon, astride the vehicle provided by the toast.

• **Angry Brigade** ▸ A radical group with anarchist sympathies, who were involved in sporadic violence, such as bombings and firearm attacks, in the UK in the late 1960s and early 1970s. Some of the leaders of the group were imprisoned for a bomb attack on the home of the secretary of state for employment in 1971.

• **Angry Young Men ▶** A journalistic name for a group of British novelists and dramatists of the late 1950s. Writers associated with the term included Kingsley Amis, Colin Wilson, and especially John Osborne, from whose play *Look Back in Anger* (1956) the term was derived. They were characterized by dissatisfaction with established social, moral, political, and intellectual values, although their protest came to look moderate in comparison with the radicalism of the 1960s. *See also*: kitchen sink; Porter, Jimmy.

> In the absence of any really firm standards among those whom they sought to replace the temptation to exploit the gullibility of the public and those who were supposed to guide them was too strong for many of the 'Angry Young Men' to resist. – BORIS FORD: *The Modern Age*.

• **animal, vegetable, or mineral ▶** Catchphrase associated with the BBC radio quiz programme Twenty Questions (1947–76). The phrase had previously been used in a US radio quiz (1946), although it had more distant origins in a parlour game dating back to the 18th century.

• **Animal Farm ▶** A satirical 'fairy story' by George Orwell (1903–50) in which an animal society is used to caricature the totalitarianism of the Soviet Union under Stalin. It describes how the pigs, by cunning, treachery, and ruthlessness, lord it over the more honest gullible hardworking farm animals. The book was first published in 1945.

• **animal house ▶** US student term for an extremely dirty and uproarious college fraternity house. Originally popular in the late 1950s, its use was revived in the 1978 film *National Lampoon's Animal House*, which starred John Belushi.

• **animal liberation** or **animal rights movement ▶** A protest movement founded to protect animals from exploitation by humans. Since the 1970s the more extreme groups, such as the Animal Liberation Front, have adopted violent methods, including car bombs, arson, and breaking into scientific research establishments, as part of their campaigns against those alleged to subject animals in their care to cruelty. *See also*: League against Cruel Sports.

• **Animated Meringue ▶** A nickname given to the romantic novelist Barbara Cartland (1901–2000) by the humorist Arthur Marshall; it reflects her extraordinary taste in clothes (very pink and very fluffy), cosmetics, and hairstyles. Cartland, the au-

thor of over 700 books, responded by sending him a telegram of thanks.

• **annus horribilis ▶** A facetious adaptation of the Latin phrase *annus mirabilis*, or 'year of wonders', to mean its opposite, a year of horrors. It was coined by Queen Elizabeth II in a speech delivered at the Guildhall in 1992, in allusion to the series of royal disasters that had marked that year. These included the Windsor Castle fire, the collapse of the marriages of three of her children, and consistently hostile coverage by the tabloid press.

• **anointing of the sick ▶** A sacrament of the Roman Catholic Church and Eastern Orthodox Church that, before 1972, was known as the sacrament of extreme unction. The somewhat alarming ancient name for this rite was changed to avoid the implication that it was only performed on patients *in extremis*, for whom there was no hope of recovery.

• **anorak ▶** A disparaging name for someone with an obsessive interest or hobby that most people consider unspeakably dull. It comes from the anoraks habitually worn by train-spotters during long periods of standing around on station platforms.

• **anorexia nervosa ▶** A psychological disorder chiefly afflicting teenage girls, in which the patient refuses to eat adequately or at all (even to the point of death) and experiences considerable emotional distress. The condition, often inspired by a girl's wholly irrational conviction that she is overweight, came into the public eye for the first time in the 1970s and 1980s. Treatment involves hospitalization, psychotherapy, sedation, and intensive nursing. *See also*: bulimia.

• **Anschluss ▶** (German, union) In a modern historical context this refers to the takeover of Austria by Germany in March 1938. After the Austrian chancellor, Kurt von Schuschnigg (1897–1977), was forced to resign because of his opposition to *Anschluss*, German troops entered Austria to rapturous acclaim. Schuschnigg was then imprisoned for the duration of the war. The Anschluss was ratified by plebiscite and Austria became part of the Nazi fatherland.

• **Antarctic Treaty ▶** A treaty signed in 1959 by 12 nations, including the UK, that restricts activities in the Antarctic to peaceful ones, such as scientific research. The treaty also prohibits all new claims on the continent, forbids its use for nuclear explosions, and bans the dumping of wastes. It provides for periodic meetings of the signatories to resolve any difficulties arising.

• **Anthony dollar►** A US dollar coin that was introduced in 1979 in honour of the US suffragette leader Susan B. Anthony (1820–1906).

• **Anthony Eden►** Popular name for the style of black homburg hat worn by Sir Anthony Eden (later Lord Avon) when he was foreign secretary in the 1930s. It was an unusual departure from the near-uniform bowler hat that was then fashionable in Whitehall.

• **Anthroposophical Society ►** An organization founded in 1912 by the Austrian philosopher and scientist Rudolph Steiner (1861–1925) to promote his doctrine of **anthroposophy**. This philosophy, intended by its creator as a more human-centred form of theosophy, holds that the key to understanding the spiritual world lies in developing certain latent human faculties. The Society's original headquarters, the twin-domed wooden Goetheanum (named after Goethe) in Dornach, Switzerland, was burnt down in 1922 and replaced by a concrete building. The British branch of the Society was founded in 1923. It shares the universal Steiner aim of creating 'a union of human beings who desire to further the life of the soul, both in the individual and in society at large, based on a true knowledge of the spiritual world.'

• **Anti-Comintern Pact►** An agreement signed by Nazi Germany and Japan on 25 November 1936, in which both countries undertook to oppose the activities of the Comintern – the Communist International. The pact gave a fillip to Japan's expansionist plans and provided a pretext for her invasion of China the following year. Italy also became a signatory in 1937, thus foreshadowing the 1940 Tripartite Pact between the three countries. Other nations regarded the pact as an ominous development.

• **anti-roman►** *See:* nouveau roman.

• **antiworld ►** A theoretical world composed of antimatter. No such astronomical body has yet been positively identified.

• **Anual►** The site of the Spanish garrison in Morocco that was overwhelmed by a Berber force under Abd al-Krim al-Khattabi in September 1921. The victory prompted his announcement of the formation of a Berber state in the Rif Mountains. The rebellion was eventually suppressed by Spanish and French forces.

• **Anvil ►** The codename for the proposed Allied landing in S France in 1944. The planned operation caused friction between the Allies, although a force of mainly US troops did eventually land, on 15 August, near St Raphael (by which time the operation had been renamed **Dragoon**).

• **Anyone for tennis? ►** A catchphrase that is generally used to encapsulate the carefree life of the well-to-do in the 1920s – a period in which wealthy young men appeared to have nothing more pressing to do than to appear at house parties in their straw hats and white flannels, inviting their friends to play lawn tennis. The phrase is often associated with the light comedies of the interwar period, although no precise use of these words has been found. Shaw's 1919 play *Misalliance* does, however, contain the line 'Anybody on for a game of tennis?'.

• **Anything can happen and probably will ►** A catchphrase associated with the enormously successful BBC radio series *Take It From Here* (1948–59). Other catchphrases to emerge from the programme included 'Black mark, Bentley!', 'Oh, Ron...' 'Yes, Eth?', and 'Wake up at the back there!'

• **anything goes►** A catchphrase meaning 'anything is permissible', heard in America from the 1930s. 'Anything Goes' was the title song of a 1934 Cole Porter musical, chosen intentionally to reflect the liberated moral climate of the times:

> In olden days, a glimpse of stocking
> Was looked upon as something shocking,
> But now, Heaven knows,
> Anything goes.

• **any time, any place, anywhere►** Trade slogan associated with the popular Italian vermouth Martini. It was coined in the early 1970s.

• **Anzac►** The Australian and New Zealand Army Corps, formed in 1915 to serve in World War I. The name was also applied to the cove and beach at Gallipoli on which they landed in April 1915.

• **Anzac Day ►** 25 April, the day on which the dead of both world wars are remembered in Australia and New Zealand. The date is that on which the Anzacs landed at Gallipoli in 1915. Sometimes also called the **One Day of the Year**.

• **Anzac Pact►** The agreement between Australia and New Zealand in 1944 to coordinate their policies on armistices with the Axis powers, the post-war settlement, and various other matters.

• **Anzio►** The site of the bridgehead established by seaborne British and US troops on the Italian coast 30 miles S of Rome in January 1944. Subsequently, the progress of the Allied forces was frustrated for four months by German resistance at the hilltop monastery of **Monte Cassino**. British and Polish troops finally captured the monastery ruins and the Allies were able to break out from Anzio to join with the Fifth Army advancing from the south.

• **AOK** ► A US abbreviation for *all* systems *OK*. It is used to indicate that something is in good working order.

• **apartheid** ► (Afrikaans, apartness) The policy of racial segregation formerly operated by the government of South Africa. It was introduced by the National Party in 1948 to codify in a series of legislative measures the already widespread practice of segregation. These included the Population Registration Act (1950) dividing South Africans into Bantus (Blacks), Coloureds (mixed race), and Whites – the category Asians (Indian and Pakistani) was added later; the Group Areas Act (1951), which designated separate residential and business sections in urban areas, enforced by the Pass Laws requiring non-Whites to carry documents authorizing their presence in restricted areas; and other laws banning mixed marriages, establishing separate education, and prohibiting non-White participation in government. The policy also promoted tribal organizations, and from 1970 enforced Black membership of a 'homeland', effectively disbarring the Black majority from South African citizenship (*see*: Bantustan). Internal opposition to apartheid from the outlawed African National Congress (ANC) and external pressure through sanctions and international isolation led to the gradual weakening of the policy during the 1980s. In 1990 the government legalized the ANC and held discussions with its figurehead, Nelson Mandela. In 1992, following a referendum in which 69% of Whites voted to abolish apartheid, wholesale reform of the constitution began. President F. W. de Klerk announced his regret for the damage done to individuals in the past by the apartheid system. South Africa's first multiracial elections were held in April 1996, resulting in victory for the ANC and Mandela.

• **APB** ► All-Points Bulletin. In US police force jargon, a message sent to all cars, patrolmen, etc., in a particular area, often beginning with the words 'Calling all cars'.

• **apehangers** ► The very high handlebars on motorbikes that were popular in the 1950s with US bikers. In the UK the term was adopted first by the rockers (*see*: mods and rockers) and later by schoolchildren in the era (1970s) of the high-handled Chopper bicycle.

• **aperturismo** ► (Spanish, opening up) The liberalization of Spanish politics and society following the death of General Franco in 1975. The term was first used in Italy in the 1960s to mark certain relaxations in Catholic teaching. *See also*: aggiornamento.

• **Apollo moon programme** ► The US space programme that culminated on 20 July 1969 with the successful first manned moon landing. The most significant missions in the programme were:

Apollo 7 (1968) first manned Apollo flight
Apollo 8 (1968) first manned moon orbit
Apollo 9 (1969) lunar module tested in earth orbit
Apollo 10 (1969) rehearsal of moon landing
Apollo 11 (1969) first manned moon landing
Apollo 12 (1969) second moon landing
Apollo 13 (1970) aborted after explosion
Apollo 14 (1971) third moon landing
Apollo 15 (1971) fourth moon landing
Apollo 16 (1972) fifth moon landing
Apollo 17 (1972) last moon landing.

• **apparatchik** ► Formerly, an official of the Soviet Communist party (Russian, *apparat*); now more loosely any bureaucrat or functionary of a public or private organization.

• **appeasement** ► *See*: Munich; peace in our time; Sudeten crisis.

• **Apple Corps** ► The company founded by the Beatles in 1968 to produce and market the group's records and other merchandise. The company's headquarters in elegant Savile Row offices became a focus of the late 1960s counterculture. Although Beatles records released on the company's Apple label proved as successful as ever, the attempt to merge fashionable values of love and peace with commerce often proved chaotic. John Lennon described the venture as an attempt 'to wrest control from the men in suits'. The Beatles' last public performance took place on the roof of the Apple Building on 30 January 1969.

• **apple polisher** ► A sycophant or toady. Derived from the idea of the model pupil presenting the teacher with a polished apple every day.

• **applesauce** ► An Americanism meaning nonsense, exaggeration, lies, or pretentious language, depending on the context. Its origin lies in the story (possibly apocryphal) that the keepers of small hotels were in the habit of serving large quantities of applesauce with their main courses to augment their small portions of meat or other expensive foods.

• **après la guerre** ► (French, after the war) A catchphrase from World War I used ironically to mean 'never', probably coined by soldiers caught in the seemingly unending stalemate of trench warfare. The true yearning behind the phrase was expressed in the contemporary song 'Après la Guerre':

Après la guerre finie
Oh, we'll go home to Blighty
But won't we be sorry to leave chère Germaine
Après la guerre finie.

• **après moi le deluge**▶ (French, after me, the deluge) The motto of 617 squadron of the RAF. Louis XV of France's comment anticipating the French Revolution was chosen after the squadron's celebrated role in the Dambusters raid of 1943. The squadron's badge depicts a wall pierced by lightning.

• **aquaplaning** ▶ (Latin, *aqua*, water; *plane*, to glide, from Latin *planum*, flat surface) The uncontrollable sliding of a vehicle on a wet road, which results when a layer of water builds up between the moving tyres and the road surface to such an exent that the tyres lose direct contact with the road. Since this phenomenon was first recognized in the early 1960s, measures investigated to combat it have included inserting narrow channels in the road for water to escape and improving the road-holding capacity of tyres. In America the phenomenon is called **hydroplaning**.

• **Aquarius**▶
   **the age of Aquarius** The astrological period, lasting 2000 years, that started at the end of the 20th century. In the 1960s the new age, with its promise of more liberal values and a new optimism, was anticipated enthusiastically by proponents of the alternative society. The phrase is best known from its use in the song 'Aquarius' from the hippie musical *Hair* (1968).

• **aquatel**▶ A marina that includes various facilities, such as restaurants and shops, for the use of travellers by boat. It is derived from the words *aquatic* and *hotel*. An alternative name is **boatel**.

• **Arab League**▶ An organization of Arab states founded in 1945 with the aim of fostering economic, political, and cultural cooperation throughout the Arab world. The League has experienced division on many issues, notably the status of Israel, the formation of a Palestinian state, the Lebanese civil war of the 1970s and 1980s, and the crisis precipitated by Iraq's invasion of Kuwait in 1990.

• **Arab Legion** ▶ A British-led force created in 1920 by Lt. Col. G. F. Peake ('Peake Pasha') from villagers of Transjordan in order to protect the region from raiding Bedouin tribes. From 1939 it was led by Major (later General) John Bagot Glubb ('Glubb Pasha') (1897–1986), who oversaw its expansion during World War II into a considerable and effective fighting unit. Glubb was dismissed by the 20-year-old King Hussein of Jordan in 1956, in part to quash rumours that the Legion's by now legendary commander was in *de facto* control of Jordan.

• **Arab Revolt**▶ An uprising against the Ottoman Turks, rulers of the Arab world since the 16th century, declared in June 1916 by Hussein, Sherif of Mecca. The revolt united Arab tribes, encouraging them to fight for national independence; it was supported by the British and French as part of the war against Turkey. T. E. Lawrence (*see*: Lawrence of Arabia) was active in the campaign, advising Hussein's third son, Feisal.

• **Arab Union**▶ A short-lived agreement for the union of Jordan and Iraq signed in February 1958. It was dissolved by Jordan's King Hussein in the following August following the overthrow of Iraq's King Feisal.

• **Arcadia**▶ The first Washington Conference between Franklin D. Roosevelt and Winston Churchill, which took place at the White House in December 1941 and January 1942. It established joint agreement on the war strategy.

• **Archer**▶ London street slang for £2000 (sometimes also called a **Jeffrey**). It is named after Jeffrey Archer, the novelist, playwright, and former deputy chairman of the Conservative Party, who was raised to the peerage as Lord Archer of Weston-super-Mare in 1992. Archer resigned from the deputy chairmanship after being accused of paying a prostitute, Monica Coughlan, hush money of £2000. In 1987 he won a libel action against *The Star*, who published the story, and received damages of £500,000. In 2000 he was chosen by the Conservative Party as their candidate for Mayor of London, but stood down before the election when evidence came to light that he had arranged for a friend to provide him with a false alibi for the night he was alleged to have spent with Coughlan. *The Star* claimed the return of the £500,000 and the police began a lengthy investigation, which culminated in Archer being convicted of five offences, including perjury and attempting to pervert the course of justice.

• **Archers, The**▶ The 'everyday story of country folk' broadcast several times a week on BBC Radio Four for the past 50 years. This national institution began broadcasting on 1 January 1951; the only member of the cast to have stayed with the programme all the way through has been Norman Painting (1924–  ), who plays Phil Archer, head of the family at the centre of the events in the fictional village of Ambridge. The Post Office produced a special set of stamps in 1989 to mark the 10,000th episode of this, the longest-running of all radio serials. *See also*: Amos 'n' Andy; Blue Peter; Coronation Street; Desert Island Discs; Sooty.

• **Archibald, certainly not!** ▶ The title of a music-hall song by Lee St John, made famous by George Robey before World War I. Until the 1920s it was a well-known catchphrase used as a mock rebuff for sexual advances.

• **Archie** ►

**aim Archie at the Armitage** Australian slang meaning to urinate (of males). Armitage ware is a well-known brand of lavatory bowl. The phrase is a variation of **point Percy at the porcelain**, both being taken from the cartoon series *Barry McKenzie* by Barry Humphries, which appeared in the magazine *Private Eye* in the 1970s.

• **Archie Bunker** ► *See*: Bunker, Archie.

• **Archie Rice** ► *See*: Rice, Archie.

• **Archies** ► In World War I anti-aircraft guns and batteries were thus nicknamed – probably from Archibald, the hero of one of George Robey's songs (*see*: Archibald, certainly not!).

• **arcology** ► A self-contained city or other environment. Designs for such structures have included cities under the sea and in space. The term arcology was coined by the architect Paolo Salieri from the words *arc*hitectural and *ec*ology.

• **Arcos Raid** ► A British police raid on the Soviet trade delegation, Arcos, which took place on 24 May 1927. Documents seized were claimed to prove that Soviet diplomats were engaged in spying but no real evidence of this was found. However, the incident provided a pretext for the UK to sever diplomatic relations with the Soviets, Soviet diplomats being expelled from London.

• **Ardennes Offensive** or **Battle of the Bulge** ► In World War II, the advance by German forces in the Ardennes region of Belgium that succeeded in breaking through Allied lines (in an attempt to reach the coast at Antwerp). The surprise attack started in foggy conditions on 16 December 1944 and by the end of the month a German salient (or 'bulge') up to 96 km (60 mi) deep had formed. By the end of January 1945 the offensive had been repulsed and the Germans driven back to their original positions. The squandering of resources in this last offensive of the war hastened Germany's defeat.

• **argie** ► British slang for an Argentinian, used in the tabloid press and by the armed forces during the Falklands Conflict in 1982.

• **Ariel** ► A series of six UK satellites launched in America between 1962 and 1979 to carry scientific instruments into space. The first Ariel, launched on 26 April 1962, was the UK's first space satellite.

• **ark** ► A large greenhouse-type structure in which a self-sufficient environment can be created, allowing food, etc., to be grown in otherwise hostile surroundings. Such self-contained environments are being developed for use in arid climates and possibly as life-support systems in space. The more complex versions can be used to provide several microclimates in which a wide range of habitats can be created.

• **Arkle** ► A near-legendary steeplechaser that captured the heart of the nation by his exploits on the race track in the 1960s. Trained by Tom Dreaper and ridden by Pat Taafe, the gelding won three Cheltenham Gold Cups, the King George VI Chase, and the Irish Grand National, among other famous victories. His owner, the Duchess of Westminster, never allowed him to race in Aintree's fearsome Grand National. His racing career was ended by injury in December 1966.

• **Armani** ► A designer clothes label, created by the Italian fashion designer Giorgio Armani (1934– ), that achieved prominence during the power-dressing yuppie era of the 1980s. After working for several years as a freelance for other manufacturers, Armani launched his first menswear collection in 1974. A year later he ventured into women's wear with a range of elegantly tailored clothes using traditional menswear fabrics. Owing largely to the rapid expansion in the number of female executives and managers at this time, these clothes enjoyed a remarkable success. Armani also became famous as the preferred wear of many Hollywood stars on Oscar night; it remains one of the most celebrated designer labels in the world.

> Fashion is what goes out of fashion. Style is timeless. – GIORGIO ARMANI, quoted in *The Guardian*, 17 June 2001.

• **armchair quarterback** or **Monday morning quarterback** ► A US expression for someone who has no active involvement in a particular field but still freely offers opinions and criticisms. Other versions include **armchair sportsman** and **armchair traveller**, all being derived from **armchair general**, a World War II term still in common use. The 'Monday morning' version refers to fans who use hindsight to point out the mistakes made by players in weekend American football matches.

• **Armistice Day** ► 11 November, the day set aside from 1919 to 1945 to commemorate the fallen in World War I, marked by a two-minute silence at 11 a.m. and appropriate civil and religious ceremonies. The armistice ending the war was signed at the eleventh hour of the eleventh day of the eleventh month in 1918. In 1946 the name was changed to Remembrance Day and in 1956 the commemoration was moved to the second Sunday in November. The custom of observing silence on 11 November itself was revived in 1996. In America and Canada, 11 November is a legal holiday, its name being changed to **Veteran's Day** in 1954.

• **Armstrong murder**► A notorious 1922 case in which Herbert Rowse Armstrong, a retired army major and solicitor of Hay-on-Wye, was convicted of murdering his wife and of attempting to murder a fellow solicitor in the town, Oswald Martin. Armstrong slowly poisoned his wife with small repeated doses of arsenic but his exploits aroused the suspicions of a local doctor, who reported Armstrong to the authorities.

• **Arnhem**► A city in the Netherlands and the site of a disastrous battle for a strategic bridge across the Rhine during September 1944. The mass parachute drop of the First British Airborne Division was part of a larger Allied assault on key river crossings. However, the planned reinforcements by a British armoured division failed to arrive as they were unable to break through German lines; in addition, bad weather prevented air reinforcement and German resistance was well organized. The British reached the northern end of Arnhem bridge but their heavy casualties made retreat inevitable. Some three-quarters of the 10,000-strong British force were killed or captured, and the defeat dashed hopes of a speedy Allied advance before the winter. The disaster is the subject of the well-known war film *A Bridge Too Far* (1977).

• **aromatherapy**► The use of plant extracts and fragrant oils to sooth tension and promote health, beauty, and mental well-being. Aromatherapy is part of the alternative medicine movement favouring natural remedies for common physical and mental ailments. The art of aromatherapy originated in classical Greece and was revived in the 1930s, when it was discovered that the oils of certain plants accelerated healing.

• **Arsène Lupin**► *See*: Lupin, Arsène.

• **Art Brut**► (French, raw art) The primitive but often striking art objects created by prisoners, children, psychiatric patients, and others outside the artistic mainstream. The term was coined by the French painter Jean Dubuffet (1901–85), who organized an exhibition of such works in 1947. Art Brut influenced many post-war painters, notably those of the Cobra group.

• **Art Deco**► The decorative style of the 1920s and 1930s in painting, glass, pottery, silverware, furniture, etc. It is distinguished by bold colours, geometrical lines and shapes, and lack of symmetry. It takes its name from the Exposition Internationale des Arts Décoratifs et Industriels Modernes held in Paris in 1925. The style arose in deliberate contrast to the earlier (1890–1910) Art Nouveau.

• **Art Nouveau**► A decorative style that pervaded the visual arts in the UK, France, Germany, Austria, Belgium, Spain, and America in the 1890s and 1900s. It was characterized by designs based on undulating lines and biomorphic shapes. In Britain it developed from the Arts and Crafts movement of William Morris and is particularly associated with the work of Charles Rennie Mackintosh (1868–1928), the Scottish architect and designer. On the Continent leading examples of Art Nouveau are the Parisian Métro designs of Hector Guimard (1867–1942), the extravagant Barcelona flats and hotels of Antonio Gaudí (1852–1926), and the Belgian stores and houses of Victor Horta (1861–1947). A parallel effect in glassware was achieved by René Lalique (*see*: Lalique glass).

• **Arthur Rank**► A bank. A British working-class rhyming-slang expression based on the name of the industrialist and film magnate J. Arthur Rank (1888–1972). However, a **J. Arthur** is rhyming slang for an incidence of masturbation (a wank). *See*: Rank Organization.

• **artificial intelligence**► (AI) The study of ways in which a computer can be built and programmed to perform tasks that, in a human being, would require intelligence. The idea of 'thinking machines' was first put forward by the mathematician Alan Turing (1912–54) who suggested what is known as the **Turing test**. In this, a person sits in a room and is told that he can communicate with a separate room through a computer keyboard. In the other room there is either a person or a computer programmed to answer questions. The subject asks a number of questions and receives replies. Would he be able to tell whether the other room contained a person or a computer? If, after a number of trials, the subject thought that the computer was a person, then it can be argued that the machine was thinking. However, answering questions in a sensible way is only one part of intelligence and a considerable amount of work has gone into the study of artificial intelligence since the 1950s. At one level, this simply consists of problem solving. Programs, known as 'expert systems', have been written to perform tasks that need logical analysis of a large amount of data – as in medical diagnosis. Programs for playing games, such as chess, have also been produced. More difficult is the production of programs that actually 'think' – for example, in solving or even postulating mathematical theorems. Even more contentious is the idea, put forward by some, that it might in principle be possible for a computer to experience emotions.

• **Art Informel** ► *See*: tachisme.

• **Aryan myth** ► The doctrine propounded by the Nazis that power was the prerogative of the Nordic-Aryan race because of its 'pure' blood. Other races were, by virtue of their 'impurity', inferior and fit only for subservient roles in society. In particular, the Jewish-Semitic race was regarded as a destructive force – a 'counter-race' – to be exterminated. Many of these ideas predated World War I, occurring in the writings of Joseph A. de Gobineau and Houston Stewart Chamberlain amongst others, but during the 1920s and 1930s they were adopted by the Nazis to create a racist ideology of the most odious kind.

• **ASDIC** ► Admiralty Submarine Detection Investigation Committee, an early form of sonar submarine detection that originated in 1917 and was used on British naval vessels towards the end of World War I.

• **ASEAN** ► *See*: SEATO.

• **ASH** ► Action on Smoking and Health. A pressure group in the UK that promotes antismoking measures.

• **ash-can school** ► A group of US painters active from *c.* 1908 to 1914, whose work concentrated on portraying the reality of urban street life. The leading member of the group was Robert Henri; other members included William James Glackens, John Sloan, George Benjamin Luks, and Everett Shinn, all of whom had worked as artist-reporters on the *Philadelphia Press*.

• **Asian flu** ► A strain of influenza caused by the myxovirus $A_2$, which is thought to have originated in China in early 1957 and by mid-year had circled the globe.

• **A side** ► In the days of vinyl records, the most commercially promising side of a pop single, *i.e.* the recording intended to enter the charts. A 'double A side' single was one with potential chart material on both sides. *See also*: B side.

• **A6 murder** ► The controversial murder case involving James Hanratty, a petty burglar, who in 1962 was convicted of murdering research scientist Michael Gregsten. The body of Gregsten was discovered in a lay-by on the A6 at Deadman's Hill near Bedford, in August 1961. Hanratty was convicted largely on the strength of his identification by Gregsten's girlfriend, Valerie Storie, who had been raped and seriously wounded by the couple's attacker. Hanratty was hanged on 4 April, in spite

of doubts about his conviction expressed by some. Concern over the outcome of the case contributed to the abolition of the death penalty in the UK. These doubts have grown over the years, with the emergence of several witnesses who claim to have seen Hanratty in north Wales at the time of the murder. After further investigation, the Criminal Cases Review Commission referred the case to the Court of Appeal in 1997. However, in 2001 DNA taken from Hanratty's exhumed corpse was found to match perfectly strands found on Storie's clothes. Campaigners for Hanratty's innocence maintain that this proves little, because some of his clothing was confiscated in 1961 and cross contamination could easily have occurred at some point in the intervening 40 years. The appeal still waits to be heard.

• **Aslan** ► *See*: Narnia.

• **asleep at the switch** ► A derisive nickname for the American Defense Medal, given to those in the armed forces on Pearl Harbor Day (7 December 1941). It derives from a US expression indicating a failure in alertness to danger. In railroad terminology, 'to switch a train' was to transfer it to another set of rails by operating a switch. Failure to do this at the right time might well lead to a catastrophe. *See*: dead man's handle.

• **asphalt jungle** ► *See*: concrete jungle.

• **aspirin** ► An analgesic in tablet or other form, consisting of acetylsalicyclic acid (derived from the bark of the willow, *Salix*). The name began life in 1899 as a tradename belonging to the German firm of Bayer, but was later ruled to have passed into the public domain. It was derived from the German *Acetylirte Spirsäure* (acetylated spiraeic acid); an alternative source of salicylic acid was the meadowsweet, *Spiraea ulmaria*.

• **Assassination is the extreme form of censorship** ► Observation by George Bernard Shaw in his play *The Shewing-Up of Blanco Posnet*. *See*: Jackal, the; Kennedy assassination; OAS; Sarajevo assassination.

• **assemblage** ► A work of art that incorporates pre-formed items, such as pieces of wood, cloth, or household refuse to create a three-dimensional collage. The first such works were the cubist collages (*see*: cubism) created by Picasso and Braque in 1910–13. The term was first used by the artist Jean Dubuffet in the 1950s.

• **assertiveness training** ► The promotion of a submissive individual's self-confidence so that he or she may adopt a more assertive role at work or in normal social intercourse. Such courses of training, which include techniques ranging from provocation to mutual support, became increasingly popular in the 1970s and 1980s, especially among the business community and women's groups.

• **asset-backed fund**► A fund in which money is invested in stocks and shares, property, works of art, etc., rather than being loaned to a bank to earn interest. In the second half of the 20th century inflation was such a dominant influence on commercial activities that pension (and other) funds needed to be asset-backed in order to keep pace with it.

• **asset stripping**► The practice of buying a company whose shares are valued at less than their asset value (*i.e.* the total value of a company's assets less its liabilities divided by the number of ordinary shares issued), with the object of selling off the company's most valuable assets and closing down the remaining shell or revitalizing its management and selling its shares at a profit. The practice was particularly prevalent in the UK and America in the decade following World War II, when rising property values made the shares of many companies look very cheap. Although the asset stripper and his associates may make enormous profits from these deals, many of the employees may lose their jobs, the other shareholders may come off badly, and the interests of the suppliers, customers, and creditors may be totally ignored. For these reasons asset stripping is now strongly deprecated by governments and company accountants have a responsibility for seeing that the assets of a business are not undervalued in their accounts.

• **Astaire, Fred** ► Frederick Austerlitz (1899–1987), the near-legendary film and stage dancer. Although Astaire's career began inauspiciously with his first audition verdict, 'Can't act. Can't sing. Slightly bald. Can dance a little', he went on to delight two generations of filmgoers with his effortless and inventive dance routines. Both Balanchine and Nureyev described him as the world's greatest dancer; the film critic C. A. Lejeune said of him '...in his loose legs, his shy grin, or perhaps the anxious diffidence of his manner, he has found the secret of persuading the world.' In many of his films he was partnered by the almost equally legendary Ginger Rogers (1911–95).

• **Astérix** ► The diminutive Gallic warrior who is the hero of the comic strip adventures originally created by Goscinny and Uderzo in 1959. With his friend Obélix, he has survived multiple translations (the English versions have been much admired), extensive commercialization, and mainly weak imitations in the cinema and on television, to become one of the most lastingly popular of cartoon characters. In 1969 a national survey reported that two-thirds of the French population had read at least one of Astérix's adventures.

• **astrobug** ► A sample of bacteria or other microscopic organisms that is sent into space for experimental purposes.

• **astrodome** ► **1.** An indoor stadium with a translucent domed roof. The first was built in Houston, Texas in 1965, and covers a playing area large enough for baseball and American football. The plastic-panelled dome has a span of 196m (642 ft), has seating for 66,000 people in six tiers, and the interior is air-conditioned to 23°C. **2.** A transparent dome on the upper side of an aircraft fuselage through which astronomical or other observations can be made.

• **astromonk** ► Any one of several monkeys sent into space in the 1950s and 1960s in order to observe the likely effects of such travel upon humans.

• **astronaut** ► (Latin, *astrum*, star; *nauta*, sailor) One who voyages in space. This word, first used in 1929, emerged from the realms of science fiction after the first manned spacecraft flight by Major Yuri Gagarin of the Soviet Union in April 1961. The first non-Soviet astronaut was the American Alan Bartlett Shepard (1923–98), who completed a 15-minute space flight in May 1961, 23 days after Gagarin's flight. *See*: cosmonaut.

• **Astroturf** ► Trademark for a type of artificial playing surface used for football pitches, etc. Such pitches were first introduced in America in the 1960s; the name is derived from the Astrodome indoor ball park in Houston, where the first such pitch was laid.

• **Aswan High Dam**► A dam 111 m (364 ft) high across the Nile at Aswan, Egypt, financed by the Soviet Union and completed in 1970. The creation of its reservoir, **Lake Nasser**, entailed the resettling of 90,000 Egyptian peasants and Sudanese Nubian nomads as well as the repositioning of the ancient Egyptian Temple of Abu Simbel. The dam allows the annual Nile flood to be controlled for irrigation and to generate prodigious amounts of electricity. It lies 6.5 km (4 mi) upstream from the earlier Aswan Dam (1902), once one of the largest dams in the world.

• **asylum seekers**► *See*: DP; economic migrant.

• **Atatürk** ► Father of the Turks. A surname adopted in 1934 by Mustapha Kemal (1881–1938), the founder of modern Turkey, when all Turks were made to assume surnames. In the 1920s and 1930s he ruthlessly set out to Westernize the republic he had established in 1923. European dress was imposed, polygamy abolished, women enfranchised, and the Roman script replaced the Arabic.

• **ATB** ► Advanced technology bomber. *See*: Stealth bomber.

• **atheists** ►
**There are no atheists in foxholes** Preaching a sermon during World War II, Father W. T. Cummings, a US army chaplain in Bataan, used the phrase 'there are no atheists in foxholes', meaning that no one can deny the existence of God in the face of imminent death. This is, of course, the view of a theist.

• **athlete's foot** ► The popular name for the skin condition tinea pedis affecting the feet and causing excessive itchiness between the toes. The name was coined during the late 1920s in the course of an advertising campaign for a product used as a remedy for the condition. It alludes to the fact that the damp floors of changing rooms and showers in gyms, sports halls, and swimming pools, where people often go barefoot, are a leading source of the infection.

• **Atlantic, Battle of the** ► The German campaign waged against Allied shipping in the Atlantic during World War II in order to disrupt vital supplies to the UK. Ships of the Merchant Navy, crewed by volunteers and with Royal Navy escorts, braved the convoy routes from Canada and America and the risk of attack by German U-boats. The battle was most intense during 1940–43, but Britain's Atlantic lifeline was kept intact, largely owing to technical improvements in radar and ASDIC and by the increasing scale of US naval protection. By 1943 German U-boat losses had reached unsustainable levels and the threat to shipping was on the wane.

• **Atlantic Charter** ► During World War II, President Roosevelt and Winston Churchill met at sea (14 August 1941) and made this eight-point declaration of the principles on which peace was to be based, consequent upon Allied victory. These included the total abolition of Nazism and the freedom of liberated peoples to choose their own governments. It can be compared with President Wilson's Fourteen Points in World War I.

• **Atlanticism** ► The tradition of close cooperation in international affairs between America and the states of Western Europe, especially the UK.

• **Atlantic Wall** ► The name given by the Germans in World War II to their defences along the Atlantic coast of Europe, built to resist invasion.

• **Atlas, Charles** ► Stagename of Angelo Siciliano (1894–1974), who became famous after winning 'The World's Most Perfectly Developed Man' title in a US body-building contest in 1922. He consolidated this success by launching mail-order body-building courses under the slogan 'You too can have a body like mine'. Charles Atlas himself was a fine advertisement for such courses, having been a 'seven stone weakling' until he devised his body-building technique, called 'Dynamic Tension', after watching a lion flexing its muscles at the zoo.

• **atom** ►
**There is no evil in the atom, only in men's souls** A remark made in 1952 by the US statesman Adlai Stevenson (1900–65). It has since been quoted many times by apologists for various nuclear programmes. *See*: Manhattan Project.

• **atom bomb** ► (A-bomb) A weapon that uses the fission of nuclear material to cause a massive explosion. The first such bombs were developed by America in World War II and dropped on the Japanese cities of Hiroshima (6 August 1945) and Nagasaki (9 August 1945). With an explosive power equivalent to 20,000 tons of TNT, the bombs killed perhaps 200,000 people and led to the rapid surrender of Japan. *See*: Manhattan Project; nuclear weapon.

• **attention all shipping** ► The words with which gale warnings and other items of maritime meteorological information are preceded in broadcasts by BBC radio.

• **Attila of Sunnybrook Farm** ► *See*: World's Sweetheart.

• **Attila the Hen** ► Nickname for Margaret Thatcher; a play on the name of the 5th-century tyrant Attila the Hun, it was probably coined by the Labour politician Denis Healey. *See*: Iron Lady.

• **attrit** ► In war, to erode the capability of a hostile force. This back formation from 'attrition' came to general attention during the Gulf War of 1991 but had been in use among US airmen since the 1960s. The word is also used as a noun to mean a casualty.

• **A₂** ► The virus identified as the cause of Asian flu.

• **ATV** ► *See*: all-terrain vehicle.

• **Aubrey holes** ► A series of 56 holes that mark the outer ring of Stonehenge. They were named in 1959 in honour of the antiquarian John Aubrey (1626–97), who was the first to identify them.

• **Aunt Edna** ► A fictional theatregoer conceived by Terence Rattigan as the epitome of the matinée audience he had to please. She later became a widely recognized personalization of all the forces that the new rebellious kitchen sink generation of writers of the 1950s sought to displace. Rattigan introduced her in his preface to the second volume of his *Collected Plays* (1953):

> A nice respectable, middle-class, middle-aged maiden lady, with time on her hands and the money to help her pass it...Let us call her Aunt Edna...Aunt Edna is universal...She is also immortal.

• **Auntie** ▸ A popular nickname for the British Broadcasting Corporation (BBC). It was acquired by the corporation in the 1950s when the apparently more adventurous commercial TV stations first started transmitting in the UK. The BBC responded, however, by adopting the nickname as a compliment rather than a criticism. The comedian Arthur Askey claimed to have been the first to use the name for the BBC. The Australian Broadcasting Commission shares the same nickname. *See also*: Beeb.

• **Aunt Jane** ▸ US slang for any enthusiastic Black female member of a church congregation, noted for her uninhibited participation in religious services. *See also*: Aunt Tom.

• **Aunt Nelly** ▸ Belly. A British rhyming-slang term, current in the 1950s when 'belly' was still considered an unmentionable word by many people.

• **Aunt Tom** ▸ A derogatory expression for a woman who does not support the aims of the feminist movement. It derives from the use of 'Uncle Tom' as a derogatory name for a Black man who behaves in a servile fashion towards Whites (from Harriet Beecher Stowe's *Uncle Tom's Cabin*, 1852).

• **au pair** ▸ (French, on equal terms) A young woman from abroad who is given free board and lodging (and sometimes a small amount of cash) in return for help around the house, looking after children, etc. The practice of taking in au pairs by middle-class families as a substitute for domestic servants became widespread after World War II; it was originally a German idea.

• **Auschwitz** or **Auschwitz-Birkenau** ▸ The largest of Nazi Germany's concentration camps, situated near the Polish town of Oświęcim in Galacia. The complex, commanded by Rudolf Franz Hoess, consisted of three camps: the first, reserved for mainly Polish prisoners-of-war, was established by Heinrich Himmler in April 1940; Auschwitz II, or Birkenau, was added in October 1942, and became the main extermination centre with large 'bathhouses' (disguised gas chambers) which could hold 2000 people at a time, cellars (*Leichenkeller*) for stor-

ing corpses, and ovens for cremating the remains; Auschwitz III was established in May 1942 to furnish the nearby chemical and synthetic rubber manufacturer I. G. Farben with slave labour. Jews were rounded up and transported here by rail from every corner of Europe. On arrival the young, old, and infirm were 'selected' for immediate extermination, while the rest earned brief respite from death in the labour gangs. Estimates of the numbers of men, women, and children who perished in this camp alone from gassing, medical experiments (*see*: Angel of Death), and forced labour vary between one and four million.

> It was a denial of God, it was a denial of man. It was the destruction of the world in miniature form. – RABBI HUGO GRYN, Auschwitz survivor, BBC interview 1982.

• **Austin 7** ▸ *See*: baby Austin.

• **Australia for the White Man** ▸ Slogan used by the Australian newspaper *The Bulletin* from 1908 to 1960, emphasizing its support for the White Australia policy.

• **auteurism** ▸ An approach to film direction that developed in the late 1950s and 1960s. In contrast to the traditional collaborative approach of Hollywood, it involved the director exercising authority over all aspects of the movie-making process in order to convey an essentially personal vision. the so-called *politique des auteurs* ('auteur policy') was first expounded by François Truffaut in the influential film journal *Cahiers du Cinéma* (Jan 1954).

• **autobahn** ▸ *See* motorway.

• **autochondriac** ▸ A facetious and usually derogatory term for a person who is obsessed with the condition or appearance of his or her car. The autochondriac is constantly hearing worrying noises when driving the car and frequently sees scratches, imaginary or otherwise, on the car's paintwork.

• **autocide** ▸ Deliberate self-destruction achieved by crashing one's car. From *automobile* and *suicide*.

• **autocue** ▸ A device, hidden from the audience, that displays a text to a speaker or performer as a memory aid. They are used mainly by politicians and television presenters to enable them to be word-perfect without having to look down at notes or a script. Closely related is the **Teleprompter**, which scrolls words on a screen situated below the television camera that the performer is addressing.

• **autogiro** ▸ An aircraft with a freely rotating horizontal wing to provide lift and a motor-driven propeller for forward motion. It was superseded by the helicopter after World War II, which, having a motorized rotor, is capable of vertical takeoff and landing.

• **automatic pilot** or **autopilot►** A device that controls an aircraft or other vehicle without the need for human intervention. Modern computerized autopilots can execute complex manoeuvres, flight plans, and even landings and takeoffs. The manufacturers of these systems claim they are fail-safe and that there is no need for concern about computer error. Such devices can also control ships, submarines, missiles and spacecraft.

A person is now said to be 'acting on autopilot' when he or she is carrying out a familiar task without much conscious thought.

• **autopia ►** An area of a city dominated by the needs of the motorist, as opposed to those of pedestrians. From *auto* and ut*opia*.

• **autopista**; **autoroute**; **autostrada ►** *See*: motorway.

• **Auxis►** *See*: Black and Tans.

• **avant-garde ►** (French, vanguard) In the forefront of new ideas or techniques, especially used of writers, artists, musicians, etc. Previously a military expression, the term was first used in this way in the 1900s and came to be particularly associated with the more adventurous European cinema directors.

• **aversion therapy►** A method used in psychiatry to break a patient's harmful habit or addiction, such as drug-taking, alcoholism, or smoking, by associating this with something painful or unpleasant. It can involve the use of mild electric shocks or the prescribing of drugs that will produce unpleasant effects if combined with alcoholic drink, heroin, etc. *See also*: behaviour therapy.

• **AWACS ►** Airborne Warning and Control System. A sophisticated radar and communications system installed in converted Boeing 707s, with a far greater range than ground-based radar stations. AWACS can detect potentially hostile air or ground

activity and coordinate the necessary offensive and defensive measures.

• **awayday ► 1.** An excursion or outing, a day trip. **2.** A single dose of LSD or other hallucinogenic drug (a pun on trip). Both senses derive from the cheap one-day excursion ticket formerly available on British Rail.

• **awful ►**
   **ooh, you are awful** Catchphrase popularized in the 1970s by a drag character called Mandy in TV shows starring the comedian Dick Emery (1917–83). The usual continuation of the phrase, accompanied by a clout with a substantial handbag, was 'but I like you'.

• **Axis►** The Rome–Berlin Axis: the alliance of the Fascist states of Germany and Italy (October 1936), described by Mussolini as 'an axis round which all European states animated by the will to collaboration and peace can also assemble.' It became the **Rome–Berlin–Tokyo Axis** in 1937. *See also*: Pact of Steel.

• **aye, aye, that's yer lot►** A catchphrase associated with the comedian and variety artist Jimmy Wheeler, who in the 1940s and 1950s used it to sign off at the end of his routine.

• **ay thang yew►** A rendering of 'I thank you', one of the many catchphrases of the British comedian Arthur Askey (1900–82), who first introduced it to a wide audience in the BBC radio show *Band Waggon*, which started in 1938. The phrase was apparently borrowed from London's bus conductors, thanking their customers for buying a ticket.

• **Azania ►** An alternative name for South Africa, sometimes used by Black political activists during the apartheid era in that country. It was originally the name of an Iron Age civilization that occupied the area between 500 AD and 1500 AD. Evelyn Waugh used the name Azania for the imaginary African kingdom in his novel *Black Mischief* (1932).

• **Aztec two-step ►** *See*: Montezuma's revenge.

# B

• **BA** ► US slang for an aggressive person, someone with a 'bad attitude': a 'bad ass'. These initials were used for the name of the aggressive Black hero B. A. Barracas, played by Mr T, in the popular TV series *The A-Team* in the 1980s.

• **Baader-Meinhof gang** ► *See:* Red Army Faction.

• **Ba'athists** ► Members of a radical Arab movement (the Arab Socialist Ba'ath Party) founded in Damascus in 1943. They advocate the formation of a single socialist Arab nation and currently hold power in both Syria and Iraq (although the Syrian and Iraqi wings have been divided since the 1970s). The Arabic word *Ba'ath* means 'renaissance'.

• **Babar the Elephant** ► The main character in a series of illustrated children's books created in 1931 by the French writer and illustrator Jean de Brunhoff (d. 1937). Babar rules over a luscious tropical kingdom with the help of his queen consort, Celeste, and his friend the Little Old Lady. His capital is at Celesteville. The books have been translated into English and many other languages.

• **Babbitt** ► The leading character in Sinclair Lewis's novel of this name (1922). He is a prosperous realtor in the western city of Zenith, a simple likeable fellow with faint aspirations to culture that are forever smothered in the futile bustle of US business life. Drive (which takes him nowhere), hustle (by which he saves no time), and efficiency (which does not enable him to do anything) are the keynotes of his life. The name is sometimes used to typify the businessman of orthodox outlook and virtues, with corresponding limitations. *See also:* Main Street.

• **Babe** ► Nickname of George Herman Ruth (1895–1948), US professional baseball player. He earned the name in his first team, which he joined when he was only 19. He was also called the **Bambino** by his fans of Italian origin. *See also:* Murderers' Row.

• **Babi Yar** ► A ravine N of Kiev in Ukraine, which in World War II became the site of a mass grave for over 100,000 victims of German exterminations. Most of the victims, killed between 1941 and 1943, were Jews (*see:* holocaust) who were unjustly blamed for a bomb attack on German troops stationed in Kiev. When the Germans retreated, the site of the mass grave was concealed and Babi Yar only came to international attention in 1961 with the publication of a poem of the same name by the acclaimed Soviet poet Yevgeny Yevtushenko. Dmitry Shostakovich subsequently set the poem to music and incorporated it in his 13th symphony (1962); both artists were reprimanded by the authorities who were reluctant to draw attention to Jewish victims of the Nazis. A memorial erected on the site in 1966 omitted any acknowledgment of the Jews killed there.

• **babushkaphobia** ► A modern woman's aversion to the traditional role of grandmother (Russian *babushka*, grandmother). It reflects the view held by increasing numbers of women who, having raised a family, wish to re-establish careers and enjoy their independence free from the constraints of baby-minding and child-rearing.

• **baby Austin** ► The nickname for a small seven-horsepower family car (the **Austin 7**), first produced in 1921 by the British engineer and industrialist Herbert Austin (later Baron Austin; 1866–1941) at his Longbridge works in Birmingham. Following the lead of Henry Ford in America, the Austin 7 was the first mass-produced car to be manufactured in Europe and greatly influenced British light-car design. *See also:* Tin Lizzie.

• **baby battering** ► *See:* child abuse.

• **Baby Bell** ► *See:* Ma Bell.

• **baby boom** ► An increase in the birth rate, especially the sharp increase in Europe and America after World War II, when servicemen returned to their wives. The children born in this period, who came to maturity during the upheavals of the 1960s and now occupy many positions of power and influence, are often known as the **baby boomers**.

• **baby bust** ► A sudden marked decline in the birthrate; a 1980s colloquial term modelled on baby boom. The post-World War II baby boom was followed in Western countries by a fall in the birthrate, which began in the mid-1960s. The adverse economic and social implications of this trend include an overall shift in the age structure of society, a declining workforce, and a potential reduction in consumer markets.

• **baby in a microwave** ► *See*: urban legends.

• **baby-kisser** ► A politician, so called from the 1940s onwards for the ubiquitous photographs seen during election campaigns of politicians making the acquaintance of various younger members of their constituencies in the belief that this will help endear them to the voting public.

• **Babylon** ► **1.** Slang for mainstream White society, seen as racist, corrupt, and oppressive. Originally the word, with all its biblical connotations, was used by the Rastafarians but its use has spread to White youths also through the widespread popularity of reggae music. **2. The Babylon** The police force, seen as the instrument of authority in a racist society. A more specific application of sense 1 above.

• **baby-sitting** ► **1.** Staying with someone to make sure they come to no harm while they are taking mind-altering drugs, particularly hallucinogens. **2.** A journalistic term for guarding an informant in order to prevent other journalists from picking up the story.

• **backdoor man** ► **1.** US expression for a secret lover, particularly a married woman's secret lover, which came originally from Black slang of the 1950s. It implies that the lover leaves by the back door as the husband arrives home at the front door. 'Back Door Man' is a well-known blues song recorded by The Doors in 1968. **2.** A heterosexual man who practises anal intercourse. **3.** Australian slang for a homosexual.

• **back end** ► A late stage in the processing of nuclear fuel in which used fuel is separated into recyclable uranium and plutonium and radioactive waste. The phrase has since been applied to the final stage of any project (especially in a financial context).

• **Backfire bomber** ► A NATO codename assigned to the Soviet-made Tupolev V-G swing-wing long-range bomber that was first deployed in the 1970s.

• **backpacking** ► Travelling cheaply with one's clothes, sleeping bag, tent, and sometimes food carried in a rucksack or other large pack (**backpack**). Backpackers are often students taking a gap year or travelling during their summer vacation. Some travel alone, while others go in small groups.

• **backroom boys** ► The unpublicized scientists and technicians in World War II, who contributed so much to the development of scientific warfare. The term has since been applied generally to any anonymous workers. The phrase comes from a speech by Lord Beaverbrook on war production (24 March 1941): 'To whom must praise be given...to the boys in the backroom.' Beaverbrook no doubt recalled Marlene Dietrich's song 'See What the Boys in the Backroom Will Have', from the film *Destry Rides Again* (1939). Nigel Balchin provided a further tribute to these workers in his novel *The Small Back Room* (1943).

• **backstage** ► The area behind or away from the stage in a theatre, including the wings, the dressing-rooms, etc. A 'backstage' film or stage show (often a musical) is one based upon life backstage.

• **backs to the wall** ► On the defensive against heavy odds. Someone beset with foes tries to get his back against a wall to prevent attack from behind.

> Every position must be held to the last man: there must be no retirement. With our backs to the wall, and believing in the justice of our cause, each of us must fight on to the end.
> – DOUGLAS HAIG, ordering his troops to resist a German attack in World War I.

The phrase is sometimes used as a jocular warning that one is in the presence of a homosexual.

• **back to basics** ► Back to first principles; a phrase first heard in the 1950s. It was adopted as a slogan by the Conservative government of John Major in the mid-1990s, to indicate their approval of a return to old-fashioned moral values. However, the campaign was fatally undermined by a series of sexual and financial scandals affecting the Conservative Party and the phrase quickly became a laughing stock (*see*: sleaze).

• **back to square one** ► Back to the starting point. The phrase was popularized by early radio commentaries on football matches; in order to make the game easier to follow, a diagram of the pitch, divided into numbered squares, was provided for listeners.

• **back to the drawing board** ► A phrase indicating that it is necessary to rethink the whole design or concept. Probably first used by aircraft designers when a plan was shown to be faulty and had to be rethought.

• **backward masking** ► In music recording, a technique for incorporating a hidden message in a song so that it can only be made out when the track is played backwards. Rock groups have sometimes included such messages (often ribald) as a joke or a gimmick. The issue hit the headlines in the 1980s, when Christian fundamentalists in America began to claim that rock groups were using the technique to smuggle Satanic messages into their songs. Although the supposed messages would be unintelligible to anyone not in the habit of playing their records backwards, campaigners argued that they could still have a 'subliminal' effect. The British rock group Judas Priest was unsuccessfully sued after two fans committed suicide while listening to an album that allegedly contained such messages.

• **bacteriophobia** ▶ An unreasoning fear of bacteria. Sufferers are obsessed with avoiding 'dirt' of any kind and wash themselves frequently. This is often interpreted as evidence of a guilt complex and is sometimes called the **Lady Macbeth syndrome**, in reference to that character's obsessive hand washing in Shakespeare's play.

• **bad** ▶ Good, excellent. Originally associated with Black US jazz musicians in the 1950s, it became widely used by the young in the 1970s and 1980s. Bad in this sense is usually pronounced 'b-a-a-d'. The superlative form is **baddest**. *See also*: wicked.

> She had on a little black cocktail number and the baddest suede, pointy, red shoes you ever saw. – BEN ELTON, *Stark* (1989).

• **Badminton horse trials** ▶ A competition held annually in April in the park of Badminton House, the seat of the dukes of Beaufort in Avon. It is a three-day event consisting of a dressage stage, a speed and endurance stage over steeplechase and cross-country courses, and a showjumping stage on the final day. The trials were started in 1952.

• **bad news** ▶ A difficult or disliked person. Originally a US expression, it has been used in the UK since the 1960s.

• **Baedeker Raids** ▶ A phrase used in Britain to describe the German air attacks on 29 April 1942. These were deliberately targeted on historic towns, such as those listed in the Baedeker series of guidebooks for tourists (*e.g.* Bath, Canterbury, Norwich).

• **Bafta awards** ▶ Awards presented annually to the film and TV industry by the British Association of Film and Television Arts. The Association was created in 1959 from the earlier British Film Academy (founded 1946).

• **bag** ▶ A person's particular taste, area of interest or expertise. This sense originated in US jazz slang, where it usually referred to a musician's personal style of playing, *e.g.* 'playing in a big band was not his bag'.

• **bagel** ▶ The Yiddish name for a hard round roll, simmered in hot water before baking and then glazed with egg white. They are eaten with lox and cream cheese, especially by Jews in New York City. The Yiddish word is derived from the German *Beugel*, a round loaf. Although bagels were well

known to European Jews, and were traditionally served with hard-boiled eggs after a funeral, their association with lox and New York Jews began in the 20th century.

• **baggies** ▶ US surfing jargon dating from the 1960s for the wide long shorts worn by surfers.

• **Baghdad Pact** ▶ A treaty for military and economic cooperation originally signed in 1955 between Iraq and Turkey. It was later joined by Iran, Pakistan, and the UK. In 1959 Iraq withdrew, America became an associate member, and the organization was renamed the **Central Treaty Organization** (CENTO). After the fall of the Shah of Iran in 1979, Iran withdrew from the pact and the organization was dissolved.

• **bag lady** ▶ A female tramp, a vagrant, characterized by the assortment of plastic carrier bags that contain her worldly possessions. The euphemism originated in the 1970s in America but is now used in the UK and elsewhere; it has also come to be used to describe any very untidy unkempt woman.

• **bag man** ▶ 1. A US underworld expression of the 1920s and 1930s for the man sent by the big gangsters to collect extortion payments. 2. A male tramp, a vagrant, characterized by his assortment of plastic carrier bags.

• **bagpipe** ▶ 1. US slang dating from the 1940s for a vacuum cleaner. 2. To indulge in sexual activity involving stimulation of the male genitals by the armpit.

• **bag system** ▶ A public welfare scheme promoted in Australia during the Great Depression. Under its terms the unemployed were given a bag of essential groceries on each dole day.

• **Bahasa Indonesia** ▶ (Malay *bahasa*, language) A form of Malay widely used as a trade language in SE Asia and adopted as the official language of Indonesia in 1972.

• **Bailey bridge** ▶ In World War II a metal bridge of great strength made of easily portable sections and capable of speedy erection. It was invented by the British engineer D. C. Bailey. Bailey bridges were a major factor in enabling the Allies to advance so rapidly in NW Europe, where many brick bridges had been destroyed by the retreating Germans.

• **bait and switch** ▶ An advertising ploy in which a customer is first lured by a cheap product and then persuaded to buy a more expensive product that has obviously superior features.

• **Bakelite** ▶ The tradename for a phenol-formaldehyde resin invented in 1908 by Leo Baekeland (1863–1944), a US chemist of Belgian birth. While searching for a substitute for shellac, which was then being used for making records for the emerging gramophone industry, he investigated the phenol-formaldehyde resins that had been discovered in 1871 by Karl Baeyer. By choosing appropriate formulation and reaction conditions he discovered a hard resin that could be both cast and machined and had unusually good electrical properties. The result, patented under the name Bakelite, formed the basis of the vast plastics industry. Shellac, however, continued to be used for 78 rpm records, until the advent of extended-play (45 rpm) and long-playing (33 rpm) records in the 1950s, which were both made from vinyl plastics.

• **Baker Street Irregulars**▸ The group of young boys that Sherlock Holmes used to gain information about London's underworld in the novels of Sir Arthur Conan Doyle (1859–1930). Holmes's rooms were at 221b Baker Street. The name was later taken by a US appreciation society dedicated to studying the Holmes novels. It was also used by the **Special Operations Executive (SOE)** – the British secret-service organization set up (1940) during World War II to train agents working in occupied territories. The SOE took the name because its original headquarters were in Baker Street.

• **balance of terror** ▸ The role of nuclear weapons in maintaining stable international relations during the Cold War. The phrase is a refinement of the more traditional 'balance of power'. *See also*: MAD.

• **Balearic**▸ A form of dance music that became popular in the 1980s. Its name was derived from the Balearic Islands (especially Majorca and Minorca and Ibiza), popular with British holiday-makers, where there are numerous clubs and discos.

• **Balenciaga** ▸ The Spanish fashion house founded by Cristóbal Balenciaga (1895–1972). Its style of elegant suits and evening dresses was enormously popular in the 1950s but fell from fashion in the more informal 1960s.

• **Balfour declaration**▸ A statement made by the British Conservative statesman Arthur Balfour (1848–1930) in 1917 (when he was foreign secretary) regarding the establishment of a national Jewish state in Palestine. The promise to support the setting up of such a state was made in a letter from Balfour to the Zionist leader Lionel Walter Rothschild (2nd Baron Rothschild; 1868–1937), and was conditional on the idea that the rights of existing non-Jewish residents in Palestine should be maintained, as should those of Jewish residents in other countries. The declaration was repudiated by the British Government in 1939. *See also*: McMahon letters; Sykes-Picot agreement.

• **Balfour's Poodle**▸ The House of Lords. From 1906 Arthur Balfour, the Conservative leader, exploited his party's majority in the House of Lords to block the legislation of the Liberal government, which had an overwhelming majority in the Commons. When the Lords rejected the Licensing Bill of 1908, Henry Chaplin MP claimed that the House of Lords was the 'watchdog of the constitution', to which Lloyd George replied, 'You mean it is Mr Balfour's poodle! It fetches and carries for him. It barks for him. It bites anybody that he sets it on to!' *See also*: People's Budget; Veto Bill.

• **Balkan League** ▸ A military alliance formed (1912) between Bulgaria, Serbia, Greece, and Montenegro to wage war against Turkey. *See*: Balkan Wars.

• **Balkan Pact**▸ A military treaty (1954) between Greece, Turkey, and Yugoslavia. Although it was never formally cancelled, the three members later quietly forgot its existence.

• **Balkan Wars**▸ Two military conflicts occurring shortly before World War I in the Balkans. The first (1912–13) was between the members of the Balkan League and the Ottoman Empire. The Empire was forced to give up most of its European territories. The second Balkan War was between members of the Balkan League – Bulgaria was defeated by Serbia, Greece, and Romania in a quarrel about the distribution of territory gained in Macedonia during the first war. At the same time, the Turks regained part of Thrace.

• **Ballets Russes** ▸ The enormously influential ballet company founded in Paris in 1909 by Sergei Diaghilev (1872–1929). It acquired almost legendary status under the choreographers Fokine, Massine, Balanchine, and Nijinsky before it was finally disbanded on Diaghilev's death.

• **Ballinspittle**▸ *See*: Our Lady of Ballinspittle.

• **balloon**▸
  **when the balloon goes up** When trouble breaks out. The phrase was first used in World War I, referring to the launching of observation balloons shortly before an attack.

• **balloon angioplasty**▸ A surgical procedure in which a blocked coronary artery (which supplies blood to the heart) is stretched by inserting into it a plastic cylinder ('balloon'), which is then inflated.

In some cases a stent (splint) is left in the artery to keep it open.

• **balloon astronomy** ▶ The use of special balloons carrying sophisticated cameras and other scientific equipment to observe astronomical features from high altitudes, where the earth's atmosphere is very thin.

• **balloon cloth** ▶ A type of cloth first used in hot-air balloons and dirigibles, but later adapted for use in the clothing industry.

• **balloon pump** ▶ A pump used in heart surgery to imitate the pulsating action of the heart, first used in the 1960s.

• **ballpark figure** ▶ An estimate, usually of a financial quantity, upon which no great reliance should be put. It comes from the slightly older phrase 'in the same ballpark' meaning that two figures are roughly of the same magnitude. In America a ballpark is a large stadium in which baseball is played.

• **balls** ▶ Testicles. The word has acquired two slang meanings on both sides of the Atlantic. 'Don't talk balls' means 'don't talk rubbish'; **balls** as a single expletive also means 'Rubbish, I don't agree'. On the other hand 'He doesn't have the balls for it' means 'He doesn't have the courage'. The term **balls-up**, used for something that has gone hopelessly awry, was first heard in the 1930s.

• **ballyhoo** ▶ A fuss, cacophony of raised voices, etc. In the film industry the word (Irish in origin) acquired the more specialized sense of promotional publicity for a film (*see also*: hype).

• **Balt** ▶ Australian slang of the 1950s for a new Australian, an immigrant. The term was originally limited to immigrants from the Baltic States, but later more widely applied. *See*: reffo.

• **Baltic Exchange** ▶ A market in the City of London for buying and selling freight space for goods to be transported by sea or air. It also deals in chartering ships and aircraft. The market formerly dealt in some commodities – grain, potatoes, and meat – but this came to an end after an IRA bomb caused severe damage to the building in 1992. These commodities have since been dealt with at the London Commodity Exchange. Forward freight is dealt with by the Baltic International Freight Futures Exchange (BIFFEX). The name comes from the fact that in the 18th century most of its business involved trade in grain through Baltic ports.

• **Bambi** ▶ A young deer, the eponymous star of a feature-length Walt Disney cartoon film (1942) based on the novel by Felix Salten (1869–1945). The character has become a symbol of gentle wide-eyed innocence. Owing to a slight facial resemblance and his rather ingenuous air, Tony Blair was often nicknamed Bambi in his earlier years as Labour Party leader.

• **Bambi Project** ▶ A US defence project involving the use of orbital satellites armed with missiles to intercept intercontinental ballistic missiles at take-off. The project was suspended in 1964, but was a forerunner of the Star Wars programme.

• **Bamboo Curtain** ▶ Especially in the 1950s and 1960s, the veil of secrecy and mistrust between Communist China and the non-Communist nations. It was named by analogy with the Iron Curtain. *See also*: Garlic Wall; Tortilla Curtain.

• **Banaban** ▶ A native of Ocean Island in the SW Pacific. In the late 1970s inhabitants of the island engaged in a lengthy battle for compensation from the British government for damage done to their home during extensive mining for phosphates (1900–79). The process culminated in the Banabans resettlement on Rabi Island in Fiji during World War II. They were finally awarded £5 million.

• **banana** ▶ **1.** A fool. This now obsolete British sense is still sometimes heard in the shortened form 'nana', used among children as a mild insult. **2.** British slang meaning penis. **3.** US slang for a light-skinned Black woman. Used by Black men, it can be either appreciative or derogatory.

• **banana belt** ▶ An area in North America that is popular for winter holidays owing to its mild climate (warm enough for bananas to be grown). The term used of other similar regions.

• **banana boat** ▶ *See*: come over with the onion boat.

• **banana republic** ▶ Any state that is dependent on one particular agricultural product, such as bananas. Usually applied to the nations of South America or Africa, the phrase has overtones of bureaucratic inefficiency, impoverishment, and easily bribed leaders. *Bananas* (1971) was a Woody Allen comedy film about such a state.

• **Bananas, Joe** ▶ *See*: Joe Bananas.

• **bananas** ▶
   **Yes, we have no bananas** A nonsensical catchphrase of the 1920s. It was taken from the chorus of a song (1923) by Frank Silver and Irving Cohn.

   I would rather have been the Author of that Banana Masterpiece than the Author of the Constitution of the United States. No one has offered any amendments to it. It's the only thing ever written in America that we haven't changed, most of them for the worst. – WILL ROGERS, *The Illiterate Digest* (1924).

The phrase was revived in the UK during World War II, when bananas disappeared completely from the shops. At the end of the war there were 5-year-old children who had never seen a real banana.

• **band-aid** ► To fix something on a temporary basis, from the tradename for an adhesive plaster. In 1984 the name **Band Aid** was adopted by the organizers of a fundraising effort launched by the pop music community to help the starving in Ethiopia and Sudan; the pun reflects what they obviously considered an inadequate response to a serious problem. Nevertheless, their recording of 'Do They Know It's Christmas' became the UK's biggest-selling single to that date, raising about £8 million. This success inspired several similar campaigns, including the **Comic Relief** events, in which leading comedians urge the public to support worthy causes by buying red plastic noses, etc. *See also*: Live Aid; telethon.

• **B and D** ► A British and Australian slang expression meaning bondage and discipline, used by prostitutes to describe the services that they offer.

• **B and K** ► The Soviet statesmen Nicolai Bulganin (1895–1975) and Nikita Khrushchev (1894–1971). It was used in newspapers during their visit to the UK in 1956. At the time, Bulganin was the Soviet prime minister and Khrushchev, who subsequently ousted Bulganin, was the first secretary of the Communist Party.

• **Bandung Conference** ► A conference (1955) attended by 29 African and Asian states at the city of Bandung in West Java, Indonesia. A strong stance against colonialism was taken and a policy of non-alignment between the Western and Communist blocs agreed.

• **bandwidth** ► A US expression of the 1990s meaning the extent of one's capacity to absorb new information. In 1993 Bill Gates, the founder of Microsoft, was described by an admirer as having 'the biggest bandwidth I've ever come across'. It derives from the use of the same term in computer systems to mean the amount of data that can be transmitted within a certain time. In analogue communications systems, such as radio, the bandwidth is the range of frequencies available on a particular channel.

• **bandy** ► A British working-class term of abuse used (by men) to describe a woman who is alleged to be 'bandy-legged' from frequent sex. It was used

by London mods (*see*: mods and rockers) and skinheads in the late 1960s.

• **bang** ► 1. To have sex. A widely used slang word since the 1960s but more common in the UK and Australia than in America. **bang like a shithouse door (in a gale)** is a colourful Australian expression meaning to be an enthusiastic sexual partner. It was popularized by the cartoon strip *Barry McKenzie* (by Barry Humphries) in the magazine *Private Eye* in the 1960s. *See also*: gang-bang. 2. US slang for a big thrill. 3. A drug abuser's term, dating from the 1940s, for an injection of illegal drugs, particularly heroin or morphine.

• **banger** ► 1. British slang for a sausage, current since the 1940s and, supposedly deriving from the noise of the sausage skin popping while it cooks. **Bangers and mash** (sausages and mashed potato) is a favourite British dish, especially when served with onion gravy, although no one would claim that it is an example of British *haute cuisine*. 2. An affectionate term for an old decrepit car.

• **banjo'd** or **banjoed** ► 1. British slang meaning completely drunk or stoned. Used mainly by young people in the 1980s, it is probably a corruption of 'banjaxed', an Irish word meaning totally overcome. 2. An army expression of the 1970s and 1980s for defeated, again probably related to 'banjaxed'. There may also be a connection with an archaic slang usage of banjo meaning a shovel or weapon.

• **bankable** ► Any project or person thought likely to prove financially profitable, applied chiefly to film stars and other celebrities since the 1960s.

• **Bankers' Ramp** ► An alleged conspiracy by British bankers (1931) to discredit the Labour government of the time by undermining the economy.

• **Ban the bomb!** ► Slogan adopted by CND in the late 1950s.

• **Bantustan** ► Formerly an area in South Africa set aside by the government for Blacks, who were allowed limited self-government. The first of these areas (also called **Bantu Homelands**) to be created was Transkei in 1963. The name came from combining 'Bantu', the indigenous people inhabiting the area, with '-stan', from Pakistan (taken as an example of a state formed from an existing state). The Bantu Homelands were reintegrated into South Africa following the multiracial elections in April 1994.

• **banzai** ► (Japanese, forward) Japanese battlecry, uttered in frontal attacks on enemy troops in World War II. Its meaning was 'May you live forever'.

• **barb** ▶ British drug-abusers' slang, first heard in the 1950s, for a barbiturate.

• **Barbarossa** ▶ The German code name for the invasion of the Soviet Union in 1941. It was taken from the nickname of the Holy Roman Emperor Frederick I (c. 1123–90), meaning 'red beard'.

> When Barbarossa commences, the world will hold its breath and make no comment. – ADOLF HITLER.

• **barber** ▶
**Every barber knows that** That is already common knowledge. A primarily US comment implying that chat between customers and their barbers is so continuous, intimate, and diverse that barbers may be expected to be extremely well informed, especially in the fields of gossip and rumour.

• **barber shop** ▶ A style of unaccompanied male close-harmony singing that is said to have emerged in the US barbers' shops of the late 19th century. Whether the originators were the customers waiting for haircuts and shaves, or the barbers themselves hoping to increase their tips by entertaining the clientele, is not clear. Perhaps it was a joint effort. In any case, the camaraderie of this form of music-making has been revived many times since in more congenial surroundings.

• **Barbican** ▶ A development in the City of London, originally planned in 1955 to replace bombed parts of the City. Officially opened in 1982, it contains many private flats as well as the Barbican Arts Centre (an exhibition gallery, theatre complex, cinemas, etc.) and the Museum of London. The name comes from a former London street on the site named after a barbican (watch tower) in the Roman city walls.

• **barbie** ▶ An Australian slang abbreviation for barbecue, dating from the 1960s, that has become widely used in the UK since the arrival of Australian soap operas on British TV.

• **Barbie doll** ▶ A US slang term for an emptyheaded but sexually attractive young woman. Barbie is the tradename for a plastic doll with a woman's figure, long combable hair, and a wardrobe of glamorous clothes. *See also*: Sindy.

• **Barbour** ▶ The tradename of a (typically green) waxed cotton coat or jacket manufactured by J. Barber and Sons Ltd of South Shields, Tyneside, established 1880. This hard-wearing waterproof and windproof article, the traditional outdoor wear of the county set and gentleman-farmers, was in the 1980s enthusiastically adopted by yuppies week-ending in the country. Its almost cult popularity, gave rise to a host of cheaper imitations.

• **Barcelona chair** ▶ A simple yet elegant chair with a stainless steel frame designed by Ludwig Mies van der Rohe in 1929. First seen on show in Barcelona, it had a fundamental effect upon contemporary design.

• **bar code** ▶ A code consisting of a series of parallel lines, of varying thickness, that can be read by a laser scanner. They are widely used for coding products for sale in shops to enable faster processing of goods at the checkout. Known as **EPOS** (electronic point of sale), this system enables stock figures to be reduced automatically as sales are made and a warning system to be activated as stocks fall below a specified figure. Such codes are also used to programme video cassette recorders, etc.

• **barefoot doctor** ▶ A medical assistant who works in remote areas of the world, usually for international charity organizations after a brief medical training. It is a rough translation of the Chinese phrase *chijiao yisheng* – many peasant doctors being literally barefooted.

• **bar fly** ▶ A US slang expression of the 1930s for a man or woman who frequents cheap bars. It was the title of a 1987 film with a script by Charles Bukowski.

• **barmy army** ▶ A nickname sometimes given to any semi-organized group, usually of football supporters or pop music fans.

• **Baruch plan** ▶ A plan, put forward in 1946, in which America agreed to destroy its stock of nuclear weapons and fissionable material provided that an international body was set up to prevent the spread of these weapons and to control the use of nuclear power. The plan, which was rejected by the Soviet Union, was proposed by Bernard Baruch (1870–1965), who was advisor to the US president and was involved in formulating US policy on atomic energy.

• **base** ▶ Crack cocaine. The term, which derives from the practice of freebasing, became part of British drug abusers' jargon in the late 1980s.

• **bash** ▶ 1. A party. 2. British term for a homeless person's shelter, made of cardboard and plastic sheeting.

> I live in a bash – a room made of pallets and cardboard, with blankets for doors. – Homeless person quoted in *The Independent on Sunday*, 20 January 1991.

• **Basic English** ▶ A radically simplified form of

English, consisting of a selected vocabulary of just 850 words, designed by the British scholar C. K. Ogden in 1926–30 as a first step in the teaching of English and as an auxiliary language. The name comes from the initials of the words British, American, Scientific, International, Commercial.

• **Basin Street ►** A street in the Storyville district of New Orleans, which was reputedly the original home of jazz music. The well-known 'Basin Street Blues' was composed by Spencer Williams in 1928: 'Basin Street is a street where Black folk meet'.

• **basket case ►** **1.** US slang for someone with both arms and legs amputated. **2.** Someone who is mentally incapacitated. Patients in psychiatric hospitals were often taught basket-weaving skills. **3.** By extension, a nervous wreck. Originally a US expression. **4.** Journalists slang for a ruined project. Derived presumably from the idea that it is fit only for the wastepaper basket.

• **Bataan ►** A peninsula in the Philippines, which witnessed some of the fiercest fighting in the Pacific theatre of World War II. US and Philippine forces surrendered to the Japanese here in 1942 after a heroic defence lasting three months; many thousands of prisoners subsequently died on a long 'death march'. Bataan was retaken by US forces later in the war. See also: Corregidor.

• **batch-process ►** A manufacturing process in which the product is made in a series of separate batches, rather than continuously.

• **bath ►**
    **take an early bath** To retire early to the players' dressing-room after being sent off the field during a match of football, rugby, etc. The term is used more widely of any situation in which someone is obliged to retire from the 'field of play' before its conclusion.

• **Bath Festival ►** An annual festival of the arts held in Bath, Somerset. Founded in 1948 as a festival of 18th-century music, it lapsed in 1956 owing to financial difficulties but was revived three years later by Yehudi Menuhin. It subsequently expanded into a festival of all the arts, with painting exhibitions, poetry readings, etc. Many notable performers have appeared in the festival.

• **bathroom record ►** A more than usually lengthy record played by a disc jockey to allow him time to visit the bathroom (i.e. lavatory) between announcements.

• **bathyscaph ►** A vessel designed by Auguste Piccard (1884–1962) and his son Jacques Piccard (1927– ) to enable them to explore the depths of the oceans. In 1960, in the bathyscaph Trieste, they reached a depth of 10,917 m (about 6.8 mi).

• **batman ►** (French bat, pack-saddle) **1.** Originally a soldier in charge of a **bat-horse** (pack-horse) and its load of officer's baggage. During World War I the name came to denote any army officer's servant through its inaccurate use by non-regular wartime officers. **2.** A person at an airport (or on an aircraft carrier) who wields a pair of lightweight bats to direct the pilot in moving the aircraft on the ground (or deck).

• **Batman ►** US comic strip hero who first appeared in 1939. In the original strip, created by Bob Kane, the **Caped Crusader** of Gotham City fought such criminal arch-fiends as The Joker, The Penguin, and Catwoman. The strip later spawned two cinema serials, (1943, 1948), a rather camp television series (1960s), and, from 1989 onwards, a series of high-tech blockbuster movies. Batman's accessories include the **Batmobile** and the **Batboat**, while **Robin** (the **Boy Wonder**) is his crime-fighting colleague in many adventures.

• **Battenberg ►** The original name of the Mountbatten family. Prince Louis of Battenberg (1854–1921) anglicized the name (German berg, mountain) to Mountbatten in 1917 because of anti-German prejudice during World War I. See also: Windsor.

• **battered baby ►** See: child abuse.

• **Battle Act ►** An act passed in America (1951) to prohibit aid being given to nations under Soviet influence. It was named after Senator Battle, who proposed it.

• **battle bowler ►** A nickname given in World War I to the soldier's steel helmet or tin hat. In World War II it was also called a 'tin topee'.

• **battle cruiser ►** Cockney rhyming slang for a boozer, a pub. It dates from the 1940s.

• **Battle of Flowers ►** An annual flower festival that takes place in St Helier, Jersey, in July. It involves a procession of flower-decorated floats and culminates in a flower-throwing contest; it was inaugurated in 1902 to mark the coronation of Edward VII and Queen Alexandra.

• **batty ►** Crazy. Possibly derived from the phrase 'to have bats in the belfry', it was first heard in the 1900s.

• **baud ►** A unit measuring the rate at which information can be transmitted. It is equal to one unit of information per second, where the unit is a bit, digit, or symbol depending on the system. The

**baud rate** measures the speed at which a computer transfers data. The unit is named after J. M. E. Baudot (1845–1903), a French inventor who patented (1874) a telegraph code (the **Baudot code**) based on sets of binary digits to replace Morse code.

• **Bauhaus** ▶ A school of architecture and design founded by the German architect Walter Gropius (1883–1969) in 1919. From 1925 to 1932 it was housed in an influential building in Dessau designed by Gropius. The full name was Staatliches Bauhaus (Public House of Building) – 'Bauhaus' was coined by inverting the German word *Hausbau* ('building of a house'). The Bauhaus school stressed the teaching of art and crafts and emphasized the mass manufacture of well-designed functional objects. The school was immensely important for its influence on 20th-century design. It was forced to close in 1933 by the Nazis. Other influential members of the school were the artists Wassily Kandinsky (1866–1944), Paul Klee (1879–1940), and László Moholy-Nagy (1895–1946) and the architect Ludwig Mies van der Rohe (1886–1969). *See*: Barcelona chair.

• **Bay of Pigs** ▶ An abortive attempt (17 April 1961) to invade Cuba made by about 1500 expatriate anti-Castro Cubans. The invasion forces were trained and financed by the CIA and landed at several sites in the south of the island, in particular Bahia de los Cochinos (the Bay of Pigs). Inadequately supported by the US military, the invaders were no match for Castro's forces and by 19 April 1100 men had been captured. They were later 'ransomed' for $53 million worth of aid. *See also*: Cuban missile crisis.

• **bazooka** ▶ A light rocket-firing tube used by the US infantry as an anti-tank weapon in World War II. The name, which was later applied to the British **PIAT** (projection, infantry anti-tank) and the German *Panzerfaust* also, was possibly taken from its earlier use to mean a trombone-type instrument used in burlesque comedy (perhaps related to kazoo, a submarine-shaped toy producing sounds of the 'comb and paper' variety).

• **bazumas** ▶ Female breasts. Presumably a corruption of 'bosoms'. *See also*: mazuma.

• **BBC** ▶ British Broadcasting Corporation. It was set up in 1922 and became a public body with responsibility to parliament under royal charter in 1927. Under its first director-general John Reith (later 1st Baron Reith; 1889–1971), the BBC acquired an international reputation for its professionalism, high ideals of public service, and independence from government. Its role in World War II further added to its high standing, although commercial pressures following the introduction of independent television companies in the 1950s, together with the rapid social changes of the 1960s and 1970s, led to a gradual evolution in both its style and its broadcasting philosophy. The BBC continues to be funded by revenue from television licences as it is not permitted to carry advertising. *See also*: Auntie; Beeb; World Service.

• **BBC English** ▶ *See*: Received Pronunciation.

• **BCS theory** ▶ *See*: superconductivity.

• **beachball** ▶ A device by which astronauts can escape from an orbiting spacecraft to another spacecraft in the event of an emergency. It consists of a circular 'bubble', which is connected to the larger craft's life-support system.

• **beach bunny** ▶ A girl who parades herself on the beach wearing a skimpy bikini.

• **Beachcomber** ▶ Pen name used by the writers of the humorous column *By The Way*, which appeared for many years in the *Daily Express*. Originally contributed by D. B. Wyndham-Lewis (who later wrote a column under the name Timothy Shy for the *News Chronicle*), it was continued by J. B. Morton (1893–1979), who developed its characteristic style of nonsensical humour. This involved a cast of fantastic characters including Mr Justice Cocklecarrot and the famous Dr Strabismus (Whom God Preserve) of Utrecht, noted for crossing a salmon with a mosquito so that fishermen could have a bite every time. Beachcomber's humour was an early outbreak of the mild comic surrealism later exemplified by the Goon Show and Monty Python's Flying Circus.

• **beached whale** ▶ A substantial person or thing left stranded in a situation from which it cannot escape, because it is out of its element. This image of an ailing whale abandoned by the tide can be applied to any reminiscent situation.

> That leaves the beached whale of the monarchy as the only remaining part of our Constitution dependent on the accident of birth. – *The Guardian*, 6 December 2000.

• **beamer** ▶ Yuppie slang for a BMW car.

• **Beam me up, Scotty** ▶ A catchphrase derived from the TV science-fiction series *Star Trek* (1966–69). To 'beam someone up' was to transfer them in dematerialized form from one location to another (usually from a planet's surface to the orbiting starship *Enterprise*); 'Scotty' was the chief engineer on the *Enterprise*. The catchphrase is usually spoken by someone in a difficult or embarrassing situation from which they would like to dematerialize. *See also*: To boldly go… *at* boldly.

• **beam weapon** ► A laser developed for use in various advanced weaponry systems. One possible application, never in fact realized, was as a component of America's Star Wars programme.

• **beanbag** ► A large cushion filled with polystyrene pellets, commonly used in the 1960s and 1970s as a substitute for an armchair, especially by students. The theory behind the beanbag was that it would mould itself to the shape of the person who sat in it. It does not, however, provide support for the back and in spite of its cheapness it has not gained in popularity.

• **Beanz Meanz Heinz** ► A slogan used in the 1960s to sell Heinz Baked Beans.

• **bear** ► US slang for a policeman. *See*: Smokey Bear.

• **Bear, the** ► *See*: Stormin' Norman.

• **beastly** ►
**Don't let's be beastly to the Germans**
The title of a song (1930) by Noël Coward, which became an ironic catchphrase in the period between the wars. After World War II it was accepted that however unspeakable the behaviour of the Germans had been during it, the Allies had to live with them. Coward's light-hearted song then carried a somewhat more serious message.

• **Beast of Belsen** ► The name given to Joseph Kramer, commandant of the infamous Belsen concentration camp.

• **Beast of Bolsover** ► Dennis Skinner (1932– ), Labour MP for Bolsover (Derbyshire). Describing himself in *Who's Who* as coming from 'good working-class mining stock' and having been himself a miner for 21 years, he was given his nickname by lobby correspondents for his aggressive behaviour in parliament. As a result of persistent and noisy interruptions, he has frequently been asked to leave the Chamber by the Speaker.

• **Beast of Exmoor** ► A mysterious puma-like creature that captured British newspaper headlines in 1983. The 'Beast' was sighted several times on the Somerset–Devon boundary and was blamed for the deaths of over 200 sheep in the area. Panic over the animal, which was described as some kind of large cat, led to a Royal Marines team equipped with night sights being detailed to find it: they failed but sightings of the creature gradually tailed off.

The Beast of Exmoor is only one of many such unidentified animals reported throughout the country in recent decades, with similar press attention being given to big cats in Cornwall (the **Beast of Bodmin**), Surrey, Derbyshire, Dorset, Buckinghamshire, Hertfordshire, Essex, and Wales in 1983 alone. One, caught in a trap in Scotland in 1980, did actually turn out to be a puma, which had presumably escaped from a zoo.

• **beat** ► A member or follower of the **Beat Generation** of US writers who emerged in the late 1950s. These writers – principally Jack Kerouac, Allen Ginsberg, and William Burroughs – adopted an ethic of spontaneous self-expression in both life and art and used their work to describe their experiments with drugs, sex, and Eastern religions. The description 'beat' seems to have been coined by Kerouac himself, but first appeared in print in John Clellan Holmes's novel *GO*. Although most people related the term to deadbeat or to beat meaning 'exhausted', Kerouac insisted that it derived from 'beatitude'.

• **beat** ►
**If you can't beat 'em, join 'em** A catchphrase, dating from the 1940s, implying that if you can't defeat your opponents it is best to cooperate with them. It is often used in a political context.

• **Beatles** ► British pop group of the 1960s that attained near-mythical status before finally disbanding in 1970. Comprising John Lennon (1940–80), Paul McCartney (1942– ), George Harrison (1943–2001), and Ringo Starr (1940– ), the group established a cult following during appearances at the **Cavern Club** in Liverpool in 1962. During the next two or three years **Beatlemania** reached such hysterical proportions in Britain and America that it became impractical for the group to perform live. Lennon was moved to remark that they were 'more popular than Jesus Christ'. The unrivalled sequence of hit records that took the group through the 1960s included the singles 'She Loves You' (1963), 'Help' (1965), 'Penny Lane' (1967), and 'Hey Jude' (1968) and the albums *Revolver* (1966), *Sergeant Pepper's Lonely Hearts Club Band* (1967), and *Abbey Road* (1969). A host of legends came to surround the band, including a peculiar rumour that McCartney had died and been replaced by a lookalike. The group's impact on British life and culture was immeasurable; with its heady energy, melodic wistfulness, and psychedelic experimentation, their music now seems a uniquely poignant evocation of a curious and confusing era. *See also*: Apple Corps; Fifth Beatle; Ringo.

• **beatnik** ► A derogatory term for a follower of the Beat Generation (*see*: beat), especially one characterized by unconventional or slovenly dress. The word derives from 'beat' and the Russian suffix -nik.

The Russian-sounding suffix...hinted at free

love and a little communism (not enough to be threatening), as well as a general oafishness. – JOYCE JOHNSON, *Minor Characters* (1983).

• **Beatty**▸ In lower-deck naval slang, an officer. It comes from Earl Beatty (1871–1936), a British admiral who took part in the Battle of Jutland and was later first sea lord.

• **beautiful game, the**▸ The name that Pelé, the star Brazilian inside forward, gave to soccer in his autobiography *My Life and the Beautiful Game* (1970). In 2000 the Andrew Lloyd Webber musical *The Beautiful Game*, with script by Ben Elton, opened in the West End. The unlikely combination of Elton, Lloyd Webber, and a storyline about a football team in Northern Ireland during the Troubles proved commercially disastrous.

• **beautiful people**▸ Originally a term applied to the hippies of the late 1960s. Later, the most fashionable and glamorous members of society.

• **beautility**▸ A design philosophy in which both beauty and utility are given equal consideration.

• **beauty**▸ In nuclear physics, a flavour of quark.

• **beaver**▸ 1. In the 1920s and 1930s anyone wearing a beard. In this period beards were so rare that a man sporting one was in danger of having 'beaver!' shouted at him in the street by schoolchildren. 2. A woman's pubic hair.

• **Beaver, the**▸ Name given in journalistic circles to Lord Beaverbrook (William Maxwell-Aitken; 1879–1964), Canadian-born politician and newspaper magnate. He served in a number of capacities in World War I and as minister of aircraft production in World War II (*see also*: backroom boys), when he was responsible for stepping up the output of the Spitfire fighter and Whitley bomber. He became minister of supply in 1941.

• **bebop**▸ A style of modern jazz that developed in New York during the 1940s. It was characterized by fast (often frenetic) tempos, unpredictable rhythms, and extended solos. Musicians associated with the style, which alienated many older jazz fans, included Thelonius Monk, Dizzy Gillespie, and Charlie Parker.

• **beddo**▸ A bed that can be adjusted by electronic means. Such beds, which can be raised, lowered, rotated, etc., were popular in Japan in the 1960s and 1970s.

• **bed of nails**▸ A self-inflicted awkward situation. Derived from the Indian fakir's spiked bed, the phrase became popular in 1966, when it was widely used of the Labour government's troubles with devaluation.

• **bedsit**▸ A combined bedroom and sitting-room, constituting a cheap form of accommodation designed for occupation by students, etc.

• **Beeb**▸ An affectionate term for the BBC, the British Broadcasting Corporation.

• **Beeching's axe**▸ Cuts in the services of the nationalized railway network (then called British Railways) made as a result of a report in 1963 by Dr Beeching (later Lord Beeching; 1913–85). Beeching, a successful industrialist from ICI, was brought in by the government in 1960 to 'make the railway service profitable'. In 1961 he was put in charge of British Railways and two years later he put forward his report (*The Reshaping of British Railways*), which recommended closing 2128 stations, cutting the rail network by 25%, and dispensing with over 65,000 jobs. Although Beeching was sacked by the government in 1964, major cuts were made in the rail network a few months later following his recommendations.

• **beef**▸

**Where's the beef?** A slogan associated with the US Democratic politician Walter Mondale. In a political context the phrase is used to imply a lack of substance in a rival's policies. Mondale popularized the phrase during his campaign (1984) to be nominated Democratic presidential candidate, having borrowed it from an advertising campaign for Wendy hamburgers, which derided the small portions of meat in a rival product. Mondale won the Democratic nomination but was defeated in the presidential election by Ronald Reagan.

• **beefalo**▸ A breed of beef cattle developed in America in the early 1970s by crossing domestic cattle with buffalo. The resultant hybrids, some three-eighths of whose genetic make up is of buffalo origin, yield a low-fat protein-rich meat.

• **beef ban**▸ The worldwide ban on exports of British beef imposed by the European Council on 27 March 1996. It was prompted by the first official government admission, made by the health minister a week earlier, that there was a possible link between eating meat from animals infected with mad cow disease and contracting the equivalent human brain disease, CJD. The ban had an immediate and catastrophic impact on the UK's beef industry, causing a collapse in beef sales and forcing the government to introduce a package of emergency financial aid.

The worldwide ban had been foreshadowed by the action of certain UK local authorities in banning beef from school meals and canteens. However, the farming industry, food retailers, and catering establishments sought to reassure their increasingly sceptical customers, and as late as December 1995 prime minister John Major was steadfast in his support for British beef, declaring 'I am advised that beef is a safe and wholesome product'.

Then came the ban, and with it stringent conditions that entailed a complete overhaul of the British beef industry. As these were implemented, and the number of infected cattle fell, customer confidence slowly returned. Even so, further restrictions on the domestic beef market were introduced, including in 1997 a controversial ban on 'beef on the bone' (which remained in force until December 1999). On 1 August 1999, the EU finally allowed limited exports of British beef to resume, although certain countries, notably France, continued to block imports. This led to the realization that it would take many years before the long-term damage to the British beef industry was repaired.

• **beefcake** ► *See*: cheesecake.

• **beef mountain** ► *See*: CAP.

• **beehive** ► A dome-shaped hairstyle of the late 1950s and early 1960s, achieved by backcombing and the application of lacquer.

• **beer and sandwiches** ► The fare supposedly offered to trade union leaders at 10 Downing Street in informal talks with the Labour government during the 1960s and 1970s. Such 'beer and sandwich' sessions were ridiculed by the Conservatives as indicative of the extraordinary influence the trade unions had on the government of the day.

• **beer-hall Putsch** ► *See*: Munich Putsch.

• **bee's knees** ► A superlative situation, person, or thing; a phrase first widely heard in the 1920s. In the 1970s it became the name of a popular US cocktail, made of lemon juice, gin, and honey.

• **Beetle** ► The name given (because of its shape) to a car first made by the Volkswagen company in 1935. Designed by Ferdinand Porsche in response to Hitler's instructions to create a 'peoples' car', it became the best-selling car ever made. Production of the traditional Beetle finally ceased in the 1980s, although a slightly bigger and more streamlined version was revived in 1999. *See also*: Porsche.

• **BEF** ► British Expeditionary Force, the seven British regiments (160,000 men; six infantry regiments and one cavalry regiment) sent to France at the start of World War I in 1914. Known as the Old Contemptibles, they suffered heavy losses at the hands of the Germans and had to be heavily reinforced. A second BEF was formed in 1939, when 10 divisions were sent to France at the start of World War II. After the Germans outflanked the Maginot Line they had to be evacuated from Dunkirk and other ports between 26 May and 4 June 1940, when 338,226 Allied troops were brought back to the UK.

• **before you came up** ► In World War I, a putdown used by a veteran soldier to an inexperienced one, who had only recently come up to the front line. It was normally used in some such formulation as: 'I'd stuck my bayonet up 25 Jerries before you came up'. Variants included 'before your number was dry' (on your kitbag) and 'before you knew what a button-stick was' (an appliance for shining buttons).

• **Befrienders International** ► *See*: Samaritans.

• **behaviourism** ► A school of psychology founded by the US psychologist J. B. Watson (1878–1958) and advocated by the US psychologist B. F. Skinner (1904–90). Behaviourists study observable behaviour rather than ideas or emotions and emphasize the effect of conditioning. *Compare*: cognitive psychology.

• **behaviour therapy** ► A method of treating patients with psychological disorders in which undesirable patterns of behaviour are replaced with less damaging ones. *See*: reinforcement therapy.

• **be-in** ► In the 1960s, an informal gathering of people in a public place at which participants were encouraged to act without inhibitions or regard for conventional modes of behaviour. *See also*: love-in; sit-in.

• **Bekaa Valley** or **Beqaa Valley** ► A fertile valley in S Lebanon between the Lebanon and the Anti-Lebanon Mountains; the scene of many armed clashes in that country's modern history, including heavy fighting between Israeli and Syrian forces in 1982. It is a stronghold of the Hizbollah, a Shiite Muslim guerrilla organization notorious for its terrorist methods.

• **Belgrade Theatre** ► A civic theatre founded in Coventry in 1958 – the first new British theatre to be opened after World War II. It was named in recognition of a gift of timber from Belgrade, Yugoslavia, that was used in its construction. The theatre continues to flourish.

• **believe it or not!** ► Slogan associated with the US cartoon strip of the same title created by Robert Leroy Ripley (1893–1949) in 1923. The strip, which later spawned a radio and TV series and a museum at Niagara Falls, presented extraordinary facts and tales, all allegedly true.

• **Belisha beacon** ► An amber-coloured globe mounted on a black and white banded pole to indicate a pedestrian crossing. Named after Leslie Hore-Belisha, minister of transport (1934–37), who introduced them.

• **Bell** ▶ A series of early US experimental rocket planes designed to test the possibility of high-speed flight at high altitudes. The Bell XS-1 was the first plane to achieve supersonic flight, at 670 mph on 14 October 1947.

• **bell-bottoms** ▶ A style of flared trousers that became popular in the 1960s and 1970s. Not dissimilar to the trousers traditionally worn in the navy, they flared out at or below the knee. Regarded as the nadir of tastelessness in the 1980s, they became fashionable once more in the early 1990s and early 2000s.

• **Belleau Wood** ▶ A forest in N France, in which US Marines halted a German attack on Paris in 1918. It was here that Sergeant Dan Daly uttered the famous rallying cry: 'Come on, you sons of bitches! Do you want to live forever?'

• **Belle Époque** ▶ (French, beautiful period) The period in Europe from the end of the 19th century up to the start of World War I, in which the affluent lived in great comfort and style.

• **bells and whistles** ▶ Marketing parlance for the special additional features possessed by a particular product. Although heavily stressed in advertising, these are usually less than essential. The phrase is particularly common in computing, where it refers to the extra facilities offered by a particular program, etc.

• **belly bomber** ▶ US slang for a small but very heavily spiced burger. A popular fast food of the 1980s, the bite-size burgers were eaten in rapid succession, producing the impression of a series of small explosions within the stomach.

• **belly landing** ▶ The landing of an aircraft on its fuselage rather than its landing gear. This was a not uncommon occurrence with fighter planes in World War II. Sometimes the retractable undercarriage was damaged in combat, sometimes it jammed for mechanical reasons, and sometimes the pilot forgot to lower it.

• **belly up** ▶ In US slang to 'go belly up' is to fail disastrously or to go bankrupt (by allusion to dead fish).

• **Bélmez, Faces of** ▶ The unexplained appearance of ghostly faces on the kitchen floor of a house in the S Spanish village of Bélmez in August 1971. The faces, which all wore unutterably sad expressions, resisted all attempts to erase them and terrified the occupants of the house, who eventually

ripped up the floor and replaced it with concrete. Three weeks later the faces reappeared. An inquiry was launched and investigators soon discovered the house stood over a medieval cemetery. The kitchen was sealed but new faces appeared elsewhere in the house and ultrasensitive microphones recorded strange cries of torment. Scientists photographed the faces but were unable to explain their origin. They eventually disappeared.

• **below-the-line** ▶ See: above-the-line.

• **Belsen** ▶ A German concentration camp during World War II, situated near the village of Belsen (north of Hanover). It was also called **Bergen–Belsen** from the nearby village of Bergen. Some 37,000 people died of starvation or disease here, including the 16-year-old diarist Anne Frank (1929–45). Belsen was one of the first camps to be liberated (by the British in 1945); the world was shocked by film of emaciated prisoners and of troops forced to use bulldozers to move piles of naked corpses into mass graves. The camp's commandant, Josef Kramer, came to be known as the Beast of Belsen.

• **Ben Barka disappearance** ▶ An unsolved mystery surrounding the disappearance of the Moroccan opposition politician Mehdi Ben Barka (b. 1920) in October 1965. Ben Barka had been exiled to France and was last seen in Paris being driven away in a French police car. It is generally assumed that he was murdered by Moroccan agents with the connivance of the French secret service.

• **bender** ▶ 1. A period of heavy drinking, or a wild spree. It may derive from the euphemism 'to bend the elbow', meaning to drink alcohol, but it may also be related to the mid-19th-century phrase 'hell-bender' meaning any exciting or outrageous event. 2. British slang for a homosexual, a euphemistic reference to one who submits to buggery. 3. In the UK an improvised tent-like structure made from hazel saplings bent into a semicircle and covered with a tarpaulin. Originally a name for the tents of travellers and gypsies, the word came into more common usage in the 1980s with the wide media coverage of the peace camp set up at Greenham Common by women, who camped in benders outside the US base there.

• **Benelux** ▶ The customs union (1948) of the three countries Belgium, The Netherlands, and Luxemburg. Although they joined the European Community in 1958, the term is still used of these three countries.

• **Benghazi cooker** ▶ In World War II an Australian name for a contrivance for heating water, made from a can containing petrol-soaked sand. It is named after the Libyan city that featured in the Africa campaign in the early 1940s.

• **Benghazi Handicap** or **Benghazi Derby**▶ The Allied (British and Australian) retreat to Tobruk in 1941, which was carried out in a state of considerable confusion and haste.

• **Benidormification**▶ The commercialization of once tranquil or exclusive holiday resorts. The exploitation of such places accompanied the rise of mass tourism and the package-holiday industry. The word, coined in the late 1980s, is based on the Spanish coastal resort of Benidorm, whose mass market appeal, particularly among the British, turned a small fishing village into a sprawling development of high-rise apartment blocks and hotels, bars, discos, and fast food outlets.

• **benign neglect**▶ Doing nothing in the belief that an already difficult state of affairs will deteriorate if a more positive course is followed. The term was first heard in America in the early 1970s in reference to race relations.

• **Benioff zone**▶ A geological zone, usually found along the edge of a continent and dipping sharply downwards, in which many earthquakes occur. It was named in 1968 after the US seismologist Victor Hugo Benioff (1899–1968).

• **Bennery**▶ The left-wing policies advocated by the British Labour MP Tony Benn (Anthony Neil Wedgwood Benn; 1925– ). As secretary of state for industry in 1974–75, he pressed for increased nationalization of industry and more government intervention in private companies. He later campaigned for the 'democratization' of the Labour Party's internal structures, Britain's withdrawal from the EC, and the disestablishment of the Church of England, amongst other causes.

• **bennie**▶ A Benzedrine pill. Benzedrine is a tradename for an amphetamine widely used and frequently abused from the 1940s to the 1960s. *See also*: bubs.

• **Be Prepared**▶ The motto of the Boy Scouts, chosen in 1908.

• **Berchtesgaden**▶ *See*: Eagle's Nest.

• **Bergen–Belsen**▶ *See*: Belsen.

• **berk** or **burk**▶ A fool. A mild term of abuse widely heard in the UK and Australia since the 1960s. Many of those who use it would be shocked to know that it comes from the Cockney rhyming slang Berkeley or Berkshire hunt for 'cunt'.

• **Berlin airlift**▶ The operation in which US and British aircraft supplied the city of West Berlin with food and other essential supplies between 26 June 1948 and 12 May 1949; a total of 195,530 flights was made, creating a so-called **airbridge** to the city. It was organized in response to the **Berlin blockade**, an attempt by the Soviet authorities to isolate West Berlin by blocking road and rail routes through the Soviet-occupied zone (later East Germany). A wide range of aircraft were used, many of them belonging to small companies that had been set up after the war by ex-RAF pilots. The Berlin airlift helped these companies to grow into fully fledged airlines.

• **Berlin by Christmas**▶ The cry of Allied servicemen at the start of World Wars I and II. In both cases the optimism evaporated rapidly. **Berlin or bust** was a more realistic variant, introduced by US soldiers in both wars.

• **Berliner**▶
**Ich bin ein Berliner!** (German, I am a Berliner!) A declaration by President John F. Kennedy made during a speech in West Berlin in June 1963. One of the most famous political statements of the 20th century, it underlined America's commitment to West Berlin's independence from the Communist bloc. Wags pointed out that the strictly correct translation was: 'I am a doughnut!' (A Berliner is a cream-filled doughnut speciality of Berlin).

> All free men, wherever they may live, are citizens of Berlin. And therefore, as a free man, I take pride in the words *Ich bin ein Berliner*. – JOHN F KENNEDY.

• **Berliner Ensemble**▶ A theatre company founded in Berlin in 1949 by the German playwright Bertolt Brecht (1898–1956). After Brecht's death, it was taken over by his widow Helene Weigel (1900–71). The company devoted itself to producing Brecht's plays and adaptations before diversifying in the 1970s. In 1992 several leading directors from the former West Germany were brought in to save the company from collapse.

• **Berlin Wall**▶ A wall built through Berlin in 1961 by the East German government to prevent the increasing flow of refugees from the Eastern sector to the West. It was heavily guarded by the East Germans and generally regarded as a symbol of Communist repression. Many East Germans were shot trying to escape over it. The Soviet policy of glasnost, introduced in 1986, led to the liberalization or breakdown of Communist regimes in eastern Europe: demolition of the wall began in 1989, heralding the unification of Germany in October 1990. German entrepreneurs subsequently set up a flourishing trade in pieces of demolished wall. *See also*: Checkpoint Charlie.

• **Bermuda shorts** ▶ Knee-length summer shorts that originated in Bermuda but became widely fashionable in the 1980s.

• **Bermuda Triangle** or **Devil's Triangle** ▶ A triangle of sea in the west Atlantic Ocean, covering 3,900,000 sq km (1,500,000 sq mi) between Bermuda, Florida, and Puerto Rico. Within this area numerous ships and aircraft are supposed to have disappeared without trace or explanation. Some have attributed these disappearances to the prevalent severe weather or dangerous sea currents, others say that no more mysterious losses have occurred here than elsewhere, while others have suggested that the area is subject to more sinister forces of unknown origin. The myth began in 1945, when five US torpedo-bombers vanished without trace; the wrecks of these aircraft were thought to have been located off Florida in 1991, but these turned out not to be the missing flight, thus leaving the myth intact.

• **Bertie** ▶ Edward VII (1841–1910; reigned 1901–10). His mother, Queen Victoria, called him Bertie, but his subjects had other nicknames for him, including **Tum-Tum** for his corpulence and **Edward the Caresser**, for his behaviour with women. He was also known, respectfully, as **Edward the Peacemaker**, for his skill in creating the Entente Cordiale with France. George VI was also known to his family as Bertie, (his first name, like Edward's, being Albert).

• **Bertram Mills Circus** ▶ A circus held every Christmas at Olympia, the London exhibition hall, from 1920 to 1966 (with the exception of the war years). It was started by a coachbuilder with a penchant for the big top – Bertram Mills (1873–1938) – and carried on after his death by his two sons. Bertram Mills Circus was a much-loved feature of the pre-war London Christmas scene.

• **Berufsverbot** ▶ (German, prohibition of vocation) The exclusion of political radicals from holding offices in the German civil service: a policy pursued by West Germany in the 1970s.

• **best by taste** or **best by test** ▶ Originally an advertising slogan for Cola soft drinks, first used in the immediate post-war years; it later became a US catchphrase describing anything regarded as highly desirable.

• **best car in the world** ▶ A trade slogan for Rolls-Royce motor cars. Among other slogans used to sell the famous Silver Ghost was the boast 'at 60 miles an hour the loudest noise in this new Rolls-Royce comes from the electric clock', which was actually an extract from an article in *The Motor*. The reaction of a Rolls-Royce official on reading the report was: 'We really ought to do something about that damned clock.'

• **best of British (luck)** ▶ Originally a World War II catchphrase used to mean 'if you think you can do it get on with it, but leave me out'. At that time the war was going badly for the Allies and British luck was down. After the war, particularly in the 1960s and 1970s, the phrase was often shortened to **and the best of British**; it was then used rather less ironically to mean little more than 'good luck'.

• **best thing since sliced bread** ▶ A catchphrase used to express approval of something for which the speaker has unadulterated admiration. It became popular in the 1960s with the rise of the supermarkets and their convenience products. More recently there has been a reaction against the blandness of many mass-produced sliced loaves, and the phrase has acquired an ironic edge.

• **beta-blocker** ▶ A drug that blocks the stimulation of the beta receptors of the sympathetic nervous system by adrenaline. These drugs are therefore used to reduce high blood pressure, treat angina, and control abnormal heart rhythms. Beta blockers in common use include propranolol, oxprenolol, and metoprolol.

• **better** ▶
    **a better 'ole** The catchphrase of **Old Bill**, a walrus-moustached disillusioned old soldier in World War I, created by Captain Bruce Bairnsfather (1887–1959), artist and journalist, in his publications *Old Bill* and *The Better 'Ole*. Cowering in a muddy shell-hole in the midst of a withering bombardment, he says to his grousing pal Bert, 'If you know of a better 'ole, go to it.'

• **Betty Boop** ▶ A US animated character created by Max Fleischer and 'Grim' Natwick in 1930. A big-eyed sexy flapper with a childlike voice, she was based on the real 'boop-a-doop' singer Helen Kane. The popularity of the Betty Boop cartoons increased after they attracted the attention of US censors; careful examination of surviving cartoons reveals the occasional lifted skirt, dropped shoulder-strap, or subliminal flash of complete nudity that the censors missed.

• **between a rock and a hard place** ▶ Caught in a difficult situation with no easy way out. The expression originated in America, but is now quite common in the UK. It might be said, for example, of a person whose life is made intolerable by a nagging wife on the one hand and a jealous mother on the other.

• **Bevanite**▶ A supporter of the left-wing Labour MP Aneurin Bevan (1897–1960). *See*: Nye.

• **Beveridge Report**▶ A report produced in 1942 by the British economist William Henry Beveridge (later Lord Beveridge; 1879–1963). Entitled *Report on Social Insurance and Allied Services*, it led to the creation of the welfare state. Although the post-war Labour government implemented many of the measures proposed by the report, and took the credit for them, Beveridge himself was a member of the Liberal party.

• **Beverly Hills**▶ A town in SW California, close to Los Angeles. It has become the home town of many of America's leading film stars and other media celebrities. Tourists can take coach tours of the area, and be shown the often palatial houses belonging to their screen idols. Beverly Hills consisted largely of beanfields until its annexation by Hollywood in the 1920s.

• **Bevin Boys**▶ Nickname for the young men directed to work in coal mines under the Emergency Powers (Defence) Act (1940). Ernest Bevin (1881–1951) was minister of labour and National Service at the time and according to this edict one in ten men called up between the ages of 18 and 25 were sent down the mines. The scheme started in 1943 and continued after the war.

• **bewdy Newk!** ▶ An Australian catchphrase used to promote a nationwide health campaign in the 1970s, in which armchair sports fans were encouraged to participate actively in sport. Television adverts showed one such fan exclaiming 'bewdy Newk!' (*i.e.* that's a beauty, Newc) in response to a fine shot by the Australian tennis player John Newcombe.

• **Beyond the Fringe**▶ An influential satirical revue staged in London in 1960. The *Beyond the Fringe* team consisted of Peter Cook and Dudley Moore as well as the show's writers, Jonathan Miller and Alan Bennett; all four were recent graduates from Oxford or Cambridge. The show had been premiered a year earlier at the Edinburgh Festival (the title alludes to the Edinburgh 'Fringe') and went on to achieve major success on Broadway. Cook and Moore later produced another touring show called *Behind the Fridge*.

• **B-52** ▶ **1.** A US heavy bomber, also called the Stratofortress. **2.** A beehive hairstyle of the early 1960s, named after the heavy bomber.

• **Bhangra**▶ A form of music combining Western rock with Punjabi folk styles, popular with the Indian community in the UK from the 1980s.

• **Bhopal** ▶ An Indian city, the capital of Madhya Pradesh, with a population of 1,063,662 (1991). It became headline news in December 1984 when over 2500 people were killed by an escape of highly poisonous methyl isocyanate gas from its US-owned Union Carbide factory. Local medical facilities collapsed when some 50,000 others, temporarily blinded or disabled by the gas, sought help. A lengthy battle for legal compensation ensued.

• **Biafra** ▶ An eastern region of Nigeria in which the Ibo people unilaterally declared independence in 1967. The state was not recognized by the Nigerian government, which finally forced it to surrender early in 1970, after the Ibo people had been decimated by war and starvation.

• **biathlon**▶ **1.** An athletic event combining cross-country skiing with marksmanship. It was first included in the Winter Olympic Games in 1960. **2.** An athletic event that consists of running and swimming contests, introduced in 1968.

• **Bible Belt**▶ The states of the US South, considered as being a hotbed of Protestant fundamentalism and intolerant social attitudes.

• **Bible-thumper** or **Bible-basher** ▶ An enthusiastic evangelist, who makes frequent reference to the Bible.

• **bidonville** ▶ (French, tin-can town) A shanty town built of metal from tin cans and other refuse materials.

• **Big Apple** ▶ New York City. The derivation of this nickname is unclear. One suggestion is that Hispanics originally nicknamed the city *la Grande Manzana* (the big street-block) because of its grid-like street pattern; the Spanish word *manzana* also means apple. Alternatively, it may simply have arisen from the idea that New York offered the opportunity for 'a bite of the apple', that is, a chance of success.

• **big band**▶ A band of musicians, usually more than 15 in number, that played the form of jazz known as swing in the 1930s and early 1940s. Functioning largely as dance bands, they made use of saxophones and several trumpets (or cornets) and trombones to provide colourful orchestration in place of the earlier solo improvisations. The US big bands included those of Glenn Miller, Benny Goodman, Artie Shaw, and Duke Ellington. Smaller and less glamorous big bands in the UK were led by Geraldo, Ambrose, and Joe Loss.

• **Big Bang** ▶ **1.** An explosion of a superdense mass of matter some $20 \times 10^9$ years ago, in which the universe is believed to have originated. Evidence for this event is thought to lie in the continuing expansion of the universe, as first suggested by the US astronomer Edwin Hubble (1889–1953) in 1929, from his observation of the redshift of the light from distant galaxies. **2.** The upheaval on the London Stock Exchange (LSE) in October 1986, when the whole manner of trading was changed, notably by the abolition of the distinction between jobbers and brokers. At the same time, the LSE was modernized by the introduction of a computerized dealing system and broadened to become a truly international market. *See also*: Chinese wall.

• **Big Bertha** ▶ The nickname for the large howitzers used by the Germans against Liège and Namur in 1914. They were made by Krupps, the German armament firm, hence the allusion to Frau Bertha Krupp. The Germans also used large guns made by Skoda known as **Slender Emmas**. In 1918 Paris was shelled from a range of 121 km (76 mi) by the 142-ton 'Paris' gun, to which the name Big Bertha was again applied. In US slang a 'Big Bertha' is any fat woman.

• **Big Bill** ▶ William Hale Thompson (1867–1944), three-times mayor of Chicago, who was noted for his anti-British views. He once threatened to punch George V on the nose if he ever visited Chicago.

• **Big Brother** ▶ **1.** In George Orwell's *Nineteen Eighty-Four* (1949) the personification of state power. Although he never appears in person, and may not even exist, he is presented as an all-seeing all-powerful figure in Party propaganda. The slogan 'Big Brother is watching you' is widely used to mean that authority, totalitarian and bureaucratic, has you under its observation from which there is no escape.

> The posters that were plastered everywhere—
> BIG BROTHER IS WATCHING YOU the caption said,
> while the dark eyes looked into Winston's own.
> – *Nineteen Eighty-Four*.

**2.** A television programme devised by the Endemol company and first shown in the Netherlands in 1999; by August 2001 versions of the show had been seen in 17 countries, including the UK. Big Brother is part game show, part docusoap, and part social experiment. A group of strangers are locked into a specially constructed house for a period of weeks. The house is installed with an extensive CCTV system with microphones everywhere and the participants are denied access to the outside world. Every day the TV broadcasts edited highlights of the CCTV footage, most of which is available live and

unedited on an official Internet site. At the end of each week the housemates secretly nominate two of their number for eviction and the viewing public then vote for one of these two to be expelled from the house (and the programme). The final survivor wins a large cash prize. When first shown in the UK in the summer of 2000 the programme attracted large audiences and obsessive coverage in both the popular and the 'quality' press. The show provoked much debate about the voyeuristic nature of the modern electronic media, the cult of celebrity for its own sake, and the kind of society that Britain – as represented by the 10 young contestants – was becoming.

• **big C** ▶ Cancer. The phrase received wide coverage when used by the US actor John Wayne (1907–79) to express his determination to cope with his cancer.

• **big crunch** ▶ The theory that, just as the universe began with a Big Bang, it will eventually collapse into a small compact core.

• **Big Cyril** ▶ Cyril Smith (1928–93), Liberal MP for Rochdale (1972–92). A vast man, weighing some 25 stones, who became a popular media personality in the 1970s.

• **Big Daddy** ▶ **1.** Stage name of Shirley Crabtree (1936–  ), British wrestler and media personality. **2.** Idi Amin (1925–  ), who as president of Uganda (1971–79) repressed the Ugandan people and instituted his own bizarre and cruel personality cult; he was finally ousted by Tanzanian forces. **3.** Lyndon B. Johnson (1908–73), US president (1963–69).

• **big enchilada** ▶ A VIP. The phrase became popular from its use in the Watergate tapes to describe the US attorney-general. An *enchilada* is a Mexican dish consisting of a tortilla filled with meat and dressed with chilli sauce.

• **Big Five** ▶ The five countries taking part in the Paris Peace Conference in 1919 following World War I: the UK, France, Italy, Japan, and America.

• **Bigfoot** ▶ A postulated 'apeman' of the mountains of the Pacific Northwest of America, several sightings of which were repoorted in the 20th century. Indistinct photographs suggest a tall hairy creature with long arms and a slightly pointed head; it is said to leave huge footprints, 43 cm (17 in) long. Also known as the **Sasquatch** (from a Salish Indian word, *saskehavas*, meaning hairy men), it was first promoted by the news media in the early 1970s, though the legend probably dates back to the late 1920s. *See also*: Abominable Snowman.

• **Biggin Hill** ▶ A former RAF airfield in Kent that

played a leading part in the Battle of Britain. It was from Biggin Hill and similar RAF airfields in southern England that the heroic Few took to the skies to defeat Goering's Luftwaffe.

• **Biggles**► The hero of several boys' adventure stories by Captain W. E. Johns. He was based upon Air Commodore Cecil George Wigglesworth (1893–1961), who served alongside Johns in World War I and became Air Officer Commanding Iceland during World War II. Biggles made his first appearance in *The Camels are Coming* (1932).

• **Big Gooseberry Season**► The silly season, the period during the summer holidays, when newspapers are glad of any subject to fill their columns; monster gooseberries exhibited at local fruit and vegetable shows will do for such a purpose.

• **Big-hearted Arthur**► Arthur Askey (1900–82), British comedian and music-hall artist, who endeared himself to the wartime British public with his radio show *Band Waggon*. He referred to himself as Big-hearted Arthur in the first edition of *Band Waggon* (in 1938) and was known by this name thereafter.

• **big house**► US underworld slang for a prison, particularly a federal prison, which came into common parlance with the 1930 Oscar-winning film of this name, starring Wallace Beery.

• **big look**► A fashion in women's clothes of the 1970s, which was based on loose-fitting designs. *See also*: layered look.

• **Big Mac**► 1. Tradename for the best-known item on the menus of McDonald's fast food outlets, consisting of a large hamburger. *See also*: McDonald's. 2. The Municipal Assistance Corporation, which was founded in 1975 to cope with New York City's huge debt problem.

• **big O**► A euphemism for an orgasm, especially a female orgasm.

• **Big One**► US nickname for the circus formed by the merger of Ringling Brothers Circus and Barnum and Bailey's in 1907. The 'Big One' finally ceased operations in 1956.

• **Big Three**► The heads of government of America, the UK, and the Soviet Union – Roosevelt, Churchill, and Stalin, respectively – at the time of the 1945 Yalta Conference, when they met towards the end of World War II to agree upon the postwar occupation of Germany.

• **Big Wind** or **Big Windy**► US nickname for Chicago, referring to the high winds that come off Lake Michigan on which the city stands.

• **bike**►
   **On your bike!** A peremptory dismissal, which is as old as the bicycle itself; it enjoyed a new lease of life after a much-discussed speech by the Conservative politician Norman Tebbit (later Lord Tebbit; 1931– ) at the party conference of 1981.

> I know all about these problems. I grew up in the thirties with an unemployed father. He didn't riot. He got on his bike and looked for work. And he found it!

• **Bikini**► An atoll in the Marshall Islands, the scene of US nuclear weapon testing in 1946 (and 1954). It gave its name to the scanty two-piece bathing outfit for women, apparently because the devastating effects of such a costume can only be compared to that of an atomic explosion.

• **Biko affair**► The death in custody of Steve Biko (1946–77), a leader of the Black Consciousness Movement in South Africa and founder (1968) of the South African Students Organization (SASO). An active opponent of apartheid, he was arrested in September 1977 and died of injuries sustained while in police custody six days later. World condemnation of this event made Biko an international symbol of the anti-apartheid struggle and a folk hero among South African Blacks. His life and death were celebrated in 'Biko' (1978), a well-known song by Peter Gabriel, and Richard Attenborough's film *Cry Freedom* (1987).

• **Bill, the** or **Old Bill, the**► The police. A British working-class slang expression that has crept into common parlance since the 1970s with its use in TV police dramas (including one called *The Bill*). Its derivation is obscure but could be related to the bill-hooks that early officers of the peace used to carry.

• **Billings method**► A method of 'natural' family planning devised by Drs John and Evelyn Billings in the 1960s. It involves daily examination of the cervical mucus in the vagina in order to observe changes in mucal consistency, which enables those days on which ovulation occurs to be identified. On these days intercourse is avoided if the woman does not wish to become pregnant or encouraged if she does. Many women find the procedure unacceptable; as a form of contraception it is regarded as unreliable.

• **Billy Bunter**► *See*: Bunter, Billy.

• **Billy Graham crusades**► The worldwide evangelical campaigns undertaken by the US preacher Dr Billy Graham (1918– ) from the 1950s onwards. The meetings were characterized by a high level of pre-publicity and were held in large stadiums. Members of the audience were invited to get out of their seats, come to the front, and make a public 'decision for Christ'.

• **Billy Williams's Cabbage Patch** ▶ The English Rugby Football Union's ground at Twickenham, the headquarters of the English game. It is so-called after W. (Billy) Williams (1860–1951), who discovered the site and through whose persistence the ground was acquired in 1907; also from the ground's former partial use as a market garden. The first match was played there on 2 October 1909. The nearby Railway Tavern changed its name to The Cabbage Patch in the early 1970s.

• **bimbo** ▶ An empty-headed but sexually attractive woman. The word originated in America around 1915–20 but in this sense, which is widely used in tabloid journalism, did not become current until the 1980s, when it spread from America to the UK and Australia. It is sometimes also applied to sexually attractive but brainless men (occasionally in the form **himbo** or **bimboy**). Originally, a bimbo (probably derived from the Italian *bambino*, a child) was a stupid, contemptible, or disreputable man; in the 1920s it was used as slang for a prostitute. A combination of these senses seems to have led to its current usage (although some argue that this is an acronym for 'body immaculate, brains optional'). A **bimbette** is a younger version of a bimbo.

> We want to love women in a way that doesn't condescend. We don't just love bimbos. – LEE EISENBERG, *The Independent on Sunday*, 9 December 1990.

• **binary weapon** ▶ A nerve gas, the lethal effects of which are released when two relatively harmless chemicals are mixed as the projectile in which they are carried reaches its target.

• **Binet test** ▶ A series of intelligence tests devised in 1903 by the French psychologist Alfred Binet (1857–1911), who based them on the responses of his two daughters to his use of objects and pictures to assess intelligence and aptitude. They have been adapted for use in many countries, the Stanford-Binet test (prepared at Stanford University, California, in 1916) being the best-known revision.

• **Bing** ▶ *See*: Old Groaner.

• **Bing Boys** ▶ The nickname of the Canadian troops in World War I from the name of their commanding officer, Lord Byng of Vimy. Also from the revue, *The Bing Boys Are Here*, which opened at the Alhambra in Leicester Square, London, in 1915.

• **bingle** ▶ Australian slang for a car crash. Earlier meanings of the word included a skirmish (in World War II) and damage done to a surfboard.

• **bingo** ▶ A game of chance, in which each player fills in the unique sequence of numbers on his or her card as they are announced at random by the 'bingo-caller'; the first to complete her sequence is the winner. The game had its origins before World War I, other names for it being 'Keno', 'Beano', 'Loo', 'Housey Housey', or 'Lotto'. Many British cinemas were converted to bingo halls in the 1960s when the game was at its most popular.

• **bint** ▶ (Arabic *bint*, daughter, young woman). A rather derogatory expression for a woman, used by British troops serving in Egypt from the 1920s to the 1960s. It is now rarely heard.

• **bioastronomy** ▶ The search for life elsewhere in the universe. Deep-space probes have been fitted with equipment to detect living processes on other planets but have so far had no success; some carry information about the probe's origins and about the earth and its inhabitants.

• **biodegradable** ▶ Describing substances that can be degraded (*i.e.* broken down into their constituents) by bacteria or other biological agents. The term was originally applied to sewage but in recent years it has been used in connection with the disposal of other pollutants: with growing concern about the build-up of domestic and industrial waste and the persistence in the environment of pesticides, there is increasing pressure for the development of packaging and products that are biodegradable. *See also*: photodegradable.

• **biofeedback** ▶ A form of therapy in which patients learn to control unconscious physiological activities, such as heart rate and brain rhythms, with the aid of machines that monitor them. By relaxing and concentrating the mind on the activity in question, while receiving feedback from the machine on changes in the activity, patients can be taught to gain some control over these bodily functions. Biofeedback has been used with some success by practitioners of alternative medicine to relieve migraine, tension headaches, and high blood pressure (hypertension); it is also said to have been helpful to cigarette smokers who want to reduce their smoking.

The techniques of biofeedback vary. In hypertension, for example, electrodes monitoring skin conductivity are taped to the patient's fingers. Damp hands (which are more conductive than dry hands) are associated with arousal and stress, factors also said to be a cause of raised blood pressure. By observing that the dial of the skin-conductivity meter is falling, the patients are taught to relax and their blood pressure falls.

• **biogas** ▶ A mixture of methane and carbon dioxide gases produced by the action of bacteria on organic matter (sewage, household and industrial waste, etc.). Some developing countries, notably India, have been using biogas – generated in special biogas plants – as a source of energy since the 1970s. With existing reserves of fossil fuels likely to become exhausted within the next hundred years, and nuclear power stations still providing only a small proportion (some 6.4%) of the world's energy, developed countries have shown interest in alternative energy sources. The large-scale production of biogas is one such solution that is being actively explored: it would serve the dual purpose of exploiting a potentially important energy source and of disposing of domestic and industrial waste.

• **Biograph Girl** ▶ The nickname given to the US actress Florence Lawrence (1886–1938), who appeared in numerous silent shorts for the Biograph film company in the 1900s. Lawrence, who like most film actors of the day appeared anonymously, became one of the first screen actors to be recognized and admired by the public. In 1910 she defected to another film company who offered her a 4000% pay rise and began to appear under her own name – thus effectively creating the Hollywood star system. Her films include *Resurrection* (1910) and *The Enfoldment* (1920).

• **biological clock** ▶ 1. The mechanism within living organisms that is assumed to control the timing of certain periodic changes of behaviour or physiology (*see*: biorhythm). These events, which include the annual migrations of birds and other animals, seem to occur more or less independently of changes in the environment: this has led biologists to postulate the existence of such a 'clock', although its method of working is not yet fully understood. 2. A childless woman's awareness that her childbearing years are limited. The phrase, often used in the form 'I hear my biological clock ticking away', became a familiar cliché in women's fiction and journalism of the 1990s.

• **biomass** ▶ The total weight of all the living organisms, or of one particular species, within a population or given area: biomass calculations are used in studies of energy flow within ecological communities. The term, which has been part of the vocabulary of ecologists since the 1930s, has come into wider and more general use in recent years in the concept of **biomass energy** – the energy derived from plants (*e.g.* sugar cane, trees) grown especially for this purpose; from sewage, farm, and domestic waste; and from other natural sources. These **biofuels** are becoming an important source of alternative energy. *See*: biogas.

• **bionic** ▶ Consisting of or possessing electronic or mechanical components whose design is based on that of comparable systems in living organisms. The term originated in the early 1960s with the evolution of **bionics** (from *biological electronics*), the study and application of bionic systems, but became much more widely known in the 1970s in connection with the popular US TV series *The Six Million Dollar Man* (1973–78). This starred Lee Majors as the eponymous 'bionic man' – an individual whose body parts had been replaced by electronic equipment, giving him superhuman strength and extraordinary powers. Since then the term has come into general use to denote superlative skill or performance.

• **biopic** ▶ Biographical picture, a movie based on the life of a real person. Biopics have tended to be unpopular with film makers, because they rarely make money and with film critics, because of their tendency to sentimental distortion. Perhaps this reputation reflects the rather poor showing that Hollywood made of its biopics in the 1930s and 1940s. For example, *Love Time* (1934; Schubert), *A Song to Remember* (1944; Chopin), *Song of Love* (1947; Liszt), *Song of my Heart* (1947; Tchaikovsky), and many others treated anecdotes in the lives of composers with a triviality reflected in their titles. Writers, scientists, inventors, and politicians fared little better. Because of this dubious track record, when Richard Attenborough tried to raise the money to fulfil a long ambition to make a biopic about Gandhi, he met with little sympathy. When, in 1982, his epic *Gandhi* finally emerged it went some way to rehabilitate the genre. Subsequent biopics have included Clint Eastwood's *Bird* (1988), about Charlie Parker, Spike Lee's *Malcolm X* (1992), Attenborough's *Shadowlands* (1994), about C. S. Lewis, and *Ali* (2001), about the boxer.

• **biorhythm** ▶ A pattern of behaviour or a metabolic activity that occurs in regular cycles controlled by a biological clock within an organism, which operates independently of external factors. Examples are the 24-hour (**circadian**) rhythms of sleeping/waking and the annual rhythms of hibernation and migration that occur in many animals. This biological term has been debased by those who postulate that human behaviour is regulated by three biorhythms of physical, emotional, and intellectual activity: there is no evidence to support this assertion.

• **bippy** ▶
   **You bet your sweet bippy!** A catchphrase popularized by the US TV comedy show *Rowan and*

*Martin's Laugh-In* in the 1960s. It was usually spoken by Dick Martin.

• **Bircher ▶** *See*: John Birch Society.

• **Bird** or **Yardbird ▶** The nickname given to Charlie Parker (1920–55), the US Black jazz saxophonist, who is now regarded as one of the most influential of all jazz performers.

• **birder ▶** A keen amateur ornithologist; a bird-watcher, especially one who is keen on spotting and identifying as many species as possible. **Twitchers** or **tickers** are birders who concentrate on spotting rare species, which they then tick off their list.

• **Birds Eye ▶** Tradename of a company noted for producing frozen foodstuffs. It takes its name from the US inventor Clarence Birdseye (1886–1956), who discovered (1915) that vegetables could be preserved by freezing them at low temperatures. He discovered this process while fur trading and trapping in Labrador. His own name is said to have been derived from an ancestor who was a page at the royal court, who attracted attention when he shot a diving hawk through the eye with an arrow.

• **bird strike ▶** A collision between a flying bird and an aircraft. These collisions can be dangerous as the bird's body or feathers may block air intakes or lead to shattered windscreens, etc. Airfields adopt various strategies to scare birds away.

• **Birmingham Six ▶** A group of six Irishmen who were imprisoned for 16 years for their supposed role in IRA pub bombings in Birmingham in which 17 people died in 1974. The heavy death toll in the attacks led to a public outcry for quick arrests. The six suspects were arrested and subsequently gaoled, although doubts were soon raised as to the quality of the evidence against them, which consisted of doubtful forensic evidence that their hands revealed traces of explosives. This evidence was later withdrawn as unsafe. There were also confessions by the men, which were later proved to have been extracted under duress. Some, but not all, of this later evidence was available to the appeal court, which failed to quash their sentences. After intense public disquiet the Director of Public Prosecutions let it be known that he would not contest another appeal and the prisoners were released on 14 March 1991 amongst a storm of vituperation at the inadequacies of British criminal law and the judges in particular. The case was considered highly damaging to the reputation of the British legal system and reforms of police procedures and legal appeals were demanded. *See also*: Chicago Seven; Guildford Four.

• **Biro ▶** A ball-point pen using a quick-drying ink, which was invented in 1938 by the Hungarian inventor Laszlo Biró (1900–85). The word has now become a generic name for any ball-point pen.

• **birth control ▶** The prevention of an unwanted pregnancy, whether by 'natural' methods or by the artificial means that only became widely available in the 20th century. Long-practised 'natural' methods include *coitus interruptus* (removal of the penis from the vagina before ejaculation) and the rhythm method (in which ejaculation into the vagina is avoided except during the woman's so-called safe period).

Both these methods are unreliable, although they are the only ones permitted to members of the Roman Catholic Church (*see*: Humanae Vitae). Artificial methods of birth control advanced in the 20th century included the condom, the diaphragm or cap (a rubber disc fitted over the cervix of the womb), the IUD (intra-uterine device, a loop or coil inserted into the uterus by a doctor), and the Pill. In a world that is grossly overpopulated, prudent **family planning** using artificial contraception is an essential aspect of responsible parenthood. *See*: Stopes clinic.

• **birth mother ▶** *See*: genetic mother; surrogate motherhood.

• **bish-bash-bosh ▶** Quickly and efficiently. A fashionable expression amongst London yuppies in the mid-1980s.

• **Bismarck ▶** A German battleship, named after Otto von Bismarck (1815–98), which sank the British ship HMS Hood in May 1941. Three days later the *Bismarck*, which had threatened to terrorize shipping in the Atlantic, was sunk by the *Dorsetshire* after being seriously damaged by aircraft from the aircraft carrier *Ark Royal* and by the *King George V* and the *Rodney*. The wreck of the *Bismarck*, in its day the most powerful battleship afloat, was located and photographed in deep water in the 1980s.

• **Bismarck Sea ▶** A region of sea around the Bismarck Archipelago – a group of some 200 islands in the SW Pacific Ocean northeast of New Guinea. Here, in 1943, US aircraft operating from aircraft carriers destroyed a Japanese troop convoy bound for New Guinea (the **Battle of the Bismarck Sea**).

• **bistable ▶** *See*: flip-flop.

• **Bisto kids ▶** Two cartoon children who appeared in advertisements by the Cerebos company for gravy browning – often with the slogan 'aah Bisto', referring to the product's appetizing smell. The slogan was first used in an advertising campaign in 1919. The name 'Bisto' is said to have been derived from 'Browns, Seasons, Thickens in One'.

• **bistro** ► A British restaurant that prides itself on its 'continental' style; in France a *bistro* is any café offering relatively low-priced food.

• **bit** ► A unit of computer information; an abbreviated form of 'binary digit'. *See also*: byte.

• **Bitch of Buchenwald** or **Witch of Buchenwald** ► Ilse Koch (d. 1967), the hated wife of the commandant of the German concentration camp at Buchenwald during World War II. A woman of unspeakable cruelty, she and her husband epitomized the degradation of the German people during the Nazi regime.

• **bite the dust** ► To die or to fail completely. The phrase, which derives from films and stories about the Wild West, originally meant to be struck off one's horse by a bullet or arrow (as in 'another Redskin bit the dust').

• **bit of fluff** ► *See at*: fluff.

• **bit of rough** ► British slang for a lover (of either sex but usually a man) from a lower social class or with rough manners. It derives from the term rough trade, meaning an uncouth male lover, either homosexual or heterosexual.

• **bitser** or **bitsa** ► A mongrel. An Australian word based on the idea that the animal's pedigree is made up of bits of this and that. It can be applied to anything made up of component parts.

• **bivvy** ► British army and Boy Scout slang meaning to bivouac, to make camp.

• **blabber** ► Australian slang for a TV remote-control device, presumably because of its ability to control the volume.

• **black** ►
 **Any colour, so long as it's black** Henry Ford's famous reply to queries about the colour range in which the Model T was available (*see*: Tin Lizzie).

• **Blackadder** ► The antihero of a BBC comedy series of the same name first shown in 1983. The show's four series present four incarnations of the devious Edmund Blackadder (Rowan Atkinson) and his faithful but stupid servant Baldrick (Tony Robinson) in historical epochs ranging from the Wars of the Roses to World War I. As played by Atkinson, Blackadder is a cowardly disaster-prone schemer with an acid wit. The final episode, screened in 1989, ended with a stunning finale in which all the main characters were mown down as they went 'over the top' on the Western Front. The witty scripts were written by Richard Curtis and Ben Elton.

• **Black and Tans** ► The irregulars enlisted by the British government in 1920 to supplement the Royal Irish Constabulary in its struggle with the IRA. They were so called from their mixed black and tan uniforms (there being a shortage of proper police uniforms). The force (subsequently reinforced by an Auxiliary Division of irregulars – the **Auxis**) was deeply resented for its brutal methods and use of indiscriminate reprisals (*see*: Bloody Sunday); they were withdrawn in 1921.

• **black bag job** ► US slang for an undercover operation carried out by a government agency. The phrase dates from the Watergate scandal of 1972.

• **Blackboard Jungle** ► Schools in a rundown urban area in which delinquency is rife and discipline is difficult to impose. The name is taken from the title of a novel by Evan Hunter (1954; filmed 1955), about a school in downtown New York. The novel was a savage indictment of certain aspects of the US state educational system.

• **black bombers** ► British slang for the very strong black amphetamine capsules containing Durophet that were popular with drug abusers in the 1960s and early 1970s.

• **Black Bottom** ► A dance popular in the late 1920s; it originated in America and involved rotating the hips.

• **black box** ► 1. An aircraft's flight recorder. 2. Any device, real or conceptual, that takes input and produces output, but whose internal workings are invisible to the outside world; often used in computer programming. 3. British derogatory slang of the 1980s for a Muslim woman wearing the traditional shapeless black ankle-length garment, the *burka*.

• **black cab** ► *See*: taxi.

• **Black Caucus** ► In America, an organization of supporters of Black civil rights in Congress, founded in 1967.

• **black-coated workers** ► Prunes. This euphemism for the prune in its laxative capacity was popularized by Charles Hill, the BBC's radio doctor of the 1940s.

• **Black Consciousness** ► A former movement in South Africa that was committed to the overthrow of apartheid and the establishment of equal civil rights for Blacks.

• **black economy** ► That part of the economic activity of a country that does not feature in national statistics because it is undisclosed. The reasons for its non-disclosure are either because it involves money earned but not returned to the tax authorities, which therefore escapes taxation, or money earned but not disclosed by those claiming state benefits. The black economy is believed to be very large in most societies, although by its nature it is unmeasurable.

• **black flag** ► **1.** In World War II, submarines, sometimes hoisted a black flag on returning to base, to indicate a 'kill'. **2.** In motor-racing, the showing of a black flag signals to a driver that he must quit the race, usually for some serious infringement of the rules.

• **Black Friday** ► 15 April 1921 was Black Friday for the British Labour Movement, this being the day on which the threatened General Strike was cancelled. *See also*: Red Friday.

• **Black Hand** ► **1.** The popular name of the Slav secret society largely responsible for contriving the assassination of the Archduke Franz Ferdinand on 28 June 1914 (*see*: Sarajevo assassination). This was the event that precipitated World War I. **2.** A criminal society, once active in New York, largely made up of Italians.

• **black hole** ► A hypothetical object in space that is believed to result from the gravitational collapse of a massive star at the end of its life, first postulated by the German astronomer Karl Schwarzchild (1873–1916) in 1916. Because the escape velocity from the object is equal to the speed of light, no radiation can escape from it and what goes on inside its boundary, called its **event horizon**, is theoretically unknowable. No black hole has been identified, although it has been postulated that they are the power sources of quasars.

• **Black is beautiful** ► Slogan adopted in the 1960s by supporters of Black civil rights in America in an attempt to improve the negative self-image and low self-confidence of many Blacks. The slogan was coined by Stokely Carmichael in 1966 and taken up by Martin Luther King the following year.

• **black knight** ► *See*: white knight.

• **black market** ► In World War II, illicit dealing in rationed goods; subsequently used of any illegal dealing. *See*: under the counter.

• **black mist** ► (Japanese *kuro kiri*) Translation of a Japanese term denoting corruption in business or politics. Several major scandals of this nature have disrupted Japanese life since the 1960s; the black mist referred to is the usual attempt made to disguise such corruption.

• **Black Monday** ► Either of the two Mondays in the 20th century on which the New York Stock Exchange opened very considerably below its level on the previous Friday. The first Wall Street Crash occurred on Monday 28 October 1929, when the 13% knocked off the Dow Jones Industrial Average led to the Great Depression of the 1930s. The second Black Monday occurred on 19 October 1987, when the Dow Jones Average fell by an alarming 23%. Although Wall Street's collapse in both cases triggered falls in stock-market prices throughout the world, in the 1987 crash careful management of international finances managed to avoid a serious slump and prices gradually recovered.

• **Black Muslims** ► A popular name for the Nation of Islam, a Black US sect noted for its fierce racial ideology. The movement dates from about 1930 when Wallace Fard Muhammed, acclaimed by his followers as the incarnate Allah, built a mosque in Detroit (he disappeared shortly afterwards in mysterious circumstances). Under Fard's successor, Elijah Muhammed, the sect developed a doctrine of racial separation, preaching that White society was the creation of devils and doomed to imminent destruction. The Black Muslims came to national prominence in the 1960s, owing mainly to their charismatic spokesman Malcolm X and the recruitment of such figures as the boxer Cassius Clay (Muhammed Ali). In the 1970s and 1980s the movement split: one faction repudiated its more extreme beliefs, merging eventually with the Islamic mainstream; the other, led by Louis Farrakhan, continued to maintain the sect's doctrines.

• **black-out** ► **1.** Originally, a period in the theatre when the whole stage is in darkness. This usage dates from the 1920s. **2.** A World War II air-raid precaution. From the outbreak of war against Germany (3 September 1939) until 23 April 1945 (coastal areas, 11 May), it was obligatory throughout Great Britain to cover all windows, skylights, etc., before dark so that no gleam of light could be seen from outside. Moving vehicles were only allowed to use masked lights. **3.** A complete loss of consciousness.

• **Black Panther** ► **1.** The name given by the popular press to the British murderer Donald Neilson. After a nine-month search he was caught and convicted of the murder of Lesley Whittle and three sub-post office officials in 1975. The name reflects his use of a black hood to conceal his identity. **1.** A member of a US Black militant organization of the late 1960s, notorious for such demands as the release of all Black prisoners from US gaols and for staging a series of shootouts with the police. The name seems to have arisen from the panther symbol used by a group of Black Power candidates who fought elections in Alabama in 1966. A Black Panther Party emerged in California the following year under the leadership of Huey Newton and Eldridge Cleaver, preaching total separation from White society and urging Blacks to take up arms in 'self defence'. By the 1970s the movement had been seriously weakened by internal rifts and the arrest, defection, or death of its leading members.

• **Blackpool illuminations ▶** The annual display of elaborate decorative street lighting that stretches for over 9 km (6 mi) along the front at Blackpool. The lights go on in the autumn and extend the 'season' by several weeks, attracting many thousands of visitors to the town. They were first erected in 1912 for a visit by Queen Victoria's daughter Princess Louise and (with a break during World War II) became an annual event from 1925.

• **Black Power ▶** A slogan first used by the US Black leader Stokely Carmichael in about 1966. The phrase implies a rejection of both integration as a political goal and of the pacifism of the civil rights movement led by Martin Luther King.

• **Black September ▶** A Palestinian terrorist group founded in 1972. It was named in commemoration of the Jordanian expulsion of Palestinians in September 1970. The seizure of Israeli athletes (and the subsequent killing of most of them) during the Olympic Games of 1972 was staged by the group, as were various sky-jackings and assassinations.

• **Blackshirts ▶** Mussolini's Italian Fascists, named after the distinguishing garments they wore. Similar shirts were adopted by the British Union of Fascists under Sir Oswald Mosley (see: Mosleyites). Also a name for the German SS, led by Himmler. See: Fascism.

• **Black Sox scandal ▶** A notorious bribery scandal that shook the US baseball world in 1920. Members of the Chicago White Sox team had been bribed to 'throw' a game in the 1919 World Series. At the subsequent trial the accused players were acquitted due to lack of evidence. However, the newly appointed first commissioner of baseball realized the threat to the sport's reputation and banned those involved from baseball for life. When news of the scandal first broke, supporters were stunned. One small boy approached his favourite star and tearfully begged him to **say it ain't so, Joe**. His words, one of the best known quotations in baseball history, are now used ironically in other situations in which a hero is suspected of having done something awful.

• **black spot ▶** A stretch of road notorious for frequent car accidents. The phrase is now also used to mean an area of high unemployment.

• **Black Wednesday ▶** Wednesday 16 September 1992, when sterling was forced out of the Exchange Rate Mechanism (see: European Monetary System), leading to a 15% fall in its value against the Deutschmark. The then chancellor of the exchequer, Norman Lamont, who had declared that any devaluation would be over his dead body, and the prime minister, John Major, who described any devaluation of sterling as 'a betrayal of our future', were both called upon to resign. Neither did so, but some nine months later Major sacked Lamont.

• **blag ▶ 1.** British slang meaning to rob, or a robbery. A familiar expression since the 1970s from its use in TV crime dramas. **2.** To scrounge, or the spoils from scrounging. The derivation of both these meanings is obscure.

• **Blairism ▶** The political ideas and policies associated with Tony Blair (1953– ), prime minister of the UK (1997– ), or his supporters, the so-called **Blairites**. The term encompasses both the reforms of the Labour Party introduced by Blair following his election as party leader in 1994 (see: New Labour), and the modernizing policies of the Blair-led Labour government (see: Third Way).

• **Blake, Nicholas ▶** The pseudonym used by the British poet C. Day Lewis (1904–72) as the author of some 20 crime novels published between 1935 and 1968. The future poet laureate turned to crime fiction when he found himself unable to pay for urgently needed repairs to his house: the pseudonym was the idea of his literary agent. Those who knew Blake's identity (a closely guarded secret) may have seen in the novels' main protagonist, the sleuth Nicholas Strangeways, a likeness to Day Lewis's friend and fellow poet W. H. Auden.

• **Blake case ▶** The trial in 1961 of the British double agent George Blake, who while working for MI6 claimed to have betrayed some 400 of his East European contacts to the KGB. Blake received a 42-year sentence, at the time the longest ever handed down by a British court. In the event, he spent less than five years in prison, escaping from Wormwood Scrubs in 1966. Bewildered officials found only an improvised rope ladder, constructed from 20 size 13 knitting needles, and a single pink chrysanthemum. It transpired that this coup had been masterminded not by a team of crack Soviet agents but by two CND activists, Michael Randle and Pat Pottle, who considered Blake's sentence excessive. It was suggested in Blake's defence that he was brainwashed by Communist agents while held captive in Korea during the 1950s. Blake himself denied this, offering instead the excuse that he only passed names to the KGB on the understanding that no one would be harmed!

In 1991 Randle and Pottle were tried for their part in the escape; although they admitted their role, they pleaded not guilty, arguing that they had acted on humanitarian grounds and that bringing the case so long after the event constituted an 'abuse of process' – a plea that the jury accepted. This perverse acquittal perhaps reflected the jury's contempt for British justice after the Birmingham Six and Guildford Four affairs.

• **bland out**▶ To lose personality, to become conventional.

• **blanket protest**▶ *See*: Maze prison.

• **Blast**▶ A magazine of the literary and artistic avant-garde founded in 1914 by Wyndham Lewis and Ezra Pound. Subtitled 'the Review of the Great English Vortex', the journal was a vehicle for vorticism. Although shortlived, it became notorious for its provocative rhetoric and experimental typography.

• **Blaue Reiter**▶ (German, blue riders) A German school of expressionist artists founded in 1911 by the Russian painter Wassily Kandinsky (1866–1944) and the German Franz Marc (1880–1916). They were later joined by the Swiss painter Paul Klee (1879–1940) and others. The artists were a breakaway group from an organization formed in 1909 – the *Neue Kunstlervereinigung* (New Artists' Association). In explaining the name, Kandinsky said: 'We both liked blue and Marc liked painting horses'. (Marc's best-known painting is *Blue Horses* (1911), in the Walker Art Center, Minneapolis). *See*: expressionism.

• **blaxploitation**▶ The exploitation of Black audiences, with their newfound confidence and growing spending power, by film makers in the early 1970s. Most blaxploitation movies were urban action thrillers featuring hip, violent, and sexually inexhaustible Black characters in stereotypical plots and huge flares. The best known were probably *Shaft* (1971) and *Superfly* (1972). *I'm Gonna Git You Sucka* (1988) is an amusing spoof of the genre.

• **bleeper**▶ A small electronic device that alerts the wearer to contact his base by telephone. Although the use of mobile phones has replaced them for some purposes, they are still widely used by medical staff in hospitals.

• **Blessed Margaret**▶ *See*: Iron Lady.

• **Bletchley Park**▶ The mansion in Buckinghamshire in which the Allied codebreakers of World War II – a motley team of mathematicians, linguists, chess players, and crossword fanatics – unpicked the workings of the German coding machine, an ingenious electro-mechanical device known as **Enigma**. Because the Enigma machine enabled any given message to be ciphered in 150 million million different ways, it was confidently considered unbreakable by the Germans. The British managed to obtain an Enigma machine in 1939 as well as several stolen code books, but these proved of limited value at first, because the keys to the various ciphers were changed daily. However, by devising and building several computing machines – most notably the world's first electronic computer, **Colossus**, in 1942 – the Bletchley codebreakers were later able to keep pace with the daily modifications of Enigma. As a result, by 1942–43 the Allies were able to decipher thousands of intercepted radio messages every day with little loss of time. This is thought to have been a deciding factor in the Battle of the Atlantic and to have shortened the war by perhaps two years.

Of almost equal importance to the breaking of the code was the Allies' success in keeping any suspicion of this breakthrough from the Germans. During the war only a handful of military and political figures on the Allied side knew that Enigma had been broken. At the end of the war the codebreakers were sworn to complete and permanent secrecy and this was maintained without a breach until the mid-1970s. As a result, many of the original codebreakers had died before their contribution to victory could receive proper recognition. Bletchley Park was eventually opened to the public as a war museum.

• **Blighty** ▶ A soldier's name for England. It was widely current in World War I but was also well known to soldiers who had served in India long before. It is derived from the Hindi *bilayati*, foreign, from Arabic *wilayet*, provincial, distant. Its use during World War I is illustrated by three popular songs of the time: 'There's a Ship That's Bound for Blighty', 'We Wish We were in Blighty', and 'Take Me Back to Dear Old Blighty'.

In the two world wars, a **Blighty one** was a wound that was not very serious but still serious enough to ensure that the sufferer was returned to Blighty to recuperate.

• **blikkeys**▶ A US slang term for the soap flakes that some drug dealers pass off as crack in order to deceive addicts.

• **blimp** ▶ Originally an observation balloon in World War I. The character **Colonel Blimp** was created by David Low, the cartoonist, between the wars, to embody the elderly dyed-in-the-wool Tory, opposing all and any change. A 'blimp' has come to mean an elderly reactionary gentleman of somewhat limited intelligence. Barrage balloons over British cities in World War II were also known as blimps.

• **blind date** ► An appointment for a person to meet someone they have never met before, with a view to starting a romantic relationship. The date may be set up by a third party such as a mutual friend or a dating agency, or arranged by the main parties themselves through the personal column of a newspaper, over the Internet, etc. The TV game show *Blind Date*, in which contestants are paired off with unseen members of the opposite sex on the basis of their answers to various questions, began broadcasting in the UK in 1985.

• **blind trust** ► A trust fund that takes over the money and financial affairs of a politician or other person in a position of influence. 'Blind' implies that the individual has no knowledge of how the money is invested, and consequently cannot be accused of using his or her position for private gain.

• **blissed out** ► In a state of euphoria after a religious experience. Probably of US origin, the expression is derived from the alternative religious cults that arose in the 1960s. It can also be used in a wider sense to mean just very happy.

• **Blitz** ► The bombing of London and other targets in the UK by the German Luftwaffe in 1940 as a precursor to the planned invasion of Britain. The name was derived from the German word **Blitzkrieg** (lightning war), which in World War II was applied to the German strategy of making a rapid advance after initial strikes by aircraft, tanks, etc. The tactic was hugely successful in the invasion of Poland, France, and the Low Countries. The Blitz on London, however, never achieved its prime objective of terrifying the population into submission. In fact, it hardened the resolve of those subjected to its nightly harassment to destroy Nazi Germany. 'London can take it' and 'business as usual' were the slogans commonly chalked up on the walls of buildings damaged in the bombing of the previous night. *See*: Britain, Battle of.

• **blitzed** ► Very drunk or stoned.

• **blob** ► **1.** British slang for a road accident victim, a corpse. It is mostly used by the police, ambulance men, and vagrants. Hence **blobwagon**, ambulance. **2.** A breast, or testicle.

• **block association** ► In America, a group of residents in a small area (*e.g.* a city block) who organize themselves to promote or defend the interests of the area. The equivalent in the UK is a residents' association.

• **blockbust** ► To force property values in a particular area to plummet by spreading rumours that Black people or other 'undesirables' are about to move in.

• **blockbuster** ► **1.** A massive bomb, first developed in World War II, that is capable of destroying a whole block of houses. **2.** Anything large and successful, especially a lavish musical or big-budget film.

• **Blonde Bombshell** ► Jean Harlow (1911–37), the US film actress and sex symbol, who starred in such films as *Hell's Angels* (1930), *Platinum Blonde* (1931), and *Bombshell* (1933). Harlow's short troubled life ended tragically with kidney failure. The phrase has since been used of any attractive blonde, particularly one with an explosive personality.

• **blood, toil, tears and sweat** ► The words used by Winston Churchill in his speech to the House of Commons on becoming prime minister (13 May 1940). 'I would say to the House, as I have said to those who have joined this Government, I have nothing to offer but blood, toil, tears and sweat.' Churchill had a number of possible sources for his famous phrase. In his *Anatomie of the World* John Donne wrote, 'Mollifie it with thy teares, or sweat, or blood', and Lord Byron has:

> Year after year they voted cent per cent,
> Blood, sweat, and tear-wrung millions—why?
> for rent!
> – *The Age of Bronze.*

Gladstone's speech in Westminster Abbey commemorating Lord Palmerston includes a reference to 'the unhappy African race, whose history is for the most part written in blood and tears' (22 February 1866).

• **Bloody Mary** ► A drink consisting of a mixture of vodka and tomato juice, usually with small amounts of other ingredients, such as Worcester sauce, Tabasco, celery salt, or lemon juice. Its name comes from the nickname of Mary I (1516–58), the Roman Catholic Queen of England (1553–58) noted for her persecution of Protestants. Bloody Mary was also a character in the popular Rodgers and Hammerstein musical *South Pacific* (1949). A **Bloody Maria** is a similar drink made with tequila rather than vodka ('Maria' being the Spanish equivalent of 'Mary'). In recent health-conscious times, a **Virgin Mary** (a Bloody Mary without the vodka) has made its appearance.

• **Bloody Sunday** ► **1.** 22 January 1905. A deputation of workers led by Father Georgy Gapon marched to the Winter Palace in St Petersburg to present a petition to the Tsar. They were fired on by police and hundreds of unarmed peasants were killed. The incident helped to spark the Russian Revolution of 1905. **2.** 21 November 1920. That morning the IRA killed 11 Englishmen thought to be spies; the Black and Tans responded by killing 12 innocent spectators at a football match in Croke Park, Dublin, the same afternoon. **3.** 30 January 1972. The dispersal of civil-rights marchers in the Bogside, Londonderry, by British paratroops, during which 13 innocent civilians were shot dead. These events, which have never been satisfactorily explained, caused great bitterness in the Catholic community and led to an escalation of violence in the province. A new inquiry into the day's events was opened in 1998.

• **Bloom, Leopold** ▶ The hero of James Joyce's *Ulysses* (1922), the complex and encyclopedic novel that is often hailed as the greatest of the modern era. According to Joyce's scheme, Bloom – a canvasser of newspaper advertisements who spends most of his day wandering between offices, pubs, libraries and other locations in central Dublin – is the modern counterpart of the legendary Ulysses, condemned to wander for seven years after the siege of Troy. As an agnostic Jew with pacifist sympathies, he is also the archetypal outsider in this fiercely Catholic and nationalist milieu. Although distinctly antiheroic in many respects, Bloom's humour, resilience, and kindness mean that he emerges from the novel as a figure of true dignity and moral value. The book ends with the famous stream of consciousness monologue of **Molly Bloom**, Leopold's unfaithful wife, who adds a shrewd feminine perspective.

The day on which the events of *Ulysses* are imagined to occur – 16 June 1904 – is now celebrated in Dublin as **Bloomsday**. Every year hundreds of people take to the streets in Edwardian dress to retrace the steps of Bloom and the other characters, while readings, dramatizations, and other special events are staged all over the city. This modern tradition began in 1954, when a group of Irish writers including Patrick Kavanagh and Flann O'Brien decided to retrace the action of *Ulysses* as part of a glorified pub crawl. Joyce is said to have chosen 16 June 1904 because it was on this day that his future wife, Nora Barnacle, first granted him a sexual favour. *See also*: Dedalus, Stephen.

• **Bloomsbury Group** ▶ A group of writers, artists, philosophers, and economists who, from about 1904, met regularly in London, mostly at the Bloomsbury homes of Clive and Vanessa Bell (née Stephen) in Gordon Square or that of Virginia and Adrian Stephen in Fitzroy Square. Virginia Stephen married Leonard Woolf and, as Virginia Woolf, became the group's best-known writer. Others prominent in the circle were Roger Fry, Duncan Grant, J. M. Keynes, David Garnett, Lytton Strachey, and to a lesser extent E. M. Forster. Seeing themselves as advocates of a new rational civilized society, many of them had met at Cambridge University and were influenced by *Principia Ethica* (1903), by the Cambridge philosopher G. E. Moore (1873–1958). The group had lost its cohesion by the end of the 1920s. Interest in the activities of the group has grown rapidly since the 1960s, with biographies, autobiographies, and other books, plays, and films contributing to a burgeoning Bloomsbury industry.

• **blooper** ▶ US slang term for a mistake, the equivalent of the British 'bloomer'. Presumably a combination of 'bloomer' and 'oops'.

• **blotto** ▶ Drunk. Used since the early years of the 20th century, it conveys the idea of absorbing liquid (like blotting paper) and that of things being blotted out.

• **blow** ▶ **1.** US slang meaning to leave. **2.** To perform fellatio. A **blow job** is an act of fellatio. **3.** To fart. **4.** US slang expression meaning to be repellent: 'his cooking really blows'. **5.** In jazz slang, to play in a jam session. **6.** To smoke, particularly cannabis, or to inhale or snort cocaine. **7.** Cannabis. A user's term common in the UK and America. *See*: pot. **8.** Tobacco. A prison term. **9.** Cocaine.

• **blow away** ▶ **1.** Slang, originally from the US underworld, meaning to kill someone. **2.** To deeply impress someone.

> Liza was so beautiful. She just blew me away.
> – *The Sun*, 26 March 1991.

• **blowdown** ▶ A sudden dangerous break or explosion of a cooling pipe in a nuclear reactor. *See also*: meltdown.

• **blower** ▶ British slang for the telephone, first heard in the 1940s. It probably derives from the action of blowing down an old telephone before speaking, or from a now archaic meaning of blow, 'to talk'.

• **blow one's mind** ▶ Amaze one utterly. If something 'blows your mind' it renders you helpless with surprise and astonishment. This 1960s expression was originally associated with the use of LSD or other hallucinogenic drugs. **Blow-your-mind roulette** was a reckless game in which drug-takers pooled all their pills and scattered them on the floor; the lights were then turned out and participants grabbed whatever pills they could find.

**• Bloxham tapes ▶** A series of recordings of 'psychic regressions' made by subjects under hypnosis by the Welsh psychic researcher Arnall Bloxham in the 1960s. Among the most remarkable recordings were an English teenager's description of her previous life in a prehistoric society, another woman's recollection of her life as the daughter of Charles I and Queen Henrietta Maria during their exile in France, and – most remarkably – a woman who told in detail of her death during a massacre of Jewish inhabitants of the city of York in the Middle Ages, after she was found hiding in a church vault. Few of Bloxham's subjects pretended to the kind of detailed historical knowledge they communicated under hypnosis and several of the stories were subsequently supported by archaeological finds. The account of the massacre in York, for instance, was scorned by historians who said that the church named had no crypt: shortly afterwards workmen stumbled upon a hitherto concealed vault. It was exactly as Bloxham's patient had described it.

**• bludger ▶** Originally (19th century) Australian slang for a pimp, but later any scrounger or one profiting without risk. In World War I 'to bludge on the flag' meant 'to slack' in the army.

**• blue ▶ 1.** Australian slang for a violent argument or fight. **2.** British drug-users' slang from the 1960s for a blue amphetamine tablet containing drinamyl. **3.** A policeman. This primarily US usage comes from the colour of the uniform. **4.** Australian nickname for a red-headed man.

**• Bluebeard ▶** The nickname of Henri Landru, a Frenchman guillotined in 1922 for the murder of 10 women and one of their sons. Unlike the Bluebeard of legend Landry did not actually marry any of his victims but he did make their acquaintance by advertising for a wife in the lonely-hearts columns of newspapers. Rather than keeping their bodies in a mysterious locked room, a practice that led to the downfall of his predecessor, he disposed of their remains in the stove of his country villa. A man of great charm, he was the inspiration behind Charles Verdoux, the dapper murderer in Charlie Chaplin's 1947 film *Monsieur Verdoux*.

**• Bluebeard of Eastbourne ▶** The nickname given by the press to Dr John Bodkin Adams in 1956, after he was suspected of poisoning a number of his patients in Eastbourne. It seemed to some a striking coincidence that the doctor should appear as a beneficiary in the wills of several of his deceased women patients. In December 1956 he was arrested for the murder of Edith Morrell, who had left the doctor a Rolls-Royce. A sensational trial ensued, in which Adams was acquitted for lack of evidence. In 1957 the **Tucker Report** into the case recommended new rules governing press reports of murder trial proceedings. Many legal experts remained unconvinced of Adams's innocence, believing that the press unwittingly helped to protect an infamous poisoner by their prejudicial reporting of the case.

**• Bluebell girls ▶** A troupe of dancers originally formed before World War II at the Folies Bergère in Paris. They were first organized by a dancer from Liverpool, Margaret Kelly, whose nickname 'Bluebell' (from the colour of her eyes) provided the name of the troupe. The group still performs in Paris variety theatres. Bluebell girls, many of whom are British, are noted for their height, statuesque figures, exotic costumes, and their elaborate seminude dance routines.

**• Bluebell line ▶** A railway line in Sussex between Haywards Heath and Horsted Keynes. Closed by British Railways in 1960, it was reopened by a group of enthusiasts. The name comes from the story that the guard used to stop the train to allow the passengers to pick bluebells.

**• Bluebird ▶** The name given to a series of racing cars, speedboats, and hydrofoils used by Sir Malcolm Campbell (1885–1948) and his son Donald Malcolm Campbell (1921–67) to set various world speed records on both land and water between 1927 and 1967. Donald was killed when the last Bluebird, a turbo-jet hydroplane, somersaulted and capsized during his attempt to break the water-speed record on Coniston Water.

**• blue cheer ▶** A US drug-user's term of the 1960s and 1970s for LSD. This probably derives from the colour of the tablets or from their ability to drive away 'the blues'.

**• blue-collar ▶** Relating to manual work or those who perform it, *e.g.* 'a blue-collar union'. The term, first heard in America *c.* 1950, refers to the blue overalls worn by factory workers. *Compare*: pink-collar; white-collar.

**• blue flu ▶** In America, organized absenteeism by policemen or (sometimes) firemen pretending to be sick as a way of taking industrial action. The expression came into use in the late 1960s and was used throughout the 1970s. *See also*: yellow flu.

**• blue helmet ▶** A member of the UN peacekeeping forces, who wear distinctive light blue headgear, including helmets.

**• blue meany ▶** A mean-minded censorious person; a kill-joy. The term derives from the villains, grotesque blue monsters who stamp out all music and fun, in the animated Beatles film *Yellow Submarine* (1967).

• **Blue Monkey** ▶ The nickname given to the Marquis Luis Augusto Pinto de Soveral (d. 1922), from his swarthy complexion and blue-black hair. Portuguese ambassador to London almost continuously from 1884 to 1909, and an intimate of King Edward VII, he was noted for his wit, discretion, and ability as a raconteur. He held a unique position in Edwardian society, being known at the German embassy as 'Soveral-Uberall' (Soveral-the-supreme).

• **blue movies** ▶ Sexually explicit films not available for general showing. Although the origin of the term has never been adequately explained, there is a traditional connection between sexual indecency and the colour blue. The Chinese, for instance, always painted their brothels blue. A link has also been suggested with the tradition that associated the Devil with the colour blue (possibly because brimstone burns with a blue flame). Perhaps the most likely explanation, however, is an association with the censor's **blue pencil** (a term that originated from the pencils used by military censors in the 19th century). The use of the term **blue joke** would also fit with this etymology.

• **Blue Orchid** ▶ A member of the Royal Australian Air Force in World War II, so called because of their uniform, which was considered more glamorous than those of the other services.

• **Blue Peter** ▶ Classic British children's television programme, first broadcast in 1958. Hosts of this popular magazine programme, which has stimulated several generations of children, included Valerie Singleton and John Noakes in the 1960s, together with a long sequence of cats, dogs, tortoises, etc. Among the familiar phrases associated with the programme are 'Here's one I made earlier' and 'sticky-backed plastic'. The programme has staged a long series of charitable appeals on behalf of such worthy causes as guide dogs for the blind, inshore lifeboats, and minibuses for the elderly.

• **Blue Riband of the Atlantic** ▶ The liner holding the record for the fastest Atlantic crossing is said to hold the 'Blue Riband of the Atlantic'. From 1907 to 1929 the title was held by the Cunard liner *Mauretania*. It then passed to the *Europa* (1930) and *Bremen* (1933) of Germany, to the *Rex* of Italy (1933), to the French liner *Normandie* (1935), and to the British Queen Mary (1938). A trophy offered in 1935 by H. K. Hales (1868–1942) was first accepted by the US-owned *United States*, which broke the *Queen Mary*'s record in 1952. The average speed of the *Mauretania* was 17.4 knots, that of the *United States* 35.69

knots. A claim by the businessman Richard Branson that he had won the title for his powerboat crossing in 1986 was dismissed on the grounds that only non-powerboats not specifically designed to win the award are eligible. In 1990 the Hales Trophy was sent to the UK after the catamaran ferry *Hoverspeed Great Britain* crossed in record time, but the organizers of the Blue Riband refused to bestow the title as the boat was not in regular Atlantic service. The same objection was raised when the Australian-built ferry *Catalonia* further reduced the record in 1998.

• **Blue Riders** ▶ *See*: Blaue Reiter.

• **blue rinse** ▶ A dyeing process in which a bluish tinge is imparted to grey hair, formerly much favoured by women of a certain age. The **blue-rinse brigade** is a derogatory term for the elderly well-groomed socially active women in any community.

• **blues** ▶ An early 20th-century form of US folk music expressing the unhappiness of the Black man in the Deep South. Blues usually consist of 12 bars in 4/4 time made up of three 4-bar phrases and are characterized by the use of **blue notes** (flattened thirds, fifths, and sometimes sevenths). They can be vocal or instrumental and have had an enormous influence on jazz and rock. *See also*: rhythm-and-blues.

• **Blues and Royals** ▶ The informal name acquired in 1969 by the Royal Horse Guards (the Blues) and the Royal Dragoons (the Royals) when they amalgamated to form the Royal Horse Guards and 1st Dragoons.

• **blueshift** ▶ A change in wavelengths to shorter wavelengths (*i.e.* to the blue end of the visible spectrum) for light or other radiation emitted by an object moving towards the observer. It is the opposite of a redshift in astronomy.

• **Blue Shirts** ▶ An Irish Fascist organization led by General Eoin O'Duffy, former Commissioner of the Garda, which developed from the Army Comrades Association in the early 1930s. A Blue Shirt battalion led by O'Duffy set off to fight for General Franco in the Spanish Civil War, but caught a train to Cork when their boat was waiting in Limerick. Unimpressed by this example of O'Duffy's leadership, about half his troops deserted.

• **Blue Water School** ▶ Nickname of a group of influential officials in the British Admiralty who, between the two world wars, argued in favour of building large ships to be deployed in distant parts of the world. A result of this policy was that, at the start of World War II, Britain had no landing craft.

• **bluie** or **bluey** ▶ 1. British slang term for a £5

note that was doomed to become obsolete when the old blue £5 notes were phased out in 1990. **2.** Slang for an airmail letter, usually written on thin blue paper. It was much used by troops during the Gulf War of 1991.

• **blurb** ► A publisher's note on the dustjacket or cover of a book purporting to tell the potential purchaser what the book is about and how good it is (with favourable press comment if it is a reprint). The word was coined by the US novelist Gelett Burgess (1866–1951) in 1906 to publicize one of his own books; he subsequently defined blurb as 'self praise, to make a noise like a publisher'. The original instance of blurb consisted of a paragraph of nonsensical text under a picture of a pretty girl, whom Burgess dubbed 'Belinda Blurb'.

• **BMEWS** ► Ballistic Missile Early Warning System; a defensive system set up by America during the Cold War with large radar installations at Clear in Alaska, Thule in Greenland, and Fylingdales in Yorkshire.

• **B-movie** ► Formerly, a motion picture made to be shown as a companion to a 'main feature' in a double-bill programme. B-movies were made on low budgets, usually with lesser-known stars, and often with formulaic plots. Although such films were derided for their feeble special effects and wooden acting, a number of actors who featured in B-movies later became stars, including the future US president Ronald Reagan.

• **BMX** ► Bicycle motorcross, a bicycle designed to be used for stunt riding or on an obstacle course. Small versions with high handlebars were very popular with children in the late 1980s.

• **BO** ► *See*: body odour.

• **Boanerges** ► The nickname given by the adventurer and writer T. E. Lawrence (*see*: Lawrence of Arabia) to the Brough Superior motorbike on which he was killed in an accident on a Dorset road in 1935. The name, meaning 'sons of thunder', was taken from the biblical tale of James and John, the sons of Zebedee, who wanted to call down 'fire from heaven' to consume the Samaritans for not 'receiving' the Lord Jesus (Luke 9:54; Mark 3:17). Lawrence's motorbike was little damaged and is still extant and in working order. The vintage car that serves as the mascot of the engineering department of the Imperial College of Science, Technology and Medicine is also called Boanerges.

• **boater** ► A flat-topped shallow-crowned straw hat, usually trimmed with a band of ribbon, popular in late-Victorian and Edwardian England and still seen until the early 1930s at cricket matches, picnics, and boating parties (hence the name). It is the established headgear of pupils at Harrow School and was formerly much favoured by butchers and fishmongers.

• **boat people** ► Refugees from Vietnam who, following the Chinese invasion (February–March 1979), escaped the country in small, often unseaworthy, boats across the South China Sea. Many died in the attempt, and those that did survive had difficulties in finding a country that would give them asylum. In the late 1980s increasingly large numbers of boat people, fleeing from the Communist regime in Vietnam, arrived in Hong Kong, where the authorities detained them in large squalid camps. The British government authorized the first forcible repatriations in 1989. In 1992 Britain signed an agreement with Vietnam to return all the boat people.

• **bob** ► A short haircut, popular among fashionable young women of the 1920s, particularly after the British actress Beatrice Lillie (1898–1989) had her hair cut this way. Variants of the style included the Irene Castle bob (Irene Castle was a popular dancer of the period).

• **Bob-a-Job-Week** ► An imaginative way of raising funds by self-help, instituted by the Boy Scouts in 1949. All kinds of jobs were undertaken, some for their publicity value, for the payment of one shilling (a 'bob'). It became an annual effort but with the declining value of the 'bob' and the advent of decimal currency, **Scout Job Week** took its place in 1972.

• **bobby-sox** ► Long white cotton socks or ankle socks worn by teenage girls in America in the early 1940s. Hence the name for the young females themselves, **bobby-soxers**.

• **Bob Hope** ► Dope, *i.e.* cannabis. This British slang term using the name of the British-born US comedian (1903–   ) was probably coined by middle-class cannabis users in imitation of Cockney rhyming slang and is therefore pronounced with a self-consciously dropped 'H'.

• **Boche** ► Derogatory term for a German or (in the phrase 'the Boche') Germans collectively. It was used in both world wars to mean the German armed forces. It comes from the French word *alboche*, which is probably a blend of *allemand* (German) and *caboche* (pate, head).

• **bodgie** ► Australian slang of the 1950s for an uncouth or delinquent youth.

• **body art** ► **1.** The practice of decorating the human body with painted designs, tattoos, and piercings, etc. **2.** An artistic genre of the 1970s in which the artist used his or her own body as the means of expression. It often involved an element of self-inflicted pain or physical endurance.

• **body bag** ▸ A plastic or rubber container with a zip fastener, used to transport a corpse. Body bags first attracted public attention during the Vietnam War, when tens of thousands of young US servicemen were sent home in body bags.

• **body building** ▸ A system of diet and exercise designed to increase muscle size. The 'sport' developed before World War II; in competitive bodybuilding men compete for such titles as 'Mr Universe'. Women also compete for similar titles. Doubts have been expressed by medical organizations about the wisdom of adopting these punishing regimes, which sometimes include the taking of anabolic steroids.

• **body count** ▸ **1.** The number of dead in a military operation or other incident. **2.** The number of people present at a particular event or location.

• **body language** ▸ The bodily movements or postures by which non-verbal information is conveyed from one person to another. Many circumstances in human relationships depend on the appropriate body language, to express support, agreement, attraction, or love on the one hand or disagreement, contempt, indifference, or hatred on the other. Body language has its own eloquence – which may be intentional or, more often, completely unconscious. Because it is difficult to fake convincingly, body language can often be a more reliable indication of someone's real feelings than their words. Although peoples of different ethnic origins may put differing interpretations on some specific gestures, in general body language is international.

• **body line** ▸ In cricket, fast bowling at the batsman rather than the wicket, with the intention of forcing him to give a catch while defending himself. The accurate but dangerous bowling of Harold Larwood (1904–95) in the infamous **Body Line Tour** of 1932–33 won the Ashes for England, but roused a storm of indignation in Australia that led to a modification in the laws of cricket. *See also*: bouncer.

• **body odour** ▸ (BO) Any offensive body smell, but chiefly that caused by stale sweat. The phrase was coined in a US publicity campaign for Lifebuoy soap (1933), designed to make people insecure about such odours.

• **body-popping** ▸ A dance popular with young people in the 1980s, employing sequences of jerky movements.

• **body scanner** ▸ Any of several pieces of medical equipment that reveal the internal structure of the body and are widely used in diagnosis. The term was coined in the 1970s, when it was used synonymously with the CT scanner (originally called a 'CAT scanner'); since then it has been used, together with **body scan** and **body scanning**, in connection with several other techniques, including the ultrasound scanner, used especially to monitor pregnancy; and magnetic resonance imaging (MRI), utilizing the phenomenon of nuclear magnetic resonance. The advantage of all these techniques over conventional X-ray examination is that they can 'scan' the soft tissues, producing images in different planes of the body. *See also*: brain scanner.

• **body shop** ▸ The job centre, the employment agency. It is used in America and the UK and reflects the depersonalized atmosphere in such places. In the UK it is an ironic contrast to the **Body Shop** chain of stores, which sell environmentally friendly cosmetics and toiletries.

• **Boer Wars** or **South African Wars** ▸ The two wars (1880–81 and 1899–1902) in which the Boers of the Transvaal challenged British rule in South Africa. The first war resulted in the Transvaal regaining its independence; the second ended in the re-establishment of British supremacy. The Second Boer War saw the humiliation of the British Army by Boer guerrillas on several occasions and British victory was only secured by harsh measures, including the confinement of Boer women and children in concentration camps, where 20,000 died. The ugliness of the war has been seen by some historians as a forewarning of the brutality of subsequent 20th-century conflicts, especially the two world wars. *See also*: mafficking; Relief of Ladysmith; Spion Kop; Vereeniging Treaty.

• **boffin** ▸ A nickname used by the RAF in World War II for research scientists or backroom boys. It passed into general use in the 1940s. It is said to derive from the practice of a certain scientist, who gave his colleagues Dickensian nicknames, Mr Boffin being a character in *Our Mutual Friend*.

• **boffo** ▸ A US slang term from the theatrical world meaning excellent. Apparently derived from 'box office' (*i.e.* box-office success), it is mainly used by journalists.

• **Bofors gun** ▸ An automatic double-barrelled anti-aircraft gun used in World War II. It was named after Bofors, a town in Sweden where it was first made.

• **Bogart** ▸ To monopolize a joint, to fail to pass on the cannabis cigarette to the next person. This expression, used in hippie circles in the late 1960s, was obviously inspired by the popular screen image of the actor Humphrey Bogart with a cigarette permanently hanging from his lip. The 1969 film *Easy Rider* featured a song by the Holy Modal Rounders called 'Don't Bogart that Joint'.

• **Bogey** ► Humphrey Bogart (1899–1957), the US film star whose portrayal of cynical tough-guys, often with a hidden streak of idealism, endeared him to audiences throughout the world. In *Casablanca* (1942), described by a critic as 'one of the outstanding entertainment experiences of cinema history', he establishes his persona with the line:

> I stick out my neck for nobody. I'm the only cause I'm interested in.

His other films include *Angels with Dirty Faces* (1938), *The Maltese Falcon* (1941), and *The African Queen* (1952). *See also*: Play it again, Sam.

• **bog standard** ► Ordinary, of rudimentary quality. The origin of the expression is uncertain but it has been suggested that it is a variation on 'box standard', *i.e.* (usually of a mechanical device) as packed by the manufacturers without modification or upgrading. Others suggest it comes from the once common abbreviation BoG, meaning British or German standards (of engineering), or that it amounts to a typical English sneer at the Irish, seen as a nation of 'bogtrotters'. Many people now use the term assuming it has some connection with the British slang word bog, meaning lavatory, although this seems not to be the case.

> The prime minister announced today that 'the day of the bog-standard comprehensive' was over and that diversity was the way forward for Britain's schools. – *The Guardian*, 12 February 2001.

• **boiler** ► British offensive slang, chiefly working-class, for an unattractive woman. The idea may be that such a woman has roughly the shape of a boiler or possibly that she resembles a boiling chicken, *i.e.* one too old and tough to roast. The phrase **dodgy boiler** implies that the woman could be a transmitter of sexual diseases.

• **boiler room** ► 1980s financial jargon for a bucket shop that specializes in selling securities over the telephone.

• **boldly** ►
**To boldly go where no man has gone before** Slogan associated with the popular US TV space adventure series *Star Trek*, first screened in 1966. The voyages of of the Starship *Enterprise* through deep space attracted millions of regular viewers, although its expressed aim 'to boldly go'

became probably the most ridiculed split infinitive of the 20th century. *See also*: Beam me up, Scotty.

• **Bolero** ► Codename for the initial planning stage (started in 1942) for a second front in Europe during World War II.

• **Bollinger Bolshevik** ► Another name for a champagne socialist.

• **Bollywood** ► A popular name for the Indian film industry. The word blends Bombay, which has been the centre of prolific Hindi film production since the 1930s, with Hollywood. Although Bombay is no longer the capital of Indian film-making – it was overtaken by Madras and several other regional centres in the 1980s – the term Bollywood is still used of the industry as a whole and of the colourful escapist melodramas that are its most typical products.

• **bolo tie** or **bola tie** ► A string or narrow leather necktie with a decorative metal clasp, associated with Western-style US dress. It is named after the *bola* – a missile used by South American gauchos, consisting of two or more weights on the end of cords thrown to entangle the legs of the quarry.

• **Bolshevik** or **Bolshevist** ► A member of the Russian revolutionary faction under Lenin that seized power in October 1917 with the objective of establishing a communist state in Russia. The Bolsheviks were so called from the fact that at the conference of the Russian Social Democratic Workers' Party held in 1903 the Leninists were the majority group (*Bolsheviki* = majority). The defeated minority were called Mensheviks. In later usage a Bolshevik was any communist, especially one from the Soviet Union.

• **Bolshie** or **Bolshy** ► A contraction of Bolshevik, originally used to denote a person with 'red' or revolutionary tendencies, but now more often used of someone (such as a child) who is difficult and uncooperative.

• **bomb** ► 1. British slang meaning to adorn a building, railway carriage, etc., with graffiti. 1. To be badly received by an audience or to fail at some test.

> If I had to go to a club and genuinely bomb, I'd faint. I do have an embarrassment threshold. – RUBY WAX, *Daily Telegraph*, 19 January 1991.

• **Bomb Alley** ► A region of Kent and Sussex in the path of the buzz bombs aimed at London in 1944 during World War II. It suffered extensive damage from bombs that fell short of their target or were shot down en route to London. The term has also been applied to other heavily bombed areas in an attacking flight path.

• **bomber** ▶ **1.** A capsule or pill containing amphetamines. **2.** A large strong cannabis cigarette. **3.** A graffiti vandal.

• **Bomber Harris** ▶ The nickname of Sir Arthur Travers Harris (1892–1984), who as head of Bomber Command from 1942 to 1945 implemented a controversial strategy of heavy bombing of German cities. Harris was the only leading British wartime leader who did not subsequently receive a peerage. The bitter controversy surrounding Harris's actions was reopened by the erection of a statue to him in the Strand, London, in 1992. *See also*: Dresden fire bombing.

• **bomber jacket** ▶ A strong well-padded short jacket that became a popular item of casual wear after World War II, during which such jackets were worn by the crews of air-force bombers.

• **bona** ▶ British slang exclamation of approval, mainly heard in London in the 1980s. It derives from the Latin *bona fide* meaning real, in good faith, or from the Spanish *buena* and the Italian *buona* meaning good.

• **Bond, James** ▶ A British secret agent created by the author Ian Fleming (1908–64). Commander Bond (code name 007) appeared in 12 novels and 7 short stories before reaching a wider audience in a series of spectacular action films (from 1962). Actors to play this archetypal male fantasy figure – suave, resourceful, sexually attractive, and high-living – include Sean Connery, Roger Moore, and Pierce Brosnan. Bond's name was taken by Fleming from that of an ornithologist who lived near his home in Jamaica. His adventures were loosely based on those of the British spy Sidney Reilly and the double-agent Dusko Popov, both notorious womanizers. *See also*: Goldfinger; M; martini, shaken not stirred; Oddjob; Q.

• **bondook** ▶ British army slang for a weapon, first heard in the 1950s, when it was confined to meaning a rifle (from Hindi).

• **bong** ▶ A water-pipe used for smoking cannabis. It is smaller than a hubble-bubble and became a typical accessory for drug users in the 1960s and 1970s. The word is used throughout the English-speaking world.

• **bonk** ▶ To have sexual intercourse. A popular euphemism for 'fuck' in the late 1980s and 1990s. Because it is vulgar without being taboo, the word has proved a godsend to tabloid journalists. 'Bonk' was originally early 20th-century slang for a hit; the sexual sense probably arose by analogy. *See* bonkers.

> Council watchdogs bugged a couple's flat after neighbours complained they were bonking too noisily. – *The Sun*, 15 March 1991.

• **bonkbuster** ▶ A style of popular novel that shamelessly courts mass appeal by including frequent and lurid descriptions of sexual encounters. The characters are generally depicted as having successful careers and glamorous lifestyles, and move between a series of exotic or bizarre locations, which form the backdrop to their liaisons. The term combines bonk (to have sex) with blockbuster, thus succinctly reflecting the content and purpose of such works. *See also*: s 'n' s.

• **bonkers** ▶ Crazy, mad. The origin is unclear, but could be related to the idea of being deranged from a 'bonk', a hit on the head ('bonce'). The term was earlier (1920s) used to mean slightly drunk.

• **Bonneville salt flats** ▶ A flat semi-desert area of NW Utah where several land-speed records have been broken since it was first identified as suitable for this purpose in 1935. The flats are the dried bed of an ancient lake.

• **Bonnie and Clyde** ▶ The US robbers Bonnie Parker (1911–34) and Clyde Barrow (1909–34) whose trail of violence and larceny across Texas, Oklahoma, New Mexico, and Missouri (1932–34) captured the US public imagination. Barrow was a small-time car thief before he met Parker in 1930; after his escape from jail using a gun she had smuggled in, the two embarked upon a series of raids on minor banks and gas stations until betrayed by a confederate and killed in a roadblock ambush by police. Despite the lethal nature of their crimes, the duo were quickly romanticized as folk heroes in the rural South, mainly owing to the popular loathing of banks during the Depression. Their short, violent, but flamboyant lives formed the basis for the celebrated film *Bonnie and Clyde* (1967; starring Warren Beatty and Faye Dunaway).

• **boo** ▶ US slang for marijuana.

• **boob** ▶ **1.** A fool, an idiot. An inoffensive shortened form of booby. **2.** A mistake, a blunder. **3.** Socially acceptable slang for a female breast.

• **boob tube** ▶ **1.** A tight-fitting strapless top for women, *i.e.* a tube to contain the breasts. **1.** In US and Canadian slang, a television set.

• **booby hatch** ▶ Slang for a mental hospital, derived from the traditional sense of booby meaning 'fool'. In the UK the phrase acquired added significance by its relation to Colney Hatch, a village near Barnet in which a mental hospital was built in 1851.

• **booby trap**▶ An explosive device that is set to go off without warning, often when it is touched. Such devices were used in World War I and reached new levels of malignity in World War II, when the Japanese even booby-trapped corpses. The IRA and other terrorist organizations have also made use of booby-trapped devices.

• **boofer**▶ US slang for a buyer of illegal drugs.

• **boogie**▶ To dance to fast pop music, especially at a disco; a common expression in the 1970s.

• **boogie box**▶ A portable tape recorder. The term was used by young Blacks in the 1970s as a synonym for ghettoblaster. It was adopted by a wider spectrum of British teenagers in the 1980s.

• **boogie-woogie**▶ A style of piano playing. The left hand maintains a heavy repetitive pattern of eight beats to the bar over which the right hand provides a syncopated improvisation. Probably developed in the Middle West by jazz musicians early in the 20th century, it owes its name to Clarence 'Pinetop' Smith's 'Pinetop's Boogie-Woogie' (1928). It did not become popular, however, until the 1930s.

• **boo-hurrah theory**▶ The philosophical theory, also known as emotivism, that moral statements are not true in any other sense than that they express the feelings of the person making them. Thus, the statement 'charity is good' merely means that the person saying it thinks that being charitable is desirable.

• **Booker Prize**▶ An annual prize for a British, Commonwealth, or Irish work of fiction written in English, first awarded in 1969. It was founded by the British engineering and trading company Booker McConnell in conjunction with the Publishers' Association; the winner is selected by a panel appointed by the Book Trust and receives a prize of £20,000. Past winners include Iris Murdoch (1978), Salman Rushdie (1981), Kingsley Amis (1986), and Graham Swift (1996). In 1999 the prize was awarded for the first time to a past winner, J. M. Coetzee (first award 1983) – a feat repeated by Peter Carey in 2001 (first award 1988). The first International Booker Prize was awarded in 1992.

• **boom corridor**▶ A strip of land under the flight path of a supersonic plane, within which the sonic boom can be heard. The term came into use with the advent of the Anglo-French supersonic airliner Concorde (1969) and the search for designated flight paths that caused minimum inconvenience.

• **boomerang kid**▶ A young adult who leaves the family home but soon returns to it, rather than set up a new home on his or her own. The phenomenon was first noticed in the 1980s.

• **boondock**▶ US slang meaning to court sexually. It is derived from *bundok* in Tagalog, the language of the Philippines, meaning mountain, an isolated place. This usage, popular among US armed forces during World War II, presumably reflects the idea of an isolated place being sought by courting couples. Hence, the use of the word **boondocks** for any remote place.

• **boondoggling**▶ Spending time, money, or energy on a futile or unnecessary project; usually with reference to the US government's expenditure in the 1930s to combat the Great Depression. It apparently derives from the Scottish word 'boondoggle', meaning a marble received as a gift.

• **bootleg**▶ An unauthorized recording of rock or pop music, distributed or sold in breach of copyright. The recordings are often made by smuggling tape recorders into concerts.

• **bootlegger**▶ One who traffics illegally in alcoholic liquor. The term apparently derives from the smuggling of flasks of liquor in the legs of smugglers' boots. Bootlegging became a major racket in America during the years of Prohibition (1920–34). Organized crime took over and the profits from bootlegging enabled a rapid and dangerous growth of the underworld under such gangsters as Capone (*see*: Scarface).

• **bootstrap**▶ In science and technology, a system that is self-acting or self-sufficient in some way. For instance, in computer science a **bootstrap program** is a short program used to load the operating system and start up the system. The word can also be used as a verb: 'to bootstrap a computer'. In nuclear physics, a **bootstrap theory** is a self-consistent theory in which fundamental nuclear particles are interconnected – composed of each other, rather than made up of more fundamental entities such as quarks. Such uses of the word come from the phrase 'pulling oneself up by one's own bootstraps'. Possibly this originated with a story by the German writer Rudolph Raspe (1737–94) in which his hero Baron Münchhausen boasts that he once found himself trapped in quicksand, lifted himself by his bootstraps, and carried himself to firm ground.

• **bop**▶ In the 1940s, another name for bebop. The word later came to be used for any dance to jazz or pop music.

• **Borley Rectory**▶ Reputedly 'the most haunted house in England', a former rectory in the village of

Borley, Essex. It laid claim to a ghostly nun, a headless coachman, and various poltergeist manifestations. The Rectory was investigated by the Society for Psychical Research, the BBC, and private ghost-hunters from all around the world before it burned down in 1938. Its reputation was largely created by the journalist and psychic researcher Harry Price, who wrote numerous articles in the press and a popular book about the alleged hauntings. When the house burned down ghostly faces were supposedly seen in the windows: later, reports of strange happenings in the church opposite led to speculation that the house's ghostly inhabitants had found a new home nearby. The legend of Borley Rectory was effectively debunked in 2000, when a 90 year-old-man named Louis Mayerling gave a detailed account of how he had helped other villagers to fake paranormal activities at the house over a period of 20 years.

• **born-again Christian** ▶ A person who has experienced a spiritual conversion and become an ardent and often evangelizing Christian. The epithet 'born-again' is now often used in non-religious contexts. For example, a **born-again golfer** is one who, having played golf occasionally for many years, becomes an ardent player on retirement.

• **born 1820 – still going strong** ▶ Trade slogan associated with Johnnie Walker whisky, coined in 1910; 1820 was the year the company was founded.

• **Borstal** ▶ A former British institution for the detention and rehabilitation of offenders between the ages of 15 and 21. Youths could be detained for up to two years with a subsequent 'parole' period of two more years. The Borstal system was introduced in 1908 and named after the first such prison at the village of Borstal, near Rochester in Kent. Borstals were abolished in 1983; offenders under 21 years of age are now sentenced to 'detention in a young offenders institution'.

• **bosey** ▶ In cricket, another (mainly Australian) name for a googly, *i.e.* a ball that appears to deviate from the leg side towards the off side but in fact does the opposite. It was so named from its inventor, the English bowler B. J. Bosanquet, who toured Australia in 1903–04. The term was also applied in World War II to a single bomb dropped from a plane.

• **Bosnywash** ▶ In America, the thickly populated and affluent eastern region of the country. It comes from the names of the three main cities in the region: *Bos*ton, *NY* (New York), and *Wash*ington. *See also*: Chippitts; Sansan.

• **boss** ▶ Excellent. This sense of the word originated among the Black youth of America in the 1960s and became fashionable with White youths some 15 years later.

• **Boss, the** ▶ 1. Franklin D. Roosevelt (1882–1945), US president, also known as the **American Dictator**, the **New Deal Caesar**, the **Sphinx**, **Franklin Deficit Roosevelt**, and **Houdini in the White House**. *See*: FDR. 2. Bess Truman (1885–1982), wife of the US president Harry S. Truman. 3. Bruce Springsteen (1949–   ), US rock star. 4. Margaret Thatcher. *See*: Iron Lady.

• **bossa nova** ▶ (Portuguese, new voice) A type of dance music, based on the samba, that originated in Brazil but subsequently became popular throughout the West.

• **Boston Strangler** ▶ A mass-murderer who killed at least 11 women in Boston, Massachusetts, in the period 1962–64. He is thought to have been Albert DeSalvo, who was sentenced to life imprisonment in 1967 for other offences involving sexual assault.

• **bottle** ▶ 1. Courage, nerve. A British slang expression used in such phrases as 'to lose one's bottle' or 'I admire his bottle.' The origin is somewhat devious; in Cockney rhyming slang 'bottle and glass' means arse, 'arse' is a taboo word for bottom, and bottom has an old-established sense meaning courage. This sense of bottle only came to be widely used in the 1970s, probably influenced by criminal and police speech in TV crime dramas. In 1985 it was used in the advertising slogan for milk, 'Milk has gotta lotta bottle'. It is usually pronounced with a medial glottal stop in an imitation of Cockney speech. 2. British slang for the money collected by street buskers. 3. To injure by hitting with a bottle or by thrusting a broken bottle into someone.

• **bottle bank** ▶ A large container provided by local authorities in a public place to enable members of the public to dispose of their used glass bottles for recycling. Three such containers are often provided, one for colourless glass, one for brown or amber glass, and one for green glass.

• **bottleneck** ▶ 1. A style of rock or blues guitar playing in which a small metal tube or similar device worn on the player's finger is moved up and down the fretboard to produce a glissando effect. It is so called because originally the neck of a glass bottle was used. This style of playing is also called **slide** or **slide guitar**. 2. A road that is frequently clogged with traffic.

• **Bottomley case** ▶ A fraud case involving Horatio Bottomley (1860–1933), former Liberal MP and editor of the ultra-patriotic magazine *John Bull*. In 1922 he was sentenced to 7 years' imprisonment for his part in issuing bogus **victory bonds**.

• **bottom line** ► The main issue at stake, the most important factor or ultimate standard by which something will be judged. The phrase became popular during the 1970s, possibly because of its use by the US secretary of state Henry Kissinger (*see*: shuttle diplomacy), who often spoke of 'the bottom line' as the eventual outcome of a negotiation. The phrase originally referred to the last line on a financial statement summarizing the net profit or loss of a company.

• **bouffant** ► A women's hairstyle, common in the 1960s, in which extra height and breadth are given by back-combing. It comes from the French *bouffer*, to puff up.

• **Boulder Dam** ► *See*: Hoover Dam.

• **boulevard cowboy** ► In US slang, a reckless taxi-driver of the type encountered in New York, Chicago, and other major cities.

• **bouncer** ► 1. In cricket, a deliberately short-pitched ball intended to bounce high enough to reach the batsman at around head height. The increasing use of the bouncer to intimidate batsmen, considered by many as 'ungentlemanly', led in the 1970s to the use of protective headgear by many professional cricketers. 2. A man employed by a pub, nightclub, etc., to prevent those considered undesirable from entering and to eject, by force if necessary, drunks or other troublemakers.

• **Bouncing Czech** ► A media nickname for the publisher Robert Maxwell (Jan Ludwig Hoch; 1923–91). Born in Czechoslovakia, he studied for the rabbinate school but later worked as a travelling salesman; with the advent of World War II he escaped from occupied Europe to serve as a captain in the British Army and to win the MC for bravery (hence his other nickname, **Captain Bob**). He later became head of the press section of the German department of the Foreign Office in Berlin (1945–47). In the post-war years he built up a remarkable network of publishing businesses, culminating in the acquisition of the *Mirror* group of newspapers in 1984. He was also Labour MP for Buckingham (1964–70). However, after his somewhat mysterious death at sea, believed by many to be suicide, his business empire collapsed as it became clear that Maxwell had supported it by criminally misappropriating huge sums from the *Mirror* pension fund. The living war hero and entrepreneur extraordinary was disgraced and discredited in death.

• **Bourbaki, Nicolas** ► A contemporary French mathematician noted for the presentation of mathematics in an original fashion, stressing its axiomatic structure. In fact, Bourbaki is not a person but a pseudonym for a group of mathematicians who came together in 1939 to write a treatise *Eléments de mathématique*. They took the name from a French general who, in the Franco–Prussian war of 1870–71, valiantly but unsuccessfully tried to break the Prussian line.

• **bovine spongiform encephalopathy** ► *See*: mad cow disease.

• **bovril** ► Australian slang for 'rubbish'; from the tradename of the beef extract, which was itself coined by combining the Latin word *bos* (ox) with 'vril' – a magical fluid with extraordinary properties in the novel *The Coming Race* (1871) by Edward Bulwer-Lytton. The word was also used as a euphemism for a brothel in the 1930s.

• **bovver** ► Trouble, aggravation. A British slang word widely used by young males, especially skinheads, in the 1970s. The word is a phonetic imitation of bother, a euphemism for extreme aggravation, spoken with a London accent. The classic skinhead taunt was 'You want bovver?' to provoke a fight. **Bovver boots** were heavy boots worn as part of skinhead dress in the late 1960s and 1970s. They were usually either ex-army boots or Doc Martens.

• **bovver-boy** ► 1. British slang for a provocatively aggressive youth, especially a skinhead. 2. A trouble-shooter. A humorous extension of the original meaning.

• **bowl game** ► An American football game between league-winning teams held after the end of the league season. *See*: Rose Bowl; Super Bowl.

• **box** ► 1. The anus. An old male homosexual term that came to be used again in the 1970s. 2. The male genitals. A British schoolboy and male homosexual usage based on the cricket box, a protective shield worn over the genitals whilst playing cricket. 3. The female genitals. This is mainly an Australian usage. 4. A coffin. 5. A safe. A sense sometimes used by the criminal world. 6. **The box**. The TV. A British colloquialism. 7. A guitar. Originally a Black US musician's term of the 1950s, it was taken up by British rock musicians in the 1960s. 8. A portable tape recorder. US slang from the 1970s.

• **Boxers** ► A branch of the White Lotus sect in China which played a prominent part in the rising against foreigners in 1900 (Boxer Rising) and was suppressed by joint European action. The Chinese name was *I Ho Chuan* or 'Righteous Harmony Fists'.

• **Boy Orator of the Platitude** ▶ *See*: Man on the Wedding Cake.

• **Boy Scouts** ▶ A successful youth movement started by General Sir Robert Baden-Powell (Lord Baden-Powell of Gilwell) in 1908. The aim was to train boys to be good citizens with high ideals of honour, service to others, cleanliness, and self-reliance. The movement, which offers training in an outdoor setting, quickly became worldwide and now has a membership of over 14 million young people. A complete Scout Group now consists of Cub Scouts (formerly Wolf Cubs), age 8 to 11; Scouts, 11 to 16; and Venture Scouts (formerly Rover Scouts), 16 to 29. These new designations, as well as that of **Scout Association** for the movement as a whole, were introduced in 1967. The first Girl Scouts were admitted in 1990. *See also*: Girl Guides.

• **boys in blue** ▶ An affectionate name for the British police; it refers, of course, to their blue uniforms.

• **Boy Wonder** ▶ *See*: Batman.

• **bozo** ▶ A fool, a stupid fellow. An inoffensive US slang term, originally dating from the 1920s, now heard frequently in the UK and Australia. It was often applied to Ronald Reagan, US president (1981–89). The derivation is uncertain.

• **bra** ▶ (French, *brassière*) A support for a woman's breasts; the name derives ultimately from the French *bras* (arm). It was invented by a US debutante, Mary Phelps Jacob, with the assistance of her French maid, who created a prototype consisting of two handkerchiefs and a ribbon. Her friends applauded her idea and she finally sold the patent in 1914 for $15,000. In the late 1960s feminists saw the garment as a symbol of women's subjugation to men, on the grounds that it was worn solely to satisfy male ideals of female beauty. Perhaps inspired by mass burnings of army draft cards during the Vietnam War, female supporters of feminism were exhorted to burn their bras.

• **Brabazon** ▶ A huge airliner built (1949) by the Bristol Brabazon company, run by Lord Brabazon of Tara (1884–1964). It was withdrawn in 1952. Lord Brabazon was the first British citizen to fly in the UK (1909).

• **Brabham** ▶ A type of racing car designed and built by the former Australian racing driver John 'Jack' Brabham (1926–   ). He started making cars in 1962 and in 1966 became the first driver to win the motor-racing championship in a car of his own construction.

• **Bradbury** ▶ A £1 note, issued by the Treasury in the period 1914–28, bearing the signature of J. S. Bradbury (first Baron Bradbury), who as joint permanent secretary to the Treasury began the issue.

• **Brahms and Liszt** ▶ Cockney rhyming slang for pissed (meaning drunk). It has been heard since the 1930s but has found much wider use in the 1970s and 1980s, promoted by the popularity of such TV situation comedies as *Only Fools and Horses*.

• **brain death** ▶ The state that exists when the region of the brain that controls vital activities, such as breathing and eye reflexes, ceases to function. Traditionally, a person was pronounced dead when his heart stopped beating and his breathing ceased. However, the use of mechanical ventilators to maintain respiration in brain-damaged patients can also enable the heart to continue beating after natural breathing has ceased. In such cases, if two doctors agree that vital brain function has nevertheless ceased, the patient is declared 'brain-dead' and organs for transplantation may be legally removed before the heart has stopped beating.

• **brain drain** ▶ A drift abroad (first noted in the early 1950s) of British-trained scientists, technologists, doctors, and university teachers (especially to America), attracted by higher salaries and often better facilities and funding for their work. *See also*: brawn drain.

• **brain gain** ▶ An increase in the pool of skilled or professional workers in a country as a result of immigration. It is thus the opposite of brain drain.

• **brain scanner** ▶ Any of several pieces of medical equipment used to detect abnormalities within the brain. These include the CT scanner, the **MRI scanner** (magnetic resonance imaging scanner), and the **PET scanner** (positron emission tomography scanner). *See also*: body scanner.

• **brainstorm** ▶ In business or marketing, to tackle a problem through an uninhibited group discussion in which people are encouraged to share their ideas, however odd or unformed these may be. Brainstorming became an accepted business technique in America in the 1930s.

• **Brains Trust** ▶ A name given by James M. Kieran of the *New York Times* to the advisers of F. D. Roosevelt in his election campaign; later it was used of the group of college professors who advised him in administering the New Deal. In Britain it became the name of a popular BBC radio programme (1941–48) in which well-known public figures (including Prof. C. E. M. Joad, Commander Campbell, and Julian Huxley) aired their views on questions submitted by listeners. Now in general use for any such panel of experts or team that answers questions impromptu.

• **brainwashing** ▶ Persuading a person to discard his own opinions in favour of a set of ideas not his own. This is sometimes achieved by various subtle psychological methods, such as repeating an idea continuously while the person concerned is in a weakened state. The notion was a favourite theme of adventure films and novels in the Cold War period; in real life, brainwashing techniques were employed by the communist North in the Korean War (1950–53) and have since been used by various repressive regimes.

• **brand awareness** ▶ The extent to which members of the public are aware of a particular consumer product, the yardstick that determines what kind of advertising a particular product requires.

> Nike isn't a maker of high-priced trainers but a world voice for sport as an agency of personal growth and achievement...The [Nike] swoosh/tick logo means precisely what the crucifix meant to an earlier generation in ghettos – it promises redemption, vindication and a way out. – PETER YORK, *The Times*, 14 November 2000.

• **brand extension** or **stretching** ▶ The practice of using a famous brandname to promote new and unrelated products made by the same company. A marketing term first heard in the early 1990s.

> The measure of a resonant modern brand is the ability to stretch – to add its magic to all kinds of products and services, not just one little category. – PETER YORK *The Times*, 14 October 2000.

• **Brands Hatch** ▶ British motor-racing circuit near Farnham, Kent, which was opened in the 1920s for use by motorcycles; from 1949 it was also used to stage car races. It held its first Grand Prix in 1964.

• **Brand X** ▶ Any unidentified competitor's product used as an example of an inferior alternative to a product being advertised. It first appeared in television advertisements in the late 1960s in which the virtues of named products, particularly soap powders, were compared with the failings of the unnamed competitor, Brand X.

• **branwagon** ▶ An allegedly healthy diet based on high-fibre foods, such as bran, that was enthusiastically adopted by health faddists during the 1980s. 'Jumping on the branwagon' was a fairly obvious variant of 'jumping on the bandwagon'.

• **Brasília** ▶ The capital of Brazil; a new city built on the country's central plateau. Building was started in 1960 on a site chosen in 1956; the principal architect was Oscar Niemeyer (1907–  ). By 1995 the population was estimated to be 1,778,000.

• **bratpack** ▶ A group of young US film stars who emerged in the mid-1980s; they included Emilio Estevez (1962–  ), Tom Cruise (1962–  ), and Demi Moore (1962–  ). They were so-called by analogy with the Rat Pack of the early 1960s, a clique of Hollywood actors and singers led by Frank Sinatra. The name is now commonly applied to any group of up-and-coming young people in a particular field.

• **Brave New World** ▶ A novel (1932) by the British author Aldous Huxley (1894–1964) with a bleak view of what the future had in store. In Huxley's Brave New World human embryos are produced and grown under laboratory conditions and pre-designed to perform certain tasks in society. The title comes from Shakespeare's *The Tempest*, in which Miranda says:

> O brave new world that has such people in it.

The phrase is now used of any real or hypothetical society that bears similarities to Huxley's invention. By the beginning of the 21st century – with advances in techniques of assisted reproduction and genetic engineering, and detailed knowledge of the human genome (*see*: Human Genome Project) – Huxley's future world did not seem too improbable.

• **brawn drain** ▶ The emigration of athletes and manual workers to other countries in search of better rewards. *See also*: brain drain.

• **Brazilian Bombshell** ▶ Carmen Miranda (1913–55). The Portuguese singer who wore strange flower- and fruit-laden hats when singing South American songs in her many wartime films.

• **bread** ▶ Money. A 1960s version of the earlier euphemism 'dough', widely used in hippie jargon as well as working-class speech. It now sounds outdated.

• **breadhead** ▶ A disparaging slang expression for someone who is only interested in money and getting rich, a capitalist. It was common in the hippie era of the 1960s and 1970s.

• **break a leg** ▶ A whimsical way of wishing an actor good luck on the opening night of a play. Actors are traditionally superstitious and the more obvious 'Good Luck' is considered highly taboo, a sure sign that the performance will be a disaster. There may be some connection to the old theatrical superstition that it is lucky to stumble or fall over on stage – especially on one's first entrance. Another theory links the saying to the fate of John Wilkes Booth, the US actor better known as the assassin of President Lincoln. Booth broke his leg after leaping from the president's box onto the stage of Ford's Theatre in Washington DC; as a result of his injury he was cornered and shot some days later.

• **breakaway** ▶ In the film industry, a prop that is designed to break easily in a fight or action scenes, thus avoiding injury to the actors. Breakaway furniture was widely used in the bar-room brawl scenes typical of the Western.

• **break dance** ▶ A dance craze of the 1980s, the distinguishing feature of which was the use of energetic acrobatic movements.

• **breaker** ▶ A person using a citizens' band radio (*see*: CB). In America, the term was used from about 1963 and derives from the idea that the person broadcasting was 'breaking in' to other people's conversations. CB radio spread to the UK in the 1970s and was for some time illegal because it was said to interfere with the short-range radio communications of the emergency services. Enthusiasts in the UK thought of themselves as 'breakers' in the sense that they were breaking the law.

• **breakfast of champions** ▶ US trade slogan for Wheaties breakfast cereal, extolling its stamina-giving qualities. Kurt Vonnegut (1922–   ) wrote a novel under the same title in 1973.

• **breathalyser** ▶ A device used by the police to estimate the amount of alcohol that a driver has recently consumed. This is done by asking the driver to blow into the device so that the amount of alcohol in the breath can be measured, which reflects the amount of alcohol in the blood. The legal limit in the UK and America is 80 milligrams of alcohol in 100 millilitres of blood. Drivers with a higher concentration of alcohol in their blood are liable to prosecution. The original breathalysers relied on a colour change in potassium dichromate crystals as a result of contact with alcohol in the driver's breath. More modern devices are electronic. Portable instruments used at the roadside give a red warning light if the limit is exceeded. Drivers who fail the preliminary test are taken to a police station and tested on a more accurate instrument, which gives a digital readout. They may then have to submit to a blood or urine test. *See also*: eyelyser.

• **Brechtian** ▶ Describing the style of left-wing theatre, associated with the German dramatist Bertolt Brecht (1898–1956). *See*: A-effect; epic theatre.

• **Brenda** ▶ The satirical magazine *Private Eye*'s nickname for Elizabeth II.

• **Bren-gun** ▶ A World War II light machine gun, fired from the shoulder. Originally made in Brno, Czechoslovakia (now the Czech Republic), it was later manufactured in Enfield, England. 'Bren' is a blend of Brno and Enfield.

• **Brest-Litovsk Treaties** ▶ Peace treaties signed in 1918 between Ukraine and Germany and between Soviet Russia and Germany. The treaties were annulled after the defeat of Germany. They were signed at Brest-Litovsk, now in Belarus, which changed its name to Brest in 1921.

• **Bretton Woods Conference** ▶ A conference, attended by America, the UK, and Canada, held in 1944 at the town of Bretton Woods in New Hampshire. The conference led to the establishment of the International Monetary Fund (IMF) and the World Bank.

• **brewer's droop** ▶ An Australian expression for the effect on the male anatomy of consuming too much beer before an intended act of sexual intercourse.

• **Brezhnev Doctrine** ▶ The policy, associated with the Soviet president Leonid Brezhnev (1906–82), that authorized the Soviet Union to intervene in the domestic affairs of satellite states in defence of socialism. *Compare*: Sinatra doctrine.

• **Brian** ▶ British slang for an ordinary working-class male, especially one considered dull or unintelligent. In the 1970s and 1980s it was often used in the phrase 'Well, Brian...' at the start of a tedious explanation, in an imitation of sportsmen interviewed by the TV commentator Brian Moore. *The Life of Brian* was a comic film about a thoroughly ordinary man mistaken for the Messiah, made by the team of Monty Python's Flying Circus. *See also*: Kevin.

• **Brideshead** ▶ The name of the fictional stately home featured in Evelyn Waugh's novel *Brideshead Revisited* (1945). The aristocratic central character, Sebastian Flyte, was based upon Hugh Lygon (1904–36), a fellow undergraduate of Waugh's at Oxford and the second son of the Earl of Beauchamp. Waugh paid several visits to the Beauchamp seat at Great Malvern, Worcestershire, and various features of this house (Madresfield Court) are accurately described in *Brideshead Revisited* (although Castle Howard in Yorkshire was used as the location in the successful ITV adaptation of the novel in the 1980s).

• **Brides in the Bath** ▶ A famous British murder case (1915) in which G. J. Smith was convicted of murdering three woman whom he had bigamously married and later drowned in the bath.

• **Bridget Jones**► *See*: Jones, Bridget.

• **Brighton trunk murders**► Two unrelated murder cases that captured national headlines in 1934. The first began with the discovery of a dismembered body in a trunk at a left-luggage office in Brighton. Subsequently, another body was found in a second trunk at the home of a petty criminal, Tony Mancini. Mancini was charged with the murders but, after a brilliant defence by the advocate Norman Birkett, acquitted, although he did subsequently admit in a newspaper (in 1976) that he had killed one of the deceased. For a time after the trial Mancini toured with a travelling fair as 'The Infamous Brighton Trunk Murder Man', pretending to cut off the head of a pretty girl with a fake guillotine. The first trunk, chief item of evidence in a crime that was never solved, is now an exhibit in Scotland Yard's Black Museum.

• **bright young things**► A phrase coined by the novelist Barbara Cartland (1902–2000) to describe the young socialites of the years following World War I. Their reaction to the horrors of the war was to dance the night away in a riot of frivolous parties in an attempt to pretend that it had never happened. *See also*: flapper.

• **brill**► A British teenager's word for excellent, wonderful. A shortened form of brilliant, it was used in the 1970s and 1980s.

• **brilliant pebbles**► A space warfare strategy, in which large numbers of small but sophisticated missiles would be deployed in orbit to keep watch for and then destroy any hostile missile that came in range. A refinement of the Star Wars project launched in the 1980s, the 'brilliant pebbles' concept started life as a far grander scheme based on bigger intercepting missiles, called **smart rocks**.

• **brinkmanship**► A term coined by the US politician Adlai Stevenson in 1956 (though he disclaimed originality), with reference to the policy of J. Foster Dulles in leading to the brink of war but not to war itself. It has since been used of any strategy that risks disastrous consequences if it goes slightly wrong. *See also*: lifemanship.

• **Brisbane Line**► A plan of defence that was put forward by the military to the Australian government in early 1942, when a Japanese invasion seemed imminent. The suggestion that the plan intended to concentrate on defending only the most crucial areas of the country, implying that all of Australia north of Brisbane would be surrendered, caused considerable public concern.

• **Britain, Battle of**► The attempt by the German Luftwaffe in their prolonged attack on SE England (August–October 1940) to defeat the RAF, as a prelude to invasion of the British Isles. Although heavily outnumbered, the RAF managed to destroy 1700 German planes for a loss of 900 British planes, a tribute to the heroism of the young fighter pilots of Hurricanes and Spitfires, whom Churchill famously eulogized as the Few. The failure of the Luftwaffe to achieve air supremacy persuaded the Germans to abandon their invasion plans. The name of the battle arose from Churchill's speech of 18 June 1940: 'What General Weygand called the "Battle of France" is over. I expect that the Battle of Britain is about to begin.'

• **Britain**►
 **I'm backing Britain** A slogan enthusiastically adopted by the British public in 1968, often in the form of stickers or posters. It was designed to encourage people to make special efforts in the national interest, particularly by doing extra work for no payment. The phrase was coined by five female typists in Surbiton, who volunteered to work an extra half hour a day free. The slogan did not survive to the end of the decade.

• **Britain can take it**► A slogan publicized by the British government in the early part of World War II; it was intended to cement the national resolve in the face of German bombing attacks. In fact, and contrary to much later mythology, the public reacted badly to this piece of bravado and the slogan was dropped in late 1941.

• **Britain's Oldest Teenager**► Nickname of the pop singer Sir Cliff Richard (Harry Rodger Webb; 1940–  ); it refers to the longevity of his career (he has enjoyed hits in every decade from the 1950s to the 2000s) and the fresh-faced boyish appearance he retained well into middle age. Born in India, he began performing in a London coffee bar and recorded his first hit single, 'Move It', at the age of 17 in 1958. A series of gold records and popular film musicals – *The Young Ones* (1961), *Summer Holiday* (1963) – followed. Richard, once criticized for his 'revolting hip-swinging' and 'vulgar antics', became a born-again Christian in the 1960s, after which he began to preach and carry out gospel tours. Although never rated highly by the rock cognoscenti – indeed, his clean-living celibate lifestyle has often made him a figure of fun – he retains a loyal fanbase. He was knighted in 1995.

• **British Academy**► A learned society founded in 1901 to promote the study of the humanities in the UK, including language, literature, archaeology, philosophy, economics, etc.

• **British Antarctic Territory** ▶ A British overseas territory established in 1962, consisting of the South Orkney and South Shetland Islands and part of the continent of Antarctica. It has an area of some 1 709 300 sq km (600 000 sq mi).

• **British Army of the Rhine** ▶ (BAOR) British forces stationed in West Germany in the post-World War II period as part of the NATO defence against any Soviet attack. The collapse of communism in E Europe and the unification of Germany in 1990 led to a reassessment of the BAOR's role.

• **British Broadcasting Corporation** ▶ See: BBC.

• **British Council** ▶ A government-supported body founded in 1934 to promote British culture and the teaching of English abroad.

• **British disease** ▶ The prevalence of strikes and other forms of industrial action in the UK during the 1970s. See also: English disease.

• **British Gazette** ▶ A government newspaper produced during the first few days of the General Strike in 1926. The editor was the then chancellor of the exchequer, Winston Churchill.

• **British Legion** ▶ The **Royal British Legion**, an organization set up in 1921 by the merger of other ex-servicemen's associations. It acts as a social and welfare organization for both ex-servicemen and women and for those still serving in the armed forces. See also: Remembrance Day.

• **British Library** ▶ A national institution created in 1972 from the amalgamation of the British Museum Library, the National Central Library, and the National Lending Library for Science and Technology. After a long delay, the library's premises in Euston Road finally opened to the public in 2001. The collection contains some 18 million volumes.

• **British Lions** ▶ The name given to the Rugby Union team selected from the players of England, Scotland, Wales, and Ireland to represent the British Isles in international matches abroad.

• **British Union of Fascists** ▶ A right-wing political party founded by Sir Oswald Mosley (1896–1980) in 1932. See also: Blackshirts; Mosleyites.

• **Britpop** ▶ The music of several British pop groups who came to prominence in the mid-1990s – notably Oasis, Blur, and Pulp. Arguably, their music had little in common, apart from a few very general characteristics. These were a return to melody and a traditional guitar-based sound after years of electronic dance music, an obvious love of the classic British pop of the 1960s (especially the Beatles, the Kinks, and the Small Faces), and lyrics reflecting the British social scene of the 1990s.

> It was the summer of Britpop [1995], Oasis and Blur were in their pomp. And laddish groups led by adenoidal singers with cheeky regional accents were the flavour of the month. – *The Times*, 20 July 2001.

• **Brixton briefcase** ▶ British slang expression for a portable tape player, a ghettoblaster. Brixton is a district in London with a large Black population.

• **Brockton Blockbuster** ▶ The nickname given to the US world heavyweight boxing champion Rocky Marciano (1923–69) whose home town was Brockton, Massachusetts.

• **bromide** ▶ **1.** A small dose of potassium bromide given as a sedative. In World War II the tea served in servicemen's canteens was said to be laced with bromide to reduce the men's libidos. **2.** A soothing remark or platitude. **3.** A person who makes such remarks. It was used in this sense by Gelett Burgess (1866–1951) in his novel *Are You a Bromide?* (1906).

• **Bronx cheer** ▶ US slang for a 'raspberry', a noise made with the tongue and lips as a sign of contempt. The Bronx is a largely working-class district of New York City.

• **Brookhaven National Laboratory** ▶ A US research establishment at Upton, Long Island, New York, noted for work on high-energy particle physics.

• **Brooklands** ▶ A former car-racing circuit near Weybridge in Surrey. It was opened in 1907 and closed down in 1946. It was famous for its steeply banked bends, which enabled cars to corner at high speeds.

• **Brookside** ▶ A Liverpool-based television soap opera broadcast by Channel 4 since 1982. The show, which centres on the inhabitants of Brookside Close, was devised by the writer Phil Redmond, who had enjoyed previous success with *Grange Hill*, a long-running children's series set in a school. Breaking with the studio-based format of many other soaps, the makers of *Brookside* film inside and around six real houses, part of a housing development that was bought by the programme-makers and modified to facilitate filming. Like its main rival EastEnders, *Brookside* confronts such unpleasant issues as murder, drug abuse, incest, domestic violence, and religious cults. It is not uncommon for helpline numbers to be shown at the end of episodes containing such storylines.

• **brothel creepers** ▶ British slang of the 1950s

for suede shoes with thick crepe soles as worn by teddy boys. **Brothel stompers** is the US equivalent.

• **Brother, can you spare a dime?** ► The title of a song with lyrics by Edgar Harburg (1896–1981) composed in the 1930s during the Great Depression. A British film made in 1975 used the same title to give a semi-documentary picture of the US Depression, in which many formerly prosperous citizens were reduced to beggars. The phrase remains characteristic of the period.

• **brown bagger** ► 1. In America, a workman who takes his lunch from a brown-paper bag rather than use the cafeteria; also a person who takes his own liquor to a club or restaurant, usually because alcoholic drinks are not available there. 2. In Britain, archaic slang for a serious student who is only interested in his course of study. The epithet derives from the brown attaché case in which students (especially non-resident students) used to carry their books.

• **Brown Berets** ► A US organization of Mexicans seeking to defend the interests of the Mexican community in America, named after the brown berets they wear.

• **Brown Bomber** ► The US boxer Joe Louis (1914–81), who was undefeated heavyweight champion of the world from 1937 until his retirement in 1949. On his return in 1950 he was defeated by Ezzard Charles. He began his career in 1934, winning 27 fights, all but four by knockouts.

• **browned off** ► A slang phrase (derivation uncertain) widely current in World War II, signifying 'fed up' or 'bored stiff'. **Cheesed off** is a similar expression.

• **brownfield site** ► *See*: greenfield site.

• **brown goods** ► Electronic products that are housed in wood, or imitation wood, cabinets. *Compare*: white goods.

• **brownie points** ► An imaginary award given to someone for doing the right thing, or for trying to please and impress somebody. Originally a US expression, it has been common in the UK since the 1970s. Some suggest it is based on the notion that Brownie Guides are awarded points for good deeds; others that it derives from a points system for employees operated by US railway companies; others still that it is based on the concept of 'arse-licking' (or 'brown nosing').

• **Brownies** ► *See*: Girl Guides.

• **brown job** ► An RAF name for a member of the army, *i.e.* a soldier in khaki.

• **brown-out** ► In World War II, Australian slang for a partial black-out, in which restricted lighting was allowed.

• **Brown Shirts** ► Hitler's Nazi *Sturmabteilung* (stormtroopers) or **SA** formed in 1921. Under Ernst Röhm the Brown Shirts (so called from the colour of their shirts) attacked and terrorized Jews and political opponents of the Nazis until 1933, when Röhm was murdered on Hitler's orders and power passed to the SS. *See*: Kristallnacht; Night of the Long Knives.

• **brown sugar** ► In America, slang term for a coarse low-grade variety of heroin originating in Asia.

• **Brücke, Die** ► (German, the bridge) A group of German artists who came together in 1905 and disbanded some eight years later. They included the expressionist painter and printmaker Ernst Kirchner (1880–1938). The artists of Die Brücke are noted for their use of bright Fauve-like colours to express a mood of angst; the school also had a lasting influence on graphic art. *See*: expressionism.

• **Bruges group** ► A British right-wing pressure group established in 1989 to oppose growing federalism in the European Community (soon to become the European Union). Its members, drawn largely from the Conservative Party, named it after the Belgian city of Bruges where, on 20 September 1988, Margaret Thatcher had made a speech attacking what she saw as the centralizing tendencies of such European leaders as Jacques Delors. The Bruges group, which contained several high vocal MPs, staunchly opposed the Maastricht Treaty, and was a persistent thorn in the side of John Major's government during the early 1990s. *See*: Eurosceptic.

• **brunch** ► A meal taken in the late morning, which replaces both breakfast and lunch.

• **Brussels Treaty** ► 1. A treaty signed in 1948 between the UK, France, and the Benelux countries, originally for mutual defence. It led to the establishment of NATO (1949) and foreshadowed the Treaty of Rome that created the EEC (*see*: European Community). 2. A treaty by which the UK, Denmark, and the Republic of Ireland became members of the European Community in 1973.

• **brutalism** ► A style of 20th-century architecture, also sometimes called **new brutalism**, characterized by monumental scale, rigorously functional design (*see*: functionalism), and the use of raw untreated concrete. The term was coined by the British architects Peter and Alison Smithson in 1953–54, in reference to the post-1930 work of

Le Corbusier (1887–1965) and certain analogous tendencies in their own work and that of their contemporaries. There was no derogatory intention behind the term, which involved a private pun on Peter Smithson's nickname, Brutus. Brutalism is now, however, used as a general term of abuse for everything most disliked about the architecture of the 20th century.

• **Brylcreem boys** ▶ The RAF fighter pilots who fought and won the Battle of Britain in 1940 (*see*: Few, the). The epithet reflects the glamour attaching to these young men and possibly the envy of those serving in less glamorous roles. It was inspired by an advertisement for **Brylcreem**, a men's hair preparation made by the Beecham group and first sold in 1928, showing a young RAF officer with oily well-ordered hair, clearly a copious user of the brand.

• **BSA** ▶ Birmingham Small Arms. A former British engineering company (founded in 1873), noted for making bicycles, motorcycles, small cars, rifles, and air guns throughout the first half of the 20th century.

• **BSE** ▶ Bovine spongiform encephalopathy. *See*: mad cow disease.

• **B side** ▶ In the days of vinyl records, the **flip side** of a pop single, *i.e.* the reverse side of the recording intended to enter the charts.

• **BST** ▶ 1. British Summer Time. The time set one hour ahead of Greenwich Mean Time. It was adopted in the UK in 1916 and now lasts from the end of March until the end of October. 2. British Standard Time. The time, set one hour ahead of Greenwich Mean Time, that was adopted all the year round in the UK from 1968 to 1971. *See*: daylight saving. 3. Bovine somatotrophin. A growth hormone of cattle, preparations of which are used to increase milk yield and beef production.

• **bubble dancing** ▶ US Black slang from the 1940s, meaning to wash the dishes.

• **bubblegum** ▶ 1. A type of chewing-gum, developed in the 1930s, that can be blown into large bubbles. 2. music A simple form of US pop music that appeared in the 1960s and was aimed at early teenage and pre-teenage youngsters. It was so-called because its fans were expected to be bubblegum-chewers.

• **bubble umbrella** ▶ A type of umbrella with a dome shape surrounding the head and shoulders of the user and made of transparent plastic so that the user can see through. The use of such an umbrella by the Queen Mother to enable sightseers a clear view of her face was much applauded by her admirers.

• **bubs** ▶ Acronym for *bloody ungrateful bastards*. A name given by British troops to Falkland Islanders, following the expulsion of the Argentinian invaders in 1982 (*see*: Falklands Conflict). During the campaign the troops called the Islanders **bennies**, an allusion to the simple-minded character of this name in the TV soap *Crossroads*. When admonished for using this uncomplimentary epithet, the British forces referred to them as **stills** (still bennies). The response of the Islanders was to call their deliverers **whennies**, because so many of them droned on about their earlier campaigns in such terms as: 'When I was in Belfast...', 'When I was in Cyprus...' The British finally resorted to 'bubs'.

• **Buchenwald** ▶ A large Nazi concentration camp set up in 1934 NW of Weimar. It held about 20,000 prisoners used as labourers in nearby factories. Although there were no gas chambers, many died through malnutrition, disease, and execution. Inmates were also used for medical research into vaccines and viral infections. The sadistic Ilsa Koch, known as the Bitch of Buchenwald, was the wife of the commandant in charge between 1939 and 1945.

• **Buchmanism** ▶ *See*: Oxford Group.

• **buck** ▶
  **The buck stops here** A slogan popularized by US President Harry S. Truman, who had it written on a sign on his desk at the White House to remind him that he was ultimately responsible for all decisions; some years later President Jimmy Carter had the motto reinstated for the same purpose. The slogan may have derived from a similar phrase used by poker players.

• **bucket shop** ▶ A shop that offers discounted airline tickets, etc., often being able to do so by taking out minimal insurance and thus exposing the customer to some risk. The epithet was originally used of US shops that sold alcoholic drink in buckets and were often on the fringes of the law. By extension, any slightly dubious business, especially a stockbroker whose standing and resources are open to question, may be described as a bucket shop.

• **bucket trading** ▶ An illegal practice on the stock exchange, which involves stockbrokers deliberately failing to obtain the best price possible for their clients. *See also*: bucket shop.

• **Buckley's hope** ▶ Australian slang for little or no chance at all, not a hope in hell. Buckley, apparently, was an escaped convict who, after 32 years on the run, gave himself up in 1955 to the authorities and then died the following year. Often shortened to **Buckley's**.

• **Buckmaster Divorce Act** ▶ The name given to a British act of parliament, the Matrimonial Causes Act (1923). It made adultery sufficient cause for divorce by either party. Up to this time, a woman could not obtain a divorce on the grounds of adultery alone – cruelty or desertion had to be involved. The act is named after the former Lord Chancellor, Lord Buckmaster, who had pressed for such reform.

• **buckminsterfullerene** ▶ A new form of carbon (in addition to diamond and graphite) discovered in 1985. It consists of molecules containing 60 carbon atoms arranged on the surface of a sphere in a framework of hexagons and pentagons. The substance is named after the architect Buckminster Fuller because of its structural resemblance to Fuller's geodesic dome. This and similar forms of carbon are called **fullerenes** or, more informally, **bucky balls**.

• **Buck Rogers** ▶ US science-fiction hero, who appeared in comic strips from 1929. First introduced in Phil Nowlan's novel *Armageddon 2419*, the character is an air-force officer who wakes up from a 500-year sleep in the 25th century, in which he has numerous adventures. Various film and television versions of the stories have been made.

• **buckshee** ▶ Free, offered without charge. The word entered the language in the 20th century as a late import from the Indian Raj; it derives from *baksheesh*, meaning a tip or gift of alms (from Persian *bakhshīsh*, from *bakhshīdan*, to give).

• **buddy** ▶ US slang for a friend. Of 19th-century origin, it was adopted in the 1980s, in both America and the UK, as a specific term for a volunteer companion of an Aids sufferer (*see*: Terrence Higgins Trust).

• **Budget leak tribunal** ▶ An official tribunal that investigated (1936) allegations that details of the budget had been leaked to a private individual who had used the information to make money. The tribunal's report led to the resignation of the then colonial secretary J. H. Thomas.

• **Buffy the Vampire Slayer** ▶ *See*: valspeak.

• **Bugger Bognor** ▶ *See*: How is the Empire? *at* Empire.

• **Bugs Bunny** ▶ **1.** Anarchic cartoon character who has appeared in over 160 films since the late 1930s. The carrot-crunching troublemaker first appeared – as a nameless hare – in Warner Brothers' *Porky's Hare Hunt* (1938). He was created by Ben 'Bugs' Hardaway (whose nickname he stole) but was later mainly drawn by the animator Tex Avery (1907–80). Bugs's Brooklyn accent was supplied by voice artist Mel Blanc, who also coined the famous catchphrase What's up, Doc? **2.** British underworld rhyming slang for money, common since the 1960s.

• **bug smasher** ▶ US airforce slang for a light aircraft, used since the 1950s.

• **Bulge, Battle of the** ▶ *See*: Ardennes Offensive.

• **bulimia** ▶ (Greek *bous*, ox, *limos*, hunger) Compulsive overeating. Originally known only as a neurological disorder, this condition, in the form of **bulimia nervosa**, became increasingly recognized during the latter part of the 20th century as a symptom of psychological disturbance, particularly affecting adolescent girls. It is sometimes seen as a phase of anorexia nervosa: the patient undergoes an orgy of overeating followed by drastic purging or self-induced vomiting.

• **Bullamakanka** ▶ Australian slang for any remote or backward place (there is no real place of the name).

• **bulldog breed** ▶ The British, especially with reference to their pugnacity. This phrase comes from Arthur Reece's music-hall song 'Sons of the Sea, All British Born' which had a tremendous vogue in late Victorian and Edwardian England. It came at the time of naval rivalry with the Kaiser's Germany and inspired the name of **Bulldog Drummond**, hero of the adventure novels of Sapper.

• **bullet** ▶
  **Every bullet has its billet** A fatalistic phrase, probably military in origin, meaning that nothing happens by chance and that there is no point in trying to evade one's destiny.

• **bullet train** ▶ A high-speed train developed in Japan since the 1970s. It proved capable of speeds over 125 mph.

• **Bullfrog of the Pontine Marshes** ▶ A dismissive reference to Benito Mussolini (1883–1945) by Winston Churchill during World War II.

• **Bull Moose** ▶ Nickname of US President Theodore Roosevelt (1858–1919).

> I am as strong as a bull moose. – THEODORE ROOSEVELT, during 1900 vice-presidential campaign.

• **bum bag** ▶ British slang for a small zipper bag attached to a belt worn around the waist with the bag part resting either at the back or in the front. Originally worn by skiers to hold their keys and money, they became part of street fashion in the late 1980s. They are worn by either sex and are a much safer alternative to a handbag, which can be snatched in the street. The US name is **fanny pack**.

• **bump** ▶ In the airline business, to move a passenger's reservation from an overbooked flight to the next available one.

• **bums on seats** ▶ A paying audience for any public event. All impressarios require sufficient bums on the seats of an auditorium to cover expenses and make a profit.

• **bum's rush** ▶ Slang for the immediate rejection of an idea, person, etc. From a US phrase for the forcible ejection of undesirables (bums), usually from a bar.

• **BUNCH** ▶ Burroughs, Univac, NCR, Control Data, and Honeywell. After IBM and the Digital Equipment Corporation, this group of companies became the biggest-selling computer manufacturers in the 1980s.

• **Bundles for Britain** ▶ An organization founded in America in January 1940, by Mrs Wales Latham, to send parcels of comforts to Britain during World War II.

• **Bungalow Bill** ▶ British slang for a rather unintelligent male, i.e. one 'with nothing going on upstairs', or a very sexually active male, i.e. 'one with a lot going on downstairs', or both. The name comes from a song by the Beatles (1968).

• **bunji-jumping** ▶ British slang for the practice of jumping from high places (such as bridges) while attached to an elastic line secured to the high place. It became popular in the late 1980s. Bunji is an adaptation of bungy, the playground word for an eraser, a rubber.

• **Bunker, Archie** ▶ A bigoted working-class character in the US TV comedy series *All in the Family*. Bunker was devised as a US counterpart to Britain's Alf Garnett, the show being essentially a reworking of the BBC's *Till Death Us Do Part*. In America and Canada the name is still used to denote an ignorant and prejudiced blue-collar male.

• **Bunny** ▶ Nickname of the British comedy actor J. Robertson Hare (1891–1979), who became a star of the Aldwych farces of the 1920s and the 1930s.

• **bunny girl** ▶ A somewhat scantily dressed waitress or attendant in a night club, equipped with a fluffy tail and a headdress with long ears to suggest a rabbit. They were introduced in the Playboy Club, London, in 1966 by Hugh Hefner and Victor Lownes.

• **bunnyhug** ▶ A jazz dance that became popular in the early 20th century; so-called because cou-ples held each other in a tight embrace while performing it.

• **Bunter, Billy** ▶ A fat greedy schoolboy created by the prolific writer Frank Richards (pen name of Charles Hamilton; 1876–1961). Bunter's exploits at the fictional Greyfriars School were recounted in the boys' comics *Gem* (1907–39) and *Magnet* (1908–40) and later in numerous books. The bespectacled Bunter was always in search of a chum who would advance him a small sum of money with which to buy tuck. The loan was always in anticipation of an expected postal order. The name Billy Bunter is now applied to any grossly overweight boy or man.

• **buppie** ▶ A US slang term of the 1980s, also heard in the UK, for a Black yuppie.

• **Burgos government** ▶ The rebel Spanish government set up in July 1936 by General Franco at Burgos, the former capital of Castile, at the start of the Spanish Civil War.

• **Burma Road** ▶ This great highway was made in 1937–39 to open up the western interior of China by communication with the sea, and ran from Lashio to Kunming in Yunnan, a distance of 770 miles. It was the chief highway for supplies to China during World War II until the Japanese cut it in 1942. It was recaptured in 1945.

• **burn, baby, burn** ▶ A slogan adopted by militant Blacks after a riot in Los Angeles in 1965, in which 34 people died and a wide area was destroyed by arsonists.

• **Burnham scale** ▶ A scale of salaries and other benefits for school teachers in England and Wales, first instituted in 1924 and named after the former newspaper owner Viscount Burnham (1862–1933), chairman of the committee that originally set it up.

• **burn rubber** ▶ To leave somewhere so fast in a car that the tyres scorch on the road.

• **Bürolandschaft** ▶ (German, office landscape) A style of open-plan flexible office design in which people work in areas delineated by small screens or rows of indoor plants, rather than by walls.

• **Burton** ▶
   **gone for a Burton** Absent, missing, or lost; dead or presumed dead. Although widely used by the services in World War II, the phrase is of uncertain origin. It is sometimes said to be an RAF coinage derived from the training of radio telegraph operators in Montagu Burton's clothing premises at Blackpool. Those who failed their tests were said to have 'gone for a Burton'. Alternatively, it may be connected with Burton beer – the impli-

cation being that the absent person has gone for a drink. Another interesting suggestion relates the phrase to council elections held in Birmingham in 1878, when George Cadbury, supporting the temperance interest, was opposed by a Dr Burton, openly backed by the licensed victuallers. The *Birmingham Post* (22 July) reported: 'During the whole of the polling day men were seen coming from Dr Burton's committee room, and, parading Steward St with jugs of beer in their hands, on which were painted papers "Vote for Burton".' This could have given rise to the expression 'he's gone for a Burton' when inquiring of someone's whereabouts.

• **Busby's babes** ► Members of the Manchester United football team managed by Sir Matt Busby (1909–94) from 1945 to 1969. *See also*: Munich air crash.

• **business as usual** ► *See*: Blitz.

• **business cycle** ► *See*: trade cycle.

• **businesspeak** ► Jargon used in business and commerce. The term is one of a number coined with the suffix '-speak' and modelled on newspeak and doublespeak in George Orwell's novel Nineteen Eighty Four (1949). There are perhaps two main styles of businesspeak: the 19th-century merchant's style, servile and garrulous, and the late 20th-century City whizz kid's double talk. An example of the former would be couched in terms of 'favouring us with an order from your good selves', while the latter might refer to shark repellents or a dead-cat bounce.

• **busing** or **crossbusing** ► The practice of transporting children by bus to a school in another area in pursuance of a policy of racial integration. The enforcing of such a policy in the southern US states in the 1960s provoked a violent backlash against the Black population.

• **busman's holiday** ► A holiday spent doing very much the same thing as one does when working – an allusion to a bus driver taking a driving holiday. As the Prince of Wales says in Shakespeare's *Henry IV Part I*:

> If all the year were playing holidays
> To sport would be as tedious as to work.

• **bust** ► 1. An arrest, especially in connection with the possession of illegal drugs. Originally US criminal or street slang, it was adopted by the hippies of the late 1960s and has since passed into everyday usage. 2. US teenage slang of the late 1980s for a great achievement. It derives from the basketball term for a good shot. 3. A wild party. 4. Australian slang for a robbery. 5. Slang for a break-out from prison. 6. To demote.

• **Butch Cassidy and the Sundance Kid** ► The nicknames of two US bandits whose exploits have become folklore; in the highly successful film with this title (1969) Paul Newman played Butch and Robert Redford was the Kid. Butch Cassidy's real name was Robert Le Roy Parker (1886–1909) – he was called Butch for the very good reason that he was an ex-butcher. The Sundance Kid, real name Harry Longbaugh (1860–1909), established his reputation by robbing a bank in Sundance, Nevada. Most of the events portrayed in the film were based on fact, including their deaths in a shoot-out in Bolivia.

• **Butcher of Baghdad** ► Epithet used for Saddam Hussein, president of Iraq, in the popular press after his annexation of Kuwait in 1990 and the atrocities performed there by his army of occupation (*see*: Gulf War). Saddam had previously established himself as a ruthless and aggressive dictator by his treatment of the Iraqi Kurdish minority and his attempted invasion of Iran.

• **Butcher of Broadway** ► Nickname given to the US drama critic Alexander Woollcott (1887–1943), who was noted for his vitriolic reviews. *See*: Whiteside, Sheridan.

• **Butcher of Lyons** ► The head of the German Gestapo in Lyons (1942–44), Klaus Barbie (1913–91), who was notorious for his cruel murder of some 4000 people, including Jews, members of the French underground, and others. He also deported 7000 Jews to death camps. He was finally brought back to Lyons from Bolivia in 1987 and sentenced by a French court to life imprisonment.

• **Butcher of Tehran** ► An acolyte of the last Shah of Iran, General Gholam Ali Oveissi, who earned the title by ordering his troops to open fire on the marching supporters of Ayatollah Khomeini in 1963 and again in 1978. He was shot in 1984.

• **Butler Act** ► An act introduced in 1944 by the then minister of education R. A. Butler (1902–82) which established a system of free universal secondary education compulsory to the age of 15. The act instituted the eleven-plus examination and divided schools into grammar, secondary modern, and technical schools.

• **Butlins** ► A chain of holiday camps set up by the businessman Sir William ('Billy') Butlin (1900–80) in 1936. Holiday camps had been started earlier (1906) by J. Fletcher Dodd at Caister-on-Sea in Norfolk. Butlin's achievement was to give them mass-appeal. His first camp was opened at Skegness in Lincolnshire; its success led to a chain of camps in which holiday makers staged in small private chalets but ate together in large dining rooms. The first camps had a somewhat institutional air, involving many communal activities and mass-entertainment organized by **redcoats**. Butlin advertised his camps in 1937 with the slogan, 'Holiday with pay! Holiday with play! A week's holiday for a week's wage.' Today, Butlins holiday camps are more luxurious and relaxed institutions, catering particularly for families with children.

• **Butskellism** ▸ The policies of the then chancellor of the exchequer R. A. Butler (1902–82) during the 1950s. The term was coined by the *Economist* to imply that there was little difference between Butler's type of conservatism and the socialism of his predecessor as chancellor, Hugh Gaitskell (1906–63).

• **butterfly effect** ▸ *See*: chaos theory.

• **butter mountain** ▸ *See*: CAP.

• **buttie** or **butty** ▸ British slang for a sandwich. Originally a Northern, particularly Liverpudlian, shortening of buttered bread, the term became widespread in the 1960s.

• **buy it** ▸ To pay with one's life; to die. Although possibly of earlier origin, this usage became very common in World War II, especially among pilots in the RAF 'Old Bloggs bought it today' is a euphemism for 'Bloggs was killed in combat today'. The implication may be that he bought a place in eternity at the cost of his earthly life. This is perhaps connected with the US pilots' ironic euphemism **to buy the farm**, *i.e.* to retire for ever.

• **buzz** ▸ **1.** A rumour. **2.** A moment of excitement, as achieved by the use of drugs, music, or some other short-lived stimulation.

• **buzz bomb** or **doodlebug** ▸ A German flying bomb used against London and SE England between June 1944 and March 1945. It was driven by a form of pulse jet, in which hinged air-intake flaps opened when the pressure of the air resulting from the bomb's passage through the atmosphere exceeded the pressure in the combustion chamber. The un-guided bombs were pointed in the direction of London from their launch site in N France with just enough fuel to reach their target. When the fuel was exhausted the engine cut out – a frightening sound for London's inhabitants, although it was said that if one heard the engine stop one was safe. They were called by the Germans **V1** weapons (V for *Vergeltungswaffe*, reprisal weapon).

• **buzz word** ▸ A word that originates in the specialized jargon of a particular field (especially business, technology, or computing), and becomes fashionable in the wider community.

• **BYOG** ▸ *See*: PBAB.

• **bypass** ▸ A main road built round a town or city to enable traffic to pass round the town without causing congestion within it. Bypasses began to be built in the 1930s in the UK as motor cars and road-haulage vehicles increased in number to such an extent that high streets designed for horse traffic in the middle ages became impassable. Many bypasses were widened into dual-carriageway roads in the late 20th century.

• **bypass surgery** ▸ An operation to bypass a diseased or narrowed blood vessel. It is used very extensively and successfully in **coronary bypass grafts**, in which coronary arteries narrowed by atheroma are bypassed by healthy mammary arteries or saphenous veins from the leg of the patient.

• **bypass variegated** ▸ Name given to certain features of 20th-century architecture by the British cartoonist and writer Osbert Lancaster (1908–86). It describes the sort of builders' houses built in large numbers along bypasses in the 1930s, usually to the same general plan but with minor differences, in an effort to introduce variety.

• **byte** ▸ A data-storage unit in a computer, comprising eight bits treated as a single entity. The term is probably an amalgamation of 'bit' and 'bite'. *See also*: megabyte.

# C

• **C** ▸ The code name used for the head of MI6. Made famous through the James Bond novels of Ian Fleming, it may have come from the name of the founder of the SIS, Mansfield Cumming. Alternatively, it may stand for 'chief' or 'control'.

• **Cabbage Patch** ▸ *See*: Billy Williams's Cabbage Patch.

• **cable television** ▸ A system using cables to relay television programmes to subscribers' homes. It was first used to improve network services in areas of poor reception. By the 1960s many areas in America had a master 'community antenna', which picked up signals from broadcasting stations and re-transmitted them by coaxial cable. Modern systems, which increasingly use fibre optics, offer a wide range of programmes, including those originated especially for cable TV or made by community groups; satellite channels can also be distributed through the cable system. In the 1990s, interactive services, such as home-banking, shopping, and accessing of data banks, were developed. Although most British towns and cities are now wired for cable television, it is far less popular than in America.

• **CAD** ▸ Computer-aided design. The use of computers in the design of products, electronic circuits, buildings, etc. The computer can display plans, elevations, or isometric views using programs based on standard design criteria and the input of specific data relating to dimensions, tolerances, factors of safety, etc. These preliminary plans can then be modified by the designer on-screen. In some appropriate cases the CAD output can be used in computer-aided manufacture (**CAM**) of components of the design.

• **caff** ▸ British slang for a café, especially a cheap one serving traditional fried food, as in the expression 'greasy caff' (*see also*: greasy spoon). The caff emerged as the meeting-place for young people in the 1950s and the word is still widely used. In 1989 London's Victoria and Albert Museum promoted itself with the slogan 'An ace caff with quite a nice museum attached.'

• **Cagoulard** ▸ (French, hooded man) A member of a secret right-wing terrorist organization in France in the mid to late 1930s. The name derives from *cagoule*, a hooded sleeveless garment, originally a monk's cowl. The name **cagoule** is now given to a light-weight, usually knee-length, anorak.

• **Caillaux affair** ▸ A scandal that rocked French politics in 1914, following the shooting of the editor of *Le Figaro*, Gaston Calmette, by the wife of the minister of finance, Joseph Caillaux. Calmette had threatened to publish letters between Caillaux and his mistress (whom he subsequently married). Madame Caillaux was acquitted at the ensuing trial, which provoked streetfighting between supporters of the political right, to which Caillaux then belonged, and the left.

• **Cairo Conference** ▸ A conference held in November 1943 between Churchill, Roosevelt, and the Chinese Nationalist leader Chiang Kai-shek (1887–1975), to establish the war policy of the Allies in the Far East.

• **Cairo Fred** ▸ A nickname given by the film industry to Omar Sharif (1932– ), the Egyptian actor who became internationally famous in such films as *Lawrence of Arabia* (1962) and *Doctor Zhivago* (1966). He was actually from Alexandria.

• **cakehole** ▸ British vulgar slang for mouth, widely used in the 1950s and 1960s in the expression 'shut your cakehole' meaning shut up. It is still sometimes heard in the school playground.

• **Calabash** ▸
  **Goodnight Mrs Calabash – wherever you are** A catchphrase used by the US comedian Jimmy ('Schnozzle') Durante (1893–1980) to end his radio and TV programmes in the 1940s and 1950s. 'Calabash' here implies to 'empty head', from the hollow calabash gourd. It is thought that 'Mrs Calabash' was Durante's pet name for his first wife, who had died in 1943.

• **Calder Hall** ▸ The world's first nuclear power station to feed appreciable quantities of electricity into a national grid. It was situated at Windscale (now Sellafield) in NW England and was opened in

1956. It was fuelled by uranium slugs in aluminium cans in a graphite moderator. The coolant was carbon dioxide. The Calder Hall reactor combined power generation with plutonium production. It was the precursor of a programme of advanced gas-cooled reactors (AGRs) developed in Britain.

• **California, here I come**▶ A catchphrase that originally referred to achieving success in the film business, based in Hollywood, California; it was the title of a song made popular by Al Jolson in the 1921 musical *Bombo*. It has since been used, on both sides of the Atlantic, by anyone who believes he or she is on his way to success.

• **Californiate** ▶ To spoil the landscape by unplanned building, industrialization, etc. The term was used in America in the 1970s and refers to the uncontrolled development of southern California. Sometimes **Californicate** is used.

• **call**▶
  **don't call us, we'll call you** A phrase supposedly used by theatre directors to say goodbye to unsuccessful applicants at auditions. The implication is, of course, that no call will be made. The phrase, which dates from the 1940s, is now used more widely, often in a jocular way, to get rid of some one offering to sell something or provide a service. It is often shortened to **don't call us**.

• **call-and-recall**▶ A system in which those who require regular medical check-ups, often for specific identified conditions, receive computer-generated reminders of the date of their next consultations. The system is particularly applicable to diagnostic tests used in preventive medicine. Call-and-recall frequently refers to smear tests for cervical cancer but also has relevance to other tests, such as mammography or blood-pressure tests, in which early detection can prevent death or serious illness.

• **callanetics**▶ A system of exercises developed in the 1970s by the US writer on fitness Callan Pinckney. It aims to improve fitness and general muscle tone without the development of unsightly muscles. Callanetics came into public prominence in 1989 when the Duchess of York (*see*: Fergie) used the method to improve her figure after the birth of her first child, Beatrice.

• **call-back**▶ In America, the recalling of a product by its manufacturer because of faults discovered after the product has been sold. The situation occurs most commonly with cars, when potentially dangerous defects can show up after a new model has been running on the road. Products may either be returned to the dealer for repairs to be carried out or may be withdrawn from sale altogether. In the UK, the term **recall** is more usual.

• **call bird**▶ A cheap article used to attract buyers into a shop, in the hope that once inside they will be tempted to make more expensive purchases.

• **call centre**▶ An office set up for the sole purpose of handling large numbers of incoming or outgoing telephone calls. Call centres can be used for cold-calling or other sales, to carry out surveys and research, or by large organizations wishing to deal with all service and other enquiries centrally. A product of the late 1980s, call centres are now a major growth industry: the UK alone has over 3500, employing well over a third of a million people. In the UK, many call centres are located in the north of the country, apparently because surveys indicate that people associate northern accents with honesty.

The rise of the call centre has not been universally welcomed. Many members of the public prefer to talk to an organization's representatives face-to-face in local branches; others resent having to navigate through as many as four submenus before being left to sit on hold for 20 minutes listening to bad muzak. Some call centres have also been criticized for providing a highly pressured and depersonalized working environment for their staff.

• **call girl**▶ A female prostitute, usually an elegant and sophisticated one, who makes her assignations on the telephone.

• **call-in** ▶ *See*: phone-in.

• **calling all cars**▶ *See*: APB.

• **call money**▶ **1.** Money repayable on demand. Money invested with a bank may be placed on the money market, either for a fixed term or to be repaid when called for. **2.** Money paid for a **call option** on a stock exchange or a commodity exchange, *i.e.* the cost of purchasing an option to buy certain shares or goods by a fixed date. A **put option** gives the buyer of the option the right to sell the shares or goods by a fixed date.

• **call off all bets**▶ Literally, to cancel all wagers in certain circumstances. A bookmaker, for example, might call off all bets if he suspected that some race or contest had been rigged. By extension, the phrase is used to mean 'repudiate a disadvantageous agreement or situation'. In particular, in US Black slang of the 1940s, it meant 'to die' – perhaps the most effective way of calling off one's bets.

• **call waiting** ▶ A service provided by British Telecom for those of their subscribers willing to pay a small fee. Without it, someone calling subscribers when they are engaged on another call will hear only the engaged signal. With call waiting, however, the caller is informed by a BT announcement that the subscriber is on another call 'but knows you are waiting'. The subscriber hears a beeping signal and can interrupt the call they are on to find out who is calling. They can then return to the original call, or not as they wish. This raises one of the more ticklish problems in modern etiquette – in what circumstances, if any, is a subscriber justified in keeping their existing caller waiting in order to take a more important or interesting call? *See also*: voicemail.

• **caló** ► A form of Mexican Spanish using many slang terms and incorporating English words. Originally an argot used in the Mexican underworld, it is now in use by youths in SW America.

• **CAM** ► Computer-aided manufacture. *See*: CAD.

• **Cambridge Complex** ► A group of research organizations associated with Harvard University, Cambridge, Massachusetts, and with the Massachusetts Institute of Technology.

• **Camden Town Group** ► A school of postimpressionist painters founded in 1911 by the British artist Walter Sickert (1860–1942). It specialized in contemporary London scenes, particularly theatre and café scenes and somewhat squalid domestic interiors. In 1913 it amalgamated with other societies to form the London Group.

• **came in** ►
**this is where we came in** Phrase said when something, such as a discussion, project, etc., starts to repeat itself, implying that the process should cease. It dates from the 1920s when cinemas started to give continuous performances – *i.e.* the programme was repeated throughout the afternoon and evening. A cinemagoer might enter the cinema part-way through the main film, watch the rest of it and the supporting programme, and then stay to see the first part of the main feature up to the point at which they came in. They would then leave.

• **Camelot** ► The site of the mythical court of King Arthur and his knights of the Round Table. The name, with its romantic associations of chivalry and heroism, was applied retrospectively to the administration (1961–63) of US President John F. Kennedy, whose glamorous image and youthful vigour had briefly inspired hopes of a golden age in America's history. At the time of Kennedy's inauguration, the Lerner–Loewe musical *Camelot*, loosely based on the Arthurian legend, had recently opened on Broadway. Shortly after Kennedy's as-

sassination, his widow told an interviewer that the president had particularly liked the title song:

Once there was a fleeting wisp of glory
Called Camelot...
Don't let it be forgot
That once there was a spot
For one brief shining moment that was known
As Camelot.

• **camel walk** ► A dance originating in the US Black community in the 1900s. It involved moving the back and shoulders in imitation of a camel.

• **Camillagate** ► A scandal concerning a tape of a sexually explicit telephone conversation between the Prince of Wales and his mistress Mrs Camilla Parker Bowles in 1989. Since the original Watergate scandal the suffix '-gate' has been widely used to form a word relating to a scandal.

Initially, the British press regarded the contents of this illegally obtained tape as too shocking to share with their readers (Charles notoriously expresses a wish to be his friend's tampon). However, when an Australian magazine published a transcript in January 1993 thousands of copies were faxed across the world to Britain and were soon circulating in offices and workplaces throughout the land. After *The Daily Sport*, *Kent Today*, and three Irish dailies published transcripts, other tabloids followed suit, claiming that loyal British subjects had a right to be aware of the sexual foibles of the heir to the throne. The continental press had a field day, with Italy's *Independente* devoting a full page to the story, under the banner headline 'Porno Prince'.

The Prince later admitted to adultery with Mrs Parker Bowles, their relationship being a major factor in the breakdown of his marriage to Princess Diana (*see*: People's Princess), which was formally dissolved in 1996. As Mrs Parker Bowles was by this time also divorced, the possibility that she might one day marry the Prince and in due course become queen began to be discussed in the media. *See also*: Squidgygate.

• **camouflage** ► The various techniques used to conceal soldiers and military equipment or installations from the enemy. Until modern times the more conspicuous and dazzling a general could make his army, the more likely it was thought that his enemy would be cowed into submission before battle was joined. Thus, soldiers were often equipped with bright uniforms and tall hats; their presence was further advertised by the blaring of bugles, the rattling of drums, and the flying of colours. However, changes in battle strategy necessitated by advances in weaponry in the 19th century meant that there were advantages to be gained in a fighting unit being inconspicuous: with an accurate rifle, a conspicuous soldier is easily shot. Early experiments with subdued colours for uniforms (such as the green jacket of the British Rifle Brigade in the Napoleonic Wars) had met with ridicule; however, by the end of the Victorian era, khaki had been adopted for most units of the British colonial forces. World War I hastened the development of camouflage techniques with the British, German, and US armies all adopting drab brown, green, or grey outfits; the light blue colour of French uniforms was blamed for increased casualties during the war. Similar thinking has since been applied to tanks, gun emplacements, aircraft, and ships (*see*: dazzle ships). Now every modern army has its specialists in the application of camouflage, which can be adapted according to the terrain in which it will be employed. The word camouflage itself was coined early in the 20th century, from the French *camoufler* (to disguise).

• **camp** ➤ Displaying effeminate mannerisms of speech or gesture; acting in a self-consciously theatrical way. The term emerged from theatrical slang after World War II. Although originally used to describe only male homosexuals, it can now be applied to either sex and has to some extent lost its sexual overtones. Its derivation is obscure; the two most likely sources are: from the French *camper*, to pose; or from the 19th-century dialect word 'kemp', meaning uncouth.

• **Campaign for Nuclear Disarmament** ➤ *See*: CND.

• **camp as a row of little pink tents** ➤ Blatantly homosexual; a pun on the double meaning of camp. A variant is **bent as a lighthouse staircase**.

• **Camp David** ➤ An official country retreat for US presidents in the Appalachian Mountains, Maryland. Originally named 'Shangri-La' by President F. D. Roosevelt, who established it in 1942, it was renamed by President Eisenhower in 1953, after his grandson. It has been the site of a number of significant international meetings. The **Camp David Agreement** of 1978 was arranged by President Jimmy Carter, between the Israeli prime minister, Menachem Begin (1913–92), and the Egyptian president, Anwar Sadat (1918–81). It led to a peace treaty between Israel and Egypt (1979).

• **Campion, Albert** ➤ A fictional detective created by the British writer Margery Allingham (1905–66). Campion first appeared in *The Crime at Black Dudley* (US title, *The Black Dudley Murder*; 1929), and continued his career through a further 21 novels. It is said that he was modelled on the author's husband, Philip Carter, who wrote two further novels featuring Campion after her death.

Campion is a bespectacled aristocrat who gives a deceptive impression of amiable foolishness that disguises a keen insight and razor-sharp brain. In this he is similar to other 'gentleman amateurs', such as Lord Peter Wimsey.

• **Canal Zone** or **Panama Canal Zone** ➤ The strip of land extending 8 km (5 mi) on either side of the Panama Canal. In 1903 the USA acquired construction rights for the canal from the newly independent Panama, retaining sovereignty over the Canal Zone. The canal itself opened for shipping in 1914. Anti-US riots led to a treaty negotiated by President Carter in 1978, in which jurisdiction over the Canal Zone passed to Panama the following year; full sovereignty over the area reverted to Panama in 2000.

• **canary** ➤ **1.** A female jazz singer. **2.** A person who gives information to the police about criminal activities. The term is usually restricted to criminals who, faced with prosecution, grass on their accomplices; *i.e.* they 'sing' to the police.

• **cancer stick** ➤ British slang for a cigarette. It has been common since the 1960s, when the link between cancer and cigarette smoking was established.

• **candid camera** ➤ An unseen camera used to photograph an unsuspecting subject. Candid-camera shots, which are often amusing, are much used in pictorial journalism. *Candid Camera* was also the name of an ITV show of the 1960s and 1970s in which unsuspecting members of the public were filmed in embarrassing or ridiculous situations that had been deliberately set up by the production team.

• **can-do** ➤ A colloquial and voguish adjective, popular from the late 1980s, meaning willing and able to face situations, however challenging and arduous (*e.g.* a can-do entrepreneur). The expression reflects the Thatcherite ideal of enterprise and initiative. It is derived from **can do**, an affirmative reply to a request or command to do something, **no can do** being the facetious negative alternative.

• **candy** ➤ US slang for illegal drugs. Originally used of cocaine and heroin, it was later applied to LSD taken on a sugar cube. **Nose-candy** is a drug that is sniffed or snorted, especially cocaine.

• **candyman** ➤ US slang for a dealer in illegal drugs, especially heroin and cocaine. Originally Black street slang, the word could also have sexual connotations; it features in many blues songs.

• **canned laughter** ► The pre-recorded laughter dubbed onto the soundtrack of a TV or radio programme that was not recorded in front of a live audience. Because the canned laughter is not always a response to something obviously funny, the term is frequently used derogatively.

• **canned music** ► Pre-recorded, as opposed to live, music. This derogatory expression is mainly applied to intrusive or annoying Muzak played in a public place such as a pub, shopping centre, etc.

• **Cannes Film Festival** ► Founded in 1946, this annual event, held in Cannes on the French Riviera in May, has become the most important of the international film festivals. As such it attracts the jetset, the media, and other hangers-on as well as leading figures from the world of the cinema. Its various awards include the prestigious Palme d'Or.

• **cannon fodder** ► Originally young soldiers with little training, who were regarded as expendable in times of war. In the late 20th century the expression was also applied figuratively to young marketing managers, insurance salespersons, and anyone else who could easily be replaced by their employers if they were less than successful.

• **can of worms** ► An unpleasant, difficult, or uncontrollable situation that is better left alone. Phrases such as 'don't open that can of worms' were first used in America in the 1950s; the expression became popular in the UK in the 1970s.

• **canteen culture** ► The prevailing attitudes and opinions in the lower ranks of an organization or company. The phrase contrasts the opinions – often reactionary, cynical, or bigoted – expressed in the staff canteen with those designed for public consumption. It was first used in connection with the British police force in the late 1980s.

• **Canutism** ► Resistance to inevitable change. The term comes from King Canute (*c.* 994–1035), who, according to legend, demonstrated the limit of his powers to his flattering courtiers by sitting on the seashore and ordering the tide to recede.

• **CAP** ► Common Agricultural Policy. A policy for food production first implemented by the EEC in 1962 in order to support farmers and ensure a regular supply of reasonably priced foodstuffs. The policy includes subsidies to farmers for modernization. More contentious is the use of a 'threshold price', below which certain foodstuffs (cereals, meat, eggs, fruit, etc.) cannot be imported into the EU. Moreover, there is a 'target price' for specified foodstuffs, which is considered to be a reasonable price for the producer. If the market price falls below this, the EU buys up surplus foodstuffs at an 'intervention price'. The system has been criticized because it is a way of paying farmers to produce food that nobody wants to buy; in the 1970s and early 1980s it also led to huge surplus stocks – the **butter mountain**, the **beef mountain**, and the **wine lake**. Measures taken to reduce these surpluses, which have proved largely successful, include the imposition of production quotas on some foodstuffs, reduction of target and intervention prices for certain products, and the introduction of setaside. To protect farm prices from normal exchange-rate fluctuations, the CAP also introduced so-called **green money** (or **green currencies**), these being the currencies of the EU member countries set at artificial exchange rates. The **green pound** is the value of the pound sterling in green money. The need for green money was greatly reduced by the advent of the European Monetary System; it is now unnecessary among those countries that use the single European currency.

• **Capcom** or **CapCom** ► Abbreviation for *Capsule Communicator*, the person at a space centre on earth, who maintains radio communication with the astronauts of a manned space flight. The capsule is the detachable pressurized compartment of a space vehicle in which the astronauts and instruments are housed. The term was coined *c.* 1970 during the US Apollo moon programme.

• **Cape Canaveral** ► *See*: Cape Kennedy.

• **Cape Coloured** or **Coloured** ► In South Africa, the population of mixed European, Hottentot, and Indian descent of Cape Province. There are approximately 3.7 million (about 9% of the total population). Under the apartheid system of South Africa they were awarded more privileges than the Bantu.

• **Caped Crusader** ► *See*: Batman.

• **capeesh** ► US slang expression meaning 'do you understand?', from an anglicization of the Italian *capisci*.

• **Cape Kennedy** ► After the assassination of President Kennedy in 1963 Cape Canaveral in Florida was renamed Cape Kennedy. It reverted to its original name in 1973 in response to pressure from the local community. It is the site of operations for the NASA space programme.

• **capitalist roader** ► A term used in China in the 1960s for those accused of wanting to take the 'capitalist road' to a market economy.

• **capital levy** ► A state tax on capital rather than income; it was first proposed in the British House of Commons in 1914. Capital levies are regarded by capitalists as a form of robbery and by socialists as a fair means of redistributing wealth. A surtax surcharge imposed by the Labour government in 1968, which taxed the highest rate of income at over 100%, is the nearest the UK has come to a capital levy.

A **capital-gains tax** was imposed in the UK in 1965. This imposes a tax on any gains made by disposing of capital assets, with certain exceptions, such as the sale of one's main dwelling house. A similar tax is used in America and several other countries.

• **capital transfer tax** ► *See*: inheritance tax.

• **Caporetto** ► (Serbo-Croat name: Kobarid) A village now in Slovenia but part of Italy until 1947. It was the scene of an Italian military disaster in October 1917, when Italian troops were forced to retreat before an Austro-German offensive. The defeat prompted Italy's allies, France and Great Britain, to send support and finally to establish the Supreme War Council to unify the Allied war effort. *See also*: Isonzo.

• **captive audience** ► An audience that cannot easily escape some message being addressed to it. For example, advertisers are justified in assuming that a cinema audience is a captive audience, just as a preacher in a place of worship has a more-or-less captive audience in his congregation.

• **car** ► Although the 20th century was often called the age of the car, the automobile was actually invented in the century before. However, Daimler's motorized dog cart bore about as much relation to the modern car as the Wright brothers' *Flyer* bears to Concorde. It was during the first decade of the 20th century that the spluttering horseless carriage came of age (*see*: Great Car Race). By the start of World War I (often called the last of the horse wars) there were some 130,000 cars registered in the UK. But it was during the inter-war years that the car established itself as a reliable and comfortable way of moving from one place to another for anyone who did not wish to use public transport. Since the start of World War II, cars have not changed greatly; they are now slightly faster, slightly more economical in fuel, and considerably more reliable. Very roughly, a new car has always cost its owner about half his or her annual income; however, some two-thirds of new cars are now company cars, *i.e.* cars bought by companies for the use of employees in addition to their salaries. At the end of the 1990s some 70% of UK homes owned one or more cars.

As mass-producers of carbon dioxide (*see*: greenhouse effect) and lead (*see*: lead-free) cars are the enemy of environmentalists, while as creators of urban congestion they have so far defeated the town planners. Yet for the man, and to a rather less extent, the woman in the street they mean much more than simply a means of transport. The car is at once a womb within which to seal oneself off from the outside world, a phallus with which to thrust oneself aggressively through it (*see*: road rage), and a symbol of the status, temperament, and aspirations of its owner.

> The car has become the carapace, the protective and aggressive shell, of urban and suburban man. – MARSHALL MCLUHAN: *Understanding Media*.

• **carbecue** ► A machine for demolishing old or wrecked cars. A US invention, the carbecue both crushes the vehicle and rotates it over a fire, the pressure and heat combined turning the vehicle into a solid mass of metal. The word, a blend of *car* and bar*becue*, was coined in the 1960s.

• **car bomb** ► A car packed with explosives with a pretimed or remote-control detonator, left by terrorists close to a suitable target. An alternative version is a small and inconspicuous explosive device, attached to the underside of the car of a target to be murdered, that explodes when the unfortunate victim switches on the ignition. Both types have been extensively used by the IRA.

• **carbon dating** ► A technique for finding the date of specimens by measuring the amount of the radioactive isotope carbon-14 present. It can be used for items made from substances of organic origin (*e.g.* wood, cloth, etc.). There is a natural abundance of carbon-14 in the atmosphere, which is incorporated into living organisms by photosynthesis. On the death of the organism, this assimilation stops and the proportion of carbon-14 slowly falls at a known rate as a result of radioactive decay. This decay enables an estimate to be made of the age of the specimen. Carbon dating is extensively used for archaeological specimens and has been applied to such controversial articles as the Turin Shroud. It is also called **radiocarbon dating**.

• **carbon fibres** ► Fine silky threads of pure carbon made by heating stretched threads of textile fibres. The crystal structure gives them immense strength enabling them to be used to produce composite materials with synthetic resins or other substances. They are found in aircraft, rockets, etc., and in such sporting equipment as tennis rackets and fishing rods.

• **car-boot sale** ► A small local sale of second-hand goods held in a hired car park or field in which the goods are sold by individuals from the boots of their cars. It has tended to increase in scale and now often includes market traders, who set up stalls beside their cars.

• **carbuncular** ▶ Describing buildings, architecture, etc., that are considered ugly or offensive. The term comes from a speech by the Prince of Wales in 1984 in which he described the proposed modern extension to the National Gallery in London as being '...like a monstrous carbuncle on the face of a much loved and elegant friend'.

• **carcass trade** ▶ The practice of econstructing old dilapidated pieces of furniture by adding new veneer or new parts in order to pass them off as genuine antiques. Recent decades have seen a rise in the demand for antiques as an investment and the carcass trade dishonestly capitalizes on this demand and the lack of knowledge of potential buyers.

• **card** ▶ Dated slang for an eccentric fellow, a 'character'. Such a person is the hero of Arnold Bennett's novel *The Card* (1911).

• **CARD** ▶ Campaign Against Racial Discrimination. An organization founded in London in 1964.

• **cardboard city** ▶ An area in an inner city in which homeless people sleep rough, often using cardboard boxes as temporary shelters. In the 1980s the name was applied particularly to an area near Waterloo station in London that was notorious for providing shelter to many such homeless people.

• **card-carrying** ▶ Denoting a person who is totally committed to a specified cause. It was originally used in the 1930s and 1940s to describe a member of the Communist Party, as opposed to someone who simply paid lip-service to its ideals and philosophy. An active supporter of the party would become a member, *i.e.* have a membership card, and could thus be described as card-carrying. In more recent times the expression has become more figurative; for example a card-carrying anti-vivisectionist would be a person deeply committed to the campaign against the use of animals in scientific and other research.

• **Cardin** ▶ The name in *haute couture* that enlivened the years following World War II, when Europe was struggling to throw off the effects of austerity. Pierre Cardin (1922–    ) opened his fashion house in Paris in 1949, establishing a reputation in the 1950s for his long slim coats with large collars and his use of oriental styles. In the 1960s he entered the ready-to-wear market for women and produced a stylish range of clothes for men.

• **cards** ▶ The National Insurance card and other documents owned by an employee but held by his or her employer. When a person leaves a job the cards are returned. Thus, to **get one's cards**, a phrase dating from the 1940s, means to be dismissed from a job. Similarly, to **give someone his cards** means to sack him. Alternatively, to **ask for one's cards** means to resign.

• **CARE** ▶ Cooperative for American Relief Everywhere Inc. A relief organization that coordinates the sending of parcels of food and clothes to areas of need. It was founded in 1945 as the Cooperative for American Remittances to Europe; in 1952 its directors decided to broaden its scope beyond Europe and its name was changed accordingly.

• **care in the community** ▶ A controversial approach to the care of the mentally ill and handicapped that has gathered momentum in the UK since the early 1960s, when Enoch Powell, then minister for health, suggested that the large, often Victorian, mental hospitals had ceased to have 'an appropriate use'. It was hoped that drug regimes for psychotic patients meant that many of them no longer needed residential care and could well lead near-normal lives in the community – calling on family or local-council care when it was needed. In political terms the concept had a double attraction – it saved a great deal of money and those who advocated it could appear as benefactors, releasing from enforced confinement a whole army of disadvantaged people.

Unfortunately the reality differed from the expectations. Although some former inmates succeeded in acquiring jobs and housing and became more-or-less integrated into the community, many of the mentally ill – lacking careful supervision – failed to take their medication on a regular basis and remained on the fringes of society, a danger to themselves and in some cases to others. These unhappy people were left asking – 'What care? What community?' The reality can be seen on any night in central London, where the sight of mentally ill people (young and old) sleeping in cardboard boxes (*see*: cardboard city) sickens both tourists and residents.

• **carelessness kills** ▶ *See*: keep death off the road *at* road.

• **careless talk costs lives** ▶ *See*: Be like dad, keep mum *at* dad.

• **Carey Street** ▶ A British colloquial term meaning bankruptcy. Carey Street is the London street in which the bankruptcy department of the Supreme Court was formerly situated.

• **Carlists** ▶ Supporters of Don Carlos (1788–1855),

second son of Charles IV of Spain, or his descendants as rightful kings of Spain. Carlist intrigues by right-wingers continued until the death of Don Carlos II in 1909. The movement was then quiescent until the 1930s, when the Carlists supported General Franco's Falange. The present Carlist pretender is Carlos Hugo de Bourbón-Parma (1930–   ).

• **Carlton Club meeting** ► See: Chanak crisis.

• **Carnaby Street** ► In the 1960s the much-publicized clothing centre for fashion-conscious young men, situated east of Regent Street in London. It became associated with trendy unisex costumes and was somewhat showily refurbished by Westminster City Council in 1973. However, its popularity had declined by 1975 when boutiques in King's Road, Chelsea, began to attract this type of trade.

• **carpet bombing** ► 1. The heavy indiscriminate bombing of a whole city or area, rather than of selected targets. 2. The sending of unsolicited (and mainly unwanted) advertising matter through the post, especially when this is done on an indiscriminate untargeted basis. The practice, which has become increasingly prevalent since the 1970s has resulted in a deluge of junk mail which reaches a crescendo in the months before Christmas.

• **carrots** ► The myth that eating carrots enabled RAF pilots to spot enemy aircraft at night better than German pilots was put out deliberately at the beginning of World War II by the Ministry of Information. It is true that carrots contain β-carotene, which forms vitamin A (retinol) in the human gut, and that this substance is required for good night vision. However, the real reason for British pilots' superior ability to 'see' enemy aircraft was the well-developed British AI radar system. Work on radar started in 1935 and thanks largely to the work of Robert Watson-Watt (1892–1973) was functioning by the start of the war. The Germans had no comparable system until later in the conflict and the British wished to minimize its value.

• **carry a torch** ► To have a long-standing but unrequited love for someone, especially one that has remained undeclared. The torch may represent the flame of love. It is thought that the phrase **torch song**, signifying a love song, may have been coined by the US nightclub singer Tommy Lyman in the 1930s. The film *Torch Singer* (1933) was about an unmarried mother who sings in a nightclub, while *Torch Song* (1953) concerned a musical comedy star's love for a blind pianist; the play *Torch Song Trilogy* (1982) by Harvey Fierstein tackled homosexual love.

• **Carry On films** ► A long-running series of bawdy low-budget British farces, which began in 1958 with *Carry on Sergeant* produced by Peter Rogers and directed by Gerald Thomas. The same team went on to produce some two films in the same vein every year until the mid-1970s, using a regular troupe of comedians that included Sid James, Kenneth Williams, Charles Hawtrey, Kenneth Connor, Hattie Jacques, Barbara Windsor, and Joan Sims. Never aspiring to be more than low lewd farce, they became a British institution with their leering humour and contrived innuendos. The films are now studied seriously for the light they shed on Britain's changing sexual mores in the 1960s and 1970s. *Carry on Columbus* (1992), an attempt to revive the series in the more knowing 1990s, proved wholly unsuccessful.

> Infamy! Infamy! They've all got it infamy! – KENNETH WILLIAMS, as Julius Caesar in *Carry on Cleo*.

• **Carry on, London** ► A catchphrase from the BBC radio programme *In Town Tonight* (1933–60). The programme was introduced by Eric Coates's 'Knightsbridge March' and a recording of the sound of London's traffic brought to a halt by a voice shouting 'Stop'. Interesting people who were visiting the capital were then introduced and interviewed. At the end of the programme the voice restored the traffic with the phrase 'Carry on, London'. In the Blitz and the later V2 and V1 attacks the phrase became a slogan expressing London-can-take-it Cockney defiance.

• **car surfing** ► Slang for riding on the roof of a moving car. An extremely dangerous craze among teenagers in the late 1980s, inspired by the US film *Teenwolf* (1985).

• **Carter, Nick** ► A US detective created in 1886 by publisher Ormond G. Smith and writer John Russell Coryell as a US counterpart to Sexton Blake. He first appeared in the novel *The Old Detective's Pupil* in which he was portrayed as a boyish clean-living all-American hero. Over 500 Nick Carter books were published, written by a stable of authors including William Wallace Cook and Johnston McCulley. He became so popular that a weekly magazine, *Nick Carter Detective Library*, was created; with films and radio plays his popularity survived two world wars. However, by the 1960s it had begun to wane so the authors decided to change his persona; Nick Carter became a 'tough guy'. A television film featuring Carter was produced in 1984.

• **cartoon** ► Originally, a preparatory sketch for a painting, fresco, tapestry, or other work of art. By the 19th century the word had acquired a second sense: namely a humorous drawing in a newspaper or magazine, as pioneered by the satirical magazine *Punch*. The early 20th century saw the introduction of the strip cartoon (or comic strip), from which the earliest American animated films (also known as cartoons) were derived. The earliest animated cartoon character, *Gertie the Dinosaur* (1909), was followed by Mutt and Jeff (from a popular comic strip) and Felix the Cat. It was, however, Walt Disney (1901–66), with his Mickey Mouse and Donald Duck, who came to dominate film animation worldwide from the late 1970s. Cartoons continue to be extremely popular – with adults as well as children – as evidenced by the enormous success of the Simpsons on TV and recent Disney features. Despite the advent of computer animation, which has had a revolutionary impact across the industry, Roy Disney, the head of the company's feature department, commented in 2001:

> We still believe in the notion of an artist with a piece of paper and a pencil in his hand.

• **carve up** ▶ 1. British slang meaning to spoil someone's chances, to have one's chances ruined, usually used in the passive form: 'he got carved up'. 2. To cut in front of another driver.

• **carving contest** ▶ *See*: cutting contest.

• **Casablanca Conference** ▶ A summit meeting between Winston Churchill and Franklin D. Roosevelt held in Casablanca, Morocco, in Jan 1943. The two leaders agreed on the invasion of Sicily, the heavy bombing of Germany, and the demand for unconditional Axis surrender.

• **Casement diaries** ▶ The diaries reputedly written by Sir Roger Casement (1864–1916), while working as a British consular official in Africa. Having retired to Ireland in 1912, Casement attempted to obtain German support for Irish nationalism during World War I. He was arrested returning to Ireland in a German submarine and subsequently tried by the British for treason, found guilty, and hanged. The diaries, which contained detailed descriptions of homosexual practices, were circulated privately by the British to prejudice his defence. They were not released until 1959, by which time their authenticity had become a controversial issue. Most scholars now accept that the diaries are genuine, although the contents often read more like sexual fantasy than fact.

• **cash-and-carry** ▶ A wholesale supplier who sells goods, usually groceries, etc., in fairly large-size packs to retail tradespeople and others engaged in small business enterprises rather than to members of the general public.

• **Cash and Carry Act** ▶ A US act passed in November 1939, concerning the sale of arms to participants in World War II. The sale was permitted provided that the purchaser paid immediately and transported the arms himself.

• **cash cow** ▶ A colloquial business name for a reliable and regular source of income, which requires very little effort or investment. It is usually a product with a brand name, well known in old-established markets.

• **cash for questions** ▶ The practice of paying an MP to ask a question in the House of Commons for the benefit of the payer. The phrase gained currency in the mid-1990s, when it was alleged that several Conservative MPs had accepted payments or gifts for their services. The highest-profile case was that of the MP for Tatton, Neil Hamilton, who allegedly received cash, gift vouchers, and a free holiday at the Ritz Hotel in Paris, in return for asking questions on behalf of Mohamed al-Fayed and his Knightsbridge store, Harrods.

The allegations against Hamilton and his colleague Tim Smith were first made by *The Guardian* newspaper and subsequently repeated by al-Fayed himself on TV. Largely as a result, Hamilton lost his seat in the 1997 general election, when he was beaten by the BBC news correspondent Martin Bell, who stood as an independent 'anti-sleaze' candidate. A report by the parliamentary Commissioner for Standards later (July 1997) concluded that Hamilton and Smith had indeed taken payments; four other MPs were criticized, while a further 20 were wholly or mainly exonerated. Nevertheless, Hamilton steadfastly maintained his innocence and somewhat recklessly sued al-Fayed for libel, leading to a much publicized High Court trial in 1999. Despite attempts to discredit al-Fayed's general probity and his reliability as a witness, Hamilton lost the case, a judgment that resulted in his financial ruin. Hamilton and his loyal and ever-present wife, Christine, have since attempted to build a new career in the media.

• **cash in one's chips** ▶ Literally, to stop gambling and exchange one's chips for money. The phrase is used figuratively in two ways. First, it means to take what one has and stop; *i.e.* to 'cut and run'. More drastically, it means to die. To **throw in one's chips** implies that one has stopped playing for ever.

• **Cassandra** ▶ Pseudonym under which Sir William Connor wrote a column for the *Daily Mirror* over many years. One of the most popular of such columnists, 'Cassandra' was one of the severest critics of P. G. Wodehouse's broadcasts from Germany during World War II. The original Cassandra was a legendary prophet of woe, who was fated never to be believed. The daughter of King Priam of Troy, she foretold the deaths of both her father and Agamemnon, her captor.

• **Cassino** ► *See*: Anzio.

• **cast of thousands** ► A jocular term implying that many people have been involved, as in 'this dictionary has been written by a cast of thousands'. It comes from the film industry, probably from the publicity for the first version of *Ben Hur* (1927), which boasted 'a cast of 125,000'. One of many apocryphal stories about the US film producer Samuel Goldwyn (1882–1974) is that he was filming *The Last Supper* and said, 'only twelve disciples!...go out and get thousands!'

• **Castroism** ► The form of communism developed in Cuba by the country's president Fidel Castro (1926–    ). It has also been called **Fidelism** and (the Spanish version) **Fidelismo**.

• **casual** ► British slang of the 1980s for a member of a working-class subgroup of young people who wore expensive designer casual clothes in the US or Italian style and listened to lightweight disco and soul music. They were the late-1980s version of the earlier mods (*see*: mods and rockers) and exhibited the right-wing, materialistic, and self-absorbed attitudes so prevalent in that era. They were epitomized by the comic character loadsamoney, created by the comedian Harry Enfield.

• **cat** ► 1. Originally, in the 1920s, Black musicians' slang for a fellow musician, usually a man. The term implies approval, being used in such phrases as 'a cool cat'. In the 1950s it became part of beat vocabulary in such phrases as hep-cat, and in the 1960s it spread to the hippie community. It is still a normal part of Black US speech, but sounds dated and self-conscious when used by Whites. 2. In America, the female genitals. *See*: pussy. 3. In Australia, the passive partner in a male homosexual relationship. Possibly, it is a shortening of 'catamite'.

• **catalytic converter** ► A device fitted to the exhaust system of a car to convert the pollutant gases in the exhaust fumes into less harmful products. Used with unleaded petrol, metal catalysts, such as platinum and palladium, can eliminate 90 per cent of the carbon monoxide and unburnt hydrocarbons, which would otherwise be expelled into the atmosphere; they also reduce the levels of nitrogen oxides. Catalytic converters were introduced in America in the 1960s as a measure to combat air pollution and smog in cities; since 1975 all new cars sold in America have converters fitted (a requirement in the UK for new cars from 1992).

• **Cat and Mouse Act** ► Popular name for the Prisoners (Temporary Discharge for Ill-Health) Act of 1913, passed during the suffragettes disturbances to prevent the imprisoned law-breakers from achieving martyrdom through hunger strikes. They were released on licence when necessary, subject to re-arrest if need arose. To **play cat and mouse** is to do what one likes with someone in one's power.

• **catastrophe theory** ► A general theory of change based on mathematical theories of topology (the analysis of general geometrical form as opposed to particular shapes). If a system depends, for example, on four factors, then any state of the system can be represented by a point in four-dimensional space. The possible states of the system can be represented by a region in this space. Catastrophe theory deals with the classification of the forms of such regions, and the way in which one can turn into another. It correlates these with sudden discontinuous changes – 'catastrophes' – in the system. Originally, it was introduced in 1972 by the French mathematician René Thom (1923–    ) to explain biological differentiation (for example, how growing animal cells can suddenly start to develop into different organs). It has subsequently been applied to many other fields, including the stability of engineering structures on the one hand and the stability of international or personal relationships on the other.

• **catch a cold** ► 1. Business slang meaning to suffer a temporary financial setback. 2. British army slang meaning to catch gonorrhoea. 3. A predominantly US slang phrase meaning that a man has his trouser zip undone. *See also*: Charlie's dead.

• **Catch-22** ► Whichever alternative you choose you can't win – you lose either way. *Catch-22* is the title of Joseph Heller's anti-war satire published in 1955. The story centres on Captain Yossarian of the 256th United States (Army) bombing squadron in World War II, whose main aim is to avoid being killed. The best way for a pilot to achieve this was to be grounded because of insanity. 'There was only one catch and that was Catch-22 which specified that concern for one's own safety in the face of dangers that were real and immediate was the process of a rational mind. Orr was crazy and could be grounded. All he had to do was to ask and as soon as he did he would no longer be crazy and would have to fly more missions'.

> How immediate is the response to a 999 call? The Catch-22 of the situation – as Chief Superintendent Eddie Gleeson of New Scotland Yard pointed out – is that the more violent and urgent the emergency, the less coherent the caller. – *Sunday Telegraph*, 24 July 1988.

• **catenaccio** ► A defensive formation used by

soccer teams, consisting of four defenders, three mid-field players, and three forwards. The term is mainly used in Italy and means 'door bolt'; the more prosaic British equivalent is 'four-three-three'.

• **Caterpillar** ▶ A type of tracked vehicle designed for travel over rough ground, such as a tractor, bulldozer, or tank. It was originally a tradename for such vehicles made by the Caterpillar Tractor Company of California, set up by the US industrialist Benjamin Holt in 1928.

• **Caterpillar Club** ▶ An unofficial club started by the Irvin Parachute Company during World War II and still in existence; the caterpillar is the silkworm that supplied the material from which parachutes were formerly made. The company presented a small gold caterpillar pin to any RAF airman who had baled out in action and could supply the number of the parachute that had saved his life. Similarly the **Goldfish Club** existed for those who had been forced to use their rubber dinghies. Since then, similar clubs have been formed to encourage the wearing of protective clothing by industrial workers.

• **cathiodermie** ▶ A deep-cleansing facial cosmetic treatment in which an electric current is passed through a specially prepared gel spread on the skin. It was invented by René Guinot, the French cosmetologist.

• **cat's eye** ▶ A self-cleaning reflector embedded in the road as a guide for motorists after lighting-up time or in fog. They were devised by the eccentric Yorkshire inventor Percy Shaw (1889–1975).

• **Cat's Eyes** ▶ Nickname of the World War II RAF fighter pilot Group Captain John Cunningham (1917–  ), noted for his successful night-time exploits.

• **cat's pyjamas** ▶ Something superlatively good; first rate; attractive. A US colloquialism in use by 1900 and current in the UK in the 1920s and 1930s. **The cat's whiskers** is used in the same way and with the same meaning.

• **cat's whisker** ▶ 1. In the original crystal wireless sets, the very fine wire that made contact with the crystal. 2. *See*: cat's pyjamas.

• **Caudillo** ▶ (Spanish, leader) The title adopted by General Franco, head of the Falangist government in Spain, in imitation of Mussolini's Duce and Hitler's Führer. *See*: Falange.

• **Cavell Memorial** ▶ The statue of nurse Edith Cavell (1865–1915) near Trafalgar Square in London. She was executed by the Germans for helping Allied soldiers to escape from Belgium during World War I. The memorial is inscribed with her last words before the firing squad: 'I realize that patriotism is not enough. I must have no hatred or bitterness towards anyone.'

• **Cavendish Laboratory** ▶ The physics laboratory at Cambridge University, founded in 1874 and named after the British scientist Henry Cavendish (1731–1810). Its director from 1919 until 1937 was the New Zealand physicist Ernest Rutherford (1871–1937). Here, in 1919, he first demonstrated the artificial disintegration of atomic nuclei (popularly known as 'splitting the atom'). Many other important discoveries have been made at the laboratory.

• **Cavern Club** ▶ *See*: Beatles.

• **CB** ▶ Citizens' band radio. A short-wave short-distance two-way radio system available for use by the general public. CB radios are particularly used by motorists and truck drivers; in the early days, they were used to warn fellow drivers of traffic jams, radar traps, etc. In America, the Citizens Radio Service was established in 1945, but only became popular in the 1970s. In the UK, CB radio was illegal until 1981 because it was said to interfere with the radio transmissions of the emergency services. CB enthusiasts, who call themselves breakers, have colourful pseudonyms (known as 'handles') and have developed their own slang. The use of CB radio declined during the 1980s and 1990s.

• **CBS** ▶ Columbia Broadcasting System. Founded in 1922 as a radio network, it became one of the main coast-to-coast TV networks in America.

• **CD** ▶ *See*: compact disc.

• **CD-I** ▶ Compact disc interactive. A type of computer game developed in the late 1980s, which allows players to take an active role in stories programmed on a compact disc. *See*: interactive fiction.

• **CD-ROM** ▶ Compact disc read-only memory (*see*: ROM). A computer storage device used to access large volumes of data, such as a dictionary, encyclopedia, or some other form of database. The present form of the CD-ROM is a 5-inch compact disc storing over 600 megabytes. The information on the disc is included during manufacture and cannot be altered or added to. *See*: electronic publishing.

• **Ceefax** ▶ (From *see* plus *facts*) An information service operated by the BBC since 1973, enabling pages of text to be displayed on a modified domestic television set. The information transmitted includes news flashes, market movements, weather reports, sports results, etc. The broadcast is transmitted with normal television programmes and makes use of two of the unused lines between picture frames. The required pages are selected for display by means of a keyboard. A similar system is operated by the Independent Broadcasting Authority under the name **teletext**.

• **ceiling inspector** ▸ A female sexual partner. An ironic description of the woman's view in the missionary position, especially if she has lost interest in what is going on. This expression is thought to have been coined by the Australian comic writer and actor Barry Humphries.

• **Cellnet** ▸ A tradename for a **cellular network** service operated in the UK jointly by British Telecom and Securicor. A cellular network enables mobile phone users to be connected to the main telephone system or to another mobile phone. It consists of a large number of adjacent cells each containing a radio transmitter/receiver connecting to the main telephone network. As the users move from one cell to another (by car, train, etc.) they are automatically switched to be in radio contact with the transmitter-receiver in the new area.

• **Cellophane** ▸ A tradename for a transparent flexible material made from wood pulp and used for wrapping. Invented in France in 1869 by the Swiss chemist Jacques Brandenberger, it was first manufactured in 1913. The name, which is used generically in America, comes from 'cellulose' (in wood pulp) plus '-phane' (meaning transparent, by analogy with 'diaphanous').

• **cell therapy** or **cellular therapy** ▸ A treatment to slow down and partially reverse the physical effects of ageing in human beings. It depends on the injection of preparations of young cells taken from the organs of embryonic animals, particularly sheep. In addition to its rejuvenating effects, the adherents of cell therapy also claim that it can cure many non-infectious illnesses. Scientifically controlled experimental studies have failed to provide any evidence in support of the claims made and the treatment is not accepted by the orthodox medical profession in Europe or America.

• **cellulite** ▸ Lumpy fatty tissue beneath the skin, especially of the thighs and buttocks, that is said by some to be resistant to conventional dieting. The name was coined in the early 1970s by the French dietician Nicole Ronsard. Orthodox medical authorities have questioned the existence of cellulite as an entity distinct from normal subcutaneous fatty tissue. Nevertheless, the female obsession with this mysterious condition (which seems to be invisible to men) has spawned a multi-million-pound

industry profferring a range of exotic and exorbitantly priced 'cures'.

• **Celtic Sea** ▸ Formally defined as 'that part of the continental shelf lying between the 200 fathom contour, S Ireland, the SW tip of Wales, Land's End, and Ushant'. The term derives from the neighbouring Celtic areas – Brittany, Cornwall, Wales, and Ireland, and was first used by E. W. L. Holt in 1921.

• **Celtic Twilight** ▸ The Irish literary revival of the late 19th and early 20th centuries, especially in its more mystical and nationalistic aspects. The phrase was adopted from the title of a collection of short stories by W. B. Yeats published in 1893, which emphasized the mysticism of the Irish and their belief in fairies. While many of the Irish literati, including Yeats himself and AE (George Russell), subscribed to the notion of Celtic Twilight it also attracted a great deal of criticism and ridicule. James Joyce was one detractor of the theory, dismissing it as 'cultic twallette'.

> In ancient shadows and twilights
> Where childhood has strayed,
> The world's great sorrows were born
> And its heroes were made.
> – AE: 'Germinal'.

• **Cenotaph** ▸ (Greek *kenos*, empty; *taphos*, tomb) A sepulchral monument raised to the memory of a person or persons buried elsewhere. By far the most noteworthy to the British is that in Whitehall, London, designed by Sir Edwin Lutyens, which was dedicated on 11 November 1920 to those who fell in World War I. It has since been adapted to commemorate the fallen of World War II and later conflicts. *See*: Armistice Day; Remembrance Day.

• **CENTO** ▸ Central Treaty Organization. *See*: Baghdad Pact.

• **Central Casting** ▸ A Hollywood casting agency maintained by the Alliance of Motion Picture and Television Producers. Those accepted onto its books were classified according to 'type' (dumb blonde, elderly hick, etc.) and allocated bit parts accordingly. The phrase **right out of central casting** is now used of anyone or anything that seems absurdly stereotyped.

• **Central Committee** ▸ Formerly, the main executive committee of the Soviet Communist Party, elected by the party congress. The main power resided in the Politburo and the Secretariat.

• **Central Intelligence Agency** ▸ *See*: CIA.

• **Central Powers** ▸ The coalition of countries opposing the Allies in World War I. Consisting of Germany, Austria-Hungary, Turkey, and Bulgaria, the Central Powers were so called because surrounded by France and Britain in the W, Russia in the E, and French and British colonies in the S. German fears of 'encirclement' by hostile powers had been a major cause of that country's belligerent policy in the lead-up to war.

• **centrefold** ▶ An illustration folded into the centre of a magazine or book or occupying the two facing pages at the centre. Since centrefold illustrations were introduced in the 'girlie' magazine *Playboy*, the term has become synonymous with the picture of a nude female. More recently, the model herself has been referred to as a centrefold. *See also*: page-three girl; pin-up.

• **Centre 42** ▶ A cultural project intended to make the arts more widely accessible, primarily through trade-union support and involvement. It was founded in 1961 by the playwright Arnold Wesker, who was also its artistic director until his decision to dissolve the movement in 1970. It was based at the Round House, a former railway building in Camden Town.

• **Century of the Common Man** ▶ The 20th century, the age of democracy. *The Century of the Common Man* (1940) was the title of a book by Henry A. Wallace, New-Dealer and US vice-president (1941–45) under F. D. Roosevelt. The phrase became popular on both sides of the Atlantic and was much favoured by Nancy, Viscountess Astor.

• **CERN** ▶ Conseil Européen pour la Recherche Nucléaire. The original name of the research centre for particle physics based in Geneva, which was formed in 1954 by most leading European nations. It operates a proton synchrotron with intersecting storage rings 300 metres in diameter and the Large Electron-Positron Collider built in a 5-mile tunnel under the Jura mountains. The centre has been renamed the **European Laboratory for Particle Physics**, but the acronym CERN is still used.

• **Ceroc** ▶ A dance craze that arrived in Britain in the mid-1990s, having originated in France some years earlier. Its devotees were mainly young professionals, who wished to dance with a partner but had never learned any formal steps. Essentially a simplified form of the jitterbug, it has been described as the 'dance equivalent to fast food' because of the ease with which it can be learned. The name is from the French *c'est le roc*.

• **Certificate of Secondary Education** ▶ *See*: CSE.

• **c'est la guerre** ▶ (French, that's war) Originally a World War I French military catchphrase offered as an excuse for any failure to perform correctly. By 1915 it had been adopted by British sol-diers. In World War II it was widely used in a civilian context to account for anything that had changed as a result of the war.

• **CFC** ▶ Chlorofluorocarbon; one of a group of chemical compounds made from hydrocarbons by replacing some of the hydrogen atoms by chlorine and fluorine atoms. Such substances have been extensively used as propellants in aerosols and as the working fluid in refrigerators. In the late 1980s conservation groups campaigned successfully to limit their use because of their effect on the ozone layer. *See also*: halon.

• **Chaco War** ▶ A bitter conflict between Bolivia and Paraguay over the disputed lowland plain known as Gran Chaco, which lies just east of the central Andes. After initial successes in 1932, the Bolivian army, consisting largely of Indian conscripts, was repulsed by the Paraguayans; by early 1935 Paraguayan forces controlled most of the Chaco. A truce was called in June 1935, by which time some 100,000 men had died. The treaty, signed at the Chaco Peace Conference in July 1938, gave the bulk of Gran Chaco to Paraguay.

• **chad** ▶ An arcane point of US electoral procedure that was brought to the world's attention by the disputed presidential election of November 2000. A 'chad' is the tiny circle of paper that is detached from the ballot paper by the punch machines that US voters use to register their choice; if the chad is partly, but not wholly, detached (because the voter did not press hard enough), this is known as a **hanging chad**; if the paper is dented, but the punch has not gone through at all, the ballot is described as 'dimpled' or 'pregnant'. All such ballots are automatically treated as void by the tally machines used to count the votes; however, some states allow the inclusion of some or all of these papers in the hand recounts that are ordered when the result is especially close (in some jurisdictions, a distinction is even made between chads that are hanging by one corner or two).

These matters suddenly acquired vital importance when it became clear that the result of the 2000 presidential election would depend on a recount of votes in the state of Florida. A first count gave George W. Bush, the Republican, a lead of less than 0.5% over Al Gore, the Democrat; this was reduced to a margin of several hundred votes in an automated recount. A number of Florida counties then began hand counts, raising the vexed question of whether imperfectly marked ballots should now be included. After a series of legal challenges from both sides, the US Supreme Court voted 5–4 in favour of halting all further counts, thus effectively handing the presidency to Bush.

• **Chad** ▸ A cartoon character whose bald head and large nose were depicted appearing over a wall and inquiring, 'Wot, no [word filled in to suit the circumstances]?', as a comment on or protest against a shortage or shortcoming. Being both easy to draw and endlessly adaptable, Chad provided humorous relief in many a difficult situation during World War II. He was the happy creation (1938) of the cartoonist 'Chat' (George Edward Chatterton). *See also*: Kilroy.

• **chain reaction** ▸ Originally a chemical or nuclear reaction that creates energy or products, which in turn cause further reactions without a need for further energy input from outside. The concept in this sense emerged in the 1930s. In the 1970s the phrase entered the non-technical language; it is now used to denote any series of events in which each event causes the next. *See also*: domino theory.

• **chair** ▸ A late 20th-century neutered term for a chairman or a chairwoman. Previously, females appointed to chair a committee, organization, etc., were content to be referred to as chairmen and to be addressed as 'madame chairman'. However, a feminist preoccupation with the etymology of words containing characteristically male sub-units led to the substitution of '-person' for '-man'. Thus, **chairpersons** and **spokespersons** made their appearance (though policepersons and seapersons did not). It was not long, however, before the predictable shortening took place and the chairperson became the chair. In this sense chair is used as an exact synonym for chairman or chairwoman. 'The chair asked for nominations' has a slightly different sense from 'questions should be addressed to the chair'; in the former the chair is a person, in the latter it is an office.

• **Challenger, Professor** ▸ George Edward Challenger, a fictional professor created by Sir Arthur Conan Doyle in *The Lost World* (1912), and appearing in other stories. Challenger is a distinguished and adventurous zoologist and anthropologist with a fiery temper. He was possibly modelled on one of Doyle's fellow medical students, George Budd.

• **Challenger disaster** ▸ A tragic accident to the US space shuttle *Challenger*, which exploded shortly after take-off on 28 January 1986 at Cape Canaveral. The disaster was later found to have been caused by leaking seals ('O rings') between stages of the rocket. All seven astronauts aboard were killed instantly, including the schoolteacher Christa McAuliffe, who had been selected as the first in a 'citizens in space' programme. Shown live on television and witnessed by the astronauts' families, the tragedy caused a massive shock, especially in America. President Reagan, speaking later, said that the crew had 'touched the face of God'. The Soviet space agency later announced that it was naming seven recently discovered asteroids after members of the crew.

• **champagne socialists** ▸ A derogatory term for those whose luxurious style of living and extravagant tastes appear to contradict their declared left-wing political ideals.

• **Chan, Charlie** ▸ Inspector Charles Chan, the fictional Chinese detective created by the US writer Earl Derr Biggers. He made his first appearance in 1925 in *The House Without a Key*. Chan lived in Honolulu with Mrs Chan and his many children. He was unfailingly dignified and polite, striving at all times to speak correct English. 'You will do me the great honour to accompany me to the station, if you please', was his usual mode of arresting criminals. He was sometimes accompanied in his work by his number one or number two son. Biggers created this gentle character as a protest against the stereotyped depiction of the Chinese in America. Eight books featuring Charlie Chan were published and over a dozen films starring Warner Oland appeared in the 1930s. Later films starred Sidney Toler, Roland Winters, and Peter Ustinov.

• **Chanak crisis** ▸ The crisis in October 1922 that caused the fall of Lloyd George's coalition government. It was started by the entry of the Turks into Chanak, on the Asiatic side of the Dardanelles, a neutral zone held by the British and the French. Their objective was to take part of Thrace from Greece. The Conservative members of Lloyd George's cabinet felt that he acted in favour of Greece by reinforcing the British garrison in Chanak. At the famous **Carlton Club Meeting**, on 19 October 1922, the Conservatives decided to withdraw from the coalition government, forcing Lloyd George's resignation. This was the occasion for the formation of the **1922 Committee** of Tory backbenchers, who were determined that the leadership of the party should not take decisions without consulting them in the future. The Committee is still a powerful force in Conservative politics.

• **chance would be a fine thing** ▸ A catchphrase meaning that someone would welcome the chance to do something but that such an opportunity is unlikely to occur. It is something a woman might say if asked whether she would consider having a relationship with a particular man – meaning 'yes, if only he would show some interest!' However, it might also be said in reply to a woman who indignantly denied that she would have such a relationship – in this case meaning 'well, you're not going to be asked!'

• **Chanel** ► The name under which a wide range of *haute couture* and beauty products have been marketed since the 1920s. The name is that of the Parisian couturier Coco Chanel (real name Gabrielle Chanel; 1883–1971), who started a fashion house in Paris in 1924. Her most characteristic innovations were her jersey suits, costume jewellery, colourful evening scarves, and perfumes, especially Chanel No 5. Although she retired before World War II she made a successful return to designing in 1954.

• **Channel** ►
   **the day the Channel caught fire** A myth of World War II that spread rapidly through the UK in the darkest days of 1940. At a time when it was widely feared that the Germans were preparing to cross the Channel, the populace was much cheered by rumours that an attempted invasion had been foiled. The story was that the Channel had been drenched with petrol, which was ignited as the German invasion fleet approached. German bodies were reported to be choking the Channel. In fact the British had conducted experiments with submerged oil pipes but had realized that such a plan was not feasible. Nevertheless for many months people recalled 'the day the Channel caught fire'.

• **channel hopping** or **channel surfing** ► Using a remote-control device to skip rapidly and aimlessly across the available television channels; the preferred mode of viewing of US adolescents in the 1980s and 1990s and now widespread among all age groups on both sides of the Atlantic.

• **Channel Tunnel** ► A rail link beneath the English Channel between the UK and France. Finance having been raised by an Anglo-French consortium, construction began in 1987 and was completed in 1994. A shuttle service (*see*: Shuttle, Le) ferrying motor vehicles through the tunnel began later that year, while Eurostar, a direct passenger service between London and Paris or Brussels, began in 1995. The link actually comprises three tunnels: two carrying trains travelling one-way and a third service and ventilation tunnel. This massive engineering feat is a manifestation of the UK's closer connection with Europe; although many Britons felt threatened by the loss of the UK's island status (raising fears of invasion by rabid animals or illegal immigrants), the tunnel is now widely popular with British holiday makers.

• **chaos theory** ► A mathematical theory concerning the unpredictable behaviour of systems because of their sensitivity to the initial conditions or because there are so many factors influencing them. Even though the laws or rules governing the system's behaviour are well-understood, the behaviour of the system as a whole is 'chaotic' because it is so complex. It was originally developed as a theory of meteorology and illustrates the difficulty of weather forecasting. It has been said that a butterfly flapping its wings in South America can be the cause of a tornado in North America – the so-called **butterfly effect**. Chaos theory has been applied to many other branches of science and social science.

• **Chappaquiddick** ► An island in New England, which in 1969 was the scene of a tragic car accident involving the US Senator Edward Kennedy; an incident that was to haunt his subsequent political career. Kennedy's car had crashed off a bridge into eight feet of water; a female passenger, Mary Jo Kopechne, aged 27, drowned. Controversy surrounded the senator's failure to save the girl, although he managed to escape from the car himself, and his failure to inform the police immediately of the accident.

• **charismatic movement** ► A Christian movement that emphasizes the charismatic gifts of speaking in tongues, healing by laying on of hands, and baptism by the Holy Spirit. Although the movement originated within the Pentecostal Church (which developed from revivalist meetings in America in 1906) many later charismatics have preferred to remain in their own churches. Since the 1960s, therefore, many charismatics have also been found in Roman Catholic, Protestant, and Orthodox Churches. In the Christian sense, charisma means a power or talent that is divinely bestowed upon a person.

• **charleston** ► A ballroom dance popular *c.* 1923–27, which originated as a dance among Black Americans. Charleston is the name of a cotton-trading seaport in South Carolina, one-third of the population of which is Black. The charleston featured in the Black musical *Runnin' Wild* (1923) and with its 4/4 syncopated rhythm and kicking toe-in steps rapidly spread throughout the world.

• **Charlie** ► 1. British slang for a fool, as in the expression 'a right Charlie'. It is derived from Cockney rhyming slang, Charlie Hunt for cunt. 2. A euphemism for cocaine; from the communications code name for its initial letter, C. It is used in such coded expressions as 'Is Charlie in tonight?', meaning is there any cocaine available here tonight. 3. A name for the Viet Cong used by US soldiers during the Vietnam War. It comes from 'Victor Charlie', the communications code names for the abbreviation VC. **4.** A slang euphemism for any unmentionable subject, as in the expression 'Charlie's come' to mean that a female's menstruation has started. **5.** Australian rhyming slang for a young woman, from Charlie Wheeler for sheila (a girl). *See also*: Checkpoint Charlie.

• **Charlie Brown** ▸ A little boy who appeared in the Peanuts cartoon strip created by Charles M. Schulz in 1950. He achieved great popularity, with his dog Snoopy and his friends Lucy and Linus. The strip had global syndication and a host of ephemera was produced. *See also*: Happiness is....

• **Charlie Chan** ▸ *See*: Chan, Charlie.

• **Charlie Farnsbarns** ▸ A person whose name one cannot remember, as in 'Mrs Thing', 'Old What-sisname', etc. It was used by the comedians Richard Murdoch and Kenneth Horne in their 1940s radio comedy *Much Binding in the Marsh*.

• **Charlie's Aunt** ▸ A nickname of Princess Margaret. One of the numerous nicknames used in the satirical magazine *Private Eye*, it is thought to have been coined (in allusion to the popular farce *Charley's Aunt* by Brandon Thomas) by the princess herself – who was, of course, the aunt of Prince Charles. *See also at*: running.

• **Charlie's dead** ▸ A slang expression meaning that a woman's petticoat is showing, or that a man's trouser zip is undone. It is often heard in the school playground, where it has been current since the 1950s. The origin of the phrase and the identity of Charlie are unknown.

• **charm** ▸ In physics, a property postulated to exist for certain quarks to account for the behaviour of some elementary particles. The term was first used in 1974 by the US physicist Sheldon Glashow (1932–    ), who used the word 'charm' because the symmetry of the theory was particularly pleasing. *See*: elementary particle.

• **Charter 88** ▸ A petition organized by leading British liberals in 1988, calling for major constitutional reforms. These included a written constitution, proportional representation, and a Freedom of Information Act. The petition's title deliberately echoed Czechoslovakia's Charter 77. This was regarded as offensively pretentious by conservative critics, who dismissed the campaign as a typical product of the chattering classes.

• **Charter 77** ▸ The manifesto of a group of Czechoslovakian dissidents formed in Prague in 1977 (designated 'Year of Rights of Political Prisoners') to monitor abuses of human rights by the Czech authorities. The Charter itself demanded the adherence of the government to UN covenants and the Helsinki accords on human rights. Hundreds of signatures were collected from people of all classes, many of whom subsequently suffered harassment, imprisonment, or exile. One of those imprisoned, the writer Václav Havel, became president of Czechoslovakia in 1989 (and of the new Czech Republic in 1993).

• **charts** ▸ Lists of best-selling records published on a weekly basis. The term is used in such phrases as **in the charts** and **top of the charts**, etc. In America lists of best-selling sheet music began to appear in *Billboard* in 1894; the magazine is still the source for the country's most authoritative record charts. In the UK the first chart listing the country's 'Top 12 Best-Selling Records' was published in the *New Musical Express* in November 1952. During the 1980s and 1990s, as the technology for gathering point-of-sale data and processing (pcs) information became cheaper and easier to use, there was a proliferation in the number of charts produced, *e.g.* for classical music, indie music, rock, pop, etc. Many record chains, radio stations, publications, etc., now publish their own charts. The compilation of charts has also been extended to other media, such as books and TV programmes.

• **chase the dragon** ▸ **1.** To smoke heroin, an expression dating from the 1970s when cheap heroin became widely available. The drug is heated on a piece of aluminium foil and the fumes inhaled through a tube. Perhaps the imaginative name derives from 'chasing' the coils of smoke across the piece of foil. **2.** To court death by taking heroin. This wider application was current among the upper- and middle-class drug users of the 1980s.

• **chatline** ▸ A telephone service that offers the caller the facility of joining in a conversation with several other callers, usually total strangers. The British Telecom version of this scheme, called Talkabout, was launched in 1983 but suspended after criticism in 1988. The main problem was that young people used the facility so frequently and for so long that their parents' telephone bills were unacceptably high. The service was also abused by people making use of it as a dating agency or for pornographic purposes. Although such services continue to be provided, people are now much more aware of the premium rates involved in making these calls (in the UK there is now an individual prefix number for premium rate services). In addition, the industry is facing stiff competition from the Internet, where chat room facilities can be enjoyed at local call rates.

• **chat room** ▶ An Internet communication channel that enables a user to take part in a real-time 'conversation' with other interested participants. Text typed and entered by one user will appear on the screens of the other users, who can then reply. The 'chat' can be either private or open. Many chat rooms are devoted to subjects of specialized interest, such as a film star, football team, etc.

• **chat show** ▶ A type of radio or television programme in which celebrity guests are invited to have light-hearted conversations with the presenter. Their content is usually somewhat trivial, hence 'chat'. These programmes are intended to appear natural and unrehearsed, although this is rarely the case.

> Genuinely spontaneous good talk is the rarest thing even in real life and almost unknown in the chat show. – MAURICE WIGAN: *The Sunday Times*.

• **chattering classes** ▶ Opinionated middle-class people who like to discuss current political and social issues. The expression is slightly derogatory, conjuring up images of self-important pseudo-intellectuals wittering away about subjects that do not truly concern or affect them.

The term was coined in the first years of Margaret Thatcher's rule as a disparaging description of the liberal and left-wing intelligentsia who impotently raged about Thatcherism around the dinner tables of north London. In this sense it was popularized by the political correspondent Alan Watkins of the *Observer*. It has since widened its meaning to include people of all political complexions.

> One fashionable expression I particularly dislike is 'the chattering classes', widely employed to describe a notional Hampstead-intellectual section of society given to fruitless prattle...The term has an unpleasant, Prussian-officer sort of feel, suggesting the existence of superior, taciturn classes who know what's best and regard any challenge or debate as insubordination. – PHILIP NORMAN: *The Independent*, 6 February 1993.

• **Chatterley, Lady** ▶ *See*: Lady Chatterley trial.

• **chauffeur** ▶ A person (male **chauffeur**, female **chauffeuse**) who is employed to drive another person's car. The word is derived from the French *chauffer*, to heat, and originally meant the stoker who fuelled the early steam cars and who occasionally took over from the driver. With the advent of the internal-combustion engine the stoker lost his job but the word remained, the chauffeur now being responsible for driving the vehicle and understanding

enough about its engine to keep it running – no mean feat in the early days of motoring.

• **Che** ▶ The name by which Ernesto Guevara (1928–67) was widely known. An Argentinian physician, writer, and guerrilla leader, he became a folk hero of socialist revolutionary movements and their sympathizers. He joined Fidel Castro and played a prominent part in the Cuban Revolution before leaving Cuba secretly in 1965. A year later he reappeared attempting to instigate a revolt in Bolivia, where he was wounded, captured, and finally shot by US-trained counter-insurgency forces. His book *Guerrilla Warfare* (1961) became required reading for all aspiring revolutionaries, while his bearded almost Christ-like face appeared on posters adorning student bedrooms throughout the Western world.

• **cheap and cheerful** ▶ A phrase indicating that something or somewhere, although inexpensive, can be quite attractive in an unsophisticated way. The garments sold by a particular chain might be described as cheap and cheerful, meaning that one should expect neither designer quality nor designer prices.

• **cheap money** or **easy money** ▶ A monetary policy in which interest rates are kept low to encourage economic expansion and investment by reducing the cost of borrowing. *See also*: dear money.

• **cheap shot** ▶ An unfair comment or action, especially one aimed at an easy target.

• **Checkpoint Charlie** ▶ The nickname given by Allied forces to a checkpoint on the border between East and West Berlin before the demolition of the Berlin Wall. It was situated at the junction of Friedrichstrasse and Zimmerstrasse and was important as the agreed crossing point for foreigners (*i.e.* non-Germans). As such, it served as a barometer indicating the political climate between East and West – at times of international tension the East German guards would cause long delays at the border. Checkpoint Charlie has also been immortalized in many spy novels and films as the place at which intelligence agents were supposed to be exchanged. At the end of the Cold War (1990), when the Berlin Wall came down, Checkpoint Charlie was removed intact to be kept as a memento in a museum. The term has been extended to mean any crossing point between divided communities.

• **Cheeky Chappie** ▶ The nickname of the music-hall comedian Max Miller (1895–1963). The epithet, which appeared on bills advertising his act from 1924, alluded to the risqué nature of his performance, in particular his use of the *double entendre*. 'Clean' gags were described as coming from his 'white book' and 'dirty' gags as coming from his 'blue book'; according to his biographer, however, the books themselves were only notional.

• **cheesecake** ▶ An originally US description of a titillating photograph of a scantily clad female. It originated in the 1930s, when such pin-up photographs became acceptable. The origin lies in the use of thin muslin veils wrapped over the camera lens to 'soften' the image and render any blemishes invisible; such muslin was primarily used to wrap cheese. The term also compares the subject herself to a slice of delectable cheesecake. Two things have happened to the word since then: on the one hand its meaning has broadened to mean female sexual attractiveness in general; on the other, it has been pounced on by feminists as sexist. The term **beefcake** is sometimes used of a photograph that displays men with muscular bodies, or of such a man.

• **Cheka** ▶ The first political police agency of the Soviet Union; it was established by Lenin in December 1917 and originally known as Vecheka. The agency was intended to investigate sabotage and counter-revolutionary activities but soon took upon itself the arrest, imprisonment, and execution of anyone considered to be an enemy of the state. It was disbanded in 1922 to be replaced by the GPU. In 1923 this organization became the notorious OGPU.

• **Chelsea Flower Show** ▶ A show held annually in May by the Royal Horticultural Society in the grounds of the Royal Hospital, Chelsea. Started in 1913, it has become the world's greatest horticultural show as well as a social event.

• **chemical warfare** ▶ The use of chemical substances to kill or disable troops or civilians or to poison food or water. In spite of a declaration by the Hague Conference (1899) agreeing to ban them, Germany (a signatory) was the first to use poisonous gases in World War I. No chemical weapons were used in World War II, although Germany manufactured large quantities of deadly nerve gases. During the Cold War large stocks of these substances were built up by America and the Soviet Union. Chemical defoliants were used by America in Vietnam and toxic gases were used by Saddam Hussein of Iraq in the war against Iran and against his own Kurdish minority. The modern range of chemical weapons is very large, from the relatively humane tear gases and other incapacitating gases, to the horrific skin-burning (mustard) gases and the lethal nerve and respiratory gases. In 1993 100 nations agreed to prohibit the production and use of chemical weapons.

• **cheque-book journalism** ▶ A phrase introduced in the mid-1960s to describe the press's misuse of its wealth to obtain rights to stories from criminals and notorious persons generally, thus financially rewarding those whom society wishes to condemn. Although this practice has been criticized by the Press Complaints Commission (formerly the Press Council), many newspaper editors would defend it on the grounds that the press should be free to provide the public with what it wants to read. The freedom of the press is regarded in the UK as a highly valued privilege; it has to be accepted, in an imperfect world, that some undesirable results will flow from it.

• **Chequers** ▶ The official country seat of British prime ministers, in Buckinghamshire near Princes Risborough. It was presented to the nation for this purpose by Sir Arthur and Lady Lee (Lord and Lady Lee of Fareham) in 1917 and first officially used by Lloyd George in 1921.

• **Chernobyl** ▶ A town in Ukraine (formerly in the Soviet Union) that leapt to fame on 26 April 1986, when the number 4 reactor in its nuclear power station blew up, causing some 250 deaths, the evacuation of 135,000 people from a 35-km (22-mi) zone surrounding Chernobyl, and increased levels of radioactivity in many parts of the world. Several countries placed restrictions on the import of food from E Europe and considerable quantities of agricultural produce had to be destroyed. Heavy rain in Wales and parts of northern England coincided with the arrival of the radioactive cloud and sheep-grazing was affected. The fire in the reactor and the escape of radioactive materials was finally brought to an end by entombing the reactor in concrete. The world's worst nuclear accident, it was caused by an unauthorized experiment that went disastrously wrong, the poor single-shell design of the reactor building, and the slow reaction of the power-station staff to the early danger signs. Western countries issued reassuring statements regarding the safety of all non-Soviet double-shelled buildings, but immense damage was done to nuclear energy programmes throughout the world, many of which were cancelled or cut back as a result of public disquiet.

• **Cheshire Homes** ▶ Homes for the incurably sick founded by Group Captain Leonard Cheshire VC (1917–92), who was so horrified at the bombing of Nagasaki in 1945, at which he was an observer, that he devoted the rest of his life to the relief of suffering. There are 79 Cheshire Homes in the UK mainly offering residential care to severely disabled adults, although a small proportion also care for mentally handicapped adults. There are over 250 Cheshire Homes and related projects in 53 countries overseas offering the same care as in the UK. The foundation that runs these homes is a charitable trust, which also runs Park House, Sandringham, a country-house hotel specially designed and equipped to provide holidays for disabled people. Cheshire's wife, Baroness (Sue) Ryder (1923–2000), ran a chain of charity shops to fund her own philanthropic work, which started with refugee relief after World War II.

• **Chesterbelloc** ▶ The name by which the partnership between G. K. Chesterton (1874–1936) and Hilaire Belloc (1870–1953) was known. Both Roman Catholics and opponents of the socialism of G. B. Shaw and H. G. Wells, they collaborated on a number of humorous books in the early part of the 20th century.

• **Chetniks** ▶ (Serbian *Četnik*, from *četa*, troop) Members of the Serbian nationalist guerrilla bands which formed during World War II to resist the Axis invaders. They also fought Tito's communist guerrillas. Several factions evolved but the most important group was that based in Serbia led by Draza Mihajlovic. By the end of the war the Chetniks had greatly reduced in number and the remainder were captured and executed by Tito's partisans.

• **chew up the scenery** ▶ An originally US phrase coined by Dorothy Parker (1893–1967). In a review she so described one notorious piece of overacting. The phrase has since entered the general language meaning to dramatize events or oneself inappropriately.

• **chewy on your boot** ▶ In Australian slang, a derisory call from the crowd to a player in Australian rules football kicking for goal. The hope is that the kicker will miss because he has 'chewy' (chewing gum) on his boot. The phrase is sometimes used more generally for any failure.

• **Chiantishire** ▶ A facetious name, coined in the 1980s, for the area of Tuscany in which the wine Chianti is made. The name arose because of the number of British who purchased farmhouses in the hills around Florence and Siena, either as holiday homes or to live in permanently.

• **Chicago piano** ▶ A World War II naval nickname for an eight-barrelled pom-pom anti-aircraft gun. The allusion is to the Chicago of the gangsters (*see*: Scarface) and the hammer action of the piano, which the back-and-forth movement of the barrels resembled. Similarly, a four-barrelled pom-pom was called a **Chicago typewriter**.

• **Chicago Seven** ▶ The people (originally eight) charged with violating the anti-riot provision of the 1968 Civil Rights Bill during the Democratic Convention in Chicago in August 1968. The charges stemmed from the rioting which ensued when police attacked hundreds of anti-war demonstrators. The label, used by their supporters and the press, set a trend for the naming of victims of legal systems on both sides of the Atlantic. Examples in the UK are the Birmingham Six and the Guildford Four. *See also*: Yippie.

• **chicane** ▶ An obstacle on a racecourse, particularly an artificial bend introduced on motor-racing tracks. This sense arose in the mid-20th century and was later broadened to include the road-narrowing obstacles used in traffic calming. Chicane is also a term used in bridge for a hand containing no trumps. The older and more general meaning of chicane is to practise chicanery (mean petty subterfuge, especially legal dodges and quibbles). The word itself is French and originally meant a dispute in games, particularly the hockey-like game known in England as pall-mall. It seems to derive ultimately from the Persian *chaugan*, the crooked stick used in polo.

• **chicano** ▶ (From Spanish *majicano*, a Mexican) A mainly US term for an American citizen of Mexican origin. The feminine equivalent is **chicana**.

• **chick** ▶ 1. A girl, girlfriend. This word has been used for hundreds of years as a term of endearment, but reappeared in the late 1950s and early 1960s, becoming part of hippie jargon in America and then in the UK. It sounds very dated in the post-feminist era and is considered rather pejorative by most women. 2. A prostitute. 3. A rare term used among homosexuals to mean a male prostitute. In US usage it is specifically a passive homosexual partner. A prison term of the 1970s and 1980s.

• **chicken** ▶ 1. Slang for a coward or cowardly. 2. A foolish game in which people dare each other to do something dangerous, for example, to stand in the path of an oncoming train. The first one to withdraw to a position of safety is the chicken, and the loser. *See*: chicken run. 3. Slang for a youth attractive to older homosexual males, known as **chickenhawks**. This usage is part of US homosexual jargon as well as police and prison jargon. 4. Slang for an under-age girl used as a sexual partner in pornography.

• **chicken run** ▶ US slang for a dangerous teenage game in which two drivers steer their cars towards each other to see which one will swerve aside first. The first one to do so is chicken, and the loser.

• **chicken switch**▶ The panic button in an aircraft that operates the ejector seat and enables the pilot to be parachuted safely to earth if something irrevocable has happened to the plane. Clearly, the moment at which to push the button is a matter of fine judgment. To push it too soon could jeopardize millions of pounds worth of aircraft unnecessarily and to push it too late could prove fatal. *See*: chicken.

• **chick fic** or **chick lit**▶ *See* Jones, Bridget.

• **Chicom**▶ In America, a derogatory term for a *Chi*nese *com*munist; mainly used in the 1950s and 1960s.

• **Chief, the**▶ The head person or boss. In America, the title was applied particularly to Herbert Hoover (1874–1964), secretary of commerce (1921–28) and 31st US president (1929–33), in connection with his role as administrator of relief operations in Europe during and after World War I.

• **chiefs**▶
  **too many chiefs and not enough Indians** or **all chiefs and no Indians** An originally US catchphrase that is now universal in English-speaking countries. It is said when a situation arises in which there are too many bosses (perhaps because there have been too many promotions) and too few workers.

• **child abuse**▶ In its broadest terms: any harm, physical or emotional, done intentionally to a child by its parents or other adults responsible for its wellbeing. This includes physical ill-treatment, sexual exploitation, and verbal or emotional assault. In the 1960s the **battered-baby syndrome** became a recognized medical condition and the 1970s witnessed growing awareness of the need to protect the rights and welfare of children. By the 1980s a heightened awareness of child sexual abuse so dominated the minds of social workers and doctors that the rights of innocent parents were sometimes overlooked (*see*: Cleveland Affair).

• **Childline**▶ A charity founded in 1986 as a result of the BBC TV programme *Childwatch*, which dealt with the abuse of children. Childline is a listening telephone service for children in distress, who wish to talk in confidence to a sympathetic adult. Some 17% of calls relate to bullying, 13% to family relationships, 20% to abuse (physical or sexual), and 6% to pregnancy. Over 900 volunteer counsellors are supervised by professionals, working from eight centres in the UK. The chairman, TV presenter Esther Rantzen, has said that of some 15,000 calls received daily, only 3500 can be answered, owing to lack of resources.

• **child migrants**▶ Some 150,000 British children from orphanages and children's homes, mostly aged 5 to 11 years, who were sent to Australia and other countries in the British Empire (and later the Commonwealth) from the end of the 19th century until the practice was stopped in 1967. Many of these children were told quite falsely that their parents were dead, while the parents were deceived into believing that their children had been adopted. Under the pretence of giving these children a new life, the British government relieved itself of the cost of bringing them up and educating them, while Australia and other recipient countries were anxious to increase their White populations. Most of the children were sent to Roman Catholic and other Christian institutions, where in many cases they were used as virtual slave labour and exposed to horrific physical and sexual abuse. The scandal was revealed by a Nottingham social worker, Margaret Humphreys, who spent years reuniting many of these children with their families in the UK. Her book *Empty Cradles* (1994) relates her experiences.

• **childproof** or **child-resistant**▶ Describing packaging, containers, etc., that are difficult for children to tamper with or open. For example, child-resistant containers, now commonly used for drugs, have tops that are not simply unscrewed, but involve two operations (*e.g.* pushing down and twisting). Their introduction in the 1970s was successful in reducing accidental poisoning of children, although many of these containers are also resistant to adults, particularly old people.

• **Children's Hour**▶ A radio programme broadcast every weekday evening by the BBC between 1922 and 1964. One of the best-loved presenters was Uncle Mac (Derek McCulloch; 1897–1967). The programme came to an end when audiences declined on account of the growth of television.

• **Child Support Agency**▶ (CSA) A UK government agency established in 1993 to collect child maintenance payments from absent parents (almost always fathers). Although the CSA was at first widely welcomed, it soon ran into bitter controversy. To its critics, the agency seemed more concerned with cutting costs to the Treasury than with ensuring proper provision for vulnerable children. Also, many of its decisions seemed to lack natural justice; the agency clearly found it easier to tighten the screws on fathers who were already making a contribution than to track down runaways. The mid-1990s saw numerous media reports of divorced men (especially those with second families) being driven to illness, breakdown, or even suicide by the demands of the CSA. Plans to reform the agency were announced in 1998.

• **chillum** ► A small cone-shaped pipe, usually made of clay but sometimes of wood or stone, used for smoking cannabis. The drug is packed on top of the 'chillum stone', a round object that fits into the narrowing end of the cone so that the contents are not sucked into the smoker's mouth. The name is an anglicization of the Hindi *cilam*.

• **China syndrome** ► A nuclear catastrophe. The term derives from the film of that name made in 1979, starring Jane Fonda and Jack Lemmon. It postulates that the heat generated by the breakdown of a nuclear reactor in America would make a hole right through the planet to China. The nuclear disaster at Chernobyl in 1986 heightened fears that the China syndrome might one day actually happen.

• **Chindit** ► A corruption of *chinthe*, the lion-headed dragon gracing the outside of Burmese pagodas. It was adopted as the device of the troops of the 3rd Indian Division raised by Major-General Orde Wingate to operate in Burma behind the Japanese lines (1943–45). The bravery of the Chindits, who sustained heavy casualties, has never been questioned, but their military value has been. Wingate himself was killed in an aircrash in March 1944.

• **Chinese** ►
  **clever chaps these Chinese** A catchphrase that seems to have originated in World War II, as a response to a complicated explanation that leaves the listener in a state of baffled incomprehension ('devils', 'buggers', etc., can be substituted for 'chaps'). It is probably a reference to the supposed inscrutability of the Chinese.

• **Chinese restaurant syndrome** ► A group of symptoms varying from sweating, burning sensations, headaches, and dizziness, to heart palpitations and temporary paralysis, first observed in the 1960s in some people after eating Chinese food. The symptoms are associated with an excessive intake of the food additive monosodium glutamate, a seasoning used in liberal quantities in Chinese restaurant cooking. The condition, thought to be an allergic reaction, is also called **Kwok's disease** after the scientist who made the connection with monosodium glutamate, Dr Robert Ho Man Kwok.

• **Chinese slavery** ► Virtual slavery; excessively hard work for negligible rewards. The phrase became widely used as a political slogan by the Liberals from 1903, when Balfour's Conservative government (1902–05) introduced indentured coolies from China to combat the shortage of Kaf-

fir labour in the Rand gold mines after the dislocation caused by the South African War. They were kept in compounds and only allowed out under permit. *See also*: terminological inexactitude.

• **Chinese wall** ► A notional barrier to the passage of information between the parts of a business that might have conflicting interests. It is used mostly to refer to the barrier that should exist between the market-making part of a stockbroker's office and the brokers. For example, brokers should not be advising clients to buy a particular share because the market-making part of the firm want to sell it. The term arose after the Big Bang of 1986, when the London Stock Exchange abandoned its two-function operation, with jobbers and brokers in separate firms. The amalgamation of these two functions into single firms necessitated the concept of a wall separating them in order not to compromise the interests of the customers. The wall was described as Chinese, either with reference to the Great Wall of China, and its former impregnability, or because Chinese walls are thought of in some contexts as being paper thin.

• **Chinese whispers** ► A parlour game in which a message is passed round a group of players in a whisper; the final version of the message is often amusingly different from the original. The term 'Chinese whispers' now refers to any situation in which a message is distorted by being passed on verbally by a number of people. It is said that in World War I a message was passed down the line in the noise of battle. The message was: 'Send reinforcements we are going to advance'. The version that arrived at the end of the line was 'Send three and fourpence we are going to a dance'.

• **chinless wonder** ► A derogatory term for an upper-class young man who has a great deal of money, no responsibilities, and little in the way of brains or personality. There is a common belief that people with weak or receding chins have weak or receding personalities. The chinlessness is often ascribed to in-breeding amongst the aristocracy. There is no evidence to support either proposition.

• **chip** ► A small piece of silicon or other semiconducting material processed to hold a large integrated circuit. The components of the circuit are formed by selectively diffusing the appropriate type of impurity into the semiconducting material. Connections between the components so formed are made by metallization. Very complex circuits can, in this way, be formed on a chip having minute dimensions.

• **Chippitts** ► In America, a name sometimes

given to the northern industrial area of the country encompassing the cities of *Chicago* and *Pittsburgh*. *See also*: Bosnywash; Sansan.

• **chippy** ▶ **1.** British slang for a fish and chip shop, common since the 1960s. **2.** British slang for a carpenter. **3.** An originally Canadian term used to describe someone who is touchy and easily angered. **4.** US and Australian slang for a prostitute or promiscuous woman.

• **Chips, Mr** ▶ Arthur Chipping, the initially aloof but later much loved schoolmaster who is the main character in *Good-Bye, Mr Chips* (1934), a novel by the British writer James Hilton (1900–54). It is said that Hilton based the character on his father, who was a headmaster, and on his old classics master, W. H. Balgarnie. The 1939 film of the same name starred Robert Donat; a musical remake in 1969 had Peter O'Toole in the title role. Graham Greene, also the son of a headmaster, wrote of the 1939 film:

> The whole picture has an assurance, bears a glow of popularity like the face of a successful candidate on election day. And it is wrong to despise popularity in the cinema.

• **chips with everything** ▶ Denoting a British working-class attitude to food in which all meals are served with fried potatoes and subsequently drenched with bottled sauce or vinegar. Originally the title of a play by Arnold Wesker (first performed in London in 1962), it is used as a catchphrase to describe to all those working-class eating habits that distinguish them from the middle classes. The middle-class evening meal is called dinner or supper, the working classes have dinner in the middle of the day and tea in the evening, on returning home from work. The middle classes have a varied repertoire of food, now often influenced by continental cuisine; the working classes have less adventurous appetites, and fried potatoes accompany most dishes. This is the theory, encapsulated in Wesker's play about class attitudes among National Servicemen in the RAF. The phrase is now used most commonly to describe the insularity of the British working-class tourist abroad. *See also*: social class.

• **chiropractic** ▶ A form of alternative medicine in which various diseases are treated by manipulation of the spine. It is based on the premise that many diseases are caused by misalignment of the skeletal bones (especially those of the spine), resulting in compression of the nerves, muscle spasms, etc.

• **chlorofluorocarbon** ▶ *See*: CFC.

• **chocaholic** ▶ Someone addicted to chocolate. Eating chocolate can release endorphins in the brain and it is apparently possible to become addicted to the pleasant mood changes that accompany this. Like similar coinages denoting addiction, the word is derived from 'alcoholic'.

• **choco** ▶ A diminutive of chocolate soldier, an Australian colloquialism applied to militiamen and conscripts in World War II.

• **choose** ▶

**I do not choose to run** A phrase used to indicate that the speaker does not want to compete or participate. It was popularized by the US politician Calvin Coolidge (1827–1933), who became president in 1923. He was noted for his frugal unpretentious character and for a policy of general inaction on domestic and international issues. In 1927 he decided not to re-stand for the office and announced the fact in a characteristically short speech:

> I do not choose to run for president in 1928.

His decision not to seek re-election caused considerable puzzlement and reporters pestered him to explain more fully why he no longer wanted to be president. He replied:

> No chance of advancement.

Coolidge's laconic utterances became famous and justified his nickname **Silent Cal**. It is said that a young lady sitting next to him at dinner told him that she had made a bet that she could get more than two words out of him. 'You lose', said Coolidge.

Coolidge's unspectacular and retiring style, exemplified by his slogan 'keep it cool with Coolidge', did inspire some jibes. Alice Roosevelt (1884–1980) said: 'He looks as if he had been weaned on a pickle', and Dorothy Parker (1893–1967), when told that he was dead, asked: 'How could they tell?'

• **chop** ▶ **1.** A customized motorcycle; an abbreviation of chopper. **2. the chop** The sack, termination of employment, as in the expression **for the chop**, meaning likely to be sacked. Previously, especially in wartime, it could mean to be killed.

• **chopper** ▶ **1.** Slang for a helicopter, widely used since World War II. It is probably derived from a corruption of the word helicopter and a description of the sound and action of the rotor blades. **2.** Slang for a customized motorcycle, especially one with high handlebars (*see*: apehangers) and extended front forks, as ridden by Hell's Angels. An abbreviation of **chopped hog**, the word is sometimes shortened further to **chop**. Choppers became popular in the early 1970s after they had featured in the biker film *Easy Rider* (1969) with Peter Fonda. A similar style of bicycle became popular amongst schoolboys at around the same time. **3.** British slang for a penis, dating from the 1940s and still in use. **4.** US slang for a submachine gun. Although no longer in current usage, this sense is widely known from films and crime fiction.

• **chop shop**▶ US slang for a workshop in which motorcycles and cars are customized or chopped. *See*: chopper.

• **chopshot**▶ Journalists' jargon for a photograph showing a death.

• **chozrim** ▶ (Hebrew, returnees) Israeli citizens who emigrate from Israel and subsequently return. *See also*: yordim.

• **Christian Aid** ▶ An aid and development agency administered by the British Council of Churches, which finances projects in over 70 countries. Its annual income is used for long-term development in the poorest of developing countries. This is channelled through local organizations to tackle the root causes of poverty, such as illiteracy, and to promote self-reliance and self-motivation against the forces of exploitation.

• **Christie disappearance**▶ *See*: Queen of Crime.

• **Christie murders**▶ A notorious series of murders committed by John Reginald Halliday Christie (1898–1953) in **Rillington Place**, Notting Hill Gate, London. In 1953 the bodies of six women, including Christie's wife, were discovered on the premises. Before he was hanged, Christie also confessed to the murder of the wife of Timothy Evans, who lived at the same address. Some four years earlier Evans had been hanged for the murder of his wife and infant daughter. Public disquiet over these events led to a judicial enquiry in 1953, which found that Christie had probably murdered the girl, but that Evans probably strangled his wife. Evans was given a posthumous free pardon for both murders in 1966. The evident frailty of human judicial procedures, so blatantly revealed by this case, convinced a majority of the members of the House of Commons (but not the public at large) that the death penalty, being irreversible, was an inappropriate punishment for anything and it ceased to be the punishment for murder in 1965.

• **Christingle** ▶ In Britain, a church service for children held around Christmas time, in which the children are given a decorated orange with a lighted candle in it. A collection is made for charity. The name comes from 'Christmas' plus 'ingle' (meaning 'fire' or 'flame'). Christingle services first became popular in the early 1970s.

• **Christmas Island**▶ **1.** Kiritimati. A coral atoll of the Line Islands in the Pacific, halfway between Tahiti and Hawaii. The first British hydrogen bomb was exploded here in 1957. **2.** An island in the Indian ocean discovered on Christmas Day 1643 by Captain Mynors. Annexed by Britain in 1888, it was occupied by the Japanese in World War II and transferred to Australia in 1958.

• **Christmas tree**▶ **1.** Slang for an amphetamine spansule containing dinamyl, a pep pill. **2.** Slang for an over-dressed woman, especially one wearing too much flamboyant jewellery.

• **Christopher Robin** ▶ Son of the playwright and author A. A. Milne (1882–1956), who was immortalized in his father's books, *When We Were Very Young*, *Now We Are Six*, *House at Pooh Corner*, and *Winnie-the-Pooh*. The Pooh books charted the adventures of a young boy, Christopher Robin, and his 'friends' Winnie-the-Pooh, Tigger, Piglet, Eeyore, Kanga, and Baby Roo. Milne based these characters on his son's favourite toys. The real Christopher Robin grew up to find his association with his father's books acutely embarrassing, although he eventually came to terms with his fictional namesake.

• **chubby chaser**▶ Slang name for someone sexually attracted to overweight people. **Chubby checker** has also been heard for a man who enjoys looking at overweight women (inspired by the name of the pop singer Chubby Checker (Ernest Evans), who originated the twist).

• **chunder**▶ In Australian slang, to be sick. It was popularized in the UK by the character Barry McKenzie in the *Private Eye* comic strip. The origin is uncertain. Possibly it is rhyming slang, from Chunder Loo (spew) – Chunder Loo being a comic character in an Australian boot-polish advertisement in the 1900s. Alternatively, it could simply be a shortening of the warning call 'watch under'.

• **Church Commissioners** ▶ The body that administers the affairs and finances of the Church of England. Chaired by the Archbishop of Canterbury, it consists of the diocesan bishops together with other representatives and functionaries. It was formed in 1948 by amalgamation of the Ecclesiastical Commissioners (established 1836) and a charitable fund for impoverished clergy known as Queen Anne's Bounty (established 1704).

• **churn**▶ To encourage or coerce people to pay for additional unnecessary services in order to increase the final fee or commission. **Churning** is particularly associated with professional organizations, such as law firms, financial advisers, and medical practices.

• **chutzpah**▶ Audacity, cheek, nerve; the word is

of Yiddish origin and pronounced 'hutspar'. Used in America by non-Jews since the 1960s, it has become widespread in the UK since the 1970s. In his *The Joys of Yiddish* (1968), Leo Rosten defines chutzpah as the quality of a man who, having killed his mother and father, throws himself on the mercy of the court because he is an orphan.

• **CIA** ▸ Central Intelligence Agency. A department of the US government set up by President Truman in 1947 to conduct intelligence operations outside America. During the Cold War period its clandestine ventures were usually designed to undermine left-wing regimes in the developing world, notably in Central and South America. The CIA lost much public support in the 1970s when US influence appeared to be diminished rather than enhanced by its activities. Its internal counter-intelligence service, operated in conjunction with the FBI, now has to be sanctioned by the attorney general, since alleged abuses in the Watergate affair.

• **ciao** ▸ An Italian word used as a greeting or as a farewell. It was adopted by English speakers in the 1960s and has continued to be widely used.

• **Cicero** ▸ Codename of Elyesa Bazna (1904–    ), the Albanian-born World War II spy. While working as valet to the British Ambassador to Turkey, Bazna photographed secret documents from the embassy safe and handed them to the Nazis. These apparently included details of the Normandy landings. However, Cicero was not fully trusted by the Nazis and it is believed that much of his information was ignored. A film of Cicero's life, *Five Fingers*, based on his autobiography, was released in 1952.

• **Cinderella of the Arts** ▸ A description of poetry, first used by the US poet and editor Harriet Monroe (1860–1936).

• **cinema novo** ▸ (Portuguese *cinema nóvo*, new cinema) A school of film-making that arose in Brazil in the 1960s, noted for fantasy and melodrama with a sharp political edge. It was suppressed by the government in the 1970s.

• **CinemaScope** ▸ The first successful widescreen film process, introduced by 20th Century-Fox in *The Robe* (1953). The system employed an anamorphic lens to compress a wide picture onto a standard 35-mm frame. When projected through a complementary lens, this produced an image width two and a half times its height. Although invented in the 1920s by Henri Chrétien, the process was not adopted by Hollywood until the 1950s, when it was used to help counter the growing threat from television. Other studios introduced their own versions of the system, variously called SuperScope, Warn-

erScope, etc. Initially, many directors disparaged the process, despite the dramatic compositional possibilities it offers; during the 1960s it was superseded by the more sophisticated Panavision.

> There was a time when all I looked for was a good story, but nowadays everything has to look the size of Mount Rushmore, and the actors in close-up look as though they belong there. – FRITZ LANG.

• **cinéma vérité** ▸ (French, truth cinema) A style of documentary film-making, developed in France in the 1960s. Light-weight hand-held cameras and synchronous sound recording are used to convey a sense of reality, unedited and unrehearsed, but hopefully enhanced by the film maker's involvement. Classic examples of the genre include Jean Rouch's *Chronique d'un été* (1961). *See also*: fly-on-the-wall.

• **cinerama** ▸ A widescreen film process in which three synchronized projectors each project one third of a film image onto a wide curved screen. The technique, which was supposed to enhance audience involvement by creating an illusion of peripheral vision, was invented by the New York photographer Fred Waller and given its first public viewing in *This Is Cinerama* (1952). The system's spectacular visual effects and stereo sound were restricted to travelogues until its first narrative use in *How The West Was Won* (1962). Because of the expense of the cumbersome projection machinery the system was superseded in the late 1960s by Panavision, which used an anamorphic lens to create similar widescreen effects more efficiently.

• **circadian rhythm** ▸ *See*: biorhythm.

• **circular file** ▸ In America, a slang term for the wastepaper basket, as in 'put it in the circular file'.

• **Citizen Kane** ▸ *See*: Kane, Citizen.

• **citizen's arrest** ▸ An arrest made by any British citizen other than a policeman. It is lawful provided that the person arrested is committing an arrestable offence (an offence that carries a fixed mandatory penalty or at least a five-year prison sentence). It is also lawful if the citizen reasonably suspects that an arrestable offence is being committed.

• **citizens' band** ▸ *See*: CB.

• **Citizens' Charter** ▸ A political concept promoted by John Major when prime minister in the early 1990s; it involved a basket of measures designed to make the public services more accountable and therefore more efficient. A keynote of the charter was to be more open government, on the grounds that the services provided could hardly be compared with the standards set for them without adequate information. However, when it came to providing this Whitehall demurred, saying that to do so would undermine traditional concepts of ministerial responsibility and the accountability of parliament. In a characteristic U-turn, Major accepted this view, although it inevitably denied the public the information that he himself said was needed to make the concept a reality.

• **City of Dreadful Knights** ▶ *See*: Honours Scandal.

• **city technology college** ▶ (CTC) In the UK, a type of senior secondary school set up in urban areas to provide a science-based education, as opposed to the more broadly based education available in other schools. Introduced in 1988, they are financed jointly by industry and the government independently of Local Education Authorities. The establishment of CTCs was an attempt to make school pupils more interested in science and technology and to prepare them for careers in industry and science.

• **civex** ▶ A US system for reprocessing nuclear fuel from fast-breeder reactors, developed in the late 1970s. The idea behind civex was that reactor technology could be sold to other countries but the reprocessing system did not allow the user to obtain pure plutonium for use in nuclear weapons. The term comes from *ci*vilian + e*x*traction, 'civilian' meaning 'non-military'.

• **Civic Trust** ▶ An independent British charity founded in 1957 by Duncan Sandys, minister of housing and local government (1954–57), to promote high standards in architecture and civil planning and to protect and improve the environment.

• **civil rights movement** ▶ The movement founded in 1950s America to end racial segregation and to ensure that Blacks received their full rights under the US Constitution. A Commission on Civil Rights was created under the Civil Rights Act (1957) and then extended under the 1960 and 1964 acts, the latter being by far the most important; the Commission had a watching brief on the development of equality for Blacks in such fields as voter registration and employment. The 1964 act, which integrated all public facilities and outlawed discrimination in the workplace, was passed in response to the mass agitation for civil rights led by Dr Martin Luther King (1929–68) in the 1950s and 1960s. *See also*: I have a dream *at* dream; NAACP.

> But in too many communities, in too many parts of the country, wrongs are inflicted on Negro citizens for which there are no remedies in law. – JOHN F. KENNEDY, June 1963.

• **CJD** ▶ Creutzfeldt-Jakob disease. A rare fatal brain disease first described by the German psychiatrists H. G. Creutzfeldt (1885–1964) and A. M. Jakob (1884–1931). It is thought to be caused by deposits of an abnormal prion protein in the brain. A variant form of CJD (**vCJD**), affecting mainly young people, appeared in the UK in the mid-1990s. Thought to have resulted from eating beef products from cattle infected with BSE (*see*: mad cow disease), it claimed over 70 lives between 1995 and 2001. Because it has a very long incubation period, experts predict that it may be many years before the full extent of the 'epidemic' is known. *See also*: beef ban.

• **clambake** ▶ A colony of marine animals living on the ocean floor in an area in which the water is heated by an underground hot spring. The term is an extension of the US name for a beach picnic at which clams are baked.

• **clam diggers** ▶ In America, trousers cut off below the knee, so-called because they were originally worn when digging clams.

• **Clapham** ▶
  **man on the Clapham omnibus** The ordinary man in the street. The phrase was invented by a senior judge, Lord Bowen, in 1903. While hearing a case for negligence, he said: 'We must ask ourselves what the man on the Clapham omnibus would think.' In those days the omnibus was still horse-drawn and Clapham was a suburb that a judge might well regard as the epitome of ordinariness – the home of unlegalistic common sense.

In fact, this was not the Clapham omnibus's only claim to fame. Some 50 years earlier a young German chemist, August Kekulé von Stradonitz, was working as a laboratory assistant at St Bartholomew's Hospital in London. While asleep on the Clapham omnibus he fell into a dream that was to revolutionize organic chemistry: '...the atoms were gambolling before my eyes...I saw how the longer ones formed a chain...(and then) the cry of the conductor "Clapham Road" awakened me from my dreaming...' Kekulé's dream led to the elucidation of the structure of many organic molecules, notably that of benzene.

Since its years of Edwardian stolidity, Clapham has gone down in the world and more recently come up again. With gentrification, it acquired the joke pronunciation 'clarm' (to rhyme with charm).

• **clapometer** ▶ An instrument used in various British and US television talent shows to measure the volume or duration of audience applause in judging the result of the contest. The word was coined by Hughie Green and Peter Dulay for the British TV show Opportunity Knocks.

• **classism** ▶ Discrimination against people on the grounds of social class; the discrimination may be against either the lower or the upper classes. The word is formed by analogy with racism, sexism, and ageism.

• **classless society** ▶ A society in which social class plays no significant role. When John Major became prime minister in 1990, he promised that under his leadership Britain would become a classless society. To the grass roots of the Conservative Party this apparent avowal of egalitarianism must have come as a surprise. After all, the phrase 'classless society' had been originated by Karl Marx to describe the ultimate goal of communist policies. Major soon qualified his statement by saying that what he really advocated was an 'opportunity society' – one in which a person from the most humble or unusual background (such as the son of an ex-circus performer turned designer of garden gnomes, perhaps) could rise to the highest of positions.

• **Clause Four** ▶ A former clause in the constitution of the British Labour Party, pledging the party to work for the common ownership of the means of production, distribution, and exchange. By 1954 Hugh Gaitskell, then the leader of the party, was doubtful that such a pledge, with its communist overtones, made sense in the context of British social institutions. However, his attempt to remove it was defeated in 1960 by socialist diehards in the party. Although the clause remained in the constitution for another 35 years most members of the Labour Party preferred to ignore it. This shibboleth of old-style socialism was finally replaced by a vaguer statement of 'aims and values' following a special conference of the Labour Party in April 1995. The era of New Labour had arrived.

• **Clause 28** or **Section 28** ▶ A clause in the Local Government Bill (1988) that prevents local authorities in the UK from presenting homosexuality in a favourable light. The bill became law despite vociferous opposition from bodies defending homosexuality and the principle of free speech. The Labour government's attempt to repeal the clause was blocked by the House of Lords in 2000.

• **clay pigeon** ▶ British bicycle or motorcycle couriers' slang for a pedestrian. In the crowded London streets, in which motorcycles are often the only vehicles able to move, pedestrians, weaving their way across a road, can easily be surprised and knocked down by a hastening courier.

• **clean, bright, and slightly oiled** ▶ An old army slogan that dates back to World War I, referring to the condition in which a soldier was ex-

pected to keep his rifle. Between the wars 'slightly oiled' became an allusion to minor drunkenness. During World War II the slogan again reverted to its military usage and it provided the title of a book of wartime short stories by Gerald Kersh (1946).

• **clear blue water** ▶ Any clear divide or separation, but especially one between two political parties or schools of thought. The phrase, which derives from the nautical use of 'clear water' to mean a discernible gap between two boats, achieved prominence in the early 1990s, and was used as the title of a pamphlet written by the British Conservative politician Michael Portillo in 1994. Because blue is traditionally the colour of the Conservative Party, political differences in other directions are sometimes spoken of as 'clear red water' or 'clear orange water', however nonsensical this may be.

> Quite early in the 1992 parliament...It was felt that the political agenda should be rewritten to sharpen the political divide. Hence the talk of 'clear blue water'. – JOHN BIFFEN, *The Independent*, 11 October 1997.

• **clearing house of the world** ▶ A description of the City of London. It comes from a speech (1904) by the British politician Joseph Chamberlain at the Guildhall in London:

> ...provided that the City of London remains, as at present, the clearing house of the World.

Although London has been able to maintain this position for nearly a century, doubts are now being expressed about its ability to remain the financial centre of the world. There are two main reasons for this: the collapse of London as a port and with it the entrepôt trade in commodities; and Britain's disinclination to join the euro economy, which has allowed other financial centres, such as Frankfurt and Paris, to challenge London.

• **Cleveland Affair** ▶ During the period April to July 1987, 121 children in Cleveland in NE England were diagnosed by Doctors Marietta Higgs and Geoffrey Wyatt as having been sexually abused. These two paediatricians, working at Middlesbrough General Hospital, based most of their diagnoses on the controversial technique known as reflex anal dilation (RAD). The number of cases was quite extraordinarily high and the rights of the parents were uncaringly swept aside, with 67 of the children being made wards of court and another 85 being separated from their families by place-of-safety orders. The uproar created by the unprecedented scale of the diagnoses led to the setting up of a judicial enquiry, conducted by Lord Justice Butler-Sloss. Her report, published in July 1988, by which time 98 of the children had been returned to their families, was highly critical of all the agencies concerned. The two doctors were severely criticized for their overconfidence in the results of RAD; the police and the social services were criticized for the poor communication between members of their staffs. Numerous detailed recommendations were made to prevent a recurrence of this tragedy and the poor judgment that caused it. Almost incredibly, however, the situation was allowed to repeat itself in 1991, when social workers in Orkney snatched nine children from their beds in a dawn raid. *See also*: child abuse.

• **cliffhanger** ▶ Figuratively, a situation full of suspense or uncertainty. From the early serial adventure films, in which the hero was often left in a situation of imminent disaster (sometimes, literally, hanging by his fingernails to the top of a cliff) in order to whet the cinema-goer's appetite for the next instalment.

• **Clio** ▶ A statuette awarded annually in America for outstanding achievement in a radio or television commercial; the advertising equivalent of the film industry's Oscar. Awards are made in several categories for acting, writing, production, etc. Clio is the name of the Muse of history.

• **clip joint** ▶ Slang for any night club or bar with over-inflated prices in which people are 'clipped' (a euphemism for swindled) out of their money. Originally a clip joint employed hostesses to invite male customers to buy them exorbitantly priced drinks in return for the promise of sexual favours, which were, in fact, rarely given.

• **clippie** ▶ A popular nickname for bus conductresses during and just after World War II, since they clipped or punched the tickets. In recent years, the bus tickets are sold by the driver and the role of the conductor or conductress has disappeared.

• **Cliveden set** ▶ The right-wing politicians and journalists who gathered for weekend parties in the late 1930s at Cliveden, the country home of Lord and Lady Astor near Marlow in Buckinghamshire. The name was coined by the left-wing journal *The Week*, which portrayed the 'set' as a tight-knit clique dedicated to the appeasement of Nazi Germany. Although some of its members certainly held such views, the legend of the Cliveden set and its sinister influence seems to have been greatly exaggerated. The idea of a Cliveden set re-emerged in the early 1960s when the Profumo affair broke; it was revealed that John Profumo (1915–99), the secretary of state for war, had been introduced to call-girl Christine Keeler by Lord Astor at Cliveden.

• **clock** ▶ **1.** British slang meaning to notice or observe. It has been in use since World War II. **2.** To put back the milometer on a car so that it shows a lower mileage than the car has actually covered; a practice frequently perpetrated by dishonest second-hand car dealers. Originally confined to car dealers' jargon, it is now in common usage, which reflects the extent of the practice. **3.** British police slang for the 36-hour period of questioning that follows a caution to the suspect in a particular inquiry.

• **clockwork orange** ▶ A person who has been brainwashed or whose individuality has been suppressed by conditioning. The term comes from the title of a novel (1962) by the British writer Anthony Burgess (1917–93), which was popularized by a film (1971) by Stanley Kubrick. Both book and film explore issues of free will and social morality through the story of Alex, a violent youth in a totalitarian society of the future, who is 'reprogrammed' to be a model citizen. The film quickly became notorious for its scenes of graphic violence and was blamed for inspiring a number of copycat incidents. As a result, Kubrick withdrew it from circulation in Britain, only reversing his decision in the weeks before his death (1999). Burgess took his book title from an earlier Cockney expression 'as queer as a clockwork orange'. *See also*: nadsat.

• **clone** ▶ **1.** A group of cells or organisms derived from a single ancestor, by any asexual means, and therefore genetically identical. The word, taken from the Greek *klōn*, twig, was first used at the beginning of the 20th century by botanists for a group of plants obtained by grafting from a single parent stock. Later it was applied to cell cultures, exact copies of a gene (**gene clone**) manufactured by techniques of genetic engineering, and replicas of entire organisms (*see*: Dolly the sheep). **2.** Slang for a person who slavishly imitates another, especially a celebrity. For example, a 'Britney Spears clone'. **3.** Slang used by gay men to describe a fellow gay man dressed in a stereotypically homosexual fashion. Originating in the Castro Street area of San Francisco, the archetypal clone uniform consists of faded, but well cared-for, denims, a leather cap, and a bushy moustache.

• **clone-zone** ▶ Male homosexual slang from the 1970s for the area of town in which gay men meet. *See*: clone.

• **closed** ▶
**We never closed** Slogan associated with the Windmill Theatre in London, which, under its proprietor Vivian Van Damm, was the only London theatre to remain open throughout the whole of the Blitz in 1940. The Windmill specialized in nude

revues and later became a proving ground for such comedians as Jimmy Edwards and Tony Hancock. It did in fact close in 1964 for conversion to a cinema and again in 1981 for further conversion.

• **closed shop**▶ A term, first used in America, to describe shops or factories from which non-union labour was excluded. In the UK trade union legislation passed in 1980, 1982, 1988, and 1992 had the effect of making closed-shop agreements unenforceable (although they are not in themselves illegal). The term is also used more widely of any institution that has a reputation for not admitting outsiders.

• **close encounter**▶ An encounter with extraterrestrial beings. Such encounters can be subdivided into various classes. A close encounter of the first kind, for example, implies a simple sighting of a UFO, while a close encounter of the third kind involves communication with the beings in question. *Close Encounters of the Third Kind* was the title of a hugely successful science-fiction film made by Steven Spielberg in 1977. *See also*: flying saucers.

• **closet queen**▶ *See*: come out.

• **close your eyes and think of England** or **lie back, open your legs, and think of England**▶ Advice supposedly given to newly wed girls in the days when they were assumed to have had no previous sexual experience nor any desire to participate actively in their first. In spite of rumours to the contrary, it is unlikely to have been said by a lady-in-waiting to Queen Victoria, or by Mrs Stanley Baldwin about her own nuptials. However, a Lady Hillingdon wrote in her *Journal* (1912): '...I endure but two calls a week [from her husband Charles] and when I hear his steps outside my door I lie down on my bed, close my eyes, open my legs and think of England.'

• **cloth-cap**▶ A British epithet for the traditional working classes, as in 'Labour has shed its cloth-cap image'. The expession derives from the cloth (or flat) caps worn by previous generations of British manual workers as part of their outdoor attire. Although the cloth cap has come to symbolize a working man, it is now mainly worn by the upper classes when out shooting. Indeed, between 12 August and 10 December, the moors abound with men in cloth caps and 12-bores under their arms. A subtle distinction between the two types of cloth cap is that the upper classes often have them made from the same material as their jackets or suits, whereas the working man's cloth cap was purchased as a single item that did not need to match anything.

• **clotheshorse**▶ A derogatory term for a person who is extremely interested in fashion and invariably looks elegant in very fashionable expensive clothes. A clotheshorse, in this sense, is not expected to have outstanding intellectual powers. The expression derives from the wooden frame on which clothes can be hung to dry.

• **cloud nine**▶ To be on cloud nine is to be very happy, so happy that one feels close to heaven. In the US classification of clouds, the type that grows tallest (cumulonimbus) is called cloud nine.

• **clowns**▶

   **send in the clowns** A phrase said when something goes wrong, meaning 'keep things going' or 'the show must go on'. It comes from the circus where, if there was an accident or other problem, the clowns were sent into the ring to divert the audience. The phrase dates from the 1930s. 'Send in the Clowns' is the title of an evocative song by the US composer Stephen Sondheim (1930–  ), first heard in his 1973 musical *A Little Night Music*.

• **Club Fed**▶ US slang for a federal prison – a pun on the Club Med (Club Mediterrané) holiday villages.

• **Club of Rome**▶ An international group of economists, businessmen, scientists, etc., formed in 1972 in Rome, who periodically issue reports about the state of the world, particularly on environmental and related issues.

• **clumsy child syndrome**▶ *See*: dyspraxia.

• **clunk, click**▶ In full, 'clunk, click, every trip', a slogan used in a series of British television advertisements of the 1970s encouraging people to use their car seatbelts; they featured the disc jockey and television presenter Jimmy Savile. The 'clunk' was the sound of the car door closing and the following 'click' was the seatbelt being fastened. The slogan inspired many jokes and variants; a museum director found 'clunk, click, every trip' written on the cases exhibiting chastity belts.

• **cluster bomb**▶ A weapon consisting of a large number of individual bombs or other projectiles that are released on impact. Cluster bombing was widely used in the Vietnam War and was used again in the so-called war on terrorism in Afghanistan. Because of the danger to civilians, some humanitarian groups have called for a ban on this type of weapon.

• **Clydesiders**▶ A loosely attached group of left-wing MPs representing Glasgow and Clydeside constituencies, who enlivened British politics and parliament from 1922 until they were much diminished in numbers by the 1931 election. Notable among them were John Wheatley, Campbell Stephen, Emmanuel Shinwell, and best known of all, James Maxton, who became chairman of the Independent Labour Party. They were notable champions of the poor and unemployed.

• **CND** ▶ Campaign for Nuclear Disarmament. An organization formed by Bertrand Russell and Canon John Collins, Dean of St Paul's Cathedral, in 1958 to campaign for the UK to cease to be a nuclear power. Its mass demonstrations and annual Aldermaston Marches were a feature of British life in the late 1950s and 1960s. In 1961 a militant group called the **Committee of 100**, which included Russell and Collins and a number of people prominent in the arts, began a campaign of direct-action protests, which led to a split in the movement and its subsequent decline.

CND revived in the 1980s with the planned deployment of US Cruise missiles in Britain, its new leaders being Roman Catholic priest Bruce Kent (chairman) and Meg Beresford (general secretary). Both resigned in 1990, after a sharp decline in membership as a result of the end of the Cold War.

• **Coathanger, the** ▶ A colloquial Australian name for the Sydney Harbour Bridge, which (shaped rather like a coathanger) arches 52 m (170 ft) above the water.

• **Cobra** ▶ **1.** An international art group founded in 1948 and named from the first letters of the cities Copenhagen, Brussels, and Amsterdam, the homes of its founders Asger Jorn (1914–73), Pierre Alechinsky (1927– ), and Karel Appel (1921– ), respectively. They aimed to revive a form of expressionism, painting in a violent semi-abstract style. The group dissolved in 1951. **2.** A German wire-guided antitank missile with a range of 1600 m.

• **Coca-Cola** ▶ Trade name for a fizzy dark-brown beverage that was first marketed at the end of the 19th century and went on to become one of the most widely consumed and advertised products in the world. Future archaeologists might be forgiven for thinking that the beverage had the properties of a panacea, so widely will remains of its packaging and advertising be found. It consists of a secret formula devised by a US druggist from Atlanta, Dr John S. Pemberton, using extracts of coca leaves and cola nuts. Originally the extract from the coca leaves included a minute quantity of cocaine – enough to enable the advertisers to claim that it was 'an esteemed brain tonic and intellectual beverage' – but all traces of the drug were removed from the formula in 1905. Nevertheless, the alternative name 'Coke', even then a street name for cocaine, remained in common use. In the 1920s the

Coca-Cola company engaged in a long battle in the courts to prevent another company, the Koke Company of America, from using the name. They won their suit, the Supreme Court ruling that the name Coke was exclusively owned by the Coca-Cola Company, which eventually registered this alternative name in 1945.

Because the second half of the name, Cola, is not registered by the Coca-Cola Company, another drugstore dispenser, Caleb D. Bradham, devised, registered, and marketed a successful rival to Coca-Cola. Called Pepsi-Cola, because it was alleged to relieve dyspepsia, this product is now marketed by Cadbury-Schweppes as a successful rival to Coca-Cola.

• **Cocacolaization** ▶ The unwelcome influence of US culture, represented by the beverage Coca-Cola, on European habits and institutions. The word was a French coinage, in response to the impact that Coca-Cola had on the consumption of wine in Europe, even in France itself. *See also*: Pepsification.

• **Coconut Grove fire** ▶ A disastrous fire at the Coconut Grove night club in Boston in 1942. The fact that exit doors opened inwards contributed to the death toll of 487, making it one of the worst fire disasters in US history.

• **cocooning** ▶ US yuppie slang of the late 1980s for leading an unadventurous life, typically staying at home with partner or family in the evenings rather than socializing, and ignoring the problems of the outside world.

• **coelacanth** ▶ *See*: Old Fourlegs.

• **coffee-table book** ▶ A large copiously illustrated book that is too heavy and cumbersome to read; it is therefore left out (typically on a coffee table) to impress visitors with its beauty and costliness. Such books are often produced for a publisher by a packager, *i.e.* a company that specializes in producing a complete book, usually typeset and printed, for the publisher to sell.

• **cognitive psychology** ▶ A relatively young branch of psychology, based on the theories of the Swiss psychologist Jean Piaget (1896–1980), that focuses on the mental processes by which we gather information, form concepts, and acquire opinions or beliefs (cognition). This approach, which gained ground in the 1940s and 1950s, contrasts most obviously with behaviourism, which deals only with an organism's observable behaviour. Modern cognitive theorists regard behaviourist theories as essentially incomplete, as they fail to explain the cognitive processes associated with the behaviours they are attempting to analyse. More recently the area has expanded, giving rise to new fields such as cognitive psychophysiology and the more general cognitive science; it has also influenced the study of information processing in computer science.

• **cohab** ▶ Short for cohabitee, *i.e.* a sexual partner with whom one lives but to whom one is not married. *See*: de facto; live-in; significant other.

• **Cointelpro** ▶ Counter-intelligence programme; a campaign mounted by the US FBI in the late 1960s to discredit people or organizations that were regarded as subversive.

• **cojones** ▶ Courage, guts, balls. The Spanish slang word for balls in both the literal and metaphorical senses, it has become widely known to English speakers through the works of Ernest Hemingway. It is pronounced 'co-honays'.

• **coke** ▶ Slang for cocaine, used throughout the English-speaking world. *See also*: Coca-Cola.

• **cold** ▶
  **come in from the cold** To come back from a lonely, isolated, or neglected position into one of safety, favour, or recognition. The phrase was popularized by the title of a novel by the British writer John Le Carré (David Cornwell, 1931– ), *The Spy Who Came in from the Cold* (1963), about a British agent in East Germany who wants to return to the West.

• **cold-calling** ▶ The practice of making unsolicited visits or telephone calls to people's homes or businesses with a view to selling them goods or services. The object is to catch the customer's interest before one is dismissed and then to use persuasive selling methods to get them to buy something that they would not otherwise have bought.

• **Cold Comfort Farm** ▶ A phrase used to imply that a particular domicile is untidy and comfortless. It comes from the humorous book (1932) of this title by Stella Gibbons.

> If she intended to tidy up life at Cold Comfort she would find herself opposed at every turn by the influence of Aunt Ada. Persons of Aunt Ada's temperament were not fond of a tidy life.
> – STELLA GIBBONS: *Cold Comfort Farm*.

*See also*: something nasty in the woodshed *at* nasty.

• **cold fusion** ▶ Nuclear fusion produced at low temperatures. All present sources of controllable nuclear energy are obtained by nuclear fission – a process in which heavy atomic nuclei are split with the release of energy. Fission needs expensive uranium fuel, which is not widely available. The opposite process, nuclear fusion, is the coming together of light nuclei, such as hydrogen or helium nuclei, to form heavier nuclei. This process also

produces energy – it is the source of energy in the Sun and in the H-bomb (*see*: nuclear weapon).

The problem is that nuclear fusion reactions can only be induced at very high temperatures and it is difficult to control them and extract the energy in a usable form. Controlled high-temperature fusion would be an immense advance; the fuel, water, is cheap and in effectively unlimited supply. Many millions of pounds (and dollars and roubles) have been spent on research using such devices as Zeta and the tokamak (*see*: nuclear reactor), so far with no practical success.

Even better would be cold fusion – fusion induced without large initial inputs of energy. Various methods of achieving this have been tried. In 1989, two scientists, Martin Fleischmann and Stanley Pons, caused a considerable stir in the world of nuclear physics by announcing that they had produced cold fusion simply by passing an electric current through heavy water using special electrodes of platinum and palladium. Unfortunately, later work failed to confirm their results.

• **Colditz** ▶ A German town on the river Mulde in Saxony, with a castle built by Augustus II poised on a cliff above the town. This castle was used during World War II as a maximum-security prison for prisoners-of-war held by the Germans, who regarded escape from it as impossible. Several attempts were made, however, by British and other servicemen; some were successful, as related in the film *The Colditz Story* (1954) and a later (1972) TV series. The castle was subsequently converted into a tourist attraction.

• **cold mooner** ▶ A person who believes that lunar craters were formed by the impact of meteorites rather than as a result of volcanic activity. Cold mooners believe that the core of the moon is cold. *See also*: hot mooner.

• **cold turkey** ▶ Originally US drug addicts' slang for the effects of sudden withdrawal from hard drugs, especially heroin. This causes the addict to suffer goose pimples, hot and cold flushes, sickness, and considerable discomfort often likened to that of a bad attack of flu. The expression is now widely used in the more general sense of withdrawal from any usual activity. It probably derives from the appearance of the goose pimples and the sufferer's resemblance to pallid cold turkey meat.

• **Cold War** ▶ The long period of hostility and tension between America and her Western allies on the one hand, and the Soviet bloc on the other, that followed the end of World War II. Owing to the ever-present threat of nuclear annihilation, the conflict was carried on by means of propaganda, threats, economic sanctions, and subversion rather than actual fighting between the superpowers. The term was first used in America in 1947 by Bernard Baruch (1870–1965), the US politician and economist, who warned: 'Let us not be deceived – we are today in the midst of a cold war.'

The Cold War came to an end in 1989–91 with the collapse of communism in Eastern Europe, the disbanding of the Warsaw Pact, and the disintegration of the Soviet Union. A **Cold Warrior** (or **Cold War Warrior**) was a politician who actively promoted or supported the Cold War.

• **Cold War Witch** ► *See*: Iron Lady.

• **collage** ► (French *coller*, to glue) A work of art made up wholly, or in part, from pieces of paper, cloth, or other materials stuck onto a flat backing. The technique was first used to real effect by the cubists (*see*: cubism), who introduced everyday objects into their easel paintings, *e.g.* Picasso's *Still Life with Chair Caning* (1912); it was also a feature of dadaism (in the form of photomontage), abstract expressionism, and the work of such pop artists as Jasper Johns. In his later works Matisse abandoned paint altogether, using instead pieces of brightly coloured paper.

• **collective bargaining** ► The process by which the members of a workforce are represented by trade-union officials to negotiate wage rates, working conditions, pay settlements, etc. Collective bargaining provides one of the main reasons for joining a union. Alone, a worker has very little ability to stand up to management in such negotiations; as a member of a large body, with the sanction of industrial action at its disposal, workers are able to negotiate better wages and work conditions. Unfortunately the weapon is double-edged. If unions become too powerful they can force managements to make uneconomic settlements that make their products uncompetitive in world markets.

• **Collins Street Farmer** ► Australian slang for a businessman who invests in farms or the farming industry. Collins Street is a principal business street in Melbourne.

• **Colombo Plan** ► An agreement to foster economic development in South and South East Asia. There are annual meetings to discuss economic development plans, such as irrigation and hydroelectric schemes, and a continuing body which helps to provide technical assistance. It was founded in 1951 at Colombo, Ceylon (now Sri Lanka).

• **Colonel Bogey** ► One of the best-known military marches, composed by Major F. J. Ricketts, bandmaster of the Argyll and Sutherland Highlanders (and from 1926 of the Royal Marines). Ricketts named it after a colonel with whom he had played golf in 1913; the colonel had a habit of whistling two notes before he played a shot (instead of calling 'Fore!') – these became the first notes of the march. A 'bogey' in golf is one shot over the standard number of strokes a good player would take for a particular hole. Ricketts did not write words for his march, but various versions were known to soldiers in both world wars. Perhaps the best known in World War II began:

> Hitler has only got one ball,
> Goering has two but they are small,
> Himmler has something similar,
> And Goebbels has no balls at all.

• **Colorado beetle** ► *Leptinotarsa decemlineata*, also known as the potato beetle or bug. The beetle is native to Colorado, USA, where it had become an important potato pest by 1874. It made its first appearance in the British Isles in 1933 and has since spread through Europe. It is 10 mm long, orange-red or yellow in colour with black stripes on its wing covers. One female can deposit 300–500 eggs on the underside of potato leaves; both the adults and the larvae eat the leaves and the larvae also consume the tubers.

• **Colossus** ► *See*: Bletchley Park.

• **colour man** ► In America, a broadcaster on radio or TV who gives interesting background information (*i.e.* vividness or 'colour') to a news story.

• **colour supplement** ► A glossy magazine using coloured illustrations, issued with a newspaper. For many years these appeared only with the so-called 'quality' Sunday papers, such as *The Sunday Times* and *The Observer*. During the 1980s, however, the Sunday editions of tabloids also published their own colour supplements, while *The Independent*, *The Times*, *The Guardian*, and *The Daily Telegraph* now issue magazine supplements on Saturdays.

• **combat neurosis** ► *See*: shell shock.

• **combo** ► **1.** A small group of jazz musicians, rather than a larger band. This term was widely used in the 1930s and 1940s. **2.** In Australia, a slang name for a couple consisting of a White man and an Aboriginal woman.

• **come** or **come off** ► Slang meaning to have an orgasm. Although neither the experience itself nor the use of this term to describe it can be said to have begun in the 20th century (citations go back to the 1600s), it is mainly in the last hundred years that orgasms have been openly talked and written about in contexts that are not pornographic. James Joyce and D. H. Lawrence were perhaps the first serious writers to use the term freely in descriptions of sexual intercourse. During the 19th century it seems to have been assumed that the experience was restricted to the male of the species. Once it became acceptable to discuss female orgasms, the editors of women's magazines of the late 1970s and 1980s found that descriptions of the experience, and how to achieve it, produced highly saleable copy. Unfortunately, the pendulum swung so far that many women came to feel deprived if they failed to achieve explosive multiple orgasms on every occasion that they made love.

• **come again?** ▶ Please repeat what you have just said: I either didn't hear you or failed to understand you. Popular at various times on both sides of the Atlantic, it probably originated in America before World War I.

• **COMECON** ▶ Council for Mutual Economic Assistance. An association set up by Stalin in 1949 to promote economic development and trade between the Soviet Union and the other communist countries of Eastern Europe (except Yugoslavia). Until 1953 the organization was largely a propaganda vehicle used by Russia to disguise the economic exploitation of its satellite states. In later years, however, it began to promote genuine mutual economic cooperation and development. East Germany left on German reunification in 1990 and the remaining members voted (1991) to replace COMECON with a looser association designed to help integrate their economies with those of Western Europe.

• **come home all is forgiven** ▶ A catchphrase spoofing the agony column advertisements formerly seen in many newspapers. Perhaps some originals on these lines were actually published, by spouses seeking the return of a missing partner or by parents revoking a decision that an offspring should never darken their door again. However, the phrase has gained wide currency in a humorous context.

• **come out** ▶ Short for **come out of the closet**, to declare oneself a homosexual. In the days when homosexuality was a criminal offence, prudence led many gays to conceal the nature of their sexual interests. They became known as **closet queens** or **closet homosexuals**, the connection with the secrecy of the closet being obvious. As anti-homosexual laws were relaxed and popular prejudice began to abate, the need for secrecy disappeared and gays were able to 'come out'. The expression is also used with no sexual connotations, to mean to state one's real position. *See also*: outing.

• **come over with the onion boat** ▶ A derogatory reference to someone regarded as an unwelcome foreigner. It originated in the 1920s, with reference to French onion sellers who crossed the Channel with their strings of onions and their bicycles, to hawk them round the towns and villages of southern England. 'You don't think I came over with the onion boats, do you?' is a commonly used form, likely to be said by someone who wishes to establish his long residency in the British Isles. Variations on this theme include 'came over with an icecream barrow' aimed at Italians, and 'came over with the banana boat' relating to those of African descent who arrived by ship from the Caribbean after World War II.

• **Comet** ▶ The first commercial jet airliner. Manufactured by the De Havilland Aircraft Company in 1952, Comet 1 was withdrawn after two tragic accidents, in which many people died, which were shown to have been caused by metal fatigue. De Havilland modified the design and introduced the extremely successful Comet 4, which entered service with BOAC in 1958.

• **come up and see me some time** ▶ A sexual innuendo associated with the US actress Mae West (1892–1980). The line first appeared in her play *Diamond Lil* (1928) but gained wider currency from the film version *She Done Him Wrong* (1933), in which Mae West says to the young Cary Grant, 'Why don't you come up some time and see me? I'm home every evening.' It may be that the phrase was used on the streets of New York before this, but it was certainly Mae West who immortalized it.

The male counterpart, **come up and see my etchings**, is probably of earlier origin; it has been used as a jokey allusion to Victorian melodrama – the villain seducing the innocent maiden – since the early years of the 20th century.

• **come with me to the Casbah** ▶ A line that Charles Boyer is supposed to have said to Hedy Lamarr in the film *Algiers* (1938). He didn't – any more than Humphrey Bogart said Play it again, Sam in *Casablanca* (1942).

• **comic strip** ▶ A sequence of drawings relating a humorous story or an adventure. They generally appear in newspapers and magazines; longer ones are sometimes published as comic books or 'graphic novels'. The first modern comic strip, 'The Yellow Kid' appeared in the *New York World* in 1896 drawn by Richard Telton Outcault. Its success encouraged many imitators on both sides of the Atlantic during the 20th century. Especially notable are the American 'Krazy Kat' (1910) by Richard Herriman, Peanuts (1950) by Charles M. Schulz, and the British Andy

Capp (1957) by Reginald Smythe. *See also*: Astérix; Jane; Peanuts; Pip, Squeak, and Wilfred; Rupert Bear.

• **Cominform** ▶ Communist Information Bureau. An international communist organization, set up in 1947 under Soviet control to publish propaganda encouraging international communist solidarity. It also coordinated the policies of the communist parties of countries not under Soviet control. The members of the Cominform were the Soviet Union, Bulgaria, Czechoslovakia, Hungary, Poland, Romania, Yugoslavia, France, and Italy. In 1948 Yugoslavia was expelled for its failure to follow Soviet instructions; the Cominform was dissolved in 1956 in order to improve relations with Yugoslavia.

• **Comintern** ▶ Communist International. An organization of world communist parties founded by Lenin in 1919 as an early stage towards the worldwide revolution of the proletariat. It was dissolved by Stalin in 1943 as a gesture towards his wartime capitalist allies.

• **commando** ▶ (Portuguese *commandar*, command) Originally armed units of Boer horsemen, who were well known for their daring during the South African War (1899–1902).

> Lord Kitchener's relentless policy of attrition was slowly breaking the hearts of the commandos. – DENEYS REITZ: *Commando*.

In World War II the name was adopted for the units of specially trained British assault troops formed from volunteers to undertake particularly hazardous tasks.

• **Committee of 100** ▶ *See*: CND.

• **Common Agricultural Policy** ▶ *See*: CAP.

• **Common Cause** ▶ A US political pressure group founded in 1970 to urge the government to respond to what it regards as the wishes of the people as a whole, rather than to the lobbying of wealthy pressure groups. In particular, it has campaigned for charges to the laws on campaign funding.

• **Common Entrance** ▶ The exam taken by British 13-year-old prep-school boys seeking entrance to a public school. The exam was instituted in 1903 and is still in force. Latin, which used to be a compulsory subject, is now optional. It is this exam, in addition to individually set scholarship exams, that enables the most prestigious public schools to select only the brightest pupils. And it is by selecting the brightest (rather than by superior teaching methods) that the same group of public schools survive at the top of the A-level tables of results.

• **Common Market** ▶ In Britain, the popular name for the European Economic Community and later the European Community. It is now rarely heard.

• **Commonwealth of Nations** ▶ A loose association of nations established in 1931 under the Statute of Westminster; until 1947 it was entitled the **British Commonwealth of Nations**. There are now 54 member states, all but one of which were formerly part of the British Empire; their populations comprise approximately 25% of the world's population. The British monarch is still recognized as the head of the Commonwealth. **Commonwealth Day** is 12 March.

• **communications satellite** ▶ An unmanned artificial earth satellite, usually in a geostationary orbit, *i.e.* one in which the satellite completes its orbit in 24 hours and thus appears to remain stationary in the sky above the same place on the earth's surface. Three such satellites suitably placed can provide a worldwide communications link enabling television broadcasting, telephone communications, and computer data to be exchanged between any points on the earth. Radio signals from a transmitting station on earth are beamed to the satellite, which retransmits them to a receiving station out of normal ground-wave or sky-wave communication with the transmitting station. The first active communications satellite was the US Telstar, launched in 1962. There are now large numbers of these satellites serving both governments and commercial interests. *See*: Intelsat.

• **communist bloc** or **Eastern bloc** ▶ After World War II many countries in Eastern Europe became communist states under the domination of the Soviet Union. These states, which included Bulgaria, Czechoslovakia, East Germany, Hungary, Poland, and Romania, signed the Warsaw Pact in 1955. Albania was a member of the Pact from 1955 until 1968, when it left. Although Yugoslavia was usually regarded as part of the communist bloc, it was not a signatory of the Warsaw Pact and managed to maintain an independent foreign policy. In 1989 mass unrest culminated in the communist parties in Poland, Hungary, Czechoslovakia, Bulgaria, Romania, and East Germany losing power. The Soviet Communist Party fell from power and was disbanded following the abortive coup of August 1991.

• **communitarianism** ▶ A somewhat vague political concept that gained currency on both sides of the Atlantic during the 1990s. Rejecting both the economic individualism of the 1980s and the social liberalism prevalent since the 1960s, communitarian thinkers stressed the importance of community life and the responsibilities that flow from it. They placed a high value on the family and civil institutions, while taking a tough view on crime and antisocial behaviour generally. Communitarianism is known to have influenced the thinking of Tony Blair and other leading figures in the 'New' Labour Party (see: New Labour; Third Way).

• **community charge** ▶ A British local tax introduced by the Conservative government in 1989–90 to replace the domestic rating system. The community charge was a flat-rate charge on every adult in the community; as such it was described (by opponents) as a **poll tax** (from Middle English *polle*, head), like that first introduced in 1377 and periodically thereafter. The government claimed that the tax was fairer than the rates, as everyone who benefited from the amenities provided by the local authority shared the bill for providing them, rather than the whole bill being paid by property owners. Opponents argued that as everyone paid the same amount, its impact was severest on the poorer members of the community (although exemptions were made for very poor families). The unpopularity of the charge contributed to the resignation in 1990 of Margaret Thatcher as prime minister. From 1993 it was replaced by the **council tax**, a charge based on property values, with various rebates depending on occupancy.

• **community medicine** ▶ The medical specialty concerned with maintaining the health of communities. Also known in the UK as public-health medicine, it did not emerge as a distinct branch of medicine until the introduction of the National Health Service after World War II. It includes such aspects of health care as preventive medicine (immunization, birth control, health visiting, mass screening tests, etc.) and monitoring special groups of the population, notably young children and the elderly.

• **community policing** ▶ A method of maintaining law and order in which the police seek to forge links with local residents and consult with community leaders on a routine basis. In the UK many such initiatives were started in the 1980s, prompted especially by Lord Scarman's report on the 1981 Brixton riots in London. This urged the need for greater cooperation by the police with the communities they serve – particularly with Black and other ethnic groups, who felt alienated from a predominantly White police force. Advocates of community policing argued that only in this way could the police effectively detect criminals, prevent crime, and protect the public. Many constabularies appointed a community liaison officer,

charged specifically with creating formal and informal links between police and community. During the 1990s, attitudes to this approach wavered, particularly with shrinking police budgets and staff cuts. However, in many British towns and cities, police officers have been moved out of central police stations to community policing teams based in offices on housing estates or in supermarkets.

• **commuter** ▶ Someone who regularly travels to a town or city centre to work. The word became common in the UK in the 1950s but has been popular in America since the late 19th century. It is derived from 'commutation ticket', the US equivalent of a British season ticket.

• **compact disc** ▶ (CD) A small plastic disc used for recording music or other sound. A 120-mm diameter disc stores more than one hour of music. The disc is made by impressing one of its sides with the master disc, thus transferring to it a series of tiny pits of varying depth in an outward spiral. This is then coated with a layer of reflective aluminium and another layer of plastic. The disc is inserted into a CD player, in which a light beam from a low-intensity laser is alternately reflected and scattered by the pits; the light-sensor converts the varying light intensity into digital signals, which are converted by the high-fidelity amplifiers into music, speech, etc. The master disc is created by a reverse process in which the minute pits are inscribed into the plastic disc by the laser of a digital recording instrument. As nothing mechanically touches the surface of the disc during playback, it does not wear with use; also, as the pits are covered by a layer of plastic, they are unaffected by scratching the surface or by deposits of dust. These two factors ensure continued high-quality sound reproduction. *See also*: CD-I; CD-ROM; DVD.

• **Companion of Honour** ▶ (CH) A British order of chivalry instituted by George V in 1917 to honour men and women who have made conspicuous contributions to the nation. Limited to the sovereign and 65 people, it confers no title.

• **comparative advertising** ▶ An advertising technique in which a competing product is mentioned by name and compared unfavourably with the advertised item. In the UK, information of this type is referred to as **knocking copy**. *See also*: Brand X.

• **compassion fatigue** ▶ Indifference to charitable appeals, especially in response to a disaster or crisis, caused by overexposure to images of suffering and distress. Media reports of calamities in every corner of the world can leave a well-disposed person feeling numbed and helpless, making them less rather than more likely to give their time or money to charity.

• **Compiègne** ▶ The town in N France on the River Oise in which Joan of Arc was captured by the English in 1430. In the 20th century the Armistice ending World War I was signed by the Germans in a railway coach in a clearing in the forest of Compiègne on 11 November 1918. On Hitler's insistence the document acknowledging the defeat of France was signed on the same spot by the generals Huntziger (France) and Keitel (Germany) on 22 June 1940.

• **complementarity principle** ▶ *See*: quantum theory.

• **complementary medicine** ▶ *See*: alternative medicine.

• **complexity theory** ▶ A general theory of the behaviour of complex systems that are self-regulating and adaptive. The approach, developed at the Santa Fe Institute in New Mexico, is interdisciplinary, including the study of such topics as liquids, neurological networks, ecological systems, and social and economic organizations. It draws on the ideas of chaos theory.

• **comprehensivization** ▶ The replacement of a selective system of secondary education with a comprehensive system, *i.e.* one in which children of all academic abilities attend the same schools (although there may be streaming within the individual school). In the UK, comprehensive schools were introduced from the mid-1960s onwards, when they replaced the grammar schools, most of which had a high level of academic achievement, and the less academic technical and secondary modern schools. The selective system, in which entry to a grammar school depended on passing the eleven-plus, was seen by many politicians and educationalists as socially divisive and bad for the country as a whole, in that it condemned the great majority of children to a poor education. On the other hand, critics of the comprehensive system argue that the abolition of the grammar schools, in which intellectually elite pupils followed an education that suited them for university, has resulted in a general decline in academic standards, making it harder for children from poorer homes to achieve a university place.

• **computer** ▶ A device, developed from principles laid down in the 19th century by Charles Babbage (1792–1871), for storing and processing information at high speeds. Babbage's mechanical contrivance (which was never actually completed until the Science Museum built it in 1991) foreshadowed an electronic model, **ENIAC** (Electronic Numerical Integrator And Calculator), developed during World War II at the University of Pennsylvania. An enormous machine using 20,000 valves, it was designed to solve a specific problem related to high-altitude trajectories. Similar valve-based machines were subsequently built in the UK and France. However, the real computer revolution began in the 1950s and 1960s, when advances in information theory and the emergence of first the transistor and then the integrated circuit transformed computer design. The first computers were massive and expensive machines owned and run by large industrial, government, or academic institutions, but during the 1970s and 1980s, silicon-chip technology enabled extremely powerful desk-top machines (*see*: personal computer) to become available at a very moderate cost. The original ENIAC device used decimal arithmetic; however, subsequent transistor-based computers have been based on binary arithmetic in which 0 and 1 are the only digits. These are represented electronically as a closed pathway and an open pathway, respectively, the transistor thus functioning as an on-off switch. The instructions that enable a computer to function are known as its programs. In general, the programs are known as computer software, while the electronic equipment itself is its hardware.

By the 1980s computers had become so ubiquitous that they had transformed many aspects of everyday life. Records of almost every kind, from the stock of tomato soup in the local supermarket to the owner of every car on the road, are now computer-held. Many processes, from bringing down an enemy missile to typesetting a book, are computer controlled. Most calculations, from one's bank balance to the orbit of spacecraft, are performed by computers. Children are made familiar with computers at six or seven, secretaries have to be able to operate computerized word processors, and doctors write their prescriptions on desk-top computers. Together with aircraft and the car, computers are perhaps the artefacts that have made the greatest impact on human beings in the last hundred years. But like cars and aircraft, their use is not without problems. Stockbrokers, for example, can program their computers to sell securites if the price falls below a specified level. In a slump, such as occurred on Black Monday, the computers can automatically fuel the decline by selling at lower and lower prices until they are stopped by overwrought stockbrokers.

• **computer animation** ▶ The creation of moving images using computer-generated graphics. The development of computer animation has gone hand in hand with advances in computer hardware and graphics software. Computer games, in which players could pit their wits and reflexes against various computer-generated monsters appeared in the late 1970s, and quickly became a boom industry. During the late 1980s and 1990s computer graphics reached new levels of sophistication, with ever more realistic pictures and high-quality sound effects. Computers were also harnessed to make animated films and create hitherto undreamt-of special effects for feature films (*see*: morphing).

There are several different ways of using a computer to make an animated film. The simplest is for the artist to create a series of images, each in a slightly different position, using graphics software; these are then played back in sequence from the computer's memory. A more sophisticated approach, employing special animation software, was used to make *Toy Story* (1995), the first feature-length film generated entirely by computer. The outlines and potential movements of the characters are specified by the animator, and the computer then generates three-dimensional models. For each scene, the animator specifies certain key poses, and the computer fills in the character's motion between these. Instructions are then given for the computer to 'shade' the models with appropriate surface colours and textures, and each scene is 'lit' to provide contrast, shadow, and other effects that would occur with normal stage lighting. All this information is then drawn together in a process called 'rendering', in which the computer draws the final image of the character. These rendered images are then transferred to film by laser scanning.

**• computer crime** ▶ Illegal activity involving computers, especially the practice of gaining access to a computer and modifying the data or program in order to transfer money for personal gain. This crime is also called **computer fraud**. Other illegal activities connected with computers include breaching computer security (*see*: hacker) or destroying data (*see*: computer virus; Trojan horse).

**• computer dating** ▶ Matchmaking using computers. Subscribers to a computer-dating agency send in details of their personal characteristics, interests, likes and dislikes, etc., which are stored in a computer and electronically matched with those of other subscribers in order to select a number of potentially suitable partners. Since the late 1960s many companies offering this type of introduction service have been set up across the world.

**• computer games** ▶ Games in which a player

or players interact with a computer, using a mouse, joystick, games pad, etc., to manipulate and respond to the images displayed on the screen. Computer games first became popular in the late 1970s, when they were generally known as **video games** and played on special machines in arcades or pubs; the first such game to capture the public imagination was Space Invaders. As ownership of personal computers grew in the 1980s, computer games became a popular form of home entertainment, being supplied on disks, CD-ROMs, games cartridges, etc. During the 1990s the games themselves gradually became more sophisticated and interesting as computer animation developed; they now range from simple hack-and-slash war games to cerebral problem-solving and simulation exercises. A notable landmark was the introduction of Sony's **PlaySta-tion** games console in 1994, the wide popularity of which is credited with dispelling the image of the typical games player as an adolescent anorak. Some 90 million original PlayStations have been sold since 1994, while the state-of-the-art *PlayStation 2* has sold 25 million since March 2000. Cult computer games of recent years include Pokemon, the *Tomb Raider* series featuring Lara Croft, and *The Sims*, in which players control the 'lives' of a computer-generated family; the last-named became the best-selling game of all time in early 2002. *See also*: interactive fiction; virtual reality.

**• computer model** ▶ A theoretical mathematical description of a complicated system used with a computer in investigating and forecasting behaviour in economics, meteorology, etc.

**• computer virus** or **electronic virus** ▶ A class of pernicious computer program designed to interfere with the operation of computer systems. Although differing in detail, all viruses share two characteristics. Once installed on a system they can lie dormant, undetected by the user, until triggered by a predetermined combination of circumstances – for example, a virus might be so triggered to become operative when the computer is switched on when the date is Friday 13th. Their effects, once triggered, range from the trivial (*e.g.* printing a message on the screen) to the disastrous (*e.g.* destroying the data held on the computer's hard disks). Their second characteristic is that, while dormant, they can replicate and run themselves on other computers via networks or 'infected' disks – hence the analogy with viruses. Computer viruses appeared in the late 1980s; so far, they have mostly been practical jokes and not especially harmful, but the potential for a major disaster clearly exists. As with real viruses, measures can be taken to prevent infection (*e.g.* only buying floppy disks from reputable sources) and, once a new type of virus has been detected, classified, and analysed, an antidote can be developed – an ever more complex task as the authors of the viruses become more devious. Computer viruses have such unlikely names as 'Jerusalem B', 'Pakistani', and 'Stoned'. *See also*: logic bomb; Trojan horse.

**• concentration camp ▸** A prison in which large numbers of people are held without trial, usually because of their politics or ethnicity. The term originated during the second Boer War (1899–1902), when the British held thousands of Afrikaners in such camps.

In Germany, the rise of the Nazis from 1933 was accompanied by the establishment of concentration camps to imprison socialists and communists and later such minorities as homosexuals, gypsies, Roman Catholics, and Jews. German camps at Dachau, Belsen, Ravensbrück, and Buchenwald were augmented by the camps at Auschwitz and Treblinka in German-occupied Poland during World War II. The cruelty of the guards, the use of slave labour, the extreme malnutrition, and the medical experiments on living prisoners have made the German concentration camps the most notorious establishments in world history. The conversion of some of them into extermination camps in which over 20 million prisoners died of disease, starvation, or deliberate murder (including 6 million Jews; *see*: holocaust) has left an ineradicable stain on German history.

**• conceptual art ▸** Art as idea rather than artefact. The term covers a variety of genres that developed in the 1960s, including minimal art (*see*: minimalism), performance art, body art, and earth art. The dadaist Marcel Duchamp (1887–1968) was the major influence on the movement, which insists that the ideas or concepts of the artist are more important than the artefacts used to convey them – which are often deliberately banal or insignificant. Conceptual art developed partly as a reaction to the marketing of artworks as commodities; ironically, works by leading conceptual artists now command very high prices.

**• concert party ▸** *See*: fan club.

**• concert pitch ▸** The pitch, internationally agreed in 1939, in which A has a pitch of 440 hertz, to which musical instruments are usually tuned. Hence figuratively **to screw oneself up to concert pitch** is to make oneself absolutely ready, prepared for anything one may have to do.

**• conchie ▸** *See*: conscientious objector.

**• Concorde ▸** The first and only supersonic airliner to be used in regular service; it is the fastest passenger aircraft in the world. Developed at considerable cost by an Anglo-French consortium consisting of Aérospatiale and the British Aircraft Corporation during the 1960s, it made its maiden flight in 1969 and entered commercial service in 1976. It cruises at Mach 2 (twice the speed of sound), carries 100–139 passengers, and can reach Paris from New York in three and a half hours flying at a height of 18,000 m. Unfortunately Concorde's impeccable safety record suffered a disastrous blow when an Air France Concorde crashed moments after take-off from Charles de Gaulle Airport, Paris, on 25 July 2000, hitting a hotel in the nearby village of Gonesse; the death toll was 115. Thereafter all Concordes in service with Air France and British Airways were grounded until late 2001. The first supersonic airliner to fly was the Soviet Tupolev Tu-144, in 1968 (often known in the West as **Concordski**). This aircraft, however, has not been in regular service since its crash at the Paris Air Show in 1973.

**• concrete jungle ▸** A tough inner-city area in which the only effective law is that of the jungle. The concrete jungle is seen as the natural habitat of pimps and prostitutes, warring gangs, and muggers seeking the wherewithal to pay for their drug habits. Since the 1960s, when the term came in, such areas have often been dominated by high-rise concrete edifices that provide a particularly unacceptable environment in which to live and bring up children. **Asphalt jungle**, an older term with much the same meaning, dates from the 1920s.

> The city is not a concrete jungle, it is a human zoo. – DESMOND MORRIS: *The Human Zoo* (1969).

**• concrete music ▸** (French *musique concrète*) A form of music in which natural or man-made sounds are recorded on tape and subsequently edited to create a composition of 'concrete' (real-life) sounds, as opposed to the 'abstract' sounds made by musical instruments. It was introduced in 1948 by the French sound technician Pierre Schaeffer (1910–95).

**• concrete poetry ▸** Poetry in which words, word elements, and individual letters are set down in patterns and shapes rather than in conventional linear arrangement, the meaning of the poem being conveyed by its visual form rather than semantically.

**• condo ▸** In America, short for 'condominium' – a block of apartments in which individuals own the separate apartments and share the upkeep of the common areas. The individual apartments are also known as 'condos'.

• **condom** ▶ A sheath-like contraceptive made from thin rubber and fitted over the penis during sexual intercourse. The condom, thought to be named after Colonel Condom, a British Guards officer, who was anxious to protect his men from venereal disease, has been in use since the early 18th century. The popularity of the condom as a standard contraceptive device declined in the 1960s with the widespread availability of the contraceptive Pill for women. However, as the undesirable side-effects of the Pill became better understood, the popularity of the condom increased in the 1980s. At the same time it was realized that barrier contraceptives provide some protection against the spread of Aids by sexual intercourse as well as against other sexually transmitted diseases. The British government therefore embarked upon an advertising programme to promote the use of condoms, especially in casual sex, as a means of controlling the spread of Aids. Increased use of the condom has led to many new nicknames for the device. To 'French letter', 'rubber', 'Johnny bag', and 'Wellie' may now be added 'American sock'.

• **condom fatigue** ▶ A weariness of hearing about condoms and their role in limiting the spread of Aids. The phrase, modelled on compassion fatigue, was sometimes used to explain the reluctance of people to change their mode of contraception (or lack of it), despite the massive publicity given to condoms and Aids in the late 1980s.

• **Confucius, he say** ▶ A 1920s catchphrase used to introduce a witty piece of advice or social comment; this was generally given in broken English, as if inadequately translated from the *Analects*, a collection of sayings and conversations attributed to the pre-Christian Chinese philosopher Confucius (c. 551–479 BC). For example: 'Confucius, he say man speaking to God, he praying; God speaking to man, he nuts.' This way of presenting a joke was popular in the 1920s and 1930s on both sides of the Atlantic; it now has a period feel to it, although it is still used.

• **connection** ▶ Slang for a drug dealer or pusher. It originated in US drug-users' jargon of the 1950s and 1960s but is now widely used in Britain, especially of heroin dealers. It was heard by a wider audience in the 1970s when the films *The French Connection I* and *II* came out.

• **connectionism** ▶ An approach to the theory of the brain, especially memory, based on the idea that information is stored by processing units consisting of extended sets of connected neurones (neural nets). It was developed in the 1980s; analogous ideas have been used in computer science. *See*: artificial intelligence.

• **conscience investment** ▶ *See*: ethical investment.

• **conscientious objector** ▶ One who takes advantage of a conscience clause in an act of parliament and so evades some particular requirement of the law in question. Once specially applied to those who had a conscientious objection to vaccination, since World War I it has come to mean one who obtains exemption from military service on grounds of conscience. Such people were also called **CO**s or **conchies**.

• **consciousness raising** ▶ (CR) The process of developing self-awareness, political awareness, social awareness, and other forms of 'awareness', often by such means as encounter groups. Consciousness-raising groups in which women were encouraged to see their personal problems in the light of feminist theory were a staple of the women's movement in the 1970s and 1980s (*see*: feminism).

• **conservation area** ▶ An area of natural, historic, or architectural interest that has been so designated under the terms of the Civic Amenities Act (1967). Once designated a conservation area, planning control is imposed on any major changes in the area, such as tree-felling, demolition of buildings, etc. In some cases government grants and loans are available to help to preserve the amenities provided by the conservation area.

• **Conservative Party** ▶ The main party of the right in the UK. Based on the legacy of such statesmen as Burke, Peel, and Disraeli, it has generally championed evolutionary rather than revolutionary change: reform where necessary, but always within the existing framework of the state and society. This makes it attractive not only to those content with the existing order but also to those suspicious of the more radical policies of its political opponents (until the 1920s the Liberal Party, thereafter the Labour Party). It is a feature of the modern Conservative Party that it has always enjoyed considerable working-class support. Often the party has vigorously opposed certain measures, only to accept them once enacted; the People's Budget (1909), the curtailment of the power of the House of Lords (1911), Irish Home Rule (1886–1922), and the welfare state (1945–51) are the principal examples in the last hundred years. At the beginning of the 20th century, the party was dominated by the landowners (including the aristocracy), whose overriding interest was the maintenance of the social and political hierarchy at home and the Empire's supremacy abroad. As the Liberal Party declined after World War I, many of its supporters, faced with the alternative of Labour's prescriptive egalitarianism, moved to the Conservatives, thus injecting into it such principles characteristic of 19th-century liberalism as personal freedom, equality of opportunity, and the merits of capitalism and free enterprise. At the end of World War II, the Conservatives were convincingly rejected by the British electorate. A new mood swept the country after the sacrifices of six years of war: the have-nots now demanded a fairer share of the country's wealth and the idealists of the Labour Party gave it to them in the form of the welfare state. As so often in the past, the Conservatives survived by adaptation; a combination of Butskellism and shrewd self-interested pragmatism enabled them to alternate with Labour in forming the governments of the 1950s, 60s, and 70s. The adaptation involved a marked change in the Conservative Party itself. The Old Etonian leaders Harold Macmillan and Alec Douglas-Home were succeeded by Heath, Thatcher, and Major – politicians educated at state schools. Under Thatcher the Conservatives enjoyed a long period in power largely by attracting the support of the new classless class of Middle Englanders who had become alienated from Labour and its cloth-cap values. By the mid-1980s it could be said that the Conservative Party had changed from a party of estate owners to one of estate agents. During the same period the party broke with the post-war consensus to embrace a radical new agenda of monetarism, privatization, and welfare reform. The party has so far failed to adjust to the hijacking of much of this agenda by New Labour, devastating electoral defeats in 1997 and 2001, and its own deep divisions on the European issue.

• **Conservative Party at prayer** ▸ A somewhat outdated description of the Church of England. The phrase comes from a speech by the Congregationalist minister Agnes Maude Royden (1887–1967), who said in 1917:

> The Church should no longer be satisfied to represent only the Conservative Party at prayer.

The traditional links between the Tory Party and the established Church weakened in the decades after World War II and can be said to have fallen away completely during the Thatcherite 1980s, when relations between the government and Church leaders became acrimonious.

• **constructivism** ▸ A Russian art movement founded between 1917 and 1920 by sculptors Vladimir Tatlin, Antoine Pevsner, and Naum Gabo. Their works, constructed from such modern materials as plastic, steel, and glass, were 'engineered' as a celebration of machinery and technology, as explained in Gabo's *Realist Manifesto* (1920). The name 'constructivist' is derived from this aspect of their work. Although proscribed under Stalin, the constructivists' functionalist and utilitarian creed spread to Europe and America, particularly influencing the Bauhaus movement in Germany and the de Stijl movement in Holland.

• **consumerism** ▸ The protection and promotion of the consumer's interests. The term was first coined in the 1940s in America and became much used from the mid-1960s with increasing public demand for safety, quality, and choice in consumer goods. In America, the movement was also known as Naderism, after its most vociferous leader, Ralph Nader (*see*: Naderite). By the early 1970s the issue of consumers' rights had become firmly established in many European countries, including the UK.

Since the 1960s the theory advocating the economic desirability of a high rate of consumption of goods and services has also been called consumerism; in this sense the word has come to be used pejoratively for a preoccupation with the acquisition of consumer goods.

• **Consumers' Association** ▸ The name by which the British Association for Consumer Research is widely known. The association, which is a registered charity, is independent of any business or company, thus allowing it the freedom to praise or criticize goods and services without bias. It publishes a monthly periodical, *Which?*, carrying detailed reports of tests on various goods and services, often indicating a 'best buy'.

• **consumer terrorism** ▸ The practice, first so-named in the 1980s, of introducing poison or other dangerous substances into consumer products, typically into foodstuffs on supermarket shelves. It is sometimes done for purely malicious reasons but often involves extortion of money from the food manufacturers. For example, in 1989, following the discovery of two jars of baby food containing broken glass, Heinz destroyed 50 million jars of food rather than give in to a blackmail demand. Similar demands were made at the time to pet-food manufacturers. The practice led to the introduction by some companies of so-called **tamper-proof** containers, which have an indicator on the lids that shows whether the container has been opened.

• **contact lens** ▸ A type of lens worn directly over the eye to correct long or short sight and astigmatism, and to provide protection in some disorders of the cornea. The first glass contact lenses were made by Adolf Fick in 1887, but the great discomfort these caused made them unpopular. Modern contact lenses, developed by Kevin Tuohy in 1948, are made of plastic and are shaped to fit the eyeball. These plastic lenses can be hard (corneal), gas-permeable (allowing oxygen to permeate the cornea), or soft (hydrophilic). They are widely used by those who prefer not to wear spectacles, for cosmetic reasons.

• **contact magazine** ▶ A publication in which those wishing to find partners for sexual activities can advertise.

• **continuity girl** or **man** ▶ The person who ensures that every detail of costume, scenery, etc., is correctly repeated in successive shots of a film. Ever since the job was created in the 1910s it has been mainly performed by women. As scenes are not necessarily shot in sequence, maintaining continuity is not always a simple matter. Sometimes, inevitably, errors occur. In *The King and I* (1956) Yul Brynner's ear-ring comes and goes in successive shots. In *Genevieve* (1953) Kenneth More's pint of beer becomes a half as he walks to his table. In *The Adventures of Robin Hood* (1938) Errol Flynn takes a bite from a whole leg of mutton; in the next shot he is holding only the bone. In *The Desk Set* (1957) a bunch of flowers held by Katharine Hepburn turns from white to pink in successive shots. In *Anatomy of a Murder* (1959) Lee Remick magically changes out of a dress into slacks as she leaves a café, while in one of the most celebrated of all British films, *Brief Encounter* (1945), Celia Johnson manages to remain completely dry after running through a downpour.

• **Contra** ▶ (Latin *contra*, against) Right-wing Nicaraguan guerrillas opposed to the socialist regime established by the Sandinista National Liberation Front after 1979. Based in Honduras and Costa Rica, the Contras organized a series of guerrilla attacks aimed at overthrowing the government of Daniel Ortega. President Reagan, who accused the Sandinistas of aiding rebels attempting to overthrow the government of El Salvador, was widely censured for his active support of the Contras, especially in the so-called Irangate affair. The Contras disbanded after the Sandinistas were voted out of office in 1990.

• **contraception** ▶ *See*: birth control.

• **contract** ▶ An agreement to pay money to have someone killed. Formerly restricted to the US underworld, it has subsequently become familiar on both sides of the Atlantic through the influence of books and films, particularly in such phrases as 'put out a contract on someone'.

• **contract marriage** ▶ A marriage in which the partners agree to stay together for a certain period, possibly with an option to renew the contract at the end of the period.

• **contraflow** ▶ A much-disliked and sometimes hazardous system used on motorways or other main roads when one carriageway is under repair. The remaining carriageway has to be used by two-way traffic, with vehicles travelling in opposite directions being separated by traffic cones.

• **contrail** ▶ *Con*densation *trail*. A vapour trail left by a high-flying aircraft, which is caused by the condensation of water vapour from the products of combustion in the aircraft's exhaust. If the temperature is sufficiently low the water vapour freezes into tiny ice crystals.

• **control freak** ▶ Someone who is overly concerned with controlling their personal or professional life, to the extent that friends and colleagues feel they are being manipulated or constrained. As most people feel they know someone like this, the term has been widely adopted and has even spawned a noun, **control freakery**.

> The Labour left has always complained that he [Tony Blair] is a control freak because he was determined to ensure that they never got anywhere near control of his party again. – *The Independent*, 23 August 1999.

• **conurbation** ▶ A large densely populated area formed by the growth and merger of adjacent towns and cities. As human populations grew, the prehistoric village developed into the town; by the middle ages, cities had appeared. The conurbation is the culmination of this process, in which uncontrolled ribbon development along the roads between a large city and its satellite towns and villages swallows up the intervening countryside. In 1770 Lambs Conduit Fields were fields on the outskirts of London; fifty years later these had been engulfed and Islington Fields, some three miles N, represented the edge of the city. Now, the old towns of Watford in the NW and Orpington in the SE (some 30 miles apart) have all been swallowed by the conurbation.

• **convenience food** ▶ Pre-packed or pre-cooked food, such as frozen or cook-chill dishes, which can be ready for eating with the minimum of preparation.

• **cook** ▶ **1.** To play jazz in an inspired way; a US Black term originating in the 1930s, used in such phrases as 'the band were really cooking'. **2.** To prepare heroin for injection by dissolving it in a spoon over a flame.

• **cook-chill** ▶ A method of catering, usually for

the mass market, in which food is cooked, fast-chilled, and later reheated before consumption. The advantages are obvious from the point of view of large institutions, such as schools, hospitals, and airlines, but some food experts are concerned that the cook-chill method of catering can lead to the spread of diseases and disorders, such as listeriosis (*see:* listeria), unless exceptional care is taken with the hygiene, temperature control, and duration of shelf-life.

• **cool** ► 1. Unflappable, unruffled by events, as in the phrase **stay cool**, meaning to keep calm. **To keep one's cool** has the same meaning; **to lose one's cool** is to become angry or emotional. **Cool it!** is an injunction to relax or calm down. **Cool out** or **chill out** is contemporary slang meaning to relax. 2. Good, marvellous, fashionable, sophisticated, stylish. This sense originated among US jazz musicians of the late 1940s, when it was used to describe a particular brand of progressive jazz (*see:* cool jazz). It became a key word in the beat culture of the 1950s and that of the hippies of the 1960s and 1970s, summing up the coolly detached attitude to life that they espoused. Unlike most other words from this era, it remains a key term of approval among today's teenagers.

> If it was ever 'cool' to support this Government, it certainly isn't any more. – WILLIAM HAGUE, quoted in *The Times*, 11 October 2000.

• **Cool Britannia** ► A phrase apparently coined by John Major but later appropriated by Tony Blair's Labour government; it refers to Britain's emergence as a hotbed of contemporary culture with the rise of a new generation of fashionable designers, pop groups, magazines, restaurants, and nightspots in the 1990s. Blair's use of the slogan during his first months in office was widely seen as an attempt to 'rebrand' Britain in the same way that New Labour had rebranded the Labour Party. Ministers were apparently worried that Britain's image abroad remained dominated by images of royalty, beefeaters, and BBC costume dramas, giving the impression of a hidebound backward-looking society rather than one characterized by its dynamism and innovation. The Cool Britannia campaign was a way for the government to promote Britain's important 'creative industries' while also burnishing its own image as new, fashionable, and 'cool'. Accordingly the stuffy-sounding Ministry for National Heritage became, under Labour, the Ministry for Culture, Media and Sport. Despite some media scorn, the slogan initially struck a chord, perhaps because it appealed both to national pride and to the widespread desire for a fresh start after 18 years of Conservative government.

Cool Britannia reached its height when, not long after his election victory, Blair hosted a glittering party at 10 Downing Street, attended mainly by personalities from the media, entertainment, and sports worlds. However, a backlash set in almost immediately, with cultural conservatives attacking the prime minister for shallow populism and the more rebellious type of rock star making it clear that they regarded Blair and his government as the very antithesis of 'cool'. The arts establishment also fell out of love with New Labour very quickly when they realized that hoped-for increases in arts funding would not be forthcoming. By 1998 'Cool Britannia' had become a mild embarrassment and the phrase was quietly dropped from government communications.

> Tony Blair's marketing of cool Britannia hasn't worked. Educated young people overseas still see the British as stuffy traditionalists, who are racially intolerant and refuse to embrace the modern world. – *The Independent*, 10 November 2000.

• **cool jazz** ► A style of jazz that originated in the late 1940s on the West Coast of America. Restrained and rhythmically relaxed, it was a reaction to the more frenetic bebop style fashionable in New York. The term reflects contemporary use of the word 'cool' to mean sophisticated or elegant in an effortless way.

• **Coordinated Universal Time** ► (UTC) *See:* Greenwich Mean Time.

• **Copenhagen interpretation** ► *See:* quantum theory.

• **copycat murder** ► A murder in which many of the details of the crime resemble those of another widely publicized recent murder. With members of the public requiring the media to give macabre details of every murder committed, it is not entirely surprising that a murderous thought should occasionally be converted into reality by some unbalanced person who has read such an account. The term is also used of killings that were allegedly inspired by acts of violence shown in films or on television. A less well-known phenomenon is **copycat suicide**, in which a well publicized and often gruesome method of killing oneself sparks off a series of further deaths by similar means.

• **Cordobes, El** ► (Spanish, man from Cordoba) The professional name of the Spanish bullfighter Manuel Benitéz Pérez (c. 1936– ). At the height of his fame in the 1960s, 'El Cordobés' was the highest paid bullfighter in history and was idolized by the Spanish people. Famous for his daring and his rapid reflexes, he broke records for the number of bulls killed in the ring. He retired in 1972 but made a comeback seven years later.

• **Corfu incident** ▸ In 1923 Italian forces under Mussolini bombarded and held Corfu in retaliation for the murder by Greek soldiers of an Italian delegation sent to define the Greek-Albanian border. Under pressure from Britain and France, the League of Nations managed to restore Corfu to the Greeks.

• **Corgi and Bess** ▸ A nickname used in broadcasting circles for the Christmas message to the British nation made by Queen Elizabeth II. The annual event is broadcast on both radio and television with the televised version usually featuring one or more of the royal household's Welsh corgi dogs. The name is a pun on Gershwin's opera *Porgy and Bess* (1935).

• **Cornish pasties** ▸ British pejorative slang of the 1980s for a style of shoes (particularly men's shoes) that are wide, solid, and sensible with heavy-duty stitching and thick soles; the shoes are so-called because they resemble the meat and vegetable pies. They are often worn by green enthusiasts or other 'alternative' types.

• **Cornwell Badge** ▸ A badge awarded to Boy Scouts for an act of bravery or sustained brave conduct, for example in overcoming a physical handicap. It is given in honour of J. T. Cornwell, a 15-year-old boy in the Royal Navy who won the VC for outstanding bravery at the Battle of Jutland (1916). He died of his wounds one year after the battle.

• **Coronation Street** ▸ A British television serial produced by Granada Television. Possibly the longest-running TV drama serial in the world, it was first broadcast on 9 December 1960; by December 2000, when the show celebrated its 40th anniversary, 4945 episodes had been broadcast. It deals with the lives of people living in a terraced street in a working-class area of Manchester. Many scenes are set in the local pub, the Rovers Return, and the corner shop. Over the decades such larger-than-life characters as Ena Sharples, Stan and Hilda Ogden, and Ken Barlow have become part of British folklore. Unlike its rivals EastEnders and Brookside, *Coronation Street* continues to present a somewhat old-fashioned picture of a tightly knit working-class community in which traditional values of neighbourliness usually prevail. *See also*: Archers, The.

• **corporate advertising** ▸ Advertising that aims to publicize not only a particular product but also the company or conglomerate that manufactures it. A company may use such advertising to project a desirable **corporate image** of itself –

reflecting, for example, its concern for the environment. Today, many companies are much preoccupied with the whole notion of **corporate identity**, and may spend vast amounts of money redesigning their logos, vehicle liveries, notepaper, etc., to create the desired public image.

• **corporate anorexia** ▸ A sickness that can befall companies as an unwelcome side effect of downsizing and outsourcing; it is the business equivalent of anorexia nervosa. When a company decides that it can or must cut costs by pruning its human resources (downsizing) and buying in some of the goods or services it formerly provided itself (outsourcing), there is a risk that its ability to create new products or expand production to meet market needs may be permanently endangered.

• **corporate raider** ▸ *See*: raider.

• **correctional facility** ▸ A US euphemism for a prison, first recommended in the 1970 report of a committee reviewing the US prison system. The prison guard became a **correctional officer**.

• **Corregidor** ▸ An island at the entrance to Manila Bay, Luzon, in the Philippines. Because of their strategic positions, Corregidor and Bataan were chosen by the American general, Douglas MacArthur, as the main defensive positions after the Japanese invasion of the Philippines in December 1941. After the fall of Bataan, on 9 April 1942, US and Philippino forces held out for 27 days on Corregidor under constant aerial and artillery bombardment, finally capitulating on 6 May. In March 1942, General MacArthur had left Corregidor with the pledge 'I shall return'. This pledge was redeemed when the island was recaptured by US forces in 1945. The island was designated a national shrine in 1954 and is the site of the Pacific War Memorial. The Malinta Tunnel, which served as hospital, shelter, and General MacArthur's headquarters, still survives.

• **corridors of power** ▸ Collectively, the ministries in Whitehall and their top-ranking civil servants. The phrase was first used by C. P. Snow in his novel *Homecomings* (1956) and gained speedy acceptance. He used it as the title of a later novel, *Corridors of Power* (1964).

> Boffins at Daggers Drawn in Corridors of Power. – *The Times*, headline, 8 April 1965.

• **Cosa Nostra** ▸ *See*: Mafia.

• **cosmic string** ▸ A theoretical one-dimensional warp, in the space-time continuum, of vast length and mass but of sub-microscopic thickness. Scientists have suggested that such warps are residues from the period during which the universe was in its infancy. The theory has been postulated that galaxies form when cosmic strings form themselves into loops.

• **cosmodog** ► A dog sent into space for experimental purposes. In March 1966 two Soviet cosmodogs, Veterok and Ugolyok, were rocketed into orbit in Cosmos 110; after 22 days they were brought back safely to earth.

• **cosmonaut** ► (Greek *kosmos*, universe; Latin *nauta*, sailor) The Russian name for an astronaut. The first manned spaceflight was made by Major Yuri Gagarin of the Soviet Union in 1961. He landed safely after orbiting the earth in 89 minutes.

• **Costa** ► (Spanish and Italian, coast) With the advent of cheap air travel and the growing affluence of the UK's working population, foreign travel has become increasingly common. Factory workers, who before the war were lucky to manage a few days in digs at damp and rather dreary British seaside towns, have since flooded to sunny Mediterranean coastal resorts, where large hotels have sprung up to accommodate them. Favourable rates of exchange with Spain encouraged resorts there to specialize in providing traditional English fare and entertainments, to ensure that the gastronomically cautious British will feel at home. The main Spanish resorts are situated on areas of coastline, which have been given these names:

**Costa Brava** The Mediterranean coast between France and Barcelona, including such resorts as Tossa del Mar, Blanes, and Palamos.

**Costa Dorada** The Mediterranean coast between Barcelona and Valencia, including Tarragona and Sagunto.

**Costa Blanca** The Mediterranean coast between Valencia and Alecante, including Javea, Denia, and Benidorm.

**Costa del Sol** The Mediterranean coast between Gibraltar and Malaga, including Marbella, Fuengirola, and Torremalinos.

**Costa de la Luz** The Atlantic coast between Gibraltar and Portugal in the Gulf of Cadiz.

The word 'costa' is also used facetiously in English. For example, the S coast of England is sometimes called the **costa geriatrica**, because so many elderly people retire there. The Costa del Sol is also known as the **costa del crime**, as many British criminals who have escaped capture live there, exploiting loopholes in extradition arrangements.

• **cost-push** ► *See*: inflation.

• **cot death** ► *See*: sudden infant death syndrome.

• **cottage** ► Male homosexual slang for a public lavatory, current in Britain since the 1950s. Public lavatories were a typical pick-up place for gay men before the anti-homosexual laws were relaxed in 1967. The practice of cruising such places for casual sexual partners, which is still some people's idea of a good time, is known as cottaging.

> There are those people who would like to see public lavatories as cosy as cottages so they can loiter with new friends. – *The Independent*, 3 November 1990.

• **Cottingley fairies** ► The 'fairies' photographed by the young cousins Elsie and Frances Wright as they played in their garden in Cottingley, near Bradford. The photographs, which show nymph-like figures dancing around the girls, caused a sensation when they were published in 1920. Among those who declared their faith in the photographs was Sir Arthur Conan Doyle, who had become increasingly interested in spiritualism since the death of his son in World War I; opposition came from an equally convinced band, including the writers Edgar Wallace and J. E. Wheelwright.

Doyle died still believing in the fairies; only in the 1980s, when the book from which the figures of the 'fairies' had been cut was identified, did the surviving sister confess to the fabrication.

• **Cotton Club** ► The jazz club in Harlem, New York, which became the world's most famous venue for hot music in the 1920s. Among the many bands that played there perhaps the best-known was that of Duke Ellington. The inspired music and the glamorous (and sometimes notorious) clientele have assured the club a permanent place in the history of jazz.

• **couch potato** ► US slang of the late 1970s for a lazy greedy person, whose favourite occupation is to slump in front of the TV all day eating and drinking. The expression is now used in most English-speaking countries.

• **Couéism** ► A form of psychotherapy, dependent upon auto-suggestion, propagated by Emile Coué (1857–1926), a French pharmacist. The key phrase of his system was: 'Every day, and in every way, I am getting better and better.'

• **coughs and sneezes spread diseases** ► A slogan dating from the early part of World War II, used in a campaign by the Ministry of Health to restrict the number of days lost by war workers as a result of minor ailments. Large amounts of money were spent to persuade the public not to sneeze on one another, especially in buses, tubes, and air-raid shelters. The associated injunction was 'trap the germs in your handkerchiefs'.

• **council house** ► A house owned by a local town

or district council, which is rented out, unfurnished, at a lower rent than it would command in the private sector. Council houses are much in demand and a waiting list exists for suitable and deserving tenants. Suitability is usually assessed by a points system. Controversially, the Conservative governments of the 1980s and 1990s sold many council houses to their tenants, thus reducing the total stock of such dwellings.

• **Council of Europe** ► A body constituted in 1949 to secure a greater measure of unity between W European countries, the member states being the UK, France, Italy, Belgium, the Netherlands, Sweden, Denmark, Norway, the Republic of Ireland, Luxembourg, Greece, Turkey, Iceland, Germany, Austria, Cyprus, Switzerland, Malta, Portugal, Spain, and Liechtenstein. The Council consists of a Consultative Assembly, a Committee of foreign ministers, a Parliamentary Assembly (with members from national parliaments), and a European Commission investigating violations of human rights. It was founded at Strasbourg, where it still has its headquarters.

• **council tax** ► *See*: community charge.

• **countdown** ► The exact timing of the start of a crucial operation by counting backwards from a given number to zero. Curiously, the countdown was invented by the German film director Fritz Lang for a rocket-launching scene in his science-fiction film *Frau im Mond* (The Woman in the Moon; 1929); after World War II it was used routinely in America in timing the launch of rockets and other missiles and – still later – in the US space programme.

• **counterculture** ► A culture with beliefs, values, and mores that are at variance with those of established society. The word, which became current in the late 1960s with the advent of the hippie movement, is applied to both a way of life that rejects the social norms and the people who adhere to it. Some aspects of the hippie counterculture, such as concern for the environment and liberal sexual attitudes, have since become part of mainstream Western thinking. *See*: alternative.

• **counter-intuitive** ► Describing an idea, theory, proposal, etc., that seems unreasonable or paradoxical; literally, it goes against the speaker's intuition. It is bureaucratic jargon, originating in the US Pentagon, for something that seems to go against all common sense but may yet be true or necessary.

• **country** ►
**Your Country Needs You** A British re-cruiting slogan of World War I, appearing as the caption to a famous poster showing the then war secretary, Lord Kitchener of Khartoum (1850–1916), pointing at the reader (*see*: Kitchener's army). The powerful image was much copied elsewhere; in America a similar poster showed Uncle Sam pointing and saying 'I want *you* for the US army'. The caption became a catchphrase and exhortation to anyone who had a difficult or dangerous job to do for the public good. Despite the success of the recruiting campaign, Kitchener lost power in the early stages of the war, and time has not been kind to his reputation. Nevertheless, in the words of Margot Asquith:

> If Kitchener was not a great man, he was, at least, a great poster.

• **country-and-western** ► A form of US music based on White folk styles of the rural South and West, deriving ultimately from the musical traditions of British and Irish settlers. The first commercial recordings of Southern string-band music were made in the 1920s but the term 'country-and-western' did not appear until the 1960s, by which time some Western cowboy songs had been incorporated. Although it embraces many regional styles, country-and-western is now most widely associated with sentimental, often mournful, ballads accompanied by electronically amplified string instruments, particularly guitars, banjos, and fiddles. Typical themes are love, divorce, and separation by distance from loved ones. The centre for country music is Nashville, Tennessee.

• **County Hall** ► A large building on the S bank of the Thames by Westminster Bridge in London, designed by Ralph Knott for the London County Council and opened in 1933, although it was not completed until 1963. It then became the home of the GLC. When the GLC was abolished in 1986 the building became empty. In the 1990s ownership of a part of it passed to a Japanese consortium; this part is now occupied by a Marriott Hotel, an aquarium, and an art gallery. Other parts of the building were bought by Frogmore Estates and converted to residential apartments and some offices.

• **Coupon Election** ► The general election of 1918, when the prime minister Lloyd George and chancellor of the exchequer Bonar Law sent a certificate or coupon to all candidates who supported the continuation of the wartime coalition. The coupon scheme was an attempt to capitalize on Lloyd George's reputation as a war leader, it being calculated that any candidate who could produce this sign of the prime minister's endorsement would achieve favour with the electorate. The coupon was rejected by those Liberals who had resigned with Asquith in 1916 and by the Labour Party. As expected, the polls saw a decisive victory for those who accepted the coupon (known as **couponeers**).

• **Courtauld Institute of Art** ▶ A gallery and college for the study of art donated to London University in 1931 by Samuel Courtauld (1876–1947), the great-nephew of the founder of the chemical manufacturing firm of that name. It was originally housed in his mansion in Portman Square, together with his collection of impressionist paintings. The collection, which has been augmented by several bequests, moved in 1958 to Woburn Square, and in 1990 to the west wing of Somerset House, which was formerly occupied by the General Register Office of births, marriages, and deaths.

• **Covent Garden** ▶ *See*: Royal Opera; Royal Ballet.

• **cover one's ass** ▶ US slang meaning to concoct an excuse or alibi in advance in order to avoid taking the blame for something. The phrase originated in the 1960s among US troops in the Vietnam War and later became part of general US slang; it became current in the UK in the 1980s.

• **covert action** or **covert operation** ▶ Secret and usually illegal activities by the police or the intelligence forces. *See also*: Cointelpro.

• **cowabunga** ▶ An Australian interjection expressing triumph or elation; originally a surfer's cry when riding a wave. The introduction of Australian soap operas to British television in the 1980s and the subsequent enthusiasm for the Australian lifestyle led to its adoption by the youth culture in the UK. It also became well-known as a catchphrase of the Teenage Mutant Ninja Turtles.

> Cowabunga! Wanna get wised up on those big green guys who live in the sewers? Check out Sarah Edghill's awesome turtle guide and you'll be the coolest dude on the block! – *TV Times*, 17–23 November 1990.

• **cowboy** ▶ 1. 1950s slang for a wild and irresponsible young man. This usage reflects the image of the Western cowboy hero as well as the 1930s gangster's use of the word to mean undercover or illegal. 2. British slang for a bad workman, someone who does a slapdash or botched-up job, as in the phrase **a cowboy builder**.

> A sign on the side of a builder's van read: Patel and Patel; Builders and Contractors – You've tried the cowboys, now give the Indians a chance.

• **cowhorns** ▶ British slang for the high curved handlebars on a chopper motorcycle or bicycle. A synonym for apehangers.

• **coyote** ▶ US slang of the 1970s and 1980s for an unscrupulous person who robs, or even kills, illegal immigrants who cross the border from Mexico into North America.

• **Crabb Affair** ▶ The disappearance in 1956 of Commander Lionel 'Buster' Crabb, a frogman with the Royal Navy, while exploring the underside of the Soviet cruiser *Ordjonikidze* in Portsmouth harbour. The cruiser was in Portsmouth having brought the Soviet leaders Bulganin and Khrushchev to England for an official visit. When the news of Crabb's disappearance broke, the British government denied any involvement, claiming that he had acted independently for motives unknown. However, reporters from *The Times* discovered that the hotel in which Crabb had stayed while working in Portsmouth had been visited by senior detectives, on the orders of the chief constable, where they had removed all record of Crabb's stay and told the staff not to discuss the matter. There was never any satisfactory explanation for the incident. Speculators suggested that Crabb had defected to the Soviet Union, drowned by accident, or been killed by British agents when it was realized that British interest in the visiting ships might prove embarrassing.

> It would not be in the public interest to disclose the circumstances in which Commander Crabb is presumed to have met his death. – ANTHONY EDEN, May 1956, in reply to repeated Opposition questions about the incident.

• **crack** ▶ 1. Slang for a purified and highly addictive form of cocaine. The name probably reflects the crackling and fizzing noise the substance makes as it burns. A **crack house** is an establishment in which crack is made or smoked. *See also*: angel dust. 2. Irish and now British slang for lively informal entertainment, a good time. Sometimes spelt in the Irish form **craic**. 3. British and Irish slang for what's happening now, the action, the news, as in the phrase **What's the crack?**

• **crackback** ▶ In American football, a block made at knee level, usually by a pass receiver blocking a defensive back from the blind side. It is a legal play, but often causes knee injuries.

• **cracker-barrel** ▶ US slang meaning unsophisticated, rustic: used in such phrases as **cracker-barrel philosophy** or **philosopher**. It derives from the habit of people in rural areas or small towns of gathering around the cracker barrel (biscuit barrel) in the general store to exchange news and gossip, philosophize, etc.

• **Cracker Night** ▶ Australian slang, originally for Empire Day (24 May), which was celebrated with fireworks (crackers) and bonfires, but later for Commonwealth Day and the Queen's birthday. However, owing to restrictions on the use of fireworks Cracker Night is now largely ignored.

• **Cranwell** ▶ A village in Lincolnshire in which the Royal Air Force College (founded 1919) is situated. Cranwell bears roughly the same relationship to the RAF as Sandhurst does to the Army and Dartmouth to the Navy.

• **crash** ▶ 1. Also **crash out**. A slang expression meaning to sleep. This was a very popular hippie expression of the 1960s and 1970s, probably because smoking cannabis can induce sleep. Originally, it was World War II forces slang. A **crash pad** is a place to sleep overnight. 2. To come down suddenly from a 'high'. 3. Short for **gatecrash**, that is to arrive uninvited at a party. This has been a popular form of entertainment with young people since the 1960s. 4. A sudden drastic failure of a computer system, usually resulting in the loss of data; also used in this sense as a verb.

• **Crawfie** ▶ Nickname for Marion Crawford, the governess of Queen Elizabeth and Princess Margaret when they were girls. Her sentimental article 'The Little Princesses', published in the magazine *Woman's Own*, was regarded by the Palace as an indiscretion and she subsequently fell from favour.

• **Crazy Gang** ▶ A group of British music-hall comedians. Their comedy and variety act, which involved mixing with the audience and riotous impromptu routines, was highly successful. The Gang comprised three pairs of comedians: Bud Flanagan (1896–1968) and Chesney Allen (1894–1982), famous for their many songs, including 'Underneath the Arches'; Jimmy Nervo (1890–1975) and Teddy Knox (1896–1974); and Charlie Naughton (1887–1976) and Jimmy Gold (1886–1967). The Crazy Gang first appeared on the stage of the London Palladium in 1932 and starred there almost continuously until 1940. After the war Chesney Allen retired, and the Gang re-formed at the Victoria Palace in 1947, with 'Monsewer' Eddie Gray (1897–1969) in his place; they finally disbanded in 1962.

• **crazy mixed-up kid** ▶ A US phrase sometimes applied to young people growing up in the aftermath of World War II. Whether owing to the traumas of that war, the sudden prospect of nuclear annihilation, or other factors altogether, members of this generation seemed to suffer disproportionately from mild psychological problems and behavioural disorders. The archetypal 'crazy mixed-up kid' is perhaps Jim Stark, the character played by James Dean in *Rebel Without a Cause* (1955).

• **cream-crackered** ▶ Rhyming slang for knackered, exhausted. A similar expression is **cattle-trucked**.

• **creative accounting** ▶ A facetious expression indicating that balance sheets or profit and loss accounts have been intentionally compiled in such a way that, without actually being fabrications, they fail to give a true indication of the state of the business concerned.

• **creative evolution** ▶ The theory propounded by Henri Bergson (1901) in his book *L'Évolution créatrice* that a life force (élan vital) is constantly urging man to accelerate his evolution, rather than to wait for what G. B. Shaw (a disciple) called the 'chapter of accidents' that brings about change in the form of natural selection, as set out in Darwin's theory. Modern biologists do not accept this concept.

• **creature-feature** ▶ A mildly derogatory insult used in the school playground. It derives from the film-business term creature-feature, meaning a horror film involving monsters.

• **cred** ▶ Short for street credibility.

• **credibility gap** ▶ A discrepancy between what is claimed or stated, especially by those in authority, and the evident facts of the case. The phrase is sometimes attributed to the future US president Gerald Ford, who used it in 1966 to refer to Lyndon Johnson's denials of deepening US involvement in the Vietnam War.

• **credit** ▶ Polonius's injunction 'neither a borrower nor lender be' (*Hamlet*, I, iii) has not been taken very seriously in the affluent countries of the West since the end of World War II. Credit is, in fact, the financial basis of much of this affluence. To buy a house, a young couple in the UK obtains credit from a building society, in which the house itself is the surety for the loan and a proportion of the couple's combined incomes is pledged to pay the interest and repayments for the next 25 years. If they have a car, it is likely that it, too, has been purchased on credit terms, i.e. a relatively small down payment and several years of pledged repayments. When the car is finally paid for it may well be virtually valueless. The furniture in the house, the television set, the cooker, and many other items that cost over £200 or so will also often have been purchased on credit. The current philosophy is that one should enjoy the trappings of affluence while one is young. It may be a great comfort to be able to buy a washing machine for cash in one's forties, but most families need one most when the children are small – and then it can only be afforded by borrowing.

This reversal of 19th-century frugality, which was based on the belief that one should only buy what one can pay for, has been encouraged by banks and credit companies for whom the credit boom has provided an enormously lucrative market. Losses that arise when borrowers fail to make repayments are offset partly by repossession of the purchased items and partly by the large profits made on the satisfactory repayers. While many have benefited by being borrowers, easy credit has been a considerable source of distress to others, especially those whose houses are repossessed by building societies when they are made redundant and are unable to finance their mortgages.

• **credit card**▸ A plastic magnetized card usually issued free to creditworthy customers, representing the holder's right to credit from a particular finance company, bank, shop, etc. (with the amount of credit extended being dependent on the individual's credit rating). Their use became widespread in the 1970s and 1980s, and they are now indispensable for certain transactions, such as ordering goods by telephone or Internet, theatre bookings, and airline reservations. They can also be used to withdraw money from automatic cash dispensing machines. Some banks, however, charge an annual fee to their cardholders, and retailers are sometimes authorized to offer discounts to cash-paying customers. *See also*: PIN.

• **credit rating**▸ The creditworthiness of an individual or company. Traditionally, banks have provided trade references in confidence but recently **credit reference agencies** have appeared, collecting information from such sources as bankruptcy proceedings, debt collectors, hire-purchase companies, etc., which they sell to anyone interested for a fee.

• **creep-up call**▸ A house call by a tradesman, deliveryman, etc. who deliberately fails to make his presence obvious to the householder. For example, they may knock only very softly, then leave a note to say they have called but received no reply. In this way they can claim to have covered their quota of calls without having done the work.

• **crew**▸ **1.** British slang for a gang of aggressive youths, such as skinheads or football hooligans, used since the 1960s by such youths themselves. **2.** US slang of the 1980s for a group of young people, used primarily of musicians, rappers, dancers, etc.

• **crew cut**▸ A form of haircut popularized by US athletes, particularly college rowing teams, in the decade following World War II. The hair is cut very short all over and brushed upright on top, rather

like a hedgehog. In the 1950s and 1960s the crew cut came to stand for a certain kind of clean-cut social conformism.

• **cricket test**▸ A notional test of an immigrant's loyalty to the UK suggested by the Tory cabinet minister Norman Tebbit in April 1990. He claimed that this could be gauged by the side such a person chose to support in a test match between England and his or her country of origin. His remarks were widely condemned as ridiculous and offensive.

• **crinklie**▸ *See*: wrinklie.

• **Crippen murder**▸ The murder of Mrs Crippen (Belle Elmor) by her husband Dr Hawley Harvey ('Peter') Crippen in 1910. Mrs Crippen was poisoned by means of hyoscine hydrobromide, after which her dismembered and filleted corpse was buried beneath the cellar of the family home in Holloway, North London. Crippen and his mistress, Ethel Le Neve, fled the country with Miss Le Neve disguising herself as a boy in the care of her uncle, 'Mr Robinson'. By a circuitous route they boarded the cargo ship *Montrose*, which was bound for Canada. However the captain of the ship suspected them of being Crippen and Le Neve and after a series of dramatic wireless messages from ship to shore and a chase across the Atlantic by Scotland Yard detectives, Crippen was arrested when the ship docked in Canada. Crippen is remembered for being the first person to be arrested by means of wireless telegraphy.

• **Cripps mission**▸ A mission to India in 1942, led by Sir Stafford Cripps (1889–1952), on behalf of Churchill's wartime coalition government. Threatened by Japanese invasion, India was offered complete independence with dominion status after the war in exchange for immediate cooperation in resisting Japan. Gandhi described the offer as 'a postdated cheque on a failing bank'; the offer was turned down by the Indian Congress Party and Gandhi and other Congress leaders were imprisoned until 1944, when they were released to discuss independence and partition.

• **Croft, Lara**▸ Digital heroine of the best-selling series of computer games *Tomb Raider*, the first of which went on sale in 1996. The success of the games established Eidos Interactive, the London-based outfit who created them, as Britain's first billion-pound computer-games company and, in 1999, the World Economic Forum's 'Most Successful Company'.

These spoils can be largely attributed to the popularity of Lara – an acrobatic gun-toting hot-pants-clad adventuress who negotiates hair-raising booby-traps while fighting off wild animals, robot assassins, and other deadly adversaries. By the late 1990s her image was everywhere – in magazine features, in comic strips and advertisements, and in shops stocking a plethora of merchandise for her seemingly insatiable fans. As a result she became the first character from the games world to be recognized by the public at large and a key figure in the gradual entry of computer games into the mainstream culture.

Although the technology may be new, the source of Lara's appeal seems to be anything but. Her popularity clearly owes little to her (nonexistent) personality and everything to her vital statistics – this unlikely action woman boasts breasts of surreal dimensions coupled with the diminutive waist and arms of a child. Unsurprisingly, the models who have played the part of Lara for marketing purposes have all proved inadequate to this male fantasy and so are continually replaced. The film of *Tomb Raider* released in 2001 starred Hollywood beauty Angelina Jolie. With her fondness for powerful motorbikes and arsenal of deadly weapons, some have claimed Lara as an icon of assertive contemporary womanhood. Others, however, argue that she is little more than the usual macho hero of computer games with the added element of sex to appeal to the main players of such games – teenage boys.

• **Croix de Guerre ▶** (French, cross of war) A French military decoration, instigated in 1915 for gallantry in battle. The different grades correspond to the level of the dispatch that records the courageous act for which it is awarded. A warship receiving the Croix may fly an appropriate pennant. During World War II several Croix were awarded: in 1939 (by the French government), in 1941 (by Pétain's Vichy government), and in 1943 (by Giraud's Fighting French in North Africa). In 1944, the French National Committee of Liberation declared that only the 1939 Croix was valid.

• **cronyism ▶** The tendency to give jobs, positions, or favours to one's friends, rather than to others who may be no less qualified and deserving. Although hardly a new concept in politics, it has come to the fore in recent years as a result of the Opposition's claims that Tony Blair's administration is particularly prone to it. 'Tony's Cronies', as the media call them, stand accused of undermining the principles of meritocracy and public service.

• **crooning ▶** A sentimental type of singing, which became popular in the early 1930s. The singing was very soft, 'somewhere near the written notes, but preferably never actually on those notes' (Eric Blom), and depended largely on electrical amplification.

• **crop circles ▶** Large circular or oval depressions of unknown origin that appear overnight in fields containing crops. There were over 100 sightings in the period 1988–90, when public interest was at its height, mostly in S England; similar phenomena have been reported in Japan, Italy, France, Canada, Brazil, Australia, and America. Suggested explanations range from UFO landings to stampeding hedgehogs. In 1992 two men in their sixties received much publicity when they claimed to have created most of the British circles as a deliberate hoax. The explanation favoured by most scientists is that the depressions are the result of air vortices.

• **crossbusing ▶** *See*: busing.

• **Cross of Lorraine ▶** The two-barred patriarchal and archiepiscopal cross, which was adopted as the emblem of the Fighting French during World War II because it had been the emblem of Joan of Arc.

• **Crouchback, Guy ▶** The divorced Roman Catholic hero of Evelyn Waugh's World War II trilogy *Sword of Honour*, comprising *Men at Arms* (1952), *Officers and Gentlemen* (1955), and *Unconditional Surrender* (1961). Both an observer and a participant in the dramatic events of the war and the matrimonial affairs of his friends, he epitomizes the patriot and gentleman that Waugh aspired to be.

• **crown-of-thorns ▶** A spiny starfish, *Acanthaster planci*, that has spread throughout the South Pacific since the mid-20th century because of the destruction of its natural predator, the Pacific triton, by shell collectors. Feeding on coral, the crown-of-thorns at one time threatened widespread destruction of coral reefs.

• **crucial ▶** Slang for excellent. Originating in Jamaican slang, it was popularized in the UK (1980s) by the comedian Lenny Henry, through his TV character Delbert Wilkins, who used the word incessantly.

• **crud ▶ 1.** Dirt, filth, or rubbish; specifically, an unwanted residue or impurity arising from a process (as in a nuclear reactor). The word has its origins in the 14th century as a variant of curds (the residue that forms on top of curdled milk); its present sense developed after World War II. **2.** A despicable person.

• **Cruella De Vil ▶** Arch-villainess of Dodie Smith's children's book *The Hundred and One Dalmatians* (1956), whose name has become a byword for glamorous ruthlessness. Although scary enough in the book, the Cruella everyone sees in their mind's eye is the terrifying witch-like figure in Disney's film version (1961). This Cruella – the creation of animator Marc Davis, who also drew the defenceless Bambi – cuts an awe-inspiring figure with her bizarre black and white hair, flaring cheekbones, extended talon-like nails, and enormous fur coat. In both book and film Cruella's plan is to murder our four-legged heroes in order to supplement her already flourishing collection of coats with one made of dalmatian pelt.

Arguably, Disney's Cruella is so potent because she offers a chic up-to-date version of one of the oldest archetypes of popular mythology – that of the evil dominant woman or Great Bitch. In more recent years many powerful women have found themselves compared to or nicknamed Cruella – most notably, perhaps, Edwina Currie, the former minister for health, who also suffered from an unfortunate slight resemblance.

I might never have known that my younger daughter regards me as South London's answer to Cruella De Vil. – *The Guardian*, 2 June 1999.

• **Cruelty, Theatre of** ▶ *See*: Theatre of Cruelty.

• **Cruise missile** ▶ A low-flying winged missile carrying a conventional or nuclear warhead and driven by an air-breathing turbofan; it has a speed of some 885 mph. Such missiles are guided by an inertial system that is updated during flight by matching the contours of the land they overfly with the contour maps stored in their computer memories. They fly so low that they are difficult to detect by radar and therefore to destroy. *See also*: Greenham Common; zero option.

• **cruising** ▶ Seeking a sexual partner in bars, etc., especially by a homosexual.

• **crumblie** or **crumbly** ▶ *See*: wrinklie.

• **crunchie** ▶ *See*: lipstick.

• **crusty** ▶ In the UK, a young person who wears filthy ragged clothes, lives by begging or off welfare benefits, and sits around in town centres drinking cheap alcohol; many also sport dreadlocks and a mangy dog on a piece of string. The term dates from the early 1990s. Crusties are also known as **swampies**, **cider punks**, and (in rural areas) **hedge punks**.

• **cry all the way to the bank** ▶ An originally US catchphrase popular in the 1950s. It is an ironic comment on someone, such as an entertainer, who has been savaged by the arbiters of taste or morality but remains hugely popular with the paying public. The phrase was popularized by the US pianist Liberace, who may have invented it. Another version is **laugh all the way to the bank**.

• **Cry Guy** ▶ *See*: Prince of Wails.

• **cryonics** ▶ The practice of freezing a corpse in the hope of being able to bring it back to life at a future time. The idea of freezing a human body until medical science develops a cure for the disease causing the death became quite popular in the late 1960s. In America, the practice has been carried out several times (the best-known case being that of Walt Disney, who died in 1966). The word comes from Greek *kruos*, cold, plus *-onics*, as in electronics.

• **cryptozoology** ▶ The study of creatures whose existence has not been scientifically proved. Cryptozoology is concerned with such phenomena as the Loch Ness Monster in Scotland, the Yeti in the Himalayas (*see*: Abominable Snowman), and the Sasquatch (*see*: Bigfoot) in Canada.

• **CSE** ▶ Certificate of Secondary Education. A former school examination taken at the age of about 16. It was introduced in 1965 as an alternative to the GCE O-level examination for pupils who were less academically inclined. Both examinations were replaced by the GCSE in 1988.

• **CS gas** ▶ An extremely effective irritant gas (2-chlorobenzalmalononitrile) developed at the British government's chemical-weapon laboratory at Porton Down in the 1950s but first manufactured in the 1920s in America; it takes its name from the initials of the surnames of its US inventors, Ben Carson and Roger Staughton. It is now used for emergency crowd control. Dispersed in the form of smoke, CS gas causes gripping chest pains, streaming eyes and nose, salivation, coughing, and retching. These effects are instantaneous, although they are not lethal and do not persist.

• **CT scanner** ▶ Computerized tomography scanner. A type of body scanner that enables images of different planes of the body to be recorded, using low doses of X-rays. It is used for the diagnosis of tumours and other abnormalities affecting the soft tissues of the body. The device is also known by its original name, **CAT scanner** (computerized axial tomography scanner), but this is misleading as it implies – incorrectly – that images can be obtained only in the axial plane of the body.

• **Cuban missile crisis** ▶ The crisis that occurred in October 1962, when America reacted furiously to the installation of Soviet nuclear rockets in Cuba; for 13 days the world trembled on the brink of nuclear war. President Kennedy finally compelled Khrushchev, by means of a naval quarantine of Soviet shipments to Cuba, to remove the rockets. Why the Soviets should have taken the drastic step of placing rockets in Cuba after repeated US warnings that such an act would not be tolerated is still a matter of some controversy. The determination to match America in nuclear weaponry that helped to bankrupt the Soviet Union's economy dates from this crisis.

> We're eyeball to eyeball and I think the other fellow just blinked. – DEAN RUSK, US secretary of state, on hearing that the Soviet ships had 'stopped dead in the water'.

> They talk about who won and who lost. Human reason won. Mankind won. – N. S. KHRUSHCHEV after the crisis.

• **cubism ▶** An early 20th-century style of painting that began as an experiment in representing three-dimensional reality on a flat canvas without using traditional illusionist techniques. The solution devised by Pablo Picasso (1881–1973) and Georges Braque (1882–1963), who jointly invented the style, was to analyse three-dimensional structures into a series of geometrical planes reflecting multiple simultaneous viewpoints. This early period (1907–12) of so-called **analytical cubism** was succeeded by one of **synthetic cubism**, in which a concern for pictorial composition became more important than the physical analysis of reality. The historical importance of the style is that it represented the first decisive break with ideas of perspective dominant since the Renaissance, and the most important catalyst in the subsequent development of abstract art. The name cubism was coined (somewhat disparagingly) by Henri Matisse in 1908.

• **cubist-realism ▶** A US form of cubism founded in about 1915 by Charles Demuth and Charles Sheeler. The movement embraced a less radical form of cubism, treating recognizably US themes.

• **cubscouts ▶** See: Boy Scouts.

• **cuisine minceur ▶** See: nouvelle cuisine.

• **Culebra Cut ▶** See: Panama Canal.

• **Cullinan diamond ▶** The largest known diamond, named after the chairman of the Premier Mine, Johannesburg, where it was found in 1905. Its uncut weight was 3025 carats (about 75g or 1lb 6oz). It was presented to King Edward VII by the South African government and was cut into a number of stones (the largest weighing some 516 carats), which now form part of the Crown Jewels.

• **cultural cringe ▶** An expression coined by the Australian writer Arthur Phillips in the early 1950s to denote his compatriots' habit of disparaging their own culture and venerating that of other countries (especially the UK). From the 1970s, however, beginning with the world acclaim for the Sydney Opera House (1973), Australians have been active

and confident in promoting their own culture. The skill and verve with which they hosted the 2000 Olympic Games in Sydney also did much to dispose of the view that Australians inhabit a backwater.

• **Cultural Revolution ▶** The 'Great Proletarian Cultural Revolution' took place in China from 1966 under the direction of Mao Tse-tung. Intended to invigorate revolutionary fervour and to avoid stagnation and revisionism, it involved replacing leaders of the old guard, abolishing the formal education system (many universities were closed), and mobilizing students as Red Guards. For several years, there was social and political turmoil in which millions of urban 'bourgeois reactionaries' were sent to the country to be 're-educated' by manual labour. Although the reign of terror abated somewhat from 1969, the policies of the Cultural Revolution remained in place until Mao's death in 1976.

• **culture ▶**
> **When I hear the word culture, I reach for my revolver** A remark often attributed to the German Nazi politician Herman Goering (1893–1946). The quotation is in fact from a work by the German novelist and dramatist Hanns Johst:

> Whenever I hear the word 'culture'...I reach for my gun. – Schlageter.

• **culture shock ▶** The unpleasant feelings of alienation, rejection, and withdrawal experienced by people when first confronted by cultures, customs, or tastes that are markedly different from their own. The phrase became common in the mid-20th century; originally used only in an anthropological or sociological context, to describe the impact of a primitive culture on those from a more advanced one (and vice versa), it is now used in a much more general sense for the effect of anything unfamiliar (music, art, etc.) on those unprepared to accept it.

• **culture vulture ▶** A person who is excessively and indiscriminately interested in the arts. The phrase originated in the mid-20th century; **culture hound** and **culture-monger** are variants.

• **Cuppie ▶** A devotee of yacht racing, especially one whose main interest is in the social aspects of the sport. Since yacht racing tends to be associated with the wealthy classes, the word is often used derogatorily. It achieved popularity when the disputed outcome of the 1987 America's Cup Race led to much media publicity for the sport (a court decision eventually deprived Australia of the trophy and awarded it to America). The word Cuppie is clearly modelled on yuppie.

• **Curly Top ▶** A 1935 film featuring the US child

star Shirley Temple (1928– ), who was herself known by this nickname. The six-year-old starlet, with tight blonde curls and an angelic smile, won her way into the hearts of mothers throughout the world, each one of whom saw in their own young daughter a reflection of this winning little tap-dancing monster. Curly Top herself was left with few childish illusions:

> I stopped believing in Santa Claus at an early age. Mother took me to see him in a department store and he asked me for my autograph.

With the passage of time, Shirley Temple ceased to be either a child or a star – a situation she coped with resourcefully. As Mrs Shirley Temple Black she served as the US ambassador to Ghana (1974–76) and Czechoslovakia (1984–92). *See also*: One-Take.

• **Curragh mutiny** ▶ A threat, in March 1914, by British cavalry officers stationed at The Curragh (a military training camp in County Kildare) to resign if they were called upon to coerce Ulster into accepting Home Rule. This threat hardly constituted a mutiny; in fact, the real threat to Asquith's government lay with Sir Edward Carson and Bonar Law, who had said that they would lead the Unionists in armed resistance to Home Rule (*see*: Ulster Volunteers). Although Asquith was alarmed by the reaction of the cavalry officers, the problems of an imminent world war were more pressing.

• **curse of Tutankhamun** ▶ A legend arising from the death of the 5th Earl of Carnarvon (1866–1923) during the excavations at Tutankhamun's tomb, which started in 1922. He died from pneumonia after contracting an infection from a mosquito bite but Sir Arthur Conan Doyle, a convinced spiritualist, suggested that his fate might be attributed to elementals created by the priests of Tutankhamun. Coincidentally there was a power failure at Cairo when Carnarvon died and his dog in England expired at the same time. Some years later Carnarvon's associate, Howard Carter (1874–1939), died at the precise moment that one of the ancient trumpets found in the tomb was being blown for the first (and only) time since Tutankhamun's death. However, the English security guard who was detailed to sleep in the tomb every night for three years after it was opened always denied that there was a curse, claiming that the newspapers had invented the story of an inscription foretelling doom to grave robbers; he himself survived into his eighties.

• **Curzon line** ▶ The demarcation line between Poland and the former Soviet Union, first proposed by the British foreign secretary Lord Curzon (1859–1925) in 1920, during the Russo-Polish war.

Poland rejected the plan because they would lose 52,000 square miles of land. However, the Soviets maintained their claim and occupied the whole of Poland during World War II. At the Yalta Conference in 1945 the Curzon line was finally recognized as the Soviet-Polish border; some minor frontier adjustments were made in 1951. It now forms Poland's boundary with Belarus and Ukraine. *See also*: Oder-Neisse line.

• **cushy** ▶ Slang for easy or comfortable: applied to jobs, positions, etc. Anglo-Indian in origin, the word derives from the Hindi *khush*, pleasant; it became part of military slang in World War I, in which context it was also used to describe trivial wounds. In World War II, a cushy job was one that did not involve danger, or too much hard work.

• **customer** ▶
   **the customer is always right** A phrase introduced into the retail trade in the 1930s by H. Gordon Selfridge (1856–1947), who came to the UK from America to start up the large department store that still bears his name. Mr Selfridge was to be seen in his store every day, up to the start of World War II – a familiar figure in silk hat and morning suit, with a flower in his buttonhole. A great salesman, he instructed his staff never to argue with or be disrespectful to his customers. Whatever the true rights and wrongs of the situation, it was to be assumed that the customer was always right.

• **cut** ▶ 1. To adulterate illegal drugs with another substance to increase the weight and thereby make more profit on the sale. 2. US euphemism for kill.

• **cut a rug** ▶ *See*: rugcutting.

• **Cuthbert** ▶ A name coined by 'Poy', the cartoonist of the *Evening News*, during World War I for the fit men of military age, especially those in government offices, who were not called up for military service or who positively avoided it. These civilians were depicted as frightened-looking rabbits.

• **cut off at the pass** ▶ To stop something at an early stage; to intercept. The phrase comes from US Western films in which a sheriff in pursuit of the baddies would often instruct his posse to 'cut them off at the pass'. It was used in 1973 by President Richard Nixon on the Watergate tapes, when he said that maybe the charge of obstruction of justice (a problem worrying his Special Counsel, John Dean) could be cut off at the pass.

• **cut-offs** or **cutaways** ▶ Long shorts made by cutting off blue jeans at the knee.

• **cutting contest** or **carving contest ▶** A friendly contest between two or more jazz musicians playing the same piece of music, in which each takes it in turn to play an improvised solo break to demonstrate their technical virtuosity and musical inventiveness. The winner of the contest is the one that gains the most vociferous reaction from the audience.

• **cyber- ▶** A prefix indicating computers and the Internet. It first appeared in English in **cybernetics**, a word coined in 1948 to mean the science of automatic control systems, from the Greek *kubernētēs*, steersman. The rapid growth of computer technology and the Internet has been accompanied by an uncontrollable proliferation of 'cyber-' words. Just a few of the better known include **cybereconomy** (the economy based on trading over the Internet), **cybercafé** (a place where people can access the Internet while taking refreshment), **cybernaut** (a person who surfs the Internet or who uses sensory devices to experience virtual reality), and **cybersex** (any kind of sexual stimulation using computer technology or the Internet).

• **cybercash ▶** Any form of currency that can be recognized by a computer and used to pay for goods and services in an electronic transaction (*see*: e-commerce; e-shopping). Cybercash, or **e-cash**, is intended to avoid the need for payment by conventional cash, cheque, or credit card, all of which are either time-consuming or pose security risks. Various systems have been devised and tested in pilot form, but none has yet to gain wide acceptance. For purchases made via the Internet, participants typically need to install an electronic wallet and account-management software on all computers involved in the transactions. The cybercash changes hands electronically and instantaneously. Ultimately, all transactions are settled through the participants' credit or bank account. Mobile phones are now being developed that will connect directly to bank accounts via the Internet, and even directly to tills using radio waves. Another source of cybercash is the so-called smart card.

• **cyberphobia ▶** Fear of computers. Although young people who have grown up with computers have no fear or hostile feelings towards them, some older people feel threatened by something that they do not understand. For these people cyberphobia is a real experience.

• **cyberpunk ▶** A subgenre of science fiction that explores the underbelly of modern technological culture. Typically, a cyberpunk film or novel will depict a nightmare future world whose population is oppressed by a dominating 'system' (governmental, corporate, or religious) that relies heavily on technology (especially computer technology) to sustain its regime. The technology frequently involves the convergence of humans and machines (in genetically engineered organs, electronic brain implants, etc.). The story's protagonists are generally loners living on the fringes of society who learn how to subvert the regime's technological tools to achieve its downfall.

Although the origins of the word 'cyberpunk' are unclear, Bruce Bethke used it as the title of a short story in 1982 and Gardner Dozois, an editor at Isaac Asimov's *Science Fiction Magazine*, applied it to an emerging school of writing soon afterwards. The quintessential cyberpunk novel is usually held to be *Neuromancer* (1984) by William Gibson (1948– ), a tale of rebellious computer hackers that won the Hugo Award (1984), the Nebula Award (1984), and the Philip K. Dick Memorial Award (1985) – making it the only book ever to have received all three top science-fiction awards. Popular works in other media have included television's *Max Headroom* (1987) and *Wild Palms* (1992) and Ridley Scott's film *Blade Runner* (1982), which has become a cult classic. During the 1980s and 1990s cyberpunk found a keen following among the computer-literate and politically disaffected generation soon to be defined as Generation X, whose world view it helped to define. Arguably, however, the technology once only imagined has become part of our daily reality so quickly that we are *all* cyberpunks now; as Gibson himself once put it, 'The future has arrived; it's just not evenly distributed.'

• **cyberspace ▶** A word invented by the US science-fiction writer William Gibson (1948– ) in 1982 and developed more fully in his 1984 novel *Neuromancer*. In popular use it has come to mean the artificial environment created by the world's interconnected computer networks, or more simply, the Internet. However, this is a pale shadow of Gibson's original concept, in which he envisaged computer-generated sensations being delivered directly into the brains of billions of human beings, producing a ubiquitous virtual landscape which they experience as reality (*see*: virtual reality).

• **cyclamates ▶** *See*: Delaney amendment.

# D

• **DA** ► **1.** British slang abbreviation for **duck's arse**, a man's hairstyle in which the hair is combed straight back and greased into a curl at the back of the neck – hence the resemblance to the rear end of a duck. It was very popular with the teddy boys of the 1950s. **2.** Abbreviation for drug addict; it has been used by drug users themselves since the late 1960s.

• **dabs** ► British criminal and police jargon for fingerprints. It has been used since the 1930s and is derived from the process of taking fingerprints, which involves pressing (dabbing) the fingers one by one onto an ink pad and then onto paper.

• **Dachau** ► A small town 12 miles north of Munich where the first of Nazi Germany's concentration camps was established on 10 March 1933, only weeks after Hitler came to power. The main camp was supplemented by a network of smaller satellite camps throughout S Germany and Austria, all called Dachau. Of the estimated 260,000 prisoners who passed through the Dachau system, 32,000 died through overwork, malnutrition, and disease, or as the result of medical experiments; many more were sent to die in extermination camps, such as Auschwitz. Dachau was the camp in which the most extensive programme of medical experiments on living prisoners was conducted, examining the effects of variations in atmospheric pressure, untried anti-malarial drugs, freezing, drinking seawater, starvation, and dehydration. After the war those doctors and scientists responsible were tried in the 'Doctors' Trial' at the Nuremberg Trials, seven of the offenders being sentenced to death. *See also*: holocaust.

• **dad** ►
**Be like dad, keep mum** A slogan originated by the British Ministry of Information in 1941, exhorting people not to talk (keep mum) about matters of national security in wartime. A similar slogan was **careless talk costs lives**. *See also*: Keep it dark; Keep it under your hat *at* hat.

• **dadaism** ► An anarchic and iconoclastic art movement that began in Zürich in 1916, arising from the despair felt by so many artists and intel-

lectuals in the aftermath of World War I. Its supporters sought to free themselves from all artistic conventions and what they considered to be cultural shams. Dadaism was influenced by cubism and futurism and after about 1922 it was succeeded by surrealism. The name Dadaism was derived from *dada*, the French word for a hobby-horse; it was selected by Tristan Tzara (1896–1963) after opening a dictionary at random. Jean Arp (1887–1966) and Max Ernst (1891–1976) were among the other leading dadaists. There was a similar movement in New York at the same time associated with Marcel Duchamp (1887–1968), Francis Picabia (1879–1953), and Man Ray (1890–1976). Although dada had no coherent style or ideology, one consistent theme was a suspicion of the traditional art-object; visitors to a dada exhibition in Cologne were actually invited to smash up the paintings on display. A plaque, showing a human navel, was unveiled at Zürich in February 1966, to commemorate the 50th anniversary of the movement.

• **Dad and Dave** ► Two figures constituting a tradition in Australian humour; the invention of A. H. Davis (Steele Rudd; 1868–1935), they first appeared in his humorous sketches *On Our Selection* (1899), which deal with the hard lives of the small farmers of the period. Dad and Dave have since been widely used in Australian broadcasting serials.

• **Daddy, what did you do in the Great War?** ► A slogan from a British World War I recruiting poster showing a man obviously pondering how to answer the daughter on his knee. It became a catchphrase as **What did you do in the Great War, Daddy?**, which was later (1966) used as the title of a film about World War II.

• **dad rock** ► A dismissive term for rock or pop music that is likely to appeal to one's parents. Coined by the British music press in the 1990s and regarded as the deadliest of insults, it was applied not just to older artistes, but also to younger bands (including some of those associated with the Britpop movement) who tried to recreate the sounds of the 1960s and 1970s.

• **Dad's Army** ► Colloquial name for the Home

Guard. It was also the title of a classic British television comedy series (1968–77) following the exploits of a bumbling platoon of the Home Guard in a small town in S England during World War II. The series, which won a Bafta award and was voted the Best Comedy Series in 1971, is still regularly repeated; it starred such actors as Arthur Lowe (as the pompous Capt. Mainwaring), John Le Mesurier, Clive Dunn, and Ian Lavender.

• **Daffy Duck** ▶ A Warner Brothers cartoon character, said to have been modelled on Harpo Marx. He was one of the stable of characters created for the Looney Tunes and Merrie Melodies cartoons by the Warners team of animators, which included Tex Avery, Chuck Jones, and Robert Clampett. The cantankerous Daffy's first real appearances came in *Porky's Duck Hunt* (1937) and *A Wild Hare* (1940); his spluttering speech was articulated by Mel Blanc, who was the voice behind nearly all the Looney Tunes characters, including Bugs Bunny, Elmer Fudd, and Sylvester the Cat.

• **daft** ▶
    **Ee, ain't it grand to be daft** The catchphrase used by Albert Modley (1901–79), the north country British comedian, who was known nationwide in the 1940s through the radio programme *Variety Bandbox*. In the 1930s and 1940s, the great age of the radio comedy, it was regarded as axiomatic that anything said in a north country accent was funny.

• **DAGMAR** ▶ Defining advertising goals for measured advertising results. The principle, first so-formulated in America in the 1960s, that the success or failure of an advertising campaign should be measured against objectives defined for it before it is embarked upon.

• **dagmars** ▶ Round protuberances on the front of some US cars of the 1950s. The name was inspired by Jennie Lewis, a US actress in TV comedies who was known as 'Dagmar' and noted for her own round protuberances.

• **Dáil Éireann** ▶ The lower chamber of the parliament of the Republic of Ireland. In Irish, *dáil* means assembly and *Éireann* means of Eire (the Irish Gaelic name for Ireland). There are 144 members of the Dáil, elected by proportional representation every five years. The first (illegal) Dáil was set up in 1918 when 73 of the 103 MPs elected to represent Ireland in Westminster were Sinn Féin members, who refused to take their seats in the British parliament. The Dáil became the lower chamber of the Irish parliament in 1921–22, when the Irish Free State was created.

• **dainties** ▶ US and Australian euphemism for women's underwear.

• **daisy-cutter** ▶ **1.** In cricket, a ball that fails to rise when delivered, and in tennis a service which behaves similarly. **2.** A very powerful bomb that is dropped from an aircraft and explodes when it is about six feet above the ground. It is designed to annihilate everything and everyone within a radius of about 100 yards. Daisy cutters were used on several occasions by US forces in the so-called war on terrorism in Afghanistan.

• **Dakar expedition** ▶ The abortive attempt by British and Free French forces to capture the port of Dakar, capital of French West Africa, that took place on 23 September 1940. The Vichy authorities who controlled Dakar refused to switch their allegiance, contrary to the expectation of the Free French leader, de Gaulle. The Dakar garrison fired on emissaries from the landing force and Vichy warships shelled the British vessels. The British called off the action when the scale of the opposition became apparent; de Gaulle's hopes of establishing a Free French enclave in West Africa were dashed by the expedition's failure.

• **Dakota** ▶ The British name for the US-built Douglas DC-3 twin-engine aircraft, one of the stalwarts of the early days of commercial flying. Introduced in 1935, the Dakota established a reputation for reliability and low operating costs, playing a major role in the expansion of the airline business around the world. The original version carried 21 passengers and could cruise at 192 mph. Military versions were widely used during World War II; after the war many were converted for passenger use. Nearly 11,000 Dakotas had been built when production ceased in 1946.

• **daks** ▶ Slang for trousers. Strictly speaking, Daks is a tradename for men's casual trousers manufactured by Simpsons, the former clothing store in Piccadilly, London; the name was coined (1934) by the second son, Alexander, of the proprietor Simeon Simpson, from a combination of 'dad' and 'slacks'. The word is now mainly heard in the phrase **to drop one's daks**, which became popular after it appeared (1960) as one of the catchphrases in *Barry McKenzie*, the cartoon strip created by Barry Humphries for the magazine *Private Eye*. At the end of the 1990s Simpsons closed and the store was bought by Waterstones, the bookselling chain, who opened it as the largest bookshop in the world.

• **Dalcroze Institute of Eurhythmics** ▶ *See*: eurhythmics.

• **Dalek** ▶ *See*: exterminate, exterminate.

• **Dallas ►** A US television soap opera set in Dallas, Texas, and concerned mainly with the Ewings, a large and powerful family involved in the oil business. The show ran from 1978 to 1991 and proved amazingly popular, its most memorable character being the villainous schemer J. R. Ewing (Larry Hagman), a Man You Love To Hate. Audiences reached a peak in 1980, when 'J.R.' was shot – as it turned out, by his sister-in-law who was pregnant with his child (see: Who shot J.R.? at J.R.). The incident proved so popular that the producers decided to have J.R. shot again when the show's viewing figures started to decline. The ludicrous plotting reached its nadir in the 1985–86 season, when Bobby Ewing (Patrick Duffy), who had been killed off some time before, returned to the show; the whole of the previous season was now explained as 'just a dream'. With its larger-than-life characters, materialistic values, and over-the-top fashions (immense shoulder pads for the women), the show now seems a curious relic of its era.

• **dallymoney ►** A US name for money ordered by a court to be paid to a former sexual partner by the other partner when it has been proved that he or she gave assurances of long-term affection and fidelity that were not fulfilled. The word is formed from the combination of 'dalliance' and 'money' on the model of alimony (money paid by a spouse to a separated wife or husband) and palimony (money paid to an unmarried partner).

• **Dalton budget leak ►** The incident as a result of which the British Labour chancellor of the exchequer, Hugh Dalton (1887–1962), was obliged to resign. Shortly before presenting his budget to the House of Commons on 13 November 1947, Dalton gave certain details of the budget to a lobby correspondent of The Star, one of London's evening papers. The paper was able to run a 'Stop Press' announcement of taxation changes before the House had been informed by the chancellor. This grave breach of protocol left Dalton with no option but to tender his resignation to the prime minister, Clement Attlee. Dalton returned to the cabinet in 1948, as chancellor of the Duchy of Lancaster.

• **Dalton Plan ►** A system of US high-school education developed by Helen Parkhurst (1887–1959) and named after the school in Parkhurst's birthplace, Dalton, Massachusetts, in which a pilot scheme was introduced in 1920. Influenced by the Montessori method, the Parkhurst system is based on learning 'contracts' in which pupils work on a particular topic for periods varying from one week to one month, organizing their own time and consulting books and teachers as necessary. The tradi-tional classroom becomes a workshop, with the teacher in a supervisory role. Dalton schools were subsequently established in many European countries, as well as Japan and China.

• **Daltons ►** The nickname, coined by the London Stock Exchange, for an issue of undated 2% Treasury stock, authorized by Hugh Dalton in 1947, when he was Labour chancellor of the exchequer. The value of the stock dived shortly after issue due to loss of stock-market confidence in the government's financial strategy. See also: Dalton budget leak.

• **Dambusters ►** The nickname of 617 Squadron of the RAF. On the night of 17 May 1943, the squadron, led by Wing-Commander Guy Gibson, attacked and destroyed the Mohne dam in the Ruhr valley and the Eder dam in the Eder valley, both highly important strategic targets in the German industrial heartland. The pilots flew low over the reservoirs behind the dams and dropped specially designed bombs at a precalculated height and distance. The so-called 'bouncing bombs' skimmed along the surface and exploded underwater at the base of the dam. The raid caused severe damage and high civilian casualties. The bombs were designed by the British aeronautical engineer Sir Barnes Wallis (1887–1979). In 1954 a popular account of the episode, and the scientific saga leading up to it, appeared in the film The Dam Busters, in which Michael Redgrave played the part of Barnes Wallis and Richard Todd was Guy Gibson; the film's stirring and much-admired musical theme (by Eric Coates) was called 'The Dambusters March'.

• **dancehall ►** A US slang euphemism either for the place in which an execution takes place or the cell in which a condemned prisoner awaits execution. It probably derives from old criminal slang **dance in the air**, meaning to be hanged. The allusion is to the dance-like foot movements of someone being hanged.

• **dangerous age ►** An epithet that is usually presumed to refer to the age of 40, although in 1967 Dudley Moore starred in a film called Thirty is a Dangerous Age, Cynthia. It seems to have an air of sexual innuendo, implying that once this milestone has been reached the trammels of marital fidelity will be thrown off in an attempt to provide reassurance that one is still sexually attractive. See also: Life begins at forty; seven-year itch.

• **D'Annunzio raid ►** The seizure of the city of Fiume (Croatian name: Rijeka) in September 1919 by a force led by the Italian Fascist novelist and poet, Gabriele d'Annunzio (1863–1938). Fiume was a Hungarian port until 1919 when, as one of the spoils of war, it was claimed by both Italy and Yugoslavia. While it was still under the control of the League of Nations, D'Annunzio led some 2600 demobbed soldiers and Fascists and took over the city, much to the delight of Italian nationalists and the embarrassment of the Italian government. He remained in control of Fiume until November 1920, when he was expelled following agreement between Italy and Yugoslavia. Fiume was briefly a free city, until its incorporation by Italy in 1923. As Rijeka, it became Yugoslavian in 1947, as reparation after World War II. Since 1991 it has been the chief seaport of independent Croatia.

• **Danny the Red** ▶ Nickname for Daniel Cohn-Bendit (1945–    ), a West German student in France who led a students' revolt at Nanterre campus in Paris in May 1968. He was later deported to West Germany.

• **DAP** ▶ Draw a person. A psychological test in which the subject is asked to make a drawing of a person. Conclusions about the personality of the subject are drawn from the type of drawing produced.

• **daps** ▶ British slang for plimsolls or tennis shoes; it has been used, especially in Wales and SW England, since the 1930s. The derivation is uncertain, but it may be related to the verb to dap, meaning to bounce or skip.

• **Dardanelles** ▶ (formerly Hellespont) A narrow strait in N Turkey linking the Aegean Sea with the Sea of Marmara. The straits have always been of strategic importance as the gateway to Istanbul and the Black Sea from the Mediterranean. In ancient history they were guarded by Troy from the Asian side (the straits are named after Dadanos, a former king of Troy). In the 4th century BC Alexander the Great crossed over using a bridge of boats on his expedition against Persia. In April 1915 Allied forces landed on the W and S sides of the Gallipoli peninsula guarding the straits, in a move to capture Istanbul and link up with Russian forces for an offensive in the east. The campaign, marked by ineptitude and indecisiveness on the part of the British commanders, quickly degenerated into a bloody stalemate and the Allied forces were forced to withdraw in January 1916. *See also*: Anzac.

• **dark matter** ▶ The hypothetical matter in the universe that cannot be observed by direct observation of the electromagnetic radiation it emits. Its existence is postulated to account for the **missing mass**, *i.e.* the difference that is believed to exist between the actual mass of the universe and that estimated by observations using all kinds of tele-

scopes. Various exotic theories have been suggested to account for this dark matter, including black holes, cosmic strings, etc.

• **dark star** ▶ An invisible star, such as a component of a multiple star, the existence of which can only be deduced from infrared or radio emissions or from its observed gravitational effects.

• **Darling Daisy** ▶ Frances, Countess of Warwick, adulterous wife of the 5th Earl of Warwick and for nine years mistress of King Edward VII, whom he often addressed as 'My Darling Daisy wife' when writing to her. In 1914 she sought to increase her income by threatening to publish her memoirs, which would have included the late King's letters. This was prevented by three prominent courtiers acting on behalf of King George V.

• **Darling of the Halls** ▶ *See*: Prime Minister of Mirth.

• **Dartington Hall** ▶ A community, near Totnes in Devon, founded in 1926 on enlightened social and economic principles. The founders were Leonard and Dorothy Elmhirst, who bought the Dartington estate in 1925. The following year they established Dartington Hall School, a coeducational day and boarding school organized on progressive lines. Pupils enjoyed considerable freedom and informality (for instance there were no compulsory games or uniforms) and were encouraged to pursue their own interests in both the arts and sciences. The Elmhirsts also founded a range of small-scale rural enterprises on the estate, such as joinery, sawmilling, cider-making, and poultry-breeding. All employees have access to the artistic and educational opportunities afforded by Dartington, with the aim of enriching the community spiritually as well as economically. Ownership of the estate was transferred to a trust in 1932. The Dartington Hall summer school for musicians has established an international reputation.

Dartington Hall School closed in 1986 after a series of sex and drugs scandals. The philosophy of the school has, however, been carried on in the new Schumacher College on the same site, named after the green economist E. F. Schumacher (*see*: small is beautiful).

• **darts** ▶ An indoor target game in which sharp weighted darts (also called 'arrows') are thrown at a circular marked board. The game evolved from military training in the Middle Ages, when 10-inch throwing 'dartes' for use in close range combat were thrown at archery targets or sawn-off tree trunks: however, the modern version of the game is less than a century old. In 1906 the first all-metal barrelled dart was patented in the UK and in a court ruling of 1908 the game was designated one of skill, not chance, and made legal in pubs. The National Darts Association was formed in 1962, and the game's most important tournaments are shown regularly on television sports programmes. These broadcasts became hugely popular in the 1980s, when leading players became household names.

• **DAT**► Digital audio tape. A system for recording digitally encoded sound on magnetic tape. The format is similar to that of a recording cassette but is capable of superior digital sound recording and reproduction. DAT technology is used widely in professional recording studios, and reasonably priced DAT machines are now available to consumers. Widespread introduction of DAT machines was delayed by attempts to reach international agreement on measures to prevent wholesale copying and piracy of compact discs.

• **database**► Organized information held on a computer in a form that enables it to be put to a number of different uses. The information has to be held in such a way that it can be easily retrieved. A special computer program, called a **database management system** (DBMS), is used for this purpose.

• **date rape**► A rape that occurs when a man takes a woman out on a date. More controversially, the term is also used to describe cases in which a woman submits to sex against her better judgement – because she has been made drunk, perhaps, or subjected to undue pressure. Such acts, which would previously have been thought of as seductions, have now been redefined as rape by many feminists – although the law has not always agreed. More recently successful prosecutions have been brought in much less ambiguous cases of date rape, when the woman has been sedated or rendered unconscious by means of so-called **date-rape drugs**, which leave their victims with no memory of the attack. Drugs that have been used for this purpose include GHB, the hypnotic Rohypnol, the sedative midazolam, and the anaesthetic ketamine.

• **Davis apparatus**► More properly known as the Davis Submerged Escape Apparatus (DSEA). Designed by Sir Robert Davis, the apparatus was introduced in the late 1920s to assist submarine crews to escape from submerged vessels. It consisted of a mouthpiece and flexible tube attached to a rubber bag, which in turn was connected to a pressurized oxygen-filled container. This enabled the submariner to breathe during the ascent to the surface. The main drawback was the need to remove the mouthpiece on reaching the surface or risk suffocation. In 1946 the Royal Navy discontinued use of the DSEA during ascent, in favour of free escape following special training.

• **Davis Cup**► The trophy awarded to the winners of the International Lawn Tennis Championship. It was donated in 1900 for the inaugural contest between America and the UK by Dwight Filley Davis (1879–1945), who himself played for the US team in the opening contests. The competition now attracts some 60 nations. Each match comprises four singles and a doubles, and the eliminating round is played in three zones, American, European, and Eastern, with a zone final in each followed by an inter-zone final to decide the winner. The most recent winners were: America (1990, 1992, 1995), France (1991, 1996, 2001), Germany (1993), Sweden (1994, 1997, 1998), Australia (1999), and Spain (2000).

• **Dawes Plan**► A scheme for reorganizing reparation payments by Germany (see: Versailles Treaty), drawn up in 1924 by a committee headed by Charles Gates Dawes (1865–1951), a US brigadier-general. The scheme was devised in the wake of France's invasion of the Ruhr in 1923 following default on payments by Germany, with the intention of obviating such military sanctions in future. Central to the plan was the establishment of a German gold reserve based on an 800 million goldmark foreign loan and a system of reparation payments that would prevent currency depreciation and link payments to German industrial growth. The total amount of reparations payable was not fixed. The Dawes Plan was superseded in 1930 by the Young Plan. Dawes himself became Republican vice-president (1925–29) and was awarded the 1925 Nobel Peace Prize (jointly with Austen Chamberlain) for the Dawes Plan, which many regarded as having saved Europe from economic collapse.

• **dawk**► In America, a person who cannot make up his or her mind about whether to approve of a war or to campaign for peace. The term, a blend of dove and hawk, plays on the slang word 'dork' or fool. It was coined by *Time* magazine during the Vietnam War, to describe Republican politicians who approved of the war in principle but opposed it for political reasons.

• **dawn raid**► Business jargon for a sudden surprise attempt to buy a company's shares as soon as the stock market opens, in order to effect a takeover. The term became current in the early 1980s during the takeover boom in the City of London. The London Stock Exchange and Council for the Securities Industry subsequently introduced regulations to limit the amount of shares that can be acquired in this way.

Takeovers are for the public good, but that's

not why I do it. I do it to make money. – SIR
JAMES GOLDSMITH, *The Sunday Times*, 8 September 1985.

• **day**▶
**Go ahead, make my day** A catchphrase meaning 'go ahead if you dare', the implication being that the outcome will benefit the speaker, not the person spoken to. It originates from a 1983 Clint Eastwood film *Sudden Impact*, in which the rogue cop 'Dirty Harry' (played by Eastwood) uses it twice, both times while pointing a gun at an armed criminal.

• **day**▶
**Have a nice day** A phrase widely used as a valediction, especially by sales staff in shops, restaurants, and garages. It originated in 1956 as 'Have a happy day' when the Los Angeles advertising agency, Carson Roberts, used it as a greeting and as a slogan on all their promotional products. In the 1970s it became 'Have a nice day'. Most of the goodwill inherent in the phrase has been drained from it by overuse.

> ...the Americanization of Western culture: *Dallas* and Coca-Cola and 'Have a nice day!' – MARK LAWSON, *The Independent*, 5 January 1991.

• **day**▶
**that'll be the day!** An ironic way of referring to an event that is never likely to happen. The catchphrase supplied the title for one of Buddy Holly's most popular hits (1957) and was more recently adapted as 'That'll be the Daewoo' to advertise Daewoo cars.

• **day care** ▶ The practice of keeping old or ill people in supervised centres during the day, *i.e.* during normal working hours, so that the people looking after them can go out to work. In America, the term is also used for nursery schools for pre-school children.

• **daylight saving** ▶ The idea of making fuller use of the hours of daylight by advancing the clock originated with Benjamin Franklin, but its introduction was due to its advocacy from 1907 by William Willett (1856–1915), a Chelsea builder. In 1916 it was adopted first in Germany and then in the UK as a wartime measure, British clocks being advanced one hour from Greenwich Mean Time. In the UK it became permanent by an Act of 1925. **Summer Time**, as it was called until 1939 (and again in 1946 and from 1948 till 1959), began on the day following the third Saturday in April (unless that was Easter Day, in which case it was the day following the second Saturday in April). It ended on the day following the first Saturday in October. In 1961 and all subsequent years Summer Time was ex-

tended by six weeks, so that it began in late March and ended in late October. During World War II it extended continuously from 25 February 1940 to October 1945. **Double Summer Time** (*i.e.* two hours in advance of GMT instead of one hour) was in force during the summers of 1941–45 and 1947 to save fuel. *See also*: BST.

In America, **Summer Time** (March to October) was in force in 1917 and 1918 and again from 1942 to 1945 (all the year round and known as **War Time**). In 1966 the Uniform Time Act re-introduced Summer Time (from the last Sunday in April until the last Sunday in October) while allowing individual states the right of option. In the years since World War II a number of other countries have adopted some form of Summer Time.

• **Daytona Beach** ▶ A city and popular beach resort on the NE Florida coast. It was named in 1876 after local landowner Mathias Day of Ohio. The hard sandy beach stretches for 37 km, and the surface has attracted motor-sport enthusiasts since 1903, including the British land-speed record holder, Sir Malcolm Campbell (1885–1948). Motor sport is also found at the Daytona International Speedway, a 4-km race track used for motorcycle, stock-car, and sports-car events.

• **Dayton anti-Darwinist trial** ▶ The test case brought in 1925 by evolutionists to challenge the anti-evolutionist campaign of religious fundamentalists then gaining momentum in many southern US states (*see*: fundamentalism). In Tennessee, such fundamentalist opinions were embodied in an Anti-Evolution Law, passed in March 1925. A biology teacher at Dayton high school, John T. Scopes, was arrested for using the standard high school text, which incorporated Darwinian theory. His arrest was contrived by a friend and anti-fundamentalist, George Rappelyea. Scopes was defended by the illustrious attorney, Clarence Darrow (1857–1938); the prosecution's case was put by William Jennings Bryan (1860–1925), leader of the fundamentalists. Darrow vehemently argued the case against religious interference in education and managed to humiliate Bryan during the course of the trial. Nevertheless, Scopes was found guilty and fined 100 dollars. On appeal the decision was reversed on a technicality. Moreover, one of the appeal judges ruled the Tennessee Anti-Evolution Law unconstitutional. Bryan died shortly after the initial trial and the tide of fundamentalism began to ebb. However, the revival of Christian fundamentalism in the later 20th century means that evolution still cannot be taught in a proper scientific fashion in many public schools in the US South.

• **dazzle gun** ► A weapon used by the Royal Navy in the Falklands Conflict in 1982 but not made publicly known until the late 1980s. It is a laser gun used to dazzle pilots of enemy aircraft or other attackers.

• **dazzle ships** ► In World War I, warships painted in zigzag patterns to confuse the enemy as to the vessel's size, speed, and course. A highly specialized application of camouflage, the patterns were designed by leading contemporary artists and are now considered to have had significant value as art in their own right.

• **DBE** ► *See*: Order of the British Empire.

• **DC aircraft** ► *See*: Douglas aircraft.

• **D-Day** ► In World War II, the day appointed for the Allied invasion of northern Europe and the opening of the long-awaited Second Front. It was eventually fixed for 5 June 1944, but owing to impossible weather conditions, it was postponed at the last moment until 6 June. Under the supreme command of Eisenhower, some 160,000 British, Canadian, and US troops were successfully landed on five beaches in Normandy – the largest amphibious operation in military history. Operation Overlord had begun.

• **DDT** ► Dichlorodiphenyltrichloroethane. A highly toxic synthetic insecticide. First made in 1874, it was first used as an insecticide in 1939 by the Swiss chemist Paul Hermann Muller. Extensive use was made of it during World War II against lice, fleas, and mosquitoes, as well as crop pests. Unfortunately many insect species become immune to the compound, which builds up in their bodies and then contaminates animals, such as birds and mammals, higher up in the food chain. As a result, in 1972 severe restrictions were imposed on its use in America, and many other countries subsequently banned it.

• **dead beat** ► Completely exhausted, absolutely 'whacked', like a dead man with no fight left in him. A **deadbeat** is a useless or idle person, a sponger or parasite. In the late 1990s the term **deadbeat dads** was widely used for the growing phenomenon of young men who impregnate their girlfriends and then take no responsibility for either mother or child.

• **dead but won't lie down** ► Catchphrase used since around 1910 in statements such as 'he's dead but he won't lie down', meaning that someone, through stupidity or courage, does not know when to give up.

• **dead-cat bounce** ► An expression that origi-

nated on the New York Stock Exchange to indicate a temporary recovery in prices (after a substantial fall) caused by speculators buying in stock they had sold at a higher level. It does not imply a sustained upward trend in the market and the fall may well continue when these buyers have covered their purchases.

• **deadhead** ► **1.** Slang for a very boring or dull person. *See also*: airhead. **2.** US slang for a scrounger or someone who avoids paying, for example by failing to buy a ticket on a train. **3.** A fan of the US rock group the Grateful Dead, whose career started in the late 1960s and ended only with the death of their leader, guitarist Jerry Garcia, in 1995. The group were known to their devoted fans, some of whom made following the group a full-time occupation, as 'The Dead'.

• **Dead Heart** ► In Australia, the central barren desert region of the country.

• **dead-in-the-water** ► Denoting a company or corporation that is making very little progress and is therefore ripe for a takeover bid. The allusion is to a dead fish, which is simply drifting in the water rather than swimming in a specific direction.

• **dead-letter box** ► A box or other receptacle in which spies are supposed to deposit messages and other information to be picked up by other agents. The term has been popularized by writers of spy fiction. *See also*: drop.

• **dead man's handle** ► A handle on the controller of an electric train, etc., so designed that it cut off the current and applied the brakes if the driver released his pressure as a result of sudden illness or some other cause. It was formerly applied to electric, diesel-electric, diesel-mechanical, and diesel-hydraulic trains but was renamed **driver's safety device**, a term with less distressing associations.

• **dead president** ► US Black slang from the 1940s for any paper money bearing the head of a deceased US president.

• **Dead Sea Scrolls** ► In 1947 a Bedouin goatherd, Muhammed the Wolf, made the first scroll discoveries in a cave at the NW end of the Dead Sea, since when 500 more have been found. Most scholars accept them as originating from the monastery of the Jewish sect of the Essenes at Qumran. There is still much controversy over their interpretation but these manuscripts (dating from the period 150 BC to 70 AD) have added considerably to the understanding of both the Old and the New Testaments. In the early 1990s a bitter controversy arose about the delay in making the scrolls' contents fully available to the public and the restrictions placed on independent scholars seeking access. It was alleged (not altogether convincingly) that one reason for this may have been the scrolls' bearing on orthodox Christian beliefs.

• **dead sheep** ▶ *See*: sheep in sheep's clothing.

• **dead soul** ▶ An expression that owes its origin to the title of the Russian author Nikolai Gogol's novel *Dead Souls* (1842); in this book a swindler, Chichikov, buys serfs who are in fact dead but officially still alive, as their names still appear in the tax register. The expression re-emerged in 1989 when 110 members of the Central Committee of the Communist Party of the Soviet Union were removed from office by President Gorbachev, whose plans for perestroika they were obstructing. It is now used to describe a person who retains a position in an organization, even though he or she is no longer making any positive contribution.

• **Dear John letter** ▶ A letter or note from a wife, girlfriend, or female partner indicating that the relationship with the recipient is over. The expression originated during World War II, the recipients of Dear John letters often being members of the armed forces whose female partners at home had formed a new relationship as they were unwilling to tolerate the long separation that overseas service entailed.

• **dear money** or **tight money** ▶ A monetary policy in which interest rates on loans are high. *See also*: cheap money.

• **dear old pals** ▶ A contemptuous catcall sometimes heard at boxing matches when it appears that the two opponents are not fighting with the aggression that the audience have paid to see. It was derived from the popular song 'Dear Old Pals, Jolly Old Pals'.

• **death duty** ▶ *See*: inheritance tax.

• **Death Row** ▶ US name for the cells of a prison in which condemned prisoners are held until their execution. Because of the protracted nature of US legal processes, prisoners can spend many years waiting for the sentence to be carried out. During the 1960s and 1970s only a few executions actually took place; most death sentences were automatically commuted to life imprisonment. However, in the more conservative political climate of the 1980s and 1990s, executions took place in many US states on a regular basis. In 2000 it was calculated that there were some 3500 prisoners on Death Row.

• **death seat** ▶ Slang for the seat next to the driver in a car, so called because it is the most vulnerable position in an accident.

• **death squad** ▶ A group of people organized, either unofficially or officially, to commit murder. The term was originally applied in the 1970s to unofficial vigilante groups in certain Latin American countries, who worked to assassinate politicians and others who opposed the current military regime. More generally, it has been applied to any group organized for assassination.

• **death star** or **throwing star** ▶ A weapon consisting of a small thin metal disc cut into the shape of a star and having sharp-edged points. Designed to be thrown, it was adopted by British football hooligans in the late 1980s. The death star is one of a range of weapons popularized by martial arts enthusiasts, who use a less dangerous rubber version.

• **death-valley curve** ▶ The ominous decline in the curve on a graph that records the use of a new company's capital. With high start-up expenses and small income from sales, the death-valley curve is likely to frighten off new investors and sources of venture capital. The decline should be halted as sales reach predicted levels and start-up expenses fall.

• **debrief** ▶ To question a member of the armed forces, spy, astronaut, etc., after a tour of duty or mission has been completed in order to obtain the maximum information from him or her as soon as possible, *i.e.* before other influences can colour the experience. It is the opposite of the briefing given before the duty or mission begins.

• **deb's delight** ▶ British slang of the 1960s for an upper-class young man, noted more for his inherited wealth than his intelligence, who nevertheless might be chosen as a suitable escort, or even a marriage partner, by a debutante's parents. It was often used disparagingly by debs themselves.

> The debs had names such as Charlotte, Eleanor, Sophie, Annabel, Samantha, Astrid, and Jokey. Their escorts – the deb's delights – were called Patrick, Hugo, and Alexander. – *The Independent*, 10 April 1991.

• **decaffeinated** ▶ Denoting coffee and some other drinks that have had their caffeine content removed in response to consumer demand for natural beverages free from potentially harmful stimulants. Decaffeinated coffee, colloquially known as **decaf**, is now widely available. There is some concern, however, about the health risks from the solvents, such as methylene chloride, used to dissolve out the caffeine. Traces of this solvent remaining in the product can make decaffeinated coffee more of a health hazard than the natural drink.

• **decathlon** ▸ An athletic contest in the modern Olympic Games consisting of ten events: 100 m sprint, long jump, putting the shot, high jump, 400 m sprint, 110 m hurdles, discus, pole vault, throwing the javelin, and 1500 m run. *See also*: pentathlon.

• **deccie** or **deccy** ▸ A derogatory slang term for someone who is constantly redecorating his or her house and who moves house frequently in order to start another round of interior decorating. The term originated in the 1980s when much gentrification of old property was taking place. This type of word, ending in '-ie' or '-y', was very popular at the time, owing to the runaway success of the term yuppie (or yuppy).

• **decimal currency** ▸ The currency introduced in the UK on 15 February 1971, the new pound consisting of 100 pence. The introduction of a decimal currency was first mooted by the Tory MP, John Croker, in 1816. The idea was again put forward in parliament in 1824, 1847, 1853, and 1855.

> During the last two years he had devoted himself to decimal coinage with a zeal only second to that displayed by Plantagenet Palliser...
> – ANTHONY TROLLOPE: *Phineas Redux* (1874).

*See also*: metrication.

• **decision tree** ▸ A diagram sometimes used in the analysis of a financial situation, especially in making investments. The diagram is used to illustrate the possible courses of action that flow from a decision; the possible courses are represented by branches at different levels arising from a series of decisions taken subsequent to the initial decision.

• **deck-access** ▸ Describing a block of flats in which there is a continuous inset balcony on each floor, onto which the front doors of the individual flats open.

• **decommissioning** ▸ *See*: Good Friday Agreement; IRA.

• **decompression chamber** ▸ A room or space in which the air pressure can be varied at a controlled rate to enable people, such as divers, who have been exposed to abnormal atmospheric pressure to be returned to normal pressure slowly, in order to avoid **decompression sickness**.

• **deconstruction** ▸ A method of reading literary and philosophical texts devised by the French philosopher Jacques Derrida (1930– ). Proceeding from a structuralist understanding of language (*see*: Structuralism), Derrida claims that the unlimited play of linguistic differences within a given text

precludes the possibility of determinate meaning. A deconstructionist reading will therefore seek to expose the ways in which a text continually undermines its own claims to coherence. In journalistic usage the term is often merely a pretentious synonym for 'analyse' or 'subvert'.

• **Dedalus, Stephen** ▸ The eponymous hero of James Joyce's novel *A Portrait of the Artist as a Young Man* (1914–15), who also appears in Joyce's *Ulysses* (1922). The earlier book, which is mainly autobiographical, relates the story of Stephen's upbringing and development in Dublin, through school and adolescence, to his student days at Trinity College. Exposed to the pressures of Irish nationalism and Catholic dogma, and afflicted by poor eyesight, Stephen struggles to retain his individuality and to create a sense of personal destiny as poet and patriot. At the end of the book he resolves to leave Dublin for Paris:

> I go to encounter for the millionth time the reality of experience, and to forge in the smithy of my soul the uncreated conscience of my race.

Despite this ringing declaration, Stephen reappears in *Ulysses* as a rather uncertain and lonely young man adrift in Dublin on one particular day – 16 June 1904 (*see*: Bloom, Leopold). Unlike his mythological Greek namesake, the inventor Daedalus who made himself a pair of wings, Stephen finds that he cannot so easily soar above the common problems of humanity.

• **de-dyke** ▸ British lesbian slang of the 1980s and 1990s meaning to remove the traces of a lesbian lifestyle from a house, usually before a parental visit. *See also*: dyke.

• **deep cover** ▸ The cover story of a spy who sustains his or her role in another country for such a long time and so intensely that the details of the invented character virtually take over from those of the real agent.

• **deepfreeze** ▸ A type of refrigerator in which food, etc., can be stored for long periods at below freezing. Most deepfreezers operate at −15°C to −20°C; these same temperatures are also achieved in the deepfreeze compartments of an ordinary domestic refrigerator.

• **deep-sea diver** ▸ British rhyming slang for a fiver, a £5 note. It was mainly used in the mid-1970s.

• **deep-six** ▸ US slang meaning to bury or dispose of, *i.e.* to kill. Used since the 1950s, it derives from the underworld euphemism **deep six**, meaning a grave, which alludes to the minimum depth (6 ft) for a grave and the minimum depth of water for burials at sea.

• **Deep Thought** ▸ A character in the cult radio series *The Hitch Hiker's Guide to the Galaxy* (1978–79) by Douglas Adams. Deep Thought is an extraordinarily intelligent supercomputer which, when asked to provide the Ultimate Answer to the meaning of Life, the Universe, and Everything, ponders for seven and half million years – and comes up with the answer of 42.

• **Deep Throat** ▸ Deep Throat was the code name of the top-secret information source within the administration of President Richard Nixon, used by *Washington Post* reporters Carl Bernstein and Bob Woodward during their investigation into the Watergate affair (1972–74). Although the journalists refused to reveal the identity of this source, some commentators have suggested possible candidates. The codename was taken from the title of a very successful pornographic film (1974) about a young lady whose clitoris is located in her throat. In interviews the film's star, Linda Lovelace, claimed to have developed a method for controlling the gagging reflex in fellatio, which accounted for her spectacular performance. Later, however, she claimed that she had been coerced into making the film by threats of beatings and violence.

• **def** ▸ British slang of the late 1980s denoting extreme approval; excellent. It is a shortening of 'definitive' and was originally part of hip-hop jargon. In 1988, BBC2 started a TV series for young people called *DEF II*.

• **de facto** ▸ Australian slang dating from the 1940s (or earlier) for a live-in partner with whom one has an enduring relationship but to whom one is not married. Although 29% of British women in the age range 18–49 were cohabiting in the year 1999, there is no widely accepted word to describe either of the partners. In most contexts, 'my partner' is used: the formal 'common-law spouse' is mainly used in legal contexts or as a joke. *See*: cohab; live-in; significant other.

• **Defense Intelligence Agency** ▸ (DIA) The organization created in 1961 to coordinate all gathering and analysis of US military intelligence. It largely took over the previously separate intelligence branches of the US Army, Navy, and Air Force. The DIA's director is responsible for supplying the defense secretary and joint chiefs of staff with military intelligence information.

• **defensive medicine** ▸ The practice by doctors of taking extreme precautions to cover themselves against possible accusations of negligence and to avoid being sued by patients or relatives of patients for supposed malpractice. Defensive medicine involves a barrage of diagnostic tests, many of which are totally unnecessary, and routine referrals to a consultant or other doctor for a specialist or second opinion when these are not needed. The tests can in fact be harmful to patients and both these and second opinions are extremely expensive and time-consuming. Originally, defensive medicine was restricted to America but from the 1980s some doctors in the UK also began to practise it in the light of an increase in negligence and malpractice suits brought against them.

• **defrosted** ▸ US slang meaning worked up, the opposite of cool and unflustered.

• **De Havilland Aircraft Company** ▸ The aircraft manufacturing company founded in the UK in 1920 by Geoffrey de Havilland (1882–1965). One of the earliest models to achieve fame was the de Havilland Moth, first produced in 1925. One was piloted by Amy Johnson on her solo flight from the UK to Australia (*see*: Queen of the Air). During the 1930s the de Havilland Tiger Moth was adopted by the RAF as their principal trainer, while the all-wooden Mosquito bomber was one of the fastest planes to fight in World War II. Perhaps the company's greatest contribution to aviation history was the Comet, the world's first jet-propelled airliner. De Havilland's companies were taken over by Hawker Siddeley in 1959.

• **Dehra Dun Academy** ▸ The military academy of the Indian army, established in 1932 at Dehra Dun, a city in NW Uttar Pradesh. From 1949 it also catered for air-force and naval officer cadets, but in 1955 all basic officer cadet training was transferred to the new National Defence Academy at Khadakvasala, near Poona. Thereafter Dehra Dun provided advanced training for newly qualified officers.

• **Delaney amendment** ▸ In America, an amendment to the Food, Drug, and Cosmetic Act prohibiting the use of substances that cause cancer. The amendment, proposed in 1970 by the US Congressman James J. Delaney, stated that 'no additive shall be deemed to be safe if it is found, after tests which are appropriate for the evaluation of food additives, to induce cancer in man and animals'. The amendment became extremely controversial in the 1970s because the US Food and Drug Administration interpreted it in a strict way, irrespective of the dose involved. For example, in 1970 they banned the use of **cyclamates**, artificial sweetening agents widely used in the food industry, on evidence that massive doses caused bladder tumours in rats. In 1977 they invoked the Delaney amendment to ban the sweetener saccharin.

• **delayed drop** ▶ A descent from an aircraft by parachute in which the opening of the parachute is delayed, usually for a predetermined period, to enable the parachutist to take part in skydiving.

• **deleted by French censor** ▶ Phrase used by the US newspaper owner James Gordon Bennett II (1841–1918) during World War I to fill empty spaces left in his paper, the *New York Herald*, when news was lacking. *See also*: Gordon Bennett.

• **Delgado murder** ▶ The violent death of Humberto Delgado, former leader of the Portuguese Opposition, whose battered body was discovered on 24 April 1965 near Badajoz, on the Spanish side of the Portuguese border. His wounds suggested that he had been clubbed to death. Delgado had been defeated in the 1958 presidential election, after which he found political asylum in Brazil. However, he remained a focus of political opposition to the Salazar dictatorship and his death took place amid growing political unrest in Portugal. He was last seen alive in Badajoz in February 1965. No perpetrator of the murder has ever been identified.

• **Delhi belly** ▶ *See*: Montezuma's revenge.

• **Delhi pact** ▶ Either of two separate pacts signed in Delhi that figure in modern Indian history. The first, signed in 1931 and also called the **Gandhi–Irwin pact**, was an agreement between the leader of the Congress Party, Mahâtma Gandhi, and Lord Irwin, viceroy of India. The pact, addressing some of Congress's grievances against the British, marked a truce in the Congress campaign of civil disobedience. It also established Congress as the principal conduit of Indian opinion in the Round Table constitutional conference. The second Delhi pact was signed in April 1950 between the Indian prime minister, Jawaharlal Nehru, and his Pakistani opposite number, Liaqat Ali Khan. The pact ensured the rights of Muslim and Hindu minorities in their respective countries; it was prompted by a massive two-way migration across the East Pakistan–Indian border following partition and fears that religious minorities in both countries would suffer persecution.

• **deli** ▶ Short for delicatessen, a shop selling unusual foods (sometimes cooked), especially those of a particular ethnic or national origin, *e.g.* a Jewish deli, an Italian deli, etc.

• **delta wing** ▶ An aircraft wing in the form of a triangle with its apex pointing in the direction of motion, which facilitates passage through the sound barrier. Experiments with delta-wing designs, also known as sweptback wings, were carried out by the Germans during the 1940s; after the war this knowledge passed to the Allies. By the early 1950s the Americans had introduced the first supersonic fighter aircraft based on the delta-wing design, the F-102. British models, such as the Hawker Hunter and the Vulcan bomber, followed later. Because of their benefits at supersonic speed, narrow delta wings were chosen for Concorde, which was designed to cruise at Mach 2; American Orbiter space shuttles have also used a similar design.

• **deltiology** ▶ The pastime of collecting picture postcards. Picture postcards became popular early in the 20th century, especially in the form of greetings cards sent by people on holiday to their friends and relations. As the cards became more diverse, some having photographs on one side depicting local scenery and some having cartoons with faintly risqué jokes, so the hobby of collecting them began to grow. The word is formed from Greek *deltion*, a diminutive of *deltos*, a writing tablet, and the suffix '-ology', as in biology.

• **delusions of grandeur** ▶ A form of megalomania in which the person concerned has a grossly inflated idea of his or her importance. Although the expression derives from the language of psychology in the early 20th century, it is now widely used in common speech to describe someone who needs to be deflated from time to time.

• **demand-pull inflation** ▶ *See*: inflation.

• **dementors** ▶ *See*: Potter, Harry.

• **demi-veg** ▶ Short for demi-vegetarian, a diet in which the major components are vegetarian but the consumption of poultry and fish is permitted. Such a regime rules out the eating of red meat, which some medical experts regard as being injurious to health.

• **demo** ▶ **1.** Slang for a street demonstration. **2.** Slang for a demonstration recording that would-be pop musicians send in to recording companies or disc jockeys, hoping to get their work known. **3.** Slang for a demolition job, either in the literal sense of knocking a building down or in the figurative sense of denigrating someone behind his or her back.

• **Demochristian** ▶ An informal term for a member of any of the European political parties that have 'Christian Democrat' in their name.

• **demographic timebomb** ▶ An expression coined at the end of the 1980s to describe an anticipated shortfall of potential workers as a result of an earlier drop in the national birth rate. The assumption is that, in the absence of enough young people to fill the jobs available, others, such as retired people or women who had not previously worked, would be required to work. The phrase was used despite the high unemployment rate current at the time.

• **demonstration model** ▶ A consumer product, such as a car or washing machine, that has been used in the showroom of a retail outlet to demonstrate the model to potential buyers. When the model being demonstrated is changed, or the demonstration model begins to show signs of use, it may be offered for sale at a discount to the normal price.

• **denim** ▶ Coloured (usually blue) twilled cotton material, the name deriving from a contraction of *serge de Nîmes*, originally made at Nîmes in the south of France. The garments themselves are known as 'denims'. Until the 1960s denim was considered only suitable for working garments, overalls, etc. but from the middle of that decade denim jeans began to be worn as fashionable casualwear by both sexes; other denim garments (shirts, jackets, etc.) are also now regarded as fashion items, especially when the fabric is artificially aged (*see*: granitewash).

• **Denning report** ▶ The report of an enquiry into the security aspects of the Profumo affair, conducted by the Master of the Rolls, Lord Denning (1899–1999). He concluded that the liaison between the UK's former war minister, John Profumo, and the call girl, Christine Keeler, had posed no threat to national security in spite of Keeler's association with a Soviet naval attaché. Denning also found no evidence to support rumours about the possible involvement of other ministers. However, Denning's criticisms of the existing security arrangements prompted the prime minister, Alec Douglas-Home, to establish a standing committee on security.

• **Denver boot** ▶ A wheel clamp; a metal clamp attached by the police, or a private firm acting for the police, to one wheel of an illegally parked car to prevent it from being driven away until the driver has paid a substantial fee to have it unlocked, plus a statutory fine. It takes its name from Denver, Colorado, where the device was first used. In the streets of New York and London (from 1983) its introduction greatly reduced illegal parking.

• **Depression** ▶ *See*: Great Depression.

• **depth charge** ▶ A drum packed with explosives, which can be timed to detonate at a pre-set depth, used by surface vessels to destroy submerged submarines. Depth charges are usually launched in groups to cover a pattern and were used with considerable success against diesel-engined sub-

marines during World War II. However, they are not so effective against nuclear submarines and are little used today.

• **Derbyite** ▶ In World War I, a soldier enlisted under the Derby Scheme of 1915. The Earl of Derby was director of recruiting and sought to promote a scheme of voluntary enlistment by age groups. The response was quite inadequate and conscription was instituted in May 1916.

• **DERL** ▶ Derived emergency reference level. The point at which action must be taken to counteract a potentially dangerous rise in radiation levels. The reference level is calculated on the basis of the most sensitive members of the public, usually children below one year of age.

• **derry** ▶ British slang for a derelict building. The term is used by tramps looking for shelter, by homeless people seeking a place in which to squat, or by people looking for derelict country properties to renovate.

• **derv** ▶ Diesel-engined road vehicles. A type of diesel oil used in road vehicles. The word was originally World War II service slang.

• **deselect** ▶ A euphemism meaning to exclude from participation or availability. It was first used in the UK in the early 1980s in the context of Labour party politics. Sitting MPs who lost the confidence of their constituency parties were faced with potential deselection, *i.e.* having their candidature rescinded before the next general election. The verb was later applied to others in a similar situation, such as local-government councillors. It has now acquired much more general application; for example, 'deselected' library books are those removed from public circulation.

• **Desert Fox** ▶ Nickname of Field Marshal Erwin Rommel (1891–1944), so called because of his intuitive strategy as commander of the German Afrika Korps in World War II. One of Hitler's most popular generals, he also enjoyed the respect of many Allied soldiers. After the success of the Allied landings in France in 1944, he became convinced that Germany would be defeated and pleaded with Hitler to end the war. He was subsequently implicated in the July 1944 bomb plot (*see*: Stauffenberg Plot) against Hitler, although he was not involved in the assassination attempt itself, preferring that Hitler should be deposed and brought to trial. In October 1944, while at home recovering from a wound received in an air raid, he was visited by two fellow generals, who gave him a choice between a public trial and suicide. He chose the latter and was given a hero's state funeral.

• **desertification** ▶ The transformation of fertile land into desert or semi-arid land. This has been brought about by soil erosion, over-intensive farming (overcultivation and overgrazing), poor soil management, and desert expansion (the constant expansion of the Sahara, for example, through a succession of droughts, has desertified large areas of North Africa in the last 50 years). Another major contributory factor is **deforestation**, the large-scale felling of forest trees to clear the land for mining or other purposes, which has had the effect of increasing soil erosion and hence desert formation. A policy of reforestation and such projects as spraying the land with synthetic water-holding resins to retain moisture and promote plant growth promise to help restore the desert to agricultural use. In the long term, however, such measures will have only limited success without major reforms in techniques of land management.

• **Desert Island Discs** ▶ A BBC radio programme, which claims the title of the longest-running record programme in the world. It was first broadcast on 29 January 1942, presented by its deviser Roy Plomley. Each celebrity 'guest' to be cast away on the mythical desert island is invited to select eight records, a book, and a luxury item to take there. When Plomley died in 1985 he was succeeded as presenter by Michael Parkinson and subsequently by Sue Lawley; the only person to be 'cast away' to the island four times was the comedian Arthur Askey. *See also*: Amos 'n' Andy; Archers, The; Blue Peter; Coronation Street; Sooty.

• **Desert Rats** ▶ The nickname of the 7th Armoured Division of the British Army, whose divisional sign is the desert rat (jerboa). The name reflects the division's 'scurrying and biting' tactics in Libya during World War II and was apparently inspired by the pet jerboa of a regimental signaller; the jerboa badge was originally sketched by the divisional commander's wife. The division served throughout the North Africa campaign, and in NW Europe from Normandy to Berlin. In 1990 the division was part of the British contingent sent to Saudi Arabia in response to the Iraqi invasion of Kuwait.

• **Desert Storm** ▶ The military codename for the US and British air attack on Iraq, which began on 17 January 1991, in response to Saddam Hussein's invasion and rape of Kuwait (August 1990). In order to protect the other Gulf States and Saudi Arabia, to force Saddam to leave Kuwait, and to achieve supremacy over the Iraqi war machine (the fourth largest in the world), a massive multinational force had previously been built up in Saudi Arabia under the code name **Desert Shield**. The short land war

(24–28 February) that followed the bombing and ended with the total rout of Iraqi forces was known as Operation **Desert Sabre**.

As a way of showing support for the forces in the Gulf, groups of women in SE England banded together to send parcels of Dundee cakes to the Gulf under the operational name 'Dessert Storm'. *See also*: Gulf War.

• **designer** ▶ A word that came into use in the 1980s to describe goods sold under the label or logo of a specific designer. Although such goods are frequently not very different from others of their kind sold on the mass market, they are considerably more expensive. First applied to clothes, especially jeans, the word spread to other goods. Eventually so many things were so designated that the word became virtually meaningless.

• **designer drug** ▶ A recreational drug produced by a chemist rather than made from a natural substance. Usually the chemist devises a formula to make the drug as potent as a similar prohibited drug but slightly different so that he and the users avoid prosecution.

• **designer socialism** ▶ A derogatory term for the UK Labour Party's attempts to present a modern nondoctrinaire image in the late 1980s and 1990s. This involved both a retreat from unpopular left-wing policies and a new emphasis on PR, media skills, and visual presentation. The latter is usually put down to the influence of Peter Mandelson (*see*: Mandy), the party's director of campaigns and communications from 1985 to 1990 and one of the architects of New Labour.

• **designer stubble** ▶ A man's one- or two-day's growth of beard that has intentionally been left unshaved to create a relaxed unsmart image.

• **designer water** ▶ An ironic description of bottled water. For many years, the idea that the British should actually buy water in bottles in their own country would have seemed ludicrous. It was the sort of thing that they felt obliged to do when venturing abroad: foreign tap water was regarded as unclean, unwholesome, and dangerous. In the 1980s, however, there was a change in attitude and home sales of bottled water increased dramatically for both carbonated and still water. There were a number of reasons for this. Perhaps the most significant was a highly successful advertising campaign for the French product **Perrier water**. This was helped by the deteriorating quality of British tap water, by a general increase in the public's awareness of health issues, and by the growing feeling that it is wise to abstain from alcohol altogether before driving or during working hours. Drinking bottled water instead of tap water is expensive but chic, hence the 'designer' label.

• **desk jockey**▶ A facetious and often derogatory description of an office worker, coined by analogy with disc jockey.

• **desktop publishing**▶ (DTP) The use of a desktop computer with page make-up software and a laser printer to produce professional-quality documents that may include graphics and photographs as well as text. The first page-layout software program, Aldus PageMaker, was released for the Apple Macintosh computer in 1985; this software and hardware combination remains the standard by which other DTP systems are judged. Because of the substantial savings in time and labour resulting from using DTP (rather than traditional typesetting), similar technology is now used at the highest level to produce books, magazines, and newspapers.

• **Desmond**▶ British student slang of the 1980s for a lower second class degree, i.e. a 2/2. It is a play on the name of the South African archbishop, Desmond Tutu. See also: Douglas; Pattie; Taiwan.

• **des res**▶ Short for desirable residence. Originally estate agents' jargon used in advertisements, it passed into common usage in the late 1980s to refer to a property with many attractive features, together with 'all mod cons' (i.e. all the usual modern conveniences).

• **de-Stalinization**▶ The reversal of the policies of the Soviet leader Joseph Stalin (1879–1953) following his death. A campaign to discredit Stalin's memory was started by his successor, Nikita Khrushchev (1894–1971), in a bitter speech at a closed session of the 20th Party Congress in March 1956. Here he denounced Stalin as a despot and brutal mass-murderer interested in 'the glorification of his own person'. It has been said that Khrushchev's speech was interrupted by a shout from the audience of 'Why didn't you stop him?'. Khrushchev glared at the delegates and shouted 'Who said that!'. Nobody spoke, and Khrushchev continued, 'Now you know why!'. A number of similar terms have been coined, for instance **de-Maoization** (or **de-Maoification**) for the reversal of the ideas of the Chinese leader Mao Tsetung (1893–1976) following his death; and **de-Thatcherization** following the resignation of the British prime minister Margaret Thatcher in 1990.

• **de Stijl**▶ (Dutch, the style) A school of Dutch artists and architects who launched a periodical of the same name in 1917; the leading members were the painter Piet Mondrian (1872–1944) and the architect Gerrit Rietveld (1888–1964). The school adhered to Mondrian's principle of neoplasticism, which stressed the use of horizontal and vertical lines and of white, black, grey, and primary colours. De Stijl had an important influence on the Bauhaus school.

• **Destour**▶ The Tunisian Liberal Constitutional Party: a nationalist political party formed in 1920 to press for Tunisian independence from French colonial rule and for reinstatement of the suspended Tunisian constitution (dustūr). After organizing strikes and boycotts in the early 1930s, Destour was banned by the French authorities in 1933. A breakaway faction, **Néo-Destour**, emerged soon after and eventually eclipsed its progenitor, in spite of several attempts to revive Destour in the 1940s and 1950s. Under Habib Bourguiba (1903–2000), Néo-Destour achieved independence for Tunisia in 1956.

• **detente**▶ The relaxing or easing of tension between nations. The word is particularly associated with the efforts to improve superpower relations that occurred in the 1970s, beginning with the Nixon–Brezhnev meetings and US rapprochement with China. The early 1980s, however, saw a return to hardline Cold-War attitudes.

• **detention centre**▶ A former institution for the short-term detention of young male offenders aged between 14 and 20. Custodial sentences were usually for between 21 days and four months. These centres operated a regime of rigid discipline, hard work, and physical exercise, in accordance with the government's 'short sharp shock' policy, announced by William Whitelaw at the 1979 Conservative Party conference. However, statistics for those committing subsequent offences after release failed to indicate that this tougher regime had had a deterrent effect and detention centres were replaced by young offender institutions.

• **detox**▶ Short for detoxification. The word has two main senses in contemporary English. One is abstention from illegal drugs or alcohol as part of a programme of treatment for those who have become physically addicted to these substances (see: detoxification centre). The other is a regime of strict dieting (usually based on organic fruits and vegetables) designed to rid the body of toxins such as caffeine, alcohol, etc.

> I can't wait to get started on my next 28-day detox and lose the pounds I've put on over Christmas she enthused. – CAROL VORDERMAN, quoted in The Sunday Times, 7 January 2001.

• **detoxification centre**▶ A clinic to which alcoholics and drug addicts go to receive professional help to reduce or eliminate their dependency by means of medical treatment, counselling, and therapy. The best-known detoxification centre is the Betty Ford Clinic (named after President Ford's wife) in America, an institution that numerous Hollywood stars and famous international figures have visited to receive treatment for various forms of addiction. In Britain, a clinic called The Priory serves a similar high-profile function. There are many similar, but less glamorous, centres throughout the Western world.

• **Deutschland ►** Either of two classes of German warship built in the 20th century. The first comprised five vessels built between 1903 and 1908, starting with the *Deutschland* itself, which was completed in 1906. Its successors were the *Hanover* (1904–07), *Pommern* (1904–07), *Schlesien* (1904–08), and *Schleswig-Holstein* (1905–08). The second Deutschland series, known as the Deutschland-Lützow class, comprised three armoured heavy cruisers built between 1929 and 1936. The *Deutschland* was launched in 1931, but renamed the *Lützow* in 1939. A bombing raid on the *Deutschland* in Ibiza harbour in 1937, resulting in the deaths of 23 men, gave Hitler the excuse he required to step up German involvement in the Spanish Civil War. Others in the trio were the *Admiral Scheer* and *Admiral Graf Spee*. All three were built using a welded steel construction method, instead of the traditional riveting, and all three were sunk by the Allies during World War II.

• **Deutschmark ►** The former standard monetary unit of Germany, divided into 100 pfennig. The Deutschmark was introduced on 21 June 1948 as a replacement for the Reichsmark. However, the new currency was forbidden to circulate in the Soviet-controlled eastern zone. This led to two different German currencies: the West German Deutschmark, or DM (West), and the Deutschmark (Ost), or Ostmark, in East Germany. With unification of East and West Germany in 1990, the DM (West) became the single currency of the united Germany. It was subsumed into the euro for all purposes other than cash transactions in January 1999 and abolished in March 2002.

• **deux-chevaux** or **2 CV ►** (French, two horses) A small French Citroen car with a two-horsepower engine. Originally designed in the 1950s to provide French farmers with a practical and inexpensive car, it became a cult car in the UK and elsewhere in the 1960s. The original advertising claimed that the car would accommodate a bale of hay and enable the driver to hold a glass of champagne without spilling any, while driving across a field.

• **developing countries ►** The countries with insufficient agricultural and industrial productive capacity to generate the savings required to sustain investment and economic growth. They are also called underdeveloped countries, less-developed countries (LDCs), and Third World countries. These countries, which make up nearly 80% of the world's population, include most of Africa, Asia, Central and South America, and the Caribbean. Common features include dependence on the export of primary products, widespread poverty and disease, illiteracy, and high birth rates. It was once thought that with economic aid from the industrialized nations, developing countries could reach the level of industrialization needed for 'take-off' into self-sustained economic growth. However, the viability of this Western model has been increasingly questioned by economists and sociologists; no real consensus exists as to the most beneficial form that either the aid itself or the means of distributing it should take. Meanwhile, unfavourable terms of trade, massive international debt, and still-growing populations that have failed to accept Western methods of family planning (and in Catholic countries have been forbidden by the Church to do so) left many developing countries worse off at the beginning of the new millennium than they have ever been.

• **Devil's Island ►** (French *Isle du Diable*) The smallest of the Isles du Salut (Safety Islands) off the coast of French Guiana. Remote and desolate, it was used by the French first as a leper colony and then a penal colony (1895–1938). The island's most famous prisoner was Alfred Dreyfus (1859–1935), who was imprisoned there for five years (1894–99) having been unjustly convicted of treason. *See*: Dreyfusard.

A graphic description of the appalling conditions on the island and the brutal treatment meted out to the unfortunates sent there can be found in *Papillon*, the autobiographical best-seller by Henri Charrière, which was made into a film (1973) starring Dustin Hoffman and Steve McQueen. The island is now a popular winter tourist resort.

• **Devil's Triangle ►** *See*: Bermuda Triangle.

• **devolution ►** The transfer of legislative powers from central government to regional assemblies. In the UK pressure for devolution in Scotland and Wales mounted during the 1970s, when the Scottish National Party (*see*: SNP) gained over 30% of the vote of the Scottish electorate and 11 parliamentary seats in the October 1974 election. The Labour Party then drew up proposals for a Scottish legislative assembly with devolved powers, which, while falling short of Nationalist demands for complete independence, were expected to satisfy most

Scots. In a referendum in March 1979, however, only a third of the total Scottish electorate voted in favour of the proposal, some way short of the 40% required for its implementation. In 1997 a new referendum to establish a Scottish Parliament with limited legislative powers was endorsed by the electorate and elections to this body took place in 1999. In Wales, the Welsh Nationalist Party Plaid Cymru has been more interested in preserving Welsh culture and language than achieving independence. Although it campaigned for devolution, only 12% of the Welsh electorate voted for an assembly in the 1979 referendum. However, a new plan to establish a Welsh Assembly was endorsed by a new referendum in 1997 and elections to this body took place in 1999. That same year devolved government was restored to Northern Ireland following the Good Friday Agreement of 1998 (see: Stormont).

**•de Wet Rebellion** or **Rebellion of 1914**▶ A rebellion among the Boers of South Africa, led in 1914 by General C. R. de Wet and C. R. Beyers, in protest at the decision of the newly formed South African government to support the UK at the outbreak of World War I. The rebellion, badly co-ordinated and lacking appreciable popular support, was quickly suppressed by Boer forces led by General L. Botha and Jan Smuts. De Wet was captured, while Beyers drowned crossing the Vaal River. By the end of 1914, the rebellion was over.

**• DEW line**▶ Distant Early Warning Line. A network of radar stations, mostly in the Arctic, intended to give America early warning of an aircraft or missile attack.

**• dex**▶ Slang for a pill or capsule containing the amphetamine Dexedrine; a pep pill. Such pills were widely abused in youth culture of the 1960s, especially by the mods (see: mods and rockers). Because of their stimulant effect the pills were sometimes known as **Dexy's Midnight Runners** – later the name of a well-known 1980s pop group.

**• DHSS**▶ Department of Health and Social Security. The British government department that was responsible for the National Health Service and social security until 1988, when it was split into the **Department of Health** (DH) and a separate **Department of Social Security** (DSS). When it was one single department it was responsible for all aspects of the welfare state and was the largest employer in Europe.

**• DI**▶ Donor insemination. Artificial insemination in which the male of a couple trying to conceive is infertile so semen from an unidentified donor is injected into the female partner. DI was originally called artificial insemination by donor (AID). However, because of the similarity between the abbreviations AID and Aids, the name for this procedure was changed; the abbreviation DI avoids any possible association with the disease. *Compare*: AIH.

**• DIA**▶ *See*: Defense Intelligence Agency.

**• diamond**▶
    **a diamond is forever** A slogan created in 1939 by B. J. Kidd of the N. W. Ayer Agency, Chicago, for the South African-based De Beers Consolidated Mines, who mine diamonds and to a large extent control the world diamond market. The advertisement was an attempt to increase the sales of diamond engagement rings. The slogan has become part of the language. Ian Fleming used a variation for the title of one of his James Bond novels, *Diamonds are Forever* (1956), which was made into a successful film in 1971; the popular theme song was belted out by Shirley Bassey.

**• diathermy**▶ (Greek *dia*, through; *thermē*, heat) The production of heat in the human body by means of a high-frequency current passed between electrodes placed on the skin. The heat produced can be used to treat deep-seated arthritic or rheumatic pain. A **diathermy knife** is an instrument used in surgery to make almost bloodless incisions. The knife used to make the incision is one electrode, the other being a pad applied to the patient's skin. As the knife is used the small blood vessels are sealed off, because the current causes the blood to coagulate.

**• dibbler**▶ A small Australian marsupial, *Antechius apicalis*. The dibbler is brown, about 20 cm (8 in) long, and has a long snout. It had been thought to be extinct since the 1800s, but was rediscovered in 1967.

**• dick**▶ 1. Slang for a detective. 2. Slang for a penis.

**• dickless Tracey**▶ Australian slang for a policewoman. It is derived from a play on the name of the popular US comic-strip detective, Dick Tracy.

**• Diehards**▶ Nickname given to the Tory rebels who, in 1911, rejected the advice of their party leader, A. J. Balfour, and pledged to 'die fighting' the constitutional changes proposed in Lloyd George's Parliament Bill. Essentially, these changes limited the power of veto exercised by the House of Lords over bills passed by the Commons. The Diehards' revolt caused Balfour to resign the Tory leadership in November 1911. *See also*: Hedgers and Ditchers; People's Budget; Veto Bill.

**• die-in**▶ In the Cold War era, a type of public demonstration in which people lay on the floor pretending to be dead, to draw attention to the dangers of nuclear or chemical warfare. The idea was an extension of the 1960s sit-in.

• **Dien Bien Phu** ► A large village in North Vietnam in an upland valley close to the Laos border. It was the site of the ignominious defeat of French forces by the Vietminh (Vietnamese nationalists) in May 1954, which ended French colonial rule in Vietnam. The French had chosen Dien Bien Phu in November 1953 as a land-air base from which to conduct offensive operations against Vietminh forces. By December, however, the Vietminh commander, General Vo Nguyen Giap, had surrounded the French garrison with over 40,000 men and heavy artillery sited in the mountains overlooking the base. The final battle began on 12 March 1954; the base was eventually taken on 7 May, the day before the opening of the international peace conference at Geneva. Although Eisenhower wisely refused French appeals for US military support, the lessons of the French defeat were unfortunately ignored by later US presidents. Two decades later, the Americans were forced to withdraw in similarly humiliating circumstances after the fall of Saigon to the Vietcong (see: Vietnam War).

• **Dieppe raid** ► An Allied assault on the German-occupied French Channel port of Dieppe that took place on 19 August 1942. The Allied force comprised 5000 Canadian and 1000 British troops, plus some US Rangers and Free French forces. The landing, codenamed Operation Jubilee, proved very costly, with over 1000 Allied troops killed. However, nearly 50 German aircraft were destroyed and Allied commanders learned valuable lessons in assault strategy. After the war, Lord Mountbatten reflected that the raid 'gave the Allies the priceless secret of victory'.

• **diesel** or **diesel dyke** ► Slang for a large, aggressive, and masculine lesbian. It reflects the rugged appearance of diesel engines and perhaps also the working clothes worn by the men who make or repair them, which are also worn by some lesbians. Originally heard in America, the word has been used in the UK since the 1980s. See also: dyke.

• **diet pill** or **slimming pill** ► Any of various drugs used to help reduce weight. Diet pills work in various ways: phentermine (Duromine, Ionamin) suppresses the appetite, methylcellulose (Celevac) induces feelings of fullness and therefore reduces food intake, and orlistat (Xenical) prevents the digestion and absorption of fatty foods. Prescribed by a doctor, these drugs are only used to treat those who are grossly overweight and are of little use for long-term weight reduction without dieting. Other drugs (amphetamines), formerly widely used as slimming pills, have now been withdrawn because of their harmful effects. The best way for the majority of slightly overweight people to reduce weight is to eat less of the fatty and sugary foods – or to eat less of everything.

• **Dietrich, Marlene** ► (1901–92) Stage name of the German-born actress and singer Maria Magdalene von Losch. She appeared in German films from the early 1920s but became an international icon with her role in Joseph von Sternberg's film (1930) *The Blue Angel*. Dietrich played Lola Frölich, a singer-prostitute in the Blue Angel nightspot, who makes an unsuitable marriage to a university professor. The film includes Dietrich's famous husky-voiced rendition of 'Falling in Love Again' – a performance that moved Lord Beaverbrook (see: Beaver, the) to remark that Dietrich in her fish-net stockings was a greater work of art than the Venus de Milo.

Although *The Blue Angel* was made in Germany and shot simultaneously in German and English, the film became an international success, and von Sternberg, by now her lover, took Dietrich to Hollywood. Here she made a number of not very remarkable films; only *Destry Rides Again* (1939), in which she robustly sang 'See What the Boys in the Back Room Will Have', remains memorable. Dietrich made few films after 1950, although she made use of her legend as a cabaret artiste. During World War II, she identified herself totally with the Allies, for which many Germans never forgave her. The last part of her life was spent in France, where her grave was desecrated by Nazi sympathizers.

• **different** ►
**And now for something completely different** A catchphrase from Monty Python's Flying Circus, the cult TV comedy of the late 1960s and 1970s. The phrase was also used as the title of the same team's first feature length film in 1971. In the TV show the line was said by John Cleese wearing evening dress, like an early BBC announcer, and seated at a table behind a microphone in totally incongruous surroundings. It was previously used on magazine programmes as a useful link phrase between unrelated items, but Monty Python made this no longer possible.

• **differently abled** ► A euphemism for disabled, first heard in America in the mid-1980s. The term was one of the first products of political correctness to achieve wide publicity. Like such phrases as **physically challenged** or **other-visioned** (blind or partially sighted), it is intended to focus attention on the 'positive' aspects of the condition in question.

• **dig** ► A slang word meaning to like, appreciate,

or understand. Its origin is uncertain but a likely explanation is that it derives from an African word *degu*, to understand. The word was used in this sense in the 1930s but re-emerged in the 1950s and 1960s as beat or hippie jargon, meaning to like or approve of. It now sounds very dated.

• **dig for victory**► A campaign run by the British Ministry of Agriculture during World War II urging garden and allotment owners to grow food to help the war effort. The campaign involved a propaganda barrage – over ten million leaflets were distributed in 1942 alone. By 1944, 25% of fresh eggs were supplied by domestic hen keepers; there was also a pig-keeping craze, with over 6900 Pig Clubs in existence by the end of the war.

• **digger**► An Australian. The name was in use before 1850, consequent upon the discovery of gold, and was applied to Anzac troops fighting both the World Wars.

• **diggers**► In America, a group of West Coast hippies who distributed free food, etc., to those who needed it. The name was derived from its use by a small group of social revolutionaries under Gerrard Winstanley (*c.* 1609–60) who began to dig the common at St George's Hill, Surrey in 1649. Their aim was to give back the land to the common people, but they were soon suppressed by the Cromwellian army leaders.

• **digital**► Describing a device or process in which data is represented as a series of discrete numerical values. Because nearly all computers are digital, in that they manipulate information in the form of groups of binary numbers, the word has also acquired the general sense 'relating to computers or computerization'.

• **digital broadcasting**► The transmission of television and radio programmes or other data as a digital signal. Compared to the traditional analogue system, digital broadcasting has several advantages. The most compelling for broadcasters is that because the signal is relatively 'compressed', it creates space for many more channels, including ones that transmit only text or graphics rather than programmes. Moreover, the quality of both sound and pictures is improved, because the signal is much less prone to distortion than analogue signals. Another feature is the capacity it provides for interactive programming, whereby viewers can use their TV sets in a host of new ways – for, example to participate directly in live broadcasts, shop over the Internet, or send e-mails (*see*: interactive television).

Digital transmission of 'terrestrial' television (DTT), received via an aerial from a ground-based transmitter, essentially uses a band of numerous carrier frequencies called a multiplex, which can be transmitted in the gaps between the existing analogue transmissions in the UHF part of the electro-magnetic spectrum. Digital audio broadcasting (DAB) employs the VHF frequency band, formerly used for TV transmissions but now empty. Satellite and cable broadcasters use different methods of transmitting the signal.

The first digital television transmissions were made in 1997 from satellites and seen by audiences in France and the USA. In the UK it is expected that the switch to digital will be completed by about 2010, when all viewers will require a set-top decoder for their TV set, or an integrated digital TV. The timetable for digital radio is less certain. One hurdle is the high cost of digital radios compared to analogue receivers.

• **digital clock**► A watch or clock featuring a readout in figures (usually the 24-hour system) as opposed to the revolving hands of a normal (analogue) clock. Early forms of digital clocks used light-emitting diode (LED) displays but these were superseded by superior liquid crystal displays (LCD). Digital read-outs are now widely used in many measuring instruments.

• **digital mapping**► A method of map making in which the points and lines that make up the map are fed into a computer in digital form and stored on magnetic tape or disk. Subsequently the map, or a selected part of it, can be displayed on a screen or printed out, to any scale or in a variety of forms of projection. Changes can also be made without needing to redraw the map. In 1973 the UK Ordnance Survey began converting its maps to the digital form.

• **digital photography**► A form of photography in which the image produced by an optical camera is stored in digital form as pixels on a computer disk. The picture can then be viewed on a computer screen or printed out by a colour printer (the quality of the print depending on the quality of the printer and the paper). Although the quality does not yet equal that of normal photography, the advantage of the process is that once converted to digital form the image can be altered in a variety of ways (cropped, retouched, etc.) or mixed with other digital images.

• **digital recording**► A method of recording sound on digital audio tape (*see*: DAT), compact discs, or DVD, in which the signal is sampled up to 30,000 times per second and its characteristics are represented by digits, in the same way that all forms of information are handled by a computer in digital form. The digits are then transmitted or recorded and reconstituted as sound in the receiver or player. This process reduces distortion and interference.

• **digital versatile disk** or **video disk** ▶ *See*: DVD.

• **Diktat** ▶ (German, something dictated, from Latin *dictatum*) An order imposed from above without consultation or consent. Hitler gave the word ominous weight by bitterly referring to the Versailles Treaty as the Versailles *Diktat*. He is reported to have told the UK's ambassador: 'Everything that comes under the Treaty of Versailles I regard as extortion.'

• **dill** ▶ A fool. US and Australian slang of the 1950s, heard in school playgrounds in the UK since the 1970s. The derivation is uncertain, but it is possibly a shortening of dill pickle cucumber.

• **Dillinger era** ▶ *See*: Public Enemy No. 1.

• **dingo baby case** ▶ The disappearance of nine-week-old baby Azaria Chamberlain at Ayers Rock, central Austrialia, which led to what is now believed to have been one of the worst miscarriages of justice in the 20th century. When the baby vanished from her parents' tent at the popular tourist site immediate suspicion fell upon the dingo population of the area – several other campers reported that their children had been threatened in such a way not long before. However, various odd details of the case coupled with general disbelief that a dingo would be capable of carrying off a sleeping infant, led to the suggestion that the baby's parents – especially the mother, Lindy Chamberlain – were to blame. Blood-stained clothing was found but forensic tests failed to provide clear evidence to support the dingo theory. Moreover the Chamberlains were devout Seventh-Day Adventists; this led to rumours that the baby had been sacrificed in some awful religious ceremony. A criminal trial of the mother followed, the prosecution's case resting on a series of circumstantial but damaging items of forensic evidence (including the discovery of blood in the couple's car). The jury ignored the doubts that surrounded these elements of the prosecution's argument and the lack of any motive for the killing and found Lindy Chamberlain guilty. She was sentenced to hard labour for life, despite being pregnant. An appeal was dismissed in 1983 but the support of a lobby of scientists and massive public concern resulted in the case being reopened in February 1986. Lindy Chamberlain was finally released and later pardoned. The couple's story was filmed as *A Cry in the Dark* (1989), with Meryl Streep in the leading role.

• **dink** ▶ Slang term used by GIs in the Vietnam War for a Vietnamese. *See also*: gook.

• **dinkie** or **dinky** ▶ Acronym formed from *double income no kids*; it refers to a couple with well-paid jobs and no family to support. It was one of a variety of neologisms coined in New York during the early 1980s and subsequently used in the UK to describe various social subgroups and relationships. *See also*: oik; oink.

• **dinkum** ▶ Australian slang for genuine, sincere, honest. The word probably derives from English country dialect. It was also used to denote the second shipment of Anzacs sent abroad in World War I. The third shipment were called 'Superdinkums'. A 'dinkum-Aussie' is a native-born Australian.

• **Dior** ▶ A French fashion house founded by the designer Christian Dior (1905–57). In 1947 he introduced his **New Look**, which used fitted bodices and long full skirts, a departure that marked a change from wartime utility to post-war femininity. Later influential styles were the **A-line** and the **H-line**, so called because of their shape.

• **dioxin** ▶ A highly poisonous chemical present in some herbicides as an impurity. The substance is extremely persistent, taking years to disappear, and minute quanities cause serious blistering of the skin. Dioxin is also thought to cause cancer, birth deformities, and other conditions. Serious dioxin contamination occurred in July 1976 in the region around Seveso near Milan following an explosion at a weedkiller factory.

• **dipstick** ▶ The word first made an appearance in the late 1920s, meaning a rod inserted into a container in order to record the level of the liquid within it. In this sense it most commonly refers to the rod used to indicate the level of oil in the sump of an engine. It later took on a figurative meaning in relation to testing the popularity of such things as foodstuffs and television programmes. It also became, for obvious reasons, a slang euphemism for penis, later becoming one of the many slang words for a fool or idiot, for less obvious reasons.

• **dirt-track racing** ▶ Motor-cycle racing on a track of cinders or similar material; introduced into the UK from Australia in 1928.

• **dirty dancing** ▶ A form of dancing performed to pop music, which involves gyratory hip-to-hip contact with one's partner. Dirty dancing was popularized by the film (1987) of the same name, starring Patrick Swayze and Jennifer Grey.

• **dirty old man** ▶ A lecherous man of any age whose practices may include exposing his genitals in public to women or children and being excessively interested in pornographic magazines or films. The expression is sometimes embellished as 'a dirty old man in a raincoat': the raincoat is regarded as an anonymous garment that does not draw attention to its wearer; it may also have slit pockets to enable the wearer to masturbate during pornographic films or striptease acts. *See also*: flasher.

• **dirty protest**▶ *See*: Maze prison.

• **dirty tricks**▶ Any deceitful or subversive activity, especially those allegedly carried out by a government or other large organization, which may even be accused of having a 'dirty tricks department'.

• **dirty weekend**▶ A weekend away from home spent with one's lover. It may be premarital, adulterous, or even spent with one's spouse – the essential quality is that it should provide an opportunity for plenty of sex in a setting removed from one's everyday responsibilities.

• **dirty work at the crossroads**▶ In general, any nefarious or questionable activity. More specifically, the phrase is often applied to illicit sexual liaisons. It probably comes from the activities of highwaymen, who were often supposed to operate at crossroads.

• **Disarmament Commission**▶ A body created by the United Nations in 1952 by merging the Atomic Energy Commission and the Conventional Armaments Commission. It was given the task of preparing proposals for the 'regulation, limitation and balanced reduction of all armed forces and all armaments in a coordinated, comprehensive programme'. A new Disarmament Commission, comprising all UN members, was established as a result of the First Special Session on Disarmament, held in 1978. (The original Commission had not met since 1965.)

• **Disarmament Conference**▶ *See*: World Disarmament Conference.

• **disaster film** or **movie**▶ A type of film that deals with the struggles of various characters to survive a natural or man-made disaster. The subgenre has been popular since Hollywood's earliest years, with such examples as *Tidal Wave* and *San Francisco* in the 1930s, *Titanic* in the 1950s, and *Krakatoa East of Java* in the 1960s. But the 1970s was the decade of the disaster movie, with such spectacular star-studded examples as *The Poseidon Adventure* (1972), *Airport '75* (1974), and *Towering Inferno* (1974); these and numerous others attracted huge audiences to the cinemas. The plots mostly featured a collection of two-dimensional characters mouthing clichés at each other while being exposed to cataclysmic explosions, floodings, or conflagrations. The same decade also spawned a number of amusing spoofs of the genre, such as *The Big Bus* (1976) and *Airplane* (1980). In the 1990s the disaster movie made a comeback as a result of new techniques in creating special effects; *Twister* and *Independence Day* (both 1996) are examples, together with the James Cameron blockbuster *Titanic* (1997).

• **disc jockey**▶ (DJ) A person who introduces and plays pop records on the radio and in clubs. Radio DJs also provide a patter of lighthearted banter, which is intended to keep the listener company, and sometimes preside over phone-ins, competitions, etc. Disc jockeys became increasingly popular during the 1950s in America and the 1960s in the UK. However, record programmes with an introducer are almost as old as broadcasting; the BBC's Christopher Stone (1882–1965) ran a very popular record programme for many years in the 1930s, which may qualify him as the first disc jockey.

In the world of contemporary dance music, DJing involves mixing the tracks as well as playing them. Some practitioners of this art, such as 'Fatboy Slim' (Norman Cook), have become star performers in their own right.

• **disclosing agent**▶ A dye that is absorbed by plaque on the teeth and is used, usually in tablet form, to disclose areas of the teeth that have not been cleaned properly.

• **disco**▶ A nightclub in which people gather to dance to recorded pop music, which is often accompanied by elaborate computer-controlled lighting effects and laser shows. Disco was also a form of dance music, and a style of dancing, popular in the 1970s. The word *discothèque* (after *bibliothèque*) originated in France in the 1950s, and was adopted in its shortened form in the UK in the 1960s.

• **Discoverer**▶ A series of unmanned space satellites launched by America from 1959. Discoverer 13, launched on 10 August 1960, carried the first capsule to be successfully recovered from orbit.

• **Discovery**▶ The ship that carried Robert Falcon Scott (1868–1912) on his first voyage of scientific exploration to the Antarctic in 1901–04 (*see*: Scott of the Antarctic). By all accounts the *Discovery* was poorly suited to Antarctic exploration. Launched in Dundee on 21 March 1901, she was probably the last big wooden sailing ship built in the UK. She had three masts, which were too short and badly positioned, and was under-rigged. The sails were supplemented by auxiliary steam engines but she did not have enough coal capacity to make long distances under steam. The person responsible for this poor design was Admiralty constructor, W. E. Smith, who also designed the Royal yacht, *Victoria and Albert*, which nearly turned turtle when launched. In 1937 the *Discovery* became a training ship for sea scouts and from 1960 she was the Royal Navy's recruiting headquarters. Formerly moored on the Victoria Embankment on the Thames in London, in 1980 she was moved down the river to St Katherine's Dock before being taken to the Victorian Dock, Dundee.

• **Discworld** ▶ A series of humorous fantasy novels by British author Terry Pratchett (1948– ). The setting is a disc-shaped world supported by four giant elephants standing on the back of a giant turtle swimming through space. The series, which began with *The Colour of Magic* (1983), is not a continuous narrative but a succession of stories featuring different groups of characters. Prominent among these are Death, Rincewind the Inept, and the three witches – Granny Weatherwax, Nanny Ogg, and Magrat. The novels satirize numerous aspects of modern society and culture, while also parodying literary forms from fairytales to Shakespeare. With some 27 Discworld novels published to date, including *Mort* (1987), *Small Gods* (1992), and *The Last Hero* (2001), Pratchett's unique blend of wit and invention has attracted a large and devoted following. Discworld fans hold conventions, publish fanzines, and can choose from an array of merchandise and games.

• **Disgusted, Tunbridge Wells** ▶ A British catchphrase that is meant to represent a signature on a letter of protest to the press, by someone who is unwilling to use his or her real name. It also plays on the image of Tunbridge Wells, a town in Kent, as a bastion of reactionary Conservative views. The origin of the phrase is uncertain. Some suggest that Richard Murdoch, who had links with the town, used it in his radio show *Much Binding in the Marsh* in the late 1940s and early 1950s. It has always been used to convey an air of self-important indignation.

Tunbridge Wells is not alone in having been selected to represent some characteristic of the English; *see*: Neasden; Wigan.

• **dish** ▶ 1. A very attractive woman or man. Originally this slang expression was mainly used of women by men; it has been heard in America and the UK since the 1930s being an example of the way in which expressions relating to food are often applied to sex (*see also*: cheesecake). In an age of feminism, however, the term is now considered rather insulting by most women. Consequently it is now more usually applied to men by women. **2.** US slang for gossip. It is taken from the expression to **dish the dirt**, meaning to pass on all the gossip.

• **dish aerial** ▶ A saucer-shaped dish, about 1 m in diameter, used to receive television signals beamed from orbiting communications satellites owned by broadcasters, such as British Sky Broadcasting. The dishes have to be placed on the outside of a building in correct alignment with the satellite, which is in geostationary orbit (*see*: satellite television). Dish aerials of much greater diameter are also used for transmitting and receiving radio waves and microwaves in radio telescopes and radar installations. For example, the steerable radio telescope at Jodrell Bank, owned by Manchester University, has a 76.2 m (250 ft) diameter dish.

• **disinformation** ▶ Misleading or inaccurate information deliberately leaked or given to the media by official sources, such as government departments, to draw attention away from the true information. It was originally used of such information disseminated in the Soviet Union but has now spread worldwide.

• **diskette** ▶ *See*: floppy disk.

• **Disneyfication** ▶ A pejorative description of the way in which historically interesting places, events, or people can be trivialized for commercial purposes. It derives from the name of Walt Disney (1901–66), the renowned US maker of cartoon films; Disneyfication, however, refers not only to Disney's films and the characters he created in them, but also to the Disneyland theme parks, which feature these characters and others in a wide variety of historical settings.

• **Disneyland** ▶ The world's most famous amusement park, opened in Anaheim, California, in 1955. Disneyland incorporates all the fantasy elements of the cartoon world created by Walt Disney. The other US Disney parks are Walt Disney World, Orlando, Florida (1971) and its companion the Experimental Prototype Community of Tomorrow (EPCOT) Center (1982), Lake Buenavista, Florida. Another Disneyland was opened in Tokyo in 1983 and the most recent, EuroDisney, opened near Paris in 1992. This is served by the Eurostar train service direct from London via the Channel Tunnel.

• **Disneyland daddy** ▶ *See*: zoo daddy.

• **displaced person** ▶ (DP) Any person forced to leave their own country because of persecution, famine, war, etc. The term was used to refer to the vast number of people who at the end of World War II found themselves in a country other than their own, in which they had no legal rights. It included survivors of the German concentration camps and people who had been deported or used as forced labour, etc. Perhaps the term was used to distinguish such people from the pre-war 'refugees' from Nazi Germany and Austria, mostly Jews and intellectuals fleeing Hitler. By the end of the war most of these refugees were established in their new homes. Since the 1950s the word 'refugee' has been widely used again and now has a particular legal status under international law; it is defined by the United Nations as 'a person who, owing to a well-founded fear of persecution for reasons of race, religion, nationality, membership of a particular social group or political opinion, is outside the country of his nationality and is unable or, owing to such fear, unwilling to avail himself of the protection of that country'. The rights of refugees seeking **political asylum** have been detailed in two international treaties. Chief among these is the principle of **non-refoulement**, which prohibits forcible repatriation of a refugee to a country in which he or she has reason to fear persecution. Despite their obligations under international law, most countries have sought ways to limit their hospitality to those seeking asylum. In the UK, public and media hostility to so-called 'bogus asylum seekers' together with the rapidly rising number of applicants, has led recent governments to tighten the applications system in various ways. Current estimates put the number of displaced persons worldwide at about 17 million – the great majority of which have fled from one developing country to another. *See also.* economic migrant.

• **diss**▸ Slang of the late 1980s and 1990s meaning to snub or put down. An abbreviation of 'disrespect' or 'dismiss', it originated amongst Black teenagers in America and spread through the hip-hop craze.

• **District, the**▸ Storyville, the area of New Orleans that witnessed the beginnings of jazz in the years 1910–17.

• **dittybop**▸ Archaic US Black slang for a pretentious young man or woman who aims to persuade others that he or she is more hip than he or she really is.

• **div**▸ Originally British prison slang for a stupid or odd person, someone who doesn't fit in. It is a shortened form of 'divvy', which is thought to be a corruption of deviant. It has been used as a mild general insult since the 1980s.

• **dive bomber**▸ An aircraft designed for precision bombing of individual surface targets by diving at them at a steep angle. The most famous dive bomber was the JU87b Stuka, used by the Germans in the *Blitzkrieg* (*see*: Blitz) against Poland at the outset of World War II. Dive bombers were also used by British, US, and Japanese air forces during the conflict. The most successful attack by a British force was the sinking of the German light cruiser *Königsberg* by the Fleet Air Arm in Bergen Fjord, in April 1940. Dive bombers also played a major role during the German siege of Malta, in the Japanese attack on Pearl Harbor and in the Pacific theatre 1942–45. After the war, the theory and practice of dive bombing was superseded by high-level blanket bombing, as used by the Americans against large-scale targets in Korea and Vietnam.

• **dive bombing**▸ 1. British slang for covering a building or train with graffiti using spray paints; it has been in use since the 1970s. 2. British slang used by tramps and down-and-outs in the 1980s for collecting cigarette ends from the street and smoking them.

• **diver**▸

**Don't forget the diver** A British catchphrase from the popular radio programme ITMA, which ran from 1939 to 1949, starring Tommy Handley. It was spoken by Horace Percival as the Diver, and is said to have originated with a memory that Handley had of a man who used to dive off the pier at New Brighton, asking for money from onlookers with this phrase. First used in 1940, it soon became a phrase of wartime public-house bonhomie.

• **Dixie**▸ Short for **Dixieland**, a style of jazz played by White musicians using a combination of trombone, clarinet, and trumpet, that developed in imitation of the Black New Orleans style. It was named after the Original Dixieland Jazz Band (known as the ODJB), which was founded in 1912.

• **Dixiecrats**▸ A breakaway faction of the US Democratic Party, also known as **States' Rights Democrats,** formed to oppose the civil-rights policies of Truman in the 1948 presidential election. Support was concentrated in the traditionally conservative Southern states, hence the nickname 'Dixiecrats'. Governor Strom Thurmond of South Carolina was nominated as their presidential candidate, with Governor Fielding Wright of Mississippi as his running mate. Despite limited success in some of their heartland states, the Dixiecrats failed in their aim of denying the main contenders outright victory in the electoral college. Thurmond's share of the Southern vote was 22.5%, compared to Truman's 50.1%.

• **Dixie Dean** ▸ Nickname of William R. Dean (1907–80), British footballer who was a famous centre forward in the 1920s and 1930s. He holds the record for the maximum number of goals scored in an English league season (60 goals in 39 games for Everton football club).

• **Dixon, Jim** ► The antihero of *Lucky Jim* (1954), the first novel by Kingsley Amis (1922–95). Jim has taken up his first job as an assistant lecturer in history at a provincial university; here he makes various floundering attempts to impress girls and his superior, the absurd Professor Welch. The character's impotent loathing of the pretension and falseness all around him made Dixon (with his near contemporary, Jimmy Porter) one of the prototype Angry Young Men of the 1950s. However, while Porter is tragically angry, Dixon's rage is comic. Both Amis's novel and the somewhat lightweight John Boulting film (1957, with Ian Carmichael as Jim) enjoyed much success.

• **DIY** ► Do-it-yourself, a post-World War II phrase applied primarily to the efforts of the amateur house-repairer, improver, and decorator, etc., but also more widely to other forms of self-help. A DIY shop is one that caters for the growing needs of the amateur decorator, furniture repairer, etc.

• **Dizzy** ► Nickname of the Black US jazz trumpeter John Birks Gillespie (1917–93). In the 1940s, with Charlie (Bird) Parker, he revolted against the dominant swing style and introduced bebop, using a smaller band.

• **DJ** ► 1. *See*: disc jockey. 2. Abbreviation for dinner jacket. In this form of evening dress a black jacket with silk lapels is worn with a dress shirt and black bow tie. An invitation to an occasion at which this form of male dress is required, now usually states 'black tie'.

• **DMs** ► British slang abbreviation for Doc Martens.

• **DMT** ► Dimethyltryptamine. A synthetic hallucinogenic drug developed in the 1970s. The effects lasted only one hour, as opposed to the four to eight hours experienced by users of LSD.

• **DMZ** ► Abbreviation for demilitarized zone.

• **DNA** ► Deoxyribonucleic acid. The complex molecule that constitutes the genetic material of living organisms. Each molecule comprises two helically coiled strands, cross-linked by bonds rather like the rungs of a ladder. Individual genes correspond to specific segments of the molecule, which forms the key component of chromosomes. The **double helix** structure of DNA was discovered by the molecular biologists James Watson (1928–  ) and Francis Crick (1916–  ) in 1953, working at the Cavendish Laboratory in Cambridge. Their model for DNA solved the mystery of the way in which living cells faithfully replicate their genes and hence how genetic information is passed on to successive generations of organisms. It proved to be one of the most significant scientific discoveries of the 20th century.

• **DNA fingerprinting** or **DNA profiling** or **genetic fingerprinting** ► The analysis of characteristic patterns in DNA to identify a particular individual; it constitutes the most significant advance in crime detection since the fingerprint. The method was invented by Professor Alex Jeffreys at Lancaster University, and relies upon the uniqueness of each person's genetic make-up as determined by the DNA molecule in each living cell. These DNA variations can be identified from small samples of blood, tissue, hair root, or semen and then photographed for purposes of comparison. This virtually infallible technique is now used extensively in criminal investigations (especially of rape, when the rapist's semen is detectable on the victim), in verification of paternity, and in immigration screening to confirm blood relationships. National and international databases of DNA fingerprints are now being established, while research continues to investigate new applications for the technique.

• **D-notice** ► Defence notice. A British government notice to news editors not to publish items on specified subjects for reasons of security. First used in 1922, the D-notice has been strictly adhered to, enabling the UK to avoid press censorship.

• **do** ►
   **Can I do you now, sir?** *See*: ITMA.

• **dock asthma** ► British police and criminal jargon for the theatrical gasps of surprise or disbelief affected by prisoners in the dock. It has been in use since the 1950s.

• **docking** ► The joining together of two orbiting spacecraft, or of a spacecraft and a space station. In July 1975, there was a symbolic joint spaceflight in which a Soviet Soyuz spacecraft docked with a US Apollo spacecraft. The astronauts moved between the two craft and carried out joint experiments.

• **Docklands** ► The area of E London formerly occupied by the docks, wharves, and warehouses of the thriving Port of London. By the late 1960s, larger ships, a growing disinclination on the part of the shipowners to lose time in negotiating a tidal estuary, and competition from the Port of Rotterdam had led to the port's gradual demise. In 1981 the London Docklands Development Corporation was set up to redevelop the area for residential and commercial use. It now has many large office blocks (the **Canary Wharf** tower is the tallest office block in Europe) and a considerable number of prestigious riverside flats and houses. The Docklands Light Railway provided a connection to the London Underground system in 1987 and the area now has other rail links as well as its own airport. During the 1980s the Docklands redevelopment was widely seen as a showpiece for Thatcherism and the emerging yuppie ethic; as such, it tended to be praised or mocked according to the prejudices of the speaker. It is now generally accepted as one more episode in London's long history of change.

• **docknie** or **dockny** ► A word formed from 'dockland' by analogy with Cockney. It denotes a person who lives in London's former Docklands, which were redeveloped and gentrified in the 1980s (*see*: gentrification). As the original Cockney inhabitants can no longer afford to live there, 'docknie' is frequently used derogatorily. *See also*: deccie; dinkie; yuppie.

• **Doc Martens** or **DMs** ► Tradename for heavy-duty lace-up shoes or boots with thick resistant soles and strong yellow stitching. Worn originally by workmen, they became fashionable as part of the skinhead uniform in the late 1960s (*see*: bovver). In the 1980s and 1990s they were fashionable among young people, both male and female, and were made in all types and colours of leather and suede.

• **Doctor Dolittle** ► The amiable and eccentric vet who was able to converse with animals; he became familiar throughout the world in the stories of the English-born US children's author Hugh Lofting (1886–1947). Dolittle, with his many friends in the animal kingdom, including the duck Dab-Dab and his parrot Polynesia, first appeared in letters sent from Lofting to his children while he was fighting on the Western Front in World War I. The first Dolittle book was published in 1920, with a new book appearing annually until 1927. An attempt by Lofting to dispose of Dolittle by sending him to the Moon in a story of 1928 resulted in such a storm of protest that he was obliged to bring him back in 1933. Film versions have been made starring Rex Harrison (1967) and Eddie Murphy (1998, 2001).

• **Doctor Feelgood** ► A US expression for a doctor or other person who supplies drugs to be used illegally for pleasure rather than as a remedy. The name was used by a popular rock group of the 1970s.

• **Dr Fritz** ► *See*: Zé Arigó.

• **Dr Kildare** ► *See*: Kildare, Dr.

• **Doctor's mandate** ► The virtual free hand sought from the British electorate by Ramsay MacDonald's National Government in the general election of October 1931. Such a 'Doctor's mandate' was deemed necessary in order to treat successfully the ailing British economy. In August, MacDonald had reached agreement with the Conservative and Liberal leaders on forming a National Government but paid the price of rejection by his own Labour Party. MacDonald stood as a National Labour Party candidate and convincingly won both his own seat and the election; the National Government was returned with 554 of the 610 seats. Labour was reduced to a rump of 52 seats.

• **Doctors' Plot** ► An alleged conspiracy by a group of leading Soviet doctors to murder prominent political and military figures in Stalin's government. The nine doctors were arrested in January 1953 and charged with poisoning a former Leningrad party leader, Andrei Zhdanov, and with acting as US intelligence agents. Fears of an anti-Jewish purge were raised because six of the accused were Jews. However, following Stalin's death on 5 March, their planned trial never took place and charges against them were dropped. Certain police officers were subsequently executed for fabricating evidence against the doctors. In 1956 Khrushchev claimed that Stalin had indeed intended the doctors' trial to be a pretext for an antisemitic purge.

• **Dr Strangelove** ► *See*: Strangelove.

• **docudrama** ► A film or television programme based on true events, presented in dramatized form. This format has been criticized for distorting historical fact but its defenders claim that docudramas are educational and thought-provoking while providing entertainment. *Compare*: faction.

• **documentary film** ► A film that depicts fact rather than fiction. The term dates from 1929, although the first major work of the kind, Robert Flaherty's *Nanook of the North* (about Canadian Eskimos), was filmed as early as 1920. The potential of the form as a tool of political propaganda was first realized during the 1930s and exploited to the full during World War II. In the 1950s the advent of hand-held cameras and lightweight sound-recording equipment enabled documentaries to become ever more spontaneous and immediate in their style – the fly-on-the-wall documentary was born. *See also*: cinéma vérité.

• **docusoap** ► A fly-on-the-wall documentary broadcast as a television serial and designed to have the same kind of addictive appeal as a soap opera. Because they are cheap to make and tend to attract huge loyal audiences, docusoaps became a staple of the television schedules in the late 1990s.

• **dog breath** ▶ British and US slang for a person who is heartily disliked. A term of abuse current since the 1980s.

• **dogface** ▶ US slang for a soldier. It has been in use since World War II and possibly reflects the 'hang dog' expression of enlisted men.

• **dogfight** ▶ Close aerial combat between military aircraft. The dogfight originated during World War I with the invention of a synchronized system for firing forward-facing machine guns through a propeller's arc, without blowing it to pieces (although some pilots had previously used handguns to take potshots at one another). The system was first used by German Fokker E IIIs and was quickly copied by the British and French. The Germans also developed the classic aerial combat strategy, which is still used by the latest supersonic fighter aircraft. This involves the dive out of the sun at the enemy plane, followed by the turn over the vertical and another dive from the opposite direction. The first dogfights also produced the first air aces – different nations adopting different criteria for what constituted a legitimate kill, and how many kills were required for a pilot to qualify as an ace. During World War I, the best known ace was the German Manfred Von Richthofen (1892–1918), known as the Red Baron, who claimed to have shot down 80 enemy planes before being killed in action. In World War II, Douglas Bader (1910–82), the legless ace, became a British national hero. He was finally shot down and imprisoned by the Germans, who were only able to prevent his escape by depriving him of his artificial legs.

• **dogfood** ▶ A US drug user's name for a dark-coloured refined heroin. It was much used in the 1950s.

• **Dogger Bank, Battle of** ▶ A naval action during World War I (January 1915) in which German vessels under Admiral Hipper confronted a British squadron led by Admiral Beatty off the East Anglian coast. The Germans, comprising three battle cruisers and a heavy cruiser, were intercepted and chased by five British battle cruisers. British guns crippled and sank the heavy cruiser *Blücher* on the Dogger Bank, but a combination of tactical errors and poor ship-to-ship communication in the British fleet enabled the remaining German vessels to escape.

• **Dogger Bank incident** ▶ The tragic and startling attack by ships of the Russian Baltic fleet on Hull trawlers off the Dogger Bank in October 1904. Two of the British vessels were sunk, with the loss of their captains. Apparently, the Russians, en route

to fight Japan, mistook the fishing boats for Japanese torpedo boats. After an international inquiry in Paris, the Russians agreed to pay Britain £65,000 in compensation for the attack.

• **doggy bag** ▶ A bag into which the leftovers from a restaurant meal are put so that the diner can take them home to feed to his or her dog.

• **dog's dinner** ▶ 1. Or **dog's breakfast**. British slang for a mess: something that has been put together in a sloppy manner or something that has been bungled. It is used in such statements as 'he made a dog's dinner of it'. 2. A slang phrase often used in such expressions as 'done up like a dog's dinner', meaning over-dressed in a vulgar attempt at chic. The expression dates from the 1920s.

• **dog-tags** ▶ Identity discs of members of the US armed forces (World War II), from their similarity to the tags attached to a dog's collar to give its name and the address of its owners.

• **do it** ▶ A euphemism for having sexual intercourse. Because 'do it' has any number of ordinary nonsexual meanings, the scope for double entendre is huge. It was used by Cole Porter (1892–1964) in the song 'Let's do it' (1928) which began:

> Birds do it, bees do it,
> Even educated fleas do it,
> Let's do it,
> Let's fall in love.

• **do-it-yourself** ▶ *See*: DIY.

• **Dolby System** ▶ Tradename of a noise-reduction system used in cassette and video recorders to reduce tape hiss. It is named after Ray Dolby (1933– ), its US inventor, who devised the system in 1965.

• **dolce vita, la** ▶ (Italian, the sweet life) A life of idle self-indulgence characterized by glittering parties, *haute couture*, expensive restaurants, and sexual promiscuity. The phrase was popularized for English speakers by Federico Fellini's 1960 film with this title, which exposes the emptiness of the high life in Rome.

• **dole-bludger** ▶ Australian slang for someone who claims unemployment benefit (dole) without being entitled to it. This phrase is sometimes used in a more general sense to mean a lazy and unreliable person.

• **doll** ▶ 1. Originally US slang for a woman. Although probably not coined by the New York writer Damon Runyon, it was popularized by the title of his collection of short stories *Guys and Dolls* in 1933. The term became popular again in the 1970s, when it was also used of men by women. Feminists see it as having a patronizing and proprietorial flavour. **2.** US slang for a pill containing either barbiturates or amphetamines, especially as used by middle-class abusers of prescribed drugs. It is thought to have been invented by the US writer Jacqueline Susann, who used it in the title of her novel *The Valley of the Dolls* (1965). It may be derived from the idea of a doll as a source of comfort.

• **dollar diplomacy** ▶ Governmental support and furtherance of commercial interests abroad for both political and economic ends. The phrase, popular with critics of US policy, stems from the Taft administration (1909–13), which fostered such policies in the Far East and Latin America. Their intention was to control as well as to promote enterprise abroad by substituting dollars for bullets and lending 'all proper support to every legitimate and beneficial American enterprise abroad'.

• **dollar shop** ▶ A shop in a communist or formerly communist country in which goods may be purchased for US dollars, or other hard foreign currency, rather than for the local currency. Such shops supply luxury goods and other items not readily obtainable in the ordinary local shops.

• **doll city** ▶ A US teenage slang expression used to describe a beautiful person, either male or female, or a beautiful place or idea. It can also be used as an exclamation of approval.

• **Dolly the sheep** ▶ A sheep born in February 1997 at the Roslin Institute, near Edinburgh – the world's first mammal to be cloned from a body cell of an adult animal (*see*: clone). The birth of the ewe lamb attracted enormous press coverage, with many commentators seeing human cloning as the next step. Such interpretations were discouraged by the scientists involved, led by Ian Wilmut. The real significance of Dolly's birth is that she was developed from cultured cells taken from the udder of a mature ewe. Prior to this, cloned mammals had all been derived from embryos, or cultured embryo cells; Dolly opened up the possibility of cloning animals using much more easily obtained tissues.

The technique used involves taking an unfertilized egg cell from a recently ovulated animal, and sucking out the chromosomes, which carry the cell's genetic instructions. This 'empty' cell is then fused with a donor cell obtained from the animal to be cloned, and containing a full set of its chromosomes. When the fused cell starts to develop like a normal embryo, it is transferred to the womb of a surrogate mother to develop into a fetus. However, only 1–2% of cloned embryos survive to become living genetic replicas of the donor animal and some of these die soon after birth. Even so, the

technique provides a relatively easy means of cloning so-called transgenic animals, for instance a sheep that has been painstakingly genetically engineered to produce a human blood-clotting factor in its milk.

A similar technique is also being used to clone endangered species, to help ensure their survival. In this case another, usually closely related, species provides the recipient egg cells and acts as the surrogate 'womb'.

• **dolphinarium** ▶ An aquarium or pool in which dolphins are kept, typically one in which the dolphins have been trained to perform tricks for public entertainment.

• **dominatrix** ▶ A Latin word meaning either a female ruler or a mistress. In the late 1980s it became associated with the idea of a woman as the provider of sexual gratification in a dominant or disciplinarian role.

• **Dominici murder** ▶ The murder of the British nutritionist Sir Jack Drummond, his wife Anne, and their ten-year-old daughter on 4 August 1952 while camping in the French Alps at Digne. A 77-year-old farmer, Gaston Dominici, was found guilty of the crime two years later, but reprieved in 1957. The mystery was never solved.

• **dominion status** ▶ A term formerly used in relation to certain countries within the British Commonwealth, meaning that they were self-governing states rather than colonies. The term 'dominion' was applied after 1919 to Canada, Newfoundland, Australia, New Zealand, and South Africa, and their status was defined in 1926 as 'autonomous communities within the British Empire, equal in status...united by a common allegiance to the Crown'. Subsequently, any such country was referred to as a 'dominion'.

• **domino operation** ▶ A surgical operation developed in the late 1980s in which the heart and lungs from a deceased person are transplanted into the body of a patient whose lungs are in need of replacement but whose heart is sound. This patient's heart is then transplanted into another patient whose lungs are healthy but whose heart is in need of replacement. The reason for this procedure is that it has been found that transplanting the lungs alone is less successful than transplanting heart and lungs together; the domino operation is also economical with transplant organs, which are often in short supply. First performed at Harefield Hospital, W London, the operation is thought to owe its name to the fact that the face of a domino piece is divided into two equal parts, rather than to any connection with the 'domino effect' (*see*: domino theory).

• **domino theory** ▸ The theory prevalent in US foreign policy during the Cold War, which justified US intervention in SE Asia to contain the spread of communism. President Eisenhower explained the theory in a press conference on 7 April 1954: 'You have a row of dominoes set up, you knock over the first one, and what will happen to the last one is that it will go over very quickly'. The theory was embraced as a moral imperative by subsequent US administrations, in the belief that if Indochina went communist, then so would Burma, Thailand, and Malaya, followed by all the other countries of SE Asia. The communists could then pose a dangerous threat to Australia and New Zealand and thereafter to the remainder of the free world. The domino theory led directly to America's disastrous involvement in Vietnam (*see*: Vietnam War).

The effect in which a row of dominoes collapses if one falls is used metaphorically in other contexts, and is often known as the **domino effect**.

• **Donald Duck** ▸ British and Australian rhyming slang for fuck, often abbreviated as in: 'fancy a Donald?' It derives, of course, from the Disney cartoon character, an irascible duck who was first seen in *The Wise Little Hen* (1934).

• **Donington Park** ▸ A motor racing circuit near Castle Donington, Derby. It was originally opened in 1931 for motor cycles and saw its first car racing event in 1933, which was organized by the Derby and District Motor Club. One of the first closed road circuits in the UK, the Donington track ran for 2 miles through wooded parkland of the former seat of Lord Hastings. During World War II Donington was used as an army vehicle depot and the circuit fell into disuse. It was not until 1977 that Donington reopened for motor cycling and automobile events. It is now a venue for saloon, sports car, and formula racing events, including Formula 3 and Formula 3000. Donington also hosts the British Motor Cycle Grand Prix.

• **donkey** ▸ British slang for a slow or clumsy person. It is often used by football fans, who make braying noises at a player (particularly one from the opposing team) who misses a ball or plays badly.

• **Donovan Report** ▸ The report of the Royal Commission on Trade Unions and Employers' Associations, chaired by Lord Donovan and published in 1968. The Report focused on ways of reducing the high incidence of unofficial strikes in British industry and recommended moving towards local plant agreements in place of national agreements between unions and employers. Donovan also advocated setting up an independent Industrial Relations Commission to investigate problem areas of industry and the establishment of Labour Tribunals to examine grievances held by individuals against either employers or unions. The report was criticized by some for rejecting criminal sanctions to curb unofficial strikes and picketing.

• **Don't just stand there, do something!** ▸ An exhortation that became a catchphrase in the 1940s, generally used humorously. The Samaritans, a voluntary organization that helps the suicidal and despairing by listening to them at length, sometimes inverts the exhortation to 'don't just do something, stand there'.

• **don't know** ▸ A person who is undecided about a particular issue, especially someone who refuses to give a definite answer either way in an opinion poll. See also floating voter.

• **doodlebug** ▸ *See*: buzz bomb.

• **doofer** ▸ **1.** A jocular term for a thing whose name has been temporarily forgotten or was never known, as in 'pass that doofer over'. **2.** Slang for a half-smoked cigarette, the other half of which will 'do for' later. This usage dates from World War II but is still heard.

• **doolally** ▸ Temporarily deranged. 'He's gone doolally', might be said of someone who has succumbed to a short-term stress by behaving in a strange way that is out of character. The word comes from the British army in the years of the Raj (until 1947). Soldiers due to return to the UK were sent to a camp in Deolali, near the port of Bombay, where they often remained for some time before being shipped home. Their restless unsettled behaviour was described as '*doolally dap*' (*dap* being Urdu for fever).

• **Dolittle, Doctor** ▸ *See*: Doctor Dolittle.

• **Doolittle, Eliza** ▸ *See*: Higgins, Professor.

• **Doolittle raid** ▸ A US bombing raid on Tokyo and other Japanese cities by planes from the carrier USS *Hornet*, which took place on 18 April 1942. The US test pilot Colonel James H. 'Jimmy' Doolittle led his force of 16 bombers more than 800 miles across the Pacific to their targets. Being unable to return over such a distance, the planes flew on into China. Two crashed in Japanese-controlled territory. Doolittle was awarded the Congressional Medal of Honour for his exploit.

• **doom-and-gloom merchant** ▸ A person who seems to enjoy bad news and can be counted on to put the worst possible interpretation on any situation.

• **Doomsday Clock** ▶ An image of a clock contained in each issue of the Bulletin of Atomic Scientists (founded 1945) that indicates the time supposedly remaining before the nuclear holocaust (imagined to take place at 12 o'clock). In 1945 the time was set to 11.52, at the height of the Cold War it was moved to 11.58, but following Gorbachov's reforms in the Soviet Union and the collapse of communism in E Europe, it was put back to 11.50.

• **Doomsday machine** ▶ A hypothetical nuclear weapon designed to destroy all human life when triggered by a nuclear attack. The idea behind the Doomsday machine is that if nuclear weapons act as a deterrent then the ultimate deterrent would be automatic destruction of everybody. The concept was first put foward by the US mathematician and 'futurologist' Herman Kahn (1922–   ).

• **doorstepping** ▶ Journalists' slang for their unpopular and unprincipled custom of waiting outside the private house of someone in the news, in order to obtain a doorstep interview the moment the person steps outside.

• **doo-wop** ▶ A type of male harmony singing popular in large US cities in the 1950s, especially among Blacks and Italians. The name, which was coined in the 1960s after the popularity of the style had declined, is derived from the 'doo-da' of Negro songs and the derogatory 'wop' for an Italian; it also reflects the nonsense sounds used in the singing.

• **dope** ▶ 1. In the 20th century this word became very familiar as a term for an illegal drug, or as a verb meaning to drug. This presumably derives from its 19th-century meaning, an additive used to improve the properties of something, which in turn comes from the Dutch *doop*, sauce. In Britain dope usually means cannabis, but in America it often means heroin. 2. A fool, stupid person. This later meaning probably derives from the drug sense, in that someone given dope would be likely to behave in a stupid way. 3. Detailed information, as in 'give me the dope on this new invention'. This sense is of US origin, but unknown derivation.

• **Doppler shift** ▶ *See*: redshift.

• **Dora** ▶ Acronym for the Defence of the Realm Acts, which imposed many temporary restrictions on individual freedoms during and after World War I. Their application to the drink trade caused particular irritation. The term passed into common speech after being used in the law courts by Mr Justice Scrutton. In numerous newspaper cartoons Dora was portrayed as a long-nosed elderly female, the personification of restriction.

• **dormitory town** ▶ A small town within commuting distance of a larger town, the majority of the residents of which work in the larger town. Because property is so expensive in the large cities of Europe and America, many people live in dormitory towns, where houses and flats are cheaper. In addition, many commuters regard their home towns as havens from the crowds, noise, and pollution of the cities.

• **Dormobile** ▶ Tradename for a type of small van equipped with living accommodation; a type of camper.

• **Dorothy Dix** or **Dorothy Dixer** ▶ In Australia, a planted question in parliament that has been pre-arranged so that the minister can make a political point from the answer. It is named after a newspaper agony column 'Dear Dorothy Dix'.

• **dosh** ▶ British slang for money. Originally a working-class term dating from the 1950s, its use was revived in the 1980s with similar words, such as 'bread' and 'spondulicks', by alternative comedians whose material frequently dealt with the current obsession with money and who therefore needed a wide range of euphemisms. This sense is thought to derive from an African colonial term 'dash' meaning a tip; it could also be derived from 'doss' meaning the price of a doss, somewhere to sleep overnight.

• **Dossena forgeries** ▶ A series of paintings and sculptures, which were accepted as genuine old masters by the artistic establishment in the 1920s but were later proved to be forgeries by the Italian restorer Alceo Dossena. Unlike many other art forgers, Dossena was equally adept at faking the work of several artists. He was so scrupulous in using old materials and so skilled in imitating the styles of the old masters that it was only the sheer number of these 'newly discovered' masterpieces that finally gave him away. Even after he was unmasked several leading museums refused to withdraw his works, so convinced were they of their authenticity: indeed some of his works are thought still to remain on display.

• **dot com** or **dot.com** ▶ A phonetic representation of the suffix '.com' used in the names of Internet domains to signify a commercial organization; an example would be 'oneborneveryminute.com'. The late 1990s saw a proliferation of dot com enterprises, which traded mainly or exclusively via the Internet, and the appellation 'dot com' came to denote anything or anybody connected with e-commerce. Hence there have been 'dot com spin-offs', 'dot com lawyers', and even a 'dot com summit' of European leaders. The 'dot com boom' of 1999–2000, in which new dot com businesses enjoyed an inflated stock-market value that could hardly be justified by their assets or performance, was followed surely enough by the 'dot com bust' of 2000–2001, in which many companies went to the wall.

> But the dot-com lure is likely to continue and big money is at stake. James Titcomb, who registered his three-letter domain for fun in 1996, is entertaining bids of $1M for the site, which, despite having no content, gets thousands of visits every week. Perhaps it's predictable: it is at www.tit.com. – *The Independent*, 25 March 2000.

• **double agent**▶ A spy who pretends to work for one country while in fact acting for a hostile country. The most famous British double agents were Harold 'Kim' Philby (1912–88), Guy Burgess (1911–63), Donald Maclean (1913–83), and Anthony Blunt (1907–83) (*see*: Magnificent Five).

• **double-bagged** ▶ US teenage slang of the 1970s describing a totally dreadful or hopelessly ugly person. It reflects the idea that the person concerned ought to wear *two* bags over his or her head. The term 'double-bagged' originated in baseball jargon, to describe a hit that enables the batter to advance two bases (or bags).

• **double-blue** ▶ British drug slang of the 1960s for a blue pill containing amphetamines or barbiturates. They were popular with the mods (*see*: mods and rockers).

• **double exposure**▶ A photographic film that has been exposed twice and therefore contains two superimposed images. The technique is used in trick photography and in cinematic special effects.

• **double helix**▶ *See*: DNA.

• **Double Summer Time** ▶ *See*: daylight saving.

• **doublethink**▶ A term used by George Orwell in his Nineteen Eighty-Four (1949) to describe the end result of total political indoctrination. It denotes the mental ability to hold and accept simultaneously two entirely conflicting views or beliefs. *See also*: newspeak.

• **double whammy** ▶ A slang expression that is now generally used to mean a double blow or disaster. It was used in this sense in a Conservative Party campaign poster during the general election of 1992, referring to Labour's tax proposals. Originally 'whammy' seems to have been a US slang word for a hex or curse:

> to put a whammy on someone is to curse them, bring them bad luck...Al Capp, in his cartoon strip *Li'l Abner*, featured a fearsome witch-like creature who could invoke a double-whammy. A triple whammy is too awful to contemplate.
> – LARRY ADLER, letter to *The Independent*, 28 March 1991.

Confusingly, there is evidence of the phrase being used in a directly opposite sense to mean a double triumph.

• **Double your pleasure, double your fun** ▶ An advertising slogan used from 1959 in America for Wrigley's doublemint chewing gum. In the UK a TV quiz show called *Double Your Money*, which started in 1955, had a signature tune that included the line 'Double your money, double your fun'.

• **dough** ▶ *See*: bread.

• **doughboy** ▶ Colloquial name for a US soldier in World War I. The nickname derived ultimately from a dough cake baked for sailors, but from the late 1840s it was given to US soldiers (until World War II, when GI generally took its place). The common explanation is that the large brass buttons of the soldier's uniform resembled the dough cake.

• **doughnutting**▶ A practice in which members of the British House of Commons form a close group or doughnut-like ring around a fellow MP, who has been chosen to address a session of parliament while it is being televised. This creates the impression that the chamber of the House is crowded, when in fact it might be very sparsely populated. Doughnutting originated in November 1989, when television cameras were first allowed to record the proceedings of the House.

• **Douglas** ▶ British student slang of the 1980s for a third class honours degree; a third. It is a play on the name of the Conservative politician Douglas Hurd. *See also*: Desmond; Pattie; Taiwan.

• **Douglas aircraft**▶ Any of the aircraft built by the Douglas Aircraft Company, founded by Donald Douglas (1892–1981) in 1921. Douglas initially built planes for the military; the series of **DC** (Douglas Commercial) models began in 1932 with the prototype DC-1, followed by its production version, the DC-2. Successive DC models were at the forefront of aviation development; the DC-3 (*see*: Dakota) was the first sleeper-transport, while the DC-4 was the world's biggest air transport. During World War II military versions of both the DC-3 (C-47) and DC-4 (C-54) saw active service. In 1951 the Douglas F4D Skyray delta wing fighter established a new world record speed of 1211 kph (753 mph). Post-war commercial airliner development continued with the

DC-6 (1947), DC-7 (1953), DC-8 (1958), and DC-9 (1965). The DC-10 airbus came on the scene in 1970, three years after the Douglas Company merged to become the McDonnell Douglas Corporation.

• **Dounreay** ▸ The site, near Thurso in Scotland, of the world's first fast-breeder reactor (see: nuclear reactor). Operation of the first experimental fast reactor at Dounreay started in 1955, while the large-scale prototype fast reactor came on stream in 1974 and was closed down in 1994. The site then became a unit for processing radioactive waste, which is due to close when its current contracts have been completed.

• **dove** ▸ A person who favours a conciliatory foreign policy rather than an aggressive one based on the threat or use of military force. The term was first used during the Vietnam War. People who take the opposite view are known as **hawks**. See also: dawk

• **Dow Jones Industrial Average** ▸ An index of prices on the New York Stock Exchange issued by the financial advisors Dow Jones & Co. It is based on 30 consistent securities, with a base value of 100 in 1928. In the Great Depression it fell to a value of 41 and now stands at well over 10,000. See also: Footsie.

• **downcycle** A downward movement of the economy as part of a cyclic process.

• **downer** ▸ 1. Drug-users' slang for a tranquillizing drug, especially a barbiturate. It is the opposite of an **upper**, or stimulant. 2. Slang for a depressing experience or person. It was originally part of US beat jargon but became widely used in all English-speaking countries in the 1960s. It now sounds rather dated.

• **Downing Street Declaration** ▸ A declaration concerning the future of Northern Ireland signed on 15 December 1993 by the British prime minister, John Major, and the prime minister of the Irish Republic, Albert Reynolds. The two governments stressed their commitment to achieving a negotiated settlement in the province and their willingness to accept any decisions regarding its future political status made by a majority of its people. They also announced their readiness to negotiate with all parties committed to peace and democracy. The Declaration was a major factor in the IRA's decision to call a ceasefire on 31 August 1994, thus potentially enabling its political wing, Sinn Féin, to participate in the talks. The Protestant paramilitaries made a similar announcement. However, progress towards substantive all-party talks broke down over the IRA's unwillingness to decommission its weapons and the British govern-

ment's insistence on making the negotiating forum an elective body. The IRA called off its ceasefire in February 1996 but resumed it in July 1997, paving the way for the Good Friday Agreement.

• **Down in the forest something stirred** ▸ A British catchphase meaning that at last something has happened. It comes from the 1915 song 'Down in the Forest' with music by Sir Landon Ronald and words by H. Simpson. The song goes on to reveal that it was only a little bird that stirred.

• **download** ▸ To transfer data from one computer to another or from a controlling computer to a remote device.

• **down-market** ▸ See: middle-market.

• **downshifting** ▸ Deliberately embracing a less affluent but more fulfilling lifestyle. The term became current in America in the mid-1990s, when journalists noticed a growing trend for successful men and women to turn their backs on conventional career advancement. A disenchantment with long hours, stress, and disruption to family life, led these 'downshifters' to seek less demanding work, even at the cost of a reduced income.

• **downside** ▸ A 1980s vogue word meaning the disadvantageous or negative aspect of something. Originally, the term was restricted to business jargon, meaning the potential loss that would be sustained if a financial investment did not do well.

• **downsizing** ▸ A commercial exercise in which a large company attempts to become a smaller but more profitable company by cutting costs. Inevitably this involves both reducing the workforce and encouraging the rump to work harder. It is claimed that this manoeuvre not only reduces overheads but increases the flexibility and adaptability of an organization. However, recent surveys suggest that the survivors of downsizing become too insecure to perform as intelligent employees, while the victims emerge onto the job market convinced that corporate loyalty is misguided (see also: corporate anorexia). More sophisticated companies, accepting that profitability is directly linked to the loyalty of their customers, are less cavalier about making long-service staff redundant; they recognize that loyal customers are almost exclusively nurtured by loyal employees.

• **downtime** ▸ The period during which a machine, particularly a computer, is inoperative, for example when it is undergoing overhaul or repairs. In common with many other technical and computing terms, 'downtime' has entered the general language and can be applied to any non-productive period, such as a holiday.

• **downtown** ▸ The business district of a US city, so called from New York, where financial houses are concentrated on the southern tip of Manhattan Island.

• **DP** ▸ *See*: displaced person.

• **Dr** ▸ *See at*: Doctor.

• **drag** ▸ 1. A single inhalation of a cigarette or joint. 2. A boring task or person. A slang term of the 1960s. 3. The wearing of women's clothes by a man. The man is said to be **in drag**, while a performer who dresses up in this way is known as a **drag artist**. 4. In US slang, power or influence. For example, a person may be described as 'having drag with the president'. 5. A mainly US term for a street or thoroughfare.

• **dragon** ▸ A newly industrialized country (**NIC**), especially one in SE Asia. Examples include Taiwan and South Korea. The term dragon reflects the fierceness of the competition they offer to the industrial world, especially in such fields as light industry and electronics.

• **dragon lady** ▸ Originally any intimidating woman, a US usage derived from such a character in 'Terry and the Pirates', a comic strip of the 1930s. Recently the expression has come to mean a woman who wields great power, not because she herself holds a powerful office, but because she is the wife of someone who does. A famous example was Imelda Marcos, wife of Ferdinand Marcos (1917–89), former dictator of the Philippines.

• **Dragoon** ▸ *See*: Anvil.

• **Drain, the** ▸ London commuters' nickname for the Waterloo and City line, the underground train line between Waterloo and Bank stations, originally so called because of the dark tunnels and the fast-travelling, rather antiquated, trains.

• **drainpipes** ▸ British slang for the very tight trousers worn by teddy boys in the 1950s. They were later fashionable with the punks of the 1970s.

• **Drake Brass Plate** ▸ During his voyage of circumnavigation (1577–80), Sir Francis Drake anchored off the Californian coast in 1579 and set up a brass plate naming the territory New Albion and claiming it in the name of Queen Elizabeth I. In 1936 the plate was said to have been found near San Francisco and the inscription seemed to be reasonably authentic although some authorities expressed doubt. A replica was, in due course, presented to Queen Elizabeth II and kept in Buckland Abbey, Drake's Devonshire property, now a museum. In 1977 a reported analysis of the composition of the brass by the Lawrence Berkeley Institute of the University of California and the Research Laboratory for Archaeology at Oxford found that it was of the 19th- or early 20th-century manufacture.

• **Drake's Drum** ▸ A drum that belonged to Sir Francis Drake, which is said to have sounded three times in the 20th century as a warning of national peril. According to tradition, the dying Drake ordered that his drum be returned to his home, Buckland Abbey near Plymouth, promising that if it was sounded in the future he would return to aid England in its hour of need. Legend has it that the drum is beaten by an unseen hand when a national crisis threatens. In 1914 it beat to herald the start of World War I. Four years later it was said to have been heard beating a victory roll aboard the flagship the *Royal Oak* as the German fleet arrived at Scapa Flow to surrender at the end of the war: an exhaustive search of the ship failed to reveal the source of the noise. Finally, in World War II, it was heard to sound once more – this time to mark the evacuation of Dunkirk in 1940.

• **drape** ▸ US Black slang from the 1930s for a stylish man's suit. The term was later adopted by the teddy boys for the long Edwardian-style jackets they wore.

• **D-ration** ▸ An emergency ration distributed to US troops. It consists of concentrated chocolate and is one of a series of such rations designated by letters of the alphabet. *See also*: K-rations.

• **draw** ▸ 1. British slang, dating from the 1950s, for tobacco. It is derived from the act of inhaling and came originally from prison jargon. 2. British slang, dating from the 1970s, for cannabis – an obvious extension of the previous meaning.

• **drawing board** ▸ *See*: back to the drawing board.

• **Drbal's pyramid** ▸ The claim by the Czech engineer Karel Drbal, in 1959, that under certain conditions small pyramids have the power to sharpen razor blades and preserve food. These alleged properties of the pyramid were studied by Drbal after he read of research by a French scientist, who suggested that the shape of the pyramids of ancient Egypt in some way contributed to the preservation of mummies placed within them. Drbal found that food placed in small pyramids could indeed be made to last longer than could be reasonably expected; he further found that razor blades lying on an east-west axis inside the pyramid were inexplicably sharpened. Speculation to account for these alleged phenomena persists; Drbal himself successfully patented his discovery and small pyramids for sharpening razor blades are still being sold around the world.

• **dreadlocks** ▶ The hairstyle worn originally by male members of the Rastafarian religion of Jamaica, in which the hair is worn in long tight ringlets that are never cut or brushed. The style has since been adopted by young people of all races and both sexes with no religious significance. The term is often shortened to **locks**.

• **Dreadnought** ▶ The 17,900-ton turbine-engined big-gun battleship completed in 1906, the first of a famous class, which greatly influenced subsequent naval construction. An earlier ship of this name was in use in the reign of Queen Elizabeth I. The name was revived in 1963 for the UK's first nuclear submarine.

• **Dreadnought hoax** ▶ A practical joke that made the Royal Navy a laughing stock in 1910. The hoax centred on the visit of a supposed party of princes from Abyssinia to HMS Dreadnought, the pride of the navy's battle fleet, as it lay at anchor in Weymouth Bay. A telegram warned the ship's captain of the visit, allowing him just enough time to assemble the Royal Marine band and make all the arrangements suitable for a royal visit. Resplendent in flowing robes and heavy beards, the guests were given an official tour of the ship, exclaiming 'Bunga, bunga!' with enthusiasm at regular intervals. They refused all offers of food, however, on religious grounds. The hoax was subsequently revealed in the papers to have been the work of the well-known practical joker William Horace de Vere Cole. The 'princes' had included a well-known cricketer, the artist Duncan Grant, and the future novelist Virginia Woolf; their disguise was the work of Sarah Bernhardt's make-up artist (who had warned them against eating anything because it might smudge their 'brown' skin).

• **dream** ▶
**I have a dream** A phrase repeated several times, with rising emotional effect, in the peroration of a speech by the Black civil rights leader Dr Martin Luther King (1929–68); the speech was delivered to some 200,000 people at the Lincoln Memorial in Washington on 27 August 1963 and is now remembered as one of the 20th century's most inspired examples of political oratory.

> I have a dream that one day this nation will rise up, live out the true meaning of its creed: we hold these truths to be self-evident, that all men are created equal. I have a dream...

King's dream of racial harmony was advanced but not realized in his own lifetime, which was brought to an early end on 4 April 1968 by a White assassin,

James Earl Ray, who shot him dead on a motel balcony in Memphis, Tennessee. Various conspiracy theories to account for the killing have been suggested but none substantiated. *See also*: civil rights movement.

• **dream factory** ▶ A film studio, or the motion-picture industry in general.

• **dream ticket** ▶ An ideal combination of two political candidates seeking office together in an election. The hope is that together they will appeal to a greater section of the electorate than either of them would individually. Mostly associated with the US elections for president and vice-president, the term has also been used in the UK of the leader and deputy leader of the Labour party.

• **Dresden fire bombing** ▶ A bombing attack starting on the night of 13–14 February 1945, on the city of Dresden in SE Germany. The attack began with 800 RAF Lancaster bombers dropping bombs and incendiaries shortly before midnight. This caused a 'fire-storm', in which hot air rising from burning buildings led to high winds, which further fanned the flames, causing immense destruction and loss of life. The next day the 8th US Air Force mounted a daylight raid with over 400 B-17 bombers and on 15 February another attack was made with 200 bombers. The result was the almost complete destruction of one of the most beautiful cities in Europe and the death of many people (estimates vary from 30,000 to 130,000). This systematic destruction of Dresden, a virtually undefended city with no obvious military significance, in the closing months of the war was justified strategically as a way of destroying a German centre of communications to aid the Soviet advance on the Eastern Front. Probably, it had little military effect and it has subsequently been criticized as a product of Air Chief Marshal Sir Arthur Harris's fanatical belief that bombing civilians could by itself destroy a country's will to continue fighting. *See*: Bomber Harris.

• **Dreyfusard** ▶ An advocate of the innocence of Capt. Alfred Dreyfus (1859–1935), a French artillery officer of Jewish descent who was convicted (1894) on a charge of betraying military secrets to Germany and sent to Devil's Island. In 1898 Clemenceau and Emile Zola took up his case, Zola writing his famous open letter *J'accuse*. In 1899 Dreyfus was re-tried, again condemned, but shortly afterwards pardoned. In 1906 the proceedings were finally quashed and Dreyfus was awarded the Légion d'Honneur. The whole affair reflected the greatest discredit on the French military hierarchy of the time.

• **Drinka Pinta Milka Day**► A British advertising slogan used by the National Milk Publicity Council of England and Wales in 1958 in a drive to persuade every man, woman, and child in the British Isles to drink at least one pint of milk every day. 'Pinta' has now become an accepted slang word for a pint of milk.

• **drink-driving**► See: breathalyser.

• **drive-by** ► Describing a murder or injury inflicted by someone shooting at the victim from a moving car. Drive-by shootings are mainly associated with feuding US gangs.

• **drive-in**► A cinema, fast-food restaurant, bank, or other venue that can be visited without leaving one's car. The US drive-in cinemas flourished in the 1950s, when they provided a haven of privacy for courting couples.

• **Drones' Club** ► The gentlemen's club frequented by Bertie Wooster and his circle in the novels of P. G. Wodehouse. Situated in Dover Street, the Drones' Club was particularly favoured by young men of good connections but limited intellect. The uninterrupted round of social pleasure enjoyed at the club included such events as the Clothes Stakes, in which bets were placed on the attire worn by the next person to enter the bar, with Claude 'Mustard' Pott making the book:

> I am offering nine to four against Blue Serge, four to one Pin-striped Grey Tweed, ten to one Golf Coat and Plus Fours, a hundred to six Gymnasium Vest and Running Shoes, twenty to one Court Dress as worn at Buckingham Palace, nine to four the field.

• **drongo**► A colloquial expression, originating in Australia, for a stupid or totally useless person. It is derived from a racehorse of this name, which was notorious for its lack of success.

• **droog**► See: nadsat.

• **drop**► A place in which secret agents leave messages or other information to be picked up by other agents. It is one of a number of terms popularized, and perhaps invented, by writers of spy fiction. See also: dead-letter box.

• **drop dead** ► 1. A phrase that originated in America in the 1930s, but is now used in all English-speaking countries. It is an emphatic way of saying 'be quiet', 'go away', or 'absolutely not'. 2. **drop-dead**. British slang of the 1990s meaning unbelievably, outstandingly (i.e. to an extent that the observer is liable to drop dead with amazement), as in such phrases as **drop-dead gorgeous**.

• **drop-dead fee**► If individuals or firms wish to take over another company using borrowed money, they often arrange a drop-dead fee to be paid to the lender if the bid fails and the loan is not required. If the bid succeeds the borrower pays interest to the lender in the usual way; the purpose of the fee is to ensure that they only incur interest charges if the takeover succeeds.

• **drop-nose**► Describing a type of aircraft design in which the nose cone of the aircraft can be pivoted downwards to give the pilot more visibility during landing. The best-known drop-nose plane is the Anglo-French supersonic airliner Concorde.

• **dropout**► A person who abandons or withdraws from something, for instance a student who drops out of a university course. In the late 1960s it became a vogue word applied to people who rejected conventional society as a whole (see: hippie). The US advocate of psychedelic drugs, Timothy Leary, coined the famous slogan 'turn on, tune in, drop out'.

• **droppies** ► A British slang coinage for self-employed people: an acronym for disillusioned relatively ordinary professionals preferring independent employment situations. It was fashionable to coin such terms in the 1980s. See also: dinkie; yuppie.

• **drum 'n' bass**► (D'n'B) A style of dance music that became fashionable in the mid-1990s; the name refers to its distinctive feture, the pronounced drum and bass lines. Also called **jungle**, D'n'B is predominantly electronic, although it sometimes also involves acoustic instruments. Typically the drum beat is fast with complex syncopation; the bass line is unusually active, reflecting the influence of dub and reggae music. Stringed-instrument sounds are also regularly incorporated although usually generated by a synthesizer. Pieces are comparatively long; Timeless by Goldie, considered to be one of the classic drum 'n' bass tracks, runs to over 20 minutes. The style emerged from London clubs in 1994 and may be said to have peaked in 1997, when Roni Size Reprazent were awarded the prestigious Mercury Music Prize in 1997 for their album New Forms.

• **druzhinnik** ► In the former Soviet Union, an auxiliary policeman. The druzhinniki assisted the official police in crowd control and similar duties. The name comes from Narodnaya Druzhina, meaning 'People's Patrol'.

• **dubbing** ► The practice of adding dialogue, music, or sound effects to the soundtrack of a film that has already been shot. The main use of dubbing is to supply dialogue in another language for the foreign release of a film.

• **Dubya** ▸ The nickname of George W. Bush (1946–   ), president of the United States (2001–   ) and former governor of Texas. It represents a Texan pronunciation of 'W', the letter that distinguishes him from his father and namesake George Bush, who was also president of the United States (1989–93). There is an apocryphal story that following Bush's disputed election victory in 2000 (see: chad), the staff of the outgoing president, Bill Clinton, doctored the computers in the West Wing of the White House so that the letter W could not be keyed.

• **Duce** ▸ (Italian, leader) The title adopted by Benito Mussolini (1883–1945), the Fascist dictator of Italy from 1922 to 1943.

> The Duce is always right. – Fascist slogan, 1922.

• **duck** ▸
**Honey, I forgot to duck** US President Ronald Reagan's reaction to his wounding in an assassination attempt in 1981, addressed to his wife Nancy as he lay recovering. His assailant, John W. Hinckley, was found to be mentally ill. The remark was not original; the president was quoting the US boxer Jack Dempsey (1895–1983), who said the same thing to his wife when he was defeated by Gene Tunney in the title fight for the World Heavyweight Championship on 23 September 1926.

• **duck** ▸
**If it looks like a duck, walks like a duck and quacks like a duck, it's a duck** Infamous test proposed in the 1950s by the US union leader Walter Reuther to determine whether someone was a communist or not. See: McCarthyism.

• **duck's arse** ▸ See: DA.

• **Dugway Proving Ground** ▸ A US test site for biological and chemical weapons in Utah.

• **Duke** ▸ 1. Nickname of the US film actor John Wayne (1907–79). He acquired it as a child from the name he gave to his dog. 2. Nickname given to the US jazz composer, band leader, and pianist Edward Kennedy Ellington (1899–1974). His 'Mood Indigo' was a worldwide success, enabling him to keep his big band together for many decades after it had ceased to be economic. His later, more extended, compositions, reveal his genius as a tone painter.

• **Duke of Edinburgh's Award** ▸ An award scheme for young people aged between 14 and 25, originally launched in the UK as two separate awards (for boys and girls) in 1962; these were merged in 1969. The scheme is administered by schools, youth clubs, voluntary organizations, etc. It aims to foster self-reliance and a spirit of voluntary service amongst young people from different backgrounds. Bronze, Silver, and Gold badges and certificates are awarded on completion of various activities. The Bronze and Silver awards have four sections: community service, expeditions, skills, and physical activity. The Gold award has a fifth section, a residential project.

• **Duma** ▸ State Deliberative Assembly: the Russian parliament established in the wake of the 1905 revolution. The proposed constitution of the first Duma was detailed by Tsar Nicholas II in his October Manifesto of 1905, as part of a declaration guaranteeing civil liberties and greater representation for the Russian people. However, before its first session started in May 1906, the Duma's powers had been curtailed: all its decisions could be vetoed by the tsar and the tsar could pass laws when it was not sitting. Nevertheless, the first Duma proved to be radically inclined and demanded land reforms inimical to the government. It was duly dissolved in July 1906. The second Duma, which convened in March 1907, lasted only until June. Changes in the electoral system ensured more conservative third and fourth Dumas (1907–12 and 1912–17), which generally supported the government. During World War I opposition to the monarchy again swelled in the Duma; after the tsar was deposed in 1917, a Duma committee formed the first provisional government but was soon disbanded. In 1993, after the break-up of the Soviet Union, the State Duma was re-established as the lower house of the bicameral Russian parliament (Federal Assembly).

• **Dumbarton Oaks Conference** ▸ A conference held in August–October 1944 between representatives of the UK, America, the Soviet Union, and China to discuss plans for setting up the organization subsequently realized as the United Nations. There was general agreement over the basic structures, such as the General Assembly, Security Council, and Secretariat. More contentious were the issues of membership – the Soviet Union wanted separate membership for all of its 16 republics – and the right of veto in the Security Council. These questions were reconsidered at the Yalta Conference in February 1945. The talks were named after the mansion in which they were held, in Georgetown, Washington DC.

• **dumb blonde** ▸ An attractive but unintelligent young woman with blonde hair (whether natural or dyed: see: peroxide; platinum blonde). The phrase dates from the early 1930s, when it came to denote a stock character in Hollywood talkies – often a starlet of dubious talent or a gangster's moll. The stereotype of the dumb or dizzy blonde still lingers; even today, women with naturally blonde hair are sometimes advised to dye it brown or black if they wish to be taken seriously in a professional role.

> The brightest dumb blonde since Queen Boadicea sliced Roman kneecaps. – VICTOR DAVIS describing the actress Goldie Hawn.

• **dumbing down** ► The process of making something – a newspaper, an academic course, or perhaps a whole culture – intellectually less demanding and sophisticated than it was. The term first became current in America in the early 1990s, when Paul Fussell's book *Bad, or the Dumbing of America* (1991) sparked a fierce debate about declining intellectual standards in US education and culture. By the late 1990s the debate had spread to Britain, where hardly a week now seems to go by without the BBC, a broadsheet newspaper, or some other national institution being accused of 'dumbing down'.

In Britain one strand of the debate has focused on the public examination boards, which have been accused of making questions easier so that students achieve higher grades in their exams. The object of this practice, if it exists, is to give the impression that the massive expansion of higher education in the 1980s and 1990s was achieved without lowering standards. The accusation is hotly denied by all the educational authorities, although some university teachers claim that students coming up to universities appear to have less ability than they used to, in spite of having higher A-level grades.

On the more general question of whether society as a whole is 'dumbing down', the evidence is (perhaps inevitably) mixed. In 2001 research published in *Psychological Review* concluded that average IQ had risen by 24 points since 1918 in America and by 27 points since 1942 in Britain. At the same time, surveys point to an alarming absence of what was once considered core historical and cultural knowledge among the young. One such survey, conducted in 2000 for *The Guardian* newspaper, reported that while 18–24 year olds knew far more than their elders about computers and pop culture, only 30% could name Churchill as prime minister during World War II, only 23% had heard of Magna Carta, and only 7% knew that Milton wrote *Paradise Lost*.

• **Dunblane massacre** ► The shooting of 16 primary schoolchildren and their teacher in the small Scottish city of Dunblane on 13 March 1996. The massacre occurred when a local misfit, Thomas Hamilton, entered the gymnasium at Dunblane Primary School and opened fire at random before killing himself. Hamilton, an organizer of boys' clubs, had long been suspected of paedophile activities, although charges had never been brought.

A member of several gun clubs, he had been licensed to own six weapons. The killings caused an outpouring of grief and horror and new public pressure for a tightening of fire-arms regulations, which culminated in legislation banning private ownership of virtually all types of handgun. In 1998 a memorial garden, funded by public donations, was opened in Dunblane Cemetery, where all the victims are buried.

• **Dungeness** ► The coastal site in Kent of two nuclear generating stations. Dungeness A uses a Magnox reactor, and Dungeness B an advanced gas-cooled reactor. The site is linked by cross-Channel cable to the French electricity grid, enabling power to be transferred between the countries.

• **Dunkirk** ► This once notorious haunt of pirates and privateers has acquired fresh associations since World War II. It is now famous for the successful evacuation (26 May–4 June 1940) of the main British Expeditionary Force (*see*: BEF), in the face of imminent disaster, by Vice-Admiral Ramsay's motley force of destroyers, yachts, and a collection of little ships manned by their private owners (with essential air cover from RAF Fighter Command). Some 338,226 Allied troops were rescued at Dunkirk, most of whom survived to fight on. The term **Dunkirk spirit** is sometimes used for the supposed British characteristic of determination and resourcefulness in the face of disaster.

> The little ships, the unforgotten Homeric catalogue of *Mary Jane* and *Peggy IV*, of *Folkestone Belle*, *Boy Billy*, and *Ethel Maud*, of *Lady Haig* and *Skylark*...the little ships of England brought the Army home. – PHILIP GUEDELLA, *Mr Churchill*.

> Our great-grandchildren, when they learn how we began this war by snatching glory out of defeat...may also learn how the little holiday steamers made an excursion to hell and came back glorious. – J. B. PRIESTLEY, radio broadcast, 5 June 1940.

• **Dunsterforce** ► The name given to the men sent to Baku in 1918 under the command of Maj-Gen L. C. Dunsterville (1865–1946) – a schoolfellow of Rudyard Kipling who provided the model for the hero of *Stalky and Co*. The purpose of this expedition was to prevent the Turks and Germans seizing the oil-wells and Dunsterforce adequately accomplished its object.

• **Durex** ► A tradename for a condom, owned by LRC International (formerly London Rubber Co). The name was coined by LRC's former chairman, A. R. Reid, who also originated the brand names 'Gossamer' and 'Fetherlite'. The implication conveyed, presumably intentionally, by the name

Durex is that the product is sufficiently durable to provide the service required of it.

• **Dust Bowl** ▸ An area of land transformed into a semi-arid state through overgrazing, intensive farming, soil erosion, etc. Historically the term applies to a section of the Great Plains in America (between Kansas and Texas), which suffered a severe drought in the 1930s; as a result most of the top soil was blown away in huge black dust storms. Thousands of families from the region had to migrate west at the height of the Great Depression and ended up in migrant camps in California. These events were movingly and accurately described in John Steinbeck's novel *The Grapes of Wrath* (1939); the film version (1940) was directed by John Ford and starred Henry Fonda. In the 1940s, with Federal Aid, the area was largely recovered as productive agricultural land by erecting windbreaks and replanting grassland.

• **dust head** ▸ Slang for a user of the drug angel dust.

• **dusty** ▸ British upper-class slang of the late 1970s for an old person. It is less widely used than wrinklie or crumblie. According to *The Official Sloane Rangers' Handbook* by A. Barr and P. York, the ages go: wrinklie, crumblie, dusty.

• **Dutch** ▸ A nickname of Ronald Reagan. *See*: Great Communicator.

• **Dutch cap** ▸ A contraceptive device used by women. It consists of a dome-shaped rubber diaphragm inserted into the vagina before intercourse so that it fits over the cervix and prevents sperm from entering the uterus. It is said to take its name from a resemblance to the traditional cap worn by Dutch women.

• **Dutch disease** ▸ The deindustrialization of a nation's economy as a result of the discovery of a new natural resource. It is named after the situation that arose in the Netherlands with the discovery of North Sea oil and gas. The new resource raised the parity of the nation's currency against those of its trading partners, which caused a drop in exports as manufactured goods became less competitive. Imports, which became cheaper, rose and the country's balance of trade was seriously disturbed. The same series of events troubled the British economy after the discovery of North Sea oil.

• **Dutch elm disease** ▸ A fungal disease of elm trees, which withers the leaves and causes the tree's eventual death. The disease is most commonly spread by the European elm bark beetle, which carries the spores from infected to healthy trees. The disease reached almost epidemic proportions in the UK in the 1970s and 1980s when millions of trees had to be felled. First described in 1919 in the Netherlands, the fungus responsible, *Ceratocystus ulmi*, blocks the vessels that carry water to the leaves.

• **dutching** ▸ The practice of sending food that would not satisfy health regulations in the UK for irradiation in a European country where this is permitted; with the poor quality of the food thus disguised, it is placed on the UK market. Dutching is so-called because the irradiation is usually carried out in the Netherlands or Belgium. The practice came to public attention in 1989, when the legalization of food irradiation in the UK was being considered.

• **DVD** ▸ Digital versatile disk or digital video disk. An optical disk that can be used to store audio, video, or computer data; it is regarded as the successor to the compact disk, being far more versatile and having a much greater storage capacity. Since they were introduced in the late 1990s DVDs have become a popular alternative to prerecorded video cassettes.

• **dweeb** ▸ US and Canadian slang for a feeble, boring, or unfashionable person; a nerd. The word was first heard amongst teenagers in the 1980s; its derivation is not known.

• **DWEM** ▸ *See*: political correctness.

• **dyarchy** or **diarchy** ▸ A system of government, literally 'dual government', introduced into India by its colonial British rulers in 1919. Government of the provinces was divided between executive councillors, appointed by the governor and in charge of 'reserved' portfolios (*e.g.* police, justice, etc.), and Indian ministers responsible to their elected legislative council and in charge of 'transferred' departments, such as public health, agriculture, and education. The system was criticized because spending control remained the prerogative of the 'reserved' arm. However, dyarchy marked the first hesitant concession towards Indian self-government; it was replaced by a more comprehensive system of provincial autonomy in 1935.

• **dyke** ▸ Slang for a lesbian. Originally used pejoratively by heterosexuals, the word conveyed the stereotypical image of the very masculine and aggressive lesbian. It is now used by gay women themselves. The derivation is unknown.

Every twentieth page or so, she treats us to some coupling, unmetaphorical, squelchy even, with a tidy spicing of perversion and peppering of dykery. – Review of a Judith Krantz novel, *The Independent*, 20 March 1991.

**• Dylan, Bob ▶** Stagename of Robert Allen Zimmerman (1941– ), the US singer and songwriter whose work helped to redefine popular music in the 1960s. After a short period on the Greenwich Village folk scene, Dylan shot to prominence in 1963–64, when his songs 'Blowin' in the Wind', 'A Hard Rain's A-Gonna Fall', and 'The Times They Are A-Changin'', were adopted as anthems by the growing civil-rights and anti-war movement. The often repeated description of Dylan as a 'spokesman for his generation' was first coined at this time. However, Dylan then outraged many of his fans by abandoning political protest for a more complex – not to say obscure – style of lyric characterized by wild impressionistic imagery and scathing wit. He also caused controversy by playing with an electric backing band (*see*: folk rock). Dylan's new style – perfected on the 1966 *Blonde on Blonde* album – influenced everyone from the Beatles down and set the main direction for White rock music for about a decade. However, in mid-1966 Dylan was involved in a somewhat mysterious motorcycle accident – believed by some to be partly or wholly a hoax – and this was followed by a long period of seclusion and semi-retirement. During this time Dylan became a venerated but largely unwilling figurehead for the hippie counterculture, with obsessive **Dylanologists** poring over his every word (and in some cases, the contents of his dustbins; *see*: garbology) in an attempt to find the 'true' meaning of his songs. The 1970s saw a return to touring and further mercurial changes of style, stance, and image – most notoriously a very public conversion to Christianity (1979) which shocked many old fans. Although critics regard his later work as erratic, subsequent decades have only enhanced Dylan's reputation as rock music's greatest enigma and – probably – its only authentic genius.

**• dynamite ▶** US drug users' slang, dating from the 1960s, for good-quality heroin. This is an extension of the colloquial use of the word for anything especially good or powerful. The term is also used for a particularly powerful marijuana cigarette, a potent mixture of cocaine and heroin, or a mixture of heroin and marijuana.

**• dyslexia ▶** Inability to read, write, and spell correctly in otherwise normally intelligent people (known as 'dyslexics'). It is often caused by an impaired ability to learn these skills and affected children require specialized education to overcome their problems. The condition is often incorrectly called **word blindness**, but this is a different problem in which a person cannot read because of an inability to recognize printed letters, symbols, and words although writing presents no difficulty.

**• dyspraxia** or **clumsy child syndrome ▶** Inability to organize and coordinate body movements. Affected children have problems with writing, catching a ball, using cutlery, etc. They are often of above-average intelligence and can benefit from physiotherapy and occupational therapy. The condition was formerly confused with dyslexia.

# E

• **E** ▶ The drug Ecstasy. A fashionable abbreviation used from about 1988, when the rave culture took off. An **E-head** is someone who takes excessive amounts of ecstasy.

• **each way** ▶ Australian slang for bisexual. A humorous extension of the betting term.

• **eager beaver** ▶ A US expression in World War II for an over-zealous recruit whose keenness was marked by volunteering on every possible occasion; it was subsequently applied in civilian life to similar enthusiasts. The phrase derives from the frantic dam-building activity of beavers.

• **eagle** ▶ *See*: krugerrand.

• **eagle** ▶
**the golden eagle lays its eggs** British slang dating from World War II, meaning 'it's pay day'. It derives from US forces slang for payday, current before and during the war: **the day the eagle shits** or **the day the eagle screams**. This alludes to the eagle emblem appearing on US banknotes and coins, and also to the eagle symbolizing the serviceman's employer, *i.e.* the US government. Payday was also known simply as **eagle day**. British forces adapted the phrase, substituting the native species of bird.

• **Eagle Day** ▶ In World War II, the day appointed for the launch of the German air attack on the UK. It fell on 13 August 1940 and marked the beginning of the Battle of Britain.

• **Eagle's Nest** ▶ The mountain lair of Adolf Hitler at **Berchtesgaden**, near Salzburg, on the Austrian border. Heavily fortified, the Eagle's Nest or Berghof was constructed 1829 m (6000 ft) up the mountain; Hitler received many important guests here.

• **Eagle Squadron** ▶ One of the most distinguished squadrons of the RAF in World War II, manned entirely by US volunteers. Having destroyed 73 German aircraft, the pilots transferred to the US 8th Air Force when America entered the war following Pearl Harbor.

• **Ealing comedies** ▶ A series of British comedy films that have enjoyed continuous popularity since their release in the 1940s and 1950s. Lacking the financial resources available to the US film industry, the film-makers at the **Ealing Studios** in west London concentrated on characterization, plotting, and scripts. Standards of production also remained consistently high. The films, which include such classics as *Kind Hearts and Coronets* (1949), *Whisky Galore* (1949), and *The Titfield Thunderbolt* (1952), present a somewhat whimsical view of the British as a nation of eccentrics and lovable rogues. The studios were virtually disused from the mid-1960s until the late 1990s, when they were bought by an Anglo-American consortium.

• **ear-basher** ▶ A mainly British and Australian slang word for someone who talks incessantly; a nag.

• **Earl's Court** ▶ An exhibition centre in London in which the annual Royal Tournament, the Boat Show, and many other major trade shows are held. The present structure was built in 1937 and was on its opening the largest reinforced concrete building in Europe, covering 12 acres. The name of the hall (and of the surrounding area) was derived from that of the courthouse of the Earls of Warwick and Holland, who were once the lords of the manor.

• **Early Bird** ▶ The first commercial communications satellite. Launched from America in 1965, it was designed to provide uninterrupted transmission by maintaining a stationary orbit, *i.e.* to rotate at the same angular speed as the earth so that its position above the earth's surface remained unchanged. *See*: Intelsat.

• **early retirement** ▶ Retirement before the statutory ages of 65 for a man and 60 for a woman. State pensions are only paid when these statutory ages have been reached, whether the person concerned has retired or not. Occupational pensions paid by an employer will usually allow early retirement on a pension below the full pension rate. If the employer is anxious to reduce staff, early retirement will be encouraged as an alternative to redundancy and the pension terms will be generous. Early retirement on health grounds is also viewed benignly in some parts of the public sector, especially those that are felt to be stressful, such as the police force. Equality of retirement age between the sexes is being introduced in the UK in 2010 – when the pension age will be 65 for both men and women. and dead

• **Early to rise and early to bed, makes a man healthy and wealthy and dead**▶ This parody of the old proverb 'Early to bed and early to rise, makes a man healthy, wealthy, and wise' was originally coined by James Thurber in 'The Shrike and the Chipmunks' from *Fables for Our Time* (1938).

• **earner**▶ British slang for a situation or activity, especially an illicit one, that will bring financial reward. Originally part of police and criminal jargon, the phrase **a nice little earner** became fashionable nationwide in the 1980s having been popularized by the TV series *Minder. See also:* 'er indoors.

• **ear'ole** ▶ British slang for a tedious person, mostly used by working-class schoolchildren in the 1970s. As a verb, it could mean to pin someone down in conversation (*i.e.* to 'buttonhole'), to scrounge, to nag, to talk endlessly, or to eavesdrop.

• **earth**▶
   **Did you feel the earth move?** More prosaically, did you have an orgasm? – a question put to a woman by her male lover after intercourse. The expression was first used in Ernest Hemingway's novel *For Whom the Bell Tolls* (1940). It is now almost always used ironically or facetiously.

• **earth art** or **land art**▶ An art movement originating in the 1960s in which artists utilize untreated natural materials, such as trees, boulders, or earth to create the desired effect. Most of this work survives only in the form of photographs. Leading exponents include the British artist Richard Long (1945–   ).

• **Earth Day**▶ A day of action chosen annually by various environmental pressure groups to focus attention on ecological matters. The first such days, usually in April, were announced in the early 1970s; they have sometimes been expanded into **Earth Weeks**.

   By the time Earth Day dawned on April 22, ecoactivists of all ages were suffused with quasi-religious fervour. – *Time*, 4 January 1971.

• **earwigging** ▶ 1. A British slang term for nagging or haranguing, based on the 19th-century use of the verb 'to wig', meaning to scold. 2. A slang word for eavesdropping.

• **East End**▶
   **Now we can look the East End in the face** Arguably the most famous royal quotation

from World War II, this was Queen Elizabeth's reaction on viewing the damage caused by a German bomb that fell on Buckingham Palace in 1940. With her husband, George VI, she made several tours of the extensively bombed East End of London during the Blitz.

• **EastEnders** ▶ A long-running BBC soap opera first aired in 1985. It concerns the mainly working-class inhabitants of Walford, a fictional area of East London. Driven mainly by issues rather than character, it has addressed such concerns as homosexuality, AIDS, murder, arson, teenage pregnancy, infidelity, and euthanasia – albeit in a more subdued manner than some of the more sensational US soaps. Unlike most British soaps, *EastEnders* has never been afraid to cast actors already known to the general public, employing a number of actors from the children's programme *Grange Hill* as well as – in more recent years – stand-up comedian Mike Reed and *Carry On* star Barbara Windsor. *See also:* Brookside.

• **Easter egg**▶ A US expression for a child born nine months after a summer romance.

• **Eastern bloc**▶ *See:* communist bloc.

• **Eastern Front**▶ The theatre of conflict on the Russian frontier in the two world wars. Operations on this front in World War I included heavy fighting in Poland and the Baltic states. In World War II the Eastern Front was created by the German invasion (reaching as far as Stalingrad) of the Soviet Union in 1941 and the subsequent Soviet counterattack through East Europe to Germany itself. Although activities on the Western Front have always attracted more attention from the Western media, fighting on the Eastern Front in both wars was often more costly and savage, with both sides suffering badly from the vicious eastern winter weather. Being sent to the Eastern Front was considered a punishment or demotion within German army circles.

• **Eastern Question**▶ The diplomatic problems arising from the disintegration of the Ottoman Empire in the 19th and 20th centuries, especially those caused by the struggle for control of the former Ottoman territories by the European powers. Throughout the 19th century recurring political instability within the Turkish domains in south-eastern Europe provoked a series of international crises including the Crimean War (1853–56) and the Balkan Crisis (1876–78) as Britain, France, Russia, Germany, and the Austro-Hungarian empire struggled to prevent one power from dominating the region. The situation was further complicated by emergent Balkan nationalism (*see*: Balkan Wars). The Eastern Question came to an end with the dissolution of the Ottoman Empire in 1918 and the foundation of the modern Republic of Turkey in 1923.

• **Easter Rising** ▸ An armed rebellion against British rule in Ireland that took place in Dublin in April 1916. The Irish Republican Brotherhood (IRB) under Patrick Pearse and James Connolly's Citizen Army – a total of around 2000 men – seized vital positions (including the Post Office) throughout Dublin and held off British troops for several days before their eventual defeat. The centre of the city was badly damaged. Although the Rising had little popular support at the time, the execution of its leaders inflamed public opinion in Ireland and helped to speed the end of British rule. *See*: Troubles, the.

• **east is east and west is west** ▸ This somewhat pessimistic observation upon cultural relations first appeared as part of a poem, 'The Ballad of East and West' (1910), by Rudyard Kipling. The full version reads:

> Oh, East is East, and West is West, and never the twain shall meet.

*East is East* is the title of a film (1999) about young Asians in the UK.

• **easy** ▸ A taunt or cry of triumph, implying that the opposing team is being defeated with great ease, heard on the terraces at British football matches since the 1960s. It is often extended to 'eeezeee' and repeated as a chant.

• **easy as you know how** ▸ A phrase meaning that something apparently difficult is actually very easy to perform, much used by members of the RAF in World War II.

• **easy lay** ▸ *See*: GHB.

• **easy listening** ▸ Undemanding music featuring simple memorable tunes and a soothing arrangement. The category embraces light classical music, favourite film and TV themes, ballads, 1930s and 1940s dance music, and relaxed pop songs. Long seen as the epitome of naff, easy listening enjoyed an unlikely revival in the mid-1990s, when ultra-fashionable metropolitan types began to attend special club evenings where they could drink martinis while listening to records by Andy Williams, Perry Como, and the James Last Orchestra.

• **easy meat** ▸ Either a gullible person, or something easily acquired. This has been a widely used phrase in the UK since the 1920s.

• **easy money** ▸ *See*: cheap money.

• **easy rider** ▸ A biker. The term was made fashionable by the 1969 film of the same name, in which two drop-out bikers (Peter Fonda and Dennis Hopper) seek fulfilment, but meet only death.

• **Easy Street** ▸ A state of financial security, in which one is not obliged to work or do anything one does not want to. In 1917 Charlie Chaplin made a silent film of the same title, although Easy Street in this case was a poverty-stricken slum.

• **eat** ▸

**You are what you eat** A phrase used by people who believe that organic food with no unnecessary additives and health foods in general lead automatically to good health. It gained in popularity as more and more people became concerned about fitness and diet in the 1970s and 1980s. The US film with this title (1969) had more to do with the hippie movement in America than diet but helped to popularize the phrase.

• **eat dirt** ▸ Originally a US expression, but now heard in the UK and Australia as well, meaning to humiliate oneself. Sometimes the expression is used as an exclamation of scorn. Variants include **eat shit**.

• **eat my shorts!** ▸ An exclamation of scorn or defiance, used mainly by teenage boys. Shorts is the US word for male underpants. In the 1990s the phrase became particularly associated with the subversive cartoon character Bart Simpson of the Simpsons.

• **Eat your heart out!** ▸ A phrase usually addressed by a lesser-known performer to an established star superstar ('Eat your heart out, Madonna!'), as if to say 'I can do this as well as you can,', or 'It's time to watch out, you have a rival'. It is almost always said ironically. This phrase became popular in the 1950s and 1960s in showbusiness.

• **e-banking** ▸ A facility offered by a bank or building society that enables account holders to carry out certain operations over the Internet. The facility, which is available 24 hours a day, seven days a week, enables the customer to view balances held and to transfer money from a cheque account to a savings account, or vice versa; standing orders and other regular transfers can also be set up, changed, or cancelled. Some banks will also arrange or amend overdrafts by e-banking. However, as cheques can neither be paid in or drawn by e-banking, this facility does not replace normal banking practices – it enables some operations to be carried out without visiting one's bank or building society or without communicating with it by post. It is similar in all respects to telephone banking.

• **E-boat alley** ▶ In World War II, the coastal convoy route, approximately off the Norfolk and Suffolk coast, which was the scene of much successful activity by German E-boats in the early years of the war. **E-boat** (enemy war motorboat) was the British name for a German motor torpedo boat.

• **e-book** ▶ *See*: electronic publishing.

• **EC** ▶ *See*: European Community.

• **e-cash** ▶ *See*: cybercash.

• **Echo 1** ▶ The first communications satellite. It was launched from America in 1960 and reflected television and radio signals in an orbit 1000 miles above the earth.

• **echovirus** ▶ Any of a group of viruses that multiply in the human intestinal tract and then migrate to the nervous system, where they cause various neurological symptoms. When first isolated in the mid-1950s, they were thought to produce pathological changes only in cell cultures and not to be associated with any disease, hence the name which is short for *e*nteric *c*ytopathic (cell-affecting) *h*uman *o*rphan (*i.e.* unrelated to any disease) *virus*.

• **eco-freak** ▶ A somewhat disparaging term for someone concerned with ecology and the environment, first used in the UK and America in the 1970s when such concerns were considered rather eccentric. *See also*: freak; green.

• **ecology** ▶ The study of the relationships between living organisms and their environment, which has acquired a new relevance in the years since World War II when man began to appreciate the widespread damage occasioned by the indiscriminate use of pesticides, unmonitored waste disposal from industrial processes, vehicle and power-station exhaust fumes, etc. If unchecked, it has been argued, such abuses of the environment could lead to mankind committing **ecocide** (mass suicide) by rendering the world uninhabitable. The prefix 'eco-' is now employed in a wide range of coinages including **ecodisaster**, **ecofeminist**, **ecofriendly**, **ecoterrorism**, **ecowarrior**, etc. Taken up by political parties throughout the Western world, and indeed beyond, ecological arguments had become by the beginning of the 21st century an integral part of every political party's manifesto. *See also*: acid rain; greenhouse effect; ozone layer.

• **e-commerce** ▶ Any form of buying and selling of goods or services using the Internet; the term is used especially of transactions between business houses. In most cases documentation of any deals is exchanged by post in the usual way. *See also*: cybercash; e-shopping.

• **economical with the truth** ▶ The words used by the British cabinet secretary Sir Robert Armstrong in the course of a trial in the Supreme Court of New South Wales in which the British government was seeking to prevent publication of *Spycatcher* by Peter Wright (a damaging book about MI5). The phrase was universally interpreted as a newly minted euphemism for 'lying'. It had in fact been used in a similar form by a British diplomat in 1942 about the character of the former Czech president Edvard Beneš and before that by Arnold Bennett, Mark Twain, Edmund Burke, and Samuel Pepys.

• **economic migrant** ▶ An emigrant from the Third World who moves to the developed countries of the West in the hope of improving his living standards. In the UK the term is often used in a hostile way, to suggest that an applicant for political asylum (*see*: displaced person) is motivated by economic considerations rather than a genuine fear of persecution.

• **Ecstasy** ▶ The street name of the stimulant hallucinogen drug 3,4-methylenedioxymethamphetamine (MDMA), which emerged in America in the 1980s. It was first manufactured in Germany in 1914. The drug, which induces short-term feelings of happiness, benevolence, and unlimited energy, became a staple of the rave culture of the later 1980s. It has the dangerous side-effect of causing overheating and intense thirst and there is some evidence that regular use may cause long-term damage to brain function. Those who use the drug are sometimes referred to as **Ecstatics** – a term recalling the ancient Greek diviners called *Ecstatici*, who used to give strange accounts of what they had seen while they were 'out of the body' (the original Greek meaning of ecstasy). The drug's name is often abbreviated to E. *See also*: eve.

• **ecu** ▶ A currency unit created in 1979 to serve as the unit of account in the European Monetary System. Derived from the initials of European Currency Unit, it had a distant antecedent in the *écu*, a silver coin used in medieval France. This in turn derived its name from the Latin *scutum* (shield), a shield being the symbol stamped on each coin. The ecu was superseded by the euro in January 1999.

• **Ecumenical Movement** ▶ The movement aiming to re-unify the various Christian Churches. It has gathered strength since the Second Vatican Council of 1962–65 and the establishment of the World Council of Churches, inaugurated at Amsterdam in 1948, which comprises most Christian bodies (but not the Roman Catholic Church).

• **Edinburgh Festival** ▸ An internationally famous festival of the arts that takes place annually in Edinburgh (in August). Founded in 1947 and lasting three weeks, it has developed its own 'fringe' tradition which now attracts as much attention as the official events. The festival has seen many notable performances by companies and artists from all over the world. *See*: fringe theatre.

• **Edwardian** ▸ 1. Belonging to the reign of King Edward VII (1901–10). 2. *See*: teddy boys.

• **Edward the Caresser** ▸ *See*: Bertie.

• **eek** ▸ 1. Face. A somewhat camp word from the London theatre slang of the 1950s; it is of obscure origin. 2. Face paint; stage make-up. This meaning obviously derives from the first.

• **E=mc²** ▸ The equation proposed by Albert Einstein (1879–1955) in his Special Theory of relativity in 1905. The best known of all scientific equations, and of immense theoretical interest to the scientific community, it linked an object's mass ($m$) multiplied by the square of the speed of light ($c^2$) to its energy ($E$). The more sinister aspects of this simple equation were revealed in July 1945 when the first atom bomb was exploded (*see*: nuclear weapon).

• **Eeyore** ▸ A character in the Winnie-the-Pooh stories of A. A. Milne. Eeyore is a melancholy donkey who suffers a series of disasters, including the loss of his tail and falling into a river, with characteristic resignation. His name is occasionally applied to people who show similar traits. Eeyore's character was based on that of Sir Owen Seaman (1861–1936), who as editor of *Punch* was Milne's employer for eight years.

• **eff** ▸ A British euphemism for fuck, sometimes also heard in Australia and America. It is mostly used in the phrases **eff off**, and **effing and blinding** meaning to curse and swear.

• **Effie** ▸ An award given annually to US advertising agencies; the name is derived from 'effective'. Such awards were first presented in 1970 for particularly striking advertising campaigns.

• **Effort, St Swithins!** ▸ An exhortation popularized by Joyce Grenfell in one of her numerous roles as a schoolmistress. Picked up by public schools everywhere, it was used (usually ironically) as a rallying cry in innumerable school matches and other contests.

• **EFTPOS** ▸ Electronic funds transfer at point of sale. A computer-based system that automatically debits the cost of goods or services to a customer's credit card or bank account. The check-out till at the point of sale has a computer and telephone link to the appropriate credit-card company or bank, which responds to the use of the customer's credit card, usually in conjunction with a PIN (personal identification number).

• **egg** ▸
   **Go to work on an egg** Slogan used in an advertising campaign mounted by the British Egg Marketing Board in the late 1950s to persuade people of the energy-giving power of eggs. The phrase caught the public fancy and was much quoted as a catchphrase. It has been ascribed to the novelist and playwright Fay Weldon, then a copy-writer with the Egg Marketing Board, although she herself does not lay claim to it. The slogan later fell into disuse, partly owing to the decline of the full English breakfast, but more importantly because eggs are a copious source of cholesterol, which is now known to clog the arteries.

• **eggbeater** ▸ 1. Slang for an old and unsophisticated motor or motor vehicle. 2. Slang term for a helicopter in America and Canada.

• **egghead** ▸ An intellectual; British slang from the 1910s that is still widely used. Scientists in particular are fancifully imagined to have large balding heads to accommodate their supposedly larger-than-normal brains.

• **egg on one's face** ▸ An appearance of discomfort as a result of having said or done something foolish or out of place. The allusion is to having an egg thrown at one at a public meeting or (less aggressively) to having a yellow egg stain around one's mouth as a result of eating one's breakfast egg carelessly.

• **ego-trip** ▸ Something undertaken to boost one's self-importance. Trip, originally a US expression from the drug culture of the 1960s, is now widely used to mean any kind of stimulating experience.

• **Egyptian PT** ▸ Army slang for sleeping. The term was adopted by British forces serving in the Middle East before World War II and referred to the widely held belief that all Arabs were irredeemably lazy: the phrase remained current for many years in both army and public-school slang.

• **Eichmann trial** ▸ The trial in 1961 at which the notorious Nazi Adolf Eichmann (1906–62) was brought before an Israeli court. Eichmann, who had been appointed to arrange the logistics of the so-called Final Solution in 1942, was accused of involvement in the mass murder of thousands of Austrian Jews, found guilty, and hanged. He was brought to trial after being kidnapped by Israeli agents in Argentina, where he was in hiding.

• **8 mm**▸ A narrow-gauge cine film used by amateur and avant-garde film-makers. Sound was impossible with 8 mm until the superior 'Super 8' gauge was developed in the 1960s. However, it has now been almost entirely replaced by home video.

• **eight to the bar**▸ The basic rhythm of the boogie-woogie style of jazz piano playing, developed in the 1930s.

• **eighty-eight**▸ 1. US slang for a piano, referring to the usual number of keys. 2. A piece of heavy but mobile German field artillery firing 88 millimetre shells, much used in World War II.

• **Ein Reich, Ein Volk, Ein Führer**▸ The slogan of the Nazi party, meaning 'One Realm, One People, One Leader'. It was first used at the Nuremberg rally in September 1934.

• **Eisenhower Doctrine**▸ The promise (5 January 1957) by US President Dwight D. Eisenhower of economic or military aid to Middle Eastern countries under threat from communist aggression. Eisenhower's commitment was a sign of America's determination to contain Soviet influence in the region during the Cold War.

• **Eisenhower jacket**▸ A short belted military jacket (also called a **battle-jacket**) as worn by General Eisenhower in World War II.

• **Eisenhower Platz** or **Little America**▸ Nickname of Grosvenor Square, London, during World War II, when all the surrounding buildings were occupied by American Military Headquarters. A statue of Eisenhower now stands in the square, which contains the US Embassy.

• **élan vital**▸ (French, vital impetus). A force that drives the evolutionary process in all living things, as described by the French philosopher Henri Bergson (1859–1941) in his *Creative Evolution* (1907, translated 1911). The concept was developed in opposition to Darwin's evolutionary theories, which Bergson considered too mechanistic. *See*: creative evolution.

• **elbow bender** ▸ British slang for a heavy drinker, from the idea of someone constantly bending their elbow to lift a glass to their lips.

• **electrification**▸
**Communism is Soviet power plus the electrification of the whole country** A political slogan adopted in the Soviet Union in 1920. It was coined by Lenin with reference to the proposed electrification programme.

• **electromagnetic smog** ▸ The electromagnetic pollution caused by the large number of electronic gadgets employed in modern households. Electromagnetic waves generated by such gadgets can interfere with the operation of other electronically controlled devices in the neighbourhood, with serious consequences (in one case electromagnetic smog is thought to have caused a fatal accident in which a computerized crane dropped its load). The phenomenon first came to attention in 1993, when the feasibility of controlling it was discussed.

• **electronic mail** ▸ *See*: e-mail.

• **electronic publishing**▸ The production and distribution of material in electronic form, using a digital code that can be read by a computer or similar device.

Since the 1980s CD-ROMs and online publishing, especially via the Internet, have become a significant part of both specialist and mass-market publishing, complementing and sometimes supplanting traditional printed media. Yet the story has not been an unmixed success, and some of the more extravagant predictions about the 'death of print' now seem absurd. Many publishers leapt onto the electronic bandwagon, only to find the costs of development alarmingly high and the market smaller than anticipated. In reality, certain areas have flourished while others have not. For example, the multimedia CD-ROM has proved an excellent medium for encyclopedias and other reference works, providing automated search for topics of interest and convenient links between text, pictures, graphics, and sound. Scientific and other academic journals now routinely publish electronic versions online, and in some cases have abandoned printed versions altogether. This enables direct inputting of materials from the author, rapid updating, and more or less instantaneous dissemination directly to the subscriber.

The phenomenal expansion of the Internet during the 1990s also brought the advent of the **electronic book**, or **e-book**. These are books that are prepared by a publisher exclusively in electronic form and posted on the publisher's website in encrypted form. Prospective readers can sample the text and chat online with others who have read the book, or perhaps with the author. A payment to the publisher then allows them to download the complete unencrypted version to their PC. The publisher thereby avoids all the traditional costs of printing and distribution. E-books can incorporate all the multimedia elements of graphics, video, and interactivity, and are especially suited to 'how-to' manuals, such as cookery and DIY books. However, no electronic product can yet match the portability and straightforward appeal of the printed book as a means of publishing novels or similar works.

• **electronic tagging**► A system for monitoring the movements of certain categories of convicted persons or persons on bail by attaching a low-powered radio transmitter to a bracelet worn on the wrist or ankle. The continuous signal emitted by the transmitter is picked up by a device attached to a telephone in the person's home, which sends a message to a controlling computer in a remote centre if the offender moves more than 75 metres from the telephone.

• **electronovision** ► A system enabling television programmes to be transferred from videotape to film for the big screen, hailed on its introduction in 1965 as a breakthrough for the cinema industry. Two cinema films were made by this method before it was discarded as artistically and financially unviable.

• **electroweak theory**► See: fundamental forces; unified-field theory.

• **elementary particle**► The fundamental constituents of which all the matter in the universe is constructed. Until J. J. Thomson (1856–1940) discovered the electron in 1897 it was assumed that matter was made from indivisible atoms. When Ernest Rutherford (1871–1937) discovered the atomic nucleus in 1906, it was thought that electrons orbited a central indestructible nucleus. By 1932, with James Chadwick's (1891–1974) discovery of the neutron, the atomic model consisted of a nucleus of protons and neutrons surrounded by sufficient negative electrons to balance the positive charge of the nucleus. Since the mid-1930s various models to account for the stability of the nucleus have been proposed, accepted, and superseded. In the current model, electromagnetic, strong, and weak forces are recognized as controlling the structure of matter (see: fundamental forces). The electromagnetic force, mediated by photons, holds the electrons in orbits around the nucleus and determines the 'chemical' properties of atoms. This is described by the theory of quantum electrodynamics. The strong force, mediated by gluons between the constituents of hadrons (protons, neutrons, and pions) is described by quantum chromodynamics. Hadrons are not themselves fundamental particles but consist of quarks between which gluons are exchanged. Weak interactions controlling radioactive decay are mediated by photons, W, and Z particles, according to quantum flavourdynamics (also called the electroweak theory or the Glashow-Weinberg-Salaam theory). The ultimate objective of particle physics is to combine these elementary particles and fundamental forces into one unified theory.

• **eleven plus**► The selection tests formerly given to schoolchildren at the age of eleven, or just over that age, throughout England and Wales as a means of judging their suitability for the various types of secondary education provided by the Education Act of 1944 (secondary modern, secondary technical, secondary grammar, etc.). The tests became a target for those who, for reasons political and social as well as educational, were seeking to replace the existing pattern of education in England with comprehensive schools (see: comprehensivization). In the 1970s the examination largely disappeared with the majority of grammar schools; in some areas it was replaced by a twelve plus examination.

• **Elginism** ► The illicit removal of items of cultural value – especially antique fireplaces – from stately homes or other sites of historical interest. The word was first used in 1986 when a rash of such thefts was reported; it derived from Lord Elgin's controversial removal of friezes from the Parthenon in Athens to the British Museum in 1816 (at a time when occupying Turkish forces were using the Parthenon for target practice).

• **Ellery Queen** ► See: Queen. Ellery.

• **Ellis hanging**► The execution of Ruth Ellis, the last woman to be hanged in the UK. She was sentenced to death for murdering her lover (who was having an affair with another woman) and was hanged at Holloway Prison on 13 July 1955. Her story provided the plot for the films *Yield to the Night* (1956) and *Dance with a Stranger* (1985).

• **Ellis Island** ► An island in Upper New York Bay that served as the main immigration station for America from 1892 to 1943 and as a detention centre for illegal aliens until it was closed in 1954. Ellis Island is close to the Statue of Liberty, whose inscription ('Give me your tired, your poor, your huddled masses...Send these, the homeless, tempest-tost to me') must have had a hollow ring for many of those detained there: the centre was infamous for its impersonal procedures and the casual brutality of its staff. It is now part of the Statue of Liberty National Museum.

• **El Niño** ► A southerly current of warm water that occurs off the western coast of South America roughly every three to seven years. It is accompanied by disturbances in weather patterns, both in the Pacific region and further afield. The Spanish name El Niño ('the Child') refers to the Infant Jesus, and was originally used for a warm current that arrives at the Peruvian and Ecuadorian coasts every December around Christmas time. However, during the 20th century, the term 'El Niño' came to refer to an irregularly recurring large-scale reversal of water currents that stretches across the tropical Pacific Ocean. Normally the easterly trade winds push warm water from east to west, causing it literally to pile up off the coast of Indonesia. This produces the heavy rainfall generally associated with Southeast Asia. However, in certain years the trade winds weaken, or even reverse their direction, and the 'pile' of warm water flows back towards the east. In such years, the normally arid east coast of South America receives much greater rainfall, while Southeast Asia experiences drier conditions. El Niño is associated with the oscillation of an air mass over tropical regions known as the Southern Oscillation, and the combined oceanic and meteorological fluctuations are termed the **El Niño–Southern Oscillation** (ENSO).

An intense and sustained El Niño can have devastating consequences for the world's climate. The occurrence in 1982–83 was particularly severe, and brought drought to Australia, Southeast Asia, and Africa, while the eastern American seaboard was hit by torrential rain and floods. Many lost their lives or homes, while the damage to crops and property was immense. Other recent occurrences have been in 1987, 1992, 1993, 1994, and 1998. Some have linked the unusual frequency of the El Niño phenomena during the 1990s with global warming. However, the events involved are highly complex, and no one has yet determined exactly how they start, and equally how they stop.

A warm El Niño event is sometimes followed by the occurrence of especially cool water in the eastern Pacific. This event, termed **La Niña** ('the little girl'), is all part of the same complex ENSO cycle.

• **el primo ▶** (Spanish, the first) The best. A US expression coined in imitation of Hispanic speech.

• **el ropo ▶** A cigar, or a joint. Derived from the idea that rough tobacco and marijuana look like, and smell like, burning rope.

• **Elstree ▶** The site near Borehamwood, in outer London, of the famous British film studios. Elstree became a centre of film-making in the 1920s and produced numerous classics of the British cinema during the next two decades. From the late 1960s activity there was greatly reduced, although the technical facilities continued to be used from time to time by top US producers. Since the 1990s there

has been a revival of film-making at Elstree; part of the site is also used by the BBC.

• **Elvis the Pelvis ▶** The nickname by which the US rock 'n' roll singer Elvis (Aaron) Presley (1935–77) became known in the late 1950s. His suggestive hip movements on stage while performing such hits as 'Hound Dog' and 'Heartbreak Hotel' (both 1956) displayed a raw sexuality never before seen in White popular music and earned him his nickname. However, in deference to his commanding stage presence, unrivalled record sales, and pivotal role in creating modern pop and rock music, Presley's millions of admirers worldwide prefer to know him as **the King of Rock 'n' Roll** or simply **the King**.

Like some other monarchs, Elvis has inspired a strangely persistent legend that his death (of a heart attack) was faked and that he is still alive and in hiding somewhere. Although there is no real evidence for such a belief, sightings of the unfortunate singer continue to be reported by his more impressionable fans. There seems little doubt that a grossly overweight Presley died of heart failure brought on by poor diet and drug dependence over many years. *See also*: Graceland.

• **e-mail ▶** A means of exchanging text messages between connected computers. The computers may be connected as part of a local area network (*e.g.* within a company's offices) or by means of the telephone network (*see*: Internet). A person wishing to send a message, letter, or data in electronic form keys the message, attaching any data file to be transmitted, and sends it to a recipient identified by a unique address. To receive a communication, someone with an e-mail address calls up the central computer, keys in a password, and receives any message or data that has arrived in his 'mail box'. The system is now widely employed by both business and private users.

• **embuggerance ▶** A complicated problem. The word was apparently used in the engineering fraternity for some years before it came to wider notice during the Falklands Conflict of 1982, when it was used by the Royal Engineers, who were faced with complicated logistical tasks.

• **Emden ▶**
**Didn't you sink the Emden?** An Australian catchphrase of World War I, used to deflate anyone indulging in excessive self-praise. The *Emden* was a German light cruiser that caused considerable damage to shipping and ports in the Pacific before it was eventually sunk by the Australian cruiser *Sydney* off the Cocos-Keeling Islands in November 1914.

• **emmet** ▶ A tourist. A Cornish dialect word, meaning an ant, that is used disparagingly of the masses of summer tourists that swarm to Cornwall each year. Grockle is another dialect word with the same meaning.

• **Emmy** ▶ A US award granted annually in various categories to television programmes that have achieved a certain standard of excellence. The awards are usually considered the Oscars of the television industry. The name is derived from 'Immy', a shortened form of image orthicon tube.

• **Empire** ▶
**How is the Empire?** The last words of George V, spoken to his private secretary in 1936. Others have it that his last words – spoken in reply to his doctor's assurance that he would soon be well enough to visit Bognor Regis – were **Bugger Bognor**. The latter may have been said by the King in 1929, in reply to the suggestion that the town be renamed Bognor Regis to commemorate his convalescence there after a serious illness.

• **Empire Day** ▶ A day instituted by the Earl of Meath in 1902, after the end of the Boer Wars, to encourage schoolchildren to be aware of their duties and responsibilities as citizens of the British Empire. The day set aside was 24 May, Queen Victoria's birthday. In 1916 it was given official recognition in the UK; it was replaced by **Commonwealth Day** (12 March) in December 1958.

• **Empire Free Trade** ▶ An unsuccessful campaign (1929–31) to establish free trade throughout the British Empire. It was spearheaded by the press barons Lords Beaverbrook and Rothermere, who argued the case with crusading zeal in their newspapers and founded the United Empire Party in an attempt to gain a parliamentary platform. The campaign foundered on the reluctance of the Dominions to give free entry to British goods and finally collapsed with the onset of the Great Depression in the 1930s.

• **Empire State Building** ▶ One of New York's best-known skyscrapers, built in Manhattan in 1930–32 by Shreve, Lamb, and Harmon at a cost of $41 million. The scene of the climax of the film King Kong (1933), in which the giant gorilla ascends the building and fights off attacking aircraft, the Empire State Building remained, at 381 m (1250 ft) high, the tallest in the world until the World Trade Center was completed in the same city in 1974. The building acquired its name by allusion to one of New York City's colloquial titles, the **Empire City** (acknowledging its wealth and importance).

• **Empress of Emotion** ▶ The nickname of the Austrian-Italian film star Elissa Landi (1904–48). A leading lady in the 1930s, she starred in such largely forgotten films as The Sign of the Cross (1932) and The Count of Monte Cristo (1934).

• **empty nest** ▶ An expression used of a household when all the children have grown up and left home. The parents, who may be left feeling bereft and directionless after all the years of taking care of the children, are known as **empty nesters**. The phrase has a particular financial relevance as these parents, who will usually have paid off their mortgage and have acquired some savings, may find themselves in possession of a substantially larger amount of disposable income than they have been accustomed to when there were more demands on their pocket.

• **EMS** ▶ See: European Monetary System.

• **emu-bobber** ▶ A worker employed to remove debris after an area of Australian bush has been cleared.

> We...went to Wingadee to work for a contractor at burning-off. This work is also known as 'stick-picking' or 'emu-bobbing'. A group of men bending to pick up the fallen timber, with heads down and tails up, look very much like a flock of emus. – H. P. TRITTON: Time Means Tucker.

An operation in which an area is cleaned up by emu-bobbers is known as an **emu parade**.

• **enchilada** ▶ See: big enchilada.

• **encounter group** ▶ A group of people who gather together to share their deepest feelings and anxieties. Participants in such sessions are encouraged to lose their inhibitions in order to achieve self-awareness and personal growth. See also: consciousness raising; group therapy; sensitivity training.

> As encounters multiplied and perspective deepened, Jane found herself kicking pillows and hurling finger paint with the worst of them – and feeling, as a result, relieved of some fossil fears. – BRAD DARRACH, 'Gropeshrink'.

• **end** ▶
**an end to the beginnings of all wars** The hope for the future expressed in the last speech of President Franklin D. Roosevelt. Broadcast the day after his death in April 1945, his words in full were: 'More than an end to war, we want an end to the beginnings of all wars.'

• **endangered species** ▶ A category of threatened species identified by the International Union for the Conservation of Nature and Natural Resources (IUCN). Populations of these species are at a critical level and are in immediate danger of extinction; the term also includes species that may already be extinct but have definitely been seen in the wild in the previous 50 years. Endangered species include:

    orang-utan (*Pongo pygmaeus*)
    mountain gorilla (*Gorilla gorilla*)
    tiger (*Panthera tigris*)
    black rhinoceros (*Diceros bicornis*)
    Indian elephant (*Elephas maximus*)
    pygmy hog (*Sus salvanius*)
    red wolf (*Canis rufus*)
    sloth bear (*Melursus ursinus*)
    blue whale (*Balaenoptera musculus*)
    crested ibis (*Nipponia nippon*)
    peregrine falcon (*Falco peregrinus*)
    Californian condor (*Gymnogyps californianus*)
    loggerhead turtle (*Caretta caretta*)
    green turtle (*Chelonia mydas*)

*See also*: extinct; threatened species; vulnerable species.

• **end of story** ▶ A phrase used to bring an argument or discussion to a close – brusquely and conclusively, if onesidedly. A child nagging a parent for some favour may be told 'End of story' if it persists in its demands longer than the parent considers acceptable.

• **end of the beginning** ▶ The words with which Winston Churchill greeted news of the Allied victory at Alamein in North Africa in November 1942. His words in full were: 'This is not the end. It is not even the beginning of the end. But it is, perhaps, the end of the beginning.'

• **endsville** ▶ A US expression for the absolute worst. It originated in the beatnik jargon of the 1950s and is still heard. The suffix '-sville' is used in a similar way in numerous other contexts.

• **Endurance** ▶ The ship in which Sir Ernest Shackleton travelled to the Antarctic in 1914. The expedition's problems began when the *Endurance* became locked fast in ice; for months the members of the team waited for the ship to free itself, but finally it sank. Living off penguin meat and seaweed, Shackleton and his fellow-explorers spent the next five months drifting on an ice floe. Two years after setting out on the voyage, they transferred to the three remaining ship's boats and eventually landed on a bleak ice-covered island. The only hope was to reach South Georgia, 800 miles away across one of the worst stretches of ocean in the world. Undaunted, Shackleton and five volunteers set off in one of the boats, just 22 feet long. Over the next two weeks the six men were constantly soaked, subjected to intense cold, and frequently threatened with being washed overboard by huge waves. Remarkably, they survived, reaching South Georgia and enabling the whole team to be rescued without a single loss of life.

    For scientific leadership give me Scott; for swift

and efficient travel, Amundsen; but when you are in a hopeless position, when there seems no way out, get down on your knees and pray for Shackleton. – Fellow-explorer of SHACKLETON's.

• **Enewetak** ▶ *See*: Eniwetok.

• **England** ▶
**If I should die, think only this of me: That there's some corner of a foreign field that is forever England** One of the best-known quotations to emerge from World War I, these lines come from 'The Soldier' by Rupert Brooke (1887–1915). Brooke died of blood poisoning on a hospital ship in the Aegean, on his way to the Dardanelles; his corner of a foreign field is on the island of Scyros. *See*: Grantchester; war poets.

• **England** ▶
**Speak for England** The resounding cry of an anguished Conservative backbencher during a parliamentary debate on the eve of World War II. At 7.30 p.m. on 2 September 1939, Neville Chamberlain disappointed the House of Commons by telling them that further negotiations were in progress to persuade Hitler to withdraw his troops from Poland. What both sides of the House wanted was an ultimatum. As Chamberlain sat down to a dismayed silence, Arthur Greenwood, acting leader of the Labour Party (Attlee was ill), rose to speak. Leo Amery reflected the mood of everyone present when he shouted from the Conservative benches: 'Speak for England, Arthur!' Greenwood's 'Every minute's delay now means the loss of life, imperilling our national interests…imperilling the very foundations of our national honour' was probably influential in persuading Chamberlain to send the ultimatum the next morning. The absence of a German reply to this ultimatum led Britain and France to declare war on Germany on 3 September.

• **English** ▶
**put on English** A US expression meaning to apply spin to the ball in billiards or baseball, presumably an allusion to the practice of spinning the ball in cricket.

• **English as she is spoke** ▶ A catchphrase used to refer to the attempts of foreigners or illiterates to speak the English language.

• **English breakfast** ▶ The large cooked morning meal beloved of the Victorians and still produced, with varying degrees of competence, at hotels and bed-and-breakfast establishments throughout the UK as well as on trains, in gentlemen's clubs, in greasy caffs, and in some private homes at weekends. Interpretations of the phrase range from a repast starting with porridge and continuing with grilled kidneys, kippers, kedgeree, and other similar dishes, to any menu including cooked food (usually bacon and egg). The US invention of breakfast cereal early in the 20th century and the later introduction of Swiss muesli have done much to undermine the institution, which has been further eroded by health warnings of the dangers of eating too much fatty food. Besides, with two wage earners and no domestic staff, very few homes have time to prepare such a lavish spread early in the morning.

• **English disease** or **English sickness** ► A variety of complaints and malaises have been ascribed to the English. Since the time of Columbus the French have described syphilis as the English disease; the English response to this insinuation was to call it the French disease. Later, after the industrial revolution, the damp climate combined with industrial smoke to create a high prevalence of bronchitis. On the continent and elsewhere, this also became known as the English disease. In the 20th century, air travel meant that physical disease could no longer be confined to particular nations and therefore could not be characterized in this way. Instead, various social ailments, including class conflict, poor industrial relations, and economic stagnation, came to be thought of as typically English: in the 1960s and 1970s, when trade union power was at its zenith, strikes were widely known as the English disease. More recently, especially since the 1980s, disgraceful behaviour at football matches, both at home and abroad, has been so described (*see*: football hooliganism).

• **English National Opera** ► (ENO) A London-based opera company that developed from the Sadler's Wells Opera Company in 1974. The company moved from the Sadler's Wells Theatre to the London Coliseum in 1969. Traditionally the ENO offers operas sung in English and has a commitment to innovative productions: these are presented less lavishly than those at the Royal Opera House, enabling seats to be more modestly priced.

• **English spliff** or **English joint** ► A US term for a joint in which the cannabis is rolled with tobacco.

• **ENIAC** ► Electronic Numerical Integrator And Calculator. *See*: computer.

• **Enigma** ► *See*: Bletchley Park.

• **Eniwetok** or **Enewetak** ► An atoll in the Republic of the Marshall Islands in the Pacific Ocean designated as a testing site for nuclear weapons shortly after World War II. Testing began in 1948; the first hydrogen bomb was exploded here in 1952, and there were further tests throughout the 1950s.

In 1980 the tiny population (88) was allowed to return until evidence of lingering contamination resulted in their re-evacuation.

• **enjoy!** ► An exclamation inviting people to sample and enjoy food, later extended to other commodities and situations. The construction is Yiddish in origin and the phrase came to the UK from America. In American Jewish speech influenced by Yiddish 'enjoy' is an intransitive verb and the imperative is usually duplicated as 'enjoy, enjoy'. This was the title of a book by Harry Cohen, published in 1960. When the phrase was brought to the attention of advertisers they used it in various slogans. It can also be used ironically. If a person complains that he has to undertake some chore, such as taking his mother-in-law out to dinner, he may be exhorted to *enjoy* the experience.

• **Enola Gay** ► The name of the US bomber that dropped the atom bomb on Hiroshima on 6 August 1945. A Superfortress, the aircraft was named in honour of the mother of the pilot, Colonel Paul W. Tibbets. The force of the explosion hit the *Enola Gay* with all the power of a near-miss by flak, although the aircraft was by then 10 miles away from the point of impact. More than 75,000 people died. Many years later members of the *Enola Gay*'s crew visited Hiroshima once more to see the rebuilt city. A Peace Memorial Park commemorates those who died. Enola Gay is also a character in the novel *London Fields* (1989) by Martin Amis.

• **enosis** ► (Greek, union) The political union of Greece and Cyprus, pursued by Greek Cypriots in the 1950s. *See*: EOKA.

• **ENSA concerts** ► In World War II, concerts provided for the British fighting forces on active service by the Entertainments National Service Association (ENSA). Many famous figures in the entertainment and musical world took part, greatly helping to boost morale. By the time of the last ENSA show in 1946, 2 million performances had been given. The US equivalent was **USO** (United Service Organizations).

• **Entente Cordiale** ► (French) A cordial understanding between nations; not amounting to an alliance but something more than a *rapprochement* (moving closer together). The term is particularly applied to the Anglo-French Entente of April 1904, sealed by King Edward VII's visit to Paris in 1906. *See also*: Triple Entente.

• **enterprise culture** ► *See*: Thatcherism.

• **E-numbers** ► Numbers, prefixed by the letter E (for European Union), that are assigned to food additives used within the EU. For example, tartrazine (a yellow colouring) is E-102; sodium benzoate (a preservative) is E-211. Additives can be identified by their E-numbers, which must be listed, with the other ingredients, on the packaging of the foodstuff.

• **environment** ► A 19th-century word derived from the Old French verb *environner*, to surround, which during the 20th century acquired the more specific sense of the surroundings in which a plant or animal lives (*see*: ecology). From the 1960s, with growing public awareness of the harmful effects of human intervention on our surroundings, the sense of the word widened to include all those attributes of the natural world that are susceptible to damage by human activities – especially by pollution and destruction of natural habitats by desertification, deforestation, etc. – leading to impoverishment of the plant and animal life they support (see threatened species; endangered species; vulnerable species). Concern for the environment, combined with an enthusiastic overuse of the word, escalated during the 1980s and 1990s; environmental – or green – issues are now embraced by most political parties, and an environment-friendly way of life is almost universally recommended.

• **EOKA** ► (Greek *Ethniki Organosis Kipriakou Agonos*) The National Organization of Cypriot Struggle, founded in 1955 to pursue the political goal of enosis. Led by Georgios Grivas, and supported by Archbishop Makarios, it conducted a guerrilla campaign against the occupying British forces. It disbanded on independence in 1959 but was re-formed in 1971.

• **epic theatre** ► A style of political theatre that emerged in Germany during the late 1920s. Deriving ultimately from the theories of Aristotle, it was developed by Bertolt Brecht (1898–1956) and the director Erwin Piscator (1893–1966). The plays they created were characterized by explicit political commitment, a loose episodic structure, and the use of the so-called A-effect to engage the audience's intellect and judgment rather than the emotions. *See also*: Berliner Ensemble.

• **epitaph** ► Strictly, an inscription on a tomb, but usually it refers to any brief verses or apt commemoration of the departed. Noted examples from the 20th century (some in jest) include:

> Hereabouts died a very gallant gentleman, Captain L. E. G. Oates of the Inniskilling Dragoons. In March 1912, returning from the Pole, he walked willingly to his death in a blizzard, to try and save his comrades, beset by hardships. – E. L. ATKINSON.

> I've played everything but the harp. – LIONEL BARRYMORE's suggested epitaph on himself.

> Over my dead body! – GEORGE S. KAUFMAN's suggested epitaph on himself.

> Free at last, free at last
> Thank God almighty
> We are free at last.
> – Epitaph of MARTIN LUTHER KING (from an anonymous spiritual).

> Beneath this slab
> John Brown is stowed.
> He watched the ads
> And not the road.
> – OGDEN NASH, *Lather as You Go*.

> He lies below, correct in cypress wood
> And entertains the most exclusive worms.
> – DOROTHY PARKER, 'Epitaph for a Very Rich Man'.

> I will return. And I will be millions. – Inscription on the tomb of EVA PERON.

• **EPOS** ► *See*: bar code.

• **Epsom salts** ► British slang for the drug Ecstasy, used from about 1989. Epsom salts are actually hydrated magnesium sulphate, a traditional remedy for indigestion and constipation.

• **EPT** ► Excess profits tax. A tax imposed in the UK during World War II. Between 1940 and 1945 any profit a company made above its pre-war profit level was payable in full to the government; 20% of it was returned when peace was restored.

• **equal** ►
**All animals are created equal but some are more equal than others** A nonsensical political slogan created by George Orwell in his political fable Animal Farm (1945). Although ironically reflecting contemporary Stalinist doctrine, Orwell was guying a statement from the Declaration of American Independence (1776) that 'All men are created equal'.

• **equalizer** ► A euphemism for a revolver. The word, derived from the view that in death all men are equal, became common currency in America in the years before World War II. Its usage has since spread to both sides of the Atlantic, largely through its adoption in crime thrillers and screenplays.

• **Equal Opportunities Commission** ► *See*: feminism.

• **equal opportunity** ► A phrase used in the business world, indicating that employees are taken on regardless of their colour, sex, or age.

• **Equal Rights Amendment** ► (ERA) A proposed amendment to the US constitution that was first pressed in 1923, passed by Congress in 1972, but failed to be ratified in 1982. Under its terms women would receive explicit constitutional protection from sex discrimination. Its opponents, who were backed by right-wing religious groups, argued that the amendment was inappropriate because it ignored the biological and psychological differences between the sexes, that it would harm the institutions of marriage and the family, and that there was protection already under the 5th and 14th Amendments.

• **equal time** ▶ *See*: fairness doctrine.

• **Equity** ▶ The actors' trade union, founded in the UK in 1929 to regulate the employment of professional actors in the theatre, radio, film, and television. The strict rules surrounding Equity membership have made the **Equity card** much sought-after. The Catch-22 of the British theatre is that in order to be given a speaking part an aspiring actor needs an Equity card, but in order to acquire an Equity card, the aspiring actor has to show that he has had previous professional engagements. The US version was founded in 1913; unlike the British union it is for stage actors only.

• **Eric** ▶ **1.** A former British schoolboy abbreviation for an erection. It is not thought to owe its derivation to F. W. Farrar's novel of school life at Harrow, *Eric, or Little by Little*. **2.** A former schoolboy expression for a stupid man or fool, possibly derived from oik.

• **'er indoors** ▶ A catchphrase popularized by the ITV series, *Minder*, which was first broadcast in 1979. The expression was used by the chief character, the roguish Arthur Daley (played by George Cole), when referring to his wife, a character who was never seen. The implication is that, although the wife is confined to the domestic sphere, she wields a considerable amount of power. *See also*: earner.

• **erk** ▶ Originally (1910s) an RAF term for an aircraftman or mechanic; it derives from 'airc', an abbreviation of aircraftman, the lowest rank in the service. The term is now applied to beginners, juniors, and underlings generally.

• **ERM** ▶ Exchange Rate Mechanism. *See*: European Monetary System.

• **ERNIE** ▶ Electronic Random Number Indicating Equipment, the electronic equipment used to select winners in the premium bonds issued by the Department of National Savings of the UK government. Premium bonds were first issued in 1956 and play on the British public's love of gambling. The prize fund is distributed to bond holders selected monthly by ERNIE; bond holders receive no interest but can cash in their bonds for the issue price at any time. It is estimated that the maximum holding of £20,000 will, on average, yield prize money of some £800 p.a. (*i.e.* about 4% tax free).

• **ersatz** ▶ (German *ersetzen*, to substitute) Describing an inferior substitute for something that is no longer available. The word was much used in Germany during and after World War I, when the country's economic collapse led to the widespread introduction of such goods; it was applied especially to coffee made from acorns. The word was subsequently adopted by most countries (including the UK) during World War II and the rationing era.

• **Erté** ▶ The pseudonym adopted by the French fashion designer and magazine illustrator Romain de Tirtoff (1892–1990). He derived it from the French pronunciation of the first letters of his Christian name and surname.

• **ERTS** ▶ Earth Resources Technology Satellite. *See*: Landsat.

• **e-shopping** ▶ The purchase of goods or services over the Internet. Using either a computer or an Internet TV, the shopper visits the website of the supplier and places an order; payment is usually by credit card or by cybercash. Small items are delivered by post or parcel service. Items ordered from a supermarket will usually be delivered by the store's own delivery service. Although on-line shopping is a fast-growing area, many consumers still have concerns about privacy and security; others like to see or handle the actual goods before deciding to buy.

• **Esky** ▶ In Australia, a tradename for a portable drinks cooler. It is an abbreviated form of 'eskimo'.

• **ESP** ▶ Extra-sensory perception, a modern term for the supposed ability of some people to acquire accurate knowledge of the outside world independently of the five senses. The subject of serious scientific research throughout the 20th century, the term covers such activities as telepathy (mind-to-mind communication), clairvoyance (knowledge of remote objects, events, or persons), precognition (foretelling the future), and retrocognition (personal knowledge of the past). The US psychologist J. B. Rhine (1895–1980) conducted experiments using special packs of cards to produce statistical evidence in favour of ESP, but the conclusion is not universally accepted.

• **Essex girl** ▶ In the early 1990s young women from Essex became the butt of a series of snobbish jokes, all stressing their supposed stupidity, lack of style, and sexual promiscuity. A 'real Essex girl' would typically sport a fake suntan, white stilettos, a short tight skirt, cheap but ostentatious jewellery, and peroxide blonde hair swept into an elaborate perm. She would speak with a pronounced Estuary accent (*see*: Estuary English).

• **Essex man** ▶ A wealthy but poorly educated

male, who typically lives in Essex, has right-wing political views, shows conspicuous bad taste in dress and decor, and has few (if any) cultural interests. The implication is that Essex man is a throw-back to a less civilized form of hominid. *See also*: loadsamoney.

...the human species known as 'Essex man': father with extensive collection of gold rings, bracelets and neck chains; wife probably aged 50 but dressed as if she was 20; sullen adolescent son in unlaced trainers, with baseball cap on back to front, lugging around a ghettoblaster. – *The Independent*, 19 January 1991.

• **Establishment, the** ▶ **1.** The Church of England in its role as the officially recognized national church. The subject of much discussion in the 19th century, the link between Church and State has remained a subject of controversy in the 20th and 21st centuries. Those who support the link are called Establishmentarians. Those who argue for its abolition are disestablishmentarians, while those who range themselves against the disestablishmentarians are adherents of antidisestablishmentarianism. **2.** Since the 1950s the term 'Establishment' has been used to designate an inner circle in the upper echelons of society that is seen as wielding long-established power and influence, often by indirect or invisible means. It is generally used to indicate reaction, privilege, and resistence to change. The term is also applied to similar groups within a particular profession or field of activity (*e.g.* 'the educational establishment').

• **estate duty** ▶ *See*: inheritance tax.

• **Estuary English** ▶ A type of spoken English that came to the attention of the media in the early 1990s. Supposedly typical of speech in the towns along the Thames Estuary, it is characterized by modified Cockney vowel sounds, lazy diction, and a colourless vocabulary.

The way people talk is much worse. Everybody has started using Estuary English, the kind that Jonathan Ross speaks. – *The Independent*, 12 June 1993.

• **ET** ▶ Abbreviation for extra-terrestrial. Steven Spielberg's hugely successful film (1982) with this title had as its central character a lovable space creature itself named ET. Most children wept copiously when ET finally abandoned his earth friends to return to his native planet, although one critic was driven to comment that he found it hard to be emotional about a collection of Hoover parts. *See also*: close encounter.

• **ETA** ▶ (*Euskadi ta Azkatasuna*, Basque Nation and Liberty). A Basque terrorist organization that operates in France and Spain. ETA emerged in the 1960s as a student movement opposed to Franco, under whose regime the Basque language and culture were heavily repressed. Since that time ETA has waged a bloody campaign to achieve independence for regions of N Spain and SW France that Basque separatists claim should be theirs. The campaign has continued for over 30 years and has resulted in some 800 deaths, including those of politicians and members of the Spanish police force. It has provoked severe countermeasures from the Spanish state, including the alleged use of illegal death squads.

Following the kidnap and murder of a politician in July 1997, millions of people across Spain mounted demonstrations demanding an end to the campaign of violence. In September 1998 a ceasefire was called. However, following the refusal of the Spanish government to discuss Basque independence, the ceasefire was officially terminated in December 1999 and the terrorist campaign resumed.

• **ethical foreign policy** ▶ A foreign policy governed by a concern for right and wrong, rather than the selfish interests of one's own country. The phrase became current following the election of the Labour government in 1997, when the new foreign secretary Robin Cook appeared to promise such a policy. Although Cook denies ever using the exact phrase, he proclaimed the new government's commitment to human rights in several speeches. For instance, in May 1997 he said: 'We have made a firm commitment not to permit the sale of arms to regimes that might use them for internal repression or international aggression.' Similarly, in July that year he asserted that he would 'put human rights at the centre of British foreign policy'.

Both the phrase and the philosophy it implied came in for a good deal of criticism. While commentators on the right denounced it as a charter for all kinds of ill-considered meddling in other countries' affairs, some on the left saw it as a hollow phrase masking the same old Realpolitik. In practice the record has been mixed. While the government did take a moral stance on some issues, such as its support for an international treaty banning landmines, and its depiction of the Kosovo crisis in terms of good and evil, critics can point to Britain's failure to halt arms sales to countries with dubious human rights records, such as Saudi Arabia, Pakistan, and Indonesia.

• **ethical investment** ▶ A financial investment in a company that has been screened to ensure that its activities are ethically acceptable. The term originated in America in the 1980s, during the drive to widen public interest in stockmarket investments.

For many new 'capitalists' the idea of using their savings to help to produce armaments or cigarettes or to boost the economies of repressive regimes was an anathema. Brokers therefore recommended investments for their clients in companies they had screened for a positive social outlook. By the late 1980s the craze for ethical investments had reached the UK and Australia; it became commonplace for unit-trust managers to launch new trusts specializing in portfolios containing investments in 'socially screened' businesses. In Australia there was even a call for legislation making it compulsory for pension funds to invest exclusively in ethical investments.

• **ethnic ►** A pejorative name for an immigrant, used chiefly in Australia and America since the 1970s. It is derived from the adjective.

• **ethnic cleansing ►** Purging an area of one or more (usually minority) ethnic groups by expulsions, terror, and murder. This repulsive expression achieved notoriety soon after the beginning of the Bosnian civil war in 1992, when it was used by Serb spokesmen to describe their inhuman policy of forcing Muslims and Croats from their homes in Serb-dominated areas. In 1998–99 a similar policy was pursued in the Serbian province of Kosovo. Here ethnic Albanians (who formed the majority of the population and were demanding independence) were subjected to 'ethnic cleansing' by Serb forces to an extent that left an estimated 10,000 dead, over 200,000 homeless, and entire villages destroyed (see: Kosovo crisis). The phrase 'ethnic cleansing' had previous been used by the Croatian fascist government in World War II, to describe their still more murderous policies towards Serbs, Jews, Gypsies, and others.

• **ethnic identity ►** While ethnic identity cannot be exclusively defined by culture, language, race, nationality, or religion, it can encompass any or all of these distinctions; essentially it defines how people see themselves in terms of the shared history, customs, and values in which they have been brought up.

Ethnicity is, unfortunately, a divisive concept – those of the older generation, in particular, can easily feel threatened by people with a different background. Intermarriage between younger members of disparate groups is often opposed by their parents because they fear that the ethnic identity of their children (and grandchildren) will be jeopardized. Religious Jews, for example, will often cut themselves off from a child who marries a non-Jew. In many cases religious differences provide a pretext for conflicts that are more accurately seen as

ethnic in origin. In Northern Ireland, for example, Protestants and Catholics are apparently unable to live together in harmony for reasons that now have little to do with religious doctrine. The same may be said of the conflicts between Muslims and Christians in the Balkans. Elsewhere, as in parts of Africa, tribal or linguistic differences may lead to ferocious antagonism between neighbouring peoples. *See also*: ethnic cleansing.

• **Eton crop ►** A short boyish hairstyle, fairly popular among English women in the 1920s, called after the famous school for boys at Eton.

• **Eureka project ►** An international science initiative launched between the European nations in the 1980s in an attempt to pool resources on projects of mutual interest. Its name refers to Archimedes' shout of 'Eureka!' (literally, I have found it) on discovering, while taking a bath, how he might test the purity of a gold crown by employing the law of displacement (now known as Archimedes' Principle). As Vitruvius says:

> When the idea flashed across his mind, the philosopher jumped out of the bath exclaiming, 'Heureka! heureka!' and, without waiting to dress himself, ran home to try the experiment.

• **eurhythmics ►** A system of exercise for health and fitness involving energetic dance routines, which became popular in the 1920s. At the **Dalcroze Institute of Eurhythmics**, founded in 1910 by the Swiss composer Emile Jacques-Dalcroze, children were encouraged to respond to music through dancing. Eurhythmics was later the name of a highly successful British pop duo (1980s).

• **euro ►** The currency unit of the European Monetary System. In May 1998 all member states of the EU except Denmark, Greece, Sweden, and the UK committed themselves to European monetary union (EMU), and their currencies were locked together. In January 1999, the euro was launched for all forms of non-cash transactions. Notes and coins denominated in euros were issued in January 2002; the various national currencies were phased out by March 2002.

Denmark voted against adopting the euro in a referendum in September 2000. On 1 January 2001 Greece became the twelfth country to enter the **eurozone**, having fulfilled the necessary criteria for EMU. In the countries that remain uncommitted – notably the UK – debate continues as to whether the economic benefits of joining can outweigh the loss of national sovereignty involved.

• **euro-ad ►** An advertisement designed so that it will be relevant in all European countries. Recent products, such as cars and electric shavers, are usually suitable for multinational advertisements. On the other hand, more traditional products, such as food, are not.

• **eurocheque** ▸ A cheque drawn on a European bank, which can be cashed at any bank displaying the sign of the European Union or used to pay for goods or services at outlets displaying this sign.

• **Eurocrat** ▸ A high-ranking civil servant working for the European Union. *See also*: globocrat.

• **eurocurrency** ▸ Any currency held in a European country other than that which issued it. For example, dollars and yen deposited in a European bank are **eurodollars** and **euroyen**, respectively.

• **Europe** ▸

**l'Europe des patries** A version of a phrase used by General de Gaulle to define his vision of the European Economic Community. First used in 1961, it was meant to distinguish de Gaulle's ideal of a loose organization of sovereign states from more ambitious schemes for European government. De Gaulle insisted that he had actually used the words '*L'Europe des états*'.

• **European Community** ▸ (EC) An organization of European states created in 1967 when the executive and legislative bodies of the European Atomic Energy Community (founded by the Treaty of Rome in 1958) and the European Coal and Steel Community (founded in 1952) merged with those of the **European Economic Community** (founded by the Treaty of Rome in 1957). The original members were Belgium, France, Italy, Luxembourg, the Netherlands, and West Germany (which became the reunified Germany in 1990). Denmark, the Republic of Ireland, and the UK joined in 1973. Greece joined in 1981 and Spain and Portugal in 1986. In 1985 Greenland left on obtaining home rule from Denmark.

Barriers to the free movement of labour, services, and capital were lifted from December 1992. Under the terms of the Maastricht Treaty (signed 1992) member states agreed a number of steps to closer political, economic, and monetary union that resulted in the creation of the European Union in 1993.

• **European Monetary System** ▸ (EMS) A system introduced in 1979 to stabilize exchange-rates between the countries of the European Community; the longer term goal was to establish a single currency unit for the member states. The system had two main elements; the **Exchange Rate Mechanism** (ERM) and a balance of payments support mechanism organized by the **European Monetary Cooperation Fund**. In the ERM, participating gov-

ernments committed themselves to maintaining the value of their currencies within agreed limits. The ERM valued each currency in ecus and a parity grid gave exchange values in ecus for each pair of currencies. If the market rate differed from the parity rate by more than the permitted percentage the relevant government had to take action. In autumn 1992, however, the British, Italian, and Spanish governments found themselves unable to support their currencies above their floor values. They then had to be allowed to float, the pound falling heavily against the Deutschmark (*see*: Black Wednesday). In August 1993 speculative pressure on the franc forced the European foreign ministers to allow wider fluctuations of the remaining currencies.

Although the EMS seemed to have failed, plans to create a single currency (the euro) and a European Central Bank by 1999 went ahead. In May 1998, 11 EU countries (all the member states with the exception of Denmark, Greece, Sweden, and the UK) committed themselves to **European Monetary Union** (EMU), having fulfilled the criteria required for participation. The European Central Bank (ECB) was set up in 1998 under the presidency of Willem Duisenberg (1935– ), a Dutch economist. In January 1999 the euro became available for non-cash transactions; notes and coins were introduced in 2002. Greece adopted the euro from 2001.

• **European Union** ▸ (EU) An organization formed by the member states of the European Community in 1993. Under the terms of the Maastricht Treaty (1992) the member states agreed to extend the scope of the EC by co-ordinating their foreign and security policies and co-operating in matters of justice and policing. Controversial moves to harmonize social policy and to create a single European currency (*see*: European Monetary System) were also approved; the euro was finally launched in January 1999. In 1995 Austria, Finland, and Sweden joined the EU, bringing the number of member states to 15.

• **Eurosceptic** ▸ Someone who is hostile to the policies of the European Union and resists steps towards closer economic and social integration of European states. Since the UK's admission to the European Community (EC) in 1973, the argument about 'Europe' has been a perennial fixture in British politics. The term 'Eurosceptic' was coined in the mid-1980s and encompassed individuals drawn from all the main political parties. Their argument essentially was that the growing powers of the EC were inexorably diminishing national sovereignty and leading to the formation of a European 'superstate'. The Conservative government elected in 1979 had, in Margaret Thatcher, an instinctively Eurosceptic leader who was continually trying to renegotiate the terms of Britain's membership. Her stance was supported by a large sector of the Conservative Party, including fellow cabinet ministers such as Norman Tebbitt, as well as many backbenchers; some of the more outspoken Eurosceptics formed the Bruges group in 1989. At the same time many Conservatives supported the principle of greater European integration – prominent **Europhiles** included Michael Heseltine and Douglas Hurd – and party unity on the issue was elusive. Meanwhile, other member states were proceeding with plans for a single market and monetary union, and this growing chasm between the prime minister's own beliefs and Britain's undertakings to her European partners contributed to Thatcher's downfall and the election of the more conciliatory John Major. In the early 1990s, the Eurosceptics gained succour from the UK's forced exit from the Exchange Rate Mechanism (*see*: European Monetary System) and intensified their attacks during negotiations over the Maastricht Treaty. The governing party's deep divisions over Europe persisted, and contributed to its humiliating defeat in the 1997 general election. Any Eurosceptics in the incoming Blair government were muffled voices; the party has contrived to avoid splits over Europe mainly by putting off any decision on the crucial issue of participating fully in European monetary union and replacing the pound with the euro.

> Deep divisions within the Conservative party will come out into the open this week when Eurosceptic fans of Lady Thatcher seek to oust Hugh Dykes, MP for Harrow East... – *The Independent on Sunday*, 24 August 1993.

• **Eurostar** ▶ A train service between London (Waterloo) and Paris (Gare du Nord) or Brussels (Midi/Zuid), travelling through the Channel Tunnel via Ashford (in Kent), Calais, and Lille. There are also Eurostar services direct from London to Disneyland Paris and to Moutiers and Bourg-St Maurice (the last two in the French Alps). The journey to Brussels takes 2 hours 40 minutes and that to Paris 3 hours. Although this is longer than the flight between London (Heathrow) and Paris (Charles de Gaulle), the actual journey time is probably shorter (considering the time required for travelling to and from airports, checking in, and baggage clearance), and passengers certainly travel in more comfort. *See also*: Golden Arrow.

• **eurotrash** ▶ The European jet set, an expression used in society circles and journalism; it is an adaptation of the US expression 'White trash', meaning worthless White people. the term is now more familiar as the title of a Channel 4 programme that presents curious mainly sex-related items from around Continental Europe for the delectation of the prurient Brits.

• **Eurotunnel** ▶ *See*: Channel Tunnel.

• **evacuees** ▶ In World War II, children from large cities in the UK who were sent to live with families in the country. Evacuation was a vast operation that had been carefully and efficiently planned by the British government to safeguard the lives of children in the event of war and the inevitable bombing of cities. The evacuation began on 1 September 1939 when it became clear that war with Germany was imminent. Although parents were under no obligation, some 3 million children were evacuated in Britain before the end of the war.

In the initial phase, children were taken by their parents to their schools, where labels were tied around their necks showing their names and destination. They carried a small suitcase or bag containing their belongings, a gas mask in its cardboard box, and sandwiches for the day. From their schools they were sent in groups to designated small towns and villages in the country, where they were met by local billeting officers. These officers had the authority to compel suitable households to accept one or more evacuees. Many of the children, separated from their parents for the first time, were not surprisingly tearful and distressed. Most found the unfamiliar environment of the countryside both bewildering and daunting. Some returned to the city after a short irreconcilably unhappy stay, but most remained and gradually settled into their new families. Michelle Magorian's book *Goodnight Mister Tom* (1981) is a moving account of a deprived East End lad who eventually flourishes in the care of an old man with whom he is compulsorily billeted. The book was later made into a convincing TV drama.

• **Evans of the Broke** ▶ Sir Edward Ratcliffe Garth Russell Evans (1881–1957), British admiral, explorer, and author. His nickname derives from his World War I exploit of sinking six German destroyers while commanding HMS *Broke* (pronounced 'brook': the ship was named after the naval hero Sir Philip Broke). This was only one incident in a colourful career: in 1909 Evans was second in command of Scott's first expedition to the Antarctic.

• **eve** ▶ The stimulant drug MDEA, which is related to Ecstasy (MDMA). Ecstasy is sometimes known as **adam**, from an anagram of MDMA; the jump to 'eve' for the related drug is not hard to understand.

• **événements** ▶ (French, events) The *événements*

of May–June 1968 were a series of violent left-wing protests, led largely by students, in the streets of Paris. The students erected barricades, occupied a number of key buildings, and briefly made common cause with striking industrial workers. The uprising caused a momentary failure of nerve in the government of Charles de Gaulle but soon burned itself out. When de Gaulle resigned the following year it was over an unrelated matter.

> During the événements of May and June, 1968, the red flag of communism and the black flag of anarchism fluttered side by side on the occupied Théâtre de l'Odéon.

• **Evenin' all**► A catchphrase popularized by the BBC TV series *Dixon of Dock Green* (1955–76), the hero of which was PC George Dixon, played by Jack Warner. His invariable opening greeting to the viewers 'Evenin' all' was accompanied by a sketchy salute. Somewhat bizarrely, the TV series was born out of the film *The Blue Lamp* (1950), in which Dixon was shot dead by the young Dirk Bogarde. Just how he recovered from this misfortune to enjoy such a long ensuing career in the police force has never been explained. By the time the programme ended, Warner was 82 – considerably past the usual police retirement age.

• **event horizon**► *See*: black hole.

• **eventide home**► A euphemism for an old people's home.

> The House of Lords is a perfect eventide home.
> – MARY STOCKS.

• **Everest syndrome**► The tendency to undertake challenging enterprises, such as climbing mountains, rowing the Atlantic, tight-rope walking across the Niagara Falls, pursuing esoteric scientific research, etc., simply for the sake of the challenge. George Mallory is said to have wished to climb Everest 'because it is there'. Everest was finally conquered on 29 May 1953 by Sir Edmund Hillary and Sherpa Tenzing Norgay; news of the climb reached the UK during celebrations of the coronation of Elizabeth II, doubling its impact.

> We done the bugger! – TENZING NORGAY, 29 May 1953.

In 1993 Rebecca Stephens became the first British woman to climb Everest.

• **Ever Readies**► Nickname of the Territorial Army Volunteer Reserve, a former (1922–67) division of the Territorial Army. The Ever Readies were called upon to supply trained and equipped men on the outbreak of war or in other sudden emergencies overseas. The name is also a tradename for a brand of battery made by Berec (formerly the British Ever Ready Electrical Company), founded in 1906.

• **everybody out**► A phrase associated with trade-union leaders when calling their members out on strike. When the British trade-union movement was at its most powerful in the 1960s and 1970s the leaders acquired a reputation for calling strikes on the slightest pretext. 'Everybody out' was the supposed automatic response to any dispute with management. It was popularized by a TV series called *The Rag Trade* in which Paddy, the shop steward (played by Miriam Karlin), shouted the phrase at the least provocation.

• **everybody's doing it**► A popular phrase of the period immediately preceding World War I, taken from the song 'Everybody's Doing It Now' by Irving Berlin. The 'it' in question was the **turkey trot**, a lively dance performed to ragtime music.

• **Every day and in every way I am getting better and better**► *See*: Couéism.

• **Evian agreement**► The treaty under which France granted Algeria independence in 1962, named after the French town in which independence talks began in 1961.

• **evil**► Youth slang, originating among US Blacks, for very good, impressive. A rarer version of bad or wicked used in the same sense.

• **Evita**► The name by which María Eva Duarte de Perón (1919–52), the second wife of Juan Perón (1895–1974), the Argentine president, was known to the adoring Argentine public. Despite abundant evidence of her ruthlessness and greed, Evita's charitable work, beauty, and early death all contributed to the popular myth surrounding her name; in 1978 her life became the subject of the successful stage musical *Evita* by Andrew Lloyd Webber and Tim Rice (filmed 1996).

> If a woman like Eva Perón with no ideals can get that far, think how far I can go with all the ideals that I have. – MARGARET THATCHER (1980).

• **excrementum bellum vincit**► (Latin) Army catchphrase from World War II; roughly translated as 'bullshit wins the war'.

• **excuse my dust**► An apology shouted by early motorists to other road-users for any dust their vehicles threw up in passing.

• **exercise is bunk**► The US car manufacturer Henry Ford's opinion of the contemporary fashion for exercising to keep healthy, since quoted by couch potatoes everywhere. Ford justified his opinion, first publicly expressed in 1920, with the further comment:

If you are healthy, you don't need it: if you are sick, you shouldn't take it.
*See also*: history is bunk.

• **exercise the ferret**▶ Australian slang meaning to have sex; a macho expression that likens the penis to the aggressive animal used to hunt rabbits, etc. from their burrows.

• **existentialism** ▶ A philosophical attitude, owing much to the writings of the Protestant thinker Søren Kierkegaard (1813–55), that developed in Germany after World War I and somewhat later in France and Italy. Atheistic existentialism was popularized in France by Jean-Paul Sartre (1905–80) and Albert Camus (1913–60) after World War II. Post-war existentialists emphasized the freedom and moral responsibility of the individual in the face of an absurd universe without meaning or the possibility of transcendence. Much of their writing is characterized by disillusionment. The term is a translation of the German *Existenz-philosophie*.

• **exit poll**▶ *See*: opinion poll.

• **Exocet**▶ An anti-ship missile developed by the French and used with great effect by the Argentinian air force in the Falklands Conflict. The most notable British casualty to this missile was HMS *Sheffield*, which was sunk. Hence, to 'Exocet' a project is to cause it to be brought to a complete standstill.

• **expanding universe**▶ The generally accepted cosmological theory that the universe is expanding. *See*: Big Bang.

• **expletive deleted**▶ A phrase widely used in the 1970s in substitution for an obscenity or blasphemous comment, especially in printed documents. It entered popular use after the publication in 1974 of transcripts of recorded exchanges between President Nixon and his advisers relating to the Watergate scandal. In these the words 'expletive deleted' were employed so frequently that it was inevitable that they should gain wider currency. Many ordinary Americans appeared to be more shocked by their president's routine use of profanities than by the political scandal itself.

• **expressionism**▶ A movement in the arts of the early 20th century in which the force of human emotion was allowed to distort the presentation of the external world. It was most important in the visual arts but also significant in cinema, theatre, literature, and music. In painting, forerunners of expressionism include Van Gogh and Edvard Munch, but the style achieved its fullest flowering in the angst-ridden work of the Brücke and Blaue Reiter groups in Germany. Many independent figures, such as Rouault, Soutine, Schiele, and Kokoschka, also worked in an expressionist style.

In the cinema, pioneers of expressionism included the German directors Fritz Lang, G. W. Pabst, and F. W. Murnau. Their work is characterized by the use of distorted perspective, unusual camera angles, and extreme contrasts of light and shade to convey abnormal states of mind. In drama, expressionism emerged as a definite movement in the German theatre of the 1910s and 1920s, when such writers as George Kaiser, Ernst Toller, and the young Brecht experimented with nonrealistic styles. In literature and music the term is used more loosely: the writing of Kafka and the early music of Berg and Schoenberg are often described as expressionist.

• **extended family**▶ *See*: nuclear family.

• **ex tenebris lux**▶ (Latin, out of darkness, light) The motto of HMS *Glow-worm*, the Royal Navy ship that in 1940 succeeded in ramming and badly damaging the German heavy cruiser *Admiral Hipper*. The *Glow-worm* exploded and sank after the impact.

• **exterminate, exterminate**▶ A catchphrase popularized by the BBC's long-running science fiction series *Dr Who* (1963–96). It was the characteristic cry of the **Daleks**, mobile metallic extraterrestrial beings equipped with ray guns. *Dr Who* was a great favourite with children, many of whom enjoyed being scared by the series, and the Daleks were the most popular of the aliens. The cry 'exterminate, exterminate' was often heard in children's games in the days of the Daleks.

• **extinct**▶ A species of animal or plant defined by the International Union for the Conservation of Nature and Natural Resources (IUCN) as not having been definitely located in the wild in the previous 50 years. Animal species that became extinct in the 20th century include:

> broad-faced potoroo (*Potorous platyops*)
> desert bandicoot (*Perameles eremiana*)
> thylacine (*Thylacinus cynocephalus*)
> Palau flying fox (*Pteropus pilosus*)
> Falkland Island wolf (*Dusicyon australis*)
> Mexican grizzly bear (*Ursus arctos nelsoni*)
> Syrian wild ass (*Equus hemionus hemippus*)
> glaucous macaw (*Anodorhynchus glaucus*)
> silver trout (*Salvelinus agassizi*)
> Texas tailed blue butterfly (*Everes comyntas texanus*)

*See also*: endangered species; threatened species; vulnerable species.

• **extra two inches**▶ The extra two inches (to their erections) that men over 40 are supposed to acquire. A well-known army myth of World War II, it implied that the sexual disappointments of one's early adulthood would be compensated for in later life.

• **eyeball** ► To stare at, often provokingly or threateningly. Used by young people and the police in the UK and Australia since the 1970s, it is thought to have originated in the Black street slang of 1940s America.

• **eyeball to eyeball** ► Person to person contact; usually with the suggestion that the contact is confrontational. The phrase has been much used in the context of diplomatic negotiations since the Cuban missile crisis of 1962.

• **eye in the sky** ► Electronic surveillance from the air. Sophisticated cameras in aircraft and satellites are reputed to be able to read a car registration plate from a distance of many miles.

• **eye it – try it – buy it** ► US trade slogan first adopted by salesmen of Chevrolet cars and heard frequently in the 1950s and 1960s.

• **eyelyser** ► A device for estimating the amount of alcohol in the blood by measuring the percentage of alcohol in the vapour given off by the eyes. The word is a coinage from 'eye' and 'breathalyser'. The device, developed in Canada by the Addiction Research Foundation, involves placing a funnel over the eyeball for 15 seconds and using a gas sensor to analyse the vapour. The main advantage claimed for the method is that it can be used on people who are unconscious.

• **eye-opener** ► A US expression for the first drink or fix of drugs of the day. *See also*: leg-opener.

• **eyes and ears of the world** ► The motto of the movie newsreel British Gaumont News, which became a more widespread catchphrase after World War II.

• **eyetie** ► An Italian. A popular expression based on a mispronunciation of the word Italian, dating from World War I and used in the UK and America. It is a less racist term than 'wop'.

# F

• **FAB** ▶ *See*: fuel air bomb.

• **Fabergé** ▶ The near legendary firm of Russian goldsmiths made famous under Peter Carl Fabergé (1846–1920). The company was founded by Fabergé's father in 1842 but it was the son who established the firm's name for *objets d'art* in gold, silver, enamel, and precious stones. Among the valuable items produced by Fabergé was a series of ingenious Easter eggs made for the Russian Tsars. The firm went out of operation after the October Revolution of 1917. Fabergé died in exile in Lausanne.

• **Fab Four** ▶ A nickname for the Beatles, especially during the early phase of Beatlemania. In the 1960s **fab** was a fashionable abbreviation for 'fabulous, wonderful'.

• **façadism** ▶ A pejorative term for the type of postmodern architecture (*see*: postmodernism) in which a modern structure is disguised by a façade in period (usually neoclassical) style. For advocates of functionalism this is the ultimate architectural heresy. Such styles have also been labelled 'bimbo architecture' (*see*: bimbo).

• **face** ▶ **1.** British slang for someone who stands out in the crowd, a stylish trendsetter. A vogue word with the mods (*see*: mods and rockers) of the 1960s, it gave its name to *The Face*, a British style magazine first published in the early 1980s. It probably derives from the idea of a famous face being instantly recognizable or from the fact that the picture cards in a pack are those with the highest values. **2.** British street slang of the 1980s for nerve or brazenness.

• **facedown** ▶ *See*: face-off.

• **faceless man** ▶ A person who is not known to the public, but who wields power behind the scenes. It is generally used in the plural; for example, one criticism of the Australian Labor Party was that it was run by a non-Parliamentary federal executive consisting of '36 faceless men'. *See also*: men in grey suits.

• **facelift** ▶ An operation to raise the sagging jowls of a person (usually a woman) who wishes to regain something of her youthful looks. When performed skilfully by a cosmetic surgeon this operation can also eliminate some of the wrinkles that come with age. However, unskilful or repeated facelifts can give the face an unnatural appearance that is far worse than the usual effects of ageing. By extension the word is now used of any other procedure designed to improve the look of something (especially superficially).

> Victoria Station's £250m facelift – Headline in *The Independent*, 25 March 2001.

• **face-off** or **facedown** ▶ A confrontation between individuals, organizations, countries, etc., in which each tries to make the other back down. The same idea of two people staring at each other is present in such phrases as eyeball to eyeball and 'who blinks first?'

• **faction** ▶ A blend of fact and fiction in a novel, film, play, etc. In a work of faction real people and events are interpreted with a good deal of dramatic licence; the result is often controversial. *Compare*: docudrama.

• **factory farming** ▶ Any system of livestock farming in which animals are kept at high densities in artifical surroundings and treated essentially as units of production. Throughout the world, millions of animals are now kept on 'factory farms', including poultry, pigs, cattle, sheep, and fish. Most are housed indoors, often in carefully controlled environments removed from the vagaries of the local climate, and fed precise amounts of feed (often by machine) in order to maximize profitability. Among the more extreme examples is the 'battery' system used for laying hens. Here the birds are kept in long tiers of cages, several birds to a cage, throughout their productive lives (this system is due to be phased out in the UK by 2012). Most pigs reared for pork and bacon are also kept indoors in densely occupied pens on concrete floors, while beef cattle and lambs are commonly reared under similar conditions.

Since the 1950s factory farming has become the norm in many countries, developing hand in hand with advances in nutrition and veterinary medicine. These have led to specially formulated feeds and feed additives, including growth promoters, and routine medication to keep disease in check. Such methods have resulted in meat, eggs, and milk produced reltively cheaply and reliably, in many cases regardless of season and weather conditions. And the quantities are huge: for example, the UK meat industry slaughters some two million chickens and 100,000 turkeys every day.

Although intensive livestock farming is subject to certain welfare codes, critics still condemn it as unethical, arguing that animals are denied the opportunity to exercise their instinctive behaviours, whether it be the hen scratching in the dirt or the pig wallowing in mud. Also, they argue that the crowded conditions in factory systems place unnatural burdens on the animals, causing them stress and making them susceptible to infections and other diseases. Consequently, factory-farmed meat, eggs, or milk are judged inferior by some, who point to instances when the products are contaminated by antibiotics, growth hormones, etc., with the attendant health risks to consumers. Moreover, factory farms often have an adverse impact on the environment, creating large amounts of manure and other wastes that create disposal problems.

Disenchantment with factory farming has led some consumers to turn to 'free-range' products, *i.e.* those produced by animals allowed free access to outdoor paddocks. This generally entails lower growth rates or yields, and consequently the product is more expensive. Yet most people continue to find the low price of factory-farmed food irresistible, despite any qualms they may have about the methods used in its production. *See*: organic farming.

• **fade** ► 1. US slang meaning to leave or go away. It was part of beatnik jargon in the 1950s, and was revived by adolescents in the 1980s. 2. US slang from the world of gambling, especially used in the dice game craps, meaning to meet a bet.

• **faff** or **faff around** ► British slang meaning to dither about in a disorganized way. It is usually said with an air of exasperation.

• **fag** ► 1. Slang for a cigarette. 2. A male homosexual; short for **faggot**.

• **fag hag** ► Slang for a woman who consorts with gay men. Originally a US expression of the 1960s, it is now also heard in the UK and Australia. It has lost its earlier pejorative overtones and may well be used by the woman herself.

• **fag tag** ► US college-student slang for the loop at the top of the back pleat of the traditional US Oxford shirt. The loop (the tag) is facetiously regarded as being helpful during a gay sexual encounter – something to hold onto, perhaps.

• **fail-safe** ► Of a system or mechanism, designed to prevent disaster in the event of human error or mechanical failure. At the height of the Cold War in the 1950s, the US Air Force introduced a fail-safe limit beyond which US bombers could not fly without specific orders; it was intended to prevent nuclear conflict by mistake or as a result of the actions of a madman. The threat of nuclear annihilation through human error or derangement is also countered by the so-called 'two-man system' ('four-man' in the former Soviet Union), in which personnel guarding, handling, or in charge of firing nuclear weapons operate in tandem. A more mundane example of a fail-safe system is the dead man's handle, a safety switch that must remain depressed by train drivers to prevent the automatic application of the brakes.

• **Fair Deal** ► In America, post-war programme of social and economic reform put forward by Harry S. Truman during his presidency (1945–53). Only a few of the recommendations, including increased retirement benefits and slum clearance, passed Congress.

• **fairness doctrine** ► In America, the principle, applied by the Federal Communications Commission, that radio and TV broadcasting stations should give reasonable coverage of opposing viewpoints on controversial issues. For example, the principle of **equal time** is that two politicians, say, in an election should have equal opportunities to air their views. In the UK, the broadcasting authorities apply the equal-time principle to the main political parties.

• **fairy** ► Slang for a male homosexual. The term is now regarded as dated as well as offensive.

• **fairy godmother** ► In 19th-century fairytales, a fairy who adopts a child at birth and protects it throughout its life. In the less fey 20th and 21st centuries, a fairy godmother is a benefactor of either sex who helps a younger person, especially by providing the necessary funds to transform her life in a way she longed for.

• **Falaise** ► A small town in Calvados, NW France. A crucial battle was fought here in August 1944, when a large contingent of the German army was almost encircled by Allied forces S of Caen. However, a number of them managed to escape through the so-called **Falaise Gap**, before it was closed. The town was virtually destroyed.

• **Falange** ▸ (Spanish, phalanx) An extreme right-wing party in Spain, formed in 1932 by José Antonio Primo de Rivera to uphold the memory of his father, the former dictator Miguel Primo de Rivera, against Republican criticism. After his victory in the Spanish Civil War General Franco made it the one official party in the state. Essentially representing a combination of European Fascism and Spanish nationalism, it was used by Franco to balance royalist, army, and Church influence. The Carlists were absorbed into the Falange in 1937 but re-emerged as a separate grouping after 1957. The Falange (latterly known as the National Movement) lost its unique position after the Caudillo's death in 1975, and was formally disbanded in 1977.

• **Falashas** ▸ An Ethiopian tribe that practises a form of biblical Judaism. During the 20th century many Falashas adopted modern Judaism and some emigrated to Israel. Israel accepts Falashas as Jews, in terms of its immigration laws, and in 1985 organized a secret airlift (known as Operation Moses) of some 7000 Falashas to Israel to escape the devastating Ethiopian famine. In 1991, during the final stages of the Ethiopian civil war, a further 15,000 Falashas were airlifted (Operation Solomon) to Israel in a few days by a fleet of airliners (some of which had been stripped of their seats to enable 1000 passengers to sit on mattresses on the cabin floor). This left behind tens of thousands of **Feres Mora**, Falashas who, having converted to Christianity, no longer qualified as Israeli immigrants under a 1962 Israeli supreme court ruling. Raramin Elazzar, head of Israel Radio's Amharic (Ethiopian Language) Service, pleading for their admission on the grounds that many of their relatives were already in Israel, commented delphically:

> They are not converted Jews, they are Jews who left Judaism.

• **Falcon, the** ▸ A character created by the novelist Michael Arlen (1895–1956). The Falcon, a suave detective with a comic but muscular servant named Goldie, appeared in some 16 second-feature films in the 1940s. Originally played by George Sanders, the detective was shot dead in *The Falcon's Brother* (1942) to enable Sanders to retire. The Falcon's brother (played by Sanders' real-life brother, Tom Conway) thereafter became the detective. In nearly all the films Goldie was played by Edward Brophy.

• **Falkland Islands, Battle of the** ▸ A naval battle of World War I, fought in December 1914, in which the Germans were decisively defeated by the British, Germany losing several ships, including the *Scharnhörst* and *Gneisenau*. In Britain it was regarded as revenge for the battle fought off the Chilean port of **Coronel** a month earlier, in which the British lost the cruisers *Monmouth* and *Good Hope*.

• **Falklands Conflict** ▸ The war between the UK and Argentina for possession of the Falkland Islands in 1982. The bleak South Atlantic islands have been a British territory since 1828, but despite the opposition of the majority of the 1800 inhabitants, Argentina has consistently asserted its claim to what it calls the Islas Malvinas. In April 1982, after British defence cuts led to the withdrawal of the only remaining Royal Navy frigate stationed at Port Stanley, Argentina launched an invasion of the islands. Much to the Argentinians' surprise, the British immediately declared a 200-mile exclusion zone around the islands and dispatched a strong military task force, which restored British sovereignty in June 1982, when Argentina was forced to surrender. This bravura military episode was regarded with pride by many British people and certainly enhanced the UK's status in the world. It also made a heroine of Margaret Thatcher, who was responsible for this prompt and determined response (*see*: Falklands factor). Others, however, questioned the economic and human costs (1000 lives lost in the conflict) involved in defending such an inhospitable and geographically remote territory; the South American writer Gabriel García Márquez famously dismissed the war as 'two bald men fighting over a comb'. Arguably, the main beneficiaries were the Argentinians, as defeat brought the restoration of democracy after many years of military rule. General Leopoldo Galtieri resigned after the surrender and – with members of his junta – was tried and imprisoned.

• **Falklands factor** ▸ The boost given to the electoral fortunes of the previously flagging Conservative Party by the success of British forces during the Falklands Conflict in 1982. The Falklands factor significantly contributed to the Conservative victory in the 1983 general election, despite the government's poor economic record. It certainly revived support for Margaret Thatcher, who thereafter commanded worldwide respect as a determined and forceful leader. The term has now passed into general usage to denote any unpredictable event that increases the popularity of a government or party.

• **fall** ▸

**Did she fall or was she pushed?** Usually a reference to a young woman who has lost her virginity. In 1908 the phrase was applied more literally in newspaper articles about the death of Violet Charlesworth, whose body was found at the foot of

Beachy Head. Thorne Smith wrote a comic novel with the title *Did She Fall?* in 1936.

• **fall guy** ▶ An expression that came into use with the popularity of professional wrestling in the early 20th century. As soon as wrestling became a spectator sport the rigging of contests began. The winner was decided beforehand; the loser was the fall guy, the contestant who agreed to take the falls. Often the fall guy may have been more prudent than unfortunate; perhaps having thought little of his chances of winning the purse, he preferred to settle for the smaller but surer fall guy's fee. His agreement with the winner may also have included a promise that no lasting damage would be inflicted on him in the ring. In modern usage, the fall guy is the one who takes the blame for some catastrophe, which may not have been of his own making. He may be a willing volunteer or an unwilling scapegoat.

• **fall-out** ▶ Radioactive particles from a nuclear explosion that are carried into the atmosphere and fall back to earth as dust or in rain. Figuratively, the indirect or delayed effects of an action, especially those that could not have been foreseen or intended.

• **family** ▶ In America, a criminal organization that is a subdivision of the Mafia. Although families are known by name – for example, the 'Luchese family' – the members are not necessarily related. *See also*: godfather; Mob, the.

• **family ganging** ▶ In America, the practice of giving unnecessary medical treatment to members of a family who accompany the actual patient. It is a way in which doctors increase their fees from the US Medicaid scheme. *See also*: ping-ponging.

• **family hour** ▶ In America, the period during the early evening up to about 9 p.m. when television programmes suitable for viewing by both parents and children are shown. In the UK there is a similar policy of no sex or excessive violence before 9 p.m. (the '9 p.m. watershed'), based on the idea that children go to bed at this time.

• **family jewels** ▶ Shameful secrets that an organization, company, political party, etc., keeps hidden. The term was first used in this sense in the late 1970s, referring to a leaked list of dirty tricks and other illicit activities indulged in by the CIA.

• **family planning** ▶ *See*: birth control.

• **family saviours** ▶ In America, a sarcastic term for right-wing fundamentalist Christians who lobby for the defence of traditional family values. According to the journalist Andrew Kopkind, who carried out research among the born-again Christian community in Illinois, family saviours support 'the death penalty, Laetrile, nuclear power, local police, Panama Canal, saccharin, FBI, CIA, defense budget, public prayer, and real-estate growth'. *See also*: moral majority.

> Fiercely, these zealots condemn promiscuity, adultery, homosexuality, masturbation, long hair and fluoride. – GORE VIDAL: *Sex is Politics* (1979).

• **family silver** ▶ *see*: sell the family silver.

• **famous last words** ▶ The following are well-known final observations by some of the great figures of the 20th century:

> BEHAN, BRENDAN (*playwright*; on having his pulse taken by a nursing nun): Bless you, Sister. May all your sons be bishops!

> CHURCHILL, SIR WINSTON (*statesman*): Oh, I am so bored with it all.

> COOPER, DAME GLADYS (*actress*; on looking into her mirror): If this is what viral pneumonia does to one, I really don't think I shall bother to have it again.

> COWARD, SIR NOËL (*playwright*): Good night, my darlings, I'll see you in the morning.

> DREISER, THEODORE (*novelist*; his intended last words): Shakespeare, I come!

> DUNCAN, ISADORA (*dancer*): Adieu my friends, I go on to glory!

> FAIRBANKS SNR, DOUGLAS (*actor*): I've never felt better!

> FERRIER, KATHLEEN (*contralto*): Now I'll have *eine kleine Pause*.

> HEATH, NEVILLE (*murderer*; on being offered a drink before his execution in 1946): You might make that a double.

> HENRY, O (*William Sidney Porter*, short-story writer; quoting a popular song): Turn up the lights, I don't want to go home in the dark.

> IBSEN, HENRIK (*playwright*; on being told by the nurse that he was feeling better): On the contrary!

> JAMES, HENRY (*novelist*): So it has come at last, the distinguished thing.

> JOYCE, JAMES (*novelist*): Does anybody understand?

> MAHLER, GUSTAV (*composer*): Mozart.

> OATES, CAPT. LAWRENCE (*explorer*; on leaving the tent occupied by fellow-members of the ill-fated Antarctic expedition led by Scott in 1912, fearing that his lameness would hinder the team's chances of survival): I am just going outside and may be some time.

> RHODES, CECIL JOHN (*statesman*): So little done, so much to do.

> RUNYON, DAMON (*writer*): You can keep the things of bronze and stone and give me one man to remember me just once a year.

SANDERS, GEORGE (*actor*; his suicide note): Dear World, I am leaving you because I am bored. I am leaving you with your worries. Good luck.

SAROYAN, WILLIAM (*playwright*): Everybody has got to die, but I have always believed an exception would be made in my case. Now what?

SMITH, LOGAN PEARSALL (*writer*): Thank heavens the sun has gone in and I don't have to go out and enjoy it.

SPENCER, STANLEY (*artist*; to the nurse who had just injected him): Beautifully done.

STRACHEY, LYTTON (*writer*): If this is dying, I don't think much of it.

THOMAS, DYLAN (*poet*): I've had eighteen straight whiskies. I think that's the record.

THURBER, JAMES (*humorist*): God bless...God damn.

TOLSTOY, LEO (*novelist*; refusing to see a priest): Even in the valley of the shadow of death, two and two do not make six.

VICTORIA (*Queen*; referring to the war in South Africa then in progress): Oh, that peace may come.

WILDE, OSCAR (*dramatist*; contemplating the room in Paris in which he lay): Either that wall paper goes, or I do.

See also: Cavell Memorial; How is the Empire? *at* Empire; Scott of the Antarctic.

• **fan club** ▶ 1. A club consisting of the admirers of a famous person, especially a pop star or film star. 2. In business jargon, a number of individuals who, independently of each other, and without collusion, decide to purchase a significant number of shares in a company. A fan club is legal, whereas the related **concert party** is an illegal combination of two or more persons who buy or sell shares in a company to influence its market value. Members of a concert party usually contrive to appear unconnected with other members; however, once their connection becomes established, the 1981 Companies Act lays down that the shares owned by all the members must be treated as if they are owned by one person, from the point of view of disclosing interests in a company's shareholding.

• **fantasy** ▶ British slang for an extremely potent hallucinogenic drug invented in the UK in 1989; it is a mixture of Ecstasy and LSD or mescaline.

• **FANY** ▶ First Aid Nursing Yeomanry. An organization of women formed in 1907. It provided amateur nursing, ambulance drivers, and other driving services in World War I. In World War II FANYs provided drivers for military cars. It was often said that a girl had to be a debutante to be accepted by this elite women's service with its elegant khaki uniform. After World War II it was amalgamated with the Women's Transport Service but is still referred to as the FANY; today its main function is in helping to maintain communications in civil and military emergencies.

• **fanzine** ▶ A neologism created from 'fan' and 'magazine' for a cheap magazine or newsletter produced by amateur followers of a particular sport, hobby, television programme, etc. The term was originally used of publications for sci-fi enthusiasts in America in the 1940s.

• **FAO** ▶ Food and Agricultural Organization. A specialized agency of the United Nations, formed in 1945 to coordinate international efforts in raising food production and nutrition levels, especially in the developing countries. It also organizes work to improve forest management, carries out research, and provides educational services. Its headquarters are in Rome.

• **farmers** ▶ British rhyming slang for piles (haemorrhoids), from the name Farmer Giles, a common personification of a country farmer.

• **far-out** ▶ A hippie term used to express extreme approval for something remarkable. It originated in America in the late 1960s and became widely used in the UK. Within 10 years it sounded very dated.

• **fascines** ▶ Bundles of faggots used to build up military defences or to fill ditches for impeding attack. They were much used in World War I for road foundations and for horse standings and also used to impede attack in World War II. See also: Fascism.

• **Fascism** ▶ Originally an Italian political movement taking its name from the old Roman *fasces* (the bound bundles of rods used as a symbol of the authority of magistrates in ancient Rome). It was founded in 1919 by Benito Mussolini (1883–1945) who took advantage of the discontent in Italy after World War I to form an authoritarian nationalist party violently opposed to left-wing socialism. In 1922 the Fascists marched on Rome and demanded power, and King Victor Emmanuel III made Mussolini prime minister. He styled himself Duce (leader) and made himself dictator in 1925, suppressing all other political parties the following year. The Fascists controlled Italy until 1943.

The term 'fascism', soon came to be applied to similar totalitarian movements in other countries, notably the Nazi party in Germany.

> Benito Mussolini provided Italy with a new theme of government which, while it claimed to save the Italian people from Communism, raised himself to dictatorial power. As Fascism sprang from Communism, so Nazism developed from Fascism. – WINSTON CHURCHILL: *The Gathering Storm.*

• **fashion statement** ▶ The use of clothing or other personal accessories to project a desired image or communicate a message. People select and wear particular clothes for all manner of reasons, such as their personality, their mood on a given day, the dictates of a certain occasion, or the weather. The signals conveyed by a person's dress are multifarious and generally subliminal. But the maker of a fashion statement knowingly chooses an outfit that reinforces a professional or social role, or identifies them as belonging to a certain social group. For example, an expensive and exquisitely tailored suit by a top designer proclaims the wearer's wealth, self-confidence, and good taste. A devotee of grunge might select a quite different ensemble, with equal care, to make a correspondingly loud fashion statement in a post-grunge era. At street level, the fashion statement is mainly about wearing the right 'designer' labels, which helpfully are often emblazoned on the outside of garments.

> Similarly, a recent Gallup poll commissioned by Motorola found that young people use pagers as a means of 'socialising and flirting'. They are also a fashion statement. – *The Independent*, 23 October 1997.

• **fashion victim** ▶ Someone who is so obsessed with the idea of being fashionable that their clothes are dictated by the latest trend rather than suitability, taste, or comfort.

> One week he's in polka dots, the next week
> he's in stripes,
> Cos he's a dedicated follower of fashion.
> – RAY DAVIES: 'Dedicated Follower of Fashion' (1966).

• **fastback** ▶ A car with a sloping rear, which forms a continuous line from roof to tail and into which the rear-view window is set.

• **fast breeder** ▶ A type of nuclear reactor that uses fast (*i.e.* high-energy) neutrons and produces fissionable plutonium as a by-product. *See*: nuclear reactor.

• **fast buck** ▶ Money made quickly, usually by speculation or illicitly, rather than by hard work. A salaried job will not usually supply a fast buck but a casual night's work might.

• **faster than a speeding bullet** ▶ *See*: Superman.

• **fast food** ▶ Food that can be prepared and served very quickly, such as hamburgers, french fries, pizzas, kebabs, etc. In the UK, fast food was once confined to fish 'n' chips or jellied eels from a market stall. Today US-style fast-food outlets have become a dominating feature of the UK's urban landscape (*see*: takeaway); they are also to be found in the high streets of many other countries. A large amount of fast food is also junk food. Apart from the fast-food outlets outside the home, there is now a vast range of food available for working housewives, old people, etc., who do not have the time, facilities, or inclination to cook a meal. This may consist of deep-frozen food or cook-chill foods. *See also*: microwave.

• **fast lane** ▶ The outermost lane of a motoway, used for overtaking or travelling at speed, in which the most powerful cars are to be found. Hence, **living in the fast lane** denotes a lifestyle that involves high living with an element of danger and excitement.

• **Fastnet** ▶ A rock and lightship off Cape Clear, SW Ireland. The **Fastnet Race**, from Ryde, Isle of Wight, to the Fastnet Rock, is one of the five races contributing to the Admiral's Cup. In the Fastnet race of 1979, 18 yachtsmen died in severe storms; 25 of the 330 yachts competing were sunk or disabled.

• **fast one** ▶ 1. US slang from the 1970s for Ritalin, a brand of amphetamine. 2. **pull a fast one**. British slang meaning to get away with a cunning but unscrupulous act.

• **fat cat** ▶ Slang for a smug, wealthy, and privileged person who flaunts his or her lifestyle even though it has been attained by exploitation or connections, rather than merit. The term is thought to have been first used of those who did well financially from World War I. Since the mid-1990s it has often been applied to senior figures in the newly privatized utilities (*see*: privatization), who awarded each other monstrous salaries as well as benefiting from share options and similar schemes.

• **fat farm** ▶ A health farm or resort to which people go specifically to lose weight. The term is mostly used by thin people.

• **Fatha** ▶ Nickname of Earl (Kenneth) 'Fatha' Hines (1905–83), Black US jazz pianist and band leader. Trained as a concert pianist, he played with several bands before forming his own (1929–48). He then joined Louis Armstrong's 'All Stars' (1948–51).

• **Father Brown** ▶ A fictional detective and East Anglian Roman Catholic priest, created by G. K. Chesterton (1874–1936). Reflecting the author's own beliefs, Father Brown regarded criminal activity as first and foremost a sin and relied on his spiritual intuition to solve the crimes he was investigating. Chesterton himself became a Catholic convert in 1922. His first Father Brown story, *The Innocence of Father Brown*, was published in 1911.

• **Father's Day** ▶ The day set aside for fathers to

receive cards and gifts from their children, in imitation of the more traditional Mother's Day. Father's Day was devised in 1910, in Spokane, Washington, but remains less well-recognized than Mother's Day on both sides of the Atlantic.

• **Fatima** ▶ *See*: Our Lady of Fatima.

• **Fats** ▶ **1.** Nickname of the Black US jazz pianist, composer, and entertainer, Thomas 'Fats' Waller (1904–43). His own compositions, which he recorded many times and in many versions, include 'Honeysuckle Rose' (1928) and 'Ain't Misbehavin' (1929). As a nightclub entertainer he could be extremely funny; perhaps this talent, and the great demand it created, detracted from full appreciation of his technical ability on the piano. A great fat man (hence his name), he has left a joyous legacy in his many recordings. **2.** Nickname of another fat Black US musician, Antoine 'Fats' Domino (1928–   ), a singer, pianist, and songwriter of the rock 'n' roll era. His rhythm-and-blues songs include 'Blueberry Hill' (1959).

• **Fatty** ▶ Nickname of Roscoe 'Fatty' Arbuckle (1887–1933), one of the great stars of silent comedy films. A man of considerable size, he is now remembered less for his films than for his role in precipitating the Hays Code (*see*: Hays Office), a film censorship code that emerged in Hollywood in the 1920s. In 1921 a case of indecent assault and manslaughter was brought against Fatty Arbuckle, who was accused of raping a starlet, who subsequently died of complications. Although he was eventually acquitted of the charges, his film career came to an end and even the films he had previously made were banned. No studio would employ him under his own name, although he tried, unsuccessfully, to make a comeback as a director under the name Will(iam) B. Good(rich). **Fatty Arbuckle** has entered the language as an epithet for any fat man.

• **fatwa** ▶ A word first widely used in English-speaking countries during the **Rushdie affair** of the late 1980s and 1990s. An Arabic word for an edict issued by a Muslim religious leader, it became familiar to a startled non-Islamic world in February 1989, when Ayatollah Khomeini (1902–89) issued a *fatwa* offering a cash reward for any Muslim who succeeded in assassinating the British author of Indian Muslim origin, Salman Rushdie (1947–   ). Rushdie was the author, and Viking Penguin the publishers, of a novel, *The Satanic Verses* (1988), in which a character identified by many Muslims as the prophet Muhammed was treated in a manner that they regarded as disrespectful.

The author of *The Satanic Verses* book, which is

against Islam, the Prophet and the Koran, and all those involved in its publication who were aware of its content, are sentenced to death. I ask all Muslims to execute them wherever they find them. – AYATOLLAH KHOMEINI, speech 14 February 1989.

The book became an international cause célèbre with fundamentalist Muslims in Tehran, Bradford, and elsewhere burning copies in the streets and calling for the death of the author, who by then had gone into hiding with a police guard, a much richer but much sadder man. Diplomatic relationships between Britain and Iran were broken off and the literary world protested that no such violent acts of religious intolerance had been seen since the days of the Inquisition. With Viking Penguin books banned in all Muslim countries, the affair dragged on. There was an unexpected development on Christmas Eve 1990, when Rushdie announced, to the dismay of his supporters, that after a meeting with Islamic scholars, he had become a Muslim. In the same announcement he cancelled plans for a paperback edition, arguing that: 'The binding of a book is not a moral principle.' His persecutors remained wholly unmoved by these concessions. On the following day, Ayatollah Khamenei, Khomeini's successor as Iran's spiritual leader, renewed the *fatwa*. An Iranian newspaper said it hoped that Rushdie would now visit a Muslim country because that would make it easier to kill him without embarrassing the British government. Subsequently, Rushdie declared that he was a 'cultural' Muslim only, and admitted that his 'conversion' statement had been chiefly tactical. During the mid-1990s he gradually adopted a more public profile in response to hints from Iran that the death sentence would not be carried out. They insisted, however, that theologically a *fatwa* can never be cancelled. In 1998 the Iranian government formally dissociated itself from the *fatwa*, thereby freeing Rushdie from a nine-year ordeal.

• **Fauves** ▶ A group of young French artists of the first decade of the 20th century, whose leader was Henri Matisse, and which included Derain, Braque, Vlaminck, Dufy, Marquet, Friez, and Rouault. There was a corresponding German movement known as the Brücke (Bridge). The French school shows the influence of Van Gogh and was characterized by the use of brilliant non-naturalistic colour, decorative simplicity, and a mood of fierce gaiety. The name *Fauves* (wild beasts) arose from a remark of the critic Vauxcelles at an exhibition of their work in 1905.

• **Fawlty Towers** ▶ A fictional West-of-England private hotel that featured in the British TV series of this name in the late 1970s. Run with manic incompetence by Basil Fawlty (John Cleese) and his nagging wife Sybil (Prunella Scales), the hotel managed to demolish a fresh set of pompous middle-class guests in every episode. The Fawltys and their Spanish waiter Manuel (Andrew Sachs) – a buffoon whose incomprehensible use of English was matched only by his inability to understand it (*qué?* – Spanish for 'what?' – he asks, every time he is addressed) – have entered British folklore. The series was also successful abroad; in Spain, however, Manuel was rewritten as an Italian waiter. The house in Buckinghamshire used for the hotel in the series burnt down in 1991. In 2000, after a repeat showing of the series, it was voted the greatest television programme of all time in a poll by the British Film Institute.

• **fax** ► Facsimile transmission. The transmission of an exact copy of a document through the telephone network or other communication link. The document to be faxed is scanned and converted into digital code by a fax machine at one end and then transmitted by a phone line or other link to the receiving fax machine, which reconstitutes the data to produce a printed copy of the original. The fax machine was once a cumbersome and expensive piece of technology, used by such organizations as police forces, who needed to transmit and disseminate text and images (*e.g.* mug shots) quickly and easily. By the early 1980s, however, small low-cost fax machines became widely available and they were soon as commonplace in offices as photocopiers. They largely replaced the telex but have themselves lost ground to e-mail during the last few years.

• **fax-napping** ► The crime of stealing someone's Filofax and demanding a 'ransom' for its return. Coined by analogy with 'kidnapping', it is also called **filonapping** or simply **filofaxing**. The loss of a Filofax can be a serious matter for its owner, causing complete breakdown of both social and business activities.

• **fax shot** ► *See*: junk mail.

• **FBI** ► Federal Bureau of Investigation. An agency of the US Department of Justice established in 1908 to investigate breaches of federal law, especially those related to security. It developed considerable autonomy under the directorship (1924–72) of J. Edgar Hoover, during which it did much to control organized crime in the 1930s and to implement McCarthyism in the 1950s. *See also*: Cointelpro.

• **FDR** ► Franklin Delano Roosevelt (1882–1945), the only US president (1933–45) to be elected four times; he died in office. His New Deal programmes

helped America to recover from the Great Depression. In World War II he introduced Lend-Lease aid to the Allies and, after the Japanese attack on Pearl Harbor, led America into the war. Paralysed from the waist down by poliomyelitis from 1921, he was filmed in newsreels in contrived sedentary poses to disguise his disability. He was widely known by his initials. *See also*: Fireside Chats; Houdini in the White House.

• **featherbed** ► To give favourable treatment to a particular group of people, especially financially. The verb is often used in connection with companies giving large wage settlements to certain trade unions or to governments favouring certain sections of the community with subsidies. The allusion is to the luxury of sleeping on a feather bed.

• **feature film** ► A fiction film of some length designed for commercial release. Most feature films run for 90 minutes or more, anything shorter than 34 minutes being defined as a 'short'. Feature films usually have at least one well-known actor and provide the main item of a cinema programme. Formerly, it was usual for most suburban and provincial cinemas to show two feature-length films, the **main feature** and a low-budget production designed to be a supporting feature (*see*: B-movie). Now, however, cinemas only show one feature film, occasionally supported by a short.

• **February Revolution** ► The first phase of the Russian Revolution, occurring in March (Old Style, February) 1917. It began with riots in Petrograd (now St Petersburg), provoked by food and fuel shortages and military incompetence in World War I, and led to the abdication of Tsar Nicholas II and the formation of a provisional government led by Prince Lvov. The February Revolution was the precursor to the October Revolution of the same year, which saw the Bolsheviks, with Lenin as their leader, seize power in Russia.

> Revolution is not the uprising against pre-existing order, but the setting up of a new order contradictory to the traditional one. – JOSE ORTEGA Y GASSET: *The Revolt of the Masses*.

• **Fed** ► Slang for the Federal Reserve System, the banking system of America that acts as its central bank. 'The Fed' consists of 12 Federal Reserve Districts, in each of which a Federal Reserve Bank acts as the lender of last resort. The whole system is controlled by the Federal Reserve Board in Washington.

• **Feds** ► US slang name, mainly used by criminals and state police, for agents of the FBI (Federal Bureau of Investigation). Feds are also known as **Feebies**, from the initials FBI.

• **feedback**▸ Originally, in electronics, the use of part of the output signal from an electronic device to modify the performance of the device. In **positive feedback** the signal augments the output (as in an oscillator); in **negative feedback** it reduces it. More specifically, feedback is a name for the whistling noise in a loudspeaker caused by the output from the loudspeaker being picked up by a microphone connected to the same amplifier. The concept of self-modification of a system has been applied in other fields; for example, the effect of a product in a biological reaction on other stages in the reaction (*see also*: biofeedback). More generally, feedback is any information about people's reaction to a product, action, or policy etc., especially when used to make improvements.

• **feederliner** ▸ An airline of moderate size designed to link small domestic airports with a main airport.

• **feeding frenzy**▸ Hostile and intensive scrutiny by the mass media, especially the press, of persons or organizations afflicted by trouble of some kind. The term alludes to the way in which a shoal of piranhas or other fish, attracted by blood, will surround a much larger victim and tear it to pieces. By the 1970s this genuine zoological term was being used to describe analogous practices in the business and financial world. Later, however, it became more associated with the activities of the tabloid press, which takes few pains to disguise its relish when reporting on the misfortunes of some celebrity, regardless of the pain and embarrassment this may cause. One of the more recent feeding frenzies by the British media involved not a person but a building – the Millennium Dome.

> I think there has been a feeding frenzy in the press at the expense of the RSC which has led to quite a number of unjust attacks on its productions and actors – ADRIAN NOBLE, artistic director of the Royal Shakespeare Company, quoted in *The Independent*, 31 March 1999.

• **feel-good factor** ▸ A general sense of well-being or good fortune, especially one that is seen as having economic or political consequences. The phrase acknowledges the fact that people's ill-defined feelings about the good or bad state of things may prove as important as more rational factors. In economics, for example, people's hopes or fears about the economy can become self-fulfilling. If people feel prosperous, or hopeful of becoming so, they will spend more of their disposable income, thus helping to create the very prosperity in question. If they feel the reverse, the opposite effect may come in to play. The absence of a feel-good factor was often cited to explain why the UK re-mained stuck in recession in the early 1990s when other indicators seemed promising. In politics, the government will always try to produce a feel-good factor among the electorate to coincide with election time, the usual strategy being to cut taxes or boost spending power in some way. However, a feel-good factor can arise from many less obvious causes, such as national success in a sporting fixture or even a spell of good weather.

> To the cynics the prospect of a millennium baby looks like a gift from the gods generating a feel-good factor that will propel Tony Blair back into Number 10 for a second term. – *The Independent on Sunday*, 21 November 1999.

• **feelie** ▸ An artistic medium in which the 'spectator' has physical contact with the work as part of his or her appreciation of it. An example would be a sculpture that the public was encouraged to touch as well as look at. The term 'feelie' was used first by Aldous Huxley (1894–1964) in his futuristic novel Brave New World (1932) for a type of film entertainment in which the viewer could actually experience the emotions and physical feelings of the people shown on the screen.

• **Felix the Cat**▸ Hero of early animated film cartoons who first appeared in 1921 in a production by Pat Sullivan. Throughout his adventures the indestructible **Felix kept on walking**, thus originating a popular catchphrase.

• **fellow-traveller**▸ A person in sympathy with a political party but not a member of that party; usually restricted to communist sympathizers. The term (Russian *poputchik*) was coined by Leon Trotsky.

> He is but one of a reputed short list of seven fellow-travellers under threat of expulsion. – *Time and Tide*, 1 May 1948, on the Labour Party's expulsion of one of its members.

• **female chauvinist pig**▸ A strident feminist, the counterpart of a male chauvinist pig. Female chauvinist pigs regard women as innately superior to men in all important respects, men being useful only as sperm donors and assemblers of flat-packed furniture.

• **feminism**▸ The belief that women should have an equal role to that of men in all areas of society. In 20th-century Britain this began with the activities of the suffragettes, who campaigned for voting rights for women. In 1903 Emmeline Pankhurst (1858–1928) and her daughters formed the Women's Social and Political Union (WSPU), which finally achieved votes for women in 1918. However, the educational and property qualifications attaching to women's suffrage were not removed for 10 years, when men and women became political equals. A second major wave of feminism began in the late 1960s, with the formation of small consciousness-raising groups in America and the Women's Liberation Workshop in London (1969). During this phase the movement was generally known as **Women's Liberation** or **Women's Lib**, although both terms now sound old-fashioned (and, in the latter case, distinctly sexist). In the early 1970s feminists campaigned for, and largely achieved, equal education and job opportunities for women and equal pay. In the UK the Equal Pay Act (1970) ensures that women are paid the same rate as men for a particular job, while the Sex Discrimination Act (1975), which set up the Equal Opportunities Commission, promotes equality of opportunity between the sexes. Despite these landmark legal reforms, some of the more controversial (and expensive) demands of the 1970s Women's Liberationists remain only partly achieved; these include free contraception, abortion on demand, and 24-hour nurseries for working mothers.

The late 1970s and 1980s saw the feminist movement turning to a wider agenda of sexual politics in which rape, pornography, and media sexism became key issues. Some radical feminists came to reject the whole basis of Western society as 'patriarchal', arguing that its structures embodied fundamentally male principles of hierarchy and violence. Some even advocated a radical form of female separatism, in which heterosexuality itself became part of the problem. On the whole, the 1990s and 2000s have seen a retreat from such sterile extremes and – especially among the young – an emphasis on women enjoying their various freedoms without guilt or ideology. For this reason, the current era is sometimes described as one of postfeminism.

• **fender-bender** ▶ A car accident in which the car is damaged ('fender' being the US term for the wing of a car). The term is also used for a driver who tends to have accidents. See also: gender-bender.

• **feng shui** ▶ (from Chinese feng, wind; shui, water – pronounced fung shway) An ancient Chinese art used to make decisions regarding the placement of buildings and their contents. Originally a method of divining the most propitious place to site graves, it subsequently had a profound influence on the Chinese traditions of town planning, architecture, and interior design. Exponents claim that adherence to its principles will enhance the natural flow of energy (chi) in any environment, leading to happiness and prosperity.

In the Far East the practice is taken very seriously; banks and other large corporations will spend huge sums on detailed feng shui consultations before building or furnishing offices – presumably in the hope that, appropriately applied, this advice will increase their profits. In the later 1990s a somewhat trivialized version of feng shui also became popular in the West, including the UK. Of the thousands of so-called feng shui consultants who have emerged, almost all lack the six-year training in a monastery that qualified practitioners in the Far East undertake. Nevertheless, companies in the City of London are estimated to have spent around £5 million on such consultations in 1999. Numerous English-language books on the subject have also been published in recent years.

A Western sceptic might conclude that feng shui combines some interesting ideas about the psychological effect of an environment on those who live and work in it with the most grotesque mumbo-jumbo (e.g. in suggesting that a wrongly positioned fishbowl can cause a company or a marriage to fail).

• **Ferdinand the Bull** ▶ A character in a children's book by Munro Leaf who was more interested in smelling flowers than in tossing matadors. The antithesis of a macho bull, he was popularized in a Walt Disney cartoon film of 1939.

• **Feres Mora** ▶ See: Falashas.

• **Fergie** ▶ The nickname of Sarah Ferguson (1959– ), who married the Queen's second son, Prince Andrew, Duke of York, in 1986. They had two daughters, Princess Beatrice (1988– ) and Princess Eugenie (1990– ), before separating in 1992. Although initially well liked for her high spirits and sense of fun, the Duchess of York soon attracted bad publicity for her extravagant spending, frequent holidays, and generally undignified behaviour. A problem with her weight also gave rise to much cruel comment ('the Duchess of Pork' was one press nickname). The marriage came to an end after Fergie had been photographed on holiday in Italy, with her financial adviser paying undue attention to her toes. Although the couple divorced in 1996, they continue to live in different parts of the same house, remaining, in the coy babytalk of the Duchess, 'the bestest of friends'.

• **fertility drug** ▶ Colloquial name for a hormonal preparation administered to women who are unable to conceive because their ovaries fail to produce egg cells. Available since the 1960s, such drugs typically act by stimulating the pituitary gland to release hormones that, in turn, cause the ovary to produce egg cells. Fertility drugs may cause the simultaneous release of several egg cells, resulting in multiple births; these drugs are used to stimulate the ovary in the technique of *in vitro* fertilization (*see*: IVF).

• **Festival Gardens** ▶ The gardens in Battersea Park in London, laid out by Osbert Lancaster and John Piper for the Festival of Britain in 1951. A pleasure garden in the style of the 18th-century Vauxhall Gardens, it had bowered walks, a grotto, and many decorative fountains.

• **Festival of Britain** ▶ An event organized in 1951 to mark the centenary of the Great Exhibition, a display of British industrial prowess mounted in the Crystal Palace (which was built especially for the occasion). The Festival of Britain was also designed to boost morale after the austerities of World War II and to demonstrate the UK's post-war developments in science, technology, architecture, and the arts. Exhibitions were held throughout the country, the main site being the South Bank of the Thames in London, organized by Hugh Casson. The Royal Festival Hall, the only building intended to be permanent, was erected here. Perhaps the most eye-catching feature was Powell and Moya's Skylon, an elongated vertical structure on wires. *See also*: Festival Gardens.

• **Festung Europa** ▶ *See*: Fortress Europe.

• **fetal alcohol syndrome** ▶ A condition affecting newborn babies whose mothers have consumed excessive amounts of alcohol during pregnancy. Affected babies may suffer from various defects, ranging from low birth weight and slow growth to facial abnormalities and mental retardation, caused by the toxic effects of the alcohol, which is carried in the mother's bloodstream across the placenta and impairs normal development in the fetus. The syndrome was first recognized in the 1970s. In the UK, most medical authorities advise women to avoid alcohol completely during the first 13 weeks of a pregnancy and to drink moderately (if they wish) thereafter; in America, the usual advice is to abstain for the whole term.

• **fetoscope** ▶ A medical instrument employing fibre optics used to observe an unborn baby in the womb. Inserted into the abdomen of a pregnant woman, it enables the fetus to be examined for the presence of any visible abnormalities and also allows samples of fetal blood to be withdrawn through a hollow needle passed through the instrument. Analysis of this blood enables the prenatal diagnosis of such disorders as haemophilia and Duchenne muscular dystrophy. Inspection of the fetus using this instrument is called **fetoscopy**.

• **Few, the** ▶ The RAF pilots of the Battle of Britain, so called after prime minister Winston Churchill's

memorable tribute to them in the House of Commons (20 August 1940):

> Never in the field of human conflict was so much owed by so many to so few.

• **Feynman diagram** ▶ A type of diagram used in particle physics to show how charged particles interact by the exchange of virtual photons (a branch of physics known as quantum electrodynamics. Such diagrams were invented by the US physicist Richard Feynman (1918–88).

• **FFI** ▶ *Forces françaises de l'intérieur* (French Forces of the Interior). The various irregular forces fighting for the liberation of France were so designated in February 1944. The FFI, which included partisans, francs-tireurs, the maquis, and others, was subsequently merged with the Fighting French (November 1944). *See*: Resistance.

• **FFL** ▶ *Forces françaises libres* (Free French forces). French forces organized by General de Gaulle after the German occupation of France (from June 1940) to continue the struggle in cooperation with the Allies. Later called the Fighting French.

• **Fianna Fáil** ▶ Irish Gaelic for Warriors of Ireland (from *fianna* warriors and *Fáil* of Ireland). The Irish political party founded by Eamon de Valera in 1926 from those opposed to the Anglo-Irish Treaty of 1921, which created the Irish Free State. It aims at the establishment of a united, independent, and self-supporting Ireland. Apart from four breaks from office during 1948–51, 1973–77, 1982–87, and 1994–97 it has been the governing party in the Republic of Ireland since 1932. Fianna Fáil has also paid particular attention to the revival of the Irish language. *See also*: Fine Gael.

• **fibre optics** ▶ The use of flexible glass or transparent plastic fibres to transmit light (or, in some cases, ultraviolet or infrared radiation) around curves. Optical fibres work by internal reflection of the light, which travels through the filaments with little loss of intensity. Fibre optics enables otherwise inaccessible sites to be viewed, as in medical examinations (*see*: fetoscope). The fibres can also transmit pulsed light in a highly efficient method of transmitting data.

• **FIDO** ▶ **1.** Fog Investigation and Dispersal Operation. The code name for a system used in World War II to clear fog from the runways of RAF airfields. It involved burning jets of petrol in specially designed burners. **2.** Film Industry Defence Organization. A body formed in 1959 by British renters and exhibitors to prevent old feature films from being sold to television companies. It collapsed in 1964.

• **Fiery Fred** ▶ Nickname of Fred Trueman (1931– ), British cricketer who played for Yorkshire and England. He acquired the name from a combination of his fast bowling and his somewhat abrasive temperament.

• **FIFA** ▶ *Fédération Internationale de Football Association*. The governing body that runs international football and organizes the World Cup.

• **fifth** ▶

**plead the fifth amendment** To refuse to answer or comment on the grounds that to do so would be embarrassing or damaging to oneself. The phrase refers to the right of US citizens to decline to give evidence against themselves, which is enshrined in the fifth amendment to the Constitution. It is now often used humorously.

• **Fifth Beatle** ▶ Sir George Martin (1926– ), producer for the EMI Parlaphone label, who recognized the talent of the Beatles in 1962, after they had been turned down by various other major record companies. He played keyboards occasionally and helped as an arranger, working closely with Lennon and McCartney in the early years of their songwriting partnership. Martin also exhibited considerable technical skills as a producer, using innovative and (for then) complex four-track recording techniques on *Sgt Pepper's Lonely Hearts Club Band* (1967). The term 'Fifth Beatle' has also been used of the group's original bass guitarist, Stuart Sutcliffe, who left the group in 1961 and died shortly afterwards.

• **fifth columnists** ▶ Traitors; those inside a country who are working for the enemy, often by assuming key positions and seeking to undermine the body politic from within. The phrase is attributed to General Mola, who, in the Spanish Civil War (1936–39), said that he had four columns encircling Madrid, and a fifth column working for him in the city.

• **Fifth Estate, the** ▶ The British Broadcasting Corporation (*see*: BBC) has jocularly been so called. The other four estates are the Lords Spiritual, the Lords Temporal, the Commons, and the press. *See also*: Auntie; Beeb.

• **fifth man** ▶ *See*: Magnificent Five.

• **Fifth Republic** ▶ The period of French history that began in 1958, when de Gaulle was recalled from retirement to become president.

• **Fighter Command** ▶ The part of the RAF that controlled its force of fighter aircraft. It was formed in 1936 under Hugh Dowding (1882–1970), with headquarters in Stanmore, NW London. It was Dowding who led Fighter Command's 55 squadrons during the Battle of Britain, and Dowding who refused to allow his main force to be distracted for other skirmishes. His resoluteness defeated the German Luftwaffe and saved the UK from invasion. Fighter Command and Bomber Command were amalgamated in 1968 to form Strike Command.

• **Fighting French** or **La France Combatante** ▶ Organized French forces who joined with the Allied nations in their war against the Axis powers after the fall of France (in June 1940). General de Gaulle and others escaped to England, where he formed the **Free French** or **FFL** with the Cross of Lorraine as their emblem. The name was later changed to the Fighting French (14 July 1942). One of their most noted feats was the march of General Leclerc's column across the Sahara, from Lake Chad, to join the British 8th Army in Libya. These men were honoured by being the first formation to enter Paris on 23 August 1944. The Fighting French supported the Allies in Africa, Italy, and elsewhere and made a valuable contribution to the liberation of France, in conjunction with the FFI.

• **film noir** ▶ (French, dark film) The US crime and gangster films of the 1940s and 1950s. The term was coined by French critics in 1946, after viewing Hollywood output since 1940 for the first time. They detected a new mood of cynicism and despair, with many films concentrating on themes of corruption and brutality. These preoccupations are epitomized by the classic *Double Indemnity* (1944), directed by Billy Wilder – a sordid tale of lust, greed, murder, and betrayal. In addition to the brooding subject-matter, film noir is characterized by sombre lighting and genuine (as opposed to studio) night shots, with strong contrasts between light and dark in the framing of each scene. The style is reminiscent of pre-war German expressionism, which is understandable, as many of the directors responsible, such as Billy Wilder, Fritz Lang, Otto Preminger, and Max Ophüls, were émigrés who began their film careers in Europe during the 1930s.

• **Filofax** ▶ Tradename for the best-selling and most prestigious brand of **personal organizer**, a portable loose-leaf ring-binder filing system using different coloured papers for recording appointments, names and addresses, useful information, etc. Possession of a bulging leather-clad Filofax became synonymous with yuppie lifestyle during the 1980s, but is now regarded as somewhat passé. As a status symbol the Filofax has largely been replaced by the electronic personal assistant (PA). *See also*: fax-napping.

• **filth, the** ▶ British slang for the police, especially

plainclothes policemen. A pejorative term widely used since the 1960s, especially by those who have reason to be apprehensive of their activities. *See also*: pig.

• **Final Solution** ► (German *Endlösung*) The euphemism used at the Wannsee Conference (1942) for the grotesque German plan to exterminate all European Jews. The schedules were laid down by the conference, which was chaired at Hitler's insistence by his brutal henchman Reinhard Heydrich; the logistics were left to Adolf Eichmann (*see*: Eichmann trial). That the 'final solution' was to be a mass extermination was not generally known in 1942, but by the time that Eichmann had organized the identification, arrest, and transportation of European Jews into death camps, there could not have been many Germans unaware of what was meant by it. *See also*: holocaust.

• **fine cut** ► *See*: rough cut.

• **Fine Gael** ► Irish Gaelic for Tribe of the Gaels (from *fine* tribe, race and *Gael* of the Gaels). The Irish political party founded by William T. Cosgrave and other members of the Dáil Éireann, who supported the Anglo-Irish Treaty of 1921 that created the Irish Free State (*see*: Free Staters). It is traditionally considered to be less nationalistic than Fianna Fáil and more concerned with reaching an accommodation with the UK. However, it was during the Fine Gael–Labour coalition government of 1948 that a republic was declared and Ireland withdrew from the Commonwealth. The Fine Gael party, led by Garrett Fitzgerald, later attempted to ease the Northern Ireland dispute by participating in the Anglo-Irish agreement of 1985 and trying to remove some of the more overtly Catholic features of the Irish constitution.

• **finest hour** ► *See at*: hour.

• **fingerlickin' good** ► Expression used since 1958 in an advertising slogan for Kentucky Fried Chicken (**It's fingerlickin' good**). It is possible that the phrase had an earlier origin in US Black slang.

• **fingerprint** ► An impression taken in ink of the whorls of lines on the finger. In no two persons are they identical, and they never change throughout life, hence their great value as a means of identification. From ancient times they were used for certifying documents by the Chinese and Japanese. Sir Francis Galton's *Finger Prints* (1892) and *Finger Print Directories* (1895) drew attention to their usefulness for identifying criminals. Sir Edward Henry, Commissioner of the Metropolitan Police (1903–18), devised a system for classifying impressions which

was widely adopted. The FBI uses his method. *See also*: DNA fingerprinting.

• **fingers** ► British slang for a pickpocket, *i.e.* someone who is light-fingered. It has been in use, especially among the police and criminals, since the 1950s.

• **Fings Ain't Wot They Used t'Be** ► Cockney version of 'things aren't what they used to be', used as the title of a musical by Frank Norman with lyrics by Lionel Bart. Put on in 1959 by Joan Littlewood (1914–  ; *see*: Theatre Workshop) at the Theatre Royal, Stratford, in E London, it was sufficiently successful for the title to become a popular catchphrase.

• **fire** ►
   **great balls of fire!** The chorus phrase from the Jerry Lee Lewis hit song of 1957, written by Jack Hammer and Otis Blackwell. It was used as an exclamation of surprise in the 1939 film *Gone with the Wind* and would therefore appear to be of southern US origin.

• **firebase** ► A military base set up to be a point from which artillery and gunfire can be used against the enemy. The term was applied to certain bases during the Vietnam War.

• **fire-break** ► In the escalation of a military conflict, a check between the use of conventional weapons and the use of nuclear weapons. The term, used in military jargon since the 1960s, was derived by analogy with the strip of land cleared between trees to check the spread of a forest fire.

• **Fireside Chats** ► The name adopted by President F. D. Roosevelt (*see*: FDR) for his broadcasts to the US people on topics of national interest and importance. They began in 1933 and became customary during his administration.

• **firestorm** ► A violent storm that can be caused by the explosion of a nuclear weapon or incendiary bomb. Hot air rising from the fireball causes strong winds to rush in, producing further damage and fanning the flames. Firestorms occurred at Hiroshima and Nagasaki as a result of nuclear bombs and in the Dresden fire bombing during World War II.

• **firewatchers** ► A force of volunteers who, during German air raids on the UK in World War II, kept watch for incendiary bombs. Very often stationed on the roofs of large buildings and equipped with only a stirrup pump, a bucket of water, and a bucket of sand, they saved many buildings from destruction.

• **First Aid Nursing Yeomanry** ► *See*: FANY.

• **first base** ▸ US teenage slang for kissing. Taken from baseball, the idea is that kissing is the first stage in a sexual encounter, just as first base is the first stage on the way to scoring a run in the ball game.

• **First Gentleman of the Screen** ▸ Nickname of the monocled George Arliss (1868–1946), a distinguished British actor, who entered the film world in middle age and unexpectedly became a star on both sides of the Atlantic. He earned his nickname from the number of films in which he was cast as a king or rajah, or at least a nobleman or millionaire.

• **First Lady of the Screen** ▸ Nickname of Norma Shearer (1900–83), a Canadian-born actress who made the big time in Hollywood. Her many films of the 1920s and 1930s ranged from the silent *The Student Prince* (1927) to *Escape* (1940), a not inconsiderable war film. She earned her nickname as one of MGM's most coveted properties and perhaps for her role in *Marie Antoinette* (1938).

• **first light** ▸ In the armed forces 'first light' denotes the earliest time (roughly dawn) at which light is sufficient for movement of ships, or for military operations to begin. Similarly **last light** is the latest time when such movements can take place. The expression became current in World War II.

• **first strike** ▸ An attack with nuclear weapons designed to destroy the enemy's ability to retaliate in kind. The expression is part of the complex jargon of nuclear strategy. First-strike weapons are usually unprotected and designed, as their name implies, to be used first, to destroy the enemy's missiles etc. **Second-strike** weapons are kept in reserve and protected (*e.g.* in missile silos) in case the enemy makes a surprise first-strike to 'take out' the first-strike weapons. Military analysts have been considerably preoccupied by first- and second-strike capabilities.

• **First World** ▸ *See*: Third World.

• **fish** ▸
   **like a fish needs a bicycle** A nonsense simile that has been attributed to the US feminist Gloria Steinem; 'a woman without a man', she is said to have said, 'is like a fish without a bicycle'. The phrase was a common graffito in the heyday of feminist separatism in the 1970s and 1980s (*see*: feminism). In 1992 a collection of quotations by women was published as *Like a Fish Needs a Bicycle* (ed. Anne Stibbs).

• **Fisher Act** ▸ The 1918 Education Act named after the historian Herbert Albert Laurens Fisher (1865–1940) who, as president of the Board of Education and a Liberal MP, was responsible for it. The Act forced pupils to remain in full-time education until aged 14, abolished all elementary school fees, and introduced nursery schools. It was not implemented until after the end of World War I.

• **fishing expedition** ▸ 1. British slang from the colonial era for the trip to India, or other outposts of the Empire, made by upper-class single women in search of husbands among the army or naval officers stationed there. 2. British slang, taken from the language of espionage, for the practice of gathering information while giving the impression of doing something else. Business corporations, for example, sometimes advertise for and interview prospective employees, not with a view to employing them but to gather any information they can about their rivals' plans.

• **fission bomb** ▸ *See*: nuclear weapon.

• **fit up** ▸ British police and underworld slang meaning to incriminate someone by planting or fabricating evidence of criminal activity. The expression is now widely known through TV crime series and, more recently, through reports in the press of examples of such police activity. Mainly used as a verb, the expression also functions as a noun, **fit-up**, as in 'he got five years, but everyone knew it was a fit-up'.

• **five** ▸
   **take five** Phrase meaning to take a short break or relax for a few minutes. It originates in the call of the director of a film or play, telling the cast to take a five-minute break. It was popularized by the composition 'Take Five' by the US jazz pianist and composer Dave Brubeck (1920– ).

• **five-mile-high club** ▸ A notional club open to those who claim to have made love on an airliner cruising at an altitude of five miles (25,000 feet), although it is not clear what proof is required either for the act having taken place or the altitude. There is also said to be a **mile-low club**, for those who have managed the same feat on a train going through the Channel Tunnel.

• **five o'clock** ▸
   **avoid five o'clock shadow** Trade slogan adopted by Gem Razors and Blades in America in the 1930s. This was apparently the first time the phrase 'five o'clock shadow' (for the growth of stubble on a man's face at the end of the day) was heard.

• **Five-Year Plans** ▸ In the former Soviet Union, plans for developing the whole of the nation's economy in a coordinated effort by a five-year programme. The first Five-Year Plan was launched by

Stalin in 1928 with the aims of making the country self-supporting, mechanizing agriculture, promoting literacy, etc. Further Five-Year Plans followed and the example was copied by other countries.

• **fix** ▶ Slang for an intravenous injection of a narcotic drug. This sense orginated in America and in the 1960s became widespread throughout the English-speaking world.

• **flag of convenience** ▶ A foreign flag under which a vessel is registered, usually to lessen taxation and manning costs. The practice became commonplace after World War II. Liberia, Honduras, and Panama are the most widely used flags of convenience; Liberia has the largest merchant fleet in the world.

• **flagpole** ▶
   **run it up the flagpole** To expose an idea, plan, etc., to some publicity to gauge the reaction to it. The full form is 'run it up the flagpole and see if anyone salutes'.

• **flak** ▶ An acronym for *Flugabwehrkanone* or *Fliegerabwehrkanone*, the German name in World War II for anti-aircraft guns. Originally used in English to describe the bursting of shells of anti-aircraft guns, as in 'our bombers passed through a heavy barrage of flak over the target area', it later became a colloquialism for any criticism or hostility.

• **flake** ▶ 1. US slang for an eccentric and unreliable person. It was formed from the adjective flaky. 2. Australian slang for shark meat. 3. US slang for cocaine. Good-quality cocaine is often sold in flake form. 4. US police slang for an arrest made to satisfy public opinion rather than on substantial evidence.

• **flak jacket** ▶ A military jacket having thin metal plates sewn into the lining, used to protect the wearer against bullets or shrapnel.

• **flaky** ▶ US slang for eccentric, unreliable, or unstable. It was not well known in the UK until President Reagan used it of the Libyan leader Colonel Gaddafi in January 1986. The word was first used in this sense in the 1960s and is possibly derived from the sense of flaky meaning crumbling.

> She did indeed have a very flaky image – she claimed that she drank her own urine. – *The Independent on Sunday*, 27 January 1991.

• **flame** An abusive or insulting e-mail or posting on an Internet newsgroup.

• **flame-thrower** ▶ A weapon that ejects a stream of burning fluid either from a hand-held device with an accompanying back pack or from a device mounted on a tank. Modern flame-throwers were developed by the Germans in the early years of the 20th century and were first used by them in 1915 during World War I. By World War II they were in use by all sides; the portable type burned oil and had a range of some 41 metres (135 ft), burning for 10 seconds. The tank-mounted units had a range of 90 metres (300 ft) and carried enough fuel for a one-minute continuous blast. A sinister development of flame-throwing was the invention of napalm, used by British and US troops towards the end of World War II and later in Korea and Vietnam.

• **Flanders poppies** ▶ Artificial poppies sold for Remembrance Day to benefit ex-service men. The poppy was established as a lasting symbol of World War I by John McCrae's poem 'Flanders Fields', which appeared in *Punch*, 8 December 1915:

> If ye break faith with us who die
> We shall not sleep, though poppies grow
> In Flanders fields.

• **flapper** ▶ 1. In the early years of the 20th century, a girl in her teens with a plaited pigtail tied at the end with a large bow. When she walked along the pigtail flapped against her back. Subsequently her hair would be put up in a bun or some other more sophisticated hairstyle. 2. In the 1920s a young woman who shocked her elders with her unconventional and uninhibited behaviour.

• **Flapper Vote** ▶ An irreverent name for the vote granted to women of 21 or over by the Equal Franchise Act of 1928, sponsored by Baldwin's Conservative government. *See*: flapper.

• **flashback** ▶ A scene in a novel, play, or film, showing events that took place before those of the main story. Always widely used in films, flashbacks became extremely popular as a narrative device in the 1930s and 1940s. In her review of *Ruthless* (1948), a labyrinthine melodrama featuring Zachary Scott, the British film critic, C. A. Lejeune, wrote:

> Beginning pictures at the end
> Is, I'm afraid a modern trend.
> But I'd find *Ruthless* much more winning
> If it could end at the beginning.

• **flasher** ▶ Slang for a man who exposes his genitals in public places, usually in the presence of young women or girls. A deviant form of sexual gratification, flashing appears to be a compulsive act, which the flasher deeply regrets after he has done it. Flashers are unlikely to have normal sexual relations and are very rarely violent. However, they do cause distress to young girls who come across them in parks, etc. *See also*: dirty old man.

• **Flash Gordon** ▶ US sci-fi hero who first appeared in a 13-part King Features newspaper comic strip in the 1930s. In 1936 he appeared in *Flash Gor-*

*don*, the first of a three-part film series, in which Flash (played by Larry 'Buster' Crabbe; *see*: King of the Serials), his companion Dr Zarkov, and sweetheart Dale Arden blast off to rescue the Earth from collision with the Planet Mongo, ruled by the evil Ming the Merciless. The two sequels, *Flash Gordon's Trip to Mars* (1938) and *Flash Gordon Conquers the Universe* (1940), were in a similar vein. A faintly pornographic spoof version, *Flesh Gordon*, appeared in 1974. In 1980 *Flash Gordon* itself was remade with Sam J. Jones and Topol in the cast. Some thought it lacked the kitsch charm of the original.

• **Flash Harry ▶ 1.** British slang for an ostentatiously dressed man, especially one whose manner inspires distrust; a wide boy or spiv. **2.** Nickname of Sir Malcolm Sargent (1895–1967), British conductor of the BBC Symphony Orchestra (1950–57) and chief conductor of the London Promenade Concerts (1957–67). Widely travelled and always immaculately dressed, an apparently fresh flower always in his buttonhole, Sargent was the epitome of a debonair man of the world. While most of his peers in the world of concert-giving musicians wore what looked like hired tail coats, Sargent's always fitted perfectly.

• **flat cap ▶** *See*: cloth-cap.

• **flat top ▶ 1.** A World War II name for an aircraft carrier. **2.** A hairstyle for men and boys that originated in America in the 1950s and has moved in and out of fashion periodically ever since. The hair is cut and shaped so that it forms a perfectly level plateau from the crown to the forehead. Some stylists use a spirit level to ensure accuracy.

• **flaunt ▶**
**When you've got it, flaunt it** An advertising slogan used in 1969 by the US airline Braniff. The poster showed pictures of famous extrovert people. The line had appeared earlier in the 1967 Mel Brooks comedy film *The Producers*, which may have been the original source.

• **flavour ▶** A property of quarks used in particle physics. Quarks come in six flavours: up, down, strange, charmed, top, and bottom.

• **flavour of the month ▶** A phrase originally used in America in an attempt to persuade people to try a different flavour of icecream each month. It has come to be used with reference to any ephemeral craze for a person, thing, theme, etc.

• **flea market ▶** A market for second-hand items usually, but not always, held in the open. The merchandise is likely to include books, bric-à-brac, old clothes, and second-hand domestic goods. The name comes from the large market on the outskirts of Paris, long known as the *marché aux puces* (flea market) because some of its merchandise was flea-ridden. *See also*: car-boot sale.

• **Flèche d'Or ▶** *See*: Golden Arrow.

• **fleet ▶**
**the fleet's lit up** A British catchphrase that originated in what can only be described as every broadcaster's nightmare. The broadcast made on 20 May 1937 was by Commander Tommy Woodrooffe (1899–1978), a leading BBC commentator, and was meant to be a 15-minute description of the illumination of the fleet after the Coronation Naval Review at Spithead. Unfortunately Woodrooffe dried up and all he could manage was a few repetitive sentences basically consisting of 'the fleet's lit up' before he was mercifully faded out. The phrase probably caught on because of the slang meaning of 'lit up', *i.e.* drunk. Many of those listening must have presumed that this was the problem with the broadcaster.

• **flesh-pressing** or **pressing the flesh ▶** Shaking hands with as many people as possible in a large gathering, as practised by politicians during election campaigns, etc.

• **flexible friend ▶** A credit card. The name comes from an advertising slogan used by Access in the 1980s: 'Access – your flexible friend'. The flexibility is understood to refer both to the bendable plastic object and to the convenience of a credit card as a means of staggering the cost of major purchases.

• **flexitime ▶** A system allowing flexibility in the time at which an employee starts and finishes work, usually operated in conjunction with a core time, an agreed minimum number of hours for which each employee has contracted to work each week. Flexitime is widely operated in both the public and private sectors, largely to ease rush-hour traffic problems and to enable employees to travel to work in greater comfort. It is also useful for those with young families. Research has indicated that the system can increase productivity by encouraging the more efficient use of an employee's time.

• **flick ▶** Old-fashioned slang for a film. It derives from the flickering effect that characterized early silent films, as a result of the slow speed at which they were projected. Both 'flick', meaning a film, and **the flicks**, meaning the cinema, were extremely widely used in the heyday of the movies, long after this defect had been righted. *See also*: skin flick.

• **flick knife ▶** A type of knife with a spring-loaded retractable blade operated by a button. It has earned itself a reputation for being the preferred weapon of the street yob and mugger. It can be carried inconspicuously and used to inflict cruel wounds.

• **flight deck** ▶ The compartment of a passenger aircraft in which the pilots, navigator, radio operator, and engineer sit. Access to the flight deck is usually prohibited during flight, except to members of the crew.

• **flight recorder** ▶ An electronic device carried by a passenger aircraft to collect and store information regarding the aircraft's performance in flight and the voices of the pilot and crew. In the event of a crash or malfunction the flight recorder can provide valuable information regarding the cause of the trouble. If the plane has crashed and killed the crew, the flight recorder may provide the only evidence of the cause. It is therefore housed in a strong metal box and is usually painted orange to make it easy to find (in spite of being known colloquially as a **black box**).

• **flight simulator** ▶ A computer-controlled ground-based training capsule, which reproduces the conditions of the flight deck of an aircraft or space vehicle. Flight simulators allow students to familiarize themselves with the hardware before potentially hazardous and expensive in-flight training. The first flight simulators appeared shortly after the Wright Brothers' invention of powered flight; in 1929 aviator Edwin A. Link produced the Link Trainer with cockpit instruments and controls, which reproduced all the movements of a proper aircraft; it was used extensively until the end of World War II. In accordance with advances in aircraft design and technology, modern simulators are even more realistic and complex, allowing every aspect of an aircraft's or spacecraft's performance to be reproduced in minute details; many now make use of virtual reality technology. Flight simulation software can also be run as a game on microcomputers; the best-known program is produced by Microsoft, who have claimed that devotees could fly solo in a real aircraft after mastering the screen simulation.

• **flimsy** ▶ **1.** A journalist's term for newspaper copy, arising from the thin paper (formerly often used with a sheet of carbon paper to take a copy) on which reporters and others typed up their matter for the press. **2.** The white £5 Bank of England note, which ceased to be legal tender in March 1961, was also known as a flimsy. **3.** In the Royal Navy the name is used for the brief certificate of conduct issued to an officer by his captain on the termination of his appointment to a ship or establishment; the name again derives from the thin-quality paper.

• **flip-flop** ▶ A component of an electronic circuit that can have two possible stable states (hence the alternative name **bistable**), and can 'flip' from one state to the other as a result of a suitable input signal. Flip-flops are an essential part of the electronic circuitry of digital computers, the two states of the elements representing bits.

• **flip-flops** ▶ Open sandals consisting of a rubber or plastic sole with loops on the front through which the toes go. They date from the 1960s and are so called because of the flip-flopping movement of the sole while the wearer is walking.

• **flip side** ▶ *See*: B side.

• **FLN** ▶ *Front de Libération Nationale*. The Algerian nationalist group that fought the war of independence (1952–62) against France. Formed in 1954 as a terrorist organization, it set up a provisional government in Tunis. In 1962 de Gaulle conceded independence to Algeria after referendums in both France and Algeria. The FLN under Ahmed Ben Bella (1916–  ) then became the sole political party; a multi-party system of government was not restored until 1989.

• **floating voter** ▶ A person who has no deep allegiance to any of the main political parties and who can be persuaded to vote for any party by the force of their arguments. *See also*: don't know; pebbledash people.

• **Float like a butterfly, sting like a bee** ▶ The catchphrase used by the US boxer Muhammed Ali (Cassius Clay; 1942–  ) to summarize his boxing style. Widely regarded as the greatest heavyweight boxer of all time, he was equally famous for his colourful personality and self-confident catchphrases (*see also*: I am the Greatest *at* greatest).

Ali's professional career began after the 1960 Olympic Games in Rome, where he won a gold medal in the light-heavyweight class. In 1964 he defeated Sonny Liston to become world heavyweight champion, the same year that he became a Black Muslim and changed his name. Ali held his title for three years, until his refusal to join the US army (because of his Black Muslim faith) caused him to be banned from the sport. He regained the title in 1974, lost it and won it back in 1978, and was finally defeated by Larry Holmes in 1980. He now suffers from Parkinson's disease, probably brought on by repeated blows to the head in the ring.

• **floppy disk** ▶ A flexible plastic disk coated with magnetic material used for storing data in small computer systems. The common type is a 3½-inch diameter disk held in a rigid plastic cover. Floppy disks are sometimes called **diskettes**. *See also*: hard disk.

• **FLOPS** ► Floating-point operations per second. A measure of the speed with which a computer can operate. A floating-point operation is an arithmetic operation (*i.e.* a multiplication, division, addition, or subtraction) between two numbers – the 'floating' implies that the position of the decimal point may change.

• **flotsam and jetsam** ► Properly, flotsam consists of wreckage or goods from a wreck found floating on the sea or washed ashore (Old French *floter*, to float) while jetsam are things thrown overboard (French *jeter*, to throw out). **Lagan**, a word of uncertain origin, applies to goods thrown overboard but tied to a float for later recovery. The term 'flotsam and jetsam' is now used of any discarded or miscellaneous objects; it is also used of vagrants, drifters, or other itinerant people.

Flotsam and Jetsam were also the names adopted by two popular entertainers of the 1930s variety stage and radio. B. C. Hilliam (1890–1968), British composer and pianist, took the name Flotsam and his partner, the Australian bass singer Malcolm McEachern (1884–1945), that of Jetsam.

• **flower people** ► In the late 1960s brightly clad hippies who advocated 'universal love' as a remedy for violence and materialism. **Flower power**, their guiding philosophy, was summed up in the slogan **make love not war**. Flowers were often worn or carried as symbols of peace, beauty, and nature.

• **flowers** ►
**Say it with flowers** An advertising slogan coined in 1917 by a Major Patrick O'Keefe for the National Publicity Committee of the Society of American Florists.

• **fluff** ► 1. A British euphemism for 'fuck' as a swear word or intensifier, mainly used in the form **fluffing**, or in the expression **fluff off**, as said by Prince Philip to journalists in October 1987. *See also*: Four-letter Annie. 2. British slang for an attractive but unintelligent young woman, usually in the phrase **a bit of fluff**. It is a derogatory expression used by men from the early 1900s.

• **fluoroplastic** ► Any of a number of synthetic plastics derived from hydrocarbons by including fluorine. Fluoroplastics tend to be stable substances; Teflon (*see*: PTFE) is a common example.

• **fly a kite** ► 1. A British and US slang expression meaning knowingly to write a worthless cheque. It derives from an earlier City use, meaning to discount a bill at a bank knowing that the person on whom it is drawn will not honour it. The phrase is now also used in the wider sense of presenting a doubtful plan for approval. 2. British slang meaning to write a begging letter asking for money. 3. British slang meaning to smuggle items into or out of prison. The items are usually drugs on the inward journey and letters on the way out.

• **fly blind** ► To pilot an aircraft solely by means of instruments; the opposite of visual navigation.

• **fly-drive** ► A holiday package-deal offered by travel agents and tour operators, which includes the cost of the return flight to a foreign airport and the provision of a hired car in the price of a holiday. This normally works out cheaper than arranging the holiday and car hire separately. In some of these packages it is not necessary to return the car to the original airport; arrangements can be made to drop the car off at another airport, from which the flight home can be arranged.

• **flying bedstead** ► Nickname of the experimental wingless and rotorless vertical take-off jet aircraft demonstrated in the UK in 1954. Built by Rolls-Royce, the craft was so christened because of its appearance. It successfully established the principles of vertical take-off (*see*: VTOL) as used in the Harrier jump jet (1966).

• **flying boat** ► A large seaplane with a boat-shaped hull for buoyancy. Flying boats were developed between the two world wars for both civil and military applications. The most famous of all flying boats is millionaire Howard Hughes's folly, the H4 *Hercules* (the *Spruce Goose*) – the largest aeroplane ever flown, with the world's largest wing span and seating for 700 passengers. It was flown only once, for a distance of about one mile at a height of 80 feet over Los Angeles Harbor, California, in November 1947. It is now a tourist attraction. In the age of jet aircraft flying boats are totally out of fashion, largely because landing a jet on a choppy sea could be extremely hazardous.

• **flying doctor** ► An airborne medical service to provide emergency aid to geographically remote communities lacking adequate health facilities. The **Royal Flying Doctor Service of Australia**, set up in 1928, both transports doctors to remote areas and has also set up a radio long-range consultation service. Similar services are run in Canada, Africa, and elsewhere.

• **Flying Duchess** ► Mary du Caurroy Russell, Duchess of Bedford (1865–1937). After making record-breaking return flights to India (1929) and South Africa (1930) with Captain Barnard, she obtained an 'A' pilot's licence in 1933 and disappeared on a solo flight over the North Sea in March 1937.

• **Flying Fortress** ▶ The name by which the US bomber the Boeing B-17 was known during World War II. It owed its name to the fact that it was exceptionally heavily armed. *See also*: Stratofortress.

• **Flying Officer X** ▶ Pen name of H. E. Bates (1905–74), the British novelist best known for *The Darling Buds of May* (1958). After working as a solicitor's clerk and provincial journalist, he joined the RAF in World War II, later writing many short stories about life in the service under this name.

• **flying picket** ▶ An industrial picket that can be moved quickly between different locations to reinforce local pickets. The use of flying pickets was a feature of the industrial strife during the UK's Winter of Discontent (1978–79). The trade union legislation of the 1980s and 1990s clarified and strengthened existing laws to make this practice clearly illegal. As a result employers can take out injunctions or extract damages under civil law to prevent flying picketing.

• **flying saucers** ▶ On 24 June 1947 a US pilot saw a group of strange objects in the sky, which he described as moving 'like saucers skipping across the water'. From this report journalists coined the phrase flying saucers, suggesting that these and similar objects sighted at around this time could be reconnaissance craft from outer space. Captain Ruppelt, the USAF intelligence officer responsible for the investigation of the flying saucer phenomenon, gave them the name UFOs (unidentified flying objects). Many people seriously believe that the US and other governments have ever since engaged in a conspiracy to prevent the public from knowing the 'truth' about flying saucers, in order to avoid panic reactions. Rumours of this kind inspired Steven Spielberg's 1978 film *Close Encounters of the Third Kind* (*see*: close encounter) and the later cult series *The X-Files* (1993–    ), about a secret department of the FBI that investigates extraterrestrial and paranormal happenings; the latter was apparently taken to be a documentary by many US viewers. Flying saucers and UFOs continue to figure prominently in popular mythology, but no evidence has ever been produced to confirm the existence of such an object, let alone any occupants. Various plausible explanations can be offered for the numerous sightings of UFOs that have been reported from all parts of the world since the term was first coined (the testing of top-secret military aircraft, unusual meteorological or astronomical phenomena, etc.). Rather more difficult to explain is the phenomenon of so-called **alien abduction**, in which people claim to have been removed from their beds at night and taken up into a UFO where they are subjected to various scientific and medical tests. Many thousands of such claims, often very similar in detail, have been reported since the 1980s. If we discount the idea that all these people are liars or lunatics, the only explanation seems to be some kind of extraordinarily vivid nightmare, perhaps with a medical cause. *See also*: Roswell incident; Warminster Thing.

• **Flying Scotsman** ▶ The steam train service run by the London and North-Eastern Railway between London (King's Cross) and Edinburgh. The record for the service was 5 hours 55 minutes. The current 125 diesel-electric train does the journey in 4 hours 30 minutes.

• **flying squad** ▶ *See*: Sweeney.

• **Flying Tigers** ▶ The nickname of a volunteer group of US airmen who supported China against Japanese aggression during World War II. Formed in August 1941, under Major-General C. L. Chennault, some months before America's entry into the war, they fought with distinction until merged with the 23rd Fighter Squadron of the USAAF in July 1942.

• **Flynn** ▶
   **in like Flynn** A phrase meaning that the person so-described does not miss a chance to seduce a woman. It is also used in a more general sense to mean that the person is quick to take advantage of anything on offer. Flynn is the Australian-born film star, Errol Flynn (1909–59), who was one of Hollywood's most swashbuckling screen lovers and a notorious womanizer off-screen. The phrase was particularly popular with the armed forces during World War II. Flynn himself was not flattered by it, despite his own partiality for boasting about his conquests.

• **fly-on-the-wall** ▶ Describing a style of documentary film-making in which the camera is used as an unobtrusive observer of people and their lives. There is little or no narration, and the 'story' is told as far as possible using only the voices and images of the subjects being filmed. The style, which was made possible by the advent of lightweight cameras and sound-recording equipment, developed in the early 1960s, chiefly in America and France (*see*: cinéma vérité). One of its earliest exponents was the US film-maker D. A. Pennebaker, whose best-known work is probably *Don't Look Back* (1966), a documentary about Bob Dylan's 1965 British tour. In the 1970s the fly-on-the-wall style was adopted for television. *An American Family* (1973), made by the PBS channel, chronicled the daily life of a Californian family, and inspired a similar series on BBC television in 1974. Entitled *The Family*, this depicted the Wilkins family of Reading, and broke new ground on UK television while also attracting a large audience. Critics of the format argue that the presence of a film crew, with their attendant equipment, is bound to alter the behaviour of the subjects, undermining the filmmaker's claims to present a slice of 'real life'. And indeed, later examples of the genre, such as the Australian series *Sylvania Waters* (1992), have often seemed to collude with the participants, who play up to their new-found celebrity with exaggerated behaviour. The same criticism has been made of the popular docusoaps of recent years – fly-on-the-wall series that follow a particular group of people, such as airport workers or 'castaways' on a remote Scottish island.

• **FM** ▶ Frequency modulation. A form of radio transmission in which the frequency of the carrier wave is varied within a narrow bandwidth of the reference frequency by the audio frequency information that is to be broadcast. It provides a better signal-to-noise ratio than **AM** (amplitude modulation), in which it is the amplitude of the carrier wave that is varied. FM is used in VHF (very high frequency) radio broadcasts, using a frequency of the order of 100 megahertz.

• **FOBS** ▶ Fractional Orbital Bombardment System. A method of delivering a nuclear bomb by a rocket travelling in a low (100-mile-high) partial orbit, which does not contravene the Outer Space Treaty (1966) prohibiting the launching of nuclear warheads into a complete orbit around the Earth. The FOBS method enables a nuclear warhead to be delivered using a retro-rocket to slow the missile at a predetermined point, causing it to drop out of orbit onto the target. This can cut the defender's radar warning time to about 3 minutes, seriously prejudicing a ballistic missile defence system. However, FOBS weapons are not sufficiently accurate to be targeted onto missile silos and were abandoned by America in 1967.

• **focus group** ▶ A small group of people brought together by a facilitator who wishes to gauge their attitude to a commercial product, a political issue, or some other matter of concern. The group, who are usually chosen to represent a very precisely targeted section of the population, will be subjected to in-depth and sometimes oblique questioning to probe their unconscious as well as their more conscious views. The focus group became a favourite tool of marketing and public relations departments in the 1990s, and is now much used in politics. New

Labour has often been accused of placing a craven reliance on focus-group findings in its search for the soul of Middle England.

• **Fog** ▶ Nickname of Capt. Mark Phillips (1948– ), ex-husband of the Princess Royal; a rather unkind epithet, probably invented at Sandhurst and taken up by *Private Eye*, for a man described as 'thick and wet'. Some accuse Prince Charles of having invented the name.

• **Fokker** ▶ One of a number of World War I aircraft designed by Anton Hermann Gerard Fokker (1890–1939), a Dutch-born aircraft designer who opened a factory in Germany in 1912. The Fokker was the first aircraft to have a machine gun that fired through the propeller, using a synchronizing method invented by Fokker. This gave the German Air Force a temporary advantage on the Western Front in Word War I.

• **folk etymology** ▶ A popular explanation of the origin of a word, which may or may not be correct, although academic etymologists believe it not to be. Examples include the explanation of **posh** – said to be an acronym formed from 'port out, starboard home', the coolest and therefore most sought-after cabins on ships between Britain and India, and spiv – 'VIPs' backwards.

• **folk rock** ▶ A type of pop music that combines folk-style melodies and lyrics with rock accompaniment. It was virtually invented by the US singer-songwriter Bob Dylan (1941– ), whose change from acoustic to electric accompaniment on his World Tour in 1966 brought boos and cat calls from traditional folk fans.

> Folk music is a bunch of fat people. – BOB DYLAN.

In the UK a different style of folk rock was pioneered by Fairport Convention (formed 1966), who performed traditional folk songs with a lively electronic backing; they were followed by other successful bands, such as Steeleye Span (1969), Jethro Tull (1968), and Lindisfarne (late 1960s).

• **folks** ▶
**That's all folks!** The phrase that appears written across the screen at the end of cartoons in the *Merry Melodies* series by Warner Bros. It was first used in 1930. Mel Blanc (1908–89), who had provided so many of the voices for the cartoon characters, chose it as his own epitaph.

• **Follow that car!** ▶ A line used in so many films and television dramas that it has become a cliché. It is said when the hero leaps into a taxi and orders the driver to chase after the villain's car.

• **F 111** ▶ (F one-eleven) A long-range bomber with

swing-wings, introduced in the 1960s and used by both the US Air Force and the US Navy. The cockpit of the plane can be ejected to become a survival capsule on land or sea. The design for the F 111 served as an almost exact model for the Sukhoi Su-24, its Soviet counterpart.

• **F₁ hybrids** ▶ Plants, especially crop plants (*e.g.* brassicas or maize), that have been grown from seed obtained by crossing two plants of dissimilar genetic make-up that have been specially selected for their desirable qualities. The offspring from this cross combine the qualities of both parental lines and, in addition, show the more vigorous growth and greater yield that is characteristic of hybrid plants. '$F_1$' denotes the first *filial* generation, *i.e.* the generation produced by crossing the two selected parental lines; the $F_2$ generation (second filial generation) would consist of the plants produced by self- or cross-fertilization of the $F_1$ hybrids.

• **food additive** ▶ Any natural or synthetic substance added by manufacturers to food products and including flavourings, preservatives, colouring agents, antioxidants, emulsifiers, stabilizers, thickeners, artificial sweeteners, flavour enhancers, etc. Increasing consumer demand for convenience foods since the 1960s has led to a great increase in food processing and the need for additives. However, despite the benefits of additives as preservatives, etc., there has been increasing concern about the possible long-term effects on health of these products. Some are thought to produce toxic, carcinogenic, or allergic effects. For example, studies indicate that tartrazine can trigger allergies and cause hyperactivity in children. The Food Labelling Regulations (1984) of the European Community introduced E-numbers to identify approved substances. Since 1986 all foods must carry a full list of additives on the package either by stating their E-number or by giving the additive's full name if it does not have an E-number. At present there are around 3800 additives in use.

• **Food and Agricultural Organization** ▶ *See*: FAO.

• **foodie** ▶ A name given by Peter York (who also coined the term Sloane Ranger) to a person whose life appears to be dominated by the buying and preparation of food, especially expensive delicacies and exotic dishes. Its appearance in the late 1980s reflects the growth of high-class delicatessens, kitchenware shops, and restaurants producing food cooked in the latest styles.

• **foot-and-mouth disease** ▶ An infectious viral disease of cattle, sheep, goats, and pigs, which causes fever, blisters on the mouth and feet, abortions, and deterioration of milk yields. Foot-and-mouth disease is a notifiable disease in many countries; infected animals are usually slaughtered and movements of herds are restricted. In the UK there was a major outbreak of the disease (the worst on record) in 2001; the government's attempt to prevent its spread through a policy of compulsory slaughter of farm animals and closing the countryside to visitors caused great controversy and hardship in rural areas.

• **football hooliganism** ▶ Uncontrolled violence by sections of the crowd at football matches. In the 1980s British fans earned an unenviable reputation for their unruly behaviour, which culminated in the death of 39 mainly Italian supporters at the 1985 European Cup Final (Liverpool vs Juventus of Turin) at the Heysels Stadium in Brussels. Subsequently English football league clubs were banned from taking part in European competitions until the 1990–91 season, when all but Liverpool were readmitted. The causes of hooliganism at football grounds are usually overcrowding, drunkenness (*see*: lager louts), unreasonable hostility towards rival supporters, and the uncontrolled aggression that can emerge from badly controlled crowds. Measures to curb football hooliganism include segregation of rival fans, banning of alcohol in and around grounds, abolition of terraces on which supporters stand in favour of all-seater stadiums, the use of closed-circuit TV, the issue of identification cards, and better policing. This behaviour has been so closely identified with the UK that it is often called the English disease. The association was reinforced in the 2000 European Championships (Euro 2000) held in Charleroi, Belgium, when English fans again disgraced themselves and their country by brawling with German fans.

• **football pools** ▶ A system of betting in which each week during the football season punters try to guess which matches will be drawn. The stakes are pooled and some 30% of the pool is distributed as prize money (40% goes in tax and 30% in running costs, including the profit of the company running the pool). The punter usually has to guess at least six score-draws (*i.e.* matches in which two or more goals were scored) and two non-score draws to qualify for a dividend. A tally of eight high-scoring draws usually wins a seven-figure jackpot. Football pools were introduced by Littlewoods in Manchester in 1923; since the advent of the National Lottery in 1995 their popularity in the UK has declined.

• **footprint** ▶ 1. The area over which the signal from a communications satellite can be received.

2. In computing, the physical space taken up by a computer device.

• **Footsie** ▶ The familiar name by which the **Financial Times Stock Exchange 100 Index**, or FTSE 100 Index, is known in the City of London and in commercial markets throughout the world. Starting with a value of 1000 in 1984, Footsie is based on the day-to-day price of 100 chosen securities and is regarded as giving the best indication of daily movement in price on the London Stock Exchange (properly known as the International Stock Exchange of the UK and Republic of Ireland Ltd). Footsie is published daily (except Sunday and Monday) in the *Financial Times*, the London commercial journal (traditionally printed on pink paper). The FT, the initials by which this paper is widely known, also has other indexes: the **Financial Times Ordinary Share Index**, representing the movements of 30 leading industrial shares, and the **Financial Times Actuaries Share Indexes**, of which there are 54, giving weighted arithmetic averages for various sectors of the market. Divided into separate industries, the Footsie is much used by portfolio managers, other large investors, and financial advisers. The equivalent indicator of price movements on the New York Stock Exchange is the Dow Jones Industrial Average.

• **Force** ▶
   **May the force be with you!** A catchphrase used as a valediction, almost as a blessing, in the hugely successful film *Star Wars* (1977) and its various sequels and prequels. The Force is the life-force of the Universe, the power of good; the phrase is therefore almost equivalent to saying 'May God go with you'. It was subsequently used as a slogan in a recruitment drive by the Cornish Police and by President Reagan, always ready to quote from Hollywood, in a speech about his Star Wars weapons programme.

• **Forces' Sweetheart** ▶ The nickname of the British singer Vera Lynn (1917-  ) used by British forces serving overseas during World War II. With her repertoire of sentimental songs, such as 'We'll Meet Again' (1944), she came to symbolize many of the qualities, freedoms, and loyalties that motivated the British people in their determination to destroy Nazi Germany. She gave her first public performance in 1924, broadcast with the Joe Loss Band for a period, and eventually became a solo star in 1940. Voted the UK's most popular singer in a *Daily Express* competition in 1939, she had her own radio show, 'Sincerely Yours' from 1941 to 1947. She was made a Dame in 1975.

• **Ford's Peace Ship** ▶ The ship on which the car manufacturer, Henry Ford (1863–1947), sailed to Europe from America with a number of similarly minded prominent pacifists in 1915. The intention of this unsuccessful mission was to bring World War I to an end by negotiation.

• **forfaiting** ▶ The financial service that has grown up in recent decades of discounting, without recourse, a promissory note, letter of credit, bill of exchange, etc., received from an overseas buyer. This enables an exporter to receive his money immediately, without waiting for the payment to become due. The word is derived from the French *forfaire*, to forfeit or surrender.

• **forgeries** ▶ *See*: Dossena forgeries; Drake Brass Plate; Hitler Diaries; Keating pictures; Piltdown Skull; Turin Shroud; Van Meegeren forgeries; Vinland Map; Wise forgeries; Zinoviev Letter.

• **Forgotten Army** ▶ The British troops serving in Burma towards the end of World War II. Following VE Day, the public at home felt that the war was over. Nor surprisingly the troops in the Far East, who knew otherwise, felt neglected and resentful. Lord Louis Mountbatten (1900–79), who was supreme Allied commander in SE Asia (1943–45), reassured his men with the words:

   You are not the Forgotten Army – nobody's even heard of you!

• **Forgotten Man** ▶ A phrase coined by W. G. Summer (1840–1910), the US sociologist, to describe the decent, hardworking, ordinary citizen. It was popularized by F. D. Roosevelt (*see*: FDR) during the presidential election campaign of 1932, although he first used the expression before his nomination. He advocated a New Deal for the 'forgotten man at the bottom of the economic pyramid'.

• **form** ▶ British police and underworld jargon for a criminal record. It is based on the horse-racing term for a horse's record of achievement. To **study form**, is to study a horse's record in previous races before placing a bet.

• **Former Naval Person** ▶ A codename by which Winston Churchill referred to himself in messages to President Roosevelt during World War II. It refers, of course, to the post of First Lord of the Admiralty, which he held (1911–15) in World War I and again (1939–40) in World War II.

• **Formica** ▶ A tradename for a plastic laminate, widely used on table tops, counters, etc. Formica was invented by two US scientists, Herb Faber and Don O'Connor, who devised it as an insulating material to be used as a substitute 'for mica'. They founded the Formica Corporation, which was subsequently taken over by the Cyanamid Co. Although the company has fought hard in the courts to protect its tradename, 'formica' is frequently used as a generic name for almost any table top with a plastic appearance.

• **Formula One** ▸ The most prestigious form of motor racing, in which specially built single-seater vehicles are raced by professional drivers for the cars' manufacturers or for private individuals. The Drivers' World Championship (Grand Prix) has been awarded since 1950 on points won in certain Formula One races. Formula One cars must weigh at least 505 kg and have a 3500 cc four-stroke engine with a maximum of 12 cylinders and no turbocharger. Championships for less powerful cars include Formula 2 and Formula 3.

• **Forsyte Saga** ▸ The trilogy of novels by John Galsworthy (1867–1933), comprising *The Man of Property* (1906), *In Chancery* (1920), and *To Let* (1921). The trilogy traces the decline over four generations of the affluent Forsyte family, headed by Soames, a successful solicitor. Although the *Forsyte Saga* has reached a wide audience in book form since its publication in 1922, it was the BBC television serial, starting in 1967, that familiarized most British and US families with the love affairs and acquisitive habits of Galsworthy's characters. A shorter version was broadcast in 2002 by ITV.

• **Fort Belvedere** ▸ A large castellated house near Sunningdale in Berkshire that became the home of the Prince of Wales from 1929 until his abdication as Edward VIII in 1936. *See*: Abdication Crisis.

• **Fort Hare** ▸ The oldest college for Black Africans in South Africa, having been founded in 1916. Under the apartheid system it was a university college for the Xhosa people of the Republic of Transkei (*see*: Bantustan).

• **Fort Knox** ▸ A US military base in N Kentucky established in 1917. In the bomb-proof vaults within the Fort, the US gold reserves are held. Said to be worth many billions of US dollars, the reserves are guarded by elaborate security measures. In the film *Goldfinger* (1964), based on the Ian Fleming novel, international gold smugglers are only foiled in their attempt to rob Fort Knox by the intrepid activities of James Bond. Fort Knox's legendary security has led to the use of the phrase **as safe as Fort Knox**.

• **Fortress Europe** ▸ Hitler's dream of Europe under German domination, so fortified that it would become impregnable against interference from the rest of the world; from the German *Festung Europa*. In the 1980s and 1990s the term was revived to express fears about the kind of exclusive and self-enclosed European Union that could emerge if certain proposals become law, including measures to limit immigration from non-EU states and to impose a degree of economic protectionism.

• **forty** ▸
   **Life begins at forty** A catchphrase taken from the title of a book by the US professor William B. Pitkin (1878–1953), which was published in 1932. The book dealt with the new-found leisure time that many people have after forty and aimed to encourage them to enjoy the second half of their lives, especially by embarking on new projects. A song with this title was written by Jack Yellen and Ted Shapiro; a rumbustious recording of it in 1937 by Sophie Tucker, who was by then 53, became a great hit.

• **Fougasse** ▸ Pen name of Kenneth Bird, the cartoonist and editor of *Punch*, in which many of his cartoons appeared. He is also remembered for his World War II posters publicizing government warnings about the dangers of careless talk. *Fougasse* is the French word for a small landmine.

• **four-colour problem** ▸ A problem in mathematical topology concerning the minimum number of colours required to colour a map so that adjacent regions have different colours. Adjacent regions are ones that have a common line boundary. It has long been known that on a flat surface or on a sphere only four colours are required to distinguish different regions. However, this was not proved mathematically until 1976 (by Appel and Haken).

• **four corners of the Earth** ▸ Generally speaking, the uttermost ends of the Earth, the remotest parts of the world. In 1965 members of the Johns Hopkins Applied Physics Laboratory named the four corners of the Earth as being in Ireland, SE of the Cape of Good Hope, W of the Peruvian coast, and between New Guinea and Japan. Each of these 'corners' (of several thousand square miles in area) is some 40 m (120 ft) above the geodetic mean and the gravitational pull is measurably greater at these locations.

• **Four Freedoms** ▸ These were defined by President F. D. Roosevelt in his message to Congress, 6 January 1941, as the freedom of speech and expression, the freedom of worship, the freedom from fear, and the freedom from want. They were to be the aims of America and ultimately the world. The occasion was his proposal to make America 'the arsenal of democracy' and to extend Lend-Lease to the UK.

• **Four-letter Annie** ▸ A nickname of the

Princess Royal in her younger days. She was reported, on one occasion, to have told unwanted members of the press corps to naff off, although some said she used a stronger four-letter word.

• **four-minute men** ▶ In America, the name given to members of a volunteer organization, some 75,000 strong, who, in 1917–18, set out to promote the sale of Liberty Loan Bonds and stir up support for the war in Europe. They gave talks of four minutes duration to church congregations, cinema audiences, lodges, etc. *See also*: minutemen.

• **four-minute mile** ▶ The running of a mile in four minutes or less was for many years the hoped-for goal of all first-class athletes. The rigorous training and timed pacing of P. J. Nurmi (Finland) achieved a time of 4 mins. 10.4 secs. in 1924 but R. G. Bannister (1929– ) was the first man to reach the goal in 1954. He achieved a sub-four-minute mile at Oxford in 1954 (3 mins. 59.4 secs.) after constant and carefully planned efforts. In July 1979 Sebastian Coe achieved a new world record of 3 mins. 49 secs. only to be beaten almost immediately by Steve Ovett, who reduced his time by one-fifth of a second. In 1981 Coe ran the mile in 3 mins. 47.33 secs. The current record (1993) of 3 mins. 44.39 secs. is held by the Algerian Noureddine Morceli.

> The four-minute mile had become rather like an Everest – a challenge to the human spirit.
> – R. BANNISTER: *The First Four Minutes.*

• **four-on-the-floor** ▶ Slang expression for flat out speed. It comes from hot rodder's (*see*: hot rod) jargon for a four-speed gear system in top gear, and was used mainly by young people in the 1980s.

• **four seven eleven** ▶ (4711) A tradename for an eau de Cologne (a fragrant liquid first made in the German city of Cologne in 1709). The name arose in 1792 when a Cologne banker, Ferdinand Muhlens, gave refuge to a monk. The monk, in gratitude, gave Muhlens a slip of paper on which were written the figures 4-7-11, which he alleged constituted a secret formula for making a cologne. The numbers were later adopted by Muhlens as a tradename, although they could not be registered in Germany until 1915, because of a rule forbidding the use of numbers in this way. The name achieved international registration in 1923.

• **Four Square Gospel** ▶ A fundamentalist Christian sect founded in Belfast in 1925 by George Jeffreys. It later amalgamated with the Elim group to form the **Elim Four Square Gospel Alliance**. They believe in baptism by total immersion, the Second Coming of Christ, and healing by anointing with holy oil.

• **Fourteen Points** ▶ The 14 conditions laid down by President Woodrow Wilson (1856–1924) as those to which the Allies should adhere when making peace with Germany on the conclusion of World War I. He outlined them in a speech to Congress on 8 January 1918 and they were later accepted as a general basis for the peace. They included the evacuation by Germany of all occupied territory, self-determination for all the peoples of Europe, freedom of the seas, reduction of armaments, open diplomacy, and a League of Nations. The settlement that eventually emerged from the Paris Peace Conference (1919) was, however, considerably less idealistic.

• **fourth dimension** ▶ A hypothetical extra dimension, whose relation to the recognized three of length, breadth, and thickness is analogous to their relation with each other. In 1921 Albert Einstein introduced time as the fourth dimension in his theory of relativity. The expression is sometimes used to describe anything beyond the limits of normal experience.

• **fourth man** ▶ A suspected fourth Soviet agent involved in the activities of Burgess, Maclean, and Philby (*see*: Magnificent Five). It was later revealed that the fourth man was Anthony Blunt.

• **Fourth Republic** ▶ The French Republic established in 1946 to replace the provisional governments that followed the collapse of the Vichy regime and the liberation of occupied France. Essentially a continuation of the Third Republic (1870–1940), it was superseded by the Fifth Republic in 1958.

• **Foxhunter** ▶ An outstanding showjumping horse owned by Lt-Col. Harry Llewellyn (1911–99). He won the King George V Cup three times in the 1950s and Llewellyn and Foxhunter were part of the British team that won the Olympic Gold Medal in Helsinki in 1952. Foxhunter died in 1959 at the age of 18.

• **foxtrot** ▶ A ballroom dance originating in America, popular from the 1920s until the 1950s. It combines slow walking steps with quick running steps in 4/4 time.

• **fractal** ▶ A class of mathematical curves or surfaces that are self-generating. The idea of fractals was developed by the Polish-born US mathematician Benoit Mandelbrot in 1975. A simple example is the **snowflake curve**, which can be generated by taking an equilateral triangle and dividing each side into three equal parts. The middle section of each side is removed and replaced by two sides of a new equilateral triangle, to produce a new star-shaped curve with six points and 12 sides. The same process is then applied to each of these sides, and the process is continuously repeated. The result is a changing snowflake-shaped figure. Fractals are described as 'self-similar' figures; each is generated from the preceding one by a fixed set of rules. The name 'fractal' comes from the fact that they have a fractional dimension between that of a one-dimensional line and a two-dimensional surface. **Fractal geometry** is the study of such figures. It is used in producing designs in computer graphics and in certain branches of science.

• **frame** ▶ To manufacture false evidence or testimony so that an innocent person appears to be guilty of a crime. It derives from the idea of a frame being made to fit neatly around a picture. There may be a connection with the photographs of known criminals held by law-enforcement officers.

• **Franglais** ▶ A type of pidgin French, containing a large number of English words, treated largely as a joke language. The humorist Miles Kington has written several books featuring Franglais.

• **Frank** ▶
  **Diary of Anne Frank** The diary (1942–43) kept by Anne Frank, a German girl of Jewish descent during World War II. She wrote her diary while in hiding with her family in an attic in Amsterdam. This moving account of a clandestine existence dominated by the fear of discovery and arrest was published in 1947 and subsequently made into a play and a film (1959), both called *The Diary of Anne Frank*. Shortly before the end of the war the family was betrayed and sent to Auschwitz (*see*: Wiesenthal Centre); Anne was subsequently transferred with her sister to Bergen-Belsen, where both died of typhus. Their father, Otto Frank, survived the war and was responsible for the publication of Anne's diary (an unexpurgated version was published in English in 1995). The house in which the family hid has been preserved as a memorial.

> In spite of everything I still believe that people are really good at heart. – ANNE FRANK: *Diary*.

• **Franks Report** ▶ A report by a commission of inquiry into Oxford University (1964–66) headed by Lord Franks (1905–92), provost of Worcester College, Oxford (1962–76). The report recommended increasing the size of the university by 30%, doubling the number of postgraduates, diminishing the autonomy of the colleges, and paying more attention to science and technology.

• **fraternize** ▶ A British and US forces euphemism meaning to have sex with the civilians in a militarily occupied country. In a more general sense it means to be friendly with an enemy or someone who sympathizes with one's enemies.

• **Fraud Squad** ▶ The section of the police force at Scotland Yard that deals with investigations concerning commercial frauds.

• **freak** ▶ **1.** Slang for someone who exhibits any form of strange or deviant behaviour, or who is very odd in their appearance. **2.** Slang for a hippie, a member of the alternative society' of the late 1960s and 1970s. The word was used pejoratively by those outside the group but was quickly adopted by the hippies themselves. **3.** As a suffix, 'freak' denotes someone enthusiastic about a specified activity, interest, etc., to the point of obsession. An eco-freak, for example, has an over-enthusiastic interest in ecology and a **health freak** is unnaturally interested in alternative health remedies and foods. *See also*: control freak; Jesus freak. **4.** Short for freak out.

• **freak out** ▶ Slang meaning to lose control and behave in a wild or disturbed way. It was first used by US hippies in the 1960s to describe the effects of such hallucinogenic drugs as LSD, but was soon used more generally to describe any loss of control, whatever the cause. To **freak someone out** means to shock or upset someone to such an extent that they freak out.

• **Fred Bloggs** ▶ *See*: Joe Bloggs.

• **Freddy Krueger** ▶ *See*: Krueger, Freddy.

• **Fred Karno's army** ▶ The nickname of the new British army raised during the war of 1914–18, in allusion to the comedian and producer of stage burlesques, Fred Karno (Frederick John Westcott; d. 1941). Fred Karno's company was a household name at the time for its chaotic slapstick performances. A well-known army chorus, sung to the tune of 'The Church's One Foundation', ran:

> We are Fred Karno's army,
> Fred Karno's infantry;
> We cannot fight, we cannot shoot,
> So what damn good are we?
> But when we get to Berlin
> The Kaiser he will say
> Hoch, hoch, mein Gott
> Vot a bloody fine lot,
> Fred Karno's infantry.

There are, of course, variants and in World War II 'Old Hitler' was substituted for 'the Kaiser'. The name is also applied derisively to other nondescript bodies. *See also*: Harry Tate's Navy; Kitchener's army.

• **freebasing** ▶ Drug users' slang for refining cocaine by mixing it with a solvent and heating; the fumes can be inhaled during the heating process and the residue is then smoked.

• **Freedom from Hunger Campaign ▶** A campaign organized by a UN special agency, the Food and Agricultural Organization (*see*: FAO), in 1960. Originally intended as a five-year rededication of FAO to its goal of eliminating hunger and malnutrition from the world, it was later extended for a second five-year period. It achieved a considerable success in publicizing the horrific problems of hunger in the developing countries.

• **free enterprise** or **free market economy ▶** An economic system in which commercial organizations compete freely in order to make a profit and the laws of supply and demand regulate prices, wages, etc., unfettered by government regulations. Although Britain is regarded as a free enterprise economy, government regulations do exist to curb what Edward Heath once referred to as the 'unacceptable face of capitalism' (*see*: Lonrho affair). However, within these regulations it is true to say that the profit motive and the laws of supply and demand do drive the economy.

• **free fall ▶ 1.** The descent of a body falling through space in which the only force acting on it is gravitational. The **acceleration of free fall** is the acceleration that results from the action of this force. The value of this acceleration has a standard value within the Earth's gravitational field of 9.806,65 m s$^{-2}$, although the actual value varies slightly with locality. **2.** The part of a parachute descent during which the parachutist falls through the air unimpeded by an open parachute. To end the free fall the parachutist pulls the rip cord and thereafter descends slowly to earth.

• **Free French ▶** *See*: Fighting French.

• **free love ▶** The practice of engaging in sexual relationships with whoever one finds attractive at the time. A person who practises free love is not bound by ties of fidelity to one partner, either within a legal marriage or outside it. In the later 20th century, the gradual erosion of religious beliefs and the sacramental view of marriage, together with the advent of efficient methods of birth control, led to a situation in which free love seemed to be an acceptable alternative to marital fidelity, in that there were no obvious ethical reasons for the community to discourage it. This philosophy is especially associated with the new morality of the so-called swinging sixties.

In the 1980s, the concept of free love received a setback in the form of the sexually transmitted disease Aids, which threatened to spread rapidly through the community if sexual promiscuity continued. This, together with the soaring divorce sta-

tistics, prompted something of a backlash against the new morality. *See also*: open marriage.

• **free lunch ▶** Economists' jargon for an apparently free benefit that has to be paid for in the end. It supposedly derives from a City tavern that offered free lunches; anyone attempting to make use of the offer without buying a drink was thrown out.

• **Freeman, Hardy, and Willis ▶** The name of a British chain of shoe shops. Freeman, Hardy, and Willis were also used by members of the Royal Navy as nicknames for the three medals – 1914–15 Star, General Service Medal, and the Victory Medal – awarded to servicemen who served throughout World War I. *See also*: Pip, Squeak, and Wilfred.

• **free market economy ▶** *See*: free enterprise.

• **Free Staters ▶** In the Irish Civil War (1922–23), supporters of the provisional government of the Irish Free State set up according to the Anglo-Irish Treaty of 1921. The Free Staters, led by Arthur Griffith (1872–1922) and Michael Collins (1890–1922), were opposed by the Republicans under De Valera, who repudiated the Treaty because it left Northern Ireland outside the Irish state and demanded an oath of allegiance to the British crown. Collins was assassinated in 1922 but the severe measures taken by the Free State government forced the Republicans to abandon the armed struggle in 1923. *See*: Troubles, the.

• **free verse ▶** Poetry that does not conform to regular metre or stanza forms and that makes little or no use of rhyme. Although Milton and Browning (among others) experimented with irregular forms, it was in the early 20th century that free verse came into its own, chiefly through the influence of Ezra Pound and T. S. Eliot. In France free verse had been pioneered somewhat earlier by the Symbolists (the term is a translation of French *vers libre*).

• **Free World ▶** Before 1990 this was a term applied collectively to all the non-communist countries of the world, even those that were not notably democratic or 'free'. The term now has little meaning, although it still figures occasionally in US political rhetoric.

• **freeze bank ▶** A term of US origin for a refrigerated stock of perishable organic substances, such as human blood and bone, kept in large modern hospitals for surgical use. *See also*: sperm bank.

• **Freikorps ▶ 1.** A post-World War I manifestation of German militarism and right-wing thuggery. First appearing in December 1918, soon after Germany's defeat, the Freikorps consisted mainly of ex-soldiers (men and officers) and unemployed youths; by 1919 there were some 65 groups spread throughout Germany. They were used by the government to beat up left-wing agitators and once they had acquired a taste for this sort of bullying violence, soon chose their own targets for plundering and vandalism. Many of the groups were later absorbed by the Nazi party and Ernst Röhm, a Freikorps commander, became head of the Nazi Brown Shirts. *See also*: Kapp Putsch. **2.** In post-World War II Germany a neo-Nazi group appeared in the West calling themselves **Freikorps Deutschland**. They were banned in 1953.

• **Frelimo** ▶ Front for the Liberation of Mozambique. The coalition of Mozambique nationalist groups, established in 1962 by Eduardo Mondlane (1920–69), that fought a successful ten-year War of Independence (1964–74) against Portuguese rule. After the granting of independence to Mozambique in June 1975, Frelimo became the only permitted party and adopted Marxist-Leninist policies. This led to a 17-year civil war with the rival **Renamo** (Mozambique National Resistance); a multi-party state was finally created in 1991–92.

• **French** ▶ **1.** Slang for cunnilingus or fellatio, based on the Anglo-Saxon belief that all such activities are foreign, dirty, and undesirable and therefore ascribable only to Gallic appetites. **2.** Short for French kiss, used as a verb.

• **French** ▶
**excuse my French** An expression used after swearing, pretending that the swear word just used was really in a foreign language.

• **French blue** ▶ Drug users' slang for a blue amphetamine tablet, the pep pill Drinamyl. The 'French' either represents the country of manufacture or is used simply to differentiate this pill from other blues.

• **French Community** ▶ (French *La Communauté*) An association of states consisting of France and certain of its former colonies, established in 1958 by the constitution of the Fifth Republic. It replaced the earlier French Union, which was itself a replacement for the French Colonial Empire.

• **French kiss** ▶ An open-mouthed kiss during which the tongues of the participants make contact. This expression has been used since the 1920s in both the UK and America; it reflects an Anglo-Saxon belief in Gallic passion.

• **Freudian slip** ▶ An error of speech or in writing or an act of omission that is motivated by an unconscious desire. In his *Psychopathology of Everyday Life* (1914), Sigmund Freud (1856–1939) tried to show that many such slips are so motivated. For example, the nervous and inexperienced chairman of a meeting who rises to his feet at its start and says: 'I would like to welcome everyone here and now declare the meeting closed', is clearly wishing that the whole thing was over. Likewise, the flustered hostess who, glancing at a guest who is making signs of leaving, says 'Oh, please can't you go – don't stay', is expressing a desire to break up the party and get to bed. However, it is clear that most everyday blunders do not fall into this category and are entirely without sinister motivation. It is only the highly improbable errors, and those that are likely to have real or long-lasting effects, that express an unconscious wish and are therefore worth investigating in psychoanalysis.

• **Friedmanism** ▶ The economic theory associated with the US economist Milton Friedman (1912– ). Friedman's ideas contradicted those of Maynard Keynes (*see*: Keynesianism), stressing regulation of the money supply and the encouragement of a free-market economy. Friedmanism was influential in determining British government policy in the early years of Margaret Thatcher's government (*see*: Thatcherism).

• **-friendly** ▶ Good for the person or thing specified. For example, user-friendly implies that a device, such as a computer, is designed in such a way that it is easy to use. **Ozone-friendly** is used to describe something, such as an aerosol can in which the propellant is not a CFC, that does not cause damage to the ozone layer. **Environment-friendly** is used more widely to describe a politician, policy, substance, or device that is kind to the environment. A returnable glass bottle with a deposit on it, for example, is considered more environment-friendly than a throw-away can.

• **friendly fire** ▶ Gun shots, rockets, bombs, etc., that accidentally kill members of one's own side, especially in battle. The expression was used by the Americans in the Gulf War of 1991 to describe the killing of nine British servicemen by the crew of an antitank aircraft, who mistook the British personnel carrier for an Iraqi vehicle. While it is obviously paradoxical to describe the fire that kills a person as friendly, the expression is intended to convey the idea that the servicemen operating the weapon are friends, who have made a tragic mistake.

• **Friends of the Earth** ▶ An organization founded in the UK in 1971 to campaign for the protection of the environment. It now has local branches throughout Britain and branches in 25 countries. Friends of the Earth organizes petitions, public meetings, demonstrations, etc., to campaign against all forms of pollution (especially nuclear power), developments which ruin the countryside, and the destruction of wildlife. *See also*: Greenpeace.

• **frighteners** ►
**put the frighteners on** To intimidate someone to make them comply with your wishes or to make them tell you something you want to know. The expression is mostly used in the underworld or by the police.

• **fringe benefits** ► Concessions and benefits given to employees, or extra 'perks' that go with a job or appointment, such as medical insurance, use of a car, pensions, etc.

• **fringe medicine** ► *See*: alternative medicine.

• **fringe theatre** ► Any form of theatre outside the commercial or subsidized mainstream. it is the British equivalent of the US 'off-off-Broadway' theatre. The term probably derives from the growth of unconventional theatrical productions on the 'fringe' of the Edinburgh Festival during the 1950s. In 1960 a team including Jonathan Miller and Alan Bennett appeared at the Edinburgh Festival in the satirical revue Beyond the Fringe, indicating that by then the limits set by the fringe had already been surpassed. Fringe productions often tackle controversial themes in a lively experimental style; they tend to attract younger audiences and to take place in small informal venues. Notable fringe theatre in London include the Bush, the Gate, and the Tricycle Theatre in Kilburn.

• **Frisbee** ► A light plastic disc, about 8 inches in diameter, which is thrown into the air with a flick of the wrist. It was first produced in California in 1957 by the Wham-O-Production Company but was based on an idea by Yale University students, who discovered the aerodynamic properties of pie plates produced by the Frisbie Pie Company of Bridgeport, Connecticut. The Frisbee is sold as a toy in the UK but on the W coast of America Frisbee throwing has reached the combined status of sport and art form.

• **Fritz** ► In World War I, the name commonly given by British soldiers to any German in the enemy lines or to Germans collectively. Fritz is the traditional German shortening for the name of Friedrich (Frederick the Great of Prussia, for instance, was called 'Old Fritz'). *See also*: Tommy.

• **frogmen** ► In World War II, strong swimmers dressed in rubber suits with paddles on their feet resembling the feet of frogs, who operated in enemy harbours by night attaching explosives to shipping, etc. Frogmen now work in salvage operations, North Sea oilrigs, etc.

• **frogspawn** ► British schoolchildren's slang for tapioca or sago pudding. This name reflects the extremely unappetizing appearance of the dish, which was formerly often served for school lunches.

• **front-end loading** ► 1. Describing a piece of earth-moving machinery in which the bucket for collecting the earth is located on a hydraulically operated arm at the front of the machine. 2. Denoting a unit trust, insurance policy, or other investment in which all charges and commissions are paid in advance when the purchase is made.

• **fruitcake** ► 1. 1960s slang for an eccentric person, often used in the phrase **nutty as a fruitcake**, which covers the whole range from being slightly odd to raving lunacy.

> Nobody interrupted. We all sat like dummies on an Underground train while the fruitcake in the corner raved on. – *The Independent*, 29 January 1991.

2. US pejorative slang for a male homosexual. An extension of 'fruit', it has been in use since the early part of the 20th century.

• **fruit machine** ► A mechanical or electronic gambling machine, operated by a lever or button, which pays out cash when images of the same type of fruit, or certain combinations of fruit, appear on a series of revolving cylinders when they come to rest. The machines, which were originally simple, have become more and more complicated as various refinements have been added. Fruit machines are found in pubs, amusement arcades, etc.

• **FT** ► *Financial Times*. *See*: Footsie.

• **FTA** ► Fuck the army, or, sometimes, free the army. A slogan coined in the US army in the 1960s and often seen as graffiti. Jane Fonda used the initials *FTA* in 1972 as the title of her anti-war film about Vietnam. Variations also abound: **FTP** (fuck the Pope) and **FTQ** (fuck the Queen) were often seen in Northern Ireland in the 1970s.

• **Fuchs spy case** ► The case of Klaus Fuchs (1911–88), a German-born British physicist, who worked on the atomic bomb during World War II in both the UK and America. In 1950 he fell under suspicion and confessed to having passed atomic secrets to Soviet agents since 1943. His motives were political and to some extent idealistic, as he had been a communist sympathizer since the 1930s. He was sentenced to 14 years imprisonment, but was released in 1959, when he emigrated to East Germany. He remained there until his death. *See*: Rosenberg spy case.

• **fuel air bomb** ► (FAB) A type of bomb giving high explosive power over a wide area. The fuel air bomb acts in two stages: first an explosion spreads a large cloud of gas over the target; secondly, this is detonated to cause widespread destruction. Fuel air bombs are conventional weapons that have a power equivalent to that of small nuclear weapons. They were first used by US forces during the Gulf War (1991) to clear minefields in Kuwait and S Iraq.

• **fuel crisis** or **petrol crisis** ▸ In the UK, a nationwide fuel shortage that brought the country to a standstill in September 2000; it was caused by the actions of farmers and others protesting against high fuel taxes. The crisis began when a few dozen farmers used their tractors to block the gates of an oil refinery in Cheshire, claiming that the high price of diesel fuel was driving them to the verge of bankruptcy. The farmers were quickly joined by hauliers from all over the country, who said that they too were likely to be put out of business. Within a few days, all 18 of the country's refineries and depots were being blockaded and the oil-company drivers were refusing to cross the picket lines. As a result, deliveries to petrol stations were soon reduced to a trickle reserved for essential services. The hauliers were also driving their trucks in procession down motorways at a snail's pace to cause the utmost congestion. Although petrol had become virtually unobtainable for the private motorist, most of the public seemed to agree that fuel prices were too high and blamed the government, rather than the protesters, for the mounting chaos – a line that was also taken by most of the press.

The government reacted slowly and failed, at first, to read the public mood. On the day that supplies of fuel ran out and widespread panic buying of food in the supermarkets began, the prime minister appeared on television to insist that the government would not give in to blackmail. When this stance was poorly received, the government quickly changed tack and agreed to listen to what the protesters were saying. Because of the potential dangers to the NHS, the press now counselled caution and the protesters decided to call off the blockade before the public mood turned against them. Although some acted on their threat to renew the blockades in 60 days time if nothing had changed, the government was now prepared and the protests soon fizzled out.

The issues that linger from this saga relate to the right to protest, the methods adopted, and the appropriate government response to such protests when they seem to enjoy overwhelming public support. Most tellingly of all, however, the crisis showed how easily our fuel-dependent society could be brought to the point of collapse within a matter of days. In the (private) words of one senior minister, the country was '24 hours away from meltdown'.

• **Führer** ▸ (German, leader) The title assumed by Adolf Hitler (1889–1945) when he acceded to supreme power in Germany on the death of Hindenburg in 1934.

• **Fulbright scholar** ▸ A postgraduate student who is able to study abroad on an international exchange programme initiated by the US senator William Fulbright (1905–90). The 1946 Fulbright Act legislated for funds to be made available for these exchanges from the sale of US surplus war materials. The programme was later taken over by the US government in association with other governments. Over 100,000 students and teachers have benefited from the scheme.

• **fullerenes** ▸ See: buckminsterfullerene.

• **full frontal** ▸ A view or depiction of a nude person in which the breasts and genital area of a woman or the penis of a man are clearly visible. The term can also be used to mean 'uninhibited' or 'undisguised' as in 'a full-frontal assault on government policy'.

• **full monty** ▸ See at: monty.

• **Fu Manchu** ▸ A sinister Chinese created by the British novelist Sax Rohmer (Arthur Sarsfield Ward; 1883–1959). Dr Fu Manchu (1913), the first of a series of novels, was a great success, encouraging the author to create more of the same. The last of the series, Emperor Fu Manchu (1959), was written while Rohmer was living in America. Reflecting the Cold War mood of the times (see: McCarthyism), for this book Fu was transformed from an inscrutable villain into a dedicated anti-communist. Fu Manchu was also an early staple of the cinema: in the 1920s he was played by the British actor Harry Agar Lyons and in Hollywood by the Swedish actor Warner Oland (who later played the Chinese detective Charlie Chan). In the 1940s Boris Karloff took over the role and in the 1960s Christopher Lee appeared in another British series. In all these films Fu Manchu was depicted as he had been described by Rohmer, with a long thin moustache hanging down on either side of the mouth. This became known as a **Fu-Manchu moustache**.

• **functionalism** ▸ 1. In architecture, the theory that the form and style of a building should be determined by its purpose. In practice this means a rejection of unnecessary ornament and of the kind of design that seeks to disguise an industrial building as e.g. a gothic church. Developed originally in the 1890s by Louis Sullivan (1856–1924), who coined the maxim 'form must follow function', the theory of functionalism found its most influential proponent in Le Corbusier. The doctrine that the most functional design for a building will also be the most beautiful was widely accepted by modernist architects but has been rejected by the adherents of postmodernism. **2.** In sociology, a perspective in which the various components of society are considered to be parallel to the workings of the different organs in a living body. The theory was devised by Emile Durkheim and subsequently developed by Talcott Parsons after World War II.

• **fundamental forces** ► The four different types of force that can exist between bodies that are not in contact. These forces (or **interactions**, as they are sometimes called) account for the way the universe is held together and for every physical event that occurs in it. The weakest of these forces is the **gravitational force**; this is $10^{40}$ times weaker than the electromagnetic force and acts between all bodies that have mass. The force is always attractive and although negligible on the atomic scale it is the force that holds the galaxies, stars, planets, etc., together. The **weak (nuclear) force**, $10^{10}$ times weaker than the electromagnetic force, occurs within certain sub-atomic particles. The **electromagnetic force** occurs between all electrically charged bodies and can be either attractive or repulsive. It controls atomic structure, chemical reactions, and all electric and magnetic phenomena. The **strong (nuclear) force**, 100 times stronger than the electromagnetic force, is the force that holds the atomic nucleus together. It acts only at very short distances (in the range $10^{15}$ metres).

The aim of physics is to unify these four fundamental forces into one theory, with one set of equations. This has not yet been achieved although the **electroweak theory** has successfully unified the electromagnetic and the weak forces. The elucidation of these fundamental forces was one of the supreme achievements of 20th-century science.

• **fundamentalism** ► The maintenance of traditional Protestant Christian beliefs based upon a literal acceptance of the scriptures. Fundamentalism arose in various US denominations from about 1919 onwards. What was new was not so much its ideas and attitudes, but the zeal of its supporters. It opposed all theories of evolution and anthropology, holding that God transcends all laws of nature and that he manifests himself by exceptional and extraordinary activities. In 1925, John T. Scopes, a science teacher of Dayton, Tennessee, was convicted of violating state laws by teaching evolution, an incident arousing controversy far beyond the religious circles of America (*see*: Dayton anti-Darwinist trial).

Fundamentalism has also been a feature of other world religions in the last hundred years, when it has often emerged as a means of holding together a faith that seemed threatened by the tides of secularism. In particular, Islamic fundamentalism has been a source of conflict and controversy since the late 1970s (*see*: fatwa). In general, religious fundamentalism has to be accepted through faith alone with no contribution from reason and imposed on waverers by edict rather than by argument. Fundamentalist teachings are, by their alleged God-given nature, true for all time. Scientific truth, based on reproducible evidence, changes and evolves as the evidence is interpreted at deeper and more generalized levels. The divergence between religious fundamentalism and science therefore tends to become wider and wider. *See also*: modernism; moral majority.

• **fundie** ► Slang for a religious fundamentalist or a purist in any cause, especially an ecological one. In the US the term was applied to Christian fundamentalists in the early 1980s. In the mid-1980s the extreme wing of the German Green Party became known as the *Fundis*, as distinct from their more pragmatic colleagues, the *Realos*.

• **Funf** ► A character who appeared as a telephone caller in the first series of the radio programme *It's That Man Again* (*see*: ITMA). Funf, a corruption of *fünf*, the German word for five, was a half-baked German spy with a muffled guttural accent (obtained by having the actor Jack Train speak into a tumbler). His catchphrase, **this is Funf speaking**, immediately caught on; many telephone conversations of the period began with this joke introduction.

• **funky music** or **funk** ► Urban Black music, especially disco or soul, characterized by strong rhythms and heavy bass; the style often incorporates elements of African music, jazz, blues, or rock. The origin of the word funky is obscure, but it became a Black American term of approval in the mid-20th century. A 'funky guy' was much the same as the earlier 'cool guy' – a person of whom one approved.

• **funny farm** ► Slang for a psychiatric hospital.

• **funny peculiar or funny ha-ha?** ► A catchphrase used to distinguish between two senses of the word funny; odd or peculiar (*e.g.* a funny way to behave) and amusing (a funny joke). It has appeared as a line in several plays, the first probably being the *Housemaster* (1938) by Ian Hay Beith.

• **fusion** ► The form of nuclear reaction in which atomic nuclei of low atomic number fuse together to form a heavier nucleus, with the release of a considerable amount of energy. For example, when two deuterium nuclei (heavy hydrogen nuclei) fuse to form a tritium nucleus (the heaviest isotope of hydrogen) $10^{13}$ joules of energy are released. Before two such positively charged nuclei can fuse, however, the repulsive electromagnetic forces between them have to be overcome. This can be achieved if the reacting nuclei have very high kinetic energies, which implies a temperature of around $10^6$ kelvins. *See also*: cold fusion; nuclear weapon.

• **futon**▶ A Japanese soft cotton mattress used as a bed; a simple and unobtrusive design, which can be folded to make seating or easily stored when not in use. The word itself is Japanese.

• **future**▶
**I have seen the future and it works** A famous declaration by the US reformer and journalist Lincoln Steffens (1879–1955), following a visit to the Soviet Union and his meeting (1919) with Lenin. It has since been widely applied, often ironically.

• **future**▶
**Your future is in your hands** A slogan from the Conservative Party campaign led by Winston Churchill in the 1950 General Election. It turned out to be a winner because although the Labour government obtained a (much reduced) majority, this was too small to be workable and the Conservatives were returned to power in 1951, with Churchill as prime minister.

• **futurism**▶ An art movement that originated in Turin in 1909 under the leadership of E. F. T. Marinetti. Its adherents sought to introduce into their paintings a dynamic 'poetry of motion' reflecting the speed and excitement of the machine age. They rejected tradition and the influence of the past, calling for all museums and libraries to be destroyed. The original futurists, who included Marinetti, Boccioni, Carra, Russolo, and Severini, exhibited at Paris in 1912. Their glorification of violence and energy led Marinetti and some others to support Fascism in the 1920s, by which time the force of the movement was in any case largely spent.

• **fuzz, the**▶ Slang for the police or a policeman. It originated in America in the late 1920s; the exact etymology is uncertain but in his *American Tramp and Underworld Slang* (1931) G. Irwin says: 'a detective; a prison guard or turnkey. Here it is likely that "fuzz" was originally "fuss", one hard to please or over-particular'. Not very likely, but in the absence of anything more convincing, it will have to do. Surprisingly, the word fuzz did not appear in the UK until the 1950s, probably in the wake of US crime TV programmes and films.

• **fuzz word**▶ A piece of fashionable jargon that serves to obscure, rather than clarify, an issue. This may or may not be intentional. From a blend of 'fuzz' and buzz word.

• **f-word**▶ A euphemism for 'fuck'. It originated in the 1980s in America and gave rise to a number of similar constructions used by people trying to avoid taboo expressions, for example, 'the T-word' (for Margaret Thatcher) or 'the L-word' (for liberal – often a term of abuse in America).

• **Fylingdales**▶ A moor to the south of Whitby in Yorkshire upon which the British station of the US Ballistic Missile Early Warning System (BMEWS) is built. It is a giant radar installation, a companion to those at Clear in Alaska and Thule in Greenland, that has continually monitored the sky in the general direction of Russia since 1963.

# G

• **G** ▸ **1.** Or **Gee**. Informal abbreviation for gram, used with reference to a quantity of an illegal drug, especially cocaine, that is sold in gram units. **2.** Abbreviation for grand, a slang word for 1000 that is usually applied to sums of money. It has largely been replaced by K, an abbreviation for kilo. **3.** A cinema certification in America for films that can be shown generally, *i.e.* to all ages.

• **gaff** ▸ **1.** British slang for a house, home, or place as in 'nice gaff you've got here'. In the 19th century gaff meant fairground but since the 1920s the usage has expanded to mean any place. In the sense 'house' it was popularized by the teddy boys in the 1950s and is still heard colloquially.

> But later in the day, the governor found me and apologised. That one thing completely changed my attitude to the gaff and to him.
> – *The Independent*, 11 February 1991.

**2.** British slang meaning to cheat or swindle, a meaning derived from the fact that cheating was a regular feature of fairground practice.

• **gaga** ▸ **1.** Slang for senile, mentally unstable. Derived from the nursery version of French *grandpère*, grandfather, it became part of upper-class English speech in the 1920s. An alternative derivation has it that the word is a corruption of 'Gauguin', the postimpressionist painter, who was somewhat eccentric and unbalanced. **2.** Emotionally unstable in a non-clinical sense. An extension of the previous meaning, it can be used of people of any age, as in 'she is completely gaga about her new boyfriend'.

• **Gaia hypothesis** ▸ The theory that the earth functions as a single self-regulating organism in which all living matter interacts to sustain the whole. It was put forward by the British scientist James Lovelock in 1969 and named after Gaia, the Greek earth goddess, on the suggestion of the novelist William Golding. In the 1980s and 1990s it was enthusiastically adopted by green activists and New Age disciples; believers sometimes describe themselves as **Gaiaists** or **Gaians**. *New Scientist* has described the theory as 'pseudoscientific idiocy'.

• **Gaiety Girl** ▸ A member of the chorus of the Old Gaiety Theatre in the Strand, London, which became a popular feature of the musical comedies staged there in late Victorian and early Edwardian times. Such productions as *The Shop Girl* (1894) and *The Circus Girl* (1896) were designed to give full reign to the singing and dancing talents of the chorus, as well as to display their good looks. Several of the Gaiety Girls, many of whom were of humble origins, married into the peerage. The New Gaiety Theatre replaced the Old Gaiety in 1903 when the latter was demolished to allow widening of the Strand; the tradition of musical comedies continued until the 1920s. *See also*: Gibson Girl.

• **gain sharing** ▸ A form of profit-sharing among employees closely linked to work performance. Under this scheme employees benefit from any savings or cost-cutting for which they are responsible.

• **galah** ▸ Australian slang for a silly person, a fool. The galah is a type of Australian cockatoo that is known for its habit of gathering in groups and chattering.

• **galah session** ▸ In Australia, a period during which the flying doctor radio network is thrown open for public use. It is so called because the chatter of the airwaves between radio users is likened to the noise of a flock of cockatoos (*see*: galah).

• **Galbraithian** ▸ Relating to the economic and social theories of the US economist Kenneth Galbraith (1908–   ); also, a supporter of these theories. Galbraith, an economist in the tradition of Keynesianism, was influential in the 1950s and 1960s and was noted for coining the phrase the Affluent Society in his book of the same name (1958); he also coined the slogan 'Private opulence and public squalor'.

• **Gallipoli** ▸ A peninsula in the Dardanelles, which in 1915 became the scene of a disastrous Allied offensive against the Turks during World War I. Initially the campaign involved naval forces, but subsequently a large contingent of Australian and New Zealand infantry (*see*: Anzac) were sent, as well as British and French troops. Allied commanders failed to order a rapid advance from the beachheads at Suvla Bay, Ari Burnu, and Cape Helles and, despite heroism from the troops themselves, the Allied forces failed to breach the Turkish lines. The final evacuation, some 10 months later, was better managed. Allied troops were taken out by ship at night and small forces were landed during the day, convincing the Turks that the Allies were continuing to reinforce their position; as a result, not a single life was lost in the evacuation. In all, though, 25,000 Allied troops died, with 13,000 missing.

• **Gallup Poll** ▶ The best known of the opinion polls, instituted by Dr George Gallup (1901–84) of the American Institute of Public Opinion in 1935. Trained interviewers interrogate a small but carefully selected cross-section of the population. For the British parliamentary election of 1945, out of 25 million voters, 1809 were interviewed, but the Gallup Poll forecast was within 1 per cent; however the forecast was wrong for the US presidential election of 1948. Notoriously, Gallup and the other polls failed to predict the Conservative victory in the British general election of 1992.

• **game of life** ▶ A mathematical game invented by the British mathematician John Conway in 1970. It is played on an infinite two-dimensional grid of squares. Each square has eight near neighbours and squares may be occupied ('alive') or empty ('dead'). There is an initial pattern of live squares, and the pattern then changes in steps, with the whole grid changing at each operation. The fate of each square depends on its neighbours. A square that has only two live neighbours is unchanged. A live square with no neighbours, one neighbour, or four or more neighbours dies. An empty square with three living neighbours is filled in the next generation (a 'birth' occurs). Depending on the original pattern, the colony may die out, grow, or switch between different patterns. The game is usually played on a computer and is highly addictive. Many millions of pounds worth of unauthorized computer time has been spent investigating its complexities.

• **gameplan** ▶ Originally, in American football, a series of tactical steps planned in advance to achieve a particular objective. The term is now used, on both sides of the Atlantic, to refer to any longer term strategy in which there are several distinct steps, such as a career plan involving a number of job changes.

• **game show** ▶ A television show in which contestants answer questions or perform other tasks to win prizes. The general format dates back to the US quiz shows of the 1950s, one of the first to offer big cash prizes being *The $64,000 Question*, launched in 1955. Such shows were cheap to make and attracted large audiences. Viewers were able to test themselves, and could readily share the excitement of contestants who sweated under the studio lights to risk a small fortune on the turn of a compere's question card. Since then, the quiz show has become a staple of schedules around the world. On British screens, some long-running favourites, such as *Mastermind*, have lured participants with little more than the prestige of winning. At the other end of the spectrum is *Who Wants to be a Millionaire?*, which in 2000 created British television's first quiz-show millionaire.

The game show has developed a host of different formats. Some test physical as well as mental prowess. For example, in French television's *Fort Boyard* teams of players face varied challenges, such as locked rooms, labyrinths, and assault-courses. The physical element is taken to extremes in the Japanese show *Endurance*, which puts its contestants through excruciating and often humiliating ordeals. Inevitably, sex has also been worked into the formula, most popularly in 'dating' formats such as Australia's *Perfect Match* and the UK's Blind Date. The current trend is for so-called **reality television** shows, such as Big Brother, in which contestants are filmed in real-life situations (albeit ones that are utterly contrived). The permutations of the game show are seemingly endless, and the genre shows no sign of taking the cheque and waving goodbye just yet.

• **gamesmanship** ▶ A word coined by Stephen Potter (1900–70), whose book *The Theory and Practice of Gamesmanship* (1947) defines the meaning in its sub-title: 'The Art of Winning Games without Actually Cheating'. *See also:* lifemanship; one-upmanship.

• **game theory** ▶ A branch of mathematics that analyses the optimum strategy to adopt in a given situation. The theory was first introduced by the French mathematician Emile Borel (1871–1956) in 1921 and was developed by the Hungarian-born US mathematician John von Neumann (1903–57) and the German-born US economist Oskar Morganstern (1907–77) in their book *The Theory of Games and Economic Behaviour* (1944). Here, they argued that the type of applied mathematics used in engineering and the physical sciences was not suitable for analysing economic activity. In the physical sciences, the subject under investigation is disinterested in the result; in economics, the individuals, companies, countries, etc., can take into account and anticipate the behaviour of other participants in the system. Consequently, economics is more like a game in which the players attempt to get the best possible result for themselves (*i.e.* to maximize their gain, or 'payoff', and to minimize their loss). Game theory (which is also known as the **theory of** games) is a formal mathematical way of analysing what the 'best' result might be. Although originally developed as a way of looking at economics, game theory has been applied in many other fields. During World War II it was used successfully to determine strategy in submarine warfare; it has subsequently been applied in politics, social science, business, biology, etc.

Games are classified in various ways. One distinction is the number of people (or parties) involved. For example, patience and solitaire are examples of 'one-person games' in which the participant is playing against chance. 'Two-person games' have two conflicting participants and 'n-person games' have three or more protagonists. Another way of classifying games is by the nature of the result. A **zero-sum game** is one in which the overall payoff is constant; one person's loss is another's gain. In a 'nonzero-sum game' all the participants may gain. Another classification is into 'cooperative' and 'noncooperative' games. Poker, for example, is an n-person zero-sum noncooperative game. Essential features of the mathematical analysis of games are that the participants should be regarded as acting rationally and, in most cases, that chance or incomplete information may affect the result.

• **G and T** ▶ An abbreviation for gin and tonic much used by those who regard this form of beverage as an essential lubricant in their lives. The drink is often associated with affluent older people of robustly Conservative views; the term **G and T belt** is sometimes used as a derogatory name for the more prosperous parts of outer London and the Home Counties.

Gin with tonic water is a somewhat less alcoholic and longer drink than its competitor, **gin and it**, in which the gin is augmented by Italian Vermouth.

• **gang-bang** ▶ Slang for an act of group sex, usually involving one woman and a number of men. A gang-bang is normally an instance of multiple rape in which the woman is forced to take part against her will.

• **gangbusters** ▶ US schoolchildren's slang used to describe something excellent, or highly approved of. It is a shortening of the phrase 'like gangbusters' meaning very energetically. Gangbusters were the law men who fought against the underworld mobs in America in the 1930s, especially as portrayed in fiction.

• **Gang of Four** ▶ **1.** Four Chinese politicians who unsuccessfully attempted to seize control of the country after the death of Mao Tse-tung in 1976.

The gang consisted of Jiang Qing (Mao's widow), Zhang Chungao, Wang Hungwen, and Yao Wenyuan. They aimed to continue the radical policies of the Cultural Revolution but were arrested and imprisoned. **2.** In the UK, the name given to the four senior MPs who left the Labour Party in 1981 to form the Social Democratic Party (SDP), namely Roy Jenkins (leader until 1983), David Owen (leader 1983–87), Shirley Williams, and William Rodgers. *See also*: Liberal Democrats.

• **gangsta** ▶ *See*: rap.

• **ganja** ▶ A highly potent form of marijuana. Derived originally from the Sanskrit *gañja*, via Hindi *gājā*, the term was popularized by Rastafarians, who regard the smoking of cannabis as a religious rite.

• **Gannex** ▶ Tradename for a type of clothing manufactured by Kagan Textiles, which was set up in 1951. The company is particularly remembered for a type of light-coloured trench coat with distinctive lapels (the **Gannex mac**) favoured by Harold Wilson during his premiership. The founder of the company, Joseph Kagan (1915–95), was knighted in 1970 and elevated to the peerage in Wilson's resignation honours list in 1976 (*see*: Lavender list). However, suspicions of what would later be called sleaze attached to Kagan's association with Wilson's government, and in 1980 he was convicted of theft and false accounting, fined, and sentenced to 10 months' imprisonment, during which he was stripped of his knighthood. Despite this disgrace, after his release Kagan resumed his seat in the House of Lords, where he regularly attended sittings.

• **gaper's block** ▶ US slang for a traffic hold-up caused by car drivers stopping or slowing down to 'gape' at a road accident, fire, or other traffic incident. Frequently gapers prevent emergency rescue vehicles, such as ambulances and fire-engines, from reaching the scene of an accident rapidly. *See also*: rubberneck.

• **gap year** ▶ A year's freedom from formal education, taken between leaving school and starting university. Typically a gap year is spent in working or travelling abroad. Some school leavers arrange to do voluntary work overseas through organizations that partly subsidize them; they raise the rest of the money they need by, for example, asking local businesses, etc., for sponsorship. Other students may choose to spend their time travelling, often backpacking, in distant countries. Usually they obtain casual jobs during their travels, which barely support them in a lifestyle that is probably the most uncomfortable and deprived that they will ever experience. Others spend their gap year in a regular job to earn enough money to support them at university.

Opinion is divided on the advisability of taking a gap year. Those in favour say that it provides a productive break from academic studies, broadens the mind, and offers an opportunity for travel and learning about other cultures that is unlikely to recur. They maintain that it can lead to independence and self-sufficiency and that it prepares the student for settling down to an academic course. The opposing view is that it distracts young people from their studies and may even persuade them to abandon plans for further education. Moreover, travelling in remote regions can be dangerous and even life-threatening.

• **garage band** ► An amateur rock or pop group that rehearses in a garage or similar makeshift premises. In 1976 the punk rock group The Clash was described by *New Musical Express* as 'the type of garage band that should be returned to the garage as soon as possible, preferably with the engine running'. They responded by writing the song 'Garage Band'.

• **garage sale** ► A sale of second-hand articles given by a householder, typically in the garage. The idea originated in America, where it is also called a **yard sale**. *See also*: car-boot sale.

• **garbage in, garbage out** or **gigo** ► An expression that originated as computer jargon meaning that what you get out of a system is dependent on the quality of what you put into it. Its usage is now much more general and can be applied to almost any kind of system.

• **garbo** ► Australian slang for a dustman, the man who collects the garbage.

• **garbology** ► A branch of social science that assumes it is possible to learn about the culture and lifestyles of people by studying what they have thrown away. Hence a **garbologist** is one who analyses refuse. The practice seems to have been originated by A. J. Weberman, an obsessive fan of the singer Bob Dylan, who made an exhaustive study of his idol's refuse in the early 1970s.

• **garbonzas** ► US slang for breasts. Like bazumas and gazungas it is a word used chiefly by adolescent males. It is very similar to the Spanish word *garbanzos*, chick peas, although the connection, if any, is unclear.

• **garden city** ► A general name for model townships specially planned to provide attractive layouts for housing and industry with a surrounding rural belt and adequate open spaces. The term garden city was first used by an American, A. T. Stew-

art, in 1869 to describe an estate development on Long Island. The garden city movement in England was led by Sir Ebenezer Howard (1850–1928), who set out the social ideals on which the concept is based in his book *To-morrow* (1898). His first garden city was founded at Letchworth, Hertfordshire, in 1903 and his second at Welwyn (1919–29). *See also*: green belt; new towns.

• **garden suburb** ► 1. A model suburb (*e.g.* Hampstead Garden Suburb) with many characteristics of a garden city. 2. The nickname applied to Lloyd George's personal secretariat, established when he became prime minister and head of the war cabinet (December 1916). The name derives from the fact that they were accommodated in huts in St James's Park. The 'Garden Suburb' was dispersed when Bonar Law assumed the premiership in 1922.

• **Garlic Wall** ► The satirical name used by Gibraltarians for the Spanish barrier that closed the frontier to the mainland at La Línea in 1969 as a consequence of Spain's claim to the Rock. Gibraltar was ceded to Great Britain by the Treaty of Utrecht, 1713. Spain reopened the frontier at La Línea in 1985. However, in 1998–99 a renewal of the dispute led the Spaniards to impose a semi-blockade on Gibraltar. *See also*: Tortilla Curtain.

• **Garnett, Alf** ► The central character in BBC TV's comedy series *Till Death Us Do Part* (first seen in 1967) and its sequels. As conceived by writer Johnny Speight and played by Warren Mitchell (1926–  ), Garnett was intended to represent the archetypal working-class bigot – racist, sexist, ignorant, and reactionary. Unfortunately many of the programme's original viewers missed the point entirely, seeing the preposterous Garnett as a purveyor of plainspoken common sense. He found a US counterpart in Archie Bunker.

• **garryowen** ► In Rugby Union, a high kick forwards in support of a charge (also known as an **up-and-under**). The word is derived from Garryowen RFC, a Limerick club founded in 1884, which has a reputation for excellent forward play. Garryowen won the Munster premier trophy more often than any other club and has provided over 30 internationals for Ireland.

• **gas guzzler** ► US slang for a car that consumes large quantities of petrol and is therefore uneconomical and environmentally unfriendly. The expression is now heard in the UK, where such a car might also be called 'juicy'.

• **gash** ► 1. British slang meaning spare, surplus to requirements. Now rarely heard, it was common among members of the forces in the 1950s.

**2.** British slang meaning broken, useless. This meaning is still heard from technicians and workmen, as in 'this computer is gash'. **3.** A derogatory slang word for a woman, especially one viewed in a sexual way. This is obviously an extension of 'gash' as a vulgar name for the vagina. In the 1980s 'gash' was used as a synonym for girlfriend among young rap music fans.

• **gasper** ▸ British slang from World War I for a cigarette. The word reflects the fact that cigarettes make one short of breath, or gasp, something that was not taken very seriously before the connection between smoking, cancer, and heart disease became clear.

• **gas pipe** ▸ US jazz slang for a trombone, dating from the 1940s.

• **Gastarbeiter** ▸ (German, guest worker) An immigrant worker in Germany (West Germany until 1990) from Turkey, North Africa, etc., allowed into the country on certain strictly defined terms to alleviate the labour shortage. The *Gastarbeiter* system has frequently been criticized as socially unjust and economically exploitative.

• **gat** ▸ US slang for a pistol, first heard in the early 1900s. It is an abbreviation of Gatling gun, the crank-operated prototype of the modern machine gun, invented by Richard Jordan Gatling (1818–1903). In the 1950s Gat was the tradename of a British air pistol.

• **Gatsby** ▸ Jay Gatsby, title character in a novel by the US writer F. Scott Fitzgerald (1896–1940), *The Great Gatsby* (1925). The character, a glamorous millionaire of somewhat mysterious antecedents, was suggested partly by one of Fitzgerald's neighbours on Long Island, the bootlegger Max Gerlack, and partly by a New York socialite and fraudster named Edward M. Fuller. Fitzgerald once said that Gatsby was based on someone he knew but then grew to be himself. The story has been filmed three times: the silent version in 1926 starred Warner Baxter, a 1949 Paramount film starred Alan Ladd, and a lavish 1974 production had Robert Redford in the name part.

• **GATT** ▸ General Agreement on Tariffs and Trade. A treaty signed by over 90 nations to regulate trade barriers and encourage free trade. The original agreement, signed by 23 nations, came into force on 1 January 1948 following talks in Geneva the previous year. A proposed UN International Trade Organization never came into being, leaving GATT as the principal regulatory framework. Fundamental principles of GATT included non-discrimination among the signatories ('most-favoured-nation'

clause); the limitation of protective measures to customs tariffs rather than import quotas or embargoes; and support for movement towards reducing and eliminating tariffs by multilateral agreements. GATT completed eight rounds of international negotiations, th last one of which took place in Uruguay in 1993. In 1996 GATT was succeeded by the **World Trade Organization** (WTO).

• **Gauleiter** ▸ (German, district leader) The head (*Leiter*) of a *Gau*, one of the administrative territories into which Germany was divided under the Third Reich. The *Gauleiter* (sometimes called the *Gaufuehrer*) was a high-ranking official, often appointed directly by Hitler; he was responsible for all economic and political activities in the area, as well as civil defence and sometimes policing. The term is now sometimes applied to any petty or local official who acts in an authoritarian manner.

• **Gaumont** ▸ Tradename for a British chain of cinemas. Gaumont, which originated in France as a production company, was named after the inventor Léon Gaumont, who developed (1901) an early method of synchronizing film with sound. The company Gaumont-British was founded in 1909 and owned some 300 movie theatres in its heyday; it was acquired by the Rank Organization in 1942.

• **gay** ▸ Originally, light-hearted, merry, in high good spirits; also bright looking, as 'she wore a gay-coloured dress'.

> Belinda smiled and all the world was gay.
> – ALEXANDER POPE: *The Rape of the Lock.*

As time went by, however, 'gay' also acquired the sense of given to pleasure and hence dissipated, as in 'he's a bit of a gay dog' and 'gay house' (formerly a common name for a brothel). In current English, the word is used to mean a homosexual; indeed it has become so identified with homosexuality that to use it in one of its previous senses is to risk serious misunderstanding. Homosexuals adopted the word as a self-description in the early 1970s, largely out of dislike for the medical connotations of 'homosexual'. In recent years, however, some radical gays have preferred the more confrontational queer. Although lesbians are sometimes referred to as gays, it is more usual to confine the term to male homosexuals (especially in its noun sense).

• **gay deceiver** ▸ Slang for a padded brassière.

• **Gay Liberation** or **Gay Lib** ▸ The campaign by lesbians and homosexual men to fight discrimination, especially in the areas of employment, criminal law, and custody rights. The symbolic beginning of the movement was on 28 June 1969 when the clientele of gay bars on Christopher Street, New

York, rioted against police raids. These events triggered the appearance of the Gay Liberation Front (GLF) in America and subsequently of similar organizations in other countries, including the UK.

• **gayola** ▶ Money extorted as blackmail from homosexuals who wish to keep their sexual proclivities secret. The word is a combination of gay and payola.

• **Gaza Strip** ▶ A belt of land on the Mediterranean coast between Egypt and Israel; it includes the city of Gaza. The Strip, some 42 km (26 mi) long and 6–10 km (3–6 mi) wide, was created in 1948 when Gaza and its surroundings were taken by Egypt following the UN proposals for the division of Palestine. It remained under Egyptian control until 1956, when it was briefly held by Israel. Israel again wrested control from Egypt in the 1967 Six-Day War. The Strip suffers from extreme overpopulation, with thousands of Palestinian refugees being housed in squalid camps. An uprising (*see*: intifada) by Palestinians living in the Gaza Strip and West Bank started in 1987, resulting in military confrontation with the Israeli occupiers. Following the Oslo Accord (1994) between Israel and the PLO, the Gaza Strip passed to a new Palestine National Authority in 1995. However, the situation remained tense and in 2000 another rising of Arab youths met with fierce Israeli reprisals, leading to the total breakdown of the peace process.

• **Gazelle Boy** ▶ In 1961, Jean-Claude Armen, travelling by camel through the Spanish Sahara in W Africa, was told by nomad tribesmen of the whereabouts of a young boy living with a herd of gazelles. In due time he sighted the boy and eventually attracted him to close quarters by playing a Berber flute. The boy fed on the same plants as the animals, sometimes eating worms and lizards. On a subsequent expedition in 1963, this time in a jeep, Armen established the speed of the boy when galloping with the herd at over 30 mph.

• **gazump** ▶ A word of unknown origin that entered the language after World War II when house prices were rising sharply. A buyer is gazumped if the seller of a house verbally agrees to sell it to him at a certain price and then accepts a higher offer from someone else. The practice is not illegal, as in England and Wales verbal contracts for the sale of land are invariably made subject to contract and subject to survey. Once contracts have been exchanged, however, the sale is binding and any attempt to gazump the buyer then would be actionable. The gazumped buyer may lose the cost of his survey and legal fees and has no recourse to claim them from the seller. In a market in which prices are falling, the opposite may occur; just before signing the contract the buyer may reduce his offer for the property, aware that the seller is anxious to sell, may have incurred legal expenses, and may also be in the process of buying another property. This became known as **gazundering** in the 1980s when the practice started. In order to prevent these two dishonest practices the authorities concerned are seeking ways of making verbal contracts binding or of shortening the time that elapses between the acceptance of an offer and the issuing of a binding written contract.

• **gazungas** ▶ A male slang term for breasts. *See also*: garbonzas.

• **Gazza** ▶ Nickname of Paul Gascoigne(1967–   ), the British footballer. Having begun his career with Newcastle United, he moved to Tottenham Hotspur in 1988. Playing for England in the 1990 World Cup, he achieved household-name status by bursting into tears when booked by the referee in the semifinal against West Germany – a decision that would have barred him from the final had England won. Gazza subsequently played for the Italian club Lazio, Glasgow Rangers, and Middlesbrough (from 1998).

• **GCE** ▶ General Certificate of Education. A secondary education certificate that was introduced in 1951 to replace the School and Higher School Certificate Examinations. There were two levels: O-level (ordinary level), taken usually at age 16 after a three- or five-year course, and A-level (advanced level), taken at 18 after an additional two-year course. The syllabuses and examinations were set by various national and regional examination boards. GCE O-level and CSE were both superseded by GCSE in 1988. A-levels continued to be taken by those in full-time education for two years after sitting GCSE exams.

• **GCHQ** ▶ Government Communications Headquarters. The establishment at Cheltenham, Gloucestershire, that is the centre for the UK government's intelligence network. Most of its work is secret and in 1946 it established a close relationship with its US equivalent, the National Security Agency. In 1984 the Conservative government informed employees (of which there were some 10,000) that they would no longer be able to belong to a trade union. This right was restored by a Labour government in 1997.

• **GCSE** ▶ General Certificate of Secondary Education. A certificate of education for 16–19 year-olds, which replaced GCE O-levels and the CSE from 1988. The GCSE is designed to allow pupils of different abilities to be regularly assessed and graded within each subject according to a variety of criteria (not only by their examination performance). These criteria include cognitive development and the acquisition and demonstration of practical, creative, and social skills, enabling the majority of pupils to attain some degree of achievement during their school years. Course work and written exams both form part of the GCSE.

• **gear►** 1. An informal term for fashionable clothing or accoutrements. 2. Slang for illegal drugs.

• **Geddes axe►** The drastic cuts in public expenditure, especially on the army, navy, and education, recommended by the Geddes Committee in 1922.

• **Gee►** 1. Codename for a radio navigation system, originally known as TR 1335, used by British bombers during World War II. Signals from three widely spaced transmitters – one 'master' and two 'slaves' – were received by the bomber. The navigator used a cathode-ray tube to display the path difference between each slave signal and the master signal, and with a special grid map could pinpoint the position of the bomber. The system was introduced operationally in 1941 but had a limited range of only 400 miles. 2. *See*: G.

• **geek►** 1. Mainly US slang for a freak, a weirdo, a crazy person. The term originally meant a performer in a freakshow, especially one who bit off the heads of live chickens or animals. It is possibly derived from the Scots word 'geck', fool. 2. US slang of the 1980s meaning to search desperately for any particles of the drug crack that might have been dropped. *See*: geek rock.

• **geek rock►** US slang of the 1980s for the drug crack. A geek is a weird or crazy person and rock is any narcotic in granule form.

• **geep►** An animal, produced by genetic engineering at Cambridge in 1984, that is a cross between a sheep and a goat; it has a sheep-like coat and goat-like horns. Such crosses cannot reproduce themselves. *See also*: beefalo.

• **gefilte fish►** A Jewish delicacy consisting of a fish cake made of a variety of chopped fish, mixed with matzo meal, eggs, onions, pepper, and salt. It can be eaten hot or cold. Widely available in Jewish delicatessen stores, especially in New York, the dish has come to be regarded as the epitome of Jewish cuisine.

> I am sitting in Mindy's restaurant putting on the gefilte fish. – DAMON RUNYON: *Guys and Dolls* (1932).

• **Geiger counter** or **Geiger-Müller counter►** A scientific instrument used to detect ionizing radiation (especially as produced by radioactive substances). It is named after the German physicist Hans Geiger (1882–1945), who invented it in 1913. It was developed in the 1920s by W. Müller, also a German physicist. It is usually known in technical circles as a **G-M counter**.

• **G8►** *See*: Group of Seven.

• **Geller, Uri►** Israeli psychic performer who became world famous in the 1970s. Born in Tel Aviv in 1946, he attracted considerable publicity with his apparent ability to influence the physical world by telepathic means. In front of incredulous audiences, including huge numbers watching on television, he bent cutlery, stopped watches, drove a car blindfolded, and controlled the movements of a cable car, amongst other feats. He has agreed to participate in many scientific investigations but none have provided conclusive evidence for or against the powers he claims.

• **Gemini►** A series of US space missions launched in the 1960s to test various manoeuvres and explore the capabilities of men under space conditions in preparation for the Apollo moon programme. Each manned Gemini mission carried a two-man crew, starting with Gemini 3 in March 1965. In June, from Gemini 4, Ed White performed the first **space walk** (extravehicular activity or EVA) by a US astronaut. Geminis 5 and 7, launched in August and December 1965, both set new records for the duration of a manned space mission. Gemini 6, also launched in December, successfully achieved a rendezvous with Gemini 7, while Gemini 8 docked with an unmanned spacecraft in March 1966. Four further Gemini missions were launched, the series ending with Gemini 12, launched in November 1966, during which mission Buzz Aldrin made a record EVA of over 5 hours duration. The success of the Gemini programme paved the way for an eventual moon landing by Apollo 11.

• **gen►** World War II RAF slang for information or the true facts. Several possible derivations have been suggested; it may be a shortened form of *gen*uine or of intelli*gen*ce, or it may be short for *gen*eral as used in the military phrase 'for the general information of all ranks'. It also appears in the verb **gen up**, as in the phrase 'I'm genned up on the project'.

• **gender-bender►** Slang term from the early 1980s for a transvestite or transexual, or anyone who adopts an androgynous style.

> Gender-bender Brenda standing for Liberals. – Headline, *The Sun*, 19 April 1991.

• **gender gap** ▸ A variation between the views and values held by males and females and between their levels of attainment in a whole range of occupations. This has been monitored, for example, in the different voting patterns of the sexes in America. In this study, women appeared to be more concerned with social and environmental issues and less with foreign affairs. The traditional explanation for this phenomenon links it to the fact that women are biologically equipped to carry and give birth to babies; the equivalent of the nest and its environment is therefore their paramount concern. Defending the family's territory, often providing for its defence, etc., is (the argument runs) the customary preoccupation of the male. Men and women are biologically different; their emotional responses are mediated by different hormones. The gender gap is therefore predictable – indeed traditional family life is based on it. However, because men and women are intellectually roughly on a par, women are able to perform as well as, and sometimes better than, men at many of the tasks usually regarded (by men) as male preserves. It is true that on average men do have heavier brains than women, but the difference (if any) that this is likely to make to average intellectual performance is small enough to be swamped by individual variation. During the 20th century it was discovered that, in spite of the gender gap, women make equally good doctors, stockbrokers, solicitors, barristers, scientists, engineers, computer programmers and analysts, etc. *See also*: feminism.

• **General Assembly** ▸ One of the six principal organs of the United Nations, the forum in which every UN member has equal influence by virtue of their single vote. The Assembly may consider any matter embraced by the UN Charter, and make recommendations to member states or the Security Council. Any issues may be discussed, including peace and security, environmental matters, and economic and social questions. The ten non-permanent members of the Security Council are elected by the Assembly, as are the 18 non-permanent members of the Economic and Social Council. Decisions on important questions require a two-thirds majority; less momentous resolutions need only a simple majority. Regular sessions, lasting three months, are held annually in New York, beginning on the third Tuesday in September. Special sessions may be called at the behest of the Security Council or a majority of member states. Main committees and special committees consider specific issues in detail and report to the Assembly.

• **generalissimo** ▸ The supreme commander, especially of a force drawn from two or more nations, or of a combined military and naval force; the equivalent of *Tagus* among the ancient Thessalians, *Brennus* among the ancient Gauls, and *Pendragon* among the ancient Welsh or Celts. The title is said to have been coined by Cardinal Richelieu on taking supreme command of the French armies in Italy, in 1629.

In modern times the title has been used by Marshal Foch (1851–1929), who commanded the Allied forces in France in 1918; by Joseph Stalin (1879–1953), who was made generalissimo of the Soviet forces in 1943; by General Franco (1892–1975), who proclaimed himself generalissimo of the Spanish army in 1939; and by Marshal Chiang Kai-shek (1888–1975), leader of the Guomindang, who was in power in China from 1927 to 1949.

• **General Strike** ▸ The national strike among vital sectors of the UK's workforce called by the Trades Union Congress (TUC) in 1926 in support of the miners' dispute with the colliery owners. A lockout of the miners on 30 April was the culmination of a long and bitter fight against threatened wage cuts and longer hours, summarized by their slogan 'Not a penny off the pay, not a minute on the day'. The strike, officially declared from midnight on 3 May, affected transport and railway workers, the iron and steel industry, building, gas, electricity, printing, and other key areas. The government, headed by Stanley Baldwin, enacted a state of emergency and introduced a range of measures to counter the effects of the strike. The country was divided into areas under the control of Civil Commissioners and troops were deployed in likely trouble spots. From the outset the TUC had promised to maintain vital food supplies, but many additional services were run by students and volunteers drawn from the middle and upper classes. With national newspapers suspended by the strike, the government produced its own *British Gazette*, belligerently edited by the then chancellor of the exchequer, Winston Churchill; he dubbed strikers 'the enemy' and called for their 'unconditional surrender'. The TUC countered with its own publication, the *British Worker*.

Government measures quickly reduced the effectiveness of the strike, which was unconditionally called off by the TUC on 12 May. The miners' lockout lasted another six months, when hunger forced them to accept their employers' terms. In 1927 the Trades Disputes Act was amended to outlaw any strike 'designed or calculated to coerce the government'. Although never invoked, it was repealed by the Labour government in 1945.

• **General Synod** ▸ The highest governing body

in the Church of England. The General Synod was introduced in 1969 to improve ecclesiastical government and admit greater lay involvement. The General Synod replaced the dual government of Convocations and the Church Assembly, and comprises members of the Upper Houses of the Convocations of Canterbury and York, a House of Clergy, and House of Laity of not more than 250 elected members. It meets at least twice each year and determines issues of doctrine, church services, and the administration of the Sacraments.

• **general theory** ▶ **1.** *See*: relativity. **2.** A theory in economics relating consumption, investment, and the behaviour of the money markets to employment levels. It was put forward in 1936 by J. M. Keynes (1883–1946) and has had a profound effect on the development of economics. *See*: Keynesianism.

• **generation gap** ▶ The difference in attitudes, social values, lifestyle, etc., between one generation and the next, typically between parents and their adolescent children. The generation gap is not an exclusively modern phenomenon. As Shakespeare pointed out:

> Crabbed age and youth cannot live together;
> Youth is full of pleasance, age is full of care;
> Youth like summer morn, age like winter
> > weather;
> Youth like summer brave, age like winter bare.
> – *The Passionate Pilgrim*, XII.

Nevertheless, interest in the differences between the generations has been a particular feature of social life from the mid-20th century, when Western youth sought to assert its own identity. The problem was spelled out by George Orwell:

> Each generation imagines itself to be more intelligent than the one that went before it, and wiser than the one that comes after it.

• **Generation X** ▶ The generation born between the mid-1960s and late 1970s, typically seen as being cynical and apathetic. The term became current in the early 1990s, when this generation was coming of age. A contrast was often drawn between disillusioned directionless Generation Xers and their parents, the idealistic ever-hopeful baby boomers (*see*: baby boom). To many who grew up in the activist 1960s, the young of the 1990s seemed to be characterized by a puzzling inertia and self-pity. This view of the so-called slacker generation can be summed up by a contemporary headline in the *Washington Post*: 'Grow Up Crybabies, You're America's Luckiest Generation'.

In fact, at this time young people's financial prospects were dim. The boom of the 1980s had been followed by the recession of the early 1990s, and this, together with record rates of higher edu-

cation, created a glut of overeducated and underemployed youngsters. Understandably, perhaps, the prevailing mood was one of apathy and anti-materialism – a sullen outlook expressed most clearly in the grunge music and fashions of the time. Disgust with 1980s-style consumerism was heightened by a new awareness of environmental problems, leading to a resentful feeling that the young were now bearing the burden of mistakes made by those who had gone before.

Generation X has now given way to those termed **Generation Y** or **Generation Why?** by the media, but has left in its wake a lasting cultural influence – mostly in film and rock music but also in books such as Douglas Coupland's novel *Generation X: Tales for an Accelerated Culture* (1991), which captures the spirit of the era.

• **generic** ▶ A product that is sold under its own name rather than a brand name of a particular manufacturer. For example Panadol is a tradename for a particular brand of the drug paracetamol. Paracetamol, the generic, can be sold more cheaply than the branded product because it can be packaged more simply and does not have to bear the cost of brand advertising.

• **generic advertising** ▶ Advertising a type of product, such as wool or milk, rather than a branded product. This is usually undertaken by a group of manufacturers or producers for the benefit of all of them.

• **generic name** ▶ The name of a branded product that has been so extensively advertised and in use for so long that it has become part of the language. Hoover is a prime example: this is now used without an initial capital letter to refer to any brand of vacuum cleaner. Similarly Biro and Walkman are now used for any brands of ball-point pen and personal stereo respectively.

• **gene therapy** ▶ A medical application of genetic engineering that seeks to replace defective human genes that cause disease by normal ones. Still in its infancy (the first clinical trial began in 1990), gene therapy is limited to non-reproductive cells, so that the new genes exert their effects only in treated patients and are not passed on to their children. (Germ-cell therapy, with its implications of 'human engineering', is considered to be ethically unacceptable and medically hazardous.) The most promising results have been achieved in treating conditions caused by single faulty genes. The replacement gene is introduced by means of a type of virus that acts as a vector. Vectors are incubated with cells taken from the patient so that the vector's DNA, into which the healthy gene has been inserted, is integrated into the patient's DNA. The patient's cells, now containing the healthy gene, are returned to his or her body. This technique has had some success in treating a type of severe immune deficiency. Another approach, which has been applied to the treatment of cystic fibrosis, is to insert the replacement genes, packaged in membranous sacs called liposomes, directly into the patient's body. Other diseases currently being investigated as candidates for gene thrapy include muscular dystrophy, certain cancers, and haemophilia.

Since many disorders involve complex interactions of a number of genes, and our understanding of these is imperfect, gene therapy has as yet very limited practical use in clinical medicine. However, it is hoped that knowledge about human genes and genetic processes revealed by the Human Genome Project will in time play a major role in the prevention and cure of many common diseases.

• **genetic code**▶ The means by which genetic information stored in the molecular structure of DNA is used for constructing proteins (the bases of living matter). This information, which determines the genetic characteristic of each individual, is transferred to messenger RNA (mRNA). The basic unit of the code (called a **codon**) consists of a group of three particular chemicals (called bases); it is the sequence of these codons in mRNA that forms the genetic code. There are four bases present in mRNA, therefore 64 codons are possible from a combination of these bases. Proteins are made up of chains of chemicals called amino acids, each of which is specified by a particular codon; different proteins have different sequences of amino acids in their chains. As the sequence of codons determines the sequence of amino acids in the protein, the genetic code directs which particular proteins are produced.

• **genetic counselling**▶ Guidance given to patients in whose families there is a history of inherited disorders, such as cystic fibrosis, muscular dystrophy, and Huntington's disease. It includes discussing the possibilities that the patient may develop the disease, the likelihood of the children of such patients being affected, and any means of prevention and management of the disease.

• **genetic engineering**▶ A late 20th-century development of genetics that allows alteration of the genetic make-up of an organism. It typically involves inserting desirable genes from one species into the DNA of another species (usually a bacterium) via an agent called a 'cloning vector'. Multiple copies of the gene (**gene clones**) are formed

when the bacterium replicates itself. In this way, human genes that control the synthesis of useful substances, such as hormones (*e.g.* insulin), enzymes, and antibodies, can be cloned in bacterial hosts to enable large quantities of such substances to be produced. Genetic engineering can similarly be applied to economically important plants to improve crop yield, disease resistance, etc. (*see*: GM food). *See also*: clone; gene therapy; transgenic.

• **genetic fingerprinting** ▶ *See*: DNA fingerprinting.

• **genetic mother** ▶ The woman who produces the egg cell from which a baby develops; the term is used in cases of assisted reproduction, in which the egg cell, after *in vitro* fertilization (*see*: IVF), is implanted into another woman's womb. The woman who gives birth to the baby is then known as the **birth mother**; she is also the legal mother unless the baby is subsequently adopted by its genetic parents or a court order is made out in favour of them. Such differentiating terms became necessary in the late 20th century with the success of new techniques to combat infertility. *See also*: surrogate motherhood.

• **Geneva Agreements**▶ The settlement signed in Geneva in 1954 between the warring parties in Indochina, which was intended to end conflict between French and Viet Minh forces in Vietnam and to ensure the evacuation of communist troops and guerrillas from Laos and Cambodia. After difficult negotiations, which also involved representatives of America, the Soviet Union, the UK, and China, the agreements were signed in the early hours of 21 July, on the 'midnight or never' deadline set by the French. Chief among the provisions agreed was the establishment of a ceasefire line along the **17th Parallel**, dividing the country into the North under Viet Minh control and the South under Emperor Bao Dai, supported by the French. A timetable was drawn up for the relocation of troops and the holding of free elections in Laos, Cambodia, and all Vietnam. The agreements stressed that the ceasefire line 'should not in any way be interpreted as constituting a political or territorial boundary'. However, neither the major powers nor the South Vietnamese regime signed the agreements and this crucial flaw left the way open for America to pursue its own policy of bolstering a separate anticommunist state south of the 17th parallel. The free elections for all of Vietnam, envisaged in the Agreements, never took place, and America was destined for protracted and costly involvement in that country's affairs (*see*: Vietnam War).

• **Geneva Protocol** ▶ Protocol for the Pacific

Settlement of International Disputes. A procedure for resolving international conflict proposed to the League of Nations in 1924 jointly by the British prime minister, Ramsay MacDonald, and the French premier, Édouard Herriot. Essentially, all disputes were to be settled by compulsory arbitration by the League's Permanent Court of International Justice or by other League bodies. The Protocol received the unanimous endorsement of the League Assembly on 2 October. Shortly after, however, MacDonald's Labour government fell in a general election and was replaced by a Conservative administration under Stanley Baldwin; the new government reversed the UK's position on the Protocol, causing its eventual demise.

• **Genevieve** ▶ The 1904 Darracq vintage car that featured in Rank's 1953 film of that name. During the annual London to Brighton Run Genevieve's owner, played by John Gregson, bets his friend, played by Kenneth More, that he can beat him in a race back to Westminster Bridge in London. Genevieve herself is to be the prize for the winner. Highlights of the chaotic return journey include a scene in which More's girlfriend, played by Kay Kendal, somewhat unexpectedly plays a dazzling trumpet solo in a restaurant. The comedy was immensely popular and holds the British reissue record.

• **Genghis Khan** ▶
  **somewhere to the right of Genghis Khan** A phrase used to describe a person whose politics are extremely right wing. Genghis Khan (c.1162–1227) was the founder of the Mongol empire, a ruthless leader whose hordes ravaged, raped, and pillaged their way across central Asia.

• **genocide** ▶ A word invented by Professor Raphael Lemkin, of Duke University, and used in the drafting of the official indictment of war criminals in 1945. It is a combination of Greek *genos*, race; and Latin *caedere*, to kill. It is defined as acts intended to destroy, in whole or in part, national, ethical, racial, or religious groups, and in 1948 was declared by the United Nations General Assembly to be a crime in international law. *See*: ethnic cleansing; holocaust.

• **Gentleman's Agreement** ▶ An informal understanding reached in 1907 between America and Japan, restricting the flow of Japanese emigrants to America. Prior to this agreement, the influx of unskilled Japanese had created racial tension and incipient racial discrimination, particularly in California.

• **gentrification** ▶ The upgrading of town houses and flats, especially those situated in areas traditionally occupied by poorer families. Typically, it occurs in terraced houses originally built for workers and usually consists of knocking two ground-floor rooms together and adding modern kitchens and bathrooms, or radically improving existing ones. The word came into use in the 1970s, by which time the practice was well established. In London whole areas, such as Islington (*see*: Islington man), have been gentrified.

• **geodesic dome** ▶ A dome-shaped structure of metal, wood, or plastic based on octahedrons or tetrahedrons, devised by the US architect Richard Buckminster Fuller (1895–1983) in the 1950s to span large areas. The best known such dome, and the one that drew attention to its versatility was that which enclosed the US Pavilion at the World Fair in Montreal (1967). The largest has a diameter of 117 m (384 ft) and was the repair shop of the Union Tank Car Co., in Baton Rouge,

• **geopolitics** ▶ The name given to the German theories of applied political geography developed by Karl Haushofer in the 1920s and earlier by F. Ratzel, whose pupil (Rudolf Kjellen) coined the term. Sir Halford Mackinder (1861–1947) and others formulated similar theories. These teachings were used by the Nazis to support their demand for Lebensraum.

• **George** ▶ Nickname for the automatic pilot in an aircraft. It is possibly derived from the use of 'George', since World War I, as forces' slang for an airman, rather like Tommy is used for a soldier.

• **George Cross** ▶ The George Cross is second only to the Victoria Cross among British decorations. It consists of a plain silver cross with a medallion showing St George and the Dragon in the centre. The words 'For Gallantry' appear round the medallion, and in the angle of each limb of the cross is the royal cipher. It hangs from a dark blue ribbon. The George Cross was founded in 1940 for acts of conspicuous heroism, primarily by civilians. It is named after King George VI, the ruling monarch. It is only awarded to service personnel for acts of heroism not covered by existing military honours. The decoration has twice been awarded collectively – to the island of Malta in 1942 (*see*: George Cross Island) and to the Royal Ulster Constabulary in 1999.

  The **George Medal** (red ribbon with five narrow blue stripes) is awarded for similar but somewhat less outstanding acts of bravery.

• **George Cross Island** ▶ The Island of Malta, which was awarded the George Cross by King George VI in April 1942, in recognition of the steadfastness and fortitude of its people while under siege in World War II. It had suffered constant aerial attacks from Italian and German bombers.

• **George Raft** ▸ British rhyming slang for a draught (of cold air). George Raft (1895–1980) was a well-known US film star who specialized in gangster parts, having himself been a nightclub gigolo with underworld connections.

• **Georgian poets** ▸ A disparate group of poets associated by virtue of publication of their works in the anthology *Georgian Poetry*; the epithet is often extended to include any poets who wrote in a generally traditional style during the period 1912 to 1922, during which the five volumes of the anthology appeared. *Georgian Poetry* was edited by Sir Edward Marsh, a scholar and patron of English poetry; preparation of the first volume coincided with the accession of George V (1910), hence 'Georgian'. Beyond that, Marsh had a vague notion of some new poetic movement emerging to replace turn-of-the-century styles; he had in mind the works of Rupert Brooke, W. H. Davies, D. H. Lawrence, Walter de la Mare, John Masefield, and others, all of whom featured in the first volume. However, the idea of 'Georgianism' as a coherent movement is not tenable; the poets had little in common except a liking for rural themes and a quietly conservative style. With the advent of literary modernism the term came to acquire a pejorative sense.

• **geothermal energy** ▸ Subterranean heat energy that makes its way to the Earth's surface in the form of steam or hot water. It is harnessed directly, or by means of heat exchangers, to drive turbines to generate electricity. This form of inexhaustible natural energy is exploited in various areas in the world, particularly North and South America, Iceland, and New Zealand, where there are large numbers of geysers and thermal springs. The oldest geothermal installation is at Lardello in Tuscany, Italy, which began to exploit local steam geysers in 1818 and still supplies a series of power stations.

• **Gerbil** ▸ An acronym for the *Great Education Reform Bill* – a controversial education bill introduced in the UK by the secretary of state for education, Kenneth Baker, in 1988. Among its measures were the creation of a National Curriculum and transference of the financial management of state schools from the local authorities to the schools themselves (*see*: LMS).

• **Gestalt** ▸ A movement in psychology, which takes its name from the German word *Gestalt*, which approximates in English to 'form' or 'shape'. Essentially it considers psychological phenomena as wholes, rather than as combinations of separate components, each to be analysed individually. The movement emerged around the turn of the 20th century, but it was Max Wertheimer who first set out the principles of Gestalt in 1912. Working with Kurt Koffka and Wolfgang Köhler at Frankfurt University, Wertheimer cited certain phenomena of visual perception to emphasize that the neural organization and perceptual experience elicited by any set of stimuli are created together as a *Gestalt* or 'whole', and cannot be analysed as the summation of sensory elements. Wholes are configurations (*Gestalten*) of different parts, with each part defined by its role in the configuration. Just as the beauty of a melody cannot be perceived by analysing the individual notes, analysis of the components individually cannot reveal the nature of the Gestalt. Starting from this view of mental processes as dynamic wholes, the concepts of Gestalt were applied to other areas of psychology, including animal behaviour, child development and education, thinking, learning, and memory. Indeed, Gestalt principles penetrated to many other intellectual fields during the 20th century, notably sociology, politics, aesthetics, and economics. The Gestalt approach to psychotherapy seeks to restore a wholeness to the individual's inner world and relationship to his or her surroundings, drawing on other psychoanalytical techniques as appropriate.

• **Gestapo** ▸ Shortened from the German *Geheime Staatspolizei*, secret state police; the organization that acquired such sinister fame in Nazi Germany after 1933. Founded by Goering and later controlled by the SS under Himmler, it was responsible for terrorizing both the Germans and the peoples of occupied territories. It was declared a criminal organization by the Nuremberg Tribunal in 1946.

• **get a life!** ▸ A contemptuous remark aimed at someone who is considered boring, narrowminded, or obsessed with unimportant details; it implies that only a person with an unimaginably dull life could possibly care about the matter in question. Someone who dares to complain about a neighbour's party going on noisily into the small hours, or who presumes to correct someone else's grammar or spelling, for example, is now almost certain to be rebuked in this way.

• **get down** ▸ US slang meaning to get on with it, get down to business. During the 1970s it was often heard as an exhortation to a group of musicians or to people dancing in a disco.

• **get into bed with** ▸ **1.** Slang euphemism meaning to have sex with. **2.** Business slang meaning to work closely with, or to merge with. This sense has been widely used since the late 1970s.

• **get it on ▸** Slang euphemism meaning to have sex. Of US origin, the expression was first used in the 1960s and is still widespread in both America and the UK.

• **get it together** or **get one's act together ▸** Slang meaning to get oneself organized. Both phrases are widely used in both the UK and America. *See*: together.

• **get off** or **get off on ▸** Slang meaning to receive stimulation or excitement from. Originally to 'get off' meant to achieve orgasm; it was then adopted by drug users in the early 1970s, as in 'I really got off on the acid yesterday'. The expression was subsequently used more generally to describe any peak of experience, be it drug-induced, sexual, or whatever.

• **get one's leg over** or **get one's leg across ▸** Vulgar British slang meaning to have sex. It is used of men by speakers of either sex.

• **G5 ▸** *See*: Group of Five.

• **Ghan, The ▸** In Australia, a weekly train from Adelaide to Alice Springs. The construction of a railway line from Adelaide to the northern coast was begun in 1877 but got no further that Oodnadatta (472 km from Alice Springs). For about 40 years camel trains conducted by Afghans carried goods and passengers from Oodnadatta to Alice. When the railway reached Alice in 1929 the train came to be known as 'The Ghan', presumably because it replaced the Afghan camel train.

• **GHB ▸** Gamma-hydroxybutyrate (*or* sodium oxybate). A drug used medically in some parts of the world as a sedative before general anaethesia, but also recreationally, as it increases libido and reduces inhibitions; its street names include **GBH**, **liquid Ecstasy**, and **liquid X**. Adverse effects of GHB can include nausea, dizziness, muscle stiffening, convulsions, collapse, and coma. As a drug of abuse it is taken primarily in clubs, mainly in liquid form, but is also used by body builders because of its stimulating effect on growth hormone. The symptoms of confusion and memory loss that often accompany it have led to its more sinister use as a date-rape drug – hence another of its street names, **easy lay**.

• **ghettoblaster ▸** A portable stereo cassette player, especially one that is playing loudly while it is being carried. Such machines are particularly associated with Black musical forms such as rap, hence 'ghetto'. Other names include boogie box and (in the UK) Brixton briefcase.

• **ghost ▸** US slang for a person who is listed as being present at work although he is not. It is also used to refer to schoolchildren who are skipping school but who appear in the register as being present. In both circumstances illicit arrangements are made by someone who is present to cover the absence of the truant.

• **ghost in the machine ▸** A phrase used by the philosopher Gilbert Ryle (1900–76) in his *The Concept of Mind* (1949) to denigrate the Cartesian dualism in which the mind (ghost) is considered to be separate from the body (machine). It was subsequently used by Arthur Koestler (1902–83) as the title of his 1967 book in which he explored these ideas.

• **GI ▸** Informal term for a member of the US Army, also used as an adjective to describe army kit, duties, standards, etc. – as in 'GI blankets', 'GI haircut' – and as a verb – as in 'you'd better GI your whole goddam' kit, private'. The term was originally used by US Army clerks to mean galvanized iron, as in 'GI can' (at the time of World War I 'GI can' was also the nickname for a German shell, owing to a physical similarity between the two objects). The meaning of GI later changed to 'general issue' or 'government issue'. During World War II, US army servicemen were affectionately known, especially to the British, as **GI Joes** (*see also*: GI Jane).

• **GI bride ▸** A woman of non-US nationality who marries a US serviceman while he is on a foreign tour of duty. During World War II about 80,000 British women became GI brides and emigrated to America after the war.

• **Gibson Girl ▸** A type of elegant young woman characteristic of the period 1890–1910 in America, as depicted by Charles Dana Gibson (1867–1944) in several series of black-and-white drawings beginning in 1896. His delineations of the ideal American girl enjoyed an enormous vogue and the series entitled *The Adventures of Mr. Pipp*, which appeared in *Collier's Weekly* (1899), formed the basis of a successful play. The Gibson Girl was portrayed in various poses and occupations, her individuality accentuated by the sweeping skirts and large hats of the period. She was based on Gibson's wife Irene (neé Langhorne) and her sisters, among whom was Nancy, Viscountess Astor. *See also*: Gaiety Girl.

• **Gideons International ▸** An international Christian organization founded in America, best known for its self-imposed mission of giving Bibles to hospitals, hotels, and other places with short-term residents. The organization was conceived in 1898, when two commercial travellers, John H. Nicholson and Samuel E. Hill, found themselves sharing a room in a hotel in Wisconsin and discovered that they were both devoted Bible readers. The two men had the immediate idea of forming a missionary society for those travelling regularly on business. The Gideons took their name from the Old Testament warrior whose forces routed a much larger army of Midianites without a fight by blowing 300 trumpets and shouting the battlecry 'the sword of the Lord and of Gideon' (Judges 6–7). The objective of placing a Bible in every hotel room in America was first adopted in 1908. This later expanded to include hospitals, gaols, military bases, colleges, and anywhere else where people are housed overnight and may be prone to feelings of loneliness and despair. The society now has 140,000 members in 175 countries and claims to distribute 56 million Bibles or Testaments worldwide every year – surely a case of supply exceeding demand by some margin. Its work is supported by voluntary donations.

• **GIFT** ▸ Gamete intra-fallopian transfer. A technique that enables some infertile women to conceive without recourse to IVF. Eggs and sperm from the couple are introduced into one of the woman's Fallopian tubes, where fertilization can occur (the success rate is about 20%). The technique, which was developed in the 1980s, has proved more acceptable to some than IVF, because fertilization occurs within the woman's body.

• **gig** ▸ 1. A club or concert performance given by a jazz or rock band. Originally used by US jazz musicians in the 1930s, the term was adopted by rock musicians in the 1960s. Its origin is unknown. 2. Slang for any event or thing of interest. This is an extension of the first meaning and was part of the hippie jargon of the 1960s. It now sounds dated. 'That's not my gig' means I'm not interested in that.

• **gigabyte** ▸ See: megabyte.

• **gigglestick** ▸ 1. Slang for a joint, a marijuana cigarette. This name reflects a typical effect of such a cigarette and was used mainly by middle-class drug users (rather than heavy drug abusers) in the 1970s. 2. Rhyming slang for prick, penis. It may also allude to the swizzlestick used to stir gigglewater.

• **gigglewater** ▸ Slang for champagne (or sometimes alcoholic spirits), so called because of the effect it can have.

• **gigo** ▸ See: garbage in, garbage out.

• **GI Jane** ▸ A nickname given in the 1980s to US army servicewomen, who at that time became eligible for all army roles except front-line combat. The term is a feminized version of 'GI Joe' (see: GI; Joe), 'jane' being US slang for a woman. The 1997 film GI Jane starred Demi Moore as a woman trying to succeed in the US military.

• **gimmick** ▸ Originally a US slang word to describe some device by which a conjurer or fairground showman worked his trick. In later usage it applied to some distinctive quirk or trick associated with a film or radio star. Its meaning has now extended to include anything designed to attract attention, publicity, or trade. Its origin is unknown.

• **ginger** ▸ British rhyming slang for a male homosexual, from gingerbeer, a queer. This expression dates from the 1930s and is now rarely heard.

• **Giovinezza, La** ▸ The official anthem of Italy's Fascist Party. As written by Giuseppe Blanc in 1909 it was originally entitled Commiato (Farewell), in which form it was adopted by Turin University. In 1926 Blanc reissued the song with words by Salvatore Gotta, under the title Giovinezza. This followed a legal battle to stop the circulation of a plagiarized version of his original, published in 1918 by Marcello Manni.

• **Gipper, the** ▸ Nickname for the American footballer George Gipp (1895–1920) and later Ronald Reagan, who once played Gipp in a biopic during his acting days. Gipp died of pneumonia at the height of his brilliant career with Notre Dame. On his deathbed he told the team's famous coach, Knute Rockne:

> Someday, when things look real tough for Notre Dame, ask the boys to go out there and win one for the Gipper.

Rockne invoked Gipp's deathbed request in 1928, before a game with Army, which Notre Dame won 12–6. The next day the New York Daily News headlined its report 'Gipp's Ghost Beats Army' and the phrase **win one for the Gipper** entered the American language. The line was spoken by Reagan, as Gipp, in the 1940 film Knute Rockne – All American. He later made frequent use of it during his political campaigns and became widely known as 'the Gipper' himself. See also: Great Communicator.

• **gippy tummy** ▸ See Montezuma's revenge.

• **Gipsy Moth IV** ▸ The 53-ft yacht in which Sir Francis Chichester (1901–72) made his solo voyage around the world in 1966–67. Chichester took the name of his boats from the Gipsy Moth biplane in which he made a solo flight from the UK to Australia in 1929. The yacht was designed specially for fast solo ocean racing. Both the yacht and her owner featured on a commemorative 1s 9d stamp issued in August 1967, the first British stamp to celebrate a living person other than the sovereign.

• **girl** ▶

**What's a nice girl like you doing in a place like this?** A chat-up line now so cliched that no-one would think of using it except as a joke. It is similar, in that sense, to 'Do you come here often?' Both were well-used lines in films and probably originated in Hollywood in the 1930s.

• **girlcott** ▶ A feminist reworking of 'boycott', which was used seriously as well as humorously in the 1980s to mean a ban agreed among a number of women.

• **Girl Guides** ▶ The feminine counterpart to Boy Scouts, organized in 1910 by General Baden-Powell and his sister Agnes. Their training and organization is essentially the same as the Scouts and is based on similar promises and laws. The three sections of the movement were called Brownies, Guides, and Rangers, but the names and groupings have now been modified to Brownie Guides (7–11 years); Guides (10–16 years); Ranger Guides (14–19 years). The Guides Association dropped the word 'Girl' from its title in 1992 but intends to remain single sex. In America, Guides are called **Girl Scouts**.

• **Girl in the Red Velvet Swing** ▶ The nickname of Evelyn Nesbit (1885–1967), a US dancer, Gibson Girl, and actress. A notorious beauty, she married an excitable industrialist, Harry K. Thaw, who accused Stanford White (1853–1906), a partner in the largest and most prestigious firm of US architects, McKim, Mead, and White, of having an affair with his wife. The argument flared into one of the most widely discussed dramas of 1906 when Thaw shot and killed White in Madison Square Garden – a New York sports stadium that White had himself designed. At the subsequent trial Thaw was found guilty but insane. The 1955 film, *The Girl in the Red Velvet Swing*, featuring Joan Collins as Miss Nesbit, was described by one critic as 'a longwinded piece of lush sensationalism'.

• **giro** ▶ A system for transferring money to people who do not have bank accounts; it originated in Austria in 1883. The word derives ultimately from Greek *guros*, circuit. In 1968 the British Post Office set up the National Girobank (now Girobank plc), used by the Department of Social Security to pay benefits. For this reason a payment of social-security benefits is often known as a giro (short for giro cheque). Being **on the giro** means being on the dole (receiving unemployment benefit). In the 1990s New Age Travellers were sometimes known as

**giro gypsies** because of their dependence on state benefits.

The **Bank Giro** is a giro system used by banks in the UK to enable customers to make payment from their accounts to anyone, whether or not they have a bank account. This is independent of Girobank.

• **gismo** or **gizmo** ▶ Slang for a thing, object, mechanical item, generally used when the correct name is unknown or has been temporarily forgotten. Originally a US forces word, it has been used in the UK since the 1960s.

• **Give 'em Hell Harry** ▶ One of the many names by which President Harry S. Truman (1884–1972) was known. He was also called **High-Tax Harry**. Truman goes down in history as the man who ordered the first atomic weapon to be used in war and the man who, lacking a second name, assumed the initial S (which doesn't stand for anything). He earned the epithet Give 'em Hell Harry during his campaign for re-election, when he told his running mate, Alben Barkly, 'I'm going to fight hard. I'm going to give 'em hell'. He served a second term!

• **give head** ▶ US vulgar slang of the 1950s and 1960s meaning to perform fellatio. It is sometimes also used of cunnilingus.

• **gi'z a job, I could do that** ▶ A catchphrase from the 1982 TV series *The Boys from the Blackstuff*, written by Alan Bleasdale. It was spoken repeatedly by the character Yosser Hughes in his tragicomic search for a job in Liverpool, an area of high unemployment; it gained popularity nationwide at a time when unemployment was rising.

• **glam** ▶ Greying, leisured, affluent, married. One of the many voguish lifestyle acronyms popular in the 1980s, coined by analogy with yuppie. Glams were considered a most important socio-economic group as a result of their economic stability and spending power. *See also*: grey population.

• **glam rock** or **glitter rock** ▶ A style of pop music that dominated the British singles charts in the early 1970s. Performers of glam rock, who wore garish androgynous clothes, face make-up, and vertiginous platform soles, included Marc Bolan, David Bowie, Gary Glitter, and Alvin Stardust.

• **Glasgow kiss** ▶ British slang for a headbutt, owing to Glasgow's reputation for being a violent place. Also known as a **Gorbals kiss**, the Gorbals being reputedly the most violent part of Glasgow (largely rebuilt in the 1980s).

• **glasnost** ▶ (Russian, openness) The policy of allowing greater freedom of information and expression and of making government more accountable, introduced from 1986 by Mikhail Gorbachov, general secretary of the Soviet Communist Party (1985–91). *Glasnost* and its complementary policy of *perestroika* (economic restructuring) were intended to operate within the existing framework of state socialism. In practice, *glasnost* encouraged reform movements throughout the communist bloc and stimulated nationalism in the constituent republics of the Soviet Union. The ultimate result was the collapse of communism in Eastern Europe, the disintegration of the Soviet Union, and the downfall of Gorbachov himself. *Glasnost* is now often used to mean any policy of openness or public accountability adopted by an organization, etc.

• **glass shot** ▶ A simple special effect used by film makers from about 1905. A background, such as a town, castle, seascape, etc., is painted on a glass slide, which is mounted in front of the camera in such a way that it blends with the live action when the scene is shot. A glass shot often saved enormous amounts of money that would otherwise have been spent on sets or location filming.

• **Glastonbury Festival** ▶ A music festival held (generally annually) on Worthy Farm at Pilton, near Glastonbury, Somerset. Taking place over a weekend in July, the event began in 1970 and is now the largest greenfield music and performing arts festival in the world. Despite such disincentives as the overflowing portaloos, overpriced inedible food, and, in some years, knee-deep mud, Glastonbury still attracts huge numbers of people and has become something of a national institution ‒ arguably as much part of the English social ‘season’ as Royal Ascot or Wimbledon. Although a product of the hippie era, Glastonbury has moved with the times and now provides dance tents alongside the more predictable ‘healing field’ for those seeking New Age remedies. Currently the festival extends over a 600-acre site and may involve 1000 performances over three days. The organizing company, headed by farmer Michael Eavis, gives most of any profits from the festival to charities, including Greenpeace and Oxfam. In recent years this has been thought to amount to around £500,000.

• **GLC** ▶ Greater London Council. Part of the two-tier administrative structure devised in 1963 to govern London ‒ the GLC (replacing the London County Council) formed one tier, while the 32 London borough councils formed the second tier. The GLC, however, was abolished in 1986 by the Conservative government as promised in their 1983 election manifesto. The GLC’s London-wide responsibilities for strategic planning, transport, housing, and other services were devolved to the borough coun-

cils, in an attempt to control local authority spending and rate increases. The abolition went ahead despite a popular campaign within the capital, mounted by the leader of the GLC, Ken Livingstone (*see*: Red Ken). In 2000 a two-tier administrative system for governing London was restored with the setting up of a **Greater London Assembly** (GLA) headed by a directly elected mayor (*see*: Mayor of London).

The building in which the GLC was housed (known as County Hall) was designed by Ralph Knott on a prestigious site on the South Bank of the river immediately to the E of Westminster Bridge. The main building was available for the London County Council in 1933 but the whole structure was not completed until 1963, when it became the home of the GLC.

• **Gleichschaltung** ▶ (German, co-ordination) The Nazi policy of integrating all aspects of German social economic life into their movement. For example, all trade unions were merged into a single body, the German Labour Front (*Deutsche Arbeitsfront*) in 1933. Various other fronts were created as part of this policy, including a German Milk Front and German Shoe Front.

• **glide path** ▶ The line of an aircraft’s descent to land. Few aircraft actually glide on their final approach to land, as it is safer to fly under power, which allows greater control over the aircraft. The pilot can assess whether he is flying on the correct glide path using simple radio beacons, checked against the aircraft altitude, or more elaborate instruments, such as the Instrument Landing System (ILS) using a pair of radio beams arranged across the glide path to register deviations on the cockpit ILS indicator. The ILS is essential when landing by instruments only. In modern aircraft the ILS is being replaced by an even more accurate system, the Microwave Landing System (MLS).

• **glitch** ▶ Slang for a technical hitch, a mechanical problem, especially with a computer. First heard in the aerospace industry in the late 1960s, it probably derived from a Yiddish word based on the German *glitschen*, to slip. It also has obvious echoes of the word ‘hitch’. In New York Yiddish, a glitch is a risky undertaking or a shady deal.

• **glitterati** ▶ A word coined in the 1980s by analogy with ‘literati’, a collective word for writers, scholars, and people interested in literature. ‘Glitterati’ is used to denote famous or fashionable people, especially members of the jet set. However, it is usually a derogatory epithet, the ‘glitter’ part of the word suggesting that the fame and glamour are flashy and superficial.

• **glitter rock** ▶ *See*: glam rock.

• **glitz** ▶ Slang for showbiz-style glamour, tacky sophistication. A combination of 'glamour' and ritzy, the word was much used by journalists in the 1980s to describe the style epitomized by the US TV soap Dallas.

• **globalization** ▶ The process by which the world economy has become dominated by large commercial organizations operating across national and geographical divides. During the 1980s and 1990s, rapid advances in communications and the growth in computer networks enabled the emergence of a truly global market in securities, commodities, and financial services. At the same time, many companies began to relocate their manufacturing away from their traditional home bases, opening plants in less developed countries to take advantage of cheaper labour and less stringent regulations. These changes have affected the ability of national governments to manage their own economic affairs. For instance, if faced with higher taxes or tougher environmental legislation, a multinational company will, it is argued, simply move its operation elsewhere, so creating unemployment by its departure. To its many critics – including the militant protestors who have made organized attempts to disrupt international summits such as those of the World Trade Organization and the Group of Eight – globalization is a pernicious process that intensifies the exploitation of the world's poor and threatens the whole planet with ecological doom. To its apologists, however, it is a powerful engine of wealth creation that will eventually benefit even the poorest countries (and is, in any case, quite unstoppable).

> Hobsbawn...describes how 'the globalization of the economy' has put all governments at the mercy of an uncontrollable 'world market'. This market does not like high taxes, high public spending, high labour costs or high inflation; it abhors nationalisation. Any country that defies it will lose capital and jobs. – *The Independent*, 9 October 1994.

• **global product** ▶ A product or service marketed throughout the world with the same brand name. Coca-Cola and McDonald's are typical examples. This practice is clearly an advantage from the point of view of advertising, although it cannot be used for all products. For example the Vauxhall Nova sold well in most European countries except Spain. The reason, it was discovered, is that in Spanish *nova* means 'no-go'.

• **global village** ▶ A term coined by the Canadian writer Marshall McLuhan (1911–81) in the late 1960s to denote the world looked upon as a relatively small community within which modern communication technology makes it possible for information of all kinds to be transmitted rapidly and easily. Air travel has also made most parts of the world accessible. *See*: McLuhanism.

• **global warming** ▶ *See*: greenhouse effect.

• **globocrat** ▶ A high-ranking official of an international organization, such as the World Health Organization or the United Nations. The word is a blend of 'global' and 'bureaucrat'. *See also*: Eurocrat.

• **Gloster Meteor** ▶ The first jet fighter to enter service with the RAF (in July 1944) and the only operational jet among Allied forces during World War II. Manufactured by the Gloster Aircraft Co., the twin-engined Meteor made its maiden flight on 5 March 1943. The Meteor F-3 was the mainstay RAF fighter in the late 1940s, followed by the Meteor F-8, introduced in 1950. Other variants included the T-7 trainer and the Armstrong-Whitworth Meteor night fighter. A world record speed of 975.67 kph (606.38 mph) was set by Group Captain H. J. Wilson piloting a Meteor F-4 in November 1945.

• **glue sniffing** ▶ The practice, indulged in by young people since the 1970s, of inhaling fumes from synthetic adhesives, cleaning fluids, aerosols, etc., to produce hallucinatory or other intoxicating effects. It is extremely dangerous because of the side effects caused. As a result many manufacturers of glues etc. have abandoned organic solvents for their products and reverted to slower-drying aqueous solutions. The more formal name is **solvent abuse**.

• **Glyndebourne** ▶ The country estate near Lewes, in Sussex, where the Glyndebourne Festival Theatre has staged operatic and musical performances since 1934. Glyndebourne remains a centre of operatic excellence, attracting world-class singers during its summer seasons. The theatre's founder John Christie (1882–1962) established it for his wife, the opera singer Audrey Mildmay (1900–53). The opera house was completely rebuilt in 1992–94. Provided the weather is fine, an evening at Glyndebourne is an expensive but memorable outing – the opera-goers wear evening dress and consume champagne picnics in the grounds during the long interval between acts.

• **G-man** ▶ US slang for an officer of the FBI. G stands in this case for government.

• **GM food** ▶ Any food derived from genetically modified organisms (GMOs), *i.e.* plants, animals, or other organisms whose genetic make-up has been altered by the techniques of genetic engineering. Such modification can change the way in which the organism's own genes function, or introduce novel genes from different, sometimes quite dissimilar, species (*see*: transgenic). GM crops underwent their first field trials in the mid 1980s, since when they have become a commercial reality in many countries, covering nearly 40 million hectares worldwide in 1999. The main GM crops are wheat, maize, cotton, soya, and canola (oilseed rape), grown chiefly in the USA, Canada, Argentina, China, and Australia. Consequently, GM flour, oil and other staple ingredients are now included in a wide range of human and animal foods. Genetic modification of crop plants can make them tolerant to herbicides, slow down ripening, or create inbuilt insect resistance. But the techniques of genetic engineering offer virtually limitless potential for modifying such characteristics as taste, colour, and nutritional quality, as well as yield and drought resistance – in effect affording the prospect of 'designer foods'.

Advocates argue that wider use of GM crops will boost production, providing food for a rapidly expanding human population, and improve the nutrition of the world's poor, who often depend on just a few staple foods. Critics contend that GM technology is still very new and requires stringent testing to assess any impact it may have on the environment. For example, they cite the possibility that pollen from GM crops might pollinate neighbouring wild plants, creating harmful 'superweeds'. There are also fears that genetic modification could contribute to the growing numbers of antibiotic-resistant bacteria, and that GM foods could produce unexpected allergic reactions in humans.

Consumers in some countries, particularly in Europe, remain wary of GM foods, and in Britain even small-scale trials of GM crops have led to fierce protests. The EU requires labelling of GM foods, so that shoppers or diners are allowed to choose between GM and non-GM food. But because GM ingredients are already so widely used in food manufacturing, it may now be virtually impossible to guarantee 100% 'GM-free' with many products.

• **GMT** ▶ *See*: Greenwich Mean Time.

• **Gnomes of Zürich** ▶ An uncomplimentary reference to the financiers of Zürich who control international monetary funds. Now seldom used, the phrase became popular after its use in November 1964 by George Brown (then the Labour minister of economic affairs) at the time of a sterling crisis.

> What most infuriated George Brown, and Labour MPs such as John Mendelson and Ian Mikardo...was that the men they disparaged as the 'gnomes of Zürich' were really giants.
> – T. R. FEHRENBACH: *The Gnomes of Zurich*.

• **goalposts** ▶
  **move the goalposts** A colloquial expression derived from football, meaning to change the conditions or rules attaching to some activity after it has already started. The implication is that to do so involves an attempt to gain some dishonest or unfair advantage.

• **gobbledygook** ▶ A term coined in 1944 by a US congressman, Maury Maverick, to denote the kind of long-winded jargon and virtually unintelligible language frequently used by bureaucrats and others in place of plain English. Some bureaucrats and minor officials think that their status will be enhanced if they use long words and an impenetrable syntax to conceal a simple instruction or observation. Lawyers often suffer from the same misapprehension. The word has its origins in the behaviour of turkeys, who strut about and gobble.

• **gobbling rods** ▶ Army slang from the Gulf War of 1991 for a soldier's knife, fork, and spoon.

• **gobsmacked** ▶ British slang for dumbstruck, or completely amazed, gaping in disbelief. Originally a Liverpudlian expression (in which 'gob' means mouth), it was taken up more widely in the late 1980s. In 1991 it was used by Chris Patten, the chairman of the Conservative Party, when told of a Labour Party comment on the Health Service. Its use by a senior member of the government provoked much press comment.

• **Gödel's proof** ▶ A proof in mathematical logic that a formal system of reasoning based on axioms, such as arithmetic, always contains statements that can neither be proved nor disproved. It was shown to be true in 1931 by the US mathematician Kurt Gödel (1906–78) and is known as **Gödel's first incompleteness theorem**. A further theorem, **Gödel's second incompleteness theorem**, states that it is impossible to prove the self-consistency of any formal logical system by using the formalization of the system itself. Gödel's proof effectively ended attempts by mathematicians to develop the whole of pure mathematics from a few basic logical axioms.

• **godfather** ▶ The head of a Mafia family, also called a **don** (ultimately from the Latin *dominus*, lord). The name was popularized by the best-selling novel *The Godfather* (1969) by Mario Puzo, which later (1972) became a hugely successful film with several sequels. The word has since been used to refer to the head of any criminal organization and, further, to any autocratic leader.

• **godfather offer** ▶ An offer made in a takeover bid for a company that is so high that, in spite of discouragement by the management of the target company, shareholders cannot resist accepting it. The name originates from the threatening use of the phrase 'make him an offer he can't refuse' (*see at*: refuse) by several mafiosi in the novel (1969) and film (1972) of *The Godfather*.

• **Godot**► *See*: Theatre of the Absurd.

• **go down**► **1.** US slang meaning to happen, a Black street expression that has been widely used since the late 1960s. 'What's going down, man?' means 'What's happening?'. **2.** Slang meaning to be sent to prison. 'Will he go down for that?' means 'Will he be sent to prison?'. This meaning is probably derived from the descent from the dock in the court room to the cells below. At the conclusion of a criminal trial, judges will sometimes instruct the warders to 'take him down' – 'him' being the prisoner who has just been sentenced.

• **go down on**► To perform fellatio or cunnilingus on.

• **God's gift**► A sarcastic way of referring to someone who has inflated ideas of their importance, ability, or sexual attractiveness; the idea is that such a person has obviously been sent by God to help lesser mortals achieve their ends. For example, 'She thinks she's God's gift to divorced men'.

• **Godslot**► A regular period of time set aside in radio or TV schedules for religious programming. *See also*: family hour.

• **God squad**► British slang, dating from the 1950s, for zealous members of religious organizations, especially those that do house-to-house visits attempting to convert people.

• **Godzilla**► A mythical prehistoric monster brought back to life by H-bomb tests who has featured in a long series of low-budget Japanese films, beginning with *Godzilla* (1954). With their primitive 'special' effects – Godzilla is quite clearly a man in a rubber suit – and inept dubbing the films have become a cult among lovers of truly dreadful movies. A big-budget Hollywood version, *Godzilla*, was released in 1998 but proved far less entertaining than the originals.

• **gofer**► Slang for a messenger or a junior assistant – someone whose job it is to 'go for' this and 'go for' that. It is also a pun on the small North American burrowing rodent, the gopher. The term originated in the US film industry but is now used in all English-speaking countries.

• **go for broke**► An expression of US origin encouraging one to invest everything, without exception, in one course of action. It is essentially a

gambling term inviting the punter to put all his money on one bet – if he succeeds he will have achieved a great coup, if he fails he will be broke.

• **go for it!**► An all-purpose exhortation that became popular in the 1980s, first in America and then in the UK. President Reagan exclaimed 'America, go for it!' in a 1985 speech on tax reform; British Airways used 'Go for it, America' as an advertising slogan (1986) to entice more Americans to visit Europe.

• **gogglebox**► British slang for a TV set. Coined in the 1950s, it was used pejoratively at first ('goggle' implying mindless watching) but later more neutrally. It is now rarely heard.

• **go-go**► Relating to a lively style of music and dancing associated with discos or nightclubs in the 1960s. A **go-go dancer** was a young man or woman employed to dance at such establishments. The term 'go-go' has been extended to describe anything lively, energetic, up-to-date, enterprising, or otherwise admirable. For example, **go-go funds** are unit trusts or other investments expected to produce high financial returns.

• **going**►
**when the going gets tough, the tough get going** A slogan said to have been coined by Joseph P. Kennedy (1888–1969), the father of President John F. Kennedy. It is an exhortation to respond to difficult situations with determined action. It was used as a tag-line for the adventure film *The Jewel of the Nile* in 1985; a hit song sung by Billy Ocean followed in 1986.

• **go-kart**► A small one-man racing vehicle propelled by a light engine. In earlier centuries a go-cart was a device for training toddlers to walk, which at the same time combined some of the features of a playpen. Introduced into England in the early 17th century, they consisted of a small framework on wheels or rollers splayed out at the base so that they could not be overturned. The top was usually in the form of a tray for containing toys with a circular opening in which the child could stand upright, and be held secure at waist height. Similar devices, now called **baby-walkers**, are still available.

• **Golan Heights**► A hilly area on the border between Syria and Israel, designated as a demilitarized buffer zone between the two countries in 1949; it was bitterly contested in subsequent Arab-Israeli conflicts (1956, 1967, and 1973). During the 1950s and 1960s Israeli settlements spread eastwards through the territory, which provoked constant armed clashes with Syria. In the 1967 War, over 100,000 Syrians fled when the Israeli army stormed the Heights. The Syrians succeeded in regaining some of the territory during the October 1973 War, with the remaining territory designated as a UN buffer zone by the Separation of Forces agreement of May 1974. However, this territory was annexed by Israel in 1982, in contravention of UN Resolution 242, and a number of Jewish settlements were established. Some commentators think that while Israel remains in occupation of the area, a lasting Middle East peace settlement will be difficult to conclude. However, from the Israeli point of view, it would be both tactically and strategically dangerous if the Syrians were allowed to occupy the high ground again, as before 1967 Syrian artillery made great use of the region to bombard the upper Jordan and Hula valleys.

• **Gold** ▶ Allied codename given to a beach NW of Bayeux, which was one of the landing sites for British and Canadian forces on D-Day. *See also*: Juno; Omaha; Sword; Utah.

• **gold-bricking** ▶ In World War II, a synonym for idling, shirking, or getting a comrade to do one's job. The term derived from 'gold brick', a US phrase meaning a swindle. This usage originated in the gold-rush days when a cheat would sell his dupe an alleged (or even a real) gold brick – in the latter case substituting a sham one before making his getaway.

• **gold card** ▶ A credit card that confers on those who hold it certain advantages and privileges not available to those in possession of ordinary credit cards. These privileges include generous overdraft facilities, but not advantageous rates of interest. The credit card companies are therefore likely to be the greatest beneficiaries from gold cards, which are only awarded to those who have high regular incomes. For this reason the gold card came to have a great snob value. In view of the cachet attached to it, the use of the term has extended beyond the credit card and became associated, for example, with travel facilities, sales offers, etc., when these are held to be of a superior nature. However, the prestige once associated with a gold card has now been somewhat eclipsed by the **platinum card**.

• **Golden Arrow** ▶ A fast train service between London Victoria and Paris, known across the Channel as the **Flèche d'Or**. It ceased to run in the late 1960s, by which time most of the traffic between the two capitals was carried by air. Since the advent of the Channel Tunnel and the Eurostar service between London and Paris or Brussels, air traffic has been considerably reduced in favour of the train.

• **Golden Foghorn** ▶ Nickname of Ethel Merman (1908–84), the US musical star, known for her ability to be heard in the next block. It was said of her that she could 'hold a note longer than the Chase Manhattan Bank', while the critic Ken Tynan once wrote that in her hands 'musical comedy became a martial art'.

• **Golden Gate Bridge** ▶ The suspension bridge, opened in 1937, that spans the Golden Gate waterway in San Francisco, California. The centre span stretches for 1280 m (4200 ft), for many years one of the world's longest single spans. Its orange-red towers and graceful lines have become a much-admired symbol of the city it serves. The bridge was designed to withstand 160 kph (100 mph) wind gusts, and swing up to 8.2 m (27 ft). The midway point, 79.2 m (260 ft) above water, is a favourite spot for suicides.

• **golden handcuffs** ▶ A large financial incentive paid to an employee, especially by a stockbroker, market maker, investment trust, etc., to persuade him or her not to be attracted away by an offer from a competitor. *See also*: golden hello.

• **golden handshake** ▶ A considerable terminal payment made to an individual, especially a business executive, whose services are prematurely dispensed with. *See also*: golden parachute.

The expression was previously applied to the final grants made to colonial dependencies on attaining their independence:

> This year promises to be an expensive one for the British taxpayer in 'golden handshakes'.
> – *The Times*, 1 June 1964.

In this sense the phrase was coined by Frederick Ellis (d. 1979), City editor of the *Daily Express*.

• **golden hello** ▶ A large financial incentive paid to a new employee, especially by a stockbroker, market maker, investment trust, etc., to attract him or her from a competitor. *See also*: golden handcuffs.

• **Golden Miller** ▶ One of the most famous steeplechasers in the history of British racing, renowned for winning both the Cheltenham Gold Cup and the Aintree Grand National in the same year (1934). Owned by the Honourable Dorothy Paget, the gelding accumulated an impressive tally of results, including five consecutive wins in the Cheltenham Gold Cup (1932–36). He was ridden to his Aintree victory by Gerry Wilson, in record time.

• **golden oldie** ▶ An old record, song, or piece of music that is either still popular or has been revived. The term was coined by disc jockeys in the 1960s. Older people, particularly those who join in the pursuits of the young, are themselves sometimes facetiously called 'golden oldies'.

• **golden palm** ▶ *See*: Palme d'Or.

• **golden parachute** ▶ A clause written into a contract of employment of a director or senior executive of a company that provides for large financial benefits if the executive is sacked or decides to leave as a result of a change in the ownership of the company. *See also*: golden handshake.

• **Golden Rose** ▶ The premier award of the annual competition for television light entertainment programmes held in Montreux, Switzerland. It is organized by the Swiss Broadcasting Corporation in conjunction with the European Broadcasting Union and the City of Montreux. Besides the Golden Rose, for the best over-all programme, Silver and Bronze Roses are awarded to the best entrants in various categories. Past British winners include *Frost Over England* (BBC, 1967); *Marty: The Best of the Comedy Machine* (ATV, 1972); *The Paul Daniels Magic Show* (BBC, 1985); *Nigel Kennedy: Four Seasons* (Zenith North and Picture Music International, 1990); *The League of Gentlemen* (BBC, 1999); and *Lenny Henry in Pieces* (BBC, 2001).

• **golden share** ▶ A share of the equity of a company that controls at least 51% of its voting rights. A golden share is often held by the government when a public company is privatized.

• **Golden Triangle** ▶ A roughly triangular area of SE Asia comprising parts of China, Myanmar (Burma), Thailand, and Laos in which opium poppies are grown. It is the source of most of the world's raw opium.

• **Goldfine affair** ▶ A US political scandal of 1958 in which a presidential assistant in the Eisenhower administration, Sherman Adams, allegedly exerted political influence in favour of his friend, the Boston industrialist Bernard Goldfine. Adams admitted receiving gifts from Goldfine, but denied putting pressure on federal agencies investigating Goldfine's affairs. In the face of mounting pressure, both from his own Republican Party and from the Democrats, Adams resigned in September. The scandal was a contributory factor in the Democrats' landslide victory in the national and state elections held two months later.

• **Goldfinger** ▶ The eponymous villain of the 1959 thriller by Ian Fleming. Goldfinger is a gold smuggler and banker for the dreaded criminal organization SMERSH, but his plan to rob America's Fort Knox of its gold is thwarted by British agent James Bond. In the 1964 film, Goldfinger was played by the German actor Gert Frobe, in one of the more convincing screen impersonations of a Bond villain. Fleming took the character's name from that of the Hungarian-born architect Ernö Goldfinger (1902–87).

• **goldfish bowl** ▶ Any situation in which a person is exposed to constant public scrutiny; like a goldfish in a bowl, one has nowhere to hide or even camouflage oneself. Celebrities, for example, often complain about having to live in a goldfish bowl in which their private lives are no longer private.

• **Goldfish Club** ▶ A notional 'club' for RAF pilots who were forced down in the sea during World War II. The **Goldfish Gang** was naval slang of the same period for the Fleet Air Arm.

• **Goldie** ▶ A golden eagle that captured British newspaper headlines in 1965 after it escaped from London Zoo. The seven-year old eagle spent nearly two weeks in the trees of Regent's Park, attracting many sightseers, before he was finally recaptured.

• **Gold Standard** ▶ A currency system based upon keeping the monetary unit at the value of a fixed weight of gold. Great Britain adopted the Gold Standard from 1821 but suspended gold payments in 1914, returned to the Gold Standard in 1925, and abandoned it in 1931 during the slump (*see*: Great Depression). Most countries of the world were on the Gold Standard from 1894 to 1914. Gold became the monetary standard of America by the Coinage Act of 1873 but the Gold Standard was abandoned in 1933.

• **Goldwater caper** ▶ The 1964 US presidential election campaign of Barry Goldwater, the Republican candidate. Goldwater's extremist right-wing platform was aimed at conservative voters in the South and Mid-West and alienated traditionally more liberal Republicans in the northern industrial centres. Goldwater was heavily defeated by Lyndon B. Johnson, split his own party, and came to be regarded by Republicans as an unmitigated disaster.

• **Goldwynisms** ▶ Malapropisms coined by Samuel Goldwyn (?1880–1974), the US film producer, who emigrated from Poland in 1895. Originally calling himself Sam Goldfish (his Polish name was unpronounceable), he obtained his first job in America as an apprentice glovemaker. By 1923 he was running his own film production company, firmly established as one of Hollywood's most powerful moguls. A non-native English speaker, he made eccentric use of his second language, perhaps not quite as naively as he pretended. 'Gentlemen, kindly include me out', 'Anyone who goes to a psychiatrist should have his head examined', 'A verbal contract isn't worth the paper it's written on', 'We have all passed a lot of water since then',

'In two words IM-POSSIBLE', and 'Directors are always biting the hand that lays the golden egg' are some of the fractured idioms attributed to him. Goldwyn appears to have been a mixture of shrewdness and absurdity. For example, when told that Radclyffe Hall's *The Well of Loneliness* was a controversial novel that would make a good film, he gave instructions that he wanted to buy the film rights. 'But you can't make that into a film', said his rights man, 'It's about lesbians'. 'That's not a problem', replied Goldwyn. 'Where he's got lesbians we'll use Austrians'. Goldwyn's showmanship was legendary:

> What we want is a story that starts with an earthquake and works its way up to a climax...

Was it subtlety or absurdity when he told the assembled press at the release of *The Best Years Of Our Lives* (1946):

> I don't care if it doesn't make a nickel, I just want every man, woman, and child in America to see it.

Lindsay Anderson said of him in 1974:

> Goldwyn is blessed with that divine confidence in the rightness (moral, aesthetic, commercial) of his own intuition – and that I suppose is the chief reason for his success.

• **gollum** ► In the game of Frisbee, a wild throw, *i.e.* one that is difficult to catch. Gollum is a rather troublesome character in J. R. R. Tolkein's books *The Hobbit* and *The Lord of the Rings*. *See*: hobbit; Lord of the Rings; Middle-earth.

• **go, man, go!** ► A catchphrase originating in US jazz clubs of the 1940s, when it was used as an exhortation to the musicians. As far back as the jazz band era of the 1920s and 1930s, to 'go' meant to 'really swing', but the catchphrase 'go, man, go' is associated more with the driving rhythms of bebop in the 1940s. It has been borrowed or adapted by many songwriters and others, including Carl Perkins in his 1956 rock 'n' roll standard, 'Blue Suede Shoes':

> Well it's one for the money, two for the show,
> three to get ready, now go cat go!
> But don't you step on my blue suede shoes.

Perhaps the most famous adaptation of the phrase is **Go, baby, go!** first used by the excited US broadcaster Walter Cronkite, at the launch of the rocket Apollo XI in 1969. Thereafter, it became a stock phrase at such events.

• **Gondwanaland** ► *See*: Pangaea.

• **gone to Lyonch** ► An advertising slogan used by the catering firm J. Lyons & Co. A combination of 'gone to lunch' and 'Lyons', it became a catchphrase of the 1930s.

• **gone with the wind** ► A phrase, meaning vanished without trace, that first appeared in a poem by Ernest Dowson (1867–1900), one of the Decadent English poets of the 1890s. Having fallen hopelessly in love with a 12-year-old Polish girl, Adelaide Foltinowicz, a waitress in her parents' Soho restaurant, he indulged in a fairly rumbustious round of wine and women after she had turned him down. She inspired his best-known poem, 'Num Sum Qualis Eram', better known as 'Cynara', which contains two famous lines:

> I have forgot much, Cynara! Gone with the
> wind.

and

> I have been faithful to thee, Cynara, in my
> fashion.

The latter has entered the language as a cynical joke, while the former achieved quite another sort of fame with the publication of Margaret Mitchell's epic *Gone With the Wind* in 1936. America's most widely read novel, it is a romance of the Civil War, set in Georgia. The book's chief characters, Scarlett O'Hara, Rhett Butler, and Ashley Wilkes, have entered US folklore. MGM's epic film (1939) of the same name starring Vivien Leigh, Clark Gable, and Leslie Howard, became one of Hollywood's greatest-ever money makers, in spite of Irving Thalberg's remark to his partner Louis B. Mayer:

> Forget it, Louis, no Civil War picture ever made a nickel.

• **gong** ► British slang for a medal or decoration, dating from the 1920s and probably suggested by the shape.

• **gonk** ► British slang for a stupid person; a contemptuous term dating from the 1960s, when Gonk was a tradename for a fat ugly egg-shaped doll, which was something of a fad at the time. 'Gonk' is also army slang for sleep, from 'conk out', to fall asleep.

• **go, no go** ► A phrase originating in the 1970s to denote the last stage of a space project at which the decision can be made to proceed with it or abort it. The expression later spread into the more general language meaning the point in any project or situation just before one commits oneself irrevocably to proceeding with it.

• **gonov** ► (From Hebrew *ganov*, thief) A Yiddish word for a crook, especially a business man who is dishonest, or one who overcharges. It was used in the UK as an underworld term for a thief or pickpocket in the 19th century, but later became New York slang for any kind of dishonest person.

• **gonzo** ► US slang for wild, eccentric, or bizzare. The word, which comes from the Italian *gonze* meaning simpleton, was introduced into English by the eccentric US journalist Hunter S. Thomson in his book *Fear and Loathing in Las Vegas* (1972). The phrase **gonzo journalism** is now often used for the type of journalism practised by Thompson, in which the writer concentrates on his own subjective impressions. The word was also popularized as the name of a strange character in the TV puppet series *The Muppets* (*see*: muppet).

• **good** ▶
**a good time was had by all** A phrase widely employed in a literal or ironic sense since the earlier 20th century. It was used by the poet Stevie Smith (1902–71) as the title of her first collection of verse, published in 1937. Bette Davis once described a rival starlet as 'the original good time had by all' (*c.* 1940).

• **good** ▶
**If you can't be good, be careful!** A catchphrase used as a valediction, generally with a distinct sexual innuendo. It is heard mostly in the UK but is also used in America. It frequently has a phrase tagged on the end, such as 'if you can't be careful, have fun', or 'name it after me'.

• **good** ▶
**you've never had it so good** A phrase used by the prime minister Harold Macmillan (later 1st Earl of Stockton; 1894–1986) in a speech at Bedford, 20 July 1957. Although he meant it as a warning that such prosperity would be difficult to maintain, it was taken out of context and used to damn him as a complacent man interested only in material comforts. As **you never had it so good** the phrase was already well known in America, having been used by the Democrats in the presidential election of 1952.

• **good field, no hit** ▶ A baseball phrase meaning a player who is a good fielder but no good at batting. It derives from a telegram sent in 1924 by a baseball coach, Miguel Gonzales, describing the Brooklyn Dodgers' player Moe Berg in these words. It was subsequently used for anyone proficient in one area but inexpert in another.

• **good for General Motors** ▶ A phrase that has become part of the common misquotation 'What's good for General Motors is good for America' – an ironic reference to the influence of big business on US political thought. In fact, what a US engineer, Charles E. Wilson (1890–1961), said in testimony before a Senate Armed Services Committee in January 1953, was:

> For many years I thought what was good for our country was good for General Motors, and vice versa.

• **Good Friday Agreement** ▶ An agreement signed on 10 April (Good Friday) 1998, proposing a settlement to the long-running conflict in Northern Ireland by establishing three new bodies: a Northern Ireland assembly with a power-sharing executive, a North–South ministerial council, and a British–Irish 'Council of the Isles'. The agreement was signed by the British and Irish governments and all the main Northern Ireland parties, including Sinn Féin. Conditions of the agreement included the release of paramilitary prisoners and the **decommissioning** of terrorist weapons, both to take place within a two-year period; by August 2000 all paramilitary prisoners had been released, but progress on the decommissioning issue remained excruciatingly slow. A referendum in May 1998 saw the agreement backed by 57.5% of the Northern Ireland electorate (71% of those who voted), and elections to the new assembly were held the following month. The assembly met for the first time in July and David Trimble (leader of the Ulster Unionists) was elected Northern Ireland's first minister. Subsequent progress proved far more difficult. Owing to disagreements over the decommissioning of IRA weapons, the executive, which was to include members of the Sinn Féin, was not established until December 1999. Lack of progress on the same issue then led the British government to suspend the new institutions in February 2000. In May 2000 the assembly and executive were re-established following a new offer from the IRA: international observers were to be allowed to inspect arms stockpiles and the IRA expressed a willingness to put its weapons 'beyond use'. However, some 15 months later no actual decommissioning had occurred, leading to a further crisis in the peace process. The IRA finally announced that it had put a quantity of weapons beyond use in October 2001.

• **good neighbour policy** ▶ A US policy of the 1930s intended to allay the fears of South American countries that America was bent on dominating the whole American continent. Its measures – withdrawal of armed forces, removal of trade barriers, and a common defence policy – were foreshadowed by President Franklin D. Roosevelt in his first inaugural address of 1933:

> In the field of world policy; I would dedicate this nation to the policy of the good neighbor.

• **Good News Bible** ▶ A new translation of the Bible published by the American Bible Society in 1976. 'Good News' is a literal translation of the word 'gospel' (Old English *godspell*, from *god* meaning 'good' and *spell* meaning 'message').

• **good night, children everywhere** ▶ The catchphrase of Uncle Mac (Derek McCulloch) on the

BBC radio programme *Children's Hour* during World War II. It was meant to include all the children who had been evacuated to the safety of the country. J. B. Priestley wrote a play with this title during the war, and Vera Lynn recorded a song with the same title in 1939.

• **Goodtime George** ▶ George Melly (1926– ), British jazz singer and writer. An expansive bon viveur usually seen in a broad-brimmed black trilby, Melly has made it clear that his omnivorous appetites (gastronomical, alcoholic, and sexual) know no bounds. He sings John Chilton's song, 'Good-time George', with evident relish.

• **good to the last drop** ▶ A US advertising slogan for Maxwell House coffee, which dates from 1907. The story goes that President Theodore Roosevelt was visiting Joel Cheek of the Maxwell House Company. Having accepted a cup of the company's product, he drank it down, smacked his lips, and proclaimed 'Good to the last drop'. With this recommendation the company had little option but to adopt it as their slogan.

• **gook** ▶ US slang for a North Vietnamese, dating from the Vietnam War. It derived from the Filipino word *gugu* (spirit). *See also*: dink.

• **goon** ▶ **1.** Slang for a stupid person, or someone who plays the fool. The word became popular in 1950s Britain with the rise to fame of the radio programme the Goon Show; it derives from the English dialect word 'gooney', meaning fool. 'Alice the Goon' was a US cartoon character created by E. C. Segar (1894–1938). **2.** US slang for a hired thug, usually of low intelligence, whose job it is to intimidate people. Often heard in the phrase **goon squad**, meaning an organized group of such thugs.

• **Goonhilly** ▶ The downs on Cornwall's Lizard peninsula where the UK's first satellite earth station was opened in 1962. Now operated by British Telecom, the station's array of dish aerials transmits and receives telephone calls, facsimiles, television pictures, and other data to and from communications satellites in space. The plateau at Goonhilly was chosen to give a good 'view' of the early satellites, such as Telstar, and because of the firm foundation of bed rock underneath. It was the first European station to transmit colour TV signals and the first to transmit a live TV programme from Europe to America.

• **Goon Show** ▶ An extremely popular British comedy radio show broadcast by the BBC from 1952 to 1960 (with an extra show in 1972). It has been repeated frequently, having become something of a cult. The Goons were Peter Sellers, Harry Secombe,

and Spike Milligan (1918–2002), who also wrote the surreal scripts; the early programmes also included Michael Bentine. The show featured a regular cast of strange characters with peculiar voices (notably Bluebottle, Bloodnok, Eccles, and the Crums) involved in crazy little sequences that owed much to the music-hall tradition. The programme gave rise to many catchphrases including: 'the dreaded lergy', 'it's all in the mind', 'you dirty rotten swine, you', and 'I don't like this game'.

• **Goose Green** ▶ A settlement in the Falkland Islands, which in May 1982 was the scene of fierce fighting during the British assault on the Argentinian occupying forces. Seventeen British paratroopers, including their commanding officer, died there before victory was secured against the defenders, who outnumbered them three to one. The Argentinians lost 250 dead and 1200 were taken prisoner. *See*: Falklands Conflict.

• **goose-step** ▶ A military step in which the legs are moved from the hips, the knees being kept rigid while each leg is swung as high as possible. (It was introduced as a form of recruit drill in the British army but never became popular; it exists in a modified form in the slow march.) The goose-step (*Stechschritt*) was first introduced as a full-dress and processional march in the German army in the time of Frederick the Great. When the Axis flourished it was also adopted by the Italian army (*il passo romano*). Many news films of the 1930s show both Hitler and Mussolini taking the salute at parades of their goose-stepping armies – a spectacle at once frightening and ridiculous. It continued to be used after World War II by armies of the communist bloc; East Germany dropped it shortly before the reunification of Germany in 1990.

• **Gorbals kiss** ▶ *See*: Glasgow kiss.

• **Gorbymania** ▶ Public adulation of the Soviet leader Mikhail Gorbachov (1913– ; general secretary 1985–91) in the West during his international visits in the late 1980s. Although fostered by the Western press, which nicknamed him **Gorby**, his popularity originated from his policy of domestic reform and his role in bringing the Cold War to an end. *See*: glasnost; perestroika.

• **Gordon Bennett** ▶ A mild expletive, equivalent to saying 'Oh Gawd'; indeed 'God and St Bennet' has been suggested as the derivation of the phrase. However, it seems more likely that the Gordon Bennett in question was an American, James Gordon Bennett (1841–1918), the editor-in-chief of the *New York Herald*, who was responsible for sending Henry Stanley to find David Livingstone in Africa (he was the son of the paper's founder who had the same name). The son also gave his name to a motor race held in the early 1900s in France, where he resided as an exile after a scandal in America. He lived in flamboyant style and is described in the *Dictionary of American Biography* as 'one of the most picturesque figures of two continents'. There is a street named Avenue Gordon-Bennett in Paris. Clearly this extrovert and extravagant man's name was well known; it is therefore not unlikely that the similarity in sound between 'Gordon' and 'Oh Gawd' provided a convenient euphemism in an age in which blasphemy, however mild, was socially unacceptable.

• **Gordonstoun School** ► A UK public school founded in 1934 at Gordonstoun House on the Moray Firth near Elgin, Morayshire. Its founder was a refugee from Nazi Germany, educationalist Kurt Hahn (1886–1974), who regarded education as a process of all-round character development, with emphasis on exploring an individual's physical and spiritual resources as well as academic pursuits. As Gordonstoun's headmaster until his retirement in 1953, Hahn encouraged pupils to pit their wits against mountain, loch, and sea in the belief that 'there is always more to us than we think'. Hahn's ideas were inspirational to the Outward Bound Trust, which started in 1945. Gordonstoun first admitted girls in 1972, and they now account for almost half the intake to the school, which has some 475 pupils in total. Fees are on a sliding scale according to parents' means – another of Hahn's principles – and the school offers a large number of scholarships and bursaries. Illustrious former pupils include the Duke of Edinburgh, who loved it, and the Prince of Wales, who hated it.

• **gorilla** ► Slang term for a sum of £1000. It was coined in the 1980s by analogy with 'monkey', a racing term for £500 that dates from the 19th century – gorillas being larger than monkeys.

• **Gormenghast** ► The huge decaying castle that provides the backdrop to the *Gormenghast* trilogy of novels by Mervyn Peake (1911–68); *Titus Groan* (1946) was followed by *Gormenghast* (1950) and *Titus Alone* (1959). The trilogy is an elaborately detailed gothic fantasy, evoking an enclosed world peopled with fantastical characters, the central figure being Titus, 77th Earl of Groan, heir to the labyrinthine Gormenghast castle. The books received relatively little critical notice or popular success until the 1960s and 1970s, when a vogue for lengthy fantasy works brought them considerable popular appeal, especially among students. They enjoyed a revival of interest in 2000, when the first two books were adapted as a BBC television serial.

• **go-slow** ► The deliberate slowing down of work or production by employees engaged in an industrial dispute. In Canada and America the term is **slowdown**. *See also*: industrial action.

• **Gosplan** ► Acronym for *Gosudarstvenny Planovyy Komitet*, the State Planning Committee of the former Soviet Union, established in 1921. In 1927 it was given the job of formulating the first of the Five-Year Plans for Soviet economic development. This was delivered in 1929, after Stalin had purged Gosplan of its more cautious members in order to obtain a more optimistic projection. The committee continued to function at the apex of the Soviet economic planning system, its strictures affecting all reaches of Soviet industry and its decisions being implemented through industry ministries.

• **gotcha!** ► The notorious front page headline in the earliest editions of the *Sun* newspaper of 4 May 1982, celebrating the sinking of the Argentine cruiser *General Belgrano* by the British submarine HMS *Conqueror* during the Falklands Conflict. Of a crew of 1093, 323 were killed. On the same day, the Argentinians managed to destroy HMS *Sheffield*, which somewhat dampened the exaltation of war that overtook the British tabloid press.

• **goth** ► A young person, of either sex, belonging to a particular subculture that originated in the late 1980s; they are identified by their taste for doomy rock music and dark clothes and frequently dye their hair black. Both sexes wear large pieces of silver jewellery; the girls use cosmetics to make their faces very pale, their eyes very black, and their lips very dark. The word is a shortened form of 'Gothic' and reflects their gloomy melodramatic appearance.

• **Gotha** ► Any of several German military aircraft of World War I built by Gothaer Waggonfabrik, notably the Gotha IV and V long-range bombers, which carried out daylight bombing raids on London in 1917. The Gotha G I, a twin-engined bomber originated by Oskar Ursinus, began production in 1915, but was succeeded by the more powerful G II and G III models in 1916. These carried a three-man crew, defensive guns fore and aft, and a payload of 14 10-kg bombs. The G IV, which appeared in 1917, had a fuselage with a wooden rather than a cloth skin, and a gallery along the fuselage connecting the rear gunner's position to the cockpit. On 25 May 1917 a squadron of 16 G IVs left Belgium for a bombing mission over London. As darkness fell they missed their target and instead released their bombs over Shornecliffe Camp in Essex, causing 100 casualties among Canadian troops stationed there. The first successful raid on London took place on 13 June 1917, when the Gothas' bombs killed 104 people in the vicinity of Liverpool Street Station. Successful air defences soon forced the Gothas to fly at night and, in the face of heavy losses, their raids ceased in May 1918.

• **go the full distance** ▸ Police and underworld expression meaning to be arrested, tried, and sent to prison. The expression comes from boxing jargon, meaning to fight to the end of the contest.

• **Government Communications Headquarters** ▸ See GCHQ.

• **government health warning** ▸ A phrase now used as a general warning, suggesting that the person, time, or activity concerned should be avoided. The phrase was used originally in 1971 in the UK on cigarette packets. 'Danger. H.M. Government health department's warning: cigarettes can seriously damage your health'. A similar notice had appeared on cigarette packets in America since 1965. The wording was strengthened when the links between cancer and other fatal diseases and smoking became irrefutable: 'Tobacco seriously damages health'.

• **government-inspected meat** ▸ US gay slang for a soldier, sailor, or airman regarded as a sexual object. It involves a play on GI, which is an abbreviation for 'government issue'.

• **goy** ▸ (From Hebrew *goy*, people) A Yiddish word for a non-Jew, a gentile. It is often, but not always, used pejoratively. The plural is *goyim* and the related adjective is *goyisher*.

• **GPU** ▸ *Gosudarstvennoye Politicheskoye Upravlenye* (State Political Administration). The Soviet state security organization, created out of the existing Bolshevik secret police, the Cheka, in 1922. Its function was to identify 'counter-revolutionaries' and monitor their activities. It was renamed **OGPU** (*Obedinennoye Gosudarstvennoye Politicheskoye Upravlenye*; United State Political Administration) in 1924 and became absorbed into the newly formed NKVD in 1934. *See also*: KGB.

• **Graceland** ▸ The two-storey mansion in Memphis, Tennessee, which was the home of singer Elvis Presley from 1957–1977. The house is now open to the public as a tourist attraction and averages about 2500 visitors every day. The tour includes visits to the singer's living room, music room, TV room, pool room, trophy room, jungle den, and automobile collection. *See*: Elvis the Pelvis.

• **Graf Spee** ▸ A German battlecruiser of the Mackensen class launched in 1917 but never completed for lack of resources. It was broken up in 1921–22. It should not be confused with the German pocket battleship *Admiral Graf Spee*, which saw action in World War II (*see*: Plate, Battle of the River).

• **Graf Zeppelin** ▸ One of the most famous airships of all time, the German LZ 127 Graf Zeppelin, launched at Friedrichshaven in 1928 (*see also*: zeppelin). This immense dirigible, 236.5 m (776 ft) long and roughly 30 m (100 ft) in diameter, was powered by five outboard engines and capable of cruising at 113 kph (70 mph) with a range of over 9650 km (6000 miles). Its maiden transatlantic crossing on 11 October 1928 was the first of 144 Atlantic crossings. The gondola suspended below the hydrogen-filled envelope contained accommodation for 20 passengers and included sleeping cabins, a lounge/dining room, and a galley. In 1929 the Graf made a round-the-world flight, travelling 31,000 miles in over 12 days, while in 1931 it was used for an aerial survey of the Arctic. During the 1930s passengers paid less than $1000 for the transatlantic round trip in the Graf, lured by the luxury and elegance of airship travel. The Graf was retired from service in 1937, and was stored in its hangar until 1940, when Goering ordered its destruction to provide valuable war materials. The name 'Graf Zeppelin' was also given to the LZ 130, an airship structurally identical to the ill-fated Hindenburg and launched in 1938. This never saw regular service and was scrapped, with its more illustrious forebear, in 1940.

• **Grammy** ▸ An award (a replica of a gold-plated gramophone record) presented annually by the US National Academy of Recording Arts and Sciences for particular achievement in the record industry. They are regarded as the US music industry's equivalent to the Oscars.

• **Grand Design** ▸ The title of a book, written by Joseph Kraft and published in 1962, that set out the Kennedy administration's view of a unified W Europe acting in economic and military alliance with America. This vision was rudely shaken by a speech made by de Gaulle early in 1963 when he made clear his anti-Americanism and his opposition to the UK's entry to the EEC.

• **Grandma Moses** ▸ Anna Mary Robertson Moses (1860–1961). A US primitive painter well known for her nostalgic depictions of rural life. Grandma Moses was born in Greenwich, New York State. From the age of 12 she worked on farms around her birthplace; in 1887 she married a dairy farmer and moved to Virginia. She began painting as a hobby, and after her husband's death in 1927, turned to embroidered pictures, although arthritis later restricted her to painting. Her talents were introduced to a wider audience thanks to New York art collector Louis Caldor, who noticed some of her works in a drugstore in Hoosick Falls, NY, in 1938. During the 1940s, by now well into her eighties, Moses painted some of her most memorable works, such as *Catching The Thanksgiving Turkey* and *Out For The Christmas Trees*. At 91 she began painting on ceramic tiles, a new medium for her, and her final paintings, *White Birches* and *Rainbow*, were done in her 101st year. She was regarded with great affection by fellow Americans; her 100th birthday, 7 September 1960, was proclaimed 'Grandma Moses Day' by New York's governor.

• **Grand Prix** ▶ (French, great prize) The various formula motor races held each year to decide the Driver's World Championship; the name usually refers to races for Formula One cars, the most powerful of several racing classes.

• **grand slam** ▶ **1.** The winning of all the major competitions or championships in a particular sport in a single season. The term usually refers to this achievement in rugby union, tennis, or golf. In rugby union a grand slam is winning all five games in the Six Nations Championship; in tennis it is winning the Wimbledon Singles championship, the Australian Open, French Open, and US Open; in golf it is winning the British and US Open tournaments, the US Masters tournament, and the US Professional Golfers' Association (PGA) tournament. **2. Grand Slam** The nickname for the heaviest conventional bomb ever used, dropped by the RAF during World War II. Measuring 7.74 m (24 ft) in length and weighing 9975 kg (22,000 lb), Grand Slam was carried by a specially modified Lancaster bomber of RAF Bomber Command 617 Squadron on 14 March 1945 (*see*: Dambusters). Dropped from about 3660 m (12,000 ft), it scored a direct hit on its target, the Bielefeld Railway Viaduct, Germany.

• **grand unified theory** ▶ (GUT) *See*: unified-field theory.

• **granite-wash** ▶ Cloth, especially blue denim, that has a pale streaking appearance. This effect is deliberately created to make articles made of the cloth look fashionably faded and worn, as though they had been washed against rough stones.

• **granny bond** ▶ Formerly, a British index-linked savings bond that was only available to savers who were over retirement age.

• **granny farm** ▶ A residential care home for the elderly, particularly one that charges very high rates but provides poor care and services. The term became popular in the second half of the 1980s when many unscrupulous people were taking advantage of the rapidly growing numbers of elderly people in need of care as a result of the decline of the extended family. Traditionally, old people who could no longer care for themselves were taken into their children's homes. With the greater mobility of people and families this practice became less practicable and many old people have no option but to seek help in residential homes. Because women tend to outlive men they represent the greater proportion of residents of such 'granny farms'. *See also*: eventide home; granny flat.

• **granny flat** ▶ A self-contained flat in, or built onto, a house that is suitable for an elderly parent or other relative. It often provides a successful arrangement, with the elderly person achieving a measure of independence within easy reach of their relatives should help be required, while at the same time being available for baby-sitting, etc.

• **Grantchester** ▶ This village, two miles south of Cambridge, has a fine old church and an idyllic riverside setting but it owes its fame to its associations with Rupert Brooke (1887–1915), who lived at the Old Vicarage. An extremely romantic figure, whose World War I poetry made him a national hero (*see*: war poets), he died before seeing active service (*see at*: England).

> But Grantchester! ah, Grantchester,
> There's peace and holy quiet there.
> – RUPERT BROOKE: 'The Old Vicarage,
> Grantchester'.

The Old Vicarage is now owned by the disgraced politician and novelist Jeffrey Archer.

• **grape** ▶
  **Beulah, peel me a grape** A quotation from the 1933 US film, *I'm No Angel*, starring Mae West. The line, delivered by West to her Black maid with an air of insouciance after her lover has just walked out, was intended to indicate her emotional self-sufficiency; it is often quoted for this reason.

• **grass** ▶ **1.** Slang for the dried leaves and flowers of the cannabis plant or hemp. *See also*: hash; pot. **2.** In criminal slang, to inform. It may derive from rhyming slang 'grasshopper' for copper. A **supergrass** is one who informs on a number of his associates.

• **gravlax** or **gravadlax** ▶ Dry-cured marinated salmon, a Scandinavian delicacy that is now widely available. The name comes from the Norwegian *grav*, to bury in a grave (because it is left to ferment in the marinade), and *laks* (or Swedish *lax*), salmon. *See also*: lox.

• **gravy train** ▶ A source of easy money that does not involve too much work. The expression is believed to have its origins in US railroad slang of the early 20th century, when it referred to an easy run that required very little work on the part of the train's crew.

• **graze** ▶ British slang from the late 1980s, meaning to consume snacks continuously, but in small quantities.

> I responded to an invitation to a 'light lunch' in a private house to find the excellent food – we grazed on the hoof as we talked – was served by a butler and three uniformed maids. – MRS D. MAY, correspondent in *The Times*, 28 December 1990.

• **grease** ▶ **1.** Slang for money. Originally from the early 20th-century criminal underworld, it was revived by the beatniks in the 1950s and early 1960s. It reflects the idea of money as a substance that makes things run more smoothly. By extension, to **grease the palm** of somebody means to bribe them with money. **2.** US slang from the 1970s meaning to kill, usually by shooting. This reflects the rather unpleasant idea of reducing someone to a pile of blubber. The word **crease** has been suggested as an alternative derivation. This is also a US euphemism meaning to kill, reflecting the idea of the victim crumpling up when shot.

• **greaser** ▶ **1.** British slang for a young motorcycle rider, usually one of a gang, who dresses in greasy black leathers with slicked-back hair and a generally untidy appearance. This was the contemptuous term used by the mods of their enemies, the rockers, in the 1960s. (*see*: mods and rockers). **2.** US offensive slang for someone of Hispanic or Mediterranean descent. This is a reference to the oily complexion they are supposed to have.

• **greasy spoon** ▶ **1.** Slang for a cheap café where most, if not all, of the food is fried in animal fat, making the atmosphere and the cutlery greasy. This expression originated in America in the 1930s but is now also widely used in the UK. **2.** In America, a restaurant serving oily food, especially a soul food restaurant.

• **Great Beast 666** ▶ A name adopted by the British occultist Aleister Crowley (1876–1947), who earned the epithet the **Wickedest Man in the World** for his practice of the black arts and his advocacy of drugs and satanic sexual rituals. He chose his name from the biblical symbol of antichrist:

> Let him that hath understanding count the number of the beast: for it is the number of a man: and his number is six hundred threescore and six. – Revelation, 13.

• **Great Car Race** ▶ An epic round-the-world car race that captured worldwide attention in 1908. It required competitors to traverse North America, cross the ice of the Bering Straits, travel through Siberia and E Europe, and complete the course in Paris. Six massive cars, three French, one German, one Italian, and one from America, set off from Times Square, cheered on their way by a crowd of 200,000, on 12 February 1908. Over the next 11 days the cars fought a desperate battle with the elements, with unmade roads, and with mechanical breakdown. Crews had to repair bridges, pull cars out of swamps, brave blizzards and snowdrifts, and fill ditches before they could proceed; when the Bering Straits proved to be unfrozen they were forced to resort to travelling by ship. France's *Moto-Bloc* was defeated by mud in Iowa; a second French car, *De Dion*, was too battered to go further than Vladivostock, while the third French car *Sizaire-Naudin* withdrew after losing its differential gear on a rock. The three remaining cars, the German *Protos*, the Italian *Zust*, and the US *Thomas Flyer*, all finished. *Protos* arrived first but the honours went to the *Thomas Flyer* after taking into account time penalties: it had covered a total distance of 12,116 miles at a rate of 108 miles a day. Perhaps the most significant achievement of the race, however, was that it proved the potential of the motor vehicle as the transport of the future.

• **Great Communicator** ▶ Nickname for the US statesman Ronald Reagan (1911–  ; president 1981–89); it originated from his skilful use of television to communicate with the US public. A less flattering epithet was the **Great Rondini**, alluding to the US escape artist Harry Houdini and to Ron's talent for extricating himself from difficult political situations.

A former Hollywood film actor, Reagan was also known as the Gipper, after a part he played in the 1940 film *Knute Rockne – All American*. In his autobiography, Reagan wrote that his family nickname was **Dutch**, from his father's comment after his birth:

> For such a little bit of a fat Dutchman, he makes a hell of a lot of noise...

• **Great Depression** ▶ The world economic crisis of the period 1929–35, triggered by the collapse of the US stock market in 1929 (the Wall Street Crash). The financial collapse ended the post-war economic boom of the 1920s, and plunged America and the other industrialized nations into an era of business failures, mass unemployment, poverty, and hardship. In America, President Franklin Roosevelt's New Deal reforms helped alleviate some of the worst economic and social effects of the depression. In

Germany the economic crisis precipitated the fall of the Weimar Republic and the rise of Hitler. World-wide recovery did not occur until World War II began.

• **Greater East Asia Co-Prosperity Sphere**► Japan's plan for a new political and economic order in SE Asia, drawn up in 1941. It envisaged concentrating industry in Japan, N China, and Manchuria, with other countries in the region supplying raw materials and forming part of the consumer market. By a combination of military conquests and political alliances the plan was embarked upon, but ultimately collapsed with Japan's defeat in World War II. It did, however, serve to fragment colonialism in the region and foster independence aspirations among such nations as Burma, Indonesia, and Netherlands East Indies.

• **Greater London Council**► See: GLC.

• **greatest**►

   **I am the greatest** A catchphrase frequently used by the US heavy-weight boxer Muhammad Ali (Cassius Clay; 1942–    ), who first became world champion in 1964. He apparently took to using the phrase after he had seen a wrestler named Gorgeous George promoting himself thus to great effect. See also: Float like a butterfly, sting like a bee.

• **Great Leap Forward**► A plan for radical economic and social reorganization in China, introduced in 1958, that was intended to transform the country into an industrialized society in the shortest possible time. The policy, which owed much to romantic Maoist notions of inspiring the peasants and harnessing their latent skills, sought to bypass the usual lengthy process of developing heavy industry and concentrate instead on labour-intensive small-scale industries and agriculture based on communes. Traditional customs and living patterns rapidly gave way to the new commune system throughout the country, but at the cost of major economic disruption. This was compounded by bad harvests and the withdrawal of Soviet technical advisers. By early 1960 the Great Leap Forward was being modified and the elements of individual incentive and land ownership reintroduced. The policy's failure continued to haunt the Chinese leadership: supporters blamed the problems on poor implementation by overzealous cadres plus bureaucratic ineptitude; opponents argued for a more conventional approach to industrialization.

• **Great Profile**► Nickname for the US film actor John Barrymore (1882–1942), reflecting his strikingly handsome face.

• **Great Rondini**► A nickname for President Ronald Reagan. See: Great Communicator.

• **Great Society**► The catchphrase used by US president Lyndon B. Johnson (see: LBJ) to describe his vision of US society, first outlined in a speech to the University of Michigan on 22 May 1964:

> The Great Society rests on abundance and liberty for all. It demands an end to poverty and racial injustice, to which we are totally committed in our time.

Johnson borrowed the phrase from the title of a 1914 book by economist Graham Wallas. In the 1964 presidential elections, the Johnson platform contained policies consistent with such social objectives, such as anti-poverty programmes, expanded social security schemes, and legislation to strengthen voting rights. He was returned in a landslide Democrat victory.

• **Great Terror**► See: Yezhovshchina.

• **Great Train Robbery**► A robbery by a well-organized gang that took place in the early hours of the morning of 8 August 1963, at Cheddington in Buckinghamshire, on the main line from London to N England. The gang stopped a mail train by changing a signal and escaped with mailbags containing over two and a half million pounds in cash. During the raid, the train driver, Jack Mills, suffered severe head injuries, which brought his career as a train driver to an end. At the time, the theft was the largest in British history. The media called it 'The Great Train Robbery', perhaps after the 1903 silent film of the same name. Most members of the gang were arrested and received long prison sentences, although one of them, Ronald Biggs, escaped from prison to Brazil, where he managed to avoid extradition until 2001, when (now terminally ill) he gave himself up to the British authorities. Of those that served their sentences, one, Charlie Wilson, died in suspicious circumstances in his villa in Marbella (Spain) and another, Buster Edwards, became a flower seller at Waterloo Station in London.

   If the robbers had dealt less viciously with the train driver, their audacity might have attracted greater public sympathy. As it is, although they have entered the mythology of the underworld, most people regard them as having got what they deserved.

• **Great War**► The war of 1914–18 was always so called until that of 1939–45, when the terms World War I or First World War largely replaced it, its successor becoming World War II or the second World War. Popular opinion of the time demanded that World War I should be the last major war – the 'war to end wars'. David Lloyd George was nearer the mark when he commented in 1916: 'This war, like the next war, is a war to end war'.

• **Great White Way** ▶ A once popular name for Broadway, the theatre district of New York City. It was inspired by the profusion of brilliant electric lighting in the area.

• **Greeks** ▶

**The Greeks Had a Word For It** The title of a play by the US poet and playwright Zoë Akins, first produced in 1929. The phrase was originally part of the dialogue but was retained only as the title of the final version. The word alluded to is ετερο (*hetero*, other, different), describing certain characters in the play with rather outlandish personalities; it is not a reference to their sexual proclivities. The phrase became popular in the 1930s, it was used to mean anything unusual or unconventional.

• **green** ▶ Describing those who are actively concerned with conserving the environment, preventing pollution, and avoiding ecological destruction; the word is also applied to issues, attitudes, etc., connected with protection of the environment. Originally regarded as eccentric or freakish, green politics spread widely in the 1980s with most countries in Europe having Green parties (whose members became known as **Greens**) and ultimately politicians of all parties claiming 'green' credentials.

• **green and blacks** ▶ Drug abusers' slang of the 1960s and 1970s for the tranquillizer Librium in capsule form. The capsules were half green and half black.

• **green audit** ▶ *See*: green labelling.

• **green belt** ▶ A stretch of country around a large urban area that has been scheduled for comparative preservation and in which building development is restricted. The concept was introduced in the 1930s to prevent conurbations from spreading uncontrollably. London's green belt was first established by the Green Belt Act of 1938.

• **Green Berets** ▶ The nickname for the US Army's Special Forces, a unit trained as specialists in unconventional warfare, such as guerrilla and undercover techniques. Named after their distinctive headgear, the Green Berets were formed in 1957 with the establishment of the Special Warfare School at Fort Bragg. Their strength was greatly increased during the 1960s in response to America's involvement in Indochina, where they were sent to advise anticommunist forces in counterinsurgency tactics and psychological warfare. Since then the Green Berets have been deployed in various parts of the world, notably Central America. Wearers of the Green Beret are trained not only in warfare but in languages, medicine, sanitation, communications, and other skills essential for liaising with indigenous forces. 'Green Berets' is also the nickname for the UK's Royal Marines, from whom most British commando units are drawn.

• **green card** ▶ **1.** In America, a green-coloured permit allowing foreign nationals to live and work in the country. **2.** In the UK, a green-coloured document issued by insurance companies to extend motor insurance to foreign countries.

• **Green Cross Code** ▶ A road safety code for children introduced by the UK Department of Transport during the 1970s. It is part of the Highway Code, which is aimed at all road users, whether on foot or in a vehicle. The Green Cross Code is valid for all pedestrians but is particularly relevant for children; it comprises 25 points describing the correct procedure for using various types of road crossing, getting on and off buses, etc.

• **greenfield site** ▶ A potential building site in the countryside or on the edge of a town that has never previously been built on. A **brownfield site**, by contrast, is one within an existing urban area; it may be wasteland of some kind or occupied by useless or derelict buildings that can be cleared away. In Britain, the ever-growing demand for private housing has led to fears that large areas of the countryside will be swallowed up unless sufficient brownfield sites can be found and reclaimed.

• **Green Goddess** ▶ **1.** The nickname for a green-coloured military fire tender first used in World War II. Green Goddesses have made subsequent appearances on British roads during Fire Service strikes and to supplement the Fire Service in emergencies. **2.** A cocktail containing crème de menthe.

• **Greenham Common** ▶ The site of a US Air Force base near Newbury, England, designated in 1981 as one of the sites for American Cruise missiles, which were installed in 1983. In September 1981 women anti-nuclear protesters set up a permanent Peace Camp outside the base; in the following years they maintained a constant vigil, harassing military convoys and breaching the perimeter fencing of the base in order to maintain public awareness of the threat from nuclear weapons. Many of the women were arrested and jailed, but the missiles were deployed on schedule in 1983. The camp remained in spite of declining public support for CND after the mid-1980s. The Cruise missiles were eventually removed in 1988–89 in accordance with the superpower arms-reduction talks in the mid-1980s.

The base closed in 1991, but the Peace Camp was not totally disbanded until 2000.

• **greenhouse effect►** An effect that occurs in the Earth's atmosphere as a result of which some of the energy of the Sun's radiation is retained by the Earth as heat, causing the temperature of the planet to rise (**global warming**). Light and ultra-violet radiation from the sun is transmitted through the Earth's atmosphere, absorbed by its surface, and re-radiated back into the atmosphere as infrared radiation. Some of this infrared radiation passes through the atmosphere back into space but some of it is absorbed by atmospheric gases, especially carbon dioxide ($CO_2$). The amount of the Sun's energy that is absorbed by the Earth's atmosphere in this way is directly related to the quantity of $CO_2$ in the atmosphere. Before the Industrial Revolution there were some 275 parts per million of $CO_2$ in the atmosphere; this has now increased to 350 ppm, causing a rise of about 1° in the average temperature of the Earth in the last 130 years. The increase in $CO_2$ in the atmosphere has two main causes, the burning of fossil fuels (about $25 \times 10^{12}$ kilograms of $CO_2$ are produced every year by burning coal, oil, and natural gas) and burning of wood in the process of deforestation (about $9 \times 10^{12}$ kg/yr of $CO_2$). Together these two causes account for 55% of global warming. The balance is provided by other so-called **greenhouse gases**, such as methane, oxides of nitrogen, etc., that are pumped into the atmosphere. The phenomenon, which is of great concern to scientists and environmentalists throughout the world, takes its name from the horticultural greenhouses in which a similar effect occurs. However, in the early 2000s there has arisen a school of thought that dismisses the whole concept. The sceptics believe that the small rise in global temperatures is not the beginning of a sustained rise but a manifestation of a natural variation. *See also*: ozone layer.

• **green labelling ►** The practice by manufacturers of labelling their products to persuade the buyer that the product will not damage the environment or that environmental damage does not result from its manufacture. Examples of green labelling are the designations of aerosols as 'ozone-friendly' (*see*: -friendly), the marking of packages as 'recycled paper' (*see*: recycling), and declarations that tinned tuna fish has been produced without endangering dolphins. Green labelling began in the late 1980s in response to the public's rising concern about green issues. Manufacturers and marketing people were quick to see that the protection of the environment could be a useful angle for selling their products. Environmental pressure groups have set up so-called **green audits** to investigate the validity of such claims.

• **green lung ►** A park or other green area in a large city. The 'lung' refers to the production of oxygen by plants.

• **greenmail►** The somewhat dubious practice of buying a large number of shares in a company on the open market and then selling them back to the company at a profit in return for a promise not to make a takeover bid for the company.

• **green money ►** *See*: CAP.

• **green monkey disease►** *See*: Marburg disease.

• **Greenpeace ►** A movement originating in Canada in 1971, aiming to persuade governments to change practices that threaten natural resources and the environment. It supports direct non-violent action and has gained wide attention by its efforts to protect whales and to prevent the killing of young seals. When acting against French nuclear tests in the South Pacific in 1985 their ship, *Rainbow Warrior*, was sunk by a French government saboteur. *See also*: Friends of the Earth.

• **green pound►** *See*: CAP.

• **greenroader►** A person who makes a hobby of driving cars or motorcycles along **green roads**. These are country roads and tracks that have not been metalled although at some time in the past they have been open to vehicles other than bicycles. The greenroaders can thus claim a precedent and drive along such roads, frequently at high speeds, even though they are now only used by walkers or cyclists.

• **Green Shield stamps►** *See*: trading stamps.

• **Greenshirt ►** A British supporter of the social credit movement established by Major Clifford Douglas in the 1920s; so named from the green uniform shirt adopted. Douglas's unorthodox economic programme, which aimed to eliminate concentrations of economic power by payment of 'social credits', found a growing number of adherents during the Great Depression. Because of its hostility to credit capitalism, which it denounced as 'usury', social credit became associated with fascism and anti-semitism in the UK (although Douglas himself did not support such views). Social credit enjoyed a more mainstream political success in Canada.

• **green stuff►** Slang for paper money. In America all bank notes are green. In the UK, £1 bank notes used to be green before they were phased out in the 1980s in favour of £1 coins.

• **green-wellie brigade ►** British slang for

upper-middle-class people who spend weekends in their second homes in the country, dressed in green Wellington boots and Barbour jackets in an attempt to look like country people.

• **Greenwich Mean Time** ▶ (GMT) The time at Greenwich, London, through which the 0° meridian passes. From 1884 until 1986 the standard times of different areas of the world were calculated using this meridian as the basis, every 15° of longitude representing one hour of time in advance or behind it. In 1986 this was replaced by **Coordinated Universal Time** (UTC), which is based on International Atomic Time and, unlike GMT, is independent of the place of observation.

• **gregory** ▶ British rhyming slang from the late 1980s for a cheque; it alludes to the US film star, Gregory Peck (1916–  ).

• **grem** or **gremmie** ▶ Australian slang for an inexperienced surfer. It is also British and Australian slang for an inexperienced skateboarder, first heard in the UK in the late 1970s. Both senses probably derive from gremlin.

• **gremlin** ▶ One of a tribe of imaginary gnomes or goblins humorously blamed by British airmen in World War II for everything that went wrong in an aircraft or an operation. The name was probably coined at the end of World War I or shortly afterwards; it was apparently in use on RAF stations in India and the Middle East in the 1930s. Its first known use in print occurred in *The Aeroplane* (10 April 1929). A common explanation is that a gremlin was the goblin that came out of a Fremlin's beer bottle (Fremlin being a brewer in Kent), although there are numerous other stories. In the film *Gremlins* (1984), small furry creatures called mogwais wreak havoc on everyone who comes into contact with them.

• **Gretna Green rail disaster** or **Quintinshill disaster** ▶ The UK's worst railway disaster, which happened on 22 May 1915 and resulted in 227 deaths. A southbound troop train, carrying members of 1/7 Royal Scots, collided with a stationary local train at Quintinshill near Gretna Green. 53 seconds later a northbound express ploughed into the wreckage, which promptly caught fire. Two other trains were also involved. The troop train was almost completely destroyed, its 194-m length being telescoped to 61 m in the first collision. Of the dead, 214 were passengers on the troop train. Two signalmen and the fireman of the local train were convicted of manslaughter.

• **grey** ▶ **1.** British colloquialism for a very conventional and conformist person: used in the 1960s, with slightly contemptuous overtones, by those who rejected the grey suits traditionally worn by professional men for more colourful clothes. A later synonym of the 1970s would be straight. Used adjectively, 'grey' had a new lease of life in the 1990s, with the election of the relatively obscure and notably uncharismatic John Major to replace Margaret Thatcher as prime minister.

> The Conservative Party happily reunited...to sing the praises of John Major, the grey man with glasses. – *The Independent*, 8 December 1990.

(*see also*: men in grey suits). **2.** US Black slang for a White man, usually used pejoratively.

• **grey area** ▶ Any ill-defined or ambiguous situation in which clear demarcations cannot easily be imposed. In morality, for example, there are many situations in which what is right and what is wrong cannot be distinguished with certainty – such a situation remains a grey area.

• **grey knight** ▶ *See*: white knight.

• **grey market** ▶ In World War II, a transaction regarded as a lesser breach of the rationing regulations than one on the black market.

• **Grey Panthers** ▶ Humorous name for members of a pressure group organized to promote the rights of retired and elderly people. The name alludes to the grey population and was formed by analogy with Black Panthers.

• **grey population** ▶ A population with an increasingly high proportion of elderly people compared to that of young people (obviously so described because elderly people tend to have grey hair). Grey populations are caused by successive falls in birth rates and higher expectation of life owing to improved medical care and nutrition. Their increasing importance in terms of spending power and political influence is reflected in such phrases as **grey power** and the **grey vote**. *See also*: glam.

> If Mr Brown's promises [on pensions] are not kept, the grey army will not easily be silenced. – ANNE ASHWORTH, *The Times*, 9 November 2000.

• **gridlock** ▶ A multiple traffic jam that occurs in urban areas in which the streets form a grid or grid-like pattern. It occurs when a traffic queue on one street blocks one or more junctions, causing further jams to form on the intersecting streets, and so on. The result can be the total paralysis of a large area of a city. The term is also used metaphorically of any situation in which all progress seems blocked.

• **grifter** ▶ US slang from the early years of the

20th century for a dishonest person, a gambler, a petty crook. The word is a combination of 'graft' in the sense of dishonest financial activities and 'drifter', with its implication of unreliability. The word enjoyed a new lease of life following the success of *The Grifters* (1990), a film about confidence tricksters.

• **Grim Grom**► Nickname for the Soviet diplomat Andrei Gromyko (1909–90; foreign secretary 1957–85). He was noted for his grim expressionless face when negotiating.

• **grip**► A person responsible for such tasks as laying camera tracks, repairing props, and moving scenery in a television or film studio. For these assorted jobs a strong grip is presumably essential. The person in charge of the grips on a set is called the **key grip**.

• **Grocer**► Nickname for the Conservative politician Edward Heath (1916–  ; prime minister 1970–74). The invention of the satirical magazine *Private Eye*, it probably arose because of his preoccupation with the price of groceries during negotiations to join the European Community (1973).

• **Grocer's Daughter**► *See*: Iron Lady.

• **grockle**► British slang for a tourist, an unwelcome visitor. Originally a Devonian word, it has now spread to all parts of the UK. *See also*: emmet.

• **groovy**► Dated slang meaning fashionable or exciting; although widely heard in the 1960s and 1970s, it is now only used sardonically. The term is related to the older (but less dated) **groove**, meaning a rhythmic pattern or riff in jazz or rock music; **to groove** or **get in the groove** is to play, dance, or listen to such music, especially in a relaxed and spontaneous way. All these words probably derive from the idea of the needle set in the groove of a gramophone record.

• **Grosvenor Squares**► British rhyming slang for flares, *i.e.* bell-bottom trousers. A term of the late 1970s, when this style of trousers was no longer fashionable and had come to seem ludicrous. Grosvenor Square is in Mayfair, London (*see*: Eisenhower Platz). Another rhyming slang name for flares is **Lionel Blairs**, after the British dancer and entertainer.

• **grotty**► British slang for awful, revolting, distasteful. It arose as a shortened form of 'grotesque' (or its Italian equivalent *grotteschi*) favoured by Liverpudlians in the 1960s. In the era of the Mersey sound, it became widely popular among young people nationwide. It has given rise to the backformation **grot** for squalor or filth.

• **ground control**► The teams of scientists, engineers, and technicians and their radar and computer systems, who monitor the takeoff and landing of an aircraft or space vehicle, and observe and maintain contact with the crew throughout the flight or mission.

• **grounded**► Teenage slang, originally US and Australian, used for being forced to stay at home as a punishment. It is taken from pilots' terminology, denoting a plane or a pilot that is prevented from flying.

• **Groundnut Scheme**► Figuratively, an expensive failure or ill-considered enterprise; from a hastily organized and badly planned British government scheme (1947) to clear large areas of hitherto unprofitable land in Africa to grow groundnuts. The venture was abandoned three years later at considerable cost to the taxpayer.

• **ground zero** ► Originally, the area on the ground directly beneath an exploding nuclear weapon. (Also called the hypocentre). Since September 11 2001 the phrase has come to mean the rubble-strewn site of the former World Trade Center in New York City, destroyed by terrorist fanatics on that date at a cost of nearly 3000 lives.

• **Group Areas Act**► Legislation introduced in 1950 by South Africa's ruling National Party in which certain residential and business areas were designated exclusively for particular racial groups. This was part of the minority White government's increasingly systematic enforcement of apartheid, and had the effect of expelling African, Coloured, and Asian citizens from many suburbs and causing expropriation of their property. For the White population the Act served to consolidate their economic and political power. The Group Areas Act was repealed in July 1991.

• **group-grope**► Slang from the early 1960s for a group petting session among teenagers. Since the 1980s it has sometimes been used contemptuously to describe group therapy sessions, especially those that involve physical contact (*see*: sensitivity training).

• **groupie**► Slang for a girl who follows a rock group or a rock star around and makes herself sexually available to them. The word originated in the 1960s, like the practice; it is normally used pejoratively. By the 1980s it had come to be used in a more general sense, to mean any admirer or a fan, *e.g.* a 'political groupie'.

• **Group of Eight**► (G8) *See*: Group of Seven.

• **Group of Five**► (G5) The five countries France, West Germany, Japan, the UK, and America, which in 1985 agreed to stabilize their exchange rates by mutual agreement.

• **Group of Seven** ▶ (G7) The group of seven countries that evolved from the first economic summit, held in 1976. They were the main industrial nations outside the communist bloc, *i.e.* Canada, France, West Germany, Italy, Japan, the UK, and America. Originally a purely economic grouping, their agenda later extended to some political issues. The beginning of a 'comprehensive and lasting' relationship between the G7 nations and post-communist Russia was announced at the so called 'G7 plus 1' conference in 1992. G7 became **G8** (**Group of Eight**) in 1998, when Russia joined the association.

• **Group of Seventy-Seven** ▶ (G77) A grouping consisting of the developing countries of the world.

• **Group of Ten** ▶ (G10) Also known as the **Paris Club**, this group of ten prosperous nations agreed at a meeting in Paris in 1962 to lend money to the International Monetary Fund (*see*: IMF) and inaugurated the concept of special drawing rights, as a standard unit of account. They were Belgium, Canada, France, Italy, Japan, Netherlands, Sweden, West Germany, the UK, and America.

• **Group of Three** ▶ (G3) The three most powerful western economies: Germany, Japan, and America.

• **group therapy** ▶ A form of psychotherapy that has been widely used since World War II, when the treatment of psychological problems by therapists, psychiatrists, and psychoanalysts became popular but extremely expensive. In group therapy a number of patients meet together, usually in the presence of a therapist, to discuss their problems with a view to understanding and overcoming them. This often involves role-play exercises or the acting out of distressing events in the patients' past. Such a group can also provide an opportunity for learning social skills or offer support to the members in overcoming a common addiction, obsession, etc. *See also*: encounter group.

• **GRU** ▶ *Glavnoye Razvedyvatelniye Upravleniye* (Central Intelligence Office). The principal intelligence organization of the former Soviet Army; the military equivalent of the KGB.

• **grumpie** ▶ One of the many words coined in the mid-1980s by analogy with yuppie. It refers to an older person who does not look favourably on the frivolities of the young and upwardly mobile, who staunchly defends the status quo, and who expresses these views in a manner that assumes that they are unquestionable.

• **grunge** ▶ A type of rock music and its associated dress style that emerged in the US in the early 1990s. Grunge music combined elements of heavy metal and punk and was characterized by a droning distorted guitar sound; the lyrics were mainly downbeat and angst-ridden. Exponents included Nirvana, Mudhoney, Screaming Trees, and Smashing Pumpkins. Grunge fashion was deliberately unglamorous, being characterized by tattered second-hand clothes, usually in grey or beige, and scruffy hair, usually worn long. In 1992–93 several mainstream fashion houses attempted to capitalize on the grunge look but failed to attract the older wealthier customers, who prefer to spend their money on clothes that make them look more, rather than less, attractive. The word derives from an earlier US slang adjective 'grungy', meaning squalid or seedy. *See also*: Generation X; heroin chic.

• **G7** ▶ *See*: Group of Seven.

• **G77** ▶ *See*: Group of Seventy-Seven.

• **G-string** ▶ A very small triangular piece of cloth attached to the body by a string around the waist and between the buttocks; it is designed to cover the genitals of striptease artistes, go-go dancers, etc. It is thought that the garment is so called because the G-string is the lowest string of a violin.

• **G suit** or **anti-G suit** ▶ A special tunic worn by jet pilots and astronauts that helps counteract the effects of high acceleration. Its name refers to the symbol, g, for the acceleration of free fall (formerly called the acceleration due to gravity). Built into the suit are air pockets that automatically inflate under high acceleration. These then press against the abdomen and thighs to lessen pooling of blood in the extremities and maintain an adequate supply of blood to the brain, so reducing the risk of blackouts.

• **GT** ▶ Gran Turismo or Grand Touring. A motoring term originally applied to a closed coupé of sporting performance, such as might be preferred for a lengthy tour of the Continent. In the 1960s there was a specific championship for GT cars, defined as distinct from 'sports cars' in international motorsport regulations. Among the most successful models on the track were the Ferrari 250 GT and GTO. In recent years the epithet 'GT' has been applied indiscriminately by car manufacturers to any model having modestly uprated performance or appointments. High-performing cars with fuel-injected engines are now often designated **GTI**, Gran Turismo Injection.

• **G10** ▶ *See*: Group of Ten.

• **G3** ▶ *See*: Group of Three.

• **Guadalcanal, Battle of** ▶ In World War II a turning point in the battle for supremacy of the Pacific. It began in August 1942 when US forces seized a large airfield on the island of Guadalcanal in the Solomon Islands, then under Japanese occupation. In the face of fierce Japanese opposition, the Americans gradually advanced over the island, while at sea the opposing navies fought air and naval battles to prevent reinforcements reaching the island. By early 1943 Japanese resistance had crumbled and on 9 February their last forces were evacuated. The battle for the island had cost the lives of over 9000 Japanese and 2000 US servicemen.

• **Guardian Angels** ▶ A group of unpaid vigilantes, founded in New York in 1979 by Curtis Sliwa to police the crime-ridden subway system. At the movement's height there were over 5000 members in America, about 20% of them women, all trained in the art of self-defence. They wore distinctive maroon berets. Moves to train a British chapter of the Angels to police the London Underground in 1989, met with coolness from Scotland Yard. In America the advent of the Angels was followed by a noticeable fall in subway crime – although this may have been due to the extra police drafted in after the publicity given to police failures to combat it.

• **Guernica** ▶ A town near Bilbao in N Spain, for centuries the symbolic centre of Basque nationalism and, until 1876, the seat of the provincial parliament. On 26 April 1937 the town was destroyed by German bombers sent by Hitler to assist Franco's Fascists in the Spanish Civil War. The town suffered repeated and indiscriminate bombing and civilian survivors were mercilessly strafed by the Germans. Goering admitted that the German objective was to test the effectiveness of saturation bombing. The resulting carnage shocked the world. Pablo Picasso commemorated the event in his famous work *Guernica*, completed two months after the attack.

• **guesstimate** ▶ An estimate based partly on guesswork and partly on calculation. It is formed from 'guess' and 'estimate'.

• **guest beer** ▶ A brand of draught beer available, usually for a temporary period, in a pub or bar in addition to the brand normally sold. Landlords of tied public houses are obliged, under their tenancy agreement, to sell the beer produced by the brewery that owns the pub. They may also 'put on' guest beers. Often these are real ales produced by small independent breweries.

• **Guggenheim Museum** ▶ The museum on New York's Fifth Avenue that houses the art collection of the US industrialist Solomon R. Guggenheim (1861–1949). The building was designed by US architect Frank Lloyd Wright and has always aroused excitement and controversy. The main exhibition space is a circular structure, within which a concrete ramp gently spirals upwards and outwards around the domed central void. The paintings hang away from the inclined and curving exterior walls. From its opening in 1959, the building has been widely admired for its brilliant harmony of material and form but criticized as a gallery space. Wright himself described his building as 'the liberation of painting by architecture'.

• **Gugnuncs** ▶ *See*: Pip, Squeak, and Wilfred.

• **guided missile** ▶ A missile that can be fired in the general direction of a target and then alter its flight path after its launch, either by means of remote control or its own internal equipment. A wide range of missile guidance systems now exists. Long-range missiles, such as ICBMs, use a form of inertial guidance in which they are aimed at a pre-programmed map reference and make in-flight computer-controlled changes of direction to reach their target. Middle- and short-range weapons, such as air-to-air, air-to-surface, and anti-tank missiles, are either steered by the operator using fine wires connected to the missile (*see*: wire-guided) or are beam riders, *i.e.* they fly along a laser beam that locks onto the target. Other guided missiles direct themselves to the target by homing onto its heat, sound, or radar emissions.

• **guide dog** ▶ A dog specially trained to act as a guide, companion, and protector to its blind owner. Dogs were systematically trained in this role in Germany during World War I to aid blind war veterans. The most common breeds used are German shepherds, labradors, and golden retrievers. In the UK, the first guide dogs were trained in 1931; the Guide Dogs for the Blind Association was established three years later and remains the only organization that trains dogs (and their owners) in the UK.

• **Guides** ▶ *See*: Girl Guides.

• **Guildford Four** ▶ The four individuals (Gerard Conlon, Paddy Armstrong, Paul Hill, and Carole Richardson) who were falsely convicted of the 1974 IRA bombing of a Guildford public house. They were released in October 1989 after 15 years in prison. Their convictions were quashed at an uncontested Appeal Court hearing; in his judgment Lord Lane accepted that police had tampered with the confessions that provided the only evidence against the Four and that the Crown prosecution and police had withheld forensic and alibi evidence from the defence (both at the time of the trial and subsequently). Had this evidence been available there is little doubt that it would have led to the acquittal, or release on appeal, of the defendants. This miscarriage of justice, one of the most scandalous in British legal history, provoked widespread indignation and unease. In particular it is unlikely that the legal establishment will ever live down the complacent and ill-judged reactions of senior legal figures to this episode.

The controversy took another turn in May 1993 when three former Surrey policemen involved in the case were acquitted of conspiring to pervert the course of justice. There was much public bemusement as to how the two verdicts could be compatible. Spokesmen for the Guildford Four complained that the policemen had not been cross-examined and that the hearing had effectively become a retrial of their own case – at which they were unable to defend themselves. See also: Birmingham Six.

• **Guild Socialism**▶ A movement, prominent in the early 20th century, that sought to reorganize industry under the control of workers' guilds. Its ideological impetus came from A. J. Penty's The Restoration of the Gild System (1906). His arguments for reviving the guilds of medieval times were taken up by A. R. Orage and S. G. Hobson, who developed them into a comprehensive system based on existing trade unions and incorporating elements of syndicalism and other contemporary ideas. Orage and Hobson envisaged workers' control of each industry through a guild chartered by the state. They argued that this would avoid the unwieldy bureaucracy associated with centralized control of industry in a socialist state.

The movement became influential before and during World War I; in 1915 the National Guilds League was formed to promulgate Guild Socialism. Support grew in many industries, including coalmining, railways, and the Post Office. However, by 1917 the trade unions were becoming increasingly politicized, and attention was diverted from shop-floor restructuring to wider issues. Moreover, after the war, the government frustrated moves towards meaningful worker participation in management, and splits appeared in the movement's leadership. The National Building Guild operated successfully for a while, building low-cost houses on contract to the government as part of the Addison housing scheme of 1919. But this too failed after government support was withdrawn, succumbing to the deepening economic depression in 1922. The National Guilds League was wound up in 1925.

• **Guinea Pig Club** ▶ A group of RAF aircrew members who suffered serious burns during World War II and were treated by the New Zealand surgeon Sir Archibald McIndoe (1900–60), who used pioneering techniques of plastic surgery involving skin grafts (hence the name 'guinea pig').

• **Guinness is good for you**▶ The advertising slogan for Guinness stout that was first used in 1929. It accurately reflects what everyone hopes to be true and is probably so memorable for that reason.

• **gulag**▶ Glavnoye Upravleniye Ispravitelno-Trudovykh Lagerey (Chief Administration of Corrective Labour Camps). The section of the KGB, the former Soviet Union's secret police department, in charge of forced labour camps for dissidents and others. The word came into the English language from The Gulag Archipelago (1973–75), a massive documentary work by Alexander Solzhenitsyn (1918–   ).

• **Gulf War**▶ 1. The conflict between Iraq and a US-led multinational force that was precipitated by Iraq's invasion of Kuwait on 2 August 1990. Under Saddam Hussein (see: Butcher of Baghdad), the Iraqis refused UN demands for their withdrawal and the allies unleashed a massive air attack on 17 January 1991 (see: Desert Storm). By the time that the allied ground forces had moved into Kuwait and S Iraq on 24 February 1991, the Iraqis were unable to offer more than token resistance and Kuwait was liberated, although not before extensive damage was done to the country's oilfields. Saddam Hussein, however, succeeded in maintaining his authority within Iraq and subsequently pursued a vindictive policy against rebellious Kurds in the N of the country and Shi'ite Muslims in the S; air-exclusion ('no-fly') zones, established to protect the threatened peoples from attack by Iraqi aircraft, have frequently been ignored. His subsequent violation of ceasefire agreements in refusing to allow UN inspections of Iraq's nuclear, biological, and chemical weapons provoked US and UK military action in 1998. 2. The name given to the Iran–Iraq War (1980–88) until the Gulf War of 1991.

• **Gulf War Syndrome**▶ An apparent medical disorder suffered by many veterans of the Gulf War (1991). The symptoms of this mysterious disease include loss of stamina, extreme fatigue, headaches, and in some cases respiratory disorders. Although some 275,000 US and British veterans claim to be persistently ill with some or all of these symptoms, the military and medical authorities in both countries refuse to accept Gulf War Syndrome as a medical diagnosis – presumably because they fear an avalanche of compensation claims. Other researchers do accept the syndrome as a genuine condition, albeit one with an uncertain aetiology.

Suggested causes include exposure to depleted uranium shells and the use of certain anti-nerve-gas vaccines. The general similarity of the symptoms to those experienced by sufferers of ME has also been noted, suggesting that a possible disorder of the immune system may be involved.

• **gumball** ▶ **1.** US drug abusers' slang from the 1980s for highly refined heroin. **2.** US slang for the flashing light on the roof of a police car, so called because it resembles a brightly coloured ball of bubble gum.

• **gumboot** ▶ A derogatory African name for a condom, so called because of the similarity between a sheath and a Wellington boot.

• **gumshoe** ▶ Early 20th-century US slang for a private detective or plain-clothes policeman, so called because of the rubber-soled shoes said to be worn by such operatives to allow them to creep up on a suspect. They are the opposite of the heavy and noisy boots worn by policemen on the beat. A film of this name starring Albert Finney was made in 1971.

• **gun** ▶
   **give it the gun** In RFC slang of World War I (also used by the RAF in World War II) to open the throttle of an aeroplane suddenly and hard. Sometimes also used of cars.

• **gun-boat diplomacy** ▶ A form of foreign policy much used in the days of the British Empire; a weak foreign power unwilling to comply with a demand by the British government could expect a visit from a gunboat. The phrase goes back only to the 1920s but the tactic itself is much older, being particularly associated with Palmerston during his period as foreign secretary in the 1840s and 1850s. The modern equivalent is, perhaps, the US or NATO airstrike.

• **guns before butter** ▶ A slogan attributed to Nazi propagandist Joseph Goebbels during World War II, although it probably dates from slightly earlier, when very similar phraseology was employed in speeches by both Goebbels and Herman Goering. In a speech in Berlin in January 1936 Goebbels said:

> We can do without butter but, despite our love of peace, not without arms. One cannot shoot with butter, but with guns.

The theme was continued by Goering in a broadcast later in the year:

> I must speak clearly. There are those in international life who are hard of hearing. They listen only if the guns go off. We have no butter, my good people, but I ask you, would you rather have butter or guns? Should we import

lard or metal ores? Let me tell it to you straight – preparedness makes us powerful. Butter merely makes us fat!

This is popularly known as Goering's 'guns-or-butter' speech.

• **gunsel** ▶ **1.** US slang for a youth (from the Yiddish *genzel*, a young goose). The word has two more specific uses: a young boy who accompanies an older tramp on the road, and a passive young male homosexual. **2.** By extension, a gunsel is also an informer or petty criminal and, because of its association with the word 'gun', a gunman.

• **guns, gas and gaiters** ▶ A naval catchphrase said to have originated at the Royal Navy's Gunnery School, Whale Island, to describe its disciplined regime. 'Guns' is slang for Gunnery Officer, while 'gas and gaiters' is a variant of 'gate and gaiters', referring to bellowing instructors ('gate' is slang for a loudmouth) and the gaiters worn by ratings and instructors alike. It was current by the 1920s.

• **gunship** ▶ British slang from the 1980s for an unmarked police car. *See also:* Q ships.

• **Guomindang** or **Kuomintang** ▶ The National People's Party, a Chinese political party formed from Sun Yat-sen's Alliance Party in 1912, following the overthrow of the Imperial government that year. Following Sun's death in 1925 the party came under the control of General Chiang Kai-shek and took over much of the country in a joint campaign with China's communists. However, civil war between the Guomindang and the communists broke out in 1927; with the exception of World War II, when the parties co-operated against Japan, this conflict lasted until 1949, when the Nationalists were driven into exile.

• **guppie** ▶ Slang for a yuppie who also aspires to be green – an environmentally aware young urban professional.

• **guru** ▶ Originally a Hindu spiritual teacher (from a Sanskrit word meaning 'serious'). However, the word is now widely used to mean any expert who commands respect for his views – whether spiritual or not. The coach of England's football team, for example, may well be referred to as 'football's guru'.

• **gutbucket** ▶ An earthy style of jazz blues. Originally played in low drinking houses in America, it is named after the small drip buckets that were placed under the liquor barrels to catch the leakages.

• **gutted** ▶ Feeling great disappointment – especially at the unsatisfactory outcome of a sporting event. Footballers questioned about a lost match frequently described themselves as gutted (*see also*: sick as a parrot). The allusion is presumably to a gutted fish or to a building gutted by fire etc.

• **gutter press**► The section of the British tabloid press that makes use of intrusive and sensationalist journalism to boost its circulation. The gutter press is characterized by an obsession with the private lives of public figures, especially media celebrities and royalty. Its techniques include relentless surveillance of its chosen victims, offers of large sums of money (*see*: cheque-book journalism) to obtain information, and even the wholesale fabrication of stories. Attempts to monitor and punish such abuses by means of the Press Complaints Commission (*see*: Press Council) have proved ineffective. There is now a growing lobby in favour of legislation to protect privacy, although many fear that such a measure would inhibit legitimate investigative journalism.

> Journalists belong in the gutter because that is where ruling classes throw their guilty secrets.
> – GERALD PRIESTLAND, 22 May 1988.

• **Guy the Gorilla** ► A nickname for the British cricketer Ian Botham (also known as **Beefy**) who played for Somerset (1973–86) and Worcestershire (1987–91). A noted all-rounder, he captained the England side (1980–81). The name comes from that of an actual gorilla, Guy, at London Zoo.

• **gymslip mum** ► Journalese for a teenage girl who becomes pregnant and has a child while still at school (a gymslip is a type of knee-length tunic formerly worn by girls as part of their school uniform). The consequences of becoming a teenage mum are nearly always unfortunate and sometimes tragic. For reasons that are not altogether clear, the UK has a much higher rate of teenage pregnancy than most other developed nations (59 conceptions per 1000 women under 20 in 1994). For some the solution is a greater emphasis on sexual abstinence among the young (as in America); for others, more sex education and free availability of the 'morning-after' pill (as in many Continental countries).

• **gynopathy** ► A condition observed in men who feel threatened by women, particularly in a workforce. It is derived from the Greek words *gunē*, woman, and *pathos*, feeling.

# H

• **H** ▶ **1.** Drug abusers' slang for heroin. **2.** A former category of film certification denoting horror films. Introduced by the British Board of Film Censors in 1932, the year after Universal's *Dracula* and *Frankenstein* were released, it was merely an advisory label to warn parents of films that might be disturbing to children. In 1951 it was superseded by the X category.

• **Habakkuk** ▶ Codename for an ambitious scheme to use icebergs as mid-Atlantic airstrips during World War II, conceived by the British aviator Geoffrey Pyke in 1942. The object was to enable aircraft to extend their range by refuelling on giant fabricated icebergs, complete with workshops, hangars, and living quarters. Secret work on prototypes began in Canada, where it was found that the addition of wood pulp would greatly increase the strength of the ice. However, when it became apparent that such a base would cost as much as a conventional aircraft carrier, the project was abandoned. The scheme was called Habakkuk after an Old Testament prophet, who said:

> For I will work a work in your days, which ye will not believe, though it be told you.

• **hack and slash** ▶ A computer game based on violence and destruction rather than on logical problem-solving. *See also*: shoot-'em-up.

• **hacker** ▶ **1.** A person who uses a computer to break into the system of a company, bank, or government department in order to obtain information, money, etc. The word conjures up the image of a solitary explorer cutting their way through the computer jungle; it became widely used after the practice was first publicized in the press in the 1980s. There have since been numerous reports of teenage computer enthusiasts hacking into the supposedly impregnable systems of governments and multinational corporations. **2.** British slang for a taxi driver. This derives from 'Hackney cab', the official name still used for London taxis. This name was kept on when the horse-drawn vehicle for hire became motorized at the beginning of the 20th century, even though the hackney was actually the horse that drew the carriage.

• **had it** ▶ A colloquial expression that became popular during World War II, when it was applied to anyone or anything considered 'finished' or 'done for'. Thus a man seriously wounded was said to have had it. The usage is reminiscent of Roman gladiatorial combats, at which the spectators cried *hoc habet* or *habet* (he has it) when a gladiator received his death-wound.

• **Hadow Reports** ▶ Any of several reports by the Consultative Committee to the Board of Education, chaired from 1920 to 1934 by Sir Henry Hadow (1859–1937), in particular the 1927 report *The Education of the Adolescent*. This introduced the terms 'primary' and 'secondary' for education before and after the age of 11 or 12, and advocated the establishment of separate schools for secondary education. Other influential reports by his committee included *The Primary School* (1931) and *Infant and Nursery Schools* (1933).

• **Haganah** ▶ (Hebrew, defence) The Jewish defence force that operated from 1920 until the declaration of the State of Israel in 1948 to defend Jewish settlements in Palestine. It was the successor to Ha-Shomer (1909–20), and generally adopted a moderate policy, eschewing the terrorist tactics of the Stern Gang and Irgun Zvai Leumi. A commando offshoot, Palmach, was formed in 1941. Under the British mandate, Haganah was proscribed, resulting in clashes with the British as well as Palestinians, especially in the run-up to the partition of Palestine after World War II. With the granting of Israeli autonomy, Haganah formed the basis of the country's armed forces.

• **Hague Conference** or **Second Hague Convention** ▶ An international peace conference held in The Hague, Netherlands, in 1907 and attended by 44 nations. It was convened at the request of US President Theodore Roosevelt in an attempt to build on the conventions adopted by the First Hague Conference, held in 1899, which had created a Permanent Court of Arbitration for international disputes. In the event, the achievements of the 1907 Conference were modest, although the principle of compulsory arbitration was accepted, and conventions were adopted on such issues as the rights and duties of neutral powers and the status of merchant shipping in a conflict. A third conference planned for 1915 never took place because by then World War I had broken out.

• **ha-ha▶** A British slang term for hashish or marijuana. It is probably based on a shortened form of hashish and 'ha-ha' meaning laughter, because of the light-hearted mood induced by the drug.

• **Haig▶**
   **Don't be vague – ask for Haig** An advertising slogan for Haig whisky used since about 1936. The phrase had appeared in several different forms: 'Don't be vague, order Haig' and 'Why be vague? Ask for Haig', but this is the one that stuck.

• **hairy▶ 1.** An informal term for frightening or dangerous. It originated as student slang in the early years of the 20th century, when it meant difficult. The present meaning comes from army slang. It probably derives from the idea that something frightening makes one's hair stand on end; however, the idea of a frightening hairy monster has also been suggested as a derivation. **2.** British slang of the early 1960s for a long-haired bearded male. It was typically used disparagingly of poets and intellectuals. It is still heard occasionally.

• **Haldane mission▶** The diplomatic mission to Berlin, undertaken by the UK's secretary of state for war, Viscount Haldane, in February 1912, in a bid to persuade the German government to reduce its programme of warship construction. No agreement was reached, prompting the First Lord of the Admiralty, Winston Churchill, to call for increased British military spending.

• **Hale's tours▶** A clever idea from the early days of cinema. The ex-chief of the Kansas City Fire Department, George C. Hale, produced it for the St Louis Exposition of 1902. He shot a film from the observation car at the rear end of a moving train, then projected the film onto a screen at the end of a small narrow theatre decorated like an observation car. The illusion was enhanced by arrangements to make the theatre rock slightly, with the sound of train whistles and clanging bells as an accompaniment to the screening. The idea was sufficiently popular for Hale to take it on tour for several years throughout America.

• **half-care▶** Partial care provided for elderly people, as in sheltered accommodation.

• **half-life▶** As a scientific term, the time taken for half the atoms of a particular radioactive substance to disintegrate. This time may vary from a fraction of a second to millions of years depending on the substance. A knowledge of this process has enabled archaeologists and geologists, etc., to date materials with considerable accuracy. *See:* carbon dating.

• **half-tone block▶** A typographic printing-block for illustrations, produced by photographing on to a prepared plate through a screen or grating, which breaks up the image into small dots of varying intensity, thus giving the lights and shades, or tones. The process has been superseded by digitizing the illustration using a computer.

• **Halifax bomber▶** A four-engined bomber built by Handley Page and used by the RAF during World War II. The Halifax Mark 1, fitted with Rolls-Royce Merlin engines, made its first operational flight in March 1941. It was followed by more powerful versions equipped with Bristol Hercules engines. The planes had gun turrets situated aft and in the tail, combined with a machine gun in the nose. The Mark II was capable of carrying up to 6000 kg (13,000 lb) of bombs. Wartime variants included paratroop and glider-tug versions; after the war modified versions of the Halifax, called Haltons, were used for civilian transport.

• **Halley's comet▶** The brightest of the comets with known periodicity, named after Edmund Halley (1656–1743), the astronomer royal who first described the elliptical orbit of comets around the Sun. Halley observed this comet in 1682 and accurately predicted its return in 1759. Halley's comet passes close to the Earth roughly every 76 years. The first definite sighting was made by Chinese astronomers in 1059–58 BC. In the 20th century it passed close to the Earth in 1910 and 1986. In the latter passage five spacecraft were launched to investigate it: two from Japan, two Soviet craft, and Giotto – the European Space Agency probe. These missions revealed a black peanut-shaped nucleus approximately 15 km long and 10 km across, giving off 25 tons of gas and 5 tons of dust every second. At its present rate of material loss, it is estimated that Halley's comet will survive for less than another 100,000 years.

• **Hallstein doctrine▶** The policy, adopted by West Germany in December 1955, that made recognition of East Germany by another state a hostile act against the Federal Republic. It was named after the West German state secretary of the Foreign Office, Dr Walter Hallstein, but was actually devised by Wilhelm Grewe, West Germany's ambassador to America. The doctrine was part of the Adenauer government's strategy of maintaining that East Germany was not a legally constituted state and that German reunification was imperative. Because of the doctrine many countries were dissuaded from establishing diplomatic relations with East Germany, particularly by the threat of losing West German economic assistance.

• **halon** ► A type of chemical compound made from hydrocarbons by replacing some of the hydrogen atoms by bromine atoms and additional chlorine and fluorine atoms. Halons are extensively used in fire extinguishers. However, as with chlorofluorocarbons (*see*: CFC) they have been implicated in depletion of the ozone layer.

• **ham** ► 1. Slang for a licensed amateur radio operator. The word is an aspirated form of the first syllable of 'amateur'. 2. Theatrical slang for a bad actor or actress, especially one who habitually overacts. Various etymologies have been suggested for this sense, which first appeared in the 19th century. It is possibly, as in sense 1 above, derived from the word 'amateur'. Alternatively it may have derived from 'ham fat', the substance formerly used to remove grease paint – thus a 'ham fatter' was an actor. A third possibility is that it is derived from the name of Hamish McCullough (1835–85), an actor who toured the Mid-West of America with his theatre company, called Ham's Actors, who apparently put on the most dreadful productions. The word is now often used in such phrases as **hamming it up** and adjectivally as **hammy**.

• **Hamas** ► Islamic Resistance Movement. An Arab organization that seeks to create an Islamic Palestinian state. Formed in 1976 as a nonmilitant group, it became increasingly violent in the 1990s and has carried out suicide bombings in Israel since 1996. It opposes all attempts by the PLO to seek a peace agreement with Israel, regarding such initiatives as surrender.

• **Hammer, Mike** ► The tough investigator who features in many of the crime thrillers written by US author Mickey Spillane (Frank Morrison Spillane; 1918–    ). Hammer, an ex-cop and war veteran, made his first appearance in *I, The Jury* (1947); in subsequent novels he established his reputation as a highly unorthodox agent of 'justice', combining the roles of judge and executioner with scant regard for legal niceties. The books have proved immensely popular and have spawned a television series. However, Hammer's predilection for sex and violence has brought criticism for his creator, the outspokenly conservative Spillane.

• **Hammer and Sickle** ► From 1923 until 1991, the emblem of the Soviet Union, symbolic of productive work in the factory and on the land.

• **Hammer horror films** ► A series of low-budget British horror films produced from the late 1950s onwards by Hammer Films, a small independent company. Hammer had been making films at its Thameside studios for the US B-movie market since the late 1940s. In 1955 it bought the film rights to a popular sci-fi TV series, which resulted in the release of *The Quatermass Xperiment* (1955). This success was soon followed by *X-the Unknown* (1957) and *Quatermass 2* (1957), which proved equally popular. Over the next 15 years Hammer specialized in making gruesome (and sometimes titillating) remakes of the original Hollywood monster movies featuring Frankenstein, Dracula, and the Mummy, the first of which was *The Curse of Frankenstein* (1956). The last Hammer horror feature film was *To the Devil a Daughter* (1976). In 2000, the by now near-moribund company was sold to a multimedia consortium, and there are plans to resume filmmaking.

• **Hampshire, HMS** ► The British cruiser that was sunk by a mine off the Orkney Islands in June 1916, while carrying the British secretary for war, Lord Kitchener, to Russia. It went down with the loss of all on board. Curiously, many years earlier, Kitchener's death by drowning had been foretold by a gipsy – a prophecy in which Kitchener himself believed.

• **Hampstead set** ► A name given in the 1950s to a group of close friends of the Labour Party leader, Hugh Gaitskell (1906–63), some of whom, like Gaitskell himself, were Oxford-educated middle-class intellectuals living in Hampstead. Members of the set included Anthony Crosland, Roy Jenkins, Douglas Jay, Denis Healey, and Frank Pakenham (later Lord Longford; *see*: Holy Fool). They were accused by some of exercising undue influence over party affairs, while others criticized Gaitskell for ill-judged favouritism.

• **handbag** ► British slang meaning (of a woman) to attack verbally, to bully. It arose in connection with Margaret Thatcher, who as prime minister frequently treated both opponents and colleagues in this way. Her use of a handbag as a prop was made much of by cartoonists. *See also*: sandbag.

> Handbag Finds Launch Pad – *The Independent*, 7 January 1991, headline of an article about Thatcher.

• **Handcuff King** ► A nickname of Harry Houdini, entertainer and expert escapologist, especially from handcuffs.

• **Handley Page bomber** ► The largest British bomber to fly operationally during World War I. The Handley Page 0/100, designed by Sir Frederick Handley Page (1885–1962), entered service in 1916 with the Royal Naval Air Service. It was a twin-engined biplane with a wingspan of 30.48 m (100 ft) and a length of 19.15 m (62 ft 10 in.); top speed was 115.87 kph (72 mph). At first the bomber was used for attacks on the coast of mainland Europe but by 1917 operations had been extended to include night attacks over German-occupied France and Belgium. A more powerful version of the 0/100, the 0/400, entered service with the RAF in 1918. This had a maximum speed of 156.9 kph (97.5 mph) and was capable of carrying 750-kg bombs. After the war, many 0/400 bombers were converted for civilian use.

• **Hand of God** ▸ Phrase used by the Argentinian footballer Diego Maradona (1960–    ) following an incident in the 1986 World Cup. Argentina met England in the quarter finals of the competition and the confrontation caused considerable interest because it was the first time the two nations had competed since the Falklands Conflict. Maradona, who at the time was regarded as one of the world's best footballers, scored two goals. The second was a brilliant solo performance, in which he took the ball through the English defence before scoring. The first was less impressive: Maradona had apparently headed the ball into the net but slow-motion replays showed that, unseen by the referee, he had knocked it in with his hand. As a result, England were knocked out of the competition. Challenged later, Maradona, unrepentant, said:

> It was a little the hand of God and a little the hand of Diego.

Possibly Maradona was trying a pun on his name ('little God'). The humour was lost on most English football fans.

• **hands-off** ▸ An adjective indicating a lack of direct involvement in a particular situation or the distancing of oneself from matters that may be thought to be under one's control. This usage became popular in the 1980s, as in 'a hands-off policy towards industry'. *See also*: hands-on.

• **Handsomest Man in the World** ▸ The nickname, almost certainly a promotional tag, of the US stage and film actor Francis X. Bushman (1883–1966), the star of many silent films. His film career began in 1911, his good looks and powerful well-built physique quickly bringing him popular acclaim as a romantic lead. His films included *Romeo and Juliet* (1915) and *Ben Hur* (1925), in which he played the role of Messala.

• **hands-on** ▸ An adjective indicating active personal involvement in situations or affairs. Specifically it implies a practical form of learning rather than a purely theoretical approach. It is often used

in the field of computers, as in 'hands-on training' or 'I have a good understanding of what computers can do but little hands-on experience'. *See also*: hands-off.

• **Handy Man** ▸ The popular name for *Homo habilis*, the species of prehistoric man thought to be the earliest member of our own genus, *Homo*. Discovery of *H. habilis* was announced in April 1964 by Louis Leakey, Phillip Tobias, and John Napier, based on the evidence of remains unearthed in the Olduvai Gorge, Tanzania. The Latin specific name, *habilis*, was proposed by Raymond Dart; it means handy, skilful. The species is thought to have lived in E Africa between about 2.5 and 1.5 million years ago. Adults were only 5 ft tall but possessed a markedly larger brain than their australopithecine ancestors. There is evidence that Handy Man built simple shelters and made rudimentary tools.

• **hang five** ▸ US surfing slang from the 1960s meaning to ride a surfboard fast with the toes of one foot hooked over the front of the board. To **hang ten** means to ride a surfboard with the toes of both feet so hooked. Both phrases are still used, the second one often in the more general sense of going dangerously fast.

• **hang-gliding** ▸ Unpowered flight in which the pilot hangs in a harness from a large cloth wing held in an aluminium frame, controlling the flight by means of a horizontal bar. Once the province of the adventurous, it is now an increasingly popular sport. The best area for flying is California, owing to its mountainous terrain and warm-air currents. *See also*: paragliding.

• **hanging on the (old) barbed wire** ▸ *See*: Mons, Battle of.

• **hang in there** ▸ A catchphrase originating in America in the 1950s, meaning hang on or, stay with it, *i.e.* an entreaty to persevere with an undertaking or persist with a point of view. It was adopted by the hippie generation in the 1960s and is still current.

• **hang loose** ▸ A slang expression originating with the hippie movement of the late 1960s, meaning to be totally relaxed and unworried. In common with much of the slang of the period, it has now become dated.

• **hang the Kaiser!** ▸ A popular slogan expressing the vengeful mood towards Germany and its leaders amongst the British public at the close of World War I. It became the rallying cry of supporters of the Lloyd George coalition in the Khaki Election of 1918. Lloyd George was swept back into office on a platform of harsh reprisals against Germany, including the execution of the Kaiser (*see*: Kaiser Bill). In the event, the former emperor was exiled to the Netherlands.

• **hang-up** ► An emotional or psychological problem relating to a particular subject, as in 'he has a big hang-up about sex'. The term originated in hippie jargon of the 1960s and is still widely used.

• **Hannah** ► In World War II, a nickname given to a Wren serving with the Royal Marines, after Hannah Snell (1723–92), who joined the marines posing as a man and took part in the attack on Pondicherry. It is said that she ultimately opened a public-house in Wapping, but retained her male attire.

• **Hannay, Richard** ► Typically British hero of a number of adventure novels by the Scottish writer John Buchan (Baron Tweedsmuir; 1875–1940). Buchan was director of information during World War I and became governor general of Canada in 1935. He first introduced Hannay in his best-known novel, *The Thirty-Nine Steps* (1915). Three film versions of the book have been made, the best being the early (1935) adaptation directed by Alfred Hitchcock. Possibly the character of Hannay was based on that of William Ironside (later Lord Ironside of Archangel; 1880–1959), whom Buchan met in South Africa. Ironside was an intelligence officer who was fluent in 14 languages (and, it has been said, made sense in none of them!).

• **Hannibal Lecter** ► *See*: Lecter, Hannibal.

• **Hanratty case** ► *See*: A6 murder.

• **happening** ► **1.** US slang of the 1970s used to describe something exciting or fashionable as in 'a really happening club'. **2.** A type of spontaneous artistic or theatrical event, usually involving considerable audience participation, that became popular in the late 1960s. They were usually outrageous or provocative in style and sometimes took the form of unannounced street theatre that spectators could mistake for a real occurrence. Both the word and the concept are now dated.

• **Happiness is...** ► A phrase completed in various ways in the work of Charles M. Schulz (1922–2000), the US creator of the Peanuts cartoon strip, starring Charlie Brown and his dog Snoopy. He was not the first to try to encapsulate the essence of happiness. Rousseau (1712–1778) said:

> Happiness: a good bank account, a good cook, a good digestion.

Archbishop Whately of Dublin (1787–1863) wrote:

> Happiness is no laughing matter.

The elusive nature of happiness was noted by Anna Pavlova (1881–1931):

> Happiness is like a butterfly which appears and delights us for one brief moment, but soon flits away.

and by Bertrand Russell (1872–1970):

> Happiness is not best achieved by those who seek it directly.

But Schulz hit on a winning formula by leaving the phrase open for anything or anyone to be included. The first such cartoon, in 1957, was 'Happiness is...a warm puppy', featuring Charlie Brown and Snoopy. A best-selling book with the title appeared in 1962. The catchphrase appeared on mugs, T-shirts, and posters, and was adopted by various companies as an advertising slogan, one of the most memorable being **Happiness is a mild cigar called Hamlet**. Having seen the caption to a photograph in a shooting magazine, John Lennon wrote, and the Beatles recorded, a song called 'Happiness Is a Warm Gun' (1968). The possibilities are endless.

• **Happy** ► The nickname of Margaretta Rockefeller, a leading lady of US society and wife of Nelson Rockefeller, governor of New York (1959–74) and US vice-president (1974–77) in Gerald Ford's administration. According to a story reported in the *New York Times*, the name was given to the infant Margaretta by her French nursemaid in 1927. On being told the news that Charles Lindbergh had achieved the first nonstop flight from New York to Paris, the baby responded with happy gurgles and smiles.

• **happy** ►
**Are you happy in your work?** An ironic question addressed to someone performing an obviously onerous or unpleasant task, or one equally clearly not to their liking. Originally a services phrase dating from World War II, it was later widely used. The Royal Navy variant was **are you happy in the Service?**

• **happy** ►
**Don't worry, be happy** A song title that became the catchphrase of George Bush Sr's successful presidential election campaign of 1988. It won a Grammy award that year for the singer Bobby Mcferrin and became the president's unofficial theme song.

• **happy clappies** ► Derogatory name for adherents of the modern Christian evangelical movement, who support the incorporation of upbeat informal music into church services. So called because such music tends to be mindlessly euphoric and to have a simple beat to which the congregation claps along.

• **Happy days are here again** ► A catchphrase

that originated as the title of a song written by US composer Milton Ager with lyrics by Jack Yellen, published in 1930. The phrase was subsequently adopted for the presidential campaign of Franklin D. Roosevelt (*see*: FDR) and became a familiar idiom on both sides of the Atlantic.

• **happy dust**▶ Drug users' slang for any narcotic in powder form, especially cocaine or angel dust.

• **happy hour**▶ A promotional ploy used by certain pubs and bars to attract customers by offering half-price drinks for a limited period (usually an hour but it can be longer) at a certain time of the day, usually in the early evening. The concept was first introduced around 1961. In cricket, the 'happy hour' is the final hour of play in a limited-overs match, when batsmen take more chances than they would do at an earlier stage of the game.

• **harakiri swap**▶ In business, a swap made without a profit margin; the term derives from the Japanese word for ritual suicide.

• **hard act to follow**▶ A phrase that originated in the US vaudeville theatre, where diverse acts would appear on the same bill, a star performer was said to be hard for subsequent turns to follow, because they would be unlikely to shine by comparison. It is now used much more widely; for example, before the events of September 11 President George W. Bush was said to be finding President Clinton a hard act to follow.

• **hardball**▶
    **play hardball** US slang meaning to behave in a tough or macho way, especially in politics or business dealings. The image is from baseball, in which male professionals play with a hard ball; women, children, and amateurs often play a modified form of the game using a softer ball.

• **hard copy**▶ The output of a computer (such as text or graphics) on paper, as opposed to data displayed on the screen. So-called because hard copy output from a printer is permanent, whereas screen output is obviously not.

• **hardcore**▶ **1.** An adjective used to describe someone who is irredeemably committed to an activity or belief, *e.g.* a hardcore criminal is never likely to reform, while a hardcore communist will remain a party member no matter what. **2.** Hardcore is also used to describe pornography that depicts unsimulated sex acts in graphic detail; it often caters to minority or deviant tastes and violence or acts with children. *Compare*: soft porn. **3.** A style of US pop music that developed out of punk in the 1980s and spread to the UK in about the middle of the decade. Anarchic, loud, and aggressive, it did not last long. *See also*: thrash.

• **hard disk**▶ A magnetic disk in a hermetically sealed unit, which can be mounted either in a computer or in a separate unit outside the computer with its own housing and power supply. Removable hard disks are available, which can be switched between computers. The magnetic storage medium in a hard disk is a rigid platter, which is more robust than the floppy disk and can store and retrieve much larger amounts of data at a much faster rate. A hard disk is essential for most modern computing applications, floppy disks being reserved for transferring data between machines and for data back-up in case of hard disk failure.

• **hard dog**▶ US police slang of the 1980s and 1990s for a dog owned by a criminal and trained to attack. Hard dogs are kept especially by drug dealers, to protect themselves and their property.

• **hard drug**▶ A drug, such as heroin or cocaine, that is both physically and psychologically addictive and seriously detrimental to the health of the user. The description 'hard' has been used of such drugs since the early 1970s; they are usually contrasted with **soft drugs**, such as cannabis and some amphetamines, whose effects on health are considered less damaging. In the UK, the law makes a distinction between class A ('hard') drugs and class B and C ('soft') drugs. While only the most extreme libertarians argue for the legalization of hard drugs, a large and perhaps growing body of opinion favours removing some or all of the restrictions on soft drugs. In 2001 the government announced changes in the law that would effectively decriminalize the possession of cannabis for one's personal use.

• **hard hat**▶ US slang for a building worker or other 'blue-collar' male who espouses right-wing political views. The term was first heard in the late 1960s when hard hats joined demonstrations against the anti-Vietnam War protestors. The term derives, of course, from the safety helmet, called a hard hat, worn by building workers.

• **Hard John**▶ US Black slang for an FBI agent, used quite persistently through the 1940s and 1950s.

• **hard landing**▶ A landing by a rocket or spacecraft in which the vehicle is destroyed on impact. *Compare*: soft landing.

• **hard rock**▶ *See*: rock.

• **hard sell**▶ The aggressive marketing of a commodity or service. Salespersons who adopt 'the hard sell' tend to use aggressive and forceful persuasion, neglect the consumer's actual requirements, and make dishonest or exaggerated claims for the product. The practice is particularly associated with holiday timeshare companies who, with the bait of quite expensive gifts, lure people into their premises, where they are often subjected to persistent pressure to buy a share in a property, which most can ill afford. *See also*: soft sell.

• **hard shoulder** ▶ The surfaced strip running along the edge of a motorway, which is used for emergency stops. It is illegal to use the hard shoulder in any other circumstances.

• **hardware** ▶ The machines and other physical components used in a computer system, as opposed to the software.

• **Hardy family** ▶ An insufferable fictional family that featured in some 15 Hollywood films between 1936 and 1946. Made by MGM on modest budgets, the films were financially extremely successful and won a special Academy Award (1942) for furthering the American way of life. The hero of the family, the son Andy Hardy, played by the bouncy Mickey Rooney, was every American's idea of the boy next door. His girlfriends, typifying the girl next door but one, included several starlets who later became major stars – Judy Garland, Lana Turner, Kathryn Grayson, and Esther Williams, among them. The paterfamilias, a small-town judge with a fund of patronizing small-town wisdom, was first played by Lionel Barrymore but subsequently by Lewis Stone. The mother was played endearingly, if oversweetly, by Fay Holden. A post-war revival of the family in *Andy Hardy Comes Home* (1958) demonstrated that the whole schmaltzy circus belonged to another era.

• **Hare Krishna** ▶ A religious movement, formally known as the International Society for Krishna Consciousness (ISKCON), founded in America in 1966 by A. C. Bhaktivedanta (religious title Swami Prabhupāda; 1896–1977) and dedicated to the worship of the Hindu deity Krishna, an incarnation of the god Vishnu. The name comes from the title of a mantra (Hindi *Hare*, god, lord) chanted by believers as part of their daily ritual. Members of the sect live in communes, are vegetarian, and observe strict prohibitions against the use of intoxicants, sex outside marriage, and gambling. They adopt Indian dress and customs and are a familiar sight in cities in Europe and America in their yellow robes, the men usually with shaven heads, soliciting funds and food.

• **Harlem toothpick** ▶ US slang for a pocket flick-knife. The term features in the English version (by Marc Blitzstein) of the Brecht-Weill song 'Mack the Knife' from *Threepenny Opera* (1928).

• **Harlot's Romp** ▶ *See*: Queen Charlotte's Ball.

• **harpoon** ▶ **1.** Drug-abusers' slang for a hypodermic syringe used for injecting drugs. **2.** Slang for a harmonica; a less common version of **harp**, which is widely used in rock-music circles for the instrument.

• **Harrier jump jet** ▶ The first operational short take-off and vertical landing (*see*: VTOL) fixed-wing fighter aircraft, developed by Hawker Siddeley in the 1960s. The Harrier made its maiden flight in 1966 and entered service with the RAF in 1969. The plane is powered by a single Rolls-Royce Pegasus turbofan engine with vectored thrust, giving it a maximum forward speed of 1184 kph (736 mph). Jet nozzles at the wing tips, nose, and tail enable the plane to manoeuvre while hovering. Initially, vertical take-off was the objective, but a short take-off was subsequently found to be preferable because it enabled the plane to carry a greater payload. The wingspan of only 8.3 m (27.25 ft) and length of 14.1 m (46.25 ft) mean that the Harrier can operate from confined areas, giving it great versatility in supporting ground troops and other operational roles. In America, the Harrier has been modified by McDonnell Douglas as the AV-8B, for use by the US Marine Corps. This was introduced in 1985. A similar plane, the Harrier GR5, has been used by the RAF as the successor to their original Harriers. The Sea Harrier is the version flown by the Royal Navy. *See also*: flying bedstead.

• **Harrow rail disaster** ▶ One of the UK's worst railway accidents, second only to the Gretna Green rail disaster in terms of casualties. It occurred at 08.18 on 8 October 1952 in Harrow, NW London. An express sleeper travelling from Perth to Euston overran signals at Harrow and ploughed into a stationary local train waiting in the station. Immediately afterwards a northbound express from Euston collided with the wreckage causing a terrible pile-up in the station, then crowded with rush-hour commuters. 112 people were killed and over 150 injured. The reasons for the crash remain unknown, the driver of the southbound express having been killed. However, it is thought that patchy fog may have affected the driver's view of the signals.

• **harry** ▶ British drug-abusers' term from the 1960s for heroin. Cocaine was personified as Charlie. *See also*: henry.

• **Harry** ▶ The suffix '-ers' is typical of British army and public school slang, *e.g.* preggers (pregnant), starkers (naked), brekkers (breakfast). For some reason, the forename Harry is often used with these '-ers' words, especially in service jargon, *e.g.* **Harry flatters** (a flat sea), **Harry flakers** (flaked out, exhausted), and **Harry pinkers** (a pink gin). This usage may have originated with the British who served in India during the Raj, whose pidgin Hindi (or Urdu) included the word *Hare*, meaning God, or the highest (*see*: Hare Krishna).

• **Harry Potter** ▶ *See*: Potter, Harry.

• **Harry Tate's Navy** ▶ A good-humoured sobriquet applied to the Royal Naval Volunteer Reserve from about the time of World War I or a little earlier. The allusion is to the music hall artist Harry Tate (Ronald Macdonald Hutchinson; 1872–1940), perhaps best known for his motoring sketches. 'Harry Tate' came to signify anything that was disorganized or chaotic. *See also*: Fred Karno's army; Wavy Navy.

• **Hartmannsweilerkopf** ▶ A mountain peak in the Vosges, near Steinbach in Alsace. During World War I it was the scene of fierce fighting between French and German forces for control of its strategic heights. In March 1915 the French wrested the heavily fortified summit from the Germans, who recaptured it briefly in April only to be driven out once more by the French. The heavy losses sustained on both sides gave a lasting and bloody fame to the name of the peak.

• **Harvey Nicks** ▶ The familiar name for the Knightsbridge store Harvey Nichols. An upmarket clothing and cosmetics store patronized by Sloane Rangers and their mothers, it not only provides most of their outfits but also functions as a congenial meeting place. The abbreviated form of the name was publicized by the BBC comedy series *Absolutely Fabulous* (1992– ), in which the two leading characters constantly refer to the store in this way.

• **Harvey Smith** ▶ A British colloquial term for a V-sign given as a gesture of contempt or abuse. The name comes from the Yorkshire-born showjumper Harvey Smith (1938– ), who was known for his outspoken and blunt manner. At a showjumping contest at Hickstead in 1971, in a moment captured by the television cameras, he made this sign. Although apparently directed disapprovingly at Douglas Bunn, Hickstead's owner, Smith maintains that it was a V for Victory salute (as popularized by Winston Churchill during World War II). The essential difference between the two gestures is that in the Churchillian salute the palm faces outwards, whereas it faces inwards when 'flicking a Harvey Smith'.

• **Harwell** ▶ The UK's main nuclear research laboratory, located near Didcot in Oxfordshire and operated by the United Kingdom Atomic Energy Authority. Harwell performs experimental work on many aspects of nuclear technology, including nuclear-waste disposal, besides basic research into nuclear physics and nuclear applications in science, medicine, and industry. Scientists at Harwell are also engaged in many other fields, including toxicology, radiological protection, and the study of various types of pollution. The laboratory has a range of particle accelerators and three experimental reactors – Gleep, Dido, and Pluto.

• **hash** ▶ Hashish, the resin form of the drug cannabis as obtained from Morocco, the Lebanon, or the Indian subcontinent. In the 1960s and 1970s this was the most widely available form of the drug in the UK. The term hash now sounds rather dated. *See*: pot.

• **Hashbury** ▶ The nickname of Haight-Ashbury, the district of San Francisco in which the hippie cult began in the mid-1960s. It involves a play on the word hash, the smoking of which was central to the hippie lifestyle.

• **hashing** ▶ A boisterous version of the popular game hare and hounds, in which a trail, usually of paper, is laid by the 'hare' for the 'hounds' to follow. The word is said to have come from Hash House, the name of a restaurant in Kuala Lumpur, which marked the end-point of the traditional hashing game, usually played by expatriate British. In this 'colonial' version, the chase was invariably followed by riotous partying.

• **hat** ▶
   **Keep it under your hat** A government slogan from World War II reminding people of the need for national security. A US variant was **Keep it under your stetson**. *See also*: Keep it dark.

• **hatchback** ▶ A car with a sloping back, which opens upwards giving access to the interior of the car; it provides a large luggage area, replacing the conventional boot. The term is also used for the back itself, which in effect provides an extra door to the vehicle. The practicality of such vehicles, often called **five-door cars**, has made them very popular thoughout the world.

• **hatchet job** ▶ A totally damning report on something or someone. It may be a review of a book, play, etc., in which the reviewer cannot say anything good about the work or it may be a character assassination – for example, by someone who is asked to provide a reference for a job applicant.

• **Hatikvah** ▸ (Hebrew, hope) A Jewish song with words by Naftali Imber (1856–1909) and music by Samuel Cohen. It was used as a rallying song by the Zionist movement from 1907 and became the national anthem of Israel in 1948, after a minor change in wording.

• **Havana Conference** ▸ A conference of American states held in Havana in 1940 to consider various issues arising from World War II. The participants agreed on the 'No Transfer' principle in which control over colonies in the Americas could not be transferred between non-American states.

• **Have a Go** ▸ The title of a popular travelling radio quiz show of the 1940s and 1950s hosted by Wilfred Pickles (1904–78) and his wife Mabel. The format was jokey and familiar, the accents north country, and the questions easy, the successful contestants being awarded small money prizes. If the question was answered correctly Pickles called out 'Give him (or her) the money, Barney'. Barney was the producer who doled out the prizes.

The phrase 'Have a go' was used in a different context in 1964 by the Assistant commissioner of Scotland Yard, Sir Ranulph Bacon. He advised members of the general public to 'have a go' (intervene) if they witnessed an armed robbery. Understandably this prompted a public outcry and was deemed foolhardy, but the phrase is still used in this sense.

> Have-a-go heroes who helped police track down an apparently armed post office raider received cash awards and bravery certificates yesterday in Carmarthen. – *Carmarthen Journal*, 9 January 1991.

• **Have a nice day** ▸ *See at*: day.

• **Hawaii** ▸ British slang for £50, based on the title of a US TV crime series *Hawaii Five-O*, which was popular in the 1970s.

• **Haw-Haw** ▸ *See*: Lord Haw-Haw.

• **hawk** ▸ *See*: dove.

• **hay** ▸
   **and that ain't hay** A US cliché, usually applied to money; it means, 'don't turn your nose up at that, it's not to be ignored'. *That Ain't Hay* was the title of an Abbot and Costello film in 1943.

• **Hays Office** ▸ The popular name for the Motion Picture Association of America (MPAA), founded in 1922 as the Motion Picture Producers and Distributors of America (MPPDA) under the directorship of the lawyer and political organizer Will H. Hays (1879–1954). The organization was established by the principal Hollywood studios to impose self-censorship on their product, a move prompted by growing public indignation at sexual boldness on the screen and the unsuitable behaviour off screen of some film stars, notably Fatty Arbuckle. One of Hays's first moves was to insert morality clauses into players' contracts, enabling them to be dismissed for transgressions in their private lives. The Hays Office registered and collated complaints from the various local censorship boards and forwarded them to the studios. In 1930 a Production Code (the **Hays Code**) was issued detailing what could and could not be shown on the screen. For example:

> Excessive and lustful kissing, lustful embracing, suggestive postures and gestures, are not to be shown.
> Miscegenation (sex relationships between Black and White races) is forbidden.

The code, formally implemented in 1934, became a constant source of friction between film producers and the Hays Office. Although it caused many tame and bowdlerized films to be produced, it had the effect of holding at bay calls for government censorship. One of the most famous concessions made by Hays was to pass the last word in Rhett Butler's line in *Gone With The Wind* (1939), addressed to Scarlett O'Hara: 'Frankly, my dear, I don't give a damn'. In time fewer and fewer people did give a damn; the code was increasingly ignored from the 1950s onwards and finally scrapped in 1968.

• **hazard lights** ▸ The yellow lamps at the back and front of a car that flash simultaneously as a warning to other motorists to keep clear. They are switched on if the car has temporarily broken down on the road.

• **Hazchem** ▸ A system of labelling road tankers and premises in which there are containers of chemicals with special codes and symbols so that, in the event of an accident, fire, etc., the emergency services know what type of chemical is involved and how to treat it. The word is short for *hazardous chemical*.

• **H-block** ▸ *See*: Maze prison.

• **H-bomb** ▸ *See*: nuclear weapon.

• **HCE** ▸ The initials of the Dublin publican, H(umphrey) C(himpden) Earwicker, whose dreams of a single night are (apparently) described in James Joyce's *Finnegans Wake*. In this perplexing and, to many, incomprehensible novel, the initials stand not only for Earwicker himself, but are punningly alluded to by a host of phrases throughout the text, for example 'Here Comes Everybody', 'Heinz cans everywhere', 'Haroun Childeric Eggeberth', and 'How Copenhagen ended'. Earwicker's wife, Anna, is similarly referred to as **ALP** – Anna Livia Plurabelle. On one level she is a personification of Dublin's River Liffey, *anna* being Irish Gaelic for river. A statue and fountain representing Anna Livia was created in central Dublin in the 1980s; it is known somewhat irreverently to locals as 'the floozie in the jacuzzi'.

• **HD**▶ The pseudonym of the US poet and novelist Hilda Doolittle (1886–1961). Originally from Bethlehem, Pennsylvania, she moved to Europe in 1911 and became a member of the Imagist movement (see: Imagism) founded by her friend Ezra Pound. Her interest in classical Greek culture and mythology is reflected in her poems.

• **head**▶ **1.** Dated slang for an anti-establishment cannabis smoker. The word was adopted by the hippies of the late 1960s from the jargon of Black musicians and became the word they used to describe themselves; it was interchangeable with freak. **2.** A suffix used to denote a habitual user of a particular drug in such words as **acidhead**, for someone who takes LSD; **snowhead**, for someone who takes cocaine; and **pothead**, a user of pot.

• **headbanger**▶ **1.** Slang for a young person, usually male, who is a fan of heavy metal music. Headbangers do not dance to the music but violently shake their heads to the beat. This practice, which was considered somewhat hazardous by the medical profession, was popular in the 1970s. **2.** Slang for a crazy or stupid person, especially someone who acts in an extreme way or adheres rigidly to extreme views.

• **head case**▶ An informal term for a person who is mentally unstable or highly eccentric. It can be used either contemptuously ('he's a head case and you can't trust him') or affectionately ('he may be a head case but you can't help liking him').

• **headhunt**▶ To seek out a person already in employment and offer him or her a post, usually at a higher level, in a company involved in the same type of business. The headhunting is usually carried out discreetly by a recruitment agency, known colloquially as **headhunters**, who are hired to find the best person for a particular job, rather than simply to select from candidates who have answered a vacancy advertisement.

• **head shop**▶ A shop selling articles associated with the drug culture of the late 1960s, such as incense sticks, hashish pipes, and psychedelic posters and fabrics etc. These shops, also known as **psychedelicatessens**, began to appear in California during the hippie era.

• **headshrink** or **headshrinker**▶ Originally US slang for a psychoanalyst or a psychiatrist. Now invariably shortened to **shrink** and used widely on both sides of the Atlantic, it is often disparaging.

• **healie-feelie**▶ An informal, and often derogatory, name for a person who believes in healing or therapy by means of handling mineral crystals, such as quartz or tourmaline. Crystal therapy is an activity on the fringes of alternative medicine.

• **health farm**▶ An establishment, usually a luxuriously appointed residential complex in the countryside, equipped with specially trained staff, saunas, swimming pools, and all the latest exercise equipment. Clients, at considerable expense, pursue a strict regime of diet and exercise to help them lose weight and restore their minds and bodies to fitness.

• **health food**▶ Food that is alleged to be 'better' for you, i.e. it prevents disease and promotes physical well-being. Ideas of what constitutes a healthy diet have changed many times in the last hundred years. It has often been claimed that the healthiest diet for the British people was that available during World War II, when food rationing was in operation. After the war, people were told that dairy products were good for them, and that they should drink more milk and eat more eggs. These are now not considered healthy foods because of the saturated fats (see: polyunsaturate) they contain. In general, health food faddists now seek nourishment that is low in calories, high in nutritional value, contains little fat (especially saturated animal fat), and makes little or no use of artificial colouring or preservatives (see: food additive). **Health-food shops**, which appeared in the UK in the 1960s, tend to concentrate on selling wholefood, vitamin pills, and a miscellaneous collection of herbal and 'natural' remedies. Since the 1980s, interest in health food has been part of a general concern with 'healthy living' in which regular exercise, jogging, aerobics, etc., play an important part. However, many medical authorities now deny that the more extreme kinds of organic wholefood have any particular nutritional merit. Moreover, they seem to exclude the element of pleasure in eating that is an essential part of the wellbeing that we derive from our food:

> Some breakfast-food manufacturer hit upon the simple notion of emptying out the leavings of carthorse nosebags, adding a few other things like unconsumed portions of chicken layer's mash and the sweepings of racing stables, packing the mixture into little bags, and selling them in health-food shops. – FRANK MUIR: *Upon My Word!*

*See also*: fast food; organic farming.

• **hear**▶
  **Can you hear me, mother?** This is reputed to be the first line from a radio show to be-

come a catchphrase. In fact, it came about by accident. The comedian Sandy Powell (1900–82) was performing a sketch for the BBC in 1932 or 1933 in which he was supposed to be broadcasting from the North Pole and trying to get in touch with his mother. The first time he used this line, he dropped his script. While he retrieved it he repeated the line several times. The following week, at a live show, the line was clearly expected by the audience, who joined in with great gusto when he repeated it.

• **heard**▶

**You ain't heard nothin' yet!** The immortal line spoken by Al Jolson in *The Jazz Singer* (1927), the first talkie feature. Although particularly resonant in this context, the line had been used as Jolson's catchphrase for some years previously. *See*: World's Greatest Entertainer.

• **heart**▶

**In your heart you know I'm** (or **he's**) **right** The slogan used by the right-wing Republican Barry Goldwater in his unsuccessful presidential election campaign (1964) against President Lyndon Johnson. Opponents countered with; 'In your guts, you know he's nuts.' *See*: Goldwater caper.

• **heartbeat**▶

**a heartbeat away from the presidency** A well-known expression describing the position of the US vice-president, who may have to assume the presidency at a moment's notice. It is normally used by political opponents to raise fears about the calibre of a presidential candidate's running mate. A book by Jules Witcover about the resignation of Spiro Agnew, vice-president under Nixon, was called *A Heartbeat Away*. When George Bush won the presidential election with the much-derided Dan Quayle as his running mate, there was a story going round Washington that Quayle was accompanied wherever he went by two armed CIA men – with orders to shoot him if anything happened to Bush. The expression arose during the Eisenhower administration, when the vice-president was Richard Nixon.

• **Heartbreak Ridge** ▶ The site of one of the bloodiest battles of the Korean War, also known as Height 1211. It is located in hilly country, W of the Hwachon Reservoir and near the 38th Parallel. The worst fighting occurred in October 1951, when troops of the US 2nd Marine Division fought to push the enemy northwards following the collapse of truce negotiations. The Americans secured the ridge on 15th October, against fierce opposition from North Korean defenders.

• **hearts and minds**▶ A slogan associated with the disastrous involvement of US forces in the Vietnam War. It refers to America's doomed attempt to win the support of the civilian population of South Vietnam. Ultimately, however, it was the administration's failure to capture the hearts and minds of the US public that led to the eventual withdrawal.

Previously the phrase was linked with President Theodore Roosevelt, who described his leadership of the US nation in terms of his ability to 'put into words what is in their hearts and minds but not in their mouths'. The Nixon White House was more cynical, adopting as its unofficial slogan 'Get them by the balls and their hearts and minds will follow'.

• **heat**▶

**If you can't stand the heat, get out of the kitchen** A saying that is usually attributed to US President Harry S. Truman, although he himself gave his aide Major-General Harry Vaughan as the original source. Truman used it in 1952 when he announced that he would not be standing again for the presidency.

• **heat, the** ▶ Slang for the police. The epithet originated in US Black street slang and was later adopted by the hippies, before becoming more widely used. The image is that of an oppressive force.

• **heat death**▶ The end that befalls a thermodynamically closed system that has attained its maximum total entropy. The concept, has been applied to the universe as a whole, on the assumptions that the universe is subject to the second law of thermodynamics, which states that entropy either remains constant or increases in an isolated system, and that the universe is, in fact, an isolated system. At present there are many hot stars cooling in space but eventually, it is suggested, this energy flow will cease and the universe will attain thermodynamic equilibrium. All change and fluctuation will then cease and the universe will be cold, still, and timeless. There is some evidence, however, that the universe is expanding and contracting, in which case its eventual heat death will be followed by a rebirth. The concept of the heat death of the universe is highly speculative. Those with a nervous disposition can be reassured that even if the concept is valid, it is an unimaginably long time away.

• **heater**▶ US slang for a handgun, first heard in the 1930s. It became well known through films and books about the underworld.

• **Heath Robinson**▶ An epithet often used to describe an absurdly complicated, ingenious, and fantastic contraption. It alludes to the cartoonist W. Heath Robinson (1872–1944), whose amusing drawings of such contrivances appeared in *Punch* and elsewhere.

• **Heaviside layer** or **Heaviside-Kennelly layer** or **E-layer** ▸ A belt in the Earth's atmosphere that contains ionized gases that act as a reflector for radio signals transmitted from Earth. It is named after the British physicist Oliver Heaviside (1850–1925). His studies of radio waves prompted him to propose (1902) the existence of such a component in the atmosphere. A similar proposal was made independently by the US engineer Arthur Edwin Kennelly (1861–1939) at the same time, hence the alternative name.

• **heavy** ▸ Slang from the youth culture of the late 1960s and early 1970s for serious, important, or meaningful, *e.g.* 'a heavy date'. It can also mean aggressive, threatening, or antagonistic.

• **heavy hitter** ▸ A colloquial expression for a person with a great deal of power, authority, or effectivess. Originating in baseball, it is usually applied to someone in the world of commerce or politics.

• **heavy metal** ▸ A form of rock music, popular since the early 1970s, that is characterized by extended guitar solos, heavy repetitive riffs, and high volume. It was developed from earlier electric blues styles in the late 1960s by such groups as Led Zeppelin and Deep Purple; later exponents have included Whitesnake and Judas Priest. With its macho posturing, the style appeals mainly to adolescent boys.

• **heavy water** ▸ Deuterium oxide, *i.e.* water in which some or all of the hydrogen has been replaced by deuterium; either HDO or $D_2O$. Heavy water is used as a moderator to slow down the neutrons in a nuclear reactor. German attempts to secure large supplies of heavy water from an industrial plant in Norway in the early 1940s convinced the Allies that the Nazis were developing an atomic weapon. The belief spurred the Anglo-American determination to build, and eventually use, the first atomic weapons.

• **hedgehopper** ▸ British slang coined during World War I for an air-force recruit; it is still used by new airmen of themselves. It is derived from the practice of flying close to the ground while still inexperienced.

• **Hedgers and Ditchers** ▸ In 1911, during the struggle against the Veto Bill proposing to curtail the powers of the House of Lords, the Conservative majority in the Lords was split. The 'Hedgers' under Lord Landsdowne were prepared to acquiesce rather than risk the creation of enough Liberal peers to ensure the bill's passage. The 'Ditchers' led by Lord Halsbury were prepared to die in the last ditch rather than yield. The Hedgers (the 'Judas group') prevailed and the bill passed, thus formally ending the power of the Lords over money bills and limiting that over other legislation to two years. *See*: Balfour's Poodle; Diehards; People's Budget.

• **heebie-jeebies** ▸ Slang for a state of nervous apprehension and fearfulness. It was coined by the US cartoonist William de Beck (1890–1942). It is now used in all English-speaking countries.

• **Heidelberg man** ▸ A form of prehistoric man first known from a fossilized lower jaw discovered in 1907 at Mauer, near Heidelberg, Germany. The thick-boned chinless mandible, about 500,000 years old, suggests that the owner had a broad projecting face, similar to *Homo erectus* ('upright man'). However, other features, such as the evenly proportioned teeth, are more characteristic of modern man (*Homo sapiens*). Heidelberg man was thus probably a type transitional between the two species and has been officially named *Homo heidelbergensis*. Since the original discovery, remains of *H. heidelbergensis* have been discovered at other sites, including Boxgrove in West Sussex (**Boxgrove man**).

• **heightism** ▸ Discrimination on the grounds of height. This can be practised against those who are considered too tall or too short for a particular job. The word was coined by analogy with other discriminative words, such as sexism and ageism.

• **hei jen** ▸ In China in the 1960s, young people who absconded from rural areas and went to live illegally in the city, with no fixed abode. The Chinese means 'black people'.

• **Heil Hitler** ▸ The salutation to the Führer used as an all-purpose greeting etc. in Nazi Germany. It was accompanied by the so-called Hitler or Nazi salute, in which the right arm was raised outstretched with the palm downward and the heels were clicked. The salutation and gesture are now used derisively of anyone perceived to be behaving in a dictatorial way.

• **Heimlich manoeuvre** ▸ An emergency technique to help a person who is choking, devised by the US physician H. J. Heimlich (1920–   ). The sufferer is clasped from behind with both arms, the clenched fist of one hand grasped by the other. The two hands are placed just below the sufferer's breastbone, enabling a sudden upward thrust of the hands and arms to dislodge the object obstructing the sufferer's airway.

• **Heimwehr** ▶ Home Defence Force: an Austrian paramilitary movement, consisting of several distinct regional forces, that was founded after World War I, partly to repel border incursions by Yugoslavs and Hungarians. The groups had strong conservative or Fascist tendencies, and gained support mainly from rural areas. During the 1920s and early 1930s the movement was increasingly courted by politicians of the right to act as a counterforce to socialist movements in Vienna and other cities. The Heimwehr leadership forged ties with Mussolini in 1930, and in 1932 the right-wing Christian Social Party gave the movement's leader, Fey, the post of national security chief in return for Heimwehr support. Although it helped in suppressing the Austrian socialists in 1934, the Heimwehr found its power draining away to the Nazis. It was dissolved by the government in 1936.

• **Heineken refreshes the parts other beers cannot reach** ▶ An advertising slogan for Heineken lager devised by Terry Lovelock of the Collett, Dickenson, Pearce Agency in 1974. The slogan is still used almost 30 years later. Since it first appeared a variety of characters, both on TV and on hoardings, have experienced the remarkable effects of the lager. 'Parts' to benefit include a policeman's feet, Concorde's nose, and those making up Frankenstein's monster. The phrase has been frequently parodied in such diverse contexts as graffiti and political speeches. At the 1980 Tory Party Conference Margaret Thatcher referred, in one of her better jokes, to her then foreign secretary, Lord Carrington, as 'the peer that reaches those foreign parts other peers cannot reach'.

• **Heinkel bomber** ▶ Any of several aircraft manufactured in Germany by Heinkel Flugzeugwerke, especially the He 111, the Luftwaffe's main medium-range bomber during World War II. The He 111 was a twin-engined development of the He 70 single-engined airliner. It first flew in 1935, and from 1936 was introduced into the Luftwaffe. The plane soon saw active service on the Nationalist side in the Spanish Civil War. More streamlined versions, the He 111P and 111H, had been developed by 1939; these had a wingspan of 22.6 m (74 ft 1 in) and a length of 16.39 m (53 ft 9 in). Many of these planes flew bombing missions over Britain during World War II, and losses were heavy during the Battle of Britain.

• **Heisenberg's Uncertainty Principle** or **Indeterminacy Principle** ▶ This states that one cannot measure precisely and simultaneously both the position and velocity of an object. It was formulated by the German physicist Werner Heisenberg (1901–76) and published in 1927. In practical terms the uncertainties involved are so small that they are significant only when considering atoms and sub-atomic particles. These uncertainties arise from the wavelike properties of such particles, i.e. they behave as both particles and waves. Position can only be determined accurately when the wave shows greatest undulation; but at this instant the wavelength is ill-defined, creating uncertainty in velocity measurement. The converse is true of precise velocity measurement. Heisenberg's principle also applies to other related pairs of physical variables, such as momentum and position, energy and time. Moreover, it has implications not only for quantum mechanics and particle physics but also for philosophy, especially arguments about cause and effect. If Heisenberg is correct, the identity of a particle can only be expressed in terms of probability and therefore its destiny cannot be stated with certainty. If one is unable to identify positively a particle and unable to be sure what will become of it in the future, one cannot say whether or not it is obeying the law of cause and effect. The breakdown of this law at the level of particles thus casts doubt on a principle that has been intuitively accepted for thousands of years – that every effect must have a cause.

• **heist** ▶ US slang for a robbery, usually an armed robbery. First used in the early years of the 20th century, it probably derives from 'hoist', meaning to lift. 'Lifting' is itself a euphemism for stealing. **Heist movies** are a popular subgenre of film in which the execution and aftermath of a robbery are seen from the viewpoint of the robbers. Examples include John Huston's *The Asphalt Jungle* (1950) and Quentin Tarantino's *Reservoir Dogs* (1992).

• **Heligoland Bight** ▶ The scene of the first naval battle of World War I, fought between the Royal Navy's Harwich Force, led by Commodore Reginald Tyrwhitt, and German vessels patrolling the waters of Heligoland Bight in the S North Sea. The intention was to lure into battle the larger German battleships anchored in nearby ports. In spite of near calamitous confusion among the British, caused by poor communications and bad visibility, several enemy ships were engaged resulting in the loss of three German light cruisers and a torpedo boat. Tyrwhitt's own cruiser, *Arethusa*, was severely crippled, and three British destroyers were damaged. The action, in August 1914, impressed the UK's naval supremacy on the Germans at the outset of the war, and prompted the Kaiser to instruct his fleet to 'hold itself back and avoid actions which can lead to greater losses'.

• **helipad** ▶ A place for helicopters to land and

take off. The word, a combination of 'helicopter' and 'pad' (a flat surface for vertical takeoff and landing), was coined in 1960. An earlier word, 'heliport', is also used.

• **heli-skiing** ▸ A form of skiing in which the skiers are transported to the top of the slopes by helicopter. Usually these slopes are remote from the usual tourist ski areas and certain to have copious snowfalls. Heli-skiing first became popular in Canada but has spread to the European ski slopes.

• **hellacious** ▸ US slang for horrifying or hellish: also sometimes used to mean extraordinary or wonderful. In Britain, the word first came to public attention during the Gulf War of 1991, when a US serviceman used it in a news broadcast.

• **Hell is other people** ▸ A much-quoted remark by the French existentialist philosopher and writer Jean-Paul Sartre (1905–80); it comes from his one-act play *Huis-clos* (1944), in which three characters find that they are condemned to torment one another for eternity. T. S. Eliot (1888–1965) did not agree:

> Hell is oneself. Hell is alone, the other figures in it
> Merely projections. There is nothing to escape from
> And nothing to escape to. One is always alone.
> – *The Cocktail Party* (1949).

• **Hello! hello! hello!** ▸ A suspicious greeting associated with the traditional, and probably mythical, British bobby. Often followed by the query 'What's going on 'ere then?', it was formerly much used by comedians to caricature a member of the uniformed constabulary. The phrase is usually delivered in grave tones, with the constable thrusting out the flaps of his tunic pockets with his thumbs, while simultaneously flexing his knees.

• **Hello playmates!** ▸ One of several catchphrases used by British comedian Arthur Askey (1900–82), originally on the BBC radio show *Band Wagon* (first broadcast January 1938). The phrase was widely mimicked by others, especially in the 1940s and 1950s.

• **Hell's Angels** ▸ Members of a gang of unruly and often trouble-making motorcyclists originating in California in the 1960s. They dress in battered, often filthy, leathers, wear their hair long and greasy, and have as their symbol a winged death's head. The group quickly became notorious for their intimidating appearance, peculiar initiation rites, and penchant for violence.

In due course Hell's Angels appeared in the UK and Europe among devotees of the motorcycle with a taste for a rootless existence on the fringe of so-

ciety. They still have a somewhat dubious image, although members claim that 'Angels' support one another and have even organized charitable fundraising efforts.

• **hell's a-poppin** ▸ A US catchphrase of the 1930s onwards describing a manifestation of immense exuberance or energy. The phrase might be used to describe a band playing with abandon or a very lively nightclub. It supplied the title of the 1942 comedy film, *Hellzapoppin*, written by Nat Perrin and directed by H. C. Potter.

• **Hell's Corner** ▸ The triangle of airspace above Kent with its apex above Dover; it was so called in World War II as it was here that much of the fiercest air combat took place during the Battle of Britain.

• **helping the police with their inquiries** ▸ A well-known police euphemism meaning that the person so described is being held as a suspect and subjected to rigorous police questioning. Since the Guildford Four and Birmingham Six cases, the phrase has taken on a somewhat sinister note.

• **helpline** ▸ A telephone line set up by special organizations to provide information, support, or counselling to groups such as the suicidal (*see*: Samaritans), Aids patients (*see*: Terrence Higgins Trust), child abuse victims (*see*: Childline), etc.

• **hen party** or **night** ▸ An evening party to which only women are invited. It usually immediately precedes a wedding and provides a last opportunity for the bride to go out on the town with her girlfriends as a single woman. Essentially an exercise in female bonding, the hen night may begin with 'pampering' at a spa or health club but invariably ends with binge drinking and much bawdy hilarity. *See also*: stag.

• **henry** ▸ **1.** British slang from the 1970s for heroin. *See also*: harry. **2.** British drug users' and dealers' slang from the 1980s for an eighth of an ounce of cannabis, based on the name Henry VIII. *See also*: Hooray Henry; louie.

• **Henry Straker** ▸ *See*: Straker, Henry.

• **hep-cat** ▸ Dated slang for a stylish or fashionable person, especially in jazz or beat culture. Possibly from the West African language Wolof, in which a *hipi-kat* is one who has opened his eyes. *See*: cat.

• **Herald of Free Enterprise** ▸ The Townsend Thoresen roll-on roll-off car ferry that capsized off the Belgian port of Zeebrugge on 6 March 1987 with the loss of 188 lives. The ferry had embarked on a routine crossing to Dover but, due to negligence on the part of the crew, the bow doors had been left open and the ship turned turtle within a mile of the harbour. Despite the high death toll, the loss of life could have been far greater if the ferry had not settled upside down on a sand bank, which allowed many of the passengers to escape.

• **herb** ► Caribbean slang for marijuana, usually pronounced in the West Indian way, 'erb'. It was used by Rastafarians and in Black music during the 1970s and has since been adopted by White users as an alternative to grass.

• **Herbert Divorce Act** ► The Matrimonial Causes Act 1937: a divorce reform act introduced to parliament as a Private Member's Bill by Sir A. P. Herbert (1890–1971), the humorist and writer who had been elected to the Commons in 1935 as an Independent MP. The Act extended the grounds for divorce to include desertion (of more than three years duration), insanity (of over five years duration), and cruelty. It also rectified discriminatory anomalies regarding adultery, and made it possible for a wife to divorce her husband for sodomy or bestiality.

• **Herero** ► A Bantu-speaking tribe native to parts of what is now Namibia and Botswana. They are traditionally herders of cattle, sheep, and goats, organized into self-governing groups comprising extended families, with an elaborate clan system.

In the late 19th century and early 20th century the Herero came into conflict with the German settlers of South West Africa, who were expropriating their land and livestock. This culminated in a full-scale rising in 1904, led by the Herero chief, Samuel Maherero. In an early exhibition of their brutality, the German forces, led by General von Trotha, implemented a policy of systematic genocide against the poorly armed tribespeople; two-thirds of the Herero men, women, and children were butchered, often in a sadistic fashion. The survivors fled to neighbouring British territory or into the Kalahari Desert.

• **Here's Johnny** ► A phrase used from 1961 onwards to introduce the US chat show host Johnny Carson on the NBC TV programme *Tonight*. His appearance was preceded by a drum roll and the 'here's' spun out to 'heeere's', the voice tone rising dramatically. Carson retired in the 1990s.

• **Here's looking at you, kid** ► The line from the film *Casablanca* (1942), starring Ingrid Bergman and Humphrey Bogart, that became the latter's catchphrase. It was based on a well-established US toast. Unlike the other catchphrase from this film, Play it again, Sam, Bogart actually said it.

• **Here we go, here we go, here we go** ► The British football fans' chant, usually sung to the tune of 'The Stars and Stripes for Ever'. The fans start chanting this when their team is doing well. It is also used provocatively by fans outside the ground and by extension in any situation in which a large crowd (*e.g.* of demonstrators) finds itself in a confrontational situation.

• **heritage coast** ► Several stretches of coastline in the British Isles that are considered to be of great natural beauty and are therefore protected from development; heritage coasts are managed by the Countryside Agency. The idea of conserving stretches of coastline arose in the 1970s. *See also*: National Parks.

• **heritage industry** ► A derogatory name for those economic activities that depend upon and perpetuate a nostalgic view of the nation's past. It is applied principally to tourism, but is also used to indict such phenomena as BBC costume drama, the trade in reproduction furniture, and the use of nostalgic imagery in advertising. It has been used scathingly of the re-creation of bygone customs or working practices (*see*: industrial tourism) to provide a tourist attraction.

Opponents of 'heritization' argue that it promotes an ersatz version of history, harmful to our understanding of both the past and the present. The term was popular with left-wing cultural commentators in the 1980s and provided the title of a book by Robert Hewison in 1987. *See also*: Disneyfication.

> There used to be coal mines in South Wales; now there's Heritage. The only working miners in the Rhondda Valley have moulded bodies and glass eyes...an organization called Heritage Projects is making glass-fibre miners for an organization called the Rhondda Heritage Park.
> – *The Independent*, 26 January 1991.

• **hero** ► Hazards of electromagnetic radiation to ordnance. This acronym refers to the risk that electromagnetic radiation will accidentally ignite the fuse of the warhead of a missile, causing it to explode.

• **heroes** ►
**a country fit for heroes** A phrase popularized by the Liberal statesman David Lloyd George in a speech on 24 November 1918, in the immediate aftermath of World War I. Although often misquoted as 'a country fit for heroes', what he actually said was:

> What is our task? To make Britain a fit country for heroes to live in.

The reality of 1920s and 1930s Britain was rather different, as suggested by Kensal Green's couplet about Lloyd George:

> Count not his broken promises as a crime

He MEANT them, HOW he meant them – at the time.

These sentiments were echoed by G. K. Chesterton in his verse 'A Land Fit for Heroes', with the ironic subtitle 'Refutation of the Only Too Prevalent Slander that Parliamentary Leaders are Indifferent to the Strict Fulfilment of their Promises and the Preservation of their Reputation for Veracity':

> They said (when they had dined at Ciro's)
> The land would soon be fit for heroes;
> And now they've managed to ensure it,
> For only heroes could endure it.

• **heroin** ▸ An addictive drug (chemical name diacetylmorphine) with harmful side-effects that first became widely used in Western societies during the hippie era. First developed from morphine in 1898 for use as a narcotic analgesic, it was subsequently banned (except for strictly controlled medical use) in many countries after its undesirable addictive and physically damaging properties became known. It can be injected, sniffed, or inhaled and causes a shortlived sensation of euphoria followed by sleep; addicts suffer severe withdrawal symptoms if they cannot obtain supplies of the drug. The injection of pure heroin can kill as well as put addicts at risk from hepatitis, Aids, and other infections. Because addicts are soon unable to work, those who are not millionaire rock stars are forced to obtain the considerable amounts of money required to feed their habit either by prostitution or criminal activities (mainly petty theft). Indeed, a major proportion of the criminal activity in many developed countries is drug related. The first heroin addicts were diagnosed in the West in the early years of the 20th century; by the end of the century the problems associated with the drug were being felt throughout the world despite severe legal penalties for use or possession of heroin and international efforts to prevent trafficking.

• **heroin baby** ▸ A baby born to a heroin addict. Heroin babies are usually born prematurely and with a dependence on the drug.

• **heroin chic** ▸ A mainly US trend of the mid-1990s in which images associated with heroin addiction became popular in fashion photography and other forms of advertising. Typical fashion spreads of the time featured gaunt glassy-eyed models posing somnambulistically in seedy locations. The most notorious purveyor of such imagery was the designer Calvin Klein, who in 1997 plucked a heroin addict from the streets as an example of the look that he wanted for his models: the same addict was even featured in subsequent campaigns. This provided a clear target for anti-drugs organizations, and eventually the campaign was discontinued.

That same year the death from a heroin overdose of Davide Sorrenti, a fashion photographer whose work had popularized heroin chic, provoked President Clinton to condemn the trend in a speech to the US Conference of Mayors (21 May 1997).

Although the extreme forms of heroin chic proved shortlived, more subtle versions of the look pervaded all branches of advertising for some time to come. To this extent, heroin chic may be seen as part of the wider grunge movement, which rebelled against the idealized images of perfection with which consumers are bombarded in the media.

> Young people adopt a heroin-chic look so that their mothers will be appalled to see how close to death they are. – *The Guardian*, 23 September 2000.

• **Herrenvolk** ▸ A German word meaning broadly master race. In Nazi usage it implied that the German peoples had an inborn superiority, especially to Jews, Slavs, and others. Largely as a result of this patently absurd belief, the German nation as a whole, during the decade starting in about 1935, showed itself to be capable of the most bestial and subhuman cruelty.

• **Herriot, James** ▸ Pen name of the writer James Alfred Wight (1916–95), who trained as a veterinary surgeon in Glasgow and began practising in N Yorkshire in 1940. The first of his many entertaining stories, drawing on his professional experiences in the Yorkshire Dales, appeared in 1970. These provided the basis of a popular TV series, *All Creatures Great and Small*, in the 1980s.

• **Hershey Bar** ▸ Tradename for a US chocolate bar, which in World War II was only available to the troops. General L. B. Hershey was director of the Selective Service System, 1941–46. Hence in US army slang the name was also used for to the narrow gold bar worn by troops on the left sleeve to indicate that they had done six months' overseas service.

• **HGV** ▸ Heavy goods vehicle. An articulated or fixed-chassis lorry used for road haulage. An HGV licence is issued in addition to the normal car licence and is graded according to the type of vehicle in which the HGV test was taken. A Class 3 licence covers two-axle rigid straight trucks; a Class 2 covers three- and four-axle straight trucks; and a Class 1 licence (the most coveted) covers articulated vehicles of any size or gross weight.

• **hiba kusha** ▸ (Japanese, explosion-affected group) A person or people who survived the atom bombs dropped on Hiroshima and Nagasaki by America in 1945. It came into English usage around 1970.

• **hidden agenda** ▶ An undisclosed motivation behind some action or policy. If a person behaves in a manner that seems out of character a hidden agenda may well be suspected. This may be personal (*e.g.* sexual attraction, desire for revenge) or political (*e.g.* an attempt to lull a rival into a false sense of security).

• **hide** ▶

**You can run, but you can't hide** A phrase associated with the US boxer Joe Louis (1914–81); although he probably didn't invent it, he used it as part of his bravado speech before his World Heavyweight Championship bout in 1946 against the nimble Billy Conn. Louis won. President Reagan used the phrase in 1985 as a warning to all international terrorists following the hijacking of a TWA airliner to Beirut.

• **Hi-de-hi!** ▶ A long-running BBC TV comedy programme, first broadcast in 1980, that was set in a 1950s holiday camp. The phrase alludes to a nonsensical chant formerly used to enthuse holidaymakers at Butlins' camps: 'Hi-de-hi! Ho-de-ho!'. The line had been used previously (1937) by the broadcaster Christopher Stone as his catchphrase on Radio Normandy. Another story concerns an army officer who trained his troops to answer 'Ho-de-ho' to his call of 'Hi-de-hi'; he was court-martialled.

• **hi-fi** ▶ The reproduction of recorded music with little distortion; also equipment that faithfully reproduces sound. The term, an abbreviation of 'high-fidelity', was first used in the late 1940s. The reproduction of music in the home has passed through a number of stages, requiring the user to buy new equipment and a new collection of recorded works several times during his or her lifetime. Recording of music began with the phonograph (invented 1877), using wax cylinders, and progressed rapidly to the gramophone (1888), using shellac records. Electrified gramophones appeared in the 1930s; called radiograms or record players, they continued to use shellac records rotating at 78 rpm until the late 1940s, when vinyl discs were introduced, using rotation speeds of 45 and 33 rpm. It was the vinyl 33 rpm discs (so called long-playing or LPs) that were first called hi-fi recordings. They were advertised as giving distortion-free reproduction between frequencies of 80 and 12,000 hertz. Later, vinyl discs had to compete with magnetic tape cassettes, which increasingly used the Dolby System. Current hi-fi systems have abandoned both vinyl and tape in favour of compact discs using digital recording and laser-driven compact-disc players. Thus a music enthusiast in his sixties is likely to have his favourite music recorded in four separate collections: shellac 78s, vinyl LPs, cassettes, and compact discs, all requiring different equipment. In the not too distant future, the hi-fi enthusiast is likely to have to re-equip with digital audio tape (*see:* DAT), a new breed of magnetic tape using digital recording.

• **Higgins, Professor** ▶ The phonetics expert in Shaw's play *Pygmalion* (1913), who tutors the Cockney flower-seller, **Eliza Doolittle**, in order that she may be passed off as a duchess. The play ends with Eliza at odds with Higgins, who persists in seeing her as an experimental subject, rather than a human being. However, for the 1938 film version, directed by Anthony Asquith and Leslie Howard, Shaw approved the scripted 'happy ending', with a reconciliation between the Professor and 'Liza (played by Howard and Wendy Hiller, respectively). This modified plot was adapted for the musical version, *My Fair Lady* (1956), which was filmed in 1964, with Higgins played by Rex Harrison. Shaw is said to have based the Higgins character on the distinguished Oxford phonetician, Henry Sweet (1845–1912).

• **high-involvement product** ▶ A product on which a purchaser will usually spend a considerable amount of time and thought before deciding to buy a particular make or model. Cars, houses, computers, DVD players, etc., are the typical high-cost items that fall into this category. Advertisements for such products will tend to provide the potential buyer with the kind of technical information required to make an informed judgment between it and its competitors.

**Low-involvement products**, on the other hand, involve the consumer in little deliberation. Such products are cheap and advertisers strive to make their advertisements interesting or funny in order to develop a brand loyalty, because they know that their product is unlikely to be much better (or worse) than its competitors.

• **high jump** ▶ To be 'for the high jump' is a British idiom meaning that the person so described is liable for a severe reprimand or punishment (often dismissal from their job). It originally meant that someone was to be executed by hanging, alluding to the victim's 'jump' into space when the trap was opened.

• **high-level language** ▶ A computer programming language that uses a notation closer to human language or mathematical symbols than a machine code. High-level languages, such as FORTRAN and Basic, are slower to execute than low-level languages, which are closer to the computer processor instructions. However, they are much easier to use and most software is written in high-level form.

• **High-oh, Silver** ▶ A catchphrase given to a grateful world by the US radio serial of the 1930s and 1940s, *The Lone Ranger*. The phrase was uttered by the show's masked hero as a means of spurring on his steed, Silver. The show later transferred to the small screen, which is how British audiences came to know the phrase in the 1960s. *See*: Lone Ranger.

• **high rise** ▶ A residential building with a large number of floors. The high rise, or tower block, came into vogue during the late 1950s and 1960s as architects followed the teaching and example of the modernist visionary Le Corbusier (1887–1965). The idea of modern, hygenic, and streamlined space-saving buildings using cheap modern concrete materials proved particularly appealing to post-war local councils faced with restricted housing budgets. The first of the UK's high-rise estates, Alton West in Roehampton, was erected by the London County Council in 1958. Hundreds of similar estates, some with slimmer and taller tower blocks, were erected in the next 20 years all over the UK. They were not, however, popular with the people housed in them. Perched high above the ground in cramped flats, young mothers longed for their own houses and back gardens in which the children could play and babies could sleep in their prams. In addition, shoddy workmanship and flawed design, such as poor waterproofing and dangerous lifts, together with lack of supervision and recreation facilities, turned many of these estates into brutal, damp, and vandalized areas, plagued by criminals and vermin; many of the buildings have now been pulled down. The architects and town planners of the period have much to answer for. *See also*: brutalism.

• **high tech** or **hi-tech** ▶ A style of domestic decor, popular in the late 1970s and 1980s, which used high-quality industrial furniture and fittings, such as metal factory shelves and tubular steel shelving, to replicate the hard metallic surfaces and textures of the industrial and technological environment. 'High-tech' is also used to describe a style of modern architecture, which regards architectural design as a branch of industrial technology. A classic example of the high-tech glass and metal style is the Lloyd's Building (1986) in London, designed by Richard Rogers (1933–   ). More generally, 'high-tech' is applied to any industry, process, product, etc., using sophisticated electronic equipment or techniques.

• **Highway Code** ▶ A code, prepared by the Driving Standards Agency and issued by the Depart-ment of Transport, for road users, both pedestrians and those using vehicles (including lorries, cars, motorcycles, and bicycles). The code contains detailed instructions on road and motorway use, and knowledge of the code is essential to pass a driving test. *See also*: Green Cross Code.

• **hijack** ▶ Illegally to take possession of a vehicle and its contents, whether goods or passengers, usually by means of force or threats of force. Hijacking can apply either to lorries, etc., or to planes, for which the word **sky-jack** has also been coined. Since the late 20th century the term has been mainly applied to the act by terrorists of taking over control of a passenger aircraft in flight and ordering the pilot at gunpoint to fly to a new destination, where political or ransom demands are made using the passengers as hostages. The word is thought to originate from the command given by robbers raiding lorries transporting illicit alcohol in America during Prohibition: 'Stick 'em up high, Jack'.

• **Hillsborough disaster** ▶ The UK's worst sports tragedy, in which 95 spectators died at the Hillsborough football ground, Sheffield, on 15 April 1989. The disaster occurred shortly after the start of the FA Cup semi-final between Liverpool and Nottingham Forest. Several hundred Liverpool fans arriving late caused severe congestion in the approaches to the Leppings Lane end of the ground, causing the police to open the turnstiles into the ground in an attempt to relieve the crush outside. However, the fans surged onto already crowded terraces, so that spectators at the front were crushed against the perimeter fencing, unable to escape onto the pitch. Besides the fatalities, some 400 fans were treated in hospital for their injuries. The official inquiry into the disaster, conducted by Lord Justice Taylor, placed the blame on inadequate policing of the crowd coupled with design flaws in the stadium. Taylor's recommendations prompted an urgent overhaul of football ground safety in the UK.

• **Hill 60** ▶ 1. A small hill SE of Ypres, Belgium, that figured in fighting on the Western Front during World War I. It was so named because of its height – 60 m. In April 1915 British forces mined and destroyed German positions and captured the hill. There followed a fierce but unsuccessful counter-attack by the Germans, whereupon both sides announced possession of Hill 60. The propaganda value of holding the hill thus came to outweigh its strategic importance; as the British still held the hill, the Germans were forced to launch a determined attack to give substance to their false claim.

On 5 May as a result of a combination of gas and heavy shelling, the British retreated. Although by now partly demolished by sheer weight of explosives, Hill 60 continued to be fought over until the Allied breakthrough of 1917. **2.** A quite different Hill 60 featured in the Gallipoli campaign, again during World War I. It is one of the foothills of the Sari Bair range on the Gallipoli peninsula.

• **Hindenburg**▸ The German airship whose tragic demise in 1937 marked the end of an era in aviation. She was built by the makers of the highly successful Graf Zeppelin I for regular service across the North Atlantic, and measured 245 m (804 ft) in length with a gas capacity of 196,000 m$^3$ (7,000,000 ft$^3$). When completed in 1936 this made her the largest airship ever built, although the record was soon to be taken by her sister ship, *Graf Zeppelin II*, with a slightly larger gas volume. The Hindenburg's scheduled transatlantic service began in 1936, between Friedrichshafen, Germany, and Lakehurst, New Jersey. On 6 May 1937, while coming in to land at Lakehurst, hydrogen gas in the airship's tail section caught fire. The flames quickly spread and the airship collapsed to the ground in a mass of burning wreckage, killing 35 of the 97 passengers and crew on board. The exact cause of the fire was never established, but the accident, combined with the growing prospect of war, effectively put paid to airship travel, and her sister ship never entered commercial service.

• **Hindenburg Line**▸ The German defensive line that formed a long section of the Western Front in the later stages of World War I; so-called because it was under the authority of the German commander, von Hindenburg (1847–1934). The line stretched some 90 miles SE from Arras to Soissons and comprised sentry posts, trench systems, dugouts, and other features forming a zone in places up to 7300 m (8000 yd) wide. Around 65,000 people were employed in its construction, between October 1916 and March 1917, including 50,000 Russian prisoners-of-war. In March 1917 the Germans started a strategic withdrawal from the existing front to the Hindenburg Line, in some places retreating a distance of over 40 km. The move enabled consolidation of both German men and materials and considerably strengthened their defensive capability. Only in September 1918 were the German forces finally ousted from large sections of the line.

• **hip** ▸ Originally US slang meaning either fashionable ('Yoga is becoming hip') or alive to, aware of, wise to ('She's hip to the lies men tell'). The alternative form **hep** is now very old-fashioned (*see*: hepcat). The word probably comes from the West African Wolof word *hipi*, meaning to open one's eyes. *See*: hippie.

• **hip-hop**▸ A form of music and a related style of dancing originated by Black and Hispanic youths in New York during the 1980s. The music, which featured rap to an electronic backing, was accompanied by rhythmical jerky dancing, such as body-popping.

• **hip-huggers**▸ Trousers or jeans that fit closely round, and hang from, the hips rather than the waist. Flared hip-huggers, also known as **hipsters**, were fashionable dress in the late 1960s and early 1970s.

• **hippie** or **hippy**▸ In the late 1960s, a young person who rejected conventional society in favour of an unstructured lifestyle based on communal living, free love, and experimentation with psychedelic drugs. Hippies wore fantastic multi-coloured clothes, often set off with flowers and bells (*see*: flower people), and preached a pacific anarchistic philosophy; many were interested in ecology and Eastern religions. The movement began in San Francisco in 1966–67 and soon spread throughout Europe and America. In the UK, social security payments enabled disaffected young people to opt out of a conventional working life; others had private means or attempted to make a living from the land.

In the 1980s the term was applied by the British tabloid press to the new phenomenon of New Age Travellers.

• **hipsters**▸ *See*: hip-huggers.

• **Hiroshima**▸ A Japanese city and military base, the target of the first atom bomb dropped in warfare (6 August 1945). Over 160,000 people were killed or injured and far more rendered homeless. The flash of the explosion was seen 170 miles away and a mushroom-shaped column of black smoke rose over the city to a height of 40,000 feet (*see*: mushroom cloud). Hiroshima remains a solemn portent of the fate over-shadowing mankind in the event of a nuclear war. *See also*: Enola Gay; hiba kusha; Nagasaki.

• **His Master's Voice**▸ A phrase once familiar to record buyers in America and Europe as the tradename of the Gramophone Company, now part of EMI. It was originally the title of a painting by Francis Barraud (1856–1924), showing the artist's terrier cross, Nipper, looking curiously at the black horn of a wax cylinder phonograph player from which the sound of 'his master's voice' is emerging. The record company agreed to purchase the work in 1899 but stipulated that the picture be altered to show a brass horn and a more up-to-date gramophone; close examination of the picture reveals the faint outline of the older model still visible. Nipper had died in 1897 but his image endured to become the most frequently reproduced dog image of all time. He was first used in an advertisement in 1900 and from 1902 the US Victor company incorporated his image on its record labels. In the UK, Nipper appeared on records from 1909, and the phrase 'His Master's Voice' became part of the logo in 1910. Nipper also appeared in an advertisement for Reid's Stout, sniffing at a glass of beer; the caption ran 'What is it that master likes so much?' More recently, the name and mascot have been revived for the HMV chain of record and video shops.

• **Hiss affair**▶ The sensation caused in 1948 by allegations that a US State Department official, Alger Hiss (1904–96), was a former communist spy. The accusation was made by Whittaker Chambers, one-time Communist Party member and a former editor of *Time* magazine, before the House Committee for Un-American Activities (*see:* McCarthyism). Hiss strenuously denied Chambers' allegations, and in August brought a suit for slander against him. When challenged for evidence to support his accusations, Chambers produced copies of State Department papers that he claimed had been supplied by Hiss. Chambers even led investigators to his Maryland farm, where he produced three rolls of microfilm hidden in a pumpkin – the infamous **pumpkin papers**. Hiss was indicted and appeared before a grand jury in 1949 on charges of perjury – for his previous denials, on oath, of passing papers to Chambers. This first trial resulted in a hung jury, but at a re-trial in 1950 Hiss was convicted and sentenced to five years imprisonment. He was released in 1954 and spent the rest of his life trying to clear his name. Many believe that Hiss fell victim to the anti-communist hysteria then widespread in America; others remain convinced of his guilt. The affair certainly boosted the career of Richard M. Nixon, then a junior member of the Un-American Activities Committee, who was instrumental in constructing the case against Hiss.

• **history is bunk**▶ A phrase often attributed to the US car manufacturer Henry Ford (1863–1947). Ford's actual words were less absolute:

> History is more or less bunk.

He went on to say:

> It's tradition. We don't want tradition. We want to live in the present and the only history that is worth a tinker's damn is the history we make today. – *Chicago Tribune*, 25 May 1916.

• **hit**▶ 1. Slang for a single puff on a marijuana cigarette or a pipe, or a single dose of an illegal drug. 2. Slang for an assassination. Originally from US underworld jargon, it is now widely used both as a noun and a verb. 3. British rhyming slang for drunk, from 'hit and missed', *i.e.* pissed. 4. Slang for to borrow, or beg, *e.g.* 'He hit me for another fiver'.

• **hit-and-run**▶ An accident involving a motor vehicle, in which the driver has neither stopped after the accident to help the victim nor informed the police. Hit-and-run drivers hope to escape the consequences of the accident but if they are caught they are dealt with very severely by the courts.

• **Hitler Diaries**▶ In April 1983 *The Sunday Times* reported the discovery of 60 volumes of Hitler's diaries which had been acquired by the Hamburg magazine *Stern* for £2,460,000 through the agency of their reporter Gert Heidemann. They were said to have been salvaged from an aircraft wrecked in 1945 and found in a hayloft. The distinguished historian Hugh Trevor-Roper (Lord Dacre) vouched for their authenticity and *The Sunday Times* (after paying *Stern* for publication rights) obtained two volumes (1932 and 1935) for testing. However, Dr Julius Grant, a chemical expert, soon proved that the paper in the diaries was of a kind not in use until after World War II and the Bonn government also declared them to be forgeries. Heidemann revealed that he had obtained them from a Stuttgart dealer in military relics, Konrad Fischer, whose real name was Konrad Kujau; he later confessed to the forgery. Both were imprisoned in May 1983, brought to trial in August 1984, and sentenced in July 1985. Kujau was jailed for 4 years 6 months for forgery and Heidemann for 4 years 8 months for fraud. *The Sunday Times* and Lord Dacre emerged from the whole episode looking rather foolish; newspapers are now somewhat more cautious about announcing scoops before they have proved them to be valid.

• **Hitlerism** ▶ The doctrine and practice of the Nazi regime of Adolf Hitler (1889–1945), who became German chancellor in 1933 and ruled Germany until his suicide. His brutal, aggressive, and expansionist policies led directly to World War II in which over 20 million people were killed. Pursuing totally spurious racial theories, he was also responsible for the holocaust, in which six million Jews were murdered on his orders. One of the most baffling mysteries of the 20th century is how virtually the entire German nation came to idolize, and obey with enthusiasm, a man accurately summed up by Churchill as 'a bloodthirsty guttersnipe'.

• **Hitlerjunge Quex** ▶ (German, Hitler Youth Quex) The title of a Nazi propaganda film produced in 1933 under the auspices of Dr Paul Joseph Goebbels, the minister for public enlightenment and propaganda. The plot concerned the real-life case of Herbert Norkus, a member of the Hitler Youth who was allegedly murdered by communists. It was a box-office flop, like the two other Goebbels-inspired movies of the same year – *SA-Mann Brand*, about Nazi stormtroopers, and *Hans Westmar*, based on the life of the Nazi 'martyr' Horst Wessel (*see*: Horst Wessel Lied).

• **Hitler-Stalin pact** ▶ A pact of nonaggression between Germany and the Soviet Union signed in Moscow on 23 August 1939 by Germany's foreign minister, von Ribbentrop, and the Soviet Commissar for foreign affairs, Molotov (it is also known as the **Ribbentrop-Molotov pact**). The two countries agreed not to support any third party that launched an attack on the other signatory, and to consult with each other on matters of mutual interest. More significant, however, was a secret protocol that effectively partitioned Europe into German and Soviet spheres. The pact was greeted triumphantly by Hitler but viewed with dismay by the UK and the other Western democracies. Hitler and Stalin had managed to swallow their long-standing rancour towards each other to win significant strategic gains: Stalin was given the defensive buffer he badly needed, while Hitler saw the final obstacle to a German invasion of Poland removed. German tanks crossed the Polish border on 1 September, and by the end of the month all of Poland was divided between the German and Soviet armies, according to the terms of the pact. The Allies were by now at war with Germany.

• **Hitler Youth** ▶ (German *Hitler Jugend*) The principal male youth organization of Nazi Germany. It was established in 1933, together with an equivalent organization for girls – the League of German Girls (*Bund Deutscher Mädel*). In 1935 Baldur von Schirach was appointed Reich Youth Leader, and the following year all youth organizations other than Hitler Youth were banned. The Hitler Youth embodied the vehement anti-intellectualism and antisemitism of the Führer, who wanted its youngsters to be 'swift as the greyhound, tough as leather, and hard as Krupp steel'. Boys were admitted to the Hitler Youth at the age of 14, normally after three or more years in the junior division, the Deutsches Jungvolk (German Young People). At 18 members graduated to the National Socialist Party, and so into the adult echelons of Nazism, having by then been thoroughly indoctrinated in Hitler's demented philosophy.

• **hit list** ▶ A list of people targeted for some form of violence, such as murder. By extension a list of people or things targeted for rigorous treatment, *i.e.*: 'a hit list of poorly performing schools'.

• **hitman** ▶ Slang for a hired killer. Originally US underworld jargon, it is now widely used in the UK.

• **hit the ground running** ▶ To start a new enterprise in such a way that one is immediately able to operate at full strength. It probably derives from the idea of troops being dropped by parachute or disembarking rapidly from helicopters (as in the Vietnam War) and going immediately into action.

• **hitting on all six** ▶ Doing well, giving a fine performance. A motor-car engine when running well is described as having the pistons in all six cylinders hitting (firing) perfectly.

• **HIV** ▶ Human immuno-deficiency virus. The virus that causes Aids. If someone is diagnosed as **HIV-positive**, he or she shows traces of the virus in their system but can remain free of Aids symptoms indefinitely. Research into the precise links between HIV infection and full-blown Aids, and into what factors induce the virus to remain dormant, is still inconclusive.

• **H-line** ▶ *See*: Dior.

• **Hoare-Laval pact** ▶ Secret proposals for ending the conflict caused by the Italian invasion of Abyssinia (Ethiopia) in 1935, formulated in early December of that year by the British foreign minister, Samuel Hoare, and his French opposite number, Pierre Laval. The proposals granted substantial territorial concessions to Italy, plus a zone of exclusive economic interest; the League of Nations would protect Abyssinian sovereignty over remaining areas. The pact was leaked to the press on 9 December causing a storm of public protest against this apparent appeasement of Italian aggression. By 18 December the British government had been forced to repudiate the pact, and Hoare resigned, to be succeeded by Anthony Eden. Unhindered, Italy proceeded to complete her conquest of Abyssinia.

• **hobbit** ▶ A member of a benevolent hospitable burrow people, two to four feet high and fond of creature comforts, created by Professor J. R. R. Tolkien. They are featured in his works *The Hobbit* (1937) and *The Lord of the Rings* (1954–55).

> I am in fact a hobbit in all but size. I like gardens, trees and unmechanized farmlands; I smoke a pipe, and like good plain food...I like, and even dare to wear in these dull days, ornamental waistcoats; I...have a very simple sense of humour...I go to bed late and get up late (when possible). I do not travel much.
> – J. R. R. TOLKIEN, letter.

• **hobble skirt** ▶ A woman's skirt of the 1910s, so tight around the ankles that the wearer was impeded in walking (much as a horse is hobbled). The fashion for this garment was at its height in 1912; by 1914, not surprisingly, it had been abandoned.

• **hobo** ▶ In US usage, a vagrant who travels in search of work – in contrast to a tramp, who travels without working, or a bum, who neither travels nor works. It derives probably from 'hoe-boy', a migratory farm worker.

• **Ho Chi Minh Trail** ▶ A network of routes running S from what was formerly North Vietnam, through E Laos into Cambodia and S Vietnam. It is named after North Vietnam's president (1954–69) and leader of the independence struggle, Ho Chi Minh (1890–1969). Parts of the trail date back to the 1940s and 1950s, when the Vietnamese were fighting for independence from the French. During the Vietnam War of the 1960s and 1970s it was greatly expanded to supply the Communist National Liberation Front (Viet Cong) with men and materials for their campaign in the South. The trail comprises a mixture of footpaths, tracks, and roads through the mountains and jungles, built and maintained largely by hand. Some stretches were suitable for trucks, but most parts were passable only by bullock cart, by bicycle, or on foot. Supplies could take up to six months to pass the full extent of the trail into South Vietnam. In spite of intensive US bombing, and efforts by the South Vietnamese army to cut Viet Cong supply lines, the North Vietnamese army and NLF kept the trail open throughout the war. This proved to be a crucial factor in their ultimate victory.

The **Sihanouk Trail**, named after the Cambodian leader, Prince Norodim Sihanouk, branched off the Ho Chi Minh Trail in S Laos to provide a route into NE Cambodia.

• **Hockey Stick** ▶ A Hollywood nickname of the British film star Julie Andrews (1935–    ). Many Americans seemed to associate her cool beauty, middle-class vowels, and no-nonsense manner with the jolly hockey sticks! tradition of British independent schools, although she never in fact attended such a school. Moss Hart, the US playwright and producer, said of her:

> She has that wonderful British strength that makes you wonder why they lost India.

This reputation, largely earned in her two governess roles (in *Mary Poppins* and *The Sound of Music*), made her a great deal of money, brought her worldwide stardom, and endeared her to several generations of children. It did not, however, please Ms Andrews herself. In 1966 she said:

> I don't want to be thought of as wholesome.

She was also in the habit of wearing a badge saying: 'Mary Poppins is a junkie'.

• **hog** ▶ **1.** US slang for a motorcyle, especially a Harley Davidson. It was first used by the Hell's Angels in America, but later became well known in the UK and Australia. *See also:* chopper. **2.** Slang for the illegal drug PCP (*see:* angel dust), which was originally developed as an animal tranquillizer and tested on pigs.

• **Hogwarts** ▶ *See:* Potter, Harry.

• **Holcomb murders** ▶ The murder in 1959 of four members of a farming family at Holcomb, Kansas. Two ex-convicts were later arrested and convicted of the brutal crime. The case occupied the attentions of US novelist Truman Capote, who used it as the basis of his book *In Cold Blood* (1966). This he described as 'a nonfiction novel': 'a new art form... that employed all the techniques of fictional art but was nevertheless immediately factual.' Serialized in *The New Yorker* magazine prior to publication, the novel attracted great attention, and no little acclaim, from critics and public alike, and became a bestseller. The British critic, Kenneth Tynan, accused Capote of being less than strenuous in his efforts to win a reprieve for the convicted men and it was undeniable that their execution helped generate interest in Capote's book. Capote retorted that the appeals procedure had been exhausted.

• **holding pattern** ▶ A repetitive circuit flown by an aircraft while waiting permission to land at an airport. The term has been extended to other states of delay or deferment.

• **holistic medicine** ▶ An approach to medical care that aims to treat the patient as a whole, rather than applying remedies to specific areas of the body or mind. The word 'holistic' was invented by Jan Smuts, prime minister of South Africa, in the mid-1920s to describe his philosophical theory of **holism**. The holistic movement in medicine arose some 40 or so years later, as part of a minority interest in homeopathy and other alternative therapies (*see:* alternative medicine); the principle is now being increasingly accepted and applied by orthodox practitioners.

• **Hollywood** ▶ A suburb of Los Angeles, California, also called **Tinsel Town** or occasionally **Sodom-by-the-sea**, famous as the centre of the US film-making industry. Founded in 1911, Hollywood quickly superseded New York as the movie capital of America and became an international byword for glitz and glamour. The **Golden Age of Hollywood** comprised the years of the studio system, roughly

1930 to 1949, when a handful of powerful producers dominated the US motion-picture output and the world mass-market entertainment business. By the mid-1950s, a combination of factors, including the rise of television, McCarthyism, and the advent of the actor-producer conspired to end the hegemony of the Hollywood 'dream factory', although the town remains the capital of US (and therefore world) cinema. See also: Beverly Hills.

> A place where they pay you $50,000 for a kiss and 50 cents for your soul. – MARILYN MONROE.

• **Hollywood Bowl** ▶ An open-air auditorium in the Hollywood area of Los Angeles, noted for its summer season of concerts given by the Los Angeles Philharmonic Orchestra. The concert platform, designed by the US architect Frank Lloyd Wright, is a fairy-tale shell-like structure, 30 m (100 ft) wide, located at the base of a natural amphitheatre capable of seating 17,500 people. The Bowl's first concert was held in 1921. Today, pop, jazz, and rock events are held in addition to the light classical performances. Los Angelinos traditionally bring picnics to consume before, and often also during, the concerts.

• **Hollywood Ten** ▶ The group of ten US screenwriters, film producers, and directors who refused to confirm or deny their affiliation to the Communist Party during the investigations of the House of Un-American Activities Committee in 1947 (see: McCarthyism): Alvah Bessie, Herbert Biberman, Lester Cole, Edward Dmytryk, Ring Lardner Jnr., John Howard Lawson, Albert Maltz, Sam Ornitz, Adrian Scott, and Dalton Trumbo. All were subsequently imprisoned for a short time for contempt of court and on their release were blacklisted and unable to work in Hollywood for several years. Many did not return to the film industry.

• **Holmes, Sherlock** ▶ The most famous figure in detective fiction, the creation of Arthur Conan Doyle (1859–1930). His ingenious solutions to a wide variety of crimes and mysteries were related in a series of 60 stories that appeared in the *Strand Magazine* between 1891 and 1927. The character was based on Dr Joseph Bell of the Edinburgh Infirmary, whose methods of rational deduction suggested the system that Holmes developed into a science – the observation of minute details and apparently insignificant circumstances scientifically interpreted. Dr Watson, Holmes's stolid friend and assistant, was a skit on Doyle himself, and Baker Street, in which the detective lived at a fictional number 221B, acquired lasting fame through the stories. Letters still arrive at the site where 221B would have been had it existed (now occupied by a bank)

asking for the detective's help: they are answered with the information that Holmes has now retired to take up bee-keeping in the country. Conan Doyle himself grew so tired of his creation that he attempted to kill him off by having him plummet over the Reichenbach Falls with his arch-enemy Moriarty. The public outcry was such that Doyle was obliged to resurrect him in a further series of stories. See also: Baker Street Irregulars; HOLMES.

> 'Excellent!' I cried. 'Elementary,' said he. – *The Crooked Man*.

• **HOLMES** ▶ A large computer maintained by the British Home Office for the investigation of crime. The acronym is for 'Home Office Large Major Enquiry System', and was coined in honour of Conan Doyle's detective Sherlock Holmes.

• **holocaust** ▶ The word originally referred to a sacrifice to the Greek gods in which the victim was burnt whole (from the Greek words *holos*, whole, and *kaustos*, burnt). It later came to mean slaughter or destruction on an immense scale and specifically the extermination of six million European Jews by the Germans under Hitler in the period 1940–45. This monstrous act of unreasoned brutality is generally seen as the most appalling crime of the 20th – or any other – century. **Holocaust Day** is observed in Israel on Nisan 27 (in April or May). See also: concentration camp; Eichmann trial; Final Solution; Wannsee conference; Wiesenthal Centre.

• **hologram** ▶ (holo-, whole; -gram, record) A permanent record on a photographic film or plate of a three-dimensional image created by the interference pattern formed by the two intersecting light beams from a split laser light source. When the developed film or plate is illuminated by laser light or, after further treatment, by ordinary white light, the 3-D image is reconstructed from the interference pattern recorded on the photographic emulsion. **Reflective holograms** that can be viewed in daylight or artificial light now appear on credit cards as a safeguard against counterfeiting.

**Holography**, the technique of producing 3-D images using a coherent beam of light or other radiation, was developed in 1947 by the Hungarian-born British scientist Dennis Gabor (1900–79), but was largely ignored until after the construction of the laser in 1960. Among its uses are the detection of defects in industrial apparatus and the production of 3-D reference models for use in building, engineering, etc.

• **holon** ▶ A distinct entity or structure that is also part of a larger entity or structure. The term (from Greek *holos*, whole) was coined by the writer Arthur Koestler (1905–83) in his book *The Roots of Co-*

*incidence* (1972). Here he put forward the theory that some paranormal phenomena, such as telepathy, might be explained by the fact that people are holons (in the sense of being integrated into some larger whole).

• **Holt drowning**▸ The mysterious death of the Australian prime minister Harold Holt on 17 December 1967. The prime minister was a keen swimmer and on the day of his death had chosen to swim off Cheviot Beach in Victoria, on a coastline known to be hazardous to bathers. The sea 'churned up' around the prime minister and he disappeared; no body was ever found. The prime minister's death caused political turmoil. Some ventured a suicide theory, but the most remarkable notion came 15 years later, in Anthony Grey's book *The Prime Minister Was a Spy*. According to Grey, Holt had been spirited away to Red China in a submarine, having completed his nefarious activities on behalf of Mao's regime. Grey's theory was based on Holt's evident desire to accommodate Chinese wishes at various points during his career; it also hinted that the Australian secret service knew more about the disappearance than was generally supposed.

• **Holy Fool**▸ A nickname given by the British tabloid press to Frank Pakenham, 7th Earl of Longford (1905–2001), a politician noted for his strong Roman Catholic beliefs and vigorous crusading for moral causes. On some occasions his obviously good intentions were made to look rather foolish, an example being his befriending of Myra Hindley (*see*: Moors murders) in prison. *See*: Lord Porn.

• **Holy Joe**▸ Forces slang for a chaplain. Used in the US Navy since the turn of the 20th century, it was common throughout the services during World War II, whence it spread into civilian use.

• **Holy Loch**▸ A loch in Scotland W of the Firth of Clyde. In 1961 it became the British base for US Polaris nuclear submarines; the base was closed in the early 1990s.

• **Homburg**▸ A soft felt hat popularized by Edward VII. Such hats were originally made at Homburg in Prussia where the king 'took the waters'.

• **home**▸
**Every home should have one** Originally, a slogan used in advertising in the 1920s. The phrase is now used humorously as a general recommendation for anything.

• **home banking**▸ *See*: e-banking; telephone banking.

• **homeboy** or **homie** ▸ US street slang for a young male from one's own neighbourhood or town; more specifically, a member of the neighbourhood gang. The term was widely publicized in the rap music of the 1980s and 1990s.

• **Home Guard**▸ In the UK, the force of volunteers raised early in World War II specifically to defend the country in the event of a German invasion. Originally known as the LDV (Local Defence Volunteers), it was renamed the Home Guard at Winston Churchill's suggestion. Its members were mainly drawn from those too old to join the regular army. Although the Home Guard never saw action, it became a highly trained military force that relieved the wartime army of many duties. The more ridiculous aspects of the Home Guard were highlighted in the 1960s TV comedy series *Dad's Army*.

• **homeland**▸ *See*: Bantustan.

• **homerta**▸ *See*: Mafia.

• **Home Rule**▸ The name given by Isaac Butt, its first leader, to the movement for establishing an independent Irish parliament under the British crown. The Home Government Association was founded in 1870 and renamed the Home Rule Association in 1873. After C. S. Parnell became leader in 1879 its policy of obstruction at Westminster became a growing bugbear to British governments. A Home Rule Bill was eventually passed in 1914 but its implementation was postponed by the advent of World War I. Following the Easter Rising of 1916, the Home Rule movement was eclipsed by the more radical activities of Sinn Féin.

• **honcho** ▸ US slang for the boss, the top man, often used in the phrase the **head honcho**. Although it sounds Spanish, the word comes from the Japanese *hancho*, meaning squad leader. It was adopted by US soldiers during the Korean War, but is now used of businessmen rather than the military.

• **honk**▸ **1.** Slang for a bad smell. It is related to the Liverpudlian dialect word 'ronk' and is widely heard in both Australia and the UK. It is also used as a verb, meaning to stink. **2.** Slang for a wildly drunken and uproarious party. This usage, popular in the UK in the 1950s, is probably derived from **honkers** and **honking**, meaning drunk. As a verb, to honk means to drink excessively and, by extension, to vomit. **3.** Prostitutes' jargon for feeling a man's genitals.

• **Honkers**▸ Dated British slang for Hong Kong. It was much used by members of the armed forces serving in the Far East and by upper-class young people who worked there, sometimes in the augmented form **Harry Honkers** (*see*: Harry).

• **honky** ▶ US Black pejorative slang for a White person. The derivation is obscure but it may be related to the noise that pigs make – the typical pig being pink-skinned. It could also be related to the long noses White people have compared to Blacks, **honker** being US slang for nose.

• **honky-tonk** ▶ A disreputable nightclub or low roadhouse. A place of cheap entertainment. A **honky-tonk piano** is one from which the felts of the hammers have been removed, thus making the instrument more percussive and giving it a different tone quality. Such pianos are also usually out-of-tune. They are still used for playing ragtime and popular melodies in public houses.

• **honours list** ▶ A list of awards made to those who have given distinguished service to the UK. The list is compiled by the prime minister's office, vetted by a committee of privy counsellors, and approved by the sovereign. An honours list is published twice every year – on New Year's Day and on the sovereign's official birthday. Additional lists may be published on other occasions, such as the resignation of a prime minister. The honours awarded include membership of the various classes of the Order of the British Empire, the orders of knighthood, and the ranks of the peerage. Over the years honours lists have attracted a good deal of controversy, both for the particular individuals chosen and for the general nature of the exercise, which is often felt to be archaic, socially divisive, and open to political abuse. *See*: Lavender list; Honours Scandal.

• **Honours Scandal** ▶ After World War I, Lloyd George, prime minister in the coalition government, made what many considered blatant misuse of the honours system to reward those who were prepared, in effect, to buy their titles. These included a number of wealthy businessmen with distinctly dubious reputations, most notoriously the South African millionaire Sir James Robinson. In 1922 Lord Salisbury alleged (correctly) that the government had fixed prices for the sale of titles, the money being put into Lloyd George's personal political fund (*see*: Lloyd George Fund). As a consequence, a Royal Commission was set up in 1922 to recommend future procedure and the Honours (Prevention of Abuses) Act was passed in 1923. Because three people connected with prominent South Wales newspapers were among the recipients of Lloyd George's honours, Cardiff was jokingly dubbed the **City of Dreadful Knights**, a punning allusion to *The City of Dreadful Night*, a poem by James Thomson (1834–82).

• **Hons, The** ▶ The name given by Jessica Mitford (1917–96) and her sister Deborah, daughters of the eccentric Lord Redesdale, to their self-styled 'society', as described in Jessica's account of their childhood, *Hons and Rebels* (1960). The two sisters were the society's only members, and conducted proceedings in 'Honnish', 'a sort of mixture of North of England and American accents'. The principal activity of the Hons was apparently the persecution of their brother, Tom – a 'Counter-Hon'. *See also*: Mitford girls.

• **hooch** ▶ US slang for illicitly distilled alcohol. The name derives from Hootchinoo, an Amerindian tribe that distilled a type of alcoholic liquor. Hooch is now the trade name of a popular alcopop.

• **hood** or **hoodlum** ▶ US slang, dating from the early 20th century, for a gangster or violent criminal. The abbreviated version, hood, became widely used in the 1940s. The derivation of hoodlum is obscure, but it is possibly related to the S German dialect word *Haderlump*, meaning a good-for-nothing person. Another possibility is that it is a version of the phrase 'huddle 'em', that was said to be the war cry of street muggers.

• **Hood, HMS** ▶ A British battle cruiser sunk by the German battleship Bismarck off the Greenland coast on 24 May 1941. A shell fired by the German guns entered the main magazine of HMS *Hood*, causing a catastrophic explosion. The British ship, the world's largest vessel in its class, sank in four minutes with the loss of all but three of her 1416-strong crew.

• **hoolivan** ▶ A police van equipped with roof-mounted video cameras to monitor the behaviour of crowds, particularly football crowds. A blend of 'hooligan' and 'van' (*see*: football hooliganism).

• **Hooray Henry** ▶ British pejorative term for an empty-headed upper-class young man noted for his loud arrogant but generally ineffectual behaviour. The term has sometimes been shortened to **Hooray**. Viscount Linley won a libel case against the *Today* newspaper, in which he had been labelled a Hooray, in March 1990.

• **hoosegow** ▶ One of many US slang names for jail. It is derived, through Mexican Spanish, from the Spanish word *juzgado*, a law court.

• **Hoover** ▶ The tradename of a firm of vacuum-cleaner makers, which has come to be used generically as both a noun and a verb. To **hoover** or **hoover up** is also a colloquial term meaning to devour greedily in the manner of a vacuum cleaner. The inventor of the machine was one J. Murray Spangler, a caretaker in an Ohio department store, who sold his rights in the invention to William Henry Hoover (1849–1932). The first vacuum cleaner made by Hoover was sold in 1908 for $70; they came on sale in the UK four years later.

The British Hoover factory, on the A40 in Perivale (outer London), has been a landmark since it was completed in 1933. Designed by Wallis Gilbert and Partners in the Art Deco style, its white façade, with bands of blue and red, is flanked by two towers. Since Hoover moved to Wales, the building has been largely occupied by a Tesco supermarket.

• **Hoover apron** ▶ A US term for a dress with a reversible double front. When one side became dirty, the other side could be turned out. It was popular in America during World War I, when Herbert Hoover (1874–1964) was Food Administrator.

• **Hoover Dam** ▶ The dam across the Colorado River on the Nevada–Arizona border, formerly known as the **Boulder Dam** or **Black Dam**. Construction of the Boulder Dam, in Black Canyon, started in 1931. Up to 5000 workers were employed on the project, and some 30 million m³ (40 million yd³) of concrete used in building the horseshoe-shaped dam. This stands 221.3 m (726 ft) high and measures 379 m (1244 ft) across. The dam is 201 m (660 ft) thick at the base, narrowing to 13.7 m (45 ft) at the crest, along which runs a two-lane highway. At the base of the dam are housed 17 electricity-generating turbines. Completed in 1935, the dam was later (1947) renamed in honour of Herbert Hoover, who was secretary of commerce (1921–28) when the project was being planned. Upstream of the dam is Lake Mead, 176 km (110 mi) long.

• **hooverers** ▶ Fishermen and fishing vessels that take up enormous numbers of fish using drift nets covering large areas of the sea. The name, used disparagingly, describes the manner in which the contents of the nets are sucked up from the sea, as if by a giant vacuum cleaner (see: Hoover). In the 1970s this method of fishing in European waters led to a serious decline in herring stocks that threatened the survival of the herring fishing industry. It is now frowned upon because of the indiscriminate way in which fish of all types and sizes, including young fish that have not yet reproduced, are caught.

• **Hoover moratorium** ▶ The concession made by US president Herbert Hoover in June 1931 allowing European nations to suspend repayment of intergovernmental war debts for one year, in order to help ease their plight during the Great Depression. The policy was implemented from 1 July 1931.

• **horizontal dancing** ▶ US slang, popular with students in the 1980s, for sexual intercourse. **Horizontal jogging** has also been heard.

• **Hornblower, Horatio** ▶ The seafarer whose adventures in the Royal Navy during the Napoleonic Wars are described in a series of 11 novels by C. S. Forester (1899–1966). Hornblower made his debut in *The Happy Return* (1937) and various episodes in his navy life were recounted in subsequent novels. For instance, in *Mr. Midshipman Hornblower* (1950) the 17-year-old Horatio is seen at the outset of his career. Others in the series include *Lord Hornblower* (1948), *Lieutenant Hornblower* (1954), and *Hornblower in the West Indies* (1958). Forester also wrote *The Hornblower Companion* (1964), which provides more general information about the characters and places encountered in the books. More recently the character has featured in a number of British TV movies.

• **horse** ▶ **1.** A slang name for heroin, popular in the 1950s but dated by the time the real drug problem affected the UK in the 1980s, when heroin was widely known as H or smack. 'Horse' probably has nothing to do with the animal but derives from the Greek word *heros*, hero, from which the name heroin itself is thought to come (because the user feels like a hero while under its influence). **2.** Rare British rhyming slang for gonorrhoea, from 'horse and trap', clap, the street name for this disease. **3.** US slang for a corrupt prison officer who carries illegal items in and out of jail. This usage probably derives from the idea of the Trojan horse.

• **horse feathers** ▶ One of the many colloquial terms for rubbish or nonsense. It was coined by the US comic-strip artist Billy de Beck in the 1920s to mean something of little consequence. The film *Horse Feathers* (1932) was an anarchic comedy starring the Marx Brothers.

• **Horses sweat, men perspire, (and) ladies only glow** ▶ A genteel adage used to rebuke anyone, lady or gentleman, who says they are sweating. With the advent of sexual equality and the modern tendency to call a spade a spade, this kind of nicety is regarded as a joke.

• **Horst Wessel Lied** ▶ Horst Wessel Song: the official marching song of the Nazi Party. It was written by a young student and stormtrooper, Horst Wessel, and adopted by the party after his murder in 1930, supposedly at the hands of the Communists. The lyrics incorporate many odious sentiments dear to the Nazis. Wessel himself was elevated to the status of martyr by Nazi propagandist Dr Goebbels. The first verse translates as:

Hold high the banner! Close the hard ranks serried!

SA marches on with sturdy stride.

Comrades, Comrades, by Red Front and
          Reaction killed, are buried,
But march with us in image at our side.

The tune was taken from a traditional fishermen's song.

**• hospice movement ▶** A movement that provides specialist care, relief from pain, and emotional support for the terminally ill and their families. The first hospice in this sense, the Dames de Calvaire, was established by Mme Jeanne Carnier in Lyon, France in 1842. The first hospices in the UK were established in the late 19th and early 20th centuries by the Irish Sisters of Charity, who had set up their first home for the sick in Dublin in 1879. The movement had a renaissance in the 1960s with the foundation of St Christopher's Hospice in 1967 by Dame Cicely Saunders (1918– ), upon which most modern hospices are modelled. There are now many hundreds of hospice services in Britain and Ireland, including special NHS-funded units, independent hospices, hospital support teams, voluntary home care services, and the homes run by the Cancer Relief Macmillan Fund and Sue Ryder Foundation.

**• hot and strong ▶** A catchphrase said to have originated in Australia in the 1940s; it is used in such phrases as 'I like my women hot and strong', *i.e.* highly stimulating sexually. The allusion is to coffee, usually preferred 'hot and strong'.

**• hot button ▶** An issue or characteristic that will produce an automatic response in certain groups of voters, consumers, etc. The phrase is now mainly heard in the context of US politics, where notorious 'hot buttons' include abortion, gun control, and taxation. Previously it was used in marketing to mean those characteristics of a product that most affected consumer choice. It was probably suggested by the idea that people's responses to some issues are as immediate and unthinking as if a button had been pushed.

**• hot dog ▶ 1.** A frankfurter sausage, heated and served in a split oblong bread roll, often with onions and ketchup or other relishes. It originated in America but its popularity spread worldwide with the rise of the fast food industry. Its invention has been ascribed to Harry Stevens, caterer to the New York stadium in 1900, but the name is thought to have been coined by a US sports cartoonist, T. A. Dorgan. **2. hot-dog** US slang meaning to show off, or to perform very well, especially in skiing or surfing. **3.** Also **hog-dog** or **hot-dogger**. US slang for a high achiever, sometimes said with a tinge of envy. It is possibly a combination of 'top dog' meaning the best and 'hot' meaning especially good.

**• hothousing ▶** Intensive methods of teaching young children, allowing little or no time for play, adopted in order to achieve high intelligence and attainment. The allusion is to the rearing of plants in a hothouse.

**• hot line ▶** A direct exclusive telephone line, especially one only to be used in times of crisis. It was used particularly of the private line between the US White House and the Soviet Kremlin established in the early 1960s, but is now used of any urgent telephone line, for example in accident services.

**• hot mooner ▶** A person who adheres to the Hot Moon theory, which proposes that the moon has or had a molten core, whose volcanic activity produced the lunar craters. **Cold mooners** believe that the craters were formed by meteorite bombardment rather than thermal or volcanic activity. Both terms were coined *c.* 1969. Hot mooners are also called **vulcanists**.

**• hot pants ▶** Provocatively short shorts, which were fashionable for young women in the early 1970s. They were usually worn skin-tight and often featured a bib and shoulder straps.

**• hot rod ▶** A motor car, especially an old one, that has been stripped down and rebuilt for extra power and speed. 'Hot-rodding' became a teenage craze in America in the late 1940s and 1950s, when many illegal race meetings were held, often on public roads.

**• hot shot ▶** US underworld slang for a fatal dose of a narcotic, usually heroin, administered deliberately as a method of murder. The victim is given either a huge overdose of the drug or one adulterated with another substance.

**• hot-wire ▶** A street expression for starting a (stolen) car without using the ignition key or switch, by altering the wiring. 'Hot' probably reflects both the slang meaning 'stolen' and the heat generated by passing the high starter current through thin wires to make a spark.

**• Houdini, Harry ▶** The stage name of Erik Weiz (1874–1926), the world's most celebrated illusionist and escapologist. Born in Budapest of Jewish parents who emigrated to New York, he began his career as a magician in 1890 but world fame began with his appearance at London in 1900. No lock could hold him, even that of the condemned cell at Washington gaol. He escaped from handcuffs, ropes, safes, etc., and was deservedly called the **Great Houdini** and the **Handcuff King**. He died from a punch in the stomach, delivered before he had tensed his muscles.

• **Houdini in the White House** ▶ Franklin D. Roosevelt (1882–1945), 32nd US president (1933–45). He acquired this nickname – one of many – because of his ability to find a way out of difficult situations. *See*: FDR.

• **Houdini of American Politics** ▶ One of the nicknames of Richard Milhous Nixon (1913–94), 37th US president (1969–74), noted for his ability to extricate himself from awkward situations. This ability failed him during the Watergate scandal. *See*: Tricky Dicky.

• **hour** ▶

   **their finest hour** The famous phrase that concluded Winston Churchill's speech of 18 June 1940, in which he prepared his listeners for the imminent Battle of Britain:

> Let us therefore brace ourselves to our duties, and so bear ourselves that, if the British Empire and its Commonwealth last for a thousand years, men will still say: 'This was their finest hour'.

• **house** ▶ *See*: acid house.

• **househusband** ▶ A married man who stays at home and undertakes the housekeeping duties traditionally the province of the wife. These may include care of small children. An analogue of 'housewife', the word was first used in America from 1970, but has since become common in the UK. Increasingly, traditional roles have become less entrenched, as working wives have built successful careers, which can make them the main income earners. *See*: New Man.

• **house sitting** ▶ The practice of living in someone else's house while they are away, in order to take care of it, tend the garden, feed the pets, etc.

• **hovercraft** ▶ Any vehicle that travels supported on a cushion of air relatively close to the surface. Hovercraft are thus distinct from both conventional surface craft, such as boats and wheeled vehicles, and aircraft, which employ aerodynamic lift to support themselves in the air. Their great advantage is their ability to move over any reasonably flat surface, land or water. The world's first working hovercraft was the SR.N1 (Saunders-Roe N1), invented by the British engineer Sir Christopher Cockerell (1910–99). This was launched in 1959 after a development programme financed by the UK's ministry of defence. Hovercraft design essentially involves a central air inlet and fan, which forces air outwards and downwards through jets around the periphery of the underside, creating the supporting air cushion. Forward thrust is provided by jets from the fan or by separate vertical propellors. An alternative arrangement underneath is the plenum chamber, in effect an entirely open bottom, which is fitted with a peripheral flexible skirt to contain the air cushion. The prototype SR.N1 was capable of carrying three people at speeds of up to 25 knots. By 1963 the payload capacity had been increased to 7 tons and the maximum speed to 50 knots. Interest in the new machines was by now spreading to other countries. However, development in the 1960s was hampered by several design hurdles, notably the high frictional wear of the skirts and the susceptibility of gas-turbine engines to saltwater-induced corrosion. By the 1970s, with these problems largely overcome, the hovercraft had created various roles for itself, including short-haul ferry, survey vehicle, and amphibious troop carrier. The largest hovercraft ever built was the SR.N4 Mk III, weighing 305 tonnes and measuring 56.38 m in length. It operated on a scheduled cross-Channel ferry service carrying up to 418 passengers and 60 cars. However, the new generation of cross-Channel ferries using catamarans are considerably more efficient than hovercraft, which therefore went out of service on this route in 2000. The hovercraft principle, therefore, is only likely to be made use of in special situations (especially military). *See also*: hovertrain.

• **hovertrain** ▶ A train that rides along a concrete track on a cushion of high-pressure air produced by powerful fans. The idea of frictionless travel by train or monorail using air-cushion suspension was first postulated in 1969, following the successful introduction of the hovercraft into public service. The first successful hovertrain was introduced in France in the 1970s between Orléans and Paris. In the UK, research has also been taking place into the use of a magnetic suspension system (*see*: maglev) with propulsion using a linear induction motor, although no commercially viable system has yet been developed.

• **How to win friends and influence people** ▶ A catchphrase that originated in America as the title of a book on business psychology, written by Dale Carnegie (1888–1955) and published in 1936. Since then the phrase has appeared in a number of variants.

• **HRT** ▶ Hormone replacement therapy. The administration of small doses of female hormones to correct hormonal imbalance in menopausal women. HRT is effective in relieving physical symptoms of the menopause, such as hot flushes and vaginal dryness; its usefulness in treating the psychological symptoms, such as irritability and fatigue, is less evident. HRT has also proved valuable in preventing osteoporosis, a brittle bone condition that is common in women over 50, and may reduce the likelihood of coronary heart disease. There is, however, some medical concern over certain adverse side effects, particularly overgrowth of the cells of the endometrium (the lining of the womb), which is stimulated by the main female hormones, oestrogens, and may progress to cancer. To prevent this, women who have not had a hysterectomy are given combined HRT of an oestrogen and a progestogen.

• **H₂S** ▶ Codename given to a secret navigational device used by Allied bombers when operating against German U-boats. Fearing that the enemy would hear about the new system, the British authorities enlisted the aid of one of the country's best-known practical jokers, Professor Reginald Jones of Aberdeen University. Jones relished the opportunity for a good hoax and accordingly arranged for the Germans to learn of a newly developed infra-red beam being used to detect their U-boats. With great haste the Germans set about painting the entire U-boat fleet with special paint to deflect the rays. Of H₂S they knew nothing: the infra-red beams were, of course, a figment of Jones's imagination. The codename was taken from the chemical formula for hydrogen sulphide ('rotten-egg gas').

• **Hubble's law** ▶ The principle in astronomy that the velocity with which distant galaxies are moving away is directly proportional to their distance; *i.e.* the more distant the galaxy, the faster it is moving. The law was discovered in 1927 by the US astronomer Edwin Hubble (1889–1953) as a result of measurements of the red shifts of galaxies. It is regarded as direct evidence that the universe is expanding (*see*: Big Bang). The constant relating the velocity to the distance is the **Hubble constant** and the reciprocal of this, the **Hubble time**, is a measure of the age of the universe, currently estimated at between 10 and 20 billion years. The **Hubble space telescope**, a powerful telescope launched into space by America in 1990, was named in his honour. The project was initially plagued by technical problems but later (1996) resulted in publication of the **Hubble Deep Field Image**, a remarkable (and remarkably beautiful) composite photograph showing some 2000 galaxies.

• **Hughie** ▶ A 20th-century Australian euphemism for God, especially in contexts that have to do with the control of the weather. **Send her down, Hughie** is a common outback exhortation to the Almighty Rainmaker.

'Don't worry about the money. Hughie looks after that, my boy'. The Corporal was diverted. 'Who's this Hughie?' he said...'Ah', Gell said, affecting a gravity which was not altogether false. 'You don't say 'God', you see, because nobody believes in God but everybody believes in Hughie. I dunno – it's just a thing you hear the boys say.' – SEAFORTH MACKENZIE: *Dead Men Rising* (1951).

• **Huks** ▶ Nickname for the Hukbalahap (Hukbo nang Bayon Laban sa Hapon: People's Army Against Japan), a communist-led Philippines guerrilla force that came close to toppling the Manila government in the late 1940s and early 1950s. The Huks were formed in 1942 in central Luzon to fight the Japanese occupiers, although the movement's origins lie in the communist-inspired peasants' struggle against the wealthy landowners of Luzon in the 1930s. By the end of World War II, the Huks controlled much of Luzon. In the 1946 election the Huk leader, Luis Taruc, won a Congressional seat, but was barred from taking office. This prompted open rebellion by the Huks, who gained in popular support. But in 1950 the government captured most of the country's leading communists in a swoop on their Manila headquarters, and won renewed military backing from America. Even more significant in the Huks' downfall was the election in 1953 of President Ramon Magsaysay, who restored popular support for the government. The nadir came with Taruc's surrender in 1954. Even so, the outlawed Huks survived through the 1950s and 1960s, reorganized as the People's Liberation Army (Hukbong Magpapalaya nang Bayan). In 1970 it was renamed the New People's Army (Bagong Hukbo nang Bayan).

• **Hula-Hoop** ▶ A light plastic hoop that is spun around the waist by swinging the hips, used by children for recreation and by adults for exercise. It was invented in 1958 by Richard P. Knerr and Arthur K. Melvin of the Wham O Manufacturing Company, San Gabriel, California, the same company that was responsible for the Frisbee. It became an instant craze and earned its inventors a considerable fortune. Hula-Hoops are now rarely seen.

• **Hulot, Monsieur** ▶ The eccentric accident-prone character who appears in the films of French director Jacques Tati (1908–82). Hulot, played by Tati himself, is a gangling pipe-smoking bachelor whose tangles with the modern machine age provide a number of very funny film sequences. In *Monsieur Hulot's Holiday* (1953) he causes havoc in a quiet seaside resort. The subsequent films – *Mon Oncle* (1958), *Playtime* (1968), and *Traffic* (1971) – have an element of social satire, with Hulot often playing a peripheral role.

• **human** ▶

**All human life is there** A slogan used to promote the *News of the World*, a British newspaper notorious for its emphasis on sex stories, in 1958–59. Incongruously enough, the phrase came originally from a story by Henry James: 'Cats and monkeys, monkeys and cats – all human life is there.' ('Madonna of the Future', 1879).

• **Humanae Vitae** ▶ 'Of Human Life': the encyclical issued by Pope Paul VI on 29 July 1968, in which he reaffirmed the Vatican's total opposition to all artificial forms of birth control and to abortion. In addition he urged restraint in the use of the rhythm method of contraception, declaring that 'each and every marriage act must remain open to the transmission of life' (*see*: Vatican roulette). The encyclical caused dismay to liberal Catholics, who had been hoping for some relaxation of the long-established ban. The Vatican's solution to poverty and misery caused by world overpopulation remains one based on economic and social reform, rather than biological intervention. In the eyes of some non-Catholics, the Pope's continued opposition to birth control reflects a cynical awareness of the reduction it would cause in the world's Catholic population.

• **Human Fly** ▶ The stage name of the US performer George Gibson Polley, who became famous throughout America for climbing skyscrapers. His first serious climb was the result of a bet in Chicago in 1910: his ascent of a lofty department store attracted such a large crowd that Polley realized he had stumbled on an entirely new form of street entertainment. Subsequently be shinned up the 500-foot Customs House in Boston, a flagpole on Rhode Island, the Woolworth Building in New York (then the tallest building in the world) and numerous department stores – in each case for a generous publicity fee. In all, before his death from a brain tumour at the age of 29, he climbed over 2000 buildings without ever falling – although his 'act' did include a deliberate slip from one ledge to another, to thrill the crowds below.

• **Human Genome Project** ▶ (HGP) A 15-year international project that began in 1988 with the aim of producing a map showing the positions of all the human genes on their respective chromosomes. Chromosomes, which occur within the nuclei of the body's cells, contain the genetic material, DNA; a gene consists of a discrete length of DNA that acts as a single unit of heredity. Individual molecules of DNA take the form of two strands coiled into a helix and linked by pairs of chemicals called bases. There are four different bases in DNA,

and it is the sequence of these bases (*i.e.* the order in which they occur in the DNA) that determines the functions of the genes.

In June 2000 representatives of the HGP announced the completion of a 'working draft' of the human genome, detailing the sequence of the approximately 3 billion base pairs it contains. This draft was published in 2001; a definitive version is expected to be available by 2003. Not all sections of the human genome correspond to genes: some sequences control gene activity, while others have different or unknown functions. So far, some 30,000 DNA sequences have been identified as genes. By 2003 the exact positions of all the genes on their chromosomes will have been pinpointed and their DNA sequences (and hence functions) determined.

The significance of mapping the human genome cannot be overemphasized. Identification of the numerous small (single-base) variations in the genome sequence that occur between individuals will be invaluable in discovering which genes are associated with disease and exactly how they contribute to complex disease processes, such as cancer, diabetes, heart disease, and schizophrenia. This will not only enable genetic testing to identify those at risk of developing such diseases but will also pave the way for new medical treatments (including gene therapy) and diagnostic techniques, heralding an era of 'personalized medicine'.

However, these advances in medical science will have far-reaching ethical, legal, and social consequences that must be explored. For example, proper safeguards must be in place to ensure the privacy of individuals whose medical records reveal details of their genetic makeup, and the limits of further genomic research must be defined. In the longer term, it raises such questions as how far prenatal selection and genetic engineering should be taken to eliminate inherited diseases and other 'undesirable' traits. All these issues must be addressed before the potential benefits of this revolution in human genetics can be put to practical use.

• **human interest** ▶ The quality of a newspaper story or television news item that focuses on the experiences of a particular person, group, or family and is presented in such a way that it evokes an emotional response in the reader or viewer – usually either sympathy with others' misfortunes or envy at their success.

• **human rights** ▶ The concept that all human beings are entitled to certain civil, political, and economic rights simply by virtue of being human.

Although human rights are usually seen as a modern preoccupation, the idea can be traced back to the Declaration of the Rights of Man (1789) proclaimed during the French Revolution, to the American Declaration of Independence (1776), and ultimately to the concept of natural law developed by Greek philosophers and Roman jurists. The modern concern for human rights developed mainly as a reaction to the terrible events of World War II, especially the Holocaust and other episodes of the mass murder of noncombatants. The victorious Allies were led to form the United Nations, envisaged as a more active and enlightened body than its predecessor, the League of Nations, and international civil servants drafted the Universal Declaration of Human Rights (1948), the cornerstone of all subsequent discussion. Although not itself legally binding, the Declaration has spawned several international conventions that are binding on their signatories. A UN High Commissioner for Human Rights was appointed in 1993.

There are also various regional conventions. In 1950 the Council of Europe set up the European Convention on Human Rights, which in turn established the European Court of Human Rights in 1959. Unlike the UN institutions, this has the power to hear individual complaints and to make rulings that will almost certainly be obeyed. The European Convention on Human Rights was incorporated into English law by the Human Rights Act (1998; enforced 2000), a move which is expected to have a profound effect on the English legal process.

• **human shield** ▶ The policy adopted by Saddam Hussein in the Gulf War of posting foreign hostages (and subsequently captured aircrew) at various strategic installations in the hope that this would deter Allied air attacks. Iraq's use of such a policy was widely condemned as contrary to the Geneva Convention. The phrase has since been applied to other cases in which similar tactics have been used.

• **Hundred Flowers policy** ▶ The short-lived period of liberalization in China instituted by Mao Tse-tung in 1957. The policy was set out in a speech given by Mao to the Supreme State conference in Peking on 27 February:

> The policy of letting a hundred flowers blossom and a hundred schools of thought contend is the policy for promoting the flourishing of the arts and the progress of science.

Mindful of the recent Hungarian Rising and of Khrushchev's denunciation of Stalin in February 1956, Mao was endeavouring to resolve the 'contradictions' becoming increasingly apparent within the Chinese communist state. Critics of the regime saw the speech as a green light and a barrage of complaint was directed at the Peking regime, especially from liberals and anti-communists. Communist Party bosses were alarmed and on 8 June a policy change was signalled by the publication of an amended version of Mao's speech. This was followed in July by a crackdown on the more outspoken critics.

• **Hungarian Rising** ▶ The popular revolt against the Soviet-backed communist regime in Hungary that cost thousands of lives in the autumn of 1956. The rising started on 23 October when police tried to break up a student demonstration in Budapest calling for the reinstatement of Imre Nagy, the reformist leader who had been ousted in April 1955 by the hard-line Stalinist, Mátyás Rákosi. Rákosi's policy of allowing some limited liberalization while strengthening ties with the Soviet Union became increasingly untenable in the face of mounting pressure for radical reforms. This was intensified by a successful workers' Revolt in Poland on 28 June, and on 18 July Rákosi was forced to resign. Pro-Moscow communists struggled to contain the situation, but the students provided the spark that set off widespread anti-Soviet protest.

In Budapest, Soviet flags were burned and Stalin's statue destroyed. The uprising was supported by Hungary's own police and army, while members of the notorious secret police (AVO) were hunted down. Imre Nagy was installed as prime minister on 24 October and promised the withdrawal of Soviet troops. But fighting was intense, especially in E Hungary, and by 30 October some 10,000 lives had been lost. Nagy attempted to negotiate with the Soviets, but the arrival of Soviet reinforcements in early November prompted Nagy to announce that Hungary had quit the Warsaw Pact and was now a neutral country. He appealed for United Nations intervention, but no outside assistance was forthcoming.

The Soviet counter-strike began on 4 November with the bombing and military takeover of Budapest. By 12 November most of the country was under Soviet control, and Hungary had a puppet government led by János Kádár. An estimated 155,000 Hungarians had fled across the border into Austria by the end of 1956. On 18 November Nagy was tricked into leaving his refuge in the Yugoslav embassy, taken to Romania, and shot. In spite of a continuing general strike, the Kádár government imposed its authority on the country, and the uprising was extinguished everywhere, except in the hearts and minds of the Hungarian people.

• **Hungerford massacre** ▶ The events of 20 August 1987, during which 13 people were killed and 15 wounded by Michael Ryan in and around the Berkshire town of Hungerford. Ryan, a deranged firearms enthusiast, whose motives have never been fathomed, ended by turning his weapon on himself: his victims included his own mother. To many in the UK, the horror of these events was all the greater for their setting, a small sleepy town that seemed to epitomize rural England.

• **hunger march** ▶ In the 1930s, one of several marches of the unemployed to call attention to their grievances, the first being that of 1932, when Wal Hannington, the leader of the National Union of Unemployed Workers, led a march on London. The biggest of the marches organized by the NUWM was that against the means test in 1936. *See also*: Jarrow march.

• **hunger strike** ▶ The refusal of prisoners to take food in order to force various concessions from the authorities or to secure release. This was a notable tactic of the suffragettes before World War I (*see*: Cat and Mouse Act). In the 1980s it was used by convicted IRA terrorists held in Northern Ireland (*see*: Maze prison); ten prisoners died before the protest was called off.

• **hunter-killer** ▶ A nuclear-powered submarine designed to stalk enemy submarines and destroy them. The key to hunter-killer ASW (anti-submarine warfare) success is speed, quietness, and powerful detection capabilities. The US Navy employs nuclear hunter-killers with torpedo tubes in the stern, which leaves the bow free for carrying sophisticated underwater listening devices, such as active sonar and passive hydrophones.

• **Huntley** ▶ British rhyming slang of the 1980s for karma (destiny or fate), from Huntley and Palmer, the well-known British biscuit company. This is a rather unique blend of the old rhyming slang tradition and a recently adopted New Age concept.

• **Hurricane** ▶ The RAF's main fighter plane during the first years of World War II, and, with the Spitfire, staunch defender of the skies during the Battle of Britain. Made by Hawker (from 1935 part of Hawker Siddeley), the Hurricane made its maiden flight in 1935 and two years later entered service with the RAF – its first monoplane fighter. The Mark I Hurricane had a wingspan of 12.19 m (40 ft) and was 9.57 m (31.42 ft) long. The single Rolls-Royce Merlin engine gave it a top speed of 521 kph (324 mph). Armament consisted of eight wing-mounted machine guns. By 1941 the Hurricane, outpaced by Germany's Messerschmitt 109 fighter, had switched roles to night fighter and fighter-bomber; versions were equipped with 12 machine-guns, cannons, or anti-tank guns, as well as bombs. The Sea Hurricane was a modified version launched by catapult from a ship or carrier. Although the Spitfire is usually thought of as the principal aircraft in the Battle of Britain, there were, in fact, twice as many Hurricanes as Spitfires in the battle and they shot down more German aircraft.

• **husband** ▶
**My husband and I** The memorable phrase which appeared repeatedly in the Queen's annual Christmas message during the 1950s and 1960s. For some reason, probably to do with her delivery, it became a joke. The Queen herself was clearly aware of this; in her speech at the Guildhall on the occasion of her silver wedding anniversary (1972), she began:

> I think that everyone will concede that – today of all days – I should begin by saying, 'My husband and I'.

• **hush money** ▶ Money paid to a person as a bribe not to disclose some piece of information.

• **Husky** ▶ Codename for the Allied invasion of Sicily during World War II. Forces of the US 7th Army and British 8th Army began the seaborne invasion on 10 July 1943, surprising the island's Italian and German defenders. By 17 August, the last Axis troops had withdrawn to mainland Italy, and Sicily was under Allied control.

• **hustler** ▶ 1. US slang for a prostitute of either sex. *Hustler* is also the name of one of America's bestselling pornographic magazines. 2. An enterprising but somewhat dubious business person, especially one who relies on forceful persuasion to sell something or solicit funds.

> In trying to analyse the psychology of why some banks lend even more money to 'hustlers', Mr Sampson goes too far. True, some bankers...may want to meet flamboyant entrepreneurs. – MS S. M. KENNEDY, correspondent in the *Independent*, 12 January 1991.

• **hutzpah** ▶ *See*: chutzpah.

• **hydroelectric power** ▶ Electricity generated by water pressure, which accounts for about 7% of the world's energy supply. A typical hydroelectric power plant (HEP) uses water stored in a high-level reservoir (usually created by damming a river), which falls through pipes to drive water turbines coupled to electricity generators at a lower level. In pumped HEP schemes, at times of low electricity demand, the turbines are reversed and used to pump water back up to the reservoir to ensure high water pressure during peak operation. The feasibility of hydroelectric power depends on the availability of suitable sites with the required fall of water. Unfortunately in the UK not many such sites are available and only some 0.2% of the country's energy is provided by hydroelectric power stations.

• **hydrofoil** ▶ A light vessel that has two or more pairs of fixed vanes (foils) attached to the hull, which produce lift (similar to wings of an aircraft) and raise the hull from the water to reduce friction and increase speed. The first successful hydrofoil to 'fly' with its hull clear of the water was invented by Professor Enrico Forlanini of Milan, whose experimental craft reached a speed of 38 knots on Lake Maggiore in 1906. Early designs were handicapped by poor rough water performance and unsatisfactory engines, but in the following decades the Germans and the Americans refined foil designs and introduced lighter and more powerful engines to develop commercial and military hydrofoil craft. In the 1960s water jet propulsion was introduced by Boeing, whose passenger-carrying **jetfoil** fleet soon began to operate on sea and inland waterways at suitable sites throughout the world. Most of the high-speed car ferries that now operate across the English Channel and the Irish Sea are jet-propelled hydrofoils.

• **hydrogen bomb** ▶ See: nuclear weapon.

• **hydronaut** ▶ A person who operates in deep submersible vessels for purposes of underwater exploration, salvage of submerged vessels, laying of cables and pipelines, etc.

• **hydrophonics** ▶ A system of cultivating plants by stimulating their growth with music or other sound. It was used in the late 1980s by the Japanese, who also investigated the effect of magnetism. The term was probably coined by analogy with hydroponics. The idea that the growth of plants can be affected by music or verbal encouragement has no scientific basis but is surprisingly widely held. In 1986, Prince Charles attracted good-natured ridicule for his remark in a TV interview:

> To get the best results, you must talk to your vegetables.

• **hydroplaning** ▶ See: aquaplaning.

• **hydroponics** ▶ A technique for cultivating plants without soil, using an inert medium, such as sand or gravel, through which a nutrient solution is circulated. (Originally the plants' roots were immersed in water to which fertilizer was added, hence the prefix *hydro-*, from Greek *hudōr*, water.) It is useful in arid regions but only commercially viable for flowers and special vegetables. See also: hydrophonics.

• **Hyman Kaplan** ▶ See: Kaplan, Hyman.

• **hype** ▶ 1. Exaggerated publicity or marketing for a product or person, typically a Hollywood blockbuster, a pop record or singer, etc. As a verb, to hype something is to promote or publicize it in an extravagant and deceptive way. In the pop-music business the word can also mean various dishonest practices used by record companies to push a particular record up the charts. The origins of the word are uncertain, but it seems probable that it derives from 'hyperbole' or 'hyperbolize', in which the Greek prefix *hyper-* means 'above' or 'abnormally high'.

> There is no reason in particular why anyone should get overexcited about the 200th anniversary of Mozart's death. But a lot of people are hoping to cash in by building up a big 'hype'. – *Independent Magazine*, 12 January 1991.

**2.** Slang meaning to stimulate or excite (someone), mainly used in the phrase **hyped up**. This usage is probably derived from sense 3 below. **3.** Also **hypo**. Slang for a hypodermic needle, as used for injecting heroin or other drugs.

• **hyperinflation** ▶ See: inflation.

• **hypermarket** ▶ A very large supermarket selling a wide range of goods in addition to food. The word is a translation of the French *hypermarché*, such stores having been more common in France than in the UK until quite recently. The first UK hypermarket opened in the early 1970s. These **superstores** are generally built on the outskirts of towns with their own extensive car parks (and often service stations); as such, they offer the customer the facility of one-stop shopping without the traffic congestion of town centres. Since their introduction, the concept of out-of-town shopping has flourished in the UK, with many large furnishing and do-it-yourself retail outlets sharing car parks with the superstores. Such developments are now discouraged by many planners, on the grounds that they encourage car use, eat into green belts and other countryside, and make it difficult for many town-centre shops to survive.

• **hypersonic** ▶ Having a speed at least five times that of sound. Only missiles and space re-entry vehicles, such as the US space shuttle, reach such speeds.

• **hypoallergenic** ▶ A word used to describe cosmetics and other products that come into contact with the skin, indicating to the consumer that their use is not likely to cause an allergic reaction.

• **hypocentre** ▶ The area directly beneath the explosion of a nuclear weapon, also called ground zero. The term was originally used to describe the central point from which an earthquake spreads.

**I**

• **IBM** ▶ International Business Machines. The world's largest computer manufacturer which has its headquarters in Armonk, New York State. IBM was incorporated in 1911 as the Computer Tabulating Recording Company and adopted its present name in 1924. In the 1920s it dominated the market in time clocks and punch-card tabulators and in the 1930s it developed the electric typewriter. Having begun to manufacture computers in 1951, IBM quickly cornered the world market owing to its massive R & D budget. In 1981 IBM introduced the personal computer (PC), a desktop micro, which became the industry standard.

• **ICBM** ▶ Intercontinental ballistic missile. During the Cold War ICBMs were defined as those missiles with a range in excess of 5500 km, i.e. capable of reaching Russia when fired from America and vice versa. The basic principles of ballistic missile design were perfected by German rocket scientists during the 1940s and first put to practical use in the V2 rocket used against London during the latter stages of World War II. Both America and the Soviet Union then employed captured German scientists on their own missile programmes and developed more sophisticated, accurate, and deadly systems. Such ICBMs as the US Minuteman III have three stages: the booster for take-off, the second-stage delivery rocket, and the unpowered re-entry vehicle. Since the late 1960s ICBMs have been equipped with multiple re-entry vehicles (**MIRVS**) carrying multiple warheads, each capable of being independently targeted. *Compare*: IRBM.

• **ice** ▶ 1. Slang for diamonds. The word is used in all English-speaking countries. 2. Slang for powdered methamphetamine, a highly addictive illegal stimulant drug. When smoked it produces a powerful and unpredictable effect on the nervous system – intensely euphoric or deeply distressing. The drug, which first appeared in Hawaii in 1989 and use of which has become epidemic in many parts of America, is particularly feared by drug enforcement agencies because it is very easy to manufacture from legally available materials. The name 'ice' refers to the translucent crystals from which the powder is produced and may have been coined by analogy with snow (cocaine). 3. US slang for an electoral bribe, apparently derived from the initial letters of 'incidental campaign expenses'. 4. US underworld slang meaning to kill. It is a shortening of 'to put someone on ice' – a reference to the refrigeration of corpses in mortuaries. The word has been popularized by TV crime series and films. If a project etc. is put **on ice** this means that no progress will be made on it for an indefinite period.

• **Iceberg** ▶ A nickname of the US film actress Grace Kelly (1929–82), reflecting her cool beauty and aloof screen persona. It was a combination of these attributes that made her a star, playing opposite Hollywood's leading men in such films as *High Noon* (1952), *The Country Girl* (1955), and *High Society* (1956). At the height of her career, however, she retired from the cinema to marry Prince Rainier III of Monaco (1956) in what was publicized as a fairytale romance. She fulfilled her royal duties in Monaco with great dignity, despite the attention paid by the press to the various romances of her children. The fairytale ended abruptly in a car accident on the winding roads above Monte Carlo.

> Writing about her is like trying to wrap up 115 pounds of smoke. – PETE MARTIN.

• **ice cream** ▶ 1. British slang from the 1950s for a man. It comes from the rhyming slang 'ice-cream freezer' for geezer (a word meaning 'fellow' probably first used by British soldiers in the Napoleonic Wars – from the Spanish *giza*, man). It is now obsolete. 2. British Black and Asian schoolchildren's derogatory name for a White person.

• **ice creamer** ▶ 1. British derogatory name for an Italian. It derives from the occupation of many Italian immigrants, in the early part of the 20th century, who opened small ice-cream businesses. 2. US slang from the 1950s for a drug user, rather than a drug addict. The term was used contemptuously by addicts – presumably because, for these dilettantes, drugs were an occasional treat rather than a necessity of everyday life.

• **iceman** ▶ 1. US slang for a jewel thief; from ice,

meaning diamonds. **2.** US slang for a hired assassin; from the use of 'ice' as a verb, meaning to kill.

• **icon►** **1.** A person or thing that is widely revered as the embodiment or symbol of a desirable quality, a popular or fashionable cultural movement, a cause, etc. For example, Oscar Wilde has been described as a 'gay icon' and Madonna as a 'feminist icon'.

> It [the Millennium Dome] has almost become an icon already and one which should be maintained. – JOHN MAXTON, Labour MP, quoted in *The Times*, 7 November 2000.

**2.** A small symbol that appears on the screen of a computer to enable the service it represents to be activated by means of a screen cursor. It saves having to tap the instruction on the keyboard. *See also*: menu.

• **ICU►** *See*: intensive care unit.

• **ID►** Short for identity or identification, as in **ID card**.

• **Identikit►** A method of identifying criminals from composite photographs based on an assemblage of individual features selected by witnesses from a wide variety of drawings. The method was developed by Hugh C. McDonald (1913–   ) and first used in Los Angeles in 1959. Photofit is an updated version using photographs and **E-fit** employs computer graphics to the same end. *See also*: DNA fingerprinting.

• **idiot box►** Slang from the 1960s for a TV set, reflecting the idea that too much television stunts the brain. It is no longer widely used, although the TV is still commonly referred to as 'the box'. *See also*: gogglebox.

• **idiot dancing►** In the late 1960s and 1970s, a style of wild, abandoned, but solitary dancing seen at rock concerts and festivals. Surprisingly, it does not take up much space because all the movement is in the top half of the body and the head. Many people found the spectacle both ridiculous and irritating, as to have one's view of the stage obscured by such a dancer was extremely frustrating. The late 1970s saw the arrival of headbangers, who adopted a more aggressive style of solitary dancing to match the more aggressive music.

• **Idlewild►** New York City airport, built on the site of Idlewild Beach golf course beside Jamaica Bay in Queens, 24 km (15 mi) from Manhattan. The new airport was opened on 1 July 1948 as the New York International, although it was still popularly called Idlewild until 24 December 1963, when it was renamed **John F. Kennedy International** (or **JFK** for short).

• **IJsselmeer►** A shallow freshwater lake in the Netherlands, which was formed in 1932 by the construction of a dam, designed by the engineer Cornelis Lely, to divide the former Zuider See from the North Sea. The project created a valuable source of fresh water for the region; it also created four polders, large areas of fertile land reclaimed from the lake by a system of dykes, which are used for agriculture, housing, and recreational facilities. Parts of the reclaimed land were flooded once more during World War II and had to be redrained after hostilities ended. The strategic value of the country's dyke system had been recognized somewhat earlier by Queen Wilhelmina (1880–1962); in reply to a threat from the German Kaiser Wilhelm II that the Dutch would be unable to resist his seven-foot tall guardsmen if they invaded, she commented: 'And when we open our dykes, the waters are ten feet deep'.

• **Ike►** Nickname of General (later President) Dwight D. Eisenhower (1890–1969). Despite graduating well down in the 1915 class at West Point and enjoying an undistinguished military career between the wars, Eisenhower advanced rapidly after the outbreak of World War II owing to his strategic knowledge, organizational skills, diplomacy, and amiability. He was given the command of the Anglo-American amphibious landings in North Africa and subsequently commanded the Allied forces in Italy (1943). In 1944 he was appointed Supreme Commander of Operation Overlord, the Allied invasion of Europe (*see*: D-Day). His war record ensured the success of his presidential candidacy in the 1952 election; despite the recurring crises during his two terms of office as a result of Cold War tensions, his presidency is remembered as a period of relative peace and prosperity.

• **Ike►**
  **I like Ike** The campaign slogan of Dwight D. (Ike) Eisenhower, used to great effect as part of his successful presidential election campaigns in 1952 and 1956. During the late 1950s and early 1960s it was often used to describe any inexplicable liking for something; it subsequently fell into disuse.

• **illywhacker►** Australian term, originating in the 1940s, for a professional trickster selling cheap goods, patent medicines, etc., especially at fairs and country shows. *Illywhacker* (1985) is a novel by the Australian writer Peter Carey.

• **Ilyushin►** Various types of Soviet civil and military aircraft produced under the auspices of Sergei Ilyushin (1894–1977), the Soviet aircraft designer. As head of the Scientific Research Committee, he directed the formulation of the requirements for new types of military aircraft for the Red Air Force

(1926–33); subsequently he became head of the Central Design Bureau (1933–70). He created the Il-2 Stormovik bomber, one of the most effective of World War II, as well as various civil aircraft, such as the Il-12 twin-engined passenger aircraft (1946) and the Il-86 airbus (1976).

• **imaging** ► A method of relieving stress that originated in America in the late 1980s; patients are taught to alleviate their stressful feelings by conjuring up mental images of pleasant and enjoyable things or situations. Stress was recognized in the 1980s as a contributing factor in many illnesses and many techniques, such as relaxation and meditation, are used to relieve the condition.

• **Imagism** ► A school of poetry founded by Ezra Pound (1885–1972) in about 1910, based in part on the aesthetic ideas of the philosopher T. E. Hulme (1883–1917). The Imagists were in conscious revolt against 19th-century romanticism, proclaiming that poetry should use the language of common speech, create new rhythms, and present clear direct images. Most Imagist poems are very short – some of the best known being only two or three lines long. The movement continued until about 1917, although Pound had abandoned it for vorticism some time before this.

• **IMF** ► International Monetary Fund. An organization established by the Bretton Woods Conference (1944) as a specialized agency of the United Nations. The main aim of the organization is to promote international trade by easing international liquidity problems and stabilizing exchange rates. Funds are made available to countries experiencing short-term balance of payments difficulties. Deposits of gold or domestic currencies are made by member countries, who can then borrow automatically up to the amount of their **reserve tranche**, which was until 1978 paid in gold and known as the **gold tranche**. In 1970 Special Drawing Rights (SDRs) were introduced to allow members to borrow in convertible currency from other member countries, and SDRs became the IMF's unit of account. Since 1978 the reserve tranche has been paid in SDRs.

• **Immaculate Heart of Mary** ► In the Roman Catholic Church, devotion to the heart of the Virgin Mary is a special form of devotion, which began in the 17th century. In 1947 Pius XII recognized 22 August as the Feast of the Immaculate Heart of Mary.

• **Immelmann turn** ► An aerobatic manoeuvre invented in World War I by the German Air Force pilot Max Immelmann, who was shot down in 1916. His celebrated 'turn' was a refinement of the classic aerial combat manoeuvre – a hawklike dive out of the sun at an enemy target – to which Immelmann added a climb with a half loop and half roll at the top to enable the attacker to gain height and dive from the reverse direction.

• **Imperial Conferences** ► The conferences between the prime ministers of the various dominions of the British Empire held in London between 1907 and 1946 inclusive. These conferences had their origin in the first Colonial Conference, which met in 1887 on the occasion of Queen Victoria's Jubilee. Since 1948, **Commonwealth Conferences** have replaced the Imperial Conferences.

• **Imperial Preference** ► A system for encouraging trade with countries within the British Empire by applying favourable rates of customs duties to goods imported from these countries; in some cases import controls were imposed on goods from outside the Empire. The system was negotiated at the Imperial Economic Conference in Ottawa (1932; *see*: Ottawa Agreements) and after 1948 also applied to trade with Commonwealth countries, when it became known as **Commonwealth Preference**. The system was gradually dismantled as a result of the anti-protectionist conditions imposed by the General Agreement on Tariff and Trade (*see*: GATT) in 1947 and by British entry into the EEC in 1973. It was finally abandoned completely in 1977.

• **implosion** ► A sudden violent collapsing inwards as a result of external pressure. A light bulb, for example, will implode if broken because of the low pressure of gas inside it. The term has been extended to a technique in psychotherapy for treating phobias. This consists of suddenly confronting the patient with the cause of the fear; for example, a patient with agoraphobia is left in the middle of a large field to come to terms with his situation.

• **impro** or **improv** ► Actors' or comedians' shorthand for improvisation. Once used mainly as a rehearsal technique, improvisation has more recently enjoyed a vogue among stand-up comedians. The performer usually asks the audience to suggest characters, situations, props, and literary styles that might be used as the basis for an improvisation: a typical outcome might be a dialogue in the manner of Noël Coward between Benito Mussolini and Britney Spears, involving a propelling pencil. Although the aim is anarchic spontaneity, the results may just as easily be laboriously unfunny.

• **impulse buying** ► The purchase of goods on the spur of the moment, without forethought. Because impulse buying is encouraged by the prominence given to goods by retailers, manufacturers often provide point-of-sale display units to enhance their sales.

• **in ▶** Fashionable, trendy; a key word of the 1960s that is still widely heard.

• **incidental music▶** Background music used for a film, television programme, etc. In some cases the music may have been written exclusively for the film or programme; in others a well-established piece of music may be used.

Examples of the latter include the use of Rachmaninov's second piano concerto in David Lean's *Brief Encounter* (1945) and Mahler's 5th Symphony in Visconti's *Death in Venice* (1971). In both cases the music provided a muted background for much of the film, with the strongly lyrical passages being used to heighten the most emotional moments. A very different use of incidental music was that of Scott Joplin's rags, especially 'The Entertainer', in *The Sting* (1975). In this case the rags experienced an enormous leap in popularity, purely as a result of being revived in the film.

Music written specially for a film or programme may either be innocuous, intended to enhance the mood of the action without being obtrusive, or it may provide a new dimension of its own. The zither music of Anton Karas (1906–85) in Carol Reed's *The Third Man* (1949) became almost as well known as the film itself, as did Mikis Theodorakis's bazouki music in *Zorba the Greek* (1964) and Vangelis's highly appropriate music to *Chariots of Fire* (1981). In some cases the music may prove more enduring than the film. The wartime *Dangerous Moonlight* (1941), for example, is now largely forgotten, but Addinsell's 'Warsaw Concerto' is still familiar.

• **include me out ▶** *See*: Goldwynisms.

• **income support▶** A form of social security payment, introduced in the UK in 1988 as a replacement for supplementary benefit; it is payable to people on low incomes, such as lone parents or the disabled (income support for the unemployed was replaced by the jobseeker's allowance in 1996).

• **Indianapolis 500 ▶** The US Grand Prix 500-mile motor race run annually in May at the Indianapolis Motor Speedway, Indiana. It was first run in 1911 and is now the fastest and most dangerous race of its kind in the world, with cars reaching speeds of up to 200 mph (321.8 kph) on the 2.25-mile (3.6-km) circuit. With prize money in excess of $1.5 million, the **Indy**, as it is called, tempts numerous entrants; it is also very popular with spectators, attracting crowds of up to 300,000 annually.

• **indie ▶** British slang for a small independent record company, as opposed to the large recording giants. Many such small companies were formed during the late 1970s to satisfy the demand for non-mainstream pop music, especially for punk. There are now separate 'indie' charts for the output of such companies. 'Indie' is also sometimes used as a label for the kind of music – mainly guitar-based, angst-ridden, and aimed at students – that dominates their output.

• **Indochina War ▶** The struggle of the Viet Minh (Vietnamese nationalist and communist guerrillas) against French colonial rule in the period 1945–54. The Viet Minh, led by Ho Chi Minh and supported by the Americans, had fought valiantly against the Japanese occupation of the region after 1940. With the collapse of the Japanese in 1945, Ho Chi Minh declared Vietnam independent but the French, with British assistance, re-established their dominion, precipitating the war. This culminated in the ignominious French defeat at Dien Bien Phu and the international Geneva Conference (April–July 1954), which agreed the partition of Vietnam into North and South along the 17th parallel (*see*: Geneva Agreements).

• **industrial action▶** Action by a workforce, usually organized in a trade union, in support of a pay claim or other demands concerned with terms and conditions of employment. The most serious industrial action, and the weapon of last resort, is the strike; other less drastic measures include an overtime ban, a go-slow, or a work to rule.

• **industrial espionage▶** The practice of spying on one's competitors to discover their trade secrets. This can be achieved by planting employees in the workforce, bribing existing workers, or making illegal use of telephone- or computer-tapping devices. The information sought usually concerns the competitor's plans for research, launching of new products, or advertising campaigns; or it may involve the competitor's manufacturing techniques, pricing policy, takeover plans, etc.

• **industrial medicine ▶** The health care provided for a workforce by the management. There are usually three facets: the first-aid and nursing care provided to cope with accidents, illness at work, etc.; the prevention of accidents, work-related diseases (*e.g.* those caused by noxious fumes or dusts), and the minimization of the factors causing stress; and a regular service of physical check-ups, especially for senior members of staff.

• **industrial tourism▶** A recent development in the tourist trade, in which factories, workshops, and other industrial sites market themselves as attractions for sightseers. For the companies involved the revenue generated is usually much less important than the public relations opportunity. In the UK, the best-known example is British Nuclear Fuels' promotion of the Sellafield nuclear power station as a holiday attraction – an all-too-obvious attempt to erase the sinister reputation the plant had acquired when it was called Windscale. The concept of industrial tourism seems to have developed in parallel with that other phenomenon of the 1980s – the repackaging of newly defunct coal mines, cotton mills, etc., as heritage centres (*see*: heritage industry).

• **Industrial Workers of the World** ▶ *See*: Wobblies.

• **Indy** ▶ Short for Indianapolis 500.

• **inertial guidance** ▶ The control of the flight path of a rocket or missile by internal instruments, as opposed to some form of external remote control. Most intermediate- and long-range missiles use inertial guidance, navigating themselves to a predetermined target (*e.g.* a map reference) by means of sophisticated internal sensing instruments and electronics, including gyroscopes, accelerometers, and gravitational computers. *See*: guided missile.

• **inertia selling** ▶ The illegal practice of sending unsolicited goods through the post and invoicing the recipient if the goods are not returned within a specified time. The practice became increasingly common during the 1960s, but is now controlled under the provisions of the Unsolicited Goods and Services Acts (1971; 1975).

• **inferiority complex** ▶ Originally a psychiatric term, made popular by the psychiatrist Alfred Adler (1870–1937), denoting unrealistic or unreasonable feelings of inadequacy brought on by actual or imagined inferiority in life. Adler's work concentrated on this area of behaviour because he believed that Freud had overemphasized the sexual element. Sufferers from this psychiatric condition may sometimes compensate for their feelings of insecurity by exhibiting markedly aggressive behavioural tendencies. The term inferiority complex has become popular in the general language, not to denote a personality disorder but to describe extreme feelings of inadequacy or insecurity, temporary or permanent, aroused in the presence of certain people or situations.

• **inflation** ▶ A continuing increase in the level of prices and fall in the purchasing power of money, which can be caused by an excessive demand for goods (**demand-pull inflation**), increased selling prices without an increase in demand (**cost-push**

inflation), or an increase in the money supply (**monetary inflation**). The opposite process is **deflation**, in which both output and employment fall. In 19th-century Europe, periods of inflation and deflation alternated regularly but it was not until more recent times that the fundamental importance of such movements was recognized. In the 20th century the rapid inflation following World War I was followed by the protracted deflation of the Great Depression. This was succeeded by a continuous period of inflation in the decades after World War II; in the UK the inflation rate rose to over 20% per annum in the mid-1970s. **Hyperinflation** is extremely high inflation, of the order of 50% or more each month. This usually causes social disorder. When the inflation rate is high consumers make strenuous efforts to convert their currency to material goods, as their notes can lose their value literally overnight. The German experience of this phenomenon after World War I, when a suitcase of notes was needed to buy even a loaf of bread, made the control of inflation a top priority for most governments. *See also*: stagflation.

• **inflationary universe** ▶ A modification to the idea of the expanding universe resulting from the Big Bang. The theory is that in the first fleeting moments of its existence the universe expanded at an ever-increasing rate to $10^{30}$ times its size. This would explain the rate at which the universe is now expanding and the fact that it is isotropic. It might also account for the formation of so much mass and energy, apparently from nothing. As the theory's originator Alan Guth said:

> They say that there is no such thing as a free lunch, but the universe is the ultimate free lunch.

• **in-flight** ▶ Referring to goods and services provided during the course of a flight. For example, **in-flight entertainment** usually refers to a film show or music provided through individual headphones with a choice of several channels.

• **infomercial** ▶ A compound of *information* and com*mercial* used to denote a short television film produced by a company to advertise its goods or services. In general, such films are longer than the usual television advertisements and more soberly informative in their style.

• **infopreneurial** ▶ Relating to the design, manufacture, and sale of electronic equipment for the distribution of information. A combination word, made up from *information* and entre*preneurial*, it is often used in the phrase **infopreneurial industry**.

• **information anxiety** ▶ (IA) Feelings of panic

or despair brought on by a surfeit of unassimilable information pumped out by the media. These may include a sense of inadequacy at one's failure to grasp matters, such as the origins of the conflict in the Middle East, that have acquired a spurious familiarity as a result of constant media exposure. The phrase, coined by the US writer Richard Wurman, points to the paradox that advances in technology and the proliferation of channels of communication may leave people feeling less able to make sense of the world around them than ever.

• **information pollution**► A large amount of information on a particular subject, especially unnecessary or redundant information, put out by the media. For instance, during the Gulf War of 1991, television companies in the UK and America had very little 'hard news', but expended vast amounts of air time in analysis by political and military pundits.

• **information superhighway** ► A phrase coined by Al Gore, the former US vice-president, in a speech (mid-1990s) referring to the development of the Internet. It points towards a worldwide system of unlimited bandwidth connections bringing unlimited amounts of data and information directly to educational institutions, businesses, and homes. A 'superhighway' is the US equivalent of a British motorway.

• **information technology** ► (IT) The use of computers, telecommunications, and microelectronics to generate, store, and distribute information.

• **infotainment** ► Any film, television programme, CD-ROM, etc., that aims to provide information about a subject by entertaining as well as instructing. The term (a compound of *information* and enter*tainment*) is now mainly used of multimedia products that combine the features of a traditional reference book with sound and video. Educational software of this type found a growing market in the 1990s (*see*: electronic publishing).

• **infrastructure**► The basic physical facilities, including roads, railways, airports, utilities, etc. that a modern industrial society requires in order to function effectively.

• **inheritance tax**► In the UK there has been a tax on property, payable on the owner's death, for over a century. Introduced in 1894 as **estate duty** at a modest maximum rate of 8%, the tax was immediately and vehemently opposed by landowners. Increases in estate duty were a major factor in the unprecedented rejection of Lloyd George's 1909 budget by the House of Lords (*see*: People's Budget).

For the first half of the century the impact of the tax varied, but it gradually became more effective, both as a source of revenue for the exchequer and as a means of breaking down class barriers by restricting inherited wealth. During Attlee's post-war Labour government the tax caused many large estates to be broken up on the death of their owners. In 1950, for example, the estate of the Duke of Devonshire attracted duty of £5 million. However, the more intelligent of the landed gentry were finding legal ways round the tax, especially by making gifts of their property to their heirs while they were still alive and by putting their property into complicated trusts. For many, estate duty came to be regarded as a voluntary tax.

This situation ended with estate duty itself, when, in March 1975, **capital transfer tax** was introduced. The impact of this tax was not limited to the value of an estate at the time of its owner's death, but applied to many of the gifts the owner had made during his or her lifetime. In March 1986 substantial changes were made to capital transfer tax and thereafter it became known as **inheritance tax**. This tax now combines many features of the former estate duty with those of the capital transfer tax. Broadly, in 2001–2002, no tax was payable on the first £242,000 of an inheritance, but a single 40% tax rate applied thereafter. Life-time gifts within a seven-year period before death are taxed on a sliding scale.

• **in joke** ► A joke shared exclusively by the members of a particular group or by people who have common interests.

• **injury time** ► In soccer, rugby, etc., extra playing time allowed by the referee to compensate for stoppages during the game to treat players' injuries. The phrase is occasionally heard in relation to other matters, such as political or business negotiations, that are extended beyond their original deadline.

• **Inkatha** ► (Inkatha Yenkululeko Yesizwe – National Cultural Liberation Movement) A Zulu political movement, led by Chief Mangosouthu Gatsha Buthelezi (1928–   ). Originally founded in 1928 as a mainly cultural organization, it was revived by Buthelezi in the 1970s as a political movement. Although it opposed apartheid, Inkatha pursued a less radical approach to South African politics than the African National Congress (*see*: ANC); it opposed sanctions and foreign disinvestment, and favoured some form of power sharing as opposed to outright Black majority rule. The political and tribal differences between Inkatha and the ANC frequently erupted into armed conflict between their supporters, especially after the ban on the ANC was lifted in 1989. Buthelezi and two other leading members of Inkatha became government ministers after the multiracial elections of 1994. Inkatha is the Zulu word for the grass coil Zulu women use to carry loads on their heads; its strength depends on the weaving together of many strands.

• **Inklings** ▶ A literary circle run by C. S. Lewis (1893–1963) at Oxford University from the 1930s to the 1960s; its other leading members were J. R. R. Tolkein (1892–1973) and Charles Williams (1886–1945). The Inklings was originally a literary club founded in 1931 by an undergraduate at University College; Lewis and his friends occasionally attended these meetings and when the club folded, Lewis decided to continue the meetings on an informal basis. Thereafter he and his small group of friends met regularly at a local pub or in Lewis's rooms, to talk and read aloud from their original literary works. See also: Middle-earth; Narnia.

• **inner city** ▶ The densely populated central part of a city. Since the 1960s the term has been associated with areas of urban squalor characterized by abandoned industrial sites, substandard housing, and social deprivation. Inner cities have also earned a reputation for vandalism, crime, and racial tension. In the UK following World War II, slum clearance outpaced house-building programmes, creating overcrowding in high-density estates and tower blocks. Rigid rules about the segregation of residential from industrial and commercial zones, together with rules prohibiting the expansion of existing industrial sites in city centres, led to the closure of many smaller firms and the relocation of others to new towns and greenfield sites. As jobs disappeared, people with skills and resources moved out to the suburbs, leaving the inner cities inhabited largely by the unemployed and disadvantaged. With sources of investment and affluence removed, the areas rapidly decayed. The problems were first recognized in the late 1960s, but little was done until a decade later when the urgency of rehabilitating these areas became a national priority. Planning policy in the UK now supports redevelopment schemes designed to enhance the status of the inner cities and encourage industry to move back. Educational facilities in inner cities have also been improved.

• **inside job** ▶ A crime, such as a burglary, committed by someone, or with the aid of someone, working or living in the organization or premises concerned. An inside job is usually one perpetrated by someone trusted by the victim.

• **insider dealing** ▶ The illegal practice of trading in stocks and shares to one's own advantage using confidential information to which one's job or position affords access. By this means profits can be made before the confidential information becomes public. The term arose in the 1960s, particularly with reference to company takeover bids. It took on a broader significance after the Big Bang, when the distinction between brokers and jobbers was ended. See: Chinese wall.

• **instant camera** ▶ A type of camera that uses special film enabling developing and processing to take place inside the camera. Finished prints can be produced within a few seconds of taking the photograph. The first instant camera was the Polaroid (or Land) camera, invented by Edwin Land (1909–91) in 1947. A colour process was developed in 1963.

• **instant karma** ▶ 1. A phrase frequently used by the hippies of the late 1960s to convey the idea that divine retribution would immediately befall the perpetrator of an evil deed or unkind act. This was based on a slightly muddled interpretation of the word karma, a concept of personal destiny from Indian religious philosophy. 'Instant Karma' was the title of a hit song by John Lennon (1970). 2. Slang from the late 1960s and early 1970s for any illegal barbiturate drug. The name is a pun on 'calmer', the required effect of a barbiturate.

• **instant zen** ▶ Slang from the late 1960s for LSD or any hallucinogenic drug. The term alludes to the Zen Buddhist concept of enlightenment through meditation. LSD was supposed to provide a path, albeit a short cut, to enlightenment.

• **integrated circuit** ▶ A miniature electronic circuit, including transistors, resistors, and capacitors, contained within a semiconductor crystal. They range in complexity from a simple logic circuit to a highly complex system containing as many as a million transistors. Integrated circuits are widely used in computers, calculators, and most electronic equipment. Small (1–8 mm), light, reliable, and fast, they are made by introducing impurities into specified regions of a semiconductor crystal. See: chip.

• **intelligent camera** ▶ A computerized security camera that can focus on suspicious activity, track a moving object, and even protect itself from attack. A prototype developed at Oxford University was unveiled in 1993.

• **intelligent terminal** ▶ A computer terminal that is itself capable of processing data without reference to the main computer of the system to which it is connected.

• **Intelsat** ▶ International Consortium for Satellite Communications. The consortium, initially of 14 countries, was founded in August 1964 with the aim of providing global communication facilities, including telephone and television, by means of a network of satellites in 24-hour synchronous orbit. Each country invested in the system in proportion to the use it expected to make of it; revenues were then shared in this proportion. Intelsat 1 (Early Bird) was launched on 4 April 1965 and made transatlantic TV possible for the first time. By 2000 over 100 countries were members. The latest Intelsats have been placed in orbit by the space shuttle.

• **intensive care unit** ▸ (ICU) A hospital unit equipped with the facilities to provide constant medical care and monitoring for critically ill patients. They were first set up in the 1960s to look after patients whose lives were at risk. An ICU is characterized by its specially trained nurses and its life-saving equipment, such as respirators and devices that continuously monitor the vital functions. Some hospitals also have specially equipped ambulances that can be sent out to deal with emergencies in the patients' homes.

• **interactive fiction** ▸ A type of computer game in which the player participates in a story by inputting a series of instructions that determine (within the limits set by the program) the events and outcome of the narrative.

• **interactive television** ▸ A development in television technology that enables viewers to interact with what they see on the screen. It has been used to provide home shopping and banking and a 'telephone' service allowing subscribers to send each other social or business messages. More sophisticated versions may also permit the viewer of e.g. a football match to choose between several camera angles, to select his own action replays, etc. Interactive television became available to some cable subscribers in Britain in 1993. See also: digital broadcasting.

• **interesting** ▸
**Very interesting...but stupid** A catchphrase from the popular US TV show of the late 1960s and early 1970s Rowan and Martin's Laugh-In. Arte Johnson, wearing glasses and dressed as a Nazi soldier, spoke the line slowly with a very strong German accent and a long pause before 'but'.

• **interferon** ▸ Any of a group of proteins produced by certain body cells, such as white blood cells and fibroblasts, that act to inhibit the reproduction of invading viruses. They can also enhance the tumour-destroying capability of the body's immune system. Interferons were discovered in 1957 by Alick Isaacs and Jean Lindemann. Since then much attention has focused on their potential in the treatment of virus infections and cancer. Progress was hampered by the minute amounts obtainable from the blood; it was only in the 1980s, when interferons could be produced in much larger quantities using genetic engineering, that the clinical value of these proteins could be assessed. They have proved effective in treating certain conditions, but can produce severe side-effects. **Interferon-alfa** is used in the treatment of some cancers (including leukaemia and Kaposi's sarcoma, a skin cancer associated with Aids), hepatitis B and C, and genital herpes. **Interferon-beta** has provided relief for some patients with multiple sclerosis by reducing the severity and frequency of relapses.

• **Interlingua** or **Latino Sine Flexione** ▸ A simplified form of Latin in which there are no inflections, developed, like Esperanto, for use as an international language. It was formulated in 1903 by the Italian mathematician, Giuseppe Peano and revived in the 1950s by the linguist Alexander Gode, for use by the international scientific community. Abstracts and summaries are published in Interlingua by several international scientific journals although its use has not spread beyond a minority of dedicated enthusiasts.

• **International Brigades** ▸ Brigades of foreign volunteers, including Europeans and Americans, who fought for the Republicans against General Franco in the Spanish Civil War. Recruitment was largely organized by the Communist Party and the membership included intellectuals and writers, adventurers, the unemployed, and ordinary workers. The seven brigades, divided by nationality, were involved in the defence of Madrid in November 1936 and subsequently reinforced Republican forces in the defence of the Jarama Valley and Guadalajara in the spring of 1937. In 1938 the brigades suffered heavy losses during fighting in the Ebro valley. Members of the British brigade included the novelist George Orwell and the poet W. H. Auden.

• **International Monetary Fund** ▸ See: IMF.

• **Internationals** ▸ Several international associations of socialist or communist parties. The first of these (1864–72) was set up under the auspices of Karl Marx as the International Working Men's Association; the Internationale was adopted as its anthem. The Second, or Social-Democratic, International was formed in 1889 and the Third, or Communist, International was set up by Lenin in 1919 and lasted until 1943. The abortive Trotskyite Fourth International dates from 1938.

• **International Style** ▸ An architectural movement that began in central Europe after World War I and spread throughout Europe and America during the late 1920s. The style favoured orthogonal forms shorn of ornamentation, open internal spaces, and the use of such modern materials as sheet glass, steel, stucco, and concrete. The movement was intended to represent an anti-eclectic, anti-bourgeois, and utilitarian fusion of art and new building technology. Its best known European exponents were the Germans Walter Gropius (1883–1969, founder of the Bauhaus) and Mies Van der Rohe (1886–1969) and the French visionary Le Corbusier (1887–1965). Their ideals were promoted in America by Philip Johnson (1906–89), who, together with the US architectural historian Henry-Russell Hitchcock, coined the term 'International Style' in 1932. *See also*: brutalism; functionalism.

• **Internet** ▶ A global network that connects other computer networks, together with software and protocols for controlling the movement of data. The Internet, often referred to as **the Net**, grew from a network called ARAPNET (Advanced Research Project Agency Network), which was initiated in 1969 by a number of universities and research groups funded by the US Department of Defense. It now covers almost every country in the world. Its organization is informal and deliberately nonpolitical.

The Internet offers users a number of basic services including data transfer, e-mail, and the ability to access information in remote databases. A notable feature is the existence of **user groups**, which allow people to exchange information about specific subjects of interest. In addition, there are a number of high-level services. The most important of these, the **World Wide Web** (known as **the Web**), was developed in the 1990s at CERN in Geneva. It is a service for distributing multimedia information, including graphics, pictures, sounds, and video as well as text. A feature of the Web is that it allows links to other related documents elsewhere on the Internet. Many commercial and public organizations now have their own **website** (specified by an address code) and publish a 'home page', giving information about the organization.

Until the mid-1990s, the major users of the Internet were academic and research organizations. In the last few years this has changed rapidly with home users linking in through commercial access providers and companies showing a growing interest in using the Internet for publicity, sales, and as a medium for electronic publishing; it is also used increasingly in the fields of education and entertainment. At the same time, the uncontrolled growth of the Internet has raised a number of un-

resolved problems, notably those of copyright and data protection; the availability of hardcore pornography, including child pornography, is also a matter of concern.

• **Interpol** ▶ International Criminal Police Commission. The organization that coordinates the police forces of over 125 countries in the fight against international crime, such as drug smuggling and counterfeiting. It was set up in Vienna in 1923 but was reformed and relocated in new headquarters in Paris in 1946. French police officials staff the General Secretariat, which administers its day-to-day functions; affiliated police forces communicate through domestic clearing houses and criminals are apprehended by means of extradition.

• **intifada** ▶ (Arabic, uprising) The revolt by the Palestinian inhabitants of the Israeli-occupied territories that began in 1987 (*see*: Gaza Strip; West Bank). The Intifada, and Israel's harsh attempts to suppress it, resulted in increased international sympathy for the Palestinians and led indirectly to the peace agreement of 1993. The term Intifada has also been applied to the second Palestinian uprising that began in 2000.

• **Invergordon Mutiny** ▶ A mutiny in the Royal Navy's Atlantic Fleet at the naval base in the Cromarty Firth, Scotland, on 15 September 1931. Ratings, led by Able Seaman Len Wincott, refused to prepare ships for sea in protest at cuts in pay ordered by the National Government, which had been announced over the radio in advance of official notification. The Board of Admiralty averted further embarrassment to the navy by agreeing to limit the cuts to below 10%. The incident contributed to the gathering mood of crisis that led to the UK's abandonment of the Gold Standard on 21 September 1931.

• **investigative journalism** ▶ Investigation by newspaper or television journalists of corruption, crime, governmental inefficiency, etc. In countries in which freedom of speech is valued, such journalism is regarded as a valuable safeguard against official complacency or abuse of the system. *See also*: muckrakers.

• **in vitro fertilization** ▶ *See*: IVF.

• **IRA** ▶ Irish Republican Army. Originally, a guerrilla force organized from the former Irish Volunteers, which confronted British forces during the Irish War of Independence (1919–21). With the creation of the Irish Free State in 1921, the IRA split between those who accepted the Anglo-Irish Treaty and those who repudiated it because Northern Ireland remained part of the UK. There followed a civil

294<< • Irangate •

war (1921–23) in which the Free State army defeated the anti-Treaty faction (who kept the name IRA). Thereafter extremists kept it in being as a secret organization dedicated to establishing a united Irish republic through terrorism. After a period of quiescence, the IRA re-emerged in 1968–69, with the eruption of the present Northern Irish Troubles. At this time the organization split into the Officials, who took an increasingly Marxist line, and the **Provisionals** or **Provos**, concerned only with expelling the British from Northern Ireland. Terrorist outrages committed by the Provisional IRA included the pub bombings in Birmingham and Guildford (1974; see: Birmingham Six; Guildford Four), the murder of Lord Mountbatten in 1979, the attempted assassination of Margaret Thatcher and her cabinet in 1984, the Remembrance Day bombing in Enniskillen (1987), and massive bomb blasts in the City of London (1992, 1993). Following the Downing Street Declaration, the IRA declared a ceasefire in August 1994; this was abandoned in February 1996, when a huge bomb exploded in London's Docklands. In 1997 the ceasefire was resumed, and in 1998 Sinn Féin (the political wing of the IRA) accepted the Good Friday Agreement. However, the IRA's reluctance to comply with the decommissioning of weapons as set out in this agreement caused repeated crises in the peace process for the next three years. The IRA finally announced that it had put a quantity of arms 'beyond use' in October 2001. IRA splinter groups hostile to the Good Friday Agreement include the **Continuity IRA** and the **Real IRA**, perpetrators of the 1998 Omagh bomb.

• **Irangate** ▶ Following Watergate, the suffix '-gate' became an indicator of political scandal involving corruption and secret transactions. 'Irangate' was used to describe a covert plan devised in 1986 by Lieut.-Col. Oliver North and members of the US administration to sell arms to Iran and use the proceeds to give military aid to the right-wing Contra rebels in Nicaragua. The gradual unravelling of the scandal in 1986–87 did much to undermine the credibility of President Reagan.

• **Iran–Iraq War** ▶ The conflict between these two countries that followed upon Iraq's invasion of W Iran in 1980. During the war the region witnessed the deaths of hundreds of thousands of combatants, toxic gas attacks by Iraq, and Iranian rocket attacks on Iraqi cities. The war ended in 1988 without appreciable benefit to either side.

• **IRBM** ▶ Intermediate range ballistic missile. A medium-range ballistic weapon, such as the US Tomahawk Cruise missile and Pershing II, or the Russian SS-20, SS-4, and SS-5. These IRBMs were exten-

sively deployed in Europe by both America and the Soviet Union during the late 1970s and early 1980s (see: Greenham Common), but were later removed in accordance with the provisions of the US–Soviet INF (Intermediate Nuclear Forces) Treaty of 8 December 1987. Compare: ICBM.

• **Irgun Zvai Leumi** ▶ (Hebrew, National Military Society) A Jewish terrorist organization founded in 1931; it was active in Palestine during 1946–48. Its most notorious act, led by Yisrael Levy (1926–90), was the bombing of the King David Hotel in Jerusalem on 22 July 1946, destroying the quarters of the British administration with the loss of 91 lives. It claimed responsibility for over 200 acts of terrorism against the British and Arabs before being disbanded in 1948, when members took an oath of loyalty to the newly founded Israeli state.

• **Irish crown jewels theft** ▶ The disappearance of the Irish crown regalia from the safe of Dublin Castle's Bedford Tower in July 1907. The theft caused a major scandal. Edward VII himself demanded the resignation of the four men responsible for the safekeeping of the jewels and a commission of inquiry was hastily set up to investigate. Lengthy recriminations ensued but were never resolved and the thief's identity was never discovered. The jewels themselves have never reappeared.

• **Irish Free State** ▶ The 26 counties of southern Ireland that were granted dominion status within the Empire under the provisions of the Anglo-Irish Treaty of 1921. Its first prime minister (president of the executive council), W. T. Cosgrave (1880–1965), was replaced in 1932 by Éamon de Valera (1882–1975). In 1937 the Irish Free State adopted a new constitution and was renamed Eire. It remained a member of the Commonwealth until 1949, when it became known officially as the Republic of Ireland. See also: Free Staters.

• **Irish National Volunteers** ▶ An irregular force raised by the Irish Republican Brotherhood (IRB) in November 1913 to counteract the Ulster Volunteers. The movement had attracted over 150,000 recruits by June 1914 but the organization soon afterwards split into two factions; the majority (the **National Volunteers**) following the moderate leadership of John Redmond and the rump (the **Irish Volunteers**) joining Eoin MacNeil, who was influenced by the radical separatists within the IRB. During World War I, however, the anti-war anti-conscription Irish Volunteers, who led the fighting in the Easter Rising of 1916, flourished at the expense of the moderates, who dwindled into insignificance. By 1919 the Irish Volunteers had evolved into the Irish Republican Army (*see*: IRA).

• **Iron Butterfly** ▶ The Hollywood nickname for Jeanette Macdonald (?1901–65), the US singer and film star best known for partnering Nelson Eddy (1901–67) in a series of screen operettas, such as *Rose Marie* (1936) and *Maytime* (1937). The pair were sometimes known as the **Singing Capon** and the Iron Butterfly by those who found their popularity inexplicable.

• **Iron Cross** ▶ A Prussian military decoration (an iron Maltese cross, edged with silver), instituted by Frederick William III in 1813 during the struggle against Napoleon. Remodelled by William I in 1870 with three grades, in civil and military divisions, the Iron Cross was awarded to some 3,000,000 servicemen in World War I. It was reinstated by Hitler in 1939.

• **Iron Curtain** ▶ The notional barrier created by the Soviet Union and its satellites along a line running from Stettin (Szczecin) to Trieste. The communist countries east of this line cut themselves off from Western Europe after World War II. The phrase was popularized by Sir Winston Churchill in his Fulton Speech (5 March 1946) but it was used previously in Germany by Count Schwerin von Krosigk on 2 May 1945 and by Lord Conesford in February of that year. It has earlier antecedents; Ethel Snowden used it in 1920 with reference to Bolshevik Russia, Lord D'Abernon used it in 1925 with regard to the proposed Locarno Treaties, and the Queen of the Belgians, in 1914, spoke of a 'bloody iron curtain' between her and the Germans. The phrase occurs in the Earl of Munster's journal as far back as 1817. The demolition of the Berlin Wall following radical political reforms in East Germany in 1989 signalled the end of the Iron Curtain as an effective barrier between East and West.

> From Stettin on the Baltic to Trieste on the Adriatic, an iron curtain has descended across Europe. – SIR WINSTON CHURCHILL.

• **Iron Guard** ▶ The title adopted by the Romanian Fascist party of the 1930s. *See*: Fascism.

• **Iron Lady** ▶ The name bestowed upon Margaret Thatcher (1925–  ; prime minister 1979–90), when she was leader of the Opposition in the House of Commons, by the Soviet defence ministry newspaper *Red Star* (24 January 1976). After her speech warning the Commons of the increasing Soviet threat to the West, the *Red Star* accused the 'Iron Lady' of trying to revive the Cold War, referring to her 'viciously anti-Soviet speech', and to 'the peace-loving policy of the Soviet Union'. Although the Russian coinage Iron Lady was probably based on an analogy to Stalin as the Man of Steel, the British press were quick to see an allusion to the Iron Maiden, a medieval instrument of torture; caricatures duly appeared in which the spiked iron devices had Thatcher faces.

Owing to a combination of her sex, her personality, and her politics, Mrs Thatcher attracted a perhaps unequalled repertoire of nicknames during her career. The Conservative minister Norman St John Stevas referred to her as **the Blessed Margaret** and **the Leaderene**; her husband, Denis Thatcher, is reputed to call her **the Boss**. Other names include **the Milk Snatcher**, referring to her decision to stop free school milk when she was education secretary, and **The Grocer's Daughter**, referring to the grocer's shop in Grantham run by her father. Most Thatcher nicknames, however, reflect her uncompromising and autocratic style: **Attila the Hen**, **TINA** (the latter from her habit of using the phrase 'There Is No Alternative!'), and **She Who Must be Obeyed** being perhaps the best known.

• **iron lung** ▶ A rigid chamber fitted over the top part of a person's body to provide prolonged artificial respiration for patients with respiratory problems by means of mechanical pumps, which force the air in and out of the lungs. The apparatus has been in use since the early 1930s but has now been largely replaced by more modern methods.

• **iron rations** ▶ Emergency rations, especially as provided in the army; usually tinned food, particularly bully beef and biscuits. Also, in World War I an ironic term for hot shell-fire.

• **Irvin suit** ▶ The flying suit worn by the RAF during World War II, which was designed by Leslie Irvin and manufactured at his factory in Letchworth, Hertfordshire.

• **ISA** ▶ (individual savings account) A form of savings account available in the UK from April 1999; they replaced personal equity plans (*see*: PEP) and Tessas. Individuals are currently (until 2006) entitled to save up to £7,000 per annum free of tax.

• **ISBN** ▶ International Standard Book Number. An internationally agreed system of numbering and registering editions of books. Every book now published carries an ISBN number on its copyright page.

• **Islington man** ▶ An affluent educated person with left-of-centre views who is imagined as living in Islington, a gentrified area of North London. Typically, Islington man works in the media or politics, has cosmopolitan tastes in food, travel, and culture, and finds no difficulty in reconciling his high-maintenance lifestyle with support for New Labour.

Tony Blair himself was a resident of Islington before his elevation to 10 Downing Street. The term is generally used in a slightly derogatory sense.

• **isometrics** ▶ A system of physical exercises to develop muscular strength; it involves brief contractions of the muscle or muscle group against the fixed resistance of an immovable object or the equal force of opposing muscles acting in the same way. Isometrics is based on the principle of isometric, or static, contraction in which tension is developed in the muscle without change in the length of the muscle fibres (the prefix 'iso-' means 'the same'). The static strength and rigidity developed by isometric exercises is required in many sports, such as gymnastics, weightlifting, and wrestling. This type of training became very popular, especially in America, in the 1960s and 1970s following reports of the significant increases in strength that could be achieved by making use of it.

• **Isonzo** ▶ A river, formerly in Italy (now in Croatia and called the Soca), that was scene of a series of fierce battles between Italian and Austrian forces between 23 June 1915 and 12 November 1917. The Italian strategy aimed at the capture of Trieste and then an advance on to Vienna, but the Austrian defences withstood all attempts to break through; in the final battle, 24 October–12 November 1917 (known as the 12th Battle of Isonzo or Caporetto), the Germans aided the Austrians in inflicting a catastrophic defeat on the Italians, who lost 305,000 men, of whom 275,000 were captured.

• **I-Spy** ▶ A series of children's educational game books, which became enormously successful in the UK after their first appearance in the 1950s. The books gave children a list of items on a particular subject (such as history) to seek out; their rewards for finding a certain number of them were badges and an 'Order of Merit' making the participant a 'Redskin of the I-Spy Tribe'. The awards were bestowed by 'Big Chief I-Spy', in reality Charles Warrell, who created the books and ran the whole enterprise until it came to an end in 1986. The Michelin company relaunched the books in 1991.

> I invented the name Big Chief I-Spy. I travelled the country holding I-Spy pow-wows – enormous gatherings. One of the last was 'I-Spy the city of Bath'. About 5,000 children and adults turned up. – CHARLES WARRELL, 1990.

• **Is you is or is you ain't?** ▶ A phrase taken from the title of the 1944 song 'Is You Is or Is You Ain't My Baby?', written by Louis Jordan and Billy Austin and meaning *are* you, or *aren't* you my girl? The phrase enjoyed a revival in the late 1980s and early 1990s, thanks largely to a series of television commercials for a leading credit card. These featured a frustrated cardholder imploring a restaurateur to accept his Access card with the line 'Does you do or does you don't take Access?'

• **It** ▶ A humorous synonym for sex appeal, popularized by the novelist Elinor Glyn in *It* (1927), though Kipling had used the word earlier in the same sense in his story 'Mrs Bathurst' (*Traffics and Discoveries*, 1904).

• **IT** ▶ *See*: information technology.

• **Italian Alp** ▶ One of the nicknames of the Italian heavyweight boxer Primo Carnera (1906–67); he was also known as the **Ambling Alp** on account of his size (almost 6 ft 6 in tall and weighing 19 stone). He was discovered while employed as a circus wrestler and strongman. Having taken up boxing professionally in 1928, he became world heavyweight champion in June 1933, when he knocked out Jack Sharkey in the sixth round. He held the title for only one year, however, being floored 11 times in as many rounds by Max Baer in 1934. He later went on to become a professional wrestler and appeared in several films.

• **It Girl** ▶ **1.** One of the most famous Hollywood nicknames; it was given to Clara Bow (1905–65), a leading actress of the silent era, who was hailed as the sexiest woman in films. She acquired the title after appearing in *It* (1927), the film based on Elinor Glyn's story (*see*: It), in which she portrayed a vivacious pouting flapper. Red-haired and exuberant, Clara Bow epitomized the Jazz Age, hence another of her nicknames, the **Jazz Baby**. In the 1930s she suffered a series of breakdowns, which ended her career. **2.** One of a group of glamorous upper-class young women who became mildly famous in the late 1990s for their frequent appearances at celebrity parties and in newspaper gossip columns. The best known was probably Tara Palmer-Tompkinson, who also wrote a gossip column in *The Sunday Times* for a time.

• **ITMA** ▶ It's That Man Again. A popular British radio series, which did much to brighten up the dreariness of the black-out years of World War II. It was devised by the comedian Tommy Handley (1896–1949), the script being written by Ted Kavanagh. It ran from 1939 until Handley's death in 1949. Mrs Mopp and Funf were among the characters in this weekly skit on English life. The show introduced many popular catchphrases, including Mrs Mopp's 'Can I do you now, sir?'

• **Ivan** ▶ Slang for a Russian man. It is based on the belief that Ivan is the most common Russian forename, much as a German is supposed to be called Fritz and an Irishman Paddy.

• **Ivan the Terrible** ▶ Ivan IV of Russia (1530–84), infamous for his cruelties but a man of great energy. He was the first to adopt the title of Tsar (1547).

In the 20th century the name was given to a notorious guard at the Treblinka concentration camp who was responsible for numerous atrocities against prisoners. In 1986 John Demjanjuk (formerly Ivan Grozny), a retired Ukrainian car worker living in Cleveland, Ohio, was identified as Ivan, extradited to Israel, and sentenced to death. However, on 30 July 1993 an Israeli court of appeal freed Demjanjuk on the grounds that there was reasonable doubt about the identification. This was a particularly hard case for the judges, as there was little doubt that, Ivan the Terrible or not, Demjanjuk had committed Nazi atrocities as a camp guard at Treblinka.

• **IVF** ▶ In vitro fertilization. The technique in which an egg is fertilized with sperm outside the body of the female. The description *in vitro* (literally 'in glass') is not strictly accurate since the process is generally performed in a metal dish. The IVF technique for humans was pioneered in the UK by gynaecologist Patrick Steptoe and physiologist Robert Edwards, in order to help women with certain types of infertility, particularly blocked or damaged Fallopian tubes. The world's first IVF baby (**test-tube baby**) was Louise Brown, born in 1978 at Oldham General Hospital, since when IVF has benefited thousands of women throughout the world. An egg is removed from the woman's ovary using a long hollow tube inserted through the abdominal wall. The egg is then introduced into a suspension of the husband's sperm under sterile conditions. When fertilization has taken place and the embryo has undergone several divisions of its cells (about 40 hours old), it is inserted into the uterus through the vagina, and allowed to implant in the wall of the womb. Often, two fertilized eggs are implanted to increase the chances of success. Failure to implant and subsequent spontaneous abortion are both common, enabling only a minority of women to be successfully treated by the technique.

In the UK, IVF and such related techniques as embryo freezing and storage, womb leasing, and egg and embryo donation, are regulated by the Human Fertilisation and Embryology Act (1990). This set up a special authority to oversee all work in this field and to issue licences to medical practitioners and researchers. In America legislation varies from state to state. Another major application of IVF has been in farm livestock breeding programmes. *See also*: AI; GIFT.

• **Ivy League** ▶ A group of old-established northeastern US colleges and universities that has acquired a reputation for academic achievement and social prestige: so-called because many of the stately college buildings are ivy-clad. The term was first used in the 1930s by sports writers; the Ivy League colleges and universities usually include Yale, Harvard, Princeton, Columbia, Dartmouth, Cornell, Pennsylvania, and Brown. **Ivy Leaguers** are students or graduates of these establishments, the use of the term now usually being confined to contexts in which their well-spoken voices and alleged snobbishness are being emphasized. The Ivy League in America is roughly equivalent to Oxbridge in the UK.

> The jerk had one of those very phoney, Ivy League voices, one of those very tired, snobby voices. – J. D. SALINGER: *Catcher in the Rye* (1951).

• **Iwo Jima** ▶ A small volcanic island in the Pacific Ocean, about 600 miles SE of the Japanese mainland. During the closing stages of World War II it was bitterly fought over as a strategic stepping stone in the Allied advance on Japan. The Americans were determined to stop the Japanese from using it as a base for their fighters intercepting US B-29 Superfortresses en route from the Marianas to bomb the Japanese mainland. After a naval and air bombardment of Japanese defences, US marines went ashore on 19 February 1945. On 23 February the US flag was raised on Mount Suribachi, the island's highest point. A second flag-raising, performed on the same day, was photographed by pressman Joe Rosenthal and transmitted to America, where it quickly assumed enormous symbolic significance. There is now a statue of the flag-raising in Washington DC. Meanwhile, the stubborn Japanese resistance on the island was gradually overcome but with heavy casualties on both sides. The marines finally secured the island at the end of March. Over 6800 marines and nearly all 22,000 Japanese defenders were killed.

• **Izvestia** ▶ (Russian, news) The official national newspaper of the former Soviet Union. It was established in Petrograd (St Petersburg) in 1917 as an organ of the Revolution, then transferred to Moscow in 1918. By 1932 it enjoyed a circulation of over 1.5 million. It represented the government's views, especially on foreign policy and international relations, reproduced official documents at length, and was intended to educate and inform the public in the light of official policy. Following the break up of the Soviet Union in 1991, *Izvestia* became an independent newspaper.

# J

• **J** ► Abbreviation for a joint, a cannabis cigarette. This has been used since the mid-1960s, both in the UK and America.

• **jack** ► **1.** British slang for alone, from the rhyming slang 'Jack Jones', alone. It is usually used in the phrase **on one's jack**. **2.** Prison slang from the 1960s for heroin. Also a single dose or injection of a narcotic, particularly a tablet of prescribed heroin or a heroin substitute given to addicts. These senses derive both from the use of jack up, meaning to inject oneself, and from the rhyming slang **Jack and Jill**, for pill. **3.** US slang for money. This meaning is also current in the UK, Ireland, and Australia. **4.** Tramps' and dossers' slang for methylated spirits. **5.** British slang for the buttocks or anus. **6.** British slang for the penis. This sense is obviously related to the US **jack off**, meaning to masturbate. It may also reflect the old rhyming slang 'Jack in the box', pox. **7.** Australian slang for bored or fed up. This is probably related to the US **jacked off**, meaning angry.

• **Jack** ►

**I'm alright Jack** A catchphrase indicating that as the self-interests of the speaker have been satisfied he has no intention of spending any effort considering the plight of others. The use of the name Jack implies a nautical origin, as does the longer form: **Pull up the ladder, Jack, I'm inboard**.

Perhaps the catchphrase reached its widest public through the Boulting Brothers film *I'm Alright Jack* (1959), in which Peter Sellers played a communist shop steward and Ian Carmichael a naive young graduate who precipitates a strike. John Boulting's swipe at the idiocies of British labour relations in the 1950s was fairly close to the mark. Indeed, Sellers' operatic performance appeared slightly underplayed by the end of the 1960s.

> It's 'Damn you, Jack – I'm all right!' with you chaps. – DAVID BONE: *The Brassbounder* (1910).

• **Jackal, The** ► The press nickname for Carlos Martinez (1949–   ), a Venezuelan known to have worked as an assassin on behalf of various terrorist organizations. The name was taken from Frederick Forsyth's novel, *The Day of the Jackal* (1970), in which a professional assassin, codenamed 'The Jackal', is hired by a group of veterans of the Algerian war to kill President de Gaulle (*see*: OAS).

• **jackboot** ► A large leather boot extending over the knee, originally worn as protective armour by troopers in the 17th and 18th centuries and still part of the uniform of the Household Cavalry. It was later adopted as part of the uniform of various military organizations, notably the Nazi stormtroopers. Because of these associations, particularly the last, the jackboot came to be used figuratively in such phrases as **under the jackboot**, to denote the repressive rule exerted by militaristic or Fascist regimes. Since the 1960s the word has been widely used to stand for any authoritarian or bullying measures or those who employ them.

• **Jackie O.** ► Jacqueline Onassis (1929–94), famous for her marriages to US president John F. Kennedy (1917–63) and the Greek shipping magnate Aristotle Socrates Onassis (1906–75). Later to become one of the world's most photographed women, she was herself a press photographer before marrying Kennedy in 1953. As first lady, her youth, beauty, and sense of style contributed greatly to the image of Kennedy's White House (*see*: Camelot); indeed, her activities became a staple of gossip columns and society journalism. When she accompanied the president on a visit to Paris in 1962 she so charmed everyone, including General de Gaulle, that when Kennedy held a press conference, he said:

> I do not think it is altogether inappropriate to introduce myself to this audience. I am the man who accompanied Jacqueline Kennedy to Paris, and I have enjoyed it.

The events of 22 November 1963, when she rode beside her husband in the Dallas motorcade (*see*: Kennedy assassination), made her the world's most celebrated widow. However, it was not long before the question of her remarriage was frequently being mooted in the press. In 1968 she married the 62-year-old Onassis, whose fabulous wealth, friendships with the famous, and stormy relationship with Maria Callas had made him a celebrity in his own right. The marriage took place on the groom's private island of Scorpios. After being widowed for the second time, Jackie O. returned to New York and a career in publishing until her death.

• **jack it in** ▶ To give up, leave, abandon something prematurely.

> There were only fifteen of us on the hunger strike, I suppose the others must have got hungry, anyway, they jacked it in. – F. NORMAN: *Bang to Rights* (1948).

• **jack up** ▶ **1.** Slang meaning to inject oneself with heroin or any other narcotic drug. **2.** British police and underworld slang meaning to put together or to organize a plan. It probably derives from the idea of jacking up a car – the preparatory stage to doing any actual work on it.

• **Jacuzzi** ▶ Tradename for a hot whirlpool bath, installed in leisure centres and some private homes as an aid to relaxation. It was developed and marketed by Roy Jacuzzi from a pump invented by his brother Candido Jacuzzi and became internationally popular from the 1970s.

• **jag** ▶ **1.** Slang for a binge, a bout of drinking, drug-taking, or any other self-indulgent activity.

> Ronnie Kray was then on a religious jag and offering only fruit juice and gramophone recordings of the Lord's Prayer. – *The Independent*, 2 February 1991.

**2.** Slang meaning to inject oneself with a drug, probably from 'jab'.

• **jalopy** or **jalloppy** ▶ A dilapidated old car. Although particularly popular in the 1950s, the term was first heard in America during the Depression era. The derivation is unknown.

• **jam** ▶ **1.** Short for **jam session**, an informal gathering of jazz, blues, or rock musicians improvising together. The word is also used as a verb meaning to improvise. A more recent and more specific sense is the improvising of rap chants.

> The gigs became almost a secondary thing to getting to the nearest jam, just getting together with whoever was in town and playing for the pure love of it. – JIM CAPALDI, rock musician, in *The Independent*, 17 January 1991.

**2.** US slang for a wild party, reflecting the idea of people being crowded into a room. **3.** Slang for an act of sexual intercourse, or a sexual partner, or the vagina. These sexual senses reflect both the close proximity of entwined bodies and the idea of jam (the conserve) as something sweet and desirable. Jam, in this sense, can also be used as a verb. **4.** Slang for an illegal drug, particularly cocaine. This again reflects the idea of jam as something sweet.

• **jam and Jerusalem** ▶ A mildly derisive catchphrase aimed (since about 1925) at the Women's Institute organizations in the UK. The popular conception of the WI is that its activities revolve around the making of jam and the singing of Parry's 'Jerusalem' at each meeting – an increasingly outdated view.

• **jamboree bags** ▶ British vulgar slang for female breasts. In the 1950s a jamboree bag was a small lucky-dip bag containing sweets and a toy. The slang sense is heard mostly among men old enough to remember these childhood delights.

• **jam jar** ▶ British rhyming slang for a car; in use since the 1920s, mainly in London.

• **jane** ▶ **1.** British and US slang for a female prostitute, probably deriving from the fact that Jane is the female form of John – the slang name for a prostitute's customer. In Britain the derivation may have been influenced by the rhyming slang Jane Shore, whore (Jane Shore being a famous mistress of King Edward IV). Female prostitutes in Britain are also known as **toms**, a slang term dating from the early 20th century and used primarily by the police and the criminal underworld. **2.** Slang for a women's lavatory. A feminized version of John, a widely used Americanism for a 'rest room'.

• **Jane** ▶ A nubile comic strip character, created by Norman Pett, who first appeared in *The Daily Mirror* in 1932 and soon became a national institution. The strip continued until 1959, Don Freeman taking over the writing in 1938 and Mike Hubbard the drawings from 1949. Although Jane generally managed to lose several items of clothing in each episode, in 1942 she emerged from her bath totally nude for the first time. On the same day the 8th Army in North Africa advanced six miles. Robert Maxwell, who was in North Africa at the time, reintroduced Jane when he bought the paper in 1985 (*see*: Bouncing Czech). The revived strip ended on 1 September 1990.

• **Jane Q. Citizen** or **Jane Q. Public** ▶ A US name for the average woman. *See*: John Q. Citizen.

• **jankers** ▶ British forces' slang for a military punishment. Widely heard during the 1950s when military service was still compulsory, it seems to have been coined during World War I. The derivation is uncertain, but the word is possibly related to an obsolete meaning of jangle, 'to complain'.

• **JAP** ▶ *See*: Jewish American Princess.

• **Japs** ▶

> **Send us more Japs!** A widely publicized remark attributed to Lt-Colonel James P. S. Dev-

ereux during the Battle of Wake Island (1941). It was allegedly the text of a defiant message sent by Devereux shortly before US forces surrendered to the Japanese and was enthusiastically taken up by the US press. However, when Devereux returned home after four years in a Japanese prisoner-of-war camp, he claimed to be totally ignorant of the whole thing:

> I did not send any such message. As far as I know, it wasn't sent at all. None of us was that much of a damn fool. We already had more Japs than we could handle.

• **Jarrow march** or **Jarrow Crusade** ▸ A protest march from Jarrow in NE England to London in October 1936 by a selection of local workers made redundant by the closure of Palmer's Shipyard on the River Tyne. The march was organized by the Jarrow town council and led by the local Labour MP, Ellen Wilkinson ('Red Ellen'), who, after 26 days on the road, presented a petition in the House of Commons to elicit government aid for the northeast and other areas afflicted by mass unemployment. The marchers attracted enormous public sympathy and the Jarrow march became one of the most famous incidents in Labour folklore. *See also*: hunger march.

• **J. Arthur** ▸ *See*: Arthur Rank.

• **Jar Wars** ▸ A campaign initiated by the Reagan administration in 1986 to deter illegal drug taking by US government employees. The campaign was so called, by analogy with the title of the space adventure film *Star Wars* (1977), because all government personnel were required to supply samples of urine to be tested for the presence of drugs. These specimens were usually taken in jars or bottles.

• **Java man** ▸ The popular name given to fossil hominid remains found at Trinil, in Java, in 1891. Formally named *Pithecanthropus erectus*, these remains were later reclassified as belonging to the species *Homo erectus*, an early form of man, which lived between 1.8 and 0.3 million years ago. *See also*: Peking man.

• **jaw-jaw** ▸ Lengthy or long-winded discussion. Although the term was used as early as 1748 in Smollett's *Roderick Random*, it gained wide currency only from the late 1950s, following a speech by Harold Macmillan on 30 January 1958, in which he coined the ugly but patently true aphorism:

> Jaw-jaw is better than war-war.

These words echoed those of Winston Churchill, spoken four years earlier at a lunch at the White House in Washington on 26 June 1954. Here he was reported to have said:

> Talking jaw to jaw is better than going to war.

• **Jaws** ▸ The hugely successful 1975 movie about a great white shark that terrorizes a small seaside resort on Cape Cod in America. Based on the bestseller by Peter Benchley, the film made the reputation of its director, Steven Spielberg and sparked off an era of 'shark mania'. It is justly celebrated for its nerve-racking underwater sequences, in which the tension is brilliantly heightened by the incidental music of John Williams. All this, however, did little for the reputation of the shark, leading several conservation groups to point out that shark attacks are rarer than the film suggests and that certain species are declining alarmingly in numbers as a result of persecution by hunters. The shark in the film was a mechanical replica, built at a cost of many thousands of dollars. The film's first sequel (of three) was released with the famous slogan **Just when you thought it was safe to go back in the water**.

• **jay-walker** ▸ A pedestrian who crosses roads carelessly, paying no attention to pedestrian crossings or traffic regulations. Originating in America in the 1910s, the term owes its derivation to the US word 'jay', meaning a simpleton or rustic, *i.e.* one who is not sufficiently sophisticated to cope with town or city traffic.

• **jazz** ▸ A type of popular music that originated in New Orleans around 1890 and went on to exert an immense influence on the musical life of the 20th century. The style developed from a combination of blues, ragtime, and brass-band music. Its main characteristics are a strong rhythmic beat, frequent use of syncopation, and improvisation on a melodic theme by trumpet, clarinet, and trombone. The word jazz (originally jass) was a New Orleans slang term for sexual intercourse; legend has it that jazz emerged in the brothels of the Storyville district, where musicians were employed to entertain the clientele waiting their turn to enjoy what they had come for.

Various styles of jazz have been popular at different times. The essentially Black New Orleans style was followed by the Dixie of White southerners, the popularity of which brought jazz to New York and thence to the entire Western world. In the 1930s Dixieland gave way to big-band swing, which was itself succeeded by the experimental style known as bebop. In the 1950s the cool jazz of Miles Davis and his contemporaries was in vogue; subsequent developments have included the use of atonality in free-form jazz and the fusion of jazz with classical, rock, and African styles.

• **Jazz Age** ▸ An epithet for the 1920s in America, popularized by the writer F. Scott Fitzgerald

(1896–1940) who captured the exhilarating hedonism of the era in his *Tales of the Jazz Age* (1922) and other works. Jazz music, wild parties, the speakeasy and the charleston – all represented a rebellion against the repressive social mores that had governed the pre-war generation. Women, in particular, enjoyed a new freedom, symbolized by the bobbed hair and short skirts of the flappers. The party ended with the Wall Street Crash of 1929, which led to the Great Depression.

> A new generation grown to find all Gods dead, all wars fought, all faiths in man shaken. – F. SCOTT FITZGERALD.

• **jazz ballet bottom** ▶ An informal medical term for an abscess between the cheeks of the buttocks. This condition is common among people performing jazz ballet exercises, many of which require the performers to sit on the floor for long periods.

• **jazz rock** ▶ Music that employs some of the instruments (such as woodwind and brass) and techniques (such as improvisation) associated with jazz while retaining the heavy beat and rhythm of rock. It enjoyed some commercial popularity in the late 1960s and early 1970s, when rock musicians were experimenting with a variety of musical influences. Well-known exponents of jazz rock at this time included the groups Soft Machine and Chicago. The later work of Miles Davis is also sometimes described as jazz rock.

• **JCB** ▶ A tradename for a multipurpose earth-moving machine, commonly used on building sites, which has a hydraulically operated shovel at the front and an excavator arm (backhoe) at the rear. The excavator is normally operated by a second set of controls situated behind the driver; most models have two sets of seats, one for driving and operating the shovel and another for the excavator. It is named after Joseph Cyril Bamford (1916–2001), its British manufacturer, whose company pioneered the development of hydraulically operated wheeled loaders and backhoe machines in the late 1940s and early 1950s.

• **Jebru, Mythical Isle of** ▶ An ironic phrase used by US soldiers in World War II. GIs would claim they were being sent there, *i.e.* 'destination unknown'.

• **jeep** ▶ A small all-purpose car first developed in America during World War II and known as a GP, *i.e.* General Purpose (vehicle), hence the name. Its four-wheel drive and high and low gearboxes gave it astonishing cross-country performance. The experimental models were also called Beeps, Peeps, and Blitz Buggies. However, it was as a jeep that it was known throughout the world from 1941 onwards. Another possible derivation of the name is from Eugene the Jeep, the family pet in the *Popeye* cartoon strips of the 1930s, which was said to be able to do 'almost everything' and made a 'jeep' noise (*see at*: spinach).

• **Jeeves** ▶ The intelligent and resourceful valet of the brainless Bertie Wooster in the comic tales and novels of P. G. Wodehouse (1881–1975; *see*: Plum). Reginald Jeeves first appeared with Wooster in a collection of stories called *The Man with Two Left Feet* (1917) and subsequently featured in a series of tales that began with *My Man Jeeves* (1919). The first Jeeves novel was *Thank You, Mr Jeeves* (1934). It is thought that he may have been based loosely upon Wodehouse's own butler, Eugene Robinson; his name was borrowed from a noted cricketer, Percy Jeeves, who was killed in action in 1916. The character was portrayed on the big screen by Arthur Treacher in two 1930s films and by Dennis Price and Stephen Fry in two television series (1960s and 1990s respectively).

• **Jeffrey** ▶ *See*: Archer.

• **Jehovah's Witnesses** ▶ A religious movement founded by Charles Taze Russell in Philadelphia in 1872, when it was known as the the International Bible Students. The present name was adopted in 1931. It does not ascribe divinity to Jesus Christ, regarding him instead as the perfect man and agent of God. Recognition of Jehovah and His word in the Bible as their sole authority led the Witnesses to refuse to salute national flags or to perform military service. They expect the end of the present world order to occur in the near future, and believe that a congregation of 144,000 true believers will then rule over the rest of mankind. The periodical *The Watch Tower* is their main publication.

• **jellies** ▶ Informal British term for the cheap clear plastic sandals, usually made in bright colours, that are worn by children and some adults, especially on the beach.

• **jelly** ▶ British underworld slang for the safe-breaker's explosive, gelignite. It originated in the 1950s and is clearly a shortening of gelignite, influenced by the jelly-like appearance of the explosive.

• **jelly beans** ▶ US drug users' slang from the 1950s for amphetamine tablets. The name reflects their use as a recreational treat rather like the children's sweets of the same name. *See also*: jolly beans.

• **jelly bomb** ▶ British soldiers' slang for a crude incendiary device containing a highly flammable substance, usually based on petrol, that ignites on impact or by means of a fuse (*see also*: Molotov cocktail). 'Jelly' here refers to the glutinous state of the liquid contained in the bomb rather than to the slang name for gelignite.

• **Jelly Roll ►** Nickname of Ferdinand Lemott Morton (1890–1941), flamboyant jazz pianist, composer, and self-styled 'Originator of Jazz Stomps and Blues'. He began his musical career playing the piano in the Storyville brothels of New Orleans in 1906; after spells as a pimp, boxing promoter, and gambling-hall manager he moved to Chicago in 1923. Here he achieved his greatest success recording the 'Red Hot Peppers' sessions for Victor records, which included many well-known songs, such as 'Sidewalk Blues'. In 1928 he moved to New York; however, the early 1930s saw the beginning of the big-band era, which eclipsed Morton's small-band New Orleans style. He spent the rest of his career in ill-health and obscurity.

• **Jemima Puddle-duck ►** The title of a children's book (1908) featuring a duck so named, written and illustrated by Beatrix Potter (1866–1943). The story of Jemima and her narrow escape from the designs of 'the gentleman with sandy whiskers', whom she fails to recognize as a fox, has become a perennial children's favourite and the focus of an enormous trade in children's toys and furnishings. *See also*: Peter Rabbit.

• **jerk ►** Slang for a stupid person, usually male. It is probably derived from the verb to **jerk off**, meaning to masturbate.

• **jerrican ►** A large (four-gallon) metal container for petrol or water designed to stand rough handling and stack easily; so-called because it was developed by the Germans for the Afrika Korps in World War II. Copied by the British in Libya, it became the standard container for fuel replenishment throughout the Allied armies.

• **Jerry ►** Since World War I a nickname for a German, or Germans collectively.

• **Jersey Lily ►** Emily Charlotte Le Breton (1852–1929), known as Lillie Langtry, was so nicknamed after her debut on the professional stage in 1881. A famous Edwardian beauty and one-time intimate of the Prince of Wales (later Edward VII), she was the wife of Edward Langtry and daughter of W. C. Le Breton, Dean of Jersey. She was the first British society hostess to become an actress. After Langtry's death she married Sir Hugo Gerald de Bathe in 1899.

• **Jerusalem Bible ►** An English translation (1966) of *La Bible de Jérusalem*, a French version of the Bible made by members of the Dominican École Biblique in Jerusalem and published in France (1948–54). Although the English text follows the French translation, the original Greek and Hebrew were also referred to. A revised version, the **New Jerusalem Bible**, appeared in 1985; this is the translation generally used in English-speaking Roman Catholic churches today.

• **jessie ►** British contemptuous term for a weak or effeminate man. Originally heard in Scotland and the N of England, it has become more widespread in the UK owing to its use by the Scottish comedian Billy Connolly. The derivation is uncertain.

• **Jesus boots** or **Jesus sandals ►** Informal name for a type of thonged sandal worn by beatniks, hippies, and others. Jesus sandals were deeply disparaged by the more sharply dressed fashion-conscious mods (*see*: mods and rockers), who wore elastic-sided Chelsea boots. The allusion is to the footwear often often worn by Christ in early paintings.

• **Jesus freak ►** Disparaging name for a born-again Christian, or a member of an evangelical Christian group. Since the late 1970s freak has been widely used as a suffix, indicating a fan or enthusiast.

• **jetfoil ►** *See*: hydrofoil.

• **jet lag ►** The physical and psychological symptoms experienced when the normal biological rhythms are disrupted by air travel involving crossing time zones. Jet lag occurs when the normal 24-hour cycle of fluctuations in hormone levels, body temperature, pulse rate, etc. (*see*: biorhythm) is disrupted by clock changes. This can affect waking and sleeping patterns, activity levels, and mood. Several days may be needed for the body to re-establish its normal rhythms; pulse rate, for example, taking up to eight days to normalize after an eight-hour shift in time zones. Crossing from west to east causes greater disruption of the biological rhythms than travel in the opposite direction. Apart from general fatigue, the effects are not apparent following a long flight from north to south as no time zones are crossed. The term was coined in the 1960s when airliners became jetpropelled. Airlines then made such tantalizing offers as 'Breakfast in New York, lunch in Paris'; to one such poster a wit added 'Luggage in Bombay'. Being jet-lagged without one's luggage is still regarded as the ultimate penalty of jet travel.

• **Jet Propulsion Laboratory ►** (JPL) The headquarters of the US space programme for unmanned spacecraft, situated near Pasadena, California. The

JPL is a subsidiary of NASA, run under contract by the California Institute of Technology; it consists of a large complex of buildings, including a Space Flight Operations Facility, which is the command and control centre, and a separate science laboratory for analysing the photographs and other data received from such craft as the Pioneer (1958–78) and Voyager space probes (1977–89).

• **jet set** ▶ Affluent socialites who can afford to fly around the world from one fashionable resort to another (*see also*: eurotrash). The phrase arose in the 1950s, when jet airliners were still a novelty and air travel of any kind was seen as a luxury. In 1980 the *Sunday Telegraph* (3 February) commented rather feebly:

> The Royal Family can hardly be said to belong to the Jet Set – all the aircraft in the Queen's Flight are prop-driven (and 15 years old).

• **jet ski** ▶ A small powered water vehicle with a flat keel shaped like a water ski. People taking part in the sport of jet skiing can stand, sit, or kneel on the ski. The sport became popular in the 1980s but is a hazard to swimmers.

• **jewel in the crown** ▶ A cliché meaning the most valuable or successful part of something. The phrase has been in use since the early 20th century, when it was mainly used in relation to the British colonies. Its popularity later received a boost from its use as the title of the 1984 TV series of Paul Scott's *Raj Quartet*, the first book of which also bears this title. The jewel referred to here, of course, was India and the crown that of Queen Victoria. The exact origins of the phrase are obscure, although a painting called 'The Jewel in Her Crown', depicting the Queen receiving a large jewel (representing India) from an Indian prince, is mentioned in Scott's novel.

• **Jewel of the Ghetto** ▶ The nickname of Ruby Goldstein, a US boxer of the early 1900s, who later became America's premier boxing referee, officiating in seven world heavyweight title fights. The 'Ghetto' of the nickname refers to his origins in Manhattan's Lower East Side.

• **Jewish** ▶
 **You don't have to be Jewish...** A US advertising slogan used in 1967 for rye bread. The rest of the slogan is '...to love Levy's real Jewish rye.' The accompanying posters showed such people as Eskimos and Chinese enjoying the bread, to emphasize the point. *You don't have to be Jewish...*was earlier used as the title of a Broadway show of Jewish humour. As with other catchphrases that use an ellipsis, there is inevitably a temptation to add a facetious ending. More generally, the form of

phrase has been imitated or parodied in numerous other contexts, most notably perhaps in a publicity slogan used by the Samaritans in the UK, 'You don't have to be suicidal to call the Samaritans'.

• **Jewish Agency** ▶ An organization created in 1929 by Chaim Weizmann to encourage Jewish settlement in Israel. Under Weizmann's conciliatory leadership during the 1930s, the agency played a variety of roles: raising funds for the Jewish National Home in Palestine, overseeing Jewish immigration, helping to resolve the resulting conflicts with Palestinian Arabs, establishing the Youth Aliyah programme to help resettle orphaned Jewish children fleeing from the Nazis, and representing Jewish interests at the League of Nations. Under the subsequent leadership (1935–48) of David Ben Gurion, the agency gradually abandoned its ancillary roles and became an uncompromising instrument of militant Zionism. In 1951 it became officially identified with the World Zionist Organization.

• **Jewish American Princess** ▶ (JAP) A mainly US expression for a rich young Jewish girl, especially one who is spoilt by her parents. Originally used affectionately by Jews themselves, it later became a derogatory term with both racist and sexist overtones. The acronym is pronounced in the same way as the slang name for a Japanese.

> Nor does she feel Jewish: 'My mission is to wipe out all Jewish American Princesses', she grins.
> – *Daily Telegraph*, 19 January 1991, referring to US comedienne Ruby Wax.

• **Jewish penicillin** ▶ Chicken soup as traditionally prepared by Jews, or descendants of Jews, from N Europe (Ashkenazim). It is regarded by Jewish mothers and many of their children as a panacea for all ailments, physical and psychological. There is, of course, no medical reason why it should be, except that it tastes good enough to cheer up the saddest patient. Mediterranean Jews (Sephardim) have various recipes for soups made with chicken but set no store by their restorative properties. Arnold Wesker's *Chicken Soup with Barley* (1958) dealt with Jewish life in London's East End, while *Chicken Soup for the Soul* was the title of a popular self-help book in the 1990s.

• **Jew Süss** ▶ Josef Süss Oppenheimer, the central character in the bestselling novel of this title by the German author Leon Feuchtwanger (1884–1958). The story, a satire about a Jew who rises from the ghetto to a position of power in 17th-century Württemberg only to discover that he is a gentile, has been filmed several times. A notorious German film *Jud Süss* (1940), directed by Veit Harlan, was used as antisemitic propaganda by the Nazis to prepare the Germans for acceptance of the Final Solution. Goebbels himself revised the script, and the actor Ferdinand Marian, who played the title role, is said to have later committed suicide as a result of his feelings of guilt for having taken part.

• **JFK** ► *See*: Idlewild.

• **jiffed** ► British army slang from the Gulf War of 1991, describing the plight of someone who has been given an unpopular task by his officers. The derivation is unclear. *See also*: spammed.

• **Jiffy Bag** ► A tradename for a padded envelope for sending fragile objects by post, available in a variety of different sizes. It was so called because it could be used quickly and easily – 'in a jiffy'.

• **jihad** ► A struggle undertaken by Muslims to achieve a certain goal, whether religious, social, or political. For pious Muslims the 'greater *jihad*' denotes the struggle of the individual to overcome personal desires and temptations. Other 'lesser' forms of *jihad* concern the relationship of Muslims to the outside world. This may take the form of charitable acts, campaigning for social justice, or, if all other means prove fruitless, armed struggle against non-believers to achieve a just and Islamic society. The term is frequently misunderstood by Western commentators to mean 'holy war', but a *jihad* may be peaceful or armed. This misunderstanding is perhaps reinforced by the name of the militant group Islamic Jihad, which is pledged to fight for an Islamic state occupying the whole of former Palestine. A person who fights a *jihad* is called a *mujahid* (*see* MUJAHEDDIN).

• **Jilleroo** ► Nickname given to Australian landgirls in World War II. It was formed by association with Jackaroo, a name used in Australia in the 19th century to denote a young Englishman newly arrived to learn farming; from tchareroo, a Queensland name for the shrike, noted for its garrulity. Later the name was applied simply to station hands.

• **Jim** ►
**I'm worried about Jim** A catchphrase used to sum up the essence of the long-running BBC radio saga *Mrs Dale's Diary* (1948–69). Jim was Mrs Dale's doctor husband, about whom she seemed to be continually anxious.

• **Jiminy Peanuts** ► *See*: President Peanuts.

• **jimmy** ► 1. British slang for an act of urination. It is a shortened version of the rhyming slang jimmy riddle, piddle. 2. Drug abusers' slang for an injection of heroin.

• **jinkai senjitsu** ► (Japanese) In business and marketing, the tactic of flooding an area with personnel or urging large numbers of people into action. The practice first came to Western notice in the early 1970s; the Japanese interest in opening up markets in North America resulted in waves of researchers and trade delegates being sent to investigate the potential of the market.

• **jitterbug** ► An energetic and acrobatic dance that originated in America in the 1930s and was spread worldwide by US troops during World War II. Performed to fast music with a syncopated rhythm, it incorporated elements from several other dances, notably the lindy hop.

• **jive** ► 1. A lively style of dance music of the 1940s, more or less synonymous with swing. **Jiving** is dancing to this music or to 1950s rock 'n' roll. The jitterbug is a form of jive. 2. A slang form of American English used by Black jazz musicians in Harlem in the 1930s. Also known as **jive talk**, it was imitated by White youths in the 1950s and became the basis for beatnik, and later hippie, slang. 3. Empty or misleading talk; by extension anything worthless or unacceptable. This sense predates senses 1 and 2 above.

• **Jix** ► The nickname of Sir William Joynson-Hicks, first Viscount Brentford (1865–1932), who was home secretary (1924–29) in Baldwin's second government. A noted puritan, he was prominent in defeating the adoption of the *Revised Prayer Book* of 1928.

> We mean to tread the Primrose Path,
> In spite of Mr. Joynson-Hicks.
> We're People of the Aftermath
> We're girls of 1926.
> – JACQUES REVAL: 'Mother's advice on Father's fears (The Woman of 1926)'.

• **job centre** ► A UK government employment agency. Formerly called **employment exchanges** and before that **labour exchanges**, they used to be involved also in registering out-of-work people for the unemployment benefit (dole). Now, however, job centres seek to find jobs for applicants, assist employers in finding suitable employees, provide training for trades in which a shortage of skilled workers exists, and offer occupational advice on retraining.

• **jobs for the boys** ► A catchphrase reflecting nepotism or cronyism, especially in government; it dates back to the 1930s or earlier. An incoming political party tends to reward its supporters with the best jobs in its administration, thus giving commentators an opportunity to make use of this phrase.

• **jobsharing** ► A system in which one full-time job is shared by two or more part-time employees.

• **jobsworth** ▶ A petty (often uniformed) official, such as a car-park attendant or commissionaire, who unreasonably refuses to cooperate beyond the limits of his or her responsibilities by invoking the phrase 'It's more than my job's worth to...'. The term was first used in the British rock-music press during the 1970s, referring to bouncers in clubs who refused journalists access to rock musicians. It has now passed into more general usage.

> And passengers will continue to suffer public-sector 'Jobsworth' attitudes to customer service, while bearing the full costs of high-risk private finance. – ANATOLE KALETSKY, on the proposed semi-privatization of London Transport, *The Times*, 30 November 2000.

• **jock** ▶ US, Canadian, and Australian slang for a young male who is obsessed with playing and watching sports, especially one who is aggressively anti-intellectual and right-wing.

> The majority of us, who are not jocks, should come out and show our disgust, our dread, our grief. – GERMAINE GREER, expressing her views on the Gulf War in the *Independent*, 2 February 1991.

• **Jodrell Bank** ▶ Site of the Nuffield Radio Astronomy Laboratories in Cheshire, which is owned by Manchester University. It contains a large steerable radio telescope, 75 mm (250 ft) in diameter, the first to be in operation. It was designed by Sir Bernard Lovell (1913–   ) and built in 1957.

• **Joe** ▶ US slang for the average man in the street, also used as a form of address for someone whose name is unknown. *See also*: GI; Joe Bloggs; Joe Public.

• **Joe Bananas** ▶ A corruption of Joseph Bonano, one-time boss of the Castellamarese crime family in New York, one of the big five of the city's Mafia gangs (the others being Gambino, Genovese, Colombo, and Lucchese). Arriving in New York from the Sicilian town of Castellamare del Golfo in 1925, he soon became the youngest **don** in America in the aftermath of the so-called Castellamarese War. He retired in 1968 after a period of bloody feuding, known as the Bonano War, with rivals in the Mafia commission (the organized crime's regulatory body). He was jailed in the mid-1980s for refusing to answer questions before a Grand Jury about Mafia operations alluded to in his autobiography *A Man of Honour* (1983). Released in November 1986 for health reasons, he was the last survivor of the five original 1930s New York bosses.

• **Joe Bloggs** or **Fred Bloggs** ▶ An average man assumed to be a typical member of the population; *i.e.* 'the man in the street' or 'the man on the Clapham omnibus'. The name is regarded as comic and perhaps slightly disparaging. Joe Bloggs has equivalents in North America and Australia, both known as **Joe Blow**.

• **Joe Lampton** ▶ *See*: Lampton, Joe.

• **Joe Palooka** ▶ A simple-minded boxer, the popular hero of a US comic strip created by Ham Fisher in 1928. The character first appeared on film in *Palooka* (1934), with Stuart Erwin playing the boxer and Jimmie Durante his trainer, Knobby Walsh. A decade later Monogram produced a series of short films starring Joe Kirkwood.

• **Joe Public** ▶ The general public personified. The use of Joe as a name for a hypothetical ordinary person originated in America and spread across the Atlantic (as in Joe Bloggs) after World War II. It is sometimes, but not always, derogatory. *See also*: John Q. Citizen.

• **jogger's nipple** ▶ A painful inflammation of the nipple caused by chafing on clothing. The condition affects both men and women. Formerly confined to professional marathon runners, it became a common problem among fun runners and joggers in the 1980s and 1990s.

• **jogging** ▶ Running at a slow steady pace, typically over a moderate distance, as a recreation or a means of improving physical condition. Jogging first became popular in America in the late 1960s, particularly among those with a sedentary lifestyle. Its popularity increased and spread to other countries with growing public awareness of the importance of physical health, especially in relation to the prevention of heart disease. There can be little doubt that the pursuit of physical fitness by jogging has done a great deal to decrease the likelihood of early heart attacks among affluent professionals with busy stressful lives. Some older enthusiasts, however, may well have run themselves into an early grave. It has also been said that no one who lives on into his nineties has ever, at any time in his life, done anything as stupid as jogging.

• **John Birch Society** ▶ An ultraconservative US secret society founded on 9 December 1958 by Robert H. W. Welch Jr (1899–1985), a retired Boston sweet manufacturer, to combat communism and other potential threats to the American way of life. It was named in honour of John Birch, a Baptist missionary and US Army intelligence officer killed by Chinese communists in August 1945. Welch regarded John Birch as the first US victim of the Cold War against international communism.

• **John Q. Citizen** or **John Q. Public** ▶ A US personification of the average man. The 'Q' reflects the American habit of including the initial of the middle name in the formal name by which a person wishes to be known. The female equivalent is **Jane Q. Citizen**.

• **joiner** ► A type of photographic collage invented in 1982 by the British artist David Hockney (1937– ), who also coined the name. A scene is photographed repeatedly from a number of different angles and over a period of time: the prints are then 'joined' together to form a composite design. This is intended to introduce a dimension of time, change, and movement that is absent from conventional photography.

• **joint** ► **1.** A cannabis cigarette. This became the usual term in the 1960s, replacing reefer, which had been current in the 1950s. A joint can either be an American-style unadulterated marijuana cigarette, usually rolled in one cigarette paper, or the more elaborate three-paper English-style cigarette, containing a mixture of marijuana and tobacco. The latter is also called a **spliff**. Among friends, both types of joint are smoked communally, being passed from one to the other. **2.** US slang for a penis, probably from the idea of a joint of meat. To **unlimber the joint** is to urinate.

• **joint** ►
   **the joint is jumping** A US phrase of the 1930s used to describe a party or club in which people were dancing to or enjoying exuberant fast-tempo jazz. The phrase was immortalized by Fats Waller in his 1937 recording 'The Joint Is Jumpin'', which he wrote in conjunction with Andy Razaf and J. C. Johnson. His exhilarating piano playing provides a fitting background to the amusing words describing the riotous atmosphere typical of Harlem rent parties of the 1920s and 1930s:

> Check your weapons at the door
> Be sure to pay your quarter
> Drag your body on the floor
> Grab anybody's daughter
> The roof is rockin'
> The neighbors are knockin'
> We're all bums when the wagon comes
> I'll say the joint is jumpin'.

• **Join the army and see the world** ► An army recruiting slogan from the 1940s, since then used ironically by soldiers to describe any humdrum posting, especially one near to home. A sharper variant, especially in anticipation of military action, is 'Join the army and see the next world', while the pacifists of the 1960s preferred 'Join the army and see the world, meet interesting people – and kill them'.

• **jolly** ► **1.** British middle-class drug-users' slang from the 1970s and 1980s for a joint. It reflects the similarity in the sound of the two words as well as the effects of the drug. 'Jolly' has always been a popular word among a certain type of hearty middle-class person. **2.** Acronym for jet-setting oldster with lots of loot: a wealthy senior citizen. One of the more contrived products of the journalistic craze for acronyms based on lifestyles, it followed the success of the term yuppie in the 1980s.

• **jolly beans** ► British drug users' slang for amphetamine pills. This is a British variant of the US jelly beans, reflecting the effect of taking them as well as their resemblance to sweets.

• **jolly hockey sticks!** ► A catchphrase associated with English girls' public schools. It is used to epitomize the regime of mandatory games, particularly hockey, which these institutions used to enforce in imitation of the boys' public schools – and also, mockingly, to deride the mistresses whose job it was to organize these activities.

The jolly-hockey-sticks mistress was caricatured inexhaustibly by Joyce Grenfell (1910–74) in such films as *The Happiest Days of Your Life* (1949), made by Frank Launder. One critic wrote of this film, in which a girls' school was mistakenly billeted on a boys' school:

> Launder couldn't have knocked another laugh out of the situation if he'd used a hockey stick.
> – *Sunday Express.*

See also: Effort, St Swithins!; Hockey Stick; St Trinian's.

• **Jolly Jack** ► The nickname of J. B. Priestley (1894–1984), British writer, literary critic, and wartime broadcaster. Although his work includes comedy (the novel *Laburnum Grove*; 1933 and the play *When We Are Married*; 1938), the description 'jolly' is generally considered to be an ironic reference to his well-known tendency for expressing dissatisfaction.

• **Jones, Bridget** ► A character created by the British author Helen Fielding, initially in a regular column for *The Independent* newspaper (from 1995) and subsequently in two best-selling novels, *Bridget Jones's Diary* (1996) and *Bridget Jones: The Edge of Reason* (1999). In 2001 the screen version of *Bridget Jones's Diary*, with Renee Zellweger in the title role, became one of the UK's most successful films. The original column continues, now in *The Daily Telegraph*.

Both the column and the novels take the form of a diary in which Bridget relates her romantic misadventures and doomed attempts at self-improvement, while listing neurotically her daily intake of calories, alcohol units, and Silk Cut cigarettes. A thirty-something unmarried professional whose ever-hopeful search for fulfilment leads to constant disappointment, Jones was quickly enshrined as the patron saint of modern single women and became the subject of endless pop-sociological analyses in the media. Although Bridget was scorned by some feminists, who found her hopelessly shallow and man-dependent, many other women found the character uncomfortably close to the bone. The success of Fielding's novels inspired numerous imitative books about young urban women, a genre for which the term **chick lit** or **chick fic** has been coined.

• **Jones Family** ► The supposedly typical US family who featured in a series of 20th Century-Fox B-movies, beginning with *Every Saturday Night* (1936) and continuing with 15 others. The series attempted, unsuccessfully, to emulate the more sentimental Hardy family films.

• **Jonestown massacre** ► The enforced mass suicide in Guyana in 1978 of followers of Jim Jones (1933–78), charismatic leader of the People's Temple Sect. The sect was founded by Jones in San Francisco but in 1977 moved to an agricultural commune in Guyana, christened Jonestown. On 14 November 1978, prompted by persistent allegations of mistreatment of sect members, the commune was visited by a US congressman, Leo Ryan, together with newsmen and a group of concerned relatives. On Jones's orders Ryan was shot, together with four other members of his party. On 18 November Jones ordered the mass suicide of all members of the sect. According to official figures, 914 people died, including 240 children, by voluntarily drinking soda pop laced with cyanide.

• **jordim** ► *See*: yordim.

• **Josephson effects** ► Two effects in physics concerning the behaviour of superconductors (*see*: superconductivity). The British physicist Brian Josephson (1940– ) showed theoretically in 1962 that if two superconductors were separated by a thin insulating layer a current can flow across the junction in the absence of an applied voltage. Moreover, if a small voltage is applied across the junction, an alternating current flows with a frequency inversely proportional to the applied voltage. The effects were later verified by experiment and the combination of superconductors and insulator is known as a **Josephson junction**. Two Josephson junctions can be connected together to form a **SQUID** (superconducting quantum interference device), which is used for measuring weak magnetic fields to a high degree of accuracy. The junctions also have applications as extremely fast switching devices in computers.

• **journey** ►
**Is your journey really necessary?** A British government slogan from World War II, aimed at discouraging civilian travel to save fuel. The campaign was promoted by posters. Whether or not these posters were effective is hard to say. More of a disincentive was that public transport was infrequent and overcrowded and petrol was severely rationed.

• **joy-firing** ► The practice of discharging live ammunition into the air as a welcome or to express delight at good news. This wasteful (and dangerous) custom seems to be particularly prevalent among Arab soldiery. The term seems to have been coined by T. E. Lawrence (*see*: Lawrence of Arabia) and has been more recently revived by Western reporters. Distressed and angry Arabs have also been known to discharge their guns into the air.

• **joy pop** ► US drug users' slang meaning to inject a narcotic occasionally and for pleasure rather than habitually as an addict.

• **J.R.** ►
**Who shot J. R.?** A promotional slogan used by the makers of the popular US soap opera Dallas in the gap between the end of the first series and the beginning of the second. In a carefully planned cliffhanger, the villain of the story, oil magnate J. R. Ewing (Larry Hagman), was shot in the final episode of the first series, with no indication of his fate or his assailant. The slogan stoked up the already high level of interest in the show on both sides of the Atlantic and when the second series began the viewing ratings were gratifyingly high. The shot – fired it transpired by an abandoned lover – was not fatal and J. R. was spared to perpetrate yet more dirty deeds. *See*: cliffhanger.

• **jubbies** ► British teenage slang for female breasts, probably from the older term 'bubbies'.

• **jubbly** ► British slang for money, often used in the phrase **lovely jubbly**. Jubbly was originally the tradename for an orange drink, popular in the 1950s and 1960s, which was advertised using the slogan 'lovely jubbly'. The phrase was revived in the 1980s with the popularity of the BBC comedy series *Only Fools and Horses*, in which it is a favourite phrase of Del Boy (David Jason).

• **Judges' Rules** ► Rules concerning the questioning of suspects by the police and the taking of statements. First formulated in 1912 and revised in 1918, they were re-formulated in 1964 and approved by a meeting of all judges of the Queen's Bench. They were superseded by the Police and Criminal Evidence Act (1984).

• **Juggernaut ▶** Originally a Hindu god, 'Lord of the World', having his temple at Puri in Orissa. Juggernaut (more properly Jagganatha) is mainly known in the West for the car festival, in which the god's image is dragged in his car (35 feet square and 45 feet high) over the sand to another temple; the car has 16 wheels, each seven feet in diameter. The belief that fanatical devotees used to cast themselves under the wheels of the car to be crushed to death is largely without foundation. However, it has led to the metaphorical use of the word juggernaut to mean any movement, institution, etc., that is regarded as unstoppable and crushing all obstacles, *i.e.* 'the juggernaut of European integration'. More literally the term 'juggernaut' is also applied to any wheeled 'monster' – most notably to the giant articulated lorries increasingly prevalent on British roads since the 1970s.

• **jukebox ▶ 1.** A machine that automatically plays a selected recording when coins are inserted. Such machines reached new levels of sophistication in the 1950s and were later much-valued by collectors. **2.** A computer storage device containing a number of CD-ROMs, which the user can select and load as required. The storage capacity is vast, it being estimated that two jukeboxes could easily store the names and addresses of everyone in the world.

• **July Plot ▶** *See*: Stauffenberg Plot.

• **jumbo ▶** (Swahili *jumbe*, chief) **1.** Slang for a large person or thing. It derives from the popular name for an elephant, a tradition deriving from the name given to a famous elephant exhibited by the circus owner P. T. Barnum. *Dumbo* was a 1941 Walt Disney film about a baby elephant who could fly using his large ears as wings. **2.** Archaic British slang for the bottom, the buttocks. **3.** US drug abusers' slang for the drug crack. **4.** British rhyming slang for a drunk, from 'jumbo's trunk'.

• **Jumbo jet ▶** The nickname of the Boeing 747 airliner, the world's first wide-bodied commercial transport aircraft, introduced in 1970 by Pan American Airways on their New York–London route. The latest models are 71 m (233 ft) long, have a wing span of 60 m (196 ft), and can carry over 400 passengers.

• **jump seat ▶** A folding seat in some aircraft used for an extra crew member. Also a folding seat in a motor vehicle, especially a London taxi.

• **jump start ▶ 1.** A method of starting a car by pushing it or rolling it downhill and then engaging the gears while it is moving in order to turn the engine. **2.** A method of starting a car using **jump leads** to connect the car's own battery to another battery, especially one in another vehicle.

• **jump suit ▶** An all-in-one garment consisting of trousers and a top, often with a zippered front fastening. Boy's one-piece suits date back to the early 19th century, when they were used as a transitional garment between the infant's dress and the trousered suit. However, the name 'jump suit' was not used until World War II, when it was applied to the one-piece garments worn by parachutists.

• **jump the gun ▶** To act prematurely. The phrase is derived from athletics, in which contestants who cross the starting line before the pistol has been fired by the starter are said to have jumped the gun.

• **jungle ▶** *See*: drum 'n' bass.

• **Jungle Jim ▶** US comic-strip hero created by Alex Raymond in the 1930s. The character also appeared in a film serial, *Jungle Jim* (1937), and was played by Johnny Weissmuller in a series of low-budget films (1948–55). He has been described as 'Tarzan with clothes'.

• **jungle juice ▶** Slang for potent, but poor-quality, alcohol. Originally a slang name for African rum, the expression was used by the armed forces during World War II for any home-made alcoholic brew.

• **junk bond ▶** A high-yielding bond that offers low security. Such bonds were popular in Wall Street from the late 1970s; they are often specifically bonds issued to raise the capital required to finance the take-over of a firm.

• **Junkers bombers ▶** A series of German military aircraft, including heavy bombers and the JU-87 Stuka divebomber, produced at the Dessau factory established by Professor Hugo Junkers (1859–1935) in 1920. Junkers JU-52 bomber-transport aircraft formed part of the Condor Legion, which aided General Franco during the Spanish Civil War (1936–39); the JU-87 divebomber and JU-88 heavy bomber were leading Luftwaffe aircraft in World War II.

• **junk food ▶** Food such as hamburgers, hot dogs, chips, potato crisps, popcorn, and fizzy drinks, which is high in calories and food additives (such as artificial flavourings and colourings) but of little nutritional value. Junk food is often eaten in addition or in preference to regular meals, especially by children. *See also*: fast food; health food; zombie food.

• **junkie** or **junky ▶** Slang for a drug addict, especially one who injects heroin or morphine. The word **junk** comes from the 15th-century Middle

English *jonke*, meaning useless old rope, hemp; it therefore came to mean drugs in general. In 19th-century America the word was used in underworld circles specifically for opium. It was first used of heroin in the early 1900s and has remained in wide use for any addictive narcotic. 'Junk' and 'junkie' also carry overtones of the dereliction and useless-ness that befall drug addicts.

• **junk mail** ▶ Unsolicited material sent through the post for advertising purposes, so called because most of it ends up in the dustbin. The volume of this type of advertising has increased steadily since the 1970s, when organizations gained access to computerized mailing lists giving the names and addresses of individuals and companies. This enabled direct-mail selling by organized **mailshots** to develop. Further technological developments in the 1980s led to the **fax shot** and **junk fax**; **cold faxing** is the practice of sending unsolicited faxes (by analogy with cold-calling). Junk faxes are even more intrusive items than junk mail; they use the recipient's toner (ink) and paper and may delay transmission of legitimate faxes. The modern phenomenon of junk e-mail threatens to become a greater menace still (*see*: spam).

• **Juno** ▶ Allied codename given to a beach NW of Caen, which was one of the main landing sites for British and Canadian forces on D-Day. *See also*: Gold; Omaha; Sword; Utah.

• **Juno space mission** ▶ An Anglo-Russian space mission that put the first Briton into space in May 1991. 13,000 applicants were considered before the confectionery technologist Helen Sharman (1964–  ) was selected for the pioneering role.

• **Jupiter-C** ▶ A four-stage rocket, which put the first US satellite, Explorer 1, into orbit on 31 January 1958. The Jupiter-C was a version of the Red-stone, a rocket developed by the captured German rocket scientist, Dr Wernher von Braun, at the Army Ballistic Missile Agency. It was based on his V2 rocket, which was used by the Germans against London during World War II.

• **just in time** ▶ (JIT) A manufacturing technique that reduces waste, queues, and bottlenecks. It depends on skilled workers taking personal responsibility for seeing that raw materials, components, etc., are only delivered and paid for when they are needed. JIT depends heavily on computer-aided manufacturing techniques.

• **Just So Stories** ▶ A book (1902) for children by Rudyard Kipling (1865–1936), comprising 10 imaginative animal fables, such as 'How the Leopard got his Spots', two whimsical stories about the origins of the alphabet and written letters, and various poems, with illustrations by Kipling himself. It remains a much-loved children's classic.

• **Jutland, Battle of** ▶ A World War I naval battle between the British and German fleets off the west coast of Jutland on 31 May 1916 – the last encounter between massed naval forces. The British Grand Fleet, commanded by Sir John R. Jellicoe, and a battle cruiser squadron under Earl Beatty lost a total of three battle cruisers, three cruisers, and eight destroyers, suffering 6784 casualties; the German High Seas Fleet, under Vice Admiral Reinhard Scheer, lost one old battleship, one battle cruiser, four light cruisers, five destroyers, and 3039 men. Although the outcome was indecisive and both sides claimed victory, the German fleet never re-emerged to engage the Grand Fleet during the remainder of the war.

> There's something wrong with our bloody ships today. – EARL BEATTY to his flag captain during the battle.

# K

• **K►** **1.** A colloquial term for one thousand, derived from the prefix 'kilo-'. In business and commercial contexts it means specifically £1000 (thus 30K would be £30,000). In computing it refers to a unit of 1024 bytes but is also used loosely to refer to a unit of 1000 bytes. **2.** Nickname of the British art historian Sir Kenneth Clark (1903–83). He was director of the National Gallery from 1935 to 1945 and chaired the Arts Council from 1953 to 1960; however, he was best known to the British public for his television lecture series *Civilisation*, broadcast in 1969, in which he examined human achievements in the arts. In 1969 he was also made a life peer, taking the title Lord Clark of Saltwood. The satirical magazine *Private Eye* dubbed him 'Lord Clark of Civilisation'. He was the father of the controversial Conservative MP Alan Clark (1923–99), who became minister of defence (1989–92); his *Diaries* (1993, 2000) specialized in both political and sexual indiscretion.

• **Kafkaesque ►** Resembling the sinister and nightmarish world portrayed in the novels of Franz Kafka (1883–1924), the Czech-born German writer, especially *The Trial* (1925) and *The Castle* (1926). The turmoil in Kafka's own life is reflected in the strange fantasy world of his fiction, in which people are isolated in an environment that is both incomprehensible and threatening. Most of his books were published after his death, and against his specific instructions, by his friend Max Brod.

> Someone must have slandered Joseph K., because one morning, without his having done anything wrong, he was arrested. – FRANK KAFKA: *The Trial*.

• **Kaiser Bill ►** Kaiser Wilhelm II (1859–1941), who ruled as emperor of Germany and king of Prussia from 1888 to 1918. The grandson of Queen Victoria, he claimed to rule by divine right but was often ineffectual and vacillating in his policies. Even before World War I the Kaiser was depicted in British newspapers (and especially by cartoonists) as a rather ludicrous and pompous militaristic figure. He abdicated after Germany's defeat in World War I, spending the rest of his life in retirement in Holland. *See*: hang the Kaiser!.

• **Kalashnikov ►** A Soviet automatic or semi-automatic assault rifle capable of firing 600 rounds per minute. Manufactured in China, North Korea, and many eastern European countries as well as in the former Soviet Union, it is used by the armies of the former communist bloc and by nationalist and guerrilla groups throughout the world. It was named after its inventor, Mikhail Timofeyevich Kalashnikov (1919–    ); it is also known as the **AK-47** (Russian *Automat Kalashnikov*, automatic Kalashnikov, 1947).

• **kalied ►** (pronounced kay-lide) Drunk; the term is used extensively in the north of England and has gained some currency elsewhere through its use in the TV soap *Coronation Street*. The origin is uncertain. One suggestion is that it comes from an old northern prefix 'kay' (or 'key') meaning left-handed; this has sometimes been used in the sense 'awry'. Another is that it comes from 'kali' (rhymes with 'pie'), which is a name for the saltwort (from the Arabic *alkali*). In the early days of the chemical industry, saltwort and similar plants were calcined to produce a whitish powder rich in potash, also known as 'kali'. In parts of the north of England, children still use the word for lemon-flavoured sugar crystals – known in the rest of the country as 'sherbet'. The word sherbet is sometimes used jokingly to mean an alcoholic drink.

• **kalimba ►** A hand-held African musical instrument consisting of a hollow wooden box with a series of metal strips inserted along its length. These strips vibrate when plucked with the thumbs or fingers. The kalimba is a modern instrument derived from the mbira or the zanza, both tribal instruments. It is tuned to play Western music and first attracted attention in the West in about 1952. The word *kalimba* is of Bantu origin.

• **kamerad ►** (German, comrade) A word used by the Germans in World War I as an appeal for quarter. It is now used in English with the meaning 'I surrender'.

• **kamikaze ►** A Japanese word meaning 'divine wind', in reference to the providential typhoon that once baulked a Mongol invasion. In World War II it was applied to the suicide aircraft attacks organized under Vice-Admiral Onishi in the Philippines between October 1944 and January 1945 (first at the Battle of Leyte Gulf). Some 5000 young pilots gave their lives when their bomb-loaded fighters crashed into their targets. In 1945 21 US ships were sunk in this way at Okinawa as the result of 3000 such sorties. The word has since been applied to any military or terrorist attack in which the assailant risks almost certain death. It also found wider usage when the British police described drivers who speed on icy or foggy motorways as **kamikaze drivers**.

• **kamikaze pricing** ▶ Financial jargon for the practice of offering loans at exceptionally low interest rates to capture a larger share of the corporate banking market.

• **Kane, Citizen** ▶ The eponymous central character in a 1941 film regarded by many critics as the greatest ever made; it was produced and directed by Orson Welles (1915–85) at the age of 26. Welles also starred as Charles Foster Kane, an enigmatic tycoon clearly based on the newspaper proprietor William Randolph Hearst. Scripted by Welles and Herman J. Mankiewicz, the film is filled with visual and audio invention, demonstrating throughout its 119 minutes the full potential of the cinematic medium. At the time, however, critics were not unanimous. The two leading British critics of the 1940s had sharply differing views:

> Probably the most exciting film that has come out of Hollywood for twenty-five years. I am not sure it isn't the most exciting film that has ever come out of anywhere. – C. A. LEJEUNE in *The Observer*.

> A quite good film which tries to run the psychological essay in harness with the detective thriller, and doesn't quite succeed. – JAMES AGATE in *The Sunday Times*.

• **kanga** ▶ Slang for a pneumatic drill. A shortened form of 'kangaroo', the word compares the bouncing movement of the machine to that of the animal. It is sometimes pronounced 'can-go', to suggest that this very powerful machine has a life of its own. Originally an Australian usage, it has also been heard in the UK.

• **kangaroo hop** ▶ The jerky movement of a car when being driven by an inexperienced driver who has not learnt how to manipulate the clutch correctly.

• **kangaroo valley** ▶ Nickname for the Earls Court district of W London because many young Australians settled here in flats and bedsits when they came to work in England in the 1960s. The area still has a large Australian community and the

name persists. Used by both the Australians and the locals, the nickname achieved wider fame after it was featured in the cartoon *The Adventures of Barry Mckenzie* by Barry Humphries and Nicholas Garland, which appeared in the satirical magazine *Private Eye* in the 1970s.

• **KANU** ▶ Kenya African National Union. Founded in 1960 as a pan-tribal national party, KANU was the successor to the Kenya African Union (KAU), established by Jomo Kenyatta (1891–1978) in 1944, which itself replaced the Kikuyu Central Association, banned by the British in 1940. Jomo Kenyatta (who had been interned by the British in April 1953) became the president of the new national party after his release in August 1961. KANU then went on to win the pre-independence elections of May 1963; Kenyatta was elected prime minister and formed a provisional government. After independence in December 1963, KANU continued to dominate the Kenyan government and legislature, being the only permitted party until 1992.

• **KAP** ▶ (Chinese *Cheng pao k'o*, Ministry for Public Security). A branch of the Chinese secret services responsible for counterespionage and the control and monitoring of overseas Chinese.

• **Kaplan, Hyman** ▶ A fictional east European immigrant to America who has difficulties with spoken English; a character created by the US humorist Leo Rosten (pen name Leonard Q. Ross) after his own experiences teaching English to immigrants. Kaplan first appeared in a series of sketches in the *New Yorker* magazine, which were then published in book form as *The Education of Hyman Kaplan* (1937). This was followed by two sequels, *The Return of Hyman Kaplan* (1938) and *O Kaplan, My Kaplan* (1979).

• **Kaposi's sarcoma** ▶ A previously rare form of malignant skin cancer, found mostly in Africans and elderly men in the S Mediterranean region, which is now common in Aids sufferers. It is named after Moritz Kohn Kaposi (1837–1902), an Austrian dermatologist, who first described the purple skin lesions that characterize the disease.

• **Kapp Putsch** ▶ An armed rising against the German government in March 1920 by the Erhardt Freikorps Brigade. The Brigade marched into Berlin in protest at the government's acceptance of the Versailles Treaty, which required the Freikorps' dissolution. The Weimar Republic was declared overthrown and a right-wing journalist, Wolfgang Kapp (1888–1922), proclaimed chancellor. However, a general strike by Berlin workers exposed the lack of public sympathy with the putsch and the regular army disassociated itself from the Freikorps. The putsch collapsed after five days and Kapp fled to Sweden.

• **kaput** ► A term derived from the German *kaputt* (done for), now commonly used in English to describe something that is ruined or broken.

• **karaoke** ► (Japanese, empty orchestra) A pastime that originated in Japan and spread to other countries, including the UK, in the late 1980s. It involves singing well-known popular songs solo to the accompaniment of a specially prepared backing audio tape. Karaoke usually takes place in bars and nightclubs with the customers taking it in turns to perform. In Japan it became a regular feature of the semi-compulsory social evenings at which male employees curry favour with their employers. The need for an employee to attend such functions perhaps seven nights a week has led to government concern in recent years at the threat thus posed to family life and the already declining national birth rate, so much so that the state named certain days to be set aside for 'family activities'.

• **Karlmarxhof** ► A block of workers' flats in Vienna designed by the chief architect of the city, Karl Ehn (1884–1957), in 1927–30. The building was commissioned by the socialist district council as part of a massive programme of public housing construction. The block later became famous as a socialist fortress during the bloody Civil War of 1934, when the socialists revolted against the administration of the Austrian chancellor Dolfuss.

• **karma** ► (Sanskrit, act) In Hinduism and Buddhism, the sum of an individual's actions, which determines the quality of his or her future life, especially after rebirth. Both the concept and the term became popular in the hippie culture of the late 1960s (*see*: instant karma). In common speech, karma is now often used somewhat inaccurately to mean destiny or fate.

• **Kashmir dispute** ► The struggle between India and Pakistan for possession of the state of Kashmir, which erupted into armed conflict in October 1947 and lasted until March 1949. The dispute began shortly after the partition of India and Pakistan, when the Maharajah of Kashmir acceded to India without consulting the Muslim population, which formed 80% of the whole. Indian troops were flown into Kashmir to suppress the resulting Muslim uprising, which was supported by Pakistan. An undeclared war raged until a ceasefire was agreed in March 1949 and the territory was partitioned by a 'ceasefire line', with the N and NW passing to Pakistani control and the remainder forming the Indian state of Jammu and Kashmir (*see also*: Ladakh

crisis). In August 1965 border skirmishes along the ceasefire line again erupted into full-scale war, which ended in January 1966 with the disengagement and withdrawal of both armies from the disputed region. A further war in 1971 was concluded by the Simla Agreement (1972), under which a 'line of control' was formally established. However, sporadic fighting and civil unrest have continued in the region ever since.

• **Kate and Sidney** ► A Spoonerism for steak and kidney pie or pudding, traditional dishes in British cuisine. It is still heard, although the dishes are now less popular than they were.

• **Katyn massacre** ► The mass execution of 5000 Polish officers in April–May 1940 by Soviet Secret Service officers in a wood near Smolensk. The officers belonged to a Polish military force of 15,000 captured and imprisoned by the Soviets after their occupation of E Poland, under the terms of the 1939 Nonaggression Pact with Hitler. The mass graves were discovered by the Germans in April 1943, in the aftermath of their invasion of the Soviet Union (1941). The Germans and the Soviets promptly accused one another of the slaughter and in 1943 the Polish government-in-exile asked the Red Cross to investigate. The Soviet government refused to cooperate, leading to the severance of diplomatic relations with the Polish government. Moscow finally admitted responsibility for the massacre in 1989, although the whereabouts of the remaining 10,000 Polish officers remains a mystery.

• **KBE** ► *See*: Order of the British Empire.

• **K-boat** ► A class of steam submarine developed by the Royal Navy during World War I. The idea was to produce a submarine capable of acting the role of a surface destroyer as part of a battle fleet. Weighing more than a conventional destroyer, they were incapable of executing a crash-dive, unlike the rival German U-boat, and were notoriously difficult to control. K-2 caught fire, K-3, K-6, and K-13 sank (the future George VI narrowly escaping from K-3), K-4 ran aground, K-5 disappeared without trace, and K-14 sprang leaks. Worse was to come, however. On 30 January 1918 a full-scale attempt was made to integrate K-boats into a major battle fleet manoeuvre in the Firth of Forth. A disastrous series of collisions ensued involving K-3, K-6, K-7, K-14, K-22, HMS *Fearless*, and HMS *Invincible*. The death toll from what became known as the **Battle of May Island** brought the total of lives lost on the project to 270; the programme was rapidly brought to an end without a single K-boat ever seeing active service.

• **Keating pictures** ▶ Drawings and paintings by Tom Keating (1918–84), a professional picture restorer, who used his skills to produce about 2000 works in the styles of Constable, Gainsborough, Turner, Rembrandt, Palmer, and others, which he then sold as originals. He admitted the forgeries in 1976, claiming that he had acted to expose the corruption of the art market rather than for personal gain. Charges against him were dropped in 1979 owing to ill-health. His paintings then became highly valued collector's items in their own right.

• **keen** ▶ US teenage slang word of the 1960s used to express approbation. Like other such words, it has subsequently gone in and out of fashion.

• **Keep Britain Tidy** ▶ A slogan adopted by the Central Office of Information to promote an anti-litter campaign in 1952. Still in occasional use, it was originally coined by the Women's Institute in the 1930s.

• **keep fit** ▶ Exercises designed to promote fitness among those who are normally inactive. Keep fit includes a variety of traditional activities, such as jogging and weight training, as well as various relatively new forms of exercise, such as aerobics and callanetics. The passion for keep fit is a product of the health craze that began in America in the 1970s and spread throughout other Western industrialized nations by the 1980s. The effectiveness of these measures continues to be debated.

• **keeping up with the Joneses** ▶ A catchphrase that sums up modern bourgeois materialism in terms of an unceasing struggle to match the apparent affluence of one's neighbours as measured by the consumer goods they possess, the holidays they take, or other lifestyle indicators. The probable origin of the phrase is a US strip cartoon of the same name, created and drawn by Arthur R. ('Pop') Momand and first published in several newspapers in 1913. Momand based it on his own experiences of living far beyond his means in a prosperous neighbourhood and his realization that all his neighbours were playing the same game. His first idea for the title, 'Keeping up with the Smiths', was abandoned in favour of the more euphonious 'Keeping up with the Joneses'.

• **Keep it dark** ▶ A slogan from World War II enjoining people to remember national security and be careful not to give away any information that could be useful to the enemy. In 1940 there was a variety show playing in London called *Shush, Keep it Dark*, and later there was a radio show featuring a character, Commander High-Price, whose catchphrase was 'Hush, keep it dark'. In 1983 the Con-

servative MP Anthony Beaumont-Dark used 'Keep it Dark' as his slogan during a successful campaign for re-election.

• **Keep it under your hat** ▶ *See at:* hat.

• **'Keep Left' group** In the later 1940s, a group of left-wing Labour MPs critical of the policies of the foreign secretary, Ernest Bevin. They began meeting in November 1946 and expressed their criticisms in a pamphlet, *Keep Left* (published by the *New Statesman* in April 1947), written by Richard Crossman, Michael Foot, and Ian Mikardo and signed by 12 other Labour MPs. The group objected to Bevin's pro-NATO stance and advocated the creation of a 'Third Force', consisting of a European socialist alliance, to hold the middle-ground between America and the Soviet Union, end Britain's dependence on America, and heal the widening breach between East and West.

• **keep on truckin'** ▶ A phrase meaning to keep going, to persevere, that was very popular among the hippies of the late 1960s and 1970s; first used in America, it quickly spread to the UK. There were a number of records with this title and the underground newspaper *International Times* featured a 'Keep On Truckin'' cartoon strip by Robert Crumb (1943– ). The main character of this strip appeared striding out with a determined loping walk, wearing his loons. The image, together with the slogan, frequently appeared on the front of T-shirts. The phrase probably derives from trucking, a dance step popular in the dance marathons of the 1930s. An alternative suggestion is that it comes from the practice by US tramps of riding or clinging on to the trucking hardware between the wheels of a train.

• **Keep the faith, baby!** ▶ A slogan adopted by US Black activists in the later 1960s, urging fellow Blacks to carry on the struggle for civil rights regardless of all setbacks. It was popularized by the US Congressman Adam Clayton Powell when he was expelled from Congress.

• **Keep your eye on the sparrow** ▶ A US catchphrase, apparently dating from the 1970s, that means 'watch out!' – especially for the unexpected. It is an allusion to the unpredictable defecatory habits of sparrows (and birds in general), and the inconvenience this may cause to the hapless people below.

• **Kellogg Pact** or **Kellogg-Briand Pact** ▶ A multilateral pact renouncing war as an instrument of policy, suggested by the French foreign minister Aristide Briand to the US secretary of state Frank B. Kellogg and signed in Paris on 27 August 1928 by America, France, Germany, Italy, Japan, and other nations. This optimistic declaration was one of several international agreements of the 1920s aimed at securing disarmament and the settlement of disputes by peaceful means under the auspices of the League of Nations. It was, however, hedged with enough caveats to render it meaningless, as demonstrated by Japan's invasion of Manchuria in 1931.

• **kelper** ▶ British slang for a Falkland Islander, first heard during the 1982 Falklands Conflict. It derives from 'kelp', a seaweed gathered from the shore and used as a fertilizer and fuel by the islanders. *See also*: bennie.

• **Kemo Sabe** ▶ The name given to the Lone Ranger by his faithful Indian companion Tonto, a man of few words. 'Kemo Sabe' means 'trusty scout' and was apparently taken from the name of a boys' camp established at Mullet Lake, Michigan, in 1911.

• **Kennedy assassination** ▶ The fatal shooting of President John F. Kennedy in Dallas, Texas, on 22 November 1963. Kennedy, who was passing through the city in a motorcade with his wife and Governor John B. Connally, was hit several times by shots fired from an upper floor of the Texas School Book Depository. He died in hospital several hours later, causing profound shock across the world. The presumed assassin was Lee Harvey Oswald (1939–63), a former US Marine with pro-Cuba views who had lived in the Soviet Union from 1959 until 1962 and married a Russian. About an hour after the assassination he was arrested in Dallas for shooting and killing a patrolman who had stopped him on suspicion. When it emerged that Oswald worked in the Depository, he was also charged with Kennedy's murder. Two days later, while being moved to a more secure jail, Oswald was gunned down by a local stripclub-owner, Jack Ruby, in full view of the television cameras. Ruby was tried and sentenced to death in February 1964 but died of cancer in 1967, while appealing for a retrial. Although Ruby claimed to have acted out of sheer rage and grief, his links with organized crime have led to speculation that he was hired by mobsters to silence Oswald, who might otherwise have revealed details of a criminal conspiracy to destroy the Kennedy presidency. Ever since, conspiracy theorists have had a field day with the circumstances of Kennedy's death, arguing variously that the CIA, the Mafia, or certain shadowy right-wing groups must have been involved.

The US government's **Warren Commission** concluded in 1964 that Oswald had fired the fatal shots and had acted alone; however, a 1979 House Select Committee on Assassinations reported that a second gunman may have been involved and that there was some evidence of a wider conspiracy.

• **Kenny polio treatment** ▶ A method of treating poliomyelitis (infantile paralysis) by physical therapy, as opposed to immobilizing the patient by using casts and splints, devised by the Australian nurse Elizabeth Kenny (1886–1952). Kenny opened a clinic in the UK in 1937, but her unorthodox methods were opposed by the British medical establishment, and still are. She achieved much wider success in America, which she toured in 1940, and, with the support of the American Medical Association, opened the Sister Kenny Foundation (1942) in Minneapolis, Minnesota, to train nurses and physiotherapists for a chain of Kenny clinics. As well as textbooks on her method, she wrote two works of autobiography, *And They Shall Walk* (1943) and *My Battle and Victory* (1955). Since the death of Sister Kenny polio has become a very rare illness, largely as a result of the widespread use of immunization (*see*: Sabin vaccine; Salk vaccine).

• **Kenyapithecus** ▶ A type of prehistoric ape dating from the early to mid Miocene Epoch, fossilized remains of which have been found in Africa. Certain features of its skull suggest similarities with the human face and jaws, causing it to be ranked as one of the earliest members of the family Hominidae, which also contains the modern great apes and extinct 'near men' as well as modern *Homo sapiens*. Fossils of *Kenyapithecus* were first discovered by the anthropologist Dr Louis Leakey in 1962 at a site called Fort Ternan in Kenya. Leakey named his hominid *Kenyapithecus wickeri*, after the owner of the site, Fred Wicker. It was shown to be some 14 million years old (mid-Miocene). Leakey later claimed that another hominid-like ape, known as *Sivapithecus africanus*, was an ancestor of his Fort Ternan hominid, and renamed it *Kenyapithecus africanus*. However, the precise relationships of these early hominids are still the subject of scientific debate.

• **kerb-crawling** ▶ The practice of driving a car very slowly beside the pavement seeking to entice someone into the car; especially as adopted by a male motorist approaching and picking up a prostitute. This activity was prohibited in England and Wales by the Sexual Offences Act (1985).

• **Kerensky government** ▶ The second provisional government in Russia (July–November 1917) in which the moderate socialist Alexander Kerensky (1881–1970) replaced Prince Lvov (1861–1925) as prime minister. Kerensky attempted to continue the war against Germany but a series of disastrous defeats, Bolshevik agitation, and the collapse of military discipline led to the October Revolution in which Lenin seized power.

• **Kermit** ▶ British student slang from the early 1980s for a French person. It alludes to the character Kermit the frog, who featured in the popular TV series *The Muppet Show* (*see*: muppet). A frog, of course, is the traditional slang name for a French person (because frogs' legs are considered a delicacy in France).

• **Kettle, Ma and Pa** ▶ A hillbilly couple, played by Marjorie Main (1890–1975) and Percy Kilbride (1888–1964), who first appeared in a film, *The Egg and I* (1947), based on the novel of the same name by Betty Macdonald. The Kettles and their numerous offspring went on to feature in a further nine cheap but popular film comedies, which continued until the late 1950s. The hayseed humour of the Kettles was later revived in the popular US television series *The Beverley Hillbillies* (1962–71).

• **Kevin** ▶ British slang for an unintelligent working-class male. It was first heard in the late 1970s, when Kevin became a particularly popular name among working-class people. It is the male equivalent of Sharon or Tracey.

> ...there was every chance their father would come steaming across the playground and chin the teacher if he thought you were picking on his 'little Kevin'. – Teacher in a working-class area, *The Independent*, 7 January 1991.

• **kewpie doll** ▶ US slang for an overdressed or over-made-up woman. In Australia the term is used as rhyming slang for 'moll', in the sense of prostitute. The name derives from the US tradename for a plump baby doll with a curl on top of its head, designed by Rose O'Neill early in the 20th century. 'Kewpie' derives from Cupid, the God of love, whom the doll was thought to resemble.

• **key grip** ▶ *See*: grip.

• **keyhole surgery** ▶ Surgery carried out through a very small incision. In the late 1980s, with the development of sophisticated fibre-optic viewing instruments, it became possible to perform what would previously have been major operations, such as gall-bladder removal, using such minimally invasive techniques.

• **Keynesianism** ▶ The economic doctrine based on the principles expounded by John Maynard Keynes (1883–1946) in *The General Theory of Employment, Interest and Money* (1936). Keynes proposed a method of solving the contemporary problem of mass unemployment by government spending to stimulate aggregate demand and employment. Keynesianism was adopted by many nations in the

1950s and 1960s but in the 1970s problems of inflation led to a reaction in favour of monetarism and the free market.

• **Keystone Comedies** ▶ The silent film comedies made in Hollywood by the Keystone Comedy Company founded by Mack Sennett (1880–1960). The first of these slapstick burlesques appeared in 1913. Charlie Chaplin worked with the company between 1913 and 1915, donning his famous Tramp outfit for the first time in *Kid Auto Races at Venice* (1914). One of the most popular features of the Keystone Comedies was the hectic chase sequences involving the **Keystone Kops**, a chaotic team of comedians (led by Ford Sterling) who executed daring comic stunts dressed in oversized police uniforms.

• **KGB** ▶ (Russian *Komitet Gosudarstvennoi Bezopasnosti*, Soviet State Security Committee) The former Soviet agency responsible for internal security, intelligence gathering, foreign operations, and border control. It was set up in 1954 after a shake-up in the Soviet intelligence services and developed into the largest and most powerful secret service in the world. At its height the KGB employed some 90,000 officers, supported by 150,000 technicians and clerical staff, controlled 250,000 border guards, and had 25,000 agents abroad. Its annual budget was between $6 and $12 billion. It was abolished in 1991.

• **KGBE** ▶ *See*: Order of the British Empire.

• **khaki** ▶ A Hindu word meaning dusty or dust-coloured, from *khak*, dust. Khaki uniform became general in the British army during the South African War of 1899–1902. It was first used some 40 years earlier by an irregular corps of guides raised by the British during the Indian Mutiny; these were known as the *Khaki Risala* (khaki squadron) and nicknamed 'the Mudlarks'. It was subsequently adopted as an active service uniform by several regiments and worn in the Omdurman campaign of 1898. By the time of World War I it was the standard uniform of most armies. *See also*: camouflage.

• **Khaki Election** ▶ 1. The general election of 1900 in which the Conservatives sought to profit from the recent military victories in the South African War (*see*: Boer Wars). The Conservatives won, although the gain in seats was very slight. 2. The general election of 1918 (also called the Coupon Election), in which the Lloyd George government successfully exploited the prevailing mood of patriotic hysteria.

• **khazi** ▶ British army slang for a latrine. It was derived from Arabic during the North African campaigns of 1940–43.

• **Khmer Rouge** ▶ A communist movement in Cambodia active from the early 1970s until the late 1990s. The Khmer are the indigenous people of the country; 'Rouge' (French for red) indicates the political colour of the movement. In 1970 the ruling Prince Sihanouk (1923–  ) was deposed and a republic, called the **Khmer Republic**, was established under General Lon Nol (1913–85). For the next few years Lon Nol, supported by America, resisted a guerrilla war waged by the Khmer Rouge under Pol Pot (1925–98). In 1974 the Khmer Rouge were victorious and a year later a new constitution was established, the country's name being changed to Democratic Kampuchea. There followed a period of upheaval in which the country's social structure was radically changed, with townspeople being deprived of their property and driven to work in agricultural cooperatives. Over two million of the country's dissenting, elderly, or sick citizens were killed, either through mass executions or indirectly through forced labour and starvation (*see*: Killing Fields). In 1979 the Vietnamese invaded Kampuchea and deposed the Khmer Rouge government. The world was shocked by photographs of piles of human skulls and reports of suffering comparable with that of the Nazi holocaust. Pol Pot was sentenced to death for genocide but escaped into the jungle. In 1988 the Vietnamese began to withdraw, leaving the country, once again named Cambodia, under the control of a pro-Vietnamese government. Meanwhile several exiled factions, including the Khmer Rouge (controlled by Pol Pot from Thailand) and the supporters of Prince Sihanouk, formed a government in exile, the Coalition Government of Democratic Kampuchea (CGDK), which gained Western support and a seat at the UN. Fighting between government forces and CGDK guerrillas continued until 1991, when UN-sponsored peace talks led to the formation of a new governing coalition that included elements of the Khmer Rouge. However, free elections held in 1993 were boycotted by the Khmer Rouge, who resumed their guerrilla activities. From 1996 the movement was subject to internal conflicts and splits, and it is now considered moribund. Pol Pot himself died after being captured by one branch of the movement in 1997.

• **khozraschot** ▶ A word derived from the Russian phrase *khozyaistvenny raschot*, meaning 'self-supporting running'. Khozraschot, meaning economic accountability, was one of the aims of the Soviet leader Mikhail Gorbachov in his efforts to reconstruct and revitalize the economy (*see also*: perestroika). It implied that commercial and industrial concerns should be responsible for their own financial state and should cease to rely heavily on subsidies from the government.

• **kibbutz** ▶ A collective agricultural, or occasionally industrial, settlement in modern Israel. In 1899 Edmond de Rothschild and Maurice de Hirsch formed a Jewish Colonization Association to establish *kvutzoth*, later called kibbutzim, in Palestine. These communally run settlements, in which children are collectively reared, prospered throughout the 20th century, in spite of opposition, often violent, from Palestinian Arabs. After the declaration (1948) of the state of Israel, the kibbutzim became an essential part of the new country's ethos and an essential part of its defence system. However, as living standards in Israel have risen, the taxing and simple life of the kibbutz has become less attractive to young Israelis, many of whom have abandoned the unsophisticated rural life for the better schools and greater comfort of the cities. The word derives from the Hebrew *qibbutz*, a gathering.

• **kibitzer** or **kibbitzer** ▶ US slang for someone who looks over the shoulder of a card player and offers unwanted advice (Yiddish, from the German *Kiebitzen*, an onlooker). By extension, any onlooker of any activity, who imagines that he knows better than the participant what the next move should be, is a kibitzer. Kibitzers cannot expect to be popular nor are they regarded as a source of useful advice.

• **kick** ▶ **1.** To give up something to which one is addicted, such as cigarettes or drugs; often used in the phrase **kick the habit**. **2.** A thrill, as in the Cole Porter song 'I Get a Kick Out of You'. In the plural, it is often used in the phrase **just for kicks**, meaning just for the fun of it. This has often been used by young people to account for apparently meaningless aggressive behaviour. **3.** A temporary enthusiasm for a particular subject or activity. For example, a **health kick** is a period during which exercise and healthy eating seem important to the person concerned.

• **kickers** ▶ US slang of the 1960s for shoes or boots. In the 1970s a French shoe company used it as a tradename for their fashionable sporty boots and shoes.

• **Kid, The** ▶ A nickname of Warren Beatty (1937–  ), the US film actor and director, who is the kid brother of the actress Shirley Maclaine (1934–  ).

• **Kidbrooke** ▶ The first British purpose-built urban comprehensive school, which was opened in Blackheath, London, by the London County Council in 1954. Kidbrooke School for Girls became the showpiece of the LCC's controversial comprehensive education policy in the mid-1950s, with parties of visitors from other local councils touring its five gymnasia, six science labs, and nine housecraft centres. *See also*: comprehensivization.

• **kidney machine** ► A piece of medical equipment, properly known as a dialyser, that functions as an artificial kidney, cleansing the blood of impurities on the principle of dialysis (selective filtration) if a patient's own kidneys have failed, either partially or completely. The patient's blood is passed through tubes consisting of thin synthetic membranes immersed in a dialysing solution. Waste products pass through the membrane and are removed from the bloodstream, while blood cells and vital protein molecules, which are too large to pass through, are retained. The first kidney machine capable of partial haemodialysis was developed in the early 1940s by the Dutch physician W. J. Kolff; the first machine capable of totally replacing the kidney function was perfected by B. H. Scribner in the 1960s.

• **kidult** ► A word coined from 'kid' and 'adult', by Neil Postman of New York University to denote the typical modern US child. The implication is that children subjected to a modern US lifestyle, especially to the excessive influence of television with all its various kinds of information and advertising, grow up too fast and become adult-like in many respects too soon; the kidult remains, however, emotionally immature, will tend to neglect education in favour of TV or computer games, and will grow up without culture and with too great a preoccupation with material possessions.

In the last few years the same term has been used with an opposite (if, perhaps, complementary) sense – to denote an adult who behaves like an overgrown kid; symptoms include the postponement of marriage, children, and a serious career until the brink of middle age and a reluctance to abandon the tastes and habits of one's childhood or adolescence.

• **kike** ► An offensive US name for a Jew, much in line with calling an Italian a wop, a German a kraut, or a Japanese a nip. The derivation is interesting. Most reference books say it is a variant of 'kiki', a duplication of the common '-ki' ending of the names of many Jews from Slav countries. Leo Rosten, however, in his *Joys of Yiddish* (1968), has a more interesting, and perhaps more credible, explanation. He says that the word came from the immigration officers on Ellis Island who, faced with Jewish immigrants who were unable to write their names in the Roman alphabet, instructed them to sign their forms with a cross. Jews, for whom the cross is a symbol of the religion that has mercilessly persecuted them for some 2000 years, often preferred to make a circle (Yiddish *kikel*), as this is a symbol of unending life. To the immigration officers, a person who asked to be allowed to make a *kikel* or a *kikeleh* (a little circle), soon became a kikee or simply a kike.

• **Kildare, Dr** ► A fictional medical hero, based on a character in the novels of Max Brand, who appeared on screen in the 1937 movie *Interns Can't Take Money* and subsequently in a further 15 films made over the next 10 years. The original Kildare, Lew Ayres, was removed from the series by MGM after declaring himself a conscientious objector in World War II (ironically, he served as a battlefield medic). The character was later resurrected in the popular US television series *Dr Kildare* (1961–66), in which he was played by the apparently ageless Richard Chamberlain. The role of his gruff but wise patron, Dr Gillespie, was played by Raymond Massey.

• **killer** ► US Black teenage slang, originally from the 1940s, for something highly approved of. It was briefly popular with the British teddy boys of the 1950s, was revived in the 1960s and 1970s in America, and made a further comeback in the 1980s.

• **killer bee** ► Originally a variety of African honeybee (*Apis mellifera adansonii*), noted for its high honey production and for its aggressive behaviour when disturbed, hence the alternative name **Mau Mau bee** (*see*: Mau Mau). Imported into Brazil in 1956, the bees interbred with native bees, producing equally aggressive varieties. These have spread to other parts of South America and into the southern states of America.

• **killer cell** ► A type of white blood cell (lymphocyte) that destroys cancer cells and cells infected with viruses. There are two kinds: **natural killer cells** and **cytotoxic T cells**. Since the early 1980s much research has been directed towards elucidating the mechanisms by which killer cells act and developing similar cells, by means of genetic engineering, that could be used in combating cancer and viral infections, notably Aids.

• **killer satellite** or **satellite killer** ► A military satellite equipped with sophisticated weapons, such as missiles and lasers, the purpose of which is to destroy other satellites and anything else within range, such as high-altitude aircraft and missiles. To date, no killer satellite has been deployed permanently, and research into and development of space laser weapons is still in its early stages. *See also*: Star Wars.

• **Killing Fields** ► A name given to the country-side around Pnomh Penh dotted with the mass graves of Cambodians killed by the Khmer Rouge during the Pol Pot regime (1975–79). After the fall of Pnomh Penh the Khmers declared 'Year Zero', forced the entire population into agricultural labour camps, and embarked on a horrifying experiment, seeking to create a classless agrarian society through political indoctrination, economic reform, and the extermination of all professionals and intellectuals. In four years over one quarter of the population died through starvation, disease, overwork, or execution. This brutal genocide was harrowingly depicted in *The Killing Fields* (1984), Roland Joffe's film (based on a true story) of one man's struggle to survive.

• **Kilroy** ► During World War II, the phrase **Kilroy was here** was found written on walls etc. wherever the Americans (particularly Air Transport Command) had been. Its origin is a matter of conjecture. One suggestion is that a certain shipyard inspector of this name at Quincy, Massachusetts, chalked up the words on material he had inspected. *See also*: Chad.

• **Kim** ► Nickname of Harold Philby (1912–1988), British intelligence officer and Soviet agent (*see*: Magnificent Five). Born in the Punjab, he was given the nickname after the hero of Rudyard Kipling's novel *Kim* (1901).

• **kindertransport** ► (German, children's transport) The trains in which some 10,000 Jewish children escaped from Germany and German-occupied countries to the UK. Before Hitler and his demented entourage had thought up the Final Solution to the Jewish 'problem', the main aim was to expel all Jews from German-occupied Europe. However, no countries were prepared to accept them; in 1938 a desperate appeal was made to all nations to at least save the Jewish children from what was soon to become the holocaust. Only the UK offered to help – all other countries, including America, stuck piously to their prearranged immigration quotas. After a debate in parliament the British government agreed to take 10,000 children and accepted the conditions imposed by Germany: £50 had to be paid for each child, the children had to be between 3 and 17, and had to be unaccompanied by parents or other adults.

The first *kindertransport* left for Holland some six weeks after Kristallnacht (9–10 November 1938) and the last two days before war was declared on 3 September 1939. The sealed and guarded trains from Berlin, Vienna, and (after March 1939) Prague, were unloaded in Holland, whence the children were shipped from Hook to Harwich. Once in England they were welcomed into the homes of Jewish and non-Jewish families all over the UK; some were sent to schools or farms and some to orphanages. Because of the mass murders of Jews in occupied Europe, some 80% of the children never saw their parents again. About 25% eventually made their way to America or Israel after the war, many to live with relatives. Most of the remainder have lived useful lives in Britain, grateful to their adopted country and foster parents for saving them from the fate of the one and a half million children who were unable to find places on the *kindertransport* or whose parents refused to allow them to travel unaccompanied.

• **kinetic art** ► Art involving movement. This is usually achieved by the use of motor-driven components or mobile parts set in motion by air currents or water. Alternatively optical effects may be used to create an impression of movement (*see*: op art). Kinetic art first appeared in the 1950s, the mobiles of the US sculptor Alexander Calder being probably the best-known examples.

• **King, the** ► *See*: Elvis the Pelvis.

• **King and Country debate** ► A famous debate that took place in the Oxford University Union on 9 February 1933 on the motion 'This House will under no circumstances fight for its King and Country'. The motion was passed by 275 to 153. Although it was given little further thought by the students themselves, the vote was widely regarded as demonstrating the degeneracy of Oxford in particular and of Young England more generally. It caused a great deal of comment in the national press and disgusted certain contemporary politicians, such as Winston Churchill.

> There is no question but that the woozy-minded Communists, the practical jokers, and the sexual indeterminates of Oxford have scored a great success... – *Daily Express*.

Six years later, when the country went to war against Germany, the young men from the universities were found to be flocking into the services; some even found a place among Churchill's cherished Few.

• **King Arthur** ► Nickname bestowed on the trade unionist Arthur Scargill (1938–   ), reflecting his power as leader of the Yorkshire miners' union (1973–81), and subsequently of the National Union of Mineworkers. His vociferous championing of the miners' cause led to frequent clashes with Conservative governments, culminating in the great miners' strike of 1984–85. The bitter dispute, in which Scargill's union confronted the government of Margaret Thatcher over the issue of threatened pit closures, lasted for over a year before splits in the union and deepening hardship forced the striking miners back to work.

• **King David Hotel bombing** ▶ *See*: Irgun Zvai Leumi.

• **Kingfish** ▶ The nickname of Huey Pierce Long (1893–1935), the US politician who became governor of Louisiana (1928–31) and state senator (1930–35). Long was a demagogue whose populist appeal derived from a series of social reforms aimed at relieving unemployment and improving standards of health and education, paid for by taxing large corporations. He built a powerful political machine and hoped to win the presidency with his Share Our Wealth programme, aimed at overhauling the taxation system to facilitate a more equitable redistribution of wealth. He was assassinated on 8 September 1935 by Dr Carl Austin Weiss.

• **King Kong** ▶ The towering ape-like monster that features in RKO's film (1933) of the same name. Although the once-thrilling special effects now seem primitive, the film has survived surprisingly well. It is mainly remembered for the scenes in which the hapless monster, clutching a beautiful woman (Fay Wray), is shot down from the top of the Empire State Building by fighter planes. A 1976 remake failed to achieve the same impact.

> It wasn't the airplanes – it was beauty that killed the beast. – Line spoken by CARL ARM-STRONG, playing Fay Wray's friend.

• **Kingledon** ▶ The name given by the *Daily Mirror* to the Wimbledon international lawn-tennis championships in 1972 in recognition of the prowess of the top-ranked US player, Billie Jean King (1943–   ), who won the ladies' singles championship for the fourth time that year.

• **King of Calypso** ▶ The nickname of the US singer Harry Belafonte (1927–   ), who spent five years of his childhood in Jamaica and became internationally famous as a calypso singer from the mid-1950s. His third LP, *Calypso*, was the first album to sell a million copies. His best known songs are the 'Banana Boat Song' (also known as 'Day-O') and 'Island in the Sun'.

• **King of Hollywood** ▶ A title conferred on the US film actor Clark Gable (1901–60), who dominated Hollywood in the 1930s. Ruggedly handsome and with an air of self-assurance, he specialized in portraying macho heroes with charm. His films include *It Happened One Night* (1934) and *Gone with the Wind* (1939), in which he played Rhett Butler. His

final film, *The Misfits*, was released in 1961, shortly after his death from a heart attack.

• **King of Swing** ▶ Benny Goodman (1909–86), the band leader and virtuoso jazz clarinettist from Chicago. In 1934, at the age of 25, he was leading his own band and caused student riots in the Palomar Ballroom, Los Angeles, with teenagers jitterbugging in the aisles (*see*: jitterbug). In 1938 his band played at Carnegie Hall, the first jazz gathering in a concert-hall setting. His mainly White band included the trumpeter Harry James and the drummer Gene Krupa, as well as (controversially for the period) such Black musicians as Lionel Hampton. He survived many changes of fashion and was still playing to critical acclaim at the end of his life.

• **King of the Cowboys** ▶ Nickname of two US stars of Hollywood cowboy films, Tom Mix and Roy Rogers (*see*: Singing Cowboy).

Tom Mix (1880–1940) was, by his own (disputed) account, a US marshal and war hero before turning to acting in 1909. His films, over 400 B-feature westerns, idealized the American West. In his private life he maintained the role of cowboy hero, invariably dressing in boots and a white suit.

• **King of the Serials** ▶ Nickname of Buster Crabbe (Clarence Linden Crabbe; 1907–83), the US film star. Crabbe won a gold medal for swimming in the 1932 Olympics, before beginning his Hollywood career. Blond and athletic, he was ideally cast in the role of comic-strip hero, playing Flash Gordon and Buck Rogers in several science-fiction film serials in the 1930s. The film serial, a phenomenon which disappeared in the early 1950s, consisted of several 15- or 20-minute action-filled episodes, only one of which was shown each week as an accompaniment to the main feature. As each episode typically ended with the hero in dire peril (*see*: cliffhanger), the film serial ensured a regular cinema-going audience avid to discover what happened next.

• **King's English** ▶ See: Received Pronunciation.

• **King's Medals** ▶ Two medals instituted in the UK in 1945. The King's Medal for Courage in the Cause of Freedom and the King's Medal for Service in the Cause of Freedom were awarded to foreign citizens, the former being given to those who had offered British forces help in occupied territory.

• **King Street** ▶ The London street (WC2) in which the Communist Party of Great Britain had its head office from its foundation in 1920 until the 1980s. King Street was also used as an epithet for the Party.

• **kinky** ▶ Applied to people, this means given to unusual sexual desires or practices, typically involving fetishism or sado-masochism. Applied to clothes, it means bizarre and provocative, in a way that might arouse people who are kinky. The adjective derives from the noun 'kink', meaning a twist or bend in a rope, hence a peculiar character trait or fixation of some kind (especially one relating to sex). However, in 1960s slang 'kink' lost most of its sexual connotation and came to mean an eccentric or rebel of almost any kind. The Kinks were a well-known British pop group of the era.

• **kinky boots** ▶ British slang for knee- or thigh-high leather boots, highly desirable and fashionable items of clothing in the mid-1960s. Often worn with a miniskirt, they have come to epitomize the swinging sixties as an era of sexual freedom. Kinky boots are particularly associated with the Diana Rigg character in the cult 1960s TV programme *The Avengers*; the actress recorded the song 'Kinky Boots' in 1965.

• **Kinsey reports** ▶ Two studies: – *Sexual Behaviour in the Human Male* (1948) and *Sexual Behaviour in the Human Female* (1951) – based on 18,500 personal interviews by Alfred C. Kinsey (1894–1956), director of the Institute for Sex Research at Indiana University. Although the reports are notable as the first serious research on the subject, they have been criticized for sampling errors and for putting too much faith in unreliable personal testimony. Nevertheless the works opened up the field of sexual response to scientific study and enabled many of the taboos surrounding the subject to be broken. Basically, Kinsey asked his subjects to tell him in some detail what they did in their sexual encounters. Twenty years later Masters and Johnson took the science of sexuality a stage further by establishing laboratory conditions to observe the specific physiological mechanisms that were involved under particular conditions of stimulation.

• **kipper** ▶ Australian slang for an Englishman, dating from World War II. It originated from the popular idea of the English breakfast, which was thought to be based exclusively on kippers. The nickname also carried the implication that the English were two-faced and gutless, just like a kipper.

• **Kipps** ▶ The hero of a semi-autobiographical comic novel of the same name (1905) by H. G. Wells (1866–1946). Kipps, a draper's assistant who inherits a fortune, fails in his attempt to join fashionable society; after losing his inheritance, he discovers true happiness in the quiet life. There is a silent film version of the novel (1921) and a later remake, starring Michael Redgrave, directed by Carol Reed (1941); a stage musical *Half a Sixpence* (1963), also based on the novel, was filmed with singer Tommy Steele in the leading role (1967).

• **Kirchner girls** ▶ Mildly suggestive postcard pin-ups produced by the Austrian-born artist Raphaël Kirchner (1875–1917). Kirchner arrived in Paris in 1901 and achieved success (especially among combatants during World War I) with a series of pin-up photographs of partially clothed girls in coy poses.

• **Kirov murder** ▶ The shooting of the popular Leningrad party chief Sergei Mironovich Kirov on 1 December 1934 by a deranged party member, Leonid Nickolaev. The murder was used by Stalin (who helped bear Kirov's ashes to his grave) as a pretext for a vicious purge of his opponents (1934–38), on the grounds that Kirov's murder had been part of a plot by counter-revolutionaries to assassinate the entire Soviet leadership. *See*: Law of December 1; Yezhovshchina.

• **kissagram** ▶ A surprise greeting service provided for birthdays and other special occasions, in which a message, together with a kiss, is delivered by an attractive young man or woman. Such services became increasingly popular during the 1980s; other types of popular greetings services available include **stripagrams** (the messenger performs a striptease), **gorillagrams** (the messenger is dressed in a gorilla outfit), and **Tarzanagrams**.

• **kiss-and-tell** ▶ Describing intimate stories sold to the more lurid tabloid newspapers by the former sexual partners of celebrities or other people in the public eye. The commercial aspects of this form of journalism are emphasized by the alternative name **kiss-and-sell stories**. It is now not unknown for someone to begin a sexual relationship with a celebrity purely for the purpose of selling their story later.

• **kissing tackle** ▶ British slang for the mouth, used by teenagers and young people in the late 1980s and 1990s.

• **kiss of death** ▶ A phrase that derives from the kiss given to Christ in Gethsemane by Judas Iscariot before he betrayed him (Luke 23:48). In Mafia circles a kiss from the boss is allegedly a sign that one's life will end shortly. The phrase is now widely used for any action, association, relationship, etc. that spells disaster.

• **kitchen cabinet** ▶ A group of influential but unofficial advisers to a political leader, especially a US president or a prime minister, who meet informally, perhaps round a kitchen table. These advisers may have a greater influence on the leader's decisions than the official cabinet. The phrase originated in America, where it was applied to the entourage of President Andrew Jackson in the 1830s, but did not become common in the UK until the premiership (1964–70) of Harold Wilson.

• **Kitchener's army** ► The volunteer army raised by Field Marshal Horatio Herbert Kitchener, 1st Earl Kitchener of Khartoum (1850–1916), at the onset of World War I. Kitchener, recognizing the deficiencies of the regular army and the Territorials, saw the urgent need for a large well-equipped well-trained volunteer force. As secretary of state for war, he orchestrated a nationwide recruitment campaign through the press and the Parliamentary Recruiting Committee, which sponsored the poster campaign 'Your Country Needs You' (*see at*: country). By 12 September 1914, 100,000 men had been recruited; the volunteers totalled three million before conscription was introduced in 1916.

> We are in Kitchener's Army
> The ragtime A.S.C.:
> We cannot fight, we cannot shoot,
> What bloody use are we?
> – FRANK RICHARDS: 'Old Soldiers Never Die' (1933).

*See also*: Fred Karno's army.

• **Kitchener wants you** ► An army catchphrase of World War I applied to anyone chosen for an unpleasant or onerous task. It was derived from the famous recruiting poster of the early war years, showing the stern features and pointing finger of the war secretary, Lord Kitchener of Khartoum, above the slogan 'Your Country Needs You' (*see at*: country).

• **kitchen sink** ► A phrase applied to a certain type of domestic drama of the late 1950s, depicting the reality of everyday life in working-class and lower middle-class households. The genre was exemplified by such plays as *Look Back in Anger* (1956) by John Osborne (*see*: Porter, Jimmy) and Shelagh Delaney's *A Taste of Honey* (1958). In part, these plays were an attack on the middle-class values represented by the drawing-room comedies of Noël Coward and Terence Rattigan (*see*: Angry Young Men).

The term had previously been applied to the **kitchen-sink school**, a group of British artists led by John Bratby (1928–92), who held several joint exhibitions in the 1950s. They painted scenes of working-class domesticity in a drably realistic style (*e.g.* Bratby's *Still Life with a Chip Frier*).

• **kite** ► 1. In lawyer's slang, a junior counsel at an assize court chosen to advocate the cause of a prisoner without other defence. 2. In RAF slang, any aircraft. 3. In Stock Exchange slang, an accommodation bill.

*See also*: fly a kite.

• **Kitemark** ► The trademark of the British Stan-

dards Institution, licensed to be used by manufacturers on products that conform to a British Standard.

• **kitsch** ► Trashy, vulgar, or in bad taste (from the German *kitsch*, rubbish). An Elvis Presley table lamp, a lurid advertising poster, or a Hollywood Biblical epic could all be labelled kitsch. Traditionally, kitsch articles were mass-produced for mass consumption and were to be avoided by the aesthetically discerning. In the 1960s, however, the distinction between high and low art became obscured by pop art, with its semi-ironic elevation of the kitsch, and by a more general reaction against the 'elitist' notion of good taste. Both tendencies have been reinforced by the postmodernism of recent decades. As a result, some kitsch articles have attained a surprising status as collectables, with a high market value.

> ...the documentary *Pumping Iron* (1977)...that allowed him [Arnold Schwarzenegger] to move bodybuilding from low camp to high kitsch and then big business. – *The Independent*, 30 January 1991.

• **Kitty Hawk** ► A town in North Carolina, USA, on the narrow dunes facing the Atlantic. It owes its fame to the Wright brothers, who made the first sustained powered flight here on 17 December 1903. To the south of the town at Kill Devil Hills is the Wright Brothers National Memorial (1927).

• **Kiwanis** ► An organization founded in America in 1915 aiming to provide idealistic leadership in business and the professions. There are many Kiwanis clubs in America and Canada. The word is thought to come from a Native American language meaning to make oneself known.

• **kiwi** ► A New Zealand bird incapable of flight. In flying circles the word is used to describe a man on the ground staff of an airfield. It is also a nickname for a New Zealander.

• **Kleenex** ► The tradename for the world's first disposable paper handkerchiefs, produced in 1924 by the Kimberley-Clarke Company in Wisconsin, USA. The soft tissues were first called Celluwipes, then renamed Kleenex-'Kerchiefs, which was later shortened to Kleenex.

• **Kleinian** ► Pertaining to the work and theories of the Austrian-born psychoanalyst Melanie Klein (1882–1960). A disciple of Sigmund Freud, she believed that complex emotional states, such as fear, anxiety, and grief, were present from early infancy and that psychoanalytic techniques could be applied successfully to very young children. She advocated the use of play as a means of allowing children to express their feelings and maintained that observing play with simple toys, drawing materials, sand, etc., provided an understanding of their behaviour and emotional needs. Although many of her theories are still controversial, the technique of 'play therapy', which she developed, is commonly used by therapists, for example in cases of suspected child abuse or in dealing with disturbed children.

• **klutz** ► Slang for a fool. Originally US Jewish, it is derived from the Yiddish *klots*, a lump, and is related to the English word 'clot', via the German *klotz*, lump. By the 1980s its use had spread throughout the English-speaking world.

• **KMT** ► Kuomintang. *See*: Guomindang.

• **knave** ► British slang for an airline passenger who has unwittingly had explosives planted in his or her luggage by terrorists. This method of terrorism was first practised in the late 1980s; the term was coined by security guards.

• **kneecapping** ► The outrageous practice of damaging a person's kneecaps, typically by blasting them with a shotgun or drilling through them with an electric drill. It became notorious through its use by the IRA as a punishment for those considered guilty of petty crime or antisocial behaviour.

• **knee-jerk** ► Describing a response (especially in the phrase **knee-jerk reaction**) that is automatic and unthinking. The term refers to the patellar reflex – the involuntary jerk of the leg caused by tapping just below the knee. It is now used in various combinations, *e.g.* a 'knee-jerk liberal' is one whose liberal response to any situation is automatic rather than thought out.

• **knees-up** ► A party, or any lively celebration; from the Cockney song 'Knees-up, Mother Brown!' (1939), popular during World War II.

• **Knesset** ► (Hebrew, Assembly) The Israeli parliament, a single chamber consisting of 120 members elected every four years by proportional representation. The first Knesset opened in Jerusalem on 16 February 1949 and elected Chaim Weizmann (1874–1952) as the first president of Israel.

• **Knickbein** ► (German, bent leg) Codename of a simple radio aid used by the Germans early in World War II to guide bombers over the UK during night raids and in bad weather. It used two radio beams, which were picked up by receivers in the aircraft: one to track the target, the other to cross the first at the bomb release point. The transmitters were positioned along the coast of Holland and N France and could guide aircraft with reasonable accuracy over central and S England. Within two months of its discovery, however, the RAF had devised effective counter-measures.

• **knickers** ►
   **get one's knickers in a twist** British slang phrase meaning to become agitated about something. It was first used in the 1950s to mean sexually excited rather than agitated or aggrieved. It is usually addressed to angry women in the form **don't get your knickers in a twist**, a patronizing remark that is intended to pacify, but can usually be counted on to have the opposite effect.

• **Knightsbridge** ► The ironic nickname given to a crossroads in the desert south of Tobruk, Libya, which was the scene of fierce tank battles during the Battle of the Gazala-Bir Hacheim Line between 28 May and 13 June 1942. It refers to Knightsbridge in W central London, a street known for its smart hotels and department stores. The British Eighth Army under Auchinleck was forced to withdraw into Egypt, after which Rommel took Tobruk and advanced on to Alamein.

• **knock, knock!** ► A catchphrase said to have been introduced to the UK by the music-hall comedian Wee Georgie Wood, who first used it in a radio programme in 1936. It was employed as a prefatory phrase in telling a joke, often of a risqué nature. By the 1960s the phrase had become part of a fairly rigid formula for a joke, of which the following is typical:

> Knock, knock!
> Who's there?
> Owl.
> Owl who?
> Owl you know unless you open the door?

• **Knock** ► *See*: Our Lady of Knock.

• **knock for knock** ► A practice adopted by British motor insurers in which they agree to pay the claims of their own policy owners, but not to counterclaim against other parties to an accident. In principle, if a motorist involved in an accident is the innocent party, his insurers could make a claim against the other party's insurers for the damage caused. In practice, the **knock-for-knock** agreement enables insurance companies to avoid this expensive and time-consuming procedure on the grounds that, in the long run, such counterclaims tend to even out. This saving in administrative costs also benefits insured motorists by keeping down the cost of premiums. However, in individual cases some motorists may lose their no-claim bonus, even though they were not to blame for an accident.

• **knocking copy** ► *See*: comparative advertising.

• **knock-on effect**▶ An effect that is a direct or indirect consequence of some previous event. When there is a whole chain of knock-on effects, this is often referred to as the **domino effect** (*see*: domino theory). *See also*: ripple effect.

• **knowledge, the** ▶ London taxi-drivers' slang for the knowledge of the streets etc. of London on which they are examined in order to become licensed black cab drivers. Would-be taxi-drivers can be seen acquiring 'the knowledge' by riding around London on mopeds following pre-arranged routes drawn out on a clipboard attached to the handlebars. This is known as being **on the knowledge**; the drivers themselves are called the **knowledge boys** irrespective of their age or gender. These terms became more widely known through a 1979 TV play, *The Knowledge*, by Jack Rosenthal.

• **Kodak**▶ Tradename for a range of cameras and films invented by the eccentric American, George Eastman (1854–1932), the first of which appeared in 1888. This first Kodak camera was compact, light, and relatively cheap; it heralded the arrival of popular photography. The box-shaped device produced 100 round photos on paper stripping film. When all the photos had been taken, the camera was returned to the factory, which replaced the film, developed the pictures, and returned the camera and snaps to the owner within 10 days. Eastman has recorded his reasons for choosing the name Kodak:

> I chose it because I knew a trade name must be short, vigorous, incapable of being misspelled to an extent that will destroy its identity, and, in order to satisfy trademark laws, it must mean nothing. The letter K had been a favourite with me – it seemed a strong, incisive sort of letter. Therefore, the word I wanted had to start with K. Then it became a question of trying out a great number of combinations of letters that made words starting and ending with K. The word *Kodak* is the result.

• **kode** ▶ Slang for a set of mainly visual signs used by gays to communicate their sexual proclivities. The code includes modes of dress (*see*: clone), key rings attached to belts, and certain coloured handkerchiefs in certain pockets, as well as the use of particular codewords in conversation.

• **kogai**▶ A Japanese word for environmental pollution. From about 1970, reports of conferences held to discuss the problem of *kogai* in Japan began to appear in Western newspapers. The term is applied to all types of environmental nuisance, including noise, water impurity, traffic congestion, obstruction of light, and air pollution.

• **Kolyma** ▶ A region in NE Siberia, site of a complex of Soviet forced-labour camps administered by Dalstroy, the Far Eastern Construction Trust. The main camps serviced the Kolyma gold mines; there were also logging camps for women prisoners. In all, over two million died under a deliberately destructive regime, which provided a starvation diet, prohibited fur clothing, and enforced outside work 10 hours a day, unless temperatures fell below –50°C.

> Labour is a matter of honour, valour and heroism. – Sign required by statute on all camp gates.

• **Komsomol** ▶ The All-Union Leninist Young Communist League, established in 1918 as a Bolshevik youth organization for agitation and propaganda.

• **Kondratieff waves**▶ Long-term cycles in economic activity with a period of about 40 years, postulated by the Russian economist N. D. Kondratieff (1892–1931). There is little substantive evidence for the theory. *See*: trade cycle.

• **Kon-Tiki expedition** ▶ The unique voyage made in 1947 by the Norwegian Thor Heyerdahl with five companions, who sailed a primitive balsa raft from Callao in Peru to Tuamotu Island in the South Pacific. Their object was to support the theory that the Polynesian race reached the Pacific islands in this fashion and were descendants of the Incas of Peru. Their raft was called *Kon-Tiki* after the Inca sun-god. Although the voyage demonstrated that such a migration was possible using prehistoric technology, modern DNA testing has shown that the theory is almost certainly wrong.

• **kook**▶ US slang for an eccentric or crazy person. It is probably derived from 'cuckoo', meaning crazy. Kook is rarely heard in the UK, although it is used in Australia.

• **Kop, the**▶ *See*: Spion Kop.

• **Köpenick hoax**▶ An incident that took place in a Berlin suburb in 1906. An ex-convict shoemaker, dressed in a guardsman's uniform, commandeered a passing platoon of soldiers and arrested the Burgomaster, before rifling his office in search of cash and a passport. He was brought to justice ten days later and identified as Wilhelm Voigt. The case, which made Prussian militarism a laughing stock, attracted wide publicity; the Kaiser was obliged to pardon the daring elderly hoaxer, who spent his remaining years in comfort on a pension given him by an admiring Berlin dowager. The episode provided the plot for the comic satire *Der Hauptmann von Köpenick* (1931) by the German dramatist and novelist Carlos Zuckmayer (1896–1977).

• **Korean War** ► (1950–53) The bitter, and ultimately inconclusive, conflict precipitated by the
surprise invasion of pro-Western South Korea by
communist North Korea on 25 June 1950. Korea
had been temporarily divided across the 38th Parallel by the Allies in 1945, after which attempts by the
UN to reunite the country failed. An international
force was raised by the UN to combat the invasion,
dominated by the Americans and led by General
Douglas MacArthur, who masterminded the successful Inchon landings (September 1950) cutting
the enemy supply lines. The UN forces then drove
the communists back to the Yalu River, the boundary between North Korea and China. MacArthur
was removed by President Truman in April 1951
for publicly advocating the bombing of China,
which had invaded in support of the North in November 1950, pushing the UN forces back to the
38th parallel. Seoul, the southern capital, fell to
the communists, but was recaptured in April 1951.
Negotiations began as the fighting continued, until
an armistice was finally signed at Panmunjon in
1953. Some 1,750,000 Koreans on both sides died in
the conflict, compared to around 55,000 Americans.

• **kosher** ► A Yiddish word (from Hebrew *kasher*,
proper) that came into use in English-speaking
countries in the 19th century to describe food that
complies with the Jewish dietary laws. Its use was
subsequently extended to describe restaurants and
butchers selling this food and even the Jews themselves. Its wider sense, in which it is used to describe anything trustworthy, genuine, or above
board, is essentially a 20th-century usage, which
originated in New York, where so many Yiddish
words entered the English language. From New
York it crossed the Atlantic to Britain, where it is
now quite common to hear such questions as 'Is
that antique kosher?' or such statements as 'You
have no need to worry, he is absolutely kosher' –
meaning not that the person concerned is Jewish,
but that he is honest, or is who he says he is.

    Interestingly, about a century before this sense
came into mainstream English, Dickens had picked
up an almost identical usage in London's East End,
where 'kosher' was used to describe a deal that was
fair. Very few Yiddish words commonly used by East
End Jews appear to have spread even a few miles
west to become part of mainstream English. This
usage of kosher, for example, simply did not exist in
20th-century English until it came back from America after World War II.

• **Kosovo crisis** ► The political and military crisis of 1998–99 caused by Serbia's repression of
the ethnic Albanian population in its southern
province of Kosovo. In 1998 demonstrations by
ethnic Albanians, who formed almost 90% of the
province's population, led to severe repression
by the Belgrade government under Slobodan
Miloševic; this in turn provoked armed resistance
from the Kosovo Liberation Army (KLA). Mounting
evidence of ethnic cleansing by Serb forces led NATO
to threaten airstrikes against the Serbs in October
1998. When subsequent talks broke down and Serbia resumed its aggression, NATO began a campaign of airstrikes against military and economic
targets in Yugoslavia in March 1999. The Serb forces
intensified their campaign of terror against ethnic
Albanians, leading to a mass exodus of some
800,000 refugees seeking shelter in Macedonia, Albania, and Montenegro; a similar number were displaced within Kosovo and at least 10,000 are
thought to have been massacred. In June 1999 the
Serbs effectively surrendered, agreeing to the complete withdrawal of their military forces, the presence of international peacekeepers, and the return
of all refugees. About 170,000 Serbs have since fled
the province. Kosovo's political status remains unresolved.

• **Kraft durch Freude** ► (KdF; German, Strength
through Joy) A popular Nazi scheme for cheap package holidays, which allowed thousands of working
Germans to visit remote areas of the country, or
take leisure cruises abroad, during the 1930s. The
scheme, based on the Italian Fascist organization
Dopo Lavoro, was initially financed from confiscated trade-union funds but later became big business, generating considerable income for the Nazis.
KdF also organized sporting and other leisure activities, such as subsidized theatre visits and travelling cabaret shows. The scheme proved a valuable
Nazi propaganda vehicle.

• **K-rations** ► US army field rations. They were
originally developed for paratroopers but became
the standard ration for US frontline troops during
World War II. There were three separate meals,
which could be eaten either hot or cold, each in a
waterproofed cardboard box: breakfast consisted
of a fruit bar, Nescafé, sugar, crackers, and a small
tin of ham and eggs; dinner and supper each comprised one can of cheese or potted meat, crackers,
orange or lemon powder, sugar, chocolate, and
chewing gum. *See also*: D-ration.

• **kraut** ► Slang for a German. It originated in
America and is now more widely used than the earlier Jerry from World War I. Kraut is a shortened
form of Sauerkraut, a German dish of pickled cabbage.

• **Kray twins** ▶ *See*: People's Villain.

• **Kremlinology** ▶ During the Cold War, the science of monitoring Soviet newspapers, TV, official photographs, etc., in an attempt to divine the internal workings of the Soviet political system. Kremlinology was practised by academics, journalists, and Western government analysts, who became adept at reading between the lines of official communiqués.

• **Kretschmer's types** ▶ Types of physique, which the German psychiatrist Ernst Kretschmer (1888–1964) believed could be correlated with certain mental disorders. In his work *Physique and Character* (1921), Kretschmer advanced the psychological theory that schizophrenia was more prevalent in tall and thin (asthenic) body types and that manic-depression is commoner in rotund (pyknic) builds. This association of body type with temperament goes back to the ancients although no convincing evidence of such a relationship has ever been confirmed.

• **Kreuger crash** ▶ The bankruptcy in 1932 of the multinational corporation created by Ivar Kreuger (1880–1932), the Swedish 'match king'. During World War I Kreuger concentrated the Swedish match industry under his control; after the war he embarked on a campaign to monopolize world match production. Backed by US investors, he made long-term loans to countries experiencing short-term balance of payments deficits in return for monopoly rights. With the onset of the Great Depression Kreuger's financial position collapsed, exposing the spurious nature of much of his empire's supposed wealth. He shot himself.

• **Krishna consciousness** ▶ *See*: Hare Krishna.

• **Krishnamurti** ▶ (1895–1986) Hindu mystic who attracted a huge following in the 1920s when he prophesied the Second Coming. In anticipation of the event, a massive amphitheatre was erected near Sydney Harbour, Australia, from which Jiddu Krishnamurti predicted that the waiting crowd of 2000 would see the Messiah approaching across the Pacific Ocean. That he had failed to do so by 1929 led to a decline in enthusiasm for Krishnamurti and his cult, the Order of the Star of the East (founded in 1911); the amphitheatre was subsequently demolished for housing. Krishnamurti himself, having been acknowledged as an incarnation of the messianic Buddha by the Theosophical Society, finally agreed that he was no such thing. He died in California, home of the Krishnamurti Foundation.

• **Kriss Kringle** ▶ A US name for Santa Claus derived from the German *Christkindl* (little Christ child).

• **Kristallnacht** ▶ (German, night of glass) The night of 9–10 November 1938 during which German mobs, led by the Nazi Brown Shirts, roamed the streets of towns and cities all over Germany and Austria smashing the windows of shops and houses belonging to Jews (hence the name). The looting of Jewish property and the torching of synagogues was for many German and Austrian Jews the last straw in the humiliating persecution they had suffered at the hands of Hitler, his Nazi party, and the many ordinary Germans and Austrians who supported him. Those Jews who were able to, fled to the UK, America, Australia, and anywhere else that would accept them. Amongst this exodus were many of the European Jewish physicists who later became the key figures in the creation of the atom bomb.

• **Kroger affair** ▶ The case of the Soviet spies Morris and Lona Cohen, alias Peter and Helen Kroger, who were both sentenced at the Old Bailey, London, on 18 March 1961 to 20 years' imprisonment for their involvement in the Portland Secrets Case (*see*: Lonsdale affair). The Cohens, owners of a bookshop in the Strand, were associates of Gordon Lonsdale (Konon Molody Trofimovich), the Soviet mole who had been receiving documents from Harry Houghton, a clerk at the top-secret Admiralty Underwater Weapons Establishment at Portland in Dorset. Special Branch officers discovered a radio transmitter in the Cohens' bungalow in the west London suburb of Ruislip, for communicating with Moscow; they also found miniature cameras, a microdot reader, false passports, and large sums of cash. It transpired that they had been part of a Soviet spy network in America since the 1940s, had left America in 1951 using false Canadian passports, and had finally settled in the UK after travelling to Australia and Switzerland. Hugh Whitemore speculated upon the impact of the Krogers on their unsuspecting British friends in his play *A Pack of Lies* (1983).

• **Kronstadt mutiny** ▶ A revolt against Bolshevik rule by sailors at the Soviet naval base at Kronstadt, on the Gulf of Finland, in March 1921. The economic privations of the Civil War, including inadequate food distribution and harsh labour regulations, provoked widespread discontent with the Bolshevik regime, which was manifested in a series of strikes by urban workers. The Kronstadt sailors established a Provisional Revolutionary Committee in support of the strikers and demanded an end to the Communist Party dictatorship, full power to the Soviets (local councils), the release of non-Bolshevik prisoners, and greater political freedoms. Although the mutiny was crushed by Trotsky and Marshal Mikhail Tukachevsky, it prompted Lenin to implement the milder New Economic Policy soon afterwards.

• **Krueger, Freddy** ► The sinister killer who stalks his victims' dreams in the horror film *A Nightmare on Elm Street* (1984), directed by Wes Craven (1949– ), and its sequels. As played by Robert Englund, Krueger quickly became one of the most recognizable figures in modern cinema; his scarred face, dirty hat, and trademark gloves with knives for fingers have terrified a generation.

In the original film, it emerges that the demonic figure scaring teenagers to death in their dreams is Fred Krueger, a child murderer who was burnt alive by vigilante parents. There were five sequels but of these only the last, *Wes Craven's New Nightmare* (1994), comes close to matching the originality of the first film. Nevertheless, as the series progressed, Englund's Krueger came increasingly to the fore, eventually claiming an enduring place in public awareness. Interestingly, the Krueger character bears a striking resemblance to Streuwelpeter, a figure from German folklore with twigs for fingers.

• **krugerrand** ► A South African gold coin introduced in 1967 and containing 1 troy ounce of gold. The coin was never intended as a currency unit but was designed as a way of enabling investors to hold gold in those countries in which there were restrictions on private hoarding. In the UK, an import licence has been necessary for krugerrands since 1975. The name comes from the standard South African monetary unit, the rand (from the gold-mining area at Witwatersrand), with the name of the Afrikaner statesman Paul Kruger (1825–1904). Krugerrands lost popularity as an investment in the late 1980s, partly for political reasons and partly because of competition from other coins, such as the **Britannia** and the **Eagle**. The Britannia, a range of four British gold coins, was introduced in 1987. They are sold in £10, £25, £50, and £100 denominations. The Eagle is a range of four US gold coins, introduced in 1986, sold in $5, $10, $25, and $50 denominations.

• **K2** ► The world's highest mountain peak (28,251 ft; 8611 m) after Everest, situated in the Karakoram Range in the Himalayas. It was discovered and measured in 1856 by Colonel T. G. Montgomery of the Survey of India and designated K2 because it was the second of the Karakoram peaks to be measured. The first successful ascent to the summit was

achieved on 31 July 1954 by two members of an Italian expedition, Achille Compagnoni and Lino Lacedelli. The peak has claimed the lives of many leading climbers.

• **Ku Klux Klan** ► (KKK) A US secret society founded at Pulaski, Tennessee, in 1866 as a social club for ex-Confederate soldiers; its fanciful ritual included the wearing of hooded white robes. The name is a corruption of the Greek *kuklos*, a circle. The Klan soon developed into a society to overawe the newly emancipated Blacks; similar societies, such as the Knights of the White Camelia, the White League, the Pale Faces, and the Invisible Circle sprang up in 1867–68. Its terrorist activities led to laws against it in 1870 and 1871. Although it had been disbanded by its leader, the Grand Wizard in 1869, local activities continued for some time.

In 1915 a new organization, The Invisible Empire, Knights of the Ku Klux Klan, was founded by the Revd William Simmonds, preacher, near Atlanta, Georgia. He adopted much of the ritual of the original, adding further puerile ceremonies, titles, nomenclature, etc., of his own. Klansmen held 'Klonvocations' and their local 'Klaverns' were ruled by an 'Exalted Cyclops', a 'Klaliff', etc. As well as anti-Black it was anti-Catholic, anti-Jewish, and xenophobic. Advocating Protestant supremacy for the native-born Whites, it grew rapidly from 1920 and gained considerable political influence in the Southern states by unsavoury methods. By 1930 it had shrunk again to small proportions but a revival began before World War II and the Klan became noted for its fascist sympathies. In 1944 it was again disbanded but continued locally; in 1965 a Congressional Committee was set up to investigate Klan activities following a resurgence of violence against Blacks and Civil Rights activists.

• **kulak** ► (Russian, fist) A prosperous Russian peasant who owned land and livestock and was capable of employing labour and leasing land. Kulaks were key figures in the traditional economic, social, and administrative structure of prerevolutionary Russian agriculture. Under Lenin, the position of the kulaks was gradually undermined although their economic and political value was exploited to maintain agricultural production along quasi-capitalist lines. However, the policy of rapid agricultural collectivization pursued by Stalin after 1929 aimed at the destruction of the kulaks as a class; by 1934 most of them had been deported to remote areas of the country, arrested or executed, and their property confiscated.

• **Kuomintang** ► *See*: Guomindang.

• **kuru** ► A fatal degenerative disease of the central

nervous system whose symptoms include tremors, excitability, loss of muscular coordination and speech, and ultimately paralysis. It is caused by the same type of agent that causes CJD, scrapie in sheep, and bovine spongiform encephalopathy (BSE) in cattle (*see:* mad cow disease). Identified in the 20th century, the disease occurs only among small groups of tribesmen in parts of New Guinea (*kuru* is a native name meaning trembling or shivering) and is probably transmitted by the practice of ritual cannibalism, which involves consuming the brains of dead relatives. As this practice has waned, outbreaks of kuru have rapidly declined.

• **Kut, Siege of ▶** The siege of a unit of the British army under Major General Charles V. F. Townshend in Kut-el-Amara at the confluence of the Tigris and Shatt-el-Hai rivers by the Turks in World War I, from 7 December 1915 to 29 April 1916. Townshend had been advancing up the Tigris towards Baghdad until the Turks inflicted heavy losses on his forces at the Battle of Ctesiphon (7–8 September); he withdrew his exhausted infantry to Kut (2 December), where he waited in vain for British reinforcements. On 29 April starvation forced the surrender of his 2070 British and 6000 Indian troops, most of whom died in captivity.

• **KVD ▶** Soviet Committee for Internal Affairs, the successor to the MVD (Ministry of Internal Affairs) in 1960.

• **kvetch ▶** US slang meaning to whine or complain, from a Yiddish word meaning to press. A person who habitually whines or complains is also called a kvetch.

# L

• **LA** ▶ Los Angeles. A city in SW California on the edge of the Mojave Desert. Originally founded by Spanish settlers in 1781 as El Pueblo de Nuestra Señora la Reina de los Angeles (Town of Our Lady the Queen of the Angels), LA is now America's third largest city, a vast 2082-square-mile urban sprawl consisting of largely indistinguishable suburbs held together by a tangle of convoluted freeways. Its three million citizens are plagued by chronic air and water pollution, traffic snarl-ups, and ethnic gang warfare; however, it is one of the world's most exciting cities – home to the faded grandeur of Hollywood, the affluence of Beverly Hills and Rodeo Drive, the Disneyland amusement park, and the even more exotic playground of Venice Beach.

• **lab** ▶ See: nab.

• **labour exchange** ▶ See: job centre.

• **Labour Party** ▶ One of the major political parties of the UK, which was formed with the aim of promoting socialism. So called from 1906, it was created as the Labour Representation Committee in 1900 from such elements as the Independent Labour Party, the trade unions, and the Fabian Society. The first Labour government was formed by Ramsay MacDonald in 1924; the second lasted from 1929 to 1931, when the party split over cuts in unemployment benefit (see: National Governments). Labour was not returned to power again until 1945, when Clement Attlee, somewhat surprisingly, won a landslide victory over the Conservatives led by the war hero Winston Churchill. Attlee's government, which is remembered chiefly for its creation of the welfare state, was defeated at the polls in October 1951, leading to another long period of Conservative rule. Labour was again in office from 1964 to 1970 under Harold Wilson and from 1974 to 1979 under Wilson and then James Callaghan. However, the Thatcherite 1980s found Labour confined to Opposition and riven by internal conflicts. Michael Foot failed to heal party divisions as leader (1980–83) and was replaced by Neil Kinnock, who began the process of making the party acceptable to the middle classes. This transformation continued under the leadership of John Smith (1992–94) and

was completed successfully under Tony Blair, enabling the so-called New Labour Party to win general elections in 1997 and 2001.

• **Lad, the** ▶ Nickname of the British comedian Tony Hancock (1924–68), who became a leading star during the 1950s in the radio programme *Hancock's Half Hour* (subsequently televised). As the lugubrious and ever-complaining tenant of 23 Railway Cuttings, East Cheam, 'the Lad' became a cult comedian with a huge following. Hancock once explained his comic persona: 'You take your own weaknesses and exploit them.'

His own weaknesses included irascibility towards his fellow-performers, who all eventually left the show, and to his long-suffering scriptwriters; they also included an increasing reliance upon alcohol – in his last television shows he was obliged to have his lines written on slips of paper around the set. In 1968, on a tour of Australia, he committed suicide in a Sydney hotel room, the quintessential example of the comic with an insupportable personal life.

• **Ladakh crisis** ▶ The surprise Chinese invasion of the remote Ladakh region of E Kashmir in N India in October 1962, signalling a dangerous flare-up in the long-running Sino-Indian border conflict. Possession of the region, as with many other areas along the 2640-mile McMahon Line (drawn up by Sir Henry McMahon in 1914 and never ratified by China), had been disputed by the two nations throughout the 1950s. On 20 October 1962 the Chinese inflicted a humiliating defeat upon the Indian Army, advancing effortlessly over the McMahon Line through the NE frontier, capturing the administrative centre of Bomdila, and threatening to sweep down the Assam Valley. On 21 November the Chinese declared a ceasefire and withdrew again, ending the crisis as suddenly as it had begun, although they retained 2500 square miles of Indian territory.

• **Ladbroke Grove train disaster** ▶ A railway accident that occurred on 5 October 1999 when a Thames train went through a red light and collided with a Great Western train at Ladbroke Grove, just outside the terminus at Paddington Station in W London. The collision resulted in the deaths of 31 people; 244 others were injured, some very severely.

Public outrage was exacerbated by the fact that there had been another high-speed collision near Paddington only four years earlier. It was also revealed that between 1993 and the 1999 crash there had been eight other incidents in which the signal in question had been passed on red; one such incident in 1998 provoked a Railtrack engineer to suggest that certain parts of the track should be one-way only – a suggestion that was ignored. In 2001 the official report on the Ladbroke Grove disaster accused Railtrack of a 'dangerously complacent attitude' and 'institutional paralysis' in its failure to respond to these warnings.

• **laddish** ▶ British term describing the behaviour of macho young males who drink absurd quantities of lager, argue interminably about football trivia, and brag about real or imagined sexual conquests. Dating from the late 1970s and associated with the concept of being **one of the lads**, the word became more widely used in the mid-1990s, when the so-called **New Lad** evolved in deliberate opposition to the New Man. Self-conscious semi-ironic **laddishness** (or **laddism**) enjoyed a considerable vogue with such varied phenomena as *Loaded* magazine (the 'lad's bible') and the sitcom *Men Behaving Badly* focusing attention on these particular features of male oafishness and ineptitude. A female who admires and apes laddishness is sometimes called a **ladette**.

> Laddish fathers may encourage the yob culture that makes even bright boys act dumb at school, an academic study suggests. – *The Times*, 27 October 2000.

• **Lady Bird** ▶ The nickname of Claudia Johnson (1912– ), wife of Lyndon Baines Johnson, 36th US president (*see*: LBJ). The nickname was given to her as an infant by her nurse and taken up by family and friends and by Claudia herself.

• **Lady Chatterley trial** ▶ The famous test case in which Penguin Books were prosecuted under the Obscene Publications Act (1959) for publishing D. H. Lawrence's last novel, *Lady Chatterley's Lover*, in an unexpurgated edition. The book was published in Italy in a limited edition in 1928, but because of Lawrence's explicit description of sexual scenes and his use of four-letter words, it had never been published in the UK and America, other than in an expurgated version. At the six-day hearing, which opened at the Old Bailey on 20 October 1960 before Mr Justice Bryne, 36 defence witnesses – including the Bishop of Woolwich, E. M. Forster, Dame Rebecca West, and Richard Hoggart – provided evidence of the book's literary and artistic merits (a further 35 defence witnesses were not called). It was the first time that expert opinion of this kind had been admitted as defence against an obscenity charge in a British court. For the prosecution, Mr Mervyn Griffith-Jones took a somewhat paternalistic view, asking, 'Is it a book you would wish your wife or your servant to read?' The jury's reply was an unanimous verdict of not guilty; the entire first impression (200,000 copies) sold out on the day of publication (10 November) and the book has since sold millions of copies. The Lady Chatterley trial proved to be a watershed in British cultural life, since it established that publication of even the most explicit material could be legal if this was judged to be in the public good.

> More to the point, would you allow your gamekeeper to read it? – Anonymous reaction to MERVYN GRIFFITH-JONES's question.

• **Lady Day** ▶ The nickname of the US jazz singer Billie Holiday (1915–59). Her individual phrasing and the emotional intensity of her singing gained her a reputation as perhaps the greatest of all female jazz vocalists and the title **First Lady of the Blues**. The nickname 'Lady Day' was given to her by the soloist Lester Young, who accompanied her on many recording sessions; it reflects the poise and dignity she possessed even in her later years when beset by drug problems.

• **Lady Macbeth strategy** ▶ Business jargon for a strategy sometimes adopted by one company in relation to another company, which is facing a hostile takeover bid from a rival. A company pursuing the Lady Macbeth strategy appears to act as a white knight in support of the other firm in combatting the hostile takeover bid, then subsequently joins the aggressor.

• **Lady Macbeth syndrome** ▶ *See*: bacteriophobia.

• **Lafayette, we are here** ▶ The words commonly attributed to US General John Pershing on his arrival in France in World War I. In fact they were said by US Colonel Charles E. Stanton (1859–1933) at the grave of the Marquis de Lafayette in Picpus cemetery, Paris, on 4 July 1917, shortly after the American Expeditionary Force landed on French soil. Lafayette (1757–1834), an honorary American citizen, had been a friend of George Washington and fought on the site of the colonists against the British in the American War of Independence.

> Here and now, in the presence of the illustrious dead, we pledge our hearts and our honour in

carrying this war to a successful issue. Lafayette, we are here.

• **lager louts** ▸ Young hooligans who create disturbances, damage property, and commit violent assaults after drinking too much lager. The term first appeared in 1988 and is often associated with football hooliganism and the yob culture.

• **Lagonda** ▸ One of the most famous marques in British motoring history, founded in 1904 by an American, Wilbur Gunn. The son of an engineer from Springfield, Ohio, Gunn came to the UK in 1897 to pursue an operatic career. Frustrated in this, he began making motorcycles in the greenhouse of his Staines home, naming them Lagonda – the Shawnee Indian for Bucks Creek, near his Ohio birthplace. The original two-wheelers were followed by a three-wheeled tricar, and in 1907 by the first four-wheeled Lagonda, a 20 hp four-cylinder model known as the 14/16. A 30 hp six-cylinder car came soon afterwards. In the 1920s the firm gave up its attempts to compete in the small-car mass-production market and turned to sports cars, launching the 2-litre 14/60 and 2.4-litre 16/65, which later became the Lagonda 3 litre. Another 3-litre model, the 16/80, was introduced in 1932, powered by a six-cylinder Crossley engine.

Lagonda managed to weather the economic slump of the 1930s but drastically slimmed its model range, leaving the 4-litre M45 as its mainstay. Launched in 1933, the M45 won the Le Mans race two years later. The late 1930s saw the unveiling of several new Lagondas designed by one of the most illustrious names in motoring, W. O. Bentley. These included the LG45, the Rapide coupe, and the V12. Immediately after World War II the company was bought by David Brown and became part of Aston Martin. The Lagonda name lived on for a time in the Bentley-designed 2.5-litre Mark I, and in a new 3-litre model introduced in 1953. Production of Lagondas was discontinued in 1958, although the Lagonda badge sporadically reappeared on certain Aston Martin models after this.

• **La Guardia** ▸ The airport for domestic flights in and out of New York City, named after Fiorello Henry La Guardia (1882–1947), US congressman and three times mayor of New York (1933–45), who had successfully campaigned for the airport's construction. La Guardia, nicknamed **Little Flower** (a literal translation of his first name), was an energetic and colourful figure. A former translator for immigrants passing through Ellis Island, he became a mayor who opposed civic corruption and organized crime, promoted social welfare policies and public works, and is remembered as the most honest and best loved incumbent of New York's City Hall. As a politician he was a habitual dissenter, supporting such issues as women's suffrage, legal aid, and the rights of trade unions.

• **laid back** ▸ Relaxed, unhurried, easygoing. The term arose in 1930s jazz parlance, when it meant a style of playing behind the main beat. It became part of the general language in the early 1970s, when it was often applied to the lifestyle and value of the hippies.

• **Laingian** ▸ Pertaining to the theories of the British psychiatrist R. D. Laing (1927–89) on the nature and origins of schizophrenia and psychotic behaviour. In his works *The Divided Self* (1960), *The Self and Others* (1961), *Sanity, Madness and the Family* (1965), and *The Politics of Experience* (1971) Laing suggested that mental illness may be a legitimate, even therapeutic, way of escaping from the alienating and constricting pressures to conform to which people are subjected in society, institutions, and even the family. As president of the Philadelphia Association (1964–82), he pursued the practical application of his radical 'anti-psychiatry', providing patients with social contexts within which they could live. Laing's explanations of psychosis remain controversial; perhaps his greatest legacy has been the stimulation of open debate, since the 1960s, on the causes and treatment of mental illness.

> Schizophrenic behaviour is a special strategy that a person invents in order to live in an unlivable situation. – *The Politics of Experience.*

• **lair** or **lare** ▸ Australian slang for a disreputable youth, a ne'er do well. Before World War II it was used to mean an overdressed young man. Although this sense is now rarely heard, the adjective **lairy** is still used in Australia and the UK to describe someone who is flashily or vulgarly dressed.

• **Lake Success** ▸ A village on Long Island in SE New York State, headquarters of the United Nations Security Council from 1946 to 1951. After the charter of the UN was signed at the San Francisco Conference in 1945 there was frenzied lobbying both by European capitals and US cities, all of which hoped to be chosen as the permanent home of the organization. New York was eventually accorded the honour, thanks mainly to John D. Rockefeller's donation of $8.5 million to purchase a site (Turtle Bay) on the East River for the new permanent headquarters. The headquarters building was not completed until 1952, and the UN held its first meeting in London early in 1946. It then occupied various temporary locations in New York, including the Waldorf Astoria Hotel, Hunter College in the Bronx, a disused skating rink at Flushing Meadow Park in

Queens, and the Sperry Gyroscope Company Building at Lake Success.

• **Lake Wobegon effect** ▶ An effect in which the standard of something or someone with which or with whom one is connected is grossly overestimated. The phrase refers to *Lake Wobegon Days* (1985), a book by the US humorist Garrison Keillor (1942–   ). The stories in the book are set in the imaginary town of Wobegon, where all the inhabitants are exceptional:

> ...the women are strong, the men good looking and all the children above average.

• **Lalique glass** ▶ A type of Art Nouveau glass designed and manufactured by the French jeweller and interior designer, René Lalique (1860–1945). Lalique was trained in London and Paris, and in his early career specialized in jewellery, textiles, and fans. His company sold designs to Cartier, made costume jewellery for the French actress, Sarah Bernhardt, and achieved some success with Art Nouveau brooches and combs at the Paris exhibition of 1900. After establishing a glass factory in 1910, Lalique mass-produced a wide range of moulded glassware, such as vases, statuettes, scent bottles, and desk accessories. These featured iced surfaces and pale opalescent hues, with elaborate relief patterns based on plant, animal, and sensuous female motifs.

• **La Lollo** ▶ Gina Lollobrigida (1927–   ), Italian actress whose ample curves featured in a series of international films from 1947. Her roles included a variety of temptresses – a trapeze artiste in *Trapeze* (1956), a glamour girl in an Italian village in *Buona Sera, Mrs Campbell* (1968), and a Munich bookseller's wife in *King, Queen, Knave* (1972).

• **lambada** ▶ A late 1980s dance craze, in which a couple embrace tightly and gyrate their hips in a lubricious manner. It is thought to have originated among sailors and prostitutes in the shanty towns of Rio de Janeiro and was long considered unfit for respectable women. The music that accompanies this performance, also called lambada, is an infectious mixture of Latin American and Caribbean styles. In the 1980s it was taken up by North African musicians in Paris, and this modified form of lambada swept through European nightclubs in the summer of 1989. The name derives from a Portuguese word meaning the crack of a whip.

• **Lambaréné** ▶ A village on an island in the Ogooué River in W Gabon, the site of the hospital built in 1913 by the German medical missionary, theologian, and musician Albert Schweitzer (1875–1965). Schweitzer was imprisoned by the French during World War I, but returned to Lambaréné in 1924, rebuilt the hospital, and founded a leper colony nearby. By 1963 the hospital had 350 patients; the leper colony treated a further 150 people. The entire complex was staffed by 35 White doctors and nurses as well as African ancillary workers. Schweitzer, called the **Saint of Lambaréné** by his admirers, died and was buried there in 1965. His writings on Bach and recordings of his recitals of Bach organ music are still highly regarded. This remarkable multitalented man was awarded the Nobel Peace Prize in 1952.

• **Lambeth Walk** ▶ A thoroughfare in Lambeth, S London, leading from Black Prince Road to the Lambeth Road. It gave its name to an immensely popular Cockney dance featured by Lupino Lane (from 1937) in the musical show *Me And My Gal* at the Victoria Palace. Purporting to imitate the strutting walk of the typical Lambeth Cockney, it came to symbolize the spirit of defiance of Londoners during the Blitz in World War II.

> Any time you're Lambeth Way
> Any evening, any day,
> You'll find us all,
> Doing the Lambeth Walk, Oi!

• **Lambretta** ▶ A motor scooter manufactured by Innocenti from the 1950s at its factory in the Lambrate district of Milan. Together with the equally well-known **Vespa** motor scooter of the same period, it provided a more genteel alternative to the motorcycle, affording greater protection from the weather and enabling the rider to dispense with the more-or-less obligatory leathers and goggles of the motorcyclist. Most models were equipped with a 125 cc two-stroke engine, providing a stately average speed of about 45 mph; there were a few larger-engined versions.

• **lame brain** ▶ Slang for a slow-witted or stupid person. Having originated in America in the 1960s, it was heard in both the UK and Australia from the 1970s.

• **lamps** ▶
**The lamps are going out all over Europe** The melancholy observation made by the British statesman Sir Edward Grey (1862–1933) just before the outbreak of World War I. His further remark 'we shall not see them lit again in our lifetime' was, arguably, a little too apocalyptic. *See also*: Belle Époque.

• **Lampton, Joe** ▶ The ruthless self-seeking antihero of John Braine's novels *Room at the Top* (1957) and *Life at the Top* (1962). From a working-class home in a small Yorkshire town, Lampton achieves his ends by discarding his long-standing but impecunious mistress, Alice Aisgill, in order to marry Susan Brown, the daughter of a wealthy man. Both books were made into films, in which Laurence Harvey took the part of Lampton: *Room at the Top* (1958; directed by Jack Clayton), *Life at the Top* (1965; directed by Ted Kotcheff). There followed a British television series entitled *Man at the Top* (1971–73) and a film of the same name (1973; directed by Mike Vardy) with Kenneth Haigh in the title role.

Braine conceived the character of Lampton after seeing the body of a baby removed from a house in Bradford into which a German bomber had crashed and wondering how the baby's life might have turned out. Years later the incident was recognized by Gareth Boyd, a public relations officer with a bus company, who it transpired had been that baby, having miraculously survived the destruction of his parents' home.

• **LAN** ▶ Local area network. A group of computer terminals situated within a reasonably restricted area, such as the same office building, and linked both to each other and to such central facilities as a laser printer.

• **Lancaster bomber** ▶ A British heavy long-range bomber that proved one of the most successful aircraft of World War II. The Avro 683 Lancaster, designed and built by A. V. Roe Ltd, was a four-engined bomber, which carried a heavier load of bigger bombs than any other aircraft in the European theatre of operations. It first went into service in April 1942 and eventually flew 156,000 sorties, dropping 608,612 tons of bombs. RAF 617 Squadron used Lancasters which had been specially modified to carry and release Barnes Wallis's 'bouncing bombs' used in the famous Dambusters raid against Germany in 1943.

• **land art** ▶ *See*: earth art.

• **Land camera** ▶ *See*: Polaroid.

• **land girls** ▶ Women recruited for farm work during the two World Wars to replace the men who were serving in the forces. In World War II they were organized as a Women's Land Army.

• **Land of Hope and Glory** ▶ A patriotic song about the UK, conceived in the heyday of imperialism; it sets words by A. C. Benson to a rousing melody by Elgar. First performed by Dame Clara Butt in 1902, it was widely used at Empire Day celebrations and other occasions. The tune was taken from the first of the *Pomp and Circumstance* marches (1901). The words were originally used in Benson's *Coronation Ode* of 1902.

> Land of Hope and Glory, Mother of the Free,
> How shall we extol thee, who are born of thee?

> Wider still and wider shall thy bounds be set;
> God who made thee mighty, make thee mightier yet.

'Land of Hope and Glory' is traditionally sung by the whole audience at the last night of the Proms (*see*: prom) in the Albert Hall. This annual outburst of jingoism is taken seriously by some but as a joke or parody by others; for most, the waving of Union Jacks, lusty singing, and high spirits amount to no more than youthful enthusiasm for a good tune stirringly orchestrated. In 1990, the conductor, Mark Elder, declared his intention of omitting 'Land of Hope and Glory' from the programme, because he thought jingoism was inappropriate with the Gulf War imminent. The prospect of breaking with tradition in this way led to such an uproar that the BBC decided to replace Elder with Andrew Davis, who conducted the song with the customary panache. In 2001 the last night of the Proms followed shortly after the shocking events of September 11; this time, the decision to replace 'Land of Hope and Glory' with more sombre and reflective music aroused little opposition.

• **landsailing** ▶ The sport of racing **land yachts**, wheeled vehicles equipped with sails. Landsailing mostly takes place on sandy beaches.

• **Landsat** ▶ A type of US orbital satellite used to obtain data about the Earth's resources. Originally called **ERTS** (Earth Resources Technology Satellite), it was introduced in 1968 and renamed Landsat (land satellite) in 1975. Landsats make cheap and accurate surveys of forestry, crop production, potential mineral resources, and fishing grounds.

• **language laboratory** ▶ A room equipped with tape recorders and other audiovisual computer-controlled apparatus for learning a foreign-language by listening and speaking. This method of providing foreign language instruction first came into use in colleges and schools in the 1960s. It enables students to progress at a rate appropriate to their ability and makes efficient use of teaching resources.

• **La Niña** ▶ *See*: El Niño.

• **Lansdowne letter** ▶ A letter sent by the Irish peer Henry Charles Petty-Fitzmaurice (1845–1927), fifth Marquess of Lansdowne, to the *Daily Telegraph* on 29 November 1917. The letter outlined Lansdowne's views on the desirability of a compromise peace with Germany, which would include offering various guarantees to Germany regarding its continuance as a political, territorial, and commercial power. Despite evidence that these views were shared by many MPs and even some members of the coalition government, the letter was violently repudiated by the government and the press as an act of disloyalty suggesting a weakening of Allied resolve to defeat Germany. As a result Lansdowne was expelled from the Tory party.

• **Lao Dong** ▶ The Vietnam Workers' Party, created by Ho Chi Minh in May 1951 to replace the Communist Party. The newly created Lao Dong absorbed the Lien Viet (National United Front), a nationalist and communist coalition, and became the ruling party of the Democratic Republic of Vietnam, which had been established in Hanoi on 2 September 1945 by Ho Chi Minh.

• **lap dancing** ▶ A striptease or erotic dance routine in which a customer pays for the dancer to perform in close proximity and at their personal invitation. Typically the dancer attends the punter's table, hence the more proper term **table dancing**. Although the performer may be pursuing his or her 'art' virtually in the lap of the punter, laws licensing such clubs often forbid physical contact. Lap dancing originated in the early 1980s in the USA, where it is now a massive industry. The UK's first table dancing venue was the Cabaret of Angels, opened in London by clubowner Peter Stringfellow in 1996; similar establishments are now common throughout the country. Britain's first gay lapdancing club opened in London in 1999. A renewed mainstream interest in erotica has created a healthy market for table dancing, and helped many such clubs to escape the traditional seedy image of the strip joint.

• **laptop** ▶ A small portable computer, usually weighing between 3 and 8lbs (1½–4 kg) and carried in a briefcase. It first appeared in 1984 and is used mostly for word processing in trains, hotels, etc.

• **Lari massacre** ▶ The slaughter of 90 people, mostly Africans, by Mau Mau terrorists at Lari in Kenya on the night of the 24 March 1953. A British-appointed Kikuyu chief and his family had relinquished land designated as 'White' in return for land at Lari, NW of Nairobi; as a result, the displaced and disgruntled Lari cultivators had joined the Mau Mau. On the night in question the Mau Mau imprisoned the Kikuyu intruders in their huts and burned them alive – those who tried to escape were hacked to pieces with machetes. Most of the men were absent, so those who died were almost exclusively women and children. The barbarity of the attack convinced the British authorities of the need to crush the Mau Mau with maximum force, an objective largely achieved in the two years following the massacre.

• **Lark Rise to Candleford** ▶ An autobiographical trilogy (1945) by Flora Thompson (1876–1947) containing a detailed evocation of her rural childhood through the experiences of the character Laura. The work was originally published as *Lark Rise* (1939), *Over to Candleford* (1941), and *Candleford Green* (1943); it is an unsentimental portrait of a lost age of agricultural customs and rural culture.

• **Larrys** ▶ Informal name for the Laurence Olivier Awards presented by the Society of London Theatre, in imitation of the Oscars awarded in the cinema. 'Larry' was the nickname of the British actor-director Laurence Olivier (1907–89), used both by those who knew him well and – with stagey familiarity – by others who aspired to be on first-name terms with one of the finest British actors. In 1947 he was knighted and in 1970 he became the first actor to be made a life peer, largely for his work as director (1961–73) of the National Theatre company. The Olivier Theatre, part of the National Theatre, was named in his honour.

• **Lascaux caves** ▶ A cave system near Montignac in the Dordogne, SW France, containing some of the most remarkable examples of prehistoric art ever found. The caves were discovered in 1940 by a group of boys after their dog disappeared through a hole, which turned out to be a hidden entrance to the grotto. The main cavern and a series of steep galleries off it contain vivid yellow, brown, red, and black paintings of various animals, including aurochs, red deer, oxen, horses, and stags' heads, which have been dated to the Upper Palaeolithic period (c. 18,000 BC). The dry atmosphere within the caves, together with a coating of calcite laid down over the centuries (which acted as a coat of varnish), had left the artwork in a remarkable state of preservation. However, when the caves were open to the public the humidity from tourists' breath and perspiration caused the paintings to deteriorate rapidly; since 1963 the caves have been closed to the public.

• **laser** ▶ A device for producing an intense narrow beam of light (or infrared, ultraviolet, or other radiation). The first laser was made by the US physicist Theodore Maiman (1927–   ) in 1960. He used a rod of ruby with partially reflective surfaces at each end. In a ruby laser, intense pulses of light are applied from surrounding sources and these excite atoms within the material. These excited atoms decay with emission of light at a particular wavelength. The light is reflected backwards and forwards through the material and stimulates further emission. The result is a narrow beam of light with a single wavelength (monochromatic), with all the light waves in phase (coherent). The name was originally an acronym: 'light amplification by stimulated emission of radiation'. Maiman's idea came from an earlier device, the **maser** (microwave amplification by stimulated emission of radiation), which had been invented in 1955 by the US physicist Charles Townes (1915–   ) and, independently, by the Soviet physicists Nicolai Basov (1922–   ) and Aleksandr Prokhorov (1916–   ). The laser was originally called an 'optical maser'. Following Maiman's invention in 1960, a number of types of laser were developed using different materials and operating in different parts of the electromagnetic spectrum. Initially, the device was regarded as something of a scientific curiosity – 'a solution without a problem'. The possibility of applying laser technology to warfare meant that early research was highly secret, stimulating the popular image of the laser as *the* weapon of the future. Subsequently, a large and diverse number of applications were found: laser light shows, measuring and surveying devices, compact discs, computer printers (*see*: laser printer), laser surgery, and, as predicted, beam weapons (*see*: Star Wars).

• **laser bomb** ► A type of bomb guided by a laser beam. An aircraft locks a laser beam onto its target; sophisticated bombs dropped by that aircraft – or accompanying aircraft – then follow the beam. First used in the Vietnam War, they were highly effective during the Gulf War of 1991 in destroying specific targets while minimizing civilian casualties.

• **laser cane** ► A type of walking stick for the blind that emits infrared laser radiation. The radiation is reflected by surrounding obstacles and detected by sensors in the cane; the signal is converted into an audible tone, which warns the user of the obstacle.

• **laser printer** ► A type of printer used with computer systems. A laser beam is scanned across an electrically charged plate and discharges the plate in regions in which the image is required. Particles of pigment adhere to the discharged region; the process is similar to that in a photocopier. Laser printers can produce type similar to that of a typesetting machine and are extensively used in desktop publishing systems.

• **laser surgery** ► Surgical treatment using light from a laser. Since the late 1960s the advantages of using a laser beam, which can be focused precisely on a minute area of tissue, have revolutionized some areas of surgery. The main benefits have been in microsurgery and ophthalmic surgery, where lasers have been used to make delicate incisions, selectively destroy damaged or tumorous tissue, seal bleeding blood vessels, weld breaks in the retina, and remove thin slices of cornea (*i.e.* to treat myopia), leaving surrounding tissue uninjured.

• **Lassa fever** ► A contagious viral disease with a high mortality rate. It was first identified in 1969 in the Nigerian village of Lassa. Symptoms include a high fever, muscle aches, skin rash, mouth ulcers, haemorrhaging under the skin, and heart infection. The disease, thought to be transmitted to humans from mice and rats, occurs chiefly in rural areas of W Africa.

• **Lasseter's gold reef** ► A seam of gold, reputed to be enormously rich, in the deserts of central Australia, which has so far eluded all searches. The seam, promising untold wealth to anyone who could find it, was apparently discovered by a prospector called Harold Bell Lasseter in 1897. By 1911 he had raised sufficient funds for an expedition, but he and his companions were driven back by the harsh conditions. In 1930 he tried again. This time he refused to turn back, even when the heat had claimed all the members of his expedition except for two camels; his starved and dehydrated body was subsequently found in a cave. The search for his gold reef continues.

• **Lassie** ► The doughty collie-dog heroine of Eric Knight's *Lassie Come Home* (1940), a novel for children, who went on to feature in a whole series of canine adventure films made by MGM in the 1940s. *Lassie Come Home* (1943) was followed by *The Courage of Lassie* (1946), *Son of Lassie* (1945), and *The Sun Comes Up* (1949). The part of Lassie was actually played by a male dog called Pal; among his co-stars were Roddy McDowell, Elizabeth Taylor, and Jeanette MacDonald. Later adaptations included *Lassie*, a popular and long-running US television series; the animated series *Lassie's Rescue Rangers* (1973–75), and the television film *Lassie: The New Beginning* (1978). Lassie returned to the big screen in the musical *The Magic of Lassie* (1978).

• **last chance trendy** ► (LCT) A disparaging epithet applied to a person, particularly a middle-aged man, who attempts to conceal his age by dressing and behaving in a manner more appropriate to a younger person. The phrase was popular in the late 1970s and 1980s. The hallmark of a last chance trendy is usually taken to be hair carefully combed or styled to hide tell-tale bald patches.

• **last hurrah** ► A final farewell appearance, a 'swan song'. The expression derives from the US film *The Last Hurrah* (1958), in which a New England political leader (played by Spencer Tracy) undertakes the last campaign of his life.

• **last night of the Proms** ▶ *See*: Land of Hope and Glory; prom.

• **last of the big spenders** ▶ An ironic jibe used to denote someone who is careful with money, or even downright mean. It is said to have originated in Australia in the late 1950s.

• **Last of the Red Hot Mommas** ▶ The nickname of the vaudeville and cabaret singer Sophie Tucker (1884–1966), born somewhere in Russia while her parents were en route to America. Her nickname, derived from the song 'I'm the Last of the Red Hot Mommas' (written by Jack Yellen), so suited her brash, often risqué, image and vigorous singing style that it was used in her billing from 1928 for the rest of her career. She was also known as **Sophie Tuckshop**, an allusion to her ample proportions.

• **last words** ▶ *See*: famous last words.

• **Las Vegas** ▶ The principal city of the US state of Nevada, a neon oasis set in the parched wasteland of the Mojave Desert. Famous for its luxury hotels and casinos, which line the 'Strip', it offers 24-hour year-round gambling and cabaret entertainment, often featuring some of the world's greatest showbusiness stars. Las Vegas means 'the Meadows' in Spanish, a reference to the artesian wells discovered here by the first Spanish settlers. Such a description, however, is no longer appropriate to this modern incarnation of glitzy vulgarity. The city owes its commercial success to the legalization of gambling by the Nevada state authorities in 1931, although it remained a shabby settlement with a few drab gambling halls, quick-wedding chapels, and legalized brothels until the first luxury casino, the Flamingo, was built with mob money in 1946. Since then it has steadily climbed up-market.

• **latchkey kid** ▶ A young child whose parents are still at work when he or she returns home after school; the child must therefore carry the key of the house or flat. The problem of children remaining unattended and unsupervised at home began to be widely recognized in the 1960s as a serious side effect of the increasing numbers of working mothers and single-parent families.

• **La Tène** ▶ A curvilinear decorative style derived from Iron-Age Celtic art. Such designs on pottery and metalwork in gold, silver, and bronze were found in the La Tène archaeological site on Lake Neuchâtel, Switzerland, in excavations between 1907 and 1917. La Tène art, which included interlaced patterns related to the Greek geometric style and stylized oriental animals, also existed in the UK and Ireland. La Tène has given its name to the second phase of the Celtic Iron Age in Europe (mid-5th century BC to the Roman conquest).

• **lateral thinking** ▶ An expression coined by the British physician Edward de Bono (1933– ) in the mid-1960s to denote a way of solving problems by the use of unorthodox or even apparently illogical means rather than by direct logical processes. The concept is explained in de Bono's *The Use of Lateral Thinking* (1967).

• **Lateran Treaty** ▶ A treaty concluded between the Holy See and the Kingdom of Italy in 1929, establishing the Vatican City as a sovereign state. In the same treaty the papacy finally recognized the loss of its temporal power over the former papal states, which had been absorbed into the unified Italy in 1870. *See*: Vatican City State.

• **Laughing Murderer of Verdun** ▶ *See*: Little Willie.

• **launch window** ▶ A short period during which a spacecraft must be launched in order to accomplish its mission successfully. This is contingent on the astronomical conditions prevailing, in particular the relative position of the planets and their satellites, which enables the craft to travel on a path requiring the minimum input of energy. A suitable launch window for a flight from Earth to Venus occurs once every 19 months; one to Mars occurs once in 26 months.

• **Launderette** ▶ A self-service laundry (called a **Laundromat** in America) in which customers can wash and dry clothes and other items in coin-operated machines. Both versions are tradenames now loosely used for any such establishments. The social life of the launderette is a feature of many districts, especially the bed-sitter areas of London. Customers are obliged to wait for periods of up to half an hour while their laundry is being washed. Conversation with other customers is usually considered preferable to sitting in silence, watching one's clothes rotate, through the glass window of the washing machine.

• **laundering** ▶ A colloquial expression originating in America to denote the process of passing money, which has been illegally obtained, through foreign banks or legitimate commercial enterprises so that it reappears in circulation in a context that makes it appear to have originated legitimately. The word is now often used in the phrase **money laundering**.

• **Laurasia** ▶ *See*: Pangaea.

• **Laurel and Hardy** ▶ Hollywood's most successful comedy team, the thin British-born Stan

Laurel (Arthur Stanley Jefferson; 1890–1965) and the chubby Oliver Norvell Hardy (1892–1957). Stan and Ollie made 104 films between 1926 and 1951, receiving an Oscar for *The Music Box* (1932), in which they suffered multiple disasters carrying a piano up a long flight of steps. Their humour ranged from subtle interplay of character to simple mayhem: in *Battle of the Century*, a record 3000 pies were thrown. The chaos often ended with Hardy's exasperated complaint to Laurel, 'Here's another nice mess you've gotten us into' (*see at*: mess). The driving force of the team was Laurel, who was awarded a special Oscar in 1960 for pioneering cinema comedy. Their characters had universal appeal: fans ranged from Winston Churchill to Joseph Stalin while in Germany they were known as 'Dick and Doof' (fat and dumb). Their films underwent a cult revival in the 1970s and remain popular on video.

• **Lausanne Treaty** ► A peace settlement signed on 24 July 1923 between Greece and the newly proclaimed Republic of Turkey, renegotiating the 1920 Treaty of Sèvres, which had been imposed on the Turks by the Allied powers after World War I. In the Lausanne Treaty the Turks agreed to surrender the non-Turkish sections of the former Ottoman Empire; Greece returned Smyrna (Izmir) to Turkey, which also regained Thrace, Adrianople, and the Dodecanese; there was an enforced exchange of national minorities between Greece and Turkey; and the Bosporos and Dardanelles were demilitarized and opened to international shipping.

• **Lavalier** or **Lavaliere** ► A pendant worn on a chain around the neck, named after the Duchess of La Vallière, a mistress of Louis XIV who wore this type of jewellery. In the 1960s, the term was extended to mean a type of microphone hung round the neck of a broadcaster and, further, to a small microphone clipped to the broadcaster's clothing.

• **Lavender list** ► The controversial resignation honours list drawn up by the Labour prime minister Harold Wilson in 1976. Among those honoured were the financier James Goldsmith (knighted); Sir Joseph Kagan (life peerage), whose company made the Gannex raincoats that were Wilson's trademark; and such nonpolitical figures as the television impressionist Mike Yarwood (OBE), whose impersonations of Wilson were legendary. The final list had been amended and typed on lavender-coloured notepaper by Wilson's political secretary Marcia Williams (ennobled as Lady Falkender); apparently Wilson's original list had contained even more controversial figures.

• **Law Commission** ► A regulatory body, established in 1965 to monitor the law in England and Wales on a continual basis with a view to its systematic development and reform. The commission, which has a permanent staff headed by the chairman (a judge) and four commissioners (two academics, two lawyers), considers the need for the codification of law, the elimination of anomalies, the repeal of obsolete enactments, and the general simplification and modernization of the law. Issues can be referred to the commission by the government and it is also empowered to investigate any question that may need reform. It produces reports, often accompanied by draft legislation, for the government to introduce into parliament. There is a separate Scottish Law Commission.

• **Law of December 1** ► A decree issued in the Soviet Union on 1 December 1934 by order of Stalin after the murder of his aide, Sergei Kirov, by a deranged gunman (*see*: Kirov murder). The decree, unprecedented in peacetime, ordered that all investigators should speed up the preparation of cases against suspected terrorists (ten days was set as the maximum preparation period); that all pending death sentences should be carried out at once; and that future executions should be carried out immediately after sentencing, with no leave for appeal. By the end of the month the decree had spurred the arrest, summary trial, and execution of more than 100 suspected 'enemies of the people'. In the next four years a series of purges finally eliminated members of the Bolshevik Old Guard, such as Kamenev and Zinoviev, and thousands of other victims of Stalin's megalomania. *See*: Yezhovshchina.

> To those who have served Russia faithfully Stalin has always been a loyal friend and generous colleague. He does not remove a man as Hitler does, nor does he kill by stealth as Mussolini. – G. D. H. COLE, British socialist historian.

• **Lawrence of Arabia** ► T. E. Lawrence (1888–1935), British soldier, writer, diplomat, and archaeologist, whose place in history rests on his role in the Arab Revolt against the Turks during World War I. Initially appointed to the Arab forces as an intelligence and liaison officer, he rose to a unique position of influence through his compelling personality, mastery of guerrilla tactics, and ability to adapt himself to Bedouin ways. The transformation of the historical Lawrence into the stuff of legend began soon after the war. The image of the romantic desert paladin was largely created by the US journalist Lowell Thomas (1892–1981), whose illustrated lectures played to huge audiences in 1919. Lawrence's sincere (if confused) attempts to escape the consequences of this fame, by entering the ranks of the RAF under an assumed name (**J. R. Ross** and later **T. E. Shaw**), only increased public fascination. To the image of the war hero was added that of the mystery man or psychological enigma. Further layers of myth have accumulated since Lawrence's death, notably the (historically untenable) view that he was a self-glorifying charlatan who invented most of his exploits. In particular, an aura of mystery has been created around the motorcycle accident in which Lawrence died (see: Boanerges). Suggestions of a murder conspiracy have hinged on sightings of a black car near the scene of the crash and false claims that at the time of his death Lawrence was seeking a private meeting with Adolf Hitler. Lawrence's life was the subject of a Terence Rattigan play, *Ross* (1960), and a David Lean film, *Lawrence of Arabia* (1962), with a script by Robert Bolt and Peter O'Toole in the title role.

• **lay** ▸ Slang meaning to have sex with. Although heard in America from the early 1900s, it has only been widely used in the UK since the 1960s. Originally, it was used by men of women, but by the 1970s it was also used by women of men. The word is also used as a noun to mean a sexual act or a sexual partner, particularly in the phrases **good lay** and an **easy lay**.

• **layered look** ▸ A fashion style of the mid-1970s, in which casual clothes of various types and sizes were worn over each other to create a layered effect. Women might for example, wear a short skirt over jeans or leggings, a large open shirt over a dress or T-shirt, and swathes of overlapping shawls, scarves, sweaters, jackets, and coats. The effect was usually completed by a shoulder bag, ethnic jewellery, and some form of headgear. A version of the look was also adopted by some men. The name itself was coined as early as 1950 by the US fashion designer Bonnie Cashin. *See also*: big book.

• **lay rubber** ▸ US slang meaning to drive away very fast, especially from a stationary position. It refers to the depositing of rubber from the rapidly spinning tyres onto the road surface.

• **LBJ** ▸ Lyndon Baines Johnson (1908–1973), 36th president of the USA (1964–68). A Southern Democrat, Johnson became president after the assassination of John F. Kennedy (see: Kennedy Assassination) on 22 November 1963. Subsequently he pushed through his Great Society legislation, an unprecedented programme of civil rights and social welfare measures designed to allieviate some of the country's most pressing racial, social, and economic problems. As a result, he was re-elected as president in 1964 by the greatest majority of the popular vote in the country's history (15 million). However, his unsurpassed domestic achievements were overshadowed by his unwise escalation of the Vietnam War, the economic and human cost of which destroyed his political credibility and crippled the Great Society programme. *See also*: Lady Bird.

• **LCD** ▸ Liquid crystal display. A device using certain materials, known as liquid crystals, which are normally transparent but become opaque when an electric field is applied. They are used in digital watches, electronic calculators, etc.

• **LCT** ▸ *See*: last chance trendy.

• **LDC** ▸ Less developed country. An epithet used by some development economists in order to avoid the pejorative implications of describing countries as *under*developed or as belonging to the Third World, both of which suggest backwardness. *See also*: developing countries.

• **LDV** ▸ Local Defence Volunteers. *See*: Home Guard.

• **LEA** ▸ Local Education Authority. LEAs were first established by the Education Act (1902) to replace the old system of school boards, introduced by the previous Act of 1870. Their numbers were then reduced and their functions more clearly defined by the Act of 1944, which also introduced a minister of education. LEAs were made exclusively responsible for the provision and funding of state schools as well as the recruitment and payment of teachers. However, the Education Reform Act (1988) reduced the authority of the LEAs by permitting schools to opt out of LEA control and receive their funds directly from central government. In such schools all management decisions are taken by parent governors, who also control the budget. These principles were later extended to all publicly maintained schools; LEAs must now delegate at least 85% of each school's budget to the school itself. The current Labour government restored the role of the LEAs in funding schools but has not otherwise reversed these changes. *See*: LMS.

• **Leadbelly** ▸ The stage name of the US blues and folk singer Huddie Ledbetter (1888–1949). The nickname, a corruption of his surname, has several possible origins: his physical strength, his hard character (he served prison terms for murder, attempted murder, and assault), or the buckshot wound in his stomach.

• **Leaderene, the** ▸ Nickname for Margaret Thatcher. *See*: Iron Lady.

• **lead-free** or **unleaded** ▸ Denoting petrol not treated with the antiknock agent tetraethyl lead. In the 1970s it was recognized that although **leaded petrol** increases the performance of petrol engines, the exhaust fumes produced were the principal cause of lead pollution in the atmosphere. Accumulation of lead in body tissues was linked with high blood pressure, brain damage, and the impairment of growth and learning abilities in children. In America, where the problem was acute, the phasing out of leaded petrol began in the mid-1970s and the production of lead additives fell by over 50% in the five years up to 1980. In the UK, lead-free petrol has been given a price advantage in carrying a lower duty than leaded petrol. Many car engines of pre-1970 cars can be converted to accept lead-free petrol and all new cars are now designed to run on it.

• **League against Cruel Sports** ► An organization founded in 1924 to campaign for the protection of wild animals and birds 'persecuted for sport'. Among its primary objectives is the abolition of blood sports involving the use of hounds, such as foxhunting, staghunting, and hare coursing. It operates by means of public-awareness campaigns, peaceful demonstrations, and pressure groups, aimed particularly at lobbying members of parliament and local authorities. It has commissioned a considerable amount of scientific research into the life history and habits of the animals it seeks to protect and publishes a periodical entitled *Wildlife Guardian*. *See also*: animal liberation.

• **League of Nations** ► An association of the world's nations having at one time about 60 members with headquarters at Geneva. Formed on 10 January 1920, in the aftermath of World War I, it had the essential aim of preventing war as well as promoting other forms of international cooperation. From the outset it was weakened by the refusal of America to participate (although President Woodrow Wilson had played a major part in its foundation) and the exclusion of the Soviet Union. Its achievements were considerable in many fields, but it failed in its primary purpose. It last met on 18 April 1946, being replaced by the United Nations, which had been established on 24 October 1945.

• **lean-burn** ► Said of an internal-combustion engine using a lean fuel mixture (an air-petrol ratio of more than 15:1). This promotes more efficient combustion, which increases fuel economy and reduces pollution from such exhaust gases as carbon monoxide.

• **lean on one's chinstraps** ► An army catchphrase, dating from World War I, meaning to be completely exhausted. For example, a long hard route march may be so draining that it leaves one's head drooping so that metaphorically, if not literally, one's chinstraps provide its only means of support.

• **leaper** ► British slang for a stimulant drug, such as an amphetamine. It has the opposite effect to a **sleeper**, one of the slang names for a tranquillizing drug. Although widely used in the 1960s, the term has largely dropped from use.

• **leaping lizards!** ► An old-fashioned US expression of surprise. It was popularized by the heroine of Harold Gray's comic strip *Little Orphan Annie*, which began in 1924; a radio series based on the strip lasted into the 1940s. The curly-haired moppet revived the expression in the 1977 Broadway musical *Annie*, which ran for more than 2000 performances and was made into a film (1982; directed by John Huston).

• **Learjet** ► A jet aircraft produced in the 1960s to carry a small number of passengers. It was designed by the US engineer William Lear (1902–78). Owning one's own Learjet has been for several decades the ultimate symbol of wealth and success. Being rich enough to hire one is rather less prestigious, but still an option available only to the privileged few.

• **learning curve** or **experience curve** ► A graph plotting the progress of an individual or group in performing a particular task against time, used in business management to monitor the progress of trainees, in psychological studies of learning, etc. The curve tends to slope sharply at the beginning, for example as a trainee gains experience of a new production process or technology, then flattens off at the level of an experienced worker. The more complex a particular operation or technology, the steeper the learning curve before achieving the **learning plateau**. The expression is now also used more generally to indicate progress in acquiring any new skill or knowledge, especially in the phrase **a steep learning curve**.

• **least-worst** ► Not very good but better than any available alternative. The combination of two superlatives adds to the emphasis, although grammatically the phrase should be 'least-bad'. It became popular in the late 1980s.

• **leather** ► 1. British slang for a middle-aged male socialite with an all-year-round suntan from a life of leisure spent mostly at ski resorts and on fashionable beaches. It is occasionally also used of women. Old and lined skin becomes leathery in the sun, giving rise to this unflattering epithet. 2. Underworld slang for a purse or a wallet.

• **leather boy** ► 1. Slang from the 1960s for a motorcycle rider; a biker. 2. Slang for a young male homosexual or a male prostitute.

• **Leather Lungs** ► The nickname of the British

singer and actress Elaine Paige (1957– ), who appeared on the London stage in the musicals *Jesus Christ Superstar* and *Grease*, before achieving stardom in Andrew Lloyd Webber's *Evita* (1978). She later triumphed on Broadway in *Sunset Boulevard* (1995).

• **leatherneck** ► A US marine. It derives from the US marine corps custom of facing the neckband of its uniform with leather.

• **leaves on the line** ► A reason used by the former British Rail (BR) to explain delays and cancellations of trains, most notoriously in the autumn of 1991. High winds and wet weather combined to deposit large quantities of leaves on adjacent tracks, putting trains at risk of skidding, according to BR. However, most rail travellers regarded this as belonging to a long tradition of feeble excuses served up by the UK's nationalized rail company in an attempt to mollify its frustrated customers. They argued that fallen leaves in autumn were hardly a new phenomenon and should not cause disruption on the scale claimed by BR. Hence, 'leaves on the line' came to represent any flimsy defence or inadequate justification; in this is stands alongside the **wrong sort of snow**, another choice example of BR spin.

• **Lebensraum** ► (German, room for living) Additional territory required by a nation for expansion, owing to its economic or demographic pressures. The concept was latched onto by Adolf Hitler in the 1930s as a justification for the expansion of Nazi Germany into central and E Europe. The Nazi interpretation of the word included the forcible removal or murder of the existing non-German population, a policy that underlaid some of the worst atrocities of the period before and during World War II.

• **Le Bourget** ► The former international Paris airport, now used only for internal domestic flights. Le Bourget was first used as a military aerodrome in 1917 and became Paris's airport after the end of World War I. It was at Le Bourget that Charles Lindbergh landed on 21 May 1927 after the first solo crossing of the North Atlantic. A new terminal was opened in 1937, which was regarded at the time as the best in the world. However, in the 1970s all major international operations were transferred to the new airport at Roissy-en-France (Charles de Gaulle airport) and to Orly. Besides handling domestic flights, Le Bourget remains the venue for the annual Salon de l'Aéronautique (Air Show), first staged there in 1953, and is also the home of a Musée de l'Air.

• **Leboyer** ► A method of childbirth that emphasizes 'birth without violence'. It was devised by the French obstetrician Frédérick Leboyer (1918– ). To create a peaceful and untraumatic atmosphere for the delivery, the birth takes place in a dark quiet room and the baby is then put in a bath kept at room temperature to simulate intrauterine conditions. This type of natural childbirth, in which the husband is an active participant, first became popular in the early 1970s.

> Birth may be a matter of a moment. But it is a unique one. – F. LEBOYER: *Birth Without Violence*.

• **lech** or **letch** ► Slang meaning to desire someone sexually, usually heard in the phrase **lech over** or **lech after**. As a noun, meaning a lecherous person, it is generally used contemptuously by women of men. The word is a shortening of 'lecherous'.

• **Leclerc** ► Assumed name of Jean de Hautecloque (1902–47), the French general whose military fame during World War II was second only to that of de Gaulle. A graduate of Saint Cyr Military Academy, he escaped to England soon after the Fall of France and joined the Free French forces under de Gaulle (*see:* Fighting French). He then changed his name to Jacques-Phillipe Leclerc to protect his family in France from Nazi reprisals. He distinguished himself as commander of the Free French Army in Chad, later fighting in Libya and supporting the Allied campaigns in North Africa. He took part in the Normandy landings and achieved lasting fame when his tank division liberated Paris in August 1944. In March 1946 he was given command of the French forces in Indochina and campaigned vigorously against the Viet Minh, although he quickly perceived that a military solution to the guerrilla war was impossible. In July 1946 he was sent to inspect of the French forces in North Africa, where he was killed in a plane crash.

• **Le Corbusier** ► Assumed name (literally 'the crow-like one') of the controversial Swiss-born French architect, Charles-Edouard Jeanneret (1887–1965). One of the dominant figures in the International Style of modern architecture, Le Corbusier is as renowned for his unfulfilled utopian urban planning, set out in his *The City of Tomorrow* (1924), as for his actual buildings. However, his urban vision was partially achieved in his designs for Chandigarh, the new capital of the Punjab, India (1951–54). His early works were based on what he called 'Purism', which sought a pristine clarity of design as reflected in the private Villa Savoye (1929–31) at Poissy, a clean white cube raised on stilts (*pilotis*), with open interiors, membranous stucco walls, and massive sliding windows. His tract

Towards an Architecture (1923) contained his definition of a house as **a machine for living in**. It also contained his revolutionary ideas on high-rise mass-produced housing, upon which he based his large-scale housing project the Unité d'Habitation at Marseilles (1946–52). After 1945 his style became more curvaceous and sculptural, as for example in the Chapel of Notre Dame Du Haut at Ronchamp (1950–55) and in the Parliament building at Chandigarh (begun 1951). These structures also reflected a move towards concrete brutalism, the style with which British architects and town planners in the 1960s and 1970s created so much municipal ugliness.

• **Lecter, Hannibal** ► A cannibalistic serial killer who features in the novels Red Dragon (1981), The Silence of the Lambs (1988), and Hannibal (1999) by US author Thomas Harris (1940–   ) and in several film adaptations. Lecter's bizarre character and gruesome killing rituals have fascinated readers and filmgoers alike, making him the quintessential serial killer character. Although Red Dragon was adapted to some acclaim as the film Manhunter in 1986, it was not until the release of the film version of The Silence of the Lambs (1990), in which Anthony Hopkins played Lecter, that the character truly infiltrated the public consciousness. There had been many previous books and films about serial killers, but none had made the murderer seem so compelling or, in a dreadful way, so attractive. A former psychiatrist, Lecter is presented as a man of great brilliance and charm as well as a terrifying psychopath. This is taken further in the film version of Hannibal (2001), in which Hopkins plays Lecter as a witty and almost avuncular figure.

> A census taker once tried to test me. I ate his liver with some fava beans and a nice Chianti.
> – HANNIBAL LECTER in the film version of The Silence of the Lambs.

• **Lee, Bruce** ► (1940–73) US film star renowned for his prowess as a practitioner of the martial arts. He starred in a series of action-packed low-budget movies, which enjoyed enormous box-office success and inspired the kung-fu cult of the 1970s. Born in San Francisco, the son of a Chinese opera star, he was brought up in Hong Kong, where he first received instruction in the martial arts. He worked briefly as a television actor in America but the films that brought him fame were all made in Hong Kong, including Fist of Fury (1972), Enter the Dragon (1973), and The Way of the Dragon (1973). After his sudden death in mysterious circumstances at the age of 33 he became something of a cult figure. There have been at least four biopics. By a macabre coincidence Lee's son, the film actor Brandon Lee

(1966–94), also died in unexplained circumstances at an early age.

• **Lee, Gypsy Rose** ► See: Queen of Burlesque.

• **Lee, Lorelei** ► The archetypal gold-digging dumb blonde; the central character of Anita Loos's satire, Gentlemen Prefer Blondes (1925) and its sequel But Gentlemen Marry Brunettes (1928). Gentlemen Prefer Blondes was adapted for the stage (1925) and for the silent screen (1928); it later provided the basis for a stage musical (1949) and was updated for a musical film starring Marilyn Monroe (1953; directed by Howard Hawks).

• **Left Book Club** ► An imprint of the publishing house of Victor Gollancz (1893–1967) launched in 1936 to encourage a left-wing response to the rise of the various forms of fascism in Europe. Its texts, bound in bright orange cloth covers, were written by many of the leading leftists of the time – Stephen Spender, J. B. S. Haldane, Hyman Levy, G. D. H. Cole, and George Orwell, amongst others. At its peak the book club had over 50 000 subscribers, but its readership declined in the war years and it finally closed in 1948.

• **left brain** ► See: right brain.

• **legal aid** ► Financial help from public funds given on an income- and capital-related scale to those who, unassisted, would not be able to meet the cost of legal advice or representation. This enabled the poorest members of the community to make use of the processes of the law, but did not benefit the large number of people who earned too much or had too much capital to qualify for legal aid but for whom risking an expenditure of many thousands, or tens of thousands, of pounds was unthinkable. To enable more people to have access to legal services, and to reduce the costs of providing legal aid, the system was reformed in 1999. Legal help and representation is now provided by a limited number of specialist lawyers, supplemented by advice and mediation services given by non-lawyer counsellors. While fewer categories of cases will qualify for legal aid, more will be conducted on a 'no win, no fee' basis.

• **legionnaire's disease** ► A form of pneumonia caused by the bacterium Legionella pneumophilia. It was first described after 182 delegates to an American Legion Convention in Philadelphia in July 1976 were struck down by a mystery illness, resulting in 29 deaths. The bacterium causing the illness was subsequently identified and named after its victims. Growth of the bacterium is encouraged by warm conditions (20–50°C), and the most common sources of infection are air-conditioning ducts, water tanks, and warm-water plumbing systems. The symptoms include headache, fever, cough, and possibly chest pain, nausea, vomiting and diarrhoea, following an incubation period of 2–10 days. Severe respiratory or renal complications may follow, especially in the sick or elderly. The illness can be successfully treated with antibiotics, especially erythromycin. Mass outbreaks are uncommon, especially now that architects and engineers are aware of the risk.

• **leg it** ▶ British slang meaning to run away or escape. Originally an expression popular with both the underworld and the police, it was used especially of running away from the scene of a crime. The expression acquired wider currency among middle-class speakers in the late 1980s, when it was fashionable to imitate earlier underworld idioms.

• **Lego** ▶ Tradename for toy plastic bricks that can be fitted together with other plastic components, such as wheels, windows, and human figures, to construct buildings, vehicles, etc. Invented in Denmark in the 1930s and marketed throughout the world since the 1950s, it takes its name from the Danish words, *leg godt*, meaning play well. The tallest Lego tower ever made was constructed in Tel Aviv in 1990: 18.15 m (59.5 ft) high, it was composed of 221,560 bricks.

• **leg-opener** ▶ Slang for an alcoholic drink, referring to its alleged ability to make women more sexually compliant. It was coined by allusion to eye-opener.

• **legs** ▶
 **Four legs good, two legs bad** The essence of 'Animalism' as described in chapter three of Animal Farm (1945), the political satire by George Orwell (1903–50). Animalism originally comprised seven commandments inspired by the teachings of old Major, the prize Middle White boar, and codified by one of the pigs, Snowball. These proved too difficult for some of the more stupid animals to understand, so Snowball reduced the commandments to this single maxim, implying that all animals (four legs) are good and all humans (two legs) are bad. Here Orwell is parodying the reduction of complex issues to simple formulas or slogans in socialist societies, which he regarded as invidious and intellectually stultifying. See also: All animals are created equal… at equal.

• **legwarmers** ▶ A pair of thick stockings without feet, normally worn over tights and usually knitted in bright colours. They are worn during dance-based exercises, such as aerobics, and for ballet and other dance rehearsals.

• **L-85** ▶ A fashion style dictated by the US government during World War II in order to save vital raw materials. Ruling L-85 laid down the styles allowed, which included narrow skirts, functional pockets only, and little in the way of frills or hems.

• **Le Mans** ▶ Capital city of the Sarthe region in NW France, site of the first Grand Prix motor race in 1906. A 24-hour event for four-seater touring cars was introduced in 1923 and has been held annually in June ever since. Originally there was no outright winner: entrants qualified for the Rudge-Whitworth Triennial Cup, which was awarded to the car that covered the greatest distance over the first three annual runnings of the event. A Biennial Cup was introduced in 1924 (and survived until the 1955–56 events); in 1928 the event became, officially, a 24-hour race. From 1949, prototypes were allowed to race, as well as production models. The event was originally established to demonstrate the reliability of touring cars; however, the latest high-tech machines produced by German and Italian manufacturers, such as Porsche and Ferrari, bear little relation to the original touring models of the early years when such entrants as Bentley, Alfa Romeo, and Bugatti introduced their sporting cars. In 1955 it was the scene of a horrific crash, the worst in motor-racing history: three cars collided at 150 mph – one of them, a Mercedes, careered into the crowd, killing 80 people. The race organizers attracted intense criticism for not stopping the race.

• **lemon law** ▶ US slang for a law that provides buyers of defective or substandard cars (whether new or secondhand) with some redress against the manufacturer or seller. Several US states passed such laws in the 1980s. A 'lemon' is a US slang term for anything that is useless or defective.

• **Lend-Lease** ▶ In World War II, the reciprocal agreements under which America lent badly needed military equipment to the UK and its allies in return for the use of Commonwealth naval and air bases. The policy began with the loan of US destroyers (*see*: rum runners) early in 1941 and was formalized by the Lend-Lease Act of March 1941. When Lend-Lease ended in 1945 America had received somewhat less than one-sixth, in monetary terms, of what she had expended in aid to her allies – over 60% of which went to Britain and the Commonwealth.

• **Lenin** ▶ Adopted name of Vladimir Ilyich Ulyanov (1870–1924), Russian revolutionary and founder of the Soviet Union. Lenin was deeply scarred by the execution of his elder brother, Alexander, in 1887, for trying to assassinate the Tsar. After leaving university he became a professional revolutionary. In 1900 he joined other Marxists in exile in Europe, waiting and preparing for the ideal moment to launch the revolution in Russia. He placed his faith in the idea of the Party as the engine of revolutionary class consciousness. At a conference of the Russian Social Democratic Workers Party in London in 1903, the majority (Bolsheviks) supported Lenin's proposals for the organization and revolutionary role of the party. After the collapse of the Tsarist government in March 1917, Lenin returned to Russia (with the connivance of Germany); with the aid of the Bolshevik-organized Red Guard, he overthrew the provisional government in October, seizing power in the name of the people (*see*: October Revolution). On his death he left behind in his writings a legacy of applied Marxism (*see*: Leninism) and a final 'testament' (*see*: Lenin's Testament), warning colleagues against the choice of Stalin as his successor. From the time of his death until the fall of Soviet Communism in 1990, Lenin was revered as a national icon in Russia, a figure of heroic strength and wisdom whose policies remained beyond criticism. His body still lies in state in a mausoleum in Red Square in Moscow, although the once lengthy queues that formed every day to file past the uncovered coffin are no more to be seen.

• **Leningrad** ▶ The former name (1924–91) of St Petersburg, the capital of Tsarist Russia founded by Peter the Great in 1703. The city was known as Petrograd between 1914 and 1924. It readopted its original name following the demise of Soviet communism.

• **Leningrad purge** ▶ The purge of the Leningrad Communist Party organization in 1949–59 following the death of the Leningrad party boss Andrei Zhdanov on 31 August 1948. The purge was carried out by Abakumov, the ruthless head of SMERSH during World War II, and was probably initiated by Georgy Malenkov and L. P. Beria to eliminate supporters of Zhdanov, who had been Malenkov's chief rival for Stalin's favour. As well as A. A. Kuznetsov, a Central Committee member, and Nikolay Voznesensky, a Politburo member, over 2000 lesser functionaries from the Leningrad party were executed.

• **Leninism** or **Marxist-Leninism** ▶ Lenin's practical adaptation of Marxist political and economic thought to the conditions of industrially underdeveloped societies, such as Russia in the early 20th century. In *Imperialism – The Highest Stage of Capitalism* (1916) he analysed the nature of imperialistic monopoly capitalism; unlike Marx, he stressed the revolutionary potential of pre-capitalist societies and the importance of a worker-peasant alliance

in achieving revolution. In *What is to be Done* (1902) he emphasized the role of a disciplined professional communist party as the 'vanguard of the proletariat'. *Left-wing Communism* (1920) has the benefit of Lenin's practical experience, emphasizing the importance of flexibility and pragmatism in achieving revolutions and then in sustaining communist authority. In this last book Lenin diverges significantly from the historical determinism of orthodox Marxism.

• **Lenin Prize** ▶ An award formerly granted for scientific, technical, and cultural achievements, established in 1950 as the Soviet counterpart to the Nobel Prizes. The winner was announced on 1 May annually. *See also*: Order of Lenin.

• **Lenin's Testament** ▶ A two-part document intended as Lenin's final instructions to his colleagues in a future Communist Party Congress, dictated on 23–25 December 1922 and 4 January 1923. The first section contained advice on necessary political reforms and the second concise portraits of six party leaders (Stalin, Trotsky, Zinoviev, Kamenev, Bukharin, and Pyatakov). In the latter he warned against Stalin's accumulation of personal power, criticized him as being too rude, and advised that he be removed as secretary general of the party. After Lenin's death in January 1924 the Testament was made known to the Central Committee, who failed to act on its recommendations; Stalin then suppressed its wider dissemination within the Soviet Union. Thirty years later, and three years after Stalin's death, Khrushchev read the text to the 20th Party Congress on 25 February 1956, thereby beginning the process of de-Stalinization.

• **Leopold and Loeb murder** ▶ A US criminal case of 1924 involving the kidnap and murder of 14-year old Bobby Franks, the son of millionaire businessman Jacob Franks, by two teenage students from prominent families, Richard Loeb and Nathan Leopold. According to Loeb, who broke down under police questioning, Leopold had relished the intellectual challenge of committing the perfect murder undetected and then enlisted Loeb's aid in coolly executing his plan. The two were defended at their trial in July 1924 by the brilliant and controversial lawyer Clarence Darrow, who successfully appealed against the imposition of the death penalty. Loeb was killed in a homosexual brawl in 1936; Leopold served 33 years and was released in 1958.

> If I were not positive that my glasses were at home, I would say these are mine. – NATHAN LEOPOLD, when shown his own glasses, which he had dropped at the scene of the crime.

• **Iergi** ▶ *See*: Iurgy.

• **letch** ▶ *See*: lech.

• **let it all hang out** ▶ An exhortation, frequently heard in the late 1960s and early 1970s, to be completely open and uninhibited. Taken literally, it invites one to be so uninhibited that, in the case of a woman, her breasts are exposed, and in the case of a man, his genitalia are open to public scrutiny. The expression is said to have originated with Black American junkies.

• **Let's blow, Crow** ▶ US catchphrase used frequently by GIs and others in the 1940s, meaning 'Let's get out of this place'. 'Blow' meaning 'to leave' dates back to the 1920s; in the late 1940s the US radio detective Sam Spade often talked of 'blowing town'. Another wartime phrase with the same meaning was **Let's take a powder**.

• **letter bomb** or **mail bomb** or **parcel bomb** ▶ A small explosive device hidden in, or disguised as, a letter or parcel. It is set to detonate when opened and posted to a victim. This tactic remains popular with terrorist groups, although the intended target is not always the victim; this can often be the secretary opening the mail or an employee of the post office.

• **Lewinsky affair** ▶ A major political crisis that arose from allegations, subsequently confirmed, that President Bill Clinton (1946–   ) had allowed himself to be fellated in the Oval Office by Monica Lewinsky, a 21-year-old member of the White House staff. The news was greeted with undisguised joy by Clinton's political opponents and with various degrees of disgust, disbelief, and hilarity around the world.

What made this private indiscretion a matter of grave public consequence was the charge that the president had not only lied about the affair, but lied on oath, and suborned Ms Lewinsky to do the same. The allegations arose from a civil action brought against the president in 1997 by one Paula Jones, who accused him of sexually harassing her in an incident six years earlier. When Jones's lawyers named Monica Lewinsky as one of several other women with whom he had had affairs, both Clinton and Lewinsky denied this in depositions. Clinton also made an emphatic (but carefully worded) denial to the US media on 26 January 1998:

> I want to say one thing to the American people. I want you to listen to me...I did not have sexual relations with that woman...I never told anybody a lie, not a single time. Never. These allegations are false.

However, damning evidence to the contrary was now mounting. The public heard that secretly made tapes of Monica's private conversations had come into the hands of Kenneth Starr, the special prosecutor in the Whitewater affair. Mention was also made of a blue dress that still bore traces of the presidential semen.

By August, the truth could no longer be hidden. Lewinsky agreed to make a full statement to Starr's grand jury investigation and Clinton himself was obliged to give detailed evidence about his private life. The president now went on US television with a somewhat different story:

> Indeed, I did have a relationship with Ms Lewinsky that was not appropriate. In fact it was wrong.

This admission left Clinton open to a perjury charge and hence to impeachment and removal from office. In September 1998 Starr delivered a full blow-by-blow report on the president's antics which concluded that there were 11 formal grounds for impeachment. Hearings began in November and on 21 December the House of Representatives voted to impeach Clinton on counts of perjury and obstruction of justice. At his subsequent trial before the Senate, however, a majority vote cleared him of all charges (February 1999). Not wishing to prolong a crisis that had paralysed US life for over a year and made the country a laughing stock abroad, the senators effectively accepted Clinton's view that fellatio was not necessarily the same thing as 'sexual relations'.

More simply, the Senate may have felt that a popular and largely successful president should not be brought down by a dispute about a blow job. Indeed, one peculiarity of the whole affair was the way in which Clinton's approval ratings soared as the crisis deepened. The American public seemed to take the view that, for all his faults, Clinton was a bigger man than his persecutors, whose motives and tactics often seemed highly questionable.

Nevertheless, the affair left a stain on Clinton's record more embarrassing than any marks on that infamous blue dress. Addressing a conference of 4500 evangelical ministers some 18 months after his acquittal, the hangdog president said:

> I am now in the second year of a process of trying to rebuild my life from a terrible mistake I made...this has to be a dynamic on-going effort...I feel much more at peace than I used to.

In a legal deal struck on his last day in office, Clinton finally admitted to lying on oath in return for a promise of non-prosecution. The president now confessed:

> I tried to walk a fine line between acting lawfully and testifying falsely but I now recognize that I did not fully accomplish this goal...

• **Lewis gun** ▶ A type of gas-operated air-cooled light machine gun, taking its name from its inventor, US army officer Isaac Newton Lewis (1858–1931). It was used widely in World War I and was the first machine gun to be attached to an aircraft.

**• Leyte Gulf, Battle of the▶** The sea and air battle on 23–26 October 1944, which crippled the Japanese Combined Fleet and enabled the US forces to recapture the Philippines. The battle was precipitated by the US amphibious assault on Leyte, the middle island in the Philippine group, on 20 October. The Japanese had formulated a plan, codenamed Sho-Go (Victory Operation), to split their fleet into four squadrons: two of these approached the Gulf through the Surigao Straits to the south, while another decoyed powerful elements of the US fleet away from the Leyte beaches allowing the remaining elements, commanded by Admiral Kurita, to attack the US invasion fleet through the San Bernardino Straits to the north. The plan nearly succeeded, but at the last moment Admiral Kurita retreated to salvage the remains of his forces, which had suffered heavy bombardment from the planes of the US navy; this enabled the superior US firepower to overwhelm the other elements of the Japanese fleet.

**• LGM▶** Little green men. Mythical creatures from other worlds coming to visit the Earth in spaceships (*see:* flying saucers). The phrase 'little green men' originated in the 1950s and was probably the result of illustrations in early science-fiction magazines. As science fiction became more sophisticated, the phrase became less common. However, in 1967 it came back into prominence in a more scientific environment – the radio-astronomy department at Cambridge University. Here the radio astronomer Antony Hewish (1924–  ) initiated a project to study the fluctuations of radio signals from space caused by ionized gas. His research student, Jocelyn Bell (1943–  ), was given the job of analysing the data from the university's radiotelescope. She noticed some unusual regular signals appearing – pulses of radio waves occurring every 1.337,301,13 seconds. One theory proposed at the time was that the source of the signals was LGM – 'little green men' from extraterrestrial civilizations attempting to make contact with the Earth. In fact, Jocelyn Bell had found the first example of a pulsar (a 'pulsating star'). Hewish, together with the Cambridge astronomer Martin Ryle (1918–  ), shared the 1974 Nobel Prize for physics for this work. There was some controversy about the fact that Bell did not share in the prize. The first pulsar might once have been called 'Bell's star', but in fact is known as CP1919.

**• Liberal Democrats▶** A UK political party of the centre, formed in 1988 from a merger of the Liberal Party and the Social Democratic Party (*see* Gang of Four). Originally called the Social and Liberal Democratic Party, the party adopted its present name in 1989. Its first leader was Paddy Ashdown, who was succeeded in 1999 by Charles Kennedy.

**• Liberal Landslide▶** The Liberal Party victory at the general election of January 1906, which represented an overwhelming public endorsement of the new Liberal government formed by Henry Campbell-Bannerman in December 1905. The Liberals, capitalizing upon the Conservative Party's disagreement on Tariff Reform, won 400 seats, giving them a technical majority of 130 over all other parties. However, they could also count on the support of the Irish Nationalist members (83) and those of the Labour Representation Committee (29), which gave the Liberals the largest working majority of any government since 1832.

**• Liberal Nationals▶** *See:* National Liberal Party.

**• Liberation Day▶** The day (9 May) on which the Channel Islands celebrate their liberation in 1945 from German occupation. The anniversary is marked throughout the islands by an annual public holiday.

**• liberation theology▶** A form of Christian theology, most widely discussed in a South American context, which insists that spiritual liberation must be linked to social and economic liberation. Because this suggests a formal connection between Christianity and Marxism, the Roman Catholic hierarchy has condemned liberation theology in spite of the good work done in its name. The name was coined by Gustavo Gutierres of Peru in his book *The Theology of Liberation* (1969).

**• Libermanism▶** A series of liberal reforms of the Soviet economy proposed by Evsei Liberman of the University of Kharkov and published in a series of articles in *Pravda* in 1962. The measures were designed to shift the emphasis away from rigid centralized planning towards the operation of market forces, allowing investment and production decisions to be made locally and rewarding workers and managers on the basis of profits. Libermanism was introduced in a hesitant and partial manner by first Khrushchev and then Kosygin, but met with opposition from powerful vested interests and was effectively smothered by the early 1970s; similar measures were later introduced by Gorbachov (*see:* perestroika).

**• Liberty bodice▶** A close-fitting sleeveless vest-like undergarment worn mainly by children. It was manufactured by R. & W. H. Symington and marketed in the 1900s under an agreement made with Liberty & Co., the London store. Apart from a modified ladies' version, production of the Liberty bodice ceased in the 1960s.

• **Liberty Island** ▶ The new name given in 1956 to Bedloe's Island in New York Bay. The 12-acre site is home to the Statue of Liberty, erected in 1886. To mark the statue's 100th anniversary, 5000 new citizens were sworn in during a ceremony on the island. The American Museum of Immigration is also here. *See also*: Ellis Island.

• **liberty ships** ▶ Standardized prefabricated cargo ships of about 10,000 tons much used by America during World War II. At one point during the war liberty ships were being built in just four days.

• **Lib-Lab** ▶ A Labour representative elected to parliament on a Liberal platform before the foundation of the Labour Party in 1906. The Lib-Labs were dominant in working-class politics during the period 1860–1880 but economic instability and unemployment, growing class-consciousness, the enfranchisement of manual workers in 1867 and 1884, and the failure of the Liberal Party to meet workers' aspirations, led to the foundation of the Labour Representation Committee in February 1900. This officially became the Labour Party after the election of 1906. The last Lib-Lab MPs joined the Labour Party in 1909.

The name was revived in the late 1970s for the **Lib-Lab pact** (1977–78), an arrangement made between the Liberal Party under the leadership of David Steel and the minority Labour government of James Callaghan. Under the pact, the Liberals agreed to support the government in return for consultation rights.

• **Librium** ▶ A tradename for the tranquillizer chlordiazepoxide, introduced in America in the 1960s by Roche Laboratories. The mock-Latin name has no meaning, but is sufficiently close to 'equilibrium' to provide the desired suggestion. The drug was widely prescribed in the 1960s and 1970s; **libs**, as the capsules were known among addicts, were also widely abused.

• **lick** ▶ 1. US drug-abusers' slang meaning to suck the smoke from a smouldering piece of crack through a small glass pipe. 2. In rock music, a short improvised solo that briefly interrupts the melody, usually on electric guitar. The word comes from 1920s jazz slang and probably derives from a 'lick' meaning a try at something. *See also*: riff.

Crafty songwriting, plenty of little stories, and new bluesy licks. – Review of a rock band in *The Independent*, 14 February 1991.

• **licorice stick** ▶ US jazz slang for a clarinet, dating from the mid-1930s. The jazz clarinet was described by one non-enthusiast as 'An ill woodwind that nobody blows good!'

• **Lidice** ▶ A mining village in the Czech Republic, NW of Prague, which was destroyed by the Germans on 10 June 1942 in reprisal for the assassination by the Czech underground of Reinhard Heydrich, Reich Protector of Bohemia and Moravia and chairman of the Wannsee Conference at which plans for the Final Solution were laid down. The assassins had no direct connection with Lidice, which was chosen at random to intimidate and subdue Czech resistance. The SS rounded up the population and shot 173 men and transported 198 women and 98 children to Ravensbrück concentration camp. Another 13 were selected as racially pure and dispersed throughout Germany to be raised as Aryan Nazis. The village was then burned and dynamited and the area levelled. After the war one of the officials responsible for the atrocity, Karl Hermann Frank, Hitler's deputy in Prague, was executed, and another, Police General Kurt Dalvege, committed suicide in a Nuremberg jail. The site was made into a memorial garden.

• **lie back and think of England** ▶ *See*: close your eyes and think of England.

• **lie detector** ▶ A device that is supposed to determine whether a person is telling the truth or not. The first lie detectors recorded the heartbeats of a person under questioning, it being assumed that a human being cannot tell a lie without an increase in pulse rate. More modern instruments, called polygraphs, also measure blood pressure, respiration rate, and skin conductivity, changes in these parameters also being believed to accompany the stress that occurs when a lie is told. Lie detectors are not usually accepted as evidence in British courts of law.

• **lie down and I'll fan you** ▶ A services catchphrase, particularly associated with the RAF, used to rebuff anyone making an unacceptably demanding or outrageous request. In use since the 1920s, it originated in India where the colonial Britons employed punka wallahs to operate the large fans used for cooling their quarters.

• **Life begins at forty** ▶ *See at*: forty.

• **lifeboat** ▶ In financial jargon, a fund set up by dealers on an exchange, *e.g.* a stock exchange or commodity exchange, to rescue any firms in danger of insolvency in the event of a collapse in the market. If such a collapse occurs, the single insolvency of a main dealer could bring many other firms down with it. It is therefore in the market's interest to protect its members against the consequences of unexpectedly large rises or falls in prices.

• **lifeboat ethics** ▶ The ethical adjustments required in certain extreme situations, in which (it is claimed) practical good can only be achieved by setting aside one's normal humanitarian instincts. The phrase alludes to the plight of passengers in an overcrowded lifeboat, faced with the choice of throwing some of their number overboard or of all sinking together. *See also*: triage.

• **Life Force** ▶ *See*: creative evolution; élan vital.

• **Life is just a bowl of cherries** ▶ A cliché now employed only with heavy irony; it started life as the title of a song by Ray Henderson (music) and Lew Brown (lyrics) for the Broadway show *George White's Scandals of 1931*.

• **lifemanship** ▶ A word and concept introduced by the British writer Stephen Potter (1900–69) in *Some Notes on Lifemanship* (1950). This applied gamesmanship to the practice of social relations. The book includes humorous guidance on the arts of Weekendmanship, Woomanship, and Newstatesmanship. *See also*: one-upmanship.

> If you have nothing to say, or, rather, something extremely stupid and obvious, say it, but in a 'plonking' tone of voice – *i.e.* roundly, but hollowly and dogmatically. – *Some Notes on Lifemanship*.

• **life peerage** ▶ Peers created since the 1958 Life Peerages Act to honour those men and women who have given outstanding service to their country. Life peerages are given as baronies to both men and women. While a life peerage carries no hereditary privileges, life peers are entitled to sit in the House of Lords. Indeed, under the government's current plans for reforming the second chamber, the House of Lords will be wholly composed of life peers.

• **lifestyle** ▶ A word that became popular in the 1980s to denote the manner in which people live their lives, with special emphasis on what they wear, eat, or otherwise consume, and how they spend their leisure. It rapidly became a buzz word, much used by pop sociologists who recognized that older kinds of classification by social class had become outdated and by advertisers trying to direct specific products at people with an appropriate style of life. **Lifestyle advertising** is advertising that attempts to make a product seem desirable by associating it with a desirable lifestyle (*i.e.* one that is affluent, successful, fashionable, etc.) rather than by explaining its benefits. **Lifestyle journal-**

**ism** is journalism that deals with such matters as fashion, food, health and beauty, foreign travel, etc., generally in an aspirational and fashion-conscious way.

> Things like *The Sunday Times*'s Lifestyle section. It's all about individualistic lifestyle, consumerism and shopping. – CANON DAVID MEARA, rector of St Brides, *The Times*, 24 November 2000.

• **life wasn't meant to be easy** ▶ A phrase widely heard in the late 1970s after its use by the Australian prime minister Malcolm Fraser, in reference to current government policies.

> It occurred to me that there are times when life is a little easier than it's meant to be. – Speech to the Liberal Party, 1977.

• **liftoff** ▶ The instant in which a rocket blasts free from its launching pad. The concept, and the word used to describe it, entered the language during the period of America's manned space flights in the 1960s. *See also*: all systems go.

• **ligger** ▶ British slang, dating from the 1970s, for a gatecrasher or freeloader, someone who habitually takes advantage of free hospitality, food, etc., especially in the media world and the entertainment industry.

• **light on the hill, the** ▶ The oft-quoted objective of the Australian Labor Party, introduced in a speech by J. B. Chifley in 1949. It is broadly synonymous with 'the light at the end of the tunnel', but in Australia, at least, acquired a particular relevance to socialism and became a standard phrase in the repertory of all that country's socialist leaders. It represents the ideal that no person should be deprived of the hope of improving his or her lot in society.

• **light pen** ▶ 1. A penlike device with a photosensor in its tip that can be touched to a computer screen to draw diagrams and shapes or to select items from a displayed menu. 2. A similar light-sensitive device used to read bar codes, such as those found on packaged products.

• **light pollution** ▶ Extraneous light from street lighting, neon signs, etc., in populated areas. Of concern to astronomers, because it interferes with telescope observations of the night sky, it is also regarded as a menace by environmentalists and regretted by many others who find that the night skies of their childhood seem to have disappeared.

• **like** ▶ A word used in a number of unusual and ungrammatical contexts; it is added without meaning to a statement, such as 'The world is like crazy' or 'Like your argument is like useless'. This usage originated amongst beatniks and jazz musicians in the 1950s and was later taken up by hippies in the 1960s and 1970s as part of their habit of making detached and often not very profound or original assertions. It has now become a compulsive speech habit among schoolchildren and teenagers. One curious development of the last few years has been the growing tendency to use 'like' as an all-purpose substitute for 'say', 'think', or 'imply', as in 'I come in and she's like Where the hell have you been?, and I'm like What's it to you?'. *See*: valspeak.

**• Likud ►** A political coalition which, under the successive leadership of Menachem Begin and Yitzhak Shamir, was the outright governing power in Israel between May 1977 and November 1984, and has subsequently formed a series of coalition governments under Shamir (1990–92), Binyamin Netanyahu (1996–99), and Ariel Sharon (2001–　). Formed in 1973, it was created from various right-wing organizations, principally the Gahal bloc, comprising the Herut (Freedom) Party, which formally emerged in 1948 (the year of Israel's independence), and the Liberal Party, itself an amalgamation formed in 1961 of the former General Zionist and Progressive parties.

**• Li'l Abner ►** The handsome hillbilly character of the long-running newspaper comic strip created by the US cartoonist Alfred G. Caplin in 1934. The character was played on screen by Granville Owen in a 1940 film; a later stage musical was also filmed (1959) with Peter Palmer in the title role. The original strip continued into the 1970s.

**• Lili Marlene ►** A German song of World War II composed by Norbert Schultze in 1938 and first recorded by the Scandinavian singer Lale Andersen. The lyric was based on a poem written by a German soldier, Hans Leip, in 1917. The song became increasingly popular during the 1940s, especially with the Afrika Korps, and the recorded version was played nightly by Radio Belgrade from the late summer of 1941 virtually until the end of hostilities. Other German stations plugged it and it was picked up and adopted by the British Eighth Army, the English version of the lyric being by T. Connor. There were French, Italian, and numerous other renderings of what became the classic song of the war. It was later performed, both in German and English, by the German-born star Marlene Dietrich, with whom it is now chiefly associated. Perhaps it was after hearing her sing 'Lili Marlene' that Ernest Hemingway wrote:

> If she had nothing but her voice, she could break your heart with it. But she also has that beautiful body and the timeless loveliness of her face.

*See also*: backroom boys.

**• Lima Declaration ►** A declaration by the Eighth International Pan-American Conference, which met in Lima, Peru, in December 1938, affirming American continental solidarity and collective security in the face of any foreign threat to its political or territorial integrity. The declaration was prompted by President Roosevelt's determination to secure the American republics against European totalitarianism, although many of the South American signatories harboured Fascist sympathies in preference to US democratic values.

**• limbo ►** A West Indian dance, popularized in the 1950s, in which dancers bend backwards to pass beneath a horizontal bar that is lowered after each try. Often the dance continues until only one dancer remains.

**• Lime, Harry ►** The unscrupulous villain played by Orson Welles in *The Third Man* (1949), a remarkable film directed by Carol Reed and scripted by Graham Greene. Lime, a shady figure who appears only briefly in the doorways, fairgrounds, and sewers of post-war Vienna, has a hospital contact who supplies him with penicillin, which he sells on the black market. As a result, the diluted penicillin left in the hospital fails to cure the sick children to whom it is administered. Lime justifies himself to his American friend Holly:

> In Italy for 30 years under the Borgias they had warfare, terror, murder, bloodshed and they produced Michelangelo, Leonardo da Vinci and the Renaissance. In Switzerland they had brotherly love, 500 years of democracy and peace and what did they produce? The cuckoo clock.

It is said that Orson Welles himself added these lines to Greene's script. The film owes its success to a combination of skills: the acting, the direction, the scriptwriting, the photography, and the haunting incidental music of Anton Karas and his zither.

**• Limehouse ►** A once common term for violent abuse of one's political opponents: from a speech by Lloyd George at Limehouse, London, on 30 July 1909, in which he poured scorn and abuse on dukes, landlords, financial magnates, etc.

In 1981 four former cabinet ministers (*see*: Gang of Four) issued the **Limehouse Declaration**, launching the Social Democratic Party.

**• limousine ►** Originally, a large car in which the driver was separated from the passengers by a partition. The name comes from the French *limousine*, a cloak (originally a hooded cloak worn by the inhabitants of Limousin). Later the name was used of any large and luxurious car, especially in North America, and was often abbreviated to **limo**. A **stretch limo** is a very long saloon car made in America by a variety of firms from Ford Lincolns. It is used worldwide as a vehicle able to transport up to 15 passengers on such special occasions as weddings. Stretch limos are also used by rock bands, film stars and their entourages, etc.

• **limousine liberal** ► A derogatory term for a person with liberal political leanings, who also has a great deal of personal wealth. The implication is that it is easy to have liberal views in the back of a chauffeur-driven limousine. Largely a US expression, it has a British counterpart in champagne socialist.

• **limp-wristed** ► A derogatory adjective used to describe a male homosexual. It is supposed to describe the camp and ineffectual wrist and hand movements of such a person.

• **Lincoln Center** ► The Lincoln Center for the Performing Arts (1957–67), a complex in New York City that includes the Metropolitan Opera House (1966), New York Philharmonic Concert Hall (1962), New York State Theatre (1964; home to the NYC Opera, NYC Ballet and other groups), and the Juilliard School of Music (1967). The buildings flank a Michelangelo-style piazza, similar in concept to the Capitoline in Rome, and were designed by a team of architects including Philip Johnson, Max Abramovitz, and Eero Saarinen, coordinated by Wallace K. Harrison.

• **Lindbergh baby murder** ► A criminal case involving the kidnap and murder of the 20-month-old baby son of the US aviator Charles A. Lindbergh (1902–74) in March 1932. Lindbergh (or 'Lindy') had become enormously famous as a result of his non-stop solo flight from New York to Paris (1927) in his monoplane Spirit of St Louis. The world was appalled by the case and a nationwide hunt resulted, with offers of help from the jailed Al Capone, among many others. In May the baby's body was found in a shallow grave – he had died from a blow to the head on the night of the kidnap. Painstaking investigation by the police led eventually to the arrest in September of a German-born carpenter, Bruno Richard Hauptmann, who had entered America illegally in 1923. Given Lindbergh's celebrity status, the trial in January 1935 was a media circus. Hauptmann was sent to the electric chair in April 1936. However, his conviction has been the subject of considerable controversy ever since and his innocence was argued by Ludovic Kennedy in his book *The Airman and the Carpenter* (1984). One theory is that the kidnap was staged by friends of Capone,

seeking his release from prison. Whatever the truth, 'Lindy' turned his back on US society and spent the next five years in Europe, an embittered man.

• **Lindbergh jacket** ► A style of waist-length jacket, which was popular in the 1930s in imitation of the flying-jacket worn by the US aviator Charles A. Lindbergh.

• **lindy hop** or **lindy** ► The vigorous jitterbug dance of the 1930s, named after transatlantic solo pilot Charles A. Lindbergh. The lindy hop was performed to swing or other fast jazz music and introduced the hip twists and pelvic gyrations that became a feature of many subsequent dances.

• **line** ► British slang for a single dose of cocaine, or other drug in powder form, that is sprinkled in a straight line on a mirror, or similar hard flat surface, and snorted into the nose through a straw or a rolled-up banknote.

• **Linear B script** ► A syllabic version of Greek (also called Mycenaen Greek), dating from c. 1400 to c. 1150 BC, most examples of which have been discovered on fragments of tablet at Knossos in Crete, Mycenae, and areas of the Greek mainland. It was so named by Sir Arthur Evans (1851–1941) to distinguish it from the hieroglyphics which preceded the linear form. The script was deciphered in 1952 by the British architect Michael Ventris (1922–56) and is thought to be either derived from, or parallel to, Linear A (c. 2000–c. 1500 BC), which cannot yet be read.

• **line dancing** ► A popular dance style of the 1990s that is faintly reminiscent of square dancing. In a line dance, the dancers form a line or lines and execute a number of simple steps to country-and-western music. The dancers (of both sexes) dress in cowboy boots and hats with various gaudy accoutrements. Line dancing seems to be popular because it offers an occasion for social dancing at which no one need be worried about not knowing the steps or not having a partner.

• **linkage** ► A political deal in which progress on one difficult issue is made dependent on progress in another (which may be otherwise unrelated). This technique was greatly favoured by US secretary of state Henry Kissinger, during his international negotiations in the 1970s. A tacit linkage between issues later formed a mainstay of the peace processes (1990s) in Northern Ireland and the Middle East, although this was often denied in public.

• **Lion of Judah** ► The title of Haile Selassie (1892–1975), emperor of Ethiopia from 1930 to 1974 except for the years of the Italian occupation

(1936–41), during which he lived in exile in the UK. In 1974 he was deposed by a military coup and Ethiopia was declared a socialist state. He is regarded by Rastafarians as the Messiah, the incarnation of God. The term 'Rastafarian' comes from Selassie's real name, Ras Tafari Makonnen. He assumed the title Haile Selassie, meaning 'Might of the Trinity', when he became emperor. The lion is the emblem of the biblical tribe of Judah, Christ sometimes being referred to as 'the lion of the tribe of Judah'.

• **liposuction**▸ A surgical method of slimming in which fat cells are permanently removed from such areas of the body as the stomach, hips, and upper arms. After administering a local anaesthetic, the surgeon makes a small incision and uses a syringe-like instrument to draw out the fat cells. The technique is generally regarded with horror by all but the most obsessive slimmers.

• **lipstick** ▸ US college slang from the 1970s for a fashionably and femininely dressed lesbian. The term gained a much wider circulation in the 1990s (*see*: Same Gender Orientation). A lipstick is the opposite of a **crunchie**, a more austerely and masculinely dressed lesbian.

• **lipsynch** ▸ To pretend to sing or talk by silently moving the lips in synchronization to a recording. Long used by Hollywood, this became an acceptable mode of performing on stage and television in the 1960s. Singers could mime to their own recordings in order to retain the original quality and certain studio sound effects that could not easily be recreated in live performance.

• **liquid crystal display**▸ *See*: LCD.

• **liquid Ecstasy** ▸ *See*: GHB.

• **liquidizer** ▸ An electrical kitchen appliance with blades that can cut, purée, mix, and blend. It is also called a **blender**, especially in America, where it was first sold in the 1960s to mix crushed-ice alcoholic drinks, such as frozen daiquiris. Modern models can blend soups, chop nuts, purée vegetables or fruit, grate cheese, and make mousses and frothy sweets. *See also*: urban legends.

• **listed building** ▸ A building in the UK officially recognized as being of 'special architectural or historic interest' according to the Town and Country Planning Act (1971). Under the act, such buildings are protected from demolition and their owners or occupiers are required to obtain consent from their local planning authority before carrying out any work that would affect the character of the building. There are three types of listing: Grade I for buildings of 'exceptional interest' (about 1% of listed buildings); Grade II*for 'particularly important buildings of more than special interest' (about 4%); and Grade II for buildings of special interest that 'warrant every effort being made to preserve them'. Some of the more unusual 'buildings' to have been listed include prefabs, ornate tombs, and various follies.

• **listeria** ▸ A bacterium belonging to a genus named after the famous British surgeon, Joseph Lister. The name usually refers to the species *Listeria monocytogenes*, which causes listeriosis in humans and animals and occurs widely in nature, for example in soil, faeces, silage, and the tissues of healthy animals. Infection in humans can cause three distinct forms of disease: a flu-like pattern of symptoms; septicaemia, caused by the organisms entering the bloodstream; and a form of meningitis. In pregnant women the organism can cross the placenta and affect the fetus, causing miscarriage, stillbirth, or birth defects. Occasionally, mass outbreaks of listeriosis occur, often traceable to contaminated food, such as soft cheeses, patés, etc. In most cases, however, infection is sporadic and from an unidentifiable source. Worries emerged in the 1980s over the risks of listeriosis caused by the presence of the highly resistant listeria organisms in cook-chill food products inadequately reheated using microwave ovens. New guidelines were introduced in the UK in 1990 to combat this risk.

• **litterbug**▸ A person who drops litter in public places. The word was coined in about 1947 in America, where it is also used as a verb, meaning to drop litter. It contains a pun on the 1940s dance craze, the jitterbug. In the UK **litter lout** is more common. *See also*: Keep Britain Tidy.

• **Little America** ▸ *See*: Eisenhower Platz.

• **Little Bighorn** ▸ British motor-cycle couriers' name for Hyde Park Corner in London, one of the capital's busiest junctions. The reference is to the Battle of Little Bighorn (1876) in America, at which General Custer's troops were massacred by the Indians and Custer himself was killed. For motorcyclists, Hyde Park Corner can be a similarly frightening and dangerous place.

• **Little Entente** ▸ The political alliance formed between Czechoslovakia, Yugoslavia, and Romania (1920–22). Originally intended to prevent the restoration of Habsburg power, it later became broader in scope. It was brought to an end by the destruction of Czechoslovakia after the Munich Agreement (1938).

• **Little Flower** ▸ *See*: La Guardia.

• **little green men** ▸ *See*: LGM.

• **Little Miss Dynamite** ► The stage name of the US singer Brenda Lee (1944– ), who was one of the few successful female rock 'n' rollers of the late 1950s and 1960s. The nickname may have been partly inspired by the song 'Dynamite', a minor hit in 1957. In the 1980s she rebuilt her career as a country singer.

• **Little Mo** ► The nickname of the US tennis champion Maureen Connolly (1934–69). One of the great tennis stars of the early 1950s, she won her first championship at 16, took three Wimbledon titles between 1952 and 1954, and was the first woman to win the tennis grand slam, taking the British, US, Australian, and French singles championships in one year.

• **Little Red Book** ► A name for the collected *Quotations of Chairman Mao Tse Tung*, a book originally produced for the indoctrination of the Chinese Army in 1964 that appeared in a regular edition from 1965. The pocket-sized book, bound in bright red plastic, contained a collection of political quotations, homilies, and aphorisms culled from Mao's writings over the decades and was designed to stimulate revolutionary awareness. It became a familiar sight during the upheavals of the Cultural Revolution, when it was brandished aloft by zealous Red Guards and workers as they heeded Mao's call to root out revisionaries among the bureaucratic and intellectual elite. It also enjoyed a vogue among the New Left in Europe and America during the same period.

> Every communist must grasp the truth, political power grows out of the barrel of a gun.

• **little ships** ► *See*: Dunkirk.

• **Little Sparrow** ► Nickname of Edith Piaf (1915–63), the French cabaret singer and entertainer. Her real name was Edith Gassion; the stage name 'Piaf' is French slang for 'sparrow', an allusion to her tiny stature. Many of her songs, '*Je m'en fous pas mal*' ('I couldn't care less'), '*Je ne regrette rien*' ('I regret nothing'), and '*La vie en rose*' ('Life through rose-coloured glasses'), are a reflection of the drug- and alcohol-induced tragedies of her own short and chaotic life. Immensely popular in her native Paris, she was mourned by virtually the whole populace, bringing traffic to a standstill on the day of her funeral. When he heard the news of her death, her friend the writer and artist Jean Cocteau suffered a fatal heart attack.

• **Little Venice** ► A picturesque tree-lined stretch of the Regent's Canal (opened in 1820 and joined to the Grand Union Canal in 1929) in London's Maida Vale. Although the name only became current after World War II, both Lord Byron and Robert Browning (who lived in nearby Warwick Crescent) noted a resemblance to Venice. Little Venice has been popular with many painters, including Feliks Topolski (1907–89) and Lucien Freud (1922– ). It has also been used as a backdrop in numerous British films and television series.

• **Little Willie** ► A nickname used by British troops in World War I for Friedrich Wilhelm, crown prince of Germany and eldest son of Kaiser Wilhelm II (*see*: Kaiser Bill). The commander of the German armies that attempted to capture Verdun, he was apparently unmoved by the enormous casualties sustained on both sides – hence another of his nicknames, the **Laughing Murderer of Verdun**.

• **Live Aid** ► Two marathon rock concerts held on 13 July 1985 in Wembley Stadium, London, and JFK Stadium, Philadelphia, to raise funds for African famine relief. The concerts, featuring such stars as U2, David Bowie, Madonna, and Mick Jagger, were watched by an estimated one and a half billion people in 160 countries. Live Aid was also the name of the charity set up to administer these funds. The venture was masterminded by the Irish rock singer Bob Geldof (1952– ), who cajoled, bullied, and blackmailed everyone from superstars to heads of state in pursuit of his aims. Geldof had previously been the moving force behind Band Aid an ad hoc supergroup that recorded a charity single in response to harrowing TV footage of the Ethiopian famine of 1984. In 1986 he was awarded an honorary knighthood. After Band Aid and Live Aid, the word 'Aid' was frequently incorporated into the titles of charity events.

> I'm not interested in the bloody system! Why has he no food? Why is he starving to death? –
> BOB GELDOF in an interview, October 1985.

• **live-in** ► Designating a sexual partner with whom one shares one's living accommodation but to whom one is not married. Live-in boyfriends, for example, may or may not own, or partly own, the accommodation and are free to go when they choose to do so. In general, they have not achieved the status of common-law husbands, who might be regarded as boyfriends who have lived-in for some years and have probably entered into some property-sharing arrangements with their partners. In 1972 only 17% of wives in the UK had started their relationships with their husbands as live-in girlfriends. By 1987 this had risen to 57%. In 1998–99 25% of all women aged between 16 and 59 were cohabiting with men to whom they were not married. *See also*: cohab; de-facto; significant other.

• **Liver bird** ► A punning name for a working-class girl from Liverpool. It derives from the effigies of mythical birds on the twin towers of the Royal Liver Exchange, known locally as the Liver birds, and the slang 'bird' meaning a girl. The name was popularized by the BBC sitcom *The Liver Birds* (1969–78).

• **living will** ▶ A document in which a legally competent person states that in the event of incurable illness, severe disability, etc., he or she would prefer not to be kept alive by artificial means. The phrase was widely heard in the 1980s, by which time many US states recognized the legal force of such documents (known formally as **advance directives**). By the mid-1990s it had been established in a number of cases in British courts that doctors should take account of patients' wishes expressed in a living will.

• **Llareggub** ▶ The small seaside town that provides the setting for Dylan Thomas's 'play for voices' *Under Milk Wood* (1954). It was based largely on Laugherne in SW Wales, where the poet spent his later years and is buried. Llareggub is 'buggerall' spelt backwards.

• **Lloyd George Fund** ▶ The controversial fund established and personally controlled by David Lloyd George (1863–1945) as prime minister (1916–22); it was set up to finance a new party organization after his split with the official Liberal Party under Asquith. Lloyd George's blatant use of the honours system to reward wealthy contributors to the fund, without regard to their personal reputations or philanthropic credentials in other spheres of life, provoked the Honours Scandal of July 1922. A commission of inquiry was set up to investigate the propriety of Lloyd George's administration of the fund; his refusal to relinquish control of it contributed to the downfall of his coalition government (*see*: Chanak crisis).

• **Lloyd George knew my father** ▶ A saying that was heard even before the death of the great Welsh Liberal prime minister in 1945. It is facetiously referred to as every Welshman's claim to fame. The originator of the phrase was reputedly Tommy Rhys Roberts QC (1910–75), of whom it was actually true as his father, Arthur Rhys Roberts, and Lloyd George had set up a solicitors' practice in London together in 1897. Tommy Rhys Roberts became famous for singing the lines 'Lloyd George knew my father, my father knew Lloyd George' to the hymn tune 'Onward Christian Soldiers' at the close of the after-dinner speeches at circuit dinners. This was the signal that a general sing-song would follow. The practice was also taken up by Welsh Rugby Clubs and by Welsh Liberal assemblies. *Lloyd George Knew My Father* is the title of a play by William Douglas Home (1972).

• **Lloyd's names** ▶ Underwriters of insurance policies at Lloyd's of London, the world's premier insurance association. Lloyd's was founded in a 17th-century London coffee shop owned by a Mr Edward Lloyd. Here marine and other insurers gathered to learn the fortune of the ships they had insured. The association was incorporated by Act of Parliament in 1871.

Lloyd's itself does not participate in underwriting policies. Its members (names) are organized into syndicates, which are run by a manager who writes the policies and stipulates the premiums. The names take no active part in the business, but they have to deposit substantial sums of money or other assets with the corporation to provide the risk capital if their syndicate makes a loss; furthermore, if this capital proves insufficient, they are called upon to provide whatever extra sums are required with unlimited liability. On the other hand, if their syndicate makes a profit, they share in it. Because Lloyd's has been regarded for nearly two centuries as a monument of reliability and financial decorum, rich men and women who could afford the deposit have queued up to become names, in the virtually certain expectation that they would make a handsome return on their investment.

However, in the period 1988–94 many syndicates made huge losses, totalling some £8 billion. This drain on the capital of names resulted in considerable financial hardship for many of them, financial ruin for some, and the suicide of several. As a result becoming a Lloyd's name is no longer regarded as an infallible source of profit. In the aftermath of this debacle, Lloyd's was forced to admit limited companies as names, thus breaking the long tradition that names accepted unlimited liability.

• **LMS** ▶ Local Management of Schools. The control of a school's finances by its own board of governors, as first introduced by the Education Reform Act of 1988 (*see*: Gerbil). This is now standard practice in state schools in England and Wales. *See also*: LEA.

• **loaded** ▶ 1. US slang meaning intoxicated by alcohol or high on drugs. In 18th-century America, a 'load' was a single measure of alcohol, as in '10 cents a load'. The use of loaded to mean drunk was extended to the effects of drug abuse in the 1950s. 2. Slang for extremely wealthy. Also originally a US expression, it is now common in all English-speaking countries.

Is your Dad rich?...He's reasonably loaded.
– COLIN MACINNES: *City of Spades* (1957).

• **loadsamoney** ► An expression coined in the mid-1980s by the comedian Harry Enfield, originally as a catchphrase and subsequently as the name of one of his characters. Loadsamoney, a coarse loudmouthed plasterer who waved a wad of banknotes in other people's faces to show off his newly acquired wealth, was intended as a broad satire on the nouveaux riches of Thatcherite Britain (dubbed the **loadsamoney society** by its critics). 'Loadsa-' subsequently became a prefix attached to other words; **Loadsabargains** are promised by shops advertising sales and comedy shows promise **loadsalaughs**. *See also*: Essex man; Lombard.

• **lobotomy** ► Strictly, surgical incision into a lobe of the brain, although a lobotomy generally refers to the surgical procedure of prefrontal lobotomy (prefrontal leucotomy) in which the nerve fibres connecting the extreme frontal (prefrontal) lobes of the cerebrum with the thalamus are severed, using a cutting instrument (leucotome) introduced through a hole drilled in the skull. The technique was pioneered in 1935 by the Portuguese surgeon António Caetanio de Egas Moniz (1874–1955) and was used to treat severe depression, schizophrenia, and other intractable emotional and behavioural disorders. Because the operation had unpredictable and sometimes adverse effects on the patient, such as marked personality changes, it is no longer practised.

• **Local Defence Volunteers** ► *See*: Home Guard.

• **Local Education Authority** ► *See*: LEA.

• **Locarno Pacts** ► A series of non-aggression agreements formulated at Locarno, in Switzerland, on 16 October 1925 and signed in London on 1 December 1925, which guaranteed the post-Versailles Treaty frontiers between Germany and France as well as those between Belgium and Germany. This settlement of Franco-German differences and the implied British and Italian military guarantee of French territorial integrity appeared to herald a new era of international peace and security (the **Locarno Spirit**). Germany was admitted to the League of Nations shortly afterwards (September 1926). Ten years later, in March 1936, Germany renounced Locarno and marched into the Rhineland.

• **Loch Ness Monster** ► In April 1933 a London surgeon driving along the shore of Loch Ness, Scotland, saw (and photographed) a strange object at some distance out, subsequently described as being about 30 ft long with two humps, a snake-like head at the end of a long neck, and two flippers about the middle of the body. This 'sighting' of some kind of monster renewed interest in a legend that has persisted since St Adamnan's 7th-century biography of St Columba mentioned that he succeeded in banishing an *aquatilis bestia* from the depths of Loch Ness. Following this revival of the legend in the 1930s, the creature has been 'seen' on numerous other occasions and has become a favourite silly season item for the British press, to whom it became known as **Nessie**. Although investigations have failed to provide convincing evidence of a prehistoric monster, local traders, for whom the monster has been a fortuitous source of income, have done their best to keep the myth alive. The extreme depth of the loch combined with the murkiness of the water meant that underwater photographs of the 'monster' taken in 1975 were indistinct; they were sufficient, however, to convince the leading naturalist Sir Peter Scott, among others, of the creature's existence. The Loch Ness Phenomena Investigation Bureau, set up in 1961, continues the quest. Sightings of a similar nature have been reported in other deep Scottish lakes, which sceptics regard as attempts to increase their tourist appeal.

• **lockdown** ► A US word (used since 1974) for the disciplinary measure of keeping a prison's inmates locked in their cells, usually for a day or more, following a disturbance in the prison or a warning of pending violence.

• **Lockerbie disaster** ► The UK's worst air disaster, in which a Pan American Boeing 747, en route from Frankfurt to New York via London, crashed over the small Scottish town of Lockerbie on 21 December 1988, killing all 259 passengers and crew and 11 people on the ground. The cause of the crash was the explosion of a terrorist bomb in one of the luggage holds; great public concern was aroused following the disclosure that warnings of terrorist attacks received some weeks earlier by airport authorities and others had neither been publicized nor heeded. In 1991 a US court indicted two Libyan intelligence officers for planting the bomb. When Libya refused to extradite these suspects for trial in America or Scotland, the UN imposed sanctions on Libya. Eventually, in 1998, Libya agreed that the men could be tried in a neutral country under Scots law. In 2001 a Scottish court sitting at Camp Zeist in the Netherlands found Abdul Baset Ali al-Megrahi guilty of multiple murders but acquitted his alleged accomplice.

• **Lockheed** ► A giant US aerospace corporation (headquarters at Burbank, California) that produces military aircraft (including the C-130 cargo planes and Stealth bombers), satellites, and submarine-launched missiles. In the mid-1970s financial difficulties and an overseas pay-off scandal threatened to sink the company; it survived, however, and remains one of the world's largest weapons manufacturers. It was founded in 1913 by aircraft designers Malcolm and Allan Loughead (they later changed the spelling) but collapsed in 1931 and was then rescued without the Lockheed brothers by a Boston bank in 1932. In the 1960s Lockheed's decision to produce the L-1011 TriStar jet, coupled with severe cost overruns on the C-5 military transport, threatened to bankrupt the company; it was only kept solvent by massive injections of Federal funds. In 1975 it was revealed that as much as $24.5 million of this money was used to bribe foreign government officials to attract overseas contracts.

• **lock-in** ▶ A form of organized protest in which the protesting group locks itself in a building. The lock-in was a tactic popular in America in the late 1960s, when it was used as a means of passive resistance. It subsequently spread to the UK, where it was sometimes used as a form of industrial action. In this case the workers lock themselves into their workplace to prevent the management from closing the company down. *See also*: lock-out.

• **lock-on** ▶ To locate and track a target by means of a radar beam. A ground-based conically scanned radar beam can be made to lock onto an enemy aircraft, which enables a guided missile to be controlled so that its flight path coincides with the beam. When the missile reaches the vicinity of the target a proximity fuse detonates it, destroying the enemy aircraft.

• **lock-out** ▶ During industrial action, the closing of a factory or workplace by the management, thus putting pressure on employees to negotiate or to accept terms. *See also*: lock-in.

• **locust years** ▶ Years of poverty or hardship, or years that have been terribly wasted. The term was applied by Sir Winston Churchill to the years of the Great Depression preceding World War II, when rearmament should have taken place but did not. It is an allusion to the Bible, Joel 2:25: 'And I will restore to you the years that the locust hath eaten...'. The phrase has also been used of the late 1960s in the UK, when the Labour government was in power.

• **logical positivism** ▶ A philosophical doctrine originating in Vienna (*see*: Vienna circle) in the 1920s and later popularized in the UK by Sir Alfred Ayer (1910–89) in his book *Language, Truth and Logic* (1936). At its core is the **verification principle**, which asserts that any non-tautological statement that cannot be verified by empirical observation is literally meaningless. On this principle, only scientific knowledge can claim to be factual; all questions of metaphysics, ethics, and religion are rendered nonsensical. Critics of the doctrine made the rather obvious point that, on these criteria, the verification principle is itself meaningless. Ayer later qualified his position in revised editions of his book (1946).

• **logic bomb** ▶ A set of secret instructions introduced into its a computer's memory that will become operative at some point in the future, leading to the breakdown of the system. By the time the breakdown takes place, the saboteur is not readily identifiable and may have left the organization concerned.

• **loi-cadre** ▶ (French, draft law) Legislation enacted by the French National Assembly on 23 June 1956 to give French overseas possessions, except Algeria, a measure of political autonomy. French territories in West Africa, such as Senegal and Sudan, and Equatorial Africa, such as Gabon, were given territorial assemblies elected by universal suffrage. The territories could also send representatives to the French National Assembly, but France retained the power of veto over the local legislatures and retained control over foreign affairs, defence, and internal security.

• **loid** ▶ Police and underworld slang for opening a locked door by using a piece of cellu*loid* (now usually a credit card). This has been a popular method of illegal entry into houses and cars since the 1930s.

• **Lolita** ▶ A sexually precocious adolescent girl under the age of sexual consent, who is attractive to older men. The word derives from the title character in *Lolita*, the 1955 novel by Vladimir Nabokov (1899–1977), which deals with the seduction of Humbert Humbert, a middle-aged academic paedophile, by the pubescent daughter of his landlady. A witty, often hilarious, satire on Middle America, the book has been filmed on two occasions, although neither attempt succeeded in capturing the full outrageousness of Nabokov's creation. Stanley Kubrick's 1962 version starred James Mason as Humbert and Peter Sellers as his rival for the 12-year-old Lolita (played as a 15-year-old by Sue Lyon). Adrian Lyne's 1997 remake, featuring Dominique Swain in the title role, was even further from catching the elusive qualities that make Nabokov's Lolita so insufferable. *See also*: nymphet.

• **lollipop lady** or **man** ▶ Name used by children for the special traffic warden who conducts them across the road on the way to and from school. It derives from the striped pole, surmounted by a brightly coloured disc, which he or she uses to direct the traffic to stop.

• **Loman, Willy** ▶ The central character in the play *Death of a Salesman* (1949) by Arthur Miller (1915–   ). Loman, a failure as a salesman and a father, kills himself in a car crash to raise insurance money for his family. The play, a sad commentary on the failure of the American Dream, won a Pulitzer Prize.

> Attention, attention must be finally paid to such a person. – *Death of a Salesman*.

• **Lombard** ▶ An acronym for *loads of money but a real dickhead* – an epithet used of those who have far more money than sense. A Lombard is also an obsolete name for a banker or money-lender, because of the number of bankers in London who came from Lombardy in N Italy. Lombard Street in the City of London, the home of many headquarters of banks, is named after them. *See also*: loadsamoney.

• **London, Treaty of** ▶ A secret alliance concluded on 26 April 1915 between the Triple Entente (the UK, France, and Russia) and Italy, which agreed terms for Italy's entry into World War I. Italy had been secretly courted by both sides after 1914; she eventually agreed to commit her forces to the Entente in return for specified territorial concessions at the end of the conflict. These included possession of S Tyrol, Trentino, Trieste, and portions of Dalmatia; recognition of Italian sovereignty over the Dodecanese; and enlarged holdings in Libya, Somalia, and Eritrea at Germany's expense. The text of the treaty was leaked by the Bolsheviks in 1917 and later published by a Swedish newspaper, which caused a degree of embarrassment at the Paris peace conference in 1919. *See also*: Sykes-Picot agreement.

• **London Eye** ▶ The world's largest Ferris wheel, erected on the south bank of the Thames in London in 1999; it is 132 metres (435 feet) in diameter and cost £35million to construct and erect. The Eye's single leg, resting on concrete foundations 12 metres (40 feet) deep, supports the wheel so that it leans over the river at an angle of 65°. Attached to the circumference are 32 air-conditioned viewing capsules, each holding up to 25 people. The wheel takes 30 minutes to complete one revolution and provides its passengers with unparalleled views of London and the surrounding countryside. Visible from the top, on a clear day, are Windsor Castle, St Albans Abbey, six racecourses, and 165 golf courses.

Commonly known as the **Millennium Wheel**, the Eye was supposed to have given its first passengers a ride on 31 December 1999. However, technical problems meant that it did not open until 1 February 2000. British Airways, the main sponsors of the project, obtained planning permission for five years from Lambeth council, but they are hoping that this will be extended to enable the wheel to become a permanent feature of London's skyline.

• **London Group** ▶ An association of London artists founded in 1913 to hold biennial (later annual) exhibitions of their work. The group's unofficial father figure was Walter Sickert (1860–1942). Although the painters in the group were very diverse, the general aim was to break free of academic tradition and to draw inspiration from French post-impressionism.

• **London marathon** ▶ A race over the classic marathon distance of 26 miles 385 yards held annually in London since 1981. The race, which starts at Blackheath and passes through Docklands and the City to finish on Westminster Bridge, was the idea of former runners Christopher Brasher and John Disley and attracted a field of 7000 in its first year; of these 6255 finished within five hours. In addition to the races for able-bodied men and women, a wheelchair race for paraplegics was introduced in 1983. The race has become one of the most popular marathon fixtures, attracting serious athletes from all over the world as well as countless 'fun runners', many of whom are sponsored on behalf of charities.

• **London season** ▶ A period of heightened social activity in summer and autumn when debutantes (daughters of marriageable age of the aristocracy and upper middle classes) 'came out' and were introduced into society at a series of social, sporting, and charitable functions, such as the Alexandra Rose Ball and the Royal Academy Summer Exhibition. The practice of presenting debutantes at court – once an essential element of the London season – ceased in 1958; another, Queen Charlotte's Ball, ended in 1976 after 200 years. The London season was once an important part of English social life for the upper classes; although its role as a marriage market is long gone, the term is still sometimes used for the calendar of social events that could be said to begin with the Chelsea Flower Show in May and end with the last night of the Proms (*see*: prom) in September.

• **London to Brighton run** ▶ 1. An annual run for veteran cars (built before 1 January 1905) from the centre of London to the Metropole Hotel in Brighton (a distance of 53 miles, or 85 km). Organized by the RAC, it is held on the first Sunday in November and commemorates the Emancipation Run, held on 14 November 1896, over the same route to commemorate the raising of the speed limit from 4 mph to 12 mph. Not a race, the run is intended to test the ability of the cars to arrive in Brighton under their own steam – an increasingly difficult task for cars approaching 100 years old. The British film Genevieve (1953), starring Kay Kendall and Kenneth More, stylishly popularized the event. **2.** An annual road running race from London to Brighton, organized since 1951 by the Road Runner's Club. The race dates back to 1899 and an amateur running race organized by the South London Harriers, which was won by Frank Randell in a time of 6 hrs 58 mins 18 secs. The first runner to break the 6-hour barrier was Arthur Newton (5 hrs 33 mins 43 secs) in 1924. As a result of road changes the course of the race has varied considerably over the years, although the distance remains about 53 miles (85 km).

• **Lone Ranger** ▶ A fictional masked law-enforcing hero of the American West. With his white horse, Silver, and Indian companion, **Tonto**, he was created in 1933 by scriptwriter Fran Striker and producer George W. Trendle for a US radio series. A valiant crusader against injustice, he became the upright hero of 17 novels written by Striker between 1936 and 1957; he was also the subject of comic strips, of cinema films – starting with *The Lone Ranger* (1938), with Lee Powell in the title role and Chief Thundercloud as Tonto – and of almost 200 television adventures (1949–57) starring Clayton Moore and Jay Silverheels. In the later 1950s two large-screen spin-offs were made with Moore: *The Lone Ranger* (1956) and *The Lone Ranger and the Lost City of Gold* (1958). The most recent full-length film, *The Legend of the Lone Ranger* (1981), starred Klinton Spilsby. *See also:* kemo sabe.

• **Lone Wolf** ▶ The central character of US writer Louis Joseph Vance's novel *The Lone Wolf* (1914) and its numerous sequels. The gentleman-thief Michael Lanyard was the subject of a clutch of silent films and reappeared in over a dozen adventure movies made by Columbia in the 1930s and 1940s. The role of the Lone Wolf was played by a number of actors, including Melvyn Douglas in *The Lone Wolf Returns* (1935), Francis Lederer in *The Lone Wolf in Paris* (1938), Warren William in *The Lone Wolf Spy Hunt* (1939), *The Lone Wolf Strikes* (1940), and six others, and Gerald Mohr in *The Notorious Lone Wolf* (1946), *The Lone Wolf in London* (1947), and *The Lone Wolf in Mexico* (1947). The last film of the series, *The Lone Wolf and his Lady* (directed by John Hoffman), was made in 1949 and starred Ron Randell.

• **longhair** ▶ A man perceived as having certain characteristics associated with long hair. In the 1960s long hair became a distinguishing feature of the male hippie. Prior to this it was the mark of the intellectual, musician, or artist, who wore his hair long to distinguish himself from the 'short back and sides' style of the forces, the business world, or the lower echelons of the establishment.

• **long hot summer** ▶ A press cliché that is invariably dragged out in response to riots in the inner city, which are always more likely to flare up when hot weather inflames existing tensions. The phrase first achieved currency in the mid-1960s, when there were five consecutive summers (1964–68) of rioting in American cities. It was Martin Luther King who made it famous:

> Everyone is worrying about the long hot summer with its threat of riots. We had a long cold winter when little was done about the conditions that create riots.

That a long hot summer unfortunately creates the ideal conditions for urban riots was borne out again in the summer of 1981, when the UK saw riots in Toxteth (Liverpool), Brixton (London), and elsewhere.

• **Long March** ▶ The epic migration in 1934–35 of 100,000 Chinese communists from Kiangsi Soviet in SE China to a new base in Yenan in the NW. The Guomindang (Nationalist) army under Chiang Kai-shek had launched a series of offensives against the Kiangsi base after 1931; in October 1934 Mao Tse Tung, Chu Teh, and Lin Piao led a breakout through Nationalist lines and marched north. They arrived in Yenan in October 1935, but after a trek of 6000 miles through rugged terrain, subjected to near starvation, freezing temperatures and Nationalist attacks, only 30,000 of the Red Army survived. In Yenan, Mao consolidated his leadership of the Communist Party and prepared the military, economic, and political foundations for the eventual communist victory in 1949.

• **Long Range Desert Group** ▶ A British military force of volunteers in World War II, who penetrated behind the enemy's lines in North Africa and carried out invaluable reconnaissance work through the uncharted desert. They helped to guide various other forces to their objectives and facilitated the exploits of the SAS. *See also:* Popski's Private Army.

• **long time no see** ▶ A greeting meaning 'It's a long time since we saw each other'. It originates from the pidgin English phrases used by the colonial British in the Far East early in the 20th century. Expatriates and servicemen imported the phrase on their visits home and it soon became well established on both sides of the Atlantic. It is now somewhat dated. The variant 'long time no see – short time buckshee (*i.e.* free)' was how servicemen hoped they would be greeted by their favourite prostitute after a long absence.

• **Lonrho affair** ► A financial scandal that shook the British establishment in 1973. The international mining and trading company Lonrho was accused of offering large bribes to business contacts, including a former Tory cabinet minister (Duncan Sandys), who accepted a golden handshake of £130,000 from the company for giving up his consultancy job. The money was to be paid into a tax-free account in the Cayman Islands. The transaction was not illegal but provided evidence of tax loopholes at the top end of the capitalist system.

> It is the unpleasant and unacceptable face of capitalism but one should not suggest that the whole of British industry consists of practices of this kind. – EDWARD HEATH, replying to a question from Jo Grimond in the House of Commons, 15 May 1973.

• **Lonsdale affair** or **Portland Secrets Case** ► The trial of Gordon Arnold Lonsdale (real name Konan Trofimovich Molody; 1923–?70) in March 1961 for the theft of secret documents from the Admiralty Underwater Weapons Establishment at Portland in Dorset. Although Soviet-born, Molody had been taken to Canada by his aunt at the age of 11 with a false passport in the name of Lonsdale; he was educated in California, served with the Red Army in World War II, and became a KGB spy in America in the early 1950s. After being posted to London in 1955, he established a reputation as a playboy businessman, and recruited a network of agents, including naval clerk Harry Houghton, who stole the Portland documents, and the Krogers, from whose bungalow Lonsdale regularly radioed Moscow (*see also*: Kroger affair). Lonsdale was sent to prison for 25 years but was exchanged for the British spy Greville Wynne in April 1964.

• **Look Back in Anger** ► *See*: Porter, Jimmy; Angry Young Men.

• **lookism** ► Forming a prejudiced opinion about somebody on the basis of his or her looks. This may take the form of assuming that a fat person is lazy and stupid, or of subjecting a beautiful woman to unwanted and inappropriate compliments. The term, an invention of the US political correctness lobby, was coined by analogy with racism, sexism, etc.

• **loons** or **loon pants** ► The tight bell-bottomed trousers widely worn in the 1970s. They were usually purple and made of cotton, although velvet and canvas versions were also worn. 'Loon' was a hippie word for a wild or unconventional person.

• **loony left** ► A derogatory term of the 1980s for those members of the Labour Party, especially the Militant Tendency (*see*: militant), who favoured extreme left-wing policies. The activities of the loony left were subsequently curtailed by Neil Kinnock in his attempt to make the Labour Party an electable alternative to the Tories.

• **looping the loop** ► The aerobatic manoeuvre that consists of describing a perpendicular circle in the air; at the top of the circle, or loop, the pilot is upside down. The expression derives from the switchback once popular at fairs in which a moving car or bicycle performed a similar circuit on a perpendicular track.

• **loose cannon** ► An originally US epithet for a dangerously unpredictable ally. The reference is to a cannon that is not properly secured to the deck of a ship, which will become a danger to the crew as the ship pitches and rolls. During the Irangate scandal of the 1980s Colonel Oliver North was widely described as a loose cannon in the Reagan administration.

• **loot** ► Informal term for money, especially in large amounts; it derives from the earlier use of the word to mean military booty or plunder. It was first heard among US jazz musicians in the 1920s and became common during World War II.

• **Loran towers** ► A shortened form of *long-range navigation towers*, a system of marine and air navigation. A ship or aircraft's position (a 'fix') is calculated by noting time differences in the reception of synchronized pulses transmitted from widely dispersed broadcasting towers.

• **Lord Haw-Haw** ► The nickname of William Joyce (1906–46), who broadcast Nazi propaganda to the British people from Germany during World War II. The name was coined by Jonah Barrington, radio correspondent for the *Daily Express*, in allusion to his exaggerated Oxford accent. Joyce's broadcasts, which were intended to threaten and demoralize, made him a figure of derision and loathing in the UK. He was hanged for treason after the war, despite the fact that he was of Irish descent and denied being a British citizen. Arguably, his broadcasts did more to bolster British determination than to undermine it.

• **Lord of the Rings** ► The title of Sauron, a godlike personification of evil, in J. R. R. Tolkien's best-selling fantasy work of the same name (three parts; 1954–55). In events occurring before the start of the main story, Sauron attempts to gain control of the Rings of Power by creating one ruling ring. He achieves this but is nevertheless defeated in battle and loses the all-powerful talisman. It is later found by accident, and *The Lord of the Rings* tells of the quest of the hobbit Frodo Baggins to destroy it, and with it Sauron himself.

Originally conceived as a sequel to Tolkien's children's story *The Hobbit*, *The Lord of the Rings* was a tale that 'grew in the telling' (Foreword), deepening and darkening from a simple adventure tale into an elaborate saga of good versus evil. The book has acquired a huge cult following – many members of which attach significances to it never envisaged by Tolkien himself – and has become a benchmark against which all subsequent attempts at epic fantasy have been judged. In 1999–2000 several nationwide readers' polls voted *The Lord of the Rings* the greatest book of the 20th century – a verdict that incensed literary critics. A film of the first part of the trilogy enjoyed great success in 2001. *See also*: Middle-earth.

• **Lord Porn** ▶ A press nickname for Frank Pakenham (1905–2001), 7th Earl of Longford (*see also*: Holy Fool). A champion of traditional Christian morality, he led an unofficial inquiry into pornography in the UK and the state of the nation's morality in 1972. He campaigned for the banning of school sex education unless parental consent was obtained, the levying of higher penalties for offences under the obscenity laws, and for a higher standard of morality to be upheld in films, television programmes, and published material.

• **Lord's Taverners** ▶ A cricket team, named after the Tavern at Lord's cricket ground, founded in 1950 by a small group of actors and their friends to raise money for charity. It is now a Commonwealth-wide organization of philanthropic 'good fellows' from the world of sport and entertainment. The money raised is administered by the National Playing Fields Association, which provides cricket fields and leisure facilities for youth organizations, village teams, etc., and also sponsors overseas tours by junior cricket sides.

• **Lorelei Lee** ▶ *See*: Lee, Lorelei.

• **lorry** ▶
   **fell off the back of a lorry** A euphemism applied to stolen goods. If someone does not wish to reveal how he acquired a particular item he may say that it fell off the back of a lorry, *i.e.* that he found it in the road. The implication is that he, or someone else, stole it.

• **Los Alamos project** ▶ *See*: Manhattan Project.

• **loss leader** ▶ A product or service offered for sale at a loss in order to attract customers to spend money on other more profitable items. The practice is technically illegal in the UK under the terms of the Resale Prices Act (1976), although 'special offers' and sales are a common feature in the retail trade.

• **Lost Generation** ▶ **1.** The young men, especially of the educated upper and middle classes, who lost their lives in World War I. In the UK Rupert Brooke became their symbol; he was 27 when he died (not in battle, but of blood-poisoning). **2.** The generation of US writers active after World War I, many of whom chose to live and work in Europe. They included Ernest Hemingway, F. Scott Fitzgerald, and Gertrude Stein.

> That's what you are. That's what you all are. All of you young people who served in the war. You are a lost generation. – GERTRUDE STEIN, 1926.

• **lotus position** ▶ A cross-legged sitting position with the feet on the thighs and the arms resting on the knees, used by Indian mystics for meditation and relaxation. The position became familiar to people in Western countries in the 1960s, as yoga and meditation became widely practised. The term is a translation from the Sanskrit *padmāsana*, from *padma*, lotus, plus *āsana*, posture. The lotus lily, a sacred plant to Hindus, symbolizes the detachment of the intellect from external matter and sensation. For most Westerners, the lotus position is excrutiatingly uncomfortable; only after long practice can it become a relaxed position in which the intellect is free to do anything.

• **Lou Gehrig's disease** ▶ *See*: Murderers' Row.

• **louie** ▶ **1.** British drug-users' slang for one sixteenth of an ounce of cannabis. It is named after King Louis XVI of France. This is the smallest quantity for sale by weight. *See also*: henry. **2.** US slang for a lieutenant.

• **lounge lizard** ▶ A well-dressed man who frequents the restaurants, bars, and hotels in which the rich gather, probably with the aim of seducing a wealthy woman. Originating in the 1920s, the expression is now rarely used.

• **Louvain** ▶ A town in Brabant province, Belgium, which suffered serious damage when invaded by Germany in both world wars. In August 1914 the Germans occupied the town, massacred hundreds of civilians as a reprisal for attacks on German soldiers, and then burnt large areas of the medieval town centre, including the 15th-century university library and Sint Pieterskirche. These sites were seriously damaged again when the town was overrun by German forces in May 1940.

• **love beads** ▶ Coloured beads worn, typically as a necklace, as a symbol of peace and love. Love beads were part of the dress of the flower people of the late 1960s.

• **love bombing ▸** A US term from the mid-1970s for a style of recruitment used by some religious and pseudo-religious cults. Members bombard potential converts, who are generally young and immature with intense feelings of care and love. This is usually accompanied by attacks on conventional society and insinuations that the victim's family and friends are corrupt or hypocritical and therefore not to be trusted.

• **love-in ▸** A gathering of hippies or flower people for the purpose of celebrating or expressing mutual love. This was one of many expressions, such as sleep-in, **laugh-in**, and **sing-in**, introduced in the 1960s by analogy with sit-in.

• **lovely grub ▸** A catchphrase, dating from service use during World War II, meaning anything agreeable or welcome, not only food.

• **lovely jubbly ▸** See: jubbly.

• **lower than a snake's hips** or **belly ▸** A catchphrase meaning contemptible, in use since at least the 1930s; for example in Leonard Mann's *Flesh in Armour* (1932):

> 'It was a dirty trick. He knew about me and her.' 'Dirty! Lower than a snake's belly.'

It should not be confused with the US slang expression **the snake's hips**, used in the 1920s and 1930s to describe a remarkable person, as in 'she was the snake's hips'.

• **low-involvement product ▸** See: high-involvement product.

• **low-level language ▸** A type of computer programming language that is closer to machine code – the actual sequence of digital instructions understood by the microprocessor itself – than to human language. Compared to a high-level language, a low-level language is much faster and more efficient in execution but can only be used by highly trained professional programmers.

• **low rider ▸ 1.** US slang for someone who drives a customized car that has had its suspension lowered. It may also be used of the car itself. Low riders were popular during the 1970s and 1980s, especially among Hispanic youths in Los Angeles who would cruise slowly in packs showing off their customized vehicles. **2.** Slang for an unpleasant person.

• **lox ▸** The Yiddish name for smoked salmon, eaten as a delicacy, usually on a bagel with cream cheese; it is mainly heard in New York City and other US cities with a large Jewish population. Unlike Scottish smoked salmon, which was until quite recently a luxury food in the UK, lox is either cured in salt (**Scandinavian lox**) or in sugar (**Nova Scotia lox**; sometimes called **Novey**). The Yiddish word is derived from the German *Lachs* (or Swedish *lax*), salmon. Although lox is usually regarded as a Jewish invention, it was unknown to the European Jews who emigrated to America and is hardly eaten in Israel. In fact, it is a delicacy that has been cultivated by the Jewish population of New York in the last 60 years. *See also*: gravlax.

• **LP ▸** Long play. The standard format for gramophone records from the late 1940s, when they were introduced by the US broadcasting company CBS. They are normally 12 inches (30 cm) in diameter, revolve at 33 rpm, contain an average of 250 grooves per inch on a vinyl plastic base, and play for about 25 minutes per side. The LP soon eclipsed the previous format (a shellac-based disc with around 100 grooves per inch, which was 10 or 12 inches in diameter and revolved at 78 rpm). LPs subsequently lost favour to tape cassettes and were finally superseded by the CD (compact disc) in the 1980s and 1990s. Like other types of gramophone record, they are now only collectors' items. *See*: digital recording.

• **LSD ▸ 1.** The former monetary units of the UK; pounds (Latin *libra*), shillings (Latin *solidus*), and pence (Latin *denarius*). They were introduced by Lombard merchants in the middle ages. LSD was replaced by decimal currency on 15 February 1971. **2.** Lysergic acid diethylamide. A synthetic crystalline compound which acts as a powerful hallucinogen. Taken in tiny doses, it can produce hallucinations, altered sensory perception, and a feeling of euphoria. It is, however, a dangerous drug to abuse; its long-term use can cause schizophrenia-like conditions and even single doses can cause fear, anxiety, and confusion.

• **LSE ▸** London School of Economics and Political Science. The LSE was founded in 1895 by the social reformer Sidney Webb (1858–1947) and admitted into the University of London in 1900, following the establishment of a Faculty of Economics and Political Science. The LSE occupies a complex of buildings in Houghton Street, off the Aldwych, in central London.

• **LS/MFT ▸** One of America's most esoteric and successful advertising slogans. The American Tobacco Company first used LS/MFT for Lucky Strike cigarettes during the 1940s, when smoking was still regarded as universally acceptable. The initials stand for 'Lucky Strike Means Fine Tobacco'. Two popular slogans used by competitors were **Call for Philip Morris** and **I'd walk a mile for a Camel**.

• **Lublin Committee** ▶ The Polish Committee of National Liberation. A group of left-wing Poles sponsored by the Soviets during World War II, as an alternative authority to the Polish government-in-exile in London. After the Red Army's liberation of E Poland in July 1944, the committee was installed in Lublin and recognized by the Soviet Union as the legitimate authority. A provisional government was proclaimed in December 1944 (of the 25 members 15 had been in the Lublin Committee), this was later recognized by the UK and America on 5 July 1945, two months after the end of the war in Europe.

• **Lubyanka** ▶ Moscow's most notorious prison of the Soviet era, reserved for political prisoners only. Thousands of NKVD victims were imprisoned, interrogated, tortured, and executed here. The Lubyanka, in Dzerzhinsky Square, was the headquarters of an insurance company until it was taken over by the Cheka in the 1920s. The NKVD offices occupied the outer section and the prison cells were located within an inner courtyard in a nine-storey building formerly used by the insurance company as a boarding house. There were around 110 small cells holding not more than 200 prisoners at a time. Executions were carried out in the basement.

• **Lucky** ▶ A common nickname for people who appear to have more than the average share of good luck, or who narrowly escape death or misfortune. Among its recipients were the Sicilian-born US gangster Salvatore Luciano (1896–1962), a leader of organized crime, who survived having his throat cut by a rival and ended his days living in luxury in Naples; and the 7th Earl of Lucan (1934–?), who acquired his nickname through his luck in gambling and disappeared without trace following the discovery of the body of his children's nanny. Widely suspected to be the murderer, 'Lucky' Lucan has been sought unsuccessfully by police forces all over the world; his friends maintained that he had committed suicide after the murder. He was finally declared dead by the High Court in 1999.

• **Lucky Jim** ▶ *See*: Dixon, Jim.

• **Lucy** ▶ Nickname given by palaeoanthropologists to skeletal remains discovered in 1974 in E Africa; the structure of the pelvis indicated that the remains were of a female. The fossil was identified as belonging to the species *Australopithecus afarensis*, an apelike hominid that lived at least 3 million years ago, probably coexisting with the earliest ancestors of modern humans. It was named after the Beatles song 'Lucy in the Sky with Diamonds', which was playing when the discovery was made.

• **Lucy ring** ▶ A spy network based in Switzerland during World War II, which channelled details of German plans for the Eastern Front to Moscow on a daily basis. 'Lucy' was the codename of the key figure in the network, Rudolph Roessler, a German publisher who moved to Switzerland after Hitler came to power. The ring was actually a Soviet-controlled organization, which employed agents of several different nationalities to glean information from a variety of sources, including anti-Fascist freelance intelligence agencies. It also made use of intercepts of German signals, from the British code-breaking operation at Bletchley Park. These were provided anonymously by the British and fed to Stalin indirectly through the Lucy ring, because he was known to mistrust any intelligence that did not come from his own networks.

• **Luftwaffe** ▶ The German airforce built up secretly after World War I and publicly unveiled to an astonished world in 1935. The Treaty of Versailles forbade the Germans to construct military aircraft; however, potential military designs, such as the Junkers 52 transport, were produced at Hugo Junkers' civilian aircraft factory at Dessau, Reichswehr personnel were trained at secret flying schools in the Soviet Union, and glider clubs were encouraged for pilot training in Germany. In 1935 the Luftwaffe was revealed as the most modern and best equipped air force in Europe, with 1888 aircraft and 20,000 trained officers and men.

• **luge** ▶ A small one- or two-seater toboggan used for racing, with each rider lying on his or her back. Toboggan racing entered the Olympics in 1928 to be replaced in 1964 by luge racing, which was dominated for many years by the East Germans.

• **Lüger** ▶ Various models of a semi-automatic hand gun invented by the Austrian George Lüger in 1898 and first manufactured for both military and commercial use in 1900. The design was partly based on the first true automatic pistol, invented by Hugo Borchardt (1893), and was adopted as a regulation weapon by many countries, notably Nazi Germany. Production ceased in 1943, but some Lüger models were again manufactured commercially in the 1970s.

• **lumpectomy** ▶ The surgical removal of a lump, especially from the breast. This technique is used in the treatment of early-stage breast cancer, and involves the excision of the tumour and surrounding tissues. Remaining breast tissue is left intact, in contrast to mastectomy, in which the entire breast is removed. It is generally combined with high-energy radiotherapy to destroy residual cancer cells.

• **Luna** ► A series of 24 Soviet moon probes launched during the years 1959–76. Luna 3 (October 1959) sent back the first pictures of the far side of the moon and Luna 9 achieved the first soft landing (3 February 1966). Luna 15 was launched on 13 July 1969 in an audacious attempt to retrieve samples of moonrock only days before the blast-off of Apollo 11, which placed the first men on the moon on 20 July 1969 (see: Apollo moon programme).

• **Lunar Orbiter** ► A series of five US space probes placed in orbit around the moon in 1966–67 to provide photographic details of the surface so that a landing site could be selected for the forthcoming Apollo moon programme.

• **lunar rover** or **lunar roving vehicle** ► A battery-driven four-wheeled vehicle used for exploratory travel on the moon's surface. Lunar rovers were used by the astronauts of Apollo missions 15, 16, and 17 in 1971 and 1972 and left behind on the moon after use. A remote-controlled television camera mounted on the vehicle beamed pictures of the lunar surface direct to Earth. Also called **moon car**, **moon crawler**, or **moon rover**.

• **lunatic fringe** ► A minority group especially within a large organization, who hold extreme or eccentric versions of the views held by the majority. The expression has been ascribed to US president Theodore Roosevelt (1913).

• **lunchtime abortion** ► An abortion carried out by vacuum aspiration in which a suction tube is used to remove the fetus. First heard in the early 1970s, the term refers to the method's quick and relatively safe procedure: though full recovery may take one or two days, some women return to work the same day after the recommended minimum half-hour rest.

• **lunchtime concerts** ► A series of daily recitals organized by the pianist Myra Hess (1890–1965) in London during World War II. Held at the National Gallery, they attracted large audiences of war-weary Londoners every day. For her tireless efforts in starting and arranging these recitals Myra Hess was made a DBE in 1941.

• **Lunokhod** ► (Russian, moonwalker) The name of two Soviet eight-wheeled unmanned vehicles used for scientific exploration of the lunar surface. The vehicles were landed by Lunik spacecraft in 1970 and 1973. Powered by solar cells and directed by radio from Earth, they travelled across the moon's surface taking pictures and measurements. The first Lunokhod was operational for 10 months; Lunokhod 2 covered a distance of over 35 km in 4 months.

• **Lupin, Arsène** ► Fictional criminal turned detective, who featured in the novels and stories of the French author Maurice Leblanc. He first appeared in *The Seven of Hearts* (1907) and has been compared to two famous characters of British fiction, the upper-crust criminal Raffles and the super-sleuth Sherlock Holmes. Films about the *cambrioleur* include a German-made series starring Paul Otto in the leading role (1910–11), a silent movie (1917), and various talkies made in the 1930s and 1940s, as well as a 1962 French film starring Jean-Claude Brialy. The character also featured in a 1970s French television series.

• **lurgy** or **lergi** ► British slang for an unspecified infectious illness, often referred to as the **dreaded lurgy**. The word, particularly popular with schoolchildren in the 1950s and 1960s, was adopted by the Goon Show. Its etymology has been traced back to the German chemical company Lurgi; alternatively, it may be a corruption of 'allergy'.

• **lush** ► 1. US slang for a drunkard or drug addict. The former sense came into popular use in the 1920s but goes back to the mid-19th century. 'Lush' was also a slang word for alcohol in late 18th-century England, probably after a London brewer named Lushington. The City of Lushington was a drinking club for actors that met at the Harp Tavern in London until about 1895. 2. Abbreviated form of luscious, indicating that someone or something is eminently desirable or attractive.

• **Lusitania** ► The Cunard liner (named after the ancient Roman province), sunk by a German U-boat off the south coast of Ireland on 7 May 1915, while en route from New York to Liverpool. The ship sank within 20 minutes with the loss of 1198 lives, including 124 Americans. Among the dead were the millionaire Alfred Vanderbilt and the theatre producer Carl Frohman. The sinking was greeted with horror and outrage by the US press and public. Although, initially, the US government maintained its policy of neutrality, the tragedy was certainly a contributory factor in its decision to enter the war against Germany in April 1917. Controversy over the sinking was revived after the war when German accusations that the *Lusitania* was carrying substantial amounts of ammunition and other war materials were partly confirmed. There has also been some speculation that Winston Churchill and the other lords of the Admiralty deliberately put the liner at risk in the hope of bringing America into the war.

> To die will be an awfully big adventure. – CARL FROHMAN, quoting from *Peter Pan* as he jumped into the sea from the *Lusitania*.

• **Lycra** ▶ The tradename (registered by E. I. du Pont de Nemours & Co.) of a shiny man-made elastic polyurethane fibre and fabric used extensively for sportswear – swimming costumes, leotards, cycling shorts, etc. – and other tight-fitting clothing.

• **Lyme disease**▶ An infectious illness first identified in 1975 among children in the Connecticut town of Old Lyme. Lyme disease, which is carried by a bacterium, can in rare cases prove fatal; it is characterized by pains in the joints, high fever, a rash, and fatigue. Research has shown that the infection is spread to humans by the bites of infected ticks.

• **Lysenkoism** or **Michurinism**▶ A movement, based on the maverick ideas of the Soviet geneticist Trofim Denisovich Lysenko (1898–1976) and the horticulturalist I. V. Michurin (1855–1935), that caused ideological and political upheaval in Soviet science from the 1930s to the 1960s. Lysenko came to prominence in 1929 with his proposals for the vernalization of winter wheat seed, which was chilled to induce it to germinate after sowing in the spring. This had the benefit of eliminating seed losses in the field due to overwintering, a problem of pressing concern to Soviet agriculture at that time. Moreover, Lysenko claimed that such environmentally induced changes in the seed could be inherited by successive generations of the plant. This contradicted prevailing scientific orthodoxy – notably the genetic theories of Mendel and others – and harked back to the early 19th-century beliefs of Jean Lamarck.

Stalin gave his backing to Lysenko, whose influence rapidly increased. The Lysenkoists integrated their theories of heredity with Marxist dogma and denounced the conflicting theories of orthodox geneticists as bourgeois and contrary to Marxist thinking. A notable critic of Lysenkoist theory was Nicolai Vavilov, president of the V. I. Lenin All-Union Academy of Agricultural Sciences; in 1938 Vavilov was succeeded in this post by Lysenko. Two years later Lysenko became director of the Genetic Institute of the Soviet Union and a key figure in Soviet agriculture and biology. Vavilov was exiled to Siberia in the same year and died in 1943. Many other dissenting Soviet geneticists shared his fate.

Lysenkoism reached its high point in 1948 with a report to the Academy of Agricultural Sciences entitled *The Position in Biological Science*. Approved by the Communist Party Central Committee, this set out the ideologically acceptable view of biology for Soviet science. Further, this meeting directed that textbooks and courses be changed in line with Lysenko's doctrines. Lysenkoism continued to prevail until the fall of Khrushchev in 1964. A committee investigating his work uncovered evidence of fraud, and he was ousted from his key administrative posts. Soviet biology was at last allowed to rejoin the mainstream of genetics research.

• **Lytton report** ▶ A report condemning Japan's invasion of Manchuria (18 September 1931) published in September 1932 by a commission appointed by the League of Nations and headed by Lord Lytton. The Japanese completely ignored the commission's findings and the major European powers proved incapable of united action. This unfortunate episode exposed the inadequacy of the League of Nations in preventing aggression.

# M

• **M** ▶ The codename of the fictional service chief in the James Bond novels of Ian Fleming. The character may have been based on the head of Military Intelligence in the UK during World War II, Maj.-Gen. Sir Stewart Menzies (1890–1968). *See also*: C; Q.

• **Maastricht Treaty** ▶ The treaty negotiated by EC heads of government in Maastricht, the Netherlands, in December 1991 and signed in February 1992. It established the European Union, committing member states to a process of ever-closer monetary and political union, while also introducing a new foreign policy and security dimension to their cooperation. On British insistence, a section dealing with the harmonization of social policy, including employees' rights and welfare (the so-called **social chapter**), was excluded from the treaty; it was, however, adopted by the other 11 states as a separate 'protocol' and was later incorporated into the Amsterdam Treaty (1997) after its adoption by the UK.

Specifically, the Maastricht Treaty set a timetable for the creation of a European Central Bank and a single currency (*see*: European Monetary System), allocated greater powers to the European parliament, and paved the way for the introduction of common citizenship. It was hailed by Chancellor Helmut Kohl of Germany as 'crossing the Rubicon' on the road to political union. However, opponents of Maastricht in the UK and elsewhere denounced it as a betrayal of national sovereignty, arguing that it would transfer power from elected governments to unelected bureaucrats.

Once signed, the treaty had to be ratified by individual states. In June 1992 the future of Maastricht was thrown into doubt when the Danish electorate rejected it in a referendum. Following a Community decision to exempt Denmark from certain of its provisions, the treaty was approved in a second referendum in May 1993. In the UK the process of ratification was also long and tortuous. It culminated in a night of parliamentary drama in July 1993, when the government was defeated by an alliance of opposition MPs pressing for the incorporation of the social chapter and Tory rebels, who saw this as an opportunity to sink the whole treaty. The government called and won a vote of confidence on the issue, securing the passage of the un-amended treaty but at a severe cost to its own authority.

• **Ma Bell** ▶ The affectionate nickname of America's Bell Telephone System, which evolved from a company formed in 1877 by the telephone's inventor, Alexander Graham Bell (1847–1922). The 22 regional operating companies, such as Southern Bell and Southwestern Bell, were owned by the American Telephone and Telegraph Co. until 1984, when the US government broke up the (80%) monopoly. The independent companies, however, remain 'Ma Bell' or – more commonly now – **Baby Bell** to their users.

> Ma Bell's babies grow big away from home. – *The Independent*, 19 February 1991.

• **Macavity** ▶ The subject of the poem 'Macavity: The Mystery Cat', by T. S. Eliot (1888–1965), published in the collection *Old Possum's Book of Practical Cats* (1939; *see*: Old Possum). A leading member of the feline underworld, Macavity is described by Eliot as 'the bafflement of Scotland Yard' and 'the Napoleon of Crime'. He is never found at the scene of the crime and always has an alibi:

> Macavity, Macavity, there's no one like
> Macavity,
> For he's a fiend in feline shape, a monster of
> depravity.
> You may meet him in a by-street, you may see
> him in the square
> But when a crime's discovered, then *Macavity's
> not there!*

Macavity appears in the Lloyd Webber musical *Cats*, based on Eliot's book. In this production the poem is read in a stage whisper.

• **McCarthyism** ▶ The anti-communist witch-hunt that led to the hounding of many alleged left-wingers from US public life in the period 1950–54; so called after its instigator, US Senator Joseph McCarthy (1909–57). His relentless investigation of prominent figures in various walks of life, from writers and film stars to members of the Democratic Party, found wide public support at first but later caused growing disquiet. Although Soviet agents were certainly active in America at this time, his claim to have the names of 205 communists employed by the State Department was never substantiated; when he went on to level criticism at the army and President Eisenhower himself in 1954 he was censured by the Senate and sacked.

• **McDonald's** ▶ The most successful fast food company in the world. About 96% of Americans eat at least once a year at McDonald's; it is also the largest such chain in the UK, Canada, Australia, Japan, and many other countries. The company opened its first restaurant in Moscow in 1990. McDonald's was started in 1940 as a single drive-in restaurant in San Bernardino, California, by the McDonald brothers, Richard and Maurice. They perfected assembly-line production, selling their hamburgers for 15 cents each. The name and technique was bought in 1955 by Ray A. Kroc, who introduced the golden-arch logo and built a $40 million Hamburger University to train employees. Kroc's perfected technology has sold some 80 billion hamburgers. He died in 1984 but lived to see his company Americanize the global food-service industry; indeed, McDonald's has now become a symbol for America's cultural and commercial dominance of the planet.

• **Mace** ▶ Tradename for a form of chemical nerve irritant used as a tear gas. Mace causes a burning sensation in the eyes, nose, and throat and temporarily incapacitates the recipient. It was used by US police for crowd control in the late 1960s and early 1970s, being particularly associated with the suppression of demonstrations against the Vietnam War. It has also been used, in aerosol form, as a means of personal protection (in the UK, Mace aerosols are considered to be offensive weapons and their use is illegal). The name is probably taken from the spice obtained from nutmeg.

• **macguffin** ▶ A word invented by the film director Alfred Hitchcock (1899–1980) to denote something that starts off the action of a film plot but subsequently turns out to be irrelevant. It later spread to the general language, meaning something that sparks off a course of action but loses its importance as events proceed. Hitchcock is on record as saying that he took both the name and the idea from a Scottish shaggy dog story in which a train passenger carrying a large odd-looking parcel was asked by other passengers what it contained. He replied that it was a macguffin; when asked what that is, he went on to explain that a macguffin is a lion in the Highlands. When it was pointed out to him that there are no lions in the Highlands, he replied that there were no macguffins either.

• **machine code** ▶ The binary code sequence that is directly understood and executed by a specific microprocessor or computer central processing unit (CPU). Computers execute instructions in machine code much faster than if they were translated into a higher level programming language, such as Basic or PASCAL. However, machine code programming is a painstaking process and requires detailed knowledge of the design of a particular microprocessor. *See also*: high-level language; low-level language.

• **machine for living in** ▶ *See*: Le Corbusier.

• **machine gun** ▶ Drug-abusers' and prison slang for a hypodermic syringe (1960s).

• **Mach number** ▶ The ratio of the flight speed of a body, aircraft, etc., to the speed of sound. The concept was devised by the Austrian physicist and psychologist, Ernst Mach (1838–1916). An aircraft flying at Mach 2 is travelling at twice the speed of sound. The first aircraft to reach the speed of sound, *i.e.* Mach 1, was the US rocket plane Bell XS-1, in 1947, which reached Mach 1.015 (1078 kph or 670 mph). *See*: supersonic.

• **macho** ▶ Showing an exaggerated pride in male characteristics such as strength or virility: from the Mexican Spanish for masculine. The noun for the concept is **machismo**. Zsa-Zsa Gabor, the Hollywood film star, is said to have remarked:

> Men who act macho aren't mucho!

• **Machu Picchu** ▶ An Inca city in Peru, widely thought to exist only in fable until it was discovered in 1911 by Hiram Bingham. The excellent condition of the city, which dates from the late 15th century, is owing to the fact that the Spaniards never found it. Built on a mountain ridge in the Urubamba valley, near Cuzco, the city contains a palace, temple, and other buildings constructed of stone blocks and is surrounded by agricultural terraces. Its original name is unknown: Machu Picchu is the name of the mountain that rises above it.

• **McKenna duties** ▶ An import tax introduced during World War I by Reginald McKenna (1863–1943), chancellor of the exchequer, and abolished in 1924. The duties were intended to restrict the import of luxury items, such as cars and watches.

• **McKenzie friend** ▶ In the UK, a person who appears in court to help and advise one of the parties on a non-professional basis. Such a person may be employed when a party cannot afford or prefers to do without legal representation. The McKenzie friend may not address the court but is entitled to make and pass notes and to confer quietly with the party. These rights were established in the case of McKenzie v. McKenzie (1970), after which the McKenzie friend is named. Although the term sometimes appeared in legal contexts in the 1970s it did not achieve wide currency until the 1980s, when an increasing number of parties began to make use of such help.

• **McLuhanism** ▶ The theories of the Canadian writer Marshall McLuhan(1911–80), concerning the impact of mass communication and modern technology on society. McLuhan saw the world becoming a global village, and predicted that the media through which information is transmitted would become more important than the information itself: 'the medium is the message.' The role of the printed word would be significantly reduced in this world of instant awareness; moreover, electronic communications technology would profoundly alter perceptions of space, time, and personal identity. These controversial ideas were propounded in such books as *The Gutenberg Galaxy* (1962) and *Understanding Media* (1964).

• **McMahon letters** ▶ Secret correspondence (1915–16) between Sir Henry McMahon, British high commissioner in Egypt, and Sherif Hussein of Mecca (c. 1854–1931). In the letters, which were published in 1938, Hussein demanded that certain Arab lands be granted independence in return for Arab help during World War I. These included what is now Saudi Arabia, Israel, Jordan, Iraq, Syria, and Lebanon. McMahon appeared to pledge British support for all but Lebanon and part of Iraq, but inserted a carefully worded get-out clause to preserve the UK's freedom of manoeuvre. His 'promise' was subsequently compromised by the Balfour declaration and the Sykes-Picot agreement; it was totally disregarded by the Allies after the war.

• **McMahon Line** ▶ The boundary between NE India and Tibet, as agreed in the Simla convention (1914). The McMahon Line follows the crest of the Himalayas, the natural boundary between the two countries. Although the convention was signed by Sir Henry McMahon for the UK and by the Tibetan representative, the Chinese government refused to recognize the McMahon Line and subsequently laid claim to much of Arunachal Pradesh on the Indian side of the boundary. Chinese troops made two unsuccessful attempts to invade this territory, crossing the McMahon Line in 1959 and in 1962 (*see*: Ladakh crisis), and the boundary remains in dispute.

• **Macpherson Report** ▶ *See*: Stephen Lawrence case.

• **macroeconomics** ▶ The study of economic fac-

tors or systems at the level of the country or economic bloc. It covers such matters as money supply, employment levels, interest rates, government spending, investment, consumption, and inflation. In particular, macroeconomics assesses the role that governments should play in an economy. *Compare*: microeconomics.

• **Mac the Knife** ▶ **1.** Nickname given to the British prime minister Harold Macmillan in July 1962; it alludes to his sacking of seven cabinet ministers, among them the Lord Chancellor, in what became known as the Night of the Long Knives. *See also*: Supermac. **2.** Nickname of the Scottish-born businessman Ian MacGregor (later Lord MacGregor; 1912–98), who earned the resentment of British trade unions in the 1980s after he was appointed to make the coal and steel industries profitable. As chairman of British Steel (1980–83) he cut the workforce by more than half, while his subsequent plan to close up to 95 coal mines provoked the great miners' strike of 1984–85 (*see*: King Arthur).

Both nicknames allude to Mack the Knife, the villain in Brecht and Weill's *The Threepenny Opera* (1929), best known from the celebrated song with this title.

• **Mac the Mouth** ▶ *See*: Superbrat.

• **Macwonder** ▶ *See*: Supermac.

• **MAD** ▶ Mutual assured destruction. A Cold War acronym for the ultimate result of any nuclear exchange between the superpowers. Advocates of nuclear deterrence argued that MAD maintained the balance of terror by virtue of the massive nuclear arsenals possessed by America and the Soviet Union. In the event of a pre-emptive strike by one side against the other, the victim would retain the capability for substantial retaliation against the aggressor. The result would be so devastating to both sides that, in theory, a nuclear strike would become totally unacceptable as a military option.

• **mad** ▶

**He went mad and they shot him** The facetious reply, often given by Australian troops during World War II, to a query (especially from an officer) as to someone's whereabouts. Another version was the more graphic **He went for a crap and the sniper got him**.

• **mad cow disease** ▶ The colloquial name for bovine spongiform encephalopathy (**BSE**), a disease of cattle thought to be caused by an abnormal protein, or prion, similar to those responsible for Creutzfeldt–Jakob disease (*see*: CJD) in humans and scrapie in sheep. First identified in the UK in 1986, it results in degeneration of brain tissue, giving it a spongy appearance, and is invariably fatal. There is evidence that the disease first arose in a single cow sometime during the 1970s, probably as a spontaneous mutation, and was spread to other cattle via feed containing bovine offal contaminated with the infectious agent. Previously it was thought that the agent might have been transmitted from sheep infected with scrapie. During the late 1980s and 1990s, the UK herd suffered an epidemic, with some 177,000 confirmed cases of BSE up to mid-2000. Fears surrounding the consumption of infected beef were realized in March 1996 when scientists concluded that a new variant form of CJD (vCJD) was likely to be caused by eating meat or meat products from animals infected with BSE. As a result, the EU imposed a global ban on exports of British beef, and the domestic beef industry was plunged into crisis (*see*: beef ban). By the time the BSE inquiry, headed by Lord Phillips, published its findings in October 2000, over 80 people had died of vCJD as a consequence of the BSE epidemic. Cases of BSE have also been confirmed in other European countries, notably France and Germany: it is feared that the disease was exported from the UK in contaminated meat-and-bone meal, shipped in the 1980s and early 1990s.

• **Mademoiselle from Armenteers** ▸ In World War I Amentières in N France was held by the British until the great German offensive of 1918. The army song 'Mademoiselle from Armenteers, Parlez-vous', which became widely known, originated in 1916. It was a modification of the much earlier song and tune 'Three Prussian Officers Crossed the Rhine'. It readily lent itself to improvisation, especially of a scurrilous nature:

> O Madam, have you any good wine?
> Parlez-vous;
> O Madam, have you any good wine?
> Parlez-vous.
> O Madam, have you any good wine?
> Fit for a soldier of the line?
> Inky-pinky, parlez-vous.

• **Madison Avenue** ▸ A street in New York City in which many advertising firms were formerly situated. In the 1940s Madison Avenue became synonymous with the advertising business itself; this sense arose when an article on the contribution of the advertising business to World War II appeared in *New Republic*, signed Madison Avenue. Most leading advertising firms have now left the Avenue.

• **Madison Square Garden murder** ▸ *See*: Girl in the Red Velvet Swing.

• **Mad Jack** ▸ Nickname of Jack Howard, 20th Earl of Suffolk and Berkshire. Renowned for his flamboyant behaviour, he was killed in 1941 while defusing a bomb; he was posthumously awarded the George Cross.

• **Mad Mike** ▸ Nickname of Mike Hoare, a South African mercenary leader who became notorious for his involvement in various escapades in the Congo in the 1960s with the Wild Geese mercenaries. He was imprisoned in 1981 following a failed coup in the Seychelles. He and 43 fellow mercenaries were detected after their cover as members of the 'Froth Blowers' club on a golfing holiday was blown – one of their golf bags came open to reveal a gun; they hijacked an Air India jet back to South Africa, where they were arrested and put on trial.

• **Mad Monk** ▸ Nickname of Gregory Efimovitch Novykh Rasputin (1871–1916), the Siberian *starets* (holy man) notorious for his influence over the Russian monarchy in its last years. He was apparently given the surname Rasputin (a word meaning 'the dissolute') by fellow villagers and did his best to live up to the epithet throughout his life. His numerous sexual conquests were furthered by his assertion that physical contact with him was itself a purification. Despite his indecencies, the Mad Monk developed an excessive familiarity with the Empress Alexandra and Tsar Nicholas II, which arose from his apparent success in healing the Tsarevich Alexis, a victim of haemophilia. Rasputin was first called to the palace in 1905; thereafter his power increased steadily until he became chief adviser to the Empress when the Tsar took personal command of the army in 1915. Although in the presence of his royal patrons he played the humble but holy peasant, in private he argued passionately that redemption was only available to sinners. As a devoted seeker of salvation he embarked on the necessary antecedent misbehaviour with relish. Because the Empress refused to believe accounts of his debauchery, a group of courtiers led by Prince Yusupov attempted to poison him. When this inexplicably failed, they shot him and threw his body into the River Neva.

• **Mad Mullah** ▸ Nickname of Mohammed bin Abdulla, a mullah who gave great trouble to the British in Somaliland at various times between 1899 and 1920. He claimed to be the Mahdi (the Islamic messiah) and made extensive raids on tribes friendly to the British. The Dervish power was not finally broken until 1920, when the Mad Mullah escaped to Ethiopia, where he died in 1921.

• **madwoman** ▸
   **all over the place like a madwoman's custard** A colourful Australian catchphrase of the period after World War II, meaning 'in total disarray'. Variants include **all over the place like a**

**madwoman's knitting** and the less polite **all over the place like a madwoman's shit**.

• **Mae West** ▶ Nickname of the inflatable life-jacket or vest worn by aircrews in World War II. It was an allusion to the generously proportioned film star Mae West. *See*: come up and see me some time.

• **mafficking** ▶ Extravagant and boisterous celebration, especially on an occasion of national rejoicing. From the uproarious scenes and unrestrained exultation that took place in the centre of London on the night of 18 May 1900, when the news of the relief of Mafeking (besieged by the Boers for 217 days) became known. The 'heroic' character of Baden-Powell's defence has since been questioned, but the impact made at the time is not in dispute.

• **Mafia** ▶ A network of Sicilian criminal organizations that became increasingly powerful during the 19th century and went on to become the most potent force in the international underworld. Extortion through blackmail, assassination, and the vendetta are its characteristic methods. The Mafia's power in Italy was largely broken under Mussolini but it soon recovered its influence after World War II. Sicilian immigrants had already introduced it into New York and other US cities, where it became a growing menace from the 1890s; indeed, Mussolini's firm measures caused a fresh influx to America, where the *mafiosi* joined the bootleggers and gangsters of the Al Capone era. These groups adopted the name **Cosa Nostra** (Italian, our thing, our affair) and soon came to control much of the drug racket, gambling, and prostitution in the big cities. Repeated campaigns to bring leading *mafiosi* to justice have been hampered by the fear of reprisals and the organization's powerful code of silence, known as **homerta**.

*Mafia* is apparently an Arabic word denoting a place of refuge, dating from the Arab conquest of Sicily in the 9th century; many Sicilian families found a *mafia* in the hills, where they duly became peasant bandits, with patriotic and family loyalties. Their resistance continued after the Norman conquest of the 11th century and later control by Spain. After the liberation and unification of Italy the Mafia came to dominate Sicilian life through a combination of blackmail and intimidation.

• **mafiaology** ▶ The study of the Mafia crime families. Since the 1960s mafiaology has been of interest to professional sociologists, criminologists, and historians investigating the origins and operation of organized crime. The activities of the Mafia have also inspired numerous popular books, films, and television programmes, which feed on the public's morbid fascination with violence and corruption. *See also*: family; godfather.

• **magical mystery tour** ▶ A long round-about journey, often when the driver is lost or taking a not very direct short cut. The phrase was used by the Beatles for the title of their 1967 television film. In the 1950s and 1960s a 'mystery tour' was a holiday excursion (usually lasting for a day) to an undisclosed destination offered by various coach companies. Passengers usually found themselves at a location they would not have dreamt of visiting in normal circumstances.

• **magic bullet** ▶ A drug designed to destroy a specific bacterium, virus, or cancer cell, without damaging healthy cells or tissue in the host. The expression was popularized by the biopic *Dr Ehrlich's Magic Bullet* (1940) in which Edward G. Robinson played the role of the German biochemist Paul Ehrlich (1854–1915), who developed chemical agents that would selectively destroy disease-causing organisms. This led to his discovery in 1910 of the antisyphilitic drug arsphenamine (marketed as Salvarsan).

• **magic circle** ▶ **1.** Any inner group of people who have control of an organization and deliberate on its management in secret. **2. The Magic Circle** is a British society of conjurors founded in 1905. Conjurors elected to the Magic Circle consider themselves to be the elite of those who entertain by magic; they are committed, on pain of expulsion, never to disclose to non-members how a particular trick is performed.

• **magic eye** ▶ A photoelectric cell used to control a circuit. In the simplest form a beam of light is directed onto the cell. When this is interrupted the circuit operates. Magic eyes are used in security devices and for the automatic opening of doors.

• **magic mushroom** ▶ Any of various species of mushroom that contain psilocybin, a hallucinogenic substance similar in effect to LSD. In the UK, eating these mushrooms is not an offence; for certain sections of the population, collecting native species of magic mushroom, such as the liberty cap, is a popular seasonal activity.

• **Maginot Line** ▶ A zone of fortifications built along the eastern frontier of France between 1929 and 1934 and named after André Maginot (1877–1932), the French minister of war who sponsored its construction. The line, which was intended mainly to protect the returned territories of Alsace-Lorraine, extended from the Swiss border to the Belgium border and lulled the French into a belief that they were secure from any German threat of invasion. In the event, Hitler's troops entered France through Belgium in 1940, leaving the Maginot line intact but totally ineffectual. *See also*: Siegfried Line.

• **maglev** ▸ *Magnetic levitation.* A system of rail transport in which the carriages are suspended above the rails by the repulsive effects of magnetic fields. The advantage of maglev transport systems is that there is no friction between the vehicle and the rail. The disadvantage is that extremely strong electromagnetic fields are required to hold the carriages in position. These can only be produced by high electric currents, which, under normal circumstances, would require an energy input over and above that gained by reducing friction. The key to maglev transport is the use of superconducting magnets, in particular the possibility of using materials that exhibit superconductivity at temperatures well above absolute zero. A number of small-scale maglev transport systems have been tried on an experimental basis. The maglev only supports the carriages above the rail; forward motion is obtained by using a linear motor.

• **magnicide** ▸ The murder of a great or prominent person, especially when the murderer has no intelligible grievance against his victim, who appears to have been selected for his or her celebrity alone. In such cases the killer's motive is thought to be a wish to share, however fleetingly, in his victim's fame. The term, coined from Latin *magnus*, great, and homi*cide*, appeared in US newspapers in the late 1960s, following the assassination of John F. Kennedy (1963), Martin Luther King (1968), and Robert Kennedy (1968).

• **Magnificent Five** ▸ The name given by Soviet intelligence to five Britons who acted as Soviet agents in the UK during World War II and the subsequent period of Cold War. They were members of a group of privileged, mainly homosexual, young men recruited at Cambridge University in the 1930s. Guy Burgess (1911–63) and Donald Maclean (1913–83) became foreign-office diplomats: Burgess was an alcoholic and a relatively minor official, whereas Maclean, as a member of MI6 with access to classified information, was a more damaging agent. In 1951 both defected to the Soviet Union, having been warned by another intelligence officer, Harold ('Kim') Philby (1912–88). Philby defected to the Soviet Union in 1963, when it was discovered that he was the so-called **third man** suspected in the affair. In 1979, the complicity of a **fourth man** in the ring was made public. He was Anthony Blunt (1907–83) – a distinguished art historian and surveyor of the Queen's pictures – who had confessed

to being an agent some 35 years earlier in return for a promise of secrecy and non-prosecution. Blunt was the man who arranged Burgess and Maclean's flight to the Soviet Union. Speculation about the identity of a **fifth man** ended with the confession of John Cairncross in 1991.

• **Magnox reactor** ▸ *See*: nuclear reactor.

• **magnum force** ▸ Extremely powerful. The phrase is derived from Magnum, a tradename for a powerful revolver patented in America in 1935. A 1973 film of this name starred Clint Eastwood.

• **Mahâtma** ▸ (Sanskrit, great soul) A title particularly associated with Mohandas Karamchand Gandhi (1869–1948), the Hindu nationalist leader who identified himself with the poor, practised prayer and fasting, and sought to achieve his political ends by non-violence (*see*: satyagraha). A passionate champion of independence for India, he was imprisoned by the British in 1922–24 for his policy of civil disobedience and again in 1930 for publicly distilling salt from seawater in defiance of the government's salt monopoly. During World War II he rejected the British offer of postwar independence in exchange for Indian help in winning the war (*see*: Cripps mission) and was again detained. On his release he played a crucial role in the postwar negotiations that led to independence and reluctantly accepted partition between India and Pakistan. When violence between Hindus and Muslims subsequently broke out, Gandhi undertook a fast to try to bring about reconciliation. This was resented by Hindu fundamentalists, one of whom assassinated this supreme Indian spiritual leader, who was by this time widely regarded as a saint.

• **Maigret** ▸ The fictional detective created by the Belgian writer Georges Simenon (1903–89). Jules Maigret's rank in the Paris police is *commissaire*, roughly equivalent to the British rank of superintendent, but in English translations of the novels he is known as Inspector Maigret. He first appeared in the early 1930s and subsequently featured in some 100 stories, such as *La Marie du port* (1938) and *Maigret et le clochard* (1963). These have been translated into many languages, making the pipe-smoking detective a household name throughout the world.

Maigret's approach to solving crime is psychological, relying on insight into the criminal's motives rather than the scientific investigation of clues and logical deduction based on them. In the late 1950s and early 1960s the detective appeared on British television in the popular series *Maigret*, with Rupert Davies in the title role. The Maigret stories have also been adapted for the cinema in French, English, German, Italian, and other languages.

Some of the detective's character traits were borrowed from the author's own father.

• **mail bomb** ▶ *See*: letter bomb.

• **mailshot** ▶ *See*: junk mail.

• **Main Drag of Many Tears** ▶ A former nickname (1940s) of 125th Street, Harlem, where poor and oppressed Blacks traditionally gathered to be distracted from their worries by cheap entertainment. In US slang 'drag' means street, a borrowing from Victorian Cockney slang.

• **mainframe** ▶ Originally a name for the central processing unit (CPU) and primary memory of a computer; however, since the development of personal and desk-top computers the term has come to denote the largest type of computer installation. Mainframe computers are used by such organizations as banks and insurance companies, which need to process massive amounts of data. They are bulky and expensive, require large clean air-conditioned rooms, have enormous storage capacities, support many input and output devices (terminals, printers, etc.), and need to be operated by highly trained personnel.

• **mainline** ▶ Drug-abusers' slang meaning to inject an illegal drug intravenously. The main line is the main blood vessel in the arm; drugs injected here take immediate effect. The image derives from fast and powerful mainline trains. The word is sometimes used metaphorically, as in 'he's put on so much weight he must have been mainlining chocolate', indicating a love of eating chocolate that approaches addiction.

• **Main Street** ▶ The principal thoroughfare in many of the smaller towns and cities of America. Sinclair Lewis's novel of this name (1920) epitomized the social and cultural life of these towns and gave the phrase a new significance; it is now often used to symbolize the conservative values of small-town America.

• **make love, not war** ▶ The ultimate pacifist slogan, coined in the mid-1960s to epitomize the philosophy of the hippie generation. It was taken up as the slogan of the anti-Vietnam War demonstrators and has been revived by protesters against subsequent military adventures.

• **makeover** ▶ A complete remodelling or repackaging of something; originally the transformation of a person's appearance by new clothes and a series of beauty treatments. This vogue word of the 1980s reflects that decade's fixation with style and image. Women's magazines of the time featured numerous articles in which ordinary people had their whole appearance altered by a team of beauticians and 'image consultants'. The term also became common in design contexts – as in the makeover of a newspaper, an interior, etc. It is also sometimes used in business to describe the restructuring of a company (a 'corporate makeover').

• **Malcolm X** ▶ The assumed name of Malcolm Little (1925–65), US Black militant leader, an influential figure in the struggle for racial equality. The son of a Baptist minister, he was converted to the faith of the Black Muslims in prison in 1952. Having changed his name to Malcolm X – he considered the surname Little to be a relic of slavery – he became actively involved in the work of the sect on his release the following year. In 1963, after a disagreement, he left the Black Muslims and founded a rival group, the Organization of Afro-American Unity, which endorsed the use of violence in the pursuit of equality. He was subsequently converted to orthodox Islam and took the name Malik El-Shabazz. The rivalry and hatred between the Black Muslims and the Organization of Afro-American Unity culminated in the assassination of Malcolm X at a rally in New York in 1965. The biopic *Malcolm X*, directed by Spike Lee, was released in 1992.

• **male chauvinist pig** ▶ (MCP) A man who regards women as inferior to men in most respects and wants them to keep to their traditional role in society, especially raising children, cooking, sewing, and looking after the home. His behaviour towards women is in accordance with these views; in particular, he sees nothing wrong with regarding women as sex objects. The term was coined during the early days of the feminist movement in the late 1960s (*see also*: female chauvinist pig).

> I enjoy fucking my wife. She lets me do it any way I want. No Women's Liberation for her. Lots of male chauvinist pig. – JOSEPH HELLER: *Something Happened* (1974).

• **Mallard** ▶ A famous British steam locomotive, which in 1938 established a long-standing record for the highest speed reached by a steam locomotive (202.8 kph, 126 mph). Immediately recognizable by its distinctive streamlined design, this Gresley A4 Pacific engine was subsequently preserved in working order as an example of rail engineering excellence.

• **mallie** or **mall rat** ▶ US slang for a female teenager who loiters in shopping malls, as somewhere to pass the time rather than a place to spend money. This phenomenon sprang up with the malls themselves in the 1980s.

• **Malvern Festival** ▶ A theatre festival founded in 1929 at Malvern in Worcestershire by the British theatre manager and director Sir Barry Jackson (1879–1961). A number of George Bernard Shaw's later plays, such as *The Apple Cart*, were first performed at the Malvern Festival. New productions also included plays by J. B. Priestley, James Bridie, and other contemporary writers. In 1939 the festival was discontinued; it enjoyed a brief revival in 1949 and was re-established in 1977 as a drama and musical festival featuring the works of Shaw and Sir Edward Elgar, who is buried at Malvern.

• **mamba** ► Acronym for *middle-aged middle-brow accomplisher*. It denotes an average middle-of-the-road person who manages to get things done and has made a success of his life. It was coined in the late 1980s when the fashion for lifestyle-based acronyms was at its height.

• **mammoplasty** ► Plastic surgery to alter the shape of the breasts. Small breasts may be enlarged by means of a silicone rubber implant. This is inserted into a pocket created behind the breast, made via an incision at the base of the breast, along the natural crease line. Some women develop scar tissue around the implant and may require further surgery to remove an excessive build-up. Improving the shape of a large or drooping breast is a more complex procedure, involving the removal of the necessary skin, fat, and underlying tissue, plus relocation of the nipple. This inevitably leaves scars, not only under the breast but also around the areola and vertically from the nipple to the base. The early 1990s saw rising concern about the possible medical and cosmetic side-effects of mammoplasty; as a result, some women chose to undergo further surgery to have their silicone implants removed (so-called 'silicone explant' operations).

• **mamser** ► *See*: momzer.

• **man** ►
　**a man's gotta do what a man's gotta do** A catchphrase used to emphasize the difficult and dangerous actions a man is forced to take in his life, now invariably used facetiously. Although the line is generally thought to originate in a John Wayne Western, nobody has been able to say which. However, it *is* spoken by Alan Ladd in the Western *Shane* (1953).
　A facetious paraphrase is sometimes used in reply to a protest made about a dog fouling the pavement: **a dog's got to do what a dog's got to do**.

• **man, the** ► 1. US slang for the police, the government, or the White establishment. Originally used contemptuously by Blacks to mean White authority in general, it is now used by disadvantaged

social groups for any part of the establishment. 2. Slang for a dealer in illegal drugs, as in 'Waiting for the Man', a song by the Velvet Underground released in 1967.

• **Manassa Mauler** ► Nickname of the US boxer Jack Dempsey (1895–1983). World heavyweight champion (1919–26), he acquired an almost legendary reputation for his ferocious punch before losing his title in controversial circumstances to Gene Tunney (*see*: We wuz robbed *at* robbed). His nickname was derived from Manassa, the town in which he was born.

• **Manchester school** ► A group of early 20th-century dramatists associated with the Gaiety Theatre in Manchester. Notable members of the Manchester school included Stanley Houghton (1881–1913), whose controversial play *Hindle Wakes* was first performed at the Manchester Gaiety in 1912; Harold Brighouse (1882–1958), author of the comedy *Hobson's Choice* (1915); and Allan Monkhouse (1858–1936). The Gaiety Theatre company, the first modern English repertory company, was founded in 1908 by Annie Horniman (1860–1937); its first production was Allan Monkhouse's *Reaping the Whirlwind*.

• **Manchukuo** ► A puppet state created by the Japanese in 1932, after the Mukden incident, from the three provinces of Manchuria in NE China. The state was largely administered by Chinese, but remained under Japanese control. Henry P'ui, the last emperor of the Manchu dynasty, emerged from retirement to become the ruler of Manchukuo until 1945, when the state was dissolved after Japan's defeat in World War II. Manchuria was subsequently redivided into the provinces of Heilungkiang, Kirin, and Liaoning.

• **Manchurian candidate** ► Someone who has been brainwashed by a foreign power to obey orders without thinking (*see*: brainwashing). The term comes from the title of a novel by Richard Condon, *The Manchurian Candidate* (1959), about a US POW who returns from Korea having been brainwashed to act as an assassin by the Chinese. This was made into a successful film (1962).

• **Mancini murder** ► *See*: Brighton trunk murders.

• **Mandates Commission** ► An organization set up by the League of Nations after World War I to supervise the administration of the former overseas possessions of Germany and Turkey. These included Iraq, Syria, Palestine, and the African colonies of Tanganyika, the Cameroons, and Togoland. Mandatory powers over these territories were assigned to the UK, France, Belgium, and other countries, who submitted annual reports to the Mandates Commission. The Commission itself consisted of representatives from Belgium, France, Holland, Italy, Japan, Portugal, Spain, Sweden, and the UK; representatives from Germany, Norway, and Switzerland joined at a later date. In 1945 it was superseded by the UN Trusteeship System.

• **Mandelbaum Gate** ▶ Formerly, the control point for traffic passing from one sector of the divided city of Jerusalem to the other. The city was divided between Israel and Jordan in 1948 and the Mandelbaum Gate remained in operation until Israel took possession of the whole of the city in 1967 (*see*: Six-Day War).

• **Mandelbrot set** ▶ An entity discovered in 1980 by the French mathematician Benoit Mandelbrot. It is generated by a simple type of quadratic equation for complex numbers and is usually plotted using computer graphics. The resulting pattern is extremely complex, containing an infinite number of repeated copies of itself. It is related to the conditions under which chaotic behaviour occurs. *See also*: chaos theory; fractal.

• **Mandy** ▶ A media nickname for Peter Mandelson (1953–  ), a leading architect of New Labour and a close associate of Tony Blair. The grandson of Herbert Morrison (Baron Morrison; 1888–1965), the home secretary in Churchill's wartime coalition, Mandelson became Labour's chief spin doctor in 1985 and an MP in 1992. During this period his reputation as a shrewd and unscrupulous master of spin earned him another press nickname – the **Prince of Darkness**.

In Blair's first administration Mandelson served initially as minister without portfolio – a position that gave him responsibility for the much maligned Millennium Dome (he was sometimes dubbed the 'dome secretary' in a snide allusion to his grandfather's high office). Mandelson then (1999) became secretary of state for trade and industry but was forced to resign later the same year, owing to the revelation that he had borrowed a large sum with which to buy a house from a fellow minister, Geoffrey Robinson, whose business affairs his department was investigating. After only a year in the wilderness Mandelson was brought back into the government as secretary of state for Northern Ireland. However, a second resignation was forced on him in 2001, when it was revealed that he had intervened in the naturalization application of an Indian businessman who had made large donations to the Millennium Dome. Whether Mandelson can defy his political obituarists by staging yet another comeback remains to be seen.

• **man for all seasons** ▶ A phrase used to describe an adaptable Renaissance man who can be regarded as dependable and competent in all situations. The phrase was popularized by Robert Bolt as the title for his 1960 play about Sir Thomas More. It was also the title of the 1966 film starring Paul Scofield. More had been described in these words by his contemporary, Robert Whittington.

• **Man from Missouri** ▶ *See*: Give 'em Hell Harry.

• **man from the Pru** ▶ Part of the 1940s advertising slogan for the Prudential Assurance Company; the full slogan was: 'Ask the man from the Pru'.

• **Manhattan eel** ▶ US slang for a used condom. It is so called because of the large number of discarded condoms that can be seen floating in New York harbour.

• **Manhattan Project** ▶ The codename given to a US project begun in the early 1940s with the aim of developing an atom bomb for use during World War II. Great secrecy and great haste were required in the race to construct such a bomb before the Germans, who were believed to be working on a similar project. Research and development took place at various laboratories, notably **Los Alamos**, New Mexico, under the direction of the physicist J. Robert Oppenheimer. The Manhattan Project culminated in the testing of the first atom bomb on 16 July 1945 and its first use in war at Hiroshima on 6 August 1945. The total expenditure on the project from start to finish was around 2000 million dollars. *See*: nuclear weapon; Oppenheimer affair.

> We knew the world would not be the same.
> – J. ROBERT OPPENHEIMER, 1945.

• **Manila Pact** ▶ The treaty signed in Manila on 8 September 1954 on the creation of the South East Asia Treaty Organization (*see*: SEATO). Signed by representatives of America, Australia, France, New Zealand, Pakistan, the Philippines, Thailand, and the UK, the treaty came into force on 19 February 1955 and was formally ended in 1977.

• **Man in Black** ▶ The supposed narrator of the BBC radio programme *Appointment With Fear*, first broadcast on 11 September 1943. The haunting tones belonged to Valentine Dyall and became a hallmark of this series of mystery and suspense stories (originally written for US radio by John Dickson Carr). Dyall's father, Franklin Dyall, narrated the second series, beginning in January 1944, but the Man in Black Junior returned to set spines tingling in later series. In 1949 Dyall was given his own series, *The Man In Black* – described as 'famous tales of mystery and fear'. *Appointment With Fear* returned in

1955 after a seven-year break, again with Dyall as narrator. The series was again resurrected in 1991, with Edward de Souza cast as the Man in Black.

• **Man in the Iron Mask** ▶ A man who agreed to imitate the historical prisoner made famous in the writings of Alexandre Dumas, following a bet made at the National Sporting Club in London in 1907. With a stake of $100,000 offered by the US millionaire John Pierpont Morgan and the British sportsman Lord Lonsdale, the young and wealthy Harry Bensley agreed to attempt to walk round the world pushing a pram: he would start out with no more than £1 and wear an iron mask for the whole time. Other rules he had to observe included finding a wife (without showing his face) and paying for his journey by selling postcards. He set out on 1 January 1908 from Trafalgar Square wearing a 4lb helmet. At Newmarket he sold a postcard to Edward VII for £5 but at Bexleyheath he only narrowly escaped imprisonment after he refused to remove his mask in the magistrates' court, having been arrested for trading without a licence. By 1914 he had traversed 12 countries and turned down 200 offers of marriage. With the outbreak of World War I, however, Bensley had to give up the challenge as he wished to join up. The sporting peers agreed to allow him to do so and gave him a reward of £4000, which he gave to charity. Bensley himself survived the war but lost his fortune, most of which was invested in Russia. He died in reduced circumstances in Brighton in 1956.

• **manky** ▶ British informal term meaning disgusting or filthy. It is derived from the Italian *mancare*, to be lacking, influenced by 'mangy'. The word is also used in the north of England to mean naughty or spoilt.

• **Mannerheim Line** ▶ A line of fortifications built in the 1930s across the Karelian Isthmus, along the border between Finland and the Soviet Union. The line successfully protected Finland from invasion by Soviet forces at the beginning of the Winter War (1939–40) but was breached in February 1940. The Mannerheim Line was named after Baron Carl Gustaf Emil Mannerheim (1867–1951), commander-in-chief of the Finnish defence forces during the Winter War and later president of Finland.

• **Man of a Thousand Faces** ▶ Nickname of the US film star Lon Chaney (1883–1930), who played numerous villains, usually in grotesque disguise. His films included *The Hunchback of Notre Dame* (1923) and *The Phantom of the Opera* (1925). *Man of a Thousand Faces* was also the title of a biopic about him made in 1957 in which James Cagney played Chaney. His son, Lon Chaney Jnr (1906–73), also starred in macabre roles – notably as a sympathetic lycanthrope in *The Wolf Man* (1941) and its sequels.

> Don't step on that spider, it might be Lon Chaney. – Joke from the 1920s.

• **Man of Steel** ▶ The English rendering of the Russian name Stalin, adopted by the dictator Joseph Dzhugashvili (1879–1953). A Bolshevik from 1903, he was frequently imprisoned and exiled in the years preceding the October Revolution of 1917. By 1922 he was general secretary of the Communist Party under Lenin; in 1929 he became dictator and began the reign of terror that made his assumed name synonymous with brutality and repression by the state (*see*: Law of December 1; Stalinism; Yezhovshchina). Treated circumspectly by the Soviet Union's allies during World War II, he became even more autocratic once the war was over, implacable in his hostility towards opposition both at home and abroad. After his death, psychiatrists conjectured that the 'man of steel' had actually suffered from a variety of psychotic conditions. Long before the liberalization of Soviet society in the late 1980s he had been stripped of his almost legendary status as a great leader of the Soviet peoples (*see*: de-Stalinization).

> What could we do? There was a reign of terror. You just had to look at him wrongly and the next day you lost your head. – NIKITA KHRUSHCHEV, 18 March 1956.

• **Man on the Wedding Cake** ▶ Nickname of Thomas E. Dewey (1902–71), governor of New York, who was unexpectedly defeated by Harry S. Truman in the presidential election of 1948. The nickname was bestowed on him by Grace Hodgson Flandrau and much repeated by Alice Roosevelt. This cruel reference to Dewey's stiff manner and lack of charisma is thought to have contributed to his defeat. Truman's victory was a major surprise to the pollsters, who had predicted an easy win for Dewey: *The Chicago Tribune* had been so confident of Dewey's success it had gone to press with the headline 'Dewey defeats Truman'. *The Washington Post*, which had been similarly caught out, invited Truman and the pollsters to dinner to eat 'humble pie'.

• **Mansion House speech** ▶ A speech made by David Lloyd George in July 1911, at the Mansion House in London, in which he issued a strong warning to Germany that the UK would support France in any conflict that might arise out of the Agadir Crisis. This declaration was notable not only for its vehemence but also for its unexpectedness: as chancellor of the exchequer Lloyd George had been largely concerned with social reform and had shown little interest in foreign policy.

• **Manson Family** ▸ A hippie group living in a commune near Los Angeles, which in 1969 was responsible for a series of drug-crazed killings that shocked US society with their brutality. Led by Charles Manson (1934– ), a failed rock musician and petty criminal who had developed bizarre messianic delusions, members of the 'Family', indulged in a quasi-religious and orgiastic lifestyle in which LSD played a major role. Their excesses reached a horrific climax when they carried out five murders in the house of the film director Roman Polanski; among the victims was Polanski's heavily pregnant wife, the actress Sharon Tate. In a previous incident they also killed supermarket millionaire Leno LaBianca and his wife. Manson's followers, after their arrest later in the year, claimed they were unaware of their victims' identities and had been inspired to kill after listening to the Beatles song 'Helter-Skelter'. During the trial Manson himself delivered wild tirades about the threat of race war; the four accused members of the gang were sentenced to death (in practice an indefinite life sentence).

• **Man Who Never Was, The** ▸ The title of a 1955 film relating the true story of a fictitious Royal Marines officer who played a key role in deceiving the Germans about the Allied invasion plans in World War II. The original book was written by a naval officer, the Hon. Ewen Montagu QC, who organized the whole affair. Montagu arranged for the body of a 'Major William Martin' to be washed up in neutral Spain in 1943; when it was found that he was carrying apparently top-secret documents, local German agents quickly passed the word to the German High Command. Among the documents found on the dead marine were a letter from the vice-chief of the Imperial General Staff to General Alexander and a letter from Lord Mountbatten to Admiral of the Fleet Sir Andrew Cunningham, both of which suggested that Sardinia, not Sicily as expected, would be the target of the Allied assault. These letters, backed up by Martin's personal documents (including two theatre ticket stubs for London shows), convinced the German agents that they had stumbled upon genuine Allied invasion plans. When the Allies were handed back the body and the documents by the Spanish authorities, scientific analysis showed that the envelopes had been opened. The plan succeeded: when the Allies finally attacked Sicily, they were opposed by the Italians and only two German divisions; Allied losses were thus greatly reduced. His duty done, 'Major Martin' was buried with full military honours in a Spanish cemetery; his real identity was not disclosed, in deference to the wishes of his family. However, de-

classification of the relevant documents in 1998 revealed that 'Martin' was really Glendwyr Michael, a Welsh down-and-out who had died after eating rat poison. His name has now been added to the gravestone in Spain.

• **Man with the Golden Flute** ▸ Nickname of the Irish flautist Sir James Galway (1939– ), in imitation of *The Man with the Golden Gun*, the title of a James Bond thriller by Ian Fleming. Galway was often pictured with his gold and silver flutes, which were made to his own specifications.

• **Man with the Orchid-Lined Voice** ▸ Nickname of the Italian tenor Enrico Caruso (1873–1921). He was the first major opera star to be recorded and the first to make a radio broadcast. Unfortunately his recordings were made in the pre-electric era and although electric remakes were produced much later, these were recorded not from live performances but from the pre-electric recordings. Nevertheless, the quality and amazing tone control of Caruso's voice can still be heard. When he died of peritonitis in Naples at the age of 48, New York's flags were flown at half mast.

• **Man you Love to Hate** ▸ Catchphrase associated originally with the actor Erich von Stroheim (1885–1957), but subsequently with many other screen villains as well as others outside the cinema world. It was first used in publicity for the 1918 propaganda film *The Heart of Humanity*, in which von Stroheim played a particularly unpleasant German officer. In 1979 a film, *The Man You Love to Hate*, commemorated the life and work of von Stroheim, who had gone on to become an admired (if notoriously extravagant) Hollywood director.

• **Mao jacket** ▸ *See*: Nehru jacket.

• **maquis** ▸ In World War II, French patriots who formed guerrilla groups in the countryside during the Occupation (1940–45), attacking German patrols, depots, etc. They were so named after the thick scrubland in Corsica and other Mediterranean coastal lands to which bandits formerly retreated to avoid capture. *See*: FFI; Resistance.

• **Marburg disease** or **green monkey disease** ▸ A disease of vervet (green) monkeys and humans caused by a virus. It is named after the town of Marburg, Germany, where the first case was reported in 1967. The patient had contracted the disease from a consignment of vervet monkeys imported from Africa. Ticks, mites, or other arthropods may act as a reservoir of the virus, which can also be transmitted from person to person. This fact, coupled with the high mortality rate of around 30%, dictates stringent isolation measures for suspected cases. The incubation period is 3–9 days, followed by the development of fever, headache, muscle pain, nausea, and vomiting. Later, a skin rash appears and, in about 50% of cases, internal bleeding.

• **Marchioness disaster** ▶ A tragedy that occurred on the River Thames in London on 20 August 1989. The *Marchioness* pleasure boat, carrying some 150 people, was rammed from behind by the dredger *Bowbelle* and sank within minutes, drowning 51 of her passengers. The accident happened near the Tower of London in the early hours of the morning. On board the *Marchioness* were partygoers celebrating the birthday of a young City businessman, Antonio Vascancellas, who was among the victims, many of whom came from the capital's fashionable social set. In 2001 the official inquiry into the disaster blamed the captains of both vessels and the companies that owned and managed them; the Department of Transport and the police were also criticized.

• **March on Rome** ▶ The arrival in Rome of Mussolini and thousands of his Blackshirts (Fascist supporters) on 28 October 1922, shortly before the establishment of Italy as a Fascist state. Mussolini and his armed followers travelled to Rome by various means and entered the city with little or no opposition from military or civilian authorities. The head of the cabinet resigned and King Victor Emmanuel III invited Mussolini to form a new government.

• **Marconi affair** ▶ A scandal in the earlier career of David Lloyd George, when he was chancellor of the exchequer. In 1912 Lloyd George had bought shares to the value of £2000 in the US Marconi company. He had obtained these shares at a preferential rate through the managing director of the company, Godfrey Isaacs, brother of the attorney general Rufus Isaacs (later 1st Marquess of Reading). Meanwhile, shares in the British Marconi company had enjoyed a sudden increase in value as the result of a government contract to build a chain of radio stations. Although the two companies were legally separate, there were inevitable rumours of corruption. The parliamentary committee set up to investigate the matter found Lloyd George and Isaacs not guilty of corruption, although the transaction was described as imprudent. Nevertheless, both ministers' reputations were damaged by the affair.

• **Marco Polo Bridge incident** ▶ An incident that renewed hostilities between China and Japan at the beginning of the Sino-Japanese War. On 7 July 1937 Japanese and Chinese troops began firing at each other at the Marco Polo Bridge on the outskirts of Peking. This was followed by further clashes in the Peking-Tientsin area. The Chinese refused to withdraw their troops but a series of attacks and counter-attacks led to their expulsion by the Japanese at the end of July.

• **mardarse** ▶ British slang for a mother's boy, a softie. It is particularly used in the north of England, where **mardie** is also used as an adjective to mean bad-tempered or (of a child) sulky and spoilt.

• **Mareth Line** ▶ A line of fortifications in S Tunisia. Originally built by the French to repel the Italians, the line was used by Rommel in the North African campaign of World War II. On 20 March 1943 the British Eighth Army under the command of General Bernard Montgomery launched an attack on the Mareth Line, which led ultimately to the surrender of the Axis forces in Tunisia.

• **marginalize** ▶ To reduce the power, influence, or importance of a person or thing. For example, to marginalize a politician is to make him or her irrelevant to the decision-making process. As with many such verbs ending in '-ize' it originated in America but became common in the UK in the second half of the 1980s.

• **Marienkirche frescoes** ▶ A series of medieval wall paintings in a church in the German port of Lübeck, which in 1952 became the subject of a major art scandal. The Marienkirche was damaged by an incendiary bomb in 1942, revealing medieval frescoes previously hidden under a layer of whitewash. However, by the time work could begin on their restoration in the post-war period, they had suffered extensive damage from exposure. Dietrich Fey, owner of a firm of art restorers, was finally awarded a contract to restore the masterpieces (for a large sum) in collaboration with the artist Lothar Malskat. Gradually, out of the public gaze, the frescoes were restored to their former glory; in 1951 Fey himself showed the completed decorations to the West German chancellor Konrad Adenauer. The German post office celebrated the restoration with a series of stamps depicting the frescoes. One year later, however, Malskat (who had received no money for his work) confessed that the frescoes were fabrications and bore no relation to the original paintings, which had been too faint to work from. Upon examination, some of the figures in the frescoes were recognized as likenesses of Rasputin, Marlene Dietrich, and members of Malskat's family. A sensational trial followed in which the German art establishment was deeply embarrassed; both Fey and Malskat were jailed.

• **Mariner** ▶ A series of space probes launched during US space programmes of the 1960s and early 1970s. Mariner 2, launched on 27 August 1962, passed within 22,000 miles of Venus, measuring the atmospheric and surface temperatures of the planet. Mariner 5, launched on 14 June 1967, came close to Venus, passing within 2500 miles of the planet. Mariner 4, launched on 28 November 1964, studied the atmosphere of Mars and photographed the surface of the planet; Mariners 6 and 7, launched in 1969, made further photographic and thermal investigations; and Mariner 9 went into orbit around the planet. Mariner 10, launched in 1974, passed Mercury three times. Mariners 11 and 12 were renamed and used in the Voyager programme (1977). Mariners 1, 3, and 8 failed to achieve their missions.

## • Marines ►

**By the grace of God and a few Marines** Catchphrase used in acknowledging that a difficult task has been fulfilled. It became widely known after General MacArthur's landing during the invasion of the Philippines in World War II; as he came ashore he was confronted by a sign put up by the US Marines, reading: 'By the grace of God and a few Marines, MacArthur returned to the Philippines'.

• **Maritime Trust ►** A British charitable organization created in 1969 and dedicated to the restoration and upkeep of vessels that have played significant roles in the nation's maritime history. Several examples of such vessels are on public display in and around the River Thames in London, including the Trust's Historic Ship Collection, located near Tower Bridge, and the 19th-century tea clipper, *Cutty Sark*, permanently moored at Greenwich. Besides its own restoration work, the Trust provides grants to other bodies engaged in similar work, such as the Mary Rose Trust.

• **market-maker ►** A person who trades in shares and bonds on a stock exchange to make a profit, rather than to earn a commission. The role of the market-maker after the deregulation of the UK stock market (the Big Bang of 1986) is roughly equivalent to that of the pre-1986 stockjobber.

• **Marks and Sparks ►** A colloquial name for the British high-street chain of clothes and food stores, Marks and Spencer. Founded in 1887 by Michael Marks (d. 1907) and Thomas Spencer (d. 1905) as a penny bazaar in Manchester, the firm was greatly expanded by Marks's son, Simon Marks (later Baron Marks; 1888–1964) and the closely related Sieff family, especially Marcus Sieff (later Baron Sieff; 1913–2001) and his brother Joseph Edward (Teddy) Sieff. For some 50 years after World War II 'M & S'

dominated the middle market for smart but 'sensible' clothes. At the end of the 1990s, however, competition from other chains and a failure to keep abreast of the trends in fashion caused a fall in profits and a decline in their status as market leaders. By the early 21st century some of their former position had been regained by new management and a severe reduction in their overseas activities. *See also*: St Michael.

• **marleys ►** Rhyming slang for piles, haemorrhoids; from Marley Tiles, a tradename for thermoplastic tiles made in a factory in Marley Lane, Riverhead, Kent.

> If it wasn't for my marleys I'd've given 'im what for. – Elderly gentleman recovering in hospital from a mugging, quoted in *The Evening Standard*.

• **Marlow, Captain ►** The narrator of *Lord Jim* (1900), *Heart of Darkness* (1902), and other novels and short stories by the Polish-born British writer Joseph Conrad (1857–1924). Marlow provides a commentary on the events and characters of the story, performing a role similar to that of the chorus in Greek drama. Sometimes he is an observer, sometimes he intervenes in the action; his reminiscences contribute to the impressionistic style of Conrad's work.

Marlow is introduced at the end of the fourth chapter of *Lord Jim* as 'a...man who sat apart from the others, with his face worn and clouded, but with quiet eyes that glanced straight, interested and clear'. Most of the remainder of the novel consists of Marlow's narrative, related 'later on, many times, in distant parts of the world,...at length, in detail and audibly'.

• **Marlowe, Philip ►** A Los Angeles private detective created by the US writer Raymond Chandler (1888–1959). Marlowe first appeared in *The Big Sleep* (1939) and subsequently in a number of other novels, such as *Farewell, My Lovely* (1940) and *The Long Goodbye* (1954). Actors to play Marlowe in the cinema include Dick Powell, Robert Mitchum, and (most famously) Humphrey Bogart.

Marlowe is a cool tough guy, attractive to women, and never short of a cynical wisecrack; he is often revealed, however, as a lonely and unexpectedly moral character. The following lines, from the Bogart version of *The Big Sleep* (1946), are typical:

> I don't mind if you don't like my manners. I don't like 'em myself. They're pretty bad. I grieve over 'em on long winter evenings.

• **Marmite ►** Tradename for a yeast and vegetable extract used as a spread and to add flavouring to casseroles, etc. Marmite, which was first manufactured in 1902, is actually a French word for a type of cooking pot, a picture of which appears on the label of the Marmite jar. Marmite soon established itself as one of those necessaries much yearned for by expatriates, being synonymous with memories of children's high tea.

• **Marne, Battles of the**▸ Two battles of World War I fought along the River Marne in NE France, both of which resulted in notable victories for the Allied armies. In the first Battle of the Marne (5–9 September 1914) the British Expeditionary Force and French troops commanded by Marshal Joffre thwarted the advance of the Germans towards Paris, forcing them back across the River Aisne.

The second Battle of the Marne (18 July 1918) was one of the last and most significant offensives of the war, consolidated by subsequent victories at Amiens and elsewhere. Marshal Foch's Allied forces succeeded in driving the Germans, commanded by Ludendorff, back to the Hindenburg Line; within three months Germany had begun peace negotiations.

• **Marple, Miss**▸ An amateur detective created by the British writer Agatha Christie (*see*: Queen of Crime). Miss Jane Marple, a matronly figure whose gentle manner disguises a capacity for powerful deductive reasoning, made her first appearance in *Murder in the Vicarage* (1930) and her last in *Sleeping Murder* (1976), although the latter was actually written in the 1940s. She has also featured in films, played by Margaret Rutherford amongst others, and a TV series, in which the veteran actress Joan Hickson endeared herself to many thousands of viewers in the title role.

• **Mars bar**▸ Tradename for a chocolate-covered bar with a double layer of a creamy toffee-like filling; it is manufactured by Mars Confections Ltd, a company established in the UK in 1932 by Forrest Mars, an immigrant American. The Mars Bar immediately became popular and has remained so ever since.

> A Mars a day helps you work, rest and play. – Advertising slogan, used on TV from about 1960.

• **Marshall Plan**▸ The popular name for the European Recovery Programme sponsored by US secretary of state G. C. Marshall, to bring economic aid to stricken Europe after World War II. It was inaugurated in June 1947. Most European states, excluding the Soviet Union and its satellites, participated. The UK ceased to receive Marshall aid in 1950. *See also*: Lend-Lease.

• **Martian invasion scare**▸ The result of a radio broadcast by Orson Welles based on H. G. Wells's science-fiction fantasy *The War of the Worlds*. The novel, first published in 1898, is the story of a Martian invasion of Britain. On 30 October 1938 the voice of Orson Welles was heard on US radio in an adaptation of the novel, in which the scene of the action was shifted to America and the invasion was reported in a simulated news broadcast. Listeners mistook this for a genuine news report of an actual Martian invasion of New Jersey and widespread panic ensued. Welles subsequently became known as 'the man who scared America to death'.

• **Martini, shaken not stirred**▸ A catchphrase associated with James Bond, the hero of Ian Fleming's novels. It did not, however, appear in the books, being a creation of the films made in the 1960s and 1970s. Although the phrase was supposed to epitomize Bond's sophisticated lifestyle and impeccable taste, experts say that shaking a dry martini renders it unappetisingly opaque; it is, in fact, much better stirred. The phrase has been much parodied and ridiculed.

> There is no hint of the agent's shaken-but-not-stirred arrogance in the mature Connery's appearance or demeanour. – Interview with Sean Connery, who played Bond, *The Independent*, 16 February 1991.

• **Marx Brothers**▸ The brothers Chico (Leonard Marx; 1886–1961), Harpo (Adolph Marx; 1888–1964), Groucho (Julius Marx; 1890–1977), Zeppo (Herbert Marx; 1901–79), and Gummo (Milton Marx; 1893–1977), who formed one of the most famous comedy teams in the history of the cinema. Zeppo and Gummo were only involved in early productions, but the other three went on to make many films, until they disbanded in 1949. The legend that Harpo (so called for his skill as a harpist) was dumb was, of course, merely put out to support the parts he played in their films. Most of the brothers' sharpest quips were spoken by the cigar-toting heavily mustachioed Groucho:

> One morning I shot an elephant in my pyjamas. How he got into my pyjamas I'll never know. – *Animal Crackers* (1930).

> GROUCHO I want to register a complaint. Do you know who sneaked into my room at three o'clock this morning?
> RECEPTIONIST Who?
> GROUCHO Nobody, and that's my complaint. – *Monkey Business* (1931).

> Look at me: I worked my way up from nothing to a state of extreme poverty. – *Monkey Business* (1931).

> WOMAN My husband is dead.
> GROUCHO I'll bet he's just using that as an excuse.
> WOMAN I was with him to the end.
> GROUCHO No wonder he passed away.

WOMAN I held him in my arms and kissed him.
GROUCHO So it was murder!
– *Duck Soup* (1933).

CHICO Hey boss, you got a woman in there?
GROUCHO If I haven't, I've been wasting thirty
minutes of valuable time.
– *A Night in Casablanca* (1945).

Groucho, too, was the greatest source of anecdotes. Resigning from a club, he sent a telegram:

I don't care to belong to any social organization
which would accept me as a member.

One year he stayed at the Hotel Danieli in
Venice. Descending in the lift from the fourth floor,
he met three priests who entered at the floor below.
One of these, recognizing Groucho, told him that
his mother was a great fan of his. 'Really', said Groucho, 'I didn't know you guys were allowed to have
mothers.'

But Chico also had his share of stories. It is said
that when his wife caught him kissing a chorus
girl, he protested that he wasn't doing any such
thing – 'I was only whispering in her mouth,' he
said.

• **Marxist-Leninism** ▶ *See*: Leninism.

• **Mary Jane** ▶ US slang for cannabis; it is a direct
translation of the Mexican Spanish name for the
hemp plant, *mariahuana*.

• **Mary of Arnhem** ▶ The name used by Helen
Sensburg in her Nazi propaganda broadcasts to
British troops in NW Europe (1944–45). Her melting
voice made her programmes very popular with the
British, but without the results for which she
hoped. *See also*: Tokyo Rose.

• **Mary Rose** ▶ An English warship from the reign
of Henry VIII that sank in 1545 in Portsmouth Harbour. One of the first true warships to be constructed (1509–10), she carried a crew of some 700
men. The cause of her sinking is unknown but may
have been due to overloading, incompetent handling, construction faults, adverse weather conditions, or a combination of all these. She went down
with a full complement of crew and equipment,
having just set off to engage the French Navy off the
Isle of Wight. In 1967 the hull was located in the
mud and a rescue operation was launched to salvage the wreck. Many Tudor artefacts were recovered from the vessel, followed by the hull itself in
1982. These are now on display in a dry dock in
Portsmouth. The Mary Rose Society was formed in
1978 to help finance restoration work and the upkeep of the vessel. *See also*: Vasa project.

• **maser** ▶ *See*: laser.

• **M\*A\*S\*H** ▶ Mobile Army Surgical Hospital; also
the title of a Robert Altman film (1970) set in such

a hospital during the Korean War and a subsequent
US (CBS) television comedy series (1972–83). Both
the film and the series appeared during the later
stages of the Vietnam War, so many obvious parallels
were drawn. In 1974 the TV *M\*A\*S\*H*, starring Alan
Alda, McLean Stevenson, and Loretta Swit, won an
Emmy as the year's outstanding comedy. The final
episode, shown on 28 February 1983, was the top-rated programme in US television history, drawing
more than 50 million viewers. However, most critics feel that the series sacrificed its original hard-edged wit to sentiment as its popularity grew and
its run extended. It has also been shown on British
television, with several repeats.

• **Mason, Perry** ▶ A fictional lawyer created by
the US writer Erle Stanley Gardner (1889–1970) in a
series of novels that combine courtroom drama
with the mystery and suspense of a detective story.
Perry Mason is a defence attorney whose clients
are always found innocent and whose investigations usually reveal the identity of the true guilty
party. The character achieved widespread recognition and popularity on both sides of the Atlantic
with the highly successful US television series *Perry
Mason* (1957–65), based on Gardner's stories, in
which Raymond Burr played the title role. In the
final episode of the series, *The Case of the Final Fade-out*, Erle Stanley Gardner made a guest appearance
as the judge.

• **massage parlour** ▶ A euphemism for an establishment that offers sexual services to men by
women posing as trained masseuses. Although such
parlours may be equipped to provide a genuine
massage, this is not why men attend them.

• **mass production** ▶ A system for producing
large quantities of a standardized item. Mass production is usually automated and capital-intensive,
the labour input being confined to simple and
repetitive tasks on the assembly line. It was Henry
Ford (1863–1947) who introduced the assembly line
into car production in 1912. Using this technique,
he had manufactured 15 million Model Ts (*see*: Tin
Lizzie) by 1928.

• **Master, the** ▶ Nickname of the British dramatist, actor, songwriter, and entertainer Sir Noël Coward (1899–1973). His status as both actor and author
was established with *The Vortex* (1924); subsequently
his 'mastery' was confirmed both as a revue artist
and in the film world. Coward himself disliked the
nickname, possibly because it had already been
given to the writer Somerset Maugham (1874–1965).
It was also associated with the US film director D.
W. Griffiths (1873–1948).

I've over-educated myself in all the things I shouldn't have known at all. – NOËL COWARD: *Wild Oats*.

• **masterclass** ▶ A session of instruction in which a person who is a master of a specific art or discipline gives advice to people who have achieved a high standard but who are still able to benefit from the master's experience. Much of the work in a masterclass takes the form of analysis and critical evaluation of the individual's work. Masterclasses in various musical disciplines and in acting have made very popular television programmes.

• **Mastermind** ▶ *See*: I've started so I'll finish *at* started.

• **Masters and Johnson** ▶ A US research team that carried out the first comprehensive study of human sexual activity under laboratory conditions. William H. Masters (1915–2001), a physician, and Virginia Johnson (1925–   ), a psychologist, began their joint research in 1954 and 10 years later established the Reproductive Biology Research Foundation in St Louis. They published their influential book, *The Human Sexual Response*, in 1966 and were married in 1971. In their physiological studies Masters and Johnson observed the process of sexual arousal in 694 male and female volunteers in the age range 18 to 89. Their conclusions, acclaimed at the time as a breakthrough in our understanding of human sexuality, now appear somewhat trite – what is known by every normal man and woman accustomed to sexual relationships. For example, they concluded:

> ...that the sexual response cycle of arousal and climax is a natural physiological property of the intact adult human being and responds predictably to adequate stimulation.

However, their physiological work did enable them to progress to sex therapy. The publication of their treatment results, with a success rate of over 80% and a relapse rate of only 5%, led to the establishment of sex-therapy clinics throughout America and to very large sales for their book *Human Sexual Inadequacy* (1970). Much of this public interest arose from a prurient concern with Masters and Johnson's use of female 'surrogate' partners as part of the therapeutic process for single males with sexual problems. Although they abandoned this form of therapy because of the 'administrative and ethical problems involved', it had progressed sufficiently for some observers to wonder how their clinic was to be distinguised from a brothel. *See also*: Kinsey reports.

• **Masters tournament** ▶ A US golf tournament played each spring at the Augusta National Golf Course, Georgia. Established in 1934, the Masters tournament is an open event at which leading international players are invited by the Augusta National Golf Club to compete for large prizes.

• **Mata Hari** ▶ The pseudonym of Margaretha Zelle (1876–1917), a Dutch dancer who was shot as a spy during World War I. Mata Hari, which means 'eye of the dawn', chose her pseudonym when she began to specialize as an exotic Indonesian dancer in the 1900s. Over the next decade her lovers included a number of government officials and high-ranking Allied officers; it is alleged that during World War I she gathered classified military information from them, and relayed it to the Germans, who had recruited her as a spy. In 1917 she was arrested, tried, and executed by the French. Her trial attracted so much public interest that 'Mata Hari' has since become an epithet for any femme fatale who acts as a spy or betrays someone. Recent research has suggested that her guilt was probably greatly exaggerated.

• **Matilda** ▶ The central character in one of the best known of Hilaire Belloc's *Cautionary Tales* (1907). Her dreadful fate, with its moral message, has since become as familiar to succeeding generations of children as those of far older traditional nursery rhymes:

> Matilda told such Dreadful Lies
> It made one Gasp and Stretch one's Eyes
> For every time she shouted 'Fire'
> They only answered 'Little Liar'...
> And therefore when her Aunt returned
> Matilda, and the House, were Burned.

• **matinee idol** ▶ An elegant, well-groomed, and handsome actor who owes his success chiefly to his popularity with female theatregoers. The term arose in the early 20th century, when matinee (afternoon) performances of plays were attended mainly by ladies. Although the tradition was continued by certain stars of the early cinema, such as Ronald Colman (1891–1958), the term and concept are now dated; a matinee idol is no longer a romantic figure – more a figure of fun.

• **Maud Committee** ▶ A committee set up in 1940 to investigate the possibility of using uranium fission to make an atom bomb. Chaired by the British physicist Sir George Paget Thomson (1892–1975), the Maud Committee presented its positive findings on the feasibility of a uranium bomb to the British government in 1941. The project was then transferred to America for further development (*see*: Manhattan Project).

The committee is said to have been named after Maud Ray, the former English governess of the Danish physicist Niels Bohr. Bohr managed to send his friends in England a telegram immediately after the German occupation of Denmark in 1940. After assuring his friends that he was safe, he added at the end of the telegram '...please inform Cockcroft and Maud Ray, Kent'. After hours of ingenious decoding, cryptographers decided that this was a secret message from Bohr telling British scientists to 'make uranium day and night'. The unfortunate Maud Ray never learnt that her former protégé was well.

• **Mau Mau** ▸ A secret political society formed by the Kikuyu tribesmen of Kenya, possibly as early as the 1940s. Their chief aim was to drive the Europeans out of Kenya by terrorist means (the word *mau* means 'get out!'); the members were bound by oaths and dire threats if these were broken. The existence of the society became known in 1952, when its members led a rebellion against the colonial government in Kenya, committing terrible acts of violence not only against White settlers but also against Blacks who refused to support the organization (*see*: Lari massacre). In 1953 Jomo Kenyatta, later president of Kenya, was sentenced to seven years' imprisonment as a suspected leader of the Mau Mau. The rebellion continued until 1960. For a time, to 'mau-mau' someone was slang meaning to harass or bully them.

• **Mau Mau bee** ▸ *See*: killer bee.

• **maven** ▸ A mainly US term for an expert or connoisseur, especially in the fashion world. It is derived from the Hebrew, meaning understanding, via Yiddish, in which it means an expert.

• **Maximum John** ▸ Nickname of the US judge John Sirica (1904–92), who became widely known during the Watergate scandal for imposing very severe sentences (1973) on those who carried out the original burglary. It was this that persuaded the Watergate burglars to name their political masters – thus unleashing a chain of events that eventually brought down a president.

• **maxiskirt** or **maxi** ▸ *See*: miniskirt.

• **mayday** ▸ A phonetic form of the French *m'aidez*, translated into English as 'help me!' Mayday is an internationally recognized distress call for people requiring help, as set down by the International Radio Telegraph Convention in 1927.

• **Mayflower II** ▸ A replica of the ship that carried the Pilgrim Fathers to America in 1620. In 1957 Mayflower II attempted to duplicate the Pilgrim Fathers' voyage, departing from Plymouth, England, on 20 April and arriving at Plymouth, Massachusetts, 53 days later (the original journey took rather longer). With a US designer and British builders, Mayflower II was a joint venture between America and the UK: the costs of constructing the 90-foot ship and the 5400-mile journey were met by contributions from both countries.

• **Mayor of London** ▸ The elected leader of the Greater London Assembly set up in 2000. For the previous 14 years London had been virtually unique among capital cities in having no citywide local government. In 1986 the Conservative government abolished the Labour-controlled Greater London Council (*see*: GLC) – largely, it seems, to curb the activities of the council's maverick leader, Ken Livingstone (*see*: Red Ken).

In 1997 the incoming Labour government held a referendum in which Londoners voted in favour of plans for a new Assembly led by a directly elected mayor. When the elections took place in 2000, the two main political parties were represented by Frank Dobson (Labour) – a former health secretary who failed to solve any of the NHS's problems – and Steven Norris (Conservative) – a former transport minister with an unfortunate reputation as a womanizer. Norris had been brought in at the last moment to replace the original Tory candidate, Lord Archer, who stood down when it was revealed that he had asked a potential witness to give false evidence in a libel case (a crime for which he was later jailed). The Liberal Democrat candidate was the little-known MP Susan Kramer. To this bunch of lacklustre official party candidates were added eight other hopefuls, including – most notably – the former leader of the GLC, Ken Livingstone, who stood as an independent. Although overwhelmingly supported by Labour Party members in London and elsewhere, Livingstone failed to become the official Labour candidate owing to the workings of a selection process that seemed designed especially to block him. Perhaps because of public anger at this, or perhaps because he had successfully cut fares on London transport in his GLC days, Livingstone was voted mayor by a comfortable majority.

• **Maze prison** ▸ A high-security prison built near Belfast in the early 1970s to hold convicted or suspected terrorists. Republicans in Ulster still refer to it by its original name, **Kesh**, or, simply, **the Kesh**. Both Loyalist and Republican prisoners were originally accommodated in Nissen huts – officially known as the Maze (Compound). In 1972 a group of Republican prisoners, led by Billy McKee, embarked on a hunger strike for prisoner-of-war status. Shortly afterwards the British government granted 'special status' to convicted prisoners in the Maze. This decision was reversed in 1976, from which time new inmates were held in eight new single-storey H-shaped blocks – the infamous **H-blocks**.

Each wing of every H-block contained 25 cells, dining room, exercise yard, and recreation room. The crosspiece of the 'H' – paradoxically known as 'the Circle' – contained offices, medical room, classrooms, etc. Other facilities within the complex – known as the Maze (Cellular) and said at the time to be the most modern in Europe – included sports hall, workshops, hospital, and two all-weather sports pitches.

The Maze was now effectively two prisons, surrounded by a 17-ft high 2-mile concrete security wall overlooked by sentry posts. In the H-blocks, prisoners were segregated on sectarian lines. Shortly after the H-blocks were opened, Republican prisoners started a campaign for the reinstatement of special political status. A refusal to wear prison uniform in which the protestors wore only prison blankets (the **blanket protest**) led to the so-called **dirty protest**, begun in 1978: prisoners confined themselves to the cells and resorted to smearing excrement over the cell walls. These protests culminated (1981) in a hunger strike during which 10 Republicans starved themselves to death. The first to die, on 5 May, was Bobby Sands, who had been elected to Parliament while in the Maze. His death, and that of Francis Hughes shortly after, sparked a wave of rioting in the province. Despite the protest, the British government refused to concede over the issue of political status for Maze prisoners. Republican prisoners were, however, later given the right to wear their own clothes and granted other privileges. The hunger strikes had the effect of increasing Irish and US sympathy for the Republican cause, and the prison, in particular the H-blocks, remained a potent symbol of 'British oppression' throughout the 1980s. As part of the Good Friday Agreement, the early release of Republican and Loyalist paramilitary prisoners from the Maze and other prisons began in 1998; in 2000 the H-blocks were demolished and the last of the Maze prisoners covered by the Agreement were released.

• **mazuma** or **mazooma** ► US slang, first hear in the early 1960s, for money. Originally from Yiddish, it reappeared in the late 1980s in the UK with a host of other slang words for money. It is said to derive ultimately from the Chaldean *m'zumon*, meaning ready, necessary. It appears in this form in the Talmud.

• **MBE** ► *See*: Order of the British Empire.

• **MCP** ► *See*: male chauvinist pig.

• **ME** ► Myalgic encephalopathy. A disease characterized by extreme fatigue, muscle pains, inability to concentrate, poor coordination, giddiness, depression, and general malaise. The cause remains controversial, with viruses, allergies, and psychological factors being variously thought to be the causative agents. For this reason the former name myalgic encephalomyelitis, with its suggestion of an infection of the muscles and the central nervous system, has now been changed to myalgic encephalopathy. In the UK the disease is also known as **post-viral fatigue syndrome**, because the condition frequently occurs as a sequel to such viral infections as glandular fever; in America, where the viral aetiology is less widely accepted, it is known as **chronic fatigue syndrome**. However, some sufferers prefer to use ME as a description of their illness, feeling that a 'fatigue syndrome' implies only that they are tired. The disorder, which is often long-lasting, was sometimes formerly called **malingerer's disease**, especially by doctors who had little experience of it. **Yuppie flu** was another name used by the tabloid press, because it frequently strikes young, energetic, and successful people. It is now recognized in the UK – notably by a report from the Chief Medical Officer (2002) – as a very real and debilitating illness.

• **meals on wheels** ► A UK welfare service that provides hot meals to elderly or housebound people, who are unable to shop or cook for themselves. The meals are prepared in central kitchens and transported by car or van to the homes of these people by voluntary workers organized by the WRVS (Women's Royal Voluntary Service). Recipients of the meals pay a token charge for the service, which is subsidized by the social services departments of local councils.

• **mean machine** ► Slang term of approval for a fast car or a motorcycle. It is also used of a very attractive fit-looking male or (occasionally) of the male sex organ. Originally part of Black US slang of the 1960s, its use later spread to the UK.

• **means test** ► The principle that evidence of need must be supplied to qualify for relief from public funds, *i.e.* a test of one's means. Such tests were introduced by the National Government in 1931 for those whose unemployment benefit was exhausted, and the resulting inquisition was much resented by those concerned. It took note of any earnings by members of the household and all monetary assets, and penalized the provident. The regulations governing public assistance were modified after World War II but some non-contributory social security benefits are still means-tested.

• **Mebyon Kernow** ► (Cornish, Sons of Cornwall) The society of Cornish nationalists, established in 1951. They advocate the use of the revived Cornish language and a degree of political devolution for Cornwall. Their flag is the emblem of St Piran (a 5th- or 6th-century saint who reputedly discovered tin in Cornwall). The flag consists of a white cross, which symbolizes tin, on a black field, which represents the ground rock from which it is extracted.

• **Meccano** ▶ The tradename of a construction set for children, first produced by Meccano Ltd of Liverpool in 1907. Meccano is a streamlined version of the original name 'Mechanics Made Easy', used by Frank Hornby for his invention in 1901. Hornby was also the inventor of Hornby model trains. The first Meccano sets consisted of green metal strips of various shapes and sizes with holes drilled in them, together with nuts, bolts, wheels, and other items that could be used to build a wide range of mechanical models of motor vehicles, cranes, etc. A plastic version, aimed at the junior end of the market, was introduced at a later date.

For more than 50 years, Meccano gave hours of educational enjoyment to generations of children and their parents and was even used in the field of engineering design. When Meccano Ltd ceased trading in the 1970s, the tradename passed through the hands of a number of other manufacturers and Meccano sets disappeared from the toyshops for several years, returning in the 1980s.

• **medallion man** ▶ A would-be macho male with a predilection for fashion accessories, most typically the neck chain and medallion suspended from it. The late 1970s were the heyday of medallion man: the trousers were tight and the shirt unbuttoned to reveal a bare but hairy (if possible) torso and the medallion – large, loud, and vaguely redolent of Olympian attributes. The John Travolta character in the 1978 film *Saturday Night Fever* is perhaps the epitome of the type – a virile Italian-American, who lives to dress and to dance, perfecting his rhythmic gyrations under the strobe lights of New York's discotheques. By the mid-1980s medallion man had been parodied into history.

> Singer Tom Jones...remains a macho sex symbol after 25 years, but now feels his Medallion Man image can be an embarrassment. – *The Times*, 13 March 1991.

• **me decade** ▶ A name for the 1970s coined in a 1976 article in the *New Yorker* magazine by the US journalist and writer Tom Wolfe (1931–   ). It refers to the narcissistic preoccupation with self-improvement and personal happiness which he regarded as characteristic of US culture in that decade. The phrase was also used in the UK of the Thatcherite 1980s. *See also*: psychobabble.

• **media** ▶ The chief agencies that disseminate information in society, including newspapers, magazines, radio, television, and now the Internet. It is, of course, a shortened form of mass media and the plural of 'medium'. Although the use of the word 'media' with a singular verb is frowned on by traditionalists, this is now very common and increasingly accepted.

• **Medicaid** ▶ The US public-health programme to provide hospital and medical care for those who cannot afford it. This was established by Congress in 1965 as a joint state-federal plan in which the federal government funds 50–80% of a state's cost, depending on its citizens' average income. Each state must meet federal standards but may choose the services it wishes to provide. Any indigent person qualifies for Medicaid, and some states include the 'medically indigent', who are unable to pay medical bills that are incompatible with their earnings. *See also*: family ganging.

• **Medicare** ▶ The US public-health insurance programme to provide hospital and medical care for persons aged 65 and older. Some disabled persons also qualify. The programme covers treatment at hospitals, nursing homes, and at home (after a deductible sum is paid each year). It also pays 80% of doctors' bills and other medical costs not covered by the hospital insurance. This Congressional programme began in 1966. In 1988, Congress added the Medicare Catastrophic Coverage Act to expand coverage, but so many elderly Americans objected to the surtax to fund its cost (more than $32 billion over five years) that the Act was repealed the next year. Medicare is financed by a tax added to social security payments.

• **Meek, Private Napoleon Alexander Trotsky** ▶ A character in the play *Too True to be Good* by George Bernard Shaw, first performed in 1932. Private Meek was based on T. E. Lawrence (*see*: Lawrence of Arabia), a friend of Shaw's. The motorcycle (*see*: Boanerges) that was to cause Lawrence's premature death in 1935 also features in the play.

• **mega-** ▶ Originally a Greek-derived prefix used to indicate a million, particularly in scientific SI units: a megavolt is $10^6$ volts, a megawatt is $10^6$ watts, etc. Since the 1980s 'mega-' has also been used more generally to mean very great or large; for example, **megabucks** (a great deal of money), **megacrowds** (a great many people), and **megastar** (a great star).

• **megabyte** ▶ (MB) In computing, loosely, one million bytes, or more accurately 1,048,576 bytes (one megabyte is 1024 kilobytes (KB) and one kilobyte is 1024 bytes). A byte is eight bits (binary elements), a bit being the basic unit of information in a computer. Memory capacity and the capacity of such storage devices as hard and floppy disks are measured in megabytes. A typical personal computer has a memory of at least one megabyte and the average hard disk will store several **gigabytes** (= a thousand megabytes).

• **megadeath** ▶ A unit representing the deaths of one million people; it was used by military bureaucrats at the height of the Cold War to calculate the likely effects of a nuclear exchange. The word is now used more loosely to mean an horrifically large number of deaths, as in a natural disaster.

• **Megan's Law** ▶ *See*: paedophile register.

• **megillah** ▶ US slang, from Yiddish, for a long written screed or (more recently) for a long verbal account that omits no details, is probably repetitive, and will certainly bore the listener. It is used in such sentences as 'He wrote me a whole megillah...' and 'Spare me a megillah, just tell me the facts'. The word came from the Hebrew, meaning scroll, and is often used in a religious context to refer to the Book of Esther.

• **Mein Kampf** ▶ (German, My Struggle) The book in which Adolf Hitler set out his political and racial theories and his misreadings of history, which in due course became the Nazi 'Bible'. It was published in two parts (1925 and 1927), the first being written when he was in prison after the abortive Munich Putsch of 1923. The original title was *Four and a Half Years of Struggle against Lies, Stupidity and Cowardice*, but the author was persuaded to think of something snappier. *See*: Hitlerism.

• **Melba toast** ▶ Toast that has been sliced down the centre and subsequently baked in the oven. According to tradition it was named after the Australian opera singer Dame Nellie Melba (Helen Porter Armstrong, née Mitchell; 1861–1931). While staying at the Savoy Hotel in London she was served dried-up fragile slices of toast that had been left too long in the oven. When the maître d'hotel apologized she cut him short, protesting how delicious it was. It was subsequently served to her, and to everyone else, in this state. *See also*: peach melba.

• **meltdown** ▶ Originally, the disastrous melting of the over-heated core of a nuclear reactor over which the operators have lost control, as happened at Chernobyl in the Soviet Union (now Ukraine) in 1986. The word has since entered the general language to describe a sudden economic or other collapse; it became particularly popular at the time of the crash of the world stock markets in 1987. Black

Monday was often referred to as **Meltdown Monday**.

• **Menin Gate** ▶ A giant war memorial erected in 1927 at Ypres in W Belgium. It stands in memory of the 55,000 British soldiers who died during World War I at the three battles that took place in and around Ypres. The names of the missing cover the entire edifice, while the graves of the identified dead stretch a great distance in all directions.

• **men in grey suits** ▶ Establishment figures who are unlikely to be seen in casual clothing and indeed are unlikely to be seen at all. They are the *éminences grises* of an organization, who make the ultimate decisions. It was the men in grey suits who were reputed to have persuaded Margaret Thatcher that her position as prime minister and leader of the Tory party was no longer tenable after the challenge from Michael Heseltine, so forcing her resignation on 22 November 1990.

• **Mensa** ▶ An international society for people who have a high IQ. Founded in the UK in 1946, the organization has no political or religious affiliations; members are of all ages and from all walks of life. Prospective members pay a small fee to take a supervised IQ test: those who achieve scores above a fixed level (approximately the top 2% of the population) are invited to join the society. Mensa organizes conferences and other events on a national basis and there are also local special-interest groups that enable members to form social and professional relationships with like-minded individuals. The name Mensa (Latin for 'table') was chosen to convey the image of a round table where all meet on equal terms.

• **Mensheviks** ▶ (Russian, minority party) The moderate Russian social democrats who initially cooperated with the Bolsheviks to overthrow the Tsarist regime but then opposed the October Revolution of 1917. *See also*: Kerensky government.

• **Men's Lib** ▶ An organization established in America in the late 1960s with the aim of freeing men from the burden of filling the traditional male role in society. It was, of course, intended as an answer to the more ubiquitous Women's Lib (*see*: feminism). Similar organizations and campaigns have continued to appear from time to time in response to the perennial male complaint that 'feminism has gone too far'. When feminists point to the continuing gender gap in earnings, male libbers reply that on average men work longer hours and for more years, suffer more illness, die sooner, and are much more likely to commit suicide.

• **menu** ▶ In computing, a list of options that usually appears on the screen at the start of a pro-gramme, showing the commands and facilities available to the user, which can then be selected by a keystroke or by using a mouse. Software making frequent use of menus is described as **menu-driven**; it is usually much more user-friendly than other forms of software. Even easier to use are computers with a **WIMP** (Windows, Icons, Menus, and Pointing devices) interface, such as that provided by the Windows operating system; these feature 'drop-down' menus (extended lists accessed by a single menu title) to control virtually every aspect of their operation. Menu options are often presented in the form of icons (*i.e.* visual mnemonics) which can be selected by a mouse.

• **MEP**▸ Member of the European Parliament. The parliament, which meets in Strasbourg or Luxem-bourg, has 626 MEPs who serve for a term of five years and are elected by universal suffrage by the EU member states. The MEPs sit in political groupings, not in national delegations (*e.g.* the European People's Party, which includes Conservatives and Christian Democrats; the Socialists, which includes the Social Democratic and Labour parties), and deliberate on the legislative proposals of the European Commission.

• **Mercedes**▸ A car produced by the original German Daimler company. The name was taken from that of a young girl, Mercedes Jellinek, whose father, Emil Jellinek, an Austrian diplomat, owned several Daimler cars, which he used for racing. In 1899 he entered one of his cars in the French Tour de Nice under the name 'Herr Mercedes'. After the Mercedes car had won the race, Jellinek bought a large number of identical cars, for which he was given the sole selling rights in Austria, Hungary, France and America, using the marque 'Mercedes'. It was not long, however, before all Daimler's cars were called Mercedes. When, in 1925, Daimler merged with Carl Benz's firm, the products of the merged company, Daimler-Benz, became known as **Mercedes-Benz** cars. Later Benz was dropped and the Merc, as it is often called in the UK, became a highly successful post-war product of West Germany.

The name Mercedes was much used for girls in 17th-century aristocratic Spanish circles but became more widely known in Europe after Dumas had so named the lover of Edmond Dantès in *The Count of Monte Cristo* (1844–45). It is said that Jellinek named his daughter after this Mercedes.

• **Merchant-Ivory films**▸ Movies made by the US director James Ivory (1930– ) and the Indian-born producer Ismail Merchant (1936– ). In the 1960s the two men made several films about India in collaboration with the German-born Ruth Prawer Jhabvala, who was married to an Indian. However, they are now mainly known for their elegant literary adaptations; the E.M. Forster films *A Room with a View* (1985) and *Howards End* (1992) were both highly acclaimed and their adaptation of *The Remains of the Day* (1993), from the novel by Kazuo Ishiguro, received four Oscar nominations. Subsequent films were less successful. The term 'Merchant-Ivory' is now sometimes used in a slightly disparaging way to denote any beautifully filmed and acted but somewhat lifeless costume drama.

• **Mercury Project**▸ The first manned flight of the US space programme. The first Mercury spacecraft, named Freedom 7, was manned by Alan Shephard and launched on 5 May 1961, less than a month after the flight of the Soviet astronaut Yuri Gagarin, the first man in space. Freedom 7 and its successor Liberty Bell 7 reached altitudes of 116 miles and 118 miles, respectively, in ballistic flights lasting approximately 15 minutes. In 1962 the first US manned orbital flights were achieved by Friendship 7, Aurora 7, and Sigma 7. After the flight of Faith 7 in 1963 the Mercury project was replaced by the Gemini programme.

• **mercy flight**▸ An aircraft or helicopter trip undertaken to relieve suffering or distress. The phrase arose from the ability of aircraft to provide rapid access to the remotest regions, making it a favoured means of bringing urgent supplies to a disaster area or transporting victims away from such an area.

• **Meredith**▸
**We're in, Meredith** A popular catchphrase derived from the very successful Fred Karno sketch, *The Bailiff*, produced in 1907. It depicted the stratagems of a bailiff and his assistant, Meredith, attempting to enter a house for purposes of distraint. The phrase was used by the bailiff each time he thought he was on the verge of success.

• **meritocracy**▸ Rule by those of superior intellect and talents. The term was popularized by Michael Young in his book *The Rise of the Meritocracy* (1958), in which he argued that educational achievement had replaced both noble birth and inherited wealth as the route to power in society. Unlike many who later used the word, Young did not see this as a wholly desirable state of affairs.

• **Mermaid Theatre**▸ A small theatre built in a blitzed Victorian warehouse in Puddle Dock in the City of London. Founded by the actor Bernard Miles (Baron Miles; 1907–91) and his wife, who had formerly run a small open-air theatre in the garden of their home in St John's Wood, the Mermaid opened in 1959. It was named after the former Mermaid Tavern, also in the City, which was the home of Sir Walter Raleigh's famous Mermaid Club. This illustrious literary club was frequented by Shakespeare, Francis Beaumont, and Ben Jonson, among others. After a series of financial and other problems the Mermaid Theatre closed its doors in 1997; its future is uncertain.

• **Merrill's Marauders** ▶ A special infantry unit of US volunteers, organized by Brig.-Gen. F. D. Merrill (1903–55) in Burma during World War II. Trained in jungle warfare, they operated in the same way as the Chindits, using guerrilla tactics to harass the enemy. The Marauders set off in February 1944 to march several hundred miles through the Burmese jungle. Although weakened by disease, hunger, and exhaustion, they brought their campaign to a triumphant conclusion with the capture of Myitkyina in August 1944, establishing a vital air base along the supply route from India to China.

• **Mers el-Kébir** ▶ A port near Oran on the Mediterranean coast of Algeria, which became a French naval base in 1935. A large number of French warships took refuge at Mers el-Kébir in June 1940, after the armistice between France and Germany. The British, anxious to prevent these vessels from falling into the hands of the Axis forces, tried in vain to negotiate with the French commander, Admiral Gensoul. After the rejection of their final ultimatum on 3 July 1940, the British had no alternative but to attack the fleet, causing considerable damage and the loss of 1300 French lives.

• **Mersey poets** ▶ The Liverpool poets Adrian Henri, Roger McGough, and Brian Patten, who often gave readings together at the peak of their popularity in the 1960s. Their work was published together in Volume 10 of the Penguin Modern Poets series, under the title *The Mersey Sound* (1967).

• **Mersey sound** ▶ The pop music produced by the Beatles and other Liverpool bands – notably the Searchers and Gerry and the Pacemakers – in the early to mid-1960s. The 'Mersey sound' was characterized by jangling guitars, catchy tunes, and exuberant vocal harmonies.

• **meshugga** ▶ (Hebrew, madness) US slang, from Yiddish, meaning crazy; a crazy person is a **meshuggener**. Like 'crazy' itself, meshugga can mean certifiably insane as well as foolish; for example: 'He's in a psychiatric hospital, poor fellow, hopelessly meshugga' or 'Don't let that meshuggener drive...'

A specific kind of eccentricity is called a **meshugaas** (or **mishegaas**). This is often no more than a fairly harmless obsession: 'His meshugaas is that he believes that in order to stay alive he has to jog three miles every morning'. The Yiddish words entered US English in New York around the turn of the 20th century, with many other Yiddishisms.

• **mess** ▶
**Here's another fine mess you've gotten me into** Oliver Hardy's catchphrase from the Laurel and Hardy comedy films of the 1920s and 1930s. When disaster inevitably overtook the duo, Hardy would fiddle with his tie, gaze helplessly into the camera, and use these words to bemoan his fate of having such a hopeless partner as Stan Laurel. One of their films was actually called *Another Fine Mess* (1930).

• **message received loud and clear** ▶ A standard phrase used in the early days of radio communications, meaning 'I understand what you are telling me'. It has since passed into more general use.

• **messenger RNA** ▶ (mRNA) A molecule found in living cells that performs a crucial role as 'messenger' of the genetic information contained in the cell's DNA. The cell manufactures proteins according to instructions carried by the DNA. These instructions are 'transcribed' with the formation of a messenger RNA molecule, whose bases form a sequence complementary to that of the DNA; it is this sequence of bases that constitutes the genetic code. The mRNA molecules can move to different parts of the cell, where the code is 'translated' by another type of RNA – ribosomal RNA – and the corresponding protein is produced. The activities of the cell are determined by the proteins it produces, hence the vital importance of the RNA messengers to the life of the cell. The role of messenger RNA was elucidated in the 1950s and 1960s through the work of many biologists.

• **Messerschmitt** ▶ Any of a number of aircraft designed by the German engineer Willy Messerschmitt (1898–1978). The Me-109 fighter, designed in 1935, won the world speed record in 1939 and was the most successful German aircraft of World War II: the Luftwaffe were supplied with some 33,675 Me-109s. The Me-262, capable of speeds up to 600 mph, was the first jet fighter to be used in military action. Fortunately for the Allies, Hitler intervened in its development to give priority to jet bombers, delaying the introduction of the Me-262 until 1944. Other less successful Messerschmitt aircraft included the Me-110, which was outclassed by the Hurricane and the Spitfire, and the single-jet Me-163.

**• Messina brothers ▶** Five members of an Italian family who were involved in procuring prostitutes and running brothels in London and other UK cities. For some 30 years in the mid-20th century the brothers made large profits from their work, at the expense of the women concerned. By the mid-1960s, after a period of imprisonment, all five had left the UK, either voluntarily or by deportation. However, some of their London brothels remained in operation, controlled from the brothers' new headquarters in Italy.

**• meter maid ▶** Originally (in the 1950s) a US name for a policewoman employed to patrol metered parking areas and report offences; it was later applied to female traffic wardens in the UK. Owing to their uniforms and their ability to inflict summary punishment, women traffic wardens have acquired a special place in male mythology, featuring either as grim-visaged gorgons or as figures of sexual fantasy. The Beatles' song 'Lovely Rita, Meter Maid' ('When it gets dark you tow my heart away') appeared in 1967.

**• Method, the ▶** An acting technique developed from the theories of Konstantin Stanislavsky (Konstantin Alekstzev; 1863–1938) and taught from 1950 onwards at the Actors' Studio, New York, under the directorship of Lee Strasberg (1901–82). Strasberg was a former pupil of Richard Boleslavsky, who had brought Stanislavsky's ideas to America in the 1920s. The most important principle of the Method technique is the actor's total understanding of and identification with his character's motivation; to grasp this, he or she is encouraged to draw on comparable experiences in his or her own life, including ones which have been buried in the subconscious. This is supposed to result in a greater realism in the actor's subsequent portrayal of the character. The technique has been widely criticized, but remains an important influence on stage and screen acting. Notable exponents of the Method include Marlon Brando, Robert De Niro, and Dustin Hoffman.

**• metrication ▶** Conversion of any of a variety of units of measurement to those based on the decimal system. The metric system was first suggested in 1585 by Simon Stevin of the Low Countries but not used until it was promoted by Napoleon and established by French laws of 1795 and 1799. It came into general usage in Europe in the 1830s. In the UK it was authorized by law in 1864, although bills to make it compulsory were defeated in 1871 and 1907. The British stuck proudly to their own unwieldly and illogical hotchpotch of units, known as the Imperial System, until 1963, when the yard and the pound were given definitions by law in terms of metric units.

The metre, the cornerstone of the metric system, was originally defined (1791) as one ten-millionth of the length of the quadrant of the Earth's meridian passing through Paris. This piece of Gallic jingoism was replaced in 1927 by a definition relating the metre to the length of a platinum-iridium bar. This in turn gave way in 1960 to a scientific definition based on the wavelength of a particular kind of light, and – in 1983 – to the distance travelled by light in a specified fraction of a second. It is on the basis of the 1960 definition of the metre that the British defined the yard: It is now 0.9144 metres exactly.

This break with the tradition of Imperial units was furthered by the setting up of a Metrication Board in 1969, with the target of completing metrication of British industry and commerce by 1975. Although decimal currency was adopted in the UK in 1972, this surge towards an alien system of units predictably petered out in 1980, when the Metrication Board was disbanded with its targets unmet. Thereafter, metrication proceeded at a leisurely pace: legislation of 1985, amended in 1994, provided for the gradual phasing out of Imperial units for trading and administrative purposes, with certain exceptions. This has created a number of anomalies. Fresh milk is sold in pint bottles, UHT milk in half-litre and litre cartons; draught beer is sold by the pint but canned beer is sold in cans of 275 ml, 440 ml, or 500 ml; the scale of maps is now metric but land distances are still measured in miles, etc. Since January 2000 it has been illegal to sell any goods (except beer and milk) in Imperial measures. Nevertheless, most customers at market stalls, for example, still ask for fruit and vegetables in terms of pounds and ounces, although prices are (or should be) quoted in pounds and pence per kilogram and goods weighed on metric scales.

Only in science and engineering has reason prevailed: all measurements are now metric and expressed in SI units.

**• Métro ▶** The universal name for the Parisian underground railway – the Chemin de Fer Métropolitain. The first Métro line, designed by Fulgence Bienvenüe, was opened in July 1900 to coincide with the 1900 World Exhibition. It ran east–west between Porte de Vincennes and Porte Maillot. Construction of an underground transit system was helped by the relatively shallow foundations of the capital's buildings and the wide boulevards, created during the rebuilding of central Paris in the late 19th century. Engineers adopted the cut-and-cover system of construction, building first the tunnel walls and roof from above. This means that the tunnels are relatively shallow and the trains easily reached from street level. The system now has 199 km (123 miles) of tunnels and some 430 stations; it is integrated with the Réseau Express Régional, opened in 1969 to provide a fast service between suburban Paris and the city centre. Métro stations reflect a range of 20th-century styles in architecture, including some prime examples of Art Nouveau, such as Porte Dauphine and Abbesses, as well as Art Deco. Other stations have design features that provide a foretaste of the district they serve; for instance, at Varenne the traveller is treated to exhibits from the nearby Rodin Museum, while Louvre Métro station shows items from the Louvre. Armchair enthusiasts of the Métro can enjoy its many delights on celluloid in the 1985 thriller *Subway*, directed by Luc Besson, in which the action takes place against the ticket barriers, tunnels, and trains of this world-famous network. *See also*: tube, the.

• **Metro-Goldwyn Mayer** ▶ *See*: MGM.

• **Metroland** ▶ A nickname for the area to the NW of the capital served by London's Metropolitan railway line. The name was coined during the 1910s, when the newly built railway enabled commuters to travel to work from this then largely undeveloped area, which also became easily accessible to day-tripping Londoners. The 1920s and 1930s saw much new housing, a good deal of it built by the railway company itself, which thus acquired a captive supply of season-ticket buyers. The name was further popularized by the fictional character of Margot Metroland (originally Margot Beste-Chetwynde), who features in a number of Evelyn Waugh's novels, notably *Decline and Fall* (1928) and *Scoop* (1938).

• **Mexican wave** ▶ An activity indulged in by an audience seated in the round – usually in sports stadiums – when they are waiting for something to begin or have become bored with the event they are watching. At a given moment, those people occupying the equivalent seats in every row stand up, raise their hands, and sit down again; as they near the high point of this cycle, their neighbours on one side begin to repeat it. The net effect is a wavelike motion that ripples round the stadium. Of course, the practical application of these rules is rather less tidy than this might suggest, but considerably more fun; the emphasis is on enthusiastic participation rather than precision. It is usual to cheer as one raises one's arms, and to boo those humourless individuals (usually in the better seats) who think it beneath their dignity to join in. A Mexican wave always seems to begin spontaneously (wherever one is sitting, it always begins somewhere else); it is never orchestrated but does not collapse in confusion (it is a mystery, for example, how it is decided whether the wave should go clockwise or anticlockwise); and it fades out when the participants lose interest. The origins of the activity are obscure, but it first came to world attention through television broadcasts of the 1986 Soccer World Cup finals from Mexico – hence the name.

• **mezoomas** ▶ Slang for breasts, probably based on bazumas, a corruption of 'bosom'.

• **mezzanine finance** ▶ Funding raised for the takeover of a company in which a number of minor unsecured loans are obtained at a high rate of interest on the understanding that these loans will only be repaid when the major loans have been repaid in case of bankruptcy. It is thus intermediate between making a straight loan and taking a share in the equity of the company, just as a mezzanine floor is intermediate between the ground floor and the first floor of a large building.

• **MFU** ▶ *See*: snafu.

• **MG** ▶ The most popular and successful British sports car, originally manufactured by Morris Garages (William Morris's old business before he moved into manufacturing) under the direction of Cecil Kimber. MG's first model was launched in 1925 and in the next decade the company went on to produce a wide range of sports and sports racing cars, becoming the largest manufacturer of sports cars in the world. In 1930 production moved to a factory at Abingdon, near Oxford, where MGs bearing the famous octagonal badge continued to be produced for over 50 years until it was finally closed down by British Leyland in 1980. The marque continued, however, in the Metros, Maestros, and Montegos manufactured by the Austin Rover Company. In fact, the turbo versions of the 2-litre injection Maestros and Montegos were the fastest MGs ever made.

• **MGB** ▶ *Ministerstvo Gosudarstvennoi Bezopasnosti*. The Soviet ministry of state security, or secret police, founded in 1946. The MGB was concerned with internal security, intelligence, and counter-intelligence. Its methods of investigation were more brutal than those of the KGB, which replaced it in 1954 after the downfall of Lavrenti Beria, head of Soviet secret police from 1938. Beria's execution in 1953 was the result of his attempt to achieve absolute political power for the MGB.

• **MGM** ▶ Metro-Goldwyn-Mayer. The Hollywood studio that dominated the film industry during its 'golden era' of the 1930s and 1940s. The company was formed in 1924 when Marcus Loew's Metro Pictures Corporation merged with Goldwyn Pictures Corporation (founded in 1916 by Samuel Goldwyn; *see*: Goldwynisms) and a company run by Louis B. Mayer (1885–1957). Goldwyn was pushed out shortly before the merger and set up again as an independent; Mayer became head of the new company and, with his executive producer Irving Thalberg, rapidly established MGM's reputation for lavishly expensive and highly successful films, notably *Ben Hur* (1926; 1959), *Mutiny on the Bounty* (1935), *The Wizard of Oz* (1939), and *Singin' in the Rain* (1952). MGM's motto was 'more stars than there are in heaven': these included Greta Garbo, Clark Gable, Spencer Tracy, Judy Garland, and the Marx Brothers. Mayer retired from MGM in 1951. The company stopped producing films in the 1970s but has since established a large cinema chain.

• **Michelin Guides** ► A famous series of guidebooks published by the Michelin Tyre Co. This French company was founded in 1888 by André Michelin (1853–1931) and his brother Édouard (1859–1940) to manufacture their newly invented pneumatic tyres. It later diversified into providing a range of maps and guidebooks for the motorist. These all carry the image of the **Michelin Man**, the trademark of the tyre company, consisting of a fat little man made of tyres. The guide books, originally of France, list hotels and restaurants using a highly regarded scale of stars – a five-star hotel or restaurant being the highest accolade its compilers can confer. Michelin guidebooks now exist for other countries, including the UK.

• **Michurinism** ► *See*: Lysenkoism.

• **mickey finn** ► Slang for a drugged drink given to an unsuspecting person, which renders the victim unconscious. It was usually made by mixing chloral hydrate with alcohol. The term originated in the early 1900s in America and is thought to have been taken from the name of a Chicago barkeeper who practised this trick. Mickey finn is now sometimes used to mean any strong mixed drink used unknowingly to intoxicate the drinker. It is often shortened to **mickey** and can be used as a verb:

> Two men...had mickey-finned his drink. – C. FRANKLIN: *Home Secretary Affair* (1971).

• **Mickey Mouse** ► The mouse-like cartoon character created by Walt Disney (1901–66) in the 1920s. Originally named Mortimer, the happy-go-lucky mouse made his debut in a 1928 short; the high-pitched voice was supplied by Disney himself. He subsequently appeared in numerous shorts, often with his girlfriend **Minnie Mouse** and his friends

Pluto and Goofy. By the 1930s he had become the most universally recognized cartoon character in the world.

The term 'Mickey Mouse' is now often used to describe something small, inferior, and trivial, for example, a Mickey Mouse project, salary, or car. This usage derives from the Mickey Mouse wristwatches introduced in America in the 1940s. These had a picture of Mickey Mouse on the dial with his outspread arms functioning as the watch-hands.

• **micro** ► Colloquial term for something very small, such as a microcomputer (*see*: personal computer) or a microskirt (*see*: miniskirt). Though long known as a prefix (from the Greek *mikros*, small), its widespread use as a noun dates only from the mid-20th century, with the tendency towards miniaturization (especially in electronics and computing technology).

• **microdot** ► **1.** A photographic image of a document reduced to the size of a pinhead for ease of transmission or for security reasons. **2.** A small dose of LSD sold as a tiny blob on a piece of paper.

• **microeconomics** ► The study of economic behaviour at the level of the individual or the firm. *See*: macroeconomics.

• **microfiche** ► A flat rectangle of plastic film bearing greatly reduced photographs of text or printed pages. It is viewed through a reader, which magnifies the text and displays it on an illuminated screen. Microfiche are widely used to provide catalogues of parts, books, etc. Instead of reproducing a whole book for updating, only individual fiche need be updated. Another use is to store historical documents, newspaper archives, etc. in a compact and accessible form.

• **microfilm** ► A reel of film with reduced photographs of printed text, pages of books or newspapers, etc. It is viewed on a reader, which magnifies the text and displays it on an illuminated screen.

• **microskirt** ► *See*: miniskirt.

• **microsurgery** ► Surgery of very fine structures requiring the use of an operating microscope. A microscope was first used as a surgical aid in 1921, for drainage of an ear infection; during the next 20 years ear surgeons developed various surgical treatments for deafness that depended on microscopy of the structures involved. The modern operating microscope was introduced in 1953 by the Carl Zeiss Company. Essentially it provides the surgeon with stereoscopic vision of the operating site, at magnifications in the range of ×4 to ×25. A beam splitter transmits the magnified image to the surgeon's eyepiece and often also to a camera and television monitor so that other theatre staff or students can follow the operation. The object field is illuminated by light transmitted through optical fibres; such fibres can also transmit laser light to make surgical incisions or destroy tissue. The microscope has enabled other micromanipulative techniques to emerge; these include the use of ultra-fine suture materials for sewing together blood capillaries, high-precision cutting techniques, and remote handling of instruments to eliminate wobble due to hand movements.

The last 40 years have seen enormous strides in microsurgery. Microtechniques are long established in ear surgery – they are now used in such operations as cochlear implants – and in eye surgery – for example cataract removal and corneal replacement. Plastic surgery has been revolutionized by modern microsurgical techniques: surgeons now successfully replace severed digits and limbs by joining blood vessels and nerves between the stump and the severed part. Similarly, progress in bone and skin grafting owes much to microsurgical restoration of blood and nerve supplies to the graft, while brain surgery now relies on microscopical techniques for precision repairs of damaged or burst blood vessels resulting from strokes.

• **microwave** ▸ A form of electromagnetic radiation with a wavelength lying between that of infrared radiation and radio waves. Microwaves have a wavelength in the range 1 millimetre to 0.3 metre. They can be generated by electronic circuits and are used in radar systems, masers (*see*: laser), and in scientific experiments. Microwaves are also used in the **microwave oven** for cooking and heating food quickly. In a conventional oven the food cooks from the outside; heat is conducted into the centre of the food. Microwave cooking is different and much faster; the radiation penetrates the whole and the food is cooked evenly and quickly. Microwave ovens were first used by commercial caterers in the late 1960s but domestic use increased in the 1980s accompanied by the availability of convenience food suitable for microwave cooking. The use of microwave ovens has led to a number of modern myths (*see*: urban legends).

• **Middle America** ▸ The majority of Americans, who believe in traditional values and reject extreme views or tastes. They also believe that they are the silent majority, as their opinions are rarely presented by the media, which tends to concentrate on either the west or east coast at the expense of the middle of the country. The term therefore has both a geographical and a sociological context. It was coined in 1968 by the US journalist Joseph Kraft,

with reference to the people whom Richard Nixon regarded as his potential supporters. *See also*: silent majority.

• **Middle-earth** ▸ A fantasy world created by J. R. R. Tolkien that forms the setting for the Lord of the Rings trilogy (1954–55) and other works. Middle-earth, also known as Endor, is inhabited by elves, dwarves, men, and hobbits, amongst other creatures: its mythology, geography, history, and languages were meticulously documented by Tolkien. Lying to the west of the Great Sea, Middle-earth contains regions and features with such poetic names as the Misty Mountains, the River Anduin, the elf-kingdom of Lothlórien, the eastern land of Hildórien (from where the first men came), and Mordor (or 'the Land of Shadow') – the realm of the evil Sauron.

> As astrology is to physics and conspiracy theory to history, so Middle Earth is to literature and learning... – JENNY TURNER, *London Review of Books*, November 2001.

• **middle eight** ▸ The middle eight bars of a popular song. Such songs are often constructed on the pattern ABABCAB, where A is the verse, B is the chorus, and C is the middle eight. This part of the song often features a change of key. A party game played by the musically minded is for each person in turn to play or hum the middle eight of a popular tune; the others then have to guess the song's title.

• **Middle England** ▸ The middle classes of England, considered as a force for political and social conservatism (with a small 'c'). Like the term Middle America, from which it is adapted, 'Middle England' has a vaguely geographical as well as a social reference. The inhabitants of this mythical domain are imagined as living outside London and other metropolitan centres, and away from the northern and Celtic fringes. The term seems to be applied particularly to those individuals and their families who were assimilated into the ever-growing middle classes during the 1980s and 1990s. These Middle Englanders are more likely to work in IT or one of the new service industries than in a traditional profession such as teaching or the law. They feel that they have outgrown the working-class values of their parents or grandparents, but have little time for the shibboleths of the old middle classes. In a word, they are aspirational but not snobs. They are more likely to take the *Daily Mail* than either *The Times* or *The Guardian*, but more likely to read *Hello!* magazine than any of these. They are far from stupid, and may well have benefited from the expansion of higher education in the 1980s and 1990s, but consider themselves too busy to have many in-

• middle management •

tellectual interests. Their tastes in clothes, decor, music, books, and films tend to the unadventurous; they think they recognize quality when they see it, but will usually be about two steps behind the latest London fashions. Their hobbies are DIY, cooking, gardening, keep fit, and shopping. Hard working and law-abiding themselves, they have no sympathy for criminals or those who are thought to be free-loading on the state; at the same time their racial and sexual attitudes are vastly more tolerant than those of 25 years ago. In politics, they probably admire Mrs Thatcher but think she 'went too far'; they probably voted for Tony Blair but sometimes wonder if he is going anywhere at all. Because the voters of Middle England are thought to have decided every general election since the mid-1980s, they are now regarded with almost superstitious awe by psephologists, opinion formers, and party politicians (see: pebbledash people). The creation of New Labour in the 1990s can be seen as perhaps the ultimate tribute to Middle England and its values – Labour politicians came to understand that they would never hold office again if they continued to alienate this huge amorphous constituency.

> Middle England is patronised as well as pampered. Focus groupies and market researchers strain to probe and manipulate its passions. Élite politicians and pundits drop their aitches and pose as its tribunes. What's left of the Left confirms its impotence by moaning from the sidelines... – *The Observer*, 1 April 2001.

• **middle management** ► Such managers as those responsible for running a single department within a large organization but who play no part in the development of policy for the organization as a whole. The concept of middle management originated in the 1950s.

• **middle-market** ► Denoting goods or services aimed at the middle range of the market, *i.e.* somewhere between **down-market** (relatively inexpensive and unglamourous goods or services) and **up-market** (relatively expensive and luxurious goods or services).

• **middle-of-the-road** ► Denoting those who tend to have moderate (rather than extreme) views and tastes. In politics, for example, middle-of-the-road party members are neither especially left-wing nor right-wing but hold the unadventurous solid views that provide the party with its stability. Because they are the most numerous, those with middle-of-the-road tastes have considerable commercial importance; in the music industry a whole category (with several subdivisions) exists to cater for their tastes, called **MOR**.

> We know what happens to people who stay in the middle of the road. They get run over.
> – ANEURIN BEVAN, 1953.

• **midi** ► Describing coats, skirts, and other garments that reach mid-calf level. Midi is also used as a prefix and a noun, particularly for the **midiskirt** (*see*: miniskirt).

• **midinette** ► A young Parisian woman employed to make or sell clothes, hats, or other fashion accessories. In the early part of the 20th century, the midinettes' youth and independence encouraged the view, especially among Englishmen, that they were sexually available. The word is thought to derive from French *midi*, noon, and *dinette*, a light lunch: the implication being that the girls were too busy to eat more than a snack at midday.

• **midi system** ► A compact stack of hi-fi equipment designed as a single unit. It plays tapes, records, and compact discs, although more recent models often do not play records.

• **midlife crisis** ► A crisis of self-confidence that occurs with the onset of middle age; it is associated with the realization that one's youth lies behind one and that what lies ahead is a decline into old age. It affects both sexes and usually passes fairly rapidly as the benefits of experience over youthful enthusiasm begin to emerge. It may, however, cause impulsive or uncharacteristic behaviour with lasting consequences – such as the abandonment of a generally happy but no longer exciting marriage or a sudden change of career.

• **Midway, Battle of** ► A battle fought during World War II at the Midway Islands, a US military base in the Pacific Ocean. A major victory for the Allies, it marked an important turning point in the war in the Pacific. The battle began on 3 June 1942 and ended on 6 June with the retirement of the Japanese. Principally an engagement between US and Japanese carrier-based aircraft, the battle resulted in the loss of one US and four Japanese aircraft carriers, causing a significant reduction in Japan's naval strength.

• **Mif** ► A word used by Nancy Mitford (*see*: Mitford girls) to describe people who pour tea into a cup after putting the 'milk in first'. In her analysis of U and Non-U language and behaviour, Mitford classified this habit as 'Non-U', a social blunder: members of the upper classes pour the tea in first. Although this kind of minor etiquette now has no significance for any class, the rationale dates back to the days in which wealthy ladies serving afternoon tea to their friends would pour the tea into the cup, which a maid would then offer to the guest on a tray containing a milk jug and a lump-sugar container. This enabled the guest to add milk and sugar to her own taste.

• **MI5** ▶ Military Intelligence, section five. The former name (from 1916) of the British government's counter-intelligence agency (the Security Service). The name MI5 is no longer in official use but remains in the popular vocabulary. The section's work involves the detection and surveillance of those known or suspected to be engaged in military or political espionage in the UK, with the aim of thwarting their mission. MI5 is answerable to the home secretary; ultimate control lies with the prime minister. *See also*: MI6.

• **MiG** ▶ Any of a series of Soviet aircraft designed by Mikoyan and Gurevich. The MiG-15, a jet fighter, was used by the Chinese Communist Air Force during the Korean War in the early 1950s, but proved to be no match for the US F-86 Sabrejet. Other MiG aircraft include the supersonic MiG-19 and the MiG-21.

• **migrant worker** ▶ A worker, often an agricultural worker, who leaves a poor country to work in a richer country. Migrant workers often send money home to support their families; this may constitute an important part of the foreign income of poor countries. *See also*: economic migrant; Gastarbeiter.

• **Mike Hammer** ▶ *See*: Hammer, Mike.

• **militant** ▶ 1. A person who is aggressive in putting his or her views or in achieving his or her aims. 2. A member of **Militant Tendency**, an extreme left-wing organization in the UK that came to prominence in the 1970s, taking its name from its weekly newspaper, *Militant*. Some members of Militant infiltrated the Labour Party but they were expelled in the mid-1980s to make the party more acceptable to the middle-of-the-road voter.

• **Military Cross** ▶ A decoration inaugurated in December 1914 and awarded to captains, lieutenants, and warrant officers in the British Army. It was formerly also bestowed on members of the Colonial and Indian forces.

• **milk round** ▶ The visit paid by the personnel managers of large companies to universities to encourage the brightest of the year's graduates to join their organizations. In the sciences and engineering, particularly, there is strong competition for students who are likely to gain first-class degrees.

• **milk-run** ▶ An expression common amongst Allied aircrews of World War II for any sortie flown regularly day after day, or a sortie against an easy target on which inexperienced pilots could be used with impunity – as simple as delivering milk.

• **Milk Snatcher** ▶ Nickname of Margaret Thatcher. *See*: Iron Lady.

• **Mille Miglia** ▶ A sports-car race formerly run in Italy, from Brescia to Rome and back, covering approximately 1000 miles on public roads (*mille miglia* is Italian for 'a thousand miles'). Inaugurated in 1927 and open to both amateurs and professionals, the Mille Miglia remained an immensely popular annual event for 30 years. The alarming number of deaths during the race caused it to be banned by Mussolini in the early 1940s, but the race continued after the war with ever-increasing risk and speed – up to 180 mph in close pursuit on badly maintained roads. The 1955 Mille Miglia was won by the British driver Stirling Moss, who covered the 1000-mile course in just 10 hours. In 1957, an accident that claimed the lives of the Spanish driver Alfonso ('Fon') de Portago, his co-driver, and 10 spectators finally brought the tradition of the Mille Miglia to an end.

• **Millennium Bridge** ▶ A footbridge across the Thames in London that links St Paul's Cathedral on the north bank to Tate Modern on the south bank. Built to commemorate the new millennium, it is the first new river crossing in central London since Tower Bridge was opened in 1894. The structure was designed by Lord Foster, in partnership with the sculptor Sir Anthony Caro, and built by Ove Arup. A sleek aluminium-decked steel suspension bridge of novel design, it has been described as a 'blade of light'. Unfortunately when this innovative structure, which cost £18million to build, was opened on 10 June 2000 it had to be closed almost immediately – because the bridge responded to the crowd of pedestrians inaugurating the new crossing by swaying ominously. The engineers proclaimed the structure safe, if somewhat unnerving, and the bridge was reopened – but caution prevailed and it was closed again after a day.

For nearly two years the bridge remained closed, while perplexed engineers sought an effective way of damping the bridge's movement without impairing its elegance. It finally reopened to the public in March 2002.

• **millennium bug** ▶ Any problem affecting computer software as a result of a failure to cope with the transition from the year 1999 to the year 2000. The problem was caused by early software using only a two-figure year date (*e.g.* 86) to timestamp information instead of a four-figure date (*e.g.* 1986); this meant that the year 2000 would be recorded as 00, possibly giving rise to confusion with the year 1900, which would also be represented as 00.

In the late 1990s there were fears that a global

emergency could arise as a result of the knock-on effect of software failures – with power stations ceasing to function, air-traffic control being thrown into confusion, and other computer-controlled public services collapsing. Governments around the world are estimated to have spent at least £400 million in dealing with and raising awareness of the issue. In the event, the transition to 2000 passed smoothly with no major hitches, presumably because adequate precautions had been taken to deal with it. However, many countries that had spent little or nothing on averting possible disaster were no more affected than countries that had spent fortunes, leading cynics to wonder how serious the problem had been to start with.

• **Millennium Dome**► The world's largest dome, sponsored by the British government to commemorate the end of the second millennium. Built on a derelict site on a U-bend in the River Thames at Greenwich in east London to designs by the Richard Rogers Partnership, the Dome rises to the height of Nelson's Column (50 metres) and covers an area equivalent to that of Trafalgar Square, including the surrounding buildings (almost 20 acres). This impressive structure consists of a Teflon-coated glass canopy suspended from 12 steel masts, each 100 metres high.

Although widely considered a triumph of British engineering, the Dome's £750 million price tag (£400 million from lottery funds, the rest from business sponsorship) caused unease from the start. Much sharper controversy came to dog the Millennium Experience, the exhibition that the Dome was built to house. The exhibition, which was opened by the Queen on 31 December 1999 and ran for a year, consisted of a central spectacle exploring the concept of time, surrounded by 12 'zones', each of which depicted an aspect of the human condition or environment. The disasters began on opening night, when poor logistics left a trainload of VIPs stranded on a deserted underground station; as this included seven national newspaper editors, terrible publicity was assured. Damning press comment was soon backed up by word-of-mouth reports that the exhibition was uninspired and overpriced, leading to a serious shortfall in the 21,500 daily visitors needed to cover running costs. As financial crisis loomed, the government, apparently still hoping it could convert a Mini into a Rolls-Royce by changing the driver, sacked the original chief executive and replaced her with an ebullient Frenchman formerly employed at EuroDisney. Predictably he failed significantly to improve the Dome's fortunes and further large injections of lottery money (some audits put this as high as £650 million) were required to keep the project afloat. By the time the Millennium Experience closed on 31 December 2000, the Dome had come to be regarded as a cross between a lame duck and a white elephant – a monumental waste of money and a hideous embarrassment to the government that had once championed it so loudly. In mid-2002 its future remains uncertain. Several high-profile bids to take it over fell through in 2000–01, while the current plan, which involves leasing the site to a US billionaire who will use it to stage sports and entertainment events, has yet to be finalized. In any case, the Dome will stand empty and unused until December 2004 at the earliest, with running costs estimated at around £500,000 a month.

> I have no doubt at all that...this country will stand proud of having the courage to own the most exciting project anywhere in the world. – MICHAEL HESELTINE, January 1998.

> If we can't make this work, we're not much of a government. – JOHN PRESCOTT, June 1997.

> Our problem will not be attracting people, but finding enough space and opportunity for them all to enter the Dome to have the time of their lives. – PETER MANDELSON, speech in the House of Commons, 16 March 1998.

> We will say to ourselves with pride: this is our Dome, Britain's Dome, And believe me, it will be the envy of the world...the benefits to Britain are huge. – TONY BLAIR, 13 April 1998.

• **Mills & Boon** ► A British publishing house, which has become a byword for sentimental romance. Founded in 1908 by Gerald Mills and Charles Boon, it originally published a range of general fiction titles, including books by Jack London, Hugh Walpole, and P. G. Wodehouse. The historical romances of Georgette Heyer made their debut under the Mills & Boon imprint and during the early 1930s the company began its specialization in romantic novels. During the Depression these proved a very popular form of escapism, especially with subscribers to the commercial 'twopenny libraries' of that time. Storylines in the 1940s reflected the more prominent roles played by women – the war inspired the birth of the still-popular Doctor/Nurse series of medical romances. In the late 1950s a small Canadian paperback publisher, Harlequin, acquired the rights to Mills & Boon titles and launched its own series of paperback romances. Its success in North America prompted the British firm to start their own paperback series in 1960. In 1972 the two companies merged, and in 1981 this transatlantic combine was acquired by the Canadian Torstar group.

Mills & Boon now publish several different series of titles, each with its own particular formula but all containing the same essential ingredients – the vicissitudes of a rugged hero and his virginal heroine, which are eventually resolved by true love. The formula has been much derided but remains very popular. Although premarital sex is no longer proscribed, little else has changed since *Punch* described the work of one of Mills & Boon's first authors, Sophie Cole:

> Her tales should appeal to every reader who does not insist on battle, murder, and divorce as essential to the best romance.

• **Mills bomb** ▶ A type of grenade developed by the British and used in both World Wars. The Mills bomb most widely used in World War I was a cast-iron fragmentation grenade weighing about 1.5 pounds (700 g), designed for use against attacking infantry from a position of cover. It could also be fired from a rifle by employing a special discharger cup and projecting cartridge. The detonator was activated by a seven-second safety fuse. During World War II the equivalent Mills-type grenades were fired from 2-in mortars and had a four-second fuse. It was named after the engineer, Sir William Mills (1856–1932), whose Birmingham factory produced the grenades during World War I.

• **Milner's Kindergarten** ▶ The nickname given to the notable group of young men gathered together by Sir Alfred (Viscount) Milner, high commissioner for South Africa, for the work of reconstruction after the Boer Wars (1899–1902). They were Robert Brand, Lionel Curtis, John Dove, Patrick Duncan, Richard Feetham, Lionel Hitchens, Philip Kerr, Douglas Malcolm, J. F. Perry, Geoffrey Robinson, and Hugh Wyndham. Among those associated with them were L. S. Amery, Basil Blackwood, John Buchan, and Basil Williams. They duly became advocates of closer imperial ties, both political and economic, and remained an important propagandist group for the imperial idea in the years before World War I. The name was probably invented by the lawyer Sir William Marriott.

• **Milton Keynes** ▶ A new town in NE Buckinghamshire, England, founded in 1967; one of the most ambitious planned in the UK since World War II. Designed for a future population of 200,000, the town contains the headquarters of the Open University, some light industry, and a number of innovative housing developments. Incorporated within the boundary of the new town, which covers an area of 9000 hectares, are the old village of Milton Keynes and the towns of Bletchley, Wolverton, and Stony Stratford. In the early years of its existence Milton Keynes, in common with many other simi-

lar developments, suffered a certain amount of criticism for the unimaginative design of some of its housing estates, its network of straight roads running parallel to each other or intersecting at right angles, and its general lack of character. Its 'concrete cows', a sculptural group suggesting a herd of cattle, became famous after being ridiculed in the national press. The town is alleged to have the highest suicide rate in the UK and the largest number of practising witches.

• **Minamata disease** ▶ A form of mercury poisoning named after the Japanese town of Minamata on the island of Kyushu. Here, between 1953 and 1960, 111 people were affected by a mystery illness, resulting in 43 deaths. Symptoms began with tiredness and irritability and gradually progressed to headache, numbness, blurred vision, and wasting. Many of the sufferers came from fishing families; the cause was eventually traced to locally caught fish containing high levels of mercury. The fish were being contaminated by mercury waste discharged into the sea by a nearby plastics factory. The organic mercury ingested was affecting the victims' brain cells, causing the neurological signs of poisoning. A similar incident occurred on Honshu island in 1965, when five people died through eating mercury-contaminated fish.

• **MIND** ▶ The UK's leading mental-health pressure group, formed in 1946 as the National Association for Mental Health. Its aims are 'to represent the interests and uphold the rights of people with mental health problems and their families, and to promote mental health.' Current priorities include ensuring adequate provision of community facilities for the mentally ill and handicapped and of support services for their families. The organization changed its name to MIND in 1970 as part of a more radical approach, in part prompted by criticism of the NAMH, as well as deficiencies in state services for the mentally ill and handicapped.

• **minder** ▶ Originally, criminal slang for a bodyguard; it has become much more widely used since the late 1970s and the popularity of a British TV series of that name, featuring the shifty Arthur Daley (George Cole) and his minder Terry (Dennis Waterman).

> Eddie Murphy was a nice guy...the first time he came in he had six huge minders guarding him. – *The Sun*, 14 February 1991.

• **mind mapping** ▶ A technique used to develop a person's use of the right-hand side of the brain and thus his or her creativity. *See*: right brain.

• **mind my bike!** ▶ Catchphrase associated with the British film and television actor Jack Warner

(1894–1981). Star of the long-running television police series *Dixon of Dock Green*, he first used the phrase in the *Garrison Theatre* radio programme during World War II and subsequently repeated it in a wide range of contexts. *See also*: Evenin' all.

• **miners' strike** ► *See*: King Arthur; Mac the Knife.

• **Ming** ► Nickname of the Australian prime minister Sir Robert Menzies (1894–1978), coined by analogy with **Ming the Merciless**, a character in the Flash Gordon comic strip; in Scottish Gaelic Menzies is pronounced 'Ming-ies'. The long Menzies premiership (1939–41 and 1949–66) inevitably came to be known as the 'Ming dynasty'.

• **mini** ► Extremely short or small – a 20th-century contraction of 'miniature'. Also widely used as a prefix (as in minipill and miniskirt) and as a noun (especially for the miniskirt).

• **Mini** ► The Austin Mini, a popular small car designed by Sir Alec Issigonis (1906–88), first unveiled on 26 August 1959. The Mini's revolutionary design featured front-wheel drive, small wheels, and a compact transverse-mounted engine, which allowed plenty of room for four adults and luggage despite measuring only 10 feet from bumper to bumper. The millionth Mini was produced in 1965 and by the mid-1980s some 5.6 million models had been sold, making it the fifth best-selling British-made car of all time. The Mini Cooper, a speeded-up version, was launched in 1961 and won the Monte Carlo Rally in 1964, 1965, and 1967.

Although the original Mini ceased production in 2000, BMW launched its so-called 'new Mini' – a much larger model with such modern features as power steering and air conditioning – in July 2001.

> You can't tell one car from another – the only one that stands out is the mini. – SIR ALEC ISSIGONIS.

• **mini-break** ► Travel agents' jargon for a short holiday of two or three days, especially a weekend package holiday.

• **minicab** ► *See*: taxi.

• **minimalism** ► 1. In art, a type of painting and sculpture that uses basic geometric forms and primary colours and eschews any expression of emotion. Also known as **reductivism**, minimal art began in New York in the late 1950s as a reaction to the emotionalism of abstract expressionism (*see*: action painting). One of the movement's leading figures, the US sculptor Carl Andre (1935–   ), was responsible for the **Tate Bricks** furore, when his *Equivalent VIII* (1976), a set of 120 bricks arranged two-deep in a rectangle, provoked severe criticism of the Tate Gallery for acquiring it at public expense. *See also*: conceptual art. 2. In music, a style characterized by intentionally simple and restricted material. Minimalist works tend to feature basic harmonies, repetitive rhythms, and to evolve at a slow pace. This type of music first attracted attention in the 1970s, with the work of the US composers Philip Glass and Steve Reich. In the 1990s the so-called 'holy minimalism' of religious composers, such as John Tavener and Henryk Górecki became unexpectedly popular. 3. In design, fashion, cookery, etc., any style that attempts to achieve elegant sophistication using few and simple elements. Minimalist styles became highly fashionable in the 1980s.

> In the early 1980s, the dread hand of minimalism was squeezing the life out of popular culture and it was fashionable to pursue the kind of reductio ad absurdum that reduced your dinner to an artful arrangement of mangetouts and your wardrobe to one perfect beige bodysuit... – *The Sunday Times*, 25 April 1993.

• **minimum lending rate** ► (MLR) Between 1971 and 1981, the minimum rate at which the Bank of England would lend to discount houses and thus the rate of interest that controlled the interest rate charged and paid by banks and building societies throughout the economy. Before 1971 this was known as the **bank rate**. After 1981 the minimum lending rate became known as the **base rate**, a change of name that was intended to signal a relaxing of government controls over the banking system. When the government suspended the MLR in 1981, it reserved the right to reintroduce it at any time if it felt it was needed. This it did for one day in January 1985. In the late 1980s and early 1990s, the government again increased interest rates in an attempt to control inflation and the balance of payments deficit. They began to fall, however, after the UK left the ERM on Black Wednesday. In 1997 the Bank of England was given responsibility for setting the base rate.

• **minipill** ► A type of contraceptive pill that contains a progestogen hormone only, in contrast to the oestrogen plus progestogen of the combined Pill. The progestogen thickens the mucus lining the cervix making it difficult for sperm to pass into the womb. It also alters the lining of the womb so that implantation of any fertilized egg is made less likely. The minipill is slightly less effective than the combined pill and must be taken every day of the menstrual cycle. However, the side-effects are generally less, making it preferable for women who cannot tolerate the combined pill and for older women. Also, it can be taken by women who are breastfeeding, since it does not interfere with milk production.

• **miniskirt** or **mini** ▸ A very short skirt, especially one in which the hemline is 4 inches or more above the knee. Although the mini first appeared in a collection by the French couturier André Courrèges (1923– ), it is chiefly associated with the British designer Mary Quant (1934– ), who marketed it in 1965. The mini quickly became ubiquitous, remaining one of the lasting symbols of 1960s style and mores. To moralists, of course, the miniskirt was anathema; it was also a source of irritation to bureaucrats as under British tax law skirts less than 24 inches long were classed as children's wear and so exempt from purchase tax. In an attempt to forestall any loss of revenue, from 1 January 1966 the bust size of dresses was also taken into account, with any bust of 32 inches or more attracting tax. Nevertheless, undeterred by either the moralists or the Customs and Excise, skirts became progressively shorter as the decade wore on, approaching vanishing point with the **microskirt**, a garment that barely covered the pelvis. The inevitable reaction set in with the appearance in 1969 of the **maxiskirt** (or **maxi**), an ankle-length skirt that had the advantage of warmth as well as being more flattering to women with indifferent legs. The **midiskirt** (or **midi**) was a calf-length skirt neither mini nor maxi. The mini and the microskirt have since enjoyed limited revivals.

• **Miniver, Mrs** ▸ A fictional diarist created by Joyce Anstruther, writing under the pen-name Jan Struther. Mrs Miniver was an upper-middle-class housewife who recorded her personal reactions to events leading up to World War II, and the daily details of life in rural England before and after the outbreak of war. The diary was originally serialized before being published in book form as *Mrs Miniver*. A Hollywood film of the same name starring Greer Garson in the title role, was released in 1942. Despite its patent sentimentality and the conventional but inaccurate Hollywood image of rural England, it made a powerful contribution to the mythology of wartime Britain. The message of the piece is summarized by the vicar's sermon in the bombed church as the film draws to a close:

> This is not only a war of soldiers in uniforms. It is a war of the people – of all the people – and it must be fought not only on the battlefield but in the cities and in the villages, in the factories and on the farms, in the home and in the heart of freedom. Well, we have buried our dead, but we shall not forget them. Instead they will inspire us with an unbreakable determination to free ourselves and those who come after us from the tyranny and terror that

threaten to strike us down. This is the people's war. It is our war. We are the fighters. Fight it, then. Fight it with all that is in us. And may God defend the right.

• **minutemen** ▸ A small secret ultra-right-wing US organization armed to conduct guerrilla warfare in the event of a communist invasion. The name was suggested by its earlier adoption by American militiamen who, at the onset of the War of Independence, promised to take up arms at a minute's notice. **Minuteman** is also the name of a US ICBM. *See also*: four-minute men.

• **Mir** ▸ *See*: Salyut.

• **miracle rice** ▸ A type of high-yield hybrid rice developed in the 1960s to boost harvests in Asia and other areas of the developing world.

• **Miranda** ▸ In America, police making an arrest must read the Miranda (Rule) to the suspect. It explains his or her legal rights during questioning, especially those of remaining silent or being represented by a lawyer. This protection is found in the Fifth and Sixth Amendments to the US Constitution but became obligatory in 1966 after the Supreme Court reversed an Arizona court's conviction of Ernesto A. Miranda. He had confessed to kidnapping and rape but had not been advised of his rights.

• **MIRV** ▸ *See*: ICBM.

• **misery index** ▸ A statistical term used as a measure of the economic problems in a particular country or society. It is based on the rates of inflation and unemployment.

• **mishegaas** ▸ *See*: meshugga.

• **MI6** ▸ Military Intelligence, section six. The former name (from 1921) of the British government's intelligence agency (the Secret Intelligence Service, SIS). The name MI6 is no longer in official use but remains in the popular vocabulary. Members of MI6 are engaged in espionage and other intelligence activities abroad, using British agents and disaffected nationals of the countries in which they operate. Answerable to the foreign secretary, with ultimate control by the prime minister, MI6 is the British equivalent of the CIA in America. *See also*: MI5.

• **Miss America** ▸ The winner of America's annual beauty pageant, which began in 1922 – it is claimed to be the oldest in the world and is held each September in Atlantic City, New Jersey. It was discontinued in 1928 for five years and revived with more emphasis on talent and less on sexual beauty. The contest was derided during the hippie era and picketed during the feminist 1970s and 1980s. Other embarrassments included the 1984 resignation of the first Black Miss America, Vanessa Williams, for posing in the nude during her reign. Despite these problems, the nationally televised event remains a beloved US institution. Parallel contests run on similar lines have proliferated since 1922 with many states having a national contest; international versions include the UK-based **Miss World** competition, which was inaugurated in 1951. There are several equivalent titles that are contested by men.

• **missing mass** ► *See*: dark matter.

• **Mission Impossible** ► The title of a US TV espionage thriller series originally broadcast between 1966 and 1972; it was also seen in the UK. The phrase became a catchphrase for any impossible task.

> Madcap tube driver Cozmik Wilson cheers up depressed commuters...with a battery of quips taken from the cult sci-fi TV series...Cozmik says he's on a 'Mission Possible' and congratulates his audience for 'navigating through the company's ticket barriers'. – *The Sport*, 5 April 1991.

The 1990s saw the release of two high-tech action movies based on the original series (1995, 1999), both starring Tom Cruise.

• **mission statement** ► A brief summary of the goals, standards, or values of a company or other organization. The mission statement, otherwise known as the **vision statement**, began to be incorporated into company literature during the late 1980s and early 1990s, and is now a standard feature for most large businesses. It is intended to communicate to employees, shareholders, or other interested parties the aims of the company, and how its members should strive to achieve those aims. However, in some quarters the 'mission statement' is still regarded as symptomatic of a management culture concerned mainly with concealing its deficiencies in a welter of trendy buzz words (favourites include 'access', 'excellence', 'benchmarks', 'outreach', and 'indicators').

> BAA's statement begins: 'Our mission is to make BAA the most successful airport company in the world. This means always focusing on our customers' needs and safety, seeking continuous improvements in the costs and quality of our services, enabling our employees to give of their best.' – *The Independent on Sunday*, 6 February 1994.

• **Miss Otis regrets** ► A catchphrase sometimes used in apologizing for not being able to attend a function, usually because one does not wish to do so. It originated in Cole Porter's song of the same name (1934), in which Miss Otis's butler coolly passes on his mistress's tragic reason for not being able to attend a lunch to which she has been invited – she has been hanged.

• **Miss World order** ► Reverse order. This was the way that Eric Morley, who started the Miss World Beauty Contest in 1951, always announced the results. He would say, 'I'll give you the results in reverse order.'

• **mistake** ►
**Did you spot this week's deliberate mistake?** A phrase that came to be used by broadcasters as a facetious way of covering up for an actual mistake in the programme. It first arose in 1938 on a BBC radio programme called *Monday Night at Seven*. After a mistake had occurred, the BBC was snowed under with listeners phoning in to make the correction. The producer decided to exploit the situation and the deliberate mistake became a feature of the programme. It has frequently been used since as a formula for small-prize competitions on radio programmes.

• **Mister** ► *See at*: Mr.

• **Mistinguett** ► The stage name of the French actress and singer Jeanne-Marie Bourgeois (1873–1956). Mistinguett was a star of the music halls of Paris between the wars, notably the Moulin Rouge and the Folies-Bergère, where she danced and sang with Maurice Chevalier. She also performed in comedy. Mistinguett was famous for her spectacular hats, her elaborate costumes, and her long shapely legs, which were said to be insured for a huge sum of money.

• **Mitford girls** ► The five daughters of the eccentric and irascible second Baron Redesdale (1878–1958), who earned himself a reputation for outstandingly poor judgment by describing Hitler as:

> ...a right-thinking man of irreproachable sincerity and honesty.

Redesdale, whose favourite sport was to hunt his terrified daughters with a bloodhound, appeared as Lord Alconleigh, also known as Uncle Matthew, in the novels *The Pursuit of Love* (1945) and *Love in a Cold Climate* (1945) by his eldest daughter Nancy Mitford (1904–73). Nancy also wrote a number of other books describing the upper-class way of life in England, including *Noblesse Oblige* (1956), which contained the original paper on U and Non-U behaviour (*see also*: Mif). Her *Wigs on the Green* (1935) consists of a pen portrait of Eugenia Malmains, based on her sister Unity Mitford (1914–48). The wayward Unity, infected by her father's enthusiasm for Hitler, became a fanatical Nazi. Accosting Hitler in his favourite Munich restaurant, the *Osteria*, she became his close friend. When the UK finally declared war on Germany, Unity used the gun Hitler had given her to shoot herself in the head. The bullet lodged in her brain but failed to kill her; Hitler arranged for his wounded admirer to be sent in a special hospital train to Geneva, whence she returned to England. Eventually she died of her self-inflicted wound. The antisemitic strain seemed to run in the family: another sister, Diana Mitford (1910–    ), married Sir Oswald Mosley, the leader of the British Union of Fascists (*see*: Mosleyites). The youngest of the sisters, Jessica Mitford (1917–96), became a writer and a US citizen. She is best known for her books *Hons and Rebels* (1960; *see*: Hons, The) and *The American Way of Death* (1963). The remaining sister, Deborah, who became the Duchess of Devonshire, was the only one not to achieve either fame or notoriety; their brother, Tom, was killed in Burma in World War II.

• **mitochondrial Eve** ▶ The hypothetical mother of the entire human species. The evidence for such an ancestral female comes not from the Bible but from a study of the DNA of mitochondria (rod-shaped structures that occur in nearly all living cells). This DNA is inherited only through the female line as sperms have no mitochondria to offer the eggs they fertilize. Recent investigations show that the mitochondrial DNA taken from a wide variety of racial and geographical sources is surprisingly uniform. This points to a 'little mother of all the people', who lived, probably in Africa, some 100,000 to 200,000 years ago.

• **Mitty, Walter** ▶ A fictional character created by the US humorist James Thurber (1894–1961) in the short story *The Secret Life of Walter Mitty* (1939). Mitty is a docile henpecked husband who escapes from his mundane lot by indulging in elaborate and heroic fantasies:

> Then, with that faint fleeting smile playing about his lips, he faced the firing squad; erect and motionless, proud and disdainful, Walter Mitty, the undefeated, inscrutable to the last.

The name of Walter Mitty has entered the English language as an epithet for anyone who takes refuge from reality in similar fantasies. *The Secret Life of Walter Mitty* was adapted for the cinema in 1947 with Danny Kaye in the title role.

• **mixed media** ▶ The combined use of live action, videotapes, photographs, music, and animation in an artistic or educational presentation. **Multimedia** is an associated term referring to specialized computer software that combines on-screen graphics, animation, music, and voice synthesis.

• **Miz Lillian** ▶ Nickname of Lillian Carter (1898–1983), mother of the US president Jimmy Carter. Of Southern stock, she became widely known for her outspoken support for her son.

• **MLR** ▶ *See*: minimum lending rate.

• **Moaning Minnie** ▶ **1.** A World War II nickname for a six-barrelled German mortar, from the rising shriek when it was fired. **2.** The air-raid warning siren used in the UK in World War II, from its repetitive wail. **3.** A colloquial epithet applied to any constant moaner or habitual grumbler.

• **Mob, the** ▶ A mainly US term for a criminal organization, especially the Mafia. A member of such a gang is a **mobster**.

• **mobile phone** ▶ A form of communication that became increasingly widespread during the 1990s. By 2000, this cordless piece of battery-operated equipment, often no larger than a spectacle case, enabled its users to be contacted instantly almost anywhere in the world, either from a landline telephone or by another mobile. The system is based on radio transmission and the cellular network service (*see*: Cellnet).

Costs are relatively low, payment being based on one of two systems. In the pay-as-you-go system, users buy time in advance but pay no rental, whereas in the rental system users pay a monthly rent for their connection to the cellular network, but are charged a lower rate for their calls.

Although once regarded as exclusive yuppie status symbols, mobile phones are now owned by over 60% of the UK population. Indeed, recent sharp falls in the profits of mobile phone companies suggest that the market may now be saturated. Because users can make and receive calls almost anywhere – in the street, on public transport, in pubs and restaurants, etc. – mobile phones have profoundly altered the ways in which we communicate and broken down some of the traditional distinctions between public and private space. The only situations in which they may not be used are those in which they could interfere with other radio communications or equipment, such as in aircraft and hospitals. There have also been growing calls for legislation specifically to penalize the dangerous practice of driving while using a mobile phone (whether hand-held or not). At present (2002) driving while using a hand-held phone is regarded as an offence under the laws against dangerous driving.

A more recent innovation has been the **WAP**

(wireless application protocol) phone, which can connect directly with the Internet. Its impact has, however, been disappointing. Paradoxically, the short message service (SMS), limited to sending 160 characters, which was introduced at the same time, unexpectedly took off. First widely used as a cheap means of communication between schoolchildren, it was later taken up by adults (some 1.5 billion text messages are sent monthly in the UK). **Texting**, as this new means of communication is called, has created its own shorthand to enable more to be said in 160 characters (*e.g.* 'cu tmoz, dont b l8' = see you tomorrow don't be late). WAP phones and texting belong to the so-called second generation of mobiles. A change of technology (the much faster packet-switching will replace the first and second generation circuit-switching) will enable third generation (3G) phones to offer a wider range of services. These will include permanent connection to the Internet, so that emails and video messages can be received instantly, and a global positioning system to establish one's whereabouts (should this be necessary).

• **mockers ▶** British and Australian slang for a curse, as in the expression to **put the mockers on** meaning to ruin something. It is thought to derive either from the English 'mock', or from the Yiddish *makeh*, meaning plague or wound.

• **mod cons ▶** Estate agents' shorthand for modern conveniences; used, especially in the phrase **all mod cons**, to confirm that a property has all the facilities (hot running water, central heating, etc.) expected in a modern home.

• **Model T ▶** *See*: Tin Lizzie.

• **modem ▶** Modulator/demodulator. An electronic device for converting digital signals from a computer into electrical signals that can be transmitted by a telephone line, and for converting these electrical signals back into digital form. Modems are used to connect a personal computer to the Internet.

• **modernism ▶** 1. A movement in the Roman Catholic Church that sought to interpret traditional doctrines with due regard to the findings of modern science, philosophy, and history. It arose in the late 19th century and was formally condemned by Pope Pius X in 1907 in the encyclical *Pascendi*, which stigmatized it as the 'synthesis of all heresies'. 2. An international movement in the arts of the earlier 20th century, characterized by the rejection of traditional subjects, attitudes, and techniques. Among the many innovations that can be labelled modernist are free verse and the stream of consciousness in literature, cubism in the visual arts, serialism in music, and functionalism in architecture. General characteristics of modernist art include formal innovation and complexity, a tone of ironic pessimism, and a rejection of 19th-century Romanticism. *See also*: postmodernism.

• **mods and rockers ▶** Two British teenage cults in the 1960s whose contrasting mores led to rivalry and violence. The **mods** affected a cool elitist image, setting great store by their smart suits and fastidious grooming. They rode scooters in their parkas, listened to rare US soul imports, and took purple hearts. In total contrast were the leather-jacketed **rockers**, who rode powerful motorcycles and cultivated a filthy dishevelled appearance. In 1964 mutual resentment between the two groups culminated in Bank Holiday clashes at a number of seaside resorts, leading to hundreds of arrests. The violence was quickly suppressed but not before a wave of outrage had swept through parliament and the press. The mod style enjoyed a brief revival in the late 1970s, when there were even a few nostalgic riots (this time with the punks).

• **Mohole ▶** A US research project to obtain rock samples from the upper mantle of the Earth, which involved boring a 7-mile hole from the ocean floor, through the Earth's crust, to the **Mohorovičić discontinuity** (the boundary between the Earth's crust and upper mantle, named after its discoverer Andrija Mohorovičić 1857–1936). Drilling began near Guadalupe, off W Mexico, but the government-funded project was abandoned in 1966 because of spiralling costs and insurmountable technological difficulties.

• **mojo ▶** Black US slang for a magic spell or a lucky charm. It is thought to be derived from a W African word. The word was frequently used in blues and rock 'n' roll songs of the 1950s and 1960s, one of the best known being Muddy Waters' 'Got my Mojo Working'. It is also a euphemism for male virility or the male sex organ – a sense popularized by its frequent use by the libidinous hero of the *Austin Powers* comedy films of the late 1990s.

• **mole ▶** A spy or traitor who obtains a position of trust in an organization, especially a government department or intelligence service. The name reflects the hidden undermining activities of such agents. The UK's most notorious mole was Kim Philby (1912–88), who worked for the Soviet Union with his fellow Cantabrigians Anthony Blunt, Guy Burgess, and Donald Maclean. *See*: Magnificent Five; sleeper.

• **Molotov ▶** Alias of the Soviet statesman Vyacheslav Mikhailovich Scriabin (1890–1986), who adopted it in 1906 to escape from the Imperial Police. He later became prime minister of the Soviet Union (1930–41) and during and after World War II served as foreign minister. In 1956 he was expelled from the Communist Party over disagreements with Khrushchev.

• **Molotov breadbasket** ▶ A canister of incendiary bombs which, on being launched from a plane, opened and showered the bombs over a wide area; named after the Soviet statesman Molotov.

• **Molotov cocktail** ▶ A home-made incendiary device, first used by the Finns against Soviet tanks in 1940 and developed in the UK as one of the weapons of the Home Guard. It consisted of a bottle filled with inflammable and glutinous liquid, with a slow match protruding from the top. When thrown at a tank the bottle burst, the liquid igniting and spreading over the plating of the tank. It was named after the Soviet statesman Molotov, who allegedly ordered the mass production of such devices during World War II. They are now mainly associated with violent rioters, who use them against police.

• **moment of truth** ▶ The moment of crisis when something or someone is put to the test. The phrase may have originated in Ernest Hemingway's novel *Death in the Afternoon* (1932), as a translation of the Spanish *momento de la verdad*, which refers to the moment in a bullfight when the matador kills the bull with his final sword-thrust.

• **momma** ▶ 1. US Black slang for a mature but attractive woman. *See also*: Last of the Red Hot Mommas. 2. Slang for a female member of a Hell's Angels chapter. The epithet implies that the woman in question is not attached to any of the males in the group; if she was, she would be known as someone's 'old lady'.

• **momzer** or **mamser** ▶ US slang, from Yiddish, for a person who is unlikable, stubborn, untrustworthy, or absolutely detestable. It came from the Hebrew *mamzer* meaning an illegitimate child, and is used much like 'bastard' in standard English.

• **Monaco Grand Prix** ▶ A motor race that takes place in May or early June on the streets of Monte Carlo. The Monaco Grand Prix is one of the few events of the Formula 1 World Championship to be raced on public roads rather than on a purpose-built track. The circuit is about 2 miles in length, including many sharp bends, narrow streets, and a long tunnel; it is comparatively slow by Formula 1 standards. The lap record for the fastest average speed stands at about 90 mph (as opposed to Silverstone's 150 mph). Only 20 cars are allowed to start the race, which consists of 78 laps.

• **Mona Lisa theft** ▶ The theft of Leonardo da Vinci's masterpiece from the Louvre in Paris, which took place on 21 August 1911. Three 'workmen', hid themselves in the museum at closing time and removed the painting with ease overnight. Subsequently the gang leader, an Italian criminal called Vincenzo Perugia, persuaded six US art collectors to part with $300,000 in the belief that they would acquire the masterpiece. Instead, they received copies painted by the master forger Yves Chaudron, who had already perpetrated a series of similar confidence tricks organized by the self-styled Marquis Eduardo de Valfierno. Chaudron and Valfierno had previously enjoyed great success with their fakes of paintings by Murillo and others; this time however, their plan went wrong when Perugia absconded with the money, attempted to sell the real painting to a dealer in Florence in November 1913, and was subsequently arrested. The painting was returned to the Louvre.

• **Monday Club** ▶ An association of Conservatives from the right wing of the party, founded in 1961 by the Marquess of Salisbury, Julian Amery, and others. The club derived its name from the fact that the members originally met for lunch on Mondays. During the 1970s it became notorious for its views on race and immigration.

• **monetarism** ▶ The economic doctrine that sees control of the money supply as the centre of policy in macroeconomics. First formulated by David Hume (1711–76), it was revived in the 1970s as an alternative doctrine to Keynesianism. Monetarists take the view that an expansion of the money supply will tend to create inflation rather than employment. The early governments of Margaret Thatcher stuck rigidly to a monetarist policy from 1979 to about 1985.

• **money** ▶
   **put one's money where one's mouth is**
To put one's stated opinions or beliefs to the test by acting on them. For example, a man who boasted about some invention of his would be putting his money where his mouth is by investing in manufacturing it. The phrase is believed to have originated in poker.

• **money laundering** ▶ *See*: laundering.

• **Money Makes the World Go Round** ▶ A song title from the musical *Cabaret* (1966) and the subsequent film (1972). It is, of course, a parody of the traditional English proverb 'Love makes the world go round'.

• **moneyman** ▸ A man whose work centres on finance, such as a company accountant, a stockbroker, or a banker. Originally a 16th-century word, it became popular in the UK in the 1980s, a decade much concerned with money-related matters.

• **money supply** ▸ The amount of money available to the economy of a nation. Since the 1970s most Western countries have accepted the central tenet of monetarism, that an increase in the money supply leads directly to inflation. In order to control the money supply it is first necessary to define it. This has been done in a variety of ways. In the UK seven definitions are used:

**M0** The notes and coins in circulation plus banks' till money and balances with the Bank of England.
**M1** The notes and coins in circulation plus private-sector current accounts and deposit accounts that can be transferred by cheque.
**M2** The notes and coins in circulation plus non-interest-bearing bank deposits plus building society deposits plus National Savings accounts.
**M3** (formerly called sterling M3) M1 plus all other private-sector bank deposits plus certificates of deposit.
**M3c** (formerly called M3) M3 plus foreign currency bank deposits.
**M4** (formerly called private-sector liquidity 1; PSL1) M1 plus most private-sector bank deposits plus holdings of moneymarket instruments.
**M5** (formerly called private-sector liquidity 2; PSL2) M4 plus building society deposits.
The choice of definition depends on the circumstances.

• **Monkees** ▸ A US–British pop group whose popular NBC Saturday-morning television series (from 1966) shot their first single, 'Last Train to Clarksville', to the top of the US charts. In 1967 'Monkeemania' went from strength to strength with the hit 'I'm a Believer' and the album *The Monkees*; for a time it seemed that the world had found the new Beatles. The Monkees were, in fact, put together for the TV series, which was about the unlikely adventures of an entirely fictional four-man pop group. Its members were the British former child star Davy Jones (1945–    ), the US former child star Mickey Dolenz (1946–    ), and the Americans Peter Tork (1945–    ) and Mike Nesmith (1942–    ). At first the group's members were allowed no say in the music and did not even play their instruments; eventually, led by Nesmith, they acquired some influence over their output before splitting up in 1968 after Tork left. They reformed in 1975 and again (minus Nesmith) in 1986. The band's most significant effect was to identify a lucrative subteenage market, the needs of which continue to dominate pop music. Subsequent attempts to imitate the success of pop's first 'man-made' group have included the creation of a whole series of 'boy bands' in the later 1990s and the formation of Hear'Say, whose members were selected by a televised competition in 2001. *See also*: Spice Girls.

• **monkey trial** ▸ *See*: Dayton anti-Darwinist trial.

• **monokini** ▸ A topless bikini, *i.e.* a pair of very brief pants used for swimming or sunbathing.

• **Monopoly** ▸ One of the most popular modern board games, in which players buy and sell property, charge rents, make a fortune – and ultimately force their oponents to go bust. It was devised in about 1930 by Charles B. Darrow, a US heating equipment engineer, who was made unemployed by the 1929 Wall Street Crash. The game proved so popular with his friends that Darrow started turning out sets full time, at $2.50 apiece. He took the street names from Atlantic City, the East Coast resort in which the Darrow family had spent their vacations. There are many similarities between Darrow's Monopoly and an earlier board game, 'The Landlord's Game', invented by Elizabeth M. Phillips of Virginia in 1924. Both games have the utilities (Electric Company and Waterworks), railway companies, and 'Go to Jail' corners. However, it was Darrow who exploited the popularity of Monopoly, producing 20,000 sets in 1934. In 1935 the US games manufacturer, Parker Brothers, bought the production rights from Darrow and were soon producing 20,000 sets a week of their own, slightly refined, version.

In 1935 the British firm John Waddington bought a licence to manufacture their English version of Monopoly, with London street names; for example, Pennsylvania Railroad was renamed Marylebone Station, while the most expensive property, Boardwalk, became Mayfair. Local placenames and currency are used in most of the many other national versions now produced. The game has maintained its popularity into the 21st century with many countries continuing to hold national championships; winners take part in the World Monopoly Championship, first held in 1973.

• **Monroe, Marilyn** ▸ (1926–62) Stagename of the US film actress Norma Jean Mortenson (later Baker) whose short and tragic life began in an orphanage, included rape as a child, marriage at 14, and death at 36 from an overdose of sleeping pills. During the last decade of her life she starred in half a dozen films that established her as the greatest sex symbol of the era.

After a short spell of modelling, Monroe attracted attention with bit parts in two films of 1950. Starring roles followed in *Gentlemen Prefer Blondes* (1953), *The Seven Year Itch* (1954), *Bus Stop* (1956), *The Prince and the Showgirl* (1957; with Laurence Olivier), and *Some Like It Hot* (1959). The director of three of these films, Billy Wilder, was less than charitable about the mythical creature he had helped to create.

> She had breasts like granite and a brain like Swiss cheese, full of holes. Extracting a performance from her is like pulling teeth.

The public, however, remained devotedly on her side, as did most of the critics, who were enchanted by her freshness, spontaneity, and instinctive comic talent.

Her marriage to baseball star Joe DiMaggio in 1954 lasted a mere nine months. From 1956 to 1961 she was married to playwright Arthur Miller, who wrote *The Misfits* for her. This 1961 film with Clark Gable proved to be her last. After her death Miller said of her:

> If she was simple it would have been easy to help her. She could have made it with a little luck.

Whether or not she intended to take her own life has never been established. In recent years, various conspiracy theorists have attempted to draw links between her death and affairs with both President John F. Kennedy and his brother Robert.

Since her death, Monroe's myth has far outstripped that of any other Hollywood goddess. Clearly, her extraordinary appeal can be partly but not wholly explained by the combination of rare beauty, blatant sexuality, and an almost childlike innocence. Although most of her problems had little to do with her choice of career, the popular imagination has also cast her as the archetypal Hollywood victim. The industry can perhaps be blamed for creating the myth, exploiting it, and failing to support the vulnerable woman around whom it was constructed.

Perhaps the last line should be hers. Asked by a columnist if she had anything on for her famous calendar pose from her modelling days, she replied:

> Oh yes, I had the radio on.

• **Mons, Battle of** ▶ A World War I battle that took place in the Belgian town of Mons; it was the first major engagement between the British Expeditionary Force and the Germans on the Western Front (23 August 1914). Greatly outnumbered, the BEF failed to halt the Germans' advance across Belgium and were forced to retreat to the River Marne, where they took part in a more successful operation, the first Battle of the Marne, on 5 September 1914.

The engagement at Mons gave rise to two catch-phrases of World War I, used in response to the question 'Where's So-and-So?'. **Gassed at Mons** or **Hanging on the (barbed) wire at Mons** meant that the person's whereabouts were either unknown or secret – the troops had encountered no barbed-wire entanglements or gas attacks in the retreat from Mons. The British war medal (the 1914 Star) given for service in France or Belgium in 1914 was also known as the **Mons Star**. *See also*: Angels of Mons.

• **Monte Bello Islands** ▶ A group of uninhabited islands off NW Australia, in the Indian Ocean: the scene of two British nuclear weapon tests in the 1950s. The first British atom bomb was detonated in a ship on 3 October 1952; the second explosion took place in 1956.

• **Monte Cassino** ▶ *See*: Anzio.

• **Montessori method** ▶ A system of training and educating young children evolved by the Italian educationist, Dr Maria Montessori (1870–1952). The method is based on a liberal classroom regime and the use of specially devised educational apparatus and didactic material. Dr Montessori's first school opened in Rome in 1907 and her method has since exercised considerable influence on work with young children. *See also*: Dalton Plan.

• **Montezuma's revenge** or **Aztec Twostep** ▶ Diarrhoea as a result of eating foreign food and drinking water of doubtful purity – a common complaint of tourists. The phrase originated in America in the 1960s and related to travelling in Mexico; Montezuma (c.1480–1520) was an Aztec ruler of Mexico during the Spanish conquest. A variant of this phrase that became widely used in the late 1970s is **Aztec two-step**, referring to the agonized hobble, not unlike a dance step, sufferers were obliged to make to the nearest lavatory. The phrase is now used internationally; variants include **Delhi belly**, **gippy tummy** (afflicting visitors to Egypt and other African countries), and **Spanish tummy**.

• **Montgomery beret** ▶ The style of beret worn by the British commander Bernard Law Montgomery in World War II. His beret was easily distinguished because, contrary to usual practice, he always wore two cap badges. *See*: Monty.

• **Montgomery bus boycott** ▶ A peaceful boycott of bus services in Montgomery, Alabama, by Blacks protesting against racial segregation on public buses. Organized by Martin Luther King, who had just begun his Baptist ministry in the town, the boycott began in December 1955. It is believed to have been sparked off by a White bus driver's offensive treatment of Mrs Rosa Parks, who refused to join her fellow Blacks at the back of the bus. The protest was successful not only in its primary aim – by the end of 1956 racial segregation on buses had been banned – but also in bringing the civil rights movement to the attention of the nation and encouraging King to take his place at the head of the campaign.

• **Montreux Convention** ▶ An agreement signed at Montreux on 20 July 1936, relating to the Turkish straits of the Dardanelles and the Bosporus. The convention maintained the right of free passage through the straits for commercial vessels of all nations in peacetime. Restrictions were placed on warships, particularly those of countries other than the Black Sea states, and on the passage of commercial vessels in wartime. In addition, Turkey was authorized to begin work immediately on the refortification of the demilitarized straits zone. The Montreux Convention replaced the International Commission of the Straits and remained in force after World War II, despite an attempt by the Soviet Union to amend it in 1946.

• **Montreux Festival** ▶ A television festival held annually at Montreux, Switzerland. The most prestigious award at the festival is the Golden Rose; Silver Roses and Bronze Roses are also awarded.

• **Monty** ▶ Nickname of Bernard Law Montgomery (1887–1976), British commander in World War II. Under his direction the British Eighth Army was victorious at Alamein and drove Rommel's forces back to Tunis (1943), making Montgomery a national hero in the UK. Subsequently he clashed with US military leaders over the command of Allied forces in the D-Day campaign and lost face at home over the defeat at Arnhem. His reputation recovered somewhat following his successful drive into Germany in 1945. His flamboyant manner, personal eccentricities, and sometimes irascible relations with other commanders guaranteed him a lasting place in the public's affections.

> Indomitable in retreat; invincible in advance; insufferable in victory. – WINSTON CHURCHILL, describing Montgomery.

He became 1st Viscount Montgomery of Alamein in 1946. After the war, he cultivated his reputation as a blimpish and reactionary old gentleman:

> This sort of thing may be tolerated by the French, but we are British – thank god. – Reaction to a parliamentary bill to relax the laws against homosexuality, 1965.

• **monty** ▶
**the full monty** An informal expression meaning that something is present in its entirety.

The expression gained wider usage in 1997 with the international success of a British comedy film, *The Full Monty*, which related the exploits of six unemployed Sheffield steel workers who set themselves up as male strippers. The full monty, in this case, referred to the culmination of the act, in which they appear totally nude.

The origin of the phrase is not known for certain but three somewhat diverse folk etymologies have been suggested: (1) that it alludes to the full English breakfast Field Marshal Montgomery apparently insisted on having wherever he was; (2) that it refers to a full three-piece suit as supplied by the high-street tailors Montague Burton; or (3) that it relates to a betting system used in roulette at the casino in Monte Carlo.

• **Monty Python's Flying Circus** ▶ A BBC television comedy series (1969–74) celebrated for its idiosyncratic blend of satire, absurdism, and elements of the English nonsense tradition. Written and performed by Graham Chapman, John Cleese, Eric Idle, Terry Jones, and Michael Palin, it also featured the distinctive work of the US animator Terry Gilliam. Favourite targets for its satire included bureaucracy, English reserve and deference, and the conventions of television itself. Introduced without fanfare in a late-night slot previously reserved for religious programmes, the show became an unexpected cult success, especially among students and the young. It later scored a still more unlikely success in America. The team made a number of films, including *Monty Python and the Holy Grail* (1975) and the spoof Bible epic *Life of Brian* (1979). The name of the show alluded to Baron Richthofen's Flying Circus, the World War I fighter group commanded by the famous Red Baron, but the relevance of this to the programme's content is as mysterious as the identity of Mr Python.

• **Monty's double** ▶ Nickname acquired by the British actor M. E. Clifton-James after he was employed to impersonate General Montgomery as part of an elaborate Allied hoax in World War II. The actor's physical similarity to the general, helped by some coaching in his mannerisms, enabled the British to mislead the Germans about Montgomery's whereabouts and plans. Clifton-James subsequently told his story in a book, filmed as *I Was Monty's Double* in 1958, with Clifton-James recreating his impersonation.

• **Monza circuit** ▶ A motor-racing track built in 1922 in the Royal Park of Monza, near Milan in N Italy. The Italian Grand Prix takes place annually at Monza in September. The scene of a number of legendary duels between some of the most famous names in motor sport, Monza is one of the fastest circuits in the Formula 1 World Championship; the lap record for the fastest average speed around the 3.6 miles of the track is over 146 mph. The original elliptical course has been modified to an open L-shape, which includes such hazards as the Ascari bend and the Parabolica.

• **mooch** ▶ A slow dance popular in the 1920s; the word was later extended to mean idling aimlessly about.

• **Moo-Cow** ▶ A nickname given to the Morris-Cowley car, first built in 1925 by Morris Motors Ltd at Cowley, Oxford. The car was also known as the **bull-nose Morris**, because of the shape of its radiator. A small reliable family car with an 11.9 HP engine, the Morris-Cowley was one of the earliest British cars produced for the mass market; at £200 it competed with Ford's Model T (*see*: Tin Lizzie).

• **Moog** ▶ Tradename for an early type of synthesizer – an electronic keyboard instrument that can produce a wide variety of musical sounds. It is named after the US engineer who invented it, Robert A. Moog (1934–   ). Moog had developed the first synthesizers in the 1950s, but it was the success of Walter Carlos's *Switched on Bach* recording in 1969, which used a Moog, that made his name synonymous with synthesized electronic sound.

• **moolah** or **moola** ▶ Slang for money. Originally an Americanism, it has been used in the UK since the 1930s.

• **Moonies** ▶ A religious sect, properly called the **Unification Church**, founded by Sun Myung Moon (1920–   ) in South Korea in 1954. It spread to America in the 1960s and subsequently to the UK, Australia, etc. Moon claimed to be the Second Messiah and that his devotees would save mankind from world communism, which he saw as the work of Satan. Funds built up by his followers, partly by selling artificial flowers and other items in the street, were used by Moon to create a large property and business organization in America, where he has lived since 1972. Tax avoidance led to his prosecution and imprisonment (1984–85). The Unification Church has attracted severe criticism for allegedly brainwashing its adherents and separating them from their families.

• **mooning** ▶ Slang for bending down and exposing one's buttocks to someone, usually as an insult. The practice originated in America in the 1950s. The derivation of the word is based on the supposed resemblance between the bare buttocks and the moon. Mooning is a traditional insult among the Maoris in New Zealand.

• **moonlighting** ▶ *See*: sunlighting.

• **moonrock** ▶ Slang name for crack (a crystalline form of cocaine) laced with heroin.

• **moonwalk** ▶ **1.** An exploratory walk on the surface of the moon. **2.** A 1980s dance step imitating the weightless movements of men walking on the moon; it was popularized by the US pop singer Michael Jackson.

• **Moorgate disaster** ▶ The worst disaster on London's Underground network, which occurred at Moorgate Station on 28 February 1975. Thirty-five people died, including the traindriver, when a tube train crashed into the end of a dead-end tunnel: the first 15 feet of train telescoped to just two feet. Speculation about the cause of the crash ranged from the suggestion that the driver was drunk to the possibility that he had suffered a sudden 'brainstorm'; a verdict of accidental death was returned, but it seems the mystery will never be satisfactorily explained.

• **Moors murders** ▶ A series of sadistic murders in the UK for which Ian Brady and his mistress Myra Hindley were sentenced to life imprisonment in 1966. At least five children were killed and buried on the Lancashire moors north of Manchester: some of the bodies have never been recovered. The horrific nature of the crimes – in some cases the dying cries of the young victims were recorded on tape – shocked the nation. Campaigns for the release of Hindley have been unsuccessful, in spite of her pleas that she acted under duress and her reported conversion to Christianity (*see*: Holy Fool). Brady, who was transferred to a psychiatric unit in the 1980s, has refused to eat for several years and is being kept alive by force feeding.

• **moped** ▶ A lightweight motorized cycle – the name is a contraction of *mo*torized *ped*al cycle. Mopeds originated in Europe after World War II, when bicycles were modified and fitted with small engines to provide an economical means of transport in the lean postwar years. They are now popular not only in Europe but in many other parts of the world, often because of generous tax concessions to owners and low legal age limit for the rider. Virtually all of them have 50 cc two-stroke engines, although the pedals are seldom now needed for pedalling.

• **Mopp, Mrs** ▶ *See*: ITMA.

• **MOR** ▶ *See*: middle-of-the-road.

• **moral majority** ▶ The members of a country or society who hold what are generally regarded as traditional moral values. The phrase became popular in America during the Reagan administration, when it was used specifically of a right-wing evangelical movement led by the Revd Jerry Falwell. The movement, which vociferously opposed abortion and rights for homosexuals, provoked the obvious rejoinder that it was neither moral nor a majority. *See*: silent majority.

• **Moral Rearmament** ▶ (MRA) A right-wing Christian movement founded in 1938 by the US evangelist Frank Buchman (1878–1961), who had earlier founded the Oxford Group. Its stated purpose was to counter modern-day materialism by persuading people to live according to the highest standards of morality and love, to obey God, and to unite in a worldwide association according to these principles.

• **Morecambe and Wise** ▶ *See*: short, fat, hairy legs.

• **Morel, Paul** ▶ The hero of the largely autobiographical novel *Sons and Lovers* (1913) by D. H. Lawrence (1885–1930). Like Lawrence himself, Morel is the son of a sometimes violent and often drunk coalminer and his puritanical and better educated wife. The novel deals with Morel's emancipation into a more cultured milieu, his loves, his mother's jealousy at the prospect of losing him, and his devastation when she finally dies. Lawrence's first major novel, it was soon established as a 20th-century classic, especially important because it was one of the earliest novels written by a working-class author about working-class life.

• **Morgenthau Plan** ▶ A plan relating to the future of Germany after World War II, drawn up by Henry Morgenthau (1891–1967), US secretary of the treasury, and the US secretary of war Henry Stimson; it was put forward at the Quebec conference between Churchill and Roosevelt in September 1944. The Morgenthau Plan proposed 'eliminating the war-making industries in the Ruhr and in the Saar' and 'converting Germany into a country primarily agricultural and pastoral in its character'. Churchill reluctantly accepted the proposal, which was later dropped.

• **morning-after pill** ▶ A contraceptive Pill that can be taken as a precautionary measure up to 72 hours *after* unprotected intercourse (followed by a second dose 12 hours later). There are two types: a progestogen-only pill and a combined oestrogen-progestogen pill. The former causes fewer side-effects (mainly nausea and vomiting).

• **Mornington Crescent** ▶ A panel game popularized during the 1980s by the BBC radio programme *I'm Sorry I Haven't A Clue*, featuring Humphrey Lyttleton, Barry Cryer, Tim Brooke-Taylor, Graeme Garden, and William Rushton. It is played by two teams, one of whom chooses a London underground station as a starting point; the two sides then alternate in making valid moves to other underground stations. The objective of the game is to reach Mornington Crescent (a station on the Northern Line) before one's opponents. Newcomers to the game are expected to pick up the rules as they go along.

• **moron** ▶ Obsolete medical terminology for an adult with a mental age of between 8 and 12 years. This term, derived from the Greek *moros*, stupid, was coined by the US physician Henry Goddard in 1910; such people are now described as suffering from a mild degree of mental retardation or handicap, or as having 'learning difficulties'. The word 'moron' is now used only colloquially, to describe someone who does stupid things, without any implication of mental deficiency in the medical sense.

• **morphing** ▶ In the cinema, an advanced computer animation technique in which film images are manipulated so that objects or actors appear to change shape magically during a scene. It was first exploited fully in James Cameron's science-fiction fantasy *Terminator 2* (1922), which starred Arnold Schwarzenegger. The film, each minute of which cost an estimated $1 million to produce, became a huge hit at the box office and earned an Oscar for its special effects.

• **Morrison shelter** ▶ The indoor air-raid shelter officially recommended by the home secretary Herbert Stanley Morrison (1888–1965) for use during the Blitz. A not dissimilar shelter recommended for use against nuclear attack in a secret government information film made in the postwar years attracted considerable public derision when it was finally shown in the 1980s: essential features of the design included large amounts of tin foil and upturned mattresses. *See also*: Anderson shelter.

• **Moscow Conference** ▶ A meeting between Churchill, Stalin, and the US ambassador Averell Harriman in Moscow (9–20 October 1944). The purpose of the conference was to discuss the partition of SE Europe at the end of World War II. The Soviet Union was given a controlling interest in Romania, Bulgaria, and Hungary; the UK was given a controlling interest in Greece; and Yugoslavia was to be a zone of counterbalanced Soviet and British influence. The last of these decisions proved to have little substance, with the rise of Tito.

• **moshing** ▶ A type of dancing performed in a packed auditorium to heavy metal or hardcore music.

Owing to the limited space, moshing amounts mainly to jumping up and down and colliding with other dancers. The word seems to be a blend of 'mash' and 'squash'.

• **Mosleyites** ▶ The supporters of Sir Oswald Mosley (1896–1980), members of the British Union of Fascists (BUF), also known as Blackshirts. The BUF was founded by Mosley in October 1932: its members took part in antisemitic demonstrations, which inevitably led to violence, in the East End of London and elsewhere. The Public Order Act (1936) restricted the activities of the Mosleyites, who are thought to have numbered about 20,000 at this time. The BUF was banned in 1940 and Mosley was interned (1940–43). His second wife was Diana Mitford (*see*: Mitford girls).

• **Mosquito** ▶ A fast twin-engined aircraft manufactured by the de Havilland company and used by the RAF during World War II. A prototype Mosquito first took to the air on 25 November 1940, and the plane entered service as a light bomber with 105 Squadron in 1942. The lightweight wooden construction and Merlin engines gave it a top speed of over 400 mph (650 kph). In the second half of the war, the Mosquito was cast in various roles, including reconnaissance plane, night fighter, fighter-bomber, and escort fighter. With a wingspan of 16.51 m (54 ft 2 in) and a length of 12.43 m (40 ft 6 in), the Mosquito could carry a payload of up to 1800 kg (4000 lb).

• **Mossad** ▶ Israel's secret intelligence service. The Committee for Illegal Immigration – *Mossad le Aliyeh Beth* – was originally formed in 1937 to arrange the illegal immigration of Jews into Palestine as part of the campaign to establish a Jewish homeland. The organization was revived after World War II and its activities expanded to direct the migration of Jews displaced by the horrors of the holocaust, initially to Allied refugee camps and thence to Palestine. This was performed by a network of Mossad agents working underground throughout Europe from a headquarters in Paris. Jewish migrants were carried from Mediterranean ports in chartered vessels and landed secretly on the Palestinian coast, in defiance of the British regulations under their Mandate. By 1948 members of Mossad were also engaged in smuggling arms and other covert activities. After the establishment of the state of Israel in 1948, Mossad formed the basis of the new country's intelligence service. As such, it has played a crucial role in Israel's struggle against Palestinian guerrilla organizations, as well as in the armed conflict with neighbouring Arab states. Mossad has become notorious for its ruthless methods, which have included murder and kidnapping.

• **most-favoured nation** ▶ In a trade agreement between two countries, a most-favoured-nation clause is one that states that each country will give to the other the same treatment as regards quotas, tariffs, and import restrictions as they extend to the most-favoured nation with which each trades. This concept is included in the European Union trade agreements and also in GATT, now the World Trade Organization.

• **MOT** ▶ The popular name for the test certificate issued by the UK's Department of Transport (originally Ministry of Transport) to road vehicles that have passed a mandatory test for roadworthiness. All cars and light goods vehicles over three years old are required to undergo an annual test at an authorized test centre – usually a garage. Such components as steering, brakes, tyres, suspension, and bodywork are examined and their condition noted. The owner is required to correct any defects before a certificate is awarded. Heavy goods vehicles must undergo similar annual tests, starting from one year old, at testing stations run by the DOT Vehicle Inspectorate. The MOT scheme was instituted by the Road Traffic Act 1960, when it applied to vehicles over five years old.

• **motel** ▶ A hotel that caters especially for motorists by being situated close to a motorway or main road, providing car parking and specializing in one-night accommodation. The motel, which originated in America in 1925, became very popular in the 1950s, when the concept spread to the UK and elsewhere. Some motels consist of single chalet-like units, each with its own parking place. The word is a combination of *mo*tor and ho*tel*.

• **mother of all battles** ▶ In the Gulf War of 1991, the fearsome battle threatened by Saddam Hussein if Allied ground forces attempted to expel his troops from occupied Kuwait. In the event his forces were routed with minimal Allied casualties. The phrase was widely imitated and ridiculed in the Western media.

> In the wake of the Gulf war George Bush, the US President, has taken to describing his wife, Barbara, as 'the mother of all Bushes.' – *The Independent*, 26 March 1991.

• **mothers** ▶
**Some mothers do 'ave 'em** Catchphrase from about 1920, implying that some mothers have stupid or clumsy sons. It was a catchphrase of the British radio comedy programme *The Jimmy Clitheroe Show* in the 1930s and was revived in the 1970s as the title of a popular television comedy series fea-

turing the disaster-prone Frank Spencer (played by Michael Crawford).

• **Mother's Day ▶** The day on which mothers traditionally receive cards and gifts from their children. In the UK the name Mother's Day, imported from America during World War II, has become synonymous with the Christian festival of Mothering Sunday, the fourth Sunday in Lent, when servants, apprentices, and other young workers living away from home were traditionally given a day's holiday to visit their mothers. In America, Mother's Day falls on the second Sunday of May, established by the US Congress in 1914 as a secular festival in honour of mothers. The commercial potential of Mother's Day is exploited to the full on both sides of the Atlantic by florists and others. *See also*: Father's Day.

• **Mothers' Union ▶** A Church of England women's society that aims to safeguard and strengthen Christian family life, to uphold the lifelong vows of marriage, and generally to play a proper part in the life of the Church. It was incorporated by Royal Charter in 1926 and generally operates as a parish institution.

• **Moto, Mr ▶** The Japanese detective hero of a popular Hollywood film series of the late 1930s, created by John P. Marquand and played by Peter Lorre (usually a classic villain). The first in the series was *Think Fast Mr Moto* (1937); the last, *Mr Moto Takes a Vacation* (1939), proved prophetic since with Pearl Harbor, America's interest in Japanese heroes disappeared overnight. (This opportunity provided a boost for the cinema's Chinese detective, Charlie Chan, who turned out 20 films in the 1940s.) A nostalgic revival, *The Return of Mr Moto*, was released in 1965 with Henry Silva in the title role.

• **motorhead ▶ 1.** Slang for a motorbike or car fan. The suffix '-head' is often used to indicate a particular interest in something (*see*: head). **2.** Slang for a person who uses amphetamine drugs. This definition is related to the first, 'motor' denoting both speed and aggression. The 1970s saw the emergence of a heavy metal band of this name, who were noted for playing very loud and very fast; their leader Lemmy once boasted 'If we moved in next door, your lawn would die'.

• **motormouth ▶** Slang for someone who talks very fast or who 'shouts their mouth off' on a variety of subjects. It originated in 1970s Black slang and has been applied to rap artists, DJs, speed takers, and others who talk incessantly or very fast. The fast-talking British comedian Ben Elton has frequently been called a motormouth.

• **motorway ▶** A main road for fast traffic with restricted access and dual carriageways, usually linking major centres of industry and population. The world's first motorway appeared in 1924 with the opening of the Milan–Varese **autostrada** in Italy. In the following decades other countries, notably Germany and America, embarked on major motorway construction programmes. In America motorways are called **expressways** or **superhighways**. In Germany, Austria, and Switzerland they are **autobahns**; in France, **autoroutes**; and in Spain, **autopistas**. In the UK the Special Roads Act (1949) provided for the building of motorways. Construction eventually began on the M1 between London and Birmingham on 24 March 1958; the first section opened on 2 November 1959. By 1997 the UK had 2535 miles of motorway.

• **motorway madness ▶** The dangerous practice of driving too fast and too close to the car in front on a motorway, which is one of the major causes of accidents and multiple pile-ups, especially in bad weather with poor visibility.

• **Motown ▶** A type of Black US music of the 1960s and 1970s that combined rhythm and blues with elements of gospel and White pop. It is the tradename of Motown Records of Detroit, which developed and popularized the sound. Major stars created by the Motown Company in the 1960s included Diana Ross and the Supremes, Smokey Robinson, and Marvin Gaye. Motown – a combination of *motor* and *town* – is the nickname of Detroit, the world's largest car-manufacturing centre.

• **mountain bike ▶** A type of sturdy bicycle originally designed for cross-country use in rough terrain. Its principal features are a strong frame, thick-rimmed wheels with heavy-duty tyres, and a large number (at least 16) of gears to cope with extreme gradients. In the 1980s the mountain bike was adopted by fashion-conscious yuppies as a healthy, ecologically sound, and status-enhancing means of getting to work. It was also an important status symbol among teenage boys. Mountain bikes, also known as **all-terrain bikes** or **ATBs**, are now perhaps the most common form of bicycle.

• **Mountbatten ▶** *See*: Battenberg.

• **Mount St Helens ▶** A volcano in the Cascade mountain range of Washington State, NW America. Its eruption in May 1980 was the biggest volcanic explosion witnessed in modern US history. The volcano, dormant since the 19th century, gave its first indication of renewed activity on 27 March 1980 with an eruption of steam. This was followed by several moderate eruptions with intervening quiet spells. However, in spite of intensive monitoring, the events of 18 May exceeded all predictions. An earthquake ruptured the entire north face of the volcano, triggering an avalanche and massive air blast, which carried ash and other debris over 20 km (12 mi) and felled vast swathes of the surrounding forest. Mudflows swept through nearby valleys, rivers steamed with the hot debris, and the sky filled with clouds of volcanic ash. The blast lifted ash to over 6000 m (18,000 ft), causing it to spread across the continent and eventually around the globe, giving red sunsets and hazy skies throughout the N hemisphere. The eruption left over 60 people dead or missing and caused over $2 billion of damage. There was a second, but less severe, eruption on 25 May, after which, with its top literally blown off, St Helens quietened down.

• **mouse** ▶ A hand-held device that controls the cursor on a computer screen. The device, a small box with buttons on top and a lead connecting it to the computer, is so-called because it is thought to resemble the animal.

• **Mouse** ▶ A German tank developed on Hitler's orders in 1944, which at 180 tons was the heaviest tank ever built. Facing the overwhelming superiority of the Soviet Union's armour, Hitler commissioned Ferdinand Porsche to design a massive tank that could withstand virtually any assault. Powered by a 1500 horsepower engine, the prototype was capable of travelling underwater and ran on three foot-wide tracks. Unfortunately it was so heavy that it could only travel at 12 mph, became bogged down on anything but the firmest ground, and shattered the roads on which it ran. The project was abandoned.

• **mouse-milking** ▶ A US business expression used to describe any project that consumes time, money, and effort but yields very little profit. Clearly milking a mouse would be laborious and unproductive.

• **Mousetrap, The** ▶ A play by Agatha Christie (*see*: Queen of Crime) which has enjoyed a record-breaking continuous run since its first performance at the Ambassador's Theatre, London, in 1952. In 1974 the play was transferred without a break to St Martin's Theatre, London, where it can still be seen. The British actor Richard Attenborough and his wife Sheila Sim were in the cast of the first production. *The Mousetrap* was originally written in 1947 as *Three Blind Mice*, a radio play for the 80th birthday of Queen Mary. It was subsequently published as a novel, under the original title, before being adapted for the stage. The play passed its 20,000th performance in 2000.

• **Mouth, The** ▶ *See*: Superbrat.

• **moved** ▶
  **We shall not be moved** A phrase used as a song or chant at demonstrations and sit-ins from the 1960s, especially during the civil rights movement. It was originally a line from a negro spiritual.

• **movers and shakers** ▶ An informal phrase for people who are powerful and influential, those with the means to organize others and to make things happen. The expression, although not with this specific meaning, derives from a poem by Arthur O'Shaughnessy:

> We are the music makers...
> We are the movers and shakers
> Of the world forever, it seems .
> – 'Ode' (1874).

• **moves** ▶
  **If it moves, shoot it, if it doesn't, chop it down** A popular Australian saying, facetiously regarded as an informal national motto. It is an ironic echo of the pioneering spirit of the first Australian settlers.

• **moving** ▶
  **Let's get America moving again** A political slogan used by John F. Kennedy in his successful campaign for the US presidency (1960). It has since been used elsewhere, by substituting the appropriate name of a country, party, etc.

• **mp3** ▶ Mpeg-1 layer 3. Software created by the Moving Picture Expert Group that enables audio files, such as those on a CD, to be compressed to about 8–10% of their original size in a few minutes. A conventional CD has a running time of about 74 minutes; in mp3 format, however, as many as 100 three- or four-minute songs can be stored on a CD. More significantly, this reduction in file size enables songs in mp3 format to be transferred across the Internet quite quickly, making them freely available to computer users all over the world. Several protracted and expensive court battles are currently being fought over whether or not such distribution contravenes copyright laws. Mp3s can be stored on hard drives or removable media, hosted on websites, or loaded onto mp3 players. Currently, hybrid players are being developed to play both conventional music CDs and data CDs containing mp3 files.

• **Mr and Mrs Wood in front** ▶ Theatrical catchphrase, first heard in the early 20th century, meaning that the auditorium is virtually empty, the performers being greeted with the sight of rows of empty wooden seats.

• **Mr Big** ► A nickname for the boss or the leader of an underworld gang. The author Ian Fleming may have originated the phrase in *Live and Let Die* (1954). This novel features a gangster named Buonaparte Ignace Gallia, whose initials happen to spell Big.

• **Mr Charley** ► US Black nickname for a White man. It became widespread in about 1960, with **Boss Charley** representing White authority figures. Older Black terms include **Whitey** and *ofay* for a White person and the man for the White establishment or one of its members.

• **Mr Chips** ► *See*: Chips, Mr.

• **Mr Clean** ► A nickname for someone who is above reproach on all levels. It was originally the tradename of a US household cleaner.

• **Mr Magoo** ► The short-sighted bumbling hero of numerous cartoon shorts and comic strips. The character was created by Stephen Bosustow for the *Mr Magoo* films produced in the early 1950s by United Productions of America. The humour largely revolves around Mr Magoo's failure to recognize everyday objects and people: he talks to hatstands and mistakes the face in a portrait for his own reflection in a mirror, for example. More recently, the character has been criticized by organizations representing the blind and partially sighted.

• **Mr Moto** ► *See*: Moto, Mr.

• **Mr Nice Guy** ► An epithet used to characterize any man who wishes to be admired for his friendliness and compassion. It is often used of politicians, usually somewhat sneeringly.

• **Mrs Miniver** ► *See*: Miniver, Mrs.

• **Mrs Mopp** ► *See*: ITMA.

• **muck** ►
  **Sing 'em muck** The advice allegedly given by the Australian soprano Dame Nellie Melba (1861–1931) to Clara Butt, who was about to carry out a tour of Australia:

  > Still, it's a wonderful country, and you'll have a good-time. What are you going to sing? All I can say is – sing 'em muck! It's all they can understand!

The phrase has since been repeated in jaundiced tones by numerous entertainers about to tour 're-mote' areas.

• **muckrakers** ► A name given to US investigative journalists and writers at the beginning of the 20th century. Their use of sensationalism to increase circulation led President Theodore Roosevelt to call them 'irresponsible'. However, many reforms were brought about as a result of articles in such magazines as *Colliers* and *McClure's* and in newspapers, led by William Randolph Hearst's *New York Journal* and Joseph Pulitzer's *New York World*. Two effective muckrakers were Ira M. Tarbell (1857–1944), whose 1904 exposé of Standard Oil encouraged legislation on monopolies, and Lincoln Steffens (1866–1936), who exposed illegal political tactics in 1902. Upton Sinclair's book *The Jungle* (1906) gave many details of insanitary practices in the meat industry, which led to the Federal Food and Drugs Act later that year. The methods of the muckraking press were also called **yellow journalism**, from Pulitzer's 'Yellow Kid' comic strip.

• **mud** ►
  **Here's mud in your eye!** A drinking toast of uncertain origin. Two possible explanations have been suggested. One is that the toast originated during World War I, when soldiers in the trenches would clearly prefer to get mud in their eyes than something more dangerous. Thus the toast was an expression of goodwill. The alternative context is the racecourse and the hope that one's own horse will be out in front kicking up mud into the eyes of the less successful horses following it. On the basis of this theory, the toast is not an expression of goodwill.

• **Mudros, Chios, and chaos** ► A British catchphrase of World War I, originating in 1915 among the men serving in the Mediterranean Expeditionary Force. It refers to the three main bases and commands in the area, two of them being on the islands of Mudros and Chios.

• **muesli-belt malnutrition** ► A dietary paradox researched by Professor Vincent Marks of the University of Surrey. It appears that parents who feed their children on a supposedly healthy diet of high-fibre low-fat foods, such as muesli, brown bread, and raw vegetables, are doing them a disservice. Marks's research showed that because the food took so long to masticate, the children were not getting enough to eat. Children consuming food that was quicker to eat, such as fish fingers and chips, turned out to be better nourished. *See*: health food.

• **mugging** ► The crime of assaulting and robbing people in the streets, on trains, in lonely parks, etc., especially at night. Muggers often hunt in packs and generally attack old or infirm people, young girls, etc., who are unable to protect themselves. This cowardly and vicious practice became a problem in urban environments during the last third of the 20th century. From the old slang use of mug, meaning to rob or swindle.

• **muggles** ▸ *See*: Potter, Harry.

• **mug shot** ▸ Originally, US slang for a frontal photograph taken of a suspect by the police. It has since spread throughout the English-speaking world and it is now also used for any head-and-shoulders portrait.

• **mujaheddin** ▸ (Arabic, fighters) A loose coalition of rebel groups formed in Afghanistan to oppose the revolutionary government of the People's Democratic Party of Afghanistan (PDPA), which came to power after a military coup in 1978. Mujaheddin guerrilla warfare intensified following the intervention in 1979 of Soviet forces in support of their PDPA allies and eventually led to the withdrawal of Soviet troops in 1988–89 and the collapse of the PDPA government in 1992. The mujaheddin, which comprised a wide range of political and ethnic factions, including Sunni and Shi'ite Muslims, Islamic traditionalists, and radical fundamentalists, then proclaimed Afghanistan an Islamic state, establishing a government and interim president. However, the political and religious diversity of the mujaheddin subsequently led to fierce fighting between rival factions; in 1995 they were defeated by the Taliban militia, which seized control of Kabul the following year and imposed strict Islamic law. By 2001 the Taliban had extended its control over 95% of the country: the mujaheddin, combined into a **Northern Alliance** of the main factions and led by General Masood, continued to mount resistance from a small stronghold in the north. In 2001 the Alliance regained control of the country during the US-led war on terrorism, which involved the destruction of the Taliban regime.

• **Mukden incident** ▸ An explosion on the South Manchurian Railway near the city of Mukden (now Shenyang) in NE China, on 18 September 1931. The Japanese blamed the explosion on the Chinese and used it as an excuse to attack and take control of the city. They set up a puppet administration there on 24 September 1931 and went on to drive the Chinese forces out of Manchuria, creating the puppet state of Manchukuo.

• **Mulberry harbour** ▸ An artificial harbour created for the Allied invasion of Normandy in 1944. Mulberry was the codename of the engineering operation that produced two of these floating harbours: they were prefabricated in England, towed across the English Channel, and sunk into position on the French coast.

• **mule** ▸ Slang for someone used to smuggle drugs into a country. Originally it referred specifically to a smuggler of South American cocaine but its meaning has been extended to anyone who is bribed, duped, or coerced into carrying drugs through customs or across a national border.

• **multimedia** ▸ *See*: mixed media.

• **multinational** ▸ A large corporation that has many branches or divisions in different countries. Companies extend their activities overseas to exploit new markets, secure supplies of raw materials, or to take advantage of lower taxes and cheaper labour. The economic and political power of the multinationals, whose interests often take precedence over the will of elected governments, has been a matter of growing concern since the 1970s. *See*: globalization.

• **Münchausen syndrome** ▸ A syndrome in which a person fakes illness or pain, telling elaborate and often harrowing stories about his or her past, in order to receive medical attention. This bizarre compulsion, which is quite distinct from hypochondria or malingering, may even lead sufferers to undergo repeated exploratory operations for complaints that they know to be fictitious. Attention-seeking behaviour of this kind can be a serious imposition on the time of medical staff and a drain on resources. Much more serious, however, is **Münchausen syndrome by proxy**, sufferers from which inflict genuine harm on others in their care in order to gain the attention they crave. The term appeared in the headlines in 1993, when Beverley Allitt, a 24-year-old nurse, was sentenced to life imprisonment on 13 charges of murder, attempted murder, and assault on young children in her care. The syndrome is named after Baron Münchausen (1720–97), an officer in the Russian army who invented extraordinary stories about his exploits.

• **munchies, the** ▸ Slang for the craving for snacks often experienced after smoking cannabis. Users talk of **having the munchies** for sweets, crisps, etc. A visit to an all-night store or garage generally follows.

• **munchkin** ▸ US slang for a sweet little child, taken from the name of the little people in the Wizard of Oz (1900), written by L. Frank Baum (1856–1919) and made into an immensely successful film in 1939. The word can also be used patronizingly of low-level employees in an organization.

• **Munich** ▸ In politics or international relations, a 'Munich' is now any potentially disastrous, humiliating, or dishonourable act of appeasement or surrender. The name alludes to the unfortunate **Munich Pact** or **Agreement**, concluded between the UK, France, Germany, and Italy (30 September 1938) in which the Sudetenland of Czechoslovakia was ceded to Germany (*see*: Sudeten crisis). The British prime minister, Neville Chamberlain, who took part in the agreement, described it as achieving 'peace for our time' (*see*: peace in our time). Six months later Hitler invaded Czechoslovakia; in another six months World War II began. The best that can be said for Chamberlain and Daladier of France is that they bought a little time in which to rearm.

• **Munich air crash ►** The accident on 6 February 1958 in which a BEA airliner crashed during take-off on a snow-covered runway at Munich airport. 23 of the 44 passengers were killed, including 12 players and staff belonging to Manchester United Football Club. The tragedy cut short the lives of several rising stars of British football – all members of the youthful Manchester team managed by Matt Busby and popularly known as Busby's babes. These included the England internationals Roger Byrne, Tommy Taylor, and David Pegg. Duncan Edwards, the English left-half, died in hospital 15 days later. The team was returning home from Belgrade after winning a European Cup semi-final place. Eight football journalists also died in the crash but manager Matt Busby recovered from his injuries to rebuild his shattered team.

• **Munich Putsch ►** An abortive attempt by Adolf Hitler (12 November 1923) to take control of Bavaria. Often called the **beer-hall Putsch**, the incident took place in Munich's largest beer hall, the Burgerbraukeller, where Gustav von Kahr, the state commissioner, was speaking. Hitler broke in, supported by his Brown Shirts, claiming that he had the support of the German war hero, Field Marshal von Ludendorff (1865–1937). Hitler and von Ludendorff were both arrested, Hitler subsequently spending time in prison, where he began to write Mein Kampf (My Struggle; 1925).

• **muppet ► 1.** One of the distinctive felt puppets created by Jim Henson (1936–90), who coined the name from marionette and puppet. The muppets first appeared in the children's television series *Sesame Street* (1969 onwards) and subsequently graduated to their own show (1976–80), which was more adult-orientated, containing songs, sketches, and special guest stars. It featured such muppet favourites as Kermit the Frog, Fozzie Bear, and Miss Piggy, who became major stars. **2.** British derogatory slang for a psychiatric patient or a person disadvantaged in some way. It is also used of unattractive teenagers by their peers. It is not known why the friendly puppets should have created this disagreeable slang sense.

• **muppie ►** A facetious acronyn for middle-aged urban professional. Such acronyms were popular in the UK in the 1980s. *See*: yuppie.

• **Murderers' Row ►** The nickname of the batting line-up of the New York Yankee baseball team in the 1920s. Among those wearing its pinstripe uniforms were two all-time baseball greats, George Herman (Babe) Ruth and Lou Gehrig (1903–41). Ruth hit a record 60 home runs in 1927 (no other player had more than 24 in a season) and retired in 1935 with 714. Gehrig, also a strong hitter, set a record of playing in 2130 consecutive games (1925–39). He died two years later from amyotrophic lateral sclerosis, now commonly called **Lou Gehrig's disease**.

• **Murphy ►** A confidence trick commonly played on men who pay to have sex with a prostitute. After payment has been made to a pimp, the punter is given a rendezvous to meet a woman, who does not turn up. The name is probably an allusion to the supposed gullibility of the Irish (Murphy being a common Irish surname). It has also been used of other con tricks.

• **Murphy, Bridey ►** The name of the woman who was 'contacted' in a celebrated hypnotic regression of a US housewife in 1952. Under hypnosis by Morey Bernstein, who later recounted the experience in a bestselling book, the subject described the life of a person called Bridey Murphy in Ireland in the previous century. Even more curiously, Bridey recalled her own funeral and life after death before her 'rebirth' in 1923. All the facts produced were checked by the author, although subsequent investigators could find no record of Bridey's birth or death. Nevertheless, many of the details given during the regression were uncannily accurate and remain unexplained by critics, who argued that most of Bridey Murphy's story was derived from the hypnotized woman's own subconscious, prompted by Bernstein's questions. Whatever the truth behind the regression, the story of Bridey Murphy greatly increased public interest in experiments using hypnosis. *See also*: Bloxham tapes.

• **Murphy's Law ►** A 'law' that can be summed up by the saying: 'anything that can go wrong, will go wrong'. It is also known as **Sod's Law**. Some typical examples of its use are: you will always find something in the last place you look; a piece of toast always lands butter-side down. Exactly who Murphy is or was is not known for certain. One explanation attributes the law and its name to George Nichols, an engineer at the US aircraft firm of Northrop in the 1940s; he is said to have taken the idea from a colleague named Murphy, who was responsible for safety trials at the company. Others point out that the US Navy once ran a series of cautionary cartoons featuring a fictitious character called Murphy, who could be relied on to get things wrong; such as attaching an aircraft propeller the wrong way round!

• **mushroom** ▶ US police slang for a law-abiding member of the public who strays into the firing-line during a shoot-out with criminals. This slightly contemptuous term alludes to the way such people appear out of nowhere and cause unnecessary complications by getting themselves shot.

• **mushroom cloud** ▶ The characteristic shape of the products of a nuclear explosion, particularly one occurring on or near the surface of the ground. The massive energy release of the explosion creates a shock wave and fireball, which render the air luminous in the form of a mushroom-shaped cloud. Such a cloud was first witnessed by scientists of the US Manhattan Project, who detonated a prototype nuclear weapon at the Alamogordo test site in New Mexico on 16 July 1945. The physicist Enrico Fermi described this first detonation:

> After a few seconds the rising flames lost their brightness and appeared as a huge pillar of smoke with an expanded head like a gigantic mushroom that rose rapidly beyond the clouds, probably to a height of the order of 30,000 feet.

Later that same year, America exploded nuclear weapons over the Japanese cities of Hiroshima and Nagasaki. Thereafter, the mushroom cloud came to symbolize the nuclear threat overshadowing all life on the planet.

• **musical medium** ▶ A British medium, Rosemary Brown, who attracted attention in the 1970s when she claimed to be in communication with Igor Stravinsky, Franz Liszt, Beethoven, and Chopin. In her home in Balham, S London, Mrs Brown took down by dictation entire new musical works from these composers, despite having only a rudimentary knowledge of music theory. The subsequent publication of some of these pieces, which included a 40-page Schubert sonata, songs by Schubert, and Beethoven's 10th and 11th symphonies, confounded music critics who had to admit they have all the hallmarks of each composer's style. No one ever succeeded in proving that Mrs Brown was faking the works; among those convinced that she was passing on genuine compositions from beyond the grave were Richard Rodney Bennett and the pianist Hephzibah Menuhin (sister of the violinist Yehudi). Bennett remarked: 'I couldn't have faked some of the Beethoven myself.'

• **music centre** ▶ An integrated home audio system that combined record turntable, cassette tape deck, radio tuner, amplifier, and speakers. Introduced in the 1970s, it was made possible by the advent of the microchip and the consequent miniaturization of many audio components. The music centre's convenience, compactness, and competitive price made it popular, although hi-fi buffs remained loyal to more expensive systems comprising separate components. By the mid-1980s the music centre had been supplanted by the even more miniaturized midi system, which was capable of playing compact discs.

• **music hall** ▶ A popular form of variety entertainment that had its origins in the 'free and easy' of the public houses and in the song and supper rooms of early Victorian London. Music halls eventually became more numerous in London and the provinces than the regular theatres. Their best days were in the early part of the 20th century, when leading performers included George Robey (see: Prime Minister of Mirth) and Marie Lloyd (see: Queen of the Halls). In the years after World War I they were gradually eclipsed by the cinema; later, radio and television sealed their fate. The halls were converted into civic theatres, cinemas, or bingo halls – although such names as Palladium, Palace, Alhambra, Coliseum, Empire, Hippodrome, etc., proclaim their former glories.

• **music, maestro, please** ▶ A phrase used by the 1950s bandleader Harry Leader when inviting his band to strike up. It comes from a song by Magidson and Wrubel, used by Flanagan and Allen in their 1938 show *These Foolish Things*.

• **Music While You Work** ▶ A daily music programme provided by the BBC as a stimulus to factory workers during World War II. A continuous selection of dance tunes (fast numbers rather than slow and romantic ones) was broadcast each day by a rota of well-known dance bands. The programmes were first broadcast in 1940 and continued throughout the war years. Whether or not they had any measurable effect on production is not known, but they proved so popular with workers that they continued for another 20 years after the war. By the 1960s the nature of popular music had changed; modern pop was regarded as too intrusive and *Music While You Work* was brought to an end in 1967.

• **musique concrète** ▶ See: concrete music.

• **muso** ▶ A derogatory term for a musician, especially one regarded as being obsessed with technique or musical equipment to the detriment of content and expression. It was coined by association with the word 'wino', for one who is addicted to drink.

> Muso...a term normally used by very bad musicians to describe very good ones. – *The Independent*, 5 February 1991.

• **mustard gas** ▶ A highly poisonous war gas (dichlorodiethyl sulphide). Mustard gas attacks the respiratory tract but also causes eye damage and blisters the skin. It was first used by the German army during World War I, notably at Passchendaele (1917). The government of Iraq used mustard gas in 1988 against Kurdish dissidents in the north of the country.

• **Mutt and Jeff** ▶ A married couple or two friends or associates who are extremely unlike each other in physical appearance. The characters originated in a comic strip drawn by the US cartoonist Bud Fisher (1884–1954) at the beginning of the 20th century. Mutt was a tall thin character, while Jeff was short and fat. 'Mutt and Jeff' is also British rhyming slang for deaf.

• **Muzak** ▶ Tradename of a system for playing background music in such public places as shops, restaurants, hairdressers, doctors' waiting rooms, etc. The name was based on Kodak, this being a short and successful tradename. It is now used generally of any bland or insipid music.

> If muzak be the food of love, no wonder it is commonly to be found...among the frozen mint-flavoured peas and the crinkle-cut chips. – *The Times*, 29 November 1968.

• **MVD** ▶ *Ministerstvo Vnutrennikh Del*. The Soviet police organization, the ministry of internal affairs, which replaced the NKVD in 1946. The official duties of the uniformed members of the MVD included general police work, the control of labour camps, the supervision of border troops, the issue of passports and visas, etc. The MVD is also believed to have been involved in the secret trial and punishment of Stalin's opponents. In 1960 the MVD was replaced by the KVD.

• **myalgic encephalopathy** ▶ *See*: ME.

• **My Lai** ▶ A Vietnamese village, also known as **Song My**, situated in Quang Ngai province; it was the scene of one of the worst atrocities committed by US forces during the Vietnam War. On 16 March 1968 C company of 1st Batallion 20th Infantry, led by Lieutenant William Calley, entered the village. Several hundred unarmed villagers were shot dead, including women and children; many of the women were raped by US soldiers. Army officers then conspired to conceal what had happened, which only came to light the following year. In March 1969 Ronald Ridenhour, a soldier serving in Vietnam, who had heard about the incident, wrote an open letter to the US army department and to members of the Senate and Congress, calling for an investigation of the events at My Lai. Later in the year, photographs of the massacred villagers, taken by army photographer Ron Haeberle, were published in a newspaper, with Haeberle's eye-witness account. On 24 November the army announced that Calley was to be court-martialled on murder charges.

Twenty-five men were charged with various crimes arising from incidents in My Lai, but only Calley was found guilty. In 1971 he was sentenced to a long prison term but after serving three years he was released on parole. Calley's defence rested on his claim that as he was 'following orders' the guilt lay with his army superiors and ultimately with the US people. For many Americans the My Lai killings confirmed their worst fears about US conduct in Vietnam. Others regarded Calley as the dupe of an incompetent and ill-disciplined command structure, or even as a martyr.

• **myxomatosis** ▶ A disease of rabbits and hares that was deliberately introduced into wild rabbits in the UK and Australia in the 1950s in an attempt to restrict their ever-growing numbers. Caused by a virus, it is usually fatal but some rabbits have developed a degree of immunity to the disease. Its introduction was welcomed by farmers whose crops were suffering damage from the rabbits; it was less popular with the general public, who were distressed by the appearance of infected rabbits with large swellings on their faces, including the eyes, making them virtually blind. The disease reduced the wild rabbit population by about 90%, but numbers have since recovered.

# N

• **NAACP** ➤ National Association for the Advancement of Colored People. The US civil-rights organization that led the campaign for equal rights for Blacks. It was formed in 1909 and fought discrimination through a combination of legal actions and public protests; by the 1940s it was using sit-in tactics to integrate White-only restaurants. In 1954 the NAACP won a historic Supreme Court ruling that segregated schools for Whites and Blacks were unconstitutional. It supported the 1955 Montgomery bus boycott led by Martin Luther King and his 'March on Washington' (1963) by more than 200,000 people. By the mid-1960s, however, it had lost ground to more radical organizations. *See:* civil rights movement.

• **NAAFI** ➤ Navy, Army, and Air Force Institute. The body that organizes canteens and shops for use by members of the British armed forces throughout the world. *See:* naff; Naffy medal.

• **nab** ➤ 1. British slang, now obsolete, for the dole. It was an acronym for National Assistance Board, the official body formerly responsible for paying the unemployment benefit. 2. Acronym for *no-alcohol beer* – a beer that has been treated to remove the alcohol. Such beverages became available in most British pubs in the late 1980s, as the campaign against drink-driving began to make headway. A **lab** is a low-alcohol beer – one that has been similarly treated to reduce the alcohol. No- and low-alcohol beers are sometimes referred to collectively as **nablabs**. Despite initial consumer resistance, the market for both is now highly profitable.

• **Naderite** ➤ A supporter of the campaigns of the US lawyer Ralph Nader (1934– ), whose battles against dubious corporate and governmental practices have led to new legislation, such as improved automobile safety standards and stricter health laws. His 1965 book, *Unsafe at Any Speed*, indicted the Detroit motor industry for putting profits before safety. His watchdog organization, Public Citizen Inc., has investigated pesticides, tax reform, health care, and the US Congress. Nader stood as Green Party candidate in the US presidential elections of 1996 and 2000. In the latter he obtained 3% of the total vote; his campaign, which focused on such issues as corporate greed and the provision of universal health care, attracted many potential Democrat votes and undoubtedly contributed to the defeat of the Democratic Party candidate, Al Gore.

• **nadsat** ➤ An invented form of teenage slang, largely based on Russian, used throughout Anthony Burgess's novel *A Clockwork Orange* (1962; filmed 1971). The story concerns Alex, a renegade teenager from the near future. Several of Burgess's coinages acquired a wider currency, notably **droog** meaning gang member (from Russian *drug*, friend). Nadsat itself derives from the Russian *pyatnádsat*, meaning fifteen. *See:* clockwork orange.

• **naff** ➤ Slang for worthless, shoddy, in bad taste, or ostentatious: a term of general disapprobation. It has been suggested that naff is armed services' slang deriving from the NAAFI, which was proverbial for providing indifferent food and poor-quality goods at its shops. Alternatively it may have begun life as an acronym for 'not available for fucking'.

> Now comes this oddly naff book, a cross between Chekhov and Georgette Heyer. - Book review, *The Independent*, 27 February 1991.

• **naff off** ➤ A euphemism for 'fuck off', as used in Keith Waterhouse's novel *Billy Liar* (1959) and in the BBC TV series *Porridge* (first shown 1974). However, it owed its widespread popularity in the early 1980s to Princess Anne's reported use of it to a group of press photographers (*see:* Four-letter Annie).

• **Naffy medal** ➤ Colloquial name for both the 1939–45 Star and the Africa Star medals awarded during World War II. This is an ironic reference to the NAAFI.

• **Nagasaki** ➤ A port in Japan, in W Kyushu, which was largely destroyed on 9 August 1945 by the dropping of the second atom bomb (*see:* nuclear weapon). Damage was somewhat less severe than at Hiroshima, but nonetheless 75,000 people were killed or wounded. Japan surrendered five days later bringing World War II to an end. The city was rapidly rebuilt after the war ended.

• **nail** ►

**another nail in my coffin** A laconic catch-phrase often uttered by smokers as they accept a cigarette offered to them. An apparent acknowledgment of the well-authenticated health risks associated with smoking, this phrase actually predates the link between smoking and cancer or heart disease. First heard in the 1920s, it originally referred to the hazard of a smoker's cough.

• **nail bomb** ► A homemade explosive device packed with nails and other sharp metal objects. The nail bomb is a popular terrorist's weapon, being designed to wound as many people as possible over the widest possible area.

• **naked ape** ► A description of the human species, first popularized by the British zoologist Desmond Morris (1928–  ) in his study of human behaviour, *The Naked Ape* (1967). Morris justifies his choice of title in the book's introduction:

> There are one hundred and ninety-three living species of monkeys and apes. One hundred and ninety-two of them are covered with hair. The exception is a naked ape self-named *Homo sapiens*.

*See also*: Dayton anti-Darwinist trial.

• **naked call writing** ► Financial jargon for selling (writing) an option on shares that one does not own. It is a dangerous strategy because if the share price rises the shares will have to be purchased at the market price in order to deliver them, thus involving an unlimited risk. Such a writer is 'naked' in the sense of being uncovered (*i.e.* not owning what one is selling).

• **'Nam** ► *See*: Vietnam War.

• **Nana** ► In Barrie's Peter Pan, the gentle and faithful old dog who always looked after the children in the Darling family. When Mr Darling played a trick on Nana by giving her unpleasant medicine, which he himself had promised to drink, the family did not appreciate his humour. This put him in a bad mood and Nana was chained up in the yard before he went out for the evening. As a consequence Peter Pan entered the children's bedroom unchallenged.

• **Nansen passport** ► A passport introduced in 1922 as a travel document for 'stateless' persons. It was named after the Norwegian explorer Fridtjof Nansen (1861–1930), who received the Nobel Peace Prize in 1922 for his humanitarian work on behalf of the League of Nations. It was Nansen who suggested such a passport as a means of helping refugees.

• **napalm** ► An explosive jelly used in incendiary bombs, which acquired a notorious reputation after its use by US forces in the Vietnam War. Consisting of a mixture of *n*apathenic acid and *palm*itic acid with petrol, it was used in bombs and flame throwers during World War II and the Korean War. Napalm carries further than petrol alone, burns at a higher temperature, and clings like a jelly to anything or anyone it touches. The horrific burns caused to civilians by napalm bombing in Vietnam intensified demands for the withdrawal of US forces from the war.

• **Napier** ► An early car, manufactured by a British company in 1902, which established a 24-hour motoring record at Brooklands in 1907. The record remained unbroken until after World War I. The Napier Company went on to manufacture aero-engines, such as the Napier Lion, which gave valuable service in World War II.

• **napoo** ► Military slang of World War I for something that is of no use or does not exist. It is an anglicized and condensed form of the French phrase *il n'y en a plus*, there is no more of it. It occurs in a popular song of 1917:

> Bonsoir old thing, cheerio, chin-chin,
> Nahpoo, toodle-oo, goodby-ee.
> – WESTON and LEE: 'Good-Bye-Ee'.

• **narc** ► US slang for a narcotics agent, possibly by allusion to the 19th-century British slang 'nark', for an informer (from the Romany *nak*, a nose).

• **Narnia** ► A magical kingdom created by C. S. Lewis in his children's novel *The Lion, the Witch and the Wardrobe* (1950); it also features in six sequels. When first seen, Narnia is ruled by the evil White Witch, who has cast a spell so that it is 'always winter but never Christmas'; it is rescued from this plight by four children from our world and by the self-sacrifice of the Christlike lion **Aslan**. The Christian allegory, though never overtly didactic, is implicit throughout: *The Magician's Nephew*, for example, has its own Garden of Eden and temptation scene involving an apple – although in this instance the temptation is refused; the series culminates with redemption at the end of the world in *The Last Battle*. The seven 'Chronicles of Narnia' have collectively become classics of children's literature that are also enjoyed by many adults.

• **NASA** ► National Aeronautics and Space Administration. The agency that, since its foundation in 1958, has coordinated America's space programme (excluding military projects). *See*: Apollo moon programme; satellite; Skylab; space probe; space shuttle.

• **Nasho** ► Australian slang for national service

(or someone fulfilling such service). National service ended in Australia in 1972.

• **Nashville** ▶ The state capital of Tennessee, famous as the centre of country-and-western music. The association with country music began in the 1920s with the success of a local hour-long radio programme, *WSM Barn Dance*, featuring banjo and fiddle music as well as Black and White gospel. In 1927 the programme was extended to three hours, renamed *The Grand Old Opry* after Nashville's main music theatre, and broadcast live from a variety of venues. The first recording studios and music publishers were established in Nashville in the 1940s; with the growth of rock 'n' roll in the 1950s, other cities abandoned country music leaving Nashville the undisputed centre of the C & W recording and music-publishing industry.

• **Nassau conference** ▶ A diplomatic meeting that took place in the Bahamas in 1962 between President John F. Kennedy and the British prime minister Harold Macmillan. Macmillan's decision during the conference to opt for the US Polaris system rather than an Anglo-French alternative greatly angered the French leader Charles de Gaulle and intensified his distrust of the UK's attitude towards Europe.

• **Nasser, Lake** ▶ *See*: Aswan High Dam.

• **nasty** ▶
  **something nasty in the woodshed** A secret horror or 'skeleton in the cupboard'. The phrase is often used when a child is believed to be disturbed on account of having witnessed illicit sexual activity; he or she 'has seen something nasty in the woodshed'. It derives from a repeated remark in Stella Gibbons's Cold Comfort Farm (1932).

• **Natal, HMS** ▶ A British cruiser that blew up without warning at anchor in Cromarty Firth on 30 December 1915, sparking off widespread speculation about a possible German sabotage campaign. The *Natal* sank in just three minutes with the loss of more than 350 lives. The immediate suspicion was that it had been attacked by a German U-boat, although the discovery by divers that the Natal's hull had exploded from within ruled out this theory. Others suggested that there might be a link with the loss of HMS *Bulwark* in suspicious circumstances in the Medway on 26 November 1914, shortly after the outbreak of World War I; it was also pointed out that German saboteurs had been active against Allied shipping in New York, successfully planting an incendiary device in the munitions ship *Phoebus*, which blew up at sea in 1915. Nonetheless, the Navy refused to accept that security could have been breached in any way. Finally, on 14 July 1917, it was announced that HMS *Vanguard* had exploded at anchor in Scapa Flow. Among the debris recovered was a German bible and some letters written in German. Upon investigation it was learnt that two mysterious civilian fitters had visited HMS *Vanguard* only hours before it sank; one of them had also boarded HMS *Natal* shortly before it was lost. The naval establishment remained tight-lipped about the whole affair but rumours spread of a secret execution. The official verdict on the *Natal* sinking was that it had gone down due to 'unavoidable causes of an uncertain nature'.

• **National Curriculum** ▶ A major change to the British educational system introduced by the Education Reform Act (1988). The Act established a curriculum of 10 subjects (11 in Wales) to be taken by children in state schools in England and Wales. Three of these – English, mathematics and science – form the **core curriculum**; the other seven – a modern language, history, geography, art, music, a technical subject, and physical education – are **foundation subjects**. The core subjects are compulsory between the ages of 5 and 16; most of the foundation subjects are compulsory from the age of 11, although some remain optional. In Wales, Welsh is a core subject in some schools and a foundation subject in others. The precise content of the subjects is determined by a series of working parties in consultation with the government. Attainment targets are specified in each subject at a series of levels. Both the content of the curriculum and the way it was implemented aroused opposition from teachers and some parents. In 1993 the main teaching unions boycotted the tests for 14-year-olds, arguing that they created unnecessary bureaucracy. As a result the government restricted testing at ages 7, 11, and 14 to the core subjects.

• **National Front** ▶ A militant racist organization founded in the UK in 1966. Professing neo-Nazi beliefs and provoking violent demonstrations in British cities, the party enjoyed a brief period of minor electoral success before splintering into numerous factions and disappearing from public view after humiliation in the general election of 1979. Adherents included many skinheads.

• **National Governments** ▶ The series of coalition governments in the UK from 1931 to 1940. The first National Government was formed on 24 August 1931 after the economic crisis had brought about the collapse of the previous Labour administration; it was headed by the Labour leader Ramsay MacDonald (1866–1937) but attracted mainly Conservative support. Subsequent National Governments were formed under the Conservative leaders Stanley Baldwin (1867–1947) and Neville Chamberlain (1869–1940). Those Liberal and Labour MPs who supported these governments called themselves the National Liberal Party and the National Labour Party, respectively. The administrations became increasingly Conservative in all but name.

• **National Health Service** ► (NHS) The 'Jewel in the Crown' of the social reforms introduced by Clement Attlee's post-war Labour government, which was established under the National Health Service Act (1946) and came into operation in July 1948. The envy of the world, it provided free primary and specialist medical care for all and was funded largely through general taxation. It was Aneurin (Nye) Bevan (1897–1960), the minister of health, who successfully unified the disorganized prewar network of local authority and voluntary hospitals into a single system and overcame the opposition of the medical establishment by allowing the continuation of private practice alongside the NHS. Bevan resigned in 1951 in protest at the government's proposals to introduce charges for false teeth and spectacles, which he regarded as a violation of the principle of an entirely free medical service. This principle has been gradually eroded since 1948. The basic problems of the NHS have been and continue to be financial. Contrary to Bevan's expectations, the cost of the service did not decline as the health of the nation improved. Instead, increasing demands were made on it by the patients whose lives it had prolonged; moreover, unexpected advances in medicine and surgery have resulted in many expensive new treatments becoming available. As a result the service seems to have become a bottomless pit that consumes the vast amounts of money poured into it without any sign of an end to the perennial problems of growing waiting lists and dilapidated buildings. Despite various attempts at reform in the 1980s and 1990s there remain too few doctors and nurses to make the NHS function as it should, while the funds available have to support a top-heavy infrastructure of administrators.

• **nationalization** ► The purchase by the state of privately owned companies, for either political or economic reasons. Until quite recently most Labour politicians governments were strong advocates of nationalization, arguing that state control brought about a sensible rationalization of resources and that the profits earned by large industries, especially those with natural monopolies (such as the railways), should be shared by the population. In some cases companies were also nationalized to prevent them collapsing. From the 1980s these measures were increasingly opposed by Conservatives, who took the view that industries become inefficient in the absence of competition and without shareholders to ensure that profits are maintained at an acceptable level. A process of wholesale privatization was undertaken by the Conservative governments of the 1980s and 1990s.

• **National Labour Party** ► (NLP) Those Labour MPs who supported the coalition National Government formed in 1931. The government was headed by Ramsay MacDonald; other prominent Labour members who joined the emergency cabinet included Philip Snowden, Sir John Sankey, and J. H. Thomas. The bulk of the Labour Party, however, remained in Opposition; MacDonald and the other NLP members were branded as traitors to the Labour movement and expelled from the party. In September 1931 the NLP consisted of about 20 MPs; after the general election of 27 October the numbers had dwindled to 13. MacDonald had hoped that the NLP would form the core of a new socialist party once the economic emergency had subsided. However, after 1931 his reputation, and that of the other National Labour members, suffered an irreversible decline and the party was wound up after the 1945 election.

• **National Liberal Party** ► A group of 25 Liberal MPs, led by Sir John Simon (1873–1954), who broke away from the main party on the issue of free trade and joined the National Government, which had resolved on protectionist measures to help British industry weather the economic depression. The party was actually called the **Liberal National Group** until 1948, when it became the National Liberal Party. In 1966 the four remaining National Liberal Party MPs were incorporated into the Conservative Party.

• **National Park** ► In England and Wales, an area of special scenic and recreational value protected by law for the enjoyment of the general public. The UK's first National Park, the Peak District, was designated in 1949; others include the Lake District, Snowdonia, and the Brecon Beacons. Scotland currently has no National Parks, although there are a number of **National Scenic Areas** which enjoy a lower level of protection. Plans to designate several Scottish National Parks, beginning with Loch Lomond and the Trossachs, were announced in 1998. *See also*: heritage coast.

• **National Plan** ► A comprehensive statement of the Labour government's strategy for the British economy over the period 1965–70, devised by the newly formed department of economic affairs under the direction of George Brown (1914–85). The plan specified a target of a 25% increase in national output by 1970 and indicated the changes in investment, expenditure, and consumption needed to achieve this target. Failure to meet the envisaged growth in exports over the period 1964–66 led to balance of payments difficulties, which prompted restrictions on domestic output after July 1966 and rendered most of the plan's other economic targets unattainable.

• **National Recovery Administration** ▶ (NRA) One of the organizations set up during the so-called first 'Hundred Days' of President Roosevelt's New Deal to tackle the social and economic crisis caused by the Great Depression. The role of the NRA was to promote industrial recovery through a series of nationwide regulatory codes to limit unfair competition, improve working conditions, establish a minimum wage, and guarantee the right to collective bargaining. Employers subscribing to the codes (which eventually amounted to 557 basic and 208 supplementary codes) were allowed to display a Blue Eagle emblem. Despite the plethora of codes and a certain confusion as to whether the NRA was intended to limit or promote corporate monopoly, it did achieve some notable successes, such as ending child labour in the cotton mills. By 1935, however, the New Deal came under increasing attack from Roosevelt's Republican opponents as 'creeping socialism', and the NRA was eventually declared unconstitutional by the Supreme Court on 27 May 1935 ('Black Monday'). Many of its provisions, however, were incorporated into later legislation.

• **National Security Agency** ▶ (NSA) An organization that coordinates the communications systems of the US government. It was established as an agency under the defense department in 1952 to bring all the communications, cryptographical, and electronic intelligence-gathering operations of the armed services, CIA, FBI, and other agencies under the control of a single body. The NSA is the largest and most secret of all US intelligence agencies, its activities being excluded from public and press scrutiny. It is often said that NSA stands for 'no such agency'.

• **Nation shall speak peace unto nation** ▶ The motto of the BBC. It was conceived by a British schoolmaster, Montague John Rendall (1862–1950), as the winning entry in a competition (1927) to provide a motto for the corporation.

• **NATO** ▶ North Atlantic Treaty Organization. An organization for collective military defence established by the North Atlantic Treaty of 4 April 1949 as a counterbalance to the power of the Soviet Union and its satellite states in E Europe. Its signatories included members of the Brussels Treaty organization (the UK, Belgium, Luxembourg, the Netherlands, and France) and Norway, Portugal, America, Canada, Denmark, and Iceland. Greece, Turkey, and West Germany joined in the early 1950s. Under the treaty members agreed to settle disputes by peaceful means and to adhere to the principle of collective security and resistance to armed aggression. The NATO military headquarters (Supreme Headquarters Allied Powers Europe – **SHAPE**) is at Chièvres, Belgium. France withdrew from NATO in July 1966 over fears that America could commit its European allies to conflict with the Soviet Union against their will. In the 1980s tension grew between the European Community and America over 'burden sharing', with the Americans seeking a greater financial commitment by EC members to their own defence. The end of the Cold War, the collapse of communism in Eastern Europe, and the disintegration of the Soviet Union have raised many questions about the future role of NATO. In 1991 the **North Atlantic Council** (NACC) was set up to forge links with the former Eastern-bloc nations; this was renamed the **Euro-Atlantic Partnership Council** in 1997. That same year Russia was given a voice in NATO business in return for accepting NATO's expansion into eastern Europe. The Czech Republic, Poland, and Hungary all joined NATO in 1999. In 1995 NATO carried out air strikes against Serb positions around Sarajevo, its first-ever aggressive action. Its first action against a sovereign state took place in 1999, when NATO undertook a major air campaign against the Federal Republic of Yugoslavia (*see*: Kosovo crisis).

• **Nauecilus** ▶ A German U-boat that was lost in a collision with a wreck on 15 November 1945. The sinking attracted unusual interest when, on 26 November 1946, a bottle containing a page apparently torn from the U-boat's log was found on the Danish coast. Sensationally, this referred to a passenger named Adolf Hitler, suggesting that the Führer had not after all died in his bunker but had perished at sea while attempting to escape war-ravaged Europe. The speculation was, however, brief and the message in the bottle was soon dismissed as a fake.

• **naughty but nice** ▶ A phrase, easily memorized because of the alliteration, that now conjures up visions of cakes oozing cream since it was used (1981–84) as a slogan in advertisements for fresh cream. It was, however, a well-established phrase before then, mostly used as an oblique reference to sex. It had also been used as the title of various films and songs.

• **Nautilus** ▶ The first nuclear-powered submarine, which was launched in 1954. It was named after the submarine in the novel *Twenty Thousand Leagues under the Sea* (1873) by Jules Verne, although an earlier *Nautilus* had been built by the US engineer Robert Fulton in 1800, with finance from Napoleon. The submarine achieved the first submerged crossing of the Arctic in 1958. It was decommissioned in 1980 and put on permanent display in 1985.

• **navy** ▶
  **The navy's here** *See*: Altmark.

• **Nazi** ▶ The German abbreviation of *National-Sozialist*, the name given to Adolf Hitler's party; subsequently adopted worldwide for the party, its supporters, and their ideology. *See*: Fascism; Führer; Hitlerism; Kristallnacht; Mein Kampf; Night of the Long Knives; Nuremberg Trials; swastika.

• **NBC** ▶ National Broadcasting Corporation. A US nationwide television network forming part of the sprawling RCA (Radio Corporation of America) empire. NBC was originally established in 1926 to create programmes that would encourage the sale of radio sets, which RCA manufactured. After experimenting with television broadcasts in the early 1930s, NBC decided in 1935 to invest $1 million in making programmes for television (RCA also manufactured TV sets); in the same year it began transmitting experimental programmes from a station in the Empire State Building. NBC's commercial debut was the broadcast of the opening ceremonies of the World's Fair in New York on 30 April 1939, during which Franklin D. Roosevelt became the first US president to appear on television.

• **near-death experience** ▶ (NDE) A type of psychic experience sometimes reported by people who have recovered from the point of death. Descriptions of this experience are remarkably uniform; in most cases there is a sensation of leaving one's body (*see*: out-of-body experience) and travelling down a tunnel towards a brilliant light. This is usually followed by an encounter with a benign presence (often interpreted as Christ or a deceased relative), who dismisses the traveller back to his or her former life. Seen by some as evidence for personal immortality, NDEs are dismissed by sceptics as hallucinations caused by freak neurological activity in the brain or by such drugs as pethidine, which is administered in hospital especially after surgery. Amongst those to experience and describe an NDE was the atheist philosopher Sir Alfred Ayer (1910–89).

• **Neasden** ▶ The NW London suburb known for its ordinariness and for being a target of the satirical magazine *Private Eye*:

Why are we all beastly to Neasden?
Just Because it lacks spires and dome?
Or is it the curse of John Betjeman
Who christened it Home of the Gnome?
– *The Times*, 11 May 1991.

In 1991 the Grange Museum – probably the only local museum to be virtually inaccessible on a roundabout amidst the London traffic – opened a section called Naff Neasden. *See*: Disgusted, Tunbridge Wells; Metroland; Wigan.

• **nebbish** ▶ US slang, from Yiddish, for an ineffectual person who is unable to stand up for himself and therefore merits one's sympathy. It is derived from the Yiddish *nebekh*, from Czech *nebohý*, unfortunate. Like many other Yiddish words, it came into British English largely from America. It is also used as an interjection conveying sympathy:

He lost his job. Nebbish, with his handicap he'll never get another.

• **necessity knows no law** ▶ The words used by the German chancellor Bethmann-Hollweg in the Reichstag on 4 August 1914, as a justification for the infringement of Belgian neutrality.

Gentlemen, we are now in a state of necessity, and necessity knows no law. Our troops have occupied Luxembourg and perhaps have already entered Belgian territory.

• **necklace killing** ▶ A particularly vicious style of unofficial execution in which a rubber tyre, often filled with petrol, is placed around the neck of the victim in the manner of a necklace and then set alight. This method of killing began in the Black townships of apartheid South Africa as a revenge against those thought to have betrayed the Black cause.

• **Neddy** ▶ The popular name for the National Economic Development Council set up by the UK government in 1962. The numerous Economic Development Committees for particular industries that subsequently appeared were called 'little Neddies'. Neddy fell into disuse during the Thatcher years and was finally abolished in 1992.

• **needle park** ▶ Any public place in which drug addicts meet to purchase or inject drugs.

• **negative equity** ▶ An asset with a market value below the amount of money borrowed to purchase it. In recessionary times, for example, when property values are falling, a house owner who needs to move may have to repay a larger sum on the mortgage than can be raised by selling the house. This can present a serious problem if a home owner with a family has to relocate as a result of changing jobs.

• **Nehru dynasty** ▶ The domination of Indian politics for more than 40 years by the family of the statesman Jawaharlal Nehru (1889–1964). A disciple of Mahâtma Gandhi, Nehru became president of the Indian National Congress in 1929 and was imprisoned nine times between 1921 and 1945 for his opposition to British rule. He became prime minister of independent India in 1947 and remained in the post until his death, providing the political stability the new country desperately needed.

He groomed his daughter Indira Gandhi (1917–84) as his successor: although she was no relation to Mahâtma Gandhi, the name gave added strength to her claim to power and undoubtedly helped her to become prime minister (1966–77; 1980–84). She too was determined to uphold the dynasty and prepared her son Sanjay Gandhi (1946–80) as her successor. When he died in an air crash she was forced to bring her other son, Rajiv Gandhi (1942–91), into the political limelight. When Indira Gandhi's suppression of Sikh unrest led to her assassination in 1984 by Sikh members of her bodyguard, she was immediately succeeded by Rajiv as prime minister.

Rajiv continued the Nehru dynasty's policy of balancing rival religious and political factions until he lost office in 1989. In the third tragedy to strike the family, he was killed during the election campaign of 1991 by a terrorist bomb. By now Indian political life had revolved around the dynasty for so long that the leaders of the Congress (I) party immediately offered the post of party president to Rajiv's Italian-born widow, Sonia Gandhi (1949–    ), despite her lack of political experience and the fact that she was not an Indian woman. She declined the offer then, but became leader of Congress (I) in 1998.

• **Nehru jacket** or **Nehru tunic** ▶ A long narrow tailored jacket, buttoned down the centre, with a high collar, as worn by the Indian prime minister Jawaharlal Nehru (1889–1964). It is commonly worn by Indian men, especially in Kashmir and the Punjab. The style became fashionable in London in 1967, the jackets usually being made of black crepe. A variation of the style, variously called the **Mao**, **oriental**, **meditation**, or **mandarin jacket**, was made from cotton, heavy linen, or velvet; this version was knee length and had side slits.

• **Neighbourhood Watch** ▶ Groups organized by local residents, in areas affected by increasing crime, especially burglary. A system of round-the-clock vigilance is organized and suspicious activities and circumstances are reported to the police. The idea, which took off in Britain during the 1980s, was copied from similar schemes in America.

• **Nell** ▶
**And did he marry poor blind Nell?** A catchphrase from the early years of the 20th century, derived from a popular sentimental ballad of the period. The question implies that 'he' certainly did not marry poor blind Nell; the phrase is generally used as a euphemism for 'like fucking hell'.

• **Nenni telegram** ▶ The telegram of support sent by John Platts-Mills, Konni Zilliacus, and 20 other members of the British Labour Party to a pro-communist candidate, Signor Nenni, at the time of the Italian general election of April 1948. The Labour Party officially supported the right-wing Italian socialists; as a result Platts-Mills was expelled from the party; Zilliacus was also subsequently expelled.

• **neorealism** ▶ An Italian cinematic movement of the 1940s, exemplified by Luchino Visconti's *Ossessione* (1942), Roberto Rossellini's *Open City* (1945), and Vittorio De Sica's *Bicycle Thieves* (1948). These films have realistic contemporary settings and characters – often played by non-professionals – who face a range of social and economic problems; they were generally shot on location and make use of unobtrusive camera and editing techniques. The style went out of favour in the early 1950s but influenced the work of later Italian directors, such as Federico Fellini and Pier Paolo Pasolini, and Indian film makers, such as Satyajit Ray in his 'Apu' trilogy (1955–57).

The term is also applied to an Italian literary movement of roughly the same period, characterized by a concern for the accurate depiction of social conditions, especially among the poor. Notable neorealist authors included the novelists Alberto Moravia (1907–90) and Cesare Pavese (1908–50).

• **NEP** ▶ *See*: New Economic Policy.

• **nerd** or **nurd** ▶ A person who invites contempt, generally because he is considered boring, conventional, or lacking in social skills.

> Some reviews you can classify as revenge of the nerds – hate mail. – *The Independent*, 7 March 1991.

• **nervous** ▶
**Not suitable for those of a nervous disposition** A warning phrase that preceded certain programmes on British television in the 1950s, which probably acted more as an enticement to watch than as a disincentive.

• **Net, the** ▶ *See*: Internet.

• **Net Book Agreement** ▸ (NBA) In the UK, an agreement between publishers and booksellers that remained in force for most of the 20th century. Its formulation was one of the first tasks of the Publishers Association, set up in 1896 by Sir Frederick Macmillan and other leading UK publishers. The NBA, dating from 1899, ensured that booksellers sold all 'net' books at their cover price without a discount. Certain ('non-net') books were allowed to be sold at a discount; these were mostly textbooks, specialist books, publishers' remainders, and books sold in a national book sale. Supporters of the NBA argued that if some large booksellers and other retail outlets (such as supermarkets and garages) were allowed to sell bestsellers at a discount, this would deprive small and specialist bookshops of the profitable sales that enabled them to stock slow-moving books. However, in 1995 the Publishers Association was forced to abandon the NBA, when three major publishers decided to withdraw from it.

• **networking** ▸ A concept that first achieved prominence in the 1980s. It involves groups of professional people consciously trying to help each other in their careers by providing information, advice, and support. Forerunners of the system include the old-boy network as well as various clubs and organizations, such as the Freemasons, which are available to men only. Modern networking has largely been undertaken by women, who did not enjoy the privileges of such social organizations.

• **Neue Kunstlervereinigung** ▸ *See*: Blaue Reiter.

• **Neuilly, Treaty of** ▸ The post-war treaty between the Allies and Bulgaria signed on 27 November 1919. Bulgaria was forced to relinquish all territory occupied during the war, lost areas on her western border to Yugoslavia, and ceded Western Thrace to Greece (although she was guaranteed economic access to the Aegean). The Bulgarian army was limited to a volunteer force of 20,000 and the nation was also committed to pay massive reparations of 2,250,000,000 gold francs to the Allies over a period of 37 years. This claim was later reduced and eventually abandoned in 1932.

• **neutrino** ▸ A fundamental particle with no electric charge and zero rest mass, thought to travel at the speed of light. The existence of neutrinos was first postulated in 1930 by the Austrian physicist Wolfgang Pauli (1879–1968). Definite evidence for their existence was first obtained in 1956. It is now known that there are three types of neutrino, depending on the radioactive decay process by which they are produced. Because of their low probability of interaction with matter, they are very difficult to detect. The US writer John Updike (1932–  ) was inspired to describe them in a poem *Cosmic Gall*:

> Neutrinos they are very small
> They have no charge and have no mass
> And do not interact at all.
> The earth is just a silly ball
> To them through which they simply pass...

It is known that every second, millions of these particles are passing through the planet and through people. Physicists find this interesting. Updike is less impressed:

> At night they enter at Nepal
> And pierce the lover and his lass
> From underneath the bed – you call
> It wonderful; I call it crass.

• **neutron** ▸ One of the fundamental constituent particles of matter. A neutral particle with a mass 1840 times that of the electron, it is present in all atomic nuclei except for that of hydrogen. The neutron was discovered in 1932 by the British physicist James Chadwick (1891–1974); for this work he received the 1935 Nobel Prize for physics.

• **neutron bomb** ▸ A type of tactical nuclear weapon developed by America in the early 1970s. The neutron bomb is delivered by missiles or by artillery shells. The blast effects of the bomb are short-range, confined to a few hundred square yards, but the bomb is designed to throw off an intense flux of neutrons and gamma-ray radiation over a large area. The radiation can penetrate defences, in particular tank armour, and disable attacking troops who are killed instantly or die within days. The neutron bomb is regarded as a fairly 'clean' weapon in that there is very little general destruction or consequent radioactive contamination; it is, however, a very efficient means of killing people. It was developed as a strategic deterrent to discourage Soviet tank attacks in Europe. So far, it has never been used.

• **neutron star** ▸ A type of star thought to have contracted under gravitational forces so that the matter within it is extremely dense. Typically, neutron stars have a diameter of about 20 km (12 miles) but a mass similar to that of the Sun. The matter within the star is largely in the form of neutrons. *See also*: black hole; pulsar.

• **Neuve Chapelle** ▸ A battle of World War I fought on 10–13 March 1915, around the village of Neuve Chapelle, SW of Armentières, France. Field Marshal Sir John French decided to launch a British assault on Neuve Chapelle independently of the French; after a massive artillery bombardment of the area, British troops led by General Sir Douglas Haig pierced the German lines and captured the village on the first day. Before allied reserves could be brought up, however, the Germans, led by General Erich von Falkenhayn, managed to contain the breakthrough and recaptured the village a few days later. *See also*: Mademoiselle from Armenteers.

• **Never again!** ► Slogan first used after World War I, the war that was to end all wars. In the 1960s it was adopted by the Jewish Defence League as its slogan to commemorate the holocaust.

• **Never chase girls or buses (there will always be another one coming along soon)** ► A catchphrase that dates from the 1920s. Perhaps sound advice in general; whether or not it is apposite in a particular circumstance may depend on what the girl looks like or how frequently the buses run.

• **never had it so good** ► *See at*: good.

• **Never knowingly undersold** ► Advertising slogan for the John Lewis Partnership department stores, coined by the founder John Spender in 1920. It means that, to the best of their knowledge, the goods in John Lewis shops cannot be purchased elsewhere at a lower price. As a catchphrase it lends itself to numerous variations:

> The industry secretary, Peter Lilley, was sparkier than usual, describing Labour's various policy proposals as 'never knowingly underlaunched'. Roy Hattersley (never knowingly underlunched) was not present to hear this... – Parliamentary Report, *The Times*, 26 March 1991.

• **never-never** ► A colloquial name for the hire-purchase system. It is so called because, although the purchaser gets the article purchased immediately, payment for it continues for so long that it seems to be never-ending.

• **Never Never Land** ► **1.** The land of the Lost Boys, also inhabited by Pirates and Red Indians, in J. M. Barrie's Peter Pan (1904). The name is now often used to mean any utopian fantasy world – 'If she believes that, she's living in Never Never Land'. **2.** The uninhabited interior of Australia. Since the publication of *We of the Never Never* (1908) by Mrs Aeneas Gunn, the name has often been restricted to a particular part of the Northern Territory.

• **New Age** ► A general term used to describe the philosophy, religion, and social attitudes of various groups of people seeking an alternative to the materialism prevailing in contemporary Western societies. **New Agers** tend to be interested in Eastern or esoteric religious traditions, meditation, alternative medicine (especially homeopathy), health foods, and ecological issues.

• **New Age Music** ► Gentle, often soporific,

mood music intended to enhance meditation. It became popular in the late 1980s.

• **New Age Travellers** ► In the UK, young people who lead a nomadic existence, travelling around the country in convoys of ramshackle vehicles; during the summer they often congregate illegally on private land to hold impromptu 'festivals'. Many took to the road as an alternative to a life of unemployment and homelessness in the inner cities; they tend to survive on benefit payments supplemented by sales of craftwork, etc. The New Age Travellers profess an antimaterialistic philosophy and scorn the values of conventional society. For its part, conventional society regards them with a mixture of resentment and fear, accusing them of all kinds of lawless and antisocial behaviour.

In the 1990s there were estimated to be about 40,000 travellers (including gypsies, didicoys, and tinkers) wandering the roads of the UK in some 12,500 vehicles. The Criminal Justice Act of 1994, which prohibited unauthorized camping in vehicles, effectively criminalized the travelling lifestyle altogether:

> Britain is surely not such a pressured society that it cannot accommodate other ways of life... Wiping out the traveller culture would be an act of small minds. – *The Independent*, 22 June 1993.

*See also*: hippie.

• **New Artists' Association** ► *See*: Blaue Reiter.

• **new brutalism** ► *See*: brutalism.

• **new classical macroeconomics** ► An economic theory of the 1970s based on the concept of 'rational expectations'. According to this view, rational people will use the economic information available to them to formulate their economic expectations. For example, if the government increases public expenditure to reduce unemployment, taxpapers will expect to pay for this with higher taxes and may decide to reduce their current expenditure accordingly. The theory that reflation of the economy will be anticipated by individuals, who will adjust their behaviour so that the economy remains unchanged in real terms, is contrary to both Keynesianism and to monetarism.

• **New Deal** ► President F. D. Roosevelt's policy of economic reconstruction, designed to save America from the worst effects of the Great Depression. He announced the policy at the start of his first presidential campaign (1932):

> I pledge you, I pledge myself, to a new deal for the American people.

A relief and recovery programme known as the **First New Deal** was inaugurated in March 1933 and a **Second New Deal** concerned with social reform in January 1935. The **Third New Deal** of 1938 sought to preserve the gains made by its predecessors. *See*: National Recovery Administration.

• **New Economic Policy** ▶ (NEP) A series of economic reforms introduced by Lenin to quell mounting discontent with the Bolshevik regime. The policy was announced at the Tenth Party Congress in March 1921 in the wake of urban riots, strikes, and the Kronstadt mutiny; it amounted to a complete reversal of the previous economic strategy. Rigid centralized planning was replaced by a mixed economy; heavy industry and banking remained in state control but agriculture and the production of consumer goods were returned to the private sector, cash wages were reinstated for industrial workers, and the profit motive encouraged to promote economic expansion. The NEP was successful in reviving the economy and restoring popular support for the Bolsheviks; the early years of the NEP (1921–28) were also associated with a flowering of Soviet art and culture. Stalin's seizure of power in the period following Lenin's death in 1924, however, signalled the end of the NEP. In 1928 he announced the first of the Five-Year Plans, which enforced a return to centralized planning.

• **New Frontier** ▶ A vague commitment to a new and challenging agenda in all areas of US society, made by John F. Kennedy (1917–63) during his 1960 presidential election campaign:

> We stand today on the edge of a new frontier. But the new frontier of which I speak is not a set of promises. It is a set of challenges.

Once elected, however, Kennedy's concrete domestic achievements were disappointing. This is largely explained by his concentration on foreign policy and the extremely narrow margin of his victory, which deprived him of a popular mandate and Congressional backing for significant reform.

• **New Labour** ▶ The transformed Labour Party under Tony Blair. Following his election as party leader in 1994, Blair began to realign Labour's political stance, dropping or amending many long-held policies (including Clause Four) in order to appeal to the voters of conservative Middle England and the business community. The transformation achieved its aim, enabling Blair's 'New' Labour to be elected to government by a very large majority in 1997 after 18 years in the political wilderness. Despite this convincing electoral victory (repeated in 2001), New Labour has not lacked critics, most of whom accuse it of putting PR above principle and the black arts of the spin doctor before practical policies.

• **New Lad** ▶ *See*: laddish.

• **New Look** ▶ *See*: Dior.

• **New Man** ▶ A man who does not conform to traditional male stereotypes. Responding positively to the aspirations of the Women's Movement, the New Man has neither sexist nor macho attitudes, is unafraid to show his more sensitive side, and is prepared to play a full part in bringing up his children and running his house. Arguably, the notion of the New Man is largely a journalists' invention. In an age in which both partners are often required to work full-time in order to pay the mortgage, there is little alternative to both sharing the care of the children and the running of the household.

> New Man must be careful – it's all very fine to be sensitive, but it would never do to be taken for gay. – *The Independent*, 31 January 1991.

• **new morality** ▶ A popular term of the 1960s implying that the hitherto publicly accepted canons of morality (especially sexual morality) were no longer relevant, owing to the changing nature of society, new roles for women, and the advent of the Pill. While many welcomed the new freedoms, or saw them as inevitable, others rumbled gloomily about the unacceptable consequences of affluence, the diminishing of individual responsibility occasioned by the welfare state, the declining influence of Christian standards, and the championship of hedonism and self-indulgence by avant-garde writers. It was Lord Shawcross who dismissed the much-heralded new morality as 'the old immorality condoned'. For better or worse, however, the **permissive society** had arrived. Premarital sex was now openly enjoyed; homosexuality and abortion were legalized; cohabitation, divorce, remarriage, and one-parent families became facts of modern life. By the 1980s a new factor – Aids – had emerged and a more prudent 'new morality' began to evolve. Both men and women became more cautious about having sexual relationships with people they did not know well.

• **New Order in Europe** ▶ The coordination of Europe under the domination of Germany as envisaged by Adolf Hitler. *See also*: Tripartite Pact.

• **New Orleans style** ▶ The earliest style of ensemble jazz playing, originating in Storyville, the redlight district of New Orleans at around the turn of the 20th century. Classical New Orleans style featured collective improvisation by a front line of trumpet, clarinet, and trombone over a rhythm section of bass, drums, guitar, and piano. As the style was developed by such performers as Sidney Bechet (1897–1959) and Louis Armstrong (*see*: Satchmo), the solo instrumentalist gained greater prominence. It was superseded by swing in the 1930s but has frequently been revived (*see*: Dixie; trad).

• **New Party** ▶ A party established by Sir Oswald Mosley (1896–1980) in 1931 after his resignation from the Labour government. Mosley resigned when his *Memorandum*, containing radical proposals to tackle the economic crisis and reduce unemployment, was rejected by the party conference in October 1930. On 6 December the *Memorandum* was published and signed by 17 Labour MPs, six of whom then joined Mosley in forming the New Party in February 1931. The party failed to win any seats in the 1931 general election; all the sitting New Party MPs lost their deposits, except Mosley himself. In 1932 the New Party was renamed the British Union of Fascists. *See*: Mosleyites.

• **news hole** ▶ The part of a newspaper that is reserved for news stories. In America, this averages about 40%, with the remaining 60% being taken up with advertisements. By tradition, advertising space is sold first and determines the extent of the news hole. Rather than eating up news space, increased advertising sales produce more pages, which enables the paper to carry more news.

• **newspeak** ▶ Deceptive euphemistic language in which words change their meaning to accord with the official political views of the state or a party. The original newspeak was the language used by the state authorities in George Orwell's Nineteen Eighty-Four (1949). *See also*: doublethink.

• **newsreels** ▶ Short films (10–20 minutes long) covering news and other items of interest, which were a regular feature of cinema programmes until they were replaced by television news in the 1950s. News events had been recorded since the earliest days of film but the first actual newsreel (sequence of news items) appeared in France in 1908. The first sound newsreel was Fox Film Corporation's Movietone News, shown in 1927, which featured stories and interviews introduced by short titles and accompanied by a voice-over narrative (*see*: talkies). During World War II (and to a lesser extent in World War I), the newsreel was a valuable source of information as well as government propaganda.

• **new towns** ▶ The specially designed towns, built in a single phase, that have been created since World War II to relieve overcrowding in large cities nearby (sometimes also known as **satellite towns**). In the UK the New Towns Act (1946) allowed for the development of 32 such towns, coordinated by development corporations and combining public and private investment. The largest project was Milton Keynes in Buckinghamshire, which was begun in

1967 and in many respects exemplified the ideals and problems shared by all the new towns. Among the disadvantages have been a lack of individuality in large-scale complexes and, perhaps as a consequence, difficulty in promoting a sense of community spirit. *See also*: garden city.

• **New Wave** ▶ 1. A new movement in French film-making that began in the late 1950s; the term is a literal translation of the French *Nouvelle vague*. Leading directors associated with the New Wave included Francois Truffaut (1932–84), Claude Chabrol (1930–  ), and Jean-Luc Godard (1930–  ), all three of whom began as film critics. In their films the group rejected many established Hollywood conventions in order to develop the more challenging narrative and editing techniques pioneered a generation earlier by such figures as Hitchcock and Jean Vigo. The first masterpiece of the New Wave was Godard's debut feature *A Bout de souffle* (*Breathless*; 1959), a fast-moving and technically adventurous piece of work that seemed to announce a radically new approach to film-making. The sense of a coherent movement was created by the release of Truffaut's *The 400 Blows* and Alain Resnais's *Hiroshima, mon amour* that same year. However, the film-makers soon developed their own highly distinctive styles and it is arguable whether the New Wave ever really existed as a defined movement. Nevertheless, it exerted a permanent and liberating influence upon European cinema – not least by proving that it was possible to produce innovative films on the smallest of budgets.

• **New Woman** ▶ In the late 19th and early 20th centuries, a woman in favour of emancipation and female independence generally. The spirited heroines of Ibsen and Shaw are usually considered to epitomize the type. In the late 20th century the term was sometimes used to describe the new post-feminist woman who was supposedly able to enjoy the changes in society brought about by the Women's Movement while also indulging her femininity. However, like New Man, New Woman turned out to be largely a journalist's invention.

• **New World Order** ▶ A phrase used by US president George Bush on various occasions in 1990–91 to describe the new international situation created by the ending of the Cold War, the collapse of communism in Eastern Europe, and the disappearance of the Soviet Union as a world power. The phrase was intended to conjure up a vision of peace, stability, and cooperation between nations. For some, however, especially those in Muslim and Third World countries, it had a more sinister ring, suggesting a world in which America, effectively the only superpower, imposed its will on weaker nations. This impression was heightened by the phrase's ominous echoes (probably unconscious) of Hitler's New Order in Europe. The utopian promise of the phrase was soon dashed by the outbreak of the Gulf War in 1991 and the intractable civil conflict in Yugoslavia.

• **newzak** ► Relentless media repetition of scenes or reports of a disaster so that it loses its impact. The word was coined in 1986 with reference to the Challenger disaster, in which seven US astronauts were killed. Frequent repetition of the film of the fatal explosion of the craft deprived the event of its horror. Formed by analogy with Muzak, the word implies that overexposure makes news events as forgettable as background music in a restaurant or shopping mall.

• **NIC** ► See: dragon.

• **nice** ►
**Have a nice day** See at: day.

• **nice** ►
**It's turned out nice again** The catchphrase of the Lancashire comedian George Formby (1904–61), which he used to open his shows. It also featured frequently in his films, especially as he rose to his feet and shook himself down after yet another mishap had befallen him.

• **nice guys finish last** ► Catchphrase associated with the legendary US baseball manager Leo Durocher. The phrase, based on comments he made about the New York Giants team in 1948, was widely seen as the ultimate summary of Durocher's philosophy – and indeed that of any unscrupulous or determined sportsman, politician, etc.

• **nice little earner** ► See: earner.

• **Nice one, Cyril!** ► A catchphrase of the 1970s. Originally a line from a 1972 TV commercial for Wonderloaf, it caught on as a phrase that could be used in almost any situation requiring a complimentary remark. It came into its own in 1973 with the popularity of the Tottenham Hotspur footballer Cyril Knowles, whose frequent goal-scoring inspired the chorus of a pop song with this title:

> Nice one, Cyril
> Nice one, son
> Nice one, Cyril
> Let's have another one.

A few years later (1978) the phrase was an obvious choice for the title of an autobiography by comedian Cyril Fletcher. It had a new lease of life in 1989, when it was used by Access, the credit card company. The advertising hoardings featured the extremely large politician, Sir Cyril Smith, attempting to touch his toes, with the slogan: 'Nice one, Cyril...but Access is more flexible' (see: flexible friend).

• **Nice place you have here** ► An observation referring ironically to any abode, however shabby. It was popularized around 1942 by the radio programme ITMA, apparently having been coined by Tommy Handley during a visit to Windsor Castle.

• **niche market** ► A specialized market that can be served by small suppliers without involving competition from larger organizations. The term is sometimes used more generally of any comparable situation:

> The Home Secretary accused lawyers of ignoring their social responsibilities to protect their niche market with the local criminal fraternity. – The Times, 28 February 2001.

• **nickelodeon** ► A former name for a cheap movie theatre. The original Nickelodeon (so-called because the admission price was only five cents) was that opened by John P. Harris and Harry Davis at McKeesport, near Pittsburgh, Pennsylvania, in 1905. The first picture shown was The Great Train Robbery. This was the first real motion-picture theatre and following its success thousands of similar nickelodeons sprang up throughout America. The name was later used for other forms of cheap mechanized entertainment, particularly a jukebox.

• **Niehan clinic** ► A clinic in Switzerland run by Dr Niehan, which in the 1950s promised to halt, or at least delay, the inexorable ageing process. It was visited by many well-known personalities who parted with considerable sums of money, which may have made them feel better. They looked much the same.

• **Nielsen rating** ► The most widely used rating system for television viewing in America. The Nielsen Survey is conducted by the A. C. Nielsen Company, which samples 1200 US families to draw a profile of the nation's viewing habits. Sampling techniques have varied from asking viewers to keep a diary to attaching an electronic recording device to the television set. The Nielsen figures give ratings to individual shows, and these are used to set advertising rates. Programmes receiving poor Nielsen results are usually cancelled.

• **Nigel** ► British nickname for a certain type of arrogant upper-class male, usually imagined as wearing country tweeds and driving a sports car. Nigel was a popular name among the upper classes and in this context is always used pejoratively.

• **nightmare scenario** ► See: worst-case.

• **Night of the Long Knives** ► The night of 30

June 1934 when the leaders of the Brown Shirts (SA) and some Catholic leaders were murdered by the Gestapo, on Hitler's orders. The shootings (mainly in Munich and Berlin) actually began on the Friday night of the 29 June and continued until Sunday. Estimates of the number killed vary between 60 and 400; the SA leaders Röhm and Schleicher were among them. Hitler had decided to rely on the Reichswehr rather than risk dependence on Röhm and the SA. After the bloody purge Himmler presented the assassins with daggers of honour inscribed with his name.

See also: Mac the Knife.

• **-nik** ▶ A suffix, copied from the Russian, that became popular in the late 1950s and 1960s following the launch of the Soviet satellite Sputnik in 1957. Neologisms incorporating this suffix were generally derogatory and often applied to antiestablishment individuals and movements, e.g. beatnik and **draftnik** (Vietnam draft dodger). See also: refusenik.

• **Nike** ▶ 1. A US army ground-to-air missile for use against high-flying attacking planes or missiles; named after the Greek winged goddess of victory. 2. Tradename for a brand of high-tech training shoes that acquired a new status as fashion footwear in the late 1980s and 1990s. Nikes and other top-selling brands of training shoe became an important status symbol among teenagers despite (or because of) their exorbitant prices (see: taxing).

• **nil carborundum** or **illegitimi nil carborundum** ▶ A mock-Latin catchphrase meaning 'don't let the bastards grind you down'. 'Carborundum' is the tradename for an extremly hard form of silicon carbide used to make grinding wheels. The phrase nil carborundum is an echo of the Latin tag from Horace nil desperandum, meaning never say die, despair of nothing. The catchphrase was widely used by the US General Vinegar Joe Stilwell during World War II and later provided the title for a play (1962) by Henry Livings.

• **Nimby** ▶ An acronym for not in my backyard, coined in the UK in 1986 to describe people who were generally in favour of nuclear power but were strongly opposed to having either nuclear power stations or the resultant nuclear waste disposal units in the vicinity of their homes. The meaning has since been extended to cover other examples of the same syndrome. For example, a person of liberal views who petitioned against having a shelter for the homeless in his street could be described as a Nimby.

> The Best Kept Village competition...has been criticized by one of its judges who thinks the exercise has become tainted with suburban values...'I've always felt this was a silly competition,' he said. 'I call it the Nimby's Charter.'
> – The Independent, 1 June 1993.

• **Nimrod** ▶ An airborne early warning system developed in the UK from the 1960s onwards as a possible key factor in NATO's future defences. The project became increasingly bogged down by technical difficulties and was eventually shelved in favour of a US system in the late 1980s. The name was derived from the biblical Nimrod, described as a 'mighty hunter before the Lord' (Genesis 10: 9).

• **9/11** ▶ (nine eleven) The usual US way of referring to the events of September 11 2001.

• **Nineteen Eighty-Four** ▶ The last completed novel of George Orwell, which was published in 1949 and depicts a nightmarish totalitarian future. In Orwell's future state human thought and action are rigidly controlled by a brutal regime that makes extensive and frightening use of propaganda and surveillance. The novel was intended as a warning against the authoritarian tendencies present in contemporary societies and 1984 was, until the actual year was reached, something of a 'doomsday' date. Orwell based some aspects of the book on his experiences working in the ministry of information during World War II; he chose the year 1984 more or less at random by juggling the date 1948, the year in which he wrote the book. See: Big Brother; doublethink; newspeak; Thought Police.

• **19th Amendment** ▶ The amendment made to the US Constitution in 1920 under which women won the vote.

• **nineteenth hole** ▶ The bar of the clubhouse of a golf course. The standard course has 18 holes, so the player who has played badly can lament his defeat at the nineteenth.

• **1922 committee** ▶ See: Chanak crisis.

• **ninety days' wonder** ▶ A variant of the traditional 'nine days' wonder' coined in World War I to describe officers emerging from military colleges after only 90 days' training. The obvious inference was that 90 days was not enough to turn them into soldiers. The phrase 'nine days' wonder' arose from an old saying that there is no wonder so great that it lasts more than nine days.

• **ninja** ▶ Originally, a type of highly trained secret agent operating in feudal Japan. Their special role was to carry out tasks prohibited by the samurai code, such as spying, sabotage, and assassinations. Ninjitsu, the martial art of the ninja, taught the arts of deception and survival as well as more lethal skills. The term became generally known in the

West as a result of the hype surrounding the Teenage Mutant Ninja Turtles, although ninja had previously featured in some comics and computer games. It is sometimes mistakenly applied to the tools of the ninja's trade – a variety of implements combining simplicity, discretion, and deadliness. Palestinians in the occupied territories now use the term to describe a kind of makeshift sabotage device for puncturing the tyres of Israeli military vehicles. This usually consists of a nail hidden in some harmless-looking object, such as an old boot or rotten vegetable.

• **nipple count** ► The number of exposed female breasts appearing in a film, tabloid newspaper, etc., used as an index of its downmarket appeal.

• **nippy** ► Colloquial name for the waitresses at the popular teashops run by J. Lyons and Company from the 1920s. The waitresses were known for their cheerful and efficient service as they 'nipped' from table to table.

• **Nissen hut** ► A semicylindrical corrugated-iron hut with a cement floor, originally used for military purposes in World War I. It takes its name from Lieutenant Colonel Peter Nissen (1871–1930), its inventor.

• **nitty-gritty** ► A colloquial expression for the basic facts of a situation, as in 'let's get down to the nitty-gritty'. It is probably derived from a combination of the words 'nits' and 'grits', nits being the eggs of lice deposited in the hair and grits being slang for particles of excrement attaching to hairs near the anus.

• **Nivelle offensive** ► A major French attack on the German defensive line on the River Aisne made in April 1917 during World War I. Led by General Nivelle, it resulted in enormous French losses and triggered a major mutiny in the French army. Nivelle was replaced by Pétain.

• **nixon** ► US slang for an underhand or illegal deal, especially one to do with drugs. It is taken from the name of the disgraced president Richard Nixon (1913–94), who was not famous for his honest dealings. See: Tricky Dicky; Watergate.

• **Nixon doctrine** ► An informal statement to journalists made by President Richard Nixon in Guam in July 1969, that in future America would expect her overseas allies to provide for their own military defence, so that US involvement in local conflicts could be avoided. The statement was intended as a clarification of his policy of Vietnamization – the gradual removal of US troops from Vietnam and the transfer of responsibility for the war to the South Vietnamese (see: Vietnam War).

However, it was subsequently elevated into a general doctrine of US foreign policy by the Nixon White House.

• **NKVD** ► (Narodnyi Komissariat Vnutrennykh Dyel; People's Commissariat for Internal Affairs) The Soviet agency responsible for state security from 1934 to 1943. Succeeding OGPU (see: GPU), it became notorious for carrying out Stalin's purges. In 1943 its state security function was taken over by another agency, the **NKGB**, but it continued to manage internal affairs, becoming a ministry – the MVD – in 1946.

• **Nobel Prizes** ► International awards established under the will of Alfred Nobel (1833–96), the Swedish chemist who invented dynamite. First awarded in 1901, the prizes are presented annually in Stockholm for the most important achievements in Chemistry and Physics (both awarded by the Swedish Academy of Sciences), Physiology or Medicine (awarded by the Karolinska Institute), and Literature (awarded by the Swedish Academy). The Peace Prize is awarded by the Norwegian Parliament (Norway and Sweden were once united). A sixth prize, for Economics, was established in 1968, based on a donation by the National Bank of Sweden, and is awarded by the Swedish Academy of Sciences. All prizewinners receive an average of $185,000 (about £142,500), a gold medal, and a diploma. Nobel Prizes are the most prestigious in the world; although the judges have sometimes been accused of poor judgement or political bias, Nobel laureates are invariably men and women of exceptional achievement.

• **NOCD** ► See: NTD.

• **no-claim bonus** ► A discount set against the annual premium of a motor insurance policy in which no claims for compensation have been made on the insurer for a specified period. Its purpose is to discourage motorists from making frequent claims for minor damage and to penalize those that do make claims. Insurers maintain that a no-claim bonus is not a no-blame bonus, i.e. a motorist who makes a claim forfeits his bonus, whether or not he is to blame for the accident that caused the claim. No-claims bonuses are also given in other forms of insurance. See also: knock for knock.

• **no comment** ► A stock phrase widely used to evade unwelcome questions from journalists. It seems to have emerged in the 1940s as journalists became increasingly invasive; Churchill, for example, discovered it after a meeting (in 1946) with President Truman. Marlin Fitzwater, a tight-lipped

White House spokesman at the time of the Gulf War, once told journalists:

> No comment and you can feel free to use that no comment wherever you need it today. – *The Guardian*, 21 February 1991.

• **nodding duck** ▶ *See*: wave power.

• **Noddy** ▶ The little 'nodding-man' with a bell on the tip of his hat in Enid Blyton's stories for small children. He first appeared in 1949, together with his friend Big Ears. Noddy's innocent unsuspecting character is underlined by his name – a 'noddy' is a much older term for a foolish or simple person.

• **noddy bike** ▶ British slang name for the Velocette motorcycle used by police patrolmen until the end of the 1960s. It was considered a laughably inferior machine by serious bikers. The allusion is to the little car driven by Enid Blyton's Noddy.

• **noddy suit** ▶ A military garment worn by soldiers and other personnel to protect them against war gases and other chemical weapons. It is cumbersome to wear and inhibits freedom of movement. Such suits were in use in the Gulf War of 1991. The connection with Noddy is that a person dressed in this garment looks somewhat foolish and even childlike.

• **no-fault** ▶ 1. A form of car insurance in America in which the victim of an accident is compensated for damages by his own insurance company, whether or not the accident was his own fault (*see also*: knock for knock). 2. An approach to divorce proceedings in which neither party has to prove the other guilty of causing the marital breakdown. In the UK, elaborate plans to reform the divorce laws on these lines were drawn up in the mid-1990s, as it was widely felt that the existing system tended to exacerbate, rather than resolve, marital conflicts. These plans passed into law in the Family Law Act (1996) but were never implemented owing to the failure of pilot schemes in 1997–99. The government now intends to repeal the law.

• **no-go area** ▶ Originally, an area barred to unauthorized individuals for security reasons. Later, however, the term came to mean an area barricaded off from the police or military authorities by a paramilitary group or hostile crowd – most notoriously those parts of Derry and West Belfast controlled by the IRA in the late 1960s and early 1970s. Certain deprived and crime-ridden areas of the inner cities are also described as no-go areas, implying that even the police are wary of entering the area except in substantial numbers. The term is sometimes used metaphorically, to mean an issue or aspect of life that the person concerned refuses to discuss, as in 'his sexuality is a no-go area'.

• **noise pollution** or **sound pollution** ▶ Contamination of the environment by noise, *i.e.* sound that is undesired by the recipient. Noise is an inevitable accompaniment to modern technological society and is now well recognized as a form of pollution, together with air and water pollution. It is not, however, entirely a modern phenomenon: Julius Caesar once tried to ban daytime chariot racing in ancient Rome because of the noise generated by flying hooves and rattling wheels. Excessive noise, especially with prolonged exposure, can cause hearing impairment and even deafness. In milder forms such symptoms as increased irritability, fatigue, and headache may arise. Levels of noise are measured in decibels, with 1 decibel (dB) corresponding to sounds just audible to the human ear. The scale is logarithmic, so an increase (or decrease) of 10 dB approximates to a doubling (or halving) in loudness. A refrigerator humming (at a distance of 2 metres) measures about 40 dB, while a pneumatic drill at 5 metres registers 100 dB. The UK's Noise Abatement Society, founded in 1959, is dedicated to reducing noise from all sources to tolerable and reasonable levels. Counterparts in America include the National Organization to Insure a Sound-Controlled Environment (NOISEP), a coalition of organizations and individuals founded in 1969 to combat jet aircraft noise.

• **Nomanhan incident** ▶ The most serious of a total of 2800 separate clashes between Japanese and Soviet forces along the border between Siberia and Manchuria during the years 1932–39. The Japanese had invaded Manchuria and established (1932) the puppet state of Manchukuo, from which they threatened to invade Siberia. In mid-1939 skirmishes between Mongolian and Manchukoan troops near the village of Nomanhan on the fringes of Outer Mongolia led to a full-scale invasion in July by the Japanese Kwantung Army. The Japanese intended to inflict a crushing defeat on Mongolian and Soviet forces but were led into a trap by the Soviets under Marshal Zhukov and suffered 17,000 casualties. An armistice was signed on 17 July 1940, which marked the end of Japan's ambitions to acquire Siberian territory.

• **no man's land** ▶ The area between hostile lines of trenches in a ground war or any space contested by two opponents and belonging to neither. The term arose on the Western Front during World War I.

• **nonaerosol** ▶ Containers that do not use a propellent, especially a CFC, under pressure to produce

• Non-Intervention Committee •

a fine spray of a liquid. These products are also described as **ozone friendly**, as the release of CFCs into the atmosphere from conventional aerosols is thought to be a major contributor to the depletion of the Earth's protective ozone layer. Nonaerosol containers achieve their objective of producing a fine spray by means of a finger pump and a fine nozzle; this is often referred to as 'pump action'.

• **Non-Intervention Committee** ▸ An international committee formed in 1936 to prevent other countries becoming involved in the Spanish Civil War. As Germany and Italy, in particular, stepped up their participation in the conflict, the proceedings of the committee became increasingly irrelevant.

• **non-ism** ▸ A policy of abstaining from all substances, activities, etc., that might be injurious to one's health. The true non-ist will renounce not only drugs, alcohol, tobacco, and caffeine but every food product that has ever received bad publicity from scientists and nutritionists (for instance, wheat and dairy products). Abstention of this kind can become a damaging psychological obsession comparable to such recognized eating disorders as anorexia nervosa. The deprivation of pleasure that follows can pose a more serious threat to mental and physical health than the substances renounced. Non-ism arose as an extreme expression of the 1980s fixation with physical fitness and healthy living. The concept first came to public attention in the US in 1990.

• **non-refoulement** ▸ See: displaced person.

• **nonstick** ▸ Describing a cooking utensil with a specially coated surface that prevents hot food from sticking to it. Nonstick saucepans are therefore easily cleaned. The most widely used nonstick coating is Teflon (see: PTFE), a plastic discovered by a US engineer, Roy J. Plunkett, in 1938, although the process of using it to coat metal saucepans was not developed until 1954 (by Marc Gregoire).

• **non-U** ▸ See: U and Non-U.

• **nookie** ▸ Slang term for sexual intercourse. It is probably derived from 'nook', which the vagina may be thought to resemble. It has been common in America since the 1920s but was not used to any significant extent in the UK until the 1960s. Unlike the older four-letter words, nookie is not regarded as being taboo or offensive.

> Hendriks said he'd picked up with a skirt that was a warm baby and he was getting his nookie every night. – J. DOS PASSOS: *42nd Parallel.*

• **no problem** ▸ A formulaic response to a request, instruction, or thanks, implying reassurance or affirmation; in practice it tends to be given irrespective of whether or not there has been, or is likely to be, a problem.

• **norks** ▸ Australian slang for breasts. Like many other Australianisms, the term first became well known in the UK through the cartoon strip *The Wonderful World of Barry McKenzie* by Barry Humphries, which appeared in Private Eye in the 1970s. The word was apparently coined from Norco, the name of a cooperative dairy company, which, in the 1950s, used a picture of a cow with a huge udder on the wrapping of its butter.

• **Norris, Arthur** ▸ The central character in Christopher Isherwood's novel *Mr Norris Changes Trains* (1935). He was based on the flamboyant Irish-born Gerald Hamilton (1888–1970), a homosexual whose many notorious escapades included being gaoled in the UK for gross indecency and attempting to negotiate peace between Germany and the Allies in 1941 (he was arrested after being unmasked on his way to Ireland, disguised as a nun).

• **Northcliffe Press** ▸ Newspapers owned or controlled by Alfred Harmsworth, Lord Northcliffe (1865–1922), the pioneer of popular journalism in the UK. Northcliffe was a flamboyant and controversial figure, who liked to be known as the **Napoleon of Fleet Street**. The first issue of his *Daily Mail* appeared on 4 May 1896 and by World War I 'The penny newspaper for one halfpenny' had achieved a readership of one million. The *Daily Mirror*, which he founded in 1903, was aimed at female readers and reached the million mark in 1912, the first paper in the world to do so. In 1904 it was turned into a picture paper and pioneered the use of illustrations in Fleet Street. In these national papers, as in his earlier local papers, such as the *London Evening News* (1894) and *Glasgow Daily Record* (1895), Northcliffe tailored the content to satisfy a new working-class readership with a taste for sensationalism. In 1905 he moved upmarket and acquired *The Observer*, which he then sold in 1911 to concentrate on *The Times*, which he had controlled since 1908. Fears that he would cheapen *The Times* proved unfounded; he actually modernized the production process and turned the paper into a profitable concern. *See also*: Press Barons; tabloid.

• **North Sea oil** ▸ Oil reserves discovered below the North Sea in the late 1960s. The area is divided into British, German, Norwegian, Danish, and Dutch sectors. The first government licences for the exploration of the British sector were issued to oil companies in 1964; the initial discoveries were of natural gas. The first oil field, Montrose, was discovered by Amoco in September 1969. The Shell-

Esso partnership discovered the Brent field NE of Shetland in July 1971 and in the following year other major discoveries included Piper (Occidental) E of Orkney and Beryl (Mobil) and Thistle (Signal group) in the East Shetland Basin. Between 1964 and 1973, 266 wells were drilled in the British sector. By 1980 the UK had become self-sufficient in oil, enabling oil revenues to help the UK's balance of payments.

• **Nose, The** ▶ Nickname of the US singer and film actress Barbra Streisand (1942–   ), referring to her distinctive profile. The epithet has also been applied to the popular US singer Barry Manilow (1946–   ). *See also*: Schnozzle.

• **nosh** ▶ Slang for food or to eat; the word is from Yiddish (ultimately from German *nachen*, to eat on the sly). Like many Yiddish words it came into British English in the 1950s from America.

• **Nostradamus** ▶ The 16th-century French prophet whose obscure verse predictions became a tool of Nazi propaganda during World War II. It was the wife of Joseph Goebbels, the minister of propaganda, who first realized that several of the Frenchman's prophecies could be adapted to current needs. Nazi leaders were impressed by Nostradamus's references to a German leader called 'Hister' – although it was felt necessary to doctor his verses somewhat to ensure that they left no doubt about an ultimate German triumph. In 1940 leaflets containing his prophecies were released over France and Belgium, predicting German victory; the Allies immediately countered with their own versions of the prophecies, which not unnaturally came to the opposite conclusion.

The verses that some have seen as referring to Hitler contain these lines:

In the mountains of Austria near the Rhine
There will be born of simple parents
A man who will claim to defend Poland and
Hungary
And whose fate will never be certain.

Other verses allegedly predict air warfare, V-bomb attacks, the rise of Franco, and the Abdication Crisis of 1936:

For not wanting to consent to the divorce,
Which afterwards will be recognized as unworthy,
The king of the islands will be forced to flee
And one put in his place who has no sign of kingship.

The atom bomb was supposedly foreseen in these verses, which can be read to refer to the destruction of Hiroshima and Nagasaki:

Near the harbour and in two cities will be two
Scourges the like of which have never been seen.

Happily, Nostradamus turned out to be wrong in his prediction of a third world war at the end of the 20th century, involving an alliance of Western powers against the East.

In the year 1999 and seven months
From the sky will come the great king of
terror...
Before and afterwards war reigns happily.

However, some might say that (give or take a couple of years) this sounds uncannily like a prediction of events since September 11 2001...

• **not just a pretty face** ▶ Originally, a somewhat patronizing expression implying that an attractive girl is also rather clever. It is now almost always used ironically. For example, a man might say of himself, 'You can trust me to get this job done, I'm not just a pretty face!'

• **Notting Hill carnival** ▶ An annual carnival, the largest in Europe, that takes place in the streets around Notting Hill Gate in London during the last weekend in August. The carnival began in the mid-1960s with local DJs playing a variety of Black music, including reggae, calypso, and jazz, from the backs of trucks, which were followed through the streets by an appreciative audience. Although it has been marred by periodic violence and muggings, the carnival survives as the major expression and celebration of Black music and culture in the UK. It now attracts huge crowds of all races from every part of London and the south-east. The 2000 carnival was attended by an estimated 1.5 million people but resulted in the worst crime figures for some years – two fatal stabbings, 69 serious injuries, and 129 arrests.

• **not waving, but drowning** ▶ A phrase used of a person whose animated convivial manner masks an underlying despair. The allusion is to a drowning swimmer whose frantic arm movements are mistaken for a cordial wave. The phrase originates from a poem of the same name by Stevie Smith (1901–71):

I was much too far out all my life
And not waving but drowning.

• **nouveau roman** ▶ (French, new novel) An experimental form of novel that emerged in France in the mid-1950s (also called **anti-roman**). The term was popularized in a series of literary essays by Alain Robbe-Grillet (1922–89), which were collected and published as *Pour un nouveau roman* in 1963. In his novels, and in those of a wide range of other modern French writers, including Nathalie Sarraute (1902–99), Michel Butor (1926–   ) and Claude Simon (1913–   ), consistent characters, sequential plot, and the use of an all-knowing narrator are rejected as alien to the reality of experience. Instead, the novels dwell on minute descriptions of sensory impressions, mental perceptions, etc., which the reader is left to interpret for him or herself.

• **nouvelle cuisine** ▶ (French, new cooking) A style of cookery developed in the 1970s by several French chefs and food critics. It was essentially a reaction against traditional French cooking with its rich heavy foods and liberal use of such allegedly unhealthy ingredients as butter, sugar, starch, and cream. For this reason the style is also called **cuisine minceur** (French, slimness cooking).

Nouvelle cuisine emphasizes fresh ingredients, light sauces, and quick cooking to retain the texture and colour of the food. The food is light, often with unusual combinations of ingredients. One of its features is that it is always arranged attractively on the plate. Portions are usually small, and it has been criticized as a highly expensive way of not getting enough to eat.

• **Nouvelle Vague** ▶ See: New Wave.

• **now and for ever** ▶ A phrase that has been used as a title for three different films (1934, 1956, 1983), perhaps to convey portentous echoes from the 'Gloria' in the Book of Common Prayer: 'As it was in the beginning is now and ever shall be...'. It was used in the late 1980s as an advertising slogan for Cats, the longest-running musical in the history of London's West End.

• **no-win situation** ▶ A set of circumstances in which a person is faced with alternative courses of action that all lead to unsatisfactory results. The concept of a no-win situation arose in the 1960s from the mathematical study of strategy known as game theory. See also: Catch-22.

• **NTD** ▶ Not top drawer. An abbreviation used as a pejorative code word among upper-class snobs. Another example of this kind of thing is **NOCD**, 'not our class, dear'. See also: PLU.

• **nuclear autumn** ▶ See: nuclear winter.

• **nuclear energy** ▶ See: nuclear reactor.

• **nuclear family** ▶ A mother, father, and children, regarded as the standard social unit in modern industrial societies. The nuclear family is often contrasted with the **extended family**, which contains such extra members as grandparents, unmarried uncles and aunts, etc. The extended family is more common in traditional pre-capitalist cultures. Sociologists have suggested that the relationship between the nuclear family and capitalism is not accidental: the capitalist system requires a degree of mobility that was not required in traditional mainly agricultural societies. Since the mid-20th century, the stability of even the nuclear family has declined, as divorce, remarriage, and single-parent families have become increasingly common.

• **nuclear fission** ▶ A process in which the nucleus of a heavy chemical element, such as uranium or plutonium, is split into two fragments of roughly equal size. Usually it is induced by the impact of a neutron and is accompanied by the evolution of large amounts of energy. Controlled nuclear fission is exploited in the nuclear reactor; uncontrolled fission reactions are used in atom bombs (see: nuclear weapon). In spite of the fact that nuclear fission was one of the most important discoveries of the 20th century, opinions differ as to when it was first achieved, and by whom. It is generally accepted that the discovery was made in 1939 by the Austrian physicist Otto Frisch (1904–79) and his aunt Lise Meitner (1878–1968). Frisch did further work on fission at Birmingham University and wrote a report to Sir Henry Tizard (1885–1959), a scientific advisor to the British government, pointing out that an explosive chain reaction could be produced with a few pounds of uranium–235. He later worked on the resulting Manhattan Project.

> MASTER They split the atom by firing particles at it at 5500 miles per second.
> BOY Good heavens! And they only split it?'
> – Exchange in the film The Ghost of St Michael's (1941) starring WILL HAY.

• **nuclear fusion** ▶ A process in which two light atomic nuclei are brought together to form heavier nuclei; for example, the fusion of two hydrogen nuclei to form a nucleus of helium. Over all, the reaction results in the evolution of a large amount of energy; however, very large quantities of energy are necessary to initiate fusion reactions. Nuclear fusion is the process responsible for the energy produced by the sun and the stars. It is also the basis of the hydrogen bomb, first tested in 1952 (see: nuclear weapon). Vast amounts of money have been spent, so far unsuccessfully, on the development of a controlled fusion reactor for producing cheap energy (see: nuclear reactor). See also: cold fusion.

• **nuclear reactor** ▶ A device for producing energy from reactions involving the nuclei of atoms. Practical nuclear reactors depend on nuclear fission as the source of energy. The fuel in a fission reactor is the element uranium, and early reactors used enriched uranium; i.e. uranium containing a high proportion of the isotope uranium–235. When bombarded with neutrons of a suitable energy, these uranium nuclei split into nuclei of lighter atoms with the production of more neutrons. These additional neutrons cause fission of other uranium nuclei, releasing more neutrons, and so on – a self-sustaining chain reaction occurs and heat is produced. The heat can be extracted using a circulating liquid or gas (the coolant), which in turn raises steam in a separate circuit to drive a turbine. This generates electricity in the same way as a conventional power station. In atom bombs (see: nuclear weapon) the chain reaction is uncontrolled – the explosion depends on producing a large amount of energy in the shortest possible time. In a nuclear reactor the chain reaction is controlled by use of a moderator. This is a substance that can slow down neutrons. The slower neutrons have a higher probability of causing nuclear fission because they are not absorbed by the uranium−238 atoms, which is the most abundant isotope of uranium in natural uranium. The energies of these slower neutrons are comparable to those that would be produced at normal temperatures; the neutrons are called 'thermal neutrons' and reactors of this type are called **thermal reactors**. The first such nuclear reactor involving a controlled chain reaction was demonstrated in 1942 by a team of scientists led by the Italian physicist Enrico Fermi (1901–54) at the University of Chicago. Here, in the sports stadium, Fermi built what was then known as an **atomic pile** – a structure of about 40,000 blocks of pure graphite drilled with holes containing enriched uranium−235. At 2.20 p.m. on 2 December 1942 the pile 'went critical' producing a self-sustaining chain reaction lasting for 28 minutes. The British physicist, Sir Arthur Compton, reported by telephone to the management committee with the news that 'the Italian navigator has just landed in the New World'. He went on to say that the natives were friendly.

The first commercial power station using this principle was built at Calder Hall in Cumbria and opened in 1956 (see: Sellafield). Since then a number of different types of nuclear reactor have been developed. Thermal reactors are named according to the type of coolant used; e.g. **gas-cooled reactors**, **boiling-water reactors**, **pressurized-water reactors**, and **heavy-water reactors**. The **Magnox reactor** is a particular type of gas-cooled reactor in which the fuel rods are encased in Magnox (a tradename for a type of magnesium alloy). A different type of nuclear fission reactor is the **fast reactor**, in which no moderator is used. In these, the uranium fuel is enriched with plutonium−239. The core of the reactor is surrounded by a blanket of natural uranium which captures neutrons and is converted into plutonium, which can be further used as a fuel. Such reactors are known as **breeder reactors**.

Energy from fission reactors (**nuclear energy**) currently accounts for some 6.4% of the world's energy production. The benefits and drawbacks of nuclear energy production are, however, a highly contentious issue. Some regard nuclear reactors as a cheap and clean method of generating energy that is preferable to the use of coal and other fossil fuels (see: greenhouse effect). Others point to the hidden costs involved in disposing of nuclear waste and decommissioning reactors, as well as the environmental and health risks, particularly if there is an accident. They cite the problems caused at Three Mile Island and at Chernobyl. In the UK no new nuclear power stations are planned and most of the existing ones are due to be shut down by 2010.

In principle, nuclear fusion is a more promising method of producing nuclear energy. Fission reactors depend on uranium and there are only limited amounts available (uranium, in the jargon of energy science, is a 'non-renewable' resource). Fusion reactors would use hydrogen as their fuel, which could be obtained from water, and would lead to the availability of large amounts of cheap and 'clean' energy.

Many millions of pounds (as well as dollars and roubles) have been spent on research into fusion reactors – so far with little success. An early attempt was an apparatus built at Harwell in the 1950s called **ZETA** (Zero Energy Thermonuclear Apparatus). Modern research is based on a similar system called the **tokamak**, which was developed in the Soviet Union in the 1960s. See also: cold fusion.

• **nuclear waste** ▶ Radioactive material produced as an undesired by-product of nuclear reactors and other radioactive processes. The safe disposal of nuclear waste – which can remain radioactive for thousands of years – has been a matter of considerable concern to environmentalists. Methods used have included sealing the waste in containers and dropping them in the sea, and underground burial. In the 1970s and 1980s, the UK developed an industry for reprocessing and disposing of nuclear waste from other countries – leading to charges that the country had become the world's 'nuclear dustbin'.

• **nuclear weapon** ▶ A type of weapon in which an explosion is produced by a nuclear reaction rather than by a chemical reaction (as in so-called 'conventional' explosives). Nuclear weapons are of two types – fission weapons and fusion weapons.

Fission weapons depend on nuclear fission for their effect; i.e. the explosive power comes from the splitting of heavy atomic nuclei, such as those of uranium and plutonium. The basic technique is to bring together sufficient quantities of fissile material (the critical mass) to allow a self-sustaining uncontrolled chain reaction to occur. The original fission bomb was tested in 1945 as a result of the Manhattan Project. At 5.30 a.m. on 16 July the director of the project, J. Robert Oppenheimer (1904–67), saw the first mushroom cloud and, as he later reported, thought of a quotation from the *Bhagavad Gita*:

I am become Death, the shatterer of worlds.

A number of senior scientists on the Manhattan Project were horrified at the monster that they had created and suggested that the bomb, known as the atom bomb, should be publicly tested to demonstrate the power of the weapon to the Japanese. Oppenheimer and senior US politicians opposed this and the atom bomb was first used at Hiroshima on 6 August 1945. Three days later another atom bomb was dropped on Nagasaki, after which the Japanese capitulated. These are the only two occasions on which nuclear weapons have been used in warfare. Subsequently, several other countries developed and tested fission weapons: the Soviet Union first tested a nuclear bomb in 1949, the UK in 1952, France 1960, China 1964, India 1974, and Pakistan 1998. These countries are known to have atomic weapons but it is thought that some other states may have nuclear weapons that they have not tested. These include Israel, South Africa, and possibly Brazil and Iraq. Another 34 countries are considered to have the ability to produce nuclear weapons.

The second type of nuclear weapon is the fusion weapon, in which the energy of the explosion results from nuclear fusion; *i.e.* the joining together of small atomic nuclei, such as those of hydrogen, to form larger nuclei. The first **fusion bomb** (also known as a **hydrogen bomb**, **H-bomb**, or **thermonuclear weapon**) was tested by the Americans at Eniwetok Atoll in the Pacific on 1 November 1952. Subsequent tests were conducted at Bikini Atoll nearby. Other countries followed: the UK tested a fusion bomb in 1957, China in 1967, and France in 1968. Fusion bombs have never been used in warfare.

The power of nuclear weapons is measured by the equivalent explosive power of TNT. Typically, fission bombs have an explosive power measured in thousands of tons of TNT (kilotons); fusion bombs have a power measured in millions of tons (megatons). The effect of nuclear weapons is not confined to their blast, but also includes the effect of radioactive fall-out. The principle of the bomb was a consequence of Einstein's equation e = mc², and Einstein himself once said:

If I had known, I would have become a watchmaker.

*See also*: CND; Doomsday machine; neutron bomb.

• **nuclear winter** ► A period of darkness and cold weather postulated as the consequence of a thermonuclear war. The term was coined in 1983 by a group of US scientists that had been studying the possible after-effects of large-scale nuclear war. They suggested that nuclear weapons would, in a global war, cause uncontrolled firestorms. The smoke, particularly from plastics and other petroleum products in burning cities, would eventually cover a significant proportion of the Northern hemisphere, blotting out the sunlight for several weeks. According to the model, the low temperatures and lack of sunlight would result in widespread loss of plant and animal life. When associated with the destruction caused by the blast, and the consequent radioactive fallout, this would result in widespread loss of human life. The theory is contentious; some scientists have suggested that the results would be less extreme – more of a **nuclear autumn**.

• **nudge nudge, wink wink, say no more** ► A catchphrase deriving from the TV comedy show Monty Python's Flying Circus, which was broadcast from 1969 to 1974. In the original sketch the words were used by a prurient character played by Eric Idle, who asked people such insinuating questions as 'Is your wife a goer, then, eh, eh?', accompanied by much elbow nudging and prodding.

• **nudzh** or **nudnik** ► US slang for a chronic complainer or pest. It was first popularly used in the late 1960s, coming from the Yiddish *nudyen*, to bore, from the Russian *nudnik*, a boring pest.

• **nuke** ► Slang meaning to attack with nuclear weapons: a shortening of 'nuclear'. Originally (1970s) an Americanism, its use has now spread throughout the English-speaking world. It is also used in a more general sense, meaning to defeat heavily or annihilate, as in a sports match. Used as a noun, it is an abbreviation for a nuclear weapon, as in the disarmament slogan 'no nukes!'.

• **Nullarbor nymph** ► An unknown blonde woman who received wide coverage in the Australian press in 1972 for her public appearances in a semi-dressed state. Speculation about her identity became rife after she was reportedly sighted, half-naked, feeding kangaroos in the bush near the town of Euda; she was tentatively identified as the missing 27-year-old daughter of a railway worker from Adelaide.

• **number cruncher▶** Originally, a person skilled at manipulating numbers or dealing with figures, *e.g.* an accountant. Now, however, the term is more likely to mean a powerful computer capable of performing complicated mathematical operations on large amounts of data.

• **numbers game** or **numbers racket▶** An illegal lottery popular among the poorer sections of US society. Since the repeal of Prohibition in 1932 the numbers game has been controlled by organized crime on a massive scale; attempts by the authorities to stamp it out have proved ineffective. The person making the bet picks a three-digit number between 000 and 999. The bet, usually a minimum of 5 cents, and the slip are taken by the 'runners' (who work on a commission basis) to the area manager, known as the 'controller', who in turn is responsible to the 'banker', usually a syndicate appointee, who finances the operation. The winning number is picked from stock market figures or other suitable statistics published in the daily newspapers.

• **number 13 ▶** US teenage slang of the 1960s and 1970s for marijuana. M (for marijuana) is the thirteenth letter of the alphabet.

• **numerati ▶** A colloquial term for those employed in the financial world, particularly financial whiz kids. It was coined by analogy with 'literati', those who are familiar with literature.

• **Nunn May affair▶** The arrest and trial of the British nuclear scientist Alan Nunn May (1911– ) in 1946 for his involvement in the Soviet Canadian spy network exposed by the defection of Igor Gouzenco in 1945 (*see*: Ottawa spy ring). A convinced communist since his days as a student and postgraduate at Cambridge University, May was included in a British scientific team pursuing atomic research in Canada (1944–45) and passed information on the Allied development of the atom bomb to the Soviet Union. He was sentenced to 10 years in prison, served six, and in 1962 took up the chair of physics at Ghana University.

• **Nürburgring▶** The famous German motor racing circuit in the Eifel Mountains, centred around the village of Nürburg, south of Bonn. It was the site of the German Grand Prix from 1927 until 1976, when it was declared unsafe after a near-fatal accident suffered by Niki Lauda. It is now used for other races, rallies, and as a test track. The German Grand Prix is now held at Hockenheim, near Heidelberg.

• **nurd ▶** *See*: nerd.

• **Nuremberg rallies▶** Mass gatherings and parades organized by the Nazi Party for propaganda purposes, which were first held in Nuremberg in January and August 1923 and then annually on Party Day (July) from 1926. The 1934 rally lasted a full week and was the subject of Leni Riefenstahl's *The Triumph of the Will*, perhaps the most impressive propaganda film ever made. Hitler reserved some of his most dramatic speeches for the rallies, which were carefully orchestrated to generate fervent, near hysterial, support for the party and its leader; they were also intended to intimidate both internal and external opponents of the Nazis. During the 1930s the staging of the gatherings became increasingly elaborate, involving such special effects as massed torchlit parades and the use of powerful anti-aircraft searchlights to surround the audience in vertical columns of light. The design of the massive Nuremberg auditorium was entrusted to Hitler's architect Albert Speer in 1934, but the grandiose structure was never completed. It now remains a bleak monument to the evil of the Third Reich.

• **Nuremberg Trials▶** The trials of 23 Nazi leaders conducted by an international military tribunal set up by the allies at Nuremberg after World War II (September 1945–May 1946). The accused faced various charges of war crimes and crimes against humanity. Three were acquitted; Goering, Ribbentrop, and ten others were condemned to death; and the remainder were sentenced to various terms of imprisonment. Perhaps the most significant conclusion of the tribunal was the ruling that claiming to have acted on orders from a superior was not a valid defence.

In the event Goering committed suicide in prison before he could be executed; Hess spent over 40 years in Spandau gaol (*see*: Prisoner of Spandau) before also taking his life. Hitler, Himmler, and Goebbels all avoided arrest and trial by committing suicide in the last days of the war.

• **nutmeg ▶** Soccer slang for passing the ball between a player's legs and running round him to collect it, thus making him look foolish. Probably derived from 'nuts' meaning testicles.

• **Nye▶** Nickname of the Welsh Labour politician Aneurin Bevan (1897–1960). The son of a Welsh miner, he became a miner himself at the age of 13. A brilliant orator, he was elected MP for Ebbw Vale in 1929. As minister of health (1945–51) in the postwar Labour government, he presided over the formation of the National Health Service in 1948. In 1955 he was defeated by Hugh Gaitskell in his attempt to become leader of the Labour Party.

• **Nylon ▶** Tradename for the world's first synthetic fibre, introduced in 1938. With countless applications in spheres ranging from the clothing industry to engineering, nylon is a product of the polymerization of diamine with a fatty acid or the polymerization of a single monomer, thus forming a polyamide. The word was coined by the Du Pont company in 1938, but it is uncertain what reasons lay behind the choice. It has been suggested that 'nyl' was taken from the initials of New York and London, while '-on' was chosen by analogy with rayon. A less likely derivation is that the name was created when one of the research chemists involved in developing nylon exclaimed: 'Now, you lousy old Nipponese!' The image of nylon was enhanced during World War II, when nylon stockings, as supplied by US servicemen arriving in the UK, became the last word in luxury and were much sought after.

• **nymphet** ► A pubescent girl who is physically mature and sexually attractive. The term was first used in this sense in Nabokov's Lolita (1955). It derives from 'nymph' in its meanings of both a beautiful young woman and an insect in the transitional pupa stage.

• **NZEF** ► New Zealand Expeditionary Force. A volunteer army raised and commanded by Major General Sir Alex Godley (1867–1957) during World War I. The NZEF fought valiantly at Gallipoli and in other theatres of the war; its actions contributed to the forging of a national identity for New Zealanders. By 1918, of the 100,444 men who had served overseas in the NZEF, 58,500 had been killed or wounded, a significant proportion of the male population of New Zealand, from which the country took many decades to recover.

# O

• **O and M** ▶ Organization and methods. A form of work study that aims to increase the efficiency of a business by improving office procedures and the ways in which these are controlled by management.

• **OAS** ▶ *Organisation de l'Armée Secrète*. A French terrorist organization founded in 1961 to oppose the establishment of an independent Algerian state. Led by General Raoul Salan (1899–1984), the OAS conducted a campaign of bombings and other outrages in both France and Algeria, culminating in the attempted assassination of President Charles de Gaulle in September 1961. This incident inspired the thriller *The Day of the Jackal* (1970; filmed 1973) by Frederick Forsyth. The OAS disintegrated in 1962 after Salan was captured. *See also*: Jackal, The.

• **oats** ▶
**get one's oats** British and US slang meaning to get sexual satisfaction, used generally of men. It is related to the older phrase 'sow one's wild oats', used of a man's sexual activities before he settles down in marriage.

> ...the bridegroom...will not forget his wedding night...He has spent the last two weeks behind bars – getting plenty of porridge, but no oats!
> – *The News of the World*, 6 January 1991.

• **OAU** ▶ Organization of African Unity. A supranational African organization, similar to the UN in its purpose and structure, which is supported by all the independent African nations. It was established in 1963 at a pan-African conference in Addis Ababa, Ethiopia, with the aim of defending the political and territorial sovereignty of its members, settling disputes by non-violent means, ending colonialism, and promoting economic, political, and cultural solidarity in Africa. In 1991 the OAU adopted plans that envisage the creation of an economic community early in the 21st century. The permanent secretariat is based in Addis Ababa.

• **OBE** ▶ *See*: Order of the British Empire.

• **Obie** ▶ The annual theatre award, established in 1955 by *The Village Voice*, for off-Broadway (OB) productions.

• **Objective Burma** ▶ A film made in Hollywood in 1945, which led to a crisis in Anglo-American relations at the close of World War II. The film, starring Errol Flynn, suggested that US forces had been solely responsible for the defeat of the Japanese in Burma. British anger at this notion led to the film being withdrawn from cinemas in the UK. *See also*: Forgotten Army.

• **objet trouvé** ▶ (French, found object) An object displayed as a work of art, often with no involvement by the 'artist' beyond the act of selection. An object that has been tampered with or tidied up is sometimes called an *objet trouvé assisté*. The most celebrated *objets trouvés* are probably the **ready-mades** of the French-born dadaist Marcel Duchamp (1887–1968), who exhibited a number of mass-produced articles as sculpture. These included a bottle rack, a bicycle wheel, and a metal urinal (given the title 'Fountain' and signed 'R. Mutt').

• **Oboe** ▶ Codename given to a secret British invention of World War II. A rudimentary direction-finding device used by RAF bombers, it operated by means of a constant note sounded in the pilot's headphones, which changed in character when the aircraft veered off its designated path.

• **Obscuranto** ▶ A word coined by analogy with Esperanto, the artificial international language; it refers to the kind of pretentious language some people or organizations use to obscure rather than clarify.

• **occupational medicine** ▶ The medical speciality concerned with the effects on health of work and the workplace. During the 20th century, many new industries created new health hazards, prompting a revolution in the research and practice of occupational medicine; London's Royal College of Physicians founded its faculty of occupational medicine in 1978. Industrial diseases are often slow to develop and the link with a specific material or process is hard to establish. For instance, asbestos has been used on a large scale since the late 1800s. It was first linked with the lung disease asbestosis in 1907, but was not identified as a cause of lung cancer until 1935; it was a further 30 or 40 years before the present stringent precautions for its manufacture and use were laid down. A similar pattern applies to radiation and radioactive materials. Many of the early radiologists suffered illness or death because of their work, including Marie Curie, who contracted bouts of radiation sickness and ultimately leukaemia; her husband and fellow radiologist, Pierre, was also affected by radiation sickness. Health in the workplace is now regulated by a host of laws and guidelines.

• **Ochrana** or **Okhrana** ▶ (Russian, guard) The Russian Imperial secret police, a special division of the department of state police under the ministry of the interior, whose role was to protect the Tsar and the government from internal and external subversion. Its main task was the infiltration and exposure of revolutionary movements and the suppression of popular dissent; to this end its permanent elite corps of 15,000 gendarmes was supplemented by an extensive network of informers and agents provocateurs. Lenin had to flee to Switzerland from the Ochrana after the abortive revolution of 1905, and thereafter the Ochrana had considerable success in infiltrating the Bolshevik movement – Lenin's close colleague, Roman Malinovskii, who was appointed the first editor of *Pravda* in 1912, was an Ochrana agent. As the hated symbol of Tsarist political oppression, the organization was liquidated in 1917 by Lenin; however, it was soon replaced by the Cheka, the Bolshevik's own secret police, whose ruthlessness and efficiency far surpassed that of its predecessor.

• **ocker** ▶ A boorish uncultivated Australian; from a character with this name in a series of sketches shown on Australian TV in the 1960s (played by Ron Frazer). The nickname 'Ocker' pre-existed the TV character – it seems to have originated as a distortion of Oscar or O'Connor and for some reason was attached to anyone with the surname Stevens.

• **OCR** ▶ Optical character recognition. The process by which printed text is scanned, recognized, and translated into a form that can be read by a computer. Modern OCR systems use inexpensive flatbed, or handheld, scanners attached to a computer; character-recognition software converts scanned text into a format that can be edited by any standard word-processing programme.

• **October Club** ▶ A left-wing political club formed at Oxford in the 1930s by communist sympathizers; it took its name from the October Revolution.

• **October Manifesto** ▶ The proclamation by Tsar Nicholas II, following the civil unrest of 1905, that he would allow the establishment of an elected Duma. *See*: Octobrists.

• **October Revolution** ▶ The Bolshevik Revolution of October 1917 (November in the Western calendar), which led to the overthrow of Kerensky and the Mensheviks and the triumph of Lenin. The Revolution established the Soviet communist regime that lasted until 1991.

> Ten days that shook the world. – Title of a book by JOHN REED (1917).

• **Octobrists** ▶ A constitutionalist centre party in Russia supported by the landlords and wealthy mercantile interests, prominent in the Duma between 1907 and 1914. It took its name from the liberal manifesto published by the Tsar in October 1905. *See*: October Manifesto.

• **octopush** ▶ A hockey-like game played underwater in swimming pools. The players – there are six on each side – use sticks to push a flat puck along the floor of the pool towards the opponents' goal. It was devised in the UK in the late 1960s and named by blending 'octopus' and 'push'.

• **OD** ▶ Abbreviation, used since the 1960s, for a drugs overdose; to OD is to take an overdose. The term is now often used in more innocent cases of over-indulgence, as in 'I've OD'd on chocolate milkshakes, I never want to see another.'

• **Oddjob** ▶ The Korean henchman of Goldfinger in the novel by Ian Fleming (1959) and the subsequent film (1964), one of the most formidable opponents of James Bond. His steel bowler hat, fitted with a sharpened rim, proved a lethal weapon.

• **Odeon** ▶ Tradename of a cinema chain founded in the UK in 1933. The name is derived from the Greek *oideion*, meaning a hall for music; in Britain, it had become almost synonymous with movie theatre itself by the time the controlling company was taken over by the Rank Organization in 1941. The flagship of the chain remains the sumptuous Art Deco Odeon in London's Leicester Square, which is used to host many prestigious premieres, awards ceremonies, etc.

• **Oder-Neisse line** ▶ The frontier between Germany and Poland established at the end of World War II. It was recognized by Poland and the former state of East Germany in 1950 but not by West Germany until the 1970s; it was confirmed by the re-united Germany in 1990. The border itself follows the Rivers Oder and Neisse; it benefited Poland by giving it a large slice of pre-war Germany. *See also*: Curzon line.

• **ODESSA** ▶ A secret organization that arranged

for leading Nazis to escape from Germany at the end of World War II. In conditions of great secrecy, several notorious wartime commanders were spirited out of the country to South America and elsewhere, where the organization continued to protect their interests. Among those thus hidden was Adolf Eichmann (*see*: Eichmann trial). The name itself was derived from *Organisation der SS-Angehörigen* (Organization of SS Members). Frederick Forsyth based his thriller *The Odessa File* (1972) on this shadowy group. ODESSA was disbanded in about 1952 and replaced by the *Kameradenwerke* (Comrade Workshop), which had similar aims.

• **ofay** ▶ Black US derogatory slang for a White person. It is thought to be derived either from a backslang rendering of 'foe', or from the Yoruba (Nigerian) *ofé*, meaning charm or fetish. The Black poet LeRoi Jones (1934– ) uses the word in his rather bitter poem about the beats:

> O, generation revered
> above all others.
> O, generation of fictitious Ofays
> I revere you...
> You are all so beautiful.

• **off** ▶ **1.** Mainly US slang meaning to kill. It is thought to be an abbreviation of 'bump off'. **2.** US slang meaning to have sex with. This is probably an abbreviation of 'to have it off (with)'.

• **off-Broadway** ▶ In New York, a type of theatrical production that developed as an alternative to the commercial theatre of Broadway in the 1950s. So-called off-Broadway theatres became popular venues for challenging low-budget plays by such dramatists as Tennessee Williams and Edward Albee. Inevitably, when the success of these productions was recognized, business interests moved in and the better-known off-Broadway theatres (including the Circle in the Square) began staging more commercial plays. By the late 1960s a new **off-off-Broadway** theatre had developed to foster the original off-Broadway experimental spirit.

• **Officer in the Tower** ▶ Nickname acquired by Lieutenant N. Baillie-Stewart, who was incarcerated in the Tower of London in 1933 after being accused of passing secrets to Nazi Germany. He returned to the Tower in 1946 to serve a second sentence for participating in propaganda broadcasts from Germany during World War II.

• **Officers' Plot** ▶ *See*: Stauffenberg Plot.

• **Official Secrets Act** ▶ A series of British parliamentary Acts (1911–89), making it an offence to publish or communicate any official information that might be useful to an enemy of the state. The Acts before 1989 (notably Section 2 of the 1911 Act,

passed in response to a German spy scare) were so broad and indiscriminate in their application that it was technically a criminal offence to disclose any information, however insignificant, contained in an official document. For decades, critics of the legislation argued that its main function was not to protect national security but to protect governments from open scrutiny of their actions. The lack of definition within Section 2 of the 1911 Act was underlined when the UK government failed to suppress publication of *Spycatcher* (1987), the memoirs of Peter Wright, a former secret-service agent. The offending section was replaced by the 1989 Act, which redefined and limited the classes of information to be protected from disclosure.

• **Official Unionists** ▶ *See*: Ulster Unionist Party.

• **off-limits** ▶ Out of bounds. An expression originating in military contexts that is now common in the general language.

• **off-piste** ▶ Describing the practice of skiing on fresh snow, away from the pistes or regular ski slopes. Experienced skiers find this more challenging and relish the chance to escape from the crowds; it is, however, more dangerous. In the 1980s it was much favoured by younger members of the British Royal Family until a member of the Prince of Wales's skiing party was killed in an off-piste accident.

• **off-roading** ▶ Driving a car, motorcycle, etc., on unsurfaced roads or over rough terrain. In the 1980s this became an increasingly popular (and organized) leisure activity; its chief attractions are the pleasure of driving away from crowded public roads and the challenge this poses to both driver and vehicle. Other countryside users, such as walkers and riders, have come to regard off-roading as a dangerous nuisance that needs to be more strictly controlled. An **off-roader** is someone who takes part in off-roading or a vehicle specially built for it.

• **offshore fund** ▶ Any sum of money held in a country that is not the country of residence of its owner. Centres for such funds usually have low rates of taxation and simple exchange-control regulations. The British dependency of the Cayman Islands is one of the most widely used offshore centres. Offshore funds may also be available for investors in the form of unit trusts based in a tax haven.

• **offside** ▶ **1.** The side of a car that is to the right hand of the driver. **2.** A type of foul in various team games, such as soccer, rugby, American football, and hockey. The rules vary with each game but the principle is that players should not gain an advantage by advancing too close to the opponents' goal in relation to the prevailing focus of play.

• **off-the-cuff** ▶ Denoting a remark or speech that is unrehearsed, or a person who speaks in this way. The phrase probably derives from the practice of speakers who talk without notes, except for a few headings written on their shirt cuffs.

• **off-the-shelf company** ▶ A company that has been formed according to UK law, is registered with the Registrar of Companies, but is not trading and has no directors. Such companies can be bought from a business broker who specializes in this trade.

• **off the wall** ▶ Eccentric or wildly creative: originally a US expression derived from such games as squash and handball, in which the ball bounces off a wall at an unpredictable angle.

• **oflag** ▶ German name for a prisoner-of-war camp for Allied officers, derived from *Offizier* (officer) and *lager* (camp). The most famous of these was undoubtedly Colditz.

• **OG** ▶ US abbreviation, used by criminals, the police, etc., in the 1980s for 'Original Gangster', in the sense of a grand old man of the gang; a respected elder of the underworld.

• **OGPU** ▶ *See*: GPU.

• **O'Hara, Scarlett** ▶ The headstrong heroine of Margaret Mitchell's bestselling novel Gone with the Wind (1936) and the subsequent Hollywood film (1939). Scarlett was based on the author's maternal grandmother, Annie Fitzgerald Stephens (1844–1934). She was the daughter of a Southern plantation owner and witnessed the burning of Atlanta in 1864 before returning to the neglected family farm. The search for an actress to play Scarlett in the hugely successful film became part of Hollywood legend: after some 90 screen tests, considerable speculation, and a good deal of wrangling, the part went to the relatively unknown Vivien Leigh.

• **oik** ▶ 1. British derogatory slang for an uncouth and uncultured youth; often used by public schoolboys for the boys at state schools or by officers in the services for other ranks. Working-class males, however, also use it deprecatingly of themselves. Its origin is uncertain but it may have been coined in imitation of uncultured vowel sounds. 2. Acronym for *one income and kids*. British slang of the 1980s, formed on the basis of dinkie and yuppie. *See also*: oink.

• **oilberg** ▶ An oil-carrying supertanker: coined from 'oil' and 'iceberg'.

• **oily rag** ▶ 1. British slang for an inexperienced or inept motor mechanic, *i.e.* one who might be given the task of cleaning up oil and grease with a rag. 2. British rhyming slang from the 1950s for a fag, a cigarette.

• **oink** ▶ Acronym for *one income no kids*. British slang of the 1980s, formed on the same basis as dinkie and yuppie. *See also*: oik.

• **Okhrana** ▶ *See*: Ochrana.

• **Okinawa** ▶ The largest of the Japanese Ryukyu Islands, which in World War II became the scene of fierce fighting between Japanese and US forces. After a huge amphibious operation, in which it faced fanatical opposition from Japanese troops and attacks by kamikaze pilots, America established control over this island. It was not returned to Japan until 1972.

• **Oklahoma bombing** ▶ A terrorist attack that took place on 19 April 1995, when a bomb was detonated at the Alfred P. Murrah federal building in Oklahoma City. The resulting blast killed 168 people, including 19 children in the building's day-care centre, making it America's worst act of mass murder before the events of September 11. A further 600 people were injured in the explosion, which damaged dozens of nearby buildings and cars and left a crater in the street.

The bomb had been planted and detonated by Timothy McVeigh, a 27-year-old ex-soldier with fanatical right-wing views. McVeigh had apparently been angry with the US government's handling of the Waco siege, in which 75 members of the Branch Davidian religious cult had been killed after federal troops were involved. The Waco siege ended two years to the day before the bombing. Although McVeigh claimed to have acted alone, suspicions of a wider conspiracy involving extreme right-wing groups have remained.

A defiant McVeigh was sentenced to death in 1997 and executed by lethal injection in 2001. In a macabre finale, live footage of the execution was beamed to an audience of some 270 survivors of the bombing and relatives of victims in Oklahoma. In 2000 a memorial garden was opened on the site once occupied by the federal building; a haunting feature of the garden is the presence of 168 empty bronze chairs.

• **Old Bill** ▶ 1. *See*: a better 'ole *at* better. 2. *See*: Bill.

• **Old Blood 'n' Guts** ▶ Nickname of US General George Smith Patton (1885–1945), commander of the US Seventh and Third Armies in World War II. He was famous for the pearl-handled revolver he always wore and his bluff attitude towards fellow-commanders, especially Montgomery. His premature death resulted from injuries received in a car crash. The US Patton tank was named in his honour.

• **Old Blue Eyes** ▶ Nickname of Frank Sinatra (1915–98), the US singer and film star. Sinatra's numerous hit records over five decades established him as perhaps the finest ever exponent of US popular song in the Tin Pan Alley tradition. His enigmatic character and wayward personal life also contributed to public fascination. David Niven once summed up Sinatra's contradictory qualities by listing 'his talent, his generosity, his ruthlessness, his kindness, his gregariousness, his loneliness, and his rumoured links with the Mob...'

• **old boiled egg** ▶ A facetious interpretation of the initials OBE (Officer of the Order of the British Empire), an honour awarded for public services. The term has been used since the 1930s in the Civil Service.

• **old-boy network** ▶ The long-established informal process by which old schoolfriends, ex-army colleagues, etc., gain employment or preferment by seeking favours based solely on the fact that they share the same background. See also: networking.

• **Old Contemptibles** ▶ The British Expeditionary Force (see: BEF) of 160,000 men that left Britain in 1914 to join the French and Belgian armies in their fight against Germany. The soldiers gave themselves this name from an army order (amost certainly apocryphal) said to have been given at Aix on 19 August by the Kaiser.

> It is my royal and imperial command that you exterminate the treacherous English, and walk over General French's contemptible little army.

It is said by some that actually he called the BEF 'a contemptibly little army', which is not nearly so disparaging.

The surviving veterans held their last parade at the garrison church of All Saints, Aldershot, on Sunday 4 August 1974, in the presence of Queen Elizabeth II, who took tea with them before their final dispersal.

• **Old Crock** ▶ Nickname of the US General Anthony C. McAuliffe (1898–1975), who commanded US forces in the Battle of the Bulge (see: Ardennes Offensive) in 1944 with considerable success. He coined his own self-deprecating nickname but became very popular among his troops when, in reply to a German demand for his surrender, he responded simply 'Nuts!'

• **Old Dun Cow** ▶ A derisive nickname given by the troops to the steamer *River Clyde* beached at Gallipoli in 1915 during World War I. It was probably a reference to the popular song containing the words 'The Old Dun Cow she's done for now', the Old Dun Cow in question being a public house that had run dry.

• **Old Dutch** ▶ Nickname of the singer and comedian Albert Chevalier (1861–1923), a star of the music hall in the early years of the 20th century. An informal Cockney expression for one's wife (an abbreviation of 'duchess'), the term became associated with Chevalier after his success with the song 'My Old Dutch'.

• **Old Fourlegs** ▶ A nickname for the coelacanth, a species of fish held to be extinct for millions of years until a specimen was caught in 1938 off East London, South Africa. Another was caught off the Comoro Islands, north of Madagascar, in 1952 and subsequently numerous others were found. The lobate fins, which could be used more or less as limbs, give rise to the name.

> My surprise would have been little greater if I had seen a dinosaur walking down the street.
> – J. L. B. SMITH, British organic chemist who identified the first specimen.

• **Old Grey Whistle Test** ▶ In Tin Pan Alley, songwriters used to play their compositions to the 'old greys', the elderly doorkeepers and other workers in the offices of the music publishers. If the 'old greys' were still whistling the tunes after a week or so, then they were likely to be worth publishing. *The Old Grey Whistle Test* subsequently became the title of a long-running rock music programme on BBC television (1970s).

• **Old Groaner** ▶ Nickname for Harry Lillis Crosby (1904–77), known worldwide as **Bing Crosby** (and in German as **Der Bingle**). The foremost 'crooner' of the 1920s and 1930s, he became one of the best-selling recording artists of all time and went on to star in some 60 films. He received the nickname Bing in allusion to a cartoon character who, like him, had large sticking-out ears.

• **Old Possum** ▶ Nickname of the poet T. S. Eliot, made widely familiar by the title of his *Old Possum's Book of Practical Cats* (1939). Years later the poems enjoyed enormous success as the basis of the Lloyd Webber musical *Cats* (1981; see: Macavity). The nickname was invented by Eliot's friend and fellow poet Ezra Pound, who saw Eliot's adoption of a highly correct and conventional public persona as a way of 'playing possum' – *i.e.* pretending to be dead or asleep when threatened.

• **Old Slow Hand** ▶ Nickname of the British blues rock guitarist Eric Clapton (1945– ), noted for his apparently effortless mastery of electric guitar technique.

• **Oldsmobile ▸** The first US mass-produced car (1901–06), made by Ransom Eli Olds (1864–1950) at his factory in Lansing, Michigan. The three horsepower curved-dash 'merry' Oldsmobile was little more than a motorized horse carriage with tiller steering, but at a price of $650 it was within the financial means of a large section of the US population and became the best-selling car in the world. Production of Oldsmobiles ceased in 2000.

• **Old soldiers never die, they simply fade away ▸** A modern proverb that was originally a line in a World War I marching song popular with the British Army. The song parodied the gospel hymn 'Kind Words Never Die'. The saying later became associated with General Douglas MacArthur, who quoted it during a valedictory speech to Congress in 1951 (*see:* American Caesar).

• **Old Timber ▸** Nickname of the British conductor Sir Henry Wood (1869–1944), who founded the London Promenade concerts (*see* prom). Every year on the last night of the Proms, a garland is placed on the shoulders of a bust of Sir Henry in the Albert Hall.

• **Old Tom ▸** The nickname given to a killer whale that established a remarkable relationship with the whalers of the township of Eden in New South Wales. Old Tom was the best known member of a pack of killer whales, who had learned to track down and weaken larger whales so that the whalers were able to kill them easily with their harpoons; the killer whales then fought over the prized tongue and lips of the carcass. Old Tom, who had made his first appearance as long ago as 1843, died in 1930, after which the collaboration ceased. Old Tom's skeleton is preserved in Eden's Museum.

• **Old Turkey Neck ▸** *See:* Vinegar Joe.

• **Olduvai Gorge ▸** A canyon in the Serengeti Plain of Tanzania, near the Ngorongoro crater, that has yielded a wealth of fossilized remains of prehistoric apes and the hominid ancestors of mankind. The most striking finds at Olduvai were made by the British anthropologists Louis and Mary Leakey. In 1959 Mary Leakey discovered the first remains of a sturdy ape, which they named *Zinjanthropus boisei*, now known as *Australopithecus boisei*. Further work by the Leakeys led to the discovery, announced in 1964, of *Homo habilis* (**Handy Man**), a probable ancestor of modern man. This early hominid was the likely user of the Oldowan tools found at the site – crude scrapers, choppers, and other artefacts made from chipped pebbles. The discovery of Handy Man and the other remains in Olduvai Gorge caused a radical re-evaluation of thinking about man's origins with the realization that man emerged much earlier than previously supposed and in Africa, rather than in Asia.

• **Old Vic ▸** The theatre in Waterloo Road, London, that became famous for its Shakespearean productions under the management of Lilian Baylis (1874–1937), who took over from her aunt, Emma Cons, in 1912. It was opened in 1818 as the Royal Coburg and was renamed the Royal Victoria in 1833. It served as the temporary home of the National Theatre company from 1964 until 1976 (*see:* Royal National Theatre). The theatre was put up for sale in 1998 but rescued by a consortium; its future remains uncertain.

• **O level ▸** *See:* GCE.

• **olim ▸** Jewish immigrants to Israel: a Hebrew plural noun meaning pilgrims (literally, 'those who ascend'). *See also:* aliyah; chozrim; yordim.

• **Olympic Games ▸** An international sporting contest held every four years. Modelled on the athletic festival of the ancient Greeks, held every fourth year at Olympia in July, the games were revived in their modern form in 1896, the first being held at Athens. The Winter Olympics were first held in 1924.

> The most important thing in the Olympic Games is not the winning but taking part...The essential thing in life is not conquering but fighting well. – PIERRE DE COUBERTIN, founder of the modern Olympics, 24 July 1908.

• **OM ▸** Order of Merit. A British order of chivalry established in 1902 by Edward VII on the occasion of his coronation. The order, which confers no title and is limited to 24 members and the sovereign, is open to both sexes and is awarded for special distinction in a particular field. Because the award is often conferred very late in life, it is sometimes jokingly styled the Order of the Morgue.

• **Omagh bomb ▸** The explosion of a terrorist bomb in the small market town of Omagh, Co. Tyrone, Northern Ireland, on 15 August 1998. Twenty-eight people, including nine children and a pregnant woman, were killed in the blast, making this the worst single atrocity of the current Troubles. The bomb was planted by the Real IRA, an IRA splinter group hostile to the Good Friday Agreement signed four months earlier, and was widely seen as a deliberate attempt to derail the peace process. As such, it was condemned from across the sectarian divide and probably had the opposite effect to that intended. No one has ever been arrested for the incident, although it is alleged that both British

Intelligence and the mainstream Republican leadership have a good idea of who ordered and executed the bombing.

• **Omaha** ▶ Allied codename given to a beach NW of Bayeux, one of the main landing sites for US forces on D-Day. It became known as 'bloody Omaha' because of the fierce German resistance encountered there. *See also*: Gold; Juno; Sword; Utah.

• **ombudsman** ▶ (Swedish, commissioner) An official appointed to protect the rights of the citizen against infringement by the government. The post originated in Sweden, which has had an ombudsman since 1809; Denmark has had one since 1955 and Norway since 1962. New Zealand was the first Commonwealth country to appoint such a commissioner (1962). The UK appointed a **Parliamentary Commissioner for Administration**, commonly known as 'the Ombudsman', in 1967. An ombudsman for local government was appointed in 1974 and ombudsmen have also been set up for insurance (1981), banking (1986), building societies (1987), unit trusts (1988), investment (1989), legal services (1990), pensions (1993), and housing (1996).

• **Omega workshops** ▶ A group of design workshops founded in 1913 by the British art critic Roger Fry (1866–1934). Following the example of William Morris, he hoped to bring a contemporary artistic sensibility to the production of useful everyday objects. Craftsmen were engaged to create furniture, textiles, pottery, etc., which were then decorated by a team of artists associated with the Bloomsbury Group (including Vanessa Bell and Duncan Grant). The workshops were run on a collective basis and the finished products identified only with an omega (Ω) sign. The project was a commercial failure and collapsed in 1919.

• **One and Only** ▶ Nickname of the US striptease artiste of the 1940s Phyllis Dixey, since applied almost universally to show-business stars, regardless of their merits. The British comedian Max Miller was also known by this nickname.

• **one-armed bandit** ▶ A gambling machine operated by the insertion of coins and the pulling of an arm or lever, so called because it frequently 'robs' one of loose change. A **fruit machine** is a one-armed bandit in which pulling the lever gives random combinations of symbols representing different fruits on the display. Certain combinations win a prize.

• **One Day of the Year** ▶ *See*: Anzac Day.

• **Onedin Line, The** ▶ A BBC TV series of the 1970s about the tall ships commanded by a 19th-century sea captain, James Onedin. The one feature of the series that everyone remembers is the use made of the ballet music from *Spartacus* (1954) by the Armenian composer Aram Khachaturian (1903–78). This rousing theme music, which was virtually unknown in the UK before *The Onedin Line*, has become immensely popular as a result of it.

• **one-hour dress** ▶ A simple dress popular in the 1920s, consisting of a chemise with kimono sleeves and short skirt. It was so called because any competent dressmaker could, it was claimed, make this dress in just one hour.

• **One Nation group** ▶ A group of liberal Conservatives, formed in 1950 soon after the general election to press for a greater financial commitment to the social services by the Conservative government. The pamphlet, *One Nation* (in homage to Disraeli's paternalistic conservativism), was published in October 1950 and, as intended, strongly influenced government social policy.

• **one-night stand** ▶ A casual sexual encounter lasting only one night. Originally this was a show-business expression denoting an engagement by a theatrical touring company for one night only.

• **one over the eight** ▶ Drunk. Apparently eight pints of beer are considered a reasonable amount for the average man to drink – one more tips the balance.

• **one small step for man** ▶ The words used by the US astronaut Neil Armstrong (1930–  ) at 3.56 a.m. British Summer Time on 21 July 1969, as he stepped off the ladder of the lunar module *Eagle*. Millions of television viewers throughout the world heard him say:

> That's one small step for man, one giant leap for mankind.

It is generally thought that he intended to say 'one small step for a man...' and that he had fluffed his lines. Armstrong himself, in his autobiography, claimed that he had used the words 'a man' rather than 'man', but that the indefinite article had been lost in the radio transmission. President Nixon, phoning the astronauts to congratulate them on the successful mission, made the extravagant claim that:

> This is the greatest week in the history of the world since the Creation.

• **One step forward, two steps back** ▶ A catchphrase reflecting on the nature of progress. It was used by Lenin as the title of his book about the state of the Communist Party in 1904.

• **one-stop** ▶ Denoting comprehensive shopping facilities provided in one large hypermarket so that all one's shopping can be completed during one stop of the car. The meaning was later extended to any business able to supply all a customer's needs within a particular field (such as financial services).

• **One-Take** ► Nickname given to a number of public figures who were noted for giving flawless performances of one kind or another. Among those to receive this accolade were Bing Crosby (*see*: Old Groaner), who rarely needed to record anything twice, and the child star Shirley Temple (*see*: Curly Top).

• **one under** ► British police slang for a person who has committed suicide by jumping under a train.

• **one-upmanship** ► An expression coined by the British humorist Stephen Potter (1900–70) for the art of making oneself appear superior to someone else. It is also the title of a book setting out the details of this art, which was published in 1952. *See also*: gamesmanship; lifemanship.

• **on-going situation** ► See: situation.

• **onion boat** ► See: come over with the onion boat.

• **on message** ► See: singing from the same hymn sheet.

• **Oomph Girl** ► Nickname of the US film actress Ann Sheridan (1915–67), reflecting the determined optimistic characters she played in such films of the 1930s and 1940s as *King's Row* (1941). She herself disliked the name, saying that Oomph was 'the sound a fat man makes when he bends over to tie his laces in a phone booth'.

• **007** ► See: Bond, James.

• **op art** ► Abstract art that exploits various forms of common optical illusion to create its effects. Op art became popular during the 1960s, when Victor Vasarely (1908–97) and Bridget Riley (1931– ) became well known for their use of repeated geometrical patterns, such as fine grids and spirals, that appear to pulsate or flicker when focused on. The term, a play on 'optical' and pop art, was coined by *Time* magazine in 1964.

• **OPEC** ► Organization of Petroleum Exporting Countries. An international cartel of oil producers formed in 1960 to combat exploitation by Western oil companies and encourage the nationalization of oil production in member countries. Current members include Venezuela, Iraq, Iran, Kuwait, Saudi Arabia, Indonesia, Libya, Qatar, United Arab Emirates, Algeria, and Nigeria. Ecuador left in 1992 and Gabon in 1995. OPEC has overseen a significant transfer of wealth from the industrialized nations to those developing countries with oil deposits.

• **open diplomacy** ► The first of Woodrow Wilson's demands in his Fourteen Points for the peace settlement in Europe after World War I: 'open covenants of peace openly arrived at, after which there shall be no private international understandings of any kind.' The reality failed to live up to the idealistic rhetoric; although the Versailles Treaty was an 'open treaty' in the sense that its terms were made public, it was negotiated in secret, ultimately by President Wilson, Clemenceau, and Lloyd George.

• **open-heart surgery** ► Surgery in which the heart is exposed, for instance to repair or replace diseased valves, to insert grafts into the coronary arteries (*see*: bypass surgery), or to repair other heart lesions. Such operations require a bloodless and motionless heart; they have been made feasible by the development of the heart-lung machine, introduced in 1953.

• **open marriage** ► A version of marriage that developed in the 1970s. In an open marriage each spouse accepts the other's right to a fully independent life, including the right to enjoy sexual and emotional relationships with other people. Although advocates of open marriage claimed that it would avoid the guilt, lies, and hurt usually associated with extramarital affairs, experience suggests that jealousy is not so easily eradicated and that most relationships require at least some attempt at fidelity if they are to survive. *See*: free love.

• **open prison** ► A low-security gaol for petty and non-violent offenders who are considered to be sufficiently trustworthy not to need to be locked up.

• **Open University** ► A British university founded in 1969 with the express objective of providing further education opportunities for part-time (usually mature) students who, because of other calls upon their time or because of their lack of formal academic qualifications, would otherwise be unable to enrol at a conventional university. The courses are organized on a non-residential basis, students taking their instruction by means of correspondence courses, combined with radio and television lectures broadcast by the BBC. In addition to degree courses in both arts and sciences, the Open University also offers a variety of vocational and training courses. With an administrative centre at Milton Keynes, the Open University, originally called the **University of the Air**, was established during Jenny Lee's term of office as minister of the arts during the 1964–70 Labour administration. It was an inspired and innovative concept, which has since been adopted in other countries. *See also*: University of the Third Age.

• **Operation Bernhard ►** A Nazi plot to wreck the British economy, planned in the later stages of World War II. This attempt to stave off German defeat hinged on flooding the UK with some £140 million of fake banknotes. The forgeries needed to be of the highest quality. As Reichbank officials refused to cooperate, Himmler, head of the Gestapo, assigned the task to a Major Bernhard Kruger, who gathered a team of engravers and printers from the concentration camps and set them to work, in exchange for various privileges, at Sachsenhausen Camp near Berlin. However, military events overtook the operation before its effect could be felt. With Germany's collapse imminent, Himmler ordered the press to provide instead forged documents and cash for escaping Nazis. Much of the money was intercepted by the Allies – some of it being found floating in the Enns River in Austria – before it could be hidden to await collection. Kruger, the mastermind of the whole operation, was never found.

• **Operation Ivy ►** Codename for the testing of the first hydrogen bomb by the Americans on Eniwetok.

• **opinion poll ►** A means of attempting to gauge public opinion by canvassing a random or representative sample of people. Probably the best known among the professional organizations that carry out such surveys are Gallup (*see*: Gallup Poll) and Mori; both organizations are associated mainly with sampling of political opinion. In an **exit poll**, those emerging from a polling station are asked how they voted in a political election. This usually gives a reliable indication of the way the voting has gone a few hours before the result is announced.

• **Oppenheimer affair ►** A scandal involving the US physicist Julius Robert Oppenheimer (1904–67) in the early 1950s. Oppenheimer was the brilliant theoretical physicist effectively in charge of the Manhattan Project to develop the atom bomb during World War II (*see also*: nuclear weapon). In 1942 Oppenheimer was investigated by the US security services, initially as a matter of routine. Later, however, Colonel Pash, the director of security at Los Alamos, began to hear criticisms of Oppenheimer's loyalty.

Under interrogation, Oppenheimer finally admitted that he had been approached by Soviet agents but, at first, refused to name the person involved on the grounds that this person was no longer operating. Eventually, in 1943, he named Haakon Chevalier, professor of Romance languages at the University of California. Chevalier was never charged but his career was ruined. Oppenheimer was cleared to continue with the project, which was concluded in 1945.

After the war, Oppenheimer continued in government service, taking responsibility for the development of the hydrogen bomb. Accusations were then made that he was trying to obstruct the programme; in 1954 a Congressional commission investigated his loyalty, reporting that:

> Dr Oppenheimer did not show the support for the Superbomb program that might have been expected of the chief adviser of the Government.

Oppenheimer consequently lost his security clearance and returned to academic work. The truth of the matter has never been clearly revealed. *See also*: McCarthyism; reds under the bed.

• **Opportunity Knocks ►** The title of a British TV talent-spotting show that ran from 1956 to 1977 hosted by Hughie Green, who used the title as his catchphrase. It was taken from the proverb 'Opportunity seldom knocks twice' – untrue in this case, as the show was revived in the late 1980s as 'Bob Monkhouse says, Opportunity Knocks'.

• **Opus Dei ►** (Latin, work of God) An international Roman Catholic organization, originally of lay people, whose members are supposed to demonstrate the principles of Christian living through the example of their own lives, in whatever career they have chosen. The organization was founded in Madrid in 1928 by José María Escrivá de Balaguer, an Aragonese priest; two years later a women's branch was established.

The organization has acquired a controversial reputation both inside and outside the Church. Its detractors accuse it of secrecy, authoritarianism, political meddling, and of controlling its adherents through techniques more often associated with pseudo-religious cults. Its requirement that members flagellate themselves has also attracted much prurient interest. Despite these criticisms, Opus Dei is highly thought of by Pope John Paul II, whose beatification (1992) and canonisation (2002) of Escrivá were not welcomed by all Catholics.

• **OR ►** Operational (or operations) research. The scientific analysis of managerial problems in civil and military organizations. It was first used by the RAF to improve radar efficiency in the early years of World War II. Similar techniques were adopted and refined by the US military establishment; in the late 1940s and 1950s they were extended to the management of civil industry. OR is now a major industry itself, employing quantitive techniques, such as linear programming and non-quantitive methods, such as modelling and game theory, to analyse man–machine relations to improve efficiency and productivity.

• **Oracle** ▶ *See*: Ceefax.

• **Oradour massacre** ▶ A tragic incident (10 June 1944) during World War II, in which German SS troops slaughtered 642 of the 652 people living in the French village of Oradour-sur-Glane, near Limoges. Germans gave the discovery of secret arms caches as justification for the massacre – not realizing that the Oradour they referred to was another village of the same name, where the Resistance had been in operation. Twenty-one of the 200 German troops responsible were tried in 1953: two men were executed. A new village was built nearby. *See also*: Lidice.

• **orange** or **orange sunshine** ▶ US drug-users' slang of the 1960s for a type of homemade LSD tablet that was orange in colour. The LSD was reputedly unadulterated and very strong.

• **Oranges and Lemons service** ▶ A church service held annually at the end of March in St Clement Danes in the Strand, London. The first Oranges and Lemons service was held in 1920, following the restoration of the famous bells in the previous year. The service was attended by pupils of the nearby St Clement Danes primary school: after rendering the nursery rhyme 'Oranges and lemons, Say the bells of St Clements' on handbells, each child received an orange and a lemon. The tradition has continued ever since, interrupted only in World War II, when the church was badly damaged during an air raid. However, the St Clements referred to in the rhyme is almost certainly not St Clement Danes in the Strand, but St Clement in Eastcheap, which is close to the wharves where cargoes of citrus fruits were once unloaded.

• **orbital** or **orbital rave** ▶ British slang of the late 1980s for an acid house party held within reach of the London orbital motorway, the M25. *See*: rave; warehouse party.

• **Order of Lenin** ▶ The highest decoration in the Soviet Union. Established by the Presidium of the Supreme Soviet in 1930, it was conferred for outstanding service in various fields, including medicine, science and technology, defence, agriculture, education, fine arts, music, film, theatre, and literature. The recipient received a gold medal and enjoyed income-tax exemption, pension rights, transport privileges, and monthly payments. *See also*: Lenin Prize.

• **Order of Merit** ▶ *See*: OM.

• **Order of the British Empire** ▶ The Most Excellent Order of the British Empire: an order of chivalry founded in 1917 by King George V, to reward distinguished wartime service by the military or civilians. Women were admitted on an equal basis in recognition of their role in the war effort. It is now conferred mainly for peacetime services. Senior positions include Sovereign of the order (the Queen), Grand Master (the Duke of Edinburgh), Prelate (the Bishop of London), King of Arms, Genealogist, and Gentleman Usher of the Purple Rod. There are five classes: Knights and Dames Grand Cross (GBE), Knights and Dames Commanders (KBE and DBE), Commanders (CBE), Officers (OBE), and Members (MBE). In 1993 the British Empire medal was merged with the MBE. Members of the two higher classes use the title 'Sir' or 'Dame'. The insignia carries the motto 'For God and Empire' and likenesses of George V and Queen Mary. Some awards reward individual achievement while others reflect an individual's status as head of a deserving organization, etc. Some regard OBE as an acronym for 'Other Buggers' Efforts' but think that MBE stands for 'My own Bloody Efforts'.

• **orders is orders** ▶ Orders must be obeyed regardless of whether or not they are considered acceptable. The phrase was widely used by NCOs in the years following World War I; it soon passed into civilian life, where it was generally used in a jocular fashion of some absurd or petty rule at work, etc. However, the phrase took a more sombre tone after the war trials that followed World War II. In these trials many war criminals attempted to justify their actions by claiming that they were 'only obeying orders'. International law no longer allows those who carry out atrocities to escape responsibility on the grounds that 'orders is orders'. *See*: Nuremberg Trials.

• **ordination of women** ▶ The conferring of holy orders on women; outside the Nonconformist churches, this has become a contentious issue. The Roman Catholic Church has never wavered on the question, steadfastly refusing to countenance the admission of women to the priesthood. Within the Church of England, however, a movement in favour of the ordination of women gathered momentum in the 1970s, when women began to be ordained in the Episcopal Church of America. The matter was given further impetus in the 1980s, when women were admitted as deacons in the Church of England; in this capacity they were permitted to fulfil all the functions of a priest, except for giving absolution and consecrating the bread and wine for Holy Communion (although they were allowed to administer it). However, despite a growing feeling in the Church as a whole that there were no valid theological grounds for excluding women from the priesthood itself, traditionalists in the Evangelical and Anglo-Catholic wings remained adamantly opposed to the change. In 1992 the General Synod voted by the necessary majority to admit women to the priesthood; some of those who could not accept the move joined the Roman Church, others simply make a point of avoiding services at which a woman presides. However, such feelings seem to be in decline; there are now many women priests in the Church of England who have earned the respect and acceptance of their parishioners.

• **organic farming** ▶ Any system of agriculture that avoids the use of synthetic fertilizers and pesticides and relies instead on natural methods of crop and animal husbandry. Central to organic farming is the health of the soil, which is nurtured by such means as crop rotation, animal and plant manures, and fertility-enhancing leguminous plants. Weeds are managed chiefly by cultivation or use of mulches, while the inherent diversity and health of the system is relied on to keep pests and diseases in check. Livestock are kept in conditions that allow them to exercise all their natural behaviours; for example, chickens and pigs are allowed free access to the outdoors, instead of being permanently housed under artificial conditions. Organic systems are also designed to fit in harmoniously with the natural environment, so that wildlife is protected.

Until the advent of artifical fertilizers, pesticides, and herbicides during the 20th century, most traditional systems were broadly 'organic'. The modern organic movement started after World War II, just as farming in many countries was undergoing a technological revolution. One of the cornerstones of the movement is the **Soil Association**, established in Britain in 1945 'to bring together all those working for a fuller understanding of the vital relationship between soil, plant, animal and man.' In 1967 it published the first set of standards for organic production, and in the ensuing decades it became the UK's main body responsible for certifying organic farms. During the same period similar bodies were founded in many other countries. The worldwide umbrella organization of the organic movement, the International Federation of Organic Agriculture Movements, now has some 760 member organizations in 105 countries.

Since the late 1980s there has been an upsurge of interest in and demand for **organic food**. This has arisen from the widely held perception that organic produce is safer and more nutritious than that from 'conventional' farms, being free of pesticide residues and genetic modification (*see*: GM food), for example. In Britain the growth in the organic sector has been encouraged by various food 'scares', notably the BSE crisis (*see*: mad cow disease). It is too early to say whether this latter-day growth in the organic movement represents a passing fad or the start of another agricultural revolution. *See*: factory farming.

• **organization and methods** ▶ *See*: O and M.

• **organization man** or **company man** ▶ A person who is totally devoted to the organization or company for whom he works, accepting its aims, methods of working, and values without question. Both expressions therefore have a derogatory flavour, being thought to describe someone who has no personal views of his own. The female equivalents are, of course, **organization** (or **company**) **women**.

• **orgasmatron** ▶ A device that induces orgasm. The name derives from the Woody Allen film *Sleeper* (1973), in which people enter a capsule to achieve sexual satisfaction instead of using the traditional biological method. Allen's idea derived in part from the **orgone boxes** marketed by the maverick psychoanalyst Wilhelm Reich (1897–1957), who claimed that such devices could capture and store the excess sexual energy in the universe, and that a person could improve his or her sex life by regularly sitting in such a box. These claims led to his prosecution for fraud.

• **Orient Express** ▶ An extremely luxurious train that enabled those who could afford it to travel in comfort from Paris to Constantinople in around 82 hours. It was the creation of the entrepreneur Georges Nagelmackers (1845–1905), founder (at the age of 24) of the Compagnie Internationale des Wagons-Lits et Grands Express Européens. The first Express left the Gare de l'Est in Paris on 4 October 1883. There was a twice-weekly service in each direction and a daily service as far as Vienna was introduced in 1885. The train made a last trip in May 1977, but was revived in the mid-1980s in opulent form as a tourist attraction. Works of fiction to use the Orient Express as a setting include Agatha Christie's *Murder on the Orient Express* (1934) and Graham Greene's *Stamboul Train* (1932).

• **Orlando** ▶ The central character of Virginia Woolf's novel (1928) of the same name. The extraordinary Orlando, whose sex changes as he moves from one historical context to another, was generally regarded as being based upon Woolf's friend Vita Sackville-West (1892–1962), to whom the book was dedicated. Vita, wife of the critic Sir Harold Nicolson, had a remarkable relationship with Woolf, which is thought to have included lesbian activities. Their friendship remained a subject of public fascination long after both women were dead; *Portrait of a Marriage* (1990), a controversial television dramatization of the Nicolsons' life together, revived the speculation.

• **Orphism** ► A movement in painting founded by the French artist Robert Delaunay (1885–1941) in about 1912; one of the first schools of abstract painting, it was characterized by patches and swirls of intense and contrasting colours.

• **Orwellian** ► Resembling or related to the totalitarian society described in Nineteen Eighty-Four, the last novel of George Orwell (Eric Arthur Blair; 1903–50), published in 1949. Such familiar Orwellian coinages as newspeak, doublethink, Thought Police, and Big Brother serve as a constant warning against the authoritarian tendencies in society.

• **Oscar** ► A gold-plated figurine awarded annually by the American Academy of Motion Picture Arts and Sciences for achievement in various categories, including Best Film, Best Director, Best Actor, and Best Actress. The Oscars, properly known as the Academy Awards, were first awarded in 1927; it is said that an award can now mean an extra $30 million in box-office receipts and a corresponding boost in a star's future fee. According to one account, the statuette owes its nickname to a long-forgotten secretary who, on seeing the newly cast figure in 1927, remarked that it reminded her of her uncle Oscar. According to another, Bette Davis named the figure after her husband, because she thought its buttocks resembled his.

• **Oscar Slater case** ► A famous case of wrongful imprisonment. Oscar Slater (c.1871–1948), a German fugitive from military service who lived by gambling and selling jewellery, was found guilty of the murder of an 82-year-old Glasgow woman, Marion Gilchrist, in 1909. Slater had been in Glasgow at the time of the murder and then sailed shortly afterwards to America on the *Lusitania*. A brooch he had pawned to pay for his passage was thought to have been owned by the victim; he was arrested on his arrival and returned to Scotland for trial. The brooch proved to have been Slater's for some time but this evidence was suppressed. As a result he was found guilty and sentenced to hang on the basis of circumstantial evidence and the dubious testimony of witnesses who claimed to have seen him outside Gilchrist's flat. After the trial 20,000 people signed a petition for clemency; his sentence was then commuted to life imprisonment. The campaign for his release was led by Sir Arthur Conan Doyle, who wrote *The Case of Oscar Slater* (1912) criticizing the verdict. Slater was finally released on appeal in 1927, after 18 years in prison. He was paid £6000 in compensation.

• **OSS** ► Office for Strategic Services. The US espionage and sabotage organization which was the forerunner of the CIA and the equivalent of the British wartime SOE (Special Operations Executive; *see*: Baker Street Irregulars). The OSS was established in June 1942 by President Roosevelt and placed under the direction of General 'Wild Bill' Donovan (1883–1959), his intelligence adviser. Its role combined information gathering and analysis with covert operations against the enemy, including guerrilla warfare, the rescue of Allied servicemen, and the support of underground resistance movements. In this latter role, Donovan modelled the OSS on the SOE.

• **Ossewa-Brandwag** ► (Afrikaans, Ox-Wagon Sentinels) A South African pro-Nazi paramilitary organization that emerged in 1938 after a symbolic re-enactment of the Great Trek; it achieved popular support in the wake of German victories in the early years of World War II. An elite inner unit, called the *stormjaers* (stormtroopers), was dedicated to sabotaging the South African war effort. Led by Hans van Rensberg, the OB included in its ranks numerous prominent Afrikaners, such as John Vorster, later prime minister (1966–78), and Hendrik van den Bergh, who became head of the Bureau of State Security (BOSS). With the defeat of Germany, the OB disintegrated and its remnants were incorporated into the National Party.

• **ossis** ► German slang term, often pejorative, for those Germans who were formerly citizens of socialist East Germany; it is used mainly by their neighbours in the richer west of the country. The *ossis* similarly refer to the former West Germans as **wessis**. The names, from the German words for east and west respectively, reflect the continuing culture clash within the outwardly reunited country. *Wessis* tend to regard *ossis* as shiftless, parasitic, and laughably unsophisticated in matters of style and taste; they are also widely seen as being ungrateful for their incorporation into a rich democracy. For their part, the *ossis* see the westerners as grasping and materialistic and accuse them of behaving with the arrogance of conquerors.

• **Ostpolitik** ► (German, eastern policy) The West German policy of normalizing relations with E European countries, which was adopted by the government (1969–74) of Willy Brandt. Previously, West German foreign policy had been constrained by the so-called **Hallstein doctrine**, prohibiting diplomatic relations with any country that recognized East Germany. *Ostpolitik* has also been used in a vaguer sense to mean any conciliatory policy by a Western nation towards the (former) communist states of E Europe.

• **Other Club** ► A dining club founded in 1911 by Sir Winston Churchill and F. E. Smith (Lord Birkenhead); apparently so called because they were not wanted at an existing fraternity known as The Club.

• **OTT** ► Abbreviation for over the top. In the early 1980s this was the name of a British TV comedy show and thereafter the abbreviation became more popular than the full phrase in many informal contexts. For example, a particularly impassioned political speech, or a person who openly insults another or dresses in very bright colours, might be described as OTT.

• **Ottawa agreements** ► The protectionist measures adopted at the Imperial Economic Conference in Ottawa (21 July–20 August 1932) at the height of the Great Depression. A series of bilateral agreements established a system of Imperial Preference, by which the UK and her dominions and colonies exchanged tariff preferences to promote trade within the empire and exclude certain classes of foreign goods.

• **Ottawa spy ring** ► An espionage network exposed in 1945 after the defection of a Soviet diplomat, Igor Gouzenko, from the Soviet Legation in Ottawa. Gouzenko, a GRU agent posing as a cipher clerk, had considerable difficulty in persuading the Canadian authorities to take him seriously because of their reluctance to embarrass their Soviet ally. A clumsy burglary at Gouzenko's apartment by the GRU finally persuaded the Canadian police to take him into custody. The documents handed over by Gouzenko revealed Soviet penetration of the Allied atom bomb programme and led to the immediate arrest of the British communist scientist Alan Nunn May and ultimately to the exposure of Klaus Fuchs and the Rosenbergs in America five years later. *See*: Nunn May affair; Rosenberg spy case.

• **Our Ginny** ► Nickname of the British tennis player Virginia Wade (1945–   ). Her victory in the women's singles championship in 1977, the year of Wimbledon's centenary and of Elizabeth II's silver jubilee, ensured her place in the affections of the nation.

• **Our Gracie** ► Nickname of the British entertainer Gracie Fields (Dame Grace Stansfield;

1898–1979) who enjoyed enormous popularity in the 1930s, when she starred in such brightly optimistic films as *Sally in Our Alley* (1931), *Sing As We Go* (1934), and *Keep Smiling* (1938). Of working-class northern origins – she was born above a fish and chip shop in Rochdale and started her working life as an employee in a cotton mill – she always sought to retain her image as the **Lassie from Lancashire** despite huge wealth and fame. At the start of World War II she achieved great success with her song 'Wish Me Luck As You Wave Me Goodbye'; however, her subsequent departure to America with her Italian-born husband, Montie Banks, who became an undesirable alien when Italy came into the war, was widely regarded as an act of betrayal. She returned to England in 1941 but never regained her previous popularity. After Banks died in 1950, she moved to Capri, where she opened a restaurant and married an Italian electrician. She made frequent visits to England and was welcomed back to her native Rochdale, where a theatre was named after her. *See also*: Forces' Sweetheart.

• **Our Lady of Ballinspittle** ► A statue of the Virgin Mary in the Irish village of Ballinspittle, near Cork, credited with miraculous powers of movement and gesture. On 22 July 1985, seven girls of the Daly and O'Mahony families were praying at the shrine when the statue – a life-sized concrete effigy weighing about half a ton – appeared to rock violently from side to side. After further reports of movements, visions, voices, and healings, crowds began to gather and an almost continuous vigil began, lasting the rest of the summer. To accommodate the daily influx of pilgrims, a stadium was built seating 7000 people. The events at Ballinspittle soon gained international publicity, much of it derisive. A variety of explanations was offered, most plausibly that the 'movements' were a hallucination produced by prolonged staring at the halo of electric lightbulbs above the Virgin's head. In 1987 it was estimated that half a million people had visited the shrine.

• **Our Lady of Fatima** ► Apparitions of the Virgin Mary that appeared to three peasant children in the Portuguese hill town of Fatima in 1917. On 13 May, Lucia Santos (10) and her cousins Francesco (9) and Jacintha (7) reported meeting a 'shining lady' while out on the hills. The visitations recurred at monthly intervals and were accompanied by a number of solemn messages to mankind. By the time of the last appearance, on 13 October, a crowd of some 30,000 had gathered, many of whom reported strange lights in the sky and other unusual phenomena. The Catholic hierarchy was initially hostile, but showed the first signs of recognizing the visions in 1927, when a national pilgrimage was organized. A year later work began on a vast basilica at the scene of the apparitions; by the time this was completed, in 1953, Fatima had established itself as one of the great pilgrimage centres of the world.

Of the original witnesses only Lucia survived childhood, becoming a Carmelite nun and living into the 2000s. In her middle age she produced a full account of the messages received from the Virgin, which included an apparent prediction of a second world war and a warning about the rise of godless communism in Russia. However, Lucia's account was only partly released by the Church authorities, the rest being placed under seal until the 1960s, when a decision was taken to postpone any further disclosures indefinitely. This reticence inspired the usual crop of conspiracy theories, alleging that the so-called **Third Secret of Fatima** concerned the date of the end of the world, the identity of the Antichrist, or details of some mysterious crime involving the Church leadership. In 1981 a former monk even hijacked a passenger jet and threatened to blow it up unless the Vatican released the Third Secret.

Speculation was finally laid to rest in May 2000, when the Vatican revealed that the 'Third Secret' concerned a 'bishop dressed in white' being shot at and apparently killed. With hindsight, many Catholics have seen this as a warning of the near-fatal assassination attempt on Pope John Paul II on 13 May 1981 – 64 years to the day after the children saw the first vision at Fatima. That the pope himself sees the matter in this light is suggested by several pieces of evidence; he has spoken several times of being saved by the direct intervention of the Virgin; he visited Fatima on the 10th anniversary of the shooting in 1991; and in 2000 he ordered a bullet taken from his body to be set in the crown of the statue of the Virgin at the main shrine there.

• **Our Lady of Knock ►** An apparition of the Virgin Mary, accompanied by St Joseph and St John, that was reported to have been seen on the gable of the Catholic church in Knock, Co Mayo, Ireland. Although this vision occurred in 1879, Knock did not become an important centre for pilgrims until the 20th century. The original appearance is said to have heralded a number of miraculous cures. A new church, to accommodate 7500 people, was opened on the site in 1974, and five years later the Pope visited the church, during the first visit of any pope to Ireland. In 1986 a new international airport was opened nearby at Charlestown, to assist in bringing to Ireland the one million pilgrims who wish to visit the site each year.

• **Our Marie ►** *See*: Queen of the Halls.

• **outasight ►** Slang meaning outstanding, extraordinary. Originating amongst US jazz musicians and beatniks of the 1950s, it was later adopted by the hippies, who used it interchangeably with 'far out'. It is now only heard in America, usually among Blacks.

• **outing ►** The practice of publicly naming prominent figures as homosexuals, as carried out by other homosexuals. This first attracted attention in 1990–91, when radical gay activists posted bills across America claiming that certain well-known entertainers were 'absolutely queer'. The practice has divided opinion amongst homosexuals. Its supporters claim that by concealing or lying about their sexuality, prominent gays help to render homosexuality invisible, reinforcing public ignorance and prejudice. They are particularly angered by the hypocrisy of politicians, who may even vote against reforms in the law affecting homosexuality, while being actively gay themselves. Others argue that while public attitudes remain unsympathetic, homosexuals have a right to privacy that overrides any of these factors. The word is derived from the phrase come out, meaning openly acknowledge one's homosexuality.

• **out-of-body experience ►** A psychic experience in which the person concerned has the distinct impression of being outside his or her body, often looking down at it from another part of the room. Such experiences have been reported by many people, often during hospital operations or in other life-threatening situations (*see*: near-death experience).

• **out of order ►** British slang meaning not following the rules as laid down by social custom. It derives from the idea of being in breach of standing orders – the rules and regulations that govern the conduct of Parliament. After the broadcasting of Parliament began in the late 1970s, the British public became increasingly familiar with the Speaker ruling MPs or their interventions 'out of order'.

> Do yourself a favour and take a little time off from the booze. It is really out of order... – *The Sun*, 6 April 1991.

• **out to lunch ►** Temporarily disorientated, or functioning below one's best. The phrase implies that one's mind has taken a break and gone out to lunch, leaving one's body to function as best it can without it.

> The captain of the team said he'd been batting

pretty well this season but his bowling was out-to-lunch – and unlikely to return until next season.

● **Outward Bound Trust** ▸ A training organization that aims to help people aged 14 and over to expand their horizons and realize their potential through a variety of challenging outdoor activities designed to develop teamwork, self-discipline, and self-awareness. The trust was formed in 1946, following the successful introduction (1941) of a course for merchant navy cadets operated at Aberdovey in North Wales.

● **Oval Office** ▸ The oval-shaped room, in the west wing of the White House, used as the office of the US president. Overlooking the Rose Garden, it was built for President Theodore Roosevelt. The elliptic design was copied from the White House's 'Blue Room'. The president's famous Oval Office desk, made from timbers of *HMS Resolute*, was a gift in 1878 from Queen Victoria to President Rutherford B. Hayes. Each president adds personal touches: on the desktop of President John F. Kennedy was the coconut shell bearing his own carved 'SOS' that led to his rescue during World War II. *See also*: The buck stops here *at* buck.

● **Ovaltine** ▸ The tradename of a milk drink containing concentrated barley malt, cocoa, eggs and vitamins, originally developed in 1904 by Dr George Wander at his laboratory in Berne, Switzerland, and launched under the name Ovomaltine. When, in 1909, a factory was opened in England the name was abbreviated to Ovaltine, reputedly because a clerical error was made at the time the company applied to register the name. The **Ovaltiney Club**, launched on Radio Luxembourg in 1935, was an immediate success with children; by 1939 there were five million members. The Sunday night broadcasts, heralded by the famous jingle 'We are the Ovaltineys', were brought to a halt by the outbreak of World War II but resumed in 1946 and continued for a number of years.

● **overkill** ▸ The state in which something is hugely overdone, often because considerably more effort and materials than were needed have been used. An extravagant advertising campaign, for example, can be said to involve overkill. The term originated in the jargon of the nuclear arms race during the Kennedy administration: nuclear overkill is having enough nuclear 'megatonnage' to annihilate the same enemy many times over. One nuclear submarine, for instance, has more destructive power than all the weapons used in World War II.

There is a limit. How many times do you have to hit a target with nuclear weapons? – JOHN F. KENNEDY.

● **Overlord** ▸ The codename given to the Allied operation for the invasion of NW Europe, which began on D-Day 1944.

● **over-paid, over-fed, over-sexed, and over here** ▸ A much-repeated catchphrase of World War II, referring to the presence of US forces in the UK. In fact, relations between the US troops and their British hosts were generally good, although the relatively high pay of the Americans and their sometimes brash manner, coupled with their evident appeal to many British women (*see*: GI bride) led to some irritation. The catchphrase was popularized by the British entertainer Tommy Trinder (1909–89). Subsequently it was also heard in Australia, when US forces were stationed there during the Vietnam War.

● **overseas blue** ▸ A shade of blue-grey adopted by the RAF for uniforms worn by personnel during World War II.

● **over the moon** ▸ A cliché used to express extreme pleasure or delight, implying that an almost impossible dream has come true. It is a particular favourite with the tabloid press. Its repetitive overuse by football players and managers, who declare themselves 'over the moon' at every victory, provided a running joke in the satirical magazine Private Eye (*see also*: sick as a parrot; We wuz robbed *at* robbed).

In 1991 it was reported in *The Sun* newspaper (6 March 1991) that a lecturer at Norton College, Sheffield, had started a course for young footballers to improve their communication skills. He told *The Sun*:

> There is no reason on earth why they can't talk to cameras without resorting to soccer-speak.

Jimmy Greaves, the well-known football commentator, reacted enthusiastically to this news:

> If the course had been around in my playing days, I'd have been over the moon.

● **over the top** ▸ An expression denoting that something goes beyond what is required or customary; excessive. It originated in World War I, when soldiers fighting trench warfare were described as going over the top when they climbed out of the trenches to attack the enemy. *See also*: OTT.

● **Ovra** ▸ The Italian Fascist secret police established in 1927 by Arturo Bocchini, Mussolini's chief of security (1926–40). The meaning of the term *Ovra* is a mystery; it may have been coined by Mussolini as a deliberately meaningless term to inspire fear in his opponents. The organization was used to spy on both known anti-Fascists and on many of the dictator's supporters, employed over 900 informers during its existence, and made frequent use of torture to terrorize its victims. Its activities, however, were never on the same scale as its German counterpart, the Gestapo.

> To govern you need only two things, policemen, and bands playing in the streets. – MUSSOLINI, on governing the Italians.

• **own goal** ► In football, accidentally kicking the ball into one's own goal, thus scoring for one's opponents. By extension, any event in which one accidentally does something to one's own detriment.

> It could be said that the Aids pandemic is a classic own-goal scored by the human race against itself. – THE PRINCESS ROYAL, January 1988.

The expression is sometimes used by police to mean an act of suicide. This sense is thought to have originated with the British forces in Northern Ireland, who use it to describe the fate of a terrorist who blows himself up with his own bomb.

• **Oxbridge** ► Oxford and Cambridge universities considered as a single entity representing the elite of the British academic world. See also: Ivy League; redbrick.

• **Oxfam** ► A charitable organization that aims to provide famine relief and other forms of aid, both emergency and long-term, wherever it is needed. Originally known as the Oxford Committee for Famine Relief (the truncated title was not officially adopted until 1965), it was founded in Oxford in 1942 in direct response to the plight of the starving civilian population of Greece during the German occupation of World War II.

• **Oxford bags** ► Very wide-bottomed flannel trousers first fashionable among Oxford undergraduates in the 1920s.

• **Oxford Group** ► The name first adopted by the followers of US evangelist Frank Buchman (1878–1961), who had a considerable following at Oxford University in the 1920s. The group was evangelical in character and also became concerned with social, industrial, and international questions. It later developed into the Moral Rearmament movement.

• **oxygen of publicity** ► Media publicity that encourages an organization or activity that is illegal, dangerous, or unacceptable. Margaret Thatcher popularized the phrase in July 1985, when she attacked the publicity given to terrorists, particularly the IRA. The result was an ill-considered and much-ridiculed broadcasting ban on Sinn Féin spokesmen,

under which the words of Gerry Adams and others had to be voiced by an actor.

• **Oz** ► Colloquial name for Australia, used mainly by Australians.

• **ozone friendly** ► See: -friendly.

• **ozone layer** ► A region of the Earth's upper atmosphere, 10–50 km (6–30 miles) above the ground, in which the gas ozone (triatomic oxygen; $O_3$) forms in greatest concentration.

Ozone molecules themselves absorb the part of the Sun's ultraviolet radiation that is dangerous to life on Earth; the ozone layer is therefore an essential attribute of the planet. However, in recent years there has been widespread concern that the ozone layer is being depleted. The main culprit has been identified as the fluorinated hydrocarbons (see: CFC) used as driver gases in aerosol cans and as refrigerants. These exceptionally stable compounds diffuse into the upper atmosphere, where they enter into photochemical reactions with the highly reactive ozone molecules, which break up and cease to function as ultraviolet absorbers. In the late 1980s holes were detected in the ozone layer over both the north and south poles. Following acceptance of the scientific evidence of this damage over 100 countries agreed, under the Montreal Protocol (December 1995), to ban the production of CFCs and other ozone-depleting substances from January 1996 and to phase out their use by 2020.

• **ozone sickness** ► A condition caused by inhaling the poisonous gas ozone, characterized by headaches, drowsiness, chest pains, and inflammation. In the late 1970s it was realized that ozone sickness was a hazard to the crews of high-flying aircraft because of ozone in the atmosphere seeping into the cabin.

• **Oz trial** ► The trial (1971) of the editors of Oz magazine on charges including 'conspiracy to corrupt the morals of liege subjects of Her Majesty the Queen by raising in their minds inordinate and lustful desires'. The magazine – a heady mixture of satire, erotica, psychedelic art, and drug-related material – had been founded in Australia by Richard Neville, who brought it to London in 1966. Motivated principally by idleness and a lack of ideas, the editors turned the April 1970 issue over to their younger readers to write and edit for themselves: the result was the notorious 'Schoolkids Oz'. The involvement of legal minors gave the authorities the perfect excuse for action against the magazine. Articles cited by the prosecution included a piece on oral sex (such as might now appear in almost any women's magazine), a comic strip featuring a priapic Rupert Bear, and a cartoon showing a cane-wielding teacher with a visible erection. The trial, held at the Old Bailey, became a theatrical confrontation – greatly relished by both sides – between the hippie underground and the guardians of traditional morality. The accused – Neville, Felix Dennis, and Jim Anderson – went for maximum publicity, posing in gymslips for the press and in the nude for a painting by David Hockney. Their supporters led a procession of chickens through the City of London (elephants having proved too expensive). Despite the evident hostility of the judge, the defendants were acquitted on the main charge (which carried a maximum life sentence).

They were, however, found guilty on the two lesser counts of obscenity and sending indecent matter through the post. The judge's decision to gaol the defendants pending psychological reports was widely commented on, as were the short haircuts gleefully imposed by prison officers. Three weeks later prison terms of between 9 and 15 months were handed down, together with deportation orders on Neville and Anderson (who were Australians). When the case went to the Court of Appeal, only the minor charge of sending indecent matter through the post was upheld and the editors were released. The *Oz* trial is said to have provoked more letters to *The Times* than the Suez crisis.

# P

• **pacemaker ▶** A device that provides electrical stimulation of the heart and so helps to correct an abnormal heart beat. The first internal pacemaker was designed in 1957; by the 1960s fully implantable units were available. These are inserted under the skin of the chest wall and connect to an electrode positioned on the surface of the left ventricle or inner wall of the right ventricle.

• **pacification ▶** The process, usually a military operation, of subduing or eliminating enemy or terrorist activity in an area by rendering it inhospitable or unusable. Unlike **peacekeeping**, in which a military presence of neutral and non-aligned forces serves to enforce a truce, pacification is carried out during a time of hostilities and typically involves securing the cooperation of the local population or removing them from the area. Buildings, food supplies, crops, animals, and ground cover that could offer support or protection to the enemy may be destroyed. During the Vietnam War US forces engaged in a policy of pacification to lower the morale of the Viet Cong and take rural areas from their control.

• **Pacific Rim ▶** Those countries situated around the rim of the Pacific Ocean, especially the nations of SE Asia, such as Thailand and Malaysia. The phrase came into use in the 1980s, when these countries were identified as a major area of economic growth. The boom continued for most of the 1990s but came to a spectacular end in 1997–98, when a financial crisis in Thailand had serious knock-on effects throughout the region. The phrase is sometimes used to include Japan and the West Coast of America.

• **package ▶** A collection or composite of various items or elements presented as or forming a complete unit. This usage derives from the idea of a parcel or package containing in one wrapping a number of different items; it generally involves the notion that each component is an essential part of the whole. A **package deal** contains a number of conditions that must be accepted or rejected in their entirety; a **package holiday** includes all travel and accommodation arrangements in the overall price. In computer terminology a **package program** comprises all the programs and documentation necessary for a particular set of applications.

• **pack drill ▶**
  **no names, no pack drill** A phrase used when refusing to identify a wrongdoer, even though the identity of the person concerned is known to the speaker. It implies that the informant does not wish to be responsible for getting the wrongdoer into trouble. The expression arose in a military context, when the punishment for a misdemeanour might be having to drill wearing a full pack for a specified time. If the wrongdoer is not identified he cannot be ordered to suffer the pack drill.

• **Pack up your troubles in your old kit-bag ▶** The opening line of one of the most memorable choruses of World War I. It was written by George Asaf (words) and Felix Powell (music) in 1915.

> Pack up your troubles in your old kit-bag,
> And smile, smile, smile.
> While you've a lucifer to light your fag,
> Smile, boys, that's the style, etc.

(A lucifer was a tradename for a type of match.)

• **Pac-Man defence ▶** A business tactic in which a company attempts to defeat an unwelcome takeover bid by buying up the bidder. It derives from **Pac-Man**, an early computer game in which a rudimentary representation of a head tried to devour its enemies or predators.

• **Pact of Steel ▶** A formal alliance between Germany and Italy, concluded in May 1939, which committed Italy to support Germany in the event of war. Mussolini coined the name after wisely abandoning his first choice, 'pact of blood'. The pact cemented the close ties between Italy and Germany known as the Rome–Berlin Axis.

• **pad ▶** Slang for a home. In the 17th century a pad was a sleeping mat, consisting of straw or rags, used by travellers. In America in the 1930s and 1940s, it was the couch in an opium den, or the den itself. This usage was extended by the beatniks in the

1950s to include any room or home, a sense taken up by the hippies in the 1960s and 1970s. It now sounds rather dated and would only be used self-consciously.

• **paddy wagon**► Slang for a police vehicle, usually a secure van of the type also known as a **black Maria**, although it can be used of a squad car. 'Paddy' refers to the many Irish policemen in New York and the New England area, in which the term originated at the end of the 19th century. Its use subsequently spread to Australia and the UK.

• **paedophile register**► An official list of paedophiles or other convicted sex offenders that contains their names and addresses and, in some cases, information about previous crimes, known contacts, etc. In England and Wales, the Sex Offenders Act of 1997 requires all those with convictions for serious sexual offences to sign the sex offenders' register for a stipulated period of time or indefinitely, depending on the severity of their crimes. The information is available to the police and to others with authorized access, such as local authorities. In America, each state now has a public register of sex offenders, with information readily available to the general public, often via a website. In New York and elsewhere this legislation is commonly referred to as **Megan's Law**, after a seven-year-old girl, Megan Kanka of New Jersey. Her rape and murder by a neighbour who, unknown to Megan's parents, was also a twice-convicted sex offender, led to a public outcry and enactment of such laws throughout the country. The sexual assault and murder of schoolgirl Sarah Payne in Sussex in 2000 fuelled a campaign for similar free access to the sex offenders' register in the UK, with sections of the press calling for a **Sarah's Law** in the young victim's memory. But others cautioned against such a move for fear of vigilante attacks, often against innocent targets, and because it might reduce compliance with the existing law, causing more offenders to go 'underground' where their activities could not be monitored by the police.

• **paedophile ring**► An organized group of people who conspire to manufacture and disseminate pornographic images of, or to commit indecent acts with, children. Paedophile rings now frequently use the Internet to transmit images to members around the world, even though in many countries it is illegal to download such material.

• **pager**► *See*: bleeper.

• **page-three girl**► A female model who poses topless, extremely scantily dressed, or nude, usually

for newspaper photographs. The UK tabloid papers, especially the *Sun*, have traditionally reserved a slot on the third page of their papers for such a photograph. *See also*: pin-up.

• **paintballing**► An adult game in which the members of two opposing teams try to hit each other with paint pellets fired from devices resembling guns. Points are gained by scoring hits and the winning team is the one that succeeds in capturing the other's flag. Before it became a sport, paintballing was used as a training exercise by the Canadian Mounted Police; it was then used as a management training technique by US and later British business firms. It has its origins in the practice of marking cattle in the American Mid-West by shooting pellets of paint at them from pistols powered by carbon dioxide.

• **pair bond**► A monogamous union between a male and a female animal of the same species. **Pair bonding** is the formation of this type of exclusive bond or the courtship and mating behaviour involved in establishing and reinforcing it. The phenomenon is relatively uncommon in the animal kingdom, a notable exception being birds, many of which form pair bonds that last throughout the mating season and often continue over a lifetime.

• **Paisleyite**► A supporter of the Revd Ian Paisley (1926– ), Presbyterian minister, Democratic Unionist MP, and militant leader of the Protestants in Northern Ireland. Since the 1960s he has presented an extreme Unionist stance, denouncing all efforts to bring Catholics and Protestants together in power-sharing bodies and opposing any form of accommodation with the Republic of Ireland. In the 1990s Paisley and his supporters were vociferous opponents of the peace process and – especially – of the the Good Friday Agreement. In elections to the Assembly established under the Agreement, Democratic Unionists won 20 seats and two portfolios in its power-sharing executive, but refused to sit in the cabinet alongside Sinn Féin ministers.

• **Paki**► **1.** British offensive slang for a Pakistani or Indian. It has been in use since the 1960s, mainly as a racist term of abuse. However, the term 'Paki' is also applied to the corner stores run by Pakistani or Asian families, which stay open for long hours; in this context the use has no pejorative sense, *e.g.* 'I'll just run round to the Paki to get some sugar.' **2.** British drug-users' slang for the black hashish from Pakistan, often known as **Paki black**. It is not particularly strong and has often been adulterated with other substances.

• **Paki bashing**► British slang term for the victimization, often brutal, of Pakistanis and other Asian people by White racist youths. This began in the late 1960s and still occurs. In the past, the police were sometimes accused of turning a blind eye to it; however, any form of racism in the police is now strongly deprecated.

• **Pakistan** ▶ The name of this state, which was formed from parts of British India in 1947, was coined by Chaudrie Rahmat Ali in 1933 to represent the areas that should be included when the time came: P – Punjab; A – Afghan border states; K – Kashmir; S – Sind; Tan – Baluchistan.

• **palimony** ▶ US slang for alimony awarded in a court case involving an unmarried couple who break up after living together, usually in a long-term relationship. The word was coined during a 1979 case involving Hollywood star Lee Marvin; it is a combination of 'pal' (*i.e.* friend) and 'alimony'. *See also*: dallymoney.

• **Palm Beach** ▶ Tradename for a lightweight fabric used in men's and women's summer suits, often with a striped design. It is named after Palm Beach, Florida, an exclusive tourist resort noted for its wealthy clientele. The famous palm trees appeared at the end of the 19th century, following the wreck of a ship with a cargo of coconuts.

• **Palme d'Or** ▶ (French, Golden Palm) The major prize (called the Grand Prix until 1975) at the annual Cannes Film Festival, which is awarded for the best film overall.

• **Palomares** ▶ The site of a nuclear accident that occurred on 17 January 1966, when four 20-megaton hydrogen bombs were lost from a US bomber, which collided while refuelling over the Spanish Mediterranean coast. Three of the bombs fell on land, close to the village of Palomares, two of them rupturing and spewing out radioactive plutonium. The fourth fell into the sea and was only located after a massive search operation had been mounted. Over 1000 tons of contaminated topsoil and vegetation were removed for disposal in America.

• **Palooka, Joe** ▶ *See*: Joe Palooka.

• **Panama Canal** ▶ The canal that connects the Atlantic and Pacific oceans through the narrow isthmus of Panama, constructed by America during the period 1904–14. Vessels are towed through the 12 locks of the 50-mile (80 km) canal by locomotives on a cog railway; it takes an average of 28 hours to pass from one side to the other. Proposals for the canal had been in existence since the time of the great explorations in the 16th century, but it was not until the late 19th century that engineering expertise enabled construction to proceed. An at-

tempt to build a sea-level canal was begun in 1880 by the French Panama Canal Company, founded by Ferdinand de Lesseps, who had supervised the construction of the Suez Canal. This was abandoned in 1891 after a financial scandal destroyed the consortium. In 1902 the Americans approved the Panama route for their own canal project; the Hay-Bunau-Vanilla treaty of November 1903, with the new Republic of Panama, provided for a US-controlled ten-mile-wide canal zone. Control over this zone eventually passed to Panama in 1979, but America retained responsibility for the management and defence of the canal itself until 31 December 1999, when full control passed to Panama. The privations suffered by the constructors of the canal, caused by malaria-carrying mosquitos, poor sanitary conditions, and consequently much disease, have passed into legend.

• **panda car** ▶ A UK police patrol car of the 1960s. The name derived from the white and black paintwork used on the vehicles at this time, reminiscent of the markings of the giant panda.

• **Pangaea** or **Pangea** ▶ The single supercontinent comprising all the Earth's land mass, first postulated by the German meteorologist Alfred Wegener (1880–1930) in 1912. He argued that the present continents originated from the break-up of this supercontinent and cited their present shapes and distribution as evidence of this process. Wegener's hypothesis, initially derided by other scientists, is now accepted as the basis of plate tectonics. Pangaea is thought to have formed by coalescence of the Earth's crustal plates about 240 million years ago and to have broken up perhaps 50 to 100 million years later to form the southern supercontinent **Gondwanaland** and the northern supercontinent **Laurasia**, separated by the Tethys sea. These supercontinents in turn divided to produce the present continental land masses of the southern and northern hemispheres, respectively.

• **panic button** ▶ The button pressed by test pilots to bring about an emergency ejection by parachute in the event of impending danger. In general language to **press the panic button** means to react, often to over-react, to a dangerous or unpredictable situation in a hysterical or hasty way. *See also*: chicken switch.

• **panic buying** ▶ Buying more than one's immediate needs of something, fearing that it will soon be in short supply or hard to find. For example, in the fuel crisis of Autumn 2000 (*see*: fuel crisis) enormous queues of panic buyers formed at petrol stations. As a result the pumps ran dry, petrol became virtually unobtainable, and it appeared that the country would grind to a total halt. In this instance, as in many others, panic buying helped to create the very shortage that the buyer's feared.

• **pansy** ▶ A male homosexual or very effeminate man. The word was first used in this sense in the 1920s; it is now seldom heard.

• **pantsuit** or **pants suit** ▶ A woman's or girl's suit of matching jacket and trousers. Pantsuits, more commonly called **trouser suits** in the UK, became fashionable in the mid-1960s. Smart and well-tailored, they helped to establish trousers as an acceptable alternative to a skirt or dress for women of all ages.

• **pantyhose** or **pantihose** ▶ A women's garment that combines underpants and hose (*i.e.* stockings): the US name for **tights**. They were invented in the early 1960s but sales really took off with the advent of the miniskirt in the latter half of the decade. Towards the end of the 1980s stockings made something of a comeback but as a glamour item rather than an everyday article of clothing.

• **paparazzo** ▶ A freelance photographer who aggressively and intrusively pursues famous people whenever they go out in public in order to take pictures that he can sell to the press. Originating in Italy, where street photographers were commonly seen in pursuit of film celebrities, the word became current in the English-speaking world in the late 1960s, with the spread of this practice to other countries: the unfortunate targets now include not only film stars but any newsworthy victims. The word is usually used in the plural, **paparazzi**, as such pests tend to hunt in packs. It came from the surname of such a photographer in Federico Fellini's 1959 film *La Dolce Vita*.

• **papers** ▶

**All I know is what I read in the papers**
A catchphrase popularized by Will Rogers, the so-called 'Cowboy Philosopher', in the later 1920s. It implies that the ordinary man in the street, who has no specialist knowledge or inside information, is as entitled to his opinion as the next man.

• **paper tiger** ▶ A person or thing that appears to be both threatening and powerful but is really neither; a paper tiger is, in fact, weak and powerless. The phrase is a translation of the Chinese *tsuh lao fu*, an expression made popular by Mao Tse-tung (1893–1976) in the mid-1940s:

> The atomic bomb is a paper tiger...All reactionaries are paper tigers. – MAO TSE-TUNG, 1946.

• **Pap test** ▶ The Papanicolaou (pronounced 'papanicolo') smear test: a diagnostic test used in the early detection of cancer, especially cervical cancer. Two samples are taken – one of cells scraped from the wall of the cervix, the other of vaginal secretions; the latter may indicate malignancy of the endometrium or ovaries as well as the cervix. A smear of the flaked-off tissue cells is fixed in alcohol and examined under a microscope for signs of malignant change. The test can also detect cancerous changes in cell samples taken from the respiratory, digestive, and genitourinary tracts. The technique is named after the US physician, George N. Papanicolaou (1883–1962), who first recognized the diagnostic importance of changes in shed tissue cells.

• **paracetamol** ▶ The generic name in the UK for *para-*acetylamino*phenol*, a drug with mild pain- and fever-relieving properties. Available without prescription, paracetamol is used in the same circumstances as aspirin for the relief of headaches, rheumatic pains, and cold and influenza symptoms. Unlike aspirin, it has no adverse side effects on the stomach, but overdosage can cause serious liver damage. The American name is **acetaminophen**.

• **paragliding** ▶ The sport, dating from the late 1960s, in which a person uses a wing-like parachute to glide from an aeroplane to a predetermined landing spot.

• **paramedic** ▶ 1. A health-care worker, especially a member of an ambulance crew, who is trained to perform life-saving medical procedures in emergencies in the absence of a doctor. 2. A health-care worker who supplements the work of doctors and nurses by providing auxiliary clinical services. Paramedics include radiographers, dieticians, physiotherapists, occupational therapists, and medical technicians.

• **paramilitary** ▶ 1. Describing a semiofficial or secret organization run on military lines. The word was first used in the early 1970s for terrorist groups in Northern Ireland. A well-known US example was the Black Panther group, which came to the fore in the late 1960s. 2. Describing civil forces or organizations that legitimately support military forces.

• **Paraquat** ▶ Tradename for a highly poisonous herbicide. A soluble yellow solid used in weed-killers, Paraquat is quick-acting but becomes inactive upon contact with the soil.

• **parasailing** ▶ The sport in which a water-skier grasps the bar of a large kite or wears a parachute and is pulled by a speedboat until airborne. It was introduced in America in 1969; land versions (**parascending**) have been successfully developed using a car or other vehicle.

• **parcel bomb ►** *See*: letter bomb.

• **Paris Club ►** *See*: Group of Ten.

• **Paris Peace Conference ►** The conference that took place in 1919–20 to arrange a peace settlement after World War I. Various treaties were concluded, the most important being the Versailles Treaty (28 June 1919) between the Allies and Germany. A series of other treaties were made to settle eastern Europe and the Middle East in the wake of the dissolution of the old Habsburg, Romanov, Hohenzollern, and Ottoman empires. Austria and Hungary were dismembered by the Treaty of St Germain and the Treaty of Trianon, respectively; the Bulgarian issue was settled by the Neuilly Treaty and the Turkish problems by the Treaty of Sevres. The Peace Conference also established the League of Nations to settle any remaining disputes or any that should arise in future.

• **Paris summit ►** An abortive meeting between Dwight D. Eisenhower, Nikita Khrushchev, Harold Macmillan, and Charles de Gaulle, which was scheduled for 16 May 1960. All four leaders arrived in Paris, but the summit was abandoned in the wake of the U-2 incident.

• **Paris Treaty ►** The treaty of 27 May 1952 in which France, West Germany, Italy, Belgium, the Netherlands, and Luxembourg agreed to the formation of the European Defence Community (EDC). Pacts were then agreed between NATO and the EDC and between the EDC and the UK. The purpose of the EDC was to incorporate West Germany into the NATO system of alliances while also establishing a unified European military command – a formula devised by the French in the hope that it would make German rearmament acceptable to French public opinion. After nearly two years of procrastination the French National Assembly refused to ratify the treaty, despite the efforts of the prime minister, Mèndes-France, and pressure from the Americans. Within a matter of months, however, a similar formula for Franco-German rapprochement, the **Western European Union**, was successfully adopted in its place.

• **parka ►** A warm weatherproof thigh-length coat with a fur-trimmed hood. It was originally an Eskimo garment made from caribou skin and seal fur, worn especially in Alaska and the Aleutian Islands (the name is Aleutian for 'skin'). The women's parkas had an extra hood, which could be used for wrapping a baby. In the 1930s the parka was adopted for skiing and winter sports, later passing into general outdoor use. It became an unlikely item of youth fashion in the 1960s, when the mods (*see*: mods and rockers) used it as a badge of identity.

• **park-and-ride ►** A system, known as **park-ride** in America, enabling motorists, especially shoppers or employees, to leave their cars in designated areas on the outskirts of congested cities and to complete their journeys by bus. The idea originated in the mid-1960s in America, where suburban commuters drove to railway stations or other car parks and then transferred to public transport.

• **Parkinson's Law ►** The famous business rule conceived by the British historian and author Cyril Northcote Parkinson (1909–93), and described in his book of the same title (1958); it states that work expands to fill the time available for its completion. Although much the best known, this is only one of Parkinson's witty and illuminating aphorisms about the business world; others include the observations that expenditure rises to meet income and that subordinates multiply at a fixed rate.

> The rise in the total of those employed is governed by Parkinson's Law and would be much the same whether the volume of work was to increase, diminish or even disappear. – *Parkinson's Law.*

• **Parliamentary Commissioner ►** *See*: ombudsman.

• **party line ►** 1. The official view or position taken by a political party, which members are expected to support in their public statements. To **toe the party line** is to follow or be coerced into following party policy. The term originated in the Communist Party, which was especially intolerant of dissenting views. *See also*: singing from the same hymn sheet. 2. A telephone line shared by two or more subscribers.

• **pass ►**
**They shall not pass!** The famous rallying cry associated with Marshal Pétain during the defence of Verdun during World War I. In fact, it was uttered by his subordinate Robert Georges Nivelle. The phrase was revived during the Spanish Civil War on the lips of the Spanish communist leader Dolores Ibarruri (1895–1989), better known as **La Pasionaria**.

• **Passchendaele ►** A village in W Flanders, Belgium, the main objective of the final thrust of the Third Battle of Ypres (31 July–6 November 1917). The British attempt to break out of the Ypres salient had progressed slowly throughout August and September, after the initial advance had become bogged down, heavy rains turning the shell-cratered ground into liquid mud. On 30 October the Canadian Third and Fourth Divisions and British Fifty-

Eighth and Sixty-Third Divisions, under Sir Douglas Haig, launched a bitter struggle with the Fifth and Eleventh Bavarian Divisions; on 6 November the Canadians succeeded in capturing the village, seven miles short of Ypres. British casualties were 380,000 and those of the Germans equally high.

• **passive smoking** ▸ The inhalation of other people's cigarette, cigar, or pipe smoke. Apart from being unpleasant, this was recognized as a potential health danger in the early 1970s; some research claims that a nonsmoking worker in an office of smokers can inhale the equivalent of several cigarettes each day. Many communities have passed laws banning smoking in public places.

• **Pass Laws** ▸ Legislation passed by the White South African government to regulate the movement of native Africans, by requiring them to carry documents authorizing their presence in restricted areas. Similar laws had been introduced in South Africa in the 18th century, obliging slaves to carry documents signed by their masters authorizing their absence from their master's premises. In the late 19th century passes were also used to regulate the movements of African workers at the Kimberley diamond mines; in the Transvaal similar laws were enacted to restrict the movement of rural Africans into urban areas, except as servants, to ensure an adequate supply of African labourers for White farmers. Under apartheid, after 1948, Pass Laws prevented rural Africans from visiting towns for longer than 72 hours without a special permit on pain of arrest and deportation. The number of those arrested for breaking these laws averaged 100,000 per annum, reaching a peak of 381,858 in 1976. The African National Congress (*see*: ANC) organized periodic anti-Pass-Law campaigns throughout the 1950s and 1960s. In 1986 the South African government finally announced the scrapping of the hated laws as part of the movement towards the dismantling of apartheid.

• **past** ▸
**The past is a foreign country: they do things differently there** The first words of *The Go-Between* (1953), a novel by L. P. Hartley (1895–1972), which have come to rank among the best known of all opening sentences.

• **Patriot missile** ▸ *See*: smart weapons.

• **patsy** ▸ A person who is easily deceived or exploited, especially by being set up as a fall guy. The derivation is uncertain, but there may be a connection with the Italian *pazzo*, a fool. Originally an Americanism, it became popular in the UK in the 1980s.

• **Pattie** ▸ British student slang of the 1980s for a first class degree. It is a rhyming allusion to the US newspaper heiress Pattie Hearst (1954– ), whose abduction by left-wing guerrillas and subsequent trial for complicity in their crimes was a *cause célèbre* in 1974–75. Her captors, a microscopic splinter-group styling themselves the Symbionese Liberation Army, kept her in a locked cupboard and subjected her to brutal and humiliating treatment. When revolutionary statements were issued in her name, coercion was naturally assumed. Doubts arose, however, when she was filmed taking an apparently active role in the armed robbery of a San Francisco bank. After several months on the run with the gang she was arrested by the FBI and charged with robbery and firearms offences. Her plea, that she had been brainwashed by her captors, was rejected and she received a seven-year sentence. The case, which went through several appeals, divided public opinion; it was argued on one side that the state was prolonging the ordeal of an innocent girl and on the other that any leniency would be an unwarranted concession to her youth, sex, and background. In 1979 she was released as a result of the intervention of President Carter. *See*: Stockholm syndrome.

• **Pauli exclusion principle** ▸ A principle in physics first formulated by the Austrian–Swiss physicist Wolfgang Pauli (1900–58) in 1924. It states that, in an atom or other system, no two electrons (or similar identical particles) can have the same set of quantum numbers. The principle is one of the fundamental tenets of quantum theory and, at the time, helped to explain the structure of the atom.

• **pavlova** ▸ A meringue cake covered with fruit and whipped cream. It was named after Anna Matveyevna Pavlova (1881–1931), the Russian-born dancer considered by many to be the greatest ballerina of all time. She settled in the UK after making her London and New York debuts (1910), featuring her famous Dying Swan solo. The pavlova cake, like its namesake, is known for its lightness and graceful appearance. The distinction of inventing and naming the sweet is claimed by both Australia and New Zealand, where the name is often shortened to **pav**.

• **Pavlov's dog** ▸ The subject of experiments by the Russian physiologist Ivan Petrovich Pavlov (1849–1936) into animal behaviour, which resulted in his discovery of conditioned reflexes. Pavlov's early research on dogs, concentrating on the physiology of digestion, had led to his discovery that the taste of food stimulates the release of gastric juices in the stomach. During his experiments he also noticed the phenomenon of 'psychic' salivation, in which a dog would salivate when confronted by a stimulus that customarily preceded feeding, *e.g.* the sight of its food dish. He called this salivation response to a stimulus associated with food the conditioned reflex. Dogs were Pavlov's favoured subjects but he also used monkeys and mice, demonstrating that the conditioned reflex occurs in all animals, including humans, and can be activated by practically any environmental factor. His work is mainly important for its contribution to research on learning processes; although behavioural psychologists have claimed that all human behaviour is due to conditioning and reinforcement, Pavlov himself rejected such an extreme interpretation of his work.

• **PAYE** ▶ Pay As You Earn. A method of collecting income tax in the UK introduced in 1944. The government effectively transferred the burden of collecting the tax to the taxpayer's employer. Each week or each month the employer has to deduct tax from its employees' wages or salaries and remit the proceeds to the Inland Revenue. This also involves the employer in calculating the amount of tax to be deducted. From the gross pay, the employer deducts the free pay (given by a code number provided by the Inland Revenue), to obtain the taxable pay. The employer then uses the correct PAYE Tax Tables to arrive at the tax that has to be deducted in that week or month from the taxable pay. Large companies have to employ wages clerks at their own expense to provide this service for the government.

• **payload** ▶ 1. The goods or passengers carried in a ship, aircraft, etc., that pay for their carriage, as opposed to the crew and equipment, etc. 2. The explosive power of a bomb or warhead carried by an aircraft or a missile.

• **payola** ▶ The practice of bribing someone to obtain special favours, especially making large payments to disc jockeys in order to secure air-time for one's records. The word, which is mainly used in America, combines 'pay' with the Spanish suffix *-ola*, meaning big or outrageous.

• **pazazz** ▶ *See*: pizazz.

• **PBAB** ▶ Please bring a bottle. A request appearing on invitations to parties, etc. The less common **BYOG** translates as Bring Your Own Grog.

• **PBS** ▶ Public Broadcasting Service. The US network of noncommercial television stations that comprise about a quarter of America's 1400 television stations. The system was established in 1967 when the US Congress created and funded an independent nonprofitmaking body, the Corporation

for Public Broadcasting (CPB). It decides policy and gives grants to stations to produce programmes that PBS schedules and distributes. PBS also buys programmes from independent producers. The non-profitmaking stations are funded primarily by viewer contributions raised during telethons. In September 1990 PBS drew a record audience for its highly praised five-part documentary *The Civil War*, with an estimated 32% of the US population seeing some part of it. Most of the BBC's major productions shown in America have been on PBS, often as *Masterpiece Theatre*. CPB also oversees National Public Radio (NPR), which was created in 1971.

• **PC** ▶ 1. *See*: personal computer. 2. *See*: political correctness.

• **PCB** ▶ Polychlorinated biphenyl. A type of organic chemical containing chlorine, first developed in the 1930s. PCBs are extremely stable compounds that have particular properties making them suitable for use as lubricants, dielectrics, plasticizers, etc. They were sold extensively until the 1970s, when it became clear that they were damaging the environment. Because of their stability, they accumulated in soil and water and entered the food chain. They are extremely toxic, even in low concentrations, causing liver damage in humans. They may also be carcinogenic. In the 1970s restrictions were placed on their manufacture and use in many countries.

• **PCP** ▶ *See*: angel dust.

• **Peace Ballot** ▶ A national ballot (27 June 1935) organized by the National Declaration Committee under the chairmanship of Lord Robert Cecil on certain questions of peace and disarmament. Over 11.5 million votes were registered in favour of adherence to the League of Nations while over 10 million voted for a reduction in armaments. The ballot was misinterpreted by the Axis powers as a sign of British weakness.

• **Peace Corps** ▶ An organization established by executive order of President John F. Kennedy in March 1961 and ratified by Congress in the Peace Corps Act (September 1961). The aim of the Peace Corps is to provide skilled manpower to aid developing countries – the first project, announced on 21 April, required engineers to help in road construction in Tanganikya (now Tanzania) – and to promote mutual understanding between the developed and developing world. Peace Corps volunteers, who work for subsistence wages, usually enter into a two-year contract of service and receive a brief training session before being sent abroad. About half the volunteers are teachers; the remainder are a mixture of agricultural experts, health workers, engineers, and those involved in community development projects.

• **peace dividend** ▸ According to certain forecasts, money that would become available to national governments for social spending as expenditure on weapons and defence was reduced after the end of the Cold War. These optimistic forecasts received a setback with the outbreak of the Gulf War (1991) and subsequent regional conflicts.

• **peace in our time** ▸ The unfortunate phrase attributed to prime minister Neville Chamberlain when he spoke to cheering crowds on returning from meeting Hitler in Munich (30 September 1938). The optimism was shortlived. In less than a year Hitler had gone back on his assurances and the UK and Germany were at war. The words echo a versicle from the Book of Common Prayer: 'Give peace in our time, O Lord'. Chamberlain's actual words were 'I believe it is peace *for* our time.' *See also*: Sudeten crisis.

• **peacekeeping** ▸ *See*: pacification.

• **Peace Pledge Union** ▸ A body pledged to renounce war, organized by Canon Dick Sheppard of St Martin-in-the-Fields in 1936.

• **peace sign** ▸ A sign made with the palm of the hand facing outwards and the first two fingers upraised in the shape of a V, used as an expression of peace or desire for peace. Formerly, this was the V for Victory sign popularized by Winston Churchill. Its current use, dating from about 1969, derives from the symbol of the Campaign for Nuclear Disarmament (*see*: CND) devised for the first ban the bomb protest march at Aldermaston in 1958. This consists of a vertical line intersected by an upside-down V enclosed in a circle. The symbol recalls representations of the World Ash Tree of Nordic mythology; ironically this was also the divisional insignia of Hitler's 3rd Panzer Division. *See also*: Harvey Smith.

• **peace studies** ▸ An educational course or programme concerning the military, political, diplomatic, legal, and ideological factors that promote peace in international relations. Such studies were introduced in the early 1950s and became a permanent part of courses in US colleges 20 years later. Similar courses were introduced in Britain in the 1980s but came under sustained attack from conservatives on both academic and political grounds.

• **peach melba** ▸ A dessert consisting of half a cooked peach containing vanilla ice cream with a clear raspberry sauce (Melba sauce) poured over it. It is named after the Australian soprano Dame Nellie Melba (1861–1931). *See also*: Melba toast.

• **Peanuts** ▸ A popular comic strip first created by the US cartoonist Charles M. Schulz in 1950. *Peanuts* features the exploits of the little round-headed boy Charlie Brown, his pet beagle Snoopy (perhaps the world's most popular cartoon dog), and Snoopy's confidant Woodstock (a small bird). Their friends – including loud-mouthed Lucy, insecure Linus, Schroeder the pianist, and the tomboy Peppermint Patty – are all members of Charlie Brown's baseball team. *See also*: happiness is….

• **Pearl Harbor** ▸ The Japanese surprise attack on the US Pacific Fleet at the Pearl Harbor naval base on the island of Oahu, Hawaii, on Sunday 7 December 1941, which brought America into World War II. For over two hours 350 Japanese carrier-borne aircraft strafed, bombed, and torpedoed the US fleet at anchor, sinking or seriously damaging seven battleships and 16 other vessels; large numbers of aircraft on nearby airbases were also destroyed on the ground. America declared war on Japan on 9 December and on Germany and Italy on 11 December. The local military commanders' failure to act on advance reports of Japanese fleet, aircraft, and submarine movements was severely criticized by a subsequent government enquiry. Ever since then in US slang a person faced with a catastrophic turn of events is sometimes said to be 'meeting his Pearl Harbor'.

• **pearlies** ▸ The coster 'kings', 'queens', 'princes', and 'princesses' of the London boroughs, so named from their glittering attire studded with innumerable pearl buttons. Since the Festival of Britain (1951) there has been an official Pearly King of London. Originally elected by the street traders of London to safeguard their rights from interlopers and bullies, they now devote their efforts to collecting and working for charities.

• **pebbledash people** ▸ A term used in the run-up to the 2001 general election for the floating voters of Middle England – the average middle-of-the-road people whose votes were expected to decide the outcome. They were imagined as living in three-bedroom (four after a loft conversion) semi-detached houses, typically with some pebbledash on the front. The Conservative Party estimated that William Hague would need to win over some 2.5 million such people in 178 constituencies in order to form a government. Most of these had voted for New Labour in 1997 but were now thought to be questioning their allegiance. In the event, the Conservatives failed to increase their share of the vote at all, suggesting that most of the pebbledash people had stayed with Blair's Labour Party or joined the growing ranks of the abstainers.

• **peckerwood** ▶ US Black slang for a White person, especially a poor one. The word was originally a dialect name for a woodpecker; it was later adopted by Southern Blacks as a name for poor 'White trash' who 'peck' for a living.

• **pecking order** ▶ (German *Hackliste*) Originally, in the 1920s, an expression used by animal behaviourists to describe the hierarchy amongst hens that permits those at the top to peck those below them without expecting any retaliation. The expression is now applied to human hierarchies in a variety of contexts. For example, a recent recruit to an organization might ask an older employee to give him an outline of the pecking order of the organization's management.

• **pedalo** ▶ A small pleasure boat driven by paddles, which are operated by foot-pedals. A common sight at the beach and on boating lakes from the 1920s onwards, pedalos have in recent years been largely superseded by the more exciting and athletic sports of water-skiing, windsurfing, and parascending (*see*: paragliding).

• **pedal pushers** ▶ Calf-length trousers worn by women and girls, originally for cycling. *See also*: clam diggers.

• **Pegasus** ▶ In Greek mythology, the winged horse on which Bellerophon rode against the Chimaera. In World War II horse and rider (in pale blue on a maroon ground) were adopted as the insignia of all British airborne troops.

• **Peking man** ▶ The popular name given to remains of a skull found near Beijing (Peking) in 1929, which in many respects showed resemblances to that of Java man. Formally named *Sinanthropus pekinensis*, it and Java man were later reclassified as *Homo erectus*, an early form of man that lived between 1.8 and 0.3 million years ago.

• **Pekingology** or **Pekinology** ▶ The close observation of the notoriously secretive internal politics of the Communist government of China. **Pekingologists** are also known as 'China watchers'. The term, which was formed on the model of Kremlinology, has largely fallen into disuse as the Wade-Giles transliteration Peking has been gradually superseded by the pinyin transliteration Beijing.

• **Pelé** ▶ Popular name of the Brazilian footballer Edson Arantes do Nascimento (1940–   ), who was probably the most widely admired player of the 20th century. An inside forward, he played for Santos (1955–74), the New York Cosmos (1975–77), and Brazil, becoming a world star at the age of 17 when Brazil won the World Cup. He scored over 1300 goals during his career.

• **Pelée, Mount** ▶ A volcano on the island of Martinique in the Caribbean, which on 8 May 1902 erupted, causing the most severe volcanic disaster of the 20th century. It took only three minutes for the town of St Pierre to be devastated, with not a single building left standing. Of the population of 30,000 only two survived; one of them was a condemned prisoner who had ironically been protected by the robustness of his death cell.

• **pelican crossing** ▶ A pedestrian crossing in the UK that is controlled by traffic lights, which the pedestrian operates by pressing a button. The crossing is marked with the black-and-white stripes of the uncontrolled **zebra crossing** or by two rows of metal studs. The name is a loose acronym taken from *pe*destrian *li*ght *con*trolled.

• **Penguin** ▶ A publishing imprint founded in 1935 by Sir Allen Lane to issue the first paperback books in the UK. Lane believed that there was an unsatisfied demand for cheap editions of serious books and aimed to meet this market without sacrificing production standards. The first Penguins, all reprints of established fiction titles, sold for 6d (equivalent to 2½p) each and proved an immediate success. Over the next decade the company expanded into most areas of general publishing, launching the topical Penguin Specials and the Pelican nonfiction series in 1937 and the Puffin children's books in 1941. Penguin dominated the market it had created to such an extent that, until the 1950s, 'Penguin' and 'paperbacks' were virtually synonymous in the UK. The company went public in 1961, following the runaway success of the unexpurgated edition of D. H. Lawrence's *Lady Chatterley's Lover* after the famous obscenity trial (*see*: Lady Chatterley trial). Lane is said to have become a millionaire overnight. The name Penguin was apparently suggested by a secretary and adopted because a highly effective penguin logo could be produced in black and white. Penguin Books Ltd, and several other publishers, are now owned by Pearson plc, a large conglomerate with banking, entertainment, and publishing interests. Penguin again became headline news in the late 1980s as a result of the Rushdie Affair (*see*: fatwa).

• **penicillin** ▶ The first of a whole range of antibiotic drugs that have saved millions of lives and eliminated an enormous amount of human suffering. That Sir Alexander Fleming (1881–1958) discovered penicillin is well-known and a firmly established item of modern folklore. What is perhaps less well known is the role of other scientists in revealing the true therapeutic value of the drug. Fleming's discovery came about by a curious accident. In 1928, working as a bacteriologist in St Mary's Hospital, London, he noticed that a dish of cultured staphylococcal bacteria had become contaminated by a mould, which had clearly destroyed the bacteria growing in its vicinity. He identified the mould as *Penicillium notatum* and demonstrated its effectiveness in killing a wide range of toxic bacteria in the test-tube by means of a metabolic product that he named 'penicillin'. From these tests, however, he concluded that penicillin (which he failed to isolate) would have little value as an antibacterial agent in living organisms. The publication of Fleming's discovery – which he himself regarded merely as a useful laboratory tool in preparing bacterial cultures – aroused little interest at the time.

It was not until 1940 that the Australian pathologist Howard Florey (1898–1968) and the German-born biochemist Ernst Chain (1906–79), working in Oxford in the search for an effective antibacterial drug, came across Fleming's paper and decided to test penicillin for this purpose. They eventually succeeded in isolating penicillin, which proved an immediate success in their first clinical trials (1941); however, they soon ran into problems with producing sufficient quantities of the drug for widespread clinical use. It was Florey and Chain who, by publicizing its enormous therapeutic potential in both the UK and America, succeeded in organizing large-scale production facilities; by 1943 penicillin was being used to save the lives of war casualties. Penicillin not only revolutionized the treatment of bacterial infections, the majority of which had hitherto relied mainly on skilled nursing care – usually with little success; it also paved the way for the isolation of a whole range of other antibiotics, enabling virtually all nonviral infectious diseases to become easily cured. When the results of penicillin treatment became widely known Fleming was hailed as a hero – he was knighted (1944) and shared the 1945 Nobel Prize with Florey (who was also knighted and later became a life peer) and Chain (who was belatedly knighted in 1969).

• **penny share** ▶ A security with a very low market value, although it is unlikely to be as low as one penny. Penny shares attract the small investor because a large number of shares can be bought for a small outlay and a rise in price of only a few pence can represent a large percentage profit. However, shares that are only worth a few pence are usually shares in unprofitable or near-bankrupt companies. Only if the company recovers, or if it is taken over

on advantageous terms, is the investor likely to do well.

• **Pentagon** ▶ A vast five-sided building erected in Arlington, Virginia, in 1941 to house 40,000 officials of the US Department of Defense; the name is now often used to stand for America's military leadership.

• **Pentagonese** ▶ A style of language characterized by euphemisms, circumlocution, and deliberate vagueness, frequently attributed to US military spokesmen. It is intended to obscure rather than clarify the relevant facts.

• **pentathlon** ▶ An athletic contest of five events, usually the jump, javelin throw, 200-metre race, discus throw, and 1500-metre flat race. In the ancient Olympic Games the contest consisted of running, jumping, throwing the discus and javelin, and wrestling. The **modern pentathlon**, first included in the Olympic Games in 1912, consists of a 5000-m cross-country ride on horseback, fencing, pistol shooting, a 300-m swim, and a 4000-m cross-country run.

• **people** ▶

**Not a lot of people know that** A catchphrase associated with the British actor Michael Caine (1933–   ), who is frequently imitated saying these words in a Cockney drawl. It is generally used after the statement of a very well known or extremely tedious fact. The phrase seems to have been invented by the British comedian Peter Cook, who used it in several sketches featuring a tedious character named E. L. Wisty (1960s); how or why it became associated with Caine is a mystery. In 1984 Caine was connected with a book for charity called *Not a Lot of People Know That*.

• **People's Budget** ▶ The Budget introduced in April 1909 by David Lloyd George (1863–1945), so-called because it proposed to raise money for old-age pensions (and rearmament) by increasing the tax burden on the landed classes. Death duties were doubled, taxes on land and unearned income raised to unprecedented levels, and a new supertax levied on all income over £5000 p.a. The Budget provoked a violent outcry from Tory landowners, who denounced it as legalized robbery. Although its measures seem modest today, this was the first time that the Budget – previously an exercise in balancing the books and little else – had been used as a direct instrument of social policy.

The 1909 Budget also had important consequences for the balance of power between the two Houses of Parliament. In November the House of Lords, with its huge inbuilt Tory majority, rejected the Budget. This had not happened for 250 years and was in clear breach of the unwritten convention that financial measures passed by the Commons should not be vetoed by the Lords. In January 1910 the Liberals went to the country seeking a popular mandate, not only for the Budget but also for the abolition of the Lords' right of veto (see: Veto Bill). This **People v. Peers** election, as it became known, returned the Liberals to power and gave the Lords little choice but to pass the Lloyd George Budget, a year late, in April 1910. The interval represented some £5 million of lost revenue for the Treasury. This still did not resolve the constitutional crisis, as the Lords continued to block the Liberal measures curtailing their powers. It took a second general election (in December 1910) and a royal undertaking to end the stalemate, by creating enough Liberal peers to carry the bill, before the Lords accepted their defeat.

• **People's Princess** ▶ Diana, Princess of Wales (1961–97). Her fairytale wedding to Prince Charles (1981), subsequent bitter divorce, and troubled search for both personal growth and a public role made Diana the most famous woman of the late 20th century, and one of the most loved. During just 16 years in the media spotlight she blossomed from a shy nursery teacher into a composed and beautiful woman, who used her formidable celebrity to benefit several good causes – notably those seeking to help the victims of AIDS and of landmines.

Born Lady Diana Spencer to the 8th Earl Spencer and his first wife, Frances Roche, she lived on the fringe of royal circles during her childhood. Her marriage to Prince Charles seemed secure at first, especially after the birth of her sons, Prince William in 1982 and Prince Harry in 1984. However, rumours of an estrangement grew during the mid-1980s and there was little surprise when the couple separated in 1992; it was by this time an open secret that the prince had resumed his affair with an old flame, Mrs Camilla Parker Bowles (see: Camillagate). That the marriage was doomed from the start became brutally clear from a controversial TV interview given by Diana in 1995. In the same broadcast she spoke candidly of her own adultery (see: Squidgygate), the eating disorders that plagued her life as a young mother, and her hatred of the Palace establishment. Although some saw this broadcast as a masterpiece of manipulation, the majority took Diana's side, and concluded that she had been deeply wronged.

After her divorce in 1996 Diana was deprived of the title 'Her Royal Highness' but allowed to continue to live in Kensington Palace. In 1997 she began an affair with Dodi Fayed, the playboy son of Mohamed Al Fayed, the Egyptian-born owner of Harrods. Attempting to flee the paparazzi who had dogged Diana's every move for years, the couple were killed in a high-speed car crash in Paris on 31 August 1997.

The premature death of this elegant, compassionate, and clearly very complex woman caused an unprecedented display of public grief. Her funeral procession in London was watched in stunned silence by a crowd of some 2 million mourners; the worldwide TV audience was said to number 2.6 billion. In Britain, the Royal Family's somewhat cool response to the tragedy caused a surge of anger. When Diana's brother, Earl Spencer, made a number of barbed remarks about the Royal Family in his funeral oration the result was not outrage but applause. Indeed, it was said that if Earl Spencer had issued a call to storm the Palace, many of the mourners would have flocked to his cause. Although the mood passed, historians and commentators continue to debate the meaning of these strange emotionally volatile days in September 1997. It is said that Diana's death and the reaction to it filled more newspaper space than any other event of the 20th century, including those of the world wars.

The feeling that Diana now belonged to the people who had loved her, rather than to the Royal Family, was clearly if tactfully implied in Tony Blair's emotional TV statement on the morning of the tragedy.

> They [Britons] liked her, they loved her, they regarded her as one of the people. She was the people's princess and that's how...she will remain in our hearts and in our memories for ever.

• **People's Villain** ▶ Reginald Kray (1934–2000), British criminal who gained notoriety as one of the infamous **Kray twins** (his psychotic brother Ronald Kray died in Broadmoor in 1995). The nickname arose when the dying Reggie was released from prison in August 2000, shortly before the anniversary of the death of Diana, Princess of Wales (see: People's Princess). The emotional public reaction led *The Times* to dub Kray the 'people's villain', observing ironically that the people of Britain had 'found a new focus for a mass outpouring of grief'.

On his release Kray was transferred to the Norwich Hospital and later moved to a nearby hotel, where he died of bladder cancer. As he arrived at the hospital, the switchboard was jammed by messages from wellwishers and the chapel was overwhelmed by some £10,000-worth of flowers – most of which were sent by total strangers and bore notes proclaiming their love for their dying hero. One note described him as a 'British legend that will never die'. Similar scenes graced Reggie's funeral a few weeks later, when much of the East End closed 'in respect' as the dead gangster was carried through the streets in a glass-sided hearse drawn by plumed horses.

The object of all this emotion was, it should hardly need saying, a protection racketeer and career criminal of the most ruthless and disgusting kind. With his brother he instigated a reign of terror in London's East End that culminated in at least two sadistic murders and left many other lives and livelihoods destroyed. The Kray twins were finally sent to prison in 1969 for the murder of Jack McVitie. Not himself a particularly savoury character, Jack 'the Hat' had upset the twins in various ways. When finally cornered, he was pinioned from behind by Ronnie while the saintly Reggie repeatedly plunged a carving knife into his face before cutting his throat. Reginald Kray never showed an iota of remorse for his criminal life and cannot possibly deserve anything but repugnance from decent people. Nevertheless, the absurd legend of the Krays as 'gentlemen' criminals who 'only harmed their own kind', 'looked after their dear old mum', and 'kept the streets safe for ordinary folk', seems to have taken on a life of its own, in defiance of the sordid and brutal facts.

• **PEP** ▶ Personal equity plan. A UK government scheme introduced in 1989 to encourage private individuals to invest in EU companies or trusts. Dividends from the holdings are not subject to income tax if they are reinvested in the scheme and capital gains tax is not incurred on an investment if it has been held for at least one calendar year. PEPs were replaced by ISAs in 1999, but existing PEPs bought before that date remain unchanged.

• **pep pill** ▶ A capsule or tablet containing a stimulant, usually a form of amphetamine. The term arose in the 1940s for such mild stimulants as caffeine tablets; its use for amphetamines began in the 1960s. Amphetamine-based pep pills are also known as **uppers**.

• **Pepsi-Cola** ▶ See: Coca-Cola.

• **Pepsification** ▶ The effect of US commercial culture on areas of the world previously untouched by it, notably eastern Europe and the developing world. The concept and term originated in the late 1980s, with the introduction of fast food outlets in Moscow, following the relaxation of trading relations with the West under perestroika. The word is derived from Pepsi-Cola (*see*: Cocacolaization).

• **pep talk** ▶ A talk given to a person or a group to stimulate their resolve to do something the person giving the talk wants them to do. Soldiers, for example, may be given a talk by their officer before going into action. Or, more intimately, a father may give his daughter a pep talk before she sits an exam.

• **Per ardua ad astra** ▶ (Latin, through difficulties to the stars) The motto of the RFC from 1913 and of the RAF from 1923.

• **Percy** ▶
   **point Percy at the porcelain** *See*: aim Archie at the Armitage *at* Archie.

• **perestroika** ▶ (Russian, restructuring) The policy of restructuring the economic and administrative system of the Soviet Union pursued by Mikhail Gorbachov from 1985 until 1991. His main targets were the endemic bureaucracy, corruption, and stagnation of Soviet life. Gorbachov first announced his plans for *perestroika* and glasnost at the 27th Party Congress in 1986. In his book *Perestroika* (1987) he described the policy as a 'revolutionary overhaul of society...a jump forward in the development of socialism'. *Perestroika* impressed Western commentators rather more than the Soviet people themselves, who found little or no improvement in the quality of their daily lives. The word is now used in English to mean any radical reform of a closed or conservative society or institution.

• **performance art** ▶ A type of live performance that usually combines such media as drama, music, dance, film, photography, and painting. The content is generally provocative or shocking. Evolving from the 1960s happenings, performance art first appeared at the beginning of the 1970s in America, the UK, and West Germany.

• **permissive society** ▶ *See*: new morality.

• **peroxide** ▶ A chemical compound containing two oxygen atoms linked together. The simplest such compound is hydrogen peroxide, $H_2O_2$, which is used as a mild antiseptic and as a bleach for hair. In the early part of the 20th century the term **peroxide blonde** came to be used for a woman who had bleached her hair in this way. It was not long before this had acquired a pejorative sense: such women were regarded as rather vulgar and common:

> An over-dressed, much behatted, peroxided young woman. – BARONESS ORCZY: *Lady Molly* (1910).

*See*: dumb blonde; platinum blonde.

• **Perrier Award** ▶ A prize for the funniest and most original cabaret, revue, or comedy act to appear at the Edinburgh Fringe Festival (*see*: Edinburgh Festival). The award, which began in 1981, is sponsored by the bottled water company Perrier. Although there is a modest cash prize (about £5000 in 2000), the award is more significant for its effect on the winner's profile, as it often brings considerable media attention to an act that might otherwise have gone unnoticed by the general public. Past winners of the award who have gone on to achieve notable success include Stephen Fry and Emma Thompson, Steve Coogan, Sean Hughes, and Frank Skinner.

• **Pershing missile** ▶ A US intermediate-range ballistic missile (IRBM), which first became operational in 1962. The Pershing II, developed during the late 1970s, has a range of 425 miles (680 km) and is ten times more accurate than its predecessor. They were deployed in W Europe in 1983 to counter the threat from Soviet medium range SS-20 missiles, but were later removed in accordance with the provisions of the US-Soviet INF (Intermediate Nuclear Forces) Treaty of 8 December 1987. They are named after US General John J. Pershing (1860–1948), who commanded the US forces in World War I.

• **persistent** ▶ Describing substances, especially pesticides and other pollutants, that are degraded relatively slowly in the environment. Consequently any harmful effects on living organisms will tend to be long-lasting and widespread, reaching many different parts of the food chain. The best known examples are the organochlorine compounds, such as DDT, lindane, and dieldrin, formerly widely used as pesticides for crops and livestock. Their use resulted in a build-up of toxic residues in the tissues of many animals, especially carnivores, with such serious consequences as infertility or poor hatchability in birds. The use of persistent compounds is now restricted or banned in most Western countries.

• **personal column** ▶ A newspaper or magazine column for private messages, announcements, and advertisements. These include invitations to share flats, appeals for money, advertisements placed by those hoping to find a new partner, and a range of private messages that are intelligible only to their intended audience. Birth, marriage, and death announcements (jokingly called the **hatch, match, and dispatch** columns) are usually separate.

• **personal computer** ▶ (PC) A type of general-purpose microcomputer for personal use that first came onto the market in the late 1970s and was used by home hobbyists for elementary programming and playing computer games. Initially such machines had limited memory and storage (most used portable cassette tape recorders) and used domestic television sets as monitors. As microchip technology progressed during the late 1970s and early 1980s, various manufacturers began producing more powerful PCs for business use. These models have larger memories, greater storage capabilities (such as hard disks), and their own monitors; they are now widely used commercially for wordprocessing, accounting, desktop publishing (DTP), computer-aided design (CAD), and many other applications. A more powerful system can be obtained by linking several personal computers in a local area network. See also: laptop.

• **personal equity plan** ▶ See: PEP.

• **personal organizer** ▶ See: Filofax.

• **Perspex** ▶ Tradename of polymethyl methacrylate (called Plexiglass and Lucite in America), a transparent plastic developed in 1924 and first marketed in 1934. Colourless, transparent, flexible, and hardwearing, it is manufactured in sheets or solid objects and is used for aircraft canopies, car windows, cheap camera lenses, spectacles, tail lights, etc.

• **perv** ▶ 1. A sexual pervert. 2. To ogle or gaze lustfully at someone, as in 'That guy keeps perving at me'.

• **pester power** ▶ The ability of children in the age range 10–13 (often now called 'tweenagers'; see: tweenie) to successfully pester their parents into buying them expensive clothes, CDs, computer games, and other consumer products. Fashion houses, in particular, have been quick to take advantage of this market by producing special brands of garments to suit pubescent figures. Tweenage advertising is skilfully directed at creating peer pressure to encourage a large market demand for the same products.

Pester power is not new. However, recent social changes have worked in favour of the young manipulators. First, divorce and separation have enabled the pesterers to play one parent against the other. It also seems that working mothers, and fathers working long hours, are more prepared to indulge their offspring because of the guilt they feel at not spending more time with them (see: quality time). Another telling factor in the pesterers' favour is that more couples now have their children later in life, when they have more funds available to spend on their children's fads.

Catherine, aged ten, is already an afficionado of designer labels...'I used to like buying Pokémon cards, but now my favourite things are clothes and CDs...' but she does not use pester power because she knows it will not work. – *The Times*, 16 August 2000.

• **Peterborough** ▶ A column in the *Daily Tele-*

graph named after the newspaper's former office address in Peterborough Court, Fleet Street; its Docklands address is now Peterborough Court, Marshwall. The column is a mixture of gossip, news, and comment, usually on politics and the arts, and is intentionally snobbish and superficial in tone. It first appeared on 17 February 1929 and was first signed 'Peterborough' in November of the same year. Perhaps Peterborough's greatest editor was Hugo Wortham, who ran the column from 1934 to 1959, peppering it with references to his favourite subjects, which included music, cricket, Eton, Egypt, horse-racing, and wine.

• **Peterlee** ▸ A new town in the mining area 10 miles (16 km) east of Durham, which was so designated on 10 March 1948. The town was intended to provide housing for a maximum of 30,000 people and to act as the commercial and social centre for 26 mining towns and villages in the region of the Durham coal fields. The establishment of new industries was also encouraged to provide an alternative source of employment to the declining coal industry. It was named after a famous local miners' leader, Peter Lee (d. 1935), secretary of the Durham Miners and later president of the Miners' Federation of Great Britain.

• **Peter Pan** ▸ The little boy who never grew up, the central character of Sir J. M. Barrie's famous children's play of this name (1904). One night Peter enters the nursery window of the house of the Darling family to recover his shadow. He flies back to Never Never Land accompanied by the Darling children, to rejoin the Lost Boys. Eventually all are captured by the pirates, except Peter, who secures their release and the defeat of the cruel Captain Hook. The children, by now homesick, fly back to the nursery with their new friends but Peter refuses to stay as he does not wish to grow up. In their absence Mr Darling lived in the dog kennel as penance for having taken Nana away, thus making possible the children's disappearance in the first instance. *See also*: Tinker Bell; Wendy house.

Frampton's statue of Peter Pan in Kensington Gardens was placed there by Barrie in 1912.

• **Peter Principle** ▸ An observation put forward by the Canadian-born US educationalist Laurence J. Peter (1919–90) in 1966: in a hierarchy every employee tends to rise to his level of incompetence, *i.e.* people are promoted until they ultimately reach a job that they are incapable of doing.

• **Peter Rabbit** ▸ The first and most popular of the animal characters created by Beatrix Potter in her children's stories. Peter's story was first privately published with the author's own watercolour illustrations in 1900. By the end of the 20th century he had become firmly established as the chief figure in a lucrative array of merchandise, ranging from soft furnishings to china figures, based on the tales.

• **Peters' projection** ▸ The map projection that shows continents and oceans in their correct relative proportions, although at the cost of some distortion to their true shapes. The older Mercator's projection gives the northern hemisphere two-thirds of the map space and thus emphasizes Europe and North America; Peters' projection gives proper attention to equatorial regions and the southern hemisphere. For this reason it is generally preferred by charities and other agencies dealing with the problems of the developing world. The revision was produced in 1973 by Arno Peters (1916–    ), a German cartographer and mathematician.

• **petrol crisis** ▸ *See*: fuel crisis.

• **PET scanner** ▸ *See*: brain scanner.

• **Peyton Place** ▸ The first major US television soap opera, based on the 1956 bestseller by Grace Metalious about the salacious goings-on in a decayed textile town in New Hampshire. The half-hour twice-weekly series ran from 15 September 1964 to 2 June 1969 (1965–70 in the UK) and attracted an audience of 60 million avid viewers (8 million in the UK). British viewers could thank the success of their own Coronation Street for inspiring the US ABC network to produce the series. ABC eventually earned $62 million from *Peyton Place*, which also launched the film careers of two of its leading characters, 19-year-old Mia Farrow and 22-year-old Ryan O'Neill; it also spawned *Return to Peyton Place* (1972–74) and two films, *Murder in Peyton Place* (1977) and *Peyton Place: The New Generation* (1985).

• **PG** ▸ Parental Guidance. A cinema certification in the UK and America indicating that a film contains some scenes that parent may consider unsuitable for younger children. America also has a **PG-13** rating, which strongly cautions parents about allowing children under that age to attend. This was introduced in 1984 in response to parental concerns about frightening scenes in several of the Steven Spielberg films of the era.

• **Phalange** ▸ A Christian paramilitary organization in Lebanon, founded in 1936 on the lines of Spain's fascist Falange movement.

• **Phantom Major** ▸ Nickname of Colonel Sir David Stirling (1915–90), founder of the SAS in World War II. His concept of small highly trained teams operating behind enemy lines was controversial but turned out to be enormously successful. Stirling abandoned the usual conventions attached to rank in the British army and SAS members called each other by their first name and adopted a less than scrupulous attitude to details of uniform, etc. Stirling's nickname was coined by his victims in the German Afrika Korps and alluded to his ability to conceal his men in the Western Desert. He was finally captured in 1943 and transferred to Colditz, having escaped four times from camps in Italy.

• **Phonecard** ▶ A plastic card issued by British Telecom to enable members of the public to use a payphone designed to accept it. The cards are valid for a specified number of units and may be purchased at post offices, newsagents, etc.

• **phone freak** ▶ **1.** Someone who uses an electronic device to make free telephone calls. With the spread of US tone dialling in the early 1970s, phone freaks acquired equipment to imitate the tones to place calls, thus bypassing the recorded billing. A few practitioners can imitate the tones with their voices alone. Their activities are so costly that some telephone companies employ detectives to trace these illegal calls. **2.** A person who regularly phones sex lines to listen to pornographic monologues or to take part in titillating conversations.

• **phone-in** ▶ A broadcast programme, particularly a radio programme, in which listeners are invited to participate by telephoning the studio to ask questions or express their opinions on air. The phone-in began in America (where it is also known as a **call-in**) and was introduced to the UK at the beginning of the 1970s. It remains a standard item in many broadcasting stations, being both popular with the public and relatively cheap to produce.

• **phoney** or **phony** ▶ Fraudulent, bogus, or insincere; a US colloquialism that became anglicized about 1920. It derives from 'fawney', an obsolete underworld term for the imitation gold ring used by confidence tricksters.

During World War II, the period of comparative inactivity from the declaration of war to the German invasion of Norway and Denmark in April 1940 was characterized by US journalists as the **Phoney War**.

• **phosgene** ▶ A poisonous gas (carbonyl chloride, $COCl_2$) with a smell of freshly cut hay. It was first used as a war gas in World War I. *See*: chemical warfare.

• **photo call** ▶ A time set aside for press photographers to take pictures of a busy politician, member of the royal family, actor, athlete, or other celebrity. This session is usually arranged and controlled by a PRO or information officer. A **photo opportunity** is an event or occasion (often one that has been specially contrived) that provides an opportunity for a politician, etc. to be photographed in a favourable or striking light. The term has been widely used since the 1980s.

• **photodegradable** ▶ Describing plastics, pesticides, and other synthetic chemicals that can be decomposed by sunlight. The use of photodegradable materials became popular in the 1970s as part of a general concern for protecting the environment. *See*: biodegradable.

• **photofinish** ▶ The end of a race so closely contested that the winner can be discovered with certainty only by means of a photograph taken at the finish. Most racecourses are equipped to take such photographs.

• **Photofit** ▶ The tradename for a police method of building up a composite photograph of a suspect's face, usually based on a description given by the victim or a witness. It was developed for Scotland Yard in 1970 by Jacques Penry. Witnesses choose facial features – nose, chin, mouth, eyes, forehead – from a range of different shapes to create the likeness. Photofit refined the Identikit system.

• **photojournalism** ▶ News coverage dominated by photographs. Initially, magazines rather than newspapers were the chief medium of photojournalism because of their higher quality paper and earlier use of colour. Two magazines that helped to define the art of photojournalism during the 1940s were the UK's *Picture Post* and America's *Life*. The latter announced:

> In using pictures first and foremost to inform, *Life* has made pictures not only a power, but a responsible new arm of journalism.

As television was later to prove all over again, realistic news images can have a uniquely powerful role in moulding public perceptions and opinion. This is demonstrated most vividly during wartime, perhaps: examples include Mathew Brady's stark photography during the US Civil War; patriotic images of World War II, such as the Iwo Jima flag-raising by US Marines; and Eddie Adams's brutal photo of the execution of a Viet Cong prisoner.

• **photo opportunity** ▶ *See*: photo call.

• **Photostat** ▶ Tradename for an early make of photocopying machine, introduced in about 1912. The name has commonly been used to mean any photocopier or copy; since the 1950s, when Xerox machines were introduced, the two words have existed side by side as generic names. The suffix

'-stat' is familiar from the names of scientific instruments, such as the thermostat, that cause something to remain constant; in the case of the Photostat it was presumably intended to suggest a scientific device that produced copies identical to the original.

• **Pianola** ▸ Tradename for a type of **player piano** invented in 1897 by the US engineer Edwin S. Votey and marketed by the Aeolian Corporation. The Pianola, like other player pianos, functioned by suction generated by pedal-operated (or later electrically driven) bellows; the reduced air pressure made the keys move in accordance with the perforations in a paper roll. The more sophisticated types of roll were able to control tempo and expression and were used to reproduce performances by famous pianists and by such composers as Ravel and Gershwin.

In bridge, a pianola is a hand so good that it 'plays itself'.

• **PIAT** ▸ *See:* bazooka.

• **picture** ▸
**Every picture tells a story** A catchphrase that originated as a trade slogan for Doane's Backache Kidney Pills in the early years of the 20th century. The original press advertisements featured a picture of a man clutching his aching back together with the slogan. The catchphrase has since been adapted to countless other situations; the singer Rod Stewart released an album with this title in 1971.

• **piece of the action** ▸ A share in the equity or profit of a venture. The phrase originated in US gamblers' slang of the 1920s; by the 1970s it had become business jargon on both sides of the Atlantic: 'If I sell you my business, I still want to keep a piece of the action'. It is now used in a wider sense to mean a share in the excitement or pleasure from something.

• **pie in the sky** ▸ Something that it is pleasant to imagine but will almost certainly never be realized. The phrase originated in America in the early years of the 20th century, when it was used in a rallying song of the Industrial Workers of the World (*see:* Wobblies) to deride the idea of a reward for the virtuous after death ('There'll be pie in the sky when you die').

• **pig** ▸ **1.** Pejorative slang for a police officer. The term became widespread in America in the late 1960s, especially among anti-Vietnam demonstrators and other young protestors. It had, however, been used much earlier in the Victorian era, as underworld slang for a policeman. **2.** Beat slang from the 1950s for a girl. This was not, surprisingly, intended to be pejorative. **3.** US college slang term from the 1980s for an ugly girl. Contests were sometimes held for the 'Pig of the Year' and the unfortunate winner awarded a prize.

• **pile it high, sell it cheap** ▸ The slogan and guiding principle adopted by Sir John Cohen (1898–1979) when building up his commercial empire based on Tesco supermarkets.

• **Pilgerism** ▸ A derogatory term for a type of campaigning left-wing journalism, characterized (in the eyes of its detractors) by selective use of facts, tendentious arguments, and a tone of strident moral indignation. It was coined by the British writer Auberon Waugh to express his distaste for the work of the Australian journalist John Pilger (1939– ).

• **Pilkington Report** ▸ A report on the future of British broadcasting produced by a committee headed by Sir Harry Pilkington and published on 27 June 1962. The report praised the 'professionalism' of the BBC, confirmed its position as the premier instrument of national broadcasting, and rejected advertising on that channel. The committee also accepted the BBC's claim to run a second channel on 625 lines UHF, which eventually became BBC 2. Commercial television, on the other hand, was heavily criticized by the committee, especially for the poor quality of its light entertainment.

> Those who say they give the public what it wants begin by underestimating public taste and end by debauching it. – *Pilkington Report*, 1962.

• **Pill, the** ▸ An orally administered preparation of synthetic sex hormones taken by women as a contraceptive (*see:* birth control). The **combined pill** consists of an oestrogen and a progestogen. Both suppress ovulation; the progestogen, moreover, alters the lining of the womb and causes mucus in the cervix to thicken, hence reducing the chances of successful fertilization in the event of ovulation. The so-called minipill contains a progestogen only. The Pill was developed in the 1950s by Gregory Pincus and Min Chuch Chang of the Worcester Foundation for Experimental Biology in Massachusetts, in conjunction with obstetrician John Rock and pharmacologist Carl Djerassi. Following trials in Haiti and Puerto Rico, the Pill was approved by the US Food and Drug Administration in 1960. The first branded product, Enovid 10, manufactured by Searle Pharmaceuticals, went on sale in the same year.

For some women, the use of the Pill involves undesirable side-effects, such as nausea, headache, and weight gain; studies have also shown a slightly increased risk of blood clots and reduced fertility with prolonged use. However, the convenience and reliability of the Pill ensured its widespread popularity, adding a new dimension to the sexual liberation of women during the 1960s and 1970s (*see*: new morality). However, by the 1980s concern over the side-effects of some brands of the Pill and the growing menace of Aids prompted a return by many to barrier methods of contraception, particularly the condom (*see*: HIV). Various types of male contraceptive pill have been devised and tested, but none has yet entered general use. Morning-after pills have also been developed for those caught unprepared the night before.

• **pillock** ▶ In Britain, a mildly abusive term for a fool or an irritating person. The word has been in use since the 1950s, but gained widespread popularity in the late 1970s and 1980s. Various etymologies have been suggested: 'pillicock' is an obsolete Scottish and Northern English word for a penis; 'pillock', meaning a little pill or ball, is also a slang term for testicle and a dialect word for a rabbit dropping.

• **pillow-biter** ▶ Slang for a male homosexual, especially the passive partner in the act of buggery. The expression is thought to have originated in Australia and to have been introduced into the UK in the 1970s by the satirical magazine *Private Eye*.

• **Piltdown Skull** or **Piltdown Man** ▶ In 1908 and 1911 Charles Dawson of Lewes 'found' two pieces of a highly mineralized human skull in a gravel bed near Piltdown Common, Sussex. By 1912 he and Sir Arthur Smith Woodward had discovered the whole skull. This was thought to provide evidence of a previously unknown species of early man called *Eoanthropus dawsoni*. It came to be accepted as such by most prehistorians, archaeologists, etc., although a few were sceptical. In 1953 J. S. Weiner, K. P. Pakley, and W. E. Le Gros Clark issued a report (*Bulletin of the British Museum* (Natural History), Vol. II, No. 3) announcing that the Piltdown mandible was a fake, in reality the jaw of a modern ape, the rest of the skull being that of *Homo sapiens*. In 1996 new evidence emerged suggesting that the hoax was the work of Martin Hinton, a curator at the Natural History Museum, who had a longstanding grudge against Sir Arthur Smith Woodward.

• **PIN** ▶ Personal Identification Number. A number given to a customer of a bank or building society who has a cash card or a credit card. The number has to be memorized by the customer and is used in conjunction with the card to obtain cash from an automatic cash dispenser or to utilize electronic funds transfer at point of sale (*see*: EFTPOS). It is necessary to keep one's PIN secret in order to avoid its misuse.

• **pina colada** ▶ (Spanish, strained pineapple) A drink made with rum, pineapple juice, and coconut milk, which became especially fashionable during the late 1960s.

• **pinball** ▶ A game of skill played on a pinball machine. The player shoots a small metal ball to the top of a sloping board and tries to keep it from rolling back by using automatic flippers to direct it into various obstructions (holes, bumpers, pins, channels, etc.). When the ball touches these, lights flash, bells ring, and scores are recorded. Pinball arcades were popular until the advent of computer and video games in the later 1970s. 'Pinball Wizard' is a well-known song by The Who, from their rock opera *Tommy* (1969).

• **pindown** ▶ In the 1980s, a form of punishment used in residential homes for children held in care by the social services in Staffordshire. The children, some as young as nine, were held, dressed only in nightclothes, in solitary confinement in their rooms, from which all personal belongings had been removed. Forbidden to talk to anyone, they had to ask permission to use the lavatory or to speak to a social worker. Some were given such absurd tasks as copying out the telephone directory.

The procedure, which was in use in four Staffordshire homes in the period 1983–89, was devised by a senior Staffordshire social worker, Tony Latham. Pindown was stopped by High Court order in 1989 when it was found that some children subjected to it had become clinically depressed, one girl attempting to commit suicide to escape the treatment by jumping out of the window. The procedure and those who operated it, were roundly condemned by an independent report in 1991.

• **ping-ponging** ▶ In America, the practice of referring a patient who attends a medical centre with one complaint to a number of other specialists. It is a way in which doctors increase their fees from the US Medicaid scheme. *See also*: family ganging.

• **pink** ▶ 1. An informal and mainly derogatory term meaning mildly left wing (red being the colour of socialism). *See also*: pinko. 2. Of or relating to male homosexuals; the term is generally used in such combinations as **the pink pound** (*e.g.* gay spending power) or **the pink vote**, etc. It probably derives from the Nazi's practice of making known homosexuals wear a pink triangle in the same way that Jews had to wear a yellow star. Pink has, however, always been a colour associated with femininity.

• **pink-collar** ▶ Denoting occupations that are usually followed by women. These include secretarial and educational jobs as well as those in retail trades. The label, which originated in America in the late 1970s, followed the earlier white-collar (1928) and blue-collar (1950) designations.

• **pinko** ▶ 1. US colloquialism for a person with political leanings to the left. *See also*: pink. 2. Australian slang meaning drunk on methylated spirits. This alcoholic substance is often dyed pink to warn people against drinking it.

• **pink triangle** ▶ The pink cloth badge in the shape of a triangle that homosexuals were forced to wear by the Nazis as a means of identification. It has since been used voluntarily as a badge of identification by gays – sometimes the triangle is no bigger than a 5p piece.

• **pin-up** ▶ A picture of an attractive person designed to be pinned up or otherwise displayed on a wall; also a person, such as a pop star or model, who regularly appears in such pictures. The term arose during World War II, when many servicemen decorated their quarters with pictures of their favourite film stars (often scantily clad). The most famous of the wartime **pin-up girls** was the actress Betty Grable (1916–73), whose legs were reputed to be insured for $1 million.

• **Pinyin** ▶ (Chinese, phonetic spelling) The present system for transliteration from the ideographic writing system of the Chinese language into romanized characters. It superseded the 19th-century **Wade-Giles** system, which did not attempt to achieve the same level of phonetic accuracy. For example, the Wade-Giles 'Peking' and 'Mao Tse-tung' are rendered in Pinyin as 'Beijing' and 'Mao Zedong'.

• **Pio, Padre** ▶ (1887–1968) Italian monk, who became world famous after his body showed the signs of the stigmata. The first occasion on which this occurred was 20 September 1915. Padre Pio never himself sought publicity but the repeated appearance on his hands, feet, and side of what were taken to be the wounds suffered by Christ on the Cross provoked a storm of interest. Although many famous instances of stigmatics have been recorded in previous centuries, that of Padre Pio, born of peasant stock in the village of Pietrelcina, near Benevento, became one of the best documented. Indeed, photographs were taken of his bleeding wounds, convincing many people that no deception was involved. Although medical experts suggested that stigmata were the product of some form of auto-suggestion, pilgrims flocked to see Padre Pio, while many others offered him enormous sums of money. The Vatican twice suspended him from his duties in an attempt to prevent embarrassment to the religious establishment. Nonetheless, tales spread of the monk's powers of clairvoyance, which included a prayer for George V even as the king, unknown to anyone in Italy, was on his deathbed. More bizarrely still, rumours began to circulate of incidents in which Pio had been seen in widely separated places at exactly the same time. Padre Pio died on 28 September 1968 and a campaign for his canonization began almost immediately. He was finally made a saint in 2002.

• **Pioneer** ▶ A series of US unmanned space probes, designed to carry various scientific instruments for planetary investigation, the first of which was launched on 11 October 1958. The first five probes (1958–60) were used to study solar energy and to give advance warning of solar flares to protect the astronauts on the moonflight programme. Pioneer 10 (launched March 1972) was the first spacecraft to fly beyond Mars, enter the Asteroid Belt, reach Jupiter (December 1973), and escape from the solar system into interstellar space (1983). Pioneer 11 (launched April 1975) flew three times closer to Jupiter and was the first spacecraft to reach Saturn (September 1979). Both Pioneer 10 and 11 carry a plaque with a diagram of the solar system showing Pioneer's route, plus drawings of a man (with his hand raised in a gesture of goodwill) and a woman, in case the probes should ever encounter intelligent life elsewhere in the universe. The final Pioneer probes, Pioneer Venus 1 (an orbiter) and 2, were launched in May and August 1978 towards Venus, the latter dropping four small probes before itself descending to the surface.

• **pip emma** ▶ World War I military usage for p.m. (post meridiem). It was originally adopted for use on the telephone; 'ten pip emma' avoids any possibility of misunderstanding. In the same way **ack emma** stood for a.m. (ante meridiem).

• **pippy** ▶ Person inheriting parents' property. A loose acronym coined in the 1980s, on the basis of similar acronyms such as yuppie, in recognition of the growing number of middle-aged people who inherited property from their parents as a result of the post-war boom in home ownership.

• **Pip, Squeak, and Wilfred** ▶ A children's comic strip, about a penguin, a dog, and a rabbit, which appeared in *The Daily Mirror* between 1919 and 1946. It was drawn by A. B. Raine and written by B. J. Lamb. A feature of the strip was a bearded anarchist called **Popski**, whose sinister black broad-brimmed hat and orb-like bomb represented the evils of communism, atheism, and any other '-ism' that was likely to threaten the existing social order. In order to increase the pressure on parents to buy the paper, the *Mirror* organized a children's club, the members of which were called **Gugnuncs**. These clubs were active in schools, holiday camps, and anywhere else that children might be expected to gather.

'Pip, Squeak, and Wilfred' also became army slang for three campaign medals of World War I: the 1914–15 Star, the British War Medal, and the Victory Medal.

• **Pirelli calendar** ► An advertising calendar sent to selected customers as a Christmas gift by the Pirelli Tyre Company, an Italian company that sells its products throughout the world. The calendar, which first appeared in 1964, has a photo of a beautiful nude (or nearly nude) woman for each month. Although inevitably titillating, the photos are taken by well-known photographers aiming to produce images that transcend the pornographic. Because they are produced in limited numbers the calendars are highly prized by their recipients and have become collectable items.

• **piss-artist** ► 1. British slang for a drunkard. 'Pissed' means drunk; '-artist' is frequently used as a slang suffix for someone accomplished at their job. (For example, a con-artist is a successful con-man.) 2. An idle, incompetent, or unreliable person, especially one who makes empty boasts or promises.

• **pisshead** ► 1. British slang for a drunkard, a synonym for piss-artist. 2. US slang for an unpleasant person.

• **piss-up** ► British vulgar slang for a drinking session or a party with a liberal supply of alcohol. The expression **he couldn't organize a piss-up in a brewery** suggests the ultimate in ineptitude. Variants include 'he couldn't organize a fuck in a brothel', and 'he couldn't sell iced-water in hell'.

• **pit bull terrier** ► A strong and potentially dangerous dog that is a crossbreed between a bulldog and a terrier. It has a white coat and resembles a Staffordshire bull terrier, although it is larger. The name is also used for several crossbreeds and is therefore not recognized by kennel clubs. Originally bred for dog-fighting, the pit bull terrier was responsible for two-thirds of the deaths from dog bites in the 1980s in America; some US communities have passed laws banning them or requiring them to be registered. In the UK, parliament banned their import in 1991; those already in the

country must be registered with the police and kept muzzled in public. *See also*: rottweiler.

• **pits, the** ► Slang for the lowest of the low, the most dreadful experience or the most awful person. Originally an Americanism, it is now widely used throughout the English-speaking world. It is thought to be a shortened form of 'armpits', an often malodorous and unattractive part of the body.

• **pizazz** or **pazazz** ► A mainly US colloquialism for flamboyant energy and style. It was apparently invented by the US fashion journalist Diana Vreeland (1902–89), who was editor of *Vogue* for most of the 1960s. Vreeland was herself the embodiment of this quality – she dressed mainly in bright red and spoke in a manner described as 'all capitals and italics'. The word is thought to derive from the sound of a racing car's engine.

• **placebo** ► (Latin, I shall please) A substance given as medication to a patient even though it has no physiological effect. Placebos may be prescribed for a patient who will feel cheated or depressed if he is not given a prescription. Indeed, in some instances the psychological benefits of taking the placebo may produce an improvement in the clinical condition of the person. This response, known as the **placebo effect**, was first documented in about 1950. Placebos are also given in the clinical trials of new drugs to assess the efficacy of the drug being tested. In a double-blind trial, neither the doctor nor the patient knows which is the drug and which is the placebo. The term 'placebo' is now often used of any measure designed purely to calm or placate.

• **Placido** ► British slang for £10, coined in the late 1980s. It alludes to the Spanish operatic tenor ('tenner') Placido Domingo (1941–   ).

• **Plaid Cymru** ► (Welsh, Party of Wales) The Welsh nationalist party, set up in 1925 with the object of achieving home rule for Wales and preserving the Welsh language. Support grew in the 1960s and the party gained three seats in the House of Commons in 1974, increasing to four in 1992, 1997, and 2001. In the first elections to the newly formed Welsh Assembly in 1999, Plaid Cymru won 17 of the 60 seats, which made it the leading opposition party to Labour. *See*: devolution.

• **Planck constant** ► A fundamental constant in physics named after the German physicist Max Planck (1858–1947). In his work on the emission of radiation, Planck suggested that the energy emitted or absorbed by a body would be proportional to the frequency of the radiation and would only occur in discrete amounts. Mathematically, $E = nh\nu$, where

$E$ is the energy, $\nu$ the frequency of the radiation, $n$ is a whole number (1, 2, 3, etc.), and $h$ is a constant, now known as the Planck constant. His theory was published in 1900 in a paper entitled 'On the Theory of the Law of Energy Distribution in the Continuous Spectrum'. The idea that energy could only be transferred in definite amounts ('quanta'), rather than continuously, was a fundamental break with the ideas of 19th-century science, now known as classical science. It led to the development of quantum theory. Planck's value for the constant:

$$h = 6.62.10^{-27} \text{ erg.sec}$$

is engraved on his tombstone in Göttingen, Germany. A more up-to-date value in SI units is $6.626\,076 \times 10^{-34}$ J s.

• **planned obsolescence** ▶ The policy of deliberately limiting the life of a product or component in order to force the consumer to replace it more frequently than he should need to. The practice can be regarded as an immoral exploitation of the consumer. Its practitioners, however, would defend it on two grounds. In the first place, in the modern world, technology advances so rapidly that very often a device, such as a camera or computer, is out-of-date long before it wears out. By designing the product in such a way that it will function well during its relatively short lifetime, the manufacturer is able to sell it more cheaply than if he had to design it to last so long that it would still function after it had become technically obsolete. Secondly, Western economies depend on a vigorous consumer demand for durables, such as cars, washing machines, etc. If they were designed to last the consumer for his lifetime, demand would fall to such a low level that unemployment would reach unacceptable proportions.

• **planning blight** ▶ A difficulty that arises in selling a property because it is either directly affected by a development plan or is adjacent to property that is so affected. For example, a residence may become unsaleable because a motorway is planned to pass close to it.

• **plastic explosive** ▶ Any of various high explosives produced in an adhesive mouldable form. The original plastic explosives were based on the substance RDX (research department explosive) mixed with various oils, waxes, and plasticizers. RDX (the chemical cyclotrimethylenetrinitramine, also called cyclonite) was invented in 1899 but was first used in World War II. Subsequently, plastic explosives became widely known because of their use by terrorist organizations. **Semtex**, which like RDX is a nitrogen-based plastic explosive, is an odourless substance, much favoured by terrorists; it was used in the Lockerbie disaster.

• **plastic money** ▶ Credit cards, debit cards, or charge cards, as distinct from cash and cheques; an increasingly important element in the cashless society that has grown up in Western cultures since World War II. Often shortened to **plastic**, as in 'I don't have cash, will you accept plastic?'

• **Plate, Battle of the River** ▶ The scuttling of the German pocket-battleship Graf Spee in December 1939 in the estuary of the River Plate (Río de la Plata) off Montevideo, Uruguay. After a naval battle in the Atlantic the Graf Spee was damaged and took refuge in Montevideo Harbour. It was refused assistance by the Uruguayan government and was scuttled on Hitler's orders. The captain, Commander Langsdorff, shot himself. The scuttling of the trapped and maimed German merchant-shipping raider disappointed many sightseers, who had hoped to see a classic naval engagement, including a party of US businessmen who had chartered a plane at the cost of £1,250 each.

• **plate tectonics** ▶ In geology, the modern theory that the Earth's crust is composed of a number of plates that move relative to each other. The main plates correspond to the American, African, Antarctic, Eurasian, Indian, and Pacific continents; where the edges of these plates meet, volcanic activity and earthquakes are common. It is the movement of these plates, either towards or away from each other, or over or under each other, that causes oceanic trenches, mountain ranges, and the formation of various other geological phenomena. *See also*: Pangaea.

• **platform sole** ▶ A thick shoe sole, usually made of cork or wood, that raises the upper an inch or more off the ground. They became fashionable for both sexes in the early 1970s, when pop stars of the glam rock era took to wearing gaudy high-heeled shoes with built-up soles. **Wedges** (or **wedgies**) are shoes in which the heel and sole form a single solid block up to 10 cm thick. They produced a grotesque hobbling gait in their wearers, who were chiefly teenage girls. Incredibly, platform soles and wedges came back into fashion in the 1990s.

• **platinum blonde** ▶ A woman whose hair has been treated to give it the silvery colour popularized by the US film star Jean Harlow in the film *Platinum Blonde* (1931). The special peroxide-and-ammonia treatment used by Harlow eventually so damaged her hair that she had to wear wigs. *See*: Blonde Bombshell.

• **platinum handshake** ► A very lavish golden handshake.

• **playgroup** ► A group of preschool-age children, particularly in the UK, who regularly meet to engage in creative play under supervision. **Playschools**, which provide this service, are usually run on a part-time voluntary basis, by or with the help of the parents, using neighbourhood facilities such as the church hall or social centre. Some receive limited funding from local councils or charitable organizations. The future of such groups has been called into question somewhat by the present government's encouragement of more structured learning for very young children, especially in nursery classes in primary schools.

• **Play it again, Sam** ► A catchphrase that is popularly supposed to come from the film *Casablanca* (1942), starring Humphrey Bogart (as Rick) and Ingrid Bergman (as Ilse). In fact, as is now well known, no such line exists in the film. What Ingrid Bergman did say was 'Play it Sam, play "As Time Goes By".' The misquotation was well enough established by 1969 for Woody Allen to use it as the title of his play (filmed in 1972) about a critic who is helped by the 'ghost' of Humphrey Bogart. Sam is the pianist in Rick's Casablanca war-time night spot, who plays and sings 'As Time Goes By' so evocatively that it reminds Rick and Ilse of their pre-war liaison in Paris. The character is played by Dooley Wilson.

• **PlayStation** ► *See*: computer games.

• **pleasure principle** ► *See*: reality principle.

• **Plexiglas** ► *See*: Perspex.

• **PLO** ► Palestine Liberation Organization. A politico-military organization founded in 1964 to represent Palestinian Arab refugees and to re-establish a Palestine state. Its terrorist activities against Israel included the murder of 11 Israeli athletes at the Munich Olympic Games (1972). Since 1967 it has been dominated by the al-Fatah guerrilla group headed by Yassir Arafat (1929–    ); Arafat became chairman of the PLO in 1968. In 1993 the PLO signed a landmark agreement with Israel, under which it renounced terrorism and recognized Israel's right to exist within secure borders. In return, Israel granted the Palestinians in the West Bank and Gaza Strip limited self-rule under PLO leadership (from 1995). A Palestine National Authority was set up to administer these regions, with Arafat as its elected president. A further land-for-security deal was signed by Israel and the PLO in 1998. However, a growing impatience with the peace process on both sides led to a recurrence of the intifada in autumn 2000 and savage Israeli reprisals, which culminated in the reoccupation of much Palestinian territory in 2002. The conflict continues.

• **plonk** ► A cheap wine for everyday or party consumption rather than for offering to wine buffs. It is thought to be a corruption of the French *vin blanc* (white wine) and dates back to World War I.

• **plonker** ► 1. British vulgar slang for a penis. It has been used since the early years of the 20th century. 2. British slang for a stupid person. It became well known during the 1980s from its frequent use by the character Del Boy (David Jason) of his slightly dim but long-suffering younger brother Rodney (Nicholas Lyndhurst) in the BBC TV comedy series *Only Fools and Horses*.

> Dazzling Dave really made a change from most mumbling pop plonkers. – *The Sun*, 6 March 1991.

3. British slang for a mistake. 4. British slang for a big wet kiss, a smacker.

• **ploughman's lunch** ► An informal lunch provided as a bar snack, usually consisting of bread and cheese with various trimmings, such as pickles and pickled onions; it is often consumed with a glass of beer. Bread and cheese is regarded as having been the staple lunch of the medieval ploughman (hence the name), although what is now offered in most pubs as a ploughman's lunch would be unlikely to have sustained a manual worker. The modern-day ploughman's lunch was promoted by the English Country Cheese Council in the 1970s.

• **PLR** ► *See*: public lending right.

• **PLU** ► People like us. Slang abbreviation used as a signal of approval among snobbish British people. *See also*: NTD.

• **plugged in** ► *Au fait* with the latest trends in fashion and popular culture. **switched on** is similarly used; both are derived from electrical appliances.

• **plugumentary** ► A film or television programme that appears to be a documentary but in fact is aimed at promoting a particular product or firm. A very common example is the TV programme that documents 'the making of' a recently released film or pop record, featuring interviews with the stars, etc. The word is a combination of 'plug' (in the sense 'promote') and 'documentary'. *See*: advertorial.

• **Plum** ► Nickname of the British comic novelist P. G. Wodehouse (1881–1975): it is a contraction of his Christian name, Pelham. The cricketer and cricket writer Sir Pelham Francis Warner (1873–1963) was also known by this name. *See also* Jeeves; Psmith; Spode, Roderick; Wooster, Bertie.

• **plus fours** ▶ Loose trousers overlapping the knee-band and thereby giving added freedom for active outdoor sports. They were particularly popular with golfers in the 1920s. The name derives from the four extra inches of cloth below the knee, tucked into long heavy socks.

• **Pluto** ▶ 1. In World War II, the codename (from the initials of *p*ipe *l*ine *u*nder *t*he *o*cean) given to the pipelines to carry oil fuel laid across the bed of the English Channel – from Sandown to Cherbourg and from Dungeness to Boulogne. 2. A cartoon dog in early Walt Disney shorts.

• **PMT** ▶ Premenstrual tension. Irritability, nervousness, anxiety, depression, and emotional instability affecting some women for up to ten days before a menstrual period is due. The condition was not recognized and named as part of a clinical syndrome until the 1920s. Associated with a premenstrual build-up of salt and water in the tissues, due to temporary hormonal imbalance, the symptoms disappear once menstruation begins.

• **pocket battleships** ▶ Small battleships built by Germany after World War I. Forbidden to build warships of over 10,000 tons by the Versailles Treaty (1919), Germany constructed several formidable so-called pocket battleships purporting to be within this limit.

• **POETS day** ▶ Friday, POETS being an acronym for 'Piss off early tomorrow's Saturday'. As an explanation of what happens on Friday afternoons in many offices, it became current in the 1960s. A similar expression from that era was **TGIF** (Thank God it's Friday) or the less polite **TFIF** (Thank Fuck its Friday). *TFI Friday* was the name of a popular Friday evening TV programme of the later 1990s, hosted by Chris Evans.

• **pogo-dancing** ▶ A somewhat basic form of dancing, originating as part of the punk culture of the 1970s, in which participants jumped up and down on the spot with their bodies rigid and their arms kept close to their sides. It developed because the crowded conditions in punk clubs allowed no room for sideways movement. The name comes from the **Pogo-stick**, a toy consisting of a spring-loaded stick with platforms for the feet, enabling a child to jump around.

• **point man** ▶ A person who spearheads a military, political, or business campaign. It is often used particularly of someone appointed to handle the opposition to a particular programme. When Presi-

dent Ronald Reagan needed support in 1986 for his Star Wars military policy, he sent Vice-President George Bush to Europe as a 'point man' to allay the gathering doubts. This sense grew out of the term's use in World War II to mean the front soldier in a military patrol.

• **point of no return** ▶ The point in an aircraft's flight at which it has not enough fuel to return to its point of departure and must continue. Hence its figurative application, a point or situation from which there is no turning back.

• **point of sale** ▶ (POS) 1. The place at which a sale is made to a consumer. It may be a shop, petrol station, market stall, mail-order house, or the doorstep (in door-to-door selling). 2. The check-out in a supermarket etc., at which payments are made and sales recorded on a cash register linked to a central computer. A **point-of-sale display** is placed at such a check-out point in order to tempt customers to make a last-minute purchase of a magazine, confectionery, etc.

• **Poirot, Hercule** ▶ The Belgian detective created by Agatha Christie (*see*: Queen of Crime) in her first crime novel, *The Mysterious Affair at Styles* (1920). The dapper slightly plump ex-policeman is famous for his fastidious grooming of his waxed moustache and his insistence that crimes are best solved by the use of one's 'little grey cells'. He made his final appearance in *Curtain* (1975), after a career in 33 books and 56 stories. He has also featured in numerous films since the 1930s, being portrayed most recently by Albert Finney in *Murder on the Orient Express* (1974) and by Peter Ustinov in *Death on the Nile* (1978), *Evil under the Sun* (1982), and *Appointment with Death* (1988). David Suchet's portrayal in the 1990–91 television series is, however, regarded by many Christie fans as definitive.

• **poison pill** ▶ A commercial spoiling tactic in which a company facing an unwanted takeover bid takes some action that will reduce the value of the company if the takeover succeeds. Examples of poison-pill measures include issuing securities with a conversion option that empowers the holder to buy the bidder's shares at a reduced price if the takeover goes through, or selling off a valuable asset to another organization at a low price on the understanding that they will sell it back if the bid fails.

• **Pokémon** ▶ Pocket-size monsters who originally featured in a Nintendo computer game but went on to conquer the world through television, feature films, and a host of merchandising tie-ins. The Pokémon computer game was created in 1995 by Satoshi Tajiri, who based it on his childhood hobby of collecting small animals. There are various complications, but the essential aim is to capture and train as many of the 150 Pokémon as possible ('Gotta catch 'em all' is the slogan). Although the game proved popular, the advent of Pokémon as a global merchandising phenomenon came with the launch of Pokémon trading cards and action toys in 1999. As with the computer game, the object is to collect all the Pokémon – a goal made frustratingly elusive by the limited supply of some monsters. This scarcity led to feverish swapping and trading of cards among obsessed youngsters. As Pokémon fever reached its height in 2000, it was reported that some young capitalists were using the demand for rare cards to make profits more usually associated with the drug trade. Incidents of theft and even violence led to bans on Pokémon products in many schools. Meanwhile parents who have not embraced Pokémon as a complex interactive learning tool have objected to its violent ethos – as well as despairing at its impact on their pockets.

• **Polaris ▶** A US submarine-launched ballistic missile (SLBM) developed during the late 1950s to help bridge the perceived missile gap between East and West. The first Polaris-equipped nuclear submarine, USS *George Washington*, was launched on 15 November 1960. In 1962 President John F. Kennedy offered Polaris technology to the British, to replace the V-bomber nuclear deterrent; the first British Polaris submarine, HMS *Renown*, was completed in 1968. The Americans replaced their Polaris with Poseidon in 1969, but the British updated their missiles with MIRV warheads (*see*: ICBM) under the Chevaline programme, completed in 1982; Polaris was finally replaced by the more advanced Trident SLBMs in the mid-1990s.

• **Polaroid ▶ 1.** Tradename for a type of plastic manufactured by the US Polaroid Corporation; it was invented by the company's founder, Edwin Land (1909–91), in 1932. The plastic sheet contains crystals that are aligned in rows and has useful optical properties. 'Normal' light is a wave motion in which electric and magnetic fields vibrate at right angles to the direction of propagation. Because of the orientation of the crystals, Polaroid film only transmits light that is vibrating in one plane aligned with the crystal orientation (the light passing through the film is said to be 'plane-polarized'). Light polarized in other directions will not pass through the Polaroid filter. Light that is reflected from surfaces is also plane-polarized on reflection; Polaroid sunglasses are therefore used to cut the reflected light and thus reduce glare. **2.** An instant camera manufactured by the Polaroid Corporation and invented by Land in 1947. The original model

produced sepia prints 60 seconds after the picture had been taken. Later models produced fast black-and-white prints, and in the 1960s instant colour cameras were introduced. The full name is the **Polaroid Land camera**, also known as the **Land camera**.

• **pole position ▶** Figuratively, a position of advantage; from its use in motor and horse-racing to denote the most favourable starting position on the grid or line. On a racecourse or running track the pole is the inside boundary fence; thus a contestant nearest to the pole gains an advantage since opponents must cover a greater distance. In motor racing the pole position is on the front row and on the inside of the first bend.

• **Polish Corridor ▶** The territory given to Poland by the Versailles Treaty (1919) to give her access to the Baltic Sea west of Danzig. The Corridor cut off E Prussia from the rest of Germany and proved to be a bone of contention from the outset. It followed roughly the line of the Vistula.

• **Politburo ▶** Formerly, the chief policy-making body of the Communist Party in the Soviet Union, first formed in 1917. It examined matters before they were submitted to the government and consisted of five members. It was superseded by the Presidium of the Central Committee of the Communist Party in 1952.

• **political asylum ▶** *See*: displaced person.

• **political correctness ▶** (PC) A concept that emerged on the college campuses of America in the late 1980s. The phrase, now almost always used pejoratively, describes an attitude that regards left-wing ultra-liberal views on race, gender, class, the environment, sexual orientation, etc., as the only acceptable ones. Exponents of PC argue that Americans must atone for their society's exploitation of Blacks, oppression of women, and persecution of homosexuals by taking positive steps to welcome the cultural diversity represented by such groups. On campus such attitudes have led to the drawing up of new curricula, which play down the cultural contributions of **DWEM**s (Dead White European Males) in favour of those of women and of people from other ethnic groups.

The most notorious aspect of PC is its practice of substituting cumbersome euphemisms for words or phrases thought to be offensive or otherwise 'incorrect'. For instance, Amerindians are now to be known as 'native Americans', the physically disabled as differently abled, and pets as 'animal companions'. When the PC phenomenon first came to media attention in the early 1990s many journalists invented ludicrous PC phrases of their own in a spirit of parody, and it is now difficult to tell which coinages were originally serious and which are purely facetious. Did anyone ever seriously suggest that short people should be described as 'vertically challenged', bald men as 'follicly challenged', or the dead as 'permanently inconvenienced'?

More worrying than these linguistic absurdities are the intolerance for other points of view and contempt for the principle of academic freedom occasionally shown by the politically correct. Questioning PC theory or practice invites the accusation that one is a racist or sexist – a slur that can blight the academic careers of both students and staff.

• **Political power grows out of the barrel of a gun** ▶ One of the political maxims proposed by Mao Tse-tung in 'Problems of War and Strategy'. Typical of his philosophy of enforcing communist doctrine by military power, it acquired an ironic echo in the practice of hippies all over the world who, when confronted by armed troops at various peace demonstrations, 'spiked' the soldiers' guns with flowers.

• **Politics is the art of the possible** ▶ A definition popularized by the British Conservative politician R. A. (Rab) Butler (1902–82) in 1971. It may have been coined much earlier, possibly by the German leader Bismarck in the previous century.

• **poll tax** ▶ See: community charge.

• **polychlorinated biphenyl** ▶ See: PCB.

• **polyester** ▶ Any of a large number of synthetic polymers used in resins, plastics, synthetic fibres, etc. Polyesters, first developed in the 1930s, are extensively used, particularly in fabrics such as Dacron and Terylene.

• **polygraph** ▶ To give someone a lie detector (polygraph) test. The instrument itself has been in use since 1923, but the use of 'polygraph' as a verb – as in 'The sheriff polygraphed two subjects' – only began in the early 1970s. Polygraphs are most frequently used in America by police.

• **polystyrene** ▶ A synthetic polymer produced from the hydrocarbon styrene (phenylethylene). Polystyrene was first produced in the 1930s. The resin itself is a clear glasslike thermoplastic material, but is usually used in the form of a rigid foam (known as **expanded polystyrene**) for ceiling tiles, insulation, packing, etc.

• **polytetrafluoroethylene** ▶ See: PTFE.

• **polythene** ▶ A synthetic plastic made by polymerizing the gas ethene ($CH_2{:}CH_2$). The original form was made by the British company ICI in the late 1930s. There are two basic forms of the plastic: high-density polythene is a tough brittle material; low-density polythene is a softer more plastic material. Both forms are used for a variety of moulded articles. The name is a contraction of 'polyethene'.

• **polyunsaturate** ▶ An oil or fat in which many of the molecules are **unsaturated**; i.e. the chain of carbon atoms contains a number of double bonds. Vegetable and fish oils have this type of structure. Animal fats, on the other hand, are saturated fats (i.e. all the bonds are single bonds). In the 1960s research indicated that saturated fats could lead to a high level of cholesterol in the body and that this could cause atheroma (a degeneration of the walls of the arteries, often resulting in arterial obstruction causing heart conditions). As a result there was a general trend towards using vegetable oils for cooking (rather than lard or dripping) and replacing butter by vegetable-based spreads. See: health food.

• **polyurethane** ▶ Any of a class of synthetic polymers used in adhesives, paints, varnishes, rubbers, and foams (in upholstery). Like many other such materials, polyurethanes were developed during the late 1940s.

• **polyvinyl chloride** ▶ See: PVC.

• **polywater** ▶ A supposedly new form of water having different properties from ordinary water, first reported by Soviet scientists in 1968. It was said to be formed by condensing water vapour in fine glass or quartz capillaries. Its properties appeared to be different from the normal properties of water; for example, it had much higher density, viscosity, boiling point, and freezing point. It was suggested that this **anomalous water**, as it was also known, was a polymeric form of water in which the molecules had linked together in some way.

The initial report caused considerable interest and scientists all over the world hurried into print with their own reports on its properties. In the early 1970s there was even concern that the new form of water might induce a change in normal water, turning the oceans solid. Possibly this idea was influenced by the science-fiction novel Ice Nine by Kurt Vonnegut (1922–   ), in which a new high-melting crystalline form of ice was discovered. In fact, it was subsequently found that polywater was not a new polymeric form of water but impure water containing a high concentration of silicate ions from the glass or quartz surface of the capillary tubes. Many scientists were made to look rather stupid as a result of this finding.

• **pommy** or **pommie** ► Australian derogatory slang for a British person, especially a British immigrant to Australia. It is now usually abbreviated to **pom**. The derivation is uncertain but two possibilities are offered. It could be a shortened form of 'pomegranate', a reference to the red cheeks thought to characterize the British. Alternatively, it could be derived from the acronym POME, meaning *prisoners of mother England* – a reference to the early British immigrants to Australia, who were convicts. The word has been in use since the beginning of the 20th century.

> Colin was a pom. He'd lived in Oz since he was 13 but that doesn't make any difference, if you're a pom, you're a pom. – BEN ELTON: *Stark* (1989).

• **pongo** ► 1. British derogatory slang, now archaic, for a Black man or a foreigner. 2. British military slang from World War I for a soldier. It is thought to derive from the Kongo word *mpongi*, ape, soldiers in uniform being thought to resemble monkeys. 3. Australian slang for a British person.

• **PONSI** ► Person of no strategic importance. Dismissive army slang, dating from the Gulf War of 1991, for any political visitor or other nonmilitary personnel at the front.

• **Pontiac fever** ► A viral disease resembling flu and characterized by headaches, fatigue, breathlessness, and bouts of coughing. The term is derived from the city of Pontiac, Illinois, in which the first known outbreak was identified. The disease has since been diagnosed elsewhere, including the UK.

• **poof** or **poofter** ► A male homosexual, especially a camp or effeminate one. The word was probably derived from 'puff', a 19th-century term for a homosexual.

> Now I'm that poof from the telly. – JULIAN CLARY, *The Independent*, 31 January 1991.

• **pop art** ► An art movement of the 1950s and 1960s characterized by the use of themes and images from popular culture and a fascination with ordinary mass-produced objects. Pop artists set out to explore the visual world of contemporary mass culture, incorporating the imagery of advertising, television, comic strips, and magazines into their work (sometimes physically). The movement began in the late 1950s as a reaction to the elitism of traditional fine art and the emotional excesses of US abstract expressionism (*see*: action painting). Largely a British and US phenomenon, its exponents included Richard Hamilton in the UK and Jasper Johns and Andy Warhol in America. The term seems to have been coined by the British critic Lawrence Alloway.

• **popcorn market** ► A derogatory expression for that large section of the cinema-going public, chiefly teenagers, whose avid consumption of popcorn is only matched by their appetite for witless and disgustingly violent movies. The deliberate exploitation of this market began in the 1980s, when film-makers discovered that 16–24-year-olds constituted a majority of filmgoers. The result was a proliferation of raucous sex comedies and blood-spattered splatter movies, usually with increasingly feeble and repetitive sequels.

• **Popeye** ► *See*: spinach.

• **pop music** ► A broad term for the various kinds of commercial youth-oriented music that have emerged since the rock 'n' roll era of the 1950s, especially those with obvious mass appeal. Pop music is sometimes contrasted with rock, a term generally reserved for the more serious (or pretentious) styles that emerged in the late 1960s and 1970s. The term **popular music** is now mainly used for pre-rock 'n' roll styles such as show tunes, Tin Pan Alley ballads, etc. *See also*: acid house; disco; folk rock; heavy metal; punk; rap; soul; etc.

• **pop one's clogs** ► A British euphemism meaning to die, implying that one may as well pawn ('pop') one's footwear as one will have no further use for it. A person who expects to die in the near future might well feel disinclined to talk about the subject in a serious way, preferring instead to make use of this jocular expression.

• **poppers** ► Drug-abusers' slang for amyl nitrate capsules; so called because the drug, a heart stimulant, comes in small glass bombs, the top of which is snapped off to enable the contents to be inhaled. A popular stimulant, it is supposed to increase sexual pleasure and is particularly associated with the gay club scene.

• **Poppy Day** ► *See*: Flanders poppies; Remembrance Day.

• **Popski's Private Army** ► A British raiding and reconnaissance force of some 120 men formed in October 1942 under Lt. Col. Vladimir Peniakoff, who had previously worked with the Libyan Arab Force. Familiarly known as 'Popski', he was born in Belgium of Russian parents, educated at Cambridge, and resident in Egypt after 1924. Popski and a small element of his force, together with the Long Range Desert Group, reconnoitred the route by which Montgomery conducted his surprise attack around the Mareth Line; he subsequently operated in Italy and Austria. *See also*: Pip, Squeak, and Wilfred.

• **popular capitalism** ▶ A slogan adopted by the British prime minister Margaret Thatcher (*see*: Iron Lady) in the 1980s. It encouraged ordinary people to become shareholders, especially in previously nationalized industries that her government had privatized. People were also encouraged to set up their own businesses – the Thatcher governments gave special tax incentives to small firms.

• **Popular Front** ▶ A political alliance of left-wing parties (communists, socialists, liberals, radicals, etc.) against a reactionary government, especially a dictatorship. The idea of an anti-Fascist Popular Front was proposed by the Communist International in 1935. Such a government was set up in Spain in 1936, but civil war soon followed. The French Popular Front government, set up by Léon Blum in 1936, lasted only until in 1938.

• **porcupine provisions** ▶ See: shark repellents.

• **porky** ▶ Shortened form of **pork pie**, British rhyming slang for a lie. The term gained popularity as a result of its use in the TV comedy series *Minder* (1979–94), set in working-class South London.

• **porridge** ▶ British slang for a term of imprisonment, chiefly used in the phrase to **do porridge**. Although the word has been in use from at least the 1950s, it became much more widely known in the mid-1970s owing to the popular television series *Porridge* (1974–77), a comedy of prison life starring Ronnie Barker.

• **Porsche** ▶ A German sports car, much prized for its speed, style, and high-quality engineering. The first Porsche, the 356, was introduced in 1948 as a sports version of the Volkswagen Beetle, having a similar bug-like appearance. The Volkswagen's designer, Ferdinand Porsche (1875–1951), had been imprisoned by the French for his association with the Nazis, and production of the new car fell to his son, Ferry, who set up the Porsche Company for this purpose. Ferdinand was cleared in 1949 but died not long afterwards, a broken man. In 1963 Ferry Porsche and his son 'Butzi' produced the Porsche 911, a slimmed-down version of the 356 that became the classic Porsche model. Its elegant but idiosyncratic appearance has been compared to many things, including a half-used bar of soap, an old-fashioned steel roller skate, and a cross between a Messerschmitt and a dodgem car. In the 1980s the Porsche was much favoured by high-salaried yuppies and became a popular symbol of their lifestyle and values.

• **Porter, Jimmy** ▶ The central character in John Osborne's play *Look Back in Anger* (1956), whose rantings were taken as typical of the Angry Young Men of the period. The frustrated product of a working-class background and a provincial university, Porter lived in a drab bedsit with his middle-class wife, Alison, who provided the butt for most of his invective.

> She's so clumsy. I watch for her to do the same things every night. The way she jumps on the bed, as if she were stamping on someone's face, and draws the curtains back with a great clatter, in that casually destructive way of hers. It's like someone launching a battleship. Have you ever noticed how noisy women are? Have you? The way they kick the floor about, simply walking over it? Or have you watched them sitting at their dressing tables, dropping their weapons and banging down their bits of boxes and brushes and lipstick?

At the time, his self-pitying harangues were thought to articulate a general disillusionment with postwar Britain. The play's dingy milieu began the vogue for kitchen sink drama. Porter, now in irritable middle age rather than angry youth, made a second appearance in Osborne's last play *Déjà vu* (1992).

• **Portland Secrets Case** ▶ See: Kroger affair; Lonsdale affair.

• **Portmeirion** ▶ A holiday resort on Tremadog Bay in Gwynedd, north Wales, built by the architect Sir Clough Williams-Ellis (1883–1978) on land he had purchased. The development of the site began in 1926, with the architecture modelled somewhat whimsically on the Italian village of Portofino. Many of the buildings have only a façade and some of the domes are incomplete (if they are not visible from the rear). The village provided a fittingly strange setting for the surreal TV series *The Prisoner*, filmed here in the late 1960s. It is, however, both picturesque and convincing. There is a hotel in which people can stay although most tourists are day visitors. The well-known Portmeirion pottery is made here. The name combines a reference to *Porto*fino and to *Merion*eth, the former Welsh county.

• **Porton Down** ▶ Site of the Chemical Defence Establishment on a 7000-acre site near Salisbury Plain, Wiltshire. It was originally established in 1916 to provide the British war machine with gas and chemical weapons for use against the Germans. Calls in the interwar period, and again after 1945, to halt the research for moral and humanitarian reasons were not complied with; Porton Down's defenders argued that research into offensive chemical and biological weapons had to proceed in order that the proper antidotes and countermeasures could be developed to protect British troops and, indeed, the British public in future conflicts.

• **posh** ▶ *See*: folk etymology.

• **postfeminism** ▶ The values and lifestyles characteristic of many women who came to adulthood after the feminist revolution of the late 1960s and 1970s. Such women are inclined to take many of the benefits of feminism (such as greater career opportunities, equal pay, etc.) for granted, while dispensing with its more militant and ideological aspects. These younger women are sometimes resented by the feminists of the 1960s and 1970s, who feel that they are reaping the rewards of earlier struggles while making no commitment or sacrifice of their own. The word enjoyed a vogue amongst journalists in the mid-to-late 1980s. *See*: New Woman.

• **postmodernism** ▶ A concept embracing all those tendencies in late 20th-century and early 21st-century culture that seem to represent a break with the style and values of modernism. Postmodernism was originally an architectural term, used from about 1975 to denote the growing reaction against the dogmas and practices of the International Style. Postmodernist buildings are characterized by an eclectic borrowing from all cultures and periods, a delight in non-functional ornament, and a knowing flirtation with kitsch. In other fields, phenomena as various as Madonna videos, the novels of Salman Rushdie, jeans commercials, and the heritage industry have all been described as postmodern. A playful ironic style, the embracing of cultural pluralism, and a concentration on style and surface at the expense of depth and authenticity are usually considered the hallmarks of postmodernist style. In a still wider sense, the word is often used to denote the general cultural condition of the West today – especially in relation to the dominance of information technology and the mass media. It is hard not to feel that the term has become a humpty-dumpty word meaning almost anything the user wishes it to mean.

• **post-traumatic stress disorder** ▶ (PTSD) A set of symptoms suffered by a person who has been involved in a traumatic event, such as a major car or plane accident or a natural disaster. The symptoms vary but can include depression, mood swings, nightmares and other sleep disorders, personality changes, and feelings of guilt. One of the major problems is that these symptoms can recur, even years after the traumatic incident occurred. The expression was coined by US psychologists treating casualties of the Vietnam War. *See also*: survivor syndrome.

• **post-viral fatigue syndrome** ▶ *See*: ME.

• **pot** ▶ Cannabis, when used as a drug for its euphoric relaxing properties. The term is used of both herbal cannabis (marijuana, grass, hemp) and cannabis resin (hashish, hash). It was the usual term in the beat culture of the 1950s and was widely adopted by the 'straight' media a decade later – by which time it was considered rather old-fashioned by those who actually used the drug. The legalization of pot has been a perennial issue since its widespread use by otherwise law-abiding people began in the 1960s. The main argument for legalization is that the drug is not very harmful and that the law, by being so widely flouted, is brought into disrepute: moreover, the fact that cannabis can only be obtained illegally is likely to lead its users into a criminal subculture in which hard drugs are also available. On the other hand, British governments have adhered to the prohibition on the grounds that pot smoking is addictive, can have long-term deleterious side effects, and is often a stepping stone to more serious drug abuse. In 2001 the government announced that it was reclassifying cannabis as a Class C rather than a Class B drug; this means that possession of the drug for one's personal use is no longer an arrestable offence.

• **Potato Jones** ▶ Captain D. J. Jones, who died in 1962 aged 92. In 1937, with his steamer *Marie Llewellyn* loaded with potatoes, he tried to run General Franco's blockade off Spain but was prevented by a British warship. Two other blockade-running captains were called Ham-and-Egg Jones and Corncob Jones.

• **pothead** ▶ Slang for a person who habitually smokes cannabis (pot). *See also*: head.

• **Potsdam Conference** ▶ The last Allied wartime conference, held from 17 July to 2 August 1945 at Potsdam near Berlin; it was attended by Stalin, Truman, Churchill, and Attlee (who became prime minister after Labour's victory in the general election and took over from Churchill during the second round of discussions). The basis of the postwar settlement in Germany was agreed, involving the division of the country and of Berlin into four zones administered by the four occupying powers – the UK, America, the Soviet Union, and France. However, the Soviet occupation of E Germany after the fall of Berlin made many of the Potsdam arrangements unenforceable, hastening the beginning of the Cold War.

• **Potter, Harry** ▶ A child wizard, the eponymous hero of J. K. Rowling's best-selling series of children's stories. Harry's adventures have captured the imaginations of millions and become the publishing phenomenon of the age. Rowling (1967–   )

wrote the first book while struggling to survive as an unemployed single parent but is now a multi-millionaire, said to be the third richest woman in the UK. Ultimately the series will consist of seven books, although currently only four are completed and available: *Harry Potter and the Philosopher's Stone* (1997), *Harry Potter and the Chamber of Secrets* (1998), *Harry Potter and the Prisoner of Azkaban* (1999), and *Harry Potter and the Goblet of Fire* (2000), which lays claim to being the fastest-selling book since records began. The film of *Harry Potter and the Philosopher's Stone* enjoyed a predictable success in 2001.

Initially the success of the books owed everything to the enthusiasm of young readers and little to publishing hype. Some critics have found Potter-mania a puzzle, arguing that the prose is undistinguished and that the plots do not always seem very original. Children, however, seem to respond instinctively to Rowling's immense narrative skill and to the stark contrasts of good and evil in the stories. The character of Harry himself also seems to tap into a universal wish-fulfilment fantasy – that of the downtrodden underdog who suddenly finds that he has extraordinary powers and a momentous destiny.

The books have introduced several terms into the modern vernacular; examples include **quidditch** (a hockey-like game for flying wizards), **muggles** (a derogatory terms for non-wizards), **Hogwarts** (the wizard school where the adventures are set), and **dementors** (evil spirits who destroy a person's self-belief).

• **Poujadists ▶** A short-lived French political party founded by the right-wing grocer-demagogue Pierre Poujade (1920–    ) in 1953. His party, Union de Défense des Commerçants et Artisans, was born out of a tax revolt by small shopkeepers and farmers in the Lot, who also felt increasingly threatened by the end of food rationing and the postwar growth of big retail businesses. His vitriolic attacks on the tax inspectorate and parliamentary government, his support for Algerie Français, and the quixotic demand for the calling of an 'estates general' to represent the voice of the little man attracted mass support. In the 1956 general election the Poujadists won a surprising 11.6% of the poll, amounting to 2.5 million votes, and returned 50 candidates to the National Assembly.

• **poverty trap ▶** An invidious situation in which low earners who manage to increase their income find themselves worse off, either as a result of loss of state benefits or because they now fall into a higher tax bracket.

• **powder one's nose ▶** A euphemism used mainly of women, meaning to go to the lavatory. The 'powder room' is itself a euphemism for the same place. The expression was first heard in the 1920s.

• **Powellism ▶** The political ideology associated with the maverick British politician Enoch Powell (1912–98), who became a Conservative MP in 1950. He is mainly notorious for his so-called **Rivers of Blood** speech made in Birmingham in April 1968, warning of the social consequences of unrestrained immigration:

> As I look ahead I am filled with foreboding. Like the Roman I seem to see 'The River Tiber foaming with much blood'.

As well as favouring strict immigration controls, Powellism involved opposition to the maintenance of a British presence 'East of Suez' during the 1960s, emphasis on the necessity of cuts in government spending, belief in the unfettered working of the free market, opposition to British membership of the EC, and support for the Unionists in Northern Ireland. Having been dismissed from Edward Heath's shadow cabinet for his Birmingham speech, Powell became the United Ulster Unionist Council MP for South Down (1974–87).

• **power dressing ▶** A style in women's fashions in the early 1980s, intended to convey such attributes as wealth, influence, and invulnerability, especially among businesswomen. It favoured sombre colours, limited use of jewellery, shoulder pads, and a 'carefully-managed' look. It was mastered by Margaret Thatcher among others. Actresses in US soap operas, notably Dallas, rapidly took the fashion to extremes. *See:* shoulder-pads.

• **power sharing ▶** A proposed solution to the problems of Northern Ireland through the creation of an executive body in which the Catholic minority have a guaranteed share of the seats. The first attempt at power sharing was shortlived. In 1972 the Stormont parliament, which had effectively excluded Catholics from any role in decision making, was replaced by direct rule from Westminster. At the time, the intention was to reinstate some form of Northern Irish government as soon as its constitution could be agreed by both communities. This approach seemed to bear fruit in 1973, when Protestant and Catholic leaders agreed to serve together in a new Northern Ireland Assembly responsible for all domestic matters except security. This announcement was followed within weeks by the Sunningdale Agreement, which proposed an additional Council of All Ireland drawing its members from both the Irish Parliament and the Northern Ireland Assembly. The Assembly opened in January 1974, under the leadership of Brian Faulkner (1921–77). From the start, however, it faced a campaign of organized disruption by Protestant extremists, led by the Revd Ian Paisley (*see:* Paisleyite), who were determined to make it unworkable. In May 1974 this object was achieved by a general strike of Protestants, backed by widespread intimidation, which reduced the province to chaos. The Assembly resigned en masse and direct rule from Westminster was resumed. Little further progress was made towards power sharing until 1998, when the Good Friday Agreement proposed a settlement involving a new Assembly with a power-sharing executive. The executive, led by the Ulster Unionist leader David Trimble and including two Sinn Féin ministers, was duly if belatedly established in December 1999; however, slow progress in the decommissioning of IRA weapons (not begun until late 2001) has put the power-sharing arrangement under repeated strain.

• **Prague Spring** ▶ The brief period of liberalization that occurred in Czechoslovakia following the election of Alexander Dubček as first secretary of the Communist Party in January 1968. In pursuit of 'socialism with a human face', Dubček relaxed state censorship and brought forward legislation to increase civil liberties; he also opened new links with Czechoslovakia's Western neighbours. These policies proved intolerable to the Soviet Union, which led a Warsaw Pact invasion of the country in August 1968 (*see:* Brezhnev doctrine) and aborted the reforms. Dubček was obliged to resign (1969) and was subsequently expelled from the Party. After 20 years in obscurity, he returned to a hero's welcome in Prague during the velvet revolution of 1989.

• **Praise the Lord and pass the ammunition** ▶ The title and chorus of a song by Frank Loesser, popular in America in 1942. A US navy chaplain is said to have used these words to a ship's gunner during the Japanese attack on Pearl Harbor in 1941, although the identity of the chaplain has not been definitely established. During the buzz bomb attacks on London in World War II, a common variation was **Praise the Lord and keep the engine running**: when the engine died the bomb would shortly hit the ground.

• **prang** ▶ World War II RAF slang meaning to bomb a target with evident success; to shoot down another aircraft or to crash one's own; and generally to collide with, or bump into, any vehicle. Hence, also, **wizard prang**, for a wonderful or extremely accurate hit, etc.

• **prawn** ▶
   **come the raw prawn** To try to fool some-

one, a phrase common among Australian forces during World War II and more widely heard subsequently. It is presumably derived from the idea of someone being deceived into accepting a raw prawn, thinking it is cooked.

• **prefab** ▶ A small house or other building constructed from prefabricated sections that were assembled on site. This method of construction was widely practised after World War II to provide temporary housing as quickly as possible. Because the housing shortage persisted long after the end of the design life of these buildings, they presented considerable problems as a result of water penetration, etc.

• **premium bond** ▶ *See:* ERNIE.

• **preppie** or **preppy** ▶ A student or graduate of a US preparatory school – an expensive private secondary school that prepares students for college. The stereotype preppie – someone rich, pampered, and well-groomed – became known in the UK from the hugely successful film *Love Story* (1970), which featured such a character as its hero.

• **prequel** ▶ A novel or film dealing with the earlier lives of characters who have already appeared in a successful novel or film. The word is an adaption of 'sequel'. The prequel is a way of extending the potential of a saga-like story, especially if a sequel is not possible, *e.g.* because a major character dies in the core novel or film.

• **President Peanuts** or **Jiminy Peanuts** ▶ Nickname of US President Jimmy Carter (1924– ), who was born into a prosperous peanut-farming Georgia family.

• **Presidium** ▶ The Presidium of the Supreme Soviet: in the former Soviet Union (1936–91), a body elected by the Supreme Soviet that fulfilled the role of constitutional head of the state. Its chairman was the nation's representative in ceremonial affairs and it issued ordinances when the Supreme Soviet was not in session. *See:* Politburo.

• **Press Barons** ▶ Those newspaper proprietors who were raised to the peerage during the 20th century. They included Alfred Harmsworth (1865–1922), who was created a baron in 1905 and became Viscount Northcliffe in 1917 (*see:* Northcliffe Press). Northcliffe's younger brother, Harold Sidney Harmsworth (1868–1940), was created a baron in 1914, becoming Viscount Rothermere in 1919; he took over the *Daily Mail* on his brother's death. William Maxwell Aitken (1879–1964) was created Baron Beaverbrook in 1917 (*see:* Beaver, the). This Scottish-Canadian self-made millionaire was the owner of the *Sunday Express*, the *Daily Express*, and the *Evening Standard*. James Gomer Berry (1883–1968), 1st Viscount Kemsley, was chairman of Kemsley Newspapers Ltd, which owned the *Sunday Times* and other papers. Roy Herbert Thomson (1894–1976), Baron Thomson of Fleet, acquired *The Scotsman* in 1953 and Kemsley Newspapers in 1959.

• **Press Council** ▸ A UK body established in 1953 and composed of 18 lay and 18 professional individuals under an independent chairman. Its stated purpose was to defend the freedom of the press while considering complaints made by the public against individual newspapers. In 1991 the Council was replaced by the **Press Complaints Commission**, which was charged with improving the general ethical standards of the press as well as dealing with individual complaints. Both bodies have been criticized for their feebleness in dealing with dishonest reporting and invasions of privacy by the press.

> Nearly everyone is happy with the Press Complaints Commission except people with complaints against the press. – RONALD STEVENS, *London Review of Books*, 7 February 2002.

• **press the flesh** ▸ *See*: flesh-pressing.

• **pressure group** ▸ A group that tries to exert pressure on governments, etc. in the interests of a particular cause. Their campaigns, often aimed at changing the law or government policy, may be conducted through letter writing, lobbying, public information, or advertising.

• **preventive detention** ▸ In UK law, the imprisonment of an offender under the Criminal Justice Act (1948) or its predecessor, the Prevention of Crime Act (1908). Under these Acts, the court could pass a further sentence of 5–14 years on a convicted offender found or admitting to be a habitual criminal, in order to prevent the repetition or continuance of his criminal activities. The 1948 Act was replaced in 1973, when the courts were authorized to extend a term of imprisonment if it was thought appropriate for the protection of the public.

In America, preventive detention refers to the imprisonment without bail of an alleged or suspected offender who, in the judge's view, may commit criminal acts before being brought to trial.

• **preventive medicine** ▸ The branch of medicine concerned with identifying possible causes of disease and rectifying or eliminating them before its onset. In its broadest sense, preventive medicine embraces all the activities of specialists in public or community health care and occupational medicine as well as the advice and treatment given by GPs and other health-care workers. In the West, most of the major communicable diseases have now been con-

trolled or eliminated by the use of vaccines and strict quarantine regulations. One notable landmark was the announcement in 1980 by the World Health Organization that smallpox had been effectively eradicated, nearly 200 years after Jenner introduced his cowpox vaccine against the disease. Vaccines developed in the 20th century include those against tuberculosis (1908), whooping cough (1923), yellow fever (1939), measles (1953), polio (1957), and rubella (1965). In developing countries, however, many easily preventable diseases are still rife owing to lack of resources and an appropriate health-care infrastructure. Infant mortality is a particular concern: in some African countries, for instance, up to 25% of all infants die before their fifth birthday, compared to 1–2% in the West. The last 20 years have also seen the spread of HIV and an enormous number of deaths from Aids, especially in central and southern Africa. Of the preventive measures that have been advocated to stem the tide of deaths from this disease, the most important is the use of condoms in both heterosexual and homosexual intercourse.

In the West much preventive medicine is now concerned with delaying the onset of non-infectious disease, such as cancer, heart disease, and stroke. This is achieved by screening and education. Regular medical check-ups are now recommended as a means of improving the early detection of disease and so increasing the chances of successful treatment. Mass screening programmes, *e.g.* for cervical and breast cancer, operate in some countries. People are encouraged to eat wisely, not smoke, drink in moderation, and take exercise – in short, to tailor their lives to healthy living.

• **prices and incomes policy** ▸ A government policy that attempts to restrict rises in both the price of goods and individual earnings in order to control inflation. The policy is difficult to enforce and will only be effective if the inflation is caused by rising costs. In the UK, prices and incomes policies were attempted by both Labour and Conservative governments in the 1970s; they are now usually regarded as an unwarranted interference with market forces.

• **primal scene** ▸ A child's first observation of sexual intercourse between his parents, as recalled by a patient undergoing Freudian analysis. The recollection, which may be either real or imaginary, is considered by some a major source of neurosis. *See also*: something nasty in the woodshed *at* nasty.

• **primal scream** ▸ A type of psychotherapy in which a patient is encouraged, often in a group setting, to relive the painful experiences of childhood and to release violent emotions about parents or others in primitive screams or aggressive physical acts. Primal therapy was originated by Arthur Janov, a US psychologist who wrote a book with this name in 1970.

• **Prime Minister of Mirth** ▶ Nickname of the British actor and music-hall performer Sir George Robey (1869–1954). He became known as the **Darling of the Halls** for an act featuring such characters as Daisy Dilwater, the Mayor of Mudcumdyke, and a red-nosed vicar with staring eyes and a lewd smile. Robey later appeared in plays and films and was in great demand as a pantomime dame.

• **prime time** ▶ The evening hours of television viewing approximately between 7 p.m. and 11 p.m. These are the peak viewing hours and therefore command the highest advertising rates. In America, the Federal Communications Commission restricted stations in large markets to three hours of prime-time network programming. This was intended to produce a variety of local programmes but has generally led to repeats of old films and game shows in the off-peak period.

• **primordial soup** or **prebiotic soup** ▶ A phrase derived from a conjectural description of the primeval oceans by the British biologist J. B. S. Haldane (1892–1964), first published in the 1920s as part of his theory for the origin of life. Haldane envisaged a starkly different oxygen-free atmosphere, containing methane, ammonia, hydrogen, and water. Energy sources, such as lightning and solar radiation, would have caused the formation of organic compounds which, he postulated, 'must have accumulated until the primitive oceans reached the consistency of hot dilute soup'. Further chemical reactions within this soup would lead eventually to the formation of rudimentary living cells. This theory, also arrived at independently by the Soviet biologist Alexander Oparin, prompted a famous experiment conducted in 1952 by Stanley Miller, a graduate student at the University of Chicago. Miller attempted to recreate these hypothetical conditions using a fully enclosed reaction vessel containing the supposed raw ingredients of the primitive atmosphere, and subjected them to repeated electric sparks. After one week he analysed the water in the flask to find that it contained, among many other materials, the amino acids glycine and alanine in appreciable amounts. As these are two of the essential building blocks of living organisms some have seized on the result as vindication of the Haldane–Oparin theory. Others have remained sceptical.

• **Prince of Darkness** ▶ *See*: Mandy.

• **Prince of Wails** ▶ Nickname of the US singer Johnnie Ray (1927– ), whose maudlin style also earned him such sobriquets as the **Cry Guy** and the **Nabob of Sob**. He established his lachrymose reputation with the double-sided single 'Cry' and 'The Little White Cloud That Cried', a million-seller in 1952. He was also known for stage performances in which he sobbed his way through many self-pitying numbers. Part Blackfoot Indian, he was sufficiently deaf to require a hearing aid.

• **Princess Royal** ▶ A title sometimes given to the eldest daughter of a British monarch; the current holder of the title, Princess Anne, was given the title in 1987. The only daughter of Elizabeth II and Prince Philip, she is an accomplished horsewoman and a former member of the British Olympic team. In 1973 she married Captain Mark Phillips (*see*: Fog); they had two children, Peter and Zara, before divorcing in 1992. In the same year she married Captain Timothy Laurence. Apart from horsemanship, the Princess Royal is known for her tirelessness in fulfilling numerous public engagements, her work for many charities (most notably the Save The Children Fund, of which she is president), and her sharp tongue (*see*: Four-letter Annie).

• **pringle** ▶ British slang of the 1980s for a type of young aggressive working-class male who wore expensive designer sportswear. Pringle is the tradename of an expensive type of woollen jumper, usually V-necked and most popular in such pastel colours as lemon and pale pink.

• **Prisoner of Spandau** ▶ Rudolf Hess (1894–1987), Hitler's wartime deputy and a prisoner in Spandau Gaol, Berlin, from 1945 until his death. From 1966 he was the prison's sole inmate. Hess fell into Allied hands following his bizarre solo flight to Scotland in May 1941, apparently intending to discuss peace terms with the Duke of Hamilton. Churchill described this episode as:

> One of those cases where imagination...is baffled by the facts as they present themselves.

Berlin Radio announced that the Deputy Führer had been suffering from 'hallucinations'. In May 1945 the Nuremberg judges (*see*: Nuremberg Trials) rejected his plea of insanity and Hess was sentenced to life imprisonment for war crimes. He appears eventually to have committed suicide.

The epithet 'Prisoner of Spandau' is used mainly by those who insist that the prisoner was not Hess but a double, substituted by the Nazis at the time of the flight to Scotland or by the Allies at some later date. These charges are based on discrepancies in the medical record, the Allies' refusal to release the prisoner long after he had become harmless, and doubts about the circumstances of his death. The problems raised by this theory seem much greater than any it purports to solve. Apart from any of his other claims to notoriety, Hess was the last prisoner to be held in the Tower of London.

• **Private Eye** ▶ A satirical magazine founded by Shrewsbury School and Oxbridge friends Christopher Booker, Richard Ingrams, Willie Rushton, and Peter Cook. The first issue (printed on yellow paper) appeared on Friday 25 October 1961. Booker edited it until 1963, then Ingrams (who wanted to call it *The Bladder*) took over until the present editor, Ian Hislop, replaced him in 1988. A product (and the only survivor) of the 1960s passion for satire, the magazine contains a mixture of gossip, satire, cartoons, and provocative articles exposing hypocrisy and corruption in the establishment. The *Eye* is famous as the persistent target of financially threatening libel suits brought against it by prominent victims. In 1966 the magazine nearly closed after it had to pay £5000 to Lord Russell of Liverpool and in 1977 it had to be helped out by readers' donations after the payment of £85,000 to businessman Sir James Goldsmith. In 1989 *Private Eye* was ordered to pay £600,000 damages to Sonia Sutcliffe, the wife of the Yorkshire Ripper. This was overturned and eventually *Private Eye* paid her £60,000 plus costs in an out-of-court settlement.

• **privatization** ▶ The process of transferring a publicly owned organization to the private sector. This may be done for economic or political reasons. Economically, privatization is only justified if increased competition leads to greater efficiency and an improved public service. Politically, it has been used to increase the number of shareholders in the community by making share offers to the public on generous terms, thus widening support for the capitalist system. In Britain, the Conservative governments of the late 1980s and 1990s sold government interests in (amongst others) British Telecom, British Gas, British Airways, the regional water and electricity companies, and British Rail. Although the subsequent Labour governments have not reversed any of these privatizations, concern over the poor performance of Railtrack led to its replacement by a non-profit trust in 2001. *See also*: nationalization.

• **Prix Goncourt** ▶ The leading French literary prize, established in 1901 in accordance with the will of the writer Edmond de Goncourt (1822–96) to commemorate himself and his brother Jules (1830–70). It is awarded annually for the best prose work in French. The winner receives a symbolic cheque for the sum of 50 francs, although the work is guaranteed to enter the bestseller lists.

• **prize money** ▶ The net proceeds of the sale of enemy shipping and property captured at sea. Prior to 1914 the distribution was confined to the ships of the Royal Navy actually making the capture; subsequently all prize money was pooled and shared out among the navy as a whole. Prize money was paid at the end of World War II for the last time.

• **PRO** ▶ Public relations officer. A person employed by a large firm, charity, or personality to deal with the media on their behalf and to provide information that shows them in a favourable light.

• **pro-am** ▶ Denoting a sporting event open to both *pro*fessional and *am*ateur players. The term is mainly used of golfing tournaments. A special case of the pro-am event is the **pro-celebrity** match, in which professionals compete with well-known names from the entertainment world, usually for charity.

• **pro-choice** ▶ *See*: pro-life.

• **professional foul** ▶ In sport, especially football, a deliberate offence committed to prevent an opponent from scoring or winning. The term is now used in other fields to denote unscrupulous tactics adopted to prevent a rival's success, *e.g.* in business.

• **Profumo affair** ▶ The resignation of John Profumo (1915–99), secretary of state for war in Harold Macmillan's Conservative government, in June 1963 because of his sexual relationship with the call girl Christine Keeler. This lady was also sleeping with Lieutenant-Commander Yevgeny Ivanov, an assistant naval attaché at the Soviet Embassy in London who was suspected of being a GRU officer. Profumo had first encountered the 19-year-old Keeler in July 1961, naked in a swimming pool at a party at Cliveden (*see*: Cliveden set), then the country estate of Lord Astor. The party was also attended by Dr Stephen Ward with whom Keeler lived. Ward, an osteopath with various famous patients to whom he occasionally supplied young women ('popsies'), had already introduced Keeler to Ivanov. MI5 learned of Profumo's association with Keeler through Ward, who was supplying them with information on the activities of the Russian. Warned by a colleague of MI5's concern at the farcical implications of having a secretary of state for war sharing a mistress with a Soviet agent, Profumo broke off his relationship with Keeler. After an unrelated shooting incident at her flat in December 1962, however, Keeler's activities began to attract the attention of the press and rumours of Profumo's relationship with her became rife. On 22 March 1963 he said in a statement in the House of Commons that his relationship with Keeler was entirely innocent. Although subsequent pressure from the Opposition on the security angle forced his resignation, it was his lie to the Commons that deprived him of support from his own party. MI5 and prime minister Harold Macmillan both declared themselves satisfied that no breach of security had taken place, a conclusion also reached by the subsequent investigation into the affair by Lord Denning (see: Denning report). Stephen Ward was brought to trial in July 1963, charged with various offences under the Sexual Offences Act (1956). When Lord Astor repudiated the evidence of Ward's mistress, the call-girl Mandy Rice-Davies, she replied somewhat archly: 'He would say that, wouldn't he?' Ward, widely regarded as the scapegoat for the whole affair, committed suicide on 3 August with an overdose of Nembutal. Profumo subsequently devoted himself to social and charity work, was awarded the CBE in 1975, and in 1982 became administrator of Toynbee Hall in London.

> I am sorry to disappoint the vultures. – STEPHEN WARD, suicide note.

• **program** ▶ A set of instructions, written in a particular computer programming language, which direct a computer to perform a specific operation. See: high-level language; low-level language; machine code.

• **Prohibition** ▶ In America, the ban on the manufacture, sale, or consumption of intoxicating liquor introduced in 1920 with the passage of the Volstead Prohibition Act and ratification of the 18th Amendment to the Constitution. The introduction of the 'noble experiment' was the result of decades of pressure from temperance groups and religious bodies. By 1906 18 states had introduced some form of restriction or ban on the sale of alcohol and many counties and cities were also 'dry' by virtue of the 'local option' made available by state legislatures. Nationwide prohibition, however, proved unenforceable; the supply of illicit liquor to a thirsty population by bootleggers spawned organized crime and widespread corruption among the police and politicians. It was finally repealed in 1933 (see: 21st Amendment).

• **pro-life** or **right-to-life** ▶ Describing people, groups, or movements that support the right of an unborn foetus to life. Pro-lifers therefore seek to limit or ban legal abortions; they also oppose experiments on embryos. The leading British anti-abortion organizations are the Society for the Protection of the Unborn Child (1966) and LIFE (1970). In America, the pro-life lobby is composed of the Catholic Church, such Protestant fundamentalist groups as the moral majority, and activists of such organizations as the National Right to Life Committee (1970), March for Life, and Right to Life. Activists have been responsible for a series of fire-bomb attacks on birth-control and abortion clinics in America since the late 1970s. In one case a doctor who performed abortions was murdered by a 'pro-life' fanatic. Those people, groups, etc. who support the right to have an abortion describe themselves as **pro-choice**.

• **prom** or **promenade concert** ▶ A concert in which some members of the audience stand in an open area of the concert-hall floor. Promenade concerts date back to the days of the London pleasure gardens, such as Vauxhall and Ranelagh. In 1895 Sir Henry Wood (see: Old Timber) began his famous Promenade Concerts at the Queen's Hall, which he conducted for over half a century and which became a regular feature of London life. In 1927 the BBC took over their management from Chappell's. The destruction of the hall by enemy action in 1941 caused a break in the concerts but they soon started again at the Royal Albert Hall and have continued there ever since. Each Prom season, from mid-July to mid-September, provides Londoners with a feast of serious music from all periods. Every concert is broadcast by the BBC; some are also televised. The **last night of the Proms** is devoted to British music and has become an immensely popular British institution. The second half of the concert always includes Elgar's Land of Hope and Glory, Parry's 'Jerusalem', and Wood's 'Fantasia on British Sea-Songs', in which the audience participate with great gusto.

• **Protocols of the Elders of Zion** ▶ Forged material published by Serge Nilus in Russia in 1905, based on an earlier forgery of 1903, purporting to outline secret Jewish plans for achieving world power by securing a monopoly in international finance, and by undermining Gentile morality, family life, and health. Their falsity was exposed by Philip Graves, The Times correspondent in Constantinople, in 1921 and later judicially, at Berne (1934–35). Their influence in inciting antisemitism, notably among the Russians, and later in providing Hitler and his associates with a pretext they knew to be false, provides tragic evidence of the power of the 'big lie'.

• **Prufrock, J. Alfred** ▶ The indecisive and introspective hero of the poem by T. S. Eliot (1888–1965), The Love Song of J. Alfred Prufrock, which was first published in the Chicago magazine Poetry *and Other Observations* (1917). The poem is in the form of a dramatic monologue, which reveals Prufrock (named after a St Louis furniture firm) as timid, sexually inhibited, bored with the Boston social round, and failing in his resolve to transform his life:

> I have measured out my life in coffee spoons...
> I grow old...I grow old...
> I shall wear the bottoms of my trousers rolled...
> Do I dare to eat a peach?

• **pseud** ▶ British colloquialism for a pretentious pseudo-intellectual. The word became popular in the 1960s through its use in the satirical magazine, *Private Eye*, which still features a column called 'Pseuds Corner' – a collection of items garnered from other publications which are thought to show laughable pretentiousness.

• **Psion** ▶ *See*: Filofax.

• **PSL** ▶ Private-sector liquidity. *See*: money supply.

• **Psmith** ▶ A character who appears in some of the earlier novels of P. G. Wodehouse, from *Enter Psmith* (1909) to *Leave it to Psmith* (1923). Psmith (originally named Smith – he adds the 'P' himself for effect) is not a monocled silly ass in the Bertie Wooster mould, and would be unlikely to join the Drones' Club. Rather, he is an ingenious and resourceful manipulator, old beyond his years. He was based on Rupert D'Oyly Carte (1876–1948), a schoolfriend of the author's cousin, who later succeeded his father as proprietor of the D'Oyly Carte Company and became chairman of the Savoy Hotel.

• **psychedelic** ▶ (Greek *psychē*, soul, mind; *dēloun*, to reveal) Denoting experiences of heightened mental and sensory awareness brought about by taking hallucinogenic drugs, such as LSD and mescaline. To the enthusiastic advocates of these drugs, who included Aldous Huxley in the 1950s and Dr Timothy Leary in the 1960s, such experiences offer a more profound view of reality rather than a mere distortion of it. The term, from the jargon of the beatniks and hippies, was imported into the UK from America in the mid-1960s. By 1967 the word **psychedelia** had been coined to refer to the whole world of psychedelic drugs and the burgeoning subculture associated with them. The impact of these drugs on the senses, in particular the distorted images and sounds and kaleidoscopic patterns of light and colour, was imitated in paintings, posters, fabric design, and music, which in turn came to be described as psychedelic.

• **psychedelic art** ▶ A type of art popular in the late 1960s, characterized by complex swirling patterns of brilliant, often jarring, colours and involving elements of op art. In the summer of 1967

designs of this type proliferated in clothing, fabrics, posters, decor, album covers, and all kinds of fashionable bric-à-brac. They also featured prominently in mixed media events (*see*: happening), which combined lightshows, 3D-art installations, and deafening psychedelic rock music to create a totally 'mind-blowing' experience. A favourite technique was to project slides containing coloured oils onto the walls and ceilings, producing vast drifting shapes like amoebas or imploding galaxies. Like other forms of psychedelic art, this was supposed to replicate the visual effects of LSD or other hallucinogens, and was perhaps best appreciated under the same influence.

• **psychobabble** ▶ A type of speech characterized by endless inconclusive analysis of one's own emotions and mental states; its vocabulary is a mixture of hippie slang and the jargon of psychoanalysis and alternative therapies. For instance, a woman might explain her marital difficulties by saying: 'My husband laid a real guilt trip on me and went into total denial when I said I needed space to find my inner child'. A product of the self-obsessed me decade, it became particularly prevalent on the West Coast of America. The term was coined in 1976 by the US writer R. D. Rosen, who later published *Psychobabble: Fast Talk and Quick Cure in the Era of Feeling* (1977). The phenomenon is satirized in Cynthia McFadden's novel *The Serial* (1976), in which the activities of a cast of solipsistic Californians are described entirely in psychobabble.

• **psychodelicatessen** ▶ *See*: head shop.

• **PTFE** ▶ Polytetrafluoroethylene. A synthetic polymer containing the element fluorine, noted for its toughness, resistance to chemical attack, and its low coefficient of friction. It was developed in the 1940s and has a variety of uses; most people know it as the coating for nonstick frying pans. It is manufactured under the tradename **Teflon**.

• **PTSD** ▶ *See*: post-traumatic stress disorder.

• **public access broadcasting** ▶ US broadcasting channels legally reserved, since 1972, for public-service use. Since a cable system can carry more than 100 channels, many communities have public-access channels devoted to local government, which provide a forum for community organizations and individual comment. This freedom of speech has even occasionally been extended, with considerable controversy, to such groups as the racialist Ku Klux Klan.

• **Public Broadcasting Service** ▶ *See*: PBS.

• **Public Enemy No. 1** ▶ The phrase used to describe the US bank robber and murderer John

Dillinger (1903–34), who was active 1933–34 in Indiana and Illinois. He was given this impressive status by the attorney general, Homer Cummings, and was finally shot dead in Chicago by FBI agents, having escaped once from police custody. The phrase 'public enemy' is thought to have been coined by the president of the Chicago Crime Commission, Frank Loesch, in an attempt to alert the public to the dangerous nature of such gangsters and to dispel the aura of glamour that the press had created around them. The James Cagney film *The Public Enemy* (1931) was one of Hollywood's first gangster movies. The phrase is now applied to anything or anyone considered a menace to society.

• **public health medicine** ▶ *See*: community medicine.

• **public lending right** ▶ (PLR) A UK government scheme, introduced in 1983, to enable authors to earn a small royalty when their books are borrowed from public libraries. Authors register with the PLR Registrar, who makes payments based on averages from some 30 libraries. Over 17,000 authors registered for the £4.16 million available for 1998–99. An annual upper limit (£6000 in 1999) on a single author's work is set to help less popular writers. Fiction accounts for nearly 70% of the money earned by authors.

• **public relations officer** ▶ *See*: PRO.

• **Pugwash** ▶ An annual international scientific conference with the aim of promoting the constructive and peaceful uses of scientific knowledge. The first was held in July 1957, at the home of Canadian philanthropist Cyrus Eaton in Pugwash, Nova Scotia. It was inspired by the Einstein-Russell Memorandum, a document describing the appalling consequences for the human race of nuclear conflict, and called for a conference of scientists from both sides of the Iron Curtain. Subsequent meetings have been held in many different countries; subjects for discussion have included nuclear disarmament, environmental issues, and the problems of the developing world. The Pugwash movement, coordinated by an International Continuing Committee, has produced various reports over the years on arms control, which have contributed to progress on disarmament since the 1970s.

• **Pulitzer Prizes** ▶ Prizes for literary work, journalism, drama, and music, awarded annually from funds left for the purpose by Joseph Pulitzer (1847–1911), a prominent and wealthy US editor and newspaper proprietor.

• **pull one's finger out** ▶ A colloquial expression meaning to get moving, to work efficiently. It is often used as a command or an exhortation to one dawdling or doing a job ineffectually. It is now widely heard, although it is regarded by some as too vulgar to use in polite society because of the possible position of the finger that needs pulling out.

• **pulsar** ▶ An extremely dense star that emits short bursts of radio waves or other radiation at precise intervals. The first pulsar was discovered in 1968 (*see*: LGM); over 300 have now been identified. It is thought that the strong magnetic field associated with the star focuses the radiation into two beams. The pulses detected are the result of the star's rotation sweeping the beams around, rather like the signal from a lighthouse.

• **pump iron** ▶ To lift weights for exercise or bodybuilding. The phrase was popularized by the film *Pumping Iron* (1970), which made a star of the Austrian-born bodybuilder Arnold Schwarzenegger (1947– ).

• **pumpkin papers** ▶ *See*: Hiss affair.

• **pumpkin time** ▶ The point at which a period of exceptional prosperity or happiness comes to an end with the status quo being suddenly re-established. The name refers to the time (midnight) when Cinderella's coach reverts to being a pumpkin after the ball.

• **pundit** ▶ Hindi for a person learned in the Sanskrit disciplines. In English the word is used to mean someone who is an authority on a particular subject. Pundits can be seen, for example, on television giving their expert ideas on such subjects as economics or military strategy.

• **punk** ▶ An anarchic youth cult of the mid-to-late 1970s in Britain and America. Its adherents followed **punk rock** bands such as the Sex Pistols and the Clash, whose energetic (if somewhat basic) music, angry lyrics, and generally provocative stance arose as a furious reaction to the dullness and complacency of the music scene at that time. Punks could be recognized by their eccentric ragged clothes and their spiky or extremely short hair, which was often dyed green or red; unusual accessories, such as safety-pins worn as jewellery, were another hallmark. The movement had fizzled out by 1979–80 but its cultural and political meaning continue to be much discussed. Although it provoked horror and outrage at the time, punk is now regarded with a good deal of nostalgia.

The word 'punk' is an archaic term for a prostitute; it later became a derogatory term for a person or thing considered worthless.

• **purges** ▶ The systematic elimination of potential

opponents by Stalin (*see*: Man of Steel), beginning in 1934 and continuing until his death in 1953. The victims included leading politicians, army officers, and party functionaries, as well as many thousands of ordinary citizens. *See also*: Doctors' Plot; Law of December 1; Leningrad Purge; Yezhovshchina.

> You can't make an omelette without breaking eggs. – Joseph STALIN, justifying his tyrannical methods.

• **purple corridors** ▶ *See*: Queen's Flight.

• **Purple Heart** ▶ **1.** A US army medal awarded for wounds received as a result of enemy action while on active service. It consists of a silver heart bearing the effigy of George Washington, suspended from a purple ribbon with white edges. **2.** The popular name of a stimulant pill (Drinamyl), so called from its shape and colour.

• **push-button war** ▶ A war fought with guided missiles controlled by pushing a button.

• **pusher** ▶ Informal for someone who supplies illegal drugs, particularly someone who knowingly supplies addictive drugs in order to create a captive market. The term is used by the police and the tabloid press, rather than by addicts or dealers themselves. Many pushers become suppliers to finance their own drug addictions. Others are essentially pimps, supplying drugs to young women addicts in return for their earnings from prostitution.

• **pussy** ▶ **1.** Slang for the female genitals, probably deriving from the resemblance of pubic hair to cats' fur. **2.** Slang for a female, viewed as a sex object.

• **Pussyfoot Johnson** ▶ Nickname of W. E. Johnson (1862–1945), the US temperance advocate. He gained his nickname from his 'cat-like' policies in pursuing law-breakers in gambling saloons, etc. in Indian territory when serving as chief special officer of the US Indian Service (1908–11). After this he devoted his energies to the cause of Prohibition and gave over 4000 lectures on temperance.

• **Put a sock in it** ▶ An instruction to be quiet. It comes from the days of the early gramophones, which had no mechanical volume controls; a convenient method of reducing the volume was to stuff a sock, or a piece of material of a similar size, in the horn.

• **put down** ▶ To humiliate. A term widely used since the 1960s. In the noun form, **put-down**, it means a belittling remark or humiliating action.

• **put the boot in** ▶ British slang meaning to kick someone. In the early 1970s this was a favourite 1960s expression of the skinheads, who wore large Doc Martens boots. It is also used in a more general sense, meaning to attack someone when they are particularly vulnerable.

• **PVC** ▶ Polyvinyl chloride. A synthetic plastic first developed in the 1930s and made by polymerizing the compound vinyl chloride (chloroethene, $CH_2{:}CHCl$). Commonly, the polymer is mixed with plasticizers, pigments, and other additives to give a flexible material used in packaging, electrical insulation, clothing (*e.g.* raincoats), etc. There is also a hard tough variety of the plastic known as **u-PVC** (unplasticized PVC), which is used as a building material (*e.g.* for door and window frames).

• **PVS** ▶ **1.** Post-Vietnam syndrome. The emotional instability and serious psychological problems encountered by many US veterans of the Vietnam War (1954–75). Many of the US soldiers serving in Vietnam were young and inexperienced conscripts, who faced appalling conditions in which over 55,000 of their compatriots were killed, a fifth accidentally by their own troops. Readjustment to civilian life was made even more difficult by the anti-war mood prevailing in America on their return. The attitude of the US people to the war had become so hostile by 1973 that America was forced to begin a withdrawal. **2.** Post-viral (fatigue) syndrome. *See*: ME.

• **PWA** ▶ Person with Aids. An abbreviation often used in preference to Aids patient or Aids victim.

• **pylon** ▶ Originally a monumental gateway (from Greek *pulon*, a gateway), especially of an Egyptian temple, consisting of two massive towers joined by a bridge over the doorway. The word now usually refers to the single structures that support the overhead cables that make up the electrical grid system.

• **Pylon Poets** ▶ A derogatory nickname for the group of young British left-wing poets – principally W. H. Auden (1907–73), Stephen Spender (1909–95), Louis MacNeice (1907–63), and C. Day Lewis (1904–72) – that emerged in the 1930s. It alludes to their sometimes naive enthusiasm for up-to-the-minute themes and imagery, seen at its most self-conscious, perhaps, in Spender's 1933 poem 'The Pylons'. Auden's idiosyncratic descriptions of industrial landscapes were widely imitated by other members of the group, giving their work a coterie flavour.

• **pyramid selling** ▶ A method of selling a product using a pyramid-like structure of part-time salespeople. At the apex of the pyramid is the holder of a franchise empowering him to sell a particular product. He sells an agreed quantity of the product to a number of regional organizers who sell off their stock to district distributors, who in turn recruit door-to-door salesmen, each of whom takes a proportion of the distributor's stock. As the franchise holder can sell more goods to his regional organizers than are actually sold to consumers at the base of the pyramid, some participants in the structure are likely to be caught with unsold, and probably unsaleable, stock. Pyramid selling is therefore illegal in the UK.

• **Pyrex** ► Tradename for a type of borosilicate glass, used domestically and in chemical apparatus for its heat-resistant properties. The name is often used generically for any kind of heatproof glassware. The first such article was produced in 1915; as it was a pie dish, the tradename 'Pie Right' was suggested: however, as the manufacturers already had a range of products with tradenames ending in '-ex', the new dish was marketed as 'Pyrex'. Any connection with the Greek *pyr*, fire, seems to be coincidental.

# Q

• **Q** ▶ **1.** The pseudonym of the British writer Sir Arthur Quiller-Couch (1863–1944). He compiled the influential first edition of the *Oxford Book of English Verse* (1900) and also wrote literary criticism, short stories, and adventure novels. **2.** The character in Ian Fleming's James Bond stories who provides the secret agent with such sophisticated gadgetry as cars that convert into submarines. In the Bond films he was played for some 35 years by the British character actor Desmond Llewellyn (1914–99).

• **QE2** ▶ Queen Elizabeth 2. A passenger liner built for the British Cunard Company as successor to the flagship Queen Elizabeth. Construction of the 293.52 m (963 ft)-long vessel began in September 1967; after completion the following year she had a gross tonnage of 65,863. She embarked on her maiden voyage in April 1969. The ship upheld the luxurious standards set by her Cunard predecessors, with four swimming pools, a casino, and a 24-hour fast food restaurant. Capable of carrying 1800 passengers, the QE2 has divided her year between plying the North Atlantic crossing and cruising to all parts of the globe. She remains the monarch of the UK's mercantile fleet and the epitome of stylish travel on the high seas. *See also*: Queen Mary.

• **QM2** ▶ *See*: Queen Mary.

• **Q-score** ▶ A rating used in the US advertising world to indicate the popular appeal or prestige of a celebrity, hence the value of his or her name in publicity, product endorsements, etc. It is arrived at by marketing research. Fictional characters have been assessed in the same way: in 1990, for example, advertising researchers correctly predicted only modest success for the film *Dick Tracy*, on the grounds that the hero had a Q-score of only 19 – some way below Wonder Woman and a children's puppet called Howdy Dowdy.

• **Q ships** ▶ In World Wars I and II, the name given to Allied gunships camouflaged as tramps. These ships were used to lure U-boats to their destruction. In the late 20th century the UK police used so-called **Q-cars**, ordinary unmarked cars containing plain-clothes police, to catch speeding motorists.

• **QSO** ▶ Quasi-stellar object. *See*: quasar.

• **Quadrant** ▶ The codename of a conference that took place at the Citadel in Quebec (11–24 August 1943) between Franklin D. Roosevelt, Winston Churchill, and other Allied leaders. The aim of the conference was to discuss preparations for the Allied invasion of Europe; there were also debates on strategy and command.

• **quadraphonics** ▶ A system for recording and reproducing music that aims to create a more spatial sound than stereo. The different voices and instruments are recorded by four microphones gathering the sound from different directions. When the music is played, four separate signals are fed to four independent speakers placed in different parts of the room. The system enjoyed a vogue in the 1970s.

• **quality of life** ▶ A phrase, originating in the 1970s, that encompasses all those aspects of everyday life that make it enjoyable or fulfilling. It was first heard in the 1970s. Annual rankings of US cities, employing different combinations of such criteria as weather, health care, education, population density, and pollution, have named such diverse cities as Seattle, Washington, and Pittsburgh as the metropolitan areas providing the best quality of life. Similar criteria have been used to rank the various cities and regions of the UK.

• **quality time** ▶ A phrase that originated in America but is now also used in the UK to describe a limited period during the day of a very busy person, when they can devote all their attention to something that is important to them. In middle-class families in which both parents work, it is often applied to the hour or so that follows their return from work, which they devote entirely to playing with their children. Conversely, it may refer to a short period early in the day, before the brain is addled by domestic or work pressures, which people can devote to a particular project or pursuit.

• **quandong** ▶ An Australian colloquialism for a professional sponger and by extension anyone who accepts drinks, hospitality, etc., without returning the favour. It is often used contemptuously of a woman who allows herself to be entertained by a man but fails to provide the expected quid pro quo. *Quandong* is an Aboriginal name for the native peach, a small semiparasitic tree that depends on a larger tree for its food and shelter.

• **quango** ► Quasi-Autonomous National (or Non-) Government Organization. An acronym for a body appointed by a minister in the British government to carry out some public duty at the public expense. Some members of a quango are usually civil servants but others are not. Although a quango is not a government agency, it is not entirely independent and is answerable to a minister. ACAS is an example of a quango.

• **quantum leap** ► A sudden breakthrough or highly significant advance. The phrase is borrowed from the field of physics, in which it means the sudden jump of a particle from one energy level to another. *See*: quantum theory.

• **quantum theory** ► A theory in physics that energy is not transferred continuously but in discrete amounts, called 'quanta' (plural of 'quantum'). It arose in 1900 as a result of work on the distribution of wavelengths of radiation emitted by hot bodies. At the time, scientists believed that they had the necessary theories to explain all phenomena and the fact that these experimental results were quite different from the theoretical expectations came as a great shock (called the **ultraviolet catastrophe**). In 1900 the German physicist Max Planck explained the result by introducing the idea of quanta of energy (*see*: Planck constant). At around the same time, other phenomena were coming to light that needed a quantum explanation. In 1905, Albert Einstein explained the photoelectric effect (the ejection of electrons from matter by light or other electromagnetic radiation) by assuming that light was composed of a stream of particles (photons) having both particle-like behaviour and wave-like behaviour. In 1913, the Danish physicist Niels Bohr (1885–1962) explained the spectrum of the hydrogen atom by suggesting that the electron orbiting the nucleus could only have certain orbits and absorbed or emitted radiation by making a 'quantum jump' from one orbit to another. In 1923, the French theoretician Louis de Broglie (1892–1987) suggested that if light waves could sometimes behave as particles then particles could, under certain circumstances, behave as waves. 1927 saw the publication of Heisenberg's Uncertainty Principle. Subsequently, various mathematical formulations of the quantum idea were developed, known as **quantum mechanics**.

Quantum mechanics has been extremely successful in describing and predicting the behaviour of atoms and subatomic particles. It does, however, have profound and, as yet, unresolved philosophical problems associated with it. For example, the idea that electrons sometimes behave as waves and sometimes as particles, depending on the experimental conditions, has caused people to ask what electrons actually are. Sir Arthur Eddington once suggested that the electron was a particle on Mondays, Wednesdays, and Fridays, and a wave on Tuesdays and Thursdays. Niels Bohr, in 1927, formulated the **complementarity principle**, in which he said that there was no point in looking for the 'underlying reality'. The only reality was the result obtained by making an observation; different types of observation produce different types of result. Evidence from different observations may not be amenable to being presented in a single model and therefore different pieces of evidence gave complementary conclusions. A consequence of this view, and of the uncertainty principle, is that our knowledge of the universe can never be absolute but always depends on probabilities.

This view of quantum mechanics is known as the **Copenhagen interpretation** (after Bohr's university) and has been highly influential among physicists, even though it seems in some ways to be unacceptable on a commonsense basis. Bohr was once reputed to have admonished a student researching quantum theory by telling him:

> We all know that your ideas are ridiculous but some of us wonder whether they are ridiculous enough!

Not everyone agreed with this uncertain view of physics. Einstein, in particular, believed until the end of his life that there is an underlying explanation:

> God does not play dice with the Universe! He may be subtle, but He is not malicious.

Other physicists have drawn attention to paradoxes in the theory (*see*: Schrödinger's cat).

• **quark** ► A subatomic particle believed to be a fundamental building block of matter. The idea of quarks was first put forward by the US theoretical physicist Murray Gell-Mann (1929– ) in 1964. He suggested that quarks have an electric charge that is a fraction of the electron's charge and that certain types of particle are composed of several quarks, of which there were originally three types. The name 'quark' was taken by Gell-Mann from a phrase in James Joyce's book *Finnegans Wake*, 'Three quarks for Muster Mark'. Protons, neutrons, and similar particles are composed of three quarks. Mesons are made of two quarks (a quark combined with an antiquark). Further extensions of the quark hypothesis have since been made, in which the quarks are characterized by various 'flavours' and 'colours'; they are held together by exchanging particles known as gluons (because they glue the quarks together).

Quark theory has been extremely successful in predicting and explaining the existence and properties of elementary particles. The only problem is that, despite many efforts, nobody has ever detected the existence of a free quark or gluon. It is probable that the energies required to separate them are too large to be obtained in current particle accelerators.

• **quartz crystal** ▶ A small crystal of quartz that is piezoelectric; *i.e.* a stress on the crystal produces an electric voltage between opposite faces. Crystals of quartz have a natural frequency of vibration and can be used to regulate the frequency of an electric circuit to a high degree of accuracy (a variation in timing of less than one tenth of a second in a year). Quartz crystal oscillators have many uses, particularly in regulating clocks and watches. Quartz watches driven by small batteries were first introduced in the 1960s, originally with a digital display but also with a conventional analog display. Their invention caused extensive redundancies in the Swiss watch industry.

• **quasar** ▶ *Quasi*-stellar object, or QSO. A distant astronomical object thought to be the nucleus of a galaxy. Quasars are the most distant observed objects in the universe, being up to $10^{10}$ light-years away. Discovered originally by radioastronomers, the US astronomer Allan Sandage (1926–  ) first observed one using an optical telescope in 1960. Quasars are pointlike objects that have very large redshifts. It is possible that they may be black holes that are attracting matter in the surrounding galaxy.

• **Quatermass** ▶ The eponymous hero of three BBC TV science-fiction series, written by Nigel Kneale and broadcast in the mid-1950s, called *The Quatermass Experiment*, *Quatermass II*, and *Quatermass and the Pit*. In the series Professor Bernard Quatermass was a rocket scientist, who battled various malevolent forces from beyond the earth. The character was played by several actors, most notably by André Morell in *Quatermass and the Pit*. In *The Quatermass Experiment* an astronaut returns to earth and begins to mutate into a fungoid creature. *Quatermass II* was about a top secret government plant, which Quatermass discovers is being used to acclimatize aliens to the Earth's atmosphere. In *Quatermass and the Pit* the discovery of a Martian spaceship reawakens supernatural forces dormant for mil-

lions of years. Intelligently scripted and imaginatively produced as well as genuinely frightening, all three series were subsequently made into Hammer horror films. A subsequent series screened by ITV in 1979 proved to be rather a disappointment, as it featured no monsters and few visual shocks.

• **queen** ▶ Slang for a male homosexual, especially one who is effeminate or a transvestite. Both 'queen' and the earlier 'quean' (derived from Old English *cwene*, woman) were formerly used to mean a whore; they were later applied to male prostitutes, effeminate males, and then to male homosexuals generally.

• **Queen, Ellery** ▶ The fictional detective hero of numerous books and films of the 1930s and 1940s; also the pseudonym used by the authors of the stories in which he appeared. These were actually written by the cousins Frederic Dannay (1905–82) and Manfred Lee (1905–71). *The Roman Hat Mystery* (1929) was followed by many more Ellery Queen stories; the popularity of the detective led to the launch of *Ellery Queen's Mystery Magazine* in 1941. A number of the stories were adapted for the cinema in the 1930s and 1940s, when Ralph Bellamy was among the actors who played the sleuth. The US actor Jim Hutton played the role of the detective in a television series of the mid-1970s.

• **Queen Charlotte's Ball** ▶ An annual event held at the Grosvenor House Hotel, London, to raise funds for Queen Charlotte's Hospital. Queen Charlotte's Birthday Ball was inaugurated in 1925 and held annually in May until 1976, as a major event of the London season, when debutantes 'came out' into society. It was revived in 1989 and is now held in September: around 150 debutantes are invited, together with representatives of the Royal Family and the media, celebrities from the world of entertainment and fashion, and consultants from Queen Charlotte's Hospital. A huge birthday cake is traditionally made for the occasion: the debutantes file past in a long procession, curtsying to the cake, before it is ceremonially cut.

• **Queen Elizabeth** ▶ Either of two illustrious British vessels of the 20th century. The battleship HMS *Queen Elizabeth*, launched in 1913, saw action in both World Wars. This 183 m (600 ft)-long vessel, of 27,500 tons displacement, gave her name to a class of fast well-armoured battleships that included *Warspite*, *Valiant*, *Barham*, and *Malaya*, all launched between 1913 and 1915. *Queen Elizabeth* went into action at the Dardanelles in February 1915; in November 1916 she became the flagship for the fleet's C-in-C, Admiral Beatty. The naval armistice with Germany was signed on board the *Queen Elizabeth* at

Rosyth on 15 November 1918. After a reconstruction (1937–41) she was commissioned into the Mediterranean fleet and took part in the action to evacuate Crete in May 1941. In December she was struck by an Italian manned torpedo in Alexandria harbour and needed extensive repairs, but later re-entered the war to serve in home waters and the Far East. She was scrapped in 1948.

Her namesake, RMS *Queen Elizabeth*, was launched in 1938, having been built by the Cunard Steamship Company as a companion to their passenger liner, Queen Mary. However, war intervened, and in 1940 the new vessel sailed secretly to New York and thence to Singapore for fitting out as a troop carrier. Only when hostilities ceased was she converted to a passenger liner – the world's largest, with an original gross tonnage of 83,673 and a length of 314 m (1031 ft). She finally embarked on her first commercial voyage on 16 October 1946, sailing from Southampton to New York. In 1968, while her successor *Queen Elizabeth 2* (*see*: QE2) was being fitted out, Cunard sold her to a US company. A plan to convert her to a convention centre and tourist attraction fell through and in 1970 she sailed from her mooring at Port Everglades, Florida, to Hong Kong, under the ownership of Taiwanese shipping tycoon, C. Y. Tung. Again, fate intervened, this time on 9 January 1972, when several fires apparently started simultaneously swept the ship and gutted this one-time denizen of the world's sealanes. Ignominiously she sank, a victim of suspected arson, and was later cut up for scrap.

• **Queen Mary** ▶ A luxury passenger liner built by the UK's Cunard Steamship Company and launched in September 1934, primarily for service on the company's transatlantic route. From 1938 until after the war she held the prestigious Blue Riband of the Atlantic for the fastest transatlantic round trip, clocking up average speeds of 30.99 knots westbound and 31.69 knots eastbound. Like her younger companion ship, Queen Elizabeth, the RMS *Queen Mary* served as a troop ship during World War II; during the latter half of the war, as a transatlantic ferry, she could carry up to 15,000 troops. Refitted as a liner after the war, she continued to offer passengers a unique blend of leisure and opulence. However, faced with growing competition from airlines, the company sold her in 1967, and she is now moored at Long Beach, California, as a floating museum and hotel.

In 2000 Cunard signed a contract with the French shipbuilder Alstom Chantiers de L'Antique for £538 million to build a successor to the Queen Mary to be called **Queen Mary 2** (**QM2**). This ship will be larger than any other and fitted out with considerable elegance. It is due to be launched in 2003.

• **Queen of Burlesque** ▶ Nickname of Gypsy Rose Lee (Rose Louise Hovick; 1914–70), US striptease artist who was noted for the wit, sophistication, and style she introduced to her craft. Together with her sister (later the actress, June Havoc), she joined her mother on the vaudeville circuit at a very early age. At 14 she had her first engagement in burlesque; within two years she was on Broadway, heading the bill at Billy Minsley's Republic Theatre. During the 1930s she was lionized by some of New York's most celebrated writers and intellectuals, becoming a regular contributor to such publications as *Harper's* and *The New Yorker*. In 1937 she announced her retirement as a stripper; she then moved to Hollywood to make her film debut, in *You Can't Have Everything*. Over the next three decades she played in a further eight, generally rather mediocre, films, emerged quite regularly from retirement to make stage appearances, and wrote two popular thrillers, *The G-string Murders* and *Mother Finds a Body*. Her autobiographical book, *Gypsy* (1957), formed the basis for a hugely successful Broadway musical of the same name (1959) and later for a rather less successful film version (1962).

> God is love, but get it in writing. – GYPSY ROSE LEE.

• **Queen of Crime** ▶ Nickname of the British detective-story writer Dame Agatha Christie (1890–1976). Born Agatha Mary Clarissa Miller, she wrote more than 70 novels and plays and created two popular amateur sleuths, Hercule Poirot and Miss Marple. Her works, many of which have been adapted for cinema and television, are characterized by complex plots in which the reader is constantly misled. They include the novels *Murder on the Orient Express* (1934) and *Death on the Nile* (1937) and the play *The Mousetrap* (1952; *see*: Mousetrap, The).

Her private life created its own mystery. In 1926 she disappeared from view for several weeks, leading to a nationwide police hunt. She was finally found in a health resort in Derbyshire, apparently suffering from amnesia. A full explanation of this episode has never been given; some regarded it as a publicity stunt, others as a genuine attack of amnesia, perhaps brought on by her failing marriage. Agatha divorced her husband, Archibald Christie, in 1928 but used his name throughout her writing career. In 1930 she married the archaeologist Max Mallowan.

• **Queen of the Air** ▶ A press nickname for the British aviator Amy Johnson (1903–41). In April 1930 she piloted a second-hand Gypsy Moth aircraft from

Croydon to Darwin in 19 days, becoming the first woman to fly solo from the UK to Australia. The 10,000-mile journey, undertaken at the age of 27 and with only a hundred hours previous flying experience, made her a national heroine and the darling of the press. She later made record-breaking flights from Siberia to Tokyo (1931) and from the UK to Cape Town (1932). In 1932 she married the aviator Jim Mollison (1905–59), with whom she flew the Atlantic in 1936, although the marriage later broke up. In 1941 she was flying a wartime mission for the Air Ministry when her plane disappeared over the Thames Estuary; she is now thought to have fallen victim to friendly fire from an anti-aircraft battery.

> Had I been a man I might have explored the Poles or climbed Mt Everest, but as it was my spirit found outlet in the air.

• **Queen of the Halls** ▶ Nickname of the British music-hall artiste Marie Lloyd (1870–1922). Born Matilda Alice Victoria Wood, she enjoyed immense popularity as a singer and comedienne for some 30 years: her alternative nickname, **Our Marie**, indicates the warmth of feeling with which she was regarded by the British public. Her most famous songs include 'Oh! Mr Porter' and the risqué 'A Little of What You Fancy Does You Good'. She died three days after collapsing on stage at the Edmonton Empire.

• **Queen's Awards** ▶ The Queen's Award to Industry was instituted by royal warrant in 1965 for outstanding achievement by a British firm. In 1976 it was replaced by two separate awards, **The Queen's Award for Export Achievement**, for a sustained increase in export earnings, and **The Queen's Award for Technological Achievement**, for a significant advance in technology. The awards are announced on the Queen's natural birthday (see: Queen's birthday), are held for five years, and enable the winners to use a special emblem on their stationery and to fly a special flag.

• **Queen's birthday** ▶ Either of two days in the calendar. The natural birthday of the monarch, currently 21 April, is celebrated by the hoisting of the Union flag over public buildings throughout the nation. A further ceremonial touch is shown by judges of the Queen's Bench Division, who mark this red-letter day literally, by wearing scarlet robes. However, full celebrations are deferred until the official birthday – not a fixed date but generally a Saturday in the middle of June (before 1958 it was fixed on the second Thursday in June). The centrepiece of the day is the trooping the colour ceremony on Horse Guards Parade in London, which until 1985

the Queen customarily attended on horseback. Announcement of the Birthday Honours list coincides with the Queen's official birthday. The official birthday was introduced during the reign of Edward VII (1901–10), who sensibly preferred to hold the outdoor ceremonials in mid-summer rather than on his natural birthday in November.

• **Queen's English** ▶ See: Received Pronunciation.

• **Queen's Flight** ▶ A fleet of aircraft used by the Queen, other members of the Royal Family, senior government ministers, and foreign dignitaries. The flight is maintained by the ministry of defence and stationed at RAF Benson, Oxfordshire. For short trips there are Wessex helicopters or Hawker-Siddeley Andovers; longer overseas flights are usually made by jet, either a BA 146-100 or a VC 10. Edward VIII created the first King's Flight in 1936; since then a special fleet has conveyed royalty at home and abroad. The royal craft are granted specially wide flight paths, known as **purple corridors**, to minimize the risk of collision with other aircraft. The sovereign and the heir to the throne never travel on the same aircraft.

• **Queen's Gallantry Medal** ▶ A decoration for outstanding bravery bestowed on civilians or service personnel. It was introduced in 1974.

• **Queen's Guide** ▶ A holder of the premier award of the Guides Association (see: Girl Guides), open to Rangers aged between 16 and 18 years. The present syllabus generally takes about two years to complete; it involves undertaking various types of community service and an enterprise test. The badge of Queen's Guide must be earned before the entrant's 19th birthday. The award was instituted in 1945 for 1st Class Guides who demonstrated qualities of service, commitment, and conduct consistent with the ideals of the Guides' founder, Lord Baden-Powell.

• **Queen's Scout** ▶ A holder of the highest award attainable by a Venture Scout, open to scouts of either sex who already possess the Venture Scout Award. Candidates must fulfil various personal and practical requirements, including planning and successfully undertaking a 4–5-day cross-country expedition, and provide evidence of regular community and social service. Award-winners receive a gold crown uniform insignia and a special Royal Certificate from the Queen. The Award was introduced by King Edward VII, as the King's Scout Award. In 1934, watched by George V and other members of the Royal Family, the first annual National Scout Service and Review was held at Windsor, which Queen's Scouts (or King's Scouts) are privileged to attend.

• **queer** ▸ Slang for a male homosexual. In the 1970s this pejorative term was largely replaced by gay. In the early 1990s, however, some gay activists decided to reclaim the word 'queer' for themselves. Their radical agenda is sometimes known as the New Queer Politics:

> Young American homosexuals want to be called queer rather than gay because it has more 'political potency'. They chant at rallies: 'We're here, we're queer – get used to it.' The trend, led by Militant Queer Nation, is also set to sweep Britain. Lesbian, Liza Powers, 34, said: 'Using a word that is offensive is a way of showing anger. Gay is white middle class.' – *The Sun*, 9 April 1991.

• **queer-basher** ▸ Slang for someone who physically attacks or victimizes male homosexuals. It can also be used figuratively for someone who is prejudiced against homosexuals.

• **Queer Hardie** ▸ Nickname of the British Labour politician (James) Keir Hardie (1856–1915). A former coal miner and active trade unionist, he was a cofounder and chairman of the Independent Labour Party and the Labour Representation Committee, which became the Labour Party in 1906. His nickname relates to his eccentricity: on his first day in Parliament, for example, he arrived in the cloth cap that was to become his trademark. For the last 15 years of his life Hardie served as MP for Merthyr Tydfil. An ardent pacifist, he died disillusioned with the Labour Party's support for World War I.

• **Quemoy crisis** ▸ Two periods of heightened international tension in the 1950s arising from the disputed sovereignty of Quemoy and Matsu, two islands just off the E China coast that had remained under Nationalist control after the Communist victory on the mainland in 1949. In 1954 the Communist Chinese premier, Chou En-lai, declared his intention of ousting the Nationalists from their last strongholds of Taiwan and nearby islands. Communist forces began an artillery bombardment of Quemoy and Matsu in September 1954, which prompted the signing, in December, of a mutual defence treaty between the Nationalists and their principal ally, America. Early in 1955 Congress authorized US military action in the event of a threatened Communist invasion of the disputed islands. The crisis flared up again in August 1958 with a renewed Communist bombardment of Quemoy, now home to a large Nationalist garrison. The Americans, wary of being drawn into a major conflict, criticized the Nationalists for their military build-up on Quemoy and effectively abandoned their policy of endorsing Nationalist hopes of recapturing the Chinese mainland. Although intermittent shelling continued on both sides, a more serious confrontation was avoided.

• **question time** ▸ The part of the timetable in both Houses of Parliament during which ministers reply to questions put by members or peers. In the House of Commons, question time commences at the start of the sitting every day except Friday, lasting for at least three-quarters of an hour, and ends not later than 3.30 p.m. Replies to questions of a complicated or personal nature are generally given in written form and sent to the member personally, besides being printed in Hansard. Members requiring oral answers must give at least two days' notice before the day on which the minister concerned is scheduled to appear. After the minister has read out the answer, the questioner usually asks one or more supplementary questions, with further responses from the minister. On Wednesdays (until 1997 on Tuesdays and Thursdays), the prime minister appears to answer questions, commencing at 3 p.m. Often this takes the form of a set piece confrontation with the leader of the Opposition on a topic of current concern. A frequent ploy used in an effort to catch the prime minister off guard is to make the original question simply an innocuous enquiry about his or her official engagements for the day. This provides the opportunity for a supplementary question on virtually any issue. With the advent of the live broadcasting of Parliament (from 1978), question time assumed a new significance in the country's political life; however, public interest in its ritualized exchanges has waned considerably since the 1990s.

• **quick and dirty** ▸ Denoting something that has been hastily put together and is therefore likely to be flawed or lacking in final polish. The phrase dates from about 1960, when it was used in US magazine publishing.

• **quickie** ▸ **1.** In film industry jargon, a cheaply produced film designed to make a quick return on the money invested. *See:* quota quickie. **2.** In everyday speech, a quick drink, as in 'Come and have a quickie', or an impromptu and rapid act of sexual intercourse, as in 'We've just got time for a quickie'.

• **quid** ▸

**not the full quid** An Australian expression meaning not fully possessed of one's faculties; half-witted or mad. It dates from the time when the pound (quid) was still used in Australia and has many common variants, such as **ten bob short of a quid**, **only tuppence in the quid**, etc.

• **quidditch** ▶ *See*: Potter, Harry.

• **quiff** ▶ A male hairstyle in which the hair at the front is worn long but brushed up and back. It usually needs to be held in place by some kind of hair preparation or by allowing the hair to remain greasy. It was a very popular style with the teddy boys and rockers (*see*: mods and rockers) of the 1950s and 1960s and is still worn today, especially by those who wish to imitate those styles.

> ...a quiff that looks as if it's been piped on like stiff black cream. – *The Independent*, 13 March 1991.

• **quill driver** ▶ A clerical member of the armed services, particularly the Royal Navy. This 19th-century term for a clerk has survived only in services slang.

• **quisling** ▶ Any traitor or collaborator. The name comes from Vidkun Quisling (1887–1945), the Norwegian admirer of Mussolini and Hitler, who acted as advance agent for the German invasion of Norway in 1940. He duly became puppet minister-president. He surrendered (9 May 1945) after the German defeat and was tried and shot (24 October).

> A vile race of quislings – to use the new word which will carry the scorn of mankind down the centuries – is hired to fawn upon the conqueror. – WINSON CHURCHILL, speech, 12 June 1941.

• **quonset hut** ▶ US name for a prefabricated building made of corrugated iron sheet. The UK equivalent is the Nissen hut. The name comes from Quonset Point, Rhode Island, where these buildings were first made in the early 1940s.

• **quota hopping** ▶ The practice of registering a business in an EU nation other than one's own in order to take advantage of that nation's more favourable production quotas. The best-known case in recent decades involved Spanish fishing boats registering as British in order to benefit from the UK fishing quota. The Merchant Shipping Act (1989) was passed to prevent this abuse.

• **quota quickie** ▶ In the 1920s and 1930s, a type of inferior B-movie churned out by British studios in order to take advantage of the **quota system**. This was a well-intentioned measure requiring British cinemas to show a certain percentage of home-produced films. In practice, however, the dearth of good British material meant that cinemas could only make up the quota by accepting substandard products. As a result, poor-quality low-budget films acquired a distribution they would never have gained on their own merits; this made them commercially attractive to produce.

• **quota system** ▶ 1. A US solution, dating from the early 1970s, to the problem of ensuring that members of minority groups have a fair chance of being employed or educated. The quota system sets a minimum percentage of people from such groups as Blacks and women who must be hired by all organizations in receipt of federal funds. This **affirmative action** has been denounced as **reverse discrimination** by some, as more highly qualified candidates who are not members of a minority may be rejected to enable the quota to be met. The practice has been subjected to repeated legal challenges and is now opposed by the Republican Party. 2. *See*: quota quickie.

• **qwerty** or **QWERTY** ▶ The standard keyboard on an English-language typewriter, wordprocessor, or computer. The name comes from the first keys of the top left row of letters. The 'querty keyboard' was introduced in the 1920s – not, as many suppose, to put the letters in the most convenient positions, but to slow the user down so that the old-fashioned mechanical typewriter did not jam as a result of being tapped too rapidly.

# R

• **R** ▶ Restricted. A US film certification introduced in 1968, meaning that persons under 17 should only see the film accompanied by a parent or guardian. *See also*: X.

• **raas** ▶ A term of abuse in Caribbean English, also used as an exclamation of anger or contempt. It is a shortened form of 'raascla', literally a cloth for wiping the arse.

• **Rab** ▶ Nickname of the British Conservative politician Richard Austen Butler (1902–82), formed from his initials. Butler held a number of important government posts, though he failed in both his attempts to become leader of the Conservative Party (Harold Wilson is said to have described him as 'the best prime minister we never had'). He is remembered for his Education Act (1944), which introduced secondary education for all without payment (*see*: Butler Act).

• **Rab's Boys** ▶ The bright young Tories who helped R. A. Butler to reshape Conservative social and economic policy after the party's electoral defeat in 1945. They were mostly members of the Conservative Research Department and the party's industrial policy committee, both headed by Butler. In particular, they are credited with changing the Conservatives' attitude to the welfare state, nationalization, and unemployment.

• **Race for the Sea** ▶ The attempt by the Allied and German armies to achieve a decisive victory on the Western Front in the autumn of 1914 by outflanking one another's lines to the north before reaching the coast of Flanders. The Battle of the Marne (5–10 September) had marked the final defeat of the famous Schlieffen Plan, by which the Germans had hoped to outflank and encircle the French by advancing through Belgium. From mid-September, both sides attempted to extend their lines northwards through Flanders, fighting a series of bitter skirmishes which culminated in the first Battle of Ypres (20 October–18 November). The BEF suffered 50,000 casualties at Ypres and was virtually wiped out but the German attempt to break through and capture the Channel Ports was decisively frustrated. The Race for the Sea therefore ended in stalemate; from November 1914 the Western Front settled into static trench warfare, which persisted until the armistice in 1918.

• **race music** ▶ From the 1920s to the 1940s, a euphemistic term for various musical styles, especially blues and rhythm-and-blues, played and appreciated by US Blacks. It was invented by record companies who, in the racial climate of the time, felt sensitive about advertising 'Negro' music. Until the 1950s most companies operated a type of musical segregation, putting out records by or appealing to Blacks on separate 'race' labels.

• **Rachmanism** ▶ The use of extortion and bullying tactics by a private landlord against his tenants. The word refers to Peter Rachman (1920–62), a Polish immigrant whose undesirable activities of this kind in the Paddington area of London were brought to light in 1962–63.

• **racism** or **racialism** ▶ Belief in the genetic superiority of a particular race (invariably one's own), leading to prejudice, discrimination, or brutality towards people of other races. 'Racialism' is the older term, dating from the early years of the 20th century, while 'racism' came into widespread use with the rise of Nazism in the 1930s. There is some disagreement as to whether the terms are exact synonyms. 'Racialism' is more likely to be used of pseudo-scientific theories purporting to show that moral or intellectual qualities are transmitted in the same way as physical characteristics, while 'racism' usually refers to the behaviour of those who practise racial discrimination. In the UK overt racism became illegal with the passing of the Race Relations Acts (1965, 1968, and 1976); subsequent Acts (1986, 1997) created offences of stirring up racial hatred and racist abuse. Despite these measures, evidence suggests that discriminatory attitudes towards non-Whites are deeply entrenched in White-dominated establishments and organizations. Described as **institutional racism**, this form of discrimination was highlighted in the Macpherson Report (1999) as the principal cause for the failure of the Metropolitan Police to bring a prosecution in the case of Stephen Lawrence, a young Black murdered by White racists in 1993 (*see*: Stephen Lawrence case). *See also*: civil rights movement; apartheid.

• **RADA** ▶ Royal Academy of Dramatic Art. The leading British drama school, founded in 1904 by Herbert Beerbohm Tree. Originally it was located at Her (then His) Majesty's Theatre, London, but moved to the present Gower Street site in 1905. For many years it was run by Sir Kenneth Barnes (1878–1957); its main theatre, the Vanbrugh, opened in 1954 and was named after his actress sisters, Irene and Violet Vanbrugh. An earlier theatre was destroyed in a bombing raid in 1941. Many of the UK's leading actors and actresses learnt their craft at RADA; among its alumni are Richard Attenborough, Alan Bates, Sir John Gielgud, Glenda Jackson, and Kenneth Branagh.

• **radar** ▶ An acronym formed from *radio detection and ranging*; originally a means of detecting the direction and range of aircraft, ships, etc., by the reflection of centimetric radio waves. It is particularly valuable at night or in fog. It was first developed by a British team led by Sir Robert Watson-Watt in 1934–35 and proved of great value during World War II, especially during the Battle of Britain. It has since been greatly extended so that automatic guidance and navigation of aircraft, missiles, ships, etc., can be achieved by computerized on-board radar equipment.

• **radar trap** ▶ A section of road or motorway monitored by police radar to catch speeding motorists. Fixed radar speed traps first came into operation in the late 1950s, but with the increasing miniaturization of electronic components the latest police radar devices are easily portable and include vehicle-mounted and handheld continuous-wave radar guns. These devices, which monitor the speed of motorists from a patrolling police vehicle, are used in tandem with ancillary video equipment to record details of the speed and direction of offenders.

• **radical chic** ▶ The late 1960s fad for members of high society to socialize and sympathize with extreme radicals, such as the Black Panthers in America. The expression was coined by the US journalist and writer Tom Wolfe (1931– ) in his 1970 book, *Radical Chic (Mau-Mauing the Flak Catchers)*.

> Tom Wolfe...satirised the glitterati's obsession with revolutionaries from the wrong side of the tracks in his essay *Radical Chic*, his account of the evening when Leonard Bernstein threw a glamorous cocktail party for the Black Panthers. – *The Times*, 1 March 2002.

• **radioastronomy** ▶ The branch of astronomy concerned with detecting radio waves from sources in space. It began with the accidental discovery in 1932 by the US radio engineer Karl Jansky (1905–50) of radio sources outside the Earth. Jansky was at that time investigating static in a radio set and trying to track down its source. From the late 1940s, it became a major research field. *See*: Jodrell Bank; LGM; pulsar; quasar.

• **radiocarbon dating** ▶ *See*: carbon dating.

• **Radio Caroline** ▶ Britain's first offshore 'pirate' radio station, which began broadcasting on Easter Sunday, 29 March 1964. The station was set up by Ronan O'Rahilly, a music agent, on an ex-Danish passenger ferry *Frederica*, which was equipped with two 10 kW transmitters and a 168 foot (51 m) radio mast; the *Frederica* was anchored outside British territorial waters, three miles off Frinton-on-Sea, Essex, to evade the British government ban on commercial broadcasting. Within three weeks the pop station attracted nearly seven million listeners and could command a rate of £190 for 60 seconds air time from advertisers. In the wake of Radio Caroline's success, numerous other pirate stations of varying quality opened, such as Radio Scotland, Radio England, and Radio Sutch (run by 'Screaming Lord Sutch', ex-pop singer and eccentric election candidate). In July 1964 one of these rivals, Radio Atlanta, joined forces with Caroline to become Radio Caroline North, anchored 3 miles off Ramsey, Isle of Man. All the pirate stations were outlawed by the Marine Broadcasting (Offences) Act, which came into operation in August 1967. In the same year the BBC introduced Radio 1 to satisfy the public appetite for non-stop pop music, employing young talents, such as Tony Blackburn, Johnny Walker, and Simon Dee, all of whom had begun their careers on Radio Caroline as pirate disc jockeys.

• **Radio City** ▶ Part of the Rockefeller Center in New York City. When it opened as a variety hall in 1932 Radio City, which seats around 6000 people, was the largest theatre in the world. From the late 1930s onwards it presented a mixture of top Hollywood films and spectacular live shows featuring the Rockettes dancers. It is now used mainly as a concert hall.

• **Radio Doctor** ▶ Dr Charles Hill (1904–89), 'the doctor with the greatest number of patients in the world' (listener research once estimated his audience at 14 million), who broadcast regular five-minute radio talks dispensing advice on common medical problems from the 1930s to 1950s. He was well known for his distinctive deep broadcasting voice and the occasional outrageousness of his comments. Hill was secretary of the BMA (1944–50), became the Liberal Conservative MP for Luton in 1950, and as Lord Hill went on to become successively chairman of the ITA (1963–67) and chairman of the governors of the BBC (1967–72).

> ...too much booze, causing you to flop down in bed like a sack of potatoes, usually on your back with your face to high heaven, and your beautifully expired air ascending to a heaven you'll never reach! Remedy obvious – the water wagon. – THE RADIO DOCTOR on the causes and treatment of snoring.

• **radiopaging** ► *See*: bleeper.

• **RAF** ► Royal Air Force. The UK's principal military aviation service, formed on 1 April 1918 by amalgamation of the Royal Flying Corps (*see*: RFC) and the Royal Naval Air Service. Headed by Viscount Trenchard, first Marshal of the RAF, the newly independent force played an important role in ending World War I by stepping up bombing raids on German industrial as well as military targets. After the war, the RAF was slimmed down and set about securing a technically advanced aircraft manufacturing industry to supply its needs. The new craft were tested in record-breaking attempts and air races around the world, and in 1927 an RAF team gained the first of several victories in the Schneider Trophy, flying planes specially built by R. J. Mitchell, who later designed the famous Spitfire. These Schneider-trophy aircraft were powered by Rolls-Royce engines, which developed into the Merlin, used throughout World War II in the Spitfire. Despite rearmament from the mid-1930s, the RAF entered the war at a great numerical disadvantage to the Luftwaffe. Nevertheless, the service soon distinguished itself, notably in providing air cover for the evacuation of Allied troops from Dunkirk in May 1940. A still more critical test came in the late summer and autumn of 1940 – the Battle of Britain (*see also*: Few, the).

Most other theatres – notably the Mediterranean, North Africa, the North Atlantic, and the Far East – saw the RAF in key roles. One outstanding action was the gallant air defence of Malta from mid-1940 to the end of 1942 by a force initially comprising three Gladiator biplanes, later reinforced by Hurricanes and Spitfires. At home, Bomber Command, led from 1942 by Bomber Harris, intensified its strategic bombing of military and industrial targets in Germany and occupied countries. From 1943 huge bomber formations were regularly making night-time sorties over Germany. Controversially, civilian areas of German towns and cities were also targeted (*see*: Dresden fire bombing). RAF casualties in World War II were over 70,000 killed and nearly 23,000 wounded. Some 13,000 airmen were captured as POWs.

Since the war, the RAF has been an important element in the NATO defences of W Europe. Bomber and Fighter Commands were merged in 1968 to form Strike Command, which is now responsible for all strategic operations. Logistical support is provided by Maintenance Command, while personnel are supplied by Training Command.

The Women's Royal Air Force (WRAF) was created in 1949 out of the Women's Auxiliary Air Force (WAAF). It provides a career structure for women in most sectors of the service, including groundcrew, aircrew, and officer branches.

• **ragga** ► A Caribbean music style combining elements of reggae and rap. The lyrical content is often aggressive or overtly sexual. The style received much media attention in Britain in 1992, following the shooting of a youth at a ragga concert in London. Followers of the style were known as **raggamuffins**.

• **raghead** ► A derogatory term for an Arab, referring to the characteristic headdress (*ha'ik*) of Arab males. It was popularized by US troops stationed in Saudi Arabia during the build-up to the Gulf War of 1991, grumbling about the privations of living in an Islamic country. Traditionally, Muslim Arabs have regarded the Western style of brimmed hat as both ridiculous and disrespectful to God.

In the UK, the term is sometimes used offensively of Sikhs and other Asian males who wear turbans.

• **ragtime** ► A style of medium tempo syncopated music of US Black origin, popular from 1890 to 1920. Although it developed from minstrel band music, many rags were published as solo piano pieces. Scott Joplin's 'Maple Leaf Rag' (1899) was one of the first of its kind to be written down. Ragtime enjoyed a substantial revival with the success of the 1973 film *The Sting*, which featured Scott Joplin's rags, especially 'The Entertainer' (1902).

• **rai** ► A style of pop music that originated in North Africa in the 1980s; it combines Arabic modal elements with Western dance rhythms. Like other world music styles, rai first came to Western attention through the activities of North African musicians in Paris in the later 1980s. *See also*: zouk.

• **raider** ► In business, a person or organization that specializes in making takeover bids for companies with assets that are undervalued in their accounts. If the bid is unwelcome to the company, this is known as a hostile bid. The use of the word raider implies that such bids will be hostile.

• **Rainbow bomb** ▶ A US H-bomb (*see*: nuclear weapon) detonated between 200 and 500 miles (320–800 km) above Johnston Island in the Pacific on 9 July 1962. Its name is derived from the spectacular aurora produced by the blast, which illuminated the Hawaiian Islands 750 miles to the southwest and was seen in New Zealand 4000 miles away. It was announced in August that radiation from the high-altitude blast had damaged the British satellite *Ariel*.

• **Rainbow Corner** ▶ In World War II, the Lyons' Corner House in London's Shaftesbury Avenue was taken over and turned into a large café and lounge for US servicemen under this name; it became a general meeting place for Americans in London. The name was a reference to both the US Rainbow Division and the rainbow insignia of SHAEF (Supreme Headquarters Allied Expeditionary Forces).

• **Rainbow Warrior** ▶ *See*: Greenpeace.

• **rain check** ▶ Originally, a receipt or the counterfoil of a ticket entitling one to see another baseball game if the match for which the ticket was purchased is rained off. The phrase, which originated in America, is now widely used to mean a promise to accept an invitation at a later date, especially in the form **to take a rain check** on something.

• **raining** ▶
**If it was raining pea soup, I'd only have a fork** An Australian expression drawing attention to some outrageous piece of bad luck. There are many common variants, including **If it was raining virgins, I'd end up with a poofter** and **If it was raining palaces, I'd be hit on the head with the handle of a dunny door**.

• **Rain is the best policeman** ▶ A catchphrase implying that rain keeps troublemakers at home. Presumably this is what every policeman hopes for before a big football match or any large and potentially troublesome gathering.

• **rainmaker** ▶ Mainly US slang for an influential businessman or similar figure – someone who is seen as altering the whole 'climate' in which business is done. The usage alludes to the American Indian medicine men, who chanted to the tribal gods in an attempt to bring rain.

• **Rambo** ▶ The brutal machine-gun toting hero played by Sylvester Stallone (1946– ) in a series of jingoistic films of the 1980s; stars to turn down the part included Paul Newman. The original Rambo film was *First Blood* (1982), an adaption of David Morrell's novel about a Vietnam veteran's battle with a small-town sheriff. Although Morrell killed off his hero, Stallone returned to the part in *Rambo: First Blood Part II* (1985), in which he rescues US prisoners-of-war held in Vietnam, and the $85-million *Rambo III* (1988), in which he takes on the Soviets in Afghanistan. The homicidal Rambo became a US folk hero, winning the keen approval of President Reagan among others. The films have added two words to the language: **Ramboesque** and **Ramboism**.

• **ram raiding** ▶ Driving a stolen car through a shop window in order to steal goods from the shop. The phrase made the headlines in the summer of 1990, following a spate of such robberies in NE England. The raids were carried out by highly organized gangs of youths, usually on shops selling clothes or electrical goods, and proved extremely difficult to prevent.

• **ranch** ▶
**Meanwhile back at the ranch** A catchphrase dating from the era of silent films, when such phrases were used as titles to link the parts of a story. The expression is now mainly used to imply that while more exciting things go on elsewhere, life jogs on in its routine way at the ranch.

> Sioux Falls, South Dakota, is the place they mean when they say 'Meanwhile back at the ranch', it's America's slow-beating downhome heart. – *The Independent*, 20 March 1991.

• **R & B** ▶ *See*: rhythm-and-blues.

• **R & D** ▶ Research and development. An important item in the budgets of large companies, involving scientific research on both production methods and materials to enable products and processes to be developed and improved. This kind of research began to be undertaken seriously at the start of the 20th century as scientists were brought into industry. Some of the first US research laboratories were opened at General Electric in 1900, Du Pont in 1902, and Bell Telephone in 1907. R & D is also a major governmental expense in the development and updating of military hardware.

• **randy** ▶ British informal term meaning eager for sex, lustful. The word is frequently used in the tabloid press, in which **Randy Andy** is the favourite epithet for any man called Andrew (it was widely applied to Prince Andrew, Duke of York, in his bachelor days). It is rarely used in America, where Randy is a popular Christian name.

• **Rangers** ▶ 1. Picked men in the US Army who carried out commando-style operations in World War II. They were named after Rogers' Rangers, an intrepid body of frontiersmen organized by Major Robert Rogers (1731–95). The Rangers first appeared at the Dieppe Raid (1942), in which a small party went as armed observers. **2.** *See:* Girl Guides.

• **Rank Organization** ▶ A commercial enterprise that dominated the British film industry in the 1940s and 1950s, founded and headed by J. Arthur Rank (1888–1972). The product of a wealthy flour-milling family with strong Methodist convictions, Rank entered the film business partly because he saw it as the most effective way of spreading his beliefs. His earliest films were instructional aids for Sunday schools and he later used his influence to promote material of a religious or edifying character, often to the dismay of his accountants. During the 1930s and 1940s he extended his activities from film production into distribution and exhibition; by the time he founded the Rank Organization in 1946, he controlled not only the leading British film studios but also two of the three biggest cinema chains. The Organization later diversified into such areas as hotels, Xerox copying, etc. Rank himself never lost his early sense of mission, claiming that if he gave a full account of his experiences in the film world 'it would be as plain to you as it is to me that I was being led by God.'

The Rank Organization's trademark, a huge metal gong struck by a bare-torsoed muscle man at the start of each film, was in reality made of cardboard.

• **rap** ▶ **1.** A long and serious conversation, as in 'Sorry I'm late. I got in a rap with my neighbour'; the word is also used as a verb, meaning to converse. A term much used by hippies and other young people from the end of the 1960s, it was originally part of US Black slang. The derivation is obscure. A **rap group** is a group of people who meet regularly to discuss their problems. **2.** A punishment for a crime. Originally a US colloquialism, it is now widely heard in such expressions as **take the rap**, meaning to take the punishment whether guilty or not, and **beat the rap**, meaning to escape punishment. In America a **rap sheet** is a criminal record. **3.** A rhythmic monologue intoned over a prerecorded instrumental backing track. This style of music originated among Black youths in the big cities of America during the early 1980s but soon spread to the UK and elsewhere. The songs often have a political or social message and can be very inventive in their use of language and imagery. **Gangsta** or **gansta rap** is a subgenre in which the words – often obscene, misogynistic, and violently anti-police – reflect life in the street gangs of US cities.

London-based jazz-rapper Galliano is a White boy with West Indian inflections – no offence in itself – whose admirably wordy raps are handicapped by a fundamental lack of vocal charisma... – *The Independent,* 28 March 1991.

• **Rapallo Treaty** ▶ Either of two treaties signed after World War I at Rapallo, a coastal resort in NW Italy. The first Rapallo Treaty, signed in November 1920, was between Italy and Yugoslavia: Italy renounced its claim to Dalmatia, the independence of Fiume was acknowledged, and the rights of Italians living in Yugoslav territory and Yugoslavs in Italian territory were established.

The second Rapallo Treaty was signed on 16 August 1922, during the Genoa Conference, by the foreign ministers of the Soviet Union and Germany. The treaty was hailed as a display of solidarity rather than an alliance: it paved the way for the immediate resumption of diplomatic relations between the two countries and enabled Germany secretly to develop and test new weapons – weapons banned by the Versailles Treaty – on Soviet territory.

• **rapid eye movement** ▶ *See:* REM.

• **rapture of the deep** ▶ Slang for the feelings of ecstasy deep-sea divers experience from breathing in compressed air that contains large amounts of nitrogen.

• **ra-ra skirt** ▶ A type of short skirt with flounces, fashionable in the early 1980s. Perhaps named after the short skirts of cheerleaders at American football games.

• **Rastafarians** ▶ Members of a Black political and religious group originating in the 1920s in Jamaica. They recognized Emperor Haile Selassie (*see:* Lion of Judah) as the living god and looked forward to his deliverance of the Black races from servitude by procuring them a homeland in Ethiopia. *Ras* means duke and *Tafari* was a family name of Haile Selassie (Might of the Trinity). There are now Rastafarians, or **Rastas**, in the Caribbean, America, Canada, and Europe. They are conspicuous by their long matted curls (dreadlocks) and often wear the Rastafarian colours of red, gold, and green.

• **Rat** ▶ A character in Kenneth Grahame's children's classic *The Wind in the Willows* (1908), best known for the opinion that 'there is nothing – absolutely nothing – half so much worth doing as simply messing about in boats'. The character was partly inspired by the rowing enthusiast Frederick James Furnivall (1825–1910), who introduced the first sculling-four and sculling-eight races to the UK and became president of the National Amateur Rowing Association. He was better known as a scholar and lexicographer, founding the Early English Texts Society (1864) and serving as one of the first editors of the *Oxford English Dictionary* (from 1861). *See also*: Toad.

• **rat**▶

**You dirty rat** A catchphrase associated with the tough-guy roles of film actor James Cagney (1899–1986), and used frequently by impersonators. In fact, he never said it. The closest he came to saying something like it was: 'a dirty double-crossing rat' (*Blonde Crazy*, 1931), and 'You dirty yellow-bellied rat' (*Taxi*, 1931).

• **Rat Pack**▶ Originally, a name given by the US actress Lauren Bacall to the group of drinking cronies (including the young Frank Sinatra) who surrounded her husband Humphrey Bogart in the 1950s. Much more famously, however, the name was revived for the clique of film actors and entertainers who associated with Sinatra in the early 1960s. This group, which included Dean Martin and Sammy Davis Jnr among others, became notorious for its hard drinking, cruel jokes, and womanizing antics. Despite the unpleasantness of much of their behaviour, the group's louche elegance and impeccable sense of cool has earned them many (chiefly masculine) admirers. *See also*: bratpack.

• **rat race**▶ The relentless struggle to get ahead of one's rivals, particularly in professional and commercial occupations.

> Just when you think you've got the rat race licked – Boom! Faster rats. – DAVID LEE ROTH, US rock star.

• **rat run**▶ A minor road used by fast heavy traffic, either as a short cut or to avoid congestion on major roads. Rat runs often pass through villages or suburbs; their use by a volume of traffic they were never designed to carry, little of which makes any concession to the speed limit, infuriates residents and is the cause of frequent accidents. The term first appeared in the 1970s and was probably suggested by rat race. It has more recently been used in a verbal sense, **rat-running**, *i.e.* availing oneself of such a route, especially during the rush hour. Various traffic-calming devices have been used to slow such traffic and to discourage it from using a particular rat run.

• **ratted** or **rat-arsed**▶ British slang for drunk.

> The last four months have been knackering... the moment that theatre opens we're all going straight down the King's Head to get absolutely ratted. – *The Independent*, 23 March 1991.

• **rattlehead**▶ UK slang from the late 1980s for someone who listens to a personal stereo, especially on public transport. It refers to the annoying tinny noise that can be overheard by those sitting close by

and which has been the subject of many irate letters to the press.

• **raunchy**▶ Earthy, bawdy, and sexually uninhibited. Originally a US slang term meaning shabby, cheap, or slovenly, the word developed strong sexual connotations in the 1960s, losing its pejorative flavour at the same time. In jazz and rock it is a term of approbation, meaning raw or unsophisticated. The back formation **raunch** now means sexually provocative behaviour or material (in a book, film, etc.), although some older speakers still use it in its former sense of untidiness. The word may derive from the Italian *rancio*, rotten.

• **rave** or **rave-up**▶ Originally, any wild or lively party, especially one involving drinking and dancing. In the late 1980s and 1990s the term 'rave' came to be applied specifically to acid-house parties – large events at which hundreds of young people danced all night to electronic music under the influence of ecstacy.

> As most raves didn't start until the wee small hours, the pub became the logical assembly point... – *The Independent*, 7 March 1991.

*See also*: orbital; warehouse party.

• **Ravensbrück**▶ A Nazi concentration camp for women, situated 50 miles (80 km) north of Berlin. It was established in 1939, shortly after the outbreak of the war; women were transported there from all over Germany and occupied Europe. Between 1943 and 1945 over 92,000 Jews and non-Jews died there, 90% of them from Allied nations. In addition to executions and brutality by staff, the main causes of death were overwork, undernourishment, overcrowding, and disease. Medical experiments were also carried out, including bone grafts and transplants and the introduction of artificial gangrene into unnecessary amputations and other deliberate wounds. In 1944 mass gassings began of those 'unproductive' prisoners who were incapable of walking. One of the inmates who witnessed these horrors was Odette Sansom (Churchill), the SOE agent, who gave evidence against the Ravensbrück staff at the Hamburg War Crimes Tribunal in 1947 and was later awarded the George Cross for her wartime espionage services.

• **ray gun**▶ An imaginary weapon that shoots rays to paralyse or kill. This fictional device has long been a feature of science-fiction epics, being vividly portrayed in cinema and television space operas. The Hollywood serials Flash Gordon (1936) and Buck Rogers (1939) both starred Buster Crabbe (1908–83), who frequently had to confront death rays and gamma bombs. Laser weapons could yet become a reality. *See*: Star Wars.

• **rayon ►** A generic name for any artificial textile fibre made from cellulose. The oldest manmade fibre, rayon was first produced commercially in 1890 and generally known as 'artificial silk' until 1924, when the new name was invented by the Retail Drygoods Association. It alludes to the long filaments, or 'rays', in which the fibre emerges from the manufacturing process – the result of forcing cellulose solution through a finely perforated nozzle, or 'spinneret'. Although *rayon* is the French word for 'ray', it was probably created as a blend of 'ray' and 'cotton'. The name is fast becoming obsolete in the UK, having been replaced in general usage by a number of tradenames. *See also*: Nylon.

• **Rayonism ►** A Russian art movement founded in 1911 by Mikhail Larionov (1881–1964) and his wife Natalia Goncharova (1881–1962); it specialized in semi-abstract compositions featuring ray-like lines of colour. There is no connection with the textile.

• **RBT ►** Random breath testing. The policy of stopping drivers at random in order to test for excess alcohol. Officially, British police can only stop a motorist for this purpose when his driving raises suspicions that he has been drinking. In practice, however, they can use a variety of pretexts to stop cars more or less as they please and then insist that the drivers take the breath test (*see*: breathalyser). Many local forces apply these procedures systematically over the Christmas and New Year period. Opponents of random testing (usually those who risk driving after having had a drink or two) claim to see it as a threat to civil liberties; supporters point out that its introduction in such countries as Sweden has led to a dramatic fall in deaths from drunken driving.

• **RCA ►** Radio Corporation of America. Founded during World War I, RCA was an early leader in radio and one of four companies that created the National Broadcasting Company (*see*: NBC) in 1926. When radio depressed the gramophone-record business, RCA bought the Victor company in 1929 and made RCA Victor a major producer of gramophone records and radio equipment. RCA also led the development of commercial television in America, launching its first important test at the 1939 World Fair in New York. RCA was bought in 1986 by General Electric, the US company that had cofounded it 70 years earlier. The NBC radio and television facilities occupy several floors of the General Electric Building (formerly RCA Building) in New York's Rockefeller Center.

• **RCs, Parsees, Pharisees, and Buckshees ►** Those who do not belong to the Church of England, or who differ from the majority in some other way. The phrase has existed in various forms in the British armed forces since the 1920s or 1930s: variants include 'Chinese, Japanese, RCs, Parsees, Standatease and One-Two-Threes' or 'Sudanese, Siamese, Breadancheese, Standatease'. It probably originated as a list of those who were not obliged to attend church parades.

• **reach for the sky ►** A phrase often used in gangster and Western films meaning 'put your hands up'. However, it is probably best known as the title of Paul Brickhill's biography of Douglas Bader (1910–82) and the subsequent film (1954); Bader was the RAF World War II hero, who continued his flying career after losing both his legs in a flying accident in 1931. In this instance the title must allude to the RAF motto Per ardua ad astra (Through adversity to the stars).

• **read ►**
**I'm sorry, I'll read that again** A stock phrase used by newsreaders or other broadcasters if they have made a mistake. It was used as the title of a radio comedy show (1964–73), starring John Cleese and others.

• **read 'em and weep ►** A phrase uttered triumphantly by the winner of a card game (such as poker) as he or she lays the winning cards on the table. It originated in the early 20th century in America. The phrase is also used in more general contexts, referring to anything written or printed that is likely to cause distress, such as bad reviews, bills, sales figures, etc.

• **Reader's Digest ►** A pocket-sized monthly magazine first published in America in 1922. It is now published internationally, with a circulation of some 28 million worldwide. There are eight English-language editions of the *Reader's Digest*, for the UK, America, Australia, New Zealand, and elsewhere, and 21 editions in 14 other languages, including French, German, Spanish, Italian, Norwegian, Chinese, Arabic, and Hindi. *Reader's Digest* is also a very successful publisher of books, especially manuals and reference books, that it sells principally to its captive magazine audience.

• **readies ►** British slang for bank notes rather than a cheque or plastic money. It is a shortened form of 'ready cash'. Those who hope to avoid or reduce the burden of tax on a payment often ask to be paid in readies.

• **read my lips ►** An expression meaning 'Listen very carefully to what I have to say because I really mean it'. The speaker generally uses it to imply that the listener is being wilfully obtuse. The phrase's present popularity began when George Bush used it in his nomination speech on 19 August 1988. He promised not to raise taxes whatever Congress tried to do to make him:

> I'll say no, and they'll push, and I'll say no, and they'll push again, and I'll say to them, 'Read my lips, no new taxes'.

Curiously, given the phrase's immediate impact in America and later celebrity, some serious British newspapers omitted the line from their transcripts of the speech, probably considering it another unfortunate example of Bush's low-brow speech patterns. When Bush did raise taxes by $25 billion in 1991, commentators referred to his earlier remark with understandable derision.

Arnold Schwarzenegger amusingly echoed the phrase in a slogan for the President's Council on Physical Fitness, of which he was head:

> Read my hips, no more fat.

• **read-only memory** ▶ *See*: ROM.

• **ready-made** ▶ *See*: objet trouvé.

• **ready-mix** ▶ Describing commercial products, from cakes to concrete, that are blended in advance for quick and convenient use. The food industry has many preparations requiring only water or milk to be added. Ready-mix cakes were first rejected by US consumers because, market research showed, housewives felt they were contributing nothing to the recipe. When companies removed the eggs from the mixtures, requiring the housewives to add them, sales increased dramatically.

• **Reaganomics** ▶ The economic policies adopted during the presidency (1980–88) of Ronald Reagan (1911–    ). Chief among these were big reductions in income tax, mandatory cuts in welfare provision and all areas of public spending except defence, and measures designed to weaken organized labour. The advocates of this programme asserted that any shortfall in government revenue resulting from tax cuts would be made up by the economic growth the cuts were sure to stimulate. In the event, the recession of 1982 was followed by only modest growth and the result was a massive federal deficit. By 1986 the national debt had more than doubled but Reagan persisted in his refusal to raise taxes. The term 'Reaganomics' was at first used derogatorily to imply that Reagan's economics were no economics at all; it was, however, later adopted by the president's supporters.

• **real** ▶

**It's the real thing** The famous advertising slogan used for Coca-Cola, implying that all the other similar drinks are poor imitations.

• **real ale** ▶ Draught beer brewed, stored, and served using traditional methods. In terms of flavour and texture, real ale is the antithesis of the bland fizzy bulk-packaged beers that came to dominate the British market in the 1950s. These are fermented, then chilled, filtered, pasteurized, carbonated, stored in metal kegs and pumped to the bar using gas pressure. Watney's Red Barrel was the first of these 'convenience' beers with long shelf lifes to appear after the war, and other brewers, such as Bass, Courage, Whitbread, and Ind Coope, quickly followed with their own varieties. A spate of mergers in the 1950s and 1960s resulted in the domination of the brewing industry by the 'Big Six'; by 1976 63% of beer was in keg form, of which 20% was in the form of lager. The near disappearance of traditional ales and the resulting decline in consumer choice prompted the foundation of such interest groups as the Society for the Preservation of Beers from the Wood in the 1960s; by far the most successful of these groups has been the Campaign for Real Ale (CAMRA) founded in 1972. Through its consumer campaigns and publications, such as *The Good Beer Guide*, CAMRA has persuaded the big brewers that real ales can be as profitable as their keg products.

• **reality principle** ▶ In Freudian psychology, the idea that external reality imposes certain constraints on one's instinctive urge to self-gratification. Its acceptance distinguishes the more-or-less sane adult from the infant or psychotic. According to Freudian theory, the reality principle governs the development of the ego, while the id is governed by the **pleasure principle**. The process by which the reality principle is learned forms the subject of Freud's *Beyond the Pleasure Principle* (1920).

• **reality television** ▶ *See*: Big Brother; docusoap; fly-on-the-wall; game show.

• **Realpolitik** ▶ (German, practical politics) Politics based on national interests or material considerations as distinct from moral or ideological objectives.

• **Rebel Without a Cause** ▶ Title of a 1955 film starring James Dean (1931–55) as a mixed-up teenager, whose affluent Californian background does nothing to prevent his slide into delinquency. The title was taken from that of a collection of case studies of juvenile delinquency published in 1944 by the psychologist Robert Lindner. The film opened only weeks after Dean's death in a car crash – an event that transformed a talented (if increasingly mannered and typecast) young actor into an icon of youthful rebellion. Ever since, Dean's performance in this powerful but clichéd melodrama has been treated as if it embodied the essence of alienated and self-destructive youth. The legend has proved surprisingly enduring; the label 'rebel without a cause' is resuscitated by the press with each new wave of teenage rebellion and Dean's image continues to glower from advertisements and the bedroom walls of his teenage fans. It was even used by the (then) National Westminster Bank in an attempt to persuade teenagers that opening a bank account is a cool and rebellious thing to do. In the 1980s a James Dean Foundation was set up by the actor's relatives to control the use of his name and image – even the imitation by others of his characteristic poses.

• **rebirthing** ▶ A type of psychotherapy developed by Otto Rank, who thought that many people's difficulties and stresses in life were caused by traumatic experiences at birth. His technique of 'continuous breathing' supposedly enables the patient to relive the moment of birth and be 'reborn' without the attendant fear. It was popular in the mid-1980s but has since become less accepted.

• **rebop** ▶ *See*: bebop.

• **recall test** ▶ A form of test used in marketing research to discover whether or not an advertisement has stuck in the minds of a group of consumers. In spontaneous tests, members of the group are asked how much they can remember about a particular advertisement, with no assistance. In a prompted test, the respondent is asked which advertisement they can remember from a series of advertisements in a campaign.

• **Received Pronunciation** ▶ (RP) The pronunciation of English most widely accepted as standard in the British Isles. It is the pronunciation used by British lexicographers in giving a pronunciation guide to the words in a dictionary. The term was coined by the English phonetician Daniel Jones (1881–1967) to describe the characteristic pronunciation of people educated in public schools and universities in the south of England. Historically, RP is derived from the language spoken by Chaucer, the Middle English of London. In the 1930s, with the rise of sound broadcasting, this pronunciation was often referred to as **BBC English** or the **Oxford accent**. The diction of such announcers and news readers as Alvar Liddell and Leslie Phillips was impeccable and certainly served as a model for many native English speakers as well as those for whom English was a second language. In his Preface to the first edition of the *BBC Pronouncing Dictionary of British Names*, G. M. Miller wrote:

> The good announcer remains, as far as the BBC is concerned, the pleasant unobtrusive speaker who does not distract attention from his subject matter by causing embarrassment, unwitting amusement, or resentment among intelligent listeners.

This policy has since been relaxed, with the introduction of news presenters and weather forecasters with a variety of regional accents, reflecting the way people actually speak as opposed to the way some feel they ought to speak.

**King's** (or **Queen's**) **English** is another description often used for the pronunciation of southern England. In fact, the royal family and many members of the upper classes do not use RP. The Duke of Edinburgh, for example, refers from time to time to his 'trisers' (trousers); the Queen talks about the 'Hise of Lords', and Prince Charles calls the London tube 'the Undergrind'. Such speech idiosyncracies occur throughout the class spectrum. It is therefore important that English dictionaries should maintain a standard of pronunciation. RP fulfils this function.

• **recombinant DNA** ▶ DNA containing segments of DNA derived from a different species. It is produced by the techniques of genetic engineering and involves cleavage of the DNA molecule and subsequent recombination of its strands to incorporate the introduced DNA fragment.

• **recreational drug** ▶ Any drug taken for pleasure or because of an addiction, rather than for medical reasons. Originally the expression signified disapproval of any non-medical drug. However, since the 1980s it has been used more neutrally to describe cannabis and other narcotics or stimulants taken to enhance one's pleasure in periods of relaxation, especially in the company of other non-addicted pleasure seekers.

• **recycling** ▶ The process in which waste materials are salvaged, sorted, and treated in order that they may be reused for manufacturing or for some other purpose. Recycling has several benefits; notably it conserves raw materials, reduces the burden on waste-disposal facilities, and lessens various forms of environmental pollution. It can be practised with many types of waste, from household rubbish to factory effluents. For instance, many items found in household dustbins can be successfully recycled, including steel and aluminium cans, paper, textiles, and glass. Most towns and cities have introduced local recycling schemes involving bottle and paper banks and encourage householders to sort newspapers and certain types of plastic from the rest of their waste for separate collection. Pressure for recycling schemes has grown since the 1980s with the greater awareness of the environmental ravages brought about by a modern consumer society and the huge amounts of waste it generates.

• **red** ►

**better red than dead** Living under a communist regime is preferable to being killed in a nuclear war. The phrase was used as a slogan in the late 1950s by British campaigners for nuclear disarmament (*see*: CND); in the words of the British philosopher and pacifist Bertrand Russell:

> If no alternative remains except communist domination or the extinction of the human race, the former alternative is the less of two evils.

Supporters of the opposite point of view reversed the elements of the phrase, producing the slogan 'Better dead than red'.

• **Red Adair** ► Nickname of Paul Adair, a US consultant on oil-well disasters chiefly known for putting out fires. He was played by John Wayne in the film *Hellfighters* (1969). In 1991 the veteran Adair was engaged to deal with the hundreds of oil-well fires deliberately started by Iraqi troops evacuating Kuwait.

• **Red Army Faction** ► (RAF; German *Rote Armee Faktion*) A West German terrorist group, known popularly as the **Baader-Meinhof gang**, created when the arsonist Andreas Baader (1943–77) was sprung from prison on 14 May 1970 by Ulrike Meinhof (1934–76), Horst Mahler, and others. The group then launched a violent campaign against the political, economic, and military organs of the West German state, which they branded as the neo-Fascist 'Strawberry Reich'. They also targeted NATO and its military personnel as the international agency of US imperialism; their attacks on the European alliance during the 1970s and 1980s were organized in league with a European network of terrorist groups, including the French Action Directe and the Italian Red Brigades. During the early 1970s their activities included bank raids, bombings, kidnappings, and the assassination of business leaders, police, and government officials. By 1972 the main leaders, Baader, Meinhof, and Gudrun Esslin, were in prison but violence continued unabated in an attempt to secure their release. In April 1977 the attorney-general, Siegfried Buback, was murdered in revenge for the suicide in Stammheim prison of Meinhof; in October of the same year Red Army members collaborated with Palestinian Red Army terrorists in the hijacking of a Lufthansa jet with 91 hostages, during which the pilot was shot. As German anti-terrorist squads stormed the plane at Mogadishu airport in Somalia, it was discovered that Baader and Esslin had also committed suicide in Stammheim; another hostage, Hans-Martin Schleyer of Daimler-Benz, kidnapped in October, was murdered as a reprisal. After these events the revolutionary appeal of the group to German students and young radicals began to wane. By the mid-1980s most of the group's leading members were either dead or imprisoned. The group formally disbanded in 1998.

> Don't argue – destroy. – Slogan of the Red Army Faction.

• **Red Arrows** ► The RAF jet aircraft aerobatics display team, regarded as the finest in the world.

• **Red Baron** ► Nickname of Manfred, Freiherr von Richthofen (1892–1918), the most celebrated German fighter pilot of World War I, reflecting his aristocratic rank and his red Fokker triplane. From 1916 he commanded Fighter Group I of the German Imperial Air Force, known to Allied airmen as **Richthofen's Flying Circus** because of its brightly coloured and whimsically decorated planes and its innovative use of team tactics. He is thought to have shot down 80 enemy planes before being brought down himself by a combination of ground fire and the guns of a Sopwith Camel flown by the Canadian ace Captain A. Roy Brown during the second Battle of the Somme. Respected as well as feared by the Allies, he was buried with full military honours by the British and Australians. The Red Baron's death was considered by Ludendorff the equivalent of losing 30 divisions. His command was taken over by Herman Goering; his cousin, Frieda von Richthofen, married the novelist D. H. Lawrence.

• **redbrick** ► Denoting a 19th-century British university, many of which were built in the redbrick Gothic revival style of such architects as Alfred Waterhouse. The term is now often applied rather loosely to all English universities built before the 1960s other than Oxford and Cambridge (*see*: Oxbridge). It was introduced by Bruce Truscot (Professor E. Allison Peers: d. 1952) in his book *Redbrick University* (1943), in which he dealt primarily with the universities of Birmingham, Bristol, Leeds, Liverpool, Manchester, Reading, and Sheffield, and expressly excluded London.

• **Red Brigades** ► (Italian *Brigate Rosse*) The Italian left-wing terrorist group that was responsible for the kidnap and murder in March 1977 of Aldo Moro, the president of the Christian Democratic Party and ex-prime minister. The organization was established in 1969, initially with the aim of attacking leaders of large corporations, such as Fiat and Pirelli, who were regarded as 'enemies of the working class'. In subsequent years they were responsible for a series of kidnappings, bombings, and the murders of police, judges, government officials, and business leaders with the aim of undermining the Italian state and initiating a Marxist revolution. The body of their most notable victim, Moro, was found in the boot of a car in Rome in May 1977, shot dead after the government refused to agree to the release of 13 Brigade leaders. The Brigades were also linked to other terrorist groups, including the German Red Army Faction. In January 1982 the Italian police achieved a major success in freeing the US Brigadier-General James Dozier, a deputy NATO commander, who had been abducted in Verona in December 1981. Leading Brigade ideologues, such as Renato Curcio (1948– ) and Alberto Fraceschini, as well as those responsible for the Moro and Dozier kidnappings, were captured and tried during the late 1970s and early 1980s. The last of the Moro kidnappers was sentenced in 1983; since then the authorities have had increasing success in penetrating and neutralizing the organization's cells in various parts of the country.

• **redcap**▶ **1.** A colloquial term for British military police, whose caps have red covers. **2.** In America, a porter at a railway or bus station.

• **red carpet**▶ A long red carpet that is unrolled in front of the door to a building, train, aircraft, etc., when an important dignitary is expected to arrive. Its practical function is to provide a dirt-free passage from one place to another; however, it also has a ceremonial significance, indicating that the visitor is of sufficient importance to merit this treatment. **Rolling out the red carpet** for someone can also be used less literally to mean that the person in question will be received with lavish hospitality, e.g. 'When my boss came to dinner we really rolled out the red carpet and served up an impressive meal.'

• **redcoat**▶ *See*: Butlins.

• **Red Dean**▶ Press nickname for Dr Hewlett Johnson (1874–1966), Dean of Canterbury and formerly Dean of Manchester. He attracted some controversy for his belief that communism, as practised in Stalin's Soviet Union, was a practical application of Christian ethics.

• **Red Devils**▶ **1.** Nickname of the British Parachute Regiment. **2.** Nickname of the Manchester United soccer team, founded in 1878, which wears a chiefly red and white strip.

• **red-eye**▶ **1.** Slang for whisky or any other strong spirit that causes the drinker's eyes to become bloodshot. **2.** Mainly US slang for a flight that takes off late at night and arrives early the next morning, thus depriving the passengers of a good night's sleep. They arrive looking exhausted with bloodshot eyes. It is usually applied to coast-to-coast flights in America.

• **red flag**▶ **1.** A flag generally used to indicate danger or as a stop signal. **2.** The symbol of international socialism; 'The Red Flag' is a socialist anthem still used, somewhat incongruously, by the British Labour Party.

> Then raise the scarlet standard high,
> Beneath its shade we'll live and die
> Though cowards flinch and traitors sneer
> We'll keep the Red Flag flying here.
> – JAMES CONNELL: 'The Red Flag' (1889).

• **Red Friday**▶ Friday 31 July 1925, when a stoppage in the coal industry, planned to meet the threat of wage cuts, was averted by the promise of government subsidies to support wages, etc. It was so called by the Labour press to distinguish it from Black Friday or 15 April 1921, when union leaders called off an impending strike of railwaymen and transport workers designed to help the miners, who were locked out.

• **Red Guards**▶ Young supporters of Mao Tsetung during the Cultural Revolution. The mobilization of the Red Guards began at a rally in Tiananmen Square, Peking, on 18 August 1966. These unruly mobs consisted chiefly of students from secondary schools, colleges, and universities: their task was to rampage the streets and the countryside of China and Tibet, harassing and attacking enemies and opponents of Mao Tse-tung, and destroying public and private property – anything that represented 'old' ideas, culture, customs, or habits. They wore red armbands and carried copies of Mao's Little Red Book.

• **Red Ken**▶ Press nickname for the Labour politician Ken Livingstone (1945– ) when he achieved notoriety as the left-wing leader of the GLC (1981–86). His outspoken views made him a bogeyman of the right-wing tabloids, one of which carried his photograph under the headline 'The Most Odious Man in Britain'. Livingstone skilfully countered this onslaught by presenting a soft-spoken downbeat image, visibly at odds with his press reputation. Meanwhile, his policies – which included handouts to unpopular fringe groups as well as a highly popular fare-cutting programme on London Transport (pensioners travelled free) – were increasingly seen as a deliberate provocation to central government. Margaret Thatcher's decision to abolish the Council, announced in October 1983, unexpectedly transformed Red Ken into something of a folk hero with Londoners, including many who had previously detested him. Following the abolition of the Council, Livingstone was elected to parliament representing Brent East. In 2000 he was elected to the newly created post of Mayor of London.

• **Red Letter** ▶ *See*: Zinoviev Letter.

• **redlining** ▶ A mainly US term for the systematic denial of loans, mortgages, and insurance to property owners, or prospective property owners, in the poorer sections of a city. Some banks and other financial institutions make use of this practice to minimize their risks, although it has been called racial discrimination, because it is in these areas that ethnic minorities usually reside. Redlining originated in the late 1960s and takes its name from the supposed practice of outlining such areas in red on a map.

• **redneck** ▶ US derogatory slang for a person from a rural community who is poorly educated, narrow-minded, and right-wing. The word was originally used to describe White Southern farmers (the backs of whose necks would be red from working in the fields under the hot sun), but its use spread in the late 1960s to describe anyone with uneducated right-wing views. The word has been used in this way in the UK since the 1980s.

• **reds** ▶ Colloquial term for socialists, radicals, or left-wingers of any kind, especially former Soviet communists. The colour red has been associated with revolution since at least 1848, when the workers of Paris manned the barricades under red banners. The words to the socialist anthem the Red Flag date from 1889. 'Reds' became a general journalistic term for communists with the Russian Civil War of 1918–22, in which Trotsky's Red Army fought the conservative White Volunteer Force. Its use was especially prevalent during the McCarthy witch-hunts in America (*see*: McCarthyism), when it was applied to alleged subversives of every kind. *See also*: pinko; better red than dead *at* red; reds under the bed.

• **redshift** ▶ An effect in which the light (or other electromagnetic radiation) emitted by a body appears to have longer wavelength if the body is moving away from the observer. There is a shift in the position of lines in the spectrum from their normal position towards the red end of the electromagnetic spectrum. The converse effect – a **blue shift** – occurs if the body is moving towards the observer. Both are examples of the so-called **Doppler shift**, named after the Austrian physicist Christian Doppler (1803–53), who discovered the effect with sound waves in 1842.

The redshift is important in astronomy. In 1929 the US astronomer Edwin Hubble investigated the spectra of a number of distant galaxies and showed that their redshifts were proportional to the distance away of the galaxy. This provides the main evidence that the universe is expanding (*see*: Big Bang).

• **reds under the bed** ▶ A reference to excessive suspicion of communists. The phrase dates from Senator McCarthy's witch-hunts of the 1950s in America, when supposed communist sympathizers were alleged to have been found in the most unlikely places (*see*: McCarthyism). Those who unreasonably or unjustifiably see a communist or left-wing influence where none exists are said to be looking for 'reds under the bed'. The phrase is now seldom heard.

• **reductivism** ▶ *See*: minimalism.

• **reefer** ▶ Slang for a hand-rolled cannabis cigarette (*see*: pot). It is now rarely heard, having been replaced by joint and **spliff** in the late 1950s to 1960s; the media nevertheless persisted in using the word well into the 1970s. There are two plausible etymologies; one derives from the nautical term 'reef', the gathered-in part of the sail, because of a similarity in shape between the furled sail and the hand-rolled cigarette. Others derive the word from *grifa*, Spanish slang for marijuana.

• **Referendum Party** ▶ A British political party founded in 1994 by the millionaire entrepreneur Sir James Goldsmith (1933–97) to press for a referendum on whether or not Britain should leave the EU. After failing to win a seat in the 1997 election the party disbanded.

• **reffo** ▶ In Australia, a derogatory term for any of the European refugees, predominantly Jewish, who arrived during or shortly before World War II. Australia was then a far more homogenous and culturally isolated society than it is today, and the reffos – also dubbed **reffujews** and **reff-raff** – provoked widespread resentment. Although the influx of refugees was unprecedented at the time, the numbers pale into insignificance beside the mass immigration that transformed Australian society in the post-war decades: between 1940 and 1964 some two million people, mainly from the UK and continental Europe, chose to start new lives in Australia. The government carefully referred to these incomers as **New Australians**, rather than immigrants, in the hope of easing assimilation. To the stubbornly xenophobic Old Australians, however, they were Balts, Naussies, emigrantos, micros, and wogs (subdivided into Pommie wogs, Yankee wogs, etc.).

• **reflexology** ▶ A technique of foot massage used to relieve tension and promote general bodily health. Like acupuncture and shiatsu, reflexology claims an ancient pedigree; it is based on the theory that channels of energy course through the body in a network of nerves linking all the body's main organs and muscles. Reflexologists hold that this energy network terminates at tiny reflex points in the feet, which mirror the body's organs, and that compression or finger massage at these specific points can help restore healthy energy flow by removing crystalline deposits clogging the energy pathways. The techniques of modern reflexology were developed during the early 20th century by the US physician William H. Fitzgerald, who established the principles of 'zone therapy', using pressure points on different areas of the body to treat common ailments. The technique was pioneered in the UK by Doreen Bayly in the 1950s; since the 1980s Bayly clinics have ministered to a growing number of believers in alternative medicine. Reflexology does not find much support in the orthodox medical profession.

• **refuse** ▶

**an offer one can't refuse** Originally, an offer of so much more than one is expecting that it would be foolish to say 'no'. In Mario Puzo's Mafia novel *The Godfather* (1969; filmed 1972) it takes on a much more sinister sense: 'I'm going to make you an offer you can't refuse' means that you are about to be told to do something by a Mafioso and will certainly do whatever it is if you don't want to be killed. It is thus the ultimate in blackmail. *See*: Godfather offer.

• **refusenik** ▶ In the former Soviet Union, a citizen who was refused an exit visa to emigrate to another country; most refuseniks were Jews wishing to emigrate to America or Israel. Until the late 1980s, under Soviet law, emigration was a state-granted privilege, although the Helsinki Accord (1975), to which the Soviet Union was a signatory, guarantees emigration as a basic human right. During the 1970s over 250,000 Soviet Jews were granted visas but many of those who were refused were branded as political dissidents and persecuted by the authorities. One of the most prominent refusenik campaigners was Anatoly Scharansky, imprisoned in 1978 for treason, who was eventually released and allowed to settle in Israel in 1986. Subsequently, restrictions on the emigration of Soviet citizens were gradually removed in accordance with Mikhail Gorbachov's policy of glasnost. Large numbers of Soviet Jews were then allowed to leave: 72,500 in 1989 and an estimated 200,000 in 1990. *See*: -nik; returnik.

• **reggae** ▶ Popular music from Jamaica with a heavily accented upbeat in each bar of four beats. It has a strong bass line and a bluesy feel. In the UK its popularity spread from the largely urban West Indian communities to young Whites during the 1970s. The derivation of the word is uncertain, but it is thought to be connected to the Jamaican 'ragerage', an argument. Many reggae musicians are Rastafarians.

• **Regulation 18b** ▶ A provision of the British Emergency Powers (Defence) Acts (1939; 1940), which was amended by parliament in 1940 to give the home secretary the power to detain, without trial, members of any organization sympathetic to an enemy power. Defence Regulation 18b(1A) was specifically targeted at the British Union of Fascists and its leader, Sir Oswald Mosley (1896–1980), who was arrested and imprisoned in Brixton on 23 May 1940. Altogether 763 BUF members (*see*: Mosleyites) were rounded up, including Mosley's wife Diana (*see*: Mitford girls), who was sent to Holloway, as well as many pro-German and pro-Italians. Mosley remained in Brixton until November 1943, when he was released for health reasons.

• **Reichsmark** ▶ (German, mark of the realm) Germany's standard monetary unit from 1924 to 1948, composed of 100 Reichspfennig. It is particularly associated with Adolf Hitler's Third Reich (1933–45). 'Mark', originally a measurement of precious metals, was the name given to German currency from 1871 until the country adopted the euro in 2002. *See*: Deutschmark; Rentenmark.

• **Reichstag fire** ▶ The destruction by arson of the Reichstag parliament building in Berlin on 27 February 1933. The fire occurred at a crucial moment in 20th-century German history, enabling the Nazis to seize absolute power. This was achieved by blaming the communists for the fire and so discrediting the left wing, who until then had blocked complete Nazi supremacy. A 24-year old Dutchman, Marius van der Lubbe, was identified as the communist who had started the blaze; before the night of 27 February was over, 5000 known communists had been arrested. The communists for their part accused the Nazis of staging the fire themselves with the object of blaming their opponents. During the trials following the war, the German chief of general staff recalled hearing Goering boast: 'The only one who really knows about the Reichstag is me, because I set it on fire.' The one person who could have solved the mystery conclusively was van der Lubbe himself, but he had been executed by the Nazis on 10 January 1934.

• **reinforcement therapy** ▶ A psychiatric treatment that rewards a patient for exhibiting the desired behaviour. These rewards – money, food, approval, etc. – encourage repetition of the behaviour. Fears, such as flying, can often be eliminated through pleasant associations; for example, having a birthday party with friends in a plane. **Negative reinforcement** is the withdrawing of rewards. Reinforcement therapy was a product of the early animal experiments by physiologists in Russia, the UK, and America and their adaptation to human behaviour by the US psychologist B. F. Skinner (1904–90) in the 1930s; the term was coined in 1969. Although reinforcement therapy has often proved successful, it is not a panacea. For example, in one study, which attempted to cure a child's fear of rabbits by giving it sweets while encouraging it to stroke a rabbit, the result was that thereafter the child invariably felt sick when given sweets.

• **reinvent the wheel** ▶ 1. Literally, to produce an invention that already exists and is in widespread use. For example: 'He has spent 3 years perfecting a computer program that does no more than one that has been available from Microsoft for over a year – talk about reinventing the wheel!'. More figuratively, to waste time and effort doing anything that has already been done. 2. To be obliged by circumstances to construct any basic device, *e.g.* 'To cross the river we had to reinvent the wheel and build a raft'.

• **Reis forgery** ▶ An ambitious forgery that threatened the economy of Portugal and the reputation of a leading British printing company in 1924. It was planned by Arthur Virgilio Alves Reis, a member of the Portuguese colonial service, who capitalized on his discovery that Portuguese banknotes were printed by a British firm, Waterlow and Sons, which was less than scrupulous about checking for notes with accidental duplicate numbers. Reis's elaborate plan involved the forging of letters from the Portuguese minister of finance and other high officials commissioning the printing of huge numbers of 500-escudo notes (worth £5 each); these, he explained, would not need new serial numbers as they would later be overprinted 'Angola' for use in that country, which was then a colony of Portugal. The overprinting, however, never happened. Instead Reis exchanged the notes for foreign stock and built up a huge financial empire, even opening his own Bank of Angola and Metropole. Sooner or later, it was inevitable that the massive fraud would be detected. In mid-1925 notes with duplicate serial numbers were discovered in Reis's bank and he was arrested. Reis eventually confessed and was sentenced to 20 years in prison; he was released in 1945 and died ten years later. He was so poor that at his own request he was buried in a sheet to enable his son to inherit his only suit.

• **Reith lectures** ▶ An annual series of broadcast lectures by leading thinkers, established by the BBC in 1947 in honour of John (Charles Walsham), 1st Baron Reith (1889–1971), the first director-general of the BBC (1927–38).

• **rejasing** ▶ *Reusing junk as something else.* US acronym for making use of old cast-off items, even rubbish, for some other purpose. Rejasing turns jam jars into paint containers and used tyres into playground obstacle courses. The movement developed in the 1970s in reaction to the disposable society.

• **relativity** ▶ A theory in physics, first proposed by the German-born physicist Albert Einstein (1879–1955), in two parts. The first, known as the **Special Theory**, was published in 1905; it arose as a result of problems in the mathematics of relative motion, particularly with reference to the speed of light. Suppose, for example, that a car travelling at 40 mph approaches another travelling at 60 mph; each driver would know his speed relative to the road but would say that the other car was approaching at 100 mph. This is the 'common-sense' view of relative motion, accepted also, until the early part of the 20th century, by most physicists.

Common sense, however, is not always a good guide to reality in physics (*see also*: quantum theory). As Einstein once said:

> Common-sense is the collection of prejudices acquired by age eighteen.

In the 19th century light was regarded as a wave motion in an all-pervading weightless elastic medium known as the 'ether'. If the Earth was moving through the ether it should be possible to confirm the existence of the ether by detecting a difference in the speed of light in the direction of the Earth's rotation compared to that at right angles to this motion. By 1887 the Michelson–Morley experiment had failed to detect this difference – a result that caused considerable uncertainty among physicists.

Einstein at the time was a technical expert (third class) in the Swiss Patent Office in Berne. As such, he was unaware of the Michelson–Morley experiment, but he was thinking about the speed of light and, in particular, the fact that the Scottish physicist James Clerk Maxwell (1831–79) had put forward in 1873 a set of equations describing light as electromagnetic waves travelling at a speed that did not depend on the relative motion of the source and observer.

At the turn of the century, mechanics – in the tradition of Galileo and Newton – was in a state of confusion. Einstein proposed that the best way to deal with the confusion was to assume that the speed of light is always the same, irrespective of the relative motion of the source and observer. For example, the drivers of the two cars approaching each other at 40 mph and 60 mph might add together their speeds to arrive at their relative speed (100 mph). However, the speed of the light emitted by their headlights would always be the same, irrespective of the speeds of the cars.

There were a number of unusual consequences to the Special Theory. For example, the mass of a body increases with its speed and becomes infinite at the speed of light, so that it is impossible to travel faster than the speed of light. Even more unusual is the idea of **time dilation**: time passes more slowly for a moving object than for a stationary object. This leads to the **twin paradox**, in which one of a pair of twins lives on Earth and the other lives in a spacecraft travelling at high speed. When they meet after many years the earthbound twin has aged in the normal way; the space traveller is still young because he has spent most of his life moving at a high speed, so time has passed more slowly.

The consequences of the Special Theory, unusual though they may seem, have been completely verified by experiment and only give results that differ from classical mechanics when objects are moving at speeds close to the speed of light. However, one consequence of the theory *does* affect our lives; this is the principle of the equivalence of mass and energy put forward by Einstein in 1905 in the equation $e = mc^2$, which is the principle upon which nuclear weapons are based.

The Special Theory only applies to objects at rest or in uniform relative motion. By 1907 Einstein was able to incorporate acceleration into the scheme to produce his **General Theory**. In this, Einstein took the view that a body's inertial mass (measured by its resistance to being accelerated) and its gravitational mass (the force it experiences in a gravitational field) were identical and that there is an equivalence between accelerating forces and gravitational forces. The final form of the General Theory, published in 1916, used the ideas of the Russian-born German mathematician Hermann Minkowski (1864–1909), who postulated that the three dimensions of space and the dimension of time formed a continuum, called **space–time**. In the General Theory, gravitation is treated as a consequence of the fact that a mass warps space–time, leading to the concept of 'curved' space.

There have been many experimental verifications of the General Theory, the most spectacular in 1919. Einstein had earlier predicted that light could be deflected by a gravitational field; in a total eclipse of the Sun the deflection of starlight just grazing the Sun should be visible. In 1919 a group led by Sir Arthur Eddington observed a solar eclipse at Principe in West Africa and were able to verify Einstein's prediction.

The result caught the public's imagination – even *The Times*, in a rare editorial on scientific matters, commented:

> The scientific conception of the fabric of the universe must be changed.

The theory of relativity was widely regarded as being incomprehensible to all but a few physicists. It was said that only three people in the world could understand it (Eddington, on hearing this, asked 'Who's the third?').

**• Relief of Ladysmith ▶** The rescue by forces led by General Sir Redvers Buller, on 28 February 1900, of General Sir George White and his Natal Defence Force from the beleaguered garrison of Ladysmith in NW Natal, which marked the turning point for British fortunes in the Boer Wars. The garrison had been under siege by General Piet Joubert and his 15,000-strong Boer army since 2 November 1899. The rescue saved Buller's military reputation, sullied by a string of defeats at the hands of the Boers in the preceding months, while General White's strategic blunder in allowing himself to be trapped in Ladysmith and encircled by Joubert's artillery cost him his health and standing. He was invalided back to England shortly afterwards. *See also*: Spion Kop.

**• REM ▶** Rapid eye movement. Denoting a stage of sleep characterized by darting movements of the eyes beneath closed eyelids, irregular breathing, increased blood flow to the brain, and increased brain temperature. In humans, during normal sleep, short periods of REM sleep (5–15 minutes) alternate with longer periods (70–80 minutes) of heavier sleep without eye movements (**non-REM sleep**). REM sleep is associated with dreaming and seems to be far more important for well-being than NREM sleep, although the reasons for this are still a mystery. Babies and infants may spend up to half their sleep in REM.

REM is also the name of a hugely successful US rock band (formed *c.* 1981).

**• Remagen ▶** A town in Germany, on the River Rhine between Coblenz and Cologne: the scene of the first Allied crossing of the Rhine in World War II. On 7 March 1945 a division of the US army discovered that the railway bridge at Remagen was fit for use – other bridges across the Rhine had been blown up as the Allies approached – and they were able to establish the first bridgehead on the east bank of the river. Further bridgeheads were established later in March as planned (Remagen had not been part of the original strategy), facilitating the Allied advance towards Berlin.

• **REME** ▶ Royal Electrical and Mechanical Engineers. A corps of engineers and technicians formed in May 1942 to maintain and repair the increasingly complex weaponry and equipment employed by the British Army. In previous wars these tasks had been performed by technicians from such units as the Royal Ordnance Corps and Royal Corps of Signals, but the need for a specialist corps became a matter of urgency; in 1942 these ROC and RCS technicians were transferred to the REME. In 1949 the REME's designation was changed to Corps of Royal Electrical and Mechanical Engineers.

• **Remember I'm your mother and get up them stairs!** ▶ A catchphrase used during both World Wars by members of the British armed forces. It was a jocular valediction to a man who was about to go on leave, exhorting him to take his wife (or girlfriend) upstairs to bed without delay.

• **Remember there's a war on** ▶ A phrase used widely during World War I in response to a request for something that was in short supply, or as a reprimand to those who were seen to be wasting time or resources or indulging in frivolous behaviour. During World War II the phrase reappeared in the form **Don't you know there's a war on?** It was often used ironically, as a justification for some undesirable state of affairs, etc.

• **Remembrance Day** or **Remembrance Sunday** ▶ In Britain, the day commemorating the fallen of both World Wars; also called **Poppy Day** from the artificial poppies (recalling the poppies of Flanders fields) sold by the British Legion in aid of ex-servicemen. From 1919 to 1945 it was called Armistice Day and observed on 11 November. From 1945 to 1956 Remembrance Day was observed on the first or second Sunday of November; in 1956 it was fixed on the second Sunday of that month. *See also*: two-minute silence.

• **remote control** ▶ A system or device that enables a distant object to be controlled, usually by radio or electrical signals. Examples of remote-controlled objects range from toy cars, television sets, videocassette players, and garage doors on the domestic scale up to guided missiles, aircraft, or spacecraft on a global scale.

• **Renaissance man** ▶ A man with a diverse range of knowledge and talents in the tradition of such giants of the Italian Renaissance as Leonardo da Vinci (1452–1519). According to the humanist ethic of the Renaissance, a man was expected to seek excellence in all aspects of his physical, intellectual, and spiritual life. The ideal is often symbolized by Leonardo's famous drawing of a perfectly proportioned man with limbs outstretched within a circle.

• **Reno divorce** ▶ A divorce that can be easily obtained in Reno, Nevada, under the liberal laws of that state. Divorces are granted in Nevada on a wider range of grounds than elsewhere to applicants who have been resident in the state for as little as six weeks. Although these laws apply throughout the state, the city of Reno is particularly famous as the place in which a number of show-business celebrities have ended their marriages, being close to the border with California.

• **rent-a-crowd** ▶ A crowd that has been specially organized or paid to appear at a rally, demonstration, political occasion, etc. For example, such a group may be organized by a politician's campaign manager to enable television audiences to see the successful and popular candidate being greeted by enthusiastic supporters. A **rent-a-mob** is a crowd specially organized to cause a disturbance or riot. Both terms were apparently coined by the right-wing satirist 'Peter Simple' (Michael Wharton) during the 1970s.

• **rent boy** ▶ British term for a young male prostitute – a youth available for 'rent'. It is an expression much favoured by the tabloid press.

> A top athletics club was rocked by a rent-boy sex scandal when their gay coach was convicted of a sex offence with a 14-year-old rent-boy.
> – *The Sun*, 6 April 1991.

• **Rentenmark** ▶ A new currency introduced on 20 November 1923 to stabilize Germany's economy and reduce inflation after World War I. Rentenmarks were issued in limited quantities for a temporary period, until the financial crisis showed signs of coming to an end. This drastic remedy was controversial but successful: in 1924 the new Reichsmark, worth 1,000,000,000,000 old marks, was introduced.

• **rent party** or **house-rent party** ▶ In the 1920s to 1940s, a type of party held by US Blacks to raise money for the rent: 'guests' were charged at the door and for their food and drink. Especially common during the Great Depression, the practice was also stimulated by Prohibition, as it provided an environment in which alcohol could be freely consumed. Such parties often lasted for days on end and were famous for the spontaneous sessions of jazz and blues that developed. Many performers survived in hard times by travelling from one rent party to the next, playing for food, drink, and a bed. 'Rent party' or 'house party' also became a term for a style of blues piano playing. *See also*: rugcutting.

• **rent strike** ▶ An organized refusal by tenants to pay their rent; for example, to protest against the dilapidated conditions of a building, unfair rent rises, lack of services, and various restrictions. It was widely used in America in the 1970s, especially in large cities and among college students.

• **repetitive strain injury** ▶ (RSI) A painful condition of particular muscles and joints caused by repeated mechanical activity. The condition was only recognized in the late 1980s, and embraces a wide range of disorders some of which, such as writer's cramp, have long been associated with certain jobs. All are the result of the prolonged repetition of specific tasks, typically performed using the hands, arms, or shoulders; common sufferers include musicians, hairdressers, machine operators, and keyboarders.

• **reserved occupation** ▶ A civilian occupation that exempts those who work in it from military service. The need to prevent workers with certain essential skills from being recruited into the armed forces was first recognized by Lloyd George during the early months of World War I, when the high levels of voluntary enlistment threatened the supply of labour to crucial industries, such as coal mining, armaments, transport, and agriculture. As well as protecting these occupations during the period 1914–18, the British government also introduced measures to make more efficient use of skilled personnel, to open up skilled jobs to the semiskilled and unskilled, and to recruit large numbers of women into industry. The same principles were applied in World War II.

• **residents' association** ▶ An organization of householders formed to act collectively on local issues, such as traffic regulation, approaching grantmaking bodies for funding for property renovation, pressurizing the local council on planning issues, organizing a Neighbourhood Watch for crime prevention, etc. Called a block association in America.

• **Resistance** ▶ An underground organization formed by the inhabitants of enemy-occupied territory in wartime: notably the **French Resistance** movement of World War II. The activities of the Resistance included sabotaging enemy operations, passing information about enemy movements to the Allies through clandestine radio communications, and hiding members of the Allied forces (such as airmen who had been shot down in action) while helping to organize their escape. From May 1943 the various Resistance groups – including former army officers, communist intellectuals, and many ordinary patriots – were coordinated as the Conseil National de la Résistance, led by Jean Moulin (until his arrest in June 1943, when he was succeeded by Georges Bidault). In February 1944 the maquis, provincial guerrilla groups operating in the countryside, became part of the newly formed Forces Françaises de l'Intérieur (FFI), which played a vital role in the liberation of France (*see also*: Fighting French). During World War II there were also active Resistance groups in Belgium, Holland, Denmark, Norway, Poland, Yugoslavia, Greece, and elsewhere.

• **Retail Price Index** ▶ (RPI) An index showing how the price of goods and services in retail shops and other outlets changes on a monthly basis. In the UK the RPI is compiled by the Department for Education and Employment and includes the prices of some 130,000 different items. The index is expressed in percentages and takes a base year as 100%, *e.g.* if 1987 is taken as 100, the RPI for mid-2001 was 173.3. In America the RPI is called the **consumer price index**.

• **retail therapy** ▶ A facetious term for the (generally female) tendency to go shopping for clothes, shoes, toiletries, or luxury items as a remedy for life's various upsets and disappointments. In practice, the term covers a range of behaviour, from the quite normal to the seriously aberrant. While it is not usually very harmful for people to spend a little money on themselves when they feel in need of a lift, this form of 'therapy' can become dangerously compulsive in those suffering from a deep emotional insecurity. The brief high that comes from spending money irresponsibly is usually followed by a feeling of guilt and depression that compounds the original problem.

• **retina identification** ▶ Identification of a person by means of the unique pattern of veins in his or her retina. It has been investigated by banks as a means of improving security at cash-point machines and by hotels, etc., as an alternative to room keys. So far, the cost of installing machinery to read such 'eye-prints' has been found prohibitive.

• **retread** ▶ A colloquial term for something – such as a film, clothes style, or pop record – that reworks old ideas, either from poverty of imagination or as a calculated appeal to nostalgia. In Australia and New Zealand there is an older use of the term to mean a pensioner who returns to his or her former employment. It is especially used of retired teachers called back to the classroom to make up a temporary shortage. In World War II, 'retread' was services slang for a World War I veteran who enlisted to fight again.

The term derives from the idea of treading over the same old ground again but it is also an allusion to the car tyres known as retreads, in which a new tread is moulded onto the casing of a worn tyre.

• **Retreat? Hell, no! We just got here!** ▶ A quotation attributed to the US army officer Lloyd S. William on his arrival at the Western Front towards the end of World War I. Captain William is said to have made this response to French troops, who were retreating and advised him to do likewise. The phrase was subsequently used in other situations, such as sporting competitions, by anybody defiantly rejecting advice to abandon what appears to be a lost cause.

• **retrorocket** ▶ A rocket motor that acts in the opposite direction to the direction of motion of a spacecraft, probe, etc. Retrorockets are used to slow down the vehicle as it enters the atmosphere or lands.

• **retrovirus** ▶ Any of a family of viruses that replicate in an unusual way. The genes of the retrovirus are in the form of RNA (rather than DNA); but what is remarkable is that by using an enzyme unique to themselves, called **reverse transcriptase**, retroviruses produce DNA versions of their own RNA genes. This is the reverse of the usual flow of genetic information – from DNA to RNA – hence the term retrovirus. This so-called DNA transcript can then combine with the DNA of the host cell, *i.e.* the cell which the virus is infecting, so that the viral genes are expressed with the genes of the host cell and are able to subvert the protein manufacturing apparatus of the host cell to assemble new virus particles. One important consequence is that certain retroviruses may introduce cancer-causing oncogenes into the host cell, transforming it into a cancer cell. These genes may be inherited by subsequent generations of the host organism, making the offspring of infected parents predisposed to certain cancers. The Aids virus, HIV, is another type of retrovirus.

• **returner** ▶ A woman who takes up her career again after an interval, usually to have and bring up children. In education and some other professions special returners' courses are now organized.

• **returnik** ▶ A former émigré from an East European country, who has returned home since the collapse of communism. A coinage of the early 1990s, modelled on refusenik.

• **reverse discrimination** ▶ *See*: quota system.

• **revisionism** ▶ A modified version of Marxism that aims to be more flexible and up-to-date in its approach. Such a policy was first advocated in 1899 in Germany by Eduard Bernstein, who argued for social reform rather than revolution; he also felt the socialist movement should include all classes and not be restricted to workers. This idea of revising and updating Marxist theory has been recurrent within communism. Strict followers of Marxist-Leninist ideology have traditionally regarded any new interpretation of doctrine to be heretical and dangerous. For this reason 'revisionist' was a bitter term of abuse among many communists before the introduction of perestroika and glasnost in the Soviet Union.

• **revolving door** ▶ Any policy, approach, etc., based on rapid cyclical activity, especially when this involves people in constant comings and goings from the same place. It is sometimes used to describe the employment policies of firms that accept a high turnover of staff, with new workers constantly arriving as others move on. It has also been used in connection with the so-called care in the community policy towards psychiatric patients, who may find themselves constantly discharged from and readmitted to hospital. The image, familiar from numerous comedy sketches, is of someone entering a building by a revolving door that carries him or her straight out again.

• **Rexists** ▶ A Belgian political party formed by Léon Degrelle in 1936 advocating Fascist methods. Markedly collaborationist during the German occupation of Belgium, it was accordingly suppressed when the Germans were expelled in 1944. The name is an adaptation of 'Christus Rex', Christ the King, the watchword of a Catholic Young People's Action Society founded in 1925.

• **Reye's syndrome** ▶ A rare but serious disease of children. First identified in 1963 by R. D. Reye (1912–77), the Australian physician after whom it was named, it typically develops during the recovery phase of a viral infection, such as influenza. Symptoms of brain damage (including swelling, delirium, and coma) are combined with those of liver failure: both require prompt treatment to prevent permanent damage to these organs. The cause has not been definitely established but evidence suggests that the disorder is caused by the toxic effects of aspirin – given to relieve the original infection – on young children. For this reason aspirin should not be given to children under 12 years of age.

• **RFC** ▶ Royal Flying Corps. The UK's first military aviation service and the forerunner of the RAF. It was created by royal warrant in 1912 from the Air

Battalion of the Royal Engineers; it was originally intended to have both army and navy wings but the naval wing quickly separated to become the Royal Naval Air Service, leaving the RFC to the army. At first the pioneer airmen relied heavily on French-designed airframes and engines, owing to the rudimentary state of the home aviation industry. Furthermore, technical progress was hampered by the RFC's preoccupation with the biplane at the expense of the faster monoplane. At the outset of World War I, squadrons of the Corps were stationed in France, chiefly for reconnaissance of enemy positions. However, by the autumn of 1915 German aircraft armed with machine guns began to take an increasing toll of RFC craft; in retaliation the Corps began to fit some of its own planes with machine guns, as well as the rifle and pistol carried by the observer. Not until May 1916 did the RFC have its first squadron of effective fighter planes – Sopwith Strutters fitted with a synchronized machine gun firing through the propellor arc. The latter part of the war also saw an increased commitment to home defence by the Corps, in an effort to combat bombing raids by German Zeppelins. Casualties were high: in April 1917, for instance, the expected duration of service for a fighter crew on the Western Front was just two months.

• **Rhayader**▶ In Paul Gallico's sentimental story *The Snow Goose* (1940), a hunchbacked recluse with a love of wild birds. His character was based on Sir Peter Scott (1909–89), the ornithologist and wildlife artist, who illustrated the first edition of the book. The two men had once been rivals for the love of the same woman, a well-known figure skater.

• **Rhodes scholars**▶ Students holding a scholarship at Oxford under the will of Cecil Rhodes (1853–1902), who accumulated a vast fortune from his mining activities in South Africa. The scholars are selected from candidates in the Commonwealth, America, and Germany.

• **rhythm-and-blues**▶ (R & B) A Black American music style that developed out of blues and gospel in the 1940s. The chief innovations were the use of amplified instruments and the addition of a strong repetitive beat. In practice, the term was used fairly loosely by the music industry to mean music by and for Blacks (*see*: race music). In the early 1950s, however, White teenagers also began to buy R & B records – despite the protestations of moralists who found them 'as bad for kids as dope'. When White musicians (most notably Elvis Presley) also became involved in making this music, it became known as rock 'n' roll. Early Black rock-'n'-roll stars who were first listed on the R & B charts included Fats Domino, Chuck Berry, Dinah Washington, Joe Turner, and The Platters.

• **rhythm section**▶ The instruments in a dance band, jazz ensemble, rock group, etc., that mainly provide the beat of the music. These are usually the bass, rhythm guitar, and drums, but may also include the piano.

• **Ribbentrop-Molotov pact**▶ *See*: Hitler-Stalin pact.

• **ribbon development**▶ Single-depth building, chiefly houses, along main roads extending out of built-up areas. Developments of this kind took place in the 1920s and 1930s but were stopped by the UK Town and Country Planning Act (1947).

• **Rice, Archie**▶ The central character in John Osborne's play *The Entertainer* (1957), a struggling survivor from the great days of music hall, partly based on the veteran comic Max Miller (1895–1963). The role was originally played by Laurence Olivier, in a notable departure from the classical repertory in which he had made his name.

• **Richter scale**▶ The scale used to measure the strength of an earthquake. It was adopted in 1935 and named after its inventor, the US seismologist Charles Richter (1900–85). The scale ranges from 0 to 8, with each number representing a tenfold increase in energy measured by ground motion. The highest recorded earthquake was 8.9 in 1933 in Japan. The 1906 San Francisco earthquake registered 8.3 (earlier measurements converted to the Richter scale); the 1989 quake in the same city registered 6.9. Although the scale measures the severity of an earthquake, it cannot predict the likely number of casualties; that is clearly also a function of the terrain experiencing the quake. For example, the 1985 Mexico City earthquake of 8.1 caused some 4200 deaths, while the 1988 earthquake in Armenia, registering 6.8 on the scale, caused more than 55,000 deaths.

• **Richthofen Flying Circus**▶ *See*: Red Baron.

• **riddle**▶
  **a riddle wrapped in a mystery inside an enigma** Winston Churchill's phrase for the ambiguities of Soviet policy in the early weeks of World War II. His words, used in a radio broadcast of 1 October 1939, were prompted by the Soviet invasion of E Poland on 18 September, some two weeks after the German invasion from the west. At the time, the Allies had little idea whether this represented active collaboration with the Nazis, an intention to resist them in some circumstances, or simple opportunism. In fact, the parti-

tion of Poland had been secretly agreed in the talks leading to the Hitler–Stalin Pact in August 1939.

Churchill's phrase has often been used out of historical context, as though it were a general comment on the Russian national character or the impenetrable secrecy of pre-glasnost Soviet politics.

• **ride man** ▶ US Black slang of the 1920s to 1940s for the lead soloist in a jazz band, especially one who improvises freely. The soloist can be said to 'ride' the accompaniment in the sense that he is carried along by it while at the same time controlling its speed and direction. The allusion is probably as much to the idea of a man 'riding' a woman in sexual intercourse as to any form of equestrianism.

A band or section of a band can also be said to 'ride' when it plays with an easy flowing rhythm. A **ride cymbal** is a cymbal used by jazz drummers to keep up a continuous rhythm, while the **ride-out** is the final chorus of a piece, usually taken in unison.

• **ride shotgun** ▶ To sit in the front passenger seat of a car. Popularized by US teenagers in the 1950s, this term was originally used in the American West, when it referred to an armed guard who rode next to the driver of a stagecoach to provide protection against robbers, hostile Indians, etc.

• **riff** ▶ In jazz and rock music, a simple ostinato figure used as a basis for improvisation. By extension, it has come to be used of speech or writing that resembles jazz riffing in its rhythms or improvisatory quality. It is also used in a derogatory sense to mean anything that is constantly reiterated, such as a phrase or argument.

The derivation is uncertain. Some accounts link it to the word 'riffle', meaning any kind of skimming or rippling motion; it may, however, be nothing more than a shortening of 'refrain'.

• **right brain** ▶ The right hemisphere of the brain, which neuropsychological research has demonstrated to be dominant for spatial awareness, creative thinking, and the production of art, music, and literature. Creative individuals can therefore be described as **right-brain thinking**. The **left brain** is usually dominant for verbal skills and mathematical and analytical thinking. Cerebral asymmetry and the localization of brain function became widely accepted in the 19th century with the discovery that damage to the left hemisphere resulted in speech impairment, whereas damage to the right had no discernible effect on speech abilities. In the early 20th century it was also discovered that the left side was dominant in controlling complex movements; the role of the right

side remained unclear until the 1950s, when research demonstrated its importance in spatial analysis.

• **right on** ▶ **1.** An expression of wholehearted agreement or encouragement that is chiefly associated with US Black speech. The phrase was already in use in the 1950s and gained wider currency in the 1960s. **2. Right-on** An adjective meaning fashionably liberal or left-wing, politically correct, as in 'His tediously right-on attitudes detract constantly from the humour'. The term is usually ironic or derogatory.

• **right stuff, the** ▶ Army slang for the qualities regarded as necessary for officer material. The phrase, often heard in the 1930s, became popular again after the US writer Tom Wolfe used it as the title of his 1979 book about the first US astronauts (filmed 1983).

• **right-to-life** ▶ See: pro-life.

• **Rillington Place** ▶ See: Christie murders.

• **Ringo** ▶ In full Ringo Starr, stage name of Richard Starkey (1940–　), drummer with the Beatles (1963–70) and subsequently a solo performer. He acquired the name in the early 1960s, when his habit of wearing several rings was far more unusual for a man than would be the case now. The surname Starr was adopted for an early stint at a Butlin's Holiday Camp.

• **ring road** ▶ A main road that encircles a city or town so that heavy through traffic can bypass the centre. London's orbital motorway, the M25, replaced an earlier ring-road network that was overtaken by the city's growth.

The US name for a ring road is a **belt** or **beltway**. The beltway round Washington, DC, has given rise to the political catchphrase **outside the beltway**, referring to public opinion in grass-roots America.

• **Rintelen spy ring** ▶ A group of German spies operating in America during World War I under the leadership of Kapitän Franz von Rintelen. The organization was highly successful, for a time, in its mission to sabotage US aid to the Allies. In August 1915 Rintelen was recalled from America by a false message; he was arrested when the Dutch ship on which he was travelling reached British waters.

• **Rin Tin Tin** ▶ An Alsatian (German shepherd) dog who became a star of the silent screen in the 1920s. Formerly a guard dog with the German army, Rin Tin Tin appeared in such films as *Jaws of Steel* (1927) and *A Dog of the Regiment* (1930), usually saving the day with a display of loyalty and resourcefulness. During his Hollywood career Rin Tin Tin enjoyed the services of a personal chef, valet, and chauffeur. This remarkable dog died in 1932, aged about 16. *See also*: Lassie.

• **Riom trials** ▶ The trials of a number of French politicians and military men, which took place in 1942 at a supreme court of justice set up by the Vichy government in the town of Riom, France. The defendants, opponents of the Vichy government, included such major figures as Edouard Daladier, Léon Blum, Paul Reynard, and Maurice Gamelin, who were blamed for the fall of France and imprisoned. The trials began in February 1942 and were suspended indefinitely in April of that year. The accused spent the remainder of World War II in prisons and concentration camps.

• **riot shield** ▶ A defensive shield, made from tough plastic, carried by police or military forces during riot control. Riot shields have been used by British troops in Northern Ireland since the early 1970s and were first issued to police forces on the mainland after the Lewisham riots in the summer of 1977. The tactic of banging on such shields to intimidate a foe was borrowed from the war customs of the Zulus and others.

• **ripcord** ▶ A cord attached to a handle that is pulled to open a parachute from its pack during descent. The first parachutes, those of the late 18th century, were dropped already opened from balloons. An American, A. L. Stevens, introduced the parachute pack and ripcord in 1908. This combination was perfected 10 years later by another American, Floyd Smith, for use in escaping from an aircraft.

• **rip off** ▶ A colloquialism meaning to steal, to swindle, to take advantage of. Originally a term from the Black street slang of large US cities, it was taken up by the hippies and has passed into more general usage, being now heard in all parts of the English-speaking world.

> In Spain, tourists used to be ripped off by souvenir shops and property speculators: nowadays they are just ripped off. – *The Independent*, 16 March 1991.

The noun form (**rip-off**) is also widely used, as in 'the price was a rip-off'. It is also used to imply that an idea has been stolen without attribution: 'His paper was a rip-off of mine!'

• **ripple effect** ▶ The series of consequences that flow from a single important event or situation. The ripple effect of the September 11 attacks in America, for example, has so far included the destruction of the Taliban regime in Afghanistan, an enhanced standing for President Bush, and major redundancies in the air industry.

• **rite of passage** ▶ A ritual or ceremony performed to mark a person's transition from one status to another. The common rites of passage are naming after birth (and/or circumcision in some communities), confirmation or some other ceremony performed at puberty, inauguration into a profession or position, marriage, and the rites associated with death and burial. In prescientific societies such rites of passage are often thought to have magical efficacy, while in modern religions the significance is a spiritual one. However, similar rites persist in even the most secular societies and communities, suggesting that they have a psychological and social importance, too. The expression was first used as the title of a French book *Les Rites de passage* (1909) by the anthropologist Arnold van Gennep.

• **Ritz Brothers** ▶ A team of US comedians of the 1930s and 1940s, comprising Al (1901–65), Jim (1903–85), and Harry (1906–86) Ritz. Beginning in nightclubs, they later appeared in such film musicals as *The Goldwyn Follies* (1938) and *The Three Musketeers* (1939). Their original family name was Joachim.

• **ritzy** ▶ Denoting an occasion, person, etc., that is fashionable and opulent. The word derives from the Ritz Hotels in Paris and London, which are identified with luxury and wealth. They were established by the Swiss hotelier, César Ritz (1850–1918). Hence 'to dine at the Ritz' may be considered to be the ultimate luxury in dining out. To **put on the Ritz** is to make an ostentatious display of opulence: the phrase predates the Irving Berlin song 'Putting on the Ritz', which was written in 1929. It was from The Ritz Hotel in Paris, currently owned by the Egyptian-born tycoon Mohammed al-Fayed, that Diana, Princess of Wales (*see*: People's Princess) and her lover, Dodi Fayed, the son of the hotel's owner, set off on their fatal drive. *See also*: glitzy.

• **Rivers of Blood** ▶ *See*: Powellism.

• **RKO** ▶ RKO Radio Pictures Inc., formerly one of the biggest Hollywood production and distribution companies. It was founded in 1921 when the Radio Corporation of America merged with the Keith-Orpheum cinema circuit. Notable RKO features included *Cimarron* (1931), *King Kong* (1933), and *Citizen Kane* (1941) but the company was best known for its low-budget and often unsuccessful films; it was in continual financial difficulties. During World War II a popular Hollywood joke ran 'In case of an air raid, go directly to RKO; they haven't had a hit in years'. In 1948 the eccentric tycoon Howard Hughes acquired a controlling share of the stock, leading to prolonged litigation, the defection of top staff, and further enormous losses; in 1953 the studios were sold off to a television company. The firm continues as RKO General, an umbrella organization controlling a number of radio and TV stations.

• **RNA** ▶ Ribonucleic acid. One of the fundamental molecules of life, responsible for interpreting the genetic information that resides in the genes of living cells. This it does in two stages: transcription and translation of the genetic message. RNA is chemically very similar to DNA; the essential difference is that it contains the sugar ribose (hence *ribo*nucleic) instead of the deoxyribose sugar of DNA. Cells contain several different types of RNA, including messenger RNA, ribosomal RNA, and transfer RNA, which all have different roles in the manufacture of proteins by the cell. In some viruses RNA is also the genetic material. Discovery of the vital roles of RNA in protein synthesis came in the 1950s through the work of many scientists, including Francis Crick, Paul Berg, and Robert Holley.

• **RNAS** ▶ Royal Naval Air Service. The air force of the Royal Navy, which was founded in 1914 to protect coastal ports and shipping and to carry out punitive raids on U-boat bases in the German-occupied Channel ports. After 1918 the RNAS was subordinated to, and controlled by, the RAF, although the Admiralty insisted that the navy should be allowed to maintain a separate specialist air service. In 1924 government permission was granted to establish the Fleet Air Arm, a carrier branch of the Royal Navy, although it was not until 1937 that the FAA was placed under sole Admiralty control.

• **road** ▶
**Keep death off the road** A British government slogan of the late 1940s and early 1950s exhorting drivers to take more care. It was used as the caption to a photograph of a haggard and distressed looking woman, with the implication that she had just been bereaved by a road accident. The campaign was criticized at the time as being too disturbing. A similar slogan was **carelessness kills**.

• **road** ▶
**one for the road** One last drink before departing, formerly a popular call at the end of a party or drinking session. However, since the introduction of strict drink-driving codes, this is now rarely heard. *See*: breathalyser.

• **road hog** ▶ Colloquial name for a selfish, reck-

less, or inconsiderate motorist, especially one who 'hogs' the road by making it difficult for others to pass. The term has been in common use since the early days of motoring.

• **roadhouse** ▶ An inn or hotel by the roadside, usually at some distance outside a town, to which people go by car for meals, dancing, etc. Roadhouses became popular with the growth in car ownership during the 1930s, but have since declined owing to strict drink-drive codes. Their other function, of providing overnight accommodation for travellers, has largely been taken over by motels.

• **roadie** ▶ A person hired by touring musicians to transport, maintain, and erect equipment for their stage shows.

• **road movie** ▶ A genre of film in which the central character takes to the road to escape the law, the past, a constricting home life, etc. His or her experiences, and those of other characters met along the way, form the substance of the film. The hero's journey usually becomes a voyage of self-discovery or an exploration of the state of a society. Classic road movies include the biker film *Easy Rider* (1969), *Badlands* (1973), and the feminist *Thelma and Louise* (1991).

This mostly rather sombre genre should certainly not be confused with the 'Road' movies of Bob Hope, Bing Crosby, and Dorothy Lamour – a series of light comedies beginning conventionally enough with *The Road to Singapore* (1940) but later developing a zany ad-libbing style of its own.

• **road rage** ▶ An uncontrollable anger that can overcome the driver of a motor vehicle if he considers that some other driver has committed either a motoring offence according to the Highway Code or an act that constitutes a personal affront. The male pronoun is here used advisedly; women tend to react less extremely to the foibles of other road users. A driver so afflicted is capable of language and behaviour that would otherwise be quite uncharacteristic; in extreme cases road rage has led to murder.

• **road show** ▶ **1.** Originally a US term for a travelling show of actors, musicians, mountebanks, etc., now used of any kind of touring attraction, especially one requiring large amounts of equipment and personnel. It is commonly used of, for example, rock bands touring with their own sound and lighting equipment, campaigning politicians with their entourage and mobile back-up facilities, or a radio or TV programme that broadcasts live from a series of outside venues; BBC TV's *The Antiques Road Show* is a notable example of the latter. **2.** In the film business, the special 'pre-release' of a major feature in selected cities before its general distribution to local cinemas nationwide.

• **robbed** ►

**We wuz robbed** A catchphrase that originated in the boxing world in America. In the 1927 world heavyweight fight between Gene Tunney and the challenger Jack Dempsey, Dempsey laid Tunney flat on the canvas – but it was six seconds before the referee could persuade Dempsey to retire to a neutral corner so that he could begin his count. The delay enabled Tunney to get to his feet, survive the round, and retain his title on points. Dempsey said afterwards, 'I was robbed of the championship'. This cry was echoed a little less grammatically by Joe Jacobs, the US manager of Max Schmeling, whom he believed had been cheated of victory in his 1932 fight against Jack Sharkey. 'We wuz robbed', he shouted into a vacant microphone. Since the 1930s, the phrase has been used by the losers and their managers in many other sports, especially football. In 1991 *The Sun*, reporting that footballers were being offered a course to help them avoid such clichés (*see*: over the moon; sick as a parrot), offered a translation:

> We were humiliated by the vastly superior technical skills of the opposition.

• **robot** ► (Czech *robota*, forced labour) In science fiction, an automaton with semi-human powers and intelligence. The word comes from the mechanical creatures in Karel Capek's play *R.U.R.* (Rossum's Universal Robots), which opened in Prague in 1921 and was successfully produced in London in 1923. The play was a warning of the dangers of uncontrolled technological development. In modern industry a robot is a computer-controlled machine that is programmed to carry out specific tasks that would otherwise be performed by a human being. Many functions in factories are now automated, *i.e.* performed by robots.

• **robot dancing** or **robotics** ► A dance style popularized in the 1980s by Black Americans; it is characterized by quick jerky movements imitating the mechanical actions of robots. 'Robotic' (resembling a robot) was a word originally coined by the US biochemist and science fiction writer Isaac Asimov (1920–92).

• **robug** ► A remote controlled device used to clean, maintain, or photograph inaccessible parts of a tall building. It uses legs with adhesive suckers to crawl up vertical surfaces and across ceilings. The name reflects its resemblance to a robotic spider. It was developed in the 1980s by Arthur Collie and Professor John Billingsley.

• **rock** ► 1. A broad term for various kinds of popular music loosely descended from rock 'n' roll. It was used more-or-less interchangeably with pop (*see*: pop music) until the early 1970s, when some critics began to insist on a distinction. Thereafter, 'rock' tended to be used of music that was more ambitious, more serious in intention, and less immediately commercial than the lightweight pop music that dominated the singles charts. In 1990 this distinction was the subject of a debate in the House of Lords, who had to rule whether a commercial radio franchise reserved for 'non-pop' broadcasting could be awarded to a company who planned to specialize in serious rock music. After a long and somewhat heated discussion, their lordships ruled that this was a distinction without a difference. Subdivisions of rock include **soft rock** (a more melodic variety) and **hard rock** (based on pounding rhythms and high volume). *See also*: acid rock; folk rock; heavy metal; punk, etc. 2. Slang for crack cocaine, because of its hard crystalline form. 3. A colloquial term for a diamond or any precious stone.

• **rock** ►

**don't knock the rock** A catchphrase of the late 1950s, used in response to hostile criticism of rock 'n' roll music. It was the title of a 1957 film featuring Bill Haley and the Comets: the title song reached No. 7 in the British charts that same year.

• **rockabilly** ► A type of popular music, originating in the southern states of America, that fuses rock 'n' roll and hillbilly country music. Popular in the 1950s, it has enjoyed several revivals, notably in the early 1990s.

• **rock 'n' roll** ► A type of popular music that emerged in the later 1950s, characterized by a heavily accented beat and simple repeated phrases. Essentially a commercialized version of rhythm-and-blues, it was the first style of popular music to become a focus for youthful rebellion and parental panic. It was accompanied by a frenetic kind of jive dancing, also known as rock 'n' roll. The term was used from about 1953 by the US disc jockey Alan Freed, who found that the racial stigma attached to rhythm-and-blues prevented this music from being accepted by White audiences. Ironically, 'rock and roll' – like so much of the popular music vocabulary – was originally Black slang for sexual intercourse.

• **Rockefeller Center** ► New York City's 22-acre business and entertainment complex of 19 buildings. It includes the 70-storey 850-foot (283-m) General Electric Building (the former RCA Building) housing the National Broadcasting Company (*see*: NBC). The building's sunken Plaza, overlooked by a gilded statue of Prometheus, becomes a garden-terrace restaurant in summer and an ice-skating rink in winter crowned with 'the world's largest Christmas tree'. Superlatives also abound in Radio City Music Hall, whose indoor cinema (6200 seats), Wurlitzer organ, and chandeliers are all listed as 'the world's largest'. The Rockefeller Center site – from 48th to 51st streets and from 5th Avenue to the Avenue of the Americas – was leased from Columbia University in 1928 by industrialist John D. Rockefeller Jr (1874–1960); the major buildings were constructed between 1931 and 1939. The family's association with the Center ended in 2000, when Rockefeller Center Properties sold the complex to US developers Jerry Speyer and Lester Crown for $1.8 billion.

• **Rockefeller Foundation** ▶ A philanthropic foundation created in 1913 by the US industrialist John Davison Rockefeller (1839–1937) and his son John D. Rockefeller Jr (1874–1960). The purpose of the foundation was 'to promote the well-being of mankind throughout the world'. Initially concerned with public health and medical education, the work of the foundation diversified after 1928, providing generous financial support for scientific research and projects connected with the social sciences and humanities.

• **rocker** ▶ See: mods and rockers.

• **Rockhampton Rocket** ▶ A press nickname for the Australian tennis player Rod Laver (1938–   ), referring to his speed about the court and his birth in Rockhampton, Queensland. Laver was the first player to win the grand slam of major tournaments twice, in 1962 and 1969; the interval represents the period during which he was barred from Wimbledon for his professional status. He was also the first player to earn £1 million in prize money.

• **rock opera** ▶ A drama set to rock music. The first of the genre was the controversial hippie musical *Hair* (1967), which ran for 1750 performances in New York. This was followed by *Tommy*, written by Pete Townshend of The Who (1969) and *Jesus Christ Superstar* (1970), with music by Andrew Lloyd Webber and lyrics by Tim Rice; both works were originally written to be listened to on records rather than experienced in the theatre, although both were later staged (and filmed). The vogue for so-called rock operas passed fairly quickly, but the genre has had a lasting influence on the development of the musical since the 1970s.

• **Roger** ▶ The word used to represent the letter R in a former version of the alphabet used in radiotelephony. 'Roger' also stood for 'received', indicating that a message had been received and understood; 'Roger and out' meant that the message had been received and there was no reply. During World War II Roger was used as a general term of acknowledgment (meaning 'right', 'OK', or 'agreed') by British and US forces; thereafter it entered the general language. In the modern telecommunications alphabet the letter R and the word 'received' are represented by the word 'Romeo'.

• **Rogers, Buck** ▶ See: Buck Rogers.

• **role model** ▶ A person whose behaviour in a particular role serves as a model for another to follow. For example, a father often functions as a role model for his son. It has often been said that the central problem with the single-parent family is that there is no father to provide a role model.

• **role play** ▶ An activity in which the participants act out designated roles in a dramatic situation; the aim is usually either therapeutic or educational. Role play was originally developed as a technique in psychotherapy by the Austrian-born US psychiatrist Jacob Moreno (1890–1974). His patients were encouraged to act out a variety of roles to gain insight into the motives, actions, and perspectives of others. The technique is now widely used in many forms of training to promote understanding and improve relationships.

• **Rolex** ▶ Tradename for the watches produced by the Rolex Watch Co. Although meaningless in itself, the name may have been chosen to suggest the 'rolling' mechanism of a watch and the idea of *excellence*. This was one of the first tradenames to use the suffix '-ex', which has since become ubiquitous. The famous **Rolex oyster**, introduced in 1926, was so-named because of its watertight design, at that time a unique feature. In the 1980s it became the yuppie watch par excellence, appearing regularly in the lists of designer accessories that fill the pages of s 'n' s novels from that era.

• **roller** ▶ British slang for a Rolls-Royce car. Originally an underworld term it became more widespread in the early 1980s and is now, perhaps, the most usual way to refer to such a vehicle.

> Duke's £38,000 bill to fix his roller. – *The Sun*, 3 April 1991.

• **roller disco** ▶ A form of disco dancing on roller skates that became a popular US pastime in the late 1970s. The most renowned performers were seen at the Empire Roller Disco in New York City's borough of Brooklyn. Indoor roller skating has remained popular in America since rinks proliferated in the 1870s.

• **Rolling Stones** ▶ The leading British rock

group of the 1960s after the Beatles. The Stones were Mick Jagger (1943–   ), Brian Jones (1942–69), who was replaced by Mick Taylor (1948–   ) and then Ron Wood (1947–   ), Keith Richard(s) (1943–   ), Charlie Watts (1941–   ), and Bill Wyman (1936–   ), who has now retired. The group was heavily influenced by rhythm-and-blues, the music of such blues singers as Muddy Waters, and the rock 'n' roll of Chuck Berry. Ironically, considering the battle between the Stones and the Beatles for the soul of British youth during the 1960s, their first top-ten hit was the Lennon and McCartney song 'I Wanna be Your Man'. The group cultivated a more rebellious and dangerous image than the Beatles, a stance reflected in the often cynical lyrics to their songs ('Satisfaction', 1965) and the blatant sexuality of Jagger's performance style. Establishment hostility culminated in a police raid in 1967, following which Jagger and Richards were briefly gaoled on drug charges. The late 1960s and early 1970s were their most creative period, with such albums as *Beggars Banquet* (1968), *Let It Bleed* (1970), and *Exile on Main Street* (1972). Hit singles from the same period included 'Jumping Jack Flash' (1968) and 'Honky Tonk Woman', which reached No. 1 in 1969, the year Brian Jones drowned in his swimming pool. Although their recordings of the past 25 years have rarely excited the critics, they continue to tour with great success.

• **Roll on, big ship** ▶ A catchphrase used by members of the British armed forces towards the end of World War I, expressing an earnest desire for the war to be over. Variants of the phrase include 'Roll on, Blighty', 'Roll on, duration' (referring to the fact that volunteers had signed up for the duration of the war), 'Roll on, that boat' (used in the RAF from the 1920s), 'I heard the voice of Moses say, Roll on, my bloody twelve' (used in the Royal Navy, referring to the service period of 12 years), 'Roll on, death, and let's have a go at the angels' (an expression of boredom or frustration), and 'Roll on, time' (used by prisoners).

In general usage the phrase 'roll on' may be followed by anything that the speaker awaits with impatience, such as 'Roll on, pay-day', 'Roll on, Christmas', etc.

• **roll-on roll-off** ▶ (RORO) Denoting a ferry that transports motor vehicles across a stretch of water and is so constructed that the vehicles can drive straight onto the vessel at the port of loading and off at the port of destination. Such vessels are widely used for transporting cars and heavy lorries across the English Channel. *See*: Herald of Free Enterprise.

• **Rolls-Royce** ▶ The supreme motor car, combining British engineering skill with both elegance and luxury. In 1904 Frederick Henry Royce (1863–1933), who ran a small Manchester engineering firm, decided that he could make a better car than any then available. His first vehicle so impressed the aristocratic car dealer Charles Stewart Rolls (1877–1910) that he persuaded Royce to set up a partnership with him as car manufacturers. Their Rolls-Royce Silver Ghost, first marketed in 1907, quickly established itself as 'the best car in the world' and, continued in production for 20 years.

The reputation of Rolls-Royce cars encouraged Royce to branch out into aeroengines. One result was the Merlin engine, which powered the legendary Hurricane and Spitfire fighter planes in World War II (*see*: Schneider Trophy).

In the 1970s, as a result of the enormous cost of developing jet engines for aircraft, the company was split into a privately owned car manufacturer and a publicly owned aeroengine company. (The latter returned to private ownership in 1987.) The Rolls-Royce motor company continued to make the best and most expensive cars in the world. By now the epithet 'Rolls-Royce' had entered the language to mean the best of anything in its class:

> ...a nine-foot Bechstein – which many people feel is the Rolls-Royce of pianos. – New Yorker, 19 September 1977.

Unfortunately, although Rolls-Royce cars continued to be sought as status symbols by the rich and famous, the company itself did not share in the financial success of its clients. In 1988 this acme of British achievement suffered the ignominy of being bought by Volkswagen, the manufacturers of Hitler's 'people's car'.

• **ROM** ▶ Read-only memory. A type of computer memory whose contents may be read but not modified and are not lost when the computer is switched off. ROM is used for storing essential programs such as that which loads the operating system (the program that controls the screen, keyboard, disk access, etc.) as soon as the computer is switched on. Because ROM is incorruptible, any changes to its contents, *e.g.* to fix errors in a program or to upgrade the operating system, have to be accomplished by replacing the ROM chips themselves. *See also*: CD-ROM.

• **roman candle** ▶ British armed forces' euphemism for the fate of a parachutist whose parachute fails to open.

• **Rome–Berlin Axis** ▶ *See*: Axis; Pact of Steel.

• **R101** ▶ British airship, the destruction of which, on 5 October 1930, signalled the end of airship development for many years. The R101 was the pride of the British aeronautical industry when it departed from England on its non-stop maiden journey to India. Bad weather, coupled with insufficient testing before the flight, caused the airship to crash in a wood near Beauvais in N France; 48 people died in the inferno resulting from the combustion of its 5 million cubic feet of hydrogen. A curious postscript to the tragedy was provided by a séance held in London three days later: a list of technical defects in the R101 was allegedly communicated through the medium; these were confirmed a year later when the results of the official enquiry were published.

• **rooinek** ▸ (Afrikaans, red-neck) A name given by the Boers to the British in the South African War; it was used later to mean any British or European immigrant to South Africa. *See also*: redneck.

• **rookie** ▸ In army and police slang, a recruit, a novice or greenhorn. In America, it is also used for a raw beginner in professional sport. It is probably a diminutive of 'recruit'.

• **rope** ▸ Marijuana, which is derived from the hemp plant (*Cannabis sativa*), also the source of fibre for rope (hence the name). The term is usually applied to marijuana in the form of a joint, perhaps because in the 1930s and 1940s a 'rope' was a facetious term for a cigar. *See also*: pot.

• **RORO** ▸ *See*: roll-on roll-off.

• **Rorschach ink-blot test** ▸ A test used in psychology, devised by the Swiss psychiatrist Hermann Rorschach (1884–1922). It consists of a series of ten ink-blots that form complex symmetrical shapes: five of the ink-blots are coloured, five are in shades of grey and black. The way in which the patients describe and interpret these shapes is supposed to reveal aspects of their personality and emotional stability (or instability); the results can be used to measure intelligence and diagnose psychological disorders. The validity of the test has been the subject of some controversy.

• **rort** ▸ An Australian colloquialism for a riotous party or drinking bout. This usage seems to have originated among Australian servicemen in World War II, probably by back formation from the slang **rorty**, meaning lively or jolly. It seems to be unrelated to the older sense of 'rort' meaning a racket, dodge, or swindle. In the Great Depression a **rorter** was a tramp who made a precarious living by peddling trashy goods from door to door. The word is used more generally to mean a small-time conman or hustler.

• **Rose Bowl** ▸ A sports stadium in Pasadena, Cal-

ifornia, which is the venue of the annual post-season US college football game between a team representing the Pacific Eight and one representing the Big Ten Conference. The first of these games was held on 1 January 1902; it became officially known as the Rose Bowl game in 1923 and has been held annually there ever since. *See also*: Super Bowl. The stadium is named after the Tournament of the Roses held there annually from 1890; this is based on the Battle of the Flowers, which takes place during the annual Lenten carnival in Nice on the French Côte d'Azur.

• **rose is a rose** ▸ A phrase meaning that something is complete and perfect in itself and therefore needs no further explanation. It is a version of a line from a poem by Gertrude Stein (1874–1946):

> Rose is a rose is a rose. – 'Sacred Emily'.

'Rose' here refers not just to the flower usually understood to be so perfect, but to work by Sir Frederick Rose, a British artist whose paintings Stein loved.

• **Roseland** ▸ South-east England outside London, regarded as a desirable place to live. 'Rose' is here an acronym for 'rest of south-east', but also conveys the idea that life is rosy in this affluent and agreeable part of the country. The acronym first appeared in the mid-1980s, when the south-east enjoyed an economic boom (and a dramatic rise in property values) while other parts of the country were still struggling out of recession.

• **Rosenberg spy case** ▸ The case of the US couple Julius (1918–53) and Ethel Rosenberg (1915–53), who were arrested in 1950 on suspicion of supplying the Soviet Union with atom bomb secrets. The case against them was based largely on the evidence of Harry Gold, a Soviet agent, and David Greenglass, Ethel Rosenberg's brother, who worked at the atomic research base at Los Alamos (*see*: Manhattan Project), both of whom had been eventually exposed by the arrest of Klaus Fuchs in 1945 (*see*: Fuchs spy case). Greenglass claimed that his espionage activities, which he admitted in return for leniency, were instigated and encouraged by the Rosenbergs, although both protested their innocence throughout their ordeal. The anti-communist hysteria generated by McCarthyism at that time combined with the outbreak of the Korean War to give the Rosenbergs little chance of acquittal. They were sentenced to death in March 1951, although a series of appeals and stays of execution prolonged the agony until 19 June 1953, when they were electrocuted in Sing Sing despite appeals for clemency and public demonstrations throughout America and Europe on their behalf. They would almost certainly have been reprieved if they had confessed to spying for the Soviet Union, which they steadfastly refused to do. The question of the guilt or innocence of the Rosenbergs has been the subject of controversy ever since. Not all the relevant FBI files have been released but some recent researchers believe that while Julius was guilty, Ethel may have been framed by the FBI in order to pressure her husband into revealing full details of his espionage activities.

> I can only say that, by immensely increasing the chance of an atomic war, the Rosenbergs may have condemned to death tens of millions of innocent people all over the world. – PRESIDENT EISENHOWER.

• **Roswell incident** ▶ The alleged crash of a flying saucer in the desert near Roswell, New Mexico, in early July 1947. This somewhat mysterious incident has become a *cause célèbre* among those conspiracy theorists who claim that evidence of UFO activity has been routinely covered up by the US government.

The facts appear to be as follows. On the night of 3 July 1947 there was an intense thunderstorm over Roswell; at least one local claimed at the time to have seen a bright saucer-shaped object hurtling through the sky at tremendous speed. The following morning a rancher named MacBrazel rode out to check his stock and came across large amounts of unidentifiable debris strewn over a wide area, pieces of which he collected and took to the county sheriff. Suspecting that this debris might be connected with secret military operations in the area, the sheriff contacted the local army air field, who sent an intelligence officer to investigate. This officer, a Major Marcel, apparently reported that the wreckage was made of a lightweight material that he could not identify, and that it would not bend or burn. Following his report, Marcel's superiors issued an astonishing press release to the local media, stating that the remains of a flying saucer had been recovered. Within hours this was rescinded by a second press release from a higher authority, claiming that the wreckage was actually that of a weather balloon and its radar reflector. A strict cordon was then placed around the area of the crash, and not lifted until all the wreckage had been removed.

Allegations that something truly extraordinary and shocking had been found by the military are based mainly on the later testimony of a local mortician, who claims to have been contacted by an army mortuary officer and asked about the availability of small hermetically sealed caskets and the best way of preserving bodies without contaminating the tissue. This man also claims to have met a nurse from the military hospital, who described assisting at an autopsy on several humanoid bodies, which she sketched for him on a napkin. The nurse has never been traced, although her celebrated sketch of small creatures with weird triangular faces remains.

The rumours about Roswell have snowballed over the years, with various new witnesses coming forward to add their 'recollections' of strange bodies and other debris found in the desert (all hastily spirited away by the military authorities).

In 1994 an exhaustive report into the incident was published by the office of the secretary of the US Air Force. This concluded that the debris found near Roswell had been the remains of a secret balloon-borne research project codenamed MOGUL. Rumours of 'alien bodies' in the desert or the military hospital were probably inspired by the anthropomorphic test dummies used in high-altitude balloon projects and confused recollections of two other incidents in which human pilots had been killed in secret tests.

• **Rotary Club** ▶ A movement among business men that takes for its motto 'Service above Self'. The idea originated with Paul Harris, a Chicago lawyer, in 1905. In 1911 it took root in the UK and there are now clubs in most towns, membership originally being limited to one member from each trade, calling, or profession. Lectures are delivered at weekly meetings by guest speakers. The name derives from the early practice of holding meetings in rotation at the business premises of its members. The Rotary Clubs are now members of one association called **Rotary International**. The Inner Wheel club is a similar organization for the wives of Rotarians and Rotaract is for younger members.

• **rotodyne** ▶ Tradename for a type of helicopter with short fixed wings to provide additional lift. The first rotodyne was constructed in 1957 by the Fairey Aviation Co. (absorbed by Westland a few years later) but only one further machine was built before the project was suspended in 1962. Similar machines (also known as convertiplanes, compound helicopters, or tilt-rotors) have been produced by other companies.

The name combines 'rotor' with 'aerodyne' – a name for any heavier-than-air machine that uses aerodynamic forces to obtain lift.

• **rotor ship** ▶ An experimental ocean-going vessel developed by Germany in 1925, which for a time promised to be a revolutionary step forward in sea transport. The *Baden-Baden*, designed by Anton Flettner, was propelled by two massive rotors, which responded to wind pressure in much the same way as a ball spinning in a breeze. Flettner claimed that it was capable of greater speeds than conventional sailing ships while being cheap and easy to run; it was also able to keep moving in the heaviest weather. It was confidently predicted that all the world's shipping would employ rotor power within years. However, the *Baden-Baden*'s dependence on the wind coupled with technical difficulties created by the continuous vibration caused by the rotors meant that even the prototypes had been scrapped within 20 years.

• **rotten** ▸ One of many Australian colloquialisms meaning drunk. It presumably describes a more advanced state of intoxication than such terms as 'ripe' and 'overripe'.

• **rottweiler** ▸ A breed of working dog with a stocky body and thick neck, named after the town of Rottweil in SW Germany. Rottweilers are thought to have been brought there by the Roman legions and were traditionally used by local butchers to carry their moneybags to market. Their characteristics include strength and aggression, making them highly suitable as guard dogs. The rottweiler became notorious in the UK in the 1980s, following a series of attacks on children and others, some fatal. A press campaign to make the dog a controlled breed seemed only to increase its popularity, especially among those young men for whom its viciousness became the chief attraction.

The word 'rottweiler' is now frequently used to mean a brutally aggressive person with no scruples or sense of fair play. In some fields, such as politics or business, the usage may be half-admiring. The word is used in such common phrases as **rottweiler tactics**, **rottweiler journalism**, etc. *See also*: pit bull terrier.

• **rough cut** ▸ The initial stage in the editing of a film. The rough cut is assembled by selecting one version of each shot and arranging them in correct narrative sequence. Many adjustments and refinements are made before the **fine cut** is submitted to the film's producers for approval and release. *See also*: rushes.

• **rough trade** ▸ 1. British male homosexual slang for an uncouth and aggressive sexual partner, usually a younger man of a lower social group, casually picked up. 2. Similarly, a macho and muscular, but socially inferior, young boyfriend of a cultured older woman.

• **round** ▸

**in the round** In the theatre, a form of staging in which plays are presented on a central stage surrounded by the audience as in an arena, without proscenium arch or curtains. This style of presentation, which allows for greater interaction between actors and audience, became fashionable in the 1960s and 1970s.

• **Round Table** ▸ An international organization that provides business and professional men under the age of 40 with an opportunity for social gatherings, with a strong emphasis on community service, charitable works, and fund raising. It was founded in 1927 as a 'Club for Young Business and Professional Men' by Louis Marchesi, the son of a Swiss-born restaurateur living in Norwich, England. The origins of the name are somewhat confused: some have attributed it to a speech made by the Prince of Wales (the future Edward VIII) in which he urged:

> The young business and professional men of this country must get together round the table, adopt methods that have proved so sound in the past, adapt them to the changing needs of the times, and wherever possible improve them.

There are now over 1250 such local groups, or 'Tables', in the UK, with more than 30,000 members, known as Tablers. The organization is also established in some 70 other countries. Tablers retiring at 40 can seek solace in the '41 Club'. The first Ladies Circle, for members' wives, was formed in Bournemouth in 1930, and the National Association of Ladies Circles was set up in 1936. *See also*: Algonquin Round Table.

• **Roy** ▸ Australian colloquialism for a rich fashionable man, especially one who drives a sports car, dresses in expensive leisure wear, and has an offensively smooth manner. He is despised by the ockers, who regard the Roys as idle, untrustworthy, and effeminate.

• **Royal Air Force** ▸ *See*: RAF.

• **Royal Ballet** ▸ The principal British ballet company, which was known as the Sadler's Wells Ballet until 1956. Founded by Ninette de Valois in 1931, it originally performed at the Sadler's Wells Theatre and the Old Vic; since 1946 it has been based at the Royal Opera House in Covent Garden (*see*: Royal Opera). In 1990 the Royal Ballet's subsidiary company moved to Birmingham, where it became known as the **Birmingham Royal Ballet**. The Royal Ballet also runs its own school of dancing.

• **Royal Festival Hall** ▸ A concert hall on the South Bank of the Thames designed by Sir Leslie Martin and Sir Robert Matthew for the Festival of Britain in 1951. It was the first significant British public building in the modern style and the only building intended to be permanent in the complex of buildings erected for the Festival. It remains one of London's premier concert halls.

• **Royal Flying Corps**► *See*: RFC.

• **Royal Green Jackets**► An infantry regiment of the British army comprising the 43rd, 52nd, King's Royal Rifle Corps, and Rifle Brigade. The regiment was created in 1966 through the amalgamation of the 1st Green Jackets, the 2nd Green Jackets (The King's Royal Rifle Corps), and the 3rd Green Jackets (The Rifle Brigade).

Honi Soit Qui Mal y Pense – Regimental motto.

• **Royal Highness**► In the UK this title, in the form His (or Her) Royal Highness (**HRH**), is confined (since 1917) to the sovereign and his or her consort, to the sons (and their wives) and daughters of the sovereign, to grandsons (and their wives) and granddaughters in the male line, and the eldest son of the eldest son of the Prince of Wales and his wife. It was formerly granted to a somewhat wider group of relations. The decision to deprive Diana, Princess of Wales of this title following her divorce from Prince Charles in 1996 caused some controversy (*see*: People's Princess).

• **Royal National Theatre**► The complex of three theatres on London's South Bank that houses the Royal National Theatre Company. It was designed by Sir Denys Lasdun and opened in 1976, when the company moved from its earlier home at the Old Vic. The complex, with terraces overlooking the Thames, has been variously called 'a great building', 'a concrete fortress', and by Prince Charles:

...a way of building a nuclear power station in the middle of London without anyone objecting.

It houses the UK's most versatile and technically advanced drama facilities and stages a great variety of classic and experimental drama. The theatres are the Olivier, holding 1160 people in its fan-shaped auditorium; the Lyttleton, a proscenium theatre that accommodates 890 people; and the Cottesloe, a venue for experimental plays with flexible seating for up to 400. The 'Royal' prefix was added to the theatre and the company in 1988.

• **Royal Observer Corps**► A volunteer civilian organization for tracking and identifying enemy aircraft flying over the UK. Since 1955 it has also been responsible for monitoring nuclear fallout and radiation levels in the event of a nuclear strike against the UK. The Observer Corps was formed in 1925, when a chain of observation posts was established across southern England. At the start of World War II the Corps' network of 1400 posts covered the entire country, a watch being maintained by some 32,000 trained volunteers. During the war the Royal Observer Corps provided warnings of impending air attacks to enable the air-raid warnings to be sounded and the RAF to launch its fighters in counterattack. The epithet 'Royal' was granted in 1941. After the war the Corps was stood down for two years, being reformed in 1947. The present Corps is affiliated to the RAF and administered by the Ministry of Defence.

• **Royal Opera**► The principal British opera company, based at the **Royal Opera House** in Covent Garden and formerly known as the Covent Garden Opera (the company was renamed in 1969). Its lavish productions cannot be financed by the sale of tickets alone and require a substantial government grant. Even so, in recent years it has suffered from serious financial difficulties and managerial problems. The Royal Opera House was closed in 1997 for refurbishment, which took two years; it reopened in 2000, to great public acclaim. *See also*: Royal Ballet.

• **Royal Shakespeare Company**► (RSC) One of the world's leading theatre companies, originally formed in 1879 as the company of Stratford-upon-Avon's newly opened Shakespeare Memorial Theatre; it was incorporated by royal charter in 1925. The name of the theatre was changed in 1961 to the 'Royal Shakespeare Theatre' and the company then adopted its present title. Although the RSC now stages a wide variety of plays in its five auditoria, the company remains faithful to its prime role – performing the works of Shakespeare. The original Shakespeare Memorial Theatre was destroyed by fire in 1926 and replaced by the present building, which opened in 1932. The company established its first London base in 1960, at the Aldwych Theatre; the Place, a London studio theatre opened in 1971. In 1982 both operations were transferred to the new Barbican Centre in the City of London, using the Barbican Theatre and The Pit. Meanwhile, Stratford had seen the opening of its own studio theatre for the RSC, The Other Place, in 1974; in 1986 this was joined by the Elizabethan-style Swan Theatre, built inside the shell of the original Shakespeare Theatre's auditorium. In 2001 the RSC announced controversial plans to restructure the company and to demolish and rebuild the main theatre in Stratford.

• **Royal Victorian Chain**► A decoration instituted in 1902 by Edward VII in honour of his mother, Queen Victoria. It is bestowed, usually on foreign sovereigns, to mark special occasions.

• **RP**► *See*: Received Pronunciation.

• **RPI**► *See*: Retail Price Index.

• **RSI** ▶ *See*: repetitive strain injury.

• **rubber bullet** ▶ A projectile made from hard rubber fired from a special weapon, used in riot control. The rubber bullet, or **baton round**, was developed at Porton Down especially for use in Northern Ireland; the idea was based on the wooden projectiles used by the Hong Kong police for riot control in the late 1960s. To minimize injuries, the rubber batons were supposed to be bounced off the ground rather than fired directly into crowds. Nevertheless, the rubber bullet and its successor the **plastic bullet** (a solid PVC cylinder), have been responsible for many deaths in Northern Ireland and elsewhere since 1970.

• **rubber-chicken** ▶ A US colloquialism describing unappetizing banquet food, especially that served to lecturers, political candidates, etc., on their travels. It is generally used in such phrases as the **rubber-chicken circuit** and a **rubber-chicken banquet**.

• **rubberneck** or **rubbernecker** ▶ 1. Contemptuous slang for an unadventurous tourist, who travels by coach to see the world but who does little more than turn the neck to take in the sights as they are enumerated by the tour guide. Hence a **rubberneck wagon** is the coach or bus containing such people. 2. Someone who gawps intrusively at some inappropriate object – such as a car crash, a topless sunbather, or a celebrity trying to enjoy a quiet meal in a restaurant.

• **Rube Goldberg machine** ▶ A complicated and contrived machine producing a simple result. The name comes from US cartoonist Reuben L. Goldberg (1883–1970), who for 40 years, starting in the 1920s, drew humorously intricate diagrams of such devices, teasing Americans about their love of gadgets. A Goldberg contraption designed to wipe a diner's chin with a napkin included such steps as lifting a spoon that pulled a string that jerked a ladle that threw a cracker biscuit past a parrot, who jumped and tilted its perch, etc., until a pendulum with a napkin attached swung past the chin. *See also*: Heath Robinson.

• **Rubik's cube** ▶ A toy puzzle invented in 1974 by Professor Erno Rubik, a Hungarian teacher of architecture and design, which was first marketed in 1977 and became a worldwide craze in the early 1980s. The puzzle was launched in the West in 1980 and sold some 20 million copies over the next two years. The two-inch cube is composed of 27 smaller cubes packed together; the aim is to restore the faces of the cube to single colours by rotating the individual layers of cubes. The number of permutations possible has been calculated as 43,252,003,274,489,856,000, but in the World Championships held during the craze, top contenders could manage a solution in less than 30 seconds. Some also fell prey to a painful medical condition, dubbed 'Cubists' (or Rubik's) Thumb', from obsessive manipulation of the toy. Rubik also invented the Magic Snake, a string of linked triangles described as a 'creative construction toy', and other brainteasing devices, but none exerted the same fascination as the cube.

• **rugcutting** ▶ US Black slang for wild ebullient dancing, especially to jazz. The term originated in the practice of giving rent parties in one's own home. These attracted keen and often expert dancers, who were excluded from commercial dance halls because of their colour or lack of means. Their athletic jitterbugging could pose a real danger to the host's furnishings.

• **Rule 43** ▶ In the UK, a prison regulation (paragraph 43 in the official rule book) under which an inmate may be segregated from other prisoners for his or her own protection. This is usually because of the crime that he or she has committed; the great majority of Rule 43 prisoners are sex offenders. The rule has existed since the 1970s but first came to media attention following the riots at Strangeways Prison in Manchester in April 1990, during which rioters broke into segregated 'E' wing and carried out horrific attacks on the Rule 43 prisoners housed there. One alleged sex offender on remand died from his injuries. A prisoner segregated under this regulation is sometimes called a Rule 43 or just a 43.

• **rumba** or **rhumba** ▶ A ballroom dance adapted in 1930 from an Afro-Cuban dance called the *son*. The modern version is danced in one spot with the feet flat on the floor and with sinuous hip movements. Rumba music has a complex syncopated rhythm in 4/4 time. In the original Cuban form, widely used as a ballroom dance in Europe and America, the dancers covered a square pattern, with little bodily contact between them.

• **Rummidge** ▶ The fictional industrial city in the West Midlands created by the British novelist David Lodge (1935– ). Bearing a close resemblance to Birmingham, it is the home of Rummidge University, the setting for such comic novels as *Small World* (1984) and *Nice Work* (1988).

• **rumpie** ▶ Slang acronym for rural upwardly mobile professional; a countrified yuppie. Rumpies typically buy large country properties after selling a smaller town house but still manage to commute to the large cities to work.

• **rum runners** ▶ During the Prohibition era in America, those engaged in smuggling illicit liquor by speedboats across the lakes from Canada or from ships outside the **three-mile limit** (where US law ceased to have effect). The limit was subsequently increased to twelve miles by agreement with other powers and enforced by US Navy destroyers. These vessels, when over-age, were passed to the UK in 1940 under the Lend-Lease arrangements. *See*: bootlegger.

• **running** ▶
**still running – like Charley's Aunt** A phrase applied to any popular and long-running play or film, or to anything or anyone else that shows a stubborn longevity. It refers to the farce *Charley's Aunt* by the British playwright Brandon Thomas (1857–1914), which was first performed in 1892, ran for four years, and was frequently revived throughout the 20th century. Since the 1960s it has been largely replaced by a phrase alluding to another record-breaking theatrical production, 'still running – like *The Mousetrap*' (*see*: Mousetrap, The).

• **running dog** ▶ Communist jargon for someone who carries out another's bidding, especially a capitalist lackey. It is a literal translation of the Chinese *zou gou*, regularly used by the Chinese communist leader Mao Tse-tung. Like some of his other picturesque phrases, such as paper tiger, it was widely taken up by readers of the Little Red Book.

• **Runnymede** ▶ The site on the south bank of the Thames, near Egham in Surrey, where King John set his seal on Magna Carta in 1215. Owned by the National Trust since 1929, this historic setting has three memorials erected in the 20th century. The first, dedicated by Elizabeth II in 1953, commemorates the men of British and Commonwealth air forces who died in World War II. The second is a domed classical temple built in recognition of Runnymede's significance in establishing fundamental liberties and civil rights now enshrined in both British and US law; it was donated by the American Bar Association in 1957. The most recent is a memorial to the US president, John F. Kennedy. Set in 1.2 ha of land given to the American people, it was unveiled by the Queen in 1965. The name Runnymede means 'the meadow in council island', reflecting its use as an ancient meeting place.

• **Rupert Bear** ▶ The subject of a long-running cartoon strip in the *Daily Express*. He was dreamt up by the wife of a news editor when the *Express* needed a rival attraction to the *Daily Mail*'s cartoon mouse, Teddy Tail. Mary Tourtel's creation, a young bear dressed in plaid trousers and matching scarf, made his debut in 1920 and quickly acquired wide popularity; Alfred Bestall took the strip over in the 1930s. Rupert's adventures, summarized in rhyming couplets, were a feature of the paper until the 1980s.

• **ruptured duck** ▶ The nickname in World War II for the US ex-service lapel button issued to all demobilized from the forces. The expression is also applied, not unkindly, to persons with some disablement.

• **Rushdie Affair** ▶ *See*: fatwa.

• **rushes** ▶ In the film industry, the initial prints of a day's shooting, 'rushed' back from the laboratory and viewed in a raw unedited form by the director, etc. *See also*: rough cut.

• **rush hour** ▶ The times during the morning and evening of a working day during which many people travel to or from their homes and workplaces in cars, trains, and buses. The expression was used as early as 1898 for passenger traffic. The rush hour has since become a daily nightmare for commuters on the roads and the overcrowded London Underground system.

• **Rushmore, Mount** ▶ A mountain in the Black Hills of Dakota, which is the site of the huge carvings of the heads of four US presidents created by the US sculptor Gutzon Borglum (1867–1941). Work on this ambitious project began in the 1920s; it consists of the heads of Washington, Jefferson, Theodore Roosevelt, and Abraham Lincoln, each head measuring 60 feet from the chin to the top of the forehead. Upon completion, Mount Rushmore was rapidly established as one of the most frequented tourist attractions in America. It was also the setting for one of Hollywood's most memorable scenes – the final confrontation between Cary Grant and Eva Marie Saint with the villainous James Mason in Alfred Hitchcock's thriller *North by Northwest* (1959). Borglum also worked on another massive carving representing General Robert E. Lee, Stonewall Jackson, Jefferson Davis, and 1200 Confederate soldiers on Stone Mountain. However, this project was plagued by disagreements and Borglum died before it could be completed.

• **Russian Revolution** ▶ *See*: February Revolution; October Revolution.

• **Russian roulette** ▶ A potentially suicidal gambling game played as a reckless act of bravado by Russian army officers in the early years of the 20th century. The player loads one chamber of a revolver, spins the cylinder, puts the revolver to his head, and pulls the trigger. In a six-chamber revolver his chance of committing suicide is 1:6. The name Russian roulette is now often given to any reckless or potentially very dangerous gamble.

• **Russo-Japanese War** ▶ (1904–05) The conflict in which the Japanese inflicted a crushing defeat on the Russians, helping to destroy the myth of White supremacy over the Oriental races. The Japanese were determined to end all Russian influence in Korea and Manchuria and to establish their own hegemony in the area. To this end, in February 1904 they launched a pre-emptive air strike against Port Arthur on the tip of Manchuria's Liaotung Peninsula, which inflicted serious damage on the Russian fleet at anchor there. Port Arthur was then besieged by Japanese land forces and surrendered in January 1905. The conflict between the opposing armies in central Manchuria was less decisive. However, in May 1905, in the Battle of Tsushima, the Japanese fleet under Admiral Togo inflicted severe losses on the Russian fleet, which brought the Russians to the conference table. By the Treaty of Portsmouth of September 1905, the Russians surrendered Port Arthur and half of Sakhalin to the Japanese as well as evacuating Manchuria, leaving Japan as the acknowledged power in the region.

> I have today seen the most stupendous spectacle it is possible for the mortal brain to conceive – Asia advancing, Europe falling back, the wall of mist and the writing thereon. – LT-GEN SIR IAN HAMILTON on the Battle of Liaoyang, *A Staff Officer's Scrap Book during the Russo-Japanese War* (1907).

• **Ruth Draper garden** ▶ A type of garden made famous by the US comedian Ruth Draper (1884–1956) in her dramatic monologue 'Showing the Garden'. An elderly English lady takes a visiting acquaintance on a tour of her country garden. Unfortunately, instead of a riot of colour, the borders are largely barren; as the tour progresses, excuse after hilarious excuse is made to explain the deficiencies. In short, a Ruth Draper garden is one that was as exquisite last month as it will be next month, although at the moment it is a shambles. By extension, the name is applied to any similar project.

> That border was a dream in June, and it's going to be again in October...could you possibly come back in October? – 'Showing the Garden'.

# S

• **SA ▶ 1.** Sex appeal. An abbreviation formerly used by people who would be embarrassed by saying the word 'sex'. **2.** *Sturmabteilung*. *See* Brown Shirts; SS.

• **Sabin vaccine ▶** An oral polio vaccine developed by Dr Albert Sabin (1906–93) of the Children's Hospital in Cincinnati in the 1950s. Sabin cultivated a preparation of live weakened (attenuated) strains of the polio virus that, when introduced into the body, did not cause the disease but did stimulate the production of antibodies to provide total long-term immunity. By the 1960s Sabin's vaccine had replaced the Salk vaccine and remains the most effective protection against the disease. It is usually administered orally on a lump of sugar.

• **sabotage ▶** Wilful and malicious destruction of machinery and plant, disruption of plans and projects, etc., by strikers, rebels, or fifth columnists. The term came into use after the great French railway strike in 1912, when the strikers cut the shoes (*sabots*) holding the railway lines.

• **saccharin ▶** A synthetic sweetener about 500 times as sweet as cane sugar. The white crystalline powder was discovered in 1879 by two US chemists and by the 1920s had become a common non-nutritive sugar substitute for diabetics. Sales boomed in the 1960s when its lack of calories appealed to a diet-conscious public. A health scare in the late 1970s prompted the US Congress to require labels saying, 'Use of this product may be hazardous to your health. This product contains saccharin which has been determined to cause cancer in laboratory animals.' *See*: Delaney amendment.

• **Sacco and Vanzetti ▶** Two Italian anarchists, Nicola Sacco and Bartolomeo Vanzetti, who were arrested for the murders on 15 April 1920 of a paymaster and his guard employed by a shoe factory in South Braintree, Massachusetts. The trial and conviction of the two immigrants by a Massachusetts court in July 1921 passed largely unnoticed by the US public but news of the case aroused the indignation of radicals around the world provoking a series of demonstrations and bomb attacks against US property in Europe and South America. This publicity turned the case into a *cause célèbre* in America, with public opinion divided between those convinced that the two men were innocent and had been condemned for their political radicalism and those who believed that their political beliefs compounded their guilt. Compelling evidence that the men were victims of mistaken identity was strengthened by the gentle and intelligent demeanour of the defendants themselves; it was given further credence by the statement of a member of the Joe Morelli gang in 1925, that Morelli had committed the crime. However, an independent investigatory commission appointed by the governor of Massachusetts upheld their conviction. They were refused clemency and executed on 23 August 1927, provoking worldwide condemnation, mass demonstrations, and bomb explosions in New York City and Philadelphia. The executions inspired a series of paintings by US artist Ben Shahn.

• **sacred cow ▶** A person, thing, custom, or institution regarded, often without good reason, as beyond reproach or criticism. The term alludes to the Hindu belief that the cow is a sacred animal that should never be slaughtered for food or otherwise mistreated.

• **Sacred Way ▶** *See*: Verdun.

• **SAD ▶** Seasonal affective disorder. A depressive condition experienced by some people in the winter months, thought to be caused by lack of sunlight. Symptoms, which include gloominess, lack of energy, and feelings of hopelessness and self-doubt – often associated with overeating and a desire to stay in bed – disappear as soon as the days get longer. Although it is now a medically recognized condition, there is no agreed physiological explanation; SAD appears to be related to increased secretion of a hormone, melatonin, by the pineal gland in the brain, which causes drowsiness and affects mood. Bright light suppresses melatonin secretion, and therefore acute sufferers may be treated by exposure to artificial sunlight. SAD first received wide publicity in the early months of 1987, a period of particularly miserable weather in the

UK; as a result, millions of people diagnosed themselves as sufferers.

• **sad sack** ▶ US armed forces' slang for a pathetic case, a depressed or inept person. It was heard before World War II but not widely used until it was adopted as the name of a cartoon character by G. Baker in the 1950s.

• **safari park** ▶ A large enclosed park in which wild animals, such as lions, tigers, giraffes, monkeys, etc., roam freely and can be viewed by the public who ride through their large enclosures in their cars or coaches. This name for a 'reverse zoo', with humans caged in their vehicles, originated in the late 1960s. A popular venue for Londoners is Whipsnade Zoo, near Dunstable.

• **safari suit** ▶ An outfit, usually of cotton or denim, modelled on the style of clothing worn on safaris, especially by the game wardens. It consists of a belted bush jacket with pleated pockets above and below the belt and matching trousers, shorts, or skirt. Safari suits became popular with both sexes in the 1970s.

• **safe havens** ▶ Designated areas in which members of a persecuted ethnic or other minority group can take refuge from their enemies. The term first gained currency in the aftermath of the 1991 Gulf War, when John Major (amongst others) proposed the creation of such havens for the Kurds of northern Iraq, who faced virtual extermination at the hands of Saddam Hussein. A number of temporary enclaves were created by Allied troops, who threatened to use force if they were violated. In 1993–95 the UN attempted (mainly unsuccessfully) to create safe havens for Muslims in parts of Bosnia and Hercegovina.

> The interpretation of 'safe haven'...varies from it being a properly defended enclave, with UN troops guaranteeing the safety of the population, to 'secure areas' away from the front-lines where refugees can go for accommodation and food and the promise of a patrolling UN presence. – *The Times*, 30 April 1993.

• **safe house** ▶ An unobtrusive house, flat, or other premises used as a secret refuge, especially by members of intelligence or terrorist organizations. The buildings are used to hide agents, political refugees, or hostages, conduct meetings and interrogations, and plan operations. They have long existed, but the term did not become widely known until the 1960s. A well-publicized case was the Symbionese Liberation Army's 1974 kidnapping of Patricia (Pattie) Hearst, who was moved from one safe house to another for over a year before being found.

The IRA have operated safe houses in London and other large cities since the late 1960s.

• **safe sex** ▶ Sexual activity that does not carry the risk of spreading Aids and other sexually transmitted diseases; in practice this means non-penetrative sex or penetration using a condom or other protective device. The advent of Aids in the early 1980s prompted a series of large-scale government campaigns urging the practice of safe sex.

• **Safety First** ▶ The complacent slogan adopted by the Conservative prime minister Stanley Baldwin (1867–1947) during the general election of May 1929, which resulted in the formation of a minority Labour government under Ramsay MacDonald. Baldwin had hoped that despite the deepening economic crisis and growing unemployment, the electorate would reject the radical economic reforms advanced by the Opposition and allow the Conservatives to continue in power on the strength of his government's existing policies.

• **safety glass** ▶ Strengthened glass, widely used for car windows and windscreens. It was developed as the result of an accident in a French laboratory in 1904, when a scientist noted that after he had knocked a glass bottle off a shelf it had shattered but remained in one piece. Inside the bottle had been a collodion solution, which had evaporated and then served to hold the splinters together as a cellulose skin on the inside of the bottle. Since then, countless road-traffic accident victims have escaped disfigurement from flying glass as a result of the use of safety glass.

• **safety razor** ▶ A shaving razor with a guarded cutting edge, first introduced in 1903. Before this men used the standard 'cut-throat' razor, with a long exposed blade, which could inflict quite serious wounds if not used with great care. The safety razor was invented by King C. Gillette, a Boston salesman, who had the idea of using a disposable blade in 1895 and spent the following eight years perfecting its design. It was a sensational success: within a year he had sold 90,000 razors and 12,400,000 blades.

• **Saint, The** ▶ The name used by Simon Templar, the debonair reformed gentleman crook who is the hero of a series of adventure novels by Leslie Charteris (1907–93), starting with *Meet the Tiger* (1928). A modern-day Robin Hood, who coolly exposes himself to hair-raising risks, he is most familiar in his various screen incarnations, having been played by Ian Ogilvie in a popular TV series of the 1980s and before that by Roger Moore. Earlier film versions date back to the 1930s, with Louis Hayward, Hugh

Sinclair, George Sanders, and Tom Conway all taking their turn as The Saint. There was even a somewhat eccentric French version starring Jean Marais. The Saint's trademark, left at the scene of crime, is a pin man with a halo.

• **St Dunstan's**▶ An organization for the care of men and women blinded during military service (in war or peacetime) or who become blind later in life as a result of injury. It was founded in 1915 at his home, St Dunstan's Lodge, by Sir Arthur Cyril Pearson (1866–1921), the newspaper proprietor, who himself became blind in 1910. The organization eschews residential care, providing instead the kind of help – such as employment retraining, the provision of special equipment, and financial support – that enables the blind to live as normal a life as possible within the sighted community.

• **St Ives group** ▶ An informal association of British artists that came to national attention in the years after World War II. It originated when the leading abstract artists Ben Nicholson, Barbara Hepworth, and Naum Gabo took refuge in and around St Ives in the west of Cornwall during the early months of the war. They were later joined by younger artists, such as Terry Frost and Patrick Heron. The group's work is essentially abstract but shows a response to the unique landscape and light conditions of the west of Cornwall. Partly to celebrate the work of this group, the Tate Gallery in London opened a subsidiary gallery in St Ives in 1993.

• **St Lawrence Seaway** ▶ A vast system of canals, locks, channels, and natural waterways, stretching for 2342 miles (3769 km), that provides access for ocean-going vessels to the Great Lakes from the Atlantic. Construction of this massive engineering project began in August 1954 and was completed in April 1959; it is navigable from early April to mid-December and is serviced by 12 ports in Canada and 66 in America.

• **St Michael** ▶ The brand name since 1928 of goods produced by Marks and Spencer (*see*: Marks and Sparks). It was originally chosen to complement the St Margaret brand name on the Corah hosiery sold in Marks and Spencer stores (itself named after the church standing next to the main Corah factory in Leicester). Various saints' names were contemplated before the chairman, Simon Marks (1888–1964), decided on Michael, the name of his father, a refugee from E Europe who started the Marks empire when he set up a penny bazaar in Leeds market.

• **Saint Mugg** ▶ The epithet applied (somewhat ironically) to British journalist, broadcaster, and writer Malcolm Muggeridge (1903–90) when, after a less than pious youth, he became an ardent Christian convert. A prolific writer on a variety of subjects, he also appeared frequently in current affairs and religious programmes, gaining a reputation as an amusing maverick. His books included *Conversion: A Spiritual Journey* (1988) and several earlier autobiographies.

• **St Nazaire Raid**▶ A British Commando raid on the port of St Nazaire, on the French Atlantic coast at the mouth of the Loire, on the night of 27–28 March 1942. The dry dock, then the largest in the world, was destroyed by ramming the lock gate with an old destroyer, HMS *Campbeltown*, which was packed with five tons of ammonal explosives timed to detonate later. Commandos then attacked the submarine pens and other repair facilities. Twelve hours after the start of the raid the *Campbeltown* exploded, killing 380 German officers and men exploring the wreckage of the ship. The operation, codenamed Chariot, successfully deprived the Germans of the only dry dock capable of accommodating such capital ships as the *Tirpitz*; the cost was heavy, however: 169 were killed and 200 captured out of a total force of 611. Five Victoria Crosses were awarded in the aftermath of the raid, the highest number for any single action in World War II.

• **St Trinian's** ▶ The anarchic girls' school created by the cartoonist Ronald Searle (1920– ) in the 1940s. The riotous adventures of the girls at the school inspired several successful films, starring Alastair Sim, Joyce Grenfell, and George Cole among others: *The Belles of Saint Trinian's* (1954), *Blue Murder at St Trinian's* (1957), *The Pure Hell of St Trinian's* (1960), and *The Great St Trinian's Train Robbery* (1966). The success of the films gave St Trinian's almost mythical status as the archetypal run-down and corrupt girls' private school.

• **St Valentine's Day Massacre**▶ The murder in America of seven members of George 'Bugsy' Moran's North Side gang on 14 February 1929, the horrific climax to a decade of slaughter that left Al Capone (*see*: Scarface) as head of the Chicago underworld. The mass killings took place at Moran's headquarters in a garage at 21222 North Clark Street. Capone's men, in the guise of uniformed and plainclothes police officers, raided the garage, lined up their victims against the wall, and then shot them to pieces with machine guns. Moran himself was late in arriving at his HQ and escaped death but his power in Chicago was effectively ended. Capone had retired to his estate in Miami, Florida, to establish an alibi, but he underestimated the impact of the massacre on public opinion, which prompted the federal authorities to redouble their efforts to convict Capone. Although he avoided capture for several more years, he was eventually imprisoned for tax evasion in 1931.

> I'm gonna send Moran a Valentine he will never forget. – AL CAPONE.

• **Saki** ▶ The pseudonym of H(ector) H(ugh) Munro (1870–1916), British humorist and author of *The Westminster Alice* (1902), *Reginald* (1904), *The Chronicles of Clovis* (1911), *The Unbearable Bassington* (1912), and numerous short stories, many featuring his effete and snobbish Edwardian heroes Clovis and Reginald. He was killed in action in World War I.

• **Salerno landing** ▶ Allied landings, codenamed Avalanche, in the Gulf of Salerno, south of Naples, on 9 September 1943. The US Fifth Army, commanded by Mark Clark and comprising the British 10th and US 6th Corps, managed to establish a beachhead but faced formidable opposition from German forces under Kesselring. On 15 September, forward units of the British Eighth Army under Montgomery, which had landed in the Calabrian peninsula 130 miles to the south a few days earlier, reached the Salerno area, forcing the Germans to withdraw to the north. *See*: Anzio.

• **sales promotion** ▶ All the activities used to boost the sale of a product or service and to break down **sales resistance** – the negative attitude of a potential buyer, which hinders or prevents the sale of a commodity. As well as advertising and publicity, a sales promotion may include a free-sample campaign, demonstrations, price reductions, and telephone, post, or door-to-door selling.

• **Salk vaccine** ▶ The first effective vaccine against polio, developed at the University of Pittsburgh School of Medicine in 1954 by Dr Jonas Edward Salk (1914–95). Salk developed a trivalent 'killed' vaccine to cover the three known strains of the polio virus. The vaccine, which has to be injected, was first released for use in 1954. It was later replaced by the oral Sabin vaccine, made from living viruses, which provided more effective longer-term protection against the disease.

• **Salò, Republic of** ▶ The short-lived Fascist regime set up by Mussolini in 1943 following the defeat of Italian forces. Mussolini had been rescued from imprisonment by German paratroopers and established the new republic (with headquarters in the town of Salò on Lake Garda) in an attempt to maintain control of that part of N Italy not yet in Allied hands. The republic collapsed ignominiously

with Mussolini's death and the final defeat of the Axis powers in 1945.

• **salsa** ▶ A type of Latin American dance music popularized in New York City in the mid-1970s. The big-band sound, usually at a fast tempo, is dominated by brass, guitars, keyboards, and percussion instruments. It combines Puerto Rican, Afro-Cuban, and other Latin American music, such as the mambo, but reflects the influence of jazz and rock. The dance itself is based on the rumba and related forms. The name comes from the American-Spanish word for sauce (salsa is also a spicy tomato sauce from Mexico).

• **SALT** ▶ Strategic Arms Limitation Talks. Discussions initiated in 1969 between the US president, Lyndon Johnson, and the Soviet leader, Leonid Brezhnev, to limit the production of strategic nuclear weapons. The talks culminated in the **SALT I** accord (1972), signed by Brezhnev and President Nixon, which agreed limitation of the build-up of nuclear weapons by both sides and significantly slowed the pace of the arms race. Further discussion, mainly between Brezhnev and President Ford, resulted in **SALT II**, signed in 1979 by Brezhnev and President Carter but repudiated by America in 1980 after the Soviet invasion of Afghanistan.

Talks were resumed in 1982 in the new form of **START** – Strategic Arms Reduction Talks. In the new era of glasnost, these discussions culminated in the signing of the **START I** treaty in 1987, under which Presidents Reagan and Gorbachov agreed to reduce intermediate-range nuclear weapons (*see*: IRBM) in Europe. Under the **START II** treaty signed by Presidents Bush and Yeltsin in 1992, both countries agreed to cut their nuclear arsenals by two thirds by 2003.

• **salvage archaeology** ▶ The urgent excavation of ancient sites to record the plans and purposes of buildings and to rescue artefacts in danger of being submerged by new construction projects or such natural disasters as floods. The name dates back to 1960, when emergency salvage work began on several building sites in London: archaeologists worked with developers who delayed work that threatened various Roman remains, including a basilica and forum, a public bath, and a palatial residence. Some sites have been preserved beneath the modern structures.

• **Salyut** ▶ A series of Soviet space stations, starting with Salyut 1, an 18-tonne prototype launched on 19 April 1971. Crew members were ferried to and from the stations by Soyuz spacecraft and spent long periods aboard, including a record-breaking 237-day stint in 1984. Salyut 7, the last to be launched (in April 1982), had a modular design, allowing the addition of further sections to increase its size. It was served by specially adapted unmanned 'Progress' space ferries, which automatically docked with the station. The Salyut series was succeeded by the permanently manned **Mir** space station, launched in 1986. Following its collision with an unmanned cargo ship in 1997, Mir was abandoned, effectively bringing Russia's manned space programme to a close. Its remains were successfully brought back to earth in 2001.

• **Samaritans** ▸ An organization founded by the Revd Chad Varah (1911–  ) in the church of St Stephen, Walbrook, London, in 1953, to help the despairing and suicidal. It now has over 200 centres in the British Isles as well as many in overseas countries affiliated to its associated organization, Befrienders International. Trained volunteers, of whom there are over 20,000 in the UK, give their help at any hour to those who make their needs known by telephone, letter, the Internet, or by a personal visit.

• **samba** ▸ A bouncy ballroom dance that evolved from a Brazilian folk-dance with African origins. It was first seen at the street carnivals in Rio de Janeiro. Samba dance music has a syncopated rhythm in duple time. It became very popular in the UK in the 1950s, when it was featured by such South American bands as that led by Edmundo Ros.

• **Same Gender Orientation** ▸ (SGO) A 1990s politically correct term describing a person who finds fulfilment chiefly in relationships with his or her own sex; such a person may or may not be actively gay. In particular, it is used of women who prefer the company of other women but dislike the stereotypical image of the lesbian. In the early 1990s the British and US media noticed the phenomenon of the beautiful highly feminine woman who has a relationship with another equally beautiful girl, with whom she likes to be seen. One such woman explained:

> If you are into yourself as an icon, a male companion will always detract the attention from you. If you match yourself up with a woman who is the right look for you, who is equally good-looking, then you double your effect; you cause traffic accidents. – *The Sunday Times*, 7 February 1993.

*See*: lipstick.

• **same-sex** or **same-sexer** ▸ A neutral term suggested as a replacement for homosexual by those who object to the view that homosexuality is a separate and life-long category of sexual identity (whether inborn or acquired) that has persisted unchanged throughout history in all cultures. It

was the French philosopher Michel Foucault (1926–84) who suggested that the compulsion of 19th-century biologists and sexologists to categorize sexual acts has itself resulted in these separate watertight sexual categories.

> In the centuries of Rome's great military and political success, there was no differentiation between same-sexers and other-sexers; there was also a lot of crossing back and forth of the sort that those Americans who *do* enjoy inhabiting category-gay or category-straight find hard to deal with. – GORE VIDAL: 'Pink Triangle and Yellow Star' (1981).

• **samizdat** ▸ Formerly, an underground press for publishing and disseminating dissident works in the Soviet Union. It is an abbreviation of the Russian *samizdatelstro*, self-publishing house. The word was first used in English in the mid-1960s.

• **sampling** ▸ In the music industry, the practice of editing snippets of earlier hits into one's own record. At its simplest, this involves straightforward quotation from a well-known hit, usually to provide a comment on the theme of the new song. However, since the mid-1980s more sophisticated and morally dubious forms of sampling have been employed. It is now possible for a producer to lift elements of a successful record – most commonly the rhythm track – and to work them into a new piece without acknowledgment or detection. For instance, the drum beat on David Bowie's song 'Let's Dance' (1983) is said to have reappeared on a dozen or so dance hits later in the decade. Computerized recording technology even allows a producer to 'sample' the style or sound of an earlier performance and to apply this to new material. In this way, it is possible to create an instrumental part in which the melody is new but the phrasing, tone, etc., are those of a master performer (who may even be dead). Defenders of sampling see it as a creative and legitimate use of the technology now available, while to others it is simple theft. The legal position has yet to be clarified.

• **sandbag** ▸ **1.** To hit with, or as if with, a sack filled with sand. The word has been used in the figurative sense 'to defeat (someone) through aggressive tactics' since the 1980s. A feminine variant, to handbag, arose during the same period, being especially applied to Mrs Thatcher's technique for dealing with any opposition. **2.** US gamblers' slang meaning to outmanoeuvre someone by pretending initially to be in a weak position. This is presumably derived from the image of hiding behind a sandbag wall and only showing oneself when the enemy has approached dangerously close. **3.** Business jargon for a stalling tactic used by the target company in a takeover bid. The management agrees to talks with an unwelcome bidder and then protracts these as long as possible in the hope that a white knight will make a more acceptable bid.

• **Sandinista** ▸ A member of the Nicaraguan leftist organization, the Sandinista National Liberation Front, that took power in 1979 and ruled until 1990. Named after August Cesar Sandino, an insurgent leader murdered in 1934, the movement was founded in 1962 as a guerrilla group opposing the corrupt regime of President Anastasio Somoza. In the late 1970s a major Sandinista offensive launched from Costa Rica and Honduras resulted in the overthrow of Somoza in 1979. In government the Sandinistas embarked on a radical policy of land redistribution. However, the new regime was undermined by America, which supported right-wing Contra rebels based in Honduras. Funds from a secret US arms sale to Iran were diverted to the Contras after Congress had banned such aid, creating the national scandal known as Irangate. The Sandinista government and the Contras held cease-fire talks in 1988. Free elections followed in 1990, resulting in the defeat of President Daniel Ortega by Violeta Barrios de Chamorro of the National Opposition Union. In his concession speech, Ortega said:

> We, the Sandinistas, have given Nicaragua this democracy and peace.

The Sandinistas continue to function as the main opposition party.

• **S & M** ▸ Sadism and masochism; sadomasochism. The abbreviation was originally a homosexual term in America and came into general use in the early 1960s. Another name for such pursuits is **sadie-maisie**.

• **s 'n' s** or **s 'n' f** ▸ Sex and shopping, or shopping and fucking. A type of popular women's fiction in which wealthy and glamorous heroines divide their time between these activities. The novels of Jackie Collins and Shirley Conran fall into this category.

> I spend most of the day going through a potential s 'n' s (sex and shopping) blockbuster that I've promised the author I will read in its entirety...The novel has everything – paedophiliac English aristocrats, long-lost French fathers, share scandals, a Russian love affair and boat chases in Monte Carlo. – *The Independent*, 25 April 1991.

• **san fairy Ann** ▸ Services slang from World War I, meaning 'it doesn't matter'. It derives from an anglicized pronunciation of the French phrase *ça ne fait rien*, which has the same meaning.

• **San Francisco earthquake** ▸ The earthquake that razed the city of San Francisco on 18 April 1906, resulting in the deaths of 700 people. The quake occurred along the infamous San Andreas fault, where the Pacific and American continental tectonic plates collide; many of the casualties were victims of the intensive three-day fires that followed. Although the tragedy etched itself upon the national consciousness, the residents refused to vacate the area; instead they rebuilt the city in the same place, instituted regular earthquake drills, and insisted that all new buildings comply with stringent safety standards. No one, however, has suggested that the entire city would survive another tremor on the same scale as 1906. A strong earthquake hit the city once more in 1989, when about 70 people died, most of them as a result of the collapse of the double-tier Oakland Bay Freeway. The 1989 earthquake made worldwide news, but seismologists warned that it was not the long-awaited 'big one', which could still strike at any time, virtually without warning.

• **Sansan** ▸ In America, a name sometimes given to the affluent strip on the West Coast between *San Francisco* and *San Diego*. *See also*: Bosnywash; Chippitts.

• **sapfu** ▸ Surpassing all previous *fuck-ups*. US acronym for a situation worse than snafu. Both terms were used by the forces during World War II. *See also*: tabu.

• **Sapper** ▸ The pseudonym of the writer Hermann Cyril McNeile (1888–1937), best known as the creator of Hugh 'Bulldog' Drummond, an amateur detective who is also the perfect upper-class Englishman. The character first appeared in the thriller *Bulldog Drummond* (1920) – subtitled 'The Adventures of a Demobilized Officer Who Found Peace Dull'. Many sequels followed; after McNeile's death the series was continued under the same pseudonym by G. T. Fairlie. Some 24 Bulldog Drummond films were made between 1922 and 1970; of these the early talkie *Bulldog Drummond* (1929), starring Ronald Colman, is perhaps the most notable.

• **Sarah** ▸
**the Divine Sarah** Sarah Bernhardt (1845–1923), French actress of international repute, most celebrated for her roles in tragedy and melodrama. Her original name was Rosine Bernard. In 1915 she had a leg amputated at the age of 70, but this did not bring her career to an end – she continued to act until her death.

• **Sarajevo assassination** ▸ The shooting of Archduke Franz Ferdinand, the heir to the Austro-Hungarian throne, and his wife in Sarajevo, the principal city of Bosnia, on 28 June 1914. The assassin was 19-year-old Gavrilo Princip (1895–1918), a member of a violent nationalist group that sought Serbian independence from Austria. The shooting is often described as 'the shot heard around the world', because it initiated a sequence of events that led directly to the outbreak of World War I. The Austrians, eager to expand their influence in the Balkans (*see*: Eastern Question), with encouragement from Germany imposed a humiliating ultimatum on the Serbian government, which was only partially accepted. The Austrians then declared war on Serbia on 28 July. This in turn prompted the mobilization of Russia, which provoked a declaration of war by Germany on Russia (1 August) and France (3 August). Germany then invaded Belgium (in accordance with the Schlieffen Plan), which prompted the British declaration of war on Germany on 4 August 1914, in defence of Belgian neutrality. *See*: Scrap of Paper.

• **SAS** ▶ Special Air Service. The crack commando unit of the British Army, renowned worldwide for its expertise in undercover military operations and anti-terrorist activities. It was created in 1941 by David Stirling, a Scots Guards subaltern serving in North Africa (*see*: Phantom Major). Stirling persuaded his C-in-C, Claude Auchinleck, to authorize the formation of a small commando unit, initially of 66 men, to operate behind enemy lines. In spite of a disastrous initial parachute raid, on 16 November 1941, from which only 22 men returned, Stirling switched to the tactic of long-range overland infiltration and embarked on a successful campaign against Axis airfields, cratering runways and blowing up aircraft. This success silenced the critics and forced Rommel to deploy troops charged with intercepting this troublesome force. In October 1942, Stirling's unit was given full regimental status, as 1st Special Air Service. The SAS soon saw action in other theatres, notably during the Allied invasion of Italy and later in front-line penetration during the Normandy invasion.

The SAS was disbanded at the end of the war, but in 1947 it was re-formed as the 21st SAS Regiment. A special SAS unit, the Malayan Scouts, was created in 1951 to combat communist insurgence in Malaya, becoming the 22nd SAS Regiment the following year. For the Malayan campaign the SAS developed new techniques, adapted both to the jungle setting and the type of operation, *i.e.* counterinsurgency. This resourcefulness also paid off later in such diverse territories as Oman, Borneo, and Aden – all troublespots calling for the special talents of the SAS. In 1969 SAS personnel were sent to Northern Ireland; the province soon became a proving ground for a whole range of secret sophisticated counterterrorist tactics. A vivid demonstration of their skills, and one witnessed by the world's media, was given on 5 May 1980 when SAS soldiers stormed the Iranian Embassy in Knightsbridge, London, to liberate the building and its staff; these had been seized at the end of April by an Iranian separatist group. A more controversial incident was the shooting by SAS soldiers of three suspected IRA terrorists in Gibraltar on 7 March 1988. The SAS cap badge incorporates the motto **Who Dares Wins** surmounted by a winged dagger; both are attributed to Jock Lewis, one of Stirling's close comrades who was killed returning from a raid in late 1941.

• **Sasquatch** ▶ *See*: Bigfoot.

• **Satchmo** ▶ Nickname of the jazz trumpeter, singer, and bandleader (Daniel) Louis Armstrong (1900–71). It was derived from Black slang **satchelmouth**, meaning a person with a big mouth. His charismatic personality, combined with his exceptional trumpet playing and his instantly recognizable singing voice, made Armstrong one of the most popular figures in the world of jazz and US entertainment generally.

• **satellite** ▶ Any artificial or natural body, such as the Moon, that orbits a planet or other celestial body. The first artificial satellite was Sputnik 1, launched by the Soviet Union in 1957. Since then several thousand satellites have been sent into space for a wide range of purposes, both peaceful and military. One key role is the relaying of telecommunications and other signals (*see*: communications satellite). Another is to survey the Earth's surface from space, monitoring vegetation cover, pollution levels, mineral resources, and other aspects of global ecology. Such earth-resources satellites include the Landsat series. Satellites also provide scientists with information about space (*see*: space probe). Modern military strategists rely heavily on information about opposition forces gleaned from spy satellites, such as the US Big Bird series. During the Cold War both superpowers drew up plans for fighting wars using satellites as space-based weapons platforms (*see*: Star Wars).

• **satellite killer** ▶ *See*: killer satellite.

• **satellite television** ▶ The use of a communications satellite to receive television signals from ground stations, which are then retransmitted to satellite dishes in viewers' homes. Each satellite covers an area on the surface of the Earth called a 'footprint'; in Europe these footprints may cross national boundaries – the UK, for example, can pick up signals from some 25 satellites, each transmitting several television channels in various languages. Telstar, launched in 1962, was the first communications satellite to relay live television pictures across the Atlantic. The first British satellite television operation was Rupert Murdoch's Sky Television, which was launched in 1989 and later merged with its rival BSB. Sky leases six channels of the Astra medium-power 16-channel satellite launched in 1988, and offers 24-hour news and current affairs, films, sport, and light entertainment. *See also*: dish aerial.

• **satellite towns** ▶ *See*: new towns.

• **Saturday night special** ▶ US slang for a small cheap handgun that is easily obtained, even by mail order. The name (first noted in 1968) refers to the use of such weapons, most frequently on Saturday nights, in urban fights and robberies. They are normally .32 calibre or less and short-barrelled. Police statistics show such guns are used in about half of all gun-related crimes. Although the US Gun Control Act of 1958 banned their importation, the parts are often imported and then assembled in America.

• **Saturn rockets** ▶ The two- and three-stage rockets, designed in America from 1958 onwards by the German rocket engineer Wernher von Braun (1912–77), that carried US command capsules into space during the 1960s and 1970s. Saturn 1 was successfully launched on 27 October 1961 and was followed by nine subsequent launches. The three-stage Saturn 5 was used for Apollo 8 and Apollo 11 manned space flights (*see*: Apollo moon programme). Weighing 3000 tons (with fuel) and 360 feet tall with the Apollo spacecraft in place, Saturn V had 11 main engines for upward thrust and another 22 for steering; the combined power of these engines was equivalent to that of 30 diesel locomotives, totalling 160 million hp. The rocket was transported to the launch pad by huge 'crawlers', the world's largest land vehicles, travelling at 2 mph (3.5 kph) under the control of a crew of 10: the roadway on which they moved sank by an inch every time it was used. The Saturn 5 (carrying 12 million gallons of liquid hydrogen, liquid helium, and liquid oxygen) reached a speed of 6000 mph (9600 kph) in the first stage, 15,000 mph (24,000 kph) in the second stage, and 25,000 mph (40,000 kph) in the third stage. The enormous cost of these unrecoverable giant rockets was the main reason for developing the space shuttle.

• **satyagraha** ▶ (Hindi, from Sanskrit, literally truth grasping) Passive resistance. Mohandas Gandhi popularized this word during his nonviolent opposition to British rule in India, especially during the periods 1920–22 and 1930–34. *See*: Mahâtma.

• **Save the Children Fund** ▶ An international voluntary organization founded in 1919 to promote child health and welfare. It operates in 20 countries and has over 100 projects in Britain. Overseas its projects promote long-term health, nutrition, education, community development, and various welfare programmes. In the UK the Fund operates family centres and schemes for the underprivileged, the disabled, the support of the families of prisoners, etc. The Princess Royal has done a great deal to promote the work of the Fund since she became its president.

• **Savoy Hill** ▶ The street, off the Strand, in London in which the first studios of the British Broadcasting Company (1922) were situated; it was the headquarters of the BBC until 1932.

• **Say it ain't so, Joe** ▶ *See*: Black Sox scandal.

• **SBS** ▶ *See*: Special Boat Squadron.

• **scam** ▶ Originally US slang for a swindle or a dubious business deal. It has been widely heard in the UK since the mid-1970s and is often used specifically of a drug-smuggling run. The derivation is uncertain but it is thought to be connected with the 18th-century use of the word 'scamp' as a verb, meaning to rob on the highway (from the Middle Dutch *schampen*).

> He proposes to beat her with a towel filled with oranges – an old insurance scam...which if done correctly leaves ugly bruises and no damage. – *The Independent*, 1 February 1991.

• **Scapa Flow** ▶ A land-locked anchorage in the Orkney Islands, which was the site of the main British naval base until it was closed down in 1957. The Grand Fleet was based there during World War I, although the lack of security from submarine attack forced the fleet to remain at sea for long periods. This vulnerability was tragically demonstrated in the opening months of World War II, when a German submarine sank the battleship *Royal Oak* with the loss of 833 lives in October 1939. Scapa Flow was also host to the German fleet, interned there after the Armistice in November 1918. On 21 June 1919 the German crews scuttled their ships as an act of defiance during the Paris Peace Conference. *See also*: Natal, HMS.

• **Scarface** ▶ The nickname of Al(phonse) Capone (1899–1947), notorious Chicago gangster and racketeer of Sicilian origin. It refers to a scar on his left cheek caused by a razor slash in a gang fight in his youth. He rose to power in the heyday of bootlegging in the 1920s (*see*: bootlegger; Prohibition) and made himself master of the rackets in the city by organizing the killing of most of his rivals. After the St Valentine's Day Massacre of 1929, when seven rival gangster leaders were machine-gunned, he was left in supreme control of the protection rackets, speakeasies, brothels, etc. The suburb of Cicero was completely dominated by him. He was imprisoned from 1931 to 1939 for tax evasion, the only charge that the police could sustain against him. He was released suffering from general paralysis resulting from advanced syphilis and died at the age of 48, a legendary symbol of evil.

• **Scarlet Pimpernel** ▶ The eponymous hero of a romantic novel by Baroness Orczy (Mrs Montague Barstow; 1865–1947), the Hungarian-born writer. Published in 1905, *The Scarlet Pimpernel* describes the adventures of Sir Percy Blakeney, leader of the League of the Scarlet Pimpernel, a group of Englishmen dedicated to the rescue of aristocratic victims of the Reign of Terror in Revolutionary France. The character appeared in ten sequels; his adventures have also been translated onto the big screen (1934; starring Leslie Howard), radio, and television. Blakeney's attractive and high-spirited wife, Marguerite, has also enjoyed a solo career in the novels of C. Guy Clayton published during the 1980s.

> They seek him here, they seek him there,
> Those Frenchies seek him everywhere.
> Is he in heaven or is he in hell,
> That demned elusive Pimpernel?

• **Scarlett O'Hara** ▶ *See*: O'Hara, Scarlett.

• **scat** ▶ In jazz, a type of singing without words, using the voice as a musical instrument. It is often said to have been invented by Louis Armstrong (*see*: Satchmo) in the 1920s, when he forgot the words to a number and improvised nonsense syllables instead; Jelly Roll Morton, on the other hand, claimed to have sung scat as early as 1906.

• **Schandband** ▶ (German, shame band) The cloth badge bearing the six-pointed **yellow star** which the Nazis forced Jews to wear after 1941; the *magen David* or Star of David is the traditional emblem of Judaism. Hans Frank, the governor-general of the 'Protectorate' of Bohemia and Moravia, first suggested the idea of introducing a system of identification for Jews within his territories in August 1941. Hitler approved the idea, and in a decree of 5 September ordered that the *Schandband* should be worn by all Jews throughout the Reich. To demonstrate his contempt for such measures, King Christian X of occupied Denmark wore a yellow star himself, to the fury of his Nazi overlords. The *Schandband* subsequently represented the shame of the whole German people for the atrocities committed in the holocaust. *See also*: pink triangle.

• **Schicklgruber** ▶ The original surname of Adolf Hitler's father, Alois Hitler (1837–1903), a civil servant in the Austrian Imperial Customs Service. Alois's mother, Maria Anna Schicklgruber, conceived him by Johann Georg Heidler, whom she eventually married in 1842. Alois, however, retained his mother's maiden name until he was nearly 40, when he adopted the name Hitler, based on the misspelling by a local priest of the name Heidler. Adolf Hitler went to considerable lengths to conceal the details of his ancestry, although they were dredged up by opponents of the Nazis during elections in the early 1930s. No concrete evidence has ever been discovered to substantiate the claim made by Hans Frank at the Nuremberg Trials, that Hitler's father was the child of a Jew from Graz, named Frankenberger, in whose household Maria Anna Schicklgruber became pregnant while working as a maid.

> HEIL SCHICKLGRUBER! – Headline in an Austrian newspaper during the German elections of July 1931.

• **schlemiel** ▶ A consistently unlucky and foolish person. A Yiddish word that entered the English language in America early in the 20th century, it is said to have originated from the Old Testament (Numbers 2): Shlumiel, the son of the leader of the tribe of Simeon, was an unfortunate general upon whom misfortune rarely failed to fall.

It is sometimes said that a schlemiel is a person who always knocks his glass over at the table; and a nebbish is the one who always mops up the mess.

• **schlep** ▶ To move in a tired and awkward way. The word, which is often used in the phrase to **schlep around**, derives from the German *schleppen*, meaning to drag, and entered the English of New York from Yiddish. Schlep also means to carry or lug something around; the *New York Post* reported in 1957:

> Queen Elizabeth will schlep along 95 pieces of baggage on her trip here.

By extension, a **schlepper** is a slow foot-dragging incompetent or someone who is too tired or lazy to care for their appearance.

> She trudges, schleps, trains, drags her load.
> – JAMES JOYCE: *Ulysses* (1922).

• **Schlieffen Plan** ▶ A German war plan devised by Count von Schlieffen (1833–1913), the German chief of staff (1890–1906). The plan envisaged a war on two fronts, against France in the west and Russia in the east. Schlieffen's strategy for a quick victory was to hold off Russia with minimal forces and then overwhelm the French armies by a massive flanking movement through neutral Belgium, thereby avoiding the formidable natural and military defences along France's eastern border. The main German forces would then be free to confront the Russians to the east, who, it was assumed, would be slow to mobilize. The plan was put into operation in August 1914 by Helmuth Von Moltke, Schlieffen's successor, and proved initially successful. Von Moltke, however, had modified Schlieffen's original plan by weakening the crucial right wing of the German advance from 90% to 60% of the total forces. At the Battle of the Marne in September, the Allied armies forced the retreat of the German First Army under General Alexander von Kluck, thereby halting the main axis of the German advance. The subsequent trench warfare caused the total collapse of Schlieffen's strategy; on 14 September the hapless Moltke was replaced by the German minister of war, Erich von Falkenhayn.

> ...only make the right wing strong. – Reputedly said by SCHLIEFFEN on his deathbed.

• **schlock** ▶ A Yiddish word for anything shoddy, from the German *Schlag*, a blow – implying that the thing in question has been knocked around so much it has lost its value. The word is often used to describe an inferior work of art:

> This is a film that will make millions of sensible people weep, and still the word that best describes it is schlock. Tear ducts have no judgement. – *The Independent*, 15 March 1991.

• **schmaltz** ▶ Originally a Yiddish word from the German *Schmaltz*, fat, especially chicken fat; it is now used of any exaggerated sentimentality, especially in the arts. Schmaltzy music is heavy with sweeping and weeping violins. Schmaltz in the cinema or the theatre is indigestibly rich, cloying, and mawkish. Not quite the same as schlock.

• **schmooze** ▶ To chat in an intimate and friendly way with someone, especially with an ulterior motive of some kind; or (as a noun) a longish friendly talk. The word, which entered American English early in the 20th century from Yiddish, comes ultimately from Hebrew *schmuos*, gossip.

• **schmuck** ▶ A stupid clumsy person. The word derives from the Yiddish *shmok*, penis; to avoid confusion with the taboo meaning it is often shortened to **schmo**.

• **Schneider Trophy** ▶ An international race for seaplanes first held in Monaco on 16 April 1913. The race was established in December 1912 by the Frenchman Jacques Schneider, who offered a trophy worth £1000 and a prize of £1000 in an annual competition to promote the development of fast and reliable water-based aircraft. From 1919 the competition was dominated by the Americans, British, and Italians, who concentrated on developing ever faster and more powerful aero engines, as opposed to reliable transport. In September 1931 the UK won the trophy outright after the victory of Flight Lieutenant J. N. Boothman in a Supermarine S.6B51595, designed by R. J. Mitchell and powered by a Rolls Royce engine – the third successive British victory in a Supermarine. The Spitfire, the UK's famous World War II fighter, also designed by Mitchell, was a direct descendant of the Supermarine design, as was the Merlin engine.

• **schnorrer** ▶ US slang for a sponger or a beggar. It derives from Yiddish and ultimately from the German *schnorren*, to beg. The semantic area covered by the word is wide – from the smoker who never seems to have a cigarette of his own to the out-and-out beggar who scrapes together a living by asking for money on the streets. A person does not have to be Jewish to be a schnorrer.

• **Schnozzle** ▶ Nickname of the US comedian Jimmy Durante (James Francis Durante; 1893–1980), who was famous for his bulbous nose (his *Schnozz* or *schnozzle*) and his gravelly New York accent. He started his show-business career as a pianist, working first at Diamond Tony's Saloon on Coney Island. Later he teamed up with Eddie Jackson and Lou Clayton, and throughout the 1920s the trio worked New York's vaudeville and nightclub circuit. From the 1930s he made periodic film appearances and his particular brand of unsophisticated humour – interspersed with songs such as 'Ink-a-Dink-a-Doo' and 'It's My Nose's Boithday Today' – became familiar to thousands as a result of his regular radio performances. In the 1950s he moved successfully into television (*see*: Goodnight Mrs Calabash... *at* Calabash).

• **school of hard knocks** ▶ A US expression for learning the hard lessons of life by experience rather than by formal education. It is the US equivalent of the mainly British **university of life**. Both expressions tend to be used defensively by those who were not fortunate enough to go to university.

• **Schrödinger's cat** ▶ An unfortunate cat that figured in a 'thought experiment' suggested by the Austrian physicist Erwin Schrödinger (1887–1961) and the Hungarian-born US physicist Eugene Wigner (1902–95) to illustrate the philosophical problem known as the 'quantum measurement problem' in quantum theory. In one interpretation of quantum mechanics, an object, such as an elementary particle, does not exist in particle form until it has been observed. Before that it has a potential existence described by a mathematical equation known as its wavefunction, which gives the probability of finding it at a particular point in space at a particular moment. When the observation is made, the properties of the entity become known and it exists as an object. In the jargon, the observation 'collapses' the wavefunction. But at what instant does the wavefunction collapse?

To answer this question Schrödinger suggested an experiment involving a box containing a piece of radioactive material, a Geiger counter to detect particles of radiation, and a cat. The counter is connected to a device that breaks a sealed tube of cyanide if a particle is detected, which kills the cat.

Nobody knows, according to quantum theory, exactly when a radioactive material will emit a particle, although it is known how many particles it will emit, on average, over a specific period of time. The experiment is run for a period that gives the cat a 50% probability of surviving. At the end of this period a person, known as **Wigner's friend**, looks in the box to observe whether or not the cat is dead. If the cat is dead, when did it die? Most people would answer that it died when the radioactive source caused the cyanide to be released. However, some interpreters of quantum mechanics would say that the cat, the cyanide, the detector, and the source were all part of the same system, which has its own wavefunction. This wavefunction collapses only when the observation is made, i.e. when Wigner's friend looks into the box. If this is the case, the cat has presumably been in an intermediate state up to this point. An additional complication is that Wigner's friend is also part of the system. Does he need an external observer to collapse his wavefunction? And so on...

• **Schrödinger wave equation** ▶ A fundamental mathematical equation in quantum mechanics (see: quantum theory). It was developed in the 1920s by Erwin Schrödinger to describe the behaviour of systems in which particles also have a wave-like characteristic.

• **schtum** ▶ Silent; especially in the phrase **to keep schtum**, to keep quiet, to say nothing. The word is of Yiddish origin, deriving from the German *stumm*, dumb. It can also be used in the imperative, meaning 'keep quiet'.

• **Schweik** ▶ The hero of the novel *The Good Soldier Schweik* (1921–23; English translation 1930), by Czech author Jaroslav Hašek (1883–1923). At his death Hašek had completed only four volumes of his projected six-volume satire on militarism, based largely on his own experiences in the Austro-Czech Army in 1915. The corpulent, drunken, and men-

dacious Schweik easily frustrates all authority and is the antithesis of a good soldier. The character became a hero to dissidents in E Europe after 1945. The book was banned in Czechoslovakia in the 1970s and was explicitly forbidden in the Czech, Polish, and Hungarian armies as 'detrimental to discipline'. The anarchic character fascinated Bertolt Brecht, who paid homage to him in the drama *Schweik in the Second World War* (1943).

• **Scientology** ▶ A quasi-religious cult developed in the 1950s by L. Ron Hubbard (1911–86), an author of pulp science fiction. In about 1949 Hubbard told a meeting of his fellow authors:

> Writing for a penny a word is ridiculous. If a man really wanted to make a million dollars, the best way to do it would be to start his own religion.

He took his first step down this road a year later, announcing the advent of a new 'science of mental health', with the tradename **dianetics**, that constituted 'a milestone for man comparable to his discovery of fire'. Hubbard claimed to have found the source of all mental and many physical ills in 'engrams', images of painful experiences that could become lodged in the mind. A course of dianetic therapy, or 'auditing', could clear the mind of engrams, restoring the sufferer to perfect health. A success rate of 100% was claimed. Dianetics enjoyed a brief fashionable success in America in 1950–51, largely because it was cheaper and simpler to grasp than orthodox psychotherapy.

The conversion of dianetics into a fully fledged 'religion' dates from 1953, when Hubbard founded the first Church of Scientology. His chief motive seems to have been the tax-exempt status enjoyed by religious organizations, but megalomania was clearly another factor. The church preached a bizarre mixture of reincarnation and science fantasy, claiming that every individual had enjoyed millions of lives on a variety of planets. The aim of scientology was to restore the believer to his or her original status as a 'thetan', an omniscient immortal being outside the realm of space and time. Hubbard himself claimed to have visited heaven on two occasions, in about 23 trillion and 24 trillion BC.

In its heyday the Scientology movement claimed some six million followers worldwide and, as he had predicted, Hubbard became a millionaire. However, its use of dubious psychological techniques to gain and hold adherents soon attracted the attentions of the FBI and foreign governments. In 1965 an Australian report concluded that Scientology was 'evil' and a 'serious threat to the community'; three years later Hubbard and his followers were banned from entering the UK. Largely to avoid this scrutiny, Hubbard appointed himself 'commodore' of a private navy of scientologists and took to the high seas for some eight years from 1967. He also ordered his followers to infiltrate US government offices and steal or destroy all documents critical of Scientology. This proved an astonishing success: many thousands of classified documents passed into Scientologist control in the late 1970s. It also led to Hubbard's downfall. In 1979 the FBI arrested leading members of the organization, including Hubbard's wife, on multiple charges relating to the theft of government documents. When guilty verdicts were returned, Hubbard, who had managed to escape direct incrimination, simply disappeared. In 1986 the body of an elderly recluse, known to his neighbours simply as 'Jack', was identified as Hubbard's.

• **sci-fi** ▶ Short for science fiction. This shortening, first heard in America in the mid-1950s, probably reflects the influence of hi-fi (for high fidelity).

• **Scone, Stone of** ▶ The great coronation stone, the Stone of Destiny, on which the Scottish kings were formerly crowned at Scone, near Perth. It is of reddish-grey sandstone and is fabled to be the stone on which Jacob lay his head when he dreamed his vision of God and the angels (Genesis 28). This biblical stone is said to have been kept at Dunstaffnage in Argyll before being removed to Scone by Kenneth MacAlpin in 843. As a sign of Scotland's subjection to the English it was removed by Edward I in 1296 and brought to Westminster Abbey, where it was placed under the Chair of St Edward, the coronation throne of English monarchs. In the 20th century the stone made headlines when it was stolen on the night of 24–25 December 1950 by Scottish nationalists, who took it north of the border. After its recovery it was restored to the Abbey in February 1952 – although there is a persistent story that the stone taken back to England was a fake, the real item remaining hidden in a Scottish cave. As a sop to Scottish nationalism the Stone of Scone was returned to Scotland in 1996 and placed in Edinburgh Castle on St Andrew's Day.

• **scoobs** ▶ British army slang for beer, dating from the Gulf War of 1991. This probably derives from 'Scooby snacks' – the treats gulped down by Scooby-doo, a cartoon dog in the popular children's TV series of the same name.

• **scorcher** ▶
**Phew! What a scorcher!** A phrase used to describe a very hot day. Since the 1960s it has appeared regularly in the satirical magazine Private Eye as a parody (or perhaps an actual quotation) of

a tabloid newspaper headline during a heatwave. The phrase has now become such common usage that it is often written as one word. It is also used as an adjective, as in 'it's really phewwhatascorcher weather!'

• **score** ▶ **1.** To pick up a casual sexual partner. **2.** To purchase an illegal drug. **3.** The real state of affairs, the true facts, as in 'What's the score with Mike and Sue these days?'

• **Scotch tape** ▶ Tradename for a brand of sticky tape, developed in America in 1952. It was the invention of some paint-sprayers who used it for masking purposes while at work. The tape acquired the name Scotch because of allegations that the adhesive was often applied too meanly and the tape refused to stick (by allusion to the traditional reputation of the Scottish for thrift).

• **Scottish National Party** ▶ See: SNP.

• **Scott of the Antarctic** ▶ Captain Robert Falcon Scott (1868–1912), the leader of the ill-fated second Antarctic expedition of 1910–12 to the South Pole. As a lieutenant in the Royal Navy, Scott successfully commanded the scientific and exploratory Antarctic expedition of 1901–04 in HMS Discovery. In June 1910 he set off in the Terra Nova on a second expedition, with the aim of reaching the South Pole using both motorized sledges and ponies. The sledge party set off from Cape Evans on 24 October 1911; after a gruelling 900-mile trek, Scott and four companions (Dr E. A. Wilson, Captain Laurence Oates, Lieutenant H. R. Bowers, and Petty Officer Edgar Evans) reached the pole on 18 January 1912, only to discover that the Norwegian, Roald Amundsen, had beaten them by about a month. Murderous blizzards hampered the return journey; they ran out of food and fuel and eventually froze to death in their tent at the end of March, only eleven miles from supplies at One Ton depot. Their bodies were discovered by a relief party in November 1912, together with Scott's diary recording the harrowing last moments of the expedition. Evans had been killed in a fall on the Beardmore Glacier, and Oates, seriously ill and frostbitten, had sacrificed himself by leaving the tent in a blizzard (see: famous last words). Although he is usually regarded as a great British hero, some have recently questioned Scott's leadership and competence.

> I do not think we can hope for better things now. We shall stick it out to the end, but we are getting weaker, of course, and the end cannot be far. It seems a pity, but I do not think I can write more. For God's sake look after our people. – Last entry in Scott's Diary, 29 March 1912.

• **Scottsboro trials** ▶ The controversial trials of

nine Black youths accused of raping two White women in a railway carriage in Scottsboro, Alabama. At their initial trial in April 1931, only three weeks after their arrest, the all-White jury found them guilty as charged, despite evidence from a doctor, who had examined the women, that no rape had occurred. The youths were then sentenced to death, which spurred protest from northern civil rights activists and other liberal and radical groups. The Supreme Court overruled the conviction in 1932, but various retrials, reconvictions, and successful appeals dragged on until the four youngest were freed and the others paroled, after spending six years in prison.

• **Scrabble** ▶ A board game in which the players attempt to make words from lettered tiles, the words being interlocked like a crossword on a 15 × 15 grid; each letter carries a different points value according to the frequency of occurrence. The game was developed in the early 1930s in America by Alfred M. Butts, who originally called his invention 'Criss-Cross'. The name was later changed to Scrabble; by the 1960s it had become established as one of the world's most popular and best-selling board games. World Tournaments have been held since the early 1970s. Top Scrabble champions have a wide knowledge of rare words containing Zs, Qs, Xs, and Js (the letters with the highest points values).

• **scramble** ▶ An emergency takeoff of military aircraft to intercept and attack enemy aeroplanes approaching their area of defence. The word is also used to alert pilots and ground crews for the operation. It was widely used by the RAF during World War II, especially during the Battle of Britain, and was later used by the US Air Force in the 1950–53 Korean War.

• **Scrap of Paper** ▶ The contemptuous description of the Treaty of London (1839) made by the German chancellor Bethmann-Hollweg on the outbreak of World War I. Under the terms of the Treaty, the UK was committed to defending Belgian neutrality, which was violated by the German invasion (in accordance with the Schlieffen Plan) on 4 August after the German declaration of war against France and Russia. On 3 August the British government had informed the German government that it would stand by the London Treaty, thus prompting Bethmann-Hollweg's dismissive comment. The German invasion allowed the UK government to justify the declaration of war on Germany as a defence of the integrity of Belgium and the Low Countries against unprovoked German aggression.

• **scratching** ▶ In the pop music of the 1980s, the incorporation of a rhythmic scratching noise by rotating a record manually on the turntable; this was often done live by a disc jockey as an accompaniment to another record being played.

• **screwball** ▶ A US colloquialism from the 1930s meaning a weird, slightly crazy, or eccentric person. The term has its origins in baseball, in which a screwball is a pitch having such a spin that its exact destination is uncertain. **Screwball comedy** was the name given to a Hollywood subgenre that developed in the mid-1930s; films of this kind generally featured slightly eccentric members of the affluent elite in a series of madcap adventures. They usually combined fast-talking verbal comedy with elements of farce, and often had a battle-of-the-sexes theme. Examples include *It Happened One Night* (1934) with Clark Gable and Claudette Colbert and *Bringing Up Baby* (1938) and *His Girl Friday* (1940), both of which starred Cary Grant.

• **Screwtape Letters** ▶ A popular religious work by C. S. Lewis (1893–1963) in which a devil, Screwtape, advises a novice devil, Wormwood, on how best to lead human beings into damnation. The letters were first published in weekly instalments from May to November 1941 in *The Guardian*, a High Church weekly, and collected in book form in 1942. They combine shrewed and often comic observations on human nature with serious moral and theological points; the book remains one of Lewis's most popular works.

> A sensible woman once said…'She's the sort of woman who lives for others – you can tell the others by their hunted expression.' – *The Screwtape Letters*.

• **scrubber** ▶ British and Australian slang for a promiscuous lower-class woman, widely used since the 1920s; probably from the menial activity of scrubbing floors.

• **scuba** ▶ Self-contained underwater breathing apparatus. **Scuba-diving** is deep-sea diving using this type of apparatus, which was developed in America in the early 1950s.

• **scud** ▶ In British army slang from the Gulf War (1991), to inflict heavy damage on an enemy. This usage was inspired by the Soviet-designed Scud ballistic missiles, which proved the most feared (though still relatively easily knocked out) weapon in the Iraqi arsenal. During the Gulf War Scuds were used as a terror weapon against Israel and Saudi Arabia. *See*: smart weapons.

• **seagull** ▶ Australian slang for a casual labourer employed in the docks, inspired by the seagull's scavenging habit.

• **Sealed Knot Society** ▶ A British society, founded in 1968 by Brigadier Peter Young, dedicated to the re-enactment of historical scenes from the English Civil War. Members engage in mock battles between 'Royalists' and 'Parliamentarians', dressing in period costume and wielding replica muskets and other weapons. Together with its sister group **The English Civil War Society**, the Sealed Knot has provided much harmless and entertaining spectacle in the name of 'living history'; similar groups in America re-enact events from the War of Independence and the Civil War; others specialize in battles of the Wars of the Roses, Viking raids, etc.

• **Sea Lion** ▶ (German *Seelöwe*) The codename for the planned German invasion of S England in 1940. The invasion was ordered in Hitler's War Directive No. 16, issued on 16 July 1940, which cited the UK's stubbornness in rejecting a negotiated settlement and refusal to recognize her hopeless military situation. Hitler instructed his army and navy chiefs to begin amassing an invasion fleet in the Channel ports; meanwhile the Luftwaffe was given the task of destroying the RAF to secure air superiority. However, the defeat of the Luftwaffe in the Battle of Britain in August and September, made the invasion plans untenable; by October Hitler had abandoned operation Sea Lion in favour of the invasion of the Soviet Union, codenamed Barbarossa.

• **search-and-destroy** ▶ A phrase from the Vietnam War describing intense military movements against guerrilla forces. Such an operation selects a limited area in which to locate the enemy and then directs concentrated firepower at this area.

• **SEATO** ▶ South East Asia Treaty Organization. An organization for mutual defence and economic co-operation, set up in Manila on 8 September 1954, whose members were Australia, the UK, France, New Zealand, Pakistan, the Philippines, Thailand, and America. SEATO was explicitly sponsored by America on the model of NATO to combat the spread of communism in SE Asia. The UK, France, and Pakistan largely abandoned their commitment after 1965 to avoid being involved in the Vietnam War; in 1975, after the communist victories in Vietnam, Laos, and Cambodia, the members agreed to end the treaty. The remaining non-communist Asian nations then formed the Association of South East Asian Nations (**ASEAN**), a non-military non-political alliance for mutual economic aid. The current members are Brunei, Indonesia, Laos, Malaysia, Myanmar (Burma), the Philippines, Singapore, Thailand, and Vietnam.

• **Second Front** ▶ The Allied invasion of German-occupied W Europe, for which various plans were drawn up after 1941, although the eventual cross-channel invasion was delayed until 6 June 1944 (*see*: D-Day). The establishment of a Second Front in the west was a matter of urgency for Stalin, who feared that his Allied partners were content to allow the Soviet Union and Germany to fight each other to extinction in the east. The Soviet foreign minister, Molotov, visited London and Washington in May 1942 and received promises that a Second Front for the relief of the Soviets would be opened soon. Churchill, however, told Roosevelt in June that US plans for an invasion of France in 1942 were unrealistic; in August he went to Moscow to explain to Stalin why these earlier promises could not be kept. Instead the Americans accepted British proposals for landings in North Africa, codenamed Operation Torch, which took place in November 1942. Churchill was determined that the invasion should not take place until success was assured and until sufficient British forces could be made available to play a major role in the campaign. At the Casablanca Conference in January 1943, plans for a full-scale invasion were postponed again, and the British plan for landings in Sicily adopted. A date for the European invasion – 1 May 1944 – was eventually agreed at the Quebec Conference in August 1943. By 1944, however, the Soviet Union had begun the drive west after the retreating German armies, so that as D-Day approached, it became clear that America and the Soviet Union would between them play the decisive roles in the liberation and postwar settlement of Europe.

• **Second International** ▶ *See*: Internationals.

• **second strike** ▶ *See*: first strike.

• **Second Vatican Council** ▶ An ecumenical council of the Roman Catholic Church opened by Pope John XXIII in October 1962 and concluded by Paul VI in December 1965. The Council formalized the policy of aggiornamento, in which Church structures and practices were updated to meet the challenge of the modern world. It called for greater participation by the laity and a firm commitment to the Ecumenical Movement; the traditional Latin mass was replaced by modern vernacular liturgies. One special feature was the presence of observers from non-Roman Catholic Churches.

• **Second World** ▶ *See*: Third World.

• **secret service** ▶ The popular name for governmental intelligence, espionage, and counter-espionage organizations. *See*: CIA; FBI; KGB; MI5; MI6; National Security Agency.

• **Section 28** ▶ *See*: Clause 28.

• **Securitate** ▶ The hated secret police of the Romanian dictator Nicolae Ceausescu (1918–89). They remained loyal to the dictator after his fall in December 1989, fighting running gun battles with the army (who had sided with the populace) and firing at random into crowded streets. They were eliminated after a week of fighting that left thousands dead.

• **Securities and Investment Board** ▶ (SIB) A regulatory body set up by the Financial Services Act (1986) to control London's financial markets. Each market has its own Self-Regulatory Organization (SRO), which reports to the SIB. Members of the SIB are appointed jointly by the secretary of state for trade and industry and the governor of the Bank of England. The SIB has the overall responsibility of ensuring that investors in London markets are protected from fraud and that the markets comply with the rules established by their individual SROs.

• **security blanket** ▶ Anything that provides emotional support and reduces anxiety, such as understanding parents, an inheritance, alcohol or drugs, or a handgun. This figurative use alludes to the objects that young children often clutch and carry for comfort and security, such as a small piece of blanket or a teddy bear. In the comic strip Peanuts the young boy Linus becomes paranoid without his blanket.

• **Security Council** ▶ The main executive organ of the United Nations, which has the primary responsibility for the maintenance of international peace and security. The UK, America, France, Russia (until 1992 the Soviet Union), and China are permanently represented while ten other nations serve two-year periods on the Council. The Council has proved more successful than the League of Nations in maintaining collective security because of its range of military, economic, and diplomatic sanctions for use against offending states. These powers have been only intermittently effective, however. During the Cold War effective action was often blocked by the superpowers' use of the Veto (available to permanent members) to prevent any action against their own interests. The UN-backed intervention in the Korean War, for example, was only possible because of the Soviet Union's absence from the Council. In the first post-Cold War test of its effectiveness, the Council successfully mobilized military support from many UN members for the US-led action against Iraq in the Gulf War (1991). However, the intractable ethnic conflicts that have blighted many parts of the world in the 1990s and 2000s have proved much more difficult to address.

• **Seddon Murder** ▶ The poisoning of Eliza Mary Barrow on 14 September 1911 by Frederick Henry Seddon, a district superintendent with the London and Manchester Industrial Insurance Company. Seddon, who was obsessed with money, had rented out rooms in his large house in Islington to Barrow, a wealthy spinster. Having persuaded her to sign over most of her assets to him, he invited her to join his family on holiday to Southend, where he poisoned her with arsenic taken from a packet of Mather's Chemical Fly Papers, which his daughter had purchased for him at a local chemist's shop. A suspicious cousin demanded the exhumation of Barrow's body, and Seddon was arrested after traces of the poison were discovered in the tissues. Seddon was tried and convicted in March 1912, although some observers believed that the guilty verdict was influenced more by his cold and dispassionate demeanour in court than any conclusive evidence against him. He was hanged at Pentonville Prison on 18 April 1912.

• **Seeadler** ▶ (German, Sea Eagle) A German warship of World War I, which was a great menace to Allied shipping in the Atlantic from December 1916 to August 1917. What made the Seeadler so effective was its elaborate disguise as a Norwegian windjammer. Built in Glasgow as the Pass of Balmaha in 1888 and captured by the Germans in 1915, it appeared to be an entirely innocent vessel until it revealed its concealed 4.2 inch guns. To complete the deception, the ship sailed under the name Maletta (the name of a similar Norwegian cargo vessel) and the crew carried Norwegian papers. Only at the last moment was the Seeadler's true identity revealed to its victims as a warship of the German Imperial Navy. In this way the Seeadler sank 12 Allied ships, totalling 40,000 tons; in true buccaneering style all the prisoners were toasted with champagne and were well treated by the crew. The Seeadler's end came in August 1917 when a freak wave, rather than an Allied shell, wrecked the ship. See also: Q ships.

• **See you later, alligator** ▶ A catchphrase that was first heard in America in the 1930s. As the title of a rock 'n' roll hit by Bill Haley and the Comets (1956), the phrase won an even wider audience. The usual response was 'In a while, crocodile'. See: alligator.

• **segue** ▶ A term, much used by disc-jockeys, for two or more pieces of music played without a break. A segue permits the disc-jockey to visit the lavatory, smoke a cigarette, etc. Pronounced 'seg-way', the word is the Italian for 'follows'.

• **self-determination** ▶ In politics, the concept that every nation, no matter how small or weak, has the right to decide upon its own form of government and to manage its own affairs. The phrase acquired this significance during the attempts to resettle Europe after World War I (*see*: Fourteen Points).

• **Self-Regulatory Organization** ▸ (SRO) One of three (originally five) organizations set up in the UK under the terms of the Financial Services Act (1986) to enforce appropriate codes of conduct in the various branches of the investment business. Since the merger of some authorities in 1994, the SROs recognized by the Securities and Investment Board (SIB) are the Securities and Futures Authority (SFA), which regulates the stock exchange and futures and options exchange; the Investment Managers Regulatory Organization (IMRO); and the Personal Investment Authority (PIA), which regulates investment business mainly for private investors.

• **self service** ▸ A largely mid-20th-century innovation in retailing in which the customer serves himself and passes through a cash point at which he pays for the goods he has taken. It was introduced in supermarkets and petrol stations but is now the norm in shops of every size and kind.

• **Sellafield** ▸ One of the UK's principal nuclear energy installations, located on the Cumbrian coast in NW England. The site was generally known as **Windscale** before 1981. In 1947 two air-cooled plutonium piles were built there, primarily to produce plutonium for the UK's atom bomb. They were joined by the country's first industrial nuclear power station, Calder Hall, which began supplying the national grid in 1956 and by 1958 comprised four Magnox reactors (*see* nuclear reactor). A facility for reprocessing spent fuel from the reactors was started in 1952, with a second line opening in 1964 (the first closed in 1973). The site also contains THORP (thermal oxide reprocessing plant), for reprocessing uranium oxide fuels, as used in AGR and PWR reactors, as well as storage tanks for high-level and intermediate-level nuclear waste and a vitrification plant for converting highly radioactive liquid wastes into a solid form. Currently, low-level solid waste is disposed of at the Drigg disposal site nearby.

The Sellafield/Windscale site has aroused considerable controversy. The worst accident was a reactor fire in October 1957, in which radioactive substances were released into the atmosphere and contaminated surrounding areas. Milk from farms covering an area of 500 sq km was deemed unfit for human consumption. The plant has also been censured for leaks of hazardous material from storage tanks into the soil and for radioactive discharges into the Irish Sea, which have attracted the attention of Greenpeace and other environmental campaigners. In 2000 Ireland and Denmark pressed for the station's closure on the grounds of marine pollution – other countries have cancelled processing contracts owing to safety concerns. *See also*: Chernobyl.

• **sell-by date** ▸ The date, as displayed on its packaging, after which a perishable food should not be offered for sale. This information is often supplemented by a **use-by date** or a **best-before date**, which is usually two or three days later than the sell-by date. The term sell-by date is now also used in an extended sense to mean the date beyond which something or somebody loses its freshness or appeal: a long-running TV series, an outmoded fashion, or a person thought to be no longer sexually attractive may all be described as past their sell-by date. *See also*: shelf life.

• **sell short** ▸ A commercial phrase meaning to sell stocks, shares, commodities, currencies, etc., that one does not currently possess, in the hope that they may be bought in at a lower price before the date on which they have to be delivered. This is also known as **bear selling**.

• **sell the family silver** ▸ Literally, to dispose of table silver or other valuable items that have been owned by a family for many generations. Selling the family silver is regarded as an act of desperation, resorted to only if there is no other way to raise a sum of money that is urgently required. Consequently, the expression is often widened to apply to a firm or even a country that is forced to sell a valuable asset that it has owned for a long time. This usage was popularized by Harold Macmillan, Lord Stockton, in a speech to the Tory Reform Group on 8 November 1985, in which he criticized the Thatcher government's policy of privatizing profitable nationalized industries:

> First of all the Georgian silver goes, and then all that nice furniture that used to be in the saloon. Then the Canalettos go.

Although Macmillan did not use the precise phrase, his remarks are often quoted or summarized as 'selling the family silver'.

• **Semtex** ▸ *See*: plastic explosive.

• **Send in the clowns** ▸ *See at*: clowns.

• **senior citizen** ▸ A popular euphemism for an elderly person, especially one receiving a state retirement pension. It originated in 1930s America, where it was taken up by advertisers and politicians. Although some older people regard it as patronizing, 'senior citizen' has become accepted on both sides of the Atlantic. Senior citizens often benefit from reduced prices in cinemas and theatres, and enjoy free use of public transport in London. These benefits bestowed by the community are, however, regarded as only a small compensation for the other effects of advancing years by most senior citizens. *See also*: third age.

• **Senoussi** ► A Muslim organization founded in the 19th century by Muhammad es-Senoussi in the region of North Africa occupied by modern Libya. It was the Senoussi Brotherhood, led by Idris Al Senoussi, that organized resistance to the Italian conquest of the provinces of Tripolitania and Cyrenaica from September 1911, and to Mussolini's African colonial regime from 1922 onwards. In 1934 Italy united Tripolitania and Cyrenaica and added a third province, Fezzan, to make up Libya. From Cairo, Idris coordinated resistance to the Italian settlement of Libya and to the Axis powers throughout World War II. When Libya was finally granted independence in December 1951, in accordance with the Allied postwar pledge of self-determination, Idris was proclaimed king. On 21 September 1969 the 70-year-old monarch was deposed in a coup by Colonel Muammar Gaddafi.

• **sense** ►
**You know it makes sense** A caption used from the late 1960s on road safety posters advising people to drive carefully. It was revived during the 1980s by Margaret Thatcher, as justification for her government's policies.

• **sensitivity training** ► A type of group therapy in which participants are encouraged to express their own feelings and to become aware of the feelings of others during sessions of physical touching. This form of therapy was in vogue during the hippie era and continued into the 1970s, when a pacesetter was the National Training Laboratories, begun by US psychologist Kurt Lewin. However, it is said to have driven some emotionally disturbed participants to seek medical treatment and is now regarded with caution.

• **Sensurround** ► Tradename for a sound system developed for use in cinemas during the mid-1970s; it used low-frequency sound waves to send detectable vibrations through a cinema audience. The object was to give a flavour of unnerving realism to such films as *Earthquake* (1974) and *Rollercoaster* (1977). The name is a blend of 'sense' and 'surround'.

• **September 11** ► The day in 2001 that saw the most murderous terrorist outrage in history, directed at key targets in New York City and Washington. That morning four airliners, fully laden with passengers, crew, and fuel, were hijacked by small teams of Islamic terrorists shortly after takeoff from airports in the vicinity of New York. After murdering the pilots, the hijackers diverted the planes from their scheduled flight paths: two were flown into the twin towers of the World Trade Center in Manhattan, causing their collapse into a pile of burning rubble, a third crashed into the Pentagon, while the fourth, thought to be heading for the White House, hit the ground near Pittsburgh, apparently as a result of the passengers' determination to thwart the hijackers' plan.

Although the number of people who lost their lives in these events turned out to be lower than early estimates suggested, the figures are still atrocious. Well over 2000 office workers and visitors died in the collapse of the World Trade Center, as did some 340 firemen who were attempting to reach survivors. A total of 265 people (including 19 terrorists) died in the hijacked aeroplanes and a further 180 were killed in the Pentagon, bringing the total death toll to about 3195. After the loss of life, it was perhaps the combination of precision planning with blind suicidal fanaticism that most shocked and stupefied the world. The terrifying destruction of the World Trade Center was witnessed by television viewers the world over as it was actually taking place; another harrowing aspect of the disaster was provided by the messages that many of those in the building or on the doomed aircraft were able to send to loved ones by e-mail or mobile phone.

Although no-one claimed responsibility for the atrocities, evidence was soon found to confirm immediate suspicions that al-Qaida, the violently anti-American terrorist network led by Osama Bin Laden, was involved. In early October, America launched the first phase of its so-called war on terrorism with air strikes against al-Qaida and Taliban targets in Afghanistan.

• **septic** ► Australian and New Zealand slang for an American, from rhyming slang 'septic tank', Yank. It was first used of visiting US soldiers during World War II and is still sometimes heard.

• **Seretse Khama affair** ► In 1949 Seretse Khama (1921–80), chief-designate of the Bamangwato tribe of the British Protectorate of Bechuanaland in S Africa, returned to the province after training as a barrister in London; he was accompanied by his English wife, a 24-year-old typist, Ruth Williams. This outraged the racial sensibilities of the South African government, which had been pressing the British government to allow the incorporation of the province into South Africa, under the terms of the South Africa Act (1909). As well as disconcerting the British and South Africans, Seretse's marriage was against the wishes of his uncle and regent, Tshekedi Khama. Despite the support of the tribe in general, it was decided by the British, South Africans, and the regent that he should be exiled for six years; he eventually returned to Bechuanaland in 1956, after renouncing the chieftainship. In 1965 he was elected head of government of the province and in 1966, when Bechuanaland became Botswana and was granted full independence, he became the first president of the new nation, which he remained until his death. He was knighted in 1966.

• **serialism** ▶ 1. In 20th-century music, the deployment of certain musical elements (most commonly pitch) according to a predetermined order. In the twelve-tone music devised by Schoenberg in the 1920s and subsequently developed by Berg and Webern, this principle is applied to the 12 notes of the chromatic scale. After World War II composers such as Pierre Boulez pioneered **total serialism**, in which duration, tempo, dynamics, etc., also adhere to a definite order. 2. An unconventional theory of 'time displacement' advanced by John William Dunne (1875–1949), aircraft designer, mathematician, and philosopher. Having analysed his own dreams, Dunne concluded that they offered glimpses of future experiences and that time itself was an unfolding of preordained events. His *An Experiment with Time* (1927) became a best-seller and started a fashion for recording dreams. In *The Serial Universe* (1934) he further refined his complex thesis; two later works, *The New Immortality* (1938) and *Nothing Dies* (1940), contained a simplified explanation of these ideas for the public at large. Dunne's serialism is not taken seriously by the scientific community; there is no solid evidence for precognitive dreaming.

• **serial killer** ▶ A murderer who kills repeatedly and compulsively, usually picking his subjects either at random or according to some bizarre pattern. The phenomenon first came to public attention in the 1960s (*see:* Zodiac murders). Public fascination with serial killers reached new heights (or depths) in the 1990s, following several horrific and well-publicized cases and the release of the film *The Silence of the Lambs* (1990), starring Anthony Hopkins as the charismatic psychopath Hannibal Lecter.

• **serious** ▶
   **You cannot be serious** *See:* Superbrat.

• **serious money** ▶ A large amount of money, as

in 'he's earning serious money now in the City'; a phrase much used during the materialistic Thatcher decade, the 1980s. Caryl Churchill's well-known play with this title (1987) was written to satirize the amoral greed of the City in the wake of Big Bang. However, it proved a huge hit with City workers, who came to see the play in large numbers.

• **SERPS** ▶ State Earnings-Related Pension Scheme. A UK government scheme introduced in 1978 with the object of providing every employed person with an earnings-related pension in addition to the basic flat-rate pension. Contributions to the scheme come from National Insurance payments and the pension, payable at the state retirement age, is calculated using a formula based on the person's earnings. Employees may contract out of SERPS provided that they subscribe to a personal pension scheme, an occupational pension scheme, or (from 2001) a stakeholder pension. The government has announced plans to replace SERPS with a pensioner credit targeted at the most needy.

• **set-aside** ▶ An agricultural practice in which a farmer is paid an agreed sum to take a piece of land out of production. The object is to reduce surpluses or to maintain the price of a particular crop, although there may also be environmental benefits. The policy was introduced in the USA and has been a key part of the European Union's Common Agricultural Policy (*see:* CAP) since 1988. In 1993 it was decreed that every farm in the EU had to set aside at least 18% of its land; this obligatory rate has since (2000) been reduced to 10%, with scope for larger amounts on a voluntary basis. New rules have also made the system more flexible and environment-friendly. For example, 10-metre-wide strips alongside watercourses, serving as wildlife habitats, can now be counted as set-aside. Also, some non-food crops, such as willow coppice for fuel, can be grown on set-aside land. However, all such land must be managed by the farmer so that it can be brought back into production if necessary.

• **seven** ▶
   **The first seven years are the worst** A cliché referring to the first years of a marriage or a new job. The implication is that if you can get through the early stages the rest will seem easy. It probably derives from World War I, 'Cheer up – the first seven years are the worst', with reference to the length of regular service in the army. *Compare:* seven-year itch.

• **17th Amendment** ▶ An amendment to the Constitution of the United States of America, which came into effect on 31 May 1913, to provide for the direct election of senators, who until then had been chosen by the individual state legislatures. The 17th Amendment therefore reduced the power and status of state governments and increased popular control over the federal legislature.

• **17th Parallel ▶** The ceasefire line agreed (July 1954) at the end of the Indochina War. *See*: Geneva Agreements.

• **seven-year itch ▶** The urge, especially on the part of men, to find a new sexual partner after seven years in a marriage or stable relationship. George Axelrod, who wrote a play with this title in 1952 (filmed, starring Marilyn Monroe, in 1955), believed that it was his use of the phrase that gave it this modern connotation. Previously it had been used to describe various itching ailments, including scabies, that only disappeared after seven years of treatment. Itch however, has been used since the 17th century as a slang word for a sexual urge and seven years is a traditional period for change:

> Time's pace is so hard that it seems the length of seven years. – WILLIAM SHAKESPEARE: *As You Like It*.

• **Seveso ▶** A town in N Italy, near Milan, which in 1976 became the scene of a major industrial accident when an explosion at a factory resulted in the discharge of a cloud of poisonous dioxin gas. The town had to be completely evacuated, domestic animals destroyed, and contaminated crops and other vegetation burned. Although the dioxin – a by-product in the manufacture of herbicides by the factory – caused no human deaths, many people heavily exposed to the gas developed chloracne, a disfiguring and persistent skin disorder.

• **sex 'n' drugs 'n' rock 'n' roll ▶** A phrase that is supposed to sum up all the ingredients of a good time for the young. It was the title of a song by Ian Dury and Chaz Jankel in 1977.

• **sex bomb** or **sex pot ▶** British slang for a very sexy woman, one who plays up her sexuality. A favourite with the tabloid press, it was first used in the 1960s and is still heard.

> They met...when they were both playing the classic sex bombs, the 'big boobed playthings'... who totter in on high heels... – *The Independent*, 10 April 1991.

• **sexism ▶** Discrimination and stereotyping on the basis of sex, especially the oppression of women by men. *See also*: feminism; male chauvinist pig; sexual politics.

• **Sex Kitten ▶** Nickname of the French film actress, Brigitte Bardot (1933–    ). The daughter of an industrialist, she worked as a model before appearing in a series of French-made sex-comedies in the early 1950s. However, it was with the release in 1956 of *Et Dieu créa la femme* (*And God Created Woman*) that she first attracted international notice and became the sex symbol of an epoch. Written and directed by her first husband, Roger Vadim, the film caused considerable moral outrage because it showed Bardot stripping on the beach at St Tropez; it was described by the Catholic Legion of Decency as 'an open violation of conventional morality'. Vadim himself commented:

> It was the first time on the screen that a woman was shown as really free on a sexual level with none of the guilt attached to nudity or carnal pleasure.

Over the next 15 years there followed a further string of films, including *Viva Maria* (1965) and *Shalako* (1968), most of which capitalized on the pouting 'Sex Kitten' image. Away from the cameras she seemed an increasingly unhappy woman. Her private life – a third marriage was dissolved in 1969 – was a continual target for scrutiny in the popular press and she is known to have made at least one suicide attempt. In 1973 she abruptly announced her retirement from the cinema and withdrew from the public glare to devote her time to promoting animal rights and welfare.

• **sex object ▶** An attractive woman valued for her sex appeal by men who have little regard for her intelligence or abilities. Although these roles can be reversed, the term almost always denotes a woman.

• **sex therapy ▶** *See*: Masters and Johnson.

• **Sex Thimble ▶** A nickname of the British comic actor and musician Dudley Moore (1935–2002). After leaving Oxford with degrees in arts and music, he was employed writing incidental music for productions at the Royal Court Theatre in London. His professional theatre debut came with *Beyond the Fringe*, a successful revue that also featured former Oxbridge students Jonathan Miller, Peter Cook, and Alan Bennett. In 1964 he teamed up with Cook for the first of three series of television comedy programmes entitled *Not Only...But Also*. Moore moved to Hollywood in the 1970s and finally achieved international stardom with a series of films in which he was promoted as a diminutive sex symbol (hence his nickname).

• **sexual politics ▶** The politics affecting relations between the sexes. The phrase was introduced by the US feminist Kate Millet in her book *Sexual Politics* (1970). It involves the idea that the struggle for sexual equality is as important in the 'private' sphere of relationships and domestic life as it is in the 'public' sphere of employment, law, and institutions. Its essence is summed up in the 1970s feminist slogan 'the personal is political'. *See also*: feminism.

• **sexual revolution** ▶ *See*: new morality.

• **Sexy Rexy** ▶ Nickname of the British stage and screen actor Rex Harrison (1908–90). The undoubted highlight of his career was the Broadway production of *My Fair Lady* (1956), in which he played Higgins, and the subsequent (1964) film. A debonair and charming man, who was six times married, he was at his best in comedy; after seeing *Blithe Spirit* (1945), Noel Coward (its author) is reputed to have said to him:

> After me, you're the best light comedian in the world.

• **SGO** ▶ *See*: Same Gender Orientation.

• **shack up** ▶ To cohabit with someone to whom one is not married. The term was first used (1930s) by itinerant workers in America, who set up temporary homes in roughly built shacks. It has been widely used in English-speaking countries since the 1960s.

• **shades** ▶ Originally US Black slang for a pair of sunglasses, an essential component of cool gear since the 1950s.

• **shag** ▶ 1. British and Australian slang meaning to have sex with, or an act of intercourse. It is thought to be related to the verb to shake, which has had sexual connotations since the 16th century. 2. A short-lived teenage dance craze of the 1960s.

• **shagged** or **shagged out** ▶ Tired out by, or as if by, excessive indulgence in sex.

• **shaggy dog story** ▶ A would-be funny story told at great length with an unexpected, usually anticlimactic, twist at the end. So called from the shaggy dog featured in many stories of this genre popular in the 1940s.

• **shamateurism** ▶ The ambiguous position of a sportsperson who manages to maintain the amateur status necessary for competing in certain events while accepting payments. This is usually achieved by setting up trust funds or by treating large sums of money received as 'expenses'. It is a combination of 'sham' and 'amateurism'.

• **shamus** ▶ US slang for a private detective or a police officer, often used in crime fiction. It is thought to be derived from the Yiddish *shamos*, from the Hebrew *shamash*, a guardian of the synagogue. It may also be related to the popular Irish Christian name Seamus, many US police officers being Irish, particularly on the East Coast.

• **Shangri La** ▶ The hidden Buddhist paradise described in James Hilton's novel *Lost Horizon* (1933). The 1937 film starring Ronald Colman was also very successful. The name was later applied to F. D. Roosevelt's mountain refuge in Maryland (now known as Camp David) and to the secret base used for the great US air raid on Tokyo in 1942.

• **SHAPE** ▶ Supreme Headquarters of the Allied Powers, Europe. *See*: NATO.

• **sharkbait** ▶ Australian slang for a swimmer who ventures further out to sea than other bathers, sometimes extended to anyone who takes more risks than might be wise.

• **shark repellents** ▶ Measures taken by a company to deter unwelcome takeover bids, such as golden parachutes, poison pills, and staggered directorships. In the last-named measure, the company adds a resolution to its articles of association that the terms of office served by its directors are to be staggered and that no director can be removed from office without good cause. This ensures that a hostile bidder will be unable to gain executive control of the company for a number of years, even after it has acquired a majority shareholding. Such measures are also known as **porcupine provisions**.

• **shark watcher** ▶ A business consultant, especially one in New York or London, who is employed by a company to identify any share purchases or manoeuvres that may be a preliminary to a takeover bid for that company.

• **Sharon** ▶ British term, first heard in the late 1970s, for a typical working-class girl. It is the female equivalent of Wayne, Gary, or Kevin. Sharon became a very popular name among working-class families from the mid-1960s and thus came to stand for an easily identifiable stereotype. Sharon would typically wear snow-washed jeans with white high heels and have her hair streaked blonde in shoulder-length wet-look curls; her best friend is **Tracey**. The snobbish stereotype took a knock in the late 1990s, when an analysis of the year's degree classes by Christian name revealed that the highest performing names were Sharon and Tracey. *See also*: Essex girl.

• **Sharpeville massacre** ▶ The mass shooting of anti-pass law demonstrators in a Black township 40 miles S of Johannesburg by the Transvaal police on 21 March 1960. Sixty-nine people were killed (many shot in the back) and 180 injured, after the police panicked when 20,000 demonstrators without passes offered themselves for arrest at the local police station. The killings provoked worldwide condemnation and led to the declaration of a state of emergency within South Africa. In the aftermath of the massacre, both the Pan-African Congress, which had called for the demonstration, and the African National Congress (*see*: ANC) were banned; 18,000 people were summarily arrested and draconian powers introduced to suppress dissent, effectively transforming the country into a police state.

• **sharpie** ► Australian slang for a skinhead, first heard in the late 1960s, from the bristly feel of closely cropped hair.

• **Shaw, T. E.** ► *See*: Lawrence of Arabia.

• **sheep in sheep's clothing** ► Someone who is weak through and through – a tongue-in-cheek alteration of the well-known proverb a 'wolf in sheep's clothing', meaning someone who appears harmless but is anything but. The phrase is often attributed to Winston Churchill, who is supposed to have used it of Clement Attlee. However, Churchill himself denied saying this and the phrase is certainly older; the British critic Edmund Gosse (1849–1928) used it when referring to the poet T. Sturge Moore, for example. In another famous jibe, Labour's Denis Healey once (July 1978) described an attack by the Conservative Geoffrey Howe as being similar to being **savaged by a dead sheep**.

• **shelf life** ► The length of time that a commodity, such as a packaged food, can be kept before it deteriorates. The term is now applied metaphorically to other phenomena – fashions, ideas, media personalities – that are not expected to last: 'Today's pop stars have a very limited shelf life'. *See also*: sell-by date.

• **shell jacket** ► A short tight-fitting undress military jacket reaching only to the waist at the back; also an officer's mess jacket.

• **shell shock** ► Psychological trauma resulting from active war service, especially prolonged exposure to being bombed and shelled. The symptoms, which can persist for many years, include loss of sight, loss of memory, terror dreams, depression, etc. The term was first used in World War I; a more modern name is **combat fatigue** or **combat neurosis**.

• **shell suit** ► A type of tracksuit with a showerproof outer nylon layer (or 'shell') and an inner cotton lining; air trapped between the layers conserves body heat. Originally designed as sportswear, shell suits became popular as all-purpose leisure garments in the late 1980s. They tend to be garishly coloured and to have an unpleasant shiny appearance. By the early 1990s they had come to be regarded as a decidedly low-status garment – the type

of thing that an Essex man or Essex girl might wear on a Saturday visit to the supermarket.

• **sheltered accommodation** ► A system of housing designed for the elderly and other vulnerable or at-risk groups, in which individuals or families live in their own self-contained flats or houses but are able to summon a warden for assistance should the need arise. Such accommodation is usually provided by local authorities or housing associations; it often has communal facilities, such as recreation rooms and laundry. Since the 1960s sheltered housing has become a popular method of enabling people, who might otherwise be forced into institutional care, to lead independent lives.

• **Shepperton studios** ► Film studios on a 60-acre site at Shepperton, Greater London, which were established in 1932 by Norman Loudon of the Sound City Film Production and Recording Company. By 1937 the lot contained seven stages, four of which could be converted to double size and had large water tanks. Despite a run of successes in the 1950s and 1960s, heavy losses forced their closure in the mid-1970s, leaving Pinewood and Elstree as the only British film studios still in use. The facilities were reopened and upgraded in 1995 and taken over by Pinewood in 2001.

• **sherbet** ► Australian slang for beer, dating from the early 20th century. It was later used in the British army and was still hear in the Gulf War of 1991. *See also*: kalied.

• **Sherlock Holmes** ► *See*: Holmes, Sherlock.

• **Sherman tank** ► The 'General Sherman' M4, a US medium tank of World War II, which was produced in various versions from February 1942. The earliest Sherman carried most of the ammunition for its 75 mm gun in hull sponsons, which were extremely vulnerable to enemy fire; for this reason it was given the nickname 'Ronson' (a cigarette) by the Germans, because it lit first time. This defect was remedied in later versions by placing the ammunition within the hull, and various other improvements were made to the armaments and the engine. In all, 30,346 Shermans were manufactured from July 1942 to February 1944; they formed an essential part of the Soviet and British, as well as the US, forces.

We'll win the war with the M4. – Allied slogan.

• **She who must be obeyed** ► A phrase used of an overbearing woman. It became popular through its use in John Mortimer's *Rumpole of the Bailey* stories (televised in the 1970s and 1980s) by the barrister Rumpole of his dragon of a wife. Denis Healey used it ironically with reference to Mrs

Thatcher in 1984. The original source was H. Rider Haggard's novel *She* (1887), about a mysterious and all-powerful African queen. *Compare:* 'er indoors.

• **shicker** ► US slang for an alcoholic drink or for a drunkard. It entered American English at the turn of the 20th century from Yiddish and derives ultimately from the Hebrew, *shikor*. It is perhaps most widely used as an adjective, as in 'he is shicker'. The Anglicized form **shickered** is widely used in Australia.

• **shimmy** ► A jazz dance that first became popular at the Cotton Club in the 1920s. Derived from the French *chemise*, shirt, the dance was so named because its energetic rhythms made shirts or blouses shake and shimmer.

• **Shipman murders** ► The murder of dozens (perhaps hundreds) of his patients by Dr Harold Shipman, a popular family GP in Greater Manchester. The victims, who were nearly all elderly women, died from morphine injections administered by the doctor, who stockpiled the drug by writing prescriptions for patients who did not need it. In order to cover up the cause of death, Shipman falsified medical records and took steps to hasten cremations, thus destroying any evidence of excessive morphine in the bodies. This killing spree continued unsuspected for years, if not decades, and the total number of victims remains unknown. Shipman was finally unmasked in 1998, after he was found to have forged the will of his last victim, Mrs Kathleen Grundy, naming himself as the beneficiary of her £400,000.

At his trial in 1999–2000 Shipman was found guilty of murdering 15 of his women patients between 1995 and 1998 and of forging Mrs Grundy's will. He received 15 life sentences, with the judge recommending that life imprisonment mean life imprisonment without chance of early release. Public horror at the ease with which Shipman eluded detection for so long increased sharply when police revealed that there was evidence to proceed against him in a further 23 cases. By the end of 2000 it was announced that some 300 deaths within his practice must now be regarded as suspicious. Finally, in 2001, the official public enquiry into the case began the grim task of examining 466 deaths over a period of 25 years.

Because Shipman has consistently denied all charges and refuses to assist the police, his motives can only be guessed at. Psychiatrists have argued that his main motive was probably a depraved enjoyment of his powers of life and death, together with the pleasure he found in outwitting the authorities.

• **Shock, horror!** ► A phrase that has been used as a parody of sensational tabloid newspaper headlines in the satirical magazine Private Eye since the 1970s. It is now often used adjectivally to imply that someone else's alarm or outrage are unwarranted, as in 'Mum had a real shockhorror reaction when I wanted to go on holiday with my boyfriend'.

• **Shoot!** ► Go ahead; say what you have to say; let's have it!

• **shoot down in flames** ► To refute the arguments of an opponent devastatingly and completely. A metaphor from aerial warfare.

• **shoot-'em-up** ► Originally, a US slang term for a film, such as a Western, dominated by gunplay and multiple shootings. It is now mainly applied to computer games in which the player attempts to obliterate a series of moving targets. *See also:* hack and slash.

• **shoot if you must this old gray head** ► A phrase used by an older person to precede a piece of unwelcome advice given to someone younger. The saying originated in America but is now heard in most English-speaking countries. It comes from a poem by John Greenleaf Whittier (1807–92) describing an incident in the American Civil War. In the poem, the Confederate general Stonewall Jackson and his troops are confronted by a 90-year-old woman waving the Union flag.

> 'Shoot if you must this old gray head
> But spare your countries flag' she said.
> – JOHN GREENLEAF WHITTIER: 'Barbara Frietchie'.

• **shooting gallery** ► US drug-users' slang for any place in which addicts **shoot up**, i.e. inject themselves with heroin or other drugs.

• **shooting war** ► A real war as distinct from a Cold War.

• **shoot oneself in the foot** ► To damage one's own cause through accident or carelessness. It is a more serious version of scoring an own goal. The phrase probably derives from the practice of shooting a bullet into one's own foot deliberately, in order to escape military service (or in time of war, to be sent home wounded). The foot is chosen because a wound here makes soldiering impossible but is unlikely to cause serious permanent damage.

• **short, fat, hairy legs** ► One of many catchphrases from the *Morecambe and Wise Show*, which ran on British television from 1961 until 1984 and became a national institution. The British comedians Eric Morecambe (1926–84) and Ernie Wise (1925–99) began their career in variety and moved into television in the 1960s. Ernie was the small 'straight' man constantly ribbed by the much taller Eric about, among other things, his 'short, fat, hairy legs' and his hair-piece (which Ernie always vehemently denied wearing).

• **shotgun wedding**► A wedding in which the groom is forced into a marriage by the irate father of the bride, literally or metaphorically under the threat of being shot at, because the groom is the putative father of the bride's forthcoming child. In the UK, where 22% of live births in 1995 were to unmarried mothers, the concept is clearly somewhat archaic. The term is sometimes used of any forced or unnatural alliance, *e.g.* 'the shotgun wedding of art and commerce'.

• **shoulder-pads**► Small pads inserted in the shoulders of women's blouses, jackets, or coats to raise the shoulder line, in imitation of male fashions. Originally fashionable in the 1940s and 1950s, they were reintroduced in the 1980s as the most characteristic element of power dressing.

• **show stopper**► 1. A song, act, etc. that provokes a particularly enthusiastic audience response, thereby halting the performance. 2. Business jargon for a legal action in which a firm seeks a permanent injunction to prevent another firm from persisting in an unwelcome takeover, on the grounds that the bid is legally defective in some way.

• **Shrieking Sisterhood**► *See:* suffragettes.

• **Shrimp, The**► Nickname of Jean Shrimpton (1941–  ), a well-known British fashion model of the 1960s. She was a close friend of the photographer David Bailey (1938–  ) and it was his photographs that made her and her sister Chrissie Shrimpton (1943–  ) symbols of the swinging sixties. Cecil Beaton, the leading fashion photographer of his time, was awed by her beauty, calling her the unicorn, the rare, almost mythological thing. In 1969 Jean Shrimpton dropped out of the London fashion circus, eventually marrying and settling down as the owner of a small Penzance hotel. *See also:* Twiggy.

• **shrink**► *See:* headshrink.

• **Shroud of Turin**► *See:* Turin Shroud.

• **shufti** ► British army slang dating from the 1930s for a quick look. It comes from the Arabic *teshuf!* (see!). Doctors and nurses sometimes refer informally to any instrument for examining the interior of any part of a patient (auriscope, sigmoidoscope, etc.) as a **shuftiscope**.

• **shutterbug** ► US slang for a keen photographer, especially an amateur.

• **Shut that door!** ► The catchphrase of the British comedian, game-show host, and compère Larry Grayson (1923–95). He claimed to have said it first on stage at the Theatre Royal, Brighton, in 1970 when he actually did feel a draught from the wings. The reaction was hilarity both from those in the wings and the audience so he decided to keep it in his act. It is usually spoken in a camp northern voice in imitation of Grayson.

• **Shuttle, Le**► The 100-mph rail shuttle that ferries motor vehicles through the Channel Tunnel linking England and France. Inaugurated in 1994, the service runs at 15-minute intervals during peak periods; the journey between the car terminals at Folkestone (England) and Coquelles (France) takes approximately 35 minutes. *See also:* Eurostar.

• **shuttle diplomacy**► Negotiations conducted by a diplomat or politician who travels back and forth to mediate between hostile countries or parties. The name was first used to describe the activities of the US secretary of state, Henry Kissinger, during his Middle East negotiations in the 1970s.

• **SIB**► *See:* Securities and Investment Board.

• **sick as a parrot**► A cliché used to describe extreme disappointment. It plays on sick meaning 'disgusted' and sick meaning 'diseased', parrots being notoriously prone to such ailments as the viral disease psittacosis (parrot fever). In the 1970s and 1980s it was a favourite expression of football players and managers, who routinely used it to describe their feelings on losing a match. This repetitive overuse was mercilessly guyed by the satirical magazine *Private Eye* and the phrase is now mostly used ironically. *See also:* over the moon; We wuz robbed *at* robbed.

• **sick-building syndrome**► A mild affliction that spreads among employees housed in an air-conditioned office building. Pathogenic microorganisms are said to circulate and recirculate through the air ducts spreading infection throughout the workforce. The general symptoms include headaches and eye irritations.

• **sicko**► A psychopath or sexual deviant: a slang term used in America from the mid-1970s and in the UK from the later 1980s.

• **sick-out** ► A form of industrial action by employees who stay away from work, claiming to be ill. It avoids a formal strike, which may be forbidden by law or result in penalties. Sick-outs have been used by various groups, including the police, teachers, postal workers, and nurses.

• **Sid**► In the UK, an ordinary person who bought

his or her first shares in one of the UK government's privatization schemes of the 1980s. It derives from the 1986 campaign to publicize the British Gas sell-off, which featured variants of the slogan 'Have you told Sid?' (*i.e.* about the share issue). The name was presumably chosen for its working-class associations, implying that anyone, even someone called Sid, could be a share-owner in Thatcherite Britain.

• **Sidney Street siege**▶ The siege by the police, Scots Guards, and Horse Artillery of a house at 100 Sidney Street, Stepney, London, on 3 January 1911. Hiding in the house were the so-called Houndsditch Gang, who had killed three policemen a few weeks previously after an unsuccessful raid on a jewellery shop in Houndsditch. The gang consisted of Latvian anarchists led by a mysterious figure named **Peter the Painter**, apparently a sign-painter from Riga. The siege was witnessed personally by Winston Churchill, then home secretary, who had authorized the use of armed troops to flush out the gang. Two anarchists died; 'Peter the Painter' escaped.

• **SIDS**▶ *See*: sudden infant death syndrome.

• **Siegfried Line**▶ The defences built by the Germans on their western frontier before and after 1939 as a counterpart to France's Maginot Line. 'The Siegfried Line', a British song popular in the early months of World War II, ended:

We're gonna hang out our washing on the
                                        Siegfried Line
    If the Siegfried Line's still there.

When Canadian troops penetrated the Line in 1945 they hung up a number of sheets with a large notice on which was written 'The Washing'.

• **signature tune**▶ A song or melody used to introduce a radio or television programme, or firmly associated with a particular dance band, singer, or other performer. The US term is **theme song**. Examples include comedian Bob Hope's 'Thanks for the Memory', and bandleader Glenn Miller's 'Moonlight Serenade'. Political signature tunes include the US Democratic Party's 'Happy Days Are Here Again'.

• **significant other**▶ A person with whom one has a lasting, or at least important, sexual relationship. The relationship may be marriage, engagement, cohabitation, or a less permanent arrangement as long as it is regarded seriously by the parties. It may be heterosexual or homosexual. The term originated in American sociologists' jargon in the 1970s, but because marriage is now by no means the only accepted lasting relationship it has become quite common on both sides of the Atlantic. In Britain, however, its use tends to be somewhat coy and facetious. *See also*: cohab; de-facto; live-in.

• **Sihanouk Trail**▶ *See*: Ho Chi Minh Trail.

• **Silent Cal**▶ *See at*: choose.

• **silent films**▶ All films made before the introduction of the talkies in 1927. The name is partly a misnomer, since they were rarely silent in performance: cinemas hired musicians to provide piano, organ, or violin accompaniment, while other staff supplied sound effects and even, occasionally, dialogue. The great silent stars included Charlie Chaplin (*see*: Tramp, The), Laurel and Hardy, Mary Pickford (*see*: World's Sweetheart), and Lillian Gish. Although the genre is now often associated with slapstick comedy, hugely ambitious and wholly serious silent films were made by D. W. Griffith in America, Eisenstein in the Soviet Union, and Fritz Lang in Germany; the UK's outstanding contribution was perhaps John Grierson's 1929 documentary, *Drifters*. The first airline film was silent: *The Lost World* was shown on an Imperial Airways flight from London in 1925.

The age of silent films effectively came to an end in 1927, when *The Jazz Singer*, with Al Jolson, became the first great talkie success:

The *Jazz Singer* definitely established the fact that talking pictures are imminent. Everyone in Hollywood can rise up and declare that they are not, and it will not alter the fact. If I were an actor with a squeaky voice I would worry.
    WELFORD BEATON in *The Film Spectator* (1927).

Alfred Hitchcock produced the first British sound film, *Blackmail*, in 1929, by immediately reshooting his original silent version (both were released).

Not everyone believed silent films would be supplanted:

The talkie is an unsuitable marriage of two dramatic forms. We cannot believe that it will endure. – *The Times* (1929).

• **silent majority**▶ The great mass of the population who are presumed to hold small 'c' conservative views that they rarely express in public; although easily ignored by liberal opinion formers, these are the people to whom any successful political candidate must have an appeal. The phrase was used by right-wingers in the 1960s and 1970s to draw a contrast between the noisy protests of a radical minority and the quiet conservatism of Middle America. It was particularly associated with Richard Nixon (1913–94), who used it in his election speech in October, 1970:

It is time for the great silent majority of Americans to stand up and be counted.
*See also*: moral majority.

• **silicon chip** ▶ *See*: chip.

• **Silicon Valley** ▶ A name originally used for Santa Clara Valley, S of San Francisco in California. Many factories here make electronic equipment, including silicon chips. Various other 'silicon valleys' have appeared in America, the UK, and elsewhere with the growth of the electronics industry.

• **silly season** ▶ A journalistic expression for the part of the year during which parliament and the law courts are not sitting (usually August and September), when, through lack of news, the papers have to fill their columns with trivial items.

• **Silly Symphony** ▶ The title given by Walt Disney to all his cartoon shorts of the 1930s that did not feature Mickey Mouse, Pluto, or Donald Duck.

• **Silver Ghost** ▶ The Rolls-Royce car produced from 1907 to 1927. The 7 litre six cylinder 40/50 hp model was first announced at the Motor Show in 1906; from 1908 to 1925 it was the only model produced by the company. It was exceptionally quiet and beautifully finished (*see*: best car in the world).

• **Silver Star** ▶ A US military decoration for gallantry in action. It consists of a bronze star bearing a small silver star in its centre.

• **Silverstone** ▶ A motor-racing circuit near Towcester in Northamptonshire, opened in 1948 on track incorporating the runways and perimeter roads of a former airfield. The circuit hosted its first British Grand Prix in 1948 and has continued as a venue for this event ever since, alternating with the Aintree circuit from 1955, and with Brands Hatch from 1964. Since 1987 all Grand Prix meetings have been held at Silverstone. From 1991 a new, slightly longer and slower, circuit was used, designed for greater safety.

• **Simpsons, the** ▶ The dysfunctional all-American family who feature in the cartoon series of the same name. Created by the animator Matt Groening, *The Simpsons* was first broadcast in 1990 and remains hugely popular on both sides of the Atlantic. The family consists of Homer (the lazy and ignorant father), Marge (the sensible mother), their son Bart (a wise-cracking troublemaker), daughter Lisa (gifted and intelligent), and baby Maggie.

Owing to its downbeat unsentimental view of small-town America, the show alienated many viewers in the US when first shown – President George Bush, for instance, declared that his mission was to make America 'more like the Waltons and less like the Simpsons'. Nevertheless, the series went on to enjoy a huge popular and critical success and the main characters are now established as modern American icons. Catchphrases from the show – notably Bart's defiant eat my shorts! and Homer's melancholy 'doh' (untranslatable, but essentially an expression of belated recognition) are now part of everyday speech.

The success of the series owes much to its intelligent writing and droll wit: many of the jokes involve ironic references to other works of popular culture, leading some critics to describe its humour as postmodern (*see*: postmodernism). Unlike most television cartoons, *The Simpsons* is not written primarily for children (although many children adore it). By attracting a large adult audience, it has raised the profile of television animation, paving the way for many other adult cartoons, such as *South Park* and *King of the Hill*.

> *The Simpsons* is a *chef-d'oeuvre* to which the work of no currently practising English-language novelist is comparable in importance or greatness... – GILBERT ADAIR, *The Independent*, 21 June 2000.

• **Simpson trial** ▶ The sensational trial of O. J. Simpson (1947–   ), a former American football star turned media celebrity, on charges of murder. On 13 June 1994 Simpson's former wife Nicole and a friend, Ronald Goldman, were murdered in a savage knife attack outside her Los Angeles home. Suspicion immediately lighted on Simpson, who had a history of domestic violence; in due course he was charged with the killings. His attempts to evade arrest, which culminated in a farcical car chase seen by millions on TV, did little to support his claim to be innocent. The subsequent trial lasted for most of 1995 and was televised in full to a huge spellbound audience. Many of those involved – as members of the legal profession, witnesses, or jurors – found themselves becoming celebrities in their own right. Ominously, opinions about the defendant's guilt or innocence tended to become polarized on racial lines (Simpson is a Black man; the murder victims were both White). Although the circumstantial and forensic evidence against Simpson was considered strong, the prosecution case was undermined by the conduct of its leading witness, a Los Angeles police officer, who revealed himself as both a racist and a perjurer. To the joy of some and the incredulity of others, Simpson was found not guilty. Both the conduct of the trial – widely seen as a grotesque media circus – and the controversial verdict raised serious doubts about the health of the US legal system.

• **Sims, The** ▶ *See*: computer games.

• **Sinatra doctrine** ▶ The principle that, in the era of glasnost, the Soviet Union would allow the communist regimes of E Europe to find their own ways to socialism – they would be permitted to 'do it their way', alluding to the song 'My Way' made famous by Frank Sinatra (*see*: Old Blue Eyes). The phrase dates from 25 October 1989, when Gennady Gerasimov, the Soviet Foreign Ministry spokesman, used it to draw a contrast with the so-called Brezhnev Doctrine. The Sinatra doctrine was quickly overtaken by the collapse of communism in E Europe in autumn 1989.

• **sin-bin** ▸ British slang for a special unit within a school to which difficult or disruptive children are sent until they are able to reintegrate. The term originated in ice hockey, where a sin-bin is the area in which a fouling player must stay until the time penalty has elapsed.

• **sindonology** ▸ *See*: Turin Shroud.

• **Sindy** ▸ Tradename of a girls' doll. First marketed in 1954, Sindy is blonde, slim, and long-legged with vacant model-girl looks. Her chief appeal is her extensive wardrobe, which contains outfits and accessories for every occasion, profession, and lifestyle. With the advent of feminism, business suits etc. have been added to the collection, but so far their popularity has not rivalled that of the wedding dress and nurse's outfit. Her success led to the creation of the **Action Man** soldier doll for boys (1965). The name was chosen after 'Cindy' emerged as the favoured choice of girls shown a photograph of the doll and asked to choose a name. The spelling was changed to Sindy to permit its registration as a tradename.

• **Singer's Singer** ▸ *See*: Velvet Fog.

• **Singing Capon** ▸ *See*: Iron Butterfly.

• **Singing Cowboy** ▸ Nickname of the US singer and film actor Roy Rogers (1912–98), who starred with his faithful horse Trigger in such movies as *The Man from Music Mountain* (1944) and *Pals of the Golden West* (1953). He once said that when he died he would like to be skinned and put on Trigger's back 'just as though nothing had happened'. In the event, Trigger predeceased him in 1965. Roy Rogers should not be confused with Will Rogers (1879–1935), the film actor and humorist known as the **Cowboy Philosopher**, or Jimmie Rodgers (1897–1933), the yodelling country and western singer.

• **singing from the same hymn sheet** ▸ A phrase used of two or more members of a political party, pressure group, or other organization, meaning that they are carefully presenting the same approved line of argument in public. If one government minister says one thing (about, for example, the euro) while another is saying something

with a different emphasis, the party's spin doctors will quickly become alarmed that ministers 'are not singing from the same hymn sheet'. Because the press is always on the lookout for real or apparent 'splits' among politicians of the same party, any perceived difference will soon become the main media story and the original message will be forgotten. In the spin- and PR-fixated world of modern politics, party managers have become obsessed with keeping all their spokesmen **on message** – even if this means that they sound like pre-programmed automata whose every word can be predicted in advance by the listener.

• **single** ▸ A pop-music record consisting of one main song and one or two supplementary numbers (*see*: A side; B side). The traditional vinyl single was seven inches in diameter and played at 45 rpm. The singles charts have been used as the measure of commercial success in the pop world since the 1950s. After the CD single was introduced in the 1980s sales of vinyl and cassette singles declined so drastically that few if any are now produced. The singles market as a whole has also shrunk since the 1970s, making it far easier for a heavily promoted record to reach the top of the charts.

• **single currency** ▸ A monetary unit that is used among a group of countries and administered by common consent. The most significant example is the euro, introduced by the European Union on 1 January 1999, when it was adopted by 11 of the 15 member states.

• **single market** ▸ A trading bloc comprising different countries that can exchange goods and services freely without restrictions or tariffs. One of the most important single markets is that involving the members of the European Union. This came into being on 1 January 1993, following a seven-year process of dismantling trade barriers across Europe initiated by the European Commission and agreed at the Milan summit meeting. However, many of its supporters claim that the single market can only be fully realized when all the member states of the EU adopt a single currency, thereby eliminating national variations in interest rates and fluctuations in exchange rates.

• **single-parent family** ▸ A phrase that has become increasingly widespread in the last 30 years. In 1999 24% of all families with one or more children under 16 were headed by a single parent (usually the mother), compared to a mere 8% in 1971. This is not in itself a new phenomenon – in the 16th and 17th centuries the proportion of single-parent families was not very different from the present figure. At that time, however, most single mothers were widows, whereas widowhood is now a rare cause of lone parenthood. Of the lone mothers of 1999, about 40% were divorced or separated but a slightly higher percentage had never been married to or lived with the father. In over 8% of cases the mother was the only registered parent, suggesting that the father plays no role at all in the child's upbringing.

The single mother with no support from a former partner faces considerable difficulties. For one thing, her disposable income is unlikely to be much more than one third of the average income of two-parent families. It is clearly very hard for anyone to care adequately for young children and do a full-time job at the same time without the support of a second adult. However, shortage of money may not be the only problem. Without a father, the children of single mothers are deprived of the kind of background enjoyed by most children of two-parent families; although studies differ, the father's influence appears to be an important component of a boy's upbringing in particular.

• **singles bar**► A bar used as a meeting place for unmarried or divorced people seeking a new sexual relationship. The singles bar evolved in America with the new sexual freedoms of the late 1960s. The danger of such casual contacts was the theme of the 1977 film *Looking for Mr Goodbar*, based on a Judith Rossner novel about a young teacher murdered by a man she picks up in a singles bar.

• **sinkansen**► (Japanese, new railroad) The Japanese system of high-speed bullet trains. Developed by Japanese National Railways, the passenger service began in 1964 with the opening of a new line between Tokyo and Osaka. The 16-car electric trains have a maximum speed of 210 kph (131 mph) and an average speed of 166 kph (103 mph). *See also*: TGV.

• **Sinn Féin**► (Irish: ourselves alone). The militant Irish separatist movement founded by Arthur Griffith in 1905. In contrast to the Home Rule movement, Sinn Féin advocated a total disengagement from British parliamentary institutions (hence the name). In 1919 it proclaimed an Irish Republic and set up an illegal government under De Valera. Following the Anglo-Irish Treaty of 1921, many Sinn Féiners refused to recognize the partition of Ireland or the legitimacy of the Irish Free State – a position maintained by a rump of diehards ever since. With the outbreak of the current Northern Irish troubles in 1969, Sinn Féin returned to prominence as the political wing of the IRA; from the mid-1980s it was also involved in electoral politics. More recently the Sinn Féin leadership has steered the Republican movement as a whole away from terrorism; the party backed the Good Friday Agreement of 1998 and several of its members now sit on the power-sharing executive set up under its terms. *See also*: Troubles, the.

• **siren suit**► A one-piece garment resembling a boiler suit but lined for extra warmth, sometimes worn in Britain during the air raids of World War II. It was much favoured by Winston Churchill and so named because of the ease with which it could be slipped on over night clothes at the first wail of an air-raid siren.

• **SIS**► Secret Intelligence Service. The formal name for the British government's intelligence agency better known as MI6.

• **sitcom**► *Situation comedy*. A comedy series on TV or radio, in which the same characters take part in a variety of everyday situations.

• **sit-down strike**► A strike in which the workers remain at their workplace but refuse to work themselves or to allow others to do so. A form of industrial action that was first used in the 1930s. *See also*: sit-in.

• **sit-in**► A form of protest in which protestors occupy certain premises with the object of redressing grievances or dictating policy. The term was first used in 1960, to note the protest of US Blacks at lunch counters that refused to serve them. *See also*: love-in; sleep-in.

• **Sittang River Disaster**► The virtual destruction of the 17th Indian Division by the demolition of the bridge over the Sittang River during the Japanese invasion of Burma on 23 February 1942. As the Japanese forces advanced towards Rangoon, the British and Commonwealth forces were ordered to fall back to the Sittang. The Japanese, having intercepted the radio transmission ordering the retreat, moved to cut them off at the bridge. Only a part of the Allied troops had crossed the bridge to the west bank when the Japanese attacked. A decision was taken to destroy the bridge to prevent it falling into Japanese hands, leaving those on the east bank cut off from retreat. Shelled by the Japanese, they tried to escape by crossing the treacherous and fast-flowing river. Hundreds were drowned or swept away and nearly all the division's transport, artillery, equipment, and personal weapons were lost. Many years later, Brigadier Noel Hugh-Jones, the commander who ordered the demolition, committed suicide because he was unable to live with the consequences of his decision.

• **sitting**►
**Are you sitting comfortably?** A catch-

phrase used to introduce a story or a speech, especially a lengthy one. It is a shortened form of 'Are you sitting comfortably? Then I'll begin...', the phrase used to introduce the regular story in the BBC children's radio programme *Listen With Mother* (first broadcast in 1950).

• **situation** ▶ A word frequently added to a noun by a speaker or writer who feels that it adds authority when in fact it is usually unnecessary, cumbersome, and ungrammatical. It is a favourite in the sententious pronouncements of bureaucrats and politicians, who wish to disguise with superfluous words their inability to make a straightforward statement. 'Disasters' are called 'disaster situations', conflicts 'conflict situations', and a sports commentator was even heard to report that 'England are in a five-yard scrum situation'. In an unsuccessful attempt to curb this ugly misuse, the satirical magazine *Private Eye* for some years ran an 'Ongoing Situations' column giving examples; this column also gave citations of the superfluous use of 'ongoing', 'at this point in time', and similar phrases.

• **SI units** ▶ Système International de Unités. The international system introduced in 1960 by the General Conference on Weights and Measures for the use of scientists. It is a metric system (*see*: metrication) based on the former metre-kilogram-second system. Its seven base units are the metre, kilogram, second, ampere, kelvin, candela, and mole; the radian and the steradian are treated as supplementary units. In Europe, including the UK, SI units are always used by scientists and engineers; in America the system is used widely but not exclusively.

• **Six, Les** ▶ A group of French composers formed in Paris in 1918, under the aegis of Jean Cocteau and Erik Satie. Their subtle, witty, and often brief works represented a reaction against 19th-century styles. The group lost its cohesion in the 1920s. The six members were Honegger, Milhaud, Poulenc, Durey, Auric, and Tailleferre.

• **Six, The** ▶ The six countries – Belgium, France, Germany, Italy, the Netherlands, and Luxembourg – who were the original participants in three European economic communities. These were: the European Coal and Steel Community, 1951; the European Economic Community or Common Market, set up by the Treaty of Rome, 1957; and the European Atomic Energy Community or Euratom, 1957. *See*: European Community.

• **six-bob-a-day tourist** ▶ Australian slang for a soldier serving in World War I, from the daily rate of pay of the Australian private (higher than in other contemporary armies).

• **Six Counties** ▶ The counties of NE Ireland that were excluded from the Irish Free State when Ireland was partitioned in 1921 – *i.e.* Armagh, Antrim, Down, Derry, Fermanagh, and Tyrone. The term is now used as a synonym for Northern Ireland, especially by Nationalists and Republicans who deny the legitimacy of partition.

• **Six-Day War** ▶ The short but bloody conflict between Israel and neighbouring Arab states in June 1967. From late 1966 a series of political moves by Egypt's president, Gamal Abdel Nasser, and other Arab leaders, raised Israeli fears of concerted action against her. In May 1967 Nasser secured the removal of UN peace-keeping troops from the Egypt–Israel border zone, closed the Gulf of Aqaba to Israeli shipping, and signed a security pact with King Hussein of Jordan. These events prompted Israel to launch a pre-emptive strike against Egypt on 5 June, in which over 400 Egyptian airforce planes were destroyed on the ground by Israeli jets. With air supremacy established, there followed a swift advance by Israeli ground forces into Sinai. By 8 June Egyptian forces were in full retreat, and a day later Israeli tanks reached the Suez Canal, after which a ceasefire was agreed. Meanwhile, Israeli forces repulsed an attack by Jordan, occupying the Old City of Jerusalem and the West Bank of the River Jordan; they also defeated Syrian attacks, securing the Golan Heights. A UN-arranged ceasefire came into effect on 11 June. The overwhelming Israeli victory dealt a severe blow to Arab military and political aspirations and enabled Israel to establish defensible borders. However, her continuing occupation of the Palestinian territories of the Gaza Strip and the West Bank created the conditions for further conflict and instability.

• **six-o'clock swill** ▶ In parts of Australia bars formerly closed at 6 p.m. Drinkers leaving their jobs at 5.30 therefore tended to have a quick drink to beat the clock. This was called the six-o'clock swill.

• **16th Amendment** ▶ An amendment to the US Constitution legitimizing the imposition of a federal income tax. A law of 1894 introducing income tax had been struck down as unconstitutional by the Supreme Court. However, the importance of allowing the national government to impose an income tax to meet extraordinary expenses, such as those arising in time of war, was recognized by the vast majority of the general public and by Congress, who approved the 16th Amendment in 1913.

• **sixty-four thousand dollar question** ► The last and most difficult question, the crux of the problem; from the prize money awarded for answering the final question in a US television quiz of the 1950s. An earlier radio quiz offered the more modest prize of sixty-four dollars. The expression is now used in all English-speaking countries. *See:* game show.

• **ska** ► A popular 1960s Jamaican dance music that was a forerunner of reggae. Dominated by saxophones and brass instruments, it blended elements of calypso, jazz, and rhythm-and-blues and featured a strongly accented off-beat. The style enjoyed a revival in the late 1970s and early 1980s.

• **Skegness is so bracing!** ► The slogan from an advertisement (1909) for the North Eastern Railway Company, recommending the seaside town of Skegness in Lincolnshire to holidaymakers. The advertisement showed a smiling fisherman in a traditional striped jersey, drawn by John Hassall (1868–1948); the image and slogan are still reproduced on postcards, posters, and mugs.

• **skid row** ► An originally US expression for the run-down area of a city where down-and-outs, vagrants, alcoholics, etc., end up. In the timber industry a skid row was a row of logs down which other felled timber was slid or skidded. Tacoma, near Seattle, flourished on its timber production and it was there that plentiful supplies of alcohol and prostitutes became available for loggers descending the skid row. This is said to be the origin of the expression, which is now used in all English-speaking countries, often in an even more metaphorical sense: the admonishment 'You'll end up on skid row' refers to an imminent state of penury and destitution rather than a physical location.

• **skiffle** ► 1. In the UK, a popular music style of the mid-1950s blending elements of jazz, blues, and folk. It was usually played by a group incorporating kazoo, washboard, and other improvised instruments, as well as guitars and drums. 2. In America, a style of jazz popular in the 1920s and 1930s; it showed the influence of US folk styles and often involved the use of improvised or unconventional instruments.

• **skin flick** ► Slang for a film in which nudity and sex predominate. This term of the late 1960s and early 1970s referred to films shown in public cinemas, such as *Deep Throat* (1972), rather than hardcore porn (*see:* blue movies).

• **skin game** ► A swindling trick. Presumably from the sense of 'skin' meaning to fleece or strip someone of their money by sharp practice or fraud. John Galsworthy wrote a play (1920) entitled *The Skin Game.*

• **skinheads** ► A British youth cult of the late 1960s and early 1970s. Skinheads cropped or shaved their hair and wore heavy boots and braces. They soon acquired a reputation for aggressive behaviour and were frequently associated with football hooliganism and racist violence. The cult represented a working-class reaction against the values and mores of the hippies.

• **skinny-dip** ► US slang for a naked swim, or to swim without a costume. It was first used in the 1960s.

• **ski trip** ► US slang for a dose of cocaine, based on a punning use of the words snow (cocaine) and trip.

• **skive** or **skive off** ► To avoid work, to shirk, or to play truant (of schoolchildren). The derivation of this British slang term is obscure, but it may relate to 'skive', meaning to shave off a sliver of leather.

• **skydiving** ► The sport of parachuting from an aeroplane and free falling for as long as possible before opening the parachute. During free-fall, the participants perform tumbling or flying manoeuvres individually or in groups.

• **sky-jack** ► *See:* hijack.

• **Skylab** ► The first US space station, launched on 14 May 1973. The station's solar panels, used to supply the craft with electricity, were damaged during the launch, threatening the mission's success at the outset. A three-man crew was launched on 25 May and, after docking with Skylab, were able to deploy a sunshield outside the craft, protecting it from overheating. They also freed a damaged solar panel, restoring adequate electricity to the station. After 28 days in space, performing telescopic observations of the Earth and other scientific investigations, the crew returned to Earth. They were followed in turn by two other crews, whose missions aboard Skylab lasted for 59 days and 84 days, the last ending in February 1974. There were no further missions. On 11 July 1979 the 75-tonne space station burnt up as it re-entered the Earth's atmosphere, scattering debris over the Australian Outback.

• **slacker** ► A US term for a young educated person who has opted out of the search for a career and spends his or her days watching TV and videos, surfing the Internet, talking nonsense with friends, etc. The term spread to the UK in the early 1990s – a period of high graduate unemployment. It was popularized by Richard Linklater's 1992 film *Slacker*, about a group of US college drop-outs.

> The camera simply tracks the progress of some 100 young residents from the college town of Austin, Texas, idling away the day with fanciful talk about alternative realities, UFOs, anarchists, Madonna's pap smear (on sale, in a bottle), movies and television – anything but work. These are the 'slackers'... – *The Times*, 3 December 1992.

*See also*: Generation X.

• **slam dancing** ▸ A style of dancing in which the participants fling themselves about so that they slam into each other, the walls, the stage, etc., to the strains of hard rock music.

• **slammer** ▸ Slang for a prison, first used in America but now also widely heard in both the UK and Australia. It is derived from the slamming of the cell door.

• **slap-and-tickle** ▸ A British euphemism, often used in the form 'a bit of slap-and-tickle', for sexual foreplay. First heard in the Edwardian era, it became popular in the 1950s but is now regarded mainly as a joke.

• **slasher movie** ▸ A variety of horror film in which the central element is explicit violence, usually involving knives, claws, or other 'slashing' implements. Such films emerged in the mid-1970s and became a mainstay of the video library in the 1980s. Examples include Tobe Hooper's notorious *The Texas Chainsaw Massacre* (1974) and John Carpenter's *Halloween* (1978) and its sequels. *See also*: splatter movie; video nasty.

• **sleaze** ▸ Dishonesty or corruption involving a public figure, especially a politician. The term **sleaze factor** was first used by US journalist Lawrence Barrett in his book *Gambling With History*, which dealt with corruption during the Reagan administration (some 225 members of which were found in breach of ethical guidelines or the criminal law). In the UK, the term became particularly prevalent during the latter days of the Conservative Party's long term in office (1979–97), when the press unearthed a rich and varied seam of human weakness, greed, and arrogance. This went beyond the usual parade of politicians caught with their pants down, and exposed behaviour that undermined the electorate's trust in the UK's political institutions. Foremost was the cash for questions scandal, which concerned several Conservative MPs accused of receiving payment in return for tabling parliamentary questions. Another high-profile scandal involved the one-time chief secretary to the Treasury, Jonathan Aitken. He embarked on a High Court libel action against the *Guardian* newspaper over various allegations, including the claim that he had allowed an Arab businessman to pay his bill at the Ritz Hotel in Paris. At a press conference in 1995 Aitken promised to demolish such accusations with 'the simple sword of truth'. This phrase came to haunt him when it was later revealed that he had been lying all along. In June 1999 Aitken was sentenced to 18 months' imprisonment for perjury and perverting the course of justice.

This tide of sleaze contributed to the overwhelming defeat of the Conservatives in the 1997 election. However, the incoming Labour government, who had committed themselves to the highest standards of public probity, quickly revealed their own susceptibility to sleaze. Following a meeting between prime minister Tony Blair and Bernie Ecclestone, the head of Formula One motor racing, a proposed government ban on tobacco sponsorship in motor sport was watered down. When it was subsequently revealed that Ecclestone had donated £1 million to the Labour Party, Blair insisted that the money was returned to Ecclestone. A weary public began to accept that sleaze is endemic in the body politic. *See also*: Mandy.

• **sleeper** ▸ **1.** An undercover agent who remains inactive and undetected within a society or organization until ordered to act by his superiors. The concept of the sleeper was much employed in the 'Red Scare' tactics of Senator Joe McCarthy and his associates in the 1950s (*see*: McCarthyism) and has since furnished writers of spy thrillers with much material. **2.** A film, often a low-budget one, that turns out to be much more successful than its producers had expected. Such films lack big advertising campaigns and tend to build up a following through word of mouth. Examples include *The Graduate* (1967) and *Four Weddings and a Funeral* (1994).

• **sleep-in** ▸ A form of action in which a group stays overnight or sleeps in a public place to protest against something or to claim squatters' rights. This mid-1960s expression was formed on the model of sit-in.

• **sleeping policeman** ▸ A low rounded hump built across a road, especially in a residential area, to deter motorists from speeding (*see*: traffic calming). Introduced in the 1970s, they are known as **speed bumps** in America.

• **sleep-learning** ▸ Absorbing information while one is asleep, especially from audio tapes or CDs. The theory that the subconscious mind can process some forms of information while a person sleeps was first exploited commercially in the early 1950s, with the marketing of a number of schemes claiming to employ the 'wasted hours' of sleep. Foreign languages have been the most popular subjects for sleep-learners. Other tapes are supposed to boost confidence by repeating assertions that the sleeper is a talented and resourceful person whose every undertaking will meet with success. The effectiveness of sleep-learning has yet to be established.

• **sleep strike** ▶ A type of industrial action in which employees deliberately go without sleep, to the point that they are unable to work efficiently or safely. It was used as a weapon by Greek air-traffic controllers in the summer of 1988.

• **slide guitar** ▶ See: bottleneck.

• **Slim** or **Slim disease** ▶ The usual African name for Aids, because serious weight loss is one of the major symptoms of the condition. Slim had been a feared and inexplicable disease in parts of sub-Saharan Africa for some time before Aids and HIV began to receive publicity in the West. Subsequently it became an epidemic of horrifying proportions in many countries of sub-Saharan Africa.

• **Slimbridge** ▶ A bird sanctuary on the Severn estuary founded in 1946 by Sir Peter Scott (1903–89), the painter and ornithologist. It holds the world's largest collection of waterfowl (such as geese, ducks, and swans) as well as flamingos, exotic ducks, and small birds. There are over 3000 species in all; the sanctuary is funded by the Wildfowl and Wetlands Trust and entrance fees.

• **slimming pill** ▶ See: diet pill.

• **Sloane Ranger** ▶ A young upper-class person, usually female, who wears informal but expensive country clothes and who lives in the vicinity of London's Sloane Square or in nearby Kensington. The name – a pun on Lone Ranger and Sloane Square – was originated by Peter York in his book *Style Wars* (1982). *The Sloane Ranger Handbook* by Ann Barr and Peter York elaborated the theme.

• **Sloppy Joe** ▶ Slang for a type of light loose-fitting sweater; they have been popular casual wear, particularly among the young, since the 1940s.

> Huge bright orange and brown hand-knitted Sloppy Joes, worn over a leather jacket and trousers. – *The Independent*, 7 February 1991.

• **slow motion** ▶ In film and television, an effect in which the action appears much slower than it would be in real life. In the cinema, this is accomplished by passing the film through the taking camera at an accelerated speed and then projecting normally. The same effect can be created for television by videodisc equipment. Slow motion is used for action replays in televised sports and for various purposes, such as dream or fantasy sequences, in the cinema.

• **sludge science** ▶ Informal name for the study of complex materials that have an irregular internal structure, as opposed to the regular structure of crystalline solids. Such materials contain polymers or small aggregates of one substance dispersed in another. They are often semisolid and include such everyday materials as plastics, grease, paints, cosmetics, jam, and mud. More formally, these are referred to as 'soft condensed matter'.

• **Slump** ▶ See: Great Depression.

• **slush fund** ▶ In politics and big business, an undeclared fund of money used for making corrupt payments and bribes. The term arose in the US Navy, where a slush fund was money accumulated from the illicit sale of 'slush', *i.e.* waste from the galley.

• **smack** ▶ Slang name used by addicts and others for heroin. It is derived from the Yiddish word *shmek*, sniff or taste, from the German *schmecken*, to taste.

• **small is beautiful** ▶ The title of a book (1973) by E. F. Schumacher (1911–77), which provided a popular slogan for those opposed to massive conglomerates in industry and centralization in government. Apparently, Shumacher himself did not coin the phrase, which was the combined inspiration of his English publishers Anthony Blond and Desmond Briggs. It has now become part of the language and can be used in almost any context:

> Small is not beautiful down at Plough Lane. – Article about crowd attendance at football matches, *The Independent*, 4 March 1991.

• **smart card** ▶ A plastic card issued by a bank, credit card company, etc., containing an integrated circuit that memorizes all transactions in which the card is used and the balance in the user's account. The smart card was developed in France in the 1980s. A **supersmart card** is equipped with its own miniature keyboard and display panel, allowing the user to check the balance of his or her account at any moment without reference to the bank.

• **smart house** ▶ A house in which the electrical circuits, telephones and answering machine, TVs and video, thermostats, security system, etc., are connected into a single computerized network. As a result, these functions can be activated by remote control, by the sound of the owner's voice, or by telephone. The scope for disaster is presumably considerable. The concept was developed in America in the later 1980s.

• **smart money** ▶ Money that has been invested by experienced and successful business people, especially those with access to inside information. **Following the smart money** is a sensible, but not infallible, guide to investment policy.

• **smart weapons** ▶ Bombs, missiles, or their delivery systems that operate by radar, laser, television, and computer technology. Although so-called **smart bombs** had been used in the Vietnam War, the expression was first widely used during the Gulf War of 1991. Examples of smart weapons are the RAF **Tornado** fighter-bomber, which uses a laser rangefinder to locate targets that appear on a head-up display (HUD) of an onboard computer screen; the **Patriot** missile, which intercepts and destroys incoming missiles by using radar guidance and computer decisions on when and where to fire; the Stealth bomber, which operates through a combination of fibre optics and computers; the AH-64A *Apache* helicopter, which has infrared technology to find tanks in the dark; and the Tomahawk cruise missile, which receives satellite data to evade enemy fire and has a video camera to help sharpen its aim by comparing its flightpath with maps programmed into its computer.

• **smear campaign** ▶ A planned or organized attempt to tarnish someone's character or reputation.

• **SMERSH** ▶ (Russian *Smeart Spionam*, death to spies) The section of the KGB that specialized in eliminating enemies outside the Soviet Union. The name ceased to be used officially after World War II but an organization with the same function continued to exist. During the Cold War, SMERSH was notorious for neutralizing its targets by blackmail, kidnapping, or murder using a variety of ingenious and lethal gadgets. Trotsky was murdered by a SMERSH agent in Mexico in 1940 under the direct orders of Stalin. SMERSH agents had less success in their encounters with the fictional British agent, James Bond, as described in Ian Fleming's *From Russia with Love* (1957).

• **Smiley, George** ▶ A spymaster of studiedly nondescript manner who appears in several novels by John Le Carré (1931– ), notably *The Looking-Glass War* (1965), *Tinker-Tailor-Soldier-Spy* (1974), and *Smiley's People* (1980). He is said to have been based on John Bingham, Baron Clanmorris, an intelligence officer who later wrote such spy thrillers as *Double Agent* (1965); his daughter is the writer Charlotte Bingham (1942– ). Le Carré worked alongside Bingham at the Foreign Office in the early 1960s. Other traits are supposed to have been supplied by an academic, the Revd Vivian Green, who taught the au-

thor at Sherborne School and later at Lincoln College, Oxford, where Green eventually became rector. In the UK, the character of Smiley is closely associated with Sir Alec Guinness's low-key performance in the role on television (1979, 1981).

• **Smith Act** ▶ The Alien Registration Act, drafted by US congressman Howard W. Smith of Virginia and passed by Congress on 28 June 1940. The Act was a response to the outbreak of World War II in Europe, which heightened fears of communist and fascist subversion in America. It required that all aliens should be registered and their fingerprints taken, while also making it illegal to belong to any organization advocating the overthrow of the US government. The constitutionality of the Act was upheld by the Supreme Court in *Dennis v. United States* (1951).

• **Smith-Connally Act** ▶ A US wartime anti-strike act passed in 1943, which gave the president authority to seize industrial plants threatened by strikes and to act against strikers. It was the first bill passed by Congress to curb the power of the unions.

• **Smith Square** ▶ The square in the City of Westminster, a few hundred yards from the Houses of Parliament, where the headquarters of the Conservative Party are located. The Labour Party also had its headquarters here (at Transport House) from 1928 until 1980.

• **smog** ▶ Polluted fog. The word, a combination of 'smoke' and 'fog', was coined in 1905 by Dr Des Voeux to describe the London phenomenon of fog mixed with coal soot. The notorious London smog of 1952 caused the deaths of some 4000 people from respiratory diseases; it resulted in the Clean Air Acts (1956, 1968), establishing smokeless zones in urban areas. Much of today's smog results from the chemical reaction between vehicle emissions and sunlight; this so-called **photochemical smog** is a growing problem in such cities as Los Angeles and Tokyo, where cyclists and even pedestrians wear masks to protect them against respiratory ailments.

• **smoker's face** ▶ A condition said to affect persistent heavy smokers, especially women. It takes the form of wrinkling about the mouth and eyes and deeper lines on the cheeks. Alleged sufferers include Brigitte Bardot (*see*: Sex Kitten).

• **smokescreen** ▶ Any ruse or ploy used to conceal one's intentions or actions from others. A smokescreen was originally a cloud of smoke used to conceal military operations or movements from the enemy.

• **smoke-stack industries** ▶ *See*: sunset industry.

• **Smokey Bear** or **smokey** or **bear** ▸ US slang for a police officer. The name is derived from the cartoon character of the same name – a bear, dressed in a forest ranger's uniform (resembling that of the police), who gave warnings about fire hazards, especially those caused by dropping lighted cigarette ends. In the 1970s the term was taken up by Citizens' Band (*see*: CB) radio enthusiasts as the codename for a police officer or a patrol car. Other CB codenames followed: **smokey beaver**, a female police officer, **smokey with camera**, police with radar; **smokey on rubber**, police in a moving patrol car; **smokey with ears**, police with CB radio.

• **snafu** ▸ Situation *normal, all fucked up* (*or fouled up*). A coinage devised by British troops in World War II that indicates the level of competence they expected of their commanders. *See also*: sapfu; tabu.

• **snarler** ▸ Australian slang for a soldier who has been sent back from active service after proving of no worth in war. It is a loose acronym of 'services *no* longer required'.

• **sneak preview** ▸ An unexpected advance showing of a feature film before its general release. This enables a studio to measure the audience's reaction and gather written comments; it can also generate local interest for a 'coming attraction'. *Gone With The Wind* (1939), received a top-secret sneak preview to keep the press from reviewing it early. The audience in the Warner Theater at Santa Barbara, California, had come to see *Alexander's Ragtime Band*, but were told they were about to see 'the biggest picture of the year' instead. Once it started, security guards blocked the exits to prevent the audience from leaving or even making telephone calls.

• **snow** ▸ 1. Cocaine; a slang term dating from the early 1900s. It derives from the powdery white form of the drug. 2. US slang meaning to mislead someone with elaborate insincere words or to confuse them with excess information. A **snow job** is the act of deliberately manipulating someone in this way, especially by flattery or cajolery.

• **snowflake's chance in hell** ▸ A phrase used to illustrate a situation in which something or someone has a very limited chance of survival. It originated in America at the turn of the century but is now in widespread use.

• **SNP** ▸ Scottish National Party. A party founded in 1928 as the National Party of Scotland by a group of disaffected Independent Labour Party (ILP) members, journalists, intellectuals, and nationalist activists. The party remained insignificant until the late 1960s, when growing disenchantment with the established parties, together with the discovery of North Sea oil, provoked increasing support for independence among Scottish voters. In the 1970 general election the SNP doubled its vote and sent one MP to Westminster. Support for the party reached its high-water mark in the general election of October 1974, when it gained 30% of the vote and 11 MPs. This threat to the traditional Scottish Labour vote prompted the Labour government to introduce devolution legislation (1976). However, the failure of these proposals to attract sufficient support in a referendum (1979) proved a major setback for the party, who lost all but two of the seats in the subsequent election. Since then support for the SNP has again grown; after the 1997 election it held six seats (five from 2001), making it the main opposition to Labour in Scotland. Since the establishment of a Scottish parliament in 1999 it has also been the official opposition in that body, holding 35 of the 129 seats. The SNP continues to campaign for total independence for Scotland as a separate country within the EU.

• **Snoopy** ▸ *See*: Happiness is…; Peanuts.

• **snuff movie** or **snuff film** ▸ An underground pornographic film that has as its climax the murder of an unsuspecting actress or actor. Although persistent rumours indicate that such films began to appear in California in the late 1960s, not one example has ever been verified. Faked snuff movies, however, have been made for commercial purposes.

• **soap opera** ▸ A long-running drama serial on radio or television, particularly one that treats domestic themes in a sentimental or melodramatic fashion. The name derives from the soap manufacturers who, in America, were the original sponsors of these programmes; it is often shortened to **soap**. Long-running British soap operas include *The Archers* (*see*: Archers, The) on radio and Coronation Street on television. Australian soaps, such as *Neighbours*, are also very popular in the UK. *See also*: Brookside; Dallas.

• **sob sister** ▸ A US journalist who conducts an 'answers to correspondents' column in a women's magazine. In the UK the more usual expression is agony aunt.

• **sob stuff** ▸ A film, newspaper article, or other story that makes use of cheap or tear-jerking emotion. *See also*: schmaltz.

• **Social and Liberal Democratic Party** ▸ (SLD) The original name (1988–89) of the Liberal Democrats.

• **social chapter** ▸ *See*: Maastricht Treaty.

• **social class** ▶ At the turn of the 20th century there was still a fairly clear and well-defined class structure in the UK: essentially, society consisted of the aristocracy, the gentry, the upper middle class (professional), the lower middle class (trade), and the working class (both industrial and agricultural). Although this scheme is somewhat arbitrary, these broad divisions were accepted and most people knew to which stratum they belonged. As Mrs Alexander wrote:

The rich man in his castle
The poor man at his gate
God makes them, high or lowly,
And order'd their estate.

This idea of an unchanging God-given hierarchy began to fall apart in the early 20th century. Traditional class barriers were undermined by the introduction of universal suffrage for men in 1918 and for women in 1928; the emergence of the Labour movement, which enabled the working classes to have their own members in parliament; and the spread of education. The two world wars also had a marked effect on social attitudes.

One influential classification of the British population was that produced in 1962 by the Institute of Practitioners in Advertising, which commissioned a survey by Research Survey Ltd. It has since been used for a variety of social and commercial purposes:

A: upper middle class (3%; professional and managerial)
B: middle class (14%; administrative and professional)
C1: lower middle class (22%; supervisory and clerical)
C2: skilled working class (29%; skilled manual workers)
D: working class (18%; semi-skilled and unskilled)
E: lowest level (14%; state pensioners and casual workers)

Another, quite different, classification is based on the type of house or accommodation that people live in (see: ACORN).

Although the advertisers' classification is almost entirely economic, it shows the influence of deep-rooted attitudes that date back to the 19th century. A particular example of this is the division of the C category into clerical and manual workers – why should a clerical officer in the Civil Service be regarded as in some way superior to a highly skilled lathe operator in an engineering company? The answer is that class distinctions are based not only on earnings, but also on how people see themselves, how they spend their money (e.g. private health care and private education), and their expectations for themselves and their children. Accent also remains important in perceptions of class (see: Received Pronunciation):

An Englishman's way of speaking absolutely
classifies him
The moment he talks he makes some other
Englishman despise him.
– ALAN LERNER: My Fair Lady.

The late 20th century saw further seismic changes, including the long-term decline of many traditional working-class occupations and the growing importance of women in the workforce. In cultural terms, television and the mass media have had an important levelling effect, with dowagers, website designers, and drug dealers all sitting down to watch the same soap operas. At the same time, inequalities in income have increased rather than diminished since 1980. Although the picture is clearly complicated, most people would agree that the UK has become less rigidly class-bound during the last hundred years. When the romantic novelist Barbara Cartland was asked in a radio interview whether she thought that class barriers had broken down she replied:

Of course they have, or I wouldn't be sitting
here talking to someone like you.

See also: classless society.

• **Social Contract** ▶ The agreement made in 1973 between the Labour Party of Harold Wilson and the trade unions. Labour agreed to initiate economic and social policies to the advantage of union members; in return the unions promised to hold down demands for wage increases. Although the promise of industrial peace helped Labour to gain re-election in 1974, this was not to last; inflation continued to grow, and the prices and incomes policy imposed in 1975 finally broke down in the chaos of the Winter of Discontent (1978–79).

The term 'social contract' was coined in the 1680s by the English philosopher John Locke: in 1762 it provided the title for a famous book by the French thinker Jean Jacques Rousseau.

• **social credit** ▶ An economic doctrine based on the ideas of an English engineer, C. H. Douglas (1879–1952), which became influential in Canada after 1930. Douglas believed that money, or 'social credit', should be distributed to allow people to purchase the goods and services produced by a capitalist economy and that lack of such credit provoked economic instability. During the Great Depression the doctrine found enough willing adherents for a Social Credit Party to be victorious in Alberta in 1935; it won nine successive elections and remained in power until 1971. A Social Credit government was elected in British Columbia in 1952, while the federal party continued to win seats and to be represented in the national parliament until 1980. Since then Social Credit has declined as a political force and the Alberta Party has been disbanded. *See also*: greenshirt.

• **Social Democratic Party** ► *See*: Gang of Four.

• **Socialism in Our Time** ► The title of a policy statement issued by the Independent Labour party in 1927. The main proposal, based on the advice of the Keynesian economist J. A. Hobson, was that a future Labour government should introduce a 'living wage' to boost demand and create full employment. Over the next two years constant pressure was placed on the Labour Party leader, Ramsay Macdonald, to adopt this policy but he favoured the more moderate policy statement, *Labour and the Nation*, adopted by the party conference in 1928. *See also*: Keynesianism.

• **socialist realism** ► The approved theory and practice of visual and literary composition in the Soviet Union from the 1930s until the glasnost era. It defined the purpose of art as promoting socialism, and insisted that the way to do this was to treat socially relevant themes in a simple realistic style. Although the application of the theory produced some interesting results in the early years, the style later degenerated into idealistic representations of the heroic successes of the Soviet economy and society, which are almost totally devoid of merit.

• **social realism** ► Art that depicts contemporary life and society in a naturalistic manner, as practised (for example) by the ash-can school in America in the early 20th century.

• **social security** ► A UK government system, run since 1988 by the Department of Social Security, for paying allowances to the unemployed (jobseekers' alowance) and the sick or injured (incapacity benefit), as well as state retirement pensions and an allowance for pregnant women (maternity allowance). It also includes various noncontributory benefits, including income support for those in need, child benefit, and family credit.

• **Sod's law** ► *See*: Murphy's Law.

• **SOE** ► *See*: Baker Street Irregulars.

• **soft drug** ► *See*: hard drug.

• **soft focus** ► In film or television, an effect in which a certain lack of sharpness is deliberately imparted to the image, usually to create a romantic or dreamy atmosphere. Another common use is to disguise the wrinkles of an ageing actor or actress in close-up. Soft focus can be accomplished by placing a gauze over the lens or using a diffusion device,

such as a fog filter. The technique is also employed by photographers for studio portraits.

• **soft landing** ► A decelerated landing by an unmanned space probe on the moon or a planet, or by a manned spacecraft on the moon. Both the Soviet Union and America achieved unmanned soft landings on the moon in 1966, before Neil Armstrong set foot there three years later. Soft landings, such as those made by the Soviet and US probes to Mars in the 1970s, are important if delicate instruments are to survive the impact. *Compare*: hard landing.

• **soft porn** ► Pornography that presents (simulated) sex in a suggestive and titillating way, rather than explicitly or violently. Soft porn is on open public sale in America and the UK, whereas the more explicit, deviant, and especially violent material is sold 'under the counter' – this is sometimes known as **hard porn** or hardcore.

• **soft rock** ► *See*: rock.

• **soft sell** ► Selling by unobtrusive methods, rather than the challenging and repetitive methods that feature in the hard sell.

• **soft touch** ► A person who is sufficiently kindhearted to give or to lend money for the asking. The term is often slightly derogatory, implying that such a person is too weak to say 'no' however outrageous the request.

• **software** ► Computer programs, as distinct from the equipment on which they are run, which is known as the hardware.

• **Soil Association** ► *See*: organic farming.

• **solar power** ► The use of light and other radiation from the Sun to produce usable energy (*see*: alternative energy). There are several ways of exploiting solar energy, the commonest being the direct heating of water in specially designed solar panels mounted on the roofs of buildings. Although the rise in temperature is not sufficient to produce water hot enough for washing or heating, it does reduce the cost of heating the water by other means. It is also possible to produce higher temperatures by using curved mirrors to focus radiation; water converted into steam in this way is then used to drive an electric generator. At present, however, such solar generators are uneconomic. Another method of generating electricity from solar radiation is by direct conversion using a solar cell. This has been used in small-scale applications, such as spacecraft, marine warning beacons, pocket calculators, etc. Large-scale commercial exploitation of solar cells for producing electricity is uneconomic because of the high cost of the silicon used in the cells.

• **So little done, so much to do** ► *See*: famous last words.

• **solvent abuse** ► *See*: glue sniffing.

• **Somebody up there likes me** ► A phrase used in the event of a miraculous escape or a lucky break. Both the autobiography of the World Middleweight Boxing champion (1947–48) Rocky Graziano, and the 1956 film made of his life, starring Paul Newman, had this title. Neil Kinnock, the former leader of the Labour Party, used the phrase in 1983, after his escape from an overturned car on the M4 motorway.

• **somewhere in France** ► A military catch-phrase of World War I, used in soldiers' letters home to avoid the possibility of furnishing the enemy with details of Allied troop movements. It was subsequently used more widely, when someone was believed to be hopelessly lost, in hiding, or otherwise untraceable.

• **Somme, Battle of the** ► The **First Battle of the Somme**, 1 July–13 November 1916, was one of the bloodiest battles of World War I. After months of preparation, the Allies launched a frontal attack on German positions along a 21-mile stretch of the Western Front north of the River Somme. In the wake of a thundering seven-day artillery bombardment, 19 Divisions of the British Fourth Army, under General Sir Henry Rawlinson, and the Third Army, under General Edmund Allenby, went 'over the top' into a storm of machine-gun fire from the entrenched German positions. The British suffered 60,000 casualties on the first day, including 19,000 killed, the greatest loss on a single day in the history of the British Army. Haig, the British Commander-in-Chief, had envisaged a swift break-through in the wake of the artillery barrage, with cavalry operating in open country to mop up the remnants of the shattered German positions. It quickly became apparent, however, that a break-through was impossible and the offensive deteriorated into a series of small but costly assaults on the well-defended German positions, which resulted in a total advance of little more than eight miles in five months. The cavalry were employed in a British attack on 13 July (the last use of mounted soldiers in such a way) but they proved easy targets for the German machine-gunners and were slaughtered en masse. On 15 September Haig authorized the use of British tanks for the first time in the war, but due to poor tactics, technical problems, and the unsuitable terrain they made little impact on the fighting. When the battle ended the British had lost 418,000, the French 195,000, and the Germans 650,000 killed or wounded. The First Battle of the Somme has gone down in history as an appalling waste of over a million young lives without any trace of tactical or strategic benefit to either side.

> I feel that every step in my plan has been taken with the Divine help. – DOUGLAS HAIG, in his diary on the eve of the Battle of the Somme.

The **Second Battle of the Somme**, 21 March–5 April 1918, marked the beginning of the last major German offensive of the war. The German commander, Erich Ludendorff, hoped to achieve a spring victory on the Western Front before the arrival of US troops to bolster the French and British forces. Three German armies struck at the British sector north of the Somme along a 60-mile-wide front between Arras and La Fère, preceded by a rolling artillery bombardment. The aim was to drive a wedge between the British and French. However, the initial German breakthrough, which gained a 40-mile-deep salient, was halted by British reserves at the beginning of April. The British lost 163,000, the French 77,000, and the Germans as many, killed or wounded.

• **sonar** ► A method of measuring the depth of water below a vessel or detecting underwater objects (submarines, shoals of fish, etc.). It is similar to radar, but uses pulses of ultrasonic sound waves rather than electromagnetic radiation. Although the method was first developed during World War I (*see*: ASDIC), the name sonar (from *so*und *na*vigation and *r*anging) came into use later.

• **son et lumière** ► (French, sound and light) Dramatic spectacles relying on the use of lighting effects and recorded sound; there may or may not be a cast of performers involved. They are usually presented after dark in an appropriate natural or historic setting.

• **Sonnenfeldt doctrine** ► The former US policy of not encouraging revolt by citizens in communist E Europe, because of the threat to regional and world peace. The doctrine was proposed in 1976 by a US official, Helmut Sonnenfeldt. After the Soviet suppression of the 1956 Hungarian Rising, in which some 7000 Hungarians were killed, Congressional hearings were critical of US foreign policy and blamed Radio Free Europe for inciting a rebellion that could not succeed. The 1968 Prague Spring was also crushed by troops from five Warsaw Pact countries. Sonnenfeldt's doctrine was thus a recognition of Western impotence in such cases. The policy began to be eroded under President Jimmy Carter's administration (1977–81).

• **Sooty** ► A glove-puppet character who first appeared on British children's television (with his creator Harry Corbett) in 1952. Sooty, a yellow teddy bear with black ears, appeared with his friends Sweep (a mischievous floppy-eared dog) and Sue (a panda). *The Sooty Show* can claim to be the longest-running programme on British television; after Harry Corbett retired in 1975, his son Matthew took over and ran the show for another ten years or more. The puppets were sold to a Japanese company in the mid-1990s. *See also*: Amos 'n' Andy; Archers, The; Blue Peter; Coronation Street; Desert Island Discs.

• **Sopwith Camel**► The standard British fighter aircraft of World War I, built by the Sopwith Aviation Company Ltd, established in 1912 by Sir Thomas Sopwith (1896–1989). Sopwith produced a number of military aircraft for use by the RFC and RNAS during the conflict. The Camel (so-called from the hump-shaped fairing over the twin Vickers machine guns in the nose) was the most successful. A single-seater fighter developed by Herbert Smith in late 1916, it was introduced into service in the following year. By April 1918, after the amalgamation of the RNAS and RFC into the RAF, the Camel was operated by 15 squadrons on the Western Front; it claimed over 3000 enemy aircraft shot down in the last 18 months of the war. The Camel had a reputation as an extremely manoeuvrable but tricky aircraft to fly, due to the fierce torque produced by the powerful 110 hp Clerget 9-cylinder rotary engine. In all, 5490 Camels were built by Sopwith and eight other companies. Smith designed an even better fighter, the Snipe, to replace the Camel but only three squadrons had them by the Armistice in November 1918; it did, however, become the RAF's standard fighter in the years immediately after the war.

• **Sorge spy affair** ► Dr Richard Sorge (1895–1944) was a German who spied for the Soviet Union and was executed by the Japanese in World War II. Sorge's brilliant assessment and analysis of military and political intelligence proved invaluable to Stalin. He had joined the German Communist Party in 1918, visited the Soviet Union as a journalist in 1925, and by 1929 was working for the GRU (Soviet military intelligence). He went to Japan in 1933 (after contriving to join the Nazi Party) as a correspondent of the *Frankfurter Zeitung*, and became friendly with Major-General Ott, the military attaché in the German Embassy in Tokyo. He also forged close links with Japanese military and political circles, and was thus able to provide crucial information to the Kremlin on both German and Japanese intentions in the period preceding the outbreak of World War II. He predicted, for example, that the Japanese would enter the war by an offensive in SE Asia, rather than an attack on the Soviet Union in Siberia, which allowed Stalin to divert troops from the east to take part in the major battles against the Germans in the west. Just before his exposure and arrest he had learned of the Japanese plan to attack Pearl Harbor, but there is no evidence that he managed to communicate his discovery to Stalin or Roosevelt. In 1964, 20 years after his death, the Russians finally acknowledged Sorge's contribution to the Soviet war effort by making him a Hero of the Soviet Union and placing his image on a postage stamp.

• **SOS**► The Morse code signal (3 dots, 3 dashes, 3 dots, •••– – –•••) used since the early years of the century by shipping, etc., in distress to summon immediate aid; hence any urgent appeal for help. The letters, in Morse a convenient combination, have been popularly held to stand for 'save our souls' or 'save our ship'.

• **soul**► A style of Black music characterized by an emotional and semi-improvised vocal style; it emerged in America in the early 1960s from a fusion of gospel, rhythm-and-blues, and White pop styles. Leading soul singers included Aretha Franklin (called 'Lady Soul' by her fans), Otis Redding, and James Brown, among others. *See also*: Motown.

• **soul food**► A style of food that has come to be considered a distinct gastronomic entity since it first emerged in the diet of poor Blacks in the southern states of America. Its delicacies include chitterlings (pig intestines), corn bread, catfish, and pig's trotters.

• **sound barrier**► *See*: supersonic.

• **sound bite**► A short extract from a speech or interview given by a politician that is designed to catch the news headlines and the attention of the public. Although modern politicians are often criticized for relying on sound bites rather than lengthy argument and analysis, they are probably only responding to wider changes in the culture as a whole. According to recent research, the amount of time for which a viewer or listener can be expected to concentrate and take in information is steadily decreasing; for example the typical TV advertisement now lasts less than 30 seconds. *See also*: three-minute culture.

• **sound pollution**► *See*: noise pollution.

• **South Bank**► The arts complex on the south bank of the River Thames in London, between Blackfriars and Westminster bridges. The first modern building on the site was the Royal Festival Hall, built by the then London County Council under the direction of architect Sir Leslie Martin for the Festival of Britain in 1951. Other buildings include the National Film Theatre, under the southern arch of Waterloo Station, which was completed in 1958; the Hayward Gallery, Queen Elizabeth Hall, and the Purcell Room (linked together in a single group), which date from 1965–68; and the Royal National Theatre, which was opened in 1977. The brutal concrete style of the South Bank complex, especially the Hayward group, has attracted much criticism. In the 1990s the South Bank was effectively extended eastwards by the reconstruction of Shakespeare's Globe Theatre in Southwark and the conversion of the disused Bankside power station into the Tate Modern art gallery.

• **South Bank religion** ▶ A journalistic label for the religious activities in the diocese of Southwark, on the south bank of the Thames in London, associated with Dr Mervyn Stockwood (1913–95), Bishop of Southwark (1959–80), Dr John Robinson (1919–83), Suffragan Bishop of Woolwich (1959–69) and author of *Honest to God* (1963), and some of their diocesan clergy. 'South Bank religion' was characterized by outspokenness on moral and political issues, often from a socialist angle, and energetic attempts to bring the Church into closer relation to contemporary society. The epithet was often used disparagingly by opponents.

> That is rather the new idea inside the Church. I should definitely say you were a South Banker.
> – AUBERON WAUGH: *Consider the Lilies* (1968).

• **southpaw** ▶ In US usage, a left-handed baseball player, especially a pitcher; also sometimes applied to any left-handed person. In both US and British usage it means a boxer who leads with his right hand.

• **Soviets** ▶
   **All power to the Soviets!** Slogan of Bolshevik forces during the October Revolution of 1917, subsequently adopted by the new Soviet state. The Soviets were the workers' councils first established in the Russian Revolution of 1905. The governmental system of the Soviet Union consisted of a pyramidal structure of such councils, with the Supreme Soviet at its apex.

• **soya** ▶ *See*: TVP.

• **Soyuz** ▶ (Russian, union) A series of Soviet-crewed spacecraft, which began with Soyuz 1, launched on 23 April 1967. Each craft consisted of an orbital module, in which the three-member crew lived and worked during the mission; an instrument assembly module, which contained the propulsion mechanism; and the descent vehicle, occupied by the crew during launch and descent and the only section to return to Earth. More ad-

vanced versions of this basic design were the Soyuz-T (introduced in 1981) and Soyuz-TM (1986). One of the principal tasks of the Soyuz craft was carrying cosmonauts to and from orbiting space stations (*see*: Salyut). The good safety record of Soyuz craft was marred in 1971 when the Soyuz 11 re-entry module depressurized during descent, killing three cosmonauts who were returning from the Salyut 1 space station.

• **space age** ▶ The present era of exploration beyond the Earth's atmosphere. General agreement marks its beginning as 4 October 1957, when the Soviet Union launched Sputnik 1. The Americans followed three months later with their satellite, *Explorer 1*. Since then, there have been many thousands of successful space launches. The first men went into space in 1961: Soviet cosmonaut Yuri Gagarin completed one orbit on 12 April and US astronaut Alan Shepard made a sub-orbital flight on 5 May. Other successful launchings have been military, weather, and communications satellites as well as space probes, moon landings, and space shuttles and stations. The European Space Agency put up its Spacelab in 1983. The same year, NASA's Pioneer became the first spacecraft to leave the solar system, passing beyond the orbit of Neptune, a feat repeated in 1989 by Voyager 2.

Space travel was predicted by two French novelists, Cyrano de Bergerac in the 17th century and Jules Verne in his novel *From the Earth to the Moon* (1873). In 1901 H. G. Wells envisaged that Englishmen would be the first men on the moon in his novel of that name. The space age first loomed as a possibility in 1926 when physicist Robert Goddard (1882–1945) began his tests on liquid propelled rockets. Although he died before the space age began, the German wartime V2 rocket was largely based on his designs, which were developed into a reliable vehicle by the German rocket scientist Wernher von Braun (1912–77). After the war von Braun went to America to work on the US space rockets, including the Saturn rockets used in the Apollo moon programme, as a result of which man set foot on the Moon.

• **spaced-out** ▶ Slang, dating from the late 1960s, for the state of being dazed or intoxicated by a drug. It later came to mean disorientated by the impact of any moving experience, such as seeing a powerful film or listening to music. The expression refers to the effects of LSD or other hallucinogens, which are said to make users feel out of touch with reality, as if flying through space. It is often shortened to **spaced**.

• **Space Invaders** ▶ Tradename for an early computer game in which the player attempted to shoot down hostile spaceships, which came attacking in different patterns across the screen.

• **space probe**▸ Any space vehicle or other device designed to investigate astronomical phenomena, either from Earth orbit or beyond. The first scientific satellites were launched in the late 1950s, starting with the Soviet Sputnik programme in 1957 and the US Explorer 1 in 1958. By orbiting above the Earth's atmosphere these early probes were able to monitor more accurately radiation from other parts of space, and so provide a wealth of new information. Since then space probes have travelled to other planets in the solar system, directed by remote control to transmit data back to Earth. Examples include the Voyager probes to Jupiter, the Viking missions to Mars, and the Pioneer spacecraft that passed close to Jupiter in the 1970s. In 1997 NASA landed the Pathfinder spacecraft on Mars, enabling the remote-controlled Sojourner buggy to send live television pictures to Earth. The Mars Odyssey Probe, launched in 2001, will spend two years orbiting the planet. *See also*: Mariner.

• **Spaceship Earth**▸ The concept of our planet as a spacecraft that carries its inhabitants as passengers. The implication is that we are travelling through space together, with our survival depending on a fragile ecology with limited natural resources and a polluted environment. This idea was popularized by the book *Operating Manual for Spaceship Earth* (1969), by R. Buckminster Fuller (1895–1983), the US architect who also developed the geodesic dome.

• **space shuttle**▸ A re-usable manned space vehicle, designed to ferry personnel and equipment to and from space. The first space shuttles were introduced in the late 1970s and 1980s by NASA. The shuttle held the promise of reduced cost and increased payload, but NASA encountered formidable development hurdles, for example heatproofing the underside of the vehicle to withstand the high temperatures encountered during re-entry. The first shuttle into space was 102 (Columbia), launched on 12 April 1981, followed by 99 (Challenger), 103 (Discovery), and 104 (Atlantis). The delta-winged orbiter vehicle is launched vertically using its own engines and two rocket boosters; the latter are jettisoned at high altitude along with a large external fuel tank. Following re-entry, the orbiter performs a conventional runway landing. Besides a flight crew of four, up to four other persons can be accommodated. The shuttles have been used to deploy various payloads, perform experiments, and even repair broken satellites. In 1986 the pro-

gramme came to an abrupt and tragic halt with the Challenger disaster; flights did not resume until 1988, with the launch of Discovery on 29 September.

A Soviet space shuttle, Buran ('blizzard'), made its first unmanned space flight on 15 November 1988 but was never used for regular flights.

• **space–time**▸ *See*: relativity.

• **space walk**▸ *See*: Gemini.

• **spaghetti junction**▸ A nickname for the Gravelly Hill interchange on the M6 in N Birmingham, so-called because an aerial view of the tangle of slip roads and flyovers suggests a plate of pasta. The name has since been applied to other complex road junctions.

• **spaghetti Western**▸ A film about the US West made by an Italian director and Italian crew, often shot in Spain. The lead actors and actresses were usually American, with English dubbed in for the Italian members of the cast. The golden era of spaghetti Westerns was the 1960s, the key director being Sergio Leone. Leone's great discovery was the US actor Clint Eastwood, who starred in such hits as the Italian-German-Spanish 1964 co-production *A Fistful of Dollars (Per un Pugno di Dollari)* and *The Good, the Bad and the Ugly (Il Buono, il Brutto, il Cattivo)* in 1967. Other 'pasta stars' have included Claudia Cardinale, Lee Van Cleef, Eli Wallach, Charles Bronson, and Rod Steiger. Although the spaghetti Westerns were sometimes ridiculed at the time, these violent, amoral, and sometimes blackly humorous films can now be seen to have breathed new life into an exhausted genre. *See*: Western.

• **Spam**▸ **1.** Tradename for a canned luncheon meat first marketed in the UK during World War II, when other meat was scarce. It was developed by George A. Hormel & Co. of Minnesota in 1936 and acquired its name as the result of a competition, for which the winner received $100; the name is short for Spiced ham. **2.** Slang for junk e-mail. This is mostly unwanted advertising material but can also include jokes and circulars, chain letters, religious messages, etc. Because it is easy and cheap to send e-mail messages to large numbers of recipients at once, spam has proliferated wildly in recent years, becoming a serious nuisance to Internet users. *See*: junk mail.

• **spammed**▸ British army slang for irritated, pissed off. Dating from the Gulf War of 1991, it is possibly by allusion to the unpopularity of tinned luncheon meat or similar convenient but unappetizing items on the menus of army field kitchens. *See also*: jiffed.

• **Spandau** ▶ *See*: Prisoner of Spandau.

• **Spanish Civil War** ▶ The bitter conflict (1936–39) in Spain between the Republican government and Nationalist rebels. For many on the left the war represented a classic struggle between the forces of good and evil – a democratically elected Popular Front government supported by urban workers, agricultural labourers, and much of the educated middle classes resisting a reactionary coalition comprising the army, Catholic Church, monarchists, industrialists, and wealthy landowners. Support for the insurgents from Hitler and Mussolini, and more limited backing for the Republicans from the Soviet Union and the left-wing volunteers from Europe and America in the International Brigades, broadened the conflict into a foretaste of the wider struggle to come. A military coup in July 1936, led by the Nationalist Generals Franco and Mola, left the rebels in control of much of the south and northwest, but Barcelona and Madrid were saved for the government by the workers' militias. There ensued a war of attrition, with the Republican forces gradually succumbing to the superior military and economic resources of the Nationalists. The Republicans were effectively deprived of support from democratic European nations by the establishment of the Non-Intervention Committee by the UK and France, to minimize the danger of international conflict. Germany and Italy were openly contemptuous of the Committee; Hitler sent the fighters and bombers of the Condor Legion, and Mussolini 100,000 Italian troops, to fight on Franco's behalf – both dictators used Spain as a testing ground for their latest weaponry. Soviet aid and the support of the International Brigades was only sufficient to enable Madrid to survive the initial Nationalist assaults in the autumn of 1936. By October 1937 Bilbao and the Basque country in the north had been bombed into submission by the Nationalists (*see also*: Guernica); they then drove eastwards to the Mediterranean, splitting the republic in two in April 1938. Catalonia was overrun by February 1939; fighting then erupted in Madrid between competing communist factions and on 28 March the city surrendered to Nationalist forces. Spain would remain under Franco's Falangist dictatorship (*see*: Falange) for nearly 40 years. Up to a million people were killed in the conflict, many of them in wholesale massacres of opponents carried out by both sides.

• **Spanish flu** ▶ A pandemic of influenza, thought to have begun in Spain, which killed an estimated 15–20 million people throughout the world during the winter of 1918–19. Spanish flu killed more people than the number of dead from all nations in World War I.

• **Spanish practices** or **customs** ▶ Irregular working practices in a particular trade or industry, usually contrived by the unions as a means of keeping wages or manning levels artificially high. Before the technological revolution of the mid-1980s the expression was often applied to the restrictive practices of the print unions in the UK newspaper industry.

• **spare-part surgery** ▶ Surgery to replace diseased or damaged parts of the body with tissues or organs from a donor or with artificial prostheses. The transplantation of most organs only became feasible from the 1940s, when the mechanisms of graft rejection became known through the work of Sir Peter Medawar (1915–87) and other immunologists. The first successful kidney transplants were performed in 1958, while the world's first heart transplant was carried out by the South African surgeon Christiaan Barnard in 1967. Since then the scope of transplantation surgery has broadened to include combined heart-and-lung transplants, liver transplants, and bone marrow transplants. The bulk of spare-part surgery concerns smaller items, such as hip replacement, corneal grafts, and heart-valve replacement, often substituting precision-bioengineered parts for the real thing.

• **Spartacists** ▶ An extreme socialist group in Germany that flourished between 1916 and 1919. It was founded by Karl Liebknecht who, with Rosa Luxemburg, led an attempted revolution in January 1919, in the suppression of which they were both killed. The movement was finally crushed by the government of Karl Ebert in April 1919. It took its name from the Thracian gladiator Spartacus, who in 73 BC led a slave rebellion against Rome.

• **speakeasy** ▶ A place in which alcoholic liquors were sold illegally in America during the years of Prohibition (1920–34). *See*: bootlegger; Scarface.

> The place of the saloon was taken by speakeasies which ranged all the way from dingy back rooms to palatial establishments, but all tolerated by the police. – L. D. BALDWIN: *The Stream of American History*, Vol. II.

• **Speakers' Corner** ▶ A wide area of pavement inside Hyde Park in London, close to Marble Arch. Here, every Sunday morning, a number of open-air soap-box orators turn out to instruct or entertain anyone willing to listen. Some have a grievance to air, some have a religious message or a pet theory to pass on, while others wish simply to hear the sound of their own voices. All, however, are exercising a British citizen's right to free speech; obscenity, blasphemy, and incitement to racial hatred or a breach of the peace are forbidden by the law – but nothing else is. If no great movements have been born at Speakers' Corner, it has, at least, served as a safety valve for Londoners who want to be heard and a free entertainment for those who want to listen (mostly, these days, tourists). The name Speakers' Corner was adopted in the 20th century, although the right of assembly here was granted in 1872.

• **speaking clock** ▶ The British Telecom service, officially Timeline, that gives callers a continuous recorded statement of the exact time at 10-second intervals. It is now sponsored by a watch company:

> At the third stroke, the time sponsored by Accurist will be...

• **speak softly and carry a big stick** ▶ An adage associated with President Theodore Roosevelt, who first used it in a speech at the Minnesota State Fair in 1901. The saying – originally, it seems, a West African proverb – summarized Roosevelt's belief in tactful diplomacy backed up by the threat of force. He used such tactics successfully (1902–04) in the Alaskan boundary dispute and the second Venezuelan crisis.

• **Special Air Service** ▶ *See*: SAS.

• **Special Boat Squadron** ▶ (SBS) A commando unit of the Royal Marines specializing in amphibious undercover operations. Before 1977 it was known as the 'Small Raids Wing' of the Royal Marines Amphibious School; the latter was created after World War II from various wartime units. The Squadron has served in several theatres of war, including Borneo and Oman. In 1972 a joint SBS-SAS team parachuted in mid-Atlantic to board and search the QE2 following a bomb threat; this turned out to be a hoax. The SBS should not be confused with the **Special Boat Service**, the amphibious arm of the SAS created during World War II.

• **special effects** ▶ In the cinema, techniques used to create effects that would otherwise be impossible, unsafe, or beyond a production budget. The undoubted father of special effects was the Frenchman George Méliès (1861–1938), a former conjuror who pioneered numerous trick effects in hit films of the 1890s. Further advances were made by Edwin S. Porter, a director for Thomas Edison's studio, whose *Dream of a Rarebit Fiend* (1906), featured a flying bed. Many of Hollywood's original techniques are still in use: breakaway bottles and chairs for fight sequences, double exposure to allow ghosts to materialize, and the use of realistic miniatures, such as model warships that sink in a studio

tank. Photographic techniques include dissolves, wipes, back projection and the use of mattes (a mask to blank part of an image to enable another image to be superimposed). For the Atlanta fire sequence in *Gone With The Wind*, the actors were filmed in front of a black backdrop: the fire, filmed weeks before, was then added using a matte process. In *Star Wars* (1977) George Lucas first acquainted filmgoers with the advanced computer-controlled special effects later seen in Spielberg's *E.T.* (1982) and other 1980s blockbusters. During the 1990s visual effects were further revolutionized by the growing use of computers to generate, enhance, and manipulate images; films to make spectacular use of such techniques include *Terminator 2* (1991), *Jurassic Park* (1993), and *The Matrix* (2000). *See*: computer animation; morphing.

• **speed** or **whizz** ▶ Drug-abusers' slang from the 1960s for the amphetamine drug, methedrine; later applied to all amphetamines. The word refers to the stimulant effects of these drugs, which appear to speed one up.

• **spend, spend, spend!** ▶ The catchphrase of Vivien Nicholson, whose husband won £152,319 on the football pools in September 1961 when she was 25. After years of scrimping and saving to bring up her children on her husband's meagre wage as a coalminer, she told a journalist that her only plans for her new-found wealth were to 'spend, spend, spend!' The phrase later supplied the title of her autobiography (1977), a TV play about her by Jack Rosenthal, and a successful West End musical (1990s). It is now used as a celebration of profligate spending; Mrs Nicholson spent all her money, worth well over £2 million today, in just four years.

• **Sperati forgeries** ▶ Postage stamps forged by the Frenchman Jean de Sperati, which in 1942 became the subject of a widely reported trial. A respected philatelist, Sperati was accused of attempting to evade export duties when sending some extremely rare and valuable stamps to a Lisbon dealer: to Sperati's acute embarrassment the only way to escape severe punishment was to confess that he had forged the stamps himself and that they were thus valueless. It subsequently emerged that he had based his illustrious 30-year career on his forgeries, which had fooled all the most eminent philatelists. He was acquitted but failed to learn his lesson: in 1952 he was gaoled for two years for a further fraud. His forgeries are now much sought after by collectors and ironically change hands for large sums.

• **sperm bank** ▶ A place in which a store of frozen human semen is kept for use in artificial insemination (see: AI), especially by women whose husbands are infertile and who wish to be inseminated by an anonymous donor (see: DI). The concept of sperm banks, or **semen banks** (the older name), dates back to the 1950s. The semen, which can be stored for years, is mainly provided by medical students for relatively small payments or in some cases by older men who have had their own families and wish to help infertile couples. Several Nobel prizewinners have also donated semen to sperm banks. The issue of whether (and in what circumstances) children born by DI should be permitted to trace their biological fathers in later life has aroused some controversy in recent years. Sperm banks now exist at infertility centres and clinics throughout the world.

• **Spice Girls ▶** An all-girl pop group that achieved huge success in the late 1990s. With its five strongly characterized members, 'Scary Spice' (Melanie Brown; 1975– ); 'Sporty Spice' (Melanie Chisholm; 1974– ); 'Ginger Spice' (Geri Halliwell; 1972– ); 'Baby Spice' (Emma Bunton; 1976– ), and 'Posh Spice' (Victoria Adams; 1974– ), the group was deliberately created to provide someone for everyone to identify with (or fancy). In 1996 the first single, 'Wannabe', went straight to the top of the charts and the group began to amass a huge fanbase, mainly among young girls for whom the band's sloganeering ('girl power', 'friendship is forever') struck a powerful chord. Despite the rapid appearance of a number of similar girl groups, the Spice Girls held onto their prime position in the market, consolidating this with a run of chart-topping singles, two albums, and a film. By the end of 1998 they had sold more than 22 million records, making them easily the most successful female group in pop history.

After Geri Halliwell left the group in mid-1998 to pursue a solo career the remaining members also took a break to follow various personal projects. Meanwhile Victoria married the England footballer David Beckham in a high-profile wedding and as **Posh and Becks** the couple remain very much in the media spotlight.

• **spinach ▶** A vegetable that has for generations been regarded as highly nutritious. In the 20th century the myth was reinforced by the amazing effect it had on the film cartoon character **Popeye**, created by Max Flischer (1889–1972) in about 1933. When Popeye, the tough sailorman, needed to defend his girlfriend Olive Oyl against the villainous Bluto, he invariably fortified himself with a tin of spinach. This idea is said to have been suggested by the marketing department of a tinned-spinach manufacturer. The theory that spinach is a good source of iron is unfortunately untrue. It does contain 4 mg of iron per 100 g of leaf (high compared to 2.5 mg/100 g of haricot beans), but this iron combines with the oxalic acid in spinach to form an insoluble oxalate. While its presence accounts for the bitter taste of spinach, having activated the taste buds it passes through the body unchanged.

• **spin doctor ▶** A public relations expert whose job is to present unpopular decisions, political policies, etc., in the most favourable light; the term alludes to the spin given to a ball in various sports in order to disguise its flight. Political spin and spin doctoring became subjects of feverish media interest in the 1990s; Tony Blair's New Labour government has often been accused of being 'all spin and no substance' – i.e. of relying on deceptive PR to conceal the ineffectiveness of its policies.

• **Spion Kop ▶** A battle during the Boer Wars, on 24 January 1900; it was the second attempt by British forces, commanded by General Sir Redvers Buller, to break through the Boer lines on the Tugela River to relieve Sir George White besieged in Ladysmith (see: Relief of Ladysmith). In the first attempt, at the Battle of Colenso on 15 December 1899, Buller had attempted to turn the left flank of the Free State General Louis Botha, but the British had suffered heavy losses from entrenched Boer sharpshooters. On 19 January, Buller sent Sir Charles Warren and 13,000 men to cross the Tugela with the aim of breaching the Boer lines west of Spion Kop, a summit at the centre of the Boer positions. Buller was to follow with the remainder of the British forces to exploit the planned breakthrough. Warren later decided on a surprise attack on the summit itself, which was successfully captured on the night of 23 January. It proved impossible, however, to reinforce the British positions with artillery, and Botha mounted a counterattack, driving the British from the summit. British casualties were 1500 killed, wounded, or captured, and Buller was forced to recross the Tugela where he had begun (a retreat that earned him the nickname 'Reverse' Buller). Many of the British dead came from Liverpool; a stand at Liverpool football ground is called **The Kop** in their honour and Liverpool's supporters are sometimes known by the same name.

• **spirit ▶**

**The spirit of the troops is excellent** A newspaper cliché dating from World War I, when it was regularly used in morale-boosting accounts of the latest fighting, regardless of how well things were really going. The public rapidly learnt to re-

gard it as an empty cipher and it subsequently acquired a wider ironic usage.

• **Spirit of St Louis** ▶ The aircraft in which
Charles A. Lindbergh (1902–74) made the first non-
stop solo flight across the Atlantic (20–21 May 1927).
Lindbergh was sponsored by a group of businessmen in St Louis, Missouri, and the aircraft was a
Ryan NYP single-engine monoplane, modified to
Lindbergh's specifications and powered by a Wright
Whirlwind 230 hp engine. It would normally have
seated five people, but most of the space was taken
up by extra fuel tanks giving it a range of 4100
miles (6600 km). The plane was returned to America by ship after the historic flight, and Lindbergh
eventually donated it to the Smithsonian Institution in Washington, DC. *See also*: Lindbergh baby
murder.

• **Spitfire** ▶ British fighter aircraft of World War
II, which remained in operational service with the
RAF into the 1950s. The design was based on the Supermarine seaplane, created by Reginald J. Mitchell
(1895–1937) during the 1920s, which won the
Schneider Trophy outright in September 1931. The
Spitfire's outstanding aerodynamics and powerful
Rolls Royce Merlin engine (designed by a team led
by A. G. Elliott) were based on Mitchell's experience
in perfecting the Supermarine. The first model of
the Spitfire, the MK1, went into production in 1937;
by the time of the Battle of Britain in August 1940,
Fighter Command was equipped with 19 Spitfire
Squadrons, which played a crucial role in the defeat
of the Luftwaffe (*see also*: Hurricane). The design was
constantly modified and upgraded throughout the
war to meet the challenge of different combat roles
and to match improvements in German fighter designs. The MKXIV, for example, which was produced
in 1944, was powered by the exceptional 2050 hp
Rolls Royce Griffon engine; it could challenge the
latest German jet fighters and was also used to intercept V-1 rockets. Although the Spitfire's last operational flight took place on 1 April 1954, the
aircraft remains one of the most cherished in the
history of aviation.

• **spitting image** ▶ A person who strongly resembles another person – often because they are related. This curious expression is a corruption of
'spit and image', 'spit' being a 19th-century slang
term for 'likeness, counterpart'. It was used as the
title of an ITV satire series (1984–96), in which
grotesque rubber puppets were used to caricature
well-known politicians and others, including the
Royal Family.

• **spiv** ▶ A flashily dressed man who earns his living by dealing in black-market goods or by various
other sharp practices. The word was frequently
heard during World War II and its aftermath, when
many things were in short supply; the spiv could
often provide them, albeit at an exhorbitant price.
The word probably comes from the dialect word
'spiff', for smartly dressed; however folk etymology
has it that it derives from VIPs backwards.

• **splashdown** ▶ The programmed landing of a
space capsule on the sea. The word, also used as a
verb, was first applied by NASA to the 1961 Atlantic
splashdown of the sub-orbital flight by astronaut
Alan Shepherd, America's first man into space.
Many later landings occurred in the Pacific Ocean,
always accompanied by NASA's live commentary of
'Splashdown!' or 'We have splashdown!'

• **splatter movie** ▶ A violent horror film in
which large numbers of people, often teenagers,
go to their deaths in spectacularly messy and unpleasant ways. *See also*: slasher movie; snuff movie.

• **splitting the atom** ▶ *See*: Cavendish Laboratory;
nuclear fission.

• **Spock baby** ▶ One of the postwar generation of
children brought up by parents influenced by the
permissive approach to childcare advocated in *The
Common-sense Book of Baby and Child Care* by the US
pediatrician, Dr Benjamin Spock (1903–98). Spock's
best-selling book, published inexpensively in paperback in 1946, sold over 30 million copies and was
important for two main reasons: it was the first to
counsel a flexible and gentle approach to childcare, as opposed to the prevailing hardline orthodoxy, and it was also the first popular medical
textbook written by experts for the general public.
During his career Spock was active in a variety of
liberal causes, including nuclear disarmament and
opposition to the war in Vietnam; his permissive
theories of parenthood were blamed by some US
conservatives for the 1960s student revolt and numerous other ills.

• **Spode, Roderick** ▶ In P. G. Wodehouse's *The
Code of the Woosters* (1938), a would-be dictator who
leads an ineffectual band of fascists called the Black
Shorts (so-named because every colour of shirt had
already been claimed). A tall mustachioed bounder
with 'the sort of eye that can open an oyster at forty
paces', he is clearly modelled to some extent on Sir
Oswald Mosley (1896–1980; *see*: Mosleyites), the
founder of the Blackshirts. Spode is memorably denounced by Bertie Wooster as 'a frightful ass...
swanking about in footer bags...a perfect perisher'.
Wodehouse himself was heavily criticized during
World War II after he made a series of ill-judged
broadcasts from Berlin to America. After the war he

settled in America, becoming an American citizen in 1955.

• **spook** ▶ 1. US slang for a Black person. Perhaps because a Black person is difficult to see in a dark place and, like a ghost, only appears to have eyes. 2. US slang for a spy. Probably a reference to the fact that spies are supposed to be as invisible as ghosts.

• **spot dance** ▶ A ballroom dance in which the couple upon which the spotlight falls when the music stops win a prize; or, when there is no spotlight, the couple on or nearest to a particular spot on the floor not previously revealed to the dancers.

• **sprechgesang** ▶ (German, speaking song) A type of vocal expression that blends singing and talking. Although the composer Engelbert Humperdinck made use of it in an opera in 1898, it is mainly a 20th-century phenomenon. Schoenberg used it in various works, including *Pierrot Lunaire* (1912), and Walton made very effective use of it in *Façade* (1926).

• **Springer empire** ▶ West German newspaper and magazine empire built up by the right-wing press magnate Axel Springer (1912–85) after 1945. His first publication was *Hör Zu!* (1946), a radio programme guide, and in 1952 he launched the tabloid *Bild Zeitung*, Europe's best-selling daily newspaper; in the following year he acquired *Die Welt*, an upmarket counterbalance to the *Bild*'s raucous populism. Springer's unbridled anti-communism and campaigns for law and order made him a target of the left during the 1960s; as a result his property was damaged in a series of attacks by terrorists of the Red Army Faction.

• **Spruce Goose** ▶ *See: flying boat.*

• **Sputnik** ▶ (Russian, travelling-companion) A Soviet man-made satellite. Sputnik I, launched 4 October 1957, was the first satellite to be projected successfully into orbit round the Earth. Weighing 84.6 kg (186 lb), it orbited the Earth in 96 minutes and made various scientific measurements; it burnt up as it re-entered the Earth's atmosphere on 4 January 1958.

• **spy satellite** ▶ *See: eye in the sky.*

• **Spy Who Came in from the Cold** ▶ *See at: cold.*

• **square** ▶ A person who is old-fashioned in his or her views, dress, habits, or tastes (especially in music). The usage dates from the 1930s and 1940s and was later associated with beat and hippie patois. There are several suggested derivations, none of which is particularly convincing; one is that it al-

ludes to the patrons of the traditional square dance as opposed to the cool devotees of modern jazz, etc.

• **Square Deal** ▶ The ambitious programme of social and economic reform introduced (1901–09) by President Theodore Roosevelt on behalf of the poorer sections of US society. The programme dictated extensive changes in working conditions, food production, and the control of monopolies; it is remembered as one of the most beneficent political projects of the 20th century.

> A man who is good enough to shed his blood for the country is good enough to be given a square deal afterwards. More than that no man is entitled to, and less than that no man shall have. – THEODORE ROOSEVELT, speech, 4 June 1903.

• **Squidgygate** ▶ A scandal concerning a tape of a telephone conversation between Diana, Princess of Wales and her friend James Gilbey, which suggested a high degree of intimacy between the speakers. On the tape Gilbey addresses Diana by the affectionate nickname 'Squidgy'. Since the Watergate affair in the 1970s, the suffix '-gate' has often been used to indicate a scandal. Transcripts of the tape were published in British newspapers in 1992, fuelling speculation that the marriage of the Prince and Princess of Wales was in trouble. The couple separated later that year and divorced in 1996. Diana confessed to adultery with Gilbey during her famous *Panorama* interview in 1995. *See also:* Camillagate; People's Princess.

• **Squiffites** ▶ Supporters of the Liberal prime minister Herbert H. Asquith (1852–1928), who followed him into opposition after he was overthrown by Lloyd George in December 1916. Asquith had been head of a coalition government since May 1915, but stalemate on the Western Front progressively weakened his political standing, and on 5 December he resigned. Asquith refused to serve under Lloyd George, but refrained from attacks on government policy for the remainder of the war. The fragmentation of the Liberals into Squiffites, followers of Lloyd George, and Independents marked the effective end of the party as a force in British politics.

• **SS** ▶ German abbreviation for *Schutzstaffel* (Protective Echelon), a corps of the Nazi Party that originated as part of Hitler's bodyguard in 1923. In 1929 Heinrich Himmler took over the SS, defining its duties as 'to find out, to fight and to destroy all open and secret enemies of the Führer, the National Socialist Movement, and our racial resurrection'. During World War II SS divisions fought with fanatical zeal. The armed unit of the SS (Waffen-SS) included the notorious *Totenkopfverbände* (Death's-Head Battalions), responsible for administering the concentration camps. *See also*: Brown Shirts.

• **St** ► *See at*: Saint.

• **stag** ► **1.** Denoting a social event, such as a prenuptial drinking session (**stag party**), to which only men are invited. *Compare*: hen party. **2.** British army slang for sentry duty, dating from World War II; possibly an allusion to the stag deer's alertness to movement.

• **stagflation** ► An economic situation in which high inflation is combined with stagnant output and employment. This deadly combination afflicted the British economy for much of the 1960s and 1970s. The term was coined by the Conservative politician Ian Macleod in 1965.

• **stagnation theory** ► The theory that depressions, and the trade cycle in general, arise because as people become more affluent in the boom periods, their opportunities for investing their savings decline. The theory was proposed in the 1940s but not widely accepted. Its supporters argued that in the boom period investment should be encouraged in such ventures as slum clearance and improvements to the infrastructure.

• **stakeholder society** ► A society in which all citizens are recognized as 'stakeholders', parties with a legitimate interest in the quality of life provided by that society. In business thought, an approach known as **stakeholder theory** began to find advocates in the 1990s. According to this, responsible businesses should consult the interests of 'stakeholders' such as employees, customers, and the wider community, as well as those of shareholders. This general approach was subsequently adopted by many centre-left figures (including, for a while at least, Tony Blair), who advocated a 'stakeholder society' as an alternative to the 'share-owning democracy' preached by Margaret Thatcher. The concept has been criticized as worthy but vague.

• **Stakhanovite** ► In the former Soviet Union, a follower of a system that encouraged increased productivity among workers by rewarding the most efficient. It was named after Alexei Stakhanov (1906–77), a Donetz coal miner who substantially increased his daily output by hard work and rationalization. In 1935 Stalin held a conference of Stakhanovites at which he extolled the working man. The term is now sometimes used to mean any obsessively hard worker.

• **stalag** ► In World War II, a German prisoner-of-war camp for NCOs and men. The word is a short-ened form of the German *Stammlager*, literally 'base camp'.

• **Stalin** ► *See*: Man of Steel.

• **Stalingrad** ► The former name (1925–61) of Volgograd, a large city on the Volga in SW Russia. Originally it was renamed to commemorate its defence (1918–20) by Stalin against the White Russians. In 1943 it was the scene of the bloody but decisive defeat by Marshal Zhukov of the German 6th Army led by Field Marshal Friedrich Paulus.

• **Stalinism** ► The ruthless version of Marxist-Leninism imposed on the Soviet Union for 30 years by Joseph Stalin (*see*: Man of Steel). It involved an extravagant personality cult; murderous purges of dissidents and rivals (*see*: Law of December 1; Leningrad purge; Yezhovshchina); and general political terror centred on a system of gulag forced-labour camps.

• **Stanislavsky system** ► *See*: Method, the.

• **star** ► A top entertainer or performer in films, television, theatre, music, sports, etc. The term is mainly associated with Hollywood, which created a powerful **star system** to increase public interest in films during the 1910s. Before about 1910 film companies tended not to identify actors and actresses by name in order to hold down their salaries. However, the popularity of the Biograph Girl (Florence Lawrence) alerted the studios to the drawing power of individual named performers. The first great international stars of the silent era were Mary Pickford (*see*: World's Sweetheart) and her husband Douglas Fairbanks. Their celebrity was soon eclipsed by that of Charlie Chaplin (*see*: Tramp, The), who became the most famous and instantly recognizable figure in human history, known and feted all over the world. In the 1920s and 1930s, the Hollywood studio system created a production line for new stars. Glamorous images were created by studio dressers and publicity departments, which even invented new names and new biographies for likely candidates. In the UK the first international star-maker was Alexander Korda (1893–1956), who made a hobby of finding star qualities among secondary performers; his successes included Merle Oberon, who also became his wife. With the collapse of the studio system, stars were able to escape from the kind of fixed images that kept Edward G. Robinson a gangster and Bette Davis a bitch queen throughout their careers. Later Hollywood stars, such as Meryl Streep and Dustin Hoffman, or Julia Roberts and Tom Hanks, have tended to be much more versatile – although some, such as Sylvester Stallone, continue in set roles.

Since the 1960s the term star has been devalued

by indiscriminate use, leading to such aggrandized versions as **superstar** and **megastar**.

• **START** ▶ *See*: SALT.

• **started** ▶

**I've started so I'll finish** The catchphrase used by the chairman, Magnus Magnusson, of the BBC TV quiz programme *Mastermind* when one of his questions was interrupted by the buzzer, indicating that the time for the round was up. He would then repeat the question, enabling the contestant to answer before the round was concluded. The expression has been widely used in a variety of contexts since 1970, when *Mastermind* was first broadcast; the last series went out in 1997.

• **Star Wars** ▶ Nickname for the Strategic Defense Initiative (SDI), a proposed system for defending America from nuclear attack using laser-beam weapons orbiting in space programmed to shoot down the enemy's guided missiles. The concept was developed in the early 1980s and won the whole-hearted support of President Reagan, despite the criticism of those who claimed that it was too expensive, would not work properly, or posed a threat to the established balance of terror. The system was nicknamed Star Wars after the hugely popular science-fiction film of that name (1977), reflecting the sci-fi aspect of the project. The scheme went into abeyance with the end of the Cold War in the late 1980s and was formally abandoned in 1993. However, plans for a somewhat similar anti-missile system were put forward by President George W. Bush in 2001; inevitably this was dubbed **Son of Star Wars** by the press.

• **stash** ▶ To hide something away, especially stolen goods, money, or drugs. The word was coined around the turn of the 20th century, by combining 'stow' or 'store' with 'cache'.

• **Stasi** ▶ Popular name for the former State Security Police (*Staatssicherheitsdienst*) in East Germany. Responsible for espionage, counterespionage, and the suppression of political dissent, they were notorious for their minute surveillance of the lives of East German citizens. They were disbanded in December 1989, a few weeks after the opening of the Berlin Wall. Several prominent Germans were later accused of having been Stasi informers.

• **Stately Homes of England** ▶ The great art-filled mansions, and the estates in which they stand, of the British aristocracy; most are now owned and managed by the National Trust. The phrase derives from a poem by Felicea Hemans (1793–1835) but is better known as the title of a song by Noël Coward:

> The stately homes of England
> How beautiful they stand,
> To prove the upper classes
> Have still the upper hand.
> – NOËL COWARD, *Operette*.

• **state-of-the-art** ▶ An expression used to describe a top of the range, advanced, and up-to-the-minute model, usually of some high-tech artefact. For example, 'his DVD player is real state-of-the-art stuff'.

• **Statue of Liberty sale** ▶ The preposterous and very nearly successful 'sale' of the Statue of Liberty by the Scottish conman Arthur Furguson in 1925. This attempted sale of America's most famous landmark to an Australian tourist – a $100,000 deposit was accepted – proved the culmination of an extraordinary career in such hoaxes. It began in London with Furguson's successful sale of Nelson's Column (complete with Landseer's lions and fountains) to a wealthy American for just £6000. Inspired by this success, Furguson went on to charge £1000 for Big Ben, £2000 for Buckingham Palace, and, following his move to America, $100,000 for a year's lease of the White House. The Statue of Liberty sale, however, proved Furguson's downfall and he served a five-year sentence following his arrest and trial. In 1930 he was freed and, undaunted, began a whole new career of similar hoaxes, successfully maintaining a luxurious lifestyle until his death in 1938.

• **Stauffenberg Plot** or **July Plot** or **Officers' Plot** ▶ The unsuccessful attempt to assassinate Hitler with a bomb on 20 July 1944. A briefcase containing the bomb was left by Count von Stauffenberg under a table at the Führer's headquarters in Rastenberg, E Prussia. A plan, known as 'Operation Valkyrie', had also been devised by the conspirators to seize key government installations in Berlin after Hitler's death. However, by an unlucky fluke – an aide moved the briefcase – Hitler escaped serious injury, although four others in the room were killed. Not unexpectedly Hitler immediately took a savage and paranoid revenge. Stauffenberg and three others were immediately shot, Rommel (*see*: Desert Fox) and General Ludwig Beck were forced to take poison, and 7000 other suspects were arrested, tried, and executed, in many cases after torture.

• **Stavisky affair** ▶ The financial scandal surrounding the affairs of Serge Alexandre Stavisky (*c.* 1886–1934), a Russian-born French swindler, which came to a head in 1933–34 and precipitated a major crisis for the Fourth Republic. Stavisky, an adept at establishing fraudulent businesses, led an extravagant lifestyle, mixing with influential society in Cannes and Deauville, until he was exposed in a 500 million franc bond swindle involving the municipal pawnshop in Bayonne in December 1933. He fled to the luxury resort of Chamonix, where he was found dead in January 1934, supposedly by his own hand, although many suspected that he had been killed by the police to protect his influential patrons in the government, judiciary, and Sûreté Générale itself. In February 1934 widespread suspicion of government corruption prompted violent anti-government and anti-parliamentary demonstrations in Paris led by the right-wing leagues Action Française and Croix Feu; this succeeded in bringing down the government and threatened the future of parliamentary democracy itself.

• **steady-state theory ▶** A theory of cosmology first proposed in 1948 by the Austrian-born US astronomer Thomas Gold (1920–    ) and the Austrian-born British mathematician Hermann Bondi (1919–    ). The British astronomer Fred Hoyle (1915–2001) was a particular supporter of the theory. It depended on what is known as the 'perfect cosmological principle' – the idea that the universe looks the same from whatever point it is observed and moreover, at whatever time. According to the steady-state theory the universe had no beginning, will never end, and contains a constant density of matter. To account for the fact that the universe appears to be expanding (*see*: redshift), Gold and Bondi made the controversial suggestion that matter was constantly being created from free space. In the 1960s it became apparent that there is a background of microwave radiation in the universe. This is best understood as a remnant of the Big Bang. The big-bang theory of the origin of the universe is therefore the one currently accepted, while the steady-state theory has been discredited.

• **Stealth bomber ▶** A US bomber plane developed in the 1980s and reputed to be virtually invisible to enemy radar on account of its innovative streamlined silhouette and high tech instruments. At a cost of £350 million each, manufacture of the Stealth bomber came under threat from the US government in the late 1980s but it subsequently proved its worth in raids on Iraqi strategic targets during the Gulf War of 1991. Its record in the Kosovo crisis (1999) was somewhat more mixed; Serb forces managed to shoot one down over Yugoslavia and displayed a photograph of the wreckage with a placard reading 'Sorry – we didn't know it was invisible'.

• **Stellenbosch ▶** A town in South Africa, 40 miles (64 km) east of Cape Town, which was the location of the main British military base during the Boer Wars (1899–1901). To be 'Stellenbosched' became a popular term for the fate of those unfortunate senior officers who were relieved of their commands for incompetence in the field and sent back to the Cape in disgrace.

• **Sten gun ▶** One of the most widely used British sub-machine guns of World War II. The name was coined with the introduction of the Mark I version in 1941, and derives from the initials of R. V. Shepherd, in charge of small arms procurement in the Army, the gun's designer, J. J. Turpin, and Enfield, the site of the Royal Small Arms Factory. Designed for simplicity and ease of production, the early versions had a tubular skeleton stock, while the later Mark V had a wooden stock. More than two million Mark II Stens were produced; several underground resistance groups, as well as the Germans, produced their own copies despite the fact that the gun was dangerously difficult to aim accurately.

• **Stephen Lawrence case ▶** The racially motivated murder of Stephen Lawrence, an 18-year-old British student, became a *cause célèbre* in the UK during the late 1990s. The son of Jamaican parents, Stephen was stabbed to death by a gang of White youths on 22 April, 1993, while waiting for a bus in Eltham, S London. Of the five prime suspects, two were arrested but released without trial, owing to lack of evidence. The case became nationally known largely owing to the persistence of the victim's parents, who brought an unsuccessful private prosecution against all five suspects in 1994–96. A subsequent inquiry, headed by Sir William Macpherson of Cluny, published its report (the **Macpherson Report**) in February 1999. The report condemned the Metropolitan Police for incompetence and an 'institutional racism' that led officers to treat the killing as an episode in a gang war, rather than the murder of an innocent man. In particular, the police failed to give first aid to the stricken youth, showed an unsympathetic attitude to the victim's family and the main witness (a Black youth), neglected to follow many basic evidence-gathering procedures, and – crucially – delayed arresting the alleged perpetrators, despite many reports from members of the public. The report, which recommended various measures to eradicate racism from the police and a number of modifications to the law, was immediately seen as a landmark in Britain's race relations.

• **sterling area ▶** An association (also called the sterling bloc, or scheduled territories) that came into existence after the UK left the gold standard in 1931, when a large number of countries agreed to stabilize their currencies in terms of the pound and to hold sterling balances as part of their international reserves. These included the British Commonwealth nations (except Canada), Jordan, Iraq, Libya, Burma, and Iceland. The sterling area declined in importance after 1945, when the progressive devaluation of sterling made it less attractive as a reserve currency. Few countries, except some current and former members of the British Commonwealth, now hold sterling as a reserve, most preferring more stable currencies, such as the Japanese yen.

• **Stern Gang ▶** A small Jewish terrorist organization, founded in Palestine in 1940, which concentrated on assassinating British personnel. It was named after an early leader, Abraham Stern (1907–42), who was killed in a gun fight with British police. On 6 November 1944 the gang murdered Lord Moyne, the minister of state for Middle East affairs, in Cairo. From 1945 it collaborated with two other terrorist groups, the Irgun Zvai Leumi and Haganah, in a guerrilla campaign to force the establishment of a Jewish state in Palestine. Although denounced by the official Zionist leadership, the activities of the Stern Gang and other terrorist groups were effective in helping to secure the British withdrawal from Palestine, which eventually led to the foundation of Israel in May 1948. A leading member of the Stern Gang, Yitzhak Shamir, became prime minister of Israel (1983–84; 1986–92).

• **Stiffkey, Rector of ▶** The Revd Harold Davidson, rector of Stiffkey (pronounced 'stookey') in Norfolk, a notorious figure of the 1930s in the UK. After a long and colourful trial at the Norwich Consistory Court in 1932, which exposed his amorous adventures to the delight of the press and public, he was unfrocked for immoral conduct. In order to make a living he then paraded his notoriety, appearing in cinemas and local fairs, exhibiting himself in a barrel on Blackpool beach, and even having himself fired from a cannon. He eventually joined a travelling menagerie and was killed by a lion in 1937.

• **stills ▶** *See*: bubs.

• **sting ▶** A robbery or con trick, especially one that is carefully planned. The use of the word in this way goes back to the turn of the 20th century and derives from the idea of being 'stung for money', *i.e.* having to pay out a certain sum. By the 1930s it was in use among criminals and the police. The word was popularized in the 1970s by the film *The Sting* (1973), featuring Robert Redford and Paul Newman in an elaborate con trick on a gangster. The music of Scott Joplin (*see*: ragtime) added considerable charm to the 1920s Chicago setting.

Top boxing manager Ambrose Mendy plotted to defraud companies of more than £650,000 in a complex bank sting... – *The Sun*, 9 April 1991.

• **stir crazy ▶** Mentally disturbed as a result of confinement in prison ('stir' for prison is thought to derive from Romany *stariben*). A 1980 comedy film with this title made extensive use of all the Hollywood prison clichés.

• **Stirling bomber ▶** The Short Brothers Ltd S 29 Stirling, a four-engined heavy bomber, which entered service with the RAF in August in 1940; it was at that time the RAF's only four-engined bomber. The Stirling was built to a 1936 specification, which limited the wing span to 100 feet (31 m) to allow it to pass through the standard width of hangar door. This drastically compromised its performance, preventing it from climbing to more than 12,000 feet (3660 m) and making it vulnerable to anti-aircraft fire from the ground as well as to bombs from above dropped by the superior Lancasters and Halifaxes, which joined it in mass bombing raids. The Stirling was also sluggish, had poor manoeuvrability, and was unable to carry bombs heavier than 4000 lb. For these reasons, by 1943, it was used mainly as a transport and carrier of ECM (Electronic Counter Measure) and spoofing devices.

• **stockbroker belt ▶** The ring of leafy outer suburbs around London, from which many City businessmen commute daily to their offices.

• **Stockholm Appeal ▶** A petition to ban the atom bomb, allegedly signed by 500 million people in over 70 countries, which was launched at a meeting of the Stockholm World Peace Conference in March 1950.

• **Stockholm syndrome ▶** A psychological condition in which hostages come to identify with their captors' political or personal causes, even to the point of justifying their crimes and taking part in them. The syndrome's name comes from a 1973 bank robbery in Stockholm, Sweden, in which several hostages gave support to the robbers. *See also*: Pattie.

• **stock shot ▶** A film sequence that can be reused in different productions to save the time and expense of reshooting. Footage of this kind is kept in the libraries of film studios and television stations or can be obtained from commercial film libraries. It is mainly used to introduce the locale in establishing shots (*e.g.* the Manhattan skyline to denote New York) or to add atmosphere (*e.g.* wildlife scenes in Tarzan films). Other favourite topics include Western landscapes, aeroplane landings, battle sequences, etc. Stock shots were used during the early years of cinema: Edwin S. Porter made a 10-minute film in 1903, *The Life of an American Fireman*, in which he inserted stock film of fires and firemen taken from Thomas Edison's files.

• **Stokes mortar** ▶ A type of light trench mortar, used in both world wars, which was invented by the civil engineer Sir Frederick Stokes (1860–1927). The weapon was originally rejected by the War Office in 1914, but Lloyd George persuaded an Indian maharajah to finance its manufacture enabling it to be introduced in the following year. The weapon consisted of a smooth-bored steel tube, 3–4 in (7–10 cm) in diameter. The projectile contained its own propellant charge, which was ignited automatically by dropping it down the tube onto a striker. The original design went through various improvements and was used for lobbing high explosives, smoke pellets, incendiary bombs, or gas into the enemy lines.

• **stomp** ▶ A jazz dance that first became popular in the 1900s, characterized by much stamping of the feet and frenetic movement; the word later came to be used of any lively dance or session of dancing.

• **stoned** ▶ Under the influence of drink, drugs, or some other stimulus. First heard among jazz musicians in the 1940s; in the 1960s it was applied especially to the effects of cannabis.

• **stone ginger** ▶ A certainty, from the New Zealand racehorse Stone Ginger, which won every race (*c.* 1910) for which it was entered.

• **Stooges, The Three** ▶ A US comedy team who appeared in a long series of film shorts from the 1930s to the 1950s. The key to their success was their skill at a rather brutal form of slapstick; with a minimum of plot or character development, their films have not survived particularly well. The original trio, Larry Fine and Moe and Jerry Howard, transferred to Hollywood from vaudeville; there were various changes in personnel before the team finally broke up.

• **Stopes clinic** ▶ The UK's first birth control clinic, opened by the pioneer birth control specialist, Marie Stopes (1880–1958), in 1922. Known as the Mothers' Clinic, it was originally housed at 61 Marlborough Road, Holloway, London, and catered mainly for married women from the capital's poorer districts. Initially the project was financed by Stopes and her husband, the aircraft manufacturer J. V. Roe (1878–1949). The clinic offered free advice and contraceptives; the most common devices were Stopes' own version of the cap and a sponge impregnated with olive oil, used as a suppository. The clinic moved to its present site, in Whitfield

Street, in 1925. It is now a registered charity, with other clinics in Leeds and Manchester, and three nursing homes in London. The UK-based Marie Stopes International supports 42 birth control projects in 21 countries, mainly in the developing world.

• **stop-go** ▶ A pejorative name for government economic policies that seek to reflate the economy when there is high unemployment and then employ straining measures when there are signs that it is overheating. Stop-go implies that the government, incapable of long-term planning to control the economy, can only respond by short-term knee-jerk reactions.

• **stop me and buy one** ▶ Advertising slogan used by the manufacturers of Wall's ice-cream; first seen around 1923, displayed on placards attached to the tricycles ridden by the company's salesman.

• **Stop yer tickling, Jock!** ▶ A catchphrase used as a lover's admonition in the first half of the 20th century; from the title of one of Sir Harry Lauder's most famous comic songs (1904).

• **Stormin' Norman** ▶ Nickname of US General H Norman Schwarzkopf (1935–   ), who was commander-in-chief of Operation Desert Storm in the Gulf War of 1991. His father, the police chief Herbert Norman Schwarzkopf (criticized in 1932 for his handling of the Lindbergh baby murder), gave him only the letter H as a first name because he disliked the family name Herbert. H Norman, credited with an IQ of 170, acquired his nickname shortly after entering the army for his ebullient manner and unpredictable temper (hence his other nickname, **The Bear**). He won two Purple Hearts and three Silver Stars for courage in battle during the Vietnam War. Conversely, he also became known for his love of ballet, opera, and amateur conjuring. He was highly praised for achieving the success of Desert Storm at a minimal cost in casualties to the allied forces.

• **Stormont** ▶ The seat of the government of Northern Ireland, set amidst 300 acres of parkland some six miles east of Belfast. The centrepiece of the site is Parliament House, designed in the 'Official Classical' style by Sir Arnold Thornley and opened in 1932 by King George V. Nearby stands Stormont Castle, formerly the official residence of Viscount Craigavon, Northern Ireland's first prime minister. The other main administrative building is Dundonald House, designed by Gibson and Taylor and opened in 1963. Stormont was the seat of the Northern Ireland Parliament from 1932 until 1972, when direct rule from Westminster was imposed; as such it came to symbolize Protestant domination in the province. Since 1998 Parliament House has been the seat of the Northern Ireland Assembly, a cross-community body set up under the Good Friday Agreement, while Stormont Castle is the official office of Northern Ireland's first minister. *See also*: power sharing.

• **stormtroopers** ▸ *See*: Brown Shirts.

• **Storyville** ▸ The red-light district of New Orleans, in which jazz was born. Black musicians congregated in the area, where they could find employment playing for the many brothels in the neighbourhood. Storyville was apparently named after a General Story, who attempted to prevent his troops from acquiring venereal diseases by confining all prostitutes to one area of New Orleans; this was marked by red lights, which his men were forbidden to pass (hence 'red-light district'). *See*: Basin Street.

• **strafe** ▸ (German *strafen*, to punish) A word borrowed in contempt from the Germans during World War I, one of their favourite slogans being *Gott strafe England!* It was applied to any sharp and sudden bombardment. During World War II it came to mean the machine-gunning of troops or civilians by low-flying aircraft.

• **Straffen murders** ▸ The crimes of a British child-murderer, John Thomas Straffen (1930–   ), a retarded 22-year-old who spent his early childhood in a school for the mentally deficient. In 1947, at the age of 17, he was institutionalized after an assault on a 13-year-old girl. On his release at the age of 21 he moved to Bath, where he strangled two young girls, in order – as he said – to annoy the police (whom he hated). At his trial at Taunton assizes, in October 1951, he was declared unfit to plead and sent to Broadmoor asylum. Six months later he escaped, and during his brief period of freedom claimed the life of another young victim, Linda Bowyer. He was tried again in July 1952, this time at Winchester, and found guilty; his death sentence was commuted to life imprisonment.

• **straight** ▸ 1. Honest or legitimate; from the jargon of criminals who are known for 'bending the rules'. 2. Heterosexual or a heterosexual. 3. Conventional or a conventional person – 'He looked a real straight in his business suit'. 4. Drug-users' slang to describe a person who does not take drugs.

• **Straker, Henry** ▸ The chauffeur of John Tanner in the play *Man and Superman* (1903) by George Bernard Shaw (1856–1950). Straker is described as the 'New Man' of the polytechnic revolution. Skilled, confident, and a scientific socialist, he is superior in every respect to his master, whose gentle-

manly class, Shaw believed, was doomed to extinction by the new economic and political forces embodied by Straker.

• **Strangelove** ▸ A fanatic or insane militarist who advocates large-scale pre-emptive nuclear strikes. The name comes from Stanley Kubrick's 1963 film *Dr Strangelove: or How I Learned to Stop Worrying and Love the Bomb*, a black comedy satirizing the nuclear arms race. The film starred Peter Sellers as Strangelove – a demented ex-Nazi scientist – and in two other parts. At one point a blustering US general, played by George C. Scott, comments:

> I don't say we wouldn't get our hair mussed,
> but I do say no more than ten to twenty million
> people killed.

• **strangeness** ▸ A property of certain elementary particles first suggested by the US physicist Murray Gell-Mann (1929–   ) in 1953. It was recognized at the time that some mesons were 'strange' in that they had abnormally long lifetimes. Gell-Mann resolved the problem by introducing a new quantum property, strangeness, possessed by such particles. *See also*: quark.

• **Stratofortress** ▸ The US Boeing **B-52** eight-engined strategic bomber, a long-serving symbol of US military might. There were eight basic variants of the initial design; the earliest version, the B-52A, went into service in August 1954, and the last, the B-52H, became operational in March 1961. The B-52D was modified for high-density bombing and used extensively during the Vietnam War from bases in Guam and the Philippines. The B-52G and H are faster (maximum speed 595 mph), have a longer range (8500–10,000 mi), are equipped with the latest electronic weapons control and digital navigation systems, and can carry sophisticated air-to-air missiles or nuclear weapons, including air-launched cruise missiles. They were still in service in the early 2000s, when they were used in airstrikes against Afghanistan.

• **streaking** ▸ Running naked in a public place, so called because the **streaker** has to run like a streak of lightning to avoid being caught. This became something of a craze in the 1970s, especially at football and cricket matches.

• **stream of consciousness** ▸ A technique of novel writing in which the continuous stream of impressions, thoughts, and feelings that pass through a character's mind are recorded with little or no explanation from the author. The term was coined by the US psychologist William James (1890) and first applied in a literary context by the British writer May Sinclair (1918). Dorothy Richardson's *Pointed Roofs* (1915) is usually considered the first stream-of-consciousness novel. The technique was subsequently developed by James Joyce, particularly in his *Ulysses* (1922), Virginia Woolf, and William Faulkner.

• **street credibility** or **street cred** ▶ A convincing command or knowledge of the styles, fashions, music, etc., current among young urban people. To be seen wearing the wrong sort of trainers, for example, might seriously damage one's street cred. The term was much used by rock journalists during the punk era of the late 1970s, when lack of street cred was considered the most serious accusation that could be levelled at a band.

• **Strength through joy** ▶ *See:* Kraft durch Freude.

• **Stresa Front** ▶ An agreement, signed in April 1935 at Stresa in Piedmont, between the UK, France, and Italy, to uphold the international status quo and to oppose further breaches of the Paris Peace settlement of 1919. The pact was concluded in response to Hitler's declaration of German rearmament in March; the three powers also agreed to defend the independence of Austria from the threat of German *Anschluss.* The Front presented no serious threat to German ambitions in Europe and collapsed only six months later, after Mussolini's invasion of Abyssinia.

• **stretch limo** ▶ *See:* limousine.

• **strides** ▶ Slang for trousers, first heard in the early years of the 20th century; later widely adopted in Australian and Cockney slang.

• **Strike Command** ▶ The RAF Command established on 30 April 1968 by the amalgamation of the historic Bomber and Fighter Commands, in accordance with a government proposal in a Defence White Paper of February 1967. In November 1968 Strike Command also absorbed the Coastal and Signals Commands, and in September 1972 Air Support Command was also incorporated. This reorganization was undertaken to improve efficiency and cut costs in the wake of the decline in the size of the RAF since 1945.

• **stripagram** ▶ *See:* kissagram.

• **striptease** ▶ A theatrical or cabaret performance in which a woman, called a **stripper**, slowly and provocatively undresses to music. This erotic entertainment was introduced to US burlesque shows from about 1920, in an attempt to compete with the growing attraction of films. The most famous of the early strippers was Gypsy Rose Lee. Towards the end of the 20th century male strippers began to perform for female audiences in pubs and clubs, etc. (*see:* the full monty *at* monty). The more in-

timate form of striptease known as lap dancing also became popular at this time.

• **Structuralism** ▶ An approach to such disciplines as linguistics, anthropology, psychology, and literature based in each case on an analysis of the structural relations between its elements. **Structural linguistics**, deriving from the work of Ferdinand de Saussure (1857–1913), regards language as a self-contained system that should be described and analysed without consideration of its comparative and historical aspects. **Structural anthropology**, deriving from the work of Claude Levi-Strauss (1908–  ), applies similar principles to the study of human cultures, which are analysed in terms of certain basic structures that are thought to underlie all human thought. **Structural psychology** offers an analysis of human thought processes in terms of the individual sensations and feelings of which they are constituted. In the 1960s and 1970s a structuralist approach to literary criticism and the analysis of popular culture was developed by such critics as Roland Barthes (1915–80) and became widely influential in the study of the humanities.

• **strut** ▶ A slow and somewhat deliberate jazz dance that was popular from the 1900s, especially among those who could not dance well.

• **Student Nonviolent Coordinating Committee** ▶ (SNCC) A civil rights organization founded by Black and White student activists in Raleigh, North Carolina, in April 1960. In the early 1960s the SNCC joined other civil rights groups, such as the Congress of Racial Equality (CORE) and Martin Luther King's Southern Christian Leadership Conference (SCLC) in organizing campaigns to desegregate lunch counters and other facilities in the South; it also campaigned to encourage Black voter registration. The SNCC originally espoused the nonviolent integrationist philosophy of King but by 1966, under the leadership of Stokely Carmichael, it had abandoned these, embracing the militant philosophy of Black Power and supporting the revolutionary tactics of the Black Panthers. The organization collapsed in 1969 when Carmichael's successor, Hubert 'Rap' Brown, was convicted of armed robbery. *See:* civil rights movement.

• **stuffed shirt** ▶ A pompous and unnecessarily formal person; the phrase conjures up the image of a slightly overweight man almost 'poured' into a starched dress shirt. Examples of its use in America go back to 1913, but it is often associated with Clare Boothe Luce (1903–87), who used it as the title of her first book (1933).

• **Stuka** ▸ (short for *Stutzkampfbomber*) The Junkers JU-87, the German dive bomber which saw action on all fronts during World War II. The first production version, JU-87 A-1, appeared in 1937. The aircraft became notorious during the first year of the war, owing to its role in the Blitzkrieg campaigns in Poland and France, when German ground and air superiority made the screaming Stukas appear to be invincible. Despite the accuracy of the dive-bombing technique, the JU-87's lack of effective armaments made it vulnerable to fighter attack and Stukas suffered severe losses during the Battle of Britain. The Stuka was less than popular among German aircrews, as the pilots often lost consciousness when they pulled out of the dive as a result of g-forces.

• **stuntman** or **stuntwoman** ▸ A skilled performer who stands in for an actor or actress in the potentially dangerous scenes in a movie. Many early stars risked their own lives in stunts, taking pride in handling difficult work or succumbing to a director's enthusiasm for realism. D. W. Griffith floated Lillian Gish on a drifting ice chunk in *Way Down East* (1920), a daring scene that almost cost her her right hand; the ice-floe sequence is famous for its excitement and realism. The comedian Harold Lloyd dislocated his shoulder in *Safety Last* (1923), when he hung from a 12-storey building with only a projecting mattress for protection. Stuntmen, too, have been seriously injured or even killed by stunts that misfired, as, for example, when a helicopter was brought down by ground explosions during filming of *Twilight Zone: The Movie* (1983). Stuntmen have become recognized macho figures in America and are the subject of at least one major film, *Hooper* (1978), starring Burt Reynolds.

• **Stupenda, La** ▸ Nickname of the Australian opera singer Joan Sutherland (1926– ). She established her reputation in coloratura roles with her Lucia in *Lucia di Lammermoor* at Covent Garden in 1959. Thereafter she appeared in all the major opera houses of Europe and America giving outstanding performances as the heroines in *Norma*, *La Traviata*, and *La fille du régiment*.

• **subtitle** ▸ In the cinema, the written dialogue superimposed at the bottom of the picture to translate a foreign-language film. In silent films the titles were not superimposed, but came in frames immediately after the unheard dialogue. These **intertitles**, as they are properly known, sometimes addressed the audience directly: 'Please read the titles to yourself', 'If Annoyed When Here Please Tell the Management' (the latter accompanied by a drawing of a man touching a woman's chin). The English captions displayed above the proscenium arch at Covent Garden and some other opera houses when a foreign-language work is being performed are known as **surtitles**.

• **subtopia** ▸ A word coined (from *suburb* and *Utopia*) by the British architectural critic Ian Nairn in 1954 to denote the sprawling suburban housing estates built to satisfy the town workers' desire for country surroundings without relinquishing the amenities of the town.

• **Suchow, Battle of** ▸ The decisive battle between the communist People's Liberation Army and the Nationalist forces, which began in Suchow, central China, on 7 November 1948. With half a million men deployed by both sides, the 56-day struggle ended in the complete annihilation of Chiang Kai-Shek's military power. This led directly to the establishment of the Chinese communist regime in Peking in October 1949.

• **sudden infant death syndrome** ▸ (SIDS) The medical name for the sudden and inexplicable death of an infant aged between seven days and two years, typically while he or she is lying in the cot (hence **cot death** – the popular name). SIDS is diagnosed when no specific cause of death can be identified; suggested possible causes have included virus infections and allergies. There is evidence that the incidence of SIDS is lower in more affluent families and in breast-fed babies; it remains a significant cause of infant mortality. In the early 1990s advice to minimize the risk of SIDS included laying the infant on its back to sleep, not smoking over the cot, not overwrapping the baby, and calling medical help if in doubt. These measures reduced SIDS by 55% in the UK.

• **Sudeten crisis** ▸ The international crisis provoked by Germany's claim to the Czech Sudetenland, which was eventually conceded to Hitler at the Munich Conference in September 1938. The Sudetenland, which had a largely German population, was placed within Czechoslovakia by the Treaty of St Germain in 1919. However, agitation by the Sudeten German (Nazi) Party in the 1930s provoked increasing demands for regional autonomy and the redress of economic grievances, which were eventually conceded by the Czech government in April 1938. Because this failed to quell the pro-Nazi agitation, in September 1938 France, the UK, Italy, and Germany met in Munich; here, to avert war, they issued an ultimatum to the Czech government to cede the Sudetenland to Germany by 10 October. The Munich Agreement marked the nadir of appeasement. Within months Hitler had occupied Prague, making it clear that the appeasement policy had failed and that a conflict was now unavoidable. After World War II the area was restored to the Czechs, who proceeded to expel most of the German population.

• **Suez crisis** ▶ The crisis in the Middle East precipitated by the nationalization of the Suez Canal by the Egyptian president, Gamal Abdel Nasser, on 26 July 1956. Nasser had acted in the wake of America's refusal to help finance the Aswan High Dam, which they had formerly promised to do. This change of policy was a result of Egypt's growing affinity with the Soviet bloc. Nasser's seizure of the canal incensed the British and the French, who feared for the safety of oil supplies to Western Europe. As diplomatic efforts to resolve the crisis continued, the UK and France prepared secret plans for the military retrieval of the canal zone and the overthrow of Nasser, who was perceived by Anthony Eden, the British prime minister, as a new Hitler. They found a ready ally in Israel, which had been in an almost continuous state of conflict with Egypt since its foundation in 1948. The Israelis invaded Egypt on 29 October 1956; British and French forces then landed at Port Said and Port Faud, on the pretext of supporting the UN call for a ceasefire, and moved to occupy the canal zone. The duplicity of the Anglo-French action distressed the Americans who threatened to support the UN's call for the imposition of economic sanctions. The British and French were therefore forced to withdraw on 22 December and the Israelis withdrew in March 1957. The episode served to underline the UK's postwar decline as an imperial power and the dependence of British foreign policy on America. It also raised Nasser to the status of an Arab nationalist hero, ensuring that British and French influence in the Middle East was deeply compromised. Egypt retained control of the Suez Canal and Eden was so widely criticized that he resigned shortly after the debacle.

• **suffragettes** ▶ The militant women who agitated for the right to vote, especially in the years 1903 to 1914. They included those who sought votes for women on the same property qualifications as applied to men at that time and those who demanded universal suffrage for all adults. From 1903 the militant members of the Women's Social and Political Union, led by Emmeline Pankhurst (1858–1928) and her daughter Christabel Pankhurst (1880–1958), chained themselves to railings, attacked property, refused to pay taxes, and held public meetings and demonstrations:

> We have taken this action, because as women... it is our duty even to break the law in order to call attention to the reasons why we do so.

– EMMELINE PANKHURST, speech in court, 21 October 1908.

The suffragettes were repeatedly sent to prison (*see*: Cat and Mouse Act), where they endangered their lives by hunger strikes and had to endure brutal forcible feeding:

> We are not ashamed of what we have done, because, when you have a great cause to fight for, the moment of greatest humiliation is the moment when the spirit is proudest. – CHRISTABEL PANKHURST, speech, 19 March 1908.

With a few exceptions, the male members of the establishment behaved badly, while the women conducted themselves with determination and dignity:

> I see some rats have got in: let them squeal, it doesn't matter. – LLOYD GEORGE, interrupting a speech when suffragettes entered the hall.

During World War I the women's organizations sensibly supported the war effort; in 1918 Lloyd George rewarded them by granting the vote to women over 30, subject to property qualifications. In 1928 these qualifications were removed and women became the political equals of men. The **Shrieking Sisterhood**, as their opponents called the suffragettes, had triumphed.

• **sugar daddy** ▶ An elderly wealthy man who lavishes expensive gifts on a much younger woman in return for sexual favours. The female equivalent, **sugar mummy**, is rarely heard (*see*: toy-boy).

• **Sugar Ray Robinson** ▶ The ring name of US boxer Walker Smith (1920–89). He acquired the name Ray Robinson when he used the amateur certificate of another boxer with this name in order to be able to take part in a contest. The epithet 'Sugar' was added later – a reference to his style, which was described as 'sweet as sugar'. In 1940 he turned professional, becoming world welterweight champion (1946–51) and middleweight champion (five times; 1951–60). He fought 202 professional contests and lost only 19 (12 of which were after he was 40).

• **suit** ▶ A 1980s term for an executive or bureaucrat, suggesting dullness, anonymity, and timeserving. It seems to have spread from advertising agencies, where the casually dressed 'creatives' refer in this way to the expensively tailored executives who deal personally with clients. The term was popularized by Heath's cartoon strip 'The Suits' in Private Eye. An **empty suit** is an executive whose specious exterior, mastery of the latest professional jargon, and air of strenuous activity mask the fact that he is doing little or no useful work. *See also*: men in grey suits.

• **Sultan of Swat** ▶ *See*: Babe.

• **Summerhill** ▸ The experimental coeducational boarding school, established first at Lyme Regis in 1924 and subsequently at Leiston, Suffolk, by the controversial writer and educationalist Alexander Sutherland Neill (1883–1973). Neill's distrust of the conventional education system, deriving from his own experience of teaching, led to his exploration of the progressive educational theories of such philosophers and psychologists as Rousseau, Freud, and Dewey. From these researches he distilled a theory of education that stressed the importance of absolute freedom from authority. Consequently, Summerhill became a self-governing community, where staff and pupils each had a vote on matters of policy and pupils could do exactly what they liked as long as they do not infringe the rights of others. Neill's ideas and motivation are explained in a number of his books, including *A Dominie's Log* (1915), *That Dreadful School* (1937), and the autobiography *Neill! Neill! Orange Peel* (1973).

• **summer time** ▸ *See*: daylight saving.

• **sun** ▸
    **a place in the sun** A favourable position that allows for development; a share in something that one has a natural right to. The phrase achieved a particular significance in the wake of the Agadir Crisis of 1901, when Wilhelm II of Germany (*see*: Kaiser Bill) spoke of his nation taking steps to ensure that 'no one can dispute with us the place in the sun that is our due.' He was referring specifically to Germany's demand for African and Asian colonies.

• **Sundance Kid** ▸ *See*: Butch Cassidy and the Sundance Kid.

• **Sunderland flying-boat** ▸ The Short Brothers Sunderland first appeared in 1938, remained in service throughout World War II, and continued to serve with the RAF until 1959. With its long-range capabilities and heavy armaments, including bombs, depth charges, and mines, the Sunderland specialized in convoy escort and antisubmarine warfare. it was the mainstay of Coastal Command's operations in the North Sea, Atlantic, and Mediterranean; it was also used during the Berlin airlift in 1948 and during the Korean War.

• **sunlighting** ▸ Slang for doing two jobs at the same time. The term derives from **moonlighting**, the practice of having an extra (often secret) job at night. High-powered sunlighters are also known as **two overcoat men**. They arrive at one office in the morning, hang up their overcoats to make it appear as if they are in the building, and then – armed with a second overcoat – travel to the offices of their other employers. Some MEPs are said to be persistent offenders.

• **Sunningdale Agreement** ▸ An agreement made at Sunningdale, Berkshire, in 1973 between the British and Irish prime ministers (Edward Heath and Liam Cosgrave, respectively) and leaders of the main Northern Irish political parties concerning the government of Northern Ireland. Protestant and Catholic leaders had already agreed to serve together in a new Northern Ireland Assembly responsible for all domestic matters except security (*see*: power sharing). The Sunningdale Agreement proposed to supplement this with a Council of All Ireland drawing its members from both the Irish Parliament and the Northern Ireland Assembly. The Agreement raised hopes of a permanent settlement in the province but was soon derailed by the hostility of rank-and-file Unionists. The Northern Ireland Assembly proved unworkable and was dissolved after only four months; the Council of All Ireland never met.

• **Sunny Jim** ▸ A name often patronizingly applied to men, whatever their name, or to naughty small boys. It comes from the advertising slogan created in the early years of the 20th century by two US women, Miss Ficken and Minnie Maud Hanff, for Force breakfast cereal. The slogan, which was accompanied by a cartoon drawing, went:

> High over the fence leaps Sunny Jim
> Force is the food that raises him.

In the 1970s the name was often used by the media for the British Labour prime minister (1976–79) James Callaghan, later Lord Callaghan (1912– ).

• **sunrise industry** ▸ A modern high-tech industry, especially one involving electronics or information technology. So called because these are seen as the industries of the future, the era that is just dawning. There is also an echo of Japan, the Land of the Rising Sun; many of these industries in the UK are Japanese-owned. *See also*: sunset industry.

• **sunset** ▸
    **ride off into the sunset** A cliché for a happy and romantic ending. It derives from the era of silent films, which often ended with the hero and heroine riding off into the sunset presumably to spend the rest of their days happily together. It is the visual equivalent of 'They lived happily ever after'.

• **sunset industry** ▸ The industries that were the mainstay of the British economy before the era of new technology; for example, coal, steel, and shipbuilding. These have been referred to as sunset industries since the 1980s because of their evident decline. Those sunset industries that have large 19th-century factories, such as steel works, cotton mills, and heavy engineering companies, are also known as **smoke-stack industries**. *See also*: sunrise industry.

• **Super Bowl** ► In US professional football, the championship game held annually in late January between the best teams of the National Football League's two conferences, the American and National. Super Bowl I (Roman numerals are used) was played in 1967 in Los Angeles with Green Bay Packers defeating Kansas City Chiefs 35-10. For the first two years, the game was officially the 'AFL-NFL World Championship Game'. The name 'Super Bowl' came from Lamar Hunt, the owner of Kansas City Chiefs, after he watched his daughter play with a 'Super Ball', and the title was adopted for the third game. About three out of every four Americans watch the telecast in addition to the millions more who are watching in other parts of the world. The price for a television commercial during ABC's Super Bowl broadcast is around a million dollars for 30 seconds. *See also*: Rose Bowl.

• **Superbrat** ► One of many epithets applied to the US tennis player John McEnroe (1959–   ); his other nicknames include **The Mouth** and **Mac the Mouth**. He became a professional while still in his teens and quickly established himself as one of the top international players, winning the Wimbledon singles title in 1981, 1983, and 1984. His career was marred by bouts of uncontrollable temper and lack of sportsmanship on court, which earned him his nicknames: he was notorious for arguing with the umpire – **You cannot be serious**, a retort to an unfavourable decision, became his best-known catchphrase.

• **superconductivity** ► The disappearance of electrical resistance in certain substances at very low temperatures (in the vicinity of absolute zero). The effect was discovered in 1911 and is now known to occur in 26 metals and many compounds and alloys. The so-called **BCS theory** explaining superconductivity is named after the three scientists who proposed it in 1957, J. Bardeen (1908–91), L. N. Cooper (1930–   ), and J. R. Schrieffer (1931–   ). According to this theory an electron moving through a crystal lattice can distort it sufficiently to affect a second passing electron. Thus, in superconductors the current carriers are not single electrons but bound pairs of electrons (called Cooper pairs). The BCS theory assumes that the flow of Cooper pairs is unchanged by interacting with the lattice and therefore continues indefinitely.

Superconducting coils can have large continuous currents passing through them creating powerful magnetic fields. These magnetic fields are made use of in some particle accelerators and other devices (*see also*: Josephson effects).

In 1986 a different type of superconductivity was discovered in which a similar phenomenon occurs at much higher temperatures (as high as 100 K). This so-called **high-temperature superconductivity**, has not yet been explained.

• **supercontinent** or **protocontinent** ► The putative huge land mass known as Pangaea that, according to the geological theory of plate tectonics, formed about 240 million years ago and subsequently broke up to produce the Earth's present continents.

• **Superfortress** ► The US B-29 high-altitude strategic bomber, which became operational in June 1944. The four-engined bomber set a new standard in terms of engine power, weight, armament, pressurization, and airborne control systems. The construction and delivery of over 3000 B-29s to the USAF by August 1945 marked one of the greatest feats in aviation history. *See*: Enola Gay.

• **supergrass** ► *See*: grass.

• **supergroup** ► A rock band formed by musicians who are already famous and successful. In the late 1960s, several well-known musicians left their groups and several bands split up altogether. When the disengaged performers recombined, the new ensembles were called supergroups. The title proved hard to live up to, and the original supergroups flourished only into the mid-1970s. Perhaps the best known was Crosby, Stills and Nash, formed in 1969 by David Crosby of the Byrds, Stephen Stills of Buffalo Springfield, and Graham Nash of the Hollies. Later joined by Neil Young of Buffalo Springfield, they produced a 1970 hit album, *Deja Vu*. Other noted supergroups included Blind Faith, Humble Pie, and Emerson, Lake and Palmer.

• **Supermac** ► A nickname of the British Conservative prime minister Harold Macmillan (1894–1986); the name stuck after the *Evening Standard*'s cartoonist Vicky drew him in the guise of Superman, the US comic-strip hero (November 1958). *See also*: Mac the Knife.

• **Superman** ► 1. A hypothetical superior human being of high intellectual and moral attainment. The term *Übermensch* was invented by the German philosopher Nietzsche (1844–1900); the English translation was popularized by George Bernard Shaw's play *Man and Superman* (1903). 2. A US comic-strip hero, who later featured on radio and television and (1978–82) in a series of blockbuster films starring Christopher Reeve. The character first appeared in *Action Comics* (1 June 1938) in a strip by Jerry Siegel and Joe Shuster. According to the story, the infant superhero was rescued from the planet Krypton shortly before it exploded and brought up on Earth by human parents. He soon discovers that he has superhuman powers, including X-ray vision, invincible strength, and the ability to fly 'faster than a speeding bullet'. While maintaining an outward identity as Clark Kent, a mild-mannered newspaper reporter, he adopts the guise of Superman to fight crime and uphold 'truth, justice, and the American way.' His Achilles' heel is his vulnerability to kryptonite, an element originating in the planet of his birth. An ironic subplot is provided by Kent's infatuation with a fellow reporter, Lois Lane, whose hero-worship of Superman leads her to slight her quiet colleague, Clark Kent. In 1991 DC Comics, publishers of the strip, announced that the two characters would finally marry, 52 years after they first met.

• **supermarket** ▶ A large self-service store carrying a wide variety of food and other products. In the UK the first such stores were opened in the 1950s by Premier Supermarkets, under the management of Patrick Galvani (1922–    ), who had been impressed with what he had seen in America. Very soon every high street in the country had its own supermarket, belonging to one of a few large chains. There are three basic principles underlying the supermarket: self service; providing a wide range of groceries, fruit and vegetables, meat, fish, etc., all in one place instead of four or five; and charging a lower price than elsewhere. Sir Jack Cohen, the founder of the Tesco chain, used as his motto Pile it high, sell it cheap.

In the 1980s the supermarket principle was extended to include the sale of a wider variety of goods in one very large out-of-town store (*see*: hypermarket).

• **super rat** ▶ A breed of rat that is immune to most poisons. It first appeared in America in the mid-1970s and has since been identified in Europe and Asia.

• **super realism** or **hyper realism** ▶ A genre of art that developed chiefly in America in the 1970s. The aim of artists working in the style was absolute verisimilitude. In painting this involved extensive use of photographs (**photorealism**) and in sculpture the making of casts direct from the human form.

• **supersonic** ▶ Denoting an aircraft that can fly faster than the speed of sound in the medium in which it is flying. The **sound barrier** is an obstacle to supersonic flight that was first overcome by the US Bell XS-1 rocket aircraft in 1947. It occurs because the pressure waves created by the aircraft cannot escape in a forward direction as the supersonic aircraft is travelling faster than the waves; the result is that shock waves build up on the aircraft's wings causing instability. The barrier is overcome by greater streamlining and swept-back wings. Concorde became the first successful commercial supersonic aircraft when put into service in 1976.

• **superstar** ▶ *See*: star.

• **superstore** ▶ *See*: hypermarket.

• **supply-side economics** ▶ An approach to macroeconomics popular with economists since the late 1970s. It emphasizes the importance of the conditions under which goods and services are supplied to the market and believes that these can be optimized by allowing the free market to operate without interference. Supply-side economists hold that employment and output will both rise if governments cut taxes and expenditure, reduce unemployment and welfare benefits, and limit the powers of trade unions. These policies, which represent a complete rejection of Keynesianism, were adopted by many Western governments in the 1980s.

• **suprematism** ▶ A school of pure abstract art founded by the Russian artist Kasimir Malevich in about 1915; it was characterized by the use of simple geometric shapes to express 'pure artistic feeling'. Malevich's earliest work in this style (1913) consisted of a black square on a white background; still more radical were the white squares on a white background he produced in 1918–19. Constructivism was an important influence on European constructivism and the Bauhaus style.

• **Supreme Soviet** ▶ The national legislature, elected every five years by citizens over the age of 18, which was notionally the supreme representative of the popular will in the former Soviet Union. It consisted of two chambers, the Soviet of the Union and the Soviet of the Nationalities (the latter giving largely symbolic representation to the various territories of the Soviet federation). Sessions took place twice a year, and matters of domestic and foreign affairs were considered by a series of elected standing commissions. The Supreme Soviet also elected the Council of Ministers (the Soviet government) and the Presidium (collective presidency). Although largely a 'rubber stamp' body for most of its existence, under Gorbachov the Supreme Soviet was more assertive in pressing for reform at local and national level.

• **surrealism**▶ A European movement in art and literature that flourished between the wars; it was launched in 1924 when its leader, the poet André Breton, published the Surrealist Manifesto in Paris. The aim of the movement was to express the irrational force of dreams and the subconscious, uncontrolled by reason or aesthetic and moral concepts. In practice surrealist painting is of two main types: hand-painted dream scenes as exemplified by the works of Chirico, Dali, and Magritte; and abstract forms created through complete spontaneity of technique, as seen in the works of Arp, Roy, and Miró. In literature, such writers as Breton, Paul Éluard, and Louis Aragon experimented with automatic writing and the free association of images. *Compare*: dadaism.

• **surrender**▶
**We shall never surrender** The climax to the speech delivered to the House of Commons on 4 June 1940, in the immediate aftermath of Dunkirk, by Winston Churchill. With Germany overrunning Europe, France on the point of collapse, and the UK apparently facing imminent invasion, Churchill pledged that whatever happened Britain would fight on, 'if necessary for years, if necessary alone'.

> We shall not flag or fail. We shall go on to the end. We shall fight in France, we shall fight with growing confidence and growing strength in the air, we shall defend our island, whatever the cost may be, we shall fight on the beaches, we shall fight on the landing grounds, we shall fight in the fields and in the streets, we shall fight in the hills; we shall never surrender.

*See also*: blood, toil, tears and sweat; their finest hour *at* hour.

• **surrogate motherhood**▶ An arrangement in which a woman agrees to undergo pregnancy in order to produce a child for another individual or a couple. The surrogate mother may be inseminated by the male of the couple (either by intercourse or by AI) or by sperm from another donor (for instance from a sperm bank). Such arrangements may be the only recourse for infertile childless couples and for gay couples, but they can be fraught with emotional and practical difficulties. In the UK, under the Surrogacy Arrangements Act (1985), all forms of commercial surrogacy service, *i.e.* those involving financial gain, are illegal and would-be surrogate mothers are unable to advertise their services. However, private surrogacy arrangements, even ones involving payment, are legal although they may prove difficult to enforce, since the bio-

logical mother has exclusive rights to the child. In America, legislation varies from state to state.

• **Surtsey**▶ An island that was spectacularly created off the S coast of Iceland on 14 November 1963. It was formed as the result of a powerful underwater volcanic eruption: within weeks the island had reached a height of 567 feet and a length of 1.3 miles. As soon as the eruption had abated the scientists arrived, realizing that this was a unique opportunity to study the processes by which flora and fauna become established. First to arrive were the birds; the seeds that came with them produced the first flower in June 1967. Within three more years four plant types and 18 mosses were found to be flourishing. The island itself was named Surtsey after a legendary Norse giant.

• **survivable**▶ US military jargon describing weapons systems, communications networks, etc., that are capable of surviving a nuclear attack and delivering a counterstrike. *See*: first strike.

• **survivalist**▶ Someone who aims to survive the nuclear doom that he or she considers inevitable by taking to the wilderness, stockpiling food and equipment, and learning survival skills, including the use of deadly weapons. Determined to survive not only the immediate catastrophe but also the 'every-man-for-himself' world that will follow, US survivalist groups have built up impressive armouries and take part in exercises of an almost paramilitary nature. The movement's ethos combines nostalgia for the values of the US frontier with social Darwinism of the most virulent kind: some adherents seem to regard a nuclear disaster as nature's way of culling that part of humanity (the vast majority) too feeble to will its own survival. Such attitudes are often combined with religious fundamentalism and an obsession with racial purity. In the 1980s and 1990s survivalism spawned a whole subculture of shops, suppliers, and 'how-to' literature, most of which lingered affectionately over the lethal properties of various types of weapon. Although many adherents are probably no more than overgrown boy scouts, the movement has an obvious appeal to the inadequate and deranged. Michael Ryan, who in 1987 shot 16 people dead in the village of Hungerford, was an avid student of survivalist literature (*see*: Hungerford massacre).

• **survivor syndrome**▶ Symptoms exhibited by survivors of a natural disaster, plane crash, massacre, etc., in which many others died. Psychological problems, such as guilt, anxiety, or depression can develop years after the event. This has most clearly been demonstrated by some survivors of the holocaust. *See also*: post-traumatic stress disorder.

• **sus** or **suss** ▶ British and New Zealand slang meaning to work out, discover. Thus to **suss out** someone or something is to discover that person or thing's true nature or character, often by intuition. The word originated in the police jargon of the mid-1920s, being a shortened form of 'suspect'; it became fashionable among beatniks in the early 1960s and has been common since the 1970s. *See also*: sus law.

• **sus law** ▶ Colloquial name for a former British law authorizing the arrest of a person *suspected* of loitering with criminal intent in a public place. The original sus law formed part of the Vagrancy Act (1824); it was repealed in 1981, mainly owing to complaints that the police used it as a charter for harassing young Blacks.

• **Susso** ▶ Australian slang from the 1940s for someone claiming government sustenance.

• **Sutton Hoo treasure** ▶ An Anglo-Saxon ship-burial of the early 7th century, discovered at Sutton Hoo near Woodbridge, Suffolk, in 1939. It is one of the richest ever found and the treasure, consisting of a sword and sheath, helmet, bowls and other objects in precious metals, is now in the British Museum. The find is of considerable archaeological and historical importance.

• **Suvla Bay** ▶ *See*: Gallipoli.

• **Suzuki method** ▶ A method for teaching young children to play a musical instrument devised by the Japanese violinist Shinichi Suzuki (1898–1998). He believed that any child can be trained to develop musical ability, just as any child can learn to speak its mother tongue. In the 1930s Suzuki began to develop his method for teaching the violin, which he called the Mother-Tongue Approach. After the war he accepted a post teaching the violin to young children at a small school in Matsumoto, basing his lessons on a sequential repertoire that presented musical and technical points in a logical manner. Within a very short period his pupils were showing both technical skill and considerable musicality. After other teachers had studied with Suzuki, his method was extended to include the cello, piano, and flute. The Suzuki method had reached America by the early 1960s and has since been taught in some 40 countries.

Ideally, children should begin to develop their musical potential in this way when 3–4 years old, but it is never too late to start. Suzuki pupils are taught to develop a basic competence on their instruments before learning to read music, in the same way that children are taught to read only after their ability to speak has been established. Moreover, just as children learn to speak in an environment filled with language, so parents should make music an important part of their children's early experiences. As Suzuki himself said, 'If a child hears fine music from the day of his birth, and learns to play it himself, he develops sensitivity, discipline and endurance. He gets a beautiful heart'.

> Perhaps it is music that will save the world. – PABLO CASALS, after hearing Suzuki-trained children playing.–

• **swastika** ▶ An elaborate cross-shaped design, also known as a gammadion or (with arms bent anticlockwise) fylfot, originally used as a charm to ward off evil and bring good luck (the word is derived from Sanskrit *svasti*, good fortune). The version with arms bent clockwise was adopted by Hitler as the Nazi emblem in about 1920, probably from the practice of the German Baltic Corps, who began to wear it on their helmets after service in Finland, where it was used as a distinguishing mark on Finnish aeroplanes. It was described by Winston Churchill as the 'crooked cross' and came to symbolize the immense evil of Nazi Germany.

• **swat team** ▶ Special weapons and tactics team. In America, a military-style police unit brought in to deal with situations that cannot be controlled by regular police officers.

• **sweater girl** ▶ A mainly 1940s term for a young woman with a well-developed bust made particularly apparent by the wearing of a clinging sweater. The original sweater girl was the Hollywood actress Lana Turner (1920–95), who in 1937–38 posed for publicity stills without a blouse beneath her tight sweater; the photograph became a favourite pin-up during World War II.

• **Sweeney** ▶ British rhyming slang for the Flying Squad (from Sweeney Todd), a high-powered division of the Metropolitan Police in London. Sweeney Todd was a fictional barber in a play by George Dibden Pitt (1799–1855), who murdered his customers. In the 1970s there was a popular and (for the time) hard-hitting TV police series called *The Sweeney*, starring John Thaw and Dennis Waterman.

• **sweetheart agreement** ▶ An agreement reached peaceably by direct negotiation between employer and employees, first heard in Australia but subsequently elsewhere.

• **swell** ▶ *Single woman earning lots of lolly.* One of the more transient acronyms of the late 1980s that proliferated following the success of the word yuppie. It plays on the word's older usage, a rich swankily dressed person.

• **swine flu** ► A disease of pigs caused by a virus that is closely related to the human flu virus and may even have originated from humans. Infected animals show respiratory signs, such as coughing, loss of appetite, and fever. Outbreaks of the disease are confined to North America, usually occurring in the autumn and winter months.

• **swine vesicular disease** ► A disease of pigs first identified in Italy in 1966 and appearing in the UK in 1972. It is caused by a virus and can be transmitted to humans. Affected animals develop blisters on the feet, which rupture, causing transient lameness. Because the signs are virtually identical to the much more serious foot-and-mouth disease, all cases of suspected swine vesicular disease have to be notified to the veterinary authorities in the UK.

• **swing** ► A form of jazz that developed in the early 1930s; it was characterized by the use of large ensembles (the so-called big bands), increasingly complex arrangements, and vibrant but steady dance rhythms.

• **swinger** ► 1. Dated slang for a fun-loving, sophisticated, and lively person. 2. Slang for someone who takes part in group sex or organized swapping of sexual partners.

• **swinging** ► Slang of the 1960s meaning lively or uninhibited. The word also acquired clear sexual connotations, reflecting the atmosphere of sexual freedom that characterized the decade (*see*: new morality). The 1960s themselves are often recalled as the **Swinging Sixties**, although many survivors of the period have questioned the reality of the popular image. In 1965 the US fashion journalist Diana Vreeland (*c*.1903–89) applied the term to London, noting the emergence of a new spirit among the traditionally staid British: **Swinging London** featured in *Time* magazine a year later, the phrase caught on, and for a few years the city was associated in the public imagination with the contemporary spirit of liberation in fashion, ideas, and sexual mores.

• **swing-wing** ► An aircraft design, also called variable-geometry wing, that enables the position of the wings to be altered during flight so they can adopt the aerodynamically most favourable position. For take-off and landing the wings are set in the straight position, while for high-speed cruising they are moved to a swept-back position. The greater aerodynamic efficiency of the swing-wing design allows the aircraft to use a less powerful, hence lighter, engine, with a reduced fuel payload, giving a weight advantage that more than offsets

the greater complexity of the swing-wing mechanism. Although the idea was pioneered by the British engineer Barnes Wallis (1887–1979), the world's first operational swing-wing aircraft was the General Dynamics F 111, introduced in the 1960s. The design was also incorporated in, among others, the European-built Tornado, and the Soviet MiG-23.

• **switched on** ► 1. Aware of contemporary fashions and ideas, thoroughly up to date and responsive to current trends and tendencies. *See also*: plugged in. 2. Under the influence of drugs. Both senses date from the 1960s and are now rarely used.

• **Sword** ► Allied codename given to a beach N of Caen, which was one of the main landing sites for British and Canadian forces on D-Day. *See also*: Gold; Juno; Omaha; Utah.

• **SWOT** ► Strengths, weaknesses, opportunities, and threats. A nmemonic used in planning the marketing of a new product, indicating the areas a company has to assess. Internal strengths needed would be a good distribution system, a strong flow of cash to support the marketing, etc. Weaknesses that need attention might include inadequate servicing facilities or poor-quality testing. Opportunities might arise from a good demand that is known to exist in a particular area of the market. Threats might include government subsidizing of an overseas competitor.

• **Sydney Opera House** ► The remarkable opera house in Sydney harbour that had become the subject of great controversy by the time of its completion in 1973. Undoubtedly the best-known building in Australia, it was designed by the Danish architect Jorn Utzon (1918–   ), winner of an international competition, who planned a series of ten huge 'shells' of concrete, which – at 26,800 tons – would constitute the heaviest roof in the world. The project should have been completed by 1961: however, endless delays and rocketing costs led to Utzon's resignation in 1966 with work still in progress. The finished building covers 4 acres and contains a concert hall, a stage for opera and ballet, a theatre, a recording hall, and a cinema. Unfortunately the final result, considered to be one of the greatest abstract sculptures of the 20th century, has been much criticized for its poor acoustic qualities; according to one critic the Opera House is 'a grand piano from the outside, a rusty xylophone inside'.

• **Sykes-Picot agreement** ► A secret pact, negotiated by Sir Mark Sykes of the UK and François Georges-Picot of France in January 1916, for dividing up the Ottoman Empire after World War I. France was given control of coastal Syria, Lebanon, and Mosul, while the UK would control southern Mesopotamia, including Baghdad, and the ports of Haifa and Akka. Palestine was to be placed under international control, and a number of independent Arab states were also to be created. The agreement was conditional on the approval of Russia, which was given in May 1916 in return for control over Turkish Armenia. The Italians had also been promised Ottoman territory in the Treaty of London, and they eventually assented to the agreement in August 1917 after they were allotted portions of Anatolia. The agreement was a source of considerable embarrassment to the Allies when it was made public by the Bolshevik government late in 1917; unfortunately it contradicted British promises made to the Jews for a national home in Palestine (in the Balfour declaration of 2 November 1917) and pledges to Hussein, the Sherif of Mecca, concerning Arab independence (*see*: McMahon letters).

• **Sylvester** ► A cartoon cat who appeared in Warner Brothers shorts from the 1940s to the 1960s, generally in vain pursuit of the distrusting bird

Tweetie Pie. Sylvester's lisping voice, provided by Mel Blanc, had many imitators.

• **synchronism** ► A form of abstract art, somewhat resembling Orphism, developed from 1913 by two Americans working in Paris, Morgan Russell and S. MacDonald Wright. It was characterized by the use of pure colour moving by gradations from the primaries to the intermediary colours.

• **syndicalism** ► (French, *syndicalisme*, trade unionism) A revolutionary socialist movement originating about 1890 in France, where it was known as *syndicalisme révolutionnaire*. It was opposed to state socialism, arguing that the means of production should be taken over by the trade unions and not by the state and that the government should comprise a federation of trade-union bodies. The syndicalists aimed to achieve their objectives by widespread strikes, go-slows, etc. Syndicalism played an important part in fomenting the trade-union unrest in the UK immediately preceding World War I; syndicalists were also a prominent element on the Republican side in the Spanish Civil War.

# T

• **table dancing** ▶ *See*: lap dancing.

• **tabloid** ▶ A newspaper that is half the size of a traditional broadsheet newspaper. Tabloids generally carry the news in a condensed and easily readable form, with large brash headlines and short paragraphs interspersed with frequent subheadings. Much of the space is devoted to celebrity gossip, titillating or sensational articles about sex or crime, and so-called 'human interest' stories. In the UK, the first papers to use these elements to appeal to a mass audience were Northcliffe's *Daily Mail* (1896) and *Daily Mirror* (1903); the latter also pioneered the tabloid format. However, Northcliffe's titles were models of taste and sobriety compared to such current publications as *The Sun*, which overtook the *Mirror* as Britain's best-selling paper in the early 1970s. British tabloids have their counterparts in other countries, most notably Germany's *Bild Zeitung*, Europe's best-selling daily newspaper. Middle-market newspapers, such as the *Daily Express*, also appear in tabloid form now; the format has also been experimented with by the British quality press, notably in their weekend editions. *See also*: gutter press; Northcliffe Press.

• **tabu** ▶ Typical *army* balls-up: army slang dating from World War II. *See also*: snafu.

• **tachisme** ▶ (French *tache*, spot) A style of abstract painting in which dabs or blotches of colour are applied in a random intuitive manner to express the mood or emotions of the artist. Tachisme was part of the more general **Art Informel** (French, art without form) movement that developed in Paris in the 1940s and 1950s and the two terms are often used synonymously. It also had much in common with the abstract expressionist movement then coming to the fore in America, particularly action painting. Like Jackson Pollock and Willem de Kooning, the tachists created large canvases containing splashes, blobs, and sweeping strokes of colour, although with greater delicacy, discipline, and concern for line and form than their US counterparts. Leading artists associated with tachisme included the French-German painters Wols and Hans Hartung.

• **tachograph** ▶ (Greek *takhos*, speed) A device used in a heavy goods vehicle to record its speed, the distance covered, rest breaks taken, etc., to ensure that the vehicle, driver, and owner are complying with regulations. Called by many drivers the 'spy-in-the-cab'.

• **tactical voting** ▶ In a political election or other ballot, casting one's vote not for one's preferred candidate but for the second-most-likely winner, in order to contribute to the defeat of the favourite. For example, in some constituencies a normally Conservative voter might vote for the Liberal Democrat candidate in an attempt to deny victory to the Labour candidate.

• **Taff Vale Judgment** ▶ The decision by the British courts in favour of the action for damages brought by the Taff Vale Railway Company against the Amalgamated Society of Railway Servants (ASRS) in 1900. In June 1900 striking ASRS members had picketed Cardiff stations; in response, the general manager of the Taff Vale Company had brought an action against the secretary of the union, claiming that the picketing contravened the Conspiracy and Protection of Property Act (1875). The decision in favour of the company, which was upheld by the House of Lords in July 1901, meant that unions could be held liable for the actions of their members in industrial disputes. In December 1902 the company was duly awarded £23,000, plus costs. This attack on the ability of the unions to mount an effective strike was an important factor in the rise of the Labour Party, because it convinced trade unionists of the need for parliamentary action to redress their grievances. In the wake of Taff Vale, trade union affiliation to the Labour Party increased dramatically and the representation of the Party in parliament increased from two to 29 members during the period 1900–06. The Taff Vale decision was eventually reversed by the Trades Disputes Act (1906).

• **tag** ▶ A type of spray-painted graffito consisting of a stylized signature or logo. Originating in the practice, common among US graffiti artists, of signing one's work with a nickname or personal symbol, tagging soon became an end in its own right. The object is to develop a stylish personal tag and to leave it in as many public places as possible, the more conspicuous or inaccessible the better. The craze began in America in the 1970s and spread to the UK and elsewhere. New York subways and London tubes have suffered much vandalism as a result of this craze. It has spawned a flourishing subculture with its own vocabulary, conventions, and etiquette.

• **tail-end Charlie** ▶ In World War II, RAF slang for the rear-gunner in the tail of an aircraft; also for the aircraft at the rear of a group or the last ship in a flotilla. **Arse-end Charlie** and **arse-hole Charlie** were common variants.

• **Tailor of Gloucester** ▶ The eponymous hero of Beatrix Potter's tale (1902), whose finest work is finished on time by mice. Potter was inspired to write the story after hearing of a notice in a tailor's window in Gloucester in 1894: 'Have your suits made by the Tailor of Gloucester, where the work is done by fairies.' Apparently, a local tailor had been startled to find that unfinished work in the shop had been completed over the weekend by unknown hands. The truth finally emerged years later; it seems that some of his employees had remained hidden in the shop all one Sunday after a lengthy drinking spree the night before. Feeling too embarrassed to reveal themselves in a dishevelled state to Gloucester's churchgoers, they stayed inside until darkness fell and completed the unfinished garments in order to pass the time.

• **Taiwan** ▶ 1980s student slang for an upper second degree ('two-one'). *See also*: Desmond; Douglas; Pattie.

• **take** ▶ 1. In film-making, one of a series of attempts to film a particular shot or scene. Even if there are no technical or artistic problems, the director will usually insist on several takes, as this increases flexibility in editing. Some directors are notorious for the number of retakes they demand; Charlie Chaplin is said to have shot one brief piece of action in *City Lights* (1931) 340 times. 2. In the music industry, one of a series of recordings made of the same piece, so that the best can be selected for release.

• **takeaway** ▶ A ready-cooked meal, packaged to be taken and consumed away from its place of sale. Although fish-and-chip shops had been providing this service in the UK for many years, the term was only coined in the late 1960s as restaurants offering takeaway Chinese, then Indian, food began to spring up in towns throughout the country. The

outlets providing this service are also known as takeaways. In America the equivalent is a **carry-out**, which is bought from a **takeout** counter. *See also*: fast food.

• **take out** ▶ To kill or destroy. A military euphemism first heard during the Vietnam War, the expression subsequently achieved wide usage.

• **Taliban** ▶ A militant Islamic movement that governed most of Afghanistan from 1996 until late 2001. It was formed in 1994 in the southern Afghan town of Kandahar, taking its name from a word meaning 'student' (many of the original members were theological students). Civil war among rival factions of mujaheddin had raged for five years when, in late 1994, the Taliban started to capture towns in the south and west of the country, proclaiming itself to stand for peace and unity. By September 1996, when it entered the capital Kabul, the Taliban also controlled eastern and central regions. The new rulers introduced strict Islamic law with capital or corporal punishment for a range of crimes, banned music, television, and cinema, and prohibited alcohol. Most offensive to Western observers was their oppression of women, who were prevented from working outside their homes and forced to wear long veils covering all the body (including woven screens to conceal the eyes). Girls' schools were closed in some areas. They also tried to erase evidence of their country's non-Islamic history, most notoriously by blowing up ancient Buddhist statues. Subsequent years saw a consolidation of the Taliban's grip on power, but continued international isolation. In October 2001 the Taliban's links with the al-Qaida organization provoked massive US air-strikes on its command centres as part of the so-called war on terrorism. The regime crumbled within weeks.

• **talkies** ▶ The earliest films with synchronized sound. As all movies are now talkies the expression is no longer used, except historically. Although experiments with sound date back to the very earliest days of cinema, the technical problems involved in synchronizing sound and image for more than a few minutes at a time proved insurmountable. A series of one-minute talkies was demonstrated at the Paris Exposition as early as 1900, but it was not until 1926 that US audiences saw a feature-length film (*Don Juan*, starring John Barrymore) with background music provided on synchronized discs rather than by a cinema pianist. In 1927 Fox Movietone newsreels introduced spoken narrative, notably for their coverage of Charles Lindbergh's triumphal return from his solo Atlantic flight (*see*: Spirit of St Louis). It was, however, the box-office triumph of Warner Brothers' *The Jazz Singer* later that year that truly inaugurated the sound era. First shown on 6 October 1927, the film included six songs performed by Al Jolson and about 350 words of spoken dialogue (*see*: You ain't heard nothing yet *at* heard). It used Vitaphone's system of synchronized discs. In 1928 Walt Disney produced the first sound cartoon, *Steamboat Willie*, featuring Mortimer Mouse (soon renamed Mickey Mouse). By 1929 all the major studios had decided to take the very expensive step of re-equipping for sound, with most opting for the sound-on-film system developed by Western Electric rather than synchronized discs, which quickly became obsolete. The era of silent films was over.

• **talking book**▶ Sound recordings of books and magazines read by professional actors. These were first produced in America in 1934 for use by the blind and introduced to the UK the following year. A vast selection of recordings of books, magazines, and periodicals is now available in libraries and shops.

• **talking head**▶ Originally, a broadcasting term for the televised 'head and shoulders' shot of a person talking, or for the type of programme that consists mainly of close-ups of a presenter or interviewee speaking directly to the camera. The phrase is now widely used, mainly disparagingly, of the people who appear in such programmes and put forward their opinions on particular topics.

• **tall, dark, and handsome**▶ A phrase used to describe the perfect hero of romantic fiction of the Mills & Boon variety; it is now a cliché. It seems to have originated in the early years of the 20th century but did not become established until Mae West used it in the film *She Done Him Wrong* (1933) to describe the character played by Cary Grant.

• **tall poppy**▶ An Australian colloquialism for a rich or prominent person. **Tall-poppy syndrome** is the tendency, said to be engrained in the Australian character, to cut such people down to size. The phrase has been current since 1931, when Jack Lang (1876–1975), the left-wing premier of New South Wales, described his egalitarian policies as 'cutting the heads off the tall poppies'. It derives from the legend that Tarquin, king of Rome, intimated his wishes respecting the captured city of Gabii by decapitating the tallest poppies in his garden; accordingly, the leading citizens were executed.

• **tamper-proof**▶ *See*: consumer terrorism.

• **Tanaka Memorial**▶ A Japanese blueprint for aggressive expansion in China, said to have been presented by the prime minister, General Tanaka Giichi (1864–1929), to the emperor in 1927. On be-

coming prime minister in April 1927, Tanaka convened a conference of top military and government officials to discuss policy towards the Asian continent, during which it was agreed that a strong stance in defence of Japanese interests in China was necessary. This conference was apparently the source of the belligerent Tanaka Memorial (memorandum), which was published throughout China in the late 1920s. The authenticity of the Memorial has yet to be proved, although Japanese aggression in China during the 1930s appears to conform to the strategy outlined in the document.

• **tango**▶ A ballroom dance in 2/4 or 4/4 time introduced into Europe from Argentina in the early years of the 20th century. The dance combines elements of Spanish flamenco with the *milonga*, a fast sensual dance popular in Buenos Aires in the 1880s, and the Cuban *habanera*, which was probably of African origin. It appears to have been created in the backstreets and bordellos of Buenos Aires, and was initially regarded as unfit for respectable people:

> ...how many other things would you willingly do in public that were first dreamed up by the clients of a Latin American brothel? – JOE JOSEPH in *The Times*, 22 May 1991.

Nevertheless, by the 1920s the tango had spread from its native Argentina to North America and Europe; in America its popularity was greatly enhanced by the film *The Four Horsemen of the Apocalypse* (1921), in which Rudolf Valentino gave a highly sensual rendition. For the British, however, it never seemed entirely suitable – the ex-public schoolboy finds it uncomfortable to look dark, Latin, and dangerous, while the demure English rose is not at her best in fishnet stockings (at least not in public). By the 1950s the tango had become little more than a formal exercise for ballroom dance enthusiasts. However, there have been several recent attempts to restore the dance to its original glory, notably in the touring show *Tango Argentino* (early 1990s) and the films *Naked Tango* (1990) and *Tango* (1998). Characterized by slow gliding movements broken by sudden changes of direction and pointing positions, the tango is very easy to caricature.

• **tango**▶
  **it takes two to tango** A common idiom dating back to the 1952 song with this title by Hofmann and Manning:

> There are lots of things you can do alone!
> But it takes two to tango.

The phrase is often used in a sexual context, to imply that it is no use blaming one partner for seducing the other when both must have been willing. It is also used more widely, especially in politics and business, to imply that in order to achieve agreement between two parties, both may have to make concessions.

• **tank** ▶ A heavily armoured motorized combat vehicle running on caterpillar tracks, first introduced on the battlefield by the British in the Battle of the Somme (1916). 'Tank' was initially used as a code word for these vehicles in order not to arouse enemy suspicions and to achieve a complete surprise.

• **tankie** ▶ In British left-wing circles, a dismissive term for an old-fashioned staunchly pro-Soviet member of the Communist Party. It derived from the refusal of such people to condemn any aspect of Soviet policy, even when this involved using tanks to crush popular movements in other Eastern bloc countries (see: Brezhnev Doctrine). It was heard in the mid-to-late 1980s.

• **tank top** ▶ A sleeveless pullover with a scoop neckline and wide shoulder straps, as worn by either sex, usually over a shirt or blouse. Tank tops became very popular in the early 1970s but are now regarded as horribly naff. They took their name from the one-piece swimming costumes with wide shoulder straps known as 'tank suits' (worn in 'swimming tanks').

• **Tannenberg** ▶ The site in Poland (then in East Prussia) of the battle fought between 26 and 30 August 1914, in which the Germans inflicted a crushing defeat on Russia. The two invading Russian armies, the First Army under General Pavel K. Rennenkampf and the Second Army under Alexander Samsonov, were initially successful against the Germans, driving them back in the initial battles of Stallupönen (17 August) and Gumbinnen (20 August). On 22 August, Prittwitz was replaced as commander of the German Eighth army by General Paul von Hindenburg, with Erich Ludendorff as his chief of staff. Following a plan devised by Colonel Max Hoffman, Ludendorff ordered that one corps should be left to hold Rennennkampf north of the Masurian Lakes, while the bulk of the German forces were moved south against Samsonov in a region of forests and lakes, near the historic town of Tannenberg. The plan was so successful that by 29 August the Russian Second Army had been encircled and destroyed, with catastrophic losses of 125,000 men and 500 guns. Samsonov disappeared into the forest and shot himself.

• **Tannoy** ▶ Tradename for a type of public-address system marketed in the 1920s by the Tannoy Audio Communications company of America and its UK subsidiary. The name, which has since been applied to any form of public-address system, refers to the use of an electrical rectifier device based on the element *tan*talum and a lead all*oy*.

• **Tante Yvonne** ▶ (French, Aunt Yvonne) Yvonne de Gaulle, the wife of President Charles de Gaulle, was so called on account of her reputation for domesticity.

• **Taranto raid** ▶ An attack by carrier-based British torpedo bombers on the main base of the Italian fleet in the Bay of Taranto on the night of 11 November 1940. Operation Judgment, as it was called, proved a brilliant success: 21 Fairey Swordfish launched from the aircraft carrier *Illustrious* disabled three Italian battleships with the loss of only two aircraft. Half the Italian battlefleet was put out of action, which effectively removed the Italian naval threat in the Mediterranean. The success of the Taranto raid was carefully noted by the Japanese, who had invested heavily in the offensive potential of carrier-based forces.

• **target-rich environment** ▶ US military jargon from the Gulf War of 1991. It meant an area in which Allied pilots would find plenty of Iraqi tanks, missile launchers, or artillery pieces to destroy with their bombs or missiles.

• **Tariff Reform** ▶ In the UK, a campaign for the reintroduction of a tariff or scale of duties on imported goods launched in 1903 by Joseph Chamberlain (1836–1914). The intention was to strengthen the bonds of the British Empire through a system of Imperial Preference. Chamberlain's campaign caused a serious split in the Unionist government of A. J. Balfour, which contained many supporters of Free Trade, and helped to ensure the Liberal Landslide of 1905. Return to protection did not take place on any scale until 1932, following the financial crisis of 1931.

• **Tarka** ▶ The principal character in the popular animal saga *Tarka the Otter* (1927) by Henry Williamson (1895–1977). Williamson had already published a number of natural history tales, but it was *Tarka* (which won the Hawthornden Prize), with its sympathetic but unsentimental portrayal of the animal world, that made his enduring reputation. A bitter and cantankerous man who alienated many former admirers with his outspoken support for Hitler, Williamson himself was sometimes known as 'Tarka the Rotter'.

• **Tarmac** ▶ A material for surfacing roads, airport runways, car parks, etc., consisting of a mixture of crushed stone and tar or bitumen. The Scottish engineer John McAdam (1756–1836) had introduced the idea of using crushed stone as a roadsurfacing material in the 19th century. In 1902, a civil engineer from Nottingham, Purnell Hooley, patented a material that he called Tarmac, made by mixing tar with crushed slag from blast furnaces. He later set up a company called the TarMacadam Syndicate. The name Tarmac has subsequently been used for any similar tar-based paving material and for any area coated with this material – especially the area surrounding an airport terminal on which the planes stand for boarding and disembarking.

• **Tarzan**▶ **1.** The hero of the jungle adventures of Edgar Rice Burroughs (1875–1950), who became a familiar and enduring figure in B-movies and TV serials. The first Tarzan story was published in 1913 and the first film, the silent *Tarzan of the Apes*, followed in 1918. By 1984, when the film *Greystoke* was released, the adventures of the jungle hero, born an aristocratic Englishman but orphaned and brought up among wild apes, had inspired over 40 films. Among the 20-or-so actors to play Tarzan have been Johnny Weissmuller (a former Olympic swimmer), Buster Crabbe, and TV's Ron Ely in the 1960s. His female companion, Jane, has been portrayed by Maureen O'Sullivan, Brenda Joyce, and Bo Derek, among others. Tarzan's halting approach to Jane with the line 'Me Tarzan, you Jane' has entered 20th-century folklore. **2.** Nickname for the Conservative politician Michael Heseltine (1933–   ), who held several senior posts under Margaret Thatcher and later became deputy prime minister under John Major (1995–97). The name derives from his Adonis-like physique and flowing mane of hair when a younger man, and his flamboyant showmanship (and occasional recklessness) as a politician.

• **Tasaday**▶ A small Stone Age tribe of about 25 people, said to have been discovered in the rain forests of Mindanao in the Philippines by neighbouring tribes in the mid-1960s; they were first encountered by anthropologists in 1971. The Tasaday were apparently cave-dwellers, knew nothing of agriculture, lived on a diet of wild yams, bananas, frogs, and insects, wore only orchid-leaf loincloths, and used only the most primitive stone tools and bamboo implements. Their existence was hailed as a major discovery with profound implications for our understanding of Neolithic culture. In 1986, however, it emerged that the whole affair was a hoax dreamed up as a publicity stunt by the regime of President Ferdinand Marcos. The Tasaday, it seems, were members of an advanced local tribe who had been put up to adopting a Neolithic lifestyle by the Philippines' presidential assistant on national minorities.

• **Tass**▶ *Telegrafnoe Agentsvo Sovetskovo Soyuza*, the former official Soviet news agency. It was established in 1925 to replace Rosta, the first Bolshevik news agency, which had taken over from the Tsarist counterpart in Petrograd during the Revolution. Tass was the main source of news for Soviet national newspapers, television, and radio. It had bureaux in over 100 countries, served all the major Western wire services, and provided bulletins in a variety of major languages. Tass pronouncements reflected the Soviet government's offical line on domestic and international affairs. Following the dissolution of the Soviet Union in 1991, Tass changed its name to Itar (January 1992).

• **Tassili cave paintings**▶ The accidental discovery of ancient cave paintings in the Saharan plateau of Tassili-n-Ajer in 1933 ranks as one of the most significant archaeological finds of the 20th century. Found by a young French army lieutenant out on patrol, the paintings record in detail the family life, hunting parties, religious beliefs, and wars of an unknown ancient dark-skinned warrior race. Many of the animals they hunted are now extinct and it seems likely this long-forgotten people eventually succumbed to their harsh surroundings (once a lush and green land) and to invasion by paler-skinned neighbours.

• **Tate Bricks**▶ *See*: minimalism.

• **Tate Modern**▶ An art gallery on the south bank of the River Thames in London, opened by the Tate Gallery in 2000 to house its international collection of modern art. Sited in the former Bankside power station, an imposing building originally designed by Sir Giles Gilbert Scott and brilliantly converted to its new purpose by the Swiss architects Jacques Herzog and Pierre de Meuron, the gallery has quickly established itself as one of London's top tourist attractions. For many visitors, however, the ingenuity of the conversion and its superb views of the Thames have proved more worthy of unreserved praise than the contents. The original Tate gallery, on the other side of the river at Millbank, is now devoted to British paintings and known as **Tate Britain**. *See also*: Millennium Bridge.

• **tax exile**▶ A wealthy person who chooses to live in a tax haven in order to avoid high taxes in his or her native country. Tax exiles from the UK are allowed to spend only a limited amount of time in the British Isles. If they exceed this period they become liable for UK taxes.

• **tax haven**▶ A country or territory in which a low rate of tax offers advantages to wealthy individuals or companies that can arrange for some of their tax liability to fall there. Individuals usually have to become tax exiles living in the territory for most of the year. Companies can generally arrange for some or all of their income to pass through an office established in the tax haven. Monaco, Liechtenstein, and the Cayman Islands are well-known tax havens.

• **taxi** ▶ **1.** A motor-cab licensed to transport passengers in return for payment. The name comes from the *taximètre* ('tariff meter') installed on French horse-drawn cabs or *fiacres* long before motor-cabs appeared on the road. In the UK this only became common with the introduction of motor-cabs and was thus associated with them. In London all taxis were originally purpose-built vehicles, the drivers of which had to demonstrate their knowledge of the city before they were given a licence. With the emergence in the 1950s of **minicabs** (any small saloon car driven by an untrained driver), the purpose-built vehicles became known as **black cabs**, because they were all black. Although 'black cabs' now come in a great variety of colours, the name has stuck. **2.** Of an aircraft, to move along the ground under its own power.

• **taxing** ▶ Slang for mugging a person and stealing some of his or her possessions, (*i.e.* forcing the victim to pay a tax). In the 1980s this sense narrowed to mugging someone in order to steal his or her fashionable training shoes. In the later 1980s sports footwear became a potent status symbol among US teenagers, with price tag and brand name the crucial factors. As top-of-the-range products by Nike and Reebok sold for upwards of £100 a pair, many who coveted them turned to some form of crime. The vogue for expensive designer trainers was undoubtedly a factor in the rise in street crime and drug dealing in US cities at this time. In 1988–89 there was a rash of killings motivated purely by a desire to own the victim's shoes. The sports-shoe craze had spread to the UK by 1989 and the first shoe-related muggings were reported soon afterwards. In 1989 a London University survey concluded that the main cause of street crime was not drugs or unemployment but a craving for designer sportswear.

• **Teamsters Union** ▶ The International Brotherhood of Teamsters, Chauffeurs, Warehousemen, and Helpers of America. The union was founded in 1899, and by 1940 had become America's largest, with over one million members. Persistent allegations of corruption and racketeering led to the union's expulsion from the American Federation of Labour–Congress of Industrial Organizations (AFL–CIO) in 1957, the year in which Jimmy Hoffa was elected leader. It was Hoffa, more than any pre-

vious leader, who made the Teamsters synonymous with violence and gangsterism. Hoffa allowed his friends in organized crime to use the Teamsters as a legitimate front for their criminal activities; in return, Hoffa and the union acquired vast wealth, enabling them to forge further links with corrupt politicians. Eventually, as a result of investigations led by the attorney general, Robert Kennedy, Hoffa was imprisoned in 1967. He was paroled in 1971 by President Nixon, and in 1975 disappeared, presumably murdered by fellow gangsters. Charges of racketeering and illegal activity continued to dog the union during the 1980s. More recently, the Teamsters have made concerted efforts to purge themselves of their criminal elements and to reform the basic structure and finances of the organization.

• **Teapot Dome scandal** ▶ In America, the long-running scandal that resulted from the discovery that President Warren Harding's secretary of the interior, Albert B. Fall, had secretly leased government oil fields to a private company. The oil fields in question formed part of the Teapot Dome Naval Oil Reserves in Wyoming, which had been transferred to Fall's department in 1921. Fall stealthily negotiated drilling rights with Harry F. Sinclair of the Monmouth Oil Company; he also granted similar rights in a reserve at Elk Hills, California, to an old friend, Edward L. Doheny. Although Fall left the cabinet in March 1923, continuing Senate investigations into his activities resulted in a series of civil and criminal court actions, which kept the affair in the headlines for the rest of the decade and made the term 'Teapot Dome' synonymous with political corruption. In November 1929 Fall was eventually found guilty of receiving at least $404,000 in bribes and was sentenced to a one-year prison term – the first US cabinet officer ever convicted of a serious crime while in office.

> If Fall isn't an honest man, then I am not fit to be president. – WARREN HARDING.

• **tear gas** ▶ A gas (or dispersed liquid or powder) that irritates the eyes and causes inflammation of the respiratory tract. Tear gas is used by police to disable people temporarily and in so-called 'crowd control'. *See:* Mace.

• **tear-jerker** or **weepie** ▶ A sentimental film, novel, or other narrative that is virtually guaranteed to bring a tear to the eye – especially one in which the emotion seems cynically contrived. The ultimate tear-jerker was probably the hugely successful film *Love Story* (1970), about a dying newlywed, to which the audience was recommended to bring a box of tissues.

• **teaser**► In advertising jargon, a poster, TV ad, or other item that is designed to stimulate interest in a new product, without giving away much detail. Teaser campaigns are often deliberately enigmatic and may not even mention the product by name.

• **Technicolor**► Tradename for a process used in making colour motion pictures. The original process, which was devised in 1915, involved simultaneous projection of both red and green versions of the film. The first such films were screened commercially in 1917–18. In 1932 a new three-colour process was introduced in the Disney cartoon *Flowers and Trees*; this set new standards for the industry and is seen to its fullest effect in the glossy MGM features of the later 1930s and 1940s, notably *Gone With the Wind* (1939). Although Technicolor lost its dominant position to Eastman Color in the 1950s, the words 'technicolour' or 'technicoloured' have entered the general language to describe anything garishly colourful.

• **techno**► A type of dance music, usually with a heavy synthesized beat, that makes full use of developments in musical and recording technology. Emerging as a distinct style in the later 1980s, it often incorporates sampling and electronic sound effects. The term is often used in such compounds as **techno-funk**, **techno-pop**, etc.

• **technobabble**► A derogatory term for abstruse technological jargon, especially when it seems designed primarily to impress or bamboozle the public. It is especially prevalent in such fields as computing and military technology. *See also*: psychobabble.

• **technocracy**► A society controlled by technical experts (technocrats). A radical US political movement advocating the control of society and the economy by engineers and scientists adopted this name in the 1930s. The movement's ideology was derived from Thorstein Veblen's *The Engineers and the Price System* (1921), which sought to replace the irrationality of the free market by an economy planned by experts in science and technology. The movement lost impetus with the improvement in social and economic conditions brought about by the New Deal after 1935.

• **technomania**► An excessive enthusiasm for modern technology. The technomaniac's zeal often overrides other considerations, such as the consequences for the environment and society.

• **technophobia**► An exaggerated fear or dislike of new technology, either because one finds it impossible to use or understand, or because of irrational worries about its effect on the environment.

• **teddy-bear**► A child's soft toy bear; so-named after Theodore (Teddy) Roosevelt, who was fond of bear-hunting. The toy acquired its name after a bearhunt was arranged for the US president in 1902: to make sure that the president made a kill, the organizers stunned a small brown bear and tied it to a tree. A pleasanter version of the story has Roosevelt sparing a bearcub that wandered into his camp.

• **teddy-bear syndrome**► A syndrome in which a person enters into a marriage or a relationship solely because he or she cannot bear to be alone and needs the constant presence of a comforter – the functions that a teddy bear fulfils for many during childhood.

• **teddy boys** or **teds**► Young men of the 1950s who affected an approximately Edwardian style of dress (they were sometimes referred to as **Edwardians**), including knee-length jackets known as 'drapes', drainpipe trousers, and brothel creeper shoes. They also sported long sideburns and wore their hair slicked up and back (*see*: DA). Of working-class origin, they were fans of early rock 'n' roll and acquired a reputation for vandalism and violence. The style has enjoyed several brief revivals, notably in the late 1970s.

• **Teenage Mutant Ninja Turtles**► A US TV cartoon series featuring four pizza-loving streetwise turtle heroes – Leonardo, Donatello, Raphael, and Michelangelo. Trained by Splinter the Rat, the foursome emerged from New York City sewers with their victory cry of **Cowabunga!** These figures became the number one children's fad of 1990, appearing in books, food and drink products, T-shirts, toothbrushes, etc. In the UK, where the name was changed to *Teenage Mutant Hero Turtles*, the mania for turtle paraphernalia was said to have saved the 1990–91 Christmas season for many shops during the depths of the recession. *See also*: ninja.

• **teeny-bopper**► A girl in her early teens, who adopts current fashions in dress and is a devotee of pop music and its star performers. *See also*: weeny-bopper.

• **Teflon**► *See*: PTFE.

• **Tehran Conference**► The meeting between the Allied leaders that took place in the Persian capital between 28 November and 1 December 1943; this was Churchill's and Roosevelt's first meeting with Stalin. Churchill hoped to delay the invasion of France, the Second Front which Stalin had so long demanded, by a continuation of the Mediterranean strategy. Roosevelt, however, agreed with Stalin on the urgent need for a cross-channel invasion; it was settled that Overlord should take place the following May and that diversionary Soviet offensives would be launched simultaneously in the east. Stalin also obtained Roosevelt's agreement to Soviet expansion into E Poland and the extension of Polish borders to include East Prussia and Danzig. The 'Big Three' also had inconclusive talks on the zoning of post-war Germany, discussed the proposed nature of the United Nations Organization, committed themselves to post-war independence of Persia, and agreed plans to increase Allied support for Tito's resistance movement in Yugoslavia.

• **tektite** ▸ A small roundish glassy object of unknown origin found only on certain areas of the Earth's surface, known as **tektite fields**. Tektites range in size from a few millimetres to about 10 cm and their chemical composition is unrelated to the geological areas in which they occur. Their origin was the subject of much scientific debate in the 20th century: some geologists believe that they are extraterrestrial and possibly lunar in origin, while others think that they were formed on the Earth at an early stage of the planet's development.

• **telecommuter** or **teleworker** ▸ A person who works from home with the aid of a computer, Internet and e-mail connections, and a telephone.

• **telephone banking** ▸ A facility offered by a bank or building society that enables account holders to carry out certain operations over the telephone, sometimes via a manned call centre but often now by means of a computerized system using touch-tone dialling or voice-recognition technology. Although cheques cannot be paid in or drawn, balances can be checked, transfers made between accounts, and direct debits etc. set up or cancelled. Like e-banking, which it closely resembles, it provides a service that is available around the clock, seven days a week.

• **Teleprompter** ▸ *See*: autocue.

• **Teletext** ▸ *See*: Ceefax.

• **telethon** ▸ A lengthy television programme screened to raise funds for a charity or some other cause. It invariably features noted entertainers, film footage of those needing help, appeals for funds, operators taking pledged donations over the telephone, and a running scoreboard on the total raised and how much is still needed to reach the stated goal. In America, local PBS stations conduct annual telethons to raise operating funds; the largest charity event is the annual 24-hour appeal for children with cerebral palsy and similar dis-

eases. In the UK, the BBC's annual *Children in Need* campaign is broadcast on both television and radio. 'Telethon' is a portmanteau word formed from *tele*vision and mara*thon*. *See also*: Live Aid.

• **Teletubbies** ▸ Four brightly coloured teddy-bear-like creatures who star in the phenomenally successful children's TV series of the same name created by Anne Wood and Andrew Davenport. Launched in 1997, it can now be seen in 120 countries and was nominated for an Emmy in 1999. The Teletubbies are – in descending size order – Tinky Winky (purple), Dipsy (green), Laa-Laa (yellow), and Po (red). They live in Teletubbyland with Noo-Noo the vacuum cleaner (whose conscientious presence is the only hint of adulthood in their world) and consume a diet of Tubby Toast and Tubby Custard. Television screens on their stomachs activate at intervals to show children's games and activities from the real world.

Unlike other programmes of its kind, *Teletubbies* was designed very deliberately to reflect the way in which very small children see and experience the world. For example, the Teletubbies' simple repetitive speech (including the ubiquitous 'eh-oh' for 'hello') echoes that of a one-year-old child. Utilizing the available research, the programme tries to encourage children's developing cognitive skills through frequent repetition, movement and dance, and simple imaginative play. Although these strategies are supposed to stimulate listening ability, encourage curiosity, and build confidence, some educationalists argue that the programme fails to stretch children mentally or emotionally. To these critics *Teletubbies* is one more symptom of the dumbing down effect of television culture.

A more bizarre controversy arose in America, where the fact that Tinky Winky (a male) carries a handbag led some right-wing groups to claim that the programme promotes homosexuality.

• **televangelists** ▸ US evangelists who preach on television, often on their own cable networks. The **electronic church** tradition goes back to radio: the celebrated preacher Oral Roberts once regularly urged listeners to lay their hands on the radio to be healed. After Billy Graham and Cardinal Fulton J. Sheen demonstrated the power of religious messages on television in the 1950s, the screen became an ever-more important medium for Christian proselytisers and fund-raisers over the next three decades. In 1977, the Revd Pat Robertson, head of the Christian Broadcasting Network, said: 'We can't really be taken seriously unless we're a $1 billion-a-year operation.' In the 1980s, however, financial and sexual scandals led to viewer disenchantment and falling revenues: Jim and Tammy Bakker, founders of the PTL (Praise the Lord) Club, lost their empire after Jim Bakker was jailed for financial misconduct and evangelist Jimmy Swaggart was caught with a prostitute. The bad publicity even affected Oral Roberts, who told viewers in 1987 that God would take him within the year if donation goals were not met (they were, and he survived). Although many of the best-known televangelists belong to the fundamentalist fringe, America's mainstream churches also employ television as a tool: in 1982, the US Catholic Conference began its National Catholic Telecommunications Network. As Pat Robertson noted: 'It would be a folly for the church not to get involved with the most formative force in America.'

• **television age** ► The post-World War II period seen as an era dominated increasingly by television. Before World War II the television – invented in 1924 by the British electrical engineer John Logie Baird (1888–1946) – was a curiosity; although the BBC began regular TV broadcasts in 1936 there were a very small number of sets to receive them. By the 1960s, however, a television set ('the box') was an essential part of the living-room furniture in most British and US homes. In 1987 the total of homes with a television set throughout the world passed 500 million, with America leading with 89,130,000 sets. A year later, however, Chinese officials announced the presence of no less than 100 million sets in their country. Some 98% of British households now have a set, with well over half of these having two or more (in 2002 a survey reported that 56% of children aged four to nine have a set in their bedroom). Recent years have also seen a proliferation of channels; in 1997–98 over 25% of British households had a satellite dish (*see*: satellite television) and about 7% subscribed to cable (*see*: cable television). Digital television (*see*: digital broadcasting) is expected to become the norm by 2010.

The effects of the penetration of television into homes throughout the world have long been the subject of anxious debate. In 1988 it was estimated that the average child in America had witnessed 26,000 murders on television by the age of 18. The average Briton watches 25 hours of television every week (1997). Audiences across the world can be enormous: 1.6 billion people (one third of the world's population) tuned in to the Live Aid concerts of 1985, while 2.5 billion watched the funeral of Diana, Princess of Wales.

The potential for television to influence huge numbers of people has led to strict control being placed on the medium, with measures ranging from total political censorship in some countries to regulations upon the degree of violence, sex, 'adult' language, etc., used on the small screen in democracies. There are also strict rules outlawing the transmission of 'subliminal messages', *i.e.* signals that are flashed on the screen so fast that the viewer is unaware that he has seen it, although his brain has registered its content.

To its advocates, television has broadened the range of public knowledge and provided more harmless enjoyment than any other medium in the last half century. Critics say it trivializes everything, undermines family life, and contributes to the breakdown of moral codes.

> Television? No good will come of this device. The word is half Greek and half Latin. – C. P. SCOTT.

> Television is more interesting than people. If it were not, we should have people standing in the corners of our rooms. – ALAN COREN, *The Times*.

• **telex** ► A system for transmitting information over telephone lines using a keyboard and a printer, originally developed in the late 1890s. The modern telex systems developed in the 1930s were widely used until the late 1980s, when fax and subsequent e-mail replaced them for nearly all purposes. The name combines *tele*printer and e*xchange*.

• **Telstar** ► The communications satellite launched in 1962 for relaying transatlantic telephone messages and television pictures.

• **ten-four** or **10-4** ► US police code for message received, message understood, message affirmed, or yes, okay, affirmative, correct. It is equivalent to the military Roger. The term was introduced in the mid-1950s and popularized in the 1970s by CB radio users, especially as depicted in films and country music. Other examples of the 'ten' codes used by US police to save air time are: **10-9** for repeat, **10-15** for civil disturbance, and **10-34** for trouble or emergency.

• **1066 and All That** ► Catchphrase taken from the title of a comic survey of British history by Robert Julian Yeatman and Walter Carruthers Sellar, published in 1930. The authors reduce British history from the Roman conquest to World War I to a breathless chronology of kings and queens, invasions, battles, wars, inventions, etc., summarized as either 'a Good Thing' or 'a Bad Thing' in a parody of traditional history textbooks familiar to every schoolchild. Familiar incidents and events are amusingly rendered; in the notorious 'Bloody Assizes', for example:

> The Rebels were ferociously dealt with by the memorable Judge Jeffreys who...made some fu-

rious remarks about the prisoners known as 'The Bloody Asides'.

• **Teresa, Mother** ▶ Albanian-born nun (Agnes Gonxha Bejaxhui; 1910–97), who attracted worldwide attention for her charitable work amongst the poor of India. She opened a hospice in the Calcutta slums in 1952 and a leper colony in 1957. A tiny stooped woman clad in a white sari and often going barefoot, she became an international celebrity in the 1970s. In her old age she pressed her case for support for India's deprived with numerous heads of state, including Queen Elizabeth II. She won the Nobel Peace Prize in 1979 and is now widely regarded as a saint.

• **terminological inexactitude** ▶ A euphemism for a lie, first used by Winston Churchill (1874–1965) in a speech in the House of Commons on 22 February 1906 (about bonded Chinese labour in South Africa):

> It cannot in the opinion of His Majesty's Government be classified as slavery in the extreme acceptance of the word without some risk of terminological inexactitude.

It is contrary to parliamentary procedure for one MP to call another a liar. A more widely used phrase now, which is less of a mouthful, is economical with the truth.

• **Terrence Higgins Trust** ▶ An organization that provides information, help, and advice on Aids and HIV infection through its helpline. The Trust was established in 1983 by the friends of Terrence Higgins, who a year earlier became one of the first people to die of Aids in the UK; it now has a government grant that covers about one quarter of its costs. The Trust's medical advice covers such issues as drug use, health education, and safe sex; its legal centre offers advice on the problems of employment, insurance, and mortgages; and its publicity department helps to promote public awareness and understanding of Aids and HIV through leaflets, campaigns in the media, lectures, and training courses. Its main contribution to the welfare of Aids sufferers is through its buddy system, in which some 400 volunteers provide practical and emotional support to those with the disease on a one-to-one basis.

• **Tessa** ▶ Tax Exempt Special Savings Account. A savings scheme in the UK introduced in 1991, which enables savers to invest £3000 in the first year and £1800 p.a. thereafter, up to a limit of £9000, in a bank or building society with tax-free interest, provided that the capital remains in the account for five years. Interest can be withdrawn but if the capital is withdrawn tax relief is forfeited. Although Tessa's were replaced by ISAs in 1998, existing Tessas will continue until their term expires.

• **Test-ban Treaty** ▶ A treaty signed by America, the Soviet Union, and the UK on 7 October 1963 agreeing to a ban on the atmospheric (but not underground) testing of nuclear weapons. The treaty represented only a small step in the direction of nuclear disarmament but was a victory for environmentalists, who feared the damaging effects of radiation dispersal in the upper atmosphere. Later, over 100 other countries endorsed the treaty, France and China being notable exceptions. Following extensive talks, a more comprehensive Test-ban Treaty was drawn up in 1996. However, this will only come into effect when signed and ratified by all 44 countries deemed to have nuclear potential. So far, it has been signed by all these countries except India, Pakistan, and North Korea, but ratified by only the UK and France.

• **test marketing** ▶ The launch of a new product in a restricted geographical area in order to test consumer reaction. This has the advantage of minimizing costs and enabling the product to be modified in the light of consumer reactions. The disadvantage is that competitors are able to see the product before its full launch.

• **test-tube baby** ▶ *See:* IVF.

• **Tethys Sea** ▶ *See:* Pangaea.

• **Tet offensive** ▶ The coordinated assault by 70,000 communist soldiers on more than 100 major cities and towns throughout South Vietnam, which was launched on 31 January 1968. The offensive broke the holiday (Tet, the lunar New Year) truce, took the US military by surprise, and came as a complete shock to the US public. For the first time in the Vietnam War, television viewers witnessed US troops fighting the Viet Cong, not deep in the countryside, but in the streets of Hue and Saigon – even within the US Embassy itself. Ever since the first commitment of US ground troops in 1965, the military had constantly assured the politicians, the press, and the general public that the communists were on the verge of collapse. The Tet offensive appeared to prove otherwise; as a result public support for the war, which had been diminishing significantly in any case, dropped sharply. Walter Cronkite, 'the most trusted face' on network TV, reported from Saigon in February that, contrary to official pronouncements, the war was going badly and was bound to end in stalemate. Although the offensive was crushed with the communists suffering severe losses, Tet represented a decisive psychological victory for the Viet Cong. The offensive also represented the last nail in the coffin of Johnson's presidency. In March 1968, faced with the growing public and political opposition to the war, even among his own staff, he announced he would not seek re-election as the Democratic candidate in the forthcoming presidential contest.

• **texting** ▸ *See*: mobile phone.

• **TGV** ▸ *Train à Grande Vitesse* (French, high-speed train). A French bullet train that can reach speeds of 236 mph (370 kph), the fastest in the world. The first TGV began service in 1983 on a specially built line between Paris and Lyon, cutting the 285-mile (460-km) journey time to two hours. A second TGV line, SW to Le Mans and Tours was opened in 1990. During the 1990s Paris was linked by TGV with the Channel Tunnel to the west and with Brussels, Amsterdam, and Cologne to the east. *See also*: sinkansen.

• **thalidomide** ▸ A drug formerly used in medicine as a sedative and to prevent vomiting. Developed in the 1950s and marketed under the tradename Distaval, it was prescribed for pregnant women until its disastrous effects on the developing foetus became widely known. Women who had taken the drug early in pregnancy gave birth to babies with a range of abnormalities typically involving the absence of limbs, the fingers or toes being attached to the trunk by a short stump. Between 1959 and 1962 over 3000 so-called 'thalidomide babies' were born in the UK, West Germany, and Canada before the drug was withdrawn. The tragedy led to stricter controls in the testing of new drugs.

• **Thatcherism** ▸ The economic and political ideology associated with Margaret Thatcher (1925–  ), prime minister of the UK (1979–90). Broadly, Thatcher favoured the unhindered operation of the free market, the privatization of public utilities, and the encouragement of share ownership to further the 'enterprise culture' she stood for. Monetarism replaced Keynesianism, direct taxation was cut, and the power of the trade unions was successfully curtailed. In foreign affairs Thatcher was resolute in her opposition to communism (*see*: Iron Lady) and support of America but resisted moves to greater unity within the European Community, which she saw as threatening British independence. Although many of these policies proved popular and successful, it was Thatcher's confrontational style of leadership and its divisive effect on the cabinet – especially over European policy and local taxation (*see*: community charge) – that brought about her downfall in November 1990.

• **That Was The Week That Was** ▸ *See*: TW3.

• **Theatre of Cruelty** ▸ A theory of drama proposed by the French director, actor, and writer Antonin Artaud (1896–1948) in his book *The Theatre and its Double* (1938). Artaud was a follower of surrealism and sought to combine its theories with Taoism and Eastern dance drama to create a ritualistic form of theatre. This was intended to be in direct opposition to the realistic theatre of the dominant rationalist culture. His aim was to shock his audiences into an awareness of basic human nature by releasing feelings usually repressed in conventional society. In the 1950s and 1960s a number of playwrights experimented with the idea of a theatre of cruelty, notably Jean Genet and Joe Orton. Peter Brook's 1964 production of Peter Weiss's play *Marat/Sade* is generally considered the definitive application of Artaud's theory.

• **Theatre of Fact** or **Documentary Theatre** ▸ A theatrical genre in which plays are based on documented historical fact. It became a recognizable theatrical form in the 1950s and 1960s, notably in the plays of Rolf Hochhuth (1931–  ), *e.g.* *The Representative* (1963) and Peter Weiss (1916–82), *e.g.* *The Investigation* (1965) and *Trotsky in Exile* (1970).

• **Theatre of the Absurd** ▸ A form of drama that jettisons the usual conventions of plot, setting, and characterization to reflect the dramatist's belief in the meaninglessness of human existence. Absurdist theatre was first fully realized in Ionesco's *The Bald Prima Donna* (1948), although Beckett's *Waiting for Godot* (1952) is usually considered the essential work in the genre. In this play, two tramps wait in vain for the mysterious **Godot**, who never appears. Like other absurdist works, it explores concepts of isolation, futility, and non-communication. The tramps' predicament is universal and the play's title has come to stand for that predicament. In his later works, Beckett reached the frontiers of the absurdist's world, with characters in increasingly bizarre settings and predicaments. For instance in *Happy Days* (1960), the main character, Winnie, is gradually immersed in sand, while *Breath* (1969) runs for just 30 seconds and includes sounds of both birth and death. Other playwrights associated with the style included Edward Albee and Harold Pinter.

• **Theatre Workshop** ▸ An experimental left-wing drama group founded in Kendal in 1945 by a group of actors dissatisfied with the mainstream theatre. From 1953 the Workshop was based in the Theatre Royal, Stratford East, London, with Joan Littlewood (1914–  ) as artistic director, Gerald Raffles as general manager, and Ewan McColl (Littlewood's husband) as writer or adapter of many of the group's dramatic productions. Theatre Workshop sought to revitalize the British theatre with challenging adaptions of the classics and new works, especially working-class plays. Many of these, including Brendan Behan's *The Quare Fellow* (1956) and Shelagh Delaney's *A Taste of Honey* (1958), later transferred to London's West End. In 1961 Littlewood left the group, disillusioned by the dilution of the radical content of its output as a result of the pressure for commercial success. She did, however, return to direct the occasional production, notably the musical *Oh, What a Lovely War!* (1963). She eventually left the UK in 1975 to work in France; the Workshop disbanded soon afterwards.

• **themed** ▶ Denoting a restaurant, pub, amusement park, etc., that is planned or designed around a single unifying theme, such as the Wild West or Sherlock Holmes. The concept arose with the advent of the **theme park**, a leisure site in which the various displays and buildings reflect a particular theme, usually a historic period or exotic place. The 1980s saw a vogue for 'theming' established pubs and restaurants with the aim of attracting a young wealthy clientele, generally to the irritation of its more conservative regular clientele. The practice has even spread to such areas as catering, so that it is possible to order a 'themed' meal for special occasions.

• **theory of games** ▶ *See*: game theory.

• **thermal reactor** ▶ *See*: nuclear reactor.

• **thermonuclear weapon** ▶ *See*: nuclear weapon.

• **think-tank** ▶ A group of people with specialized knowledge and ability, set up to carry out research into particular problems (usually social, political, and technological) and to provide ideas and possible solutions. The idea originated in America in the 1940s; in the UK the term was first used for the Central Policy Review Staff, set up by Edward Heath in 1970 under the directorship of Lord Rothschild (1910–90). Its function was to provide the cabinet and individual ministers with advice on strategy. It was abolished in 1983 by Margaret Thatcher.

• **Thin Man, the** ▶ An epithet now associated with Nick Charles, the wisecracking detective hero of a series of films in the 1930s and 1940s (and later of a TV series). In the first of these films, *The Thin Man* (1934), as in the original Dashiell Hammet novel, the Thin Man was actually the first of the murder victims and not the detective. However, a string of sequels followed, all with 'Thin Man' somewhere in the title; as a result the hero (played by William Powell) became firmly identified with the phrase.

• **third age** ▶ The years after middle age, a term borrowed from the French *troisième âge*. *See also*: University of the Third Age.

• **third man** ▶ A suspected third Soviet agent involved in the defection of Burgess and Maclean to Russia in 1951 (*see*: Magnificent Five). In 1963 it became apparent that the third man was journalist Kim Philby, who also fled to Moscow. The name alludes to the title of the Graham Greene and Carol Reed film *The Third Man* (1949). *See*: Lime, Harry.

• **Third Programme** ▶ One of the three postwar BBC radio channels (the others being the Light Programme and the Home Service) which went on the air for the first time on 29 September 1946. The Third Programme was devoted to serious, often avant-garde, music, drama, literature, lectures, and intelligent discussion. Exact programme timings were avoided to ensure a free-flowing schedule and items broadcast during the first week included Bach's *Goldberg Variations*, Shaw's *Man and Superman*, talks by Field Marshal Smuts and Max Beerbohm, and a humorous programme devised by Joyce Grenfell and Stephen Potter. The darling of intellectuals, 'the Third', as it was called, was sneered at by the uneducated and by some others who ought to have known better:

> I have listened attentively to all programmes and nothing will confirm me more in my resolution to emigrate. – EVELYN WAUGH.

• **Third Reich** ▶ The offical name of the Nazi regime in Germany, from January 1933 to May 1945. The Third Reich was deemed to be the successor to two previous periods of German power: the First Reich being the medieval Holy Roman Empire and the Second Reich the empire of the Kaisers (1871–1918). *Reich* is German for empire or realm.

• **Third Republic** ▶ The government of France between the defeat of the Second Empire by Prussia in 1870 and the fall of France to Nazi Germany in 1940. The Third Republic was notable for its political instability, especially after 1918, when government ministries came and went with great rapidity. The period was also punctuated by a series of crises that threatened the French parliamentary system itself; these included the Dreyfus affair in the 1890s and the Stavisky affair in the 1930s. In spite of these shortcomings, the Third Republic proved to be France's longest-lived system of government since the Revolution of 1789.

• **Third Way** ▶ A political approach developed by centre-left parties during the 1990s; although somewhat ill-defined, it can be seen as an attempt to modernize social democracy in the light of changing social and economic conditions. The idea was highly influential in the policy-making of Tony Blair's New Labour government in the UK and Bill Clinton's 'New Democrats' in the USA.

As the name suggests, the Third Way attempts to provide an alternative to traditional ideologies of both left and right, arguing that these have become outdated in an era of rapid technological advance, globalization of business and information, and fragmentation of social classes. Its proponents endorse the role of the free market as the basis for creating a 'new mixed economy', while seeking to construct a new social contract on the principle of 'no rights without responsibilities'. They also uphold traditional family values (while accepting that family structures have changed), are 'tough on crime' (but also 'tough on the causes of crime'), and have introduced measures aimed at reducing the scale and cost of the welfare state (while insisting that the principles behind it are intact).

Critics have condemned Third Way thinking as ideologically incoherent and totally inadequate to the real challenges posed by globalization. In the UK, many traditional leftwingers regard it scornfully as a capitulation by the Labour Party to the values of Thatcherism.

• **Third World** ▸ The underdeveloped countries of Africa, Asia, and Latin America in which agricultural and industrial production are insufficient to sustain investment and economic growth. The term was coined during the Cold War era to distinguish these countries from both the capitalist Western nations (the **First World**) and the communist bloc (the **Second World**). Although it is still used, the term **developing world** is now generally preferred.

• **Thirteen Plots of May 13** ▸ The dramatic and secretive plotting and counterplotting that returned Charles de Gaulle (1890–1979) to power in France in May 1958. De Gaulle had resigned the premiership in 1946 in disgust at what he perceived as the harmful vacillation and factionalism of parliamentary politics. By 1958, however, a powerful body of Gaullist supporters had begun secretly plotting to secure his return to power. They consisted of malcontents within the army and among White French settlers in Algeria, angered by what they regarded as inadequate political support from the mainland, and right-wing opponents of the government in metropolitan France. On 13 May, as a new prime minister, Pierre Pflimin, was about to be appointed, a large crowd attacked and occupied the government offices in Algiers, establishing a Committee of Public Safety. The army generals sup-

ported the Committee's call for de Gaulle's return to power, and on 15 May de Gaulle dramatically announced that he would be willing to assume power if invited. Meanwhile the rebellion in Algeria escalated; on 24 May Algerian-based troops occupied Corsica and it was widely rumoured that the generals were planning to occupy Paris on 27 May. It was against this background of political crisis, heightened by fears of an imminent military coup and the threat of civil war, that Pflimin agreed to step down in favour of de Gaulle. On 1 June the national assembly confirmed de Gaulle's appointment as premier, gave him full powers for six months, and left him with the task of elaborating a new constitution. De Gaulle was certainly aware of the plots to secure his return but he wisely refused to commit himself until the collapse of the Fourth Republic was certain; this enabled him to assume power on his own terms.

• **38th Parallel** ▸ The dividing line between North and South Korea agreed by the Soviet Union and America in August 1945. It was originally intended as a temporary measure to facilitate the surrender of Japanese forces in the region; the Soviets would be responsible for the Japanese surrender north of the 38th Parallel and the Americans responsible south of the line. The division was hastily suggested by the Americans as the Soviet forces moved into the north of Korea in the last days of the war. Stalin surprisingly agreed, although the absence of US forces in the area at that time would not have prevented him moving further south. As a result America was left in control of the capital Seoul, two-thirds of the population, and the main agricultural region, while the Soviet Union controlled the industrial north. As the wartime alliance between the Soviet Union and America dissolved into Cold War rivalry, the prospects for unification receded and civil war escalated into full-scale international confrontation in the Korean War (1950–53). The post-war armistice left the boundary unchanged; the division of Korea into North and South along the 38th Parallel remains.

• **thirty-something** ▸ Any age between 30 and 40, when the conflicting impulses of youth and oncoming middle age can precipitate a crisis of identity. The phrase is often used to avoid giving one's exact age; its association with a vague spiritual malaise was reinforced in the 1980s when it was used as the title of a highly successful US TV series about a group of affluent but troubled young people in their thirties. Britain's most famous thirty-something is undoubtedly the neurotic Bridget Jones. The terms twenty-something, forty-something, etc., are now also common.

• **Thought Police** ▶ The sinister and murderous guardians of Party orthodoxy described by George Orwell (1903–50) in his Nineteen Eighty-Four (1949). In this nightmarish vision of a totalitarian future, society is divided into the Party and the Proles. The Proles are insignificant, but the Party is divided into the Inner Party, the privileged class, and the Outer Party, who are constantly monitored by the Thought Police for deviation from prescribed thinking (**thought crimes**). Those caught harbouring improper thoughts are arrested, tortured at the Ministry of Love, and then vaporized. The term is now often used for any agency (real or imagined) that attempts to impose official thinking or political correctness.

• **Thousand Days** ▶ The three-year administration of President John F. Kennedy (1917–63), from his election on 9 November 1960 to his assassination on 22 November 1963. It was taken as the title of one of the best inside accounts of Kennedy's presidency, A Thousand Days: John F. Kennedy in the White House (1965), by the historian Arthur Schlesinger Jr, one of the 'Best and Brightest' whom Kennedy selected to implement his promised New Frontier. See also: Camelot.

• **thrash** ▶ A type of rock music that combines the speed and violence of hardcore with the high-volume guitar style of heavy metal. It originated in New York in the late 1980s. Exponents rejoiced in such names as Anthrax, Napalm Death, and Millions of Dead Cops. It is also known as **speed metal**, **thrash metal**, **thrashcore**, and **deathcore**.

• **threatened species** ▶ A species of animal or plant that is in danger of becoming extinct if nothing is done to halt the decline in its wild population. Reasons for the decline may include exploitation of the species (e.g. the killing of elephants to obtain their tusks) or destruction of its habitat (e.g. the burning of tropical rain forests). The International Union for the Conservation of Nature and Natural Resources (IUCN) has identified several categories of threatened species. These include (in ascending order of vulnerability): rare species (those with small populations considered to be at risk); vulnerable species; and endangered species. See also: extinct.

• **3-D** ▶ Three-dimensional cinematography. From the 1920s onwards various stereoscopic techniques were used to create an illusion of realistic depth on the cinema screen, mainly in short films. It was not, however, until competition from television became a serious threat in the 1950s that the studios paid serious attention to 3-D processes with such tradenames as Natural Vision 3-D and Dynoptic

3-D. The first 3-D feature film, Bwana Devil in 1952, promised 'A lion in your lap'; Warner Brothers' House of Wax (1953) was perhaps the most successful of the 30 or so features that followed in the next couple of years. The anaglyphic process used required the audience to wear polarized glasses, which blended two simultaneously projected images of the same scene shot by separate cameras. The public's thrill at ducking spears and boulders soon waned in favour of well-scripted films that did not require glasses.

• **Three Mile Island** ▶ The site near Harrisburg, Pennsylvania, of America's most serious nuclear reactor accident on 28 March 1979. Owing to human and technological failure, the fissionable core, normally immersed in water, became accidentally exposed to the air and began to melt, releasing radioactive gases into the air. Complete meltdown of the reactor core (see: China syndrome) was avoided but the accident provoked a national debate on the safety of nuclear power. This effectively brought the US nuclear reactor programme to a halt and provided support for the anti-nuclear power lobby elsewhere. See also: Chernobyl.

• **three-mile limit** ▶ See: rum runners.

• **three-minute culture** ▶ A culture in which the constant supply of miscellaneous information by means of television, magazines, etc., has led to the average viewer or reader being unable to concentrate on a single topic for more than a few minutes. As evidence for the damaging influence of such a culture, commentators point to the diminishing length of newspaper articles and the phenomenon of the sound bite, etc. See also: dumbing down.

• **throwaway** ▶ A disposable artefact, especially one designed to be discarded after a single use. Throwaway cameras, for example, are sold containing a film; after the film has been exposed and developed, the camera is thrown away. The proliferation of such items has led to accusations that the West has become a wasteful 'throwaway society'.

• **throw a wobbly** or **wobbler** ▶ To be overcome by a fit of uncontrollable rage. Although a number of derivations have been suggested for this slang phrase (such as the idea that it refers to throwing a 'wobbly' ball in cricket), it probably combines the idiom 'to throw a fit' with the idea of somebody trembling (wobbling) with anger. The term was popular with teenagers in the 1980s and 1990s, who used it chiefly to make the anger of parents or teachers seem ridiculous.

• **Thunderthighs** ▶ A nickname for an obese or

heavily built woman, especially one who is intimidating to men. In the late 1970s it was the media's nickname for Christina Onassis, heiress of the Greek shipping magnate Aristotle Onassis (1906–75), referring to her evident weight problem. It presumably refers to 'thunder' in the sense of moving heavily or noisily.

• **Tiananmen Square massacre** ▸ The massacre by the Chinese army of thousands of unarmed civilians in Beijing's Tiananmen Square during pro-democracy demonstrations in June 1989. Protests had started in late April during the funeral of the liberal Hu Yaobang, a deposed former general secretary of the Chinese Communist Party. About 150,000 students gathered in Tiananmen Square shouting anti-government slogans. By mid-May more than one million demonstrators, including some government officials, held the largest protest gathering in communist China's history. This occurred during a visit by the reforming Soviet leader, Mikhail Gorbachov, who made a point of interrupting his schedule to lay a wreath in Tiananmen Square. Students occupied the square permanently and erected a Statue of Freedom based on New York's Statue of Liberty; some of them staged hunger strikes. Martial law was imposed on 20 May and on 3 June about 10,000 troops of the People's Liberation Army entered the city; the next day tanks and armoured personnel carriers moved in to kill the fleeing students. The massacre provoked worldwide condemnation and trade reprisals. However, Deng Xiaoping, China's veteran leader, made it clear that he would continue to crush the 'counter-revolutionary rebellion'. Mass arrests and executions followed.

• **ticker** ▸ See: birder.

• **tidal power** ▸ A method of generating electricity by using the ebb and flow of the tides. Water is collected behind a barrage at high tide and released at low tide to drive a turbine, which in turn drives a generator. The first successful scheme to exploit tidal power was the La Rance power station opened in 1967 in the Gulf of Saint-Malo in France. Several UK sites, especially the Severn estuary, are thought to be suitable for tidal power generation. See also: alternative energy.

• **Tiger, the** ▸ Nickname of the French statesman and journalist Georges Clemenceau (1841–1929), who, as prime minister, led his country to victory in World War I and negotiated the Versailles Treaty (1919). A determined fighter, single-minded in achieving his objectives, he gained an early reputation for destructive political power by bringing down one ministry after another using his newspaper La Justice.

• **tights** ▸ See: pantyhose.

• **time and motion study** ▸ A widely used method of analysing a complex operation by breaking it into small steps and timing each step. This enables standards of performance to be set so that the operation can be incorporated into a larger process, which can be timed and costed accurately.

• **time capsule** ▸ A box or other container enclosing items related to the present period, which is buried or hidden for rediscovery and reopening in the distant future. Such capsules, usually containing daily newspapers, everyday objects, etc., have been 'planted' at numerous sites throughout the UK since the 1960s, often with civic ceremony. The ultimate in time capsules must, however, be the summaries of human achievement carried on board the Pioneer and Voyager space probes.

• **time dilation** ▸ See: relativity.

• **time-lapse photography** ▸ A method of filming used to record such slow processes as plant growth. A series of single exposures of the subject is made over a period of time using a film or video camera adapted to taking single shots. When this film is shown at a normal speed the rate of change is greatly speeded up. For example, if one photograph per day is taken of a plant, the growth from seedling to mature plant over a period of several weeks can be seen in a few seconds.

• **time share** ▸ 1. An arrangement for sharing ownership in a furnished holiday house or flat, with each owner occupying the property for a certain period during the year. Popularized in the mid-1970s, time share has since come into disrepute because of the high-pressure selling methods associated with it (see: hard sell). For example, people are often telephoned by a company and told that they have 'won' a foreign holiday; however, in order to collect this prize they have to attend a long presentation during which they are subjected to the full repertoire of hard-sell techniques. Those who withstand this battery and try to claim their 'prize' without signing up for an expensive time-share arrangement meet with short shrift. Action to end the worst such abuses was taken in the early 1990s. 2. The apparently simultaneous use of a central computer by operators at separate terminals. This is possible because of the computer's high speed of processing data.

• **TINA** ▸ A nickname of Margaret Thatcher. See: Iron Lady.

• **tin fish** ▶ Naval slang for a torpedo.

• **Tinker Bell** ▶ In J. M. Barrie's children's play Peter Pan (1904), a female fairy who accompanies Peter and the Darling children on their adventures. When she 'dies', the audience is required to declare its belief in fairies in order to bring her back to life. The name is sometimes applied to effeminate or oversensitive males.

• **Tin Lizzie** ▶ Nickname of the Ford Model T motor car, designed by Henry Ford and manufactured by the Ford Motor Company in the early 20th century. The Model T was the first mass-produced motor car: 15 million had been manufactured and sold by 1927, when the model was discontinued. The first Model T car was made in 1908, and mass production began five years later on a specially designed assembly line housed in a purpose-built factory at Highland Park, Michigan. With its four-cylinder 2898 cc engine, the Model T was capable of speeds up to 40 mph; in accordance with Ford's specifications it was durable, easy to operate and maintain, and equally suitable for town and country driving. A reduction in the price of the Model T to $500, or £110, brought motoring within the reach of the average citizen in America and the UK. *See at*: black.

• **Tin Pan Alley** ▶ The district of New York City, originally in the area between 5th Avenue and Broadway, where many songwriters and music publishers were formerly based. In England, Denmark Street, off Charing Cross Road, was also so called as the centre of the popular music industry. The name has been said to derive from the rattling of pans by aggrieved neighbours when a performance was too loud or too protracted. The 'Alley' is now largely deserted by songwriters and music publishers who have moved to bigger premises. *See*: Old Grey Whistle Test.

• **tinsel town** ▶ *See*: Hollywood.

• **tip and run raid** ▶ During World War II, a hurried and often indiscriminate air raid in which the enemy sped homeward after jettisoning their bombs. So called from the light-hearted form of cricket in which the batsman has to run every time he hits the ball.

• **Tipperary** ▶ A song inseparably associated with World War I, composed by Jack Judge (d. 1938), of Oldbury, Birmingham, with words by Harry J. Williams of Temple Balsall, Warwickshire (who has the first line of the refrain engraved on his tombstone). The two men wrote the song in 1912, in response to a bet that they could not write a song and perform it the same day; it became popular in the music hall in 1914 after it was sung by troops embarking for France and on the Front.

> It's a long way to Tipperary,
> It's a long way to go,
> It's a long way to Tipperary,
> To the sweetest girl I know,
> Goodbye, Piccadilly;
> Farewell, Leicester Square;
> It's a long, long way to Tipperary,
> But my heart's right there.

• **tired and emotional** ▶ A euphemism for drunk that has proved useful to the press who have to be mindful of the libel laws when reporting people's exploits. The expression is thought to have originated in the satirical magazine Private Eye in the 1960s, when it was frequently used to describe the demeanour of George Brown, a notoriously bibulous Labour politician. It is sometimes abbreviated to **t and e**.

• **Titanic** ▶ The sinking of RMS *Titanic* on 14 April 1912 ranks as perhaps the most notorious shipwreck of all time. The large number of deaths, together with the shock caused by the loss of the world's newest and most luxurious ocean-liner on her maiden voyage, made an impression on the world's imagination that has never faded. The *Titanic* set sail from Southampton with 3000 people aboard, including at least six millionaires and many prominent members of British and US society. At 11.45 p.m. on 14 April, however, the claims that the ship was unsinkable were put to the severest test when she hit an iceberg, which tore a 300-foot gash below the waterline. When the *Titanic* went down two hours and 40 minutes later – its band still playing – 1513 people drowned. The high death toll was largely owing to the criminally small number of lifeboats provided (only 16) and a failure to load these to their proper capacity.

Curiously, the loss of the *Titanic* appears to have been foretold some years earlier by Morgan Robertson in his novel *Futility*. In this work of fiction, a great liner on its maiden voyage – with many society figures among its 3000 passengers – sinks when it rams an iceberg: the death toll is high because there are not enough lifeboats. The *Titan* is also called 'unsinkable'.

This was not the only forewarning of the tragedy. The journalist and spiritualist W. T. Stead had in 1892 published another story closely parallel to the *Titanic*'s; he was one of those to die in the disaster in 1912.

The sinking has inspired several films and novels, notably James Cameron's epic *Titanic* (1997), which had the distinction of being both the most expensive and the most successful movie made to that date. By contrast Lew Grade's big-budget *Raise the Titanic!* (1980) was such a disaster in box-office terms that it nearly 'sank' its production company; Grade later joked that it would have been cheaper to lower the Atlantic. The wreck itself was located and photographed in 1985; divers recovered various items and shots of it were used in Cameron's film.

> Over the mirrors meant
> To glass the opulent
> The sea-worm crawls – grotesque, slimed,
>                         dumb, indifferent.
> – THOMAS HARDY: 'The Convergence of the Twain'.

• **Titan rocket**► A US liquid-fuelled ICBM developed during the 1950s and replaced by the Minuteman in the early 1960s. Titan I had a range of 8000 miles (12,800 km) and Titan II 9000 miles (14,400 km); both carried a 10 megaton nuclear warhead. The Titan was also modified as a two-stage space launch vehicle, proving to be one of the most reliable of NASA's rockets; Titan II successfully launched all ten of the Gemini two-man spacecraft in the early 1960s. Until the development of the space shuttle, the Titan IIIE-Centaur was the heaviest US launch vehicle, capable of placing 13,600 kg into Earth orbit. First tested in 1974, it was used to launch the Viking I spacecraft to Mars in August of the following year.

• **Titoism**► The pragmatic form of communism implemented in Yugoslavia after 1945 by Josip Broz Tito (1892–1980). Tito rejected the Soviet model of communist social and economic development, imposed by Stalin in the eastern bloc countries, believing instead in the possibility of 'separate roads to socialism'. His policies included decentralized profit-sharing workers' councils and a non-aligned stance in international affairs. Regarding Titoism as a dangerous threat to his authority, Stalin expelled Yugoslavia from the Cominform in 1948. A purge was then carried out of suspected Titoist heretics throughout the communist parties and governments of E Europe. Surprisingly, Tito survived Stalin's wrath, although similar national and reformist movements in Hungary and Czechoslovakia, which were partially inspired by the Yugoslavian example, were later crushed by Soviet tanks *(see:* Hungarian Rising; Prague Spring).

• **TLC** ► Tender loving care. The abbreviation is widely used in medical contexts to denote the unspecific treatment that a person may require in some circumstances.

• **Toad** ► A character in the popular children's book, *The Wind in the Willows* (1908), by Kenneth Grahame (1859–1932). Mr Toad, the master of Toad Hall, is a bumptious egotist with a passion for driving at reckless speeds. The work was later dramatized by A. A. Milne as *Toad of Toad Hall* (1929). *See also*: Rat.

• **Tobruk** ► The best harbour in Cyrenaica (Libya), North Africa, which was the scene of fierce battles during World War II. In January 1941 it was captured from the Italians by British and Australian troops; by February the whole of Cyrenaica was in British hands after the total collapse of the Italian forces. The Germans then entered the Mediterranean campaign and by April Tobruk was encircled by Rommel's Panzer divisions after German forces had met only thin resistance from the British as they drove eastward from El Agheila through Benghazi. The Royal Navy and the RAF managed to supply the besieged garrison with food, weapons, and fresh troops, until on 11 December the 242-day-long siege ended when Commonwealth troops broke out of the city to join with the British Eighth Army units at nearby Acroma. In his second offensive in Libya, Rommel inflicted another series of defeats on the Eighth Army, until on 20 June 1942 Tobruk was finally captured, along with 33,000 troops. In the following weeks the Eighth Army retreated all the way to El Alamein, where Rommel's advance was finally halted in July.

• **Toc H** ► An interdenominational Christian association for social service. It developed from Talbot House, a servicemen's club founded (December 1915) at Poperinghe in Belgium, by the Revd P. B. (Tubby) Clayton (1885–1972), who made it a famous rest and recreation centre. The club was named in memory of Gilbert Talbot (1885–1915), son of the Bishop of Winchester, who had been killed at Hooge in the preceding July; it became known as Toc H from the army telegrapher's code for the initials T and H. In 1920 Clayton founded a similar centre in London, also known as Toc H, which developed into a wider social movement.

• **Today is the first day of the rest of your life** ► A saying attributed to the US founder of an anti-heroin clinic, Charles Dederich. Heroin addicts who are really determined to overcome their habit have to make a clean break with their past lives – refusing to see any of their addicted friends or drug sources, who will do all they can to undermine their reform. Entering a clinic, if it is to serve any purpose, needs to constitute a new start – the first day of a new life.

• **Todt Organization**► The Nazi construction organization headed by Fritz Todt (1891–1942), a civil engineer who had joined the Nazi Party in 1922. He was made inspector-general of the road and highway system in 1933, was put in charge of the Four-

Year-Plan (1936–40), and was Reich minister for munitions from 1940 until his death in a plane crash. The Todt Organization was responsible for the construction of the autobahn system, the 400-mile long Siegfried Line, and the Atlantic Wall, the French coastal defences erected after the German occupation in 1940.

• **together** ▶ Self-possessed, free of emotional problems. In the late 1960s this was a popular term in the hippie lexicon, indicating a vague idea of being at peace with oneself and the world (especially in the exhortation get it together). In the work- and efficiency-obsessed 1980s its meaning dwindled to competent or well-organized.

• **tokamak** ▶ *See*: nuclear reactor.

• **tokenism** ▶ The practice by some companies, schools, sports teams, etc., of accepting a token representation of a minority group, such as Blacks or women, in order to give the appearance of operating an equal-opportunities policy. This early-1960s Americanism spread to the UK a decade or so later. A **showcase nigger** is Black slang for a token Black given high visibility in the company's front office.

> I was the showcase Jew with the agency. I tried to look Jewish desperately, used to read my memos from right to left all the time. They fired me finally 'cos I took off too many Jewish holidays. – WOODY ALLEN.

*See*: quota system.

• **tokus** or **tochis** ▶ Bottom or backside, from the Yiddish *tokhes* and originally Hebrew *tahath*, under. A common expression in New York is **get off your tokus**, *i.e.* get up and do something. Like many other Yiddish words it has crossed the Atlantic since World War II.

• **Tokyo Rose** ▶ The nickname given by US servicemen to a mysterious sultry voiced young woman who broadcast propaganda from Japan during World War II. 'Tokyo Rose' has never been satisfactorily identified and it now seems that she was either a composite of several broadcasters or completely mythical. After the war several American-Japanese women were suspected of taking part in these broadcasts but only one, Iva Ikuko Toguri D'Aquino (1916–   ), was charged. Although there is good evidence that D'Aquino was pro-Allied in her sympathies, and that her broadcasts (for a Channel run by POWs) were intended as lighthearted send-ups of Japanese propaganda, she was found guilty of being the notorious 'Tokyo Rose' and sentenced to 10 years in prison. After her release in 1956 a campaign to clear her name gathered momentum; she was finally given a presidential pardon in 1977. *See also*: Lord Haw-Haw.

• **tom** ▶ *See*: jane.

• **Tom and Jerry** ▶ Two cartoon characters who have featured in numerous MGM shorts since the early 1940s; Tom, a vindictive but accident-prone cat, and Jerry, a clever little mouse. They were created by William Hanna and Joe Barbera and first seen in *Puss Gets the Boot* (1940). The characters are famous for the extreme slapstick violence they mete out on each other, while remaining indestructible.

They may have been named after a couple of roistering young men about town featured in Pierce Egan's *Life in London; or, The Day Night Scenes of Jerry Hawthorn, Esq., and his Elegant Friend Corinthian Tom* (1821).

• **Tommy** ▶ The usual nickname given to British soldiers fighting in the two world wars. In fact the name Tommy or **Tommy Atkins** had been used for the British private soldier for many years before this. From 1815 and throughout the 19th century 'Thomas Atkins' was the name used in the specimen form, accompanying the official manual issued to all army recruits, showing them how their own form, requiring details of name, age, date of enlistment, etc., should be filled in. *See also*: Fritz.

• **Tommy-cooker** ▶ A small individual stove using solid fuel invented during World War I and issued to Allied troops in World War II. It was also the name given by the Germans to the Sherman tank, which caught fire very easily when hit.

• **Tommy gun** ▶ A Thompson short-barrelled sub-machine-gun.

• **tomography** ▶ (Greek *tōmos*, slice, section; *graphein*, to write) A technique for obtaining an X-ray or ultrasound picture of a specific plane of the body or of any other solid object. The tomography machine is so designed that the radiation or ultrasound is focused only on a selected plane; clear images are obtained of structures in that plane, while overlying structures appear blurred. Tomography, which was developed in the 1930s, is widely used in medical diagnosis as it enables the imaging of soft and deep-seated tissues and organs, which cannot be visualized using conventional X-ray machines. It is often used in the form of computerized tomography (*see*: CT scanner). *See also*: body scanner; brain scanner.

• **ton** ▶ A speed of 100 mph. In the late 1950s, 'doing a ton' became a goal for every young motorcyclist, being regarded as the ultimate test of both machine and rider. Organized speed trials were held on public roads, their illegality supplying an extra frisson of excitement. The activities of the

**ton-up kids**, as they were dubbed, became the subject of outraged comment in the press.

In darts and cricket a ton is a personal score of 100, while in betting and underworld slang it means a sum of £100.

• **tong** ▶ (Cantonese *tohng*, meeting place) Chinese fraternal organizations that originated in the benevolent and protective associations formed by Chinese immigrants to the West, especially America, in the second half of the 19th century. By the turn of the century, competition for scarce economic opportunities led to open warfare between the tong societies. During the 1930s, these 'tong wars' were serious enough for the US government to arrest and deport large numbers of Chinese. Although many of the tongs developed into fronts for criminal activities, including gambling, prostitution, and drug-pushing, the modern tong societies are largely respectable. Their main function is promoting the economic and political well-being of the Chinese comunity.

• **Tonkin Gulf incident** ▶ Attacks by North Vietnamese motor torpedo boats on the US destroyer *Maddox* on 2 August 1964, and on the *Maddox* and *C. Turner Joy* on 4 August off the North Vietnamese coast. The incident provoked America to bomb North Vietnamese oil refineries and naval bases in retaliation. On 7 August a receptive Congress approved the vaguely worded Southeast Asia Resolution (**Tonkin Gulf Resolution**), granting President Lyndon Johnson emergency powers to take any action necessary to repel or prevent any further attacks on US forces. This amounted to carte blanche to wage an undeclared war in Southeast Asia. It is now known that the *Maddox* was on a spying mission in North Vietnamese waters, gathering information to aid the clandestine campaign of commando raids against North Vietnamese coastal installations, which South Vietnamese forces (with US help) had been pursuing since partition in 1954. These had been stepped up since Johnson assumed office in late 1963. The action of the North Vietnamese MTBs against the *Maddox* on 2 August had therefore been largely defensive in nature. It is also highly likely that the attack of 4 August never took place, being the product of spurious sonar readings produced by atmospheric disturbances. It is also known that plans for bombing North Vietnam, implemented after the incident, had been drawn up in the early part of 1964, in anticipation of a major escalation in the US involvement.

• **Tonto** ▶ *See*: Kemo Sabe; Lone Ranger.

• **Tontons Macoute** ▶ (Creole, Uncle Knapsack) In Haitian folklore a tonton macoute is a bogeyman who hunts naughty children and captures them in his sack (*macoute*). The name was applied to the fearsome private militia and secret police created by François 'Papa Doc' Duvalier (1907–71) as president of Haiti after 1957. The Tontons Macoute were Duvalier loyalists, who in return for weapons, and occasionally money, were licensed to terrorize, torture, and murder those perceived as enemies of the Duvalier regime. Many of the recruits (known officially after 1960 as the Volunteers for National Security – VSN) were ex-soldiers, many were criminals; all could be easily identified by their unofficial uniform – smart suit, dark glasses, and bulging hip holsters. Duvalier also encouraged the connection between the tontons and voodooism, in order to oppress and terrorize the population. When Duvalier died the tontons remained under his son, the new president, Jean-Claude 'Baby Doc' Duvalier, whose regime was toppled by a revolution in 1986.

• **Tony Awards** ▶ America's best-known theatre awards. First bestowed in 1947, Tonys are presented each spring for the best play, musical, actors, actresses, directors, authors, designers, producers, etc., on Broadway since the previous autumn. The award was named after Antoinette Perry (1888–1946), a Broadway producer and director.

• **Tonypandy riots** ▶ Violent disturbances caused by striking miners in the village of Tonypandy in Rhondda Valley, S Wales, in November 1910. The episode is mainly remembered for the myth that Winston Churchill, then Liberal home secretary, authorized troops to fire on the strikers, killing a number of them. In fact, no miners died and it was Churchill who was largely responsible for preventing bloodshed. On 10 November the chief constable of Glamorgan had requested the local army commander to take military action to control the rioters. When Churchill was informed that a small force of troops were on their way to the area, he insisted that they be held in reserve and that extra unarmed constables be sent instead. The police then managed to restrain the rioters without causing serious injuries.

• **too much** ▶ Outstanding or excellent; overpoweringly good. An expression originating in the Black jazz culture of the 1920s and 1930s, later adopted by hippies as a favourite term of enthusiasm.

> One day 'too much' will sound as old-fashioned as 'ripping'. – *Scottish Daily Mail*, January 1968.

• **top-hat scheme** ▶ A pension plan for a senior executive of a company.

• **topless** ▶ Describing an item of women's clothing that leaves the breasts and upper part of the body uncovered. The term is also used to describe a woman who is unclothed above the waist or a place in which women are allowed or encouraged to be topless. The 1960s saw the arrival of topless bars, nightclubs, etc., in which topless waitresses and dancers were employed for the titillation of men. Quite different are topless beaches, which enable women of all ages to obtain 'strapless' suntans.

• **topless radio** ▶ Slang for a radio phone-in programme that discusses sexual topics. Topless implies the sexually explicit nature of such a programme.

• **top secret** ▶ Describing military or governmental information about which the greatest secrecy is to be observed. In service and civil-service jargon there is a hierarchy of epithets for information that is 'classified' (*i.e.* for restricted circulation): 'top secret' is for the eyes and ears of only a very few, 'secret' may be shared a little more widely, and 'restricted' is available to a larger number still.

• **Torch** ▶ The codename for the Allied plan for the North African landings which began on 8 November 1942.

• **torch song** ▶ *See*: carry a torch.

• **Tornado** ▶ *See*: smart weapons.

• **Torrey Canyon** ▶ The oil tanker on charter to British Petroleum that ran aground on Seven Stones Reef, between Land's End and the Scilly Isles, on 18 March 1967. In an attempt to contain the leakage of her 120,000 tonnes of crude oil, naval vessels sprayed detergent onto the surrounding seas. On 26 March, however, she broke her back and oil polluted over 80 miles of the Cornish coastline. Subsequently Royal Navy Buccaneers were used to bomb the wreck to burn off the remaining oil and prevent further spillage. More recent tanker disasters include the *Exxon Valdez* off Alaska in 1989, the *Braer* off the Shetland Islands in 1993, and the *Sea Empress* off South Wales in 1996.

• **Tortilla Curtain** ▶ Slang for the fences built along the US–Mexican border to keep illegal immigrants out of America. The phrase is, of course, an adaptation of Iron Curtain; a tortilla is a cornmeal pancake – a staple of the Mexican diet. *See also*: Garlic Wall.

• **total quality management** ▶ (TQM) An approach to business management, pioneered in America and Japan, that encourages workers and managers to understand customers' requirements and to supply the right quality the first time. This is achieved by training, developing a corporate philosophy that encompasses all employees, and accepting that cheap inputs usually result in shoddy outputs. The approach is often criticized as being too costly, unworkable in practice, or a statement of the patently obvious disguised by jargon. The UK Post Office's attempt to split its workers into 'motivated teams' in furtherance of TQM led to strikes in 1996; this reflects a similar experience in America, where the Postal Service abandoned its attempt to utilize TQM after it led to a sharp decline in productivity and an even sharper increase in customer complaints.

• **Totenkopfverbände** ▶ *See*: SS.

• **Tour de France** ▶ The world's most prestigious bicycle race, established in 1903 by Henri Desgrange (1865–1940), the French cyclist and journalist. The route covers some 4000 km (2500 miles) of flat and mountainous terrain, mostly through France and Belgium, and is divided into 21 daily stages. The finishing line is always in Paris. There are normally around 120 contestants in the annual competition, each stage of the race is timed, and the rider with the lowest aggregate time for all stages is the winner. A **yellow jersey** is awarded to the rider with the fastest time in each stage of the race. Competitors ride in teams, which are sponsored by the manufacturer of a particular product; in addition to contending with the gruelling pace, riders are plagued by sponsors following them and journalists and TV crews speeding ahead of them, often choking the race leaders with exhaust fumes. The 1998 race nearly had to be abandoned after nearly half the riders withdrew, protesting at 'over-zealous' enforcement of the rules against drug use.

• **toy boy** ▶ The young male lover of an older woman. The term is usually derogatory, implying that the man is a brainless sexual athlete kept like a toy by the woman in return for his services. Its popularity in the 1980s and 1990s reflected a social trend in which middle-aged female celebrities began to do what successful men had always done, *i.e.* use their wealth and status to attract younger lovers.

• **Tracey** ▶ *See*: Sharon.

• **Tracy, Dick** ▶ The detective hero of a comic strip created by Chester Gould in 1931. His trademarks were his jutting jaw, fedora hat, and trench coat. The character appeared in a number of film serials and B-movies from the early 1930s; more recently, he was played by Warren Beatty in the stylish *Dick Tracy* (1990).

• **Trachtenberg System** ▶ A system of speedy

mathematical calculation based upon simple counting according to prescribed keys or formulae, which need to be memorized. It enables complicated calculations to be rapidly handled. The system was devised by Jakow Trachtenberg during his seven years in a Nazi concentration camp. He was born at Odessa and trained as an engineer, becoming a refugee in Germany after the Russian Revolution.

• **trad** ▸ Jazz in the traditional New Orleans style, especially as revived by White musicians during the 'trad boom' of the late 1950s and early 1960s. *See also*: Dixie.

• **trade cycle** or **business cycle** ▸ The cycle in an economy consisting of boom, recession, depression, recovery, and boom. Although it first appeared in the 19th century, the 20th century saw the greatest fluctuations and the most widespread consequences of the cycle. The Great Depression of the 1930s was a protracted world slump, causing great hardship in Western democracies. There is no single clear theory to explain the phenomenon, although the role of politicians has been stressed by a number of economists. Karl Marx suggested that during a boom workers became sufficiently powerful to demand higher wages, which capitalists countered by engineering a recession to create unemployment in order to undermine the workers' strength. More recent theories point to the stringent measures often imposed by a government shortly after its election and the way in which these are usually relaxed to stimulate demand before the next election. These changes can themselves make a strong contribution to the creation of a cycle. A simpler economic theory is that booms generate over-investment in new plant and equipment, which produces greater quantities of goods than the market can absorb. This causes price-cutting, redundancies, and a contraction in demand, as those made redundant cease to be affluent consumers. As more people are made redundant, the level of consumption falls, and more redundancies are required; this vicious circle leads to recession and eventually to slump. *See also*: stagnation theory.

• **trading stamps** ▸ Stamps given to customers by shops as an incentive to buy goods. They can be collected and later exchanged for goods or money. The trading-stamp company sells the stamps to the retailer, who gets his money back by the increased custom. The idea originated in America, where the company Sperry & Hutchinson produced what were popularly known as **green stamps**. In the UK a separate company produced **Green Shield stamps** from 1957. Trading stamps were extremely popular in the 1960s but their use has since declined. The

loyalty cards issued by supermarkets and other major chains now fulfill much the same function.

• **traffic calming** ▸ A policy of impeding motorists in residential streets in order to ensure that they drive slowly. Sleeping policemen are a common measure. These, however, cannot always be used on bus routes and are unpopular with ambulance drivers. **Build-outs** to narrow a road to a single lane are another device but these tend to increase congestion unless the traffic flow is very light.

• **trahison des clercs** ▸ (French, treachery of the intellectuals) The betrayal of intellectual principles by the intelligentsia. In particular, the phrase refers to the incursion of the intelligentsia, who should be concerned with the pursuit of truth and be guided by abstract thought, into partisan politics and propaganda. It comes from the title of Julien Benda's work *La Trahison des clercs* (1927), in which he attacked intellectuals who seek to govern the world.

• **trail** ▸
  **There's a long, long trail awinding** The refrain and title of one of the best-known songs of World War I. Peculiarly appropriate to the slogging warfare of the trenches, it was written by the then-unknown US songwriter Alonzo Elliott in 1913. The war he had in mind was not the terrible conflagration to come but Napoleon's retreat from Moscow in 1812.

• **Tramp, The** ▸ The famous character created by Charlie Chaplin (1889–1977), the British-born US comedian, film actor, and director. The shuffling downtrodden little vagabond with baggy trousers, bowler hat, moustache, and cane is one of the most endearing and enduring images of the 20th century. According to legend, Chaplin borrowed a pair of Fatty Arbuckle's trousers from a wardrobe in the male dressing room at the Keystone Studios in February 1914; film historians differ over whether this was during *Kid Auto Races at Venice, California* or *Mabel's Strange Predicament* (both 1914). Chaplin claimed to have based the character's outsize trousers and curious gait on an old man who held the horses outside a South London pub run by his uncle. The Tramp finally bowed out in Chaplin's last silent film *Modern Times* (1936).

• **tranny** or **trannie** ▸ 1. Short for transistor radio; a type of light compact radio introduced in the late 1950s. Before long, cheap portable trannies were ubiquitous in the streets and on beaches, etc., to such an extent that many regarded them as a public nuisance. The term is rarely heard now. The tiny outdoor tranny, with its small loudspeaker and tinny sound, has been superseded by the Walkman (with headphones) and the ghettoblaster (with stereo and relatively large speakers). **2.** Shortened form of photographic transparency, widely used by photographers and layout artists. **3.** Shortened form of transsexual or transvestite.

• **transcendental meditation (TM)** ▶ A method of meditation and relaxation devised by the Maharishi Mahesh Yogi; he began to teach his technique in India in 1955 but it did not become popular in Europe and America until the 1960s. The method involves the silent repetition of Sanskrit mantras so that the meditator's thoughts are withdrawn from surface concerns to a deeper level of consciousness. TM students are formally instructed by teachers, who then allocate them their mantras according to their temperament and lifestyle. The physical and mental benefits of TM can, it is claimed, be obtained by two 20-minute meditation periods per day. More controversially, advocates of TM claim that meditation by large numbers of people can influence world events.

In 1992 the movement launched the so-called Natural Law Party, which contested almost every seat in the British general election of that year. Its manifesto promised a swift end to the world's problems through organized meditation and 'the first government in the world based on sound scientific principles'. The party became something of a laughing stock through its advocacy of yogic flying.

• **transformational grammar** or **transformational-generative grammar** ▶ In linguistics, a system of grammar that devises rules for basic sentence structure and assumes that every possible sentence in the language can be generated from them. The system also indicates how intended meanings (the deep structure) are converted into specific language units (surface structures) by using these rules or transformations. The theory of transformational grammar was primarily developed by the US linguist, Noam Chomsky (1928–   ).

• **transgenic** ▶ Denoting animals and plants whose genetic makeup has been altered by genetic engineering. The potential value of transgenic plants and animals in agriculture, the food industry, and medicine is considerable; however, there is still much consumer resistance to their use on environmental and other grounds. *See*: GM food.

• **Trans-Siberian Railway** ▶ The railway line between Moscow and Vladivostok, linking European Russia with the Pacific Coast across Siberia. The route runs for a distance of 9297 km (5778 mi), which takes about eight days to cover, making this the longest railway journey in the world both by distance and time. Construction began simultaneously

from both ends in 1891 and was completed in 1904. The first line made use of the Chinese Eastern Railway from Chita to Vladivostock, but in 1916 an all-Russia line was completed via Khabarovsk. It was the construction of the railway that opened up Siberia to economic development and colonization.

• **Traven, B.** ▶ The pen name of an author of best-selling adventure novels and short stories, the most popular of which are *The Death Ship* (1925), published in Germany, and *The Treasure of the Sierra Nevada* (1934), published in Mexico. Because 'Traven' avoided contact with his publishers and refused to provide any personal details, his true identity is still a mystery. According to W. Wyatt's *The Man Who was B. Traven* (1980), the man behind the pseudonym was probably Albert Otto Max Feige (1882–1969), who also used the name Ret Marut. Born in the Polish town of Swiebodzin (then in Germany), Feige was an actor and radical pamphleteer, who was involved in the anarchist movement during the German Revolution of 1918–19 and later (1924) moved to Mexico.

• **Treblinka** ▶ A Nazi concentration camp that opened in July 1942 at a railway junction on the Bug River in Poland, 45 miles (72 km) NE of Warsaw. The sole purpose of Treblinka was to systematically exterminate the Jews of central Poland (*see*: Final Solution; holocaust), including the 350,000 survivors of the Warsaw Ghetto, who were transported here in batches of 5000 per day. The new arrivals were segregated by sex, stripped, and then herded along the Himmelstrasse ('Heavenly Way') towards the 30 chambers initially fed with carbon monoxide gas from diesel engines and later with specially manufactured cyanide (Zyklon B). On 2 August 1943 about 700 Jewish forced labourers, whose task was to sort the clothes of the victims and burn corpses, rose in revolt, shooting 15 Ukranian guards. Most of the insurgents were killed in the camp; of the 150 that managed to escape, all but 12 were hunted down and killed. It is estimated that 850,000 Jews were murdered at Treblinka before it was shut down in October 1943.

• **Treetops** ▶ The most famous hotel in Kenya, built high in cape chestnut trees in the Aberdare National Park so that guests can observe the abundant wildlife in comfort and safety. The first Treetops Hotel, which was burned down by the Mau Mau in 1954, is famous as the place where Princess Elizabeth, on vacation with Prince Philip in February 1952, learned of the death of her father and became Queen.

• **trench coat** ▶ A style of raincoat influenced by British army officers' uniform coats of World War

I and later. These waterproof coats with various flaps and deep pockets are particularly associated with US private detectives, probably because of the battered trench coat worn by Humphrey Bogart in several of his films (*see also*: Tracy, Dick). They became fashionable again in the 1950s.

• **trench fever▸** A remittent or relapsing fever affecting men living in trenches, dug-outs, etc.; it is transmitted by the excrement of lice. It first appeared in World War I, in the static warfare on the Western Front.

• **trendy▸** Fashionable, up-to-date, following the latest trend or style. When first used in the 1960s, the term was one of approbation, often contrasting what was lively and new with what seemed old, dull, and square. In the 1980s it re-emerged as a derogatory term implying studied adherence to the latest fads and fashions. As a noun, it is almost always used scornfully, as in 'middle-aged trendy' and last chance trendy.

• **triage▸** The principle that if circumstances restrict the amount of help that can be given to those in distress, then the sufferers most likely to benefit from it should be chosen to receive the help, rather than those in the greatest need of it. The principle is similar to that involved in so-called lifeboat ethics.

The word 'triage' is derived from the Old French *trier*, 'to select', and was used in the 18th century to refer to sorting a sample of a commodity according to quality. Its modern meaning derives from the battlefields of World War I, where overstretched medical orderlies had to sort casualties into those that could be helped and those that could not. The latter were left to die. A similar medical usage has arisen in Britain's National Health Service. Overcrowded accident and emergency departments, where patients can wait several hours before seeing a doctor, usually have a specially trained triage nurse to decide the order in which patients receive medical attention. Clearly, 'first come first served' is not an appropriate system. The job of the triage nurse is to ensure that patients who may deteriorate (or even die) while they are waiting are seen first, leaving those with stable conditions to wait, even if they are in pain.

Triage is also used in the context of international aid. Help may be withdrawn from a desperately poor country with a 'basket-case' economy in order to target limited resources at another country that is considered more likely to benefit. Here, as elsewhere, the principle of triage involves a dispassionate pragmatism that may not come easily to a person or organization used to putting humanitarian criteria above all others.

At the very least, many Americans are now being forced to exercise 'family triage'. For example, a parent may save up to pay for a child's dental treatment before finding the money for his wife's mammogram. – *The Times*, 3 May 1991.

• **Trianon adventure▸** The extraordinary experience of Charlotte Moberly, principal of St Hugh's College, Oxford, and her companion Eleanor Jourdain, the vice-principal, while visiting the gardens of the Petit Trianon at Versailles on 10 August 1901. They claimed to have entered some form of time warp, which transported them back to 1789, and to have encountered a number of people in period dress, including a woman sketching, who, they decided later, was probably Marie Antoinette. Their experience, which was described in a book, *An Adventure* (1911), provoked considerable debate.

• **trick cyclist▸** A derisive term for a psychiatrist, based on a mispronunciation of the word. It is common among the British police, who frequently refer to criminal psychiatrists in this way. *See also*: headshrink.

• **trick or treat▸** The traditional Halloween cry of US children who, disguised as ghosts, witches, monsters, etc., visit neighbouring houses to ask for sweets. Their friendly threat is to play a prank on any resident who does not fill their bags. In the early 20th century, teenagers often played such tricks as turning over lawn furniture and soaping windows. Little of this occurs today, however, largely because trick-or-treaters are now mostly preteenagers and households keep a supply of sweets for the occasion. The trick-or-treat custom found a foothold in the UK in the 1980s and is now an established seasonal ritual, despite the disapproval of some; many householders treat their visitors with pennies in the tradition of Guy Fawkes Day (five days later).

• **Tricky Dicky▸** A nickname of Richard Milhous Nixon (1913–94), US president from 1969 until his resignation in 1974, when the Watergate scandal led to moves for his impeachment. He was first given the name by Helen Gahagan Douglas, his opponent in the 1950 senatorial election in California, whom he defeated in a campaign marked by innuendo about her supposed communist sympathies.

The name stuck to Nixon through the 1950s and 1960s owing to persistent controversies about his campaign funding and a somewhat shifty demeanour that did him no favours in the new era of television politics. Although his first term as president was in many ways a success, public doubts about Nixon's probity were revived with a vengeance as details of the Watergate conspiracy and the subsequent cover-up emerged in 1972–73. He resigned in disgrace on 8 August 1974. *See also*: Houdini of American Politics.

> Would you buy a used car from this man?
> – Caption to photograph of Nixon, *c.* 1952.

• **Trident ▶** The codename of the Anglo-American conference held in Washington between 12 and 25 May 1943. Churchill pressed for the continuation of the Mediterranean Strategy, with an attack on Sicily followed by an invasion of Italy. Roosevelt, on the other hand, insisted on a British commitment to the opening of the Second Front with a cross-channel invasion. A compromise was reached, with the Americans agreeing to preparations for an invasion of Italy, while Churchill was committed to the scheduling of Overlord for 1 May 1944. The US Pacific strategy against Japan was approved; a combined Anglo-American bombing offensive was also planned to destroy German military, industrial, and economic capabilities as a prelude to the cross-channel invasion. It was also secretly agreed that the development of the atom bomb should be a joint enterprise (*see*: Manhattan Project).

• **Trident missile ▶** US submarine-launched ballistic missile (SLBM) system developed as a replacement for Poseidon in America and Polaris in the UK. Development of Trident I started in America in the late 1960s; by the early 1980s it had replaced the Poseidon SLBM, which had succeeded Polaris in 1969. It carries eight 100-kiloton MIRVs with a range of up to 6900 miles (11,000 km). Trident II, with greater accuracy and more powerful warheads, was developed for deployment by both the Americans and the British in the early 1990s.

• **triffid ▶** Any large plant, whether a houseplant or a garden weed, that seems to be growing unusually strongly and is threatening to take over. The word comes from the science-fiction novel by John Wyndham, *The Day of the Triffids* (1951), in which a species of plant, created by scientists, grew to gigantic proportions, moving about and stinging people to death.

• **trigger happy ▶** Ready to shoot at the slightest provocation. Originating in World War II, the expression is now used metaphorically to describe any kind of reckless overeagerness: 'trigger-happy journalists rushed into print before the true facts emerged.'

• **trip ▶** Slang (1960s) for a hallucinatory experience – good or bad – undergone by someone who has taken LSD or a similar drug. By extension it came to mean any stimulating or 'mind-blowing' experience. In more recent use, a trip is any interest or enthusiasm that occupies a person to the point of obsession, such as a **health trip**.

• **Tripartite Pact ▶** The extension of the Rome-Berlin Axis to include Japan on 27 September 1940, which committed the signatories to a ten-year military alliance. Japan had initially (May 1939) refused Hitler's invitation to join the Pact of Steel but reversed the decision after the outbreak of war, when German successes against France and Belgium rendered their Far Eastern colonies vulnerable to Japanese attack. Japan also hoped that support from Germany and Italy would deter the Soviet Union and America from interfering in her plans for southern expansion. In the event, there was no attempt to coordinate German and Japanese strategy after 1940, although in March 1941 Hitler unwisely promised to support Japan if she attacked America. After Pearl Harbor Germany declared war on America, which effectively guaranteed her defeat. Other countries that later joined the Axis were Hungary, Bulgaria, Romania, Slovakia, and Croatia.

• **Triple Entente ▶** In the early 20th century, the informal agreement between the UK, France, and Russia to seek means of settling their outstanding colonial differences. The agreement was based on the Anglo-French Entente Cordiale of April 1904, which settled differences over Egypt and Africa, and the Anglo-Russian agreement of August 1907, which settled differences over Persia, Tibet, and Afghanistan. The Triple Entente became a military pact in 1914, forming the nucleus of the Allied powers in World War I.

• **Tripolitan War ▶** The conflict between Italy and Turkey in 1911–12, in which Turkey sought to conquer Libya and establish a presence in North Africa to counterbalance French power in Algeria, Tunisia, and Morocco. The Italians won fairly easy victories against Turkish forces, who were inferior both in numbers and training. By the Treaty of Ouchy (15 October 1912) Turkey was forced to cede Libya, Rhodes, and the Dodecanese to Italy.

• **Trivial Pursuit ▶** A board game in which contestants have to supply the answers to general knowledge questions printed on a series of cards (coloured by subject). Invented in 1979 by two Canadian journalists, Chris Hanes and Scott Abbott, it became a huge fashionable success in the mid-1980s, making its originators multimillionaires.

• **trog ▶** A boorish or unintelligent person; a lout. The word is a shortened form of troglodyte, a caveman. In the 1950s it was jazz slang for someone who was considered unsophisticated or square, especially in their musical taste. The 1960s British rock group The Troggs played a deliberately basic form of rock 'n' roll, earning the encomium 'They're so far behind, they're in front.' The term is often used self-deprecatingly by potholers and speleologists.

• **Troika Plan ►** The Soviet demand, first made by Nikita Khrushchev on 23 September 1962, that the secretary-general of the United Nations be replaced by a three-man team or troika. Throughout the 1950s the Soviet Union regarded the UN as a tool of the capitalist West and the secretary-general, Dag Hammarskjold, as a NATO puppet. Khrushchev's attempt to replace the secretariat with a troika, consisting of representatives of the West, the Soviet bloc, and the Third World, was rejected as an assault on the concept of an impartial international body and a ploy to extend Soviet influence in the UN. A troika was originally a Russian vehicle pulled by a team of three horses.

• **Trojan horse ►** An apparently trustworthy computer program that, in reality, contains a hidden instruction designed to wreak havoc on the system in which it is used. The name comes from the wooden horse in which the Greeks concealed themselves in order to gain entry to the city of Troy. *See also*: computer virus; logic bomb.

• **troppo ►** Deranged. The term originated among Australian troops in World War II, who applied it to cases of sunstroke or nervous collapse brought on by service in the tropics. It is mainly used in the phrase **to go troppo**, which can now refer to any kind of excessive behaviour (perhaps influenced by the French *trop*, too much).

• **Trot ►** An informal term for a Trotskyite (see Trotskyism). In the UK it is applied rather loosely to any extreme left-wing activist, especially one who rejects the model of state communism as formerly practised in the Soviet Union and its satellites. The epithet owes some of its derogatory implications to its resemblance to 'the trots', a British colloquialism for diarrhoea.

• **Trotskyism ►** The theory of world revolution advanced by Leon Trotsky (1879–1940), in opposition to the theory of building 'socialism in one country', supported by Stalin. Trotsky held that the long-term success of the October Revolution could only be guaranteed by promoting revolutions in the nations of W Europe, to prevent the encirclement and isolation of the Soviet state by hostile capitalist nations. After his defeat by Stalin in the power struggle that followed Lenin's death in 1924, Trotsky accused his rival of betraying the world revolution in the interests of Russian nationalism and of creating an oppressive bureaucratic state based on the exploitation of the Soviet people. Trotsky went into exile in Mexico, where he was murdered by a Stalinist agent in 1940. Sixty years later various Trotskyite parties continue to agitate for the implementation of his internationalist and anti-bureaucratic revolutionary ideas.

• **Troubles, the ►** 1. The civil conflict in Ireland between January 1919 and April 1923. Following its sweeping successes in the general election of 1918, Sinn Féin set up an independent Irish parliament, the Dáil Éireann, and elected as president Eamon De Valera, one of the survivors of the abortive Easter Rising of 1916. Official British rule from Dublin Castle was ignored, and the Republican administration effectively extended its authority throughout the country. The rebellion turned into civil war in January 1919, when the newly constituted Irish Republican Army (*see*: IRA), led by Michael Collins (another survivor of the Easter Rising), embarked on a guerrilla campaign against the British authorities. In 1920 the British introduced the Black and Tans, a force of irregulars, to augment the regular army and the armed police, the Royal Irish Constabulary, in the fight against the IRA. There followed a bitter struggle characterized by murder and brutality on both sides. Although the **Anglo-Irish War**, as it is known in Ireland, was concluded by treaty in 1921, a committed minority of Republicans refused to accept the partition of Ireland into North and South and the continuing role of the British monarch in the Irish Free State. A second and still more bloody conflict, the so-called **Irish Civil War**, then broke out between the Free State forces led by Collins and the rump of the IRA. This ended with the defeat of the Republicans in April 1923 but left a legacy of bitterness that survived for decades. **2.** The bitter strife between the Protestant and Catholic communities in Northern Ireland that erupted into open violence in 1969, leading the British to commit regular troops to the province. The Good Friday Agreement of 1998 and associated terrorist ceasefires have produced a welcome reduction in the annual death toll, although sectarian incidents continue with depressing regularity. It is clearly too soon to say that the Troubles are over. *See also*: Downing Street Declaration; power sharing; Stormont; Sunningdale Agreement.

• **trouble-shooter ►** Someone trained to locate a source of trouble and to give advice on how to repair the situation. The trouble may be of any kind, from mechanical failure to industrial relations.

• **trousersuit ►** *See*: pantsuit.

• **trucking** ▶ A jazz dance step resembling an exaggerated strutting walk that originated at the Cotton Club in 1933. Trucking later came to mean walking in such a manner or walking generally. Because the dance could be kept up over long periods, it became a staple of the competitive dance marathons of the 1930s. This may be why the word came to acquire a further sense of persevering (see: keep on truckin'). In the late 1960s West Coast hippies used the term to describe a curious laid-back style of walking fashionable at the time: this involved taking long loping strides while leaning dangerously far backwards from the waist. It had no resemblance to the original dance.

• **Truman Doctrine** ▶ An anticommunist strategy formulated in 1947 by the administration of President Harry S. Truman, under which US aid was guaranteed to countries that resisted communist intervention and aggression. The primary concern at the time was to keep Greece and Turkey free of Soviet influence and dominance. Truman felt that the best defence against communist expansion was to help in the financial rehabilitation of friendly nations weakened by World War II. The year before the doctrine was announced, Congress approved a loan of more than $3.7 million to the UK.

• **trunk** ▶ Describing the main lines of railway, postal, and telephone systems, from which branch lines radiate. A **trunk call** was the former name for a telephone call on a trunk line from one town to another. A **trunk road** is a major highway used for long-distance journeys.

• **truth drug** ▶ The alkaloid scopolamine. A US doctor, R. E. House (1875–1930), used this drug to induce a state of lethargic intoxication in which the patient lost many of his defences and spoke the truth concerning matters about which he would normally have lied or prevaricated. The value of this and other truth drugs in penology has by no means been established.

• **Tschiffley's Ride** ▶ A journey of 13,350 miles (21,484 km) undertaken by a Swiss-born Argentinian, A. F. Tschiffley, by horse between Buenos Aires and Washington DC between 1925 and 1927. He used only two horses on his epic journey in order to demonstrate the stamina of a certain Argentinian breed.

• **tsuris** ▶ US slang for troubles or problems, from the Yiddish *tsores*, originally from Hebrew *saroth*, troubles. The word was common in New York and Hollywood entertainment circles in the 1970s and has since crossed the Atlantic.

• **Tsushima** ▶ In the Russo-Japanese War, a naval battle fought on 27 May 1905, in which the Russian Baltic fleet, commanded by the incompetent Admiral Rozhdestvenski, was decisively defeated by the Japanese fleet commanded by Togo. The Russians lost all their eight battleships, seven out of eight cruisers, and four out of nine destroyers and suffered 10,000 casualties; the Japanese lost three torpedo boats and less than 1000 men.

• **TTFN** ▶ Ta-ta for now. An abbreviation used as a catchphrase in the radio programme ITMA; it was the parting remark of the character Mrs Mopp, played by Dorothy Summers, and was widely used during the war years and after. A more recent version, popular during the late 1960s and 1970s, was **BFN** – bye for now – used by the disc jockey Jimmy Young to sign off at the end of his show.

• **TT races** ▶ The Isle of Man Auto-Cycle Union touring trophy, the world's oldest motorcycle race and one of the most dangerous. The first competition was held in 1907 over the existing motor racing circuit, which was shortened and made easier for the purpose. There were two races, one for single-cylinder machines and the other for two-cylinder machines. In 1911 the race was run for the first time over the full length of the course round the island, which included a stiff climb up Snaefell mountain. Until the 1950s, British motorcycles, such as Nortons and Triumphs, largely dominated the event. In the 1960 race Honda made their first entry and the Japanese machines have dominated ever since.

• **tube, the** ▶ 1. A television set; a colloquial name originating in America at the end of the 1950s. It is a shortening of cathode-ray tube, the component that produces the images in a television set. 2. The London Underground railway system, from the tubular tunnels through which much of it runs. London was the first city in the world to have an underground rail system. The first such railway (1863) running between Paddington and Farringdon was built using the cut and cover method (cutting a trench from above and filling in over the railway tunnel). The first tube line opened in 1890 and ran between the City and Stockwell. The Underground network now consists of 257 miles (415 km) of track, most of which is tube, although some older overground lines are included. Publicly owned for all its life, the Tube is now suffering from overcrowding in the rush hours and years of persistent underfunding. The Labour government's early 21st-century plans to privatize the network have met with considerable opposition (led by the Mayor of

London), largely because of the disastrous experience of privatizing the mainline railways.

• **Tube Alloys**▶ Codename of the committee established in October 1941 to supervise British research into nuclear power during World War II. It was constituted as a division of the Department of Scientific and Industrial Research, under the general direction of the Lord President of the Council, Sir John Anderson; the Tube Alloys committee itself was headed by Wallace Akers, research director of ICI, and his assistant Michael Perrin. At the Trident Anglo-American conference in May 1943 it was secretly agreed that the development of the atom bomb should be a joint effort between Tube Alloys and the US Manhattan Project.

• **tubular**▶ US teenage slang (1980s–90s) for wonderful, awesome, marvellous. It originated amongst surfers, who consider a tubular (*i.e.* highly curved) wave the most exciting to ride on. In the 1980s the expression spread to US youth in general; it came to Britain in 1989–1990 through the cult of the Teenage Mutant Ninja Turtles, who used it as a favourite term of approbation.

• **Tucker Report**▶ *See*: Bluebeard of Eastbourne.

• **Tuesday Club**▶ Regular meetings betwen UK civil servants, City journalists, economists, and representatives of finance and industry to exchange information and ideas on the direction of national economic policy. The Club evolved from dinner parties given by Oswald Toynbee Falk, a treasury official and friend of the economist John Maynard Keynes (1883–1946), who became a founder member. The first meeting took place on 19 July 1917 at the Café Royal; occasional Tuesday Club meetings in the Reform Club still take place.

• **tug of love**▶ A conflict of affections, especially a battle for the custody of a child. The phrase came into use in the 1970s.

• **tummy tuck** ▶ Colloquialism for a cosmetic operation to tighten a sagging stomach; abdominal fat is removed, excess skin trimmed away, and what is left is sewn back into place.

• **Tum-Tum**▶ *See*: Bertie.

• **Tupperware** ▶ Tradename for a range of moulded dishes, storage containers, etc., made of plastic. Introduced in America in 1945 by an engineer, Earl Tupper, the product was first sold in the UK in 1960. A feature of Tupperware is that it is sold directly by agents working on commission at **Tupperware parties**, held in their own homes.

• **Turing machine** ▶ A hypothetical computer developed by Alan Mathison Turing (1912–54) in 1936. Its purpose is to determine whether or not a mathematical problem can be solved by algorithm (a computational procedure). Turing postulated a computer with an infinitely long tape storing characters in discrete locations. The computer passes through a series of active states scanning and altering characters until it settles into a passive state if the problem is soluble. Although purely conceptual, the Turing machine represented an important advance in computer logic.

• **Turin Shroud**▶ The shroud of twill linen kept in Turin Cathedral and claimed to be that used to wrap the body of Christ after the crucifixion. It bears the impression of a human body resembling the crucified Christ. The pope agreed to carbon dating in 1987 and in 1988 the Archbishop of Turin appointed the Oxford Research Laboratory for Archaeology, the department of physics of Arizona University, and the Swiss Federal Institute of Technology at Zurich to date the shroud. The results, announced later that year, dated the cloth between 1260 and 1390. As there is no historical evidence that it was known before the 14th century, the general conclusion is that the shroud is a medieval forgery. However, the markings on the shroud remain unexplained and many people continue to see in its haunting facial image an authentic likeness of Christ. Further dating tests, including pollen dating, have thrown some doubt on the finding that the shroud is of medieval origin. The study of the Turin Shroud is known as **sindonology**.

• **turkey trot**▶ A US ballroom dance popular in the early 20th century; the precursor of the foxtrot. Danced to ragtime music, its contortions shocked many older and more conservative people. It was adapted in England as the **one-step**, having long quick steps.

• **Turner Prize**▶ An annual prize, inaugurated in 1984 and worth £20,000, that aims to promote awareness of contemporary British art. The prize is awarded by a jury under the auspices of the Tate Galleries and there is an accompanying exhibition. With their clear preference for avant-garde and conceptual art, the awards have frequently provoked controversy – perhaps most notably when the 1995 winner, Damien Hirst, displayed the severed halves of a cow and calf that had been preserved in giant tanks of formaldehyde. In 1999 *My Bed*, an entry by Tracey Emin, featured an unmade bed surrounded by such intimate relics of its former occupant as soiled underwear, condoms, and empty vodka bottles. Although Emin did not win the prize, this gem of contemporary British art was subsequently bought by Charles Saatchi for a six-figure sum.

Other winners of the prize have included Gilbert and George, Anish Kapoor, Rachel Whiteread, Anthony Gormley, and Chris Ofili.

• **turn-off** ▶ Something that repels, bores, or quenches sexual ardour; also used as a verb to mean repel or discourage. The opposite of turn-on.

• **turn-on** ▶ Something that is attractive, stimulating, or sexually arousing. In hippie parlance, 'to turn on' meant to liberate one's mind from conventions, materialism, negative thinking, etc., especially through the use of mind-altering drugs. **Turn on, tune in, drop out** was the slogan of the LSD-guru Dr Timothy Leary (1920–96). The term derives from the idea of turning on a light or other electrical apparatus.

• **TVA** ▶ Tennessee Valley Authority. The US federal corporation created in 1933 to develop the basin of the Tennessee River, mostly to build dams for flood control and to provide cheap electric power. It was one of President Franklin D. Roosevelt's first projects to reverse the Great Depression and tackle unemployment. Critics called it socialistic, which made TVA a controversial issue for many years; private electricity companies especially opposed the federal competition. It is now highly regarded, however: TVA's 39 dams on the Tennessee River and about 160 nonprofit-making electric power distributors provide cheap electricity (one-third cheaper than the US average) to consumers within 210,000 sq km (80,000 sq mi). The river, which once flooded regularly, has been converted into a series of lakes along the Tennessee Valley, which extends 105,956 sq km (40,910 sq mi).

• **TV movie** ▶ A film made specifically for showing on television rather than in the cinema. Such productions, which proliferated from the 1960s onwards, have often been distinguished by low standards in production and facile plots and characterization. Indeed, the made-for-TV movie has often been seen as the successor to the B-movie. On the other hand the development of the genre did much to restore Hollywood's finances and helped the careers of both up-and-coming and no longer fashionable stars. The quality of movies made for television has improved greatly in more recent years, notably in the UK, where independent production companies have created some innovative and accomplished films.

• **TVP** ▶ Textured vegetable protein (also called textured soya protein, **TSP**). A meat substitute developed in the 1970s, TVP is similar in appearance, texture, and taste to meat but is generally cheaper. It comes in tins (sausages or slices) or in dried form (small lumps or granules), which usually has to be soaked before use. It is widely available in health food stores and is also used in ready-made vegetarian meals and soup powders.

• **TVR** ▶ Television rating. The popularity of a particular television programme as determined by equipment attached to sets in selected homes that records the times and channels during which the set is on. Diary panels are used to record the number of people watching a particular set. Audience research is clearly of great value to programme producers and advertisers. In the UK audience research is carried out by the Broadcasters Audience Research Board (BARB).

• **tweenie** ▶ A young person, especially a girl, between the ages of 10 and 15. The word is most often used by those in the media and marketing industries, who have recognized tweenies as an important new consumer group with tastes and interests of their own (and the spending power to gratify them). To take just one example, television (notably Channel 4) increasingly shows programmes for and advertisements aimed at tweenies between 6pm and 7pm – their peak viewing time. The word itself is clearly a diminutive of 'between' but may owe something to the obsolete 'tweeny' or 'between maid' (a domestic servant who helped both the cook and parlour maid). More recently the word **tweenager** has also become a favourite with journalists. This appears to differ slightly from 'tweenie' in that it refers mainly to 'pre-teens' in the 9–13 year-old range. However, the distinction is somewhat sophisticated and many use the terms interchangeably.

> Affluent, aspirational and apparently sophisticated, tweenies are a marketer's dream. Little girls of nine and 10 running around in cropped tops and body tattoos, watching *EastEnders* and *Friends*, getting up to who-knows-what with God-knows-who in Internet chat rooms. – *The Guardian*, 3 December 2000.

• **twelve-tone music** ▶ The compositional system devised in the early 1920s by the Austrian composer Arnold Schoenberg (1874–1951), which had a profound impact on Western music. As an alternative of orthodox tonality, Schoenberg based his compositions on fixed sequences that used all 12 notes of the chromatic scale in a particular order. As long as the sequence was maintained, the tones could be used harmonically (in chords) or melodically (successively); the series could also be transposed, inverted, or reversed. The principles of the system were later employed by Schoenberg's disciples, Alban Berg and Anton Webern, and also to a certain extent by Stravinsky. *See also*: serialism.

• **21st Amendment ►** The 1933 amendment to the US Constitution that repealed Prohibition. This 'Noble Experiment' had resulted in illegal distilling and brewing, the growth of speak-easy bars and nightclubs, and gangland warfare. As some states wished to keep Prohibition, the 21st Amendment promised federal help to enforce their anti-drinking laws. Various states still have 'dry counties', which are supposedly alcohol-free.

• **Twenty Questions ►** An immensely popular BBC radio panel game based on the old parlour game in which someone chooses an object, which the others have to identify with only twenty questions (animal, vegetable, or mineral, etc.). The programme was borrowed from US radio and first broadcast on 28 February 1947. The regular panellists, who included Richard Dimbleby, Joy Adamson, Jack Train, and Anona Winn, all became celebrities, as did the chairman, Stewart MacPherson, and the Mystery Voice, Norman Hackforth. This family entertainment became a weekly ritual that helped to lighten the gloom of postwar Britain; it eventually ran for over a quarter of a century, with audiences that rarely fell below 15 million.

• **22nd Amendment ►** The 1947 amendment to the US Constitution that limited the US president to two terms in office. This was in reaction to Franklin D. Roosevelt's successful election to four terms (though he died in the first year of the last term). No other president has served more than two terms. If a vice president or another person has served more than two years in place of an elected president, he can only be elected once thereafter. However, if he has replaced the president for only two years, his maximum time in office could be 10 years, which is the longest possible presidency under the 22nd Amendment.

• **Twiggy ►** The professional name of Lesley Hornby (1946– ), one of the best known British models of the 1960s. She was born in Neasden, an unfashionable part of NW London. Her nickname refers to the thinness of her stick-like legs, which was often accentuated by the shortest of mini skirts. By the later 1960s she had become an internationally recognized icon of 'Swinging London' (*see*: swinging). Despite her emaciated look and somewhat whiney Cockney voice, her exceptionally beautiful face enabled her to embark on a second career as a stage and film actress. Amongst her other awards and honours, she is an honorary colonel of the Tennessee Army.

• **twilight sleep ►** A state of semiconsciousness produced by injection of scopolamine and mor-phine in which a woman can undergo childbirth with comparatively little pain. *See also*: truth drug.

• **twin paradox ►** *See*: relativity.

• **twist ►** A dance popular in the early 1960s, so called from the twisting contortions performed by the dancers. It was popularized by the songs 'The Twist' and 'Let's Twist Again' by Chubby Checker.

• **twitcher ►** *See*: birder.

• **twoccing ►** Police slang word for stealing cars for joyriding, later adopted by those who engage in the practice (mostly teenage boys). If they are caught they are charged with Taking Without Owner's Consent – to twoc, present participle twoccing. It was first heard in the 1990s.

• **Two Cultures, the ►** The controversial phrase coined by the scientist, novelist, and government administrator C. P. Snow (1905–80) to describe the division in Western culture between those educated in the sciences and those educated in the humanities. The concept was first introduced in an article, 'The Two Cultures', in the *New Statesman* (1956); it was later expanded as *The Two Cultures and the Scientific Revolution*, delivered as the Rede Lecture at Cambridge University in May 1959, and subsequently published in book form. Snow asserted that science was fundamentally progressive and confident whereas the arts were reactionary and defensive, making communication between the two cultures practically impossible. This failure of communication, Snow believed, had serious consequences for Western civilization, which he regarded as the product largely of scientific progress, although it was still dominated politically by non-scientists. Snow's attack on the humanities provoked a fierce reaction, especially from the literary critic F. R. Leavis, whose counter-attack in the Richmond Lecture at Cambridge in 1962 was later published as *Two Cultures? The Significance of C. P. Snow*.

• **two-minute silence ►** The period of silence when all traffic and all other activities stopped for two minutes at 11 am on 11 November to commemorate those who died in World War I. First observed in 1919, it remained a central feature of Armistice Day until 1945, when the commemoration was moved to Remembrance Day. The practice of observing a short silence on 11 November was revived in 1996.

• **two-overcoat men ►** *See*: sunlighting.

• **Two-Ton Tessie ►** The nickname of the variety artist Tessie O'Shea (1917–95), an allusion to her size. In 1945 an RAF bomb weighing 22,000 lbs was named 'Ten-Ton Tessie' after her.

• **TW3** ▸ *That Was The Week, That Was*, a live late-night satirical BBC television programme first broadcast on Saturday 24 November 1962. TW3 was partly inspired by the satirical revue *Beyond The Fringe*, which was a success at the Edinburgh Festival in 1960 and transferred to London's West End in May 1961. The same year saw the launch of Private Eye and the opening of London's first satirical nightclub, *The Establishment*. Many of the comedy-writing talents involved in these ventures, such as Peter Cook and Willie Rushton, produced material for TW3, the BBC's contribution to the comedy revolution of the early 1960s. The show was produced by Ned Sherrin and made stars of its leading performers, including David Frost (the compere), Bernard Levin, Lance Percival, and Millicent Martin. The material included merciless lampoons of leading political figures and humorous sketches and songs making fun of such sacrosanct topics as religion, the royal family, the police, and big business. The show was suspended in November 1963 because of the forthcoming general election; it reappeared in the following year as *Not So Much a Programme, More a Way of Life*, also hosted by Frost.

# U

• **U** ▶ A category of film classification indicating that in the opinion of the British Board of Film Censors the movie concerned is suitable for even the youngest children as it does not contain scenes of violence, sex, etc. It is short for 'universal'.

• **U and Non-U** ▶ In Britain, a distinction between the upper classes and everyone else based on the usage of certain words. Devised by Professor A. S. C. Ross in an article 'Linguistic Class Indicators in Present-day English' in 1954, it was publicized by Nancy Mitford (*see*: Mitford girls) in her book *Noblesse Oblige* (1956). For example, it is 'U' (upper-class) to say luncheon, napkin, and cycle but 'Non-U' (non-upper-class) to say lunch (or worse, 'dinner'), serviette, and bike. This kind of snobbery is not usually taken very seriously. *See*: social class.

• **UB40** ▶ In the UK, a registration and attendance card formerly issued by the Department of Employment to those out of work and claiming unemployment benefit. It was also used as an informal term for someone in this position. A British reggae group of the 1980s adopted the name.

• **U-boat** ▶ A German submarine; from the German *Unterseeboot* (underwater vessel).

• **UDI** ▶ Unilateral Declaration of Independence. The announcement of Southern Rhodesia's independence from the UK made by Ian Smith on 11 November 1965, as an alternative to accepting Black majority rule. The move had no legal validity and provoked British and Commonwealth trade sanctions. Despite predictions by the British prime minister, Harold Wilson, that Smith's rebel regime would collapse in 'weeks rather than months', Rhodesia did not return to legality until 1979, when a transition to majority rule was agreed at the Lancaster House Talks in London.

• **UFO** ▶ Unidentified Flying Object. An object, the exact nature of which is uncertain, that is sighted in the sky (*see*: flying saucers) or picked up on radar screens. Study and observation of UFOs is known as **ufology** by its enthusiasts.

• **Ugandan discussions** or **discussing Ugandan affairs** ▶ British euphemism for illicit sex.

The term first appeared in the gossip columns of the satirical magazine Private Eye in March 1973 and became one of its longstanding jokes. The magazine reported that when a female journalist had to explain herself after being found upstairs with an African diplomat while at a party, she said, 'We were discussing Ugandan affairs' (Uganda was a country much in the news at the time).

> That they should be there together doesn't surprise her. Everyone knows about them now: Rosemary has even been mentioned in *Private Eye* as 'discussing Ugandan Affairs with a gorgeous young American don'. – ALISON LURIE: *Foreign Affairs* (1984).

• **Ulster Covenant** ▶ The pledge by Ulster Protestants led by Sir Edward Carson (1854–1935) that they would resist the imposition of all-Ireland Home Rule signed in Belfast on 28 September 1912. The 'solemn covenant' echoed the earlier anti-Papist Solemn League and Covenant signed by Scottish Presbyterians in the 17th century. The ceremonial signing at Belfast City Hall was led by Carson and two other prominent Unionists, Lord Londonderry and Sir James Craig MP; the queue of Ulster Protestants eager to add their names to the document stretched for three-quarters of a mile. The covenant eventually amassed 471,414 signatures, many inscribed in the signers' own blood. *See also*: Ulster Volunteers.

• **Ulster Unionist Party** ▶ A political party of Northern Ireland, whose members support continued union with the UK. Descended from various Protestant political clubs of the late 19th century, it provided a long sequence of prime ministers of Northern Ireland until direct rule was imposed in 1972. In 1974 the party's name was changed to Official Unionist Party, to distinguish it from the Democratic Unionist Party (*see*: Paisleyite), and members are still sometimes known as **Official Unionists**. A narrow majority of Ulster Unionists support the Good Friday Agreement of 1998; their leader since 1995, David Trimble, is first minister of the Northern Ireland Assembly.

• **Ulster Volunteers** ▶ A private army founded in 1913 by the lawyer and politician Sir Edward Carson

(1854–1935) to resist Home Rule for Ireland. In 1912 Carson led a parliamentary campaign to obstruct the passage of the Home Rule Bill (1912), which would have granted self-governing status to the whole of Ireland, and organized mass signings of the Ulster Covenant. The following year the Ulster Volunteer Force, who claimed over 100,000 members, began to drill publicly. Carson's threats convinced the British government that special provision would have to be made for the Protestant North; in 1914 the outbreak of World War I led to the whole question being shelved for the duration. *See also*: Curragh mutiny; Irish National Volunteers.

The present-day Ulster Volunteer Force (UVF) is a Protestant terrorist organization, illegal since 1966. It declared a ceasefire in the late 1990s but occasional violence has continued.

• **ultrasound scanner** ▶ A device used to examine internal structures in the body using ultrasound, *i.e.* pressure waves with a frequency above 30,000 hertz (sound consists of pressure waves with a maximum frequency of 20,000 hertz). An ultrasound beam is directed into the body in such a way that reflections from the organ to be examined are used to form an electronic image on a screen, which can be photographed. The technique is widely used in pregnancy to examine the foetus without fear of the damage that could be caused by X-rays.

• **ultraviolet catastrophe** ▶ *See*: quantum theory.

• **unacceptable face of capitalism** ▶ *See*: Lonrho affair.

• **unbundling** ▶ Taking over a large organization with a view to keeping the central part of the business and selling off some of the more peripheral concerns in order to help pay for the takeover.

• **uncertainty principle** ▶ *See*: Heisenberg's Uncertainty Principle.

• **Uncle Joe** ▶ A British World War II nickname for Joseph Stalin, head of the Soviet Government (1941–53). *See*: Man of Steel.

• **Uncle Mac** ▶ British rhyming slang from the 1970s for heroin, from smack, heroin. Uncle Mac, a figure totally unconnected with this aspect of life, was a presenter of children's radio programmes from the 1930s to the 1960s.

• **under cover** ▶ Working out of sight, in secret. An undercover agent is someone, such as a spy or policeman, who pursues his enquiries or work unknown to any but his employer.

• **underground, the** ▶ 1. A political or military movement carried on in secret against an oppressor government or an occupying enemy administration, especially in World War II. *See*: Resistance. **2.** An artistic or social movement that exists outside the mainstream of society, especially the alternative society of the late 1960s and early 1970s. **3.** *See*: tube, the.

• **under the counter** ▶ A phrase that became current in World War II, to denote a common practice of dishonest tradesmen. Articles in short supply were kept out of sight, or under the counter, for sale to favoured customers, often at enhanced prices. *See also*: black market.

• **UNESCO** ▶ United Nations Educational, Scientific, and Cultural Organization. An autonomous UN agency, based in Paris, that promotes an exchange among nations of ideas and achievements. UNESCO-sponsored activities have included literacy programmes, teacher training, science conferences, and advice on how to preserve national monuments. The agency also helped found CERN. UNESCO was established in 1945 at a United Nations conference in London and began operating the next year with the British scientist Sir Julian Huxley as its first director-general. About 160 nations currently belong; America withdrew in 1984, complaining of wasteful management and anti-Western bias; the UK followed suit in 1985 but rejoined in 1997.

• **unfair dismissal** ▶ Under the UK Employment Protection (Consolidation) Act (1978) and the Employment Rights Act (1996), employees have the right not to be dismissed unfairly if they have been continuously employed for at least two years, although other considerations (such as age) may be taken into account. Unfair dismissal does not apply if the employer can demonstrate the employee's incapability, bad conduct, or lack of qualifications; nor does it generally apply in cases of redundancy. The employer has an obligation to show that he has acted reasonably (within the terms of the Act) in dismissing an employee, otherwise the employee may apply to an industrial tribunal for reinstatement or compensation.

• **unflappable** ▶ Imperturbable, remaining calm in a crisis; from 'flap', a state of excitement, panic, or confusion. The epithet was originally (1958) applied to the British prime minister Harold Macmillan (*see*: Supermac) by Quintin Hogg (Lord Hailsham).

• **unhappy teddy** ▶ British army slang from the Gulf War of 1991 for a depressed or disgruntled soldier.

• **UNICEF** ▶ United Nations Children's Fund; originally the United Nations International Children's Emergency Fund. An autonomous UN agency, established in 1946, to provide food, clothing, and medicine to children suffering in the wake of World War II. It was made a permanent body in 1953 and now provides financial aid, education, and health care to children, young people, and mothers in more than 100 nations, especially in developing countries and in disaster areas. Its work includes help in family planning. It is based in the United Nations Building in New York but funding comes from voluntary contributions, with three-quarters being provided by governments. UNICEF was awarded the 1965 Nobel Peace Prize.

**• Unification Church ▶** *See*: Moonies.

**• unified-field theory ▶** A theory in physics that would encompass the four fundamental interactions (electromagnetic, gravitational, weak, and strong) in one set of equations. Unification has not yet been achieved although the **electroweak theory** (1967) of Steven Weinberg (1933– ) and Abdus Salam (1926–96) has successfully combined the electromagnetic and weak interactions. It is not known whether or not complete unification is feasible; indeed problems remain in attempting to make use of relativistic quantum field theory to cover the four interactions and the known elementary particles.

Theories that seek to unite the strong, weak, and electromagnetic interactions are known as **grand unified theories** (GUTs). A number of such theories exist, most of which postulate that these interactions merge at energies over $10^{15}$ GeV, which is above the range of existing accelerators.

**• Union of Democratic Control ▶** (UDC) In the UK, an ad hoc coalition of socialists, radicals, and pacifists formed in September 1914, shortly after the outbreak of World War I. The main aims of the UDC were to secure parliamentary control over foreign policy, to open negotiations for a peace settlement offering reasonable terms for all participants, and to promote more open conduct of international diplomacy to prevent a repetition of the secret alliances and agreements that had precipitated the conflict. Founding members of the UDC included Ramsay MacDonald, Bertrand Russell, E. D. Morel, Charles Trevelyan, and Joseph Rowntree. In the hysteria of the period, when pacifists and other opponents of the war were regarded as cowards and traitors, UDC public meetings were often broken up by soldiers on leave. Morel, the secretary, was imprisoned and Russell was fined for a pamphlet in which he allegedly discouraged recruiting. Much of the UDC platform was adopted by the Labour Party after 1917; the organization remained active until World War II.

**• unisex ▶** Not distinguishing or differentiating between the sexes; designed for or applicable to both males and females. The term was applied to the fashions of the late 1960s and early 1970s when women increasingly wore trousers or jeans, men had long hair, and unisex boutiques sold clothing that could be worn by either sex. The unisex style, while abhorred at the time by many of the older generation, has since become the norm, particularly for leisure wear. The late 1990s saw a vogue for unisex lavatories in the workplace and in fashionable nightclubs, etc.

**• UNITA ▶** *União Nacional para a Indepencia Total de Angola* (Portuguese, National Union for the Total Independence of Angola). An Angolan guerrilla organization led by Dr Jonas Savimbi (1934–2002). In the 1960s it was in the forefront of the struggle against Portuguese rule in Angola. However, following Portugal's withdrawal in 1975, it began a long civil war against the rival MPLA, a Marxist group that gained control of the country in 1976. UNITA's acceptance of South African backing discredited it in the eyes of many Black Africans. A ceasefire was agreed in 1991 and multiparty elections held the following year. However, when these resulted in victory for the MPLA, UNITA resumed its guerrilla activities. There was a further ceasefire in 1996 but fighting broke out once more when negotiations broke down in 1999. Savimbi's death during a clash with government troops in early 2002 left the future of the movement uncertain.

**• United Nations ▶** (UN) The successor to the league of nations as a world organization primarily concerned with the maintenance of peace but with numerous other functions and agencies. It sprang from the Dumbarton Oaks Conference (1944) between America, the UK, and the Soviet Union and was formally inaugurated on 24 October 1945 when 51 founder members joined it. Most countries are now members of the UN, with Switzerland and Taiwan being the chief exceptions. The organization's main deliberative organ is the General Assembly, while the Security Council bears the chief responsibility for maintaining peace. Its headquarters are in New York City.

**• United Nations Day ▶** The birthday of the United Nations; 24 October.

**• Unit One ▶** A group of British artists formed in 1933 to promote the ideas of international modernism. Its leading members were Paul Nash (1889–1946), Henry Moore (1898–1986), Ben Nicholson (1894–1982), and Barbara Hepworth (1903–75). The writer and critic Herbert Read (1893–1968) became the chief spokesman for the group.

• **unit trust** ▶ A trust that manages a substantial sum of money invested in stock-exchange securities, in which members of the public can buy units. Thus the unit trust provides the small investor with an opportunity to own a part of a diverse and professionally managed holding of securities. The trustees are usually a commercial bank and it is part of their responsibility to show that the terms laid down in the trust deed are rigidly adhered to by their managers. Many trusts are now available, including those investing in home companies and those making overseas investments; some trusts seek high income for their unit holders while others attempt to maximize capital gains.

• **Universal Declaration of Human Rights** ▶ A document adopted by the General Assembly of the United Nations in 1948 setting forth basic rights and fundamental freedoms to which all are entitled. They include the right to life, liberty, freedom from servitude, fair trial, marriage, ownership of property, freedom of thought and conscience, and freedom of expression. They also include the right to vote, to work, and to be educated. *See*: human rights.

• **university of life** ▶ *See*: school of hard knocks.

• **University of the Third Age** ▶ (U3A) A 'university' for retired people, founded in France by Pierre Vellus in 1973. It was introduced into the UK by Peter Laslett in 1983 and now has some 100 thriving British branches. Learning is for pleasure; there are no qualifications, examinations, or age limits. Teaching and the organization of lectures, classes, etc., are on a voluntary basis.

• **Unknown Prime Minister** ▶ An epithet bestowed on A. Bonar Law (1858–1923), who briefly held office as Conservative leader in 1922-23. It was coined by H. H. Asquith, who remarked at Bonar Law's funeral in Westminster Abbey: 'It is fitting that we should have buried the Unknown Prime Minister by the side of the Unknown Warrior'.

• **Unknown Warrior** ▶ The body of an unknown British soldier who died in Flanders in World War I. The body was chosen at random by a blindfolded senior officer from a number of unidentifiable corpses; lying in soil brought from the battlefield it was brought to London to be 'buried among the kings' in Westminster Abbey (11 November 1920). Part of the inscription on the gravestone reads:

> Thus are commemorated the many multitudes who during the Great War of 1914–1918 gave the most that man can give, Life itself...

Similar tombs were set up in the National Cemetery at Arlington, Virginia; beneath the Arc de Triomphe at Paris; and in the Unter den Linden, Berlin.

In 1958 the bodies of two more unknown servicemen were placed in the **Tomb of the Unknowns** at Arlington – one who died in World War II, and one in the Korean War.

• **unleaded** ▶ *See*: lead-free.

• **unorthodox medicine** ▶ *See*: alternative medicine.

• **unreal** ▶ Fantastically good or outrageously bad, depending on intonation and context. Originally part of beatnik jargon, the word was widely used by teenagers in America in the 1960s and later spread to the UK and Australia.

• **unsocial hours** ▶ Hours of work outside the normal working day; the term is especially used by shift workers and others because of the disruptive effect working such hours has on family and social life. It has been used as a factor in pay bargaining between union representatives and employers.

• **up against the wall** ▶ Catchphrase used by radical Black groups of the 1960s, usually with the word 'motherfucker' added. An imitation of the usual order of police officers when making an arrest or searching a suspect, it was chanted during demonstrations against racist oppression.

• **up-and-under** ▶ *See*: garryowen.

• **upfront** ▶ 1. Originally, open or honest; now widened to mean confident, extrovert, or showing leadership qualities. Both senses derive from the idea of someone standing up boldly and openly in front of others. 2. Paid in advance, as in **money upfront**.

• **up-market** ▶ *See*: middle-market.

• **upper** ▶ *See*: downer.

• **uptight** ▶ Originally US slang describing a person in a tense, anxious, or irritable state. It can also be used to describe someone who is strait-laced or stiffly formal.

• **upwardly mobile** ▶ Moving to a higher social class or economic position. When the term was introduced in the late 1940s, upward mobility usually involved the acquisition of manners and habits belonging to the classes above one. However, as class structures have become less rigid, it has come to be measured more and more in terms of financial success. The yuppie, who epitomized the 1980s concept of upward mobility, was primarily concerned with the enhanced status acquired through wealth.

• **urban guerrilla** ▶ One who employs the methods of guerrilla warfare in cities and towns. The term has been in use since the late 1960s to describe the members of organizations who use kidnapping, bombing, and other violent methods to intimidate and coerce governments.

• **urban legends**▸ A body of largely apocryphal stories that constitutes a major component of modern folklore. Such stories dwell on the macabre and often surreal, with just enough plausibility to ensure their retelling. Many are connected with technological innovations, such as electric saws, microwave ovens (into which a baby is inadvertently placed), and liquidizers (into which a frog falls). Others are elaborations of actual events; for example, the discovery of venomous spiders in imported yucca plants and the presence of alligators in the sewers of New York. Perhaps the best-known urban legend relates to the family who take a motoring holiday in France with Granny. The heat proves too much for poor Granny, who expires in the car. The family stop at the next town to report the death at the local police station, leaving the deceased Granny covered with a rug. When they emerge from the police station, they find that the car, and Granny with it, has been stolen. On their return home they are unable to inherit because they have no body with which to establish the death. In another version, the family attempts to avoid foreign red tape by wrapping Granny in a carpet and hiding her on the roof-rack; the same consequences ensue. An urban legend is invariably introduced with the claim that this really happend to 'a friend of a friend'.

• **urban renewal**▸ The redevelopment of urban areas in response to changing economic and social needs. In principle, urban renewal programmes concentrate on the renovation and adaptation of existing buildings, particularly substandard buildings in inner city areas, rather than the wholesale demolition of slums. The term is US in origin; in the UK it was first used officially in the heading of Title I of the Housing Act of 1949: 'Slum Clearance and Urban Renewal'.

• **urban sprawl**▸ The expansion of urban areas into the surrounding countryside in a haphazard and largely uncontrolled manner (*see also*: ribbon development). A problem accentuated by car ownership, urban sprawl became a political and environmental issue in the 1960s. At its worst, urban sprawl results in piecemeal developments of houses, shopping complexes, and industrial sites on the outskirts of towns and cities. The result of this sprawling unplanned growth is that adjacent developments merge into a vast conurbation. *See also*: green belt.

• **Urdd Gobaith Cymru**▸ (Welsh, Order of the Hope of Wales) A Welsh youth organization whose members dedicate themselves to the service of Wales, humanity, and Christ. It is particularly concerned with preserving the Welsh language. Founded in 1922 by Sir Ifan al Owen Edwards (1895–1970), it now has some 40,000 members. It organizes eisteddfods and Welsh-language summer schools as well as the usual range of sporting and social events.

• **user-friendly**▸ Denoting a computer or other device that is easy to use and understand. User-friendly computer systems can be relied upon to give the operator plenty of on-screen instructions, usually in the form of menus, and clear guidance on how to correct errors. *See also*: -friendly.

• **U-65 haunting**▸ The alleged haunting of the ill-fated German U-boat U-65 by its second officer. U-65's short history was a series of misfortunes. These began even before its launch in 1916, when a falling steel girder killed two workmen. On the day of the launch itself, a further three workmen died when they inhaled poisonous fumes: no explanation for the accident was given at the subsequent inquest. Before the U-65's first dive, a rating went up on deck to check that all was secure – and simply stepped off the casing into the sea; the dive itself nearly ended in disaster for the entire crew when the submarine refused to return to the surface for 12 hours.

Subsequently, the second officer and four others died when a torpedo exploded. When members of the crew (including the captain) reported seeing the second officer's ghost on the casing, talk of a jinx rapidly spread. After docking in Bruges, the captain was killed in an air-raid. To stem the mounting panic, German officials held an inquiry followed by an exorcism of the vessel; this served only to convince the crew that something was seriously wrong.

U-65's career ended finally off the Irish coast, on 10 July 1918, when the US submarine L-2 spotted it on the surface. Before the L-2 could fire, the German target inexplicably blew up. Just before the explosion, the US commander reported seeing a lone figure on the casing, staring thoughtfully out to sea.

• **Utah** ▸ Allied codename for a beach N of Carentan in Normandy, which was one of the landing sites for US forces on D-Day. *See also*: Gold; Juno; Omaha; Sword.

• **utility** ▸ The official name given during and after World War II to clothing, furniture, etc., made according to government specification and sold at controlled prices. The name was a sign of the austerity of the times, in which practical qualities were more important than ornamentation.

• **U-turn** ▶ Literally, a U-shaped turn made by a vehicle so that its direction is completely reversed. The term is also used metaphorically of a total change of policy or opinion, as by a minister, government, etc. In November 1971 the phrase was widely used to describe the Heath government's decision to abandon its previous anti-inflationary policy and spend £160 million of public money in an attempt to reduce unemployment. In October 1980, Margaret Thatcher denied rumours that her government would perform a similar about-turn when she told the Conservative Party Conference:

> U-turn if you want to. The Lady's not for turning.

The phrase, inspired by the play title *The Lady's Not For Burning* (1948) by Christopher Fry, was supplied by the playwright Sir Ronald Millar, who wrote Thatcher's speech; he was knighted in the same year.

• **U-2** ▶ A US high-altitude photoreconnaissance aircraft built by the Lockheed company. The U-2 has a highly specialized lightweight design with some characteristics of a glider, allowing it to fly at 75,000 ft (22,860 metres) at a speed of about 500 mph (800 kph). It has a single-turbine engine with a range of about 3000 miles (4830 km). The U-2 was used from 1956 to 1960 by the CIA for photosurveillance of the Soviet Union and has been employed to gather data on the weather and on fallout from nuclear tests.

On 1 May 1960 a U-2 reconnaissance aircraft was shot down over the Soviet Union; its pilot, Francis Gary Powers, was captured and confessed to spying. This event (known as the **U-2 incident**) gave the first intimation of US spy missions over the Soviet Union, which President Dwight Eisenhower now admitted had taken place for four years. The incident came a fortnight before representatives from America, the UK, France, and the Soviet Union were due to meet at the Paris summit to discuss the status of Berlin. The Soviet leader, Nikita Khrushchev, demanded Eisenhower's apology and a promise to punish those responsible for the flights. When this was refused, Khrushchev cancelled the conference and Eisenhower's coming visit to the Soviet Union. In 1962, the Soviets returned the U-2 pilot in exchange for a Soviet spy held in America.

# V

• **Valentine State** ► One of the names by which Arizona is known, because it was admitted as a state of the USA on St Valentine's Day (14 February) 1912.

• **Valentino** ► The screen-name of the legendary US star of silent films Rodolpho de Valentina d'Antonguolla (1895–1926). Of Italian origin, he became a romantic idol for thousands of cinema-goers in such films as *The Four Horsemen of the Apocalypse* (1921), *The Sheik* (1921), *Blood and Sand* (1922), and *Son of the Sheik* (1926). His intense looks and animal magnetism established the legend of the great lover. Ironically, he was rejected for military service on grounds of poor physique and probably failed to consummate either of his marriages. His sudden death from peritonitis led to mass hysteria and precipitated several suicides. His life and death have been the subject of many studies, including the film biography *Valentino* (1967), with Rudolf Nureyev in the title role.

> His acting is largely confined to protruding his large, almost occult eyes until the vast areas of white are visible, drawing back the lips of his wide, sensuous mouth to bare his gleaming teeth, and flaring his nostrils. – ADOLPH ZUKOR, Hungarian-born Hollywood producer.

• **Valium** ► A proprietary name for the drug diazepam, a tranquillizer and muscle relaxant commonly prescribed for the short-term relief of tension and anxiety. The drug is potentially habit-forming and since its introduction in 1963 there have been well-publicized cases of prolonged use leading to psychological dependence. *See also*: Librium.

• **valley girl** ► A pampered teenage girl from S California's San Fernando valley. The quintessential valley girl comes from a wealthy suburban background, often with parents in the music business or the media, and has sufficient money and leisure to indulge her passion for shopping. Her distinguishing characteristic is the idiosyncratic argot, valspeak, which she uses to communicate with other valley girls. The valley girl phenomenon first became widely known through the success of the satirical record 'Valley Girl' (1982), made by the rock musician Frank Zappa and featuring his daughter, Moon Unit, in an improvised monologue in valspeak. The phenomenon was further highlighted by an article in the magazine *Harpers and Queen* in 1983. In America, the girls have their own handbook, *The Valley Girl's Guide to Life* (1982), by Mimi Pond. *See also*: Jewish American Princess; Sloane Ranger.

• **Valley of Ten Thousand Smokes** ► A volcanic valley in the region of Mount Katmai, Alaska. Shortly before Mount Katmai erupted on 6 June 1912 there were many bursts of molten matter in the valley; these fissures have since discharged hot gases, hence the name of the valley. It has been a National Monument since 1918.

• **valspeak** ► US slang for the patois spoken by the valley girls of S California. Based on a mixture of high-school slang, psychobabble, and surf-talk, it is spoken in a laid-back Californian drawl with frequent exaggerated emphases. Two particular quirks are the use of 'so' as an all-purpose intensifer and 'like' to mean almost anything. A valley girl might, for instance, report the ending of a relationship by saying 'So I'm like *hello-o*, *pur-lease*, you are *so* totally not my boyfriend, jerk!' Although the lingo might seem inane, it gives considerable scope for elaborate deadpan bitchiness. An up-to-date version of valspeak was heard in the hit film *Clueless* (1995), a reworking of Jane Austen's *Emma* set in a Californian high school, and further popularized in the highly successful TV series *Buffy the Vampire Slayer* (from 1997), about a valley girl who combines a normal valley-girl routine of shopping, dating, and schoolwork with an ongoing battle against the supernatural forces of darkness. Owing largely to the popularity of this series, valspeak has penetrated into general teenage argot on both sides of the Atlantic.

• **vamp** ► A woman who uses her feminine charms and sexual attraction to entice and exploit men. The vamp (short for vampire) was a popular stock character of silent films, the best known exponent of the type being the actress Theda Bara (1890–1955). The term seems to have arisen from Bara's performance in *A Fool There Was* (1914), a film based on Kipling's poem 'The Vampire'. Vamps still appear in TV movies and the less subtle television soap operas.

• **Van Allen belts** ▶ Radiation belts that surround the Earth, consisting of high-energy charged particles trapped in the Earth's magnetic field. The lower belt, containing electrons and protons, extends from 1000 to 5000 km above the equator. An outer belt, containing mostly electrons, extends from 15,000 to 25,000 km above the equator. They were discovered in 1958 by James Van Allen (1914– ), as a result of radiation detectors carried by Explorer satellites.

• **Van de Graaff generator** ▶ A machine used to generate an electrostatic charge. A continuously moving belt collects charge from an external voltage source and transfers this to a hollow metal sphere. The very high voltages produced within the dome are often used to accelerate electrons, protons, etc., for research in particle physics. It was invented by the US physicist R. J. Van de Graaff (1901–67).

• **Van Meegeren forgeries** ▶ Notorious art forgeries perpetrated by the Dutch artist Hans Van Meegeren (1889–1947) in the 1930s and 1940s, which caused acute embarrassment to the numerous prominent art critics who had authenticated them. Van Meegeren's forgeries were exposed after the close of World War II, when a painting purporting to be Vermeer's *The Woman Taken in Adultery* was found among the works of art obtained illegally by Herman Goering. The sale to Goering was traced to Van Meegeren, who had been paid the equivalent of £150,000 (ironically enough, in forged banknotes). Accused of collaborating with the Nazis and facing a possible death sentence, the artist confessed to his long series of forgeries. It subsequently emerged that he had forged 14 masterpieces by such artists as Hals, Hooch, and Vermeer, including the latter's *Christ and the Disciples at Emmaus*, which had been hailed by the art establishment on its discovery in 1937. The authorities dismissed his confession and challenged him to produce another Vermeer of equal quality. Van Meegeren was locked into a studio with a panel of experts and he began his *Young Christ Teaching in the Temple*. His mastery of faking the effects of time upon the painting was so sophisticated that he did not even have to complete the work to convince the judges. The collaboration charges were dropped but charges of falsifying signatures brought the artist a sentence of one year in prison: he died of a heart attack before he could begin his term. Van Meegeren's motive, it seems, was to revenge himself upon the art establishment;

his own work had been derided by a critic when, as a young man, he had refused to buy a good review with a bribe.

• **Vasa project** ▶ The raising of the Swedish sailing ship *Vasa*, which sank in a sudden squall in Stockholm harbour before it began its maiden voyage in 1628. This feat of engineering, completed in 1961, was initiated by Anders Franzen, a salvage expert who believed that the *Vasa* might well be largely intact on the seabed, the Baltic being free of the destructive shipworm (*teredo navalis*) that is prevalent elsewhere in the world. It took four years to find the wreck and a further five years to prepare the *Vasa* for its perilous ascent to the surface, using inflatable pontoons and hydraulic jacks. The ship was brought up in an extraordinary well-preserved condition; it was subsequently housed in a specially built museum, in which it was constantly sprayed to prevent the timbers warping. This triumph of marine salvage inspired several similar projects (*see*: Mary Rose).

• **VAT** ▶ Value Added Tax. An indirect tax on goods or services calculated by adding a percentage (currently 17½% in the UK) to the value of a product at each stage in its production. Each trader has to remit the tax to the Customs and Excise after deducting the amount of tax he has paid for goods or services (but not labour costs). Thus the tax is not borne by traders but by consumers. It replaced **purchase tax** in 1973 to conform with the similar tax levied in the European Community. Some products, *e.g.* food and books, are zero-rated for VAT or taxed at a special reduced rate.

• **Vatican City State** ▶ The area of Rome occupied by the city of the Vatican, recognized by the Lateran Treaty (1929) as constituting the territorial extent of the temporal power of the Holy See. It consists of the Papal palace, the Vatican Library, archives and museums, the Piazza of St Peter, and contiguous buildings including a railway station – in all an area of just under a square mile. It has about 900 inhabitants. Certain other buildings outside the Vatican enjoy extraterritorial rights.

• **Vatican roulette** ▶ Slang for the rhythm method of contraception, which is based on avoiding intercourse during the middle of the menstrual cycle when ovulation is most likely to occur. It is not a reliable method of birth control, but the Vatican still forbids contraception by any other method. The phrase alludes to Russian roulette, a potentially suicidal game of chance played with a gun. It is said jokingly that couples who play Vatican roulette are called 'parents'.

• **Vatican II** ► *See*: Second Vatican Council.

• **VC** ► *See*: Victor Charlie; Viet Cong.

• **VDU** ► Visual display unit. The part of a computer system on which words, pictures, diagrams, etc., are displayed. It consists of a cathode-ray tube and is usually connected to a keyboard and personal computer. In larger computer systems, however, the cathode-ray tube, its controlling electronics, and the keyboard may be referred to collectively as the VDU.

• **VE Day** ► The day on which hostilities in Europe ended in World War II, 8 May 1945. *See also*: VJ Day.

• **veganism** ► A strict form of vegetarianism in which all food of animal origin is renounced. Vegans refuse not only meat but also eggs, dairy products, and even honey. Adherents of this strict regime coined the term in 1944, to distinguish themselves from mere vegetarians (sometimes referred to as **ovolactarians**, *i.e.* egg-and-milk eaters). Vegans argue that theirs is the only logical form of vegetarianism, since commercial production of milk and eggs could not be carried on without the market for beef and chicken. They use a milk-substitute manufactured from beans. The diet is not self-sufficient; vegans require certain dietary supplements to remain healthy.

• **Velcro** ► Tradename for a 'touch and close' fabric fastener. The device was invented in 1957 in Switzerland by Georges de Mestral, who devised the name as a combination of the French words *velours* (velvet) and *croché* (hooked). It consists of two strips of nylon, one having a large number of tiny hooks and the other with an equal number of loops, into which the hooks fit when the two strips are pressed together.

• **Velvet Fog** ► A nickname for the US singer Mel Tormé (1923–99), in allusion to the smooth crooning style that characterized his singing of the late 1940s and 1950s.

• **velvet revolution** ► The overthrow of communism in Czechoslovakia during November–December 1989; so-called because of the peaceful nature of the transition. Following a week of mass demonstrations in Prague and elsewhere, the entire ruling politburo resigned on 24 November. A majority non-communist government was sworn in on 10 December.

• **Venlo incident** ► The arrest of two British agents by German counter-intelligence in Venlo, on the German–Dutch border, on 8 November 1939. Their capture was a disaster for British intelligence and compromised its network of agents throughout Europe. The British agents, Captain Sigismund Payne Best and Major R. H. Stevens, were part of an MI6 network seeking contacts with the anti-Nazi movement in Germany, with the ultimate aim of removing Hitler from power and securing an end to the war. They were contacted by a 'Captain Schaemmel', actually Major Walter Schallenburg of Nazi counter-espionage, who claimed to be a representative of the anti-Nazi movement. After several meetings, the MI6 agents agreed to arrange the airlift from Venlo to London of the movement's leader who, Schallenburg claimed, wanted urgent talks with the British government. Hitler ordered that the British agents should be seized on Dutch soil, kidnapped, and transported to Germany, where they remained prisoners until released by US forces in 1945.

• **venture capital** ► Capital used by an investor to buy shares in a new company or an expanding business, when he is well aware that the investment carries a substantial risk. Venture capital is an investment rather than a loan.

• **Venture Scouts** ► *See*: Boy Scouts.

• **Verdun** ► The fortress region in E France that saw one of the longest and bloodiest battles of World War I (21 February–18 December 1916). The Germans launched a major offensive here in the belief that French determination to hold the region at all costs would fatally sap their resources. The initial German artillery barrage was one of the most devastating ever launched and enabled the German Fifth Army to advance through the outer defences and capture Fort Douaumont on 25 February. The French then mounted a counterattack using reinforcements transported to the front along the secondary road from Bar-le-Duc, which became known as the **Sacred Way**. This halted the German advance and during March and April the German commander, Erich von Falkenhayn, focused his attacks on the eastern and western flanks. The offensive settled into a war of attrition, with frequent attacks and counterattacks and the capture and recapture of territory around the Meuse Heights. At the nearest, the Germans came to within 5 km (3 mi) of Verdun itself but in October the French, under Generals Nivelle and Pétain, mounted a series of counterattacks, which successfully recovered much of the lost territory, including Fort Douaumont (24 October) and Vaux (2 November). The long and bitter struggle became a symbol of French determination to resist and survive (*see*: They shall not pass! *at* pass). The French losses were estimated at 542,000, against the Germans' 434,000.

• **Verdun pigeon** ▶ A pigeon that performed invaluable service for the French army by carrying vital messages during the Battle of Verdun in 1916. Pigeons were a key factor in the Allied communications network in World War I; in World War II they were also dropped in crates by parachute to Resistance fighters to facilitate the sending of secret messages to London. The Verdun pigeon won particular praise for its heroism in braving fierce artillery fire and was greatly mourned when it died from wounds received on one of these missions; in recognition of its courage, it was posthumously awarded the Légion d'Honneur.

• **Vereeniging Treaty** ▶ The treaty that ended the second Boer War, signed in Pretoria on 31 May 1902, after the Boers had agreed to the British terms at Vereeniging. The South African Republic and the Orange Free State were placed under British military administration but were promised eventual self-government. A general amnesty was declared, the burghers were disarmed, and the sum of £3,000,000 was allocated for the payment of war debts and to provide for the economic reconstruction of the Transvaal. The issue of native voting rights was left for settlement after the granting of self-government, an ignoble concession by the British, which guaranteed African disfranchisement after the formation of the Union of South Africa in 1910 (see: apartheid). See: Boer Wars.

• **verification principle** ▶ See: logical positivism.

• **Versailles Treaty** ▶ The peace treaty between the Allies and Germany concluded at the Paris Peace Conference in 1919; separate treaties were concluded between the Allies and the other defeated nations. The terms were fixed in Paris by President Wilson of America; Clemenceau, prime minister of France; Lloyd George, the British prime minister; and Orlando, the prime minister of Italy. There were no German representatives and the Germans were forced to sign under threat of the resumption of the war. The Versailles Treaty included the covenant of the League of Nations, as did all the other peace treaties. Germany lost one eighth of its European territory, including Alsace-Lorraine, the Rhineland, which was to be occupied by Allied troops, and the Saar, which was placed under League of Nations control for 15 years after which a referendum would decide the future of the population. Germany also lost Malmédy and Eupen to Belgium and North Schleswig to Denmark. The Poles were given access to the Baltic along a 'corridor' at the head of which was Danzig, declared a free city under League control. Austrian independence was assured and Germany also forfeited all her colonies, which

became mandates of the League. The military terms were also harsh. Germany was to disarm, abolish military service, maintain an army of not more than 100,000 men, and reduce the size of her navy. In Article 231, the famous War Guilt Clause, Germany had to accept responsibility for the war and to pay crippling reparations for the damages caused to Allied nations. The amount of reparations was later reduced by the Dawes Plan and the Young Plan, while various military clauses were circumvented during the 1930s. Nevertheless, the treaty was a focus for German disaffection throughout the life of the Weimar Republic and thus played a crucial role in the rise of the Nazis and the outbreak of World War II.

• **Vespa** ▶ See: Lambretta.

• **vet** ▶ A US abbreviation for 'veteran soldier', most often heard in the phrase **Vietnam vet**, widely used after the Vietnam War. See also: PVS.

• **veteran car** ▶ A car from the early days of motoring. The UK Veteran Car Club is interested in any car built before the end of 1918, although the strict definition of a veteran car is one built before the end of 1904. To qualify for the London to Brighton run a car has to comply with this strict definition. Some enthusiasts call vehicles built between the beginning of 1905 and the end of 1918 **Edwardian cars**. See also: vintage car.

• **Veteran's Day** ▶ See: Armistice Day.

• **Veto Bill** ▶ The controversial parliamentary bill, introduced by the Liberal Government and passed on 10 August 1911. The bill asserted the supremacy of the House of Commons, stipulated that bills passed by the Commons in three successive parliamentary sessions should become law in spite of the Lords' opposition, removed the authority of the Lords to veto money bills, and limited the Lords' powers to delay other legislation; it also reduced the duration of parliament from seven years to five. In July 1911 the Liberal prime minister, Asquith, secured the backing of King George V to the creation of 500 new peers if necessary to force the bill through the upper house. This finally persuaded the Lords to accept the legislation, thereby preserving the chamber from more radical changes in its constitution and function. See also: Diehards; Hedgers and Ditchers; People's Budget.

• **V for Victory** ▶ On 14 January 1941 Victor de Lavaleye, a member of the exiled Belgian government in London, proposed in a broadcast to Belgium that the letter V, standing for Victory in all European languages, be substituted for the letters RAF, which were being chalked up on walls, etc., in occupied Belgium as a sign of defiance. The plan was immediately adopted and the Morse code V (• • • –) was featured in every BBC broadcast to Europe followed by the opening bar of Beethoven's 5th Symphony (which has the same rhythm). Colonel Britton (D. E. Ritchie), director of the BBC European news service, was responsible for the diffusion of the V-sign propaganda, which gave hope to those under the Nazi yoke. Winston Churchill greatly popularized the sign of two upraised fingers in the form of a V; it has subsequently been adopted by various movements all over the world (*see*: peace sign). *See also*: Harvey Smith.

• **Viagra** ▶ Tradename for a drug used to treat impotence in men by enhancing the erectile response to sexual stimulation. Whereas previous treatments for impotence involved injections or mechanical devices that most sufferers found uncomfortable, embarrassing, or difficult to use in a natural and spontaneous way, Viagra is taken in simple tablet form. It is also extremely effective. The active substance, sildenafil, was originally developed by Pfizer in the USA as a treatment for hypertension. Its other effects were discovered by men taking it during trials and only came to the notice of the drug company when these guinea pigs proved strangely reluctant to return unused tablets. In the UK Viagra is available only on prescription and is supplied by the NHS to certain classes of patients. It has become the world's fastest selling prescription drug.

• **vibes** ▶ 1. Short for 'vibrations', in the sense of an emotional atmosphere emanating from a person, place, or thing that is sensed intuitively. As in 'I'm getting some bad vibes about the meeting next week'. 2. In jazz, short for 'vibraphone'; a person who plays this instrument is known as a **vibrist**.

• **Vichy** ▶ A town in the department of Allier, in central France, formerly fashionable on account of its thermal and medicinal springs. Vichy acquired a new significance during World War II as the seat of Marshal Pétain's collaborationist government (1940–44) after the fall of France to Germany. Vichy's authority extended over unoccupied (*i.e.* central and southern) France and the French colonies. From 1942, when Pierre Laval became the dominant political figure, it was run on increasingly authoritarian lines and collaborated enthusiastically in the persecution of the Jews, some 70,000 of whom were sent to their deaths in Germany. The regime collapsed with the Allied liberation of France in 1945.

• **Vicky** ▶ The pseudonym of Victor Weisz (1913–66), the political cartoonist famous for his caricatures in the *Evening Standard* in the late 1950s and 1960s. He was born in Berlin of Hungarian parents, suffered harassment from the Nazis for his precocious political cartoons, and settled in England with his parents in 1935. He quickly learned English, became a self-taught expert on the nature of British humour, and in 1941 was given a job as a political cartoonist on the *News Chronicle*. Throughout the war he was frequently denounced by the political establishment as an enemy alien because of his mordant and satirical talents. After a spell on the *Daily Mirror* he joined the *Evening Standard* in 1958; thereafter he produced six cartoons a week for the *Standard*, as well as a weekly cartoon for the *New Statesman*. His impudent caricatures of contemporary politicians and statesmen, such as de Gaulle, Churchill, Eden, and Macmillan (*see*: Supermac), became very well known. He committed suicide with an overdose of sleeping pills in February 1966.

• **Victor Charlie** ▶ US military slang from the late 1960s for the Viet Cong or a Viet Cong guerrilla. 'Victor' and 'Charlie' are communications code for the letters V and C. The Viet Cong were later referred to simply as the **VC**.

> He...was told about being shot out of a helicopter by Victor Charlie. – *The New Yorker*, 18 June 1966.

• **victory bonds** ▶ *See*: Bottomley case.

• **Victory Medal** ▶ A bronze medal with a winged figure of Victory on the obverse; it was awarded in 1919 to all Allied service personnel who had served in a theatre of war, also to certain women's formations.

• **victory roll** ▶ An aerobatic manoeuvre in which the pilot executes a complete roll of the aircraft; pilots in both world wars sometimes executed a roll to celebrate a 'kill' in the air.

• **video game** ▶ *See*: computer game.

• **video nasty** ▶ A straight-to-video film, characterized by violence and horrific special effects, sometimes also having a strong pornographic content. Such films proliferated in the early 1980s as video recorders became more common in the home and sparked a moral panic in the press and Parliament. Notorious examples included *Cannibal Holocaust*, *I Spit on Your Grave*, and *The Driller Killer*.

• **video recorder** ▶ A device used for playing prerecorded video tapes on television equipment or recording from the television for viewing at a later time. Both the vision and sound signals are recirded on a magnetic tape contained in a closed plastic cassette. As the video (vision) signal contains frequencies in the megahertz range, a video tape cannot be used in the same way as an audio (sound) tape, in which the signals have kilohertz frequencies. To avoid the need for excessive tape speeds, the signal is recorded diagonally on the tape (each diagonal line representing one line on the picture) and the tape runs slowly over a drum on which the recording and reading heads rotate rapidly. Since the early 1980s video recorders have been widely used by the British public; in 1990 64% of homes owned a recorder while by 2000 the figure was around 80%. **Video cameras** (camcorders) are also widely owned and have now almost entirely replaced the use of 8mm or 16mm film in home movie-making.

• **Vienna circle** ▶ A group of philosophers, scientists, and mathematicians that formed around the figure of Moritz Schlick (1882–1936), professor of philosophy at the University of Vienna, during the 1920s. The circle included Otto Neurath (1882–1945), Rudolph Carnap (1891–1970), Kurt Gödel (1906–78), and others. In 1922 the group described themselves as logical positivists and dedicated their researches to separating true science from metaphysics. To this end they were influenced by the scientific phenomenalism of Ernst Mach, Schlick's predecessor in the chair of philosophy at the university, the New Logic developed by Frege, Bertrand Russell, and Alfred Whitehead, and by Wittgenstein's *Tractatus* (1921). The group issued a manifesto, *The Vienna Circle: Its Scientific Outlook* (1929); published a journal, *Erkenntnis*; and held a number of annual congresses in various European capitals. The circle made Vienna the centre of philosophy in the 1920s and early 1930s but with the rise of totalitarianism in Europe threatening a new Dark Age, its members (many of whom were Jewish) dispersed into exile after 1935. In 1936 Schlick was murdered on the steps of the university library by an insane student, a crime never fully investigated by the authorities, who reviled Schlick's empiricist and phenomenalist teachings. A radical version of the logical positivism of the Vienna circle was popularized by Alfred Ayer, who had studied in Vienna.

• **Viet Cong** ▶ Communist guerrilla forces who fought the government of South Vietnam and its US allies in the Vietnam War (1954–75). After the Geneva Agreements of 1954, which divided the country into North and South, about 10,000 communist Viet Minh insurgents stayed in the South and renamed themselves the Viet Cong (short for *Viet Nam Cong San*, Vietnamese Communists). Their political organization, the National Liberation Front (NLF), was established in 1960. By the mid-1960s, US soldiers usually referred to the enemy as the **VC** (*see*: Victor Charlie).

• **Viet Minh** ▶ The communist-led Vietnamese guerrilla organization that resisted Japanese occupation during World War II and fought French rule after 1945. The Viet Minh League, a coalition of communist and nationalist parties headed by the communist leader Ho Chi Minh, was organized in 1941. After ousting the Japanese-sponsored regime in 1945, they went on to defeat the French forces at Dien Bien Phu. In 1954 they became the ruling government of the Democratic Republic of Vietnam (North Vietnam) and three years later began military support for the Viet Cong. The name Viet Minh is derived from *Viet Nam Doc-lap Dong Minh* ('Revolutionary League for the Independence of Vietnam').

• **Vietnam War** ▶ The war (1954–75) in which communist Viet Cong guerrillas, supported by troops from North Vietnam, fought the government of South Vietnam, supported from 1961 by America. US forces suffered about 58,000 combat deaths and 365,000 wounded during this gruelling jungle war; the total number of Vietnamese killed was around 1.3 million.

As part of its commitment to support regimes threatened by communism, America sent its first 'military advisers' to South Vietnam in 1961. By 1965 US troops had become active combatants in a still undeclared war. As their involvement deepened, graphic television coverage of the war's horrors – including napalm bombing of Vietnamese villages – together with a growing sense that the conflict was going badly and was perhaps unwinnable (*see*: Tet offensive), gave rise to a powerful anti-war movement that began on college campuses, especially within the hippie culture. The US military presence reached a maximum of 543,400 in April 1969; seven months later 250,000 anti-war activists demonstrated in Washington, DC. With no prospect of a military breakthrough in sight, President Richard Nixon's administration signed a ceasefire agreement in 1973 and US troops began to withdraw; the South Vietnamese government finally fell on 30 April 1975. The country was officially reunited on 2 July 1976, as the Socialist Republic of Vietnam. About 6.5 million refugees fled from South Vietnam, with more than 165,000 being accepted into America.

The Vietnam War has often been said to mark the death of American innocence; certainly such incidents as the My Lai massacre and the secret and illegal bombing of Cambodia (1972) seemed hard to square with any idealistic purpose. There was also the fact of defeat itself; for the first time in history America had lost a foreign war – and lost it, moreover, to a small undeveloped nation with a fraction of the manpower and resources. The burden of guilt, bitterness, and disillusion lasted for two decades and almost certainly inhibited further military adventures. It took America's speedy and almost casualty-free victory in the Gulf War of 1991 to lay the ghosts of Vietnam. *See also*: PVS.

• **Vimy Ridge** ▶ A hill in N France, on the ridge of Nótre Dame de Lorette, NE of Arras, which was captured by Allied troops in World War I during the Battle of Arras (9–14 April 1917). The capture of the German stronghold by the Canadian Corps under General Sir Julian Byng was the only success of the battle; it cost 11,285 lives.

• **Vinegar Joe** ▶ Nickname of General Joseph W. Stilwell (1883–1946), US Commander of troops in China during World War II. Another of his nicknames was **Old Turkey Neck**.

• **Vinland Map** ▶ A supposedly 15th-century map showing the NE coast of America, as explored by the Vikings in the 10th century. According to the Norse Saga, *Flateyjarbók*:

> When spring came they made ready and left, and Leif named the land after its fruits, and called it *Vinland*.

The discovery of the map in 1957 was hailed as the most exciting cartographic find of the century. Supposedly drawn in about 1440, if genuine it would have substantially preceded the voyages of Columbus (1492) and of John Cabot (1497), thus conclusively establishing the extent of the Viking explorations. It was presented to Yale University by an anonymous donor in 1965. In 1974 Yale announced that it was a fake; the pigment of the ink with which it was drawn had been found to contain titanium dioxide, first used in the 1920s.

• **vintage car** ▶ Broadly, any car built between the beginning of 1905 (earlier models are called veteran cars) and the start of World War II. However, the strict definition of a vintage car is one built between 1905 and 1930. The supreme example of a vintage car is the 1927 Bugatti Royale of which only six were sold. One survivor sold for £5.5 million pounds in 1987. The expression **classic car** is used for any sought-after model built after 1930 that had a good reputation in its day.

• **VIP** ▶ Very Important Person. This now widespread usage was coined by a station commander of Transport Command in 1944; this officer was responsible for the movement of a plane-load of important individuals, including Lord Mountbatten, to the Middle East and so described them in his movement orders to avoid disclosing their identity.

• **Virgin Mary** ▶ *See*: Bloody Mary.

• **virtual reality** ▶ A computer simulation in which high-quality graphics give the user the experience of moving through, and interacting with, an artificial environment. In the strict sense of the term, virtual reality involves the user wearing a visor, which has two small screens to give a three-dimensional image, and special gloves. Sensors in the helmet feed signals to the computer to change the image as the head is moved, while the gloves sense the hand and arm movements and allow the wearer to 'move' objects in his field of view. This kind of virtual reality now has established applications in flight simulation, medical teaching, building design, etc.; contrary to many predictions made in the early 1990s, however, it has never become widespread among ordinary computer users. The term virtual reality is now used in a wider and weaker sense to refer to any highly realistic interactive computer game involving 3-D graphics.

> Mr Saenz, 33, a former cartoonist for Marvel Comics, runs Reactor Inc in Chicago which markets one of the first interactive cybersex software packages, called Virtual Valerie. Just slip a CD-ROM into your disk-drive and an animated Virtual Valerie will appear on screen and obey your every command – or at least every command for which she has been programmed. – *The Times*, 11 February 1993.

• **virus** ▶ *See*: computer virus.

• **vision statement** ▶ *See*: mission statement.

• **vital statistics** ▶ Properly, population statistics concerned with births, marriages, deaths, divorces, etc. It is also used to refer (in inches) to a woman's bust, waist, and hip measurements: 'Her vital statistics are 34-24-34'.

• **Viyella** ▶ Tradename for a soft woven fabric used for shirts, blouses, etc. It is manufactured by William Hollins & Co., originally in the Via Gellia valley in Derbyshire. The Via Gellia was a Roman road that ran through the valley, between Buxton and Nottingham. Pronounced locally 'Vi Jella', this was the source for the tradename.

• **VJ Day** ▶ The day on which hostilities ended in Japan and the rest of the Far East in World War II, 15 August 1945. *See also*: VE Day.

• **vogueing** ▶ A style of dance of the late 1980s, in which participants strutted and posed like models on a catwalk. It was named after the fashion magazine *Vogue*. The style was popularized by Madonna's hit single 'Vogue' (1990) and the video that accompanied it.

• **voicemail** ▶ Any electronic system in which telephone messages are stored centrally until 'collected' by the recipient. In its simplest forms, such as BT's Callminder, voicemail offers essentially the same service as a telephone answering machine; calls received when the user is out, or otherwise occupied, can be stored and dealt with at his or her convenience. However, more sophisticated forms of voicemail enable the user to transfer spoken messages across the Internet in the same way as e-mail. This means that messages can be recorded and sent out at a later time (perhaps because the recipient is in a different time zone) or sent out to a number of people simultaneously.

• **Voice of America** ▶ (VOA) The official overseas radio broadcasting network of the United States Information Agency. Founded in 1942 within the Office of War Information for propaganda purposes, VOA now seeks to promote a favourable image of America by broadcasting balanced news and entertainment throughout the world. The programmes, originating from Washington, DC, go out in English and 41 other languages. They reach an estimated weekly audience of 120 million people. VOA is often confused with **Radio Free Europe/ Radio Liberty**, the Munich-based organization funded by Congress but run by private US citizens.

• **voice-over** ▶ A commentary accompanying film or television pictures, spoken by an unseen narrator or announcer. The technique is common in documentaries and advertisements, which often feature the recognizable voices of well-known personalities. In fiction films a leading character will often think aloud, reminisce, or sum up in voice-over.

• **voiceprint** ▶ An electronically constructed graphic representation of a person's voice. A voiceprint, more formally called a **speech spectogram**, consists of a pattern of lines and whorls, showing distinctions in pitch, loudness, and duration of speech obtained by running a tape recording of a voice through a **sound spectrograph**. Like a fingerprint, a voiceprint pattern is said to be unique to each individual and of possible value in police work. They have been used as evidence in court cases but, like polygraphs, their validity has been challenged. The sound spectrograph was devised in the 1940s by three US scientists at the Bell Research Laboratories; the US physicist Lawrence G. Kersta developed it for identification purposes.

• **V1** ▶ See: buzz bomb.

• **vorticism** ▶ A shortlived artistic movement which began in the UK in 1914; somewhat akin to both cubism and futurism, it embraced both art and literature. The movement was wilfully iconoclastic and regarded the question of representation as ir-

relevant. Vorticist works tended to feature angular patterns of straight lines and to show a fascination with the energy and violence of the modern machine age. P. Wyndham Lewis and Edward Wadsworth were the most notable exponents of the style. The name was bestowed by Ezra Pound, the movement's chief propagandist. Its mouthpiece was the magazine Blast.

• **Vostok** ▶ (Russian, East) A series of six Soviet manned spacecraft launched during the two-year period 1961–63. Vostok 1, launched on 12 April 1961, took the first man into space: cosmonaut Yuri A. Gagarin made a single orbit of the Earth before re-entry, a total flight time of 1 hour 48 minutes. Vostok 2 (6 August 1961) carried Major Herman Titov in 17 orbits around the Earth; Vostok 3 and 4 (launched together on 11 August 1962) made 48 joint orbits, the first double manned flight. This mission also produced the first TV pictures from space and demonstrations of weightlessness seen by the public. Vostok 5, launched on 14 June 1963, was followed two days later by Vostok 6, which carried the first woman into space, Valentina V. Tereshkova.

• **Votes for Women** ▶ See: suffragettes.

• **vox pop** ▶ (Latin vox populi, voice of the people) Public opinon, the popular verdict. The expression was taken up by the British broadcasting media in the 1960s to refer to the opinions elicited from the man or woman in the street when stopped and questioned by reporters. It derives from the maxim Vox populi vox Dei (the voice of the people is the voice of God).

• **Voyager** ▶ Two unmanned US space probes designed for interplanetary travel and exploration of the outer solar system. Voyager 1 was launched on 5 September 1977, reaching Jupiter in March 1979 and Saturn in November 1980. Data transmitted back from its planetary encounters included the discovery of three moons of Saturn, two moons of Jupiter, Jupiter's ring, and fine details of the structure of Saturn's ring system. Voyager 2 was launched on 20 August 1977, before its twin; travelling more slowly than Voyager 1, it passed Jupiter in July 1979, Saturn in August 1981, Uranus in January 1986, and Neptune in August 1989. Voyager 2 achieved the first flybys of Uranus and Neptune as well as discovering the 14th moon of Jupiter and 10 moons and two rings of Uranus. Both probes are now heading into deep space, carrying recordings of terrestrial culture, including Earth sounds, music, and greetings in 60 languages, should they ever encounter alien life forms.

• **VSO** ▶ Voluntary Service Overseas. A UK organization founded in 1958 by Alexander Dickson (1914– ) to allow skilled people to contribute voluntarily to improving the economic and social infrastructure of developing countries. VSO does not administer its own projects but provides volunteers with the desired qualifications in response to requests by the host countries. Skills required include those used in teaching, agriculture, technology, and business development; volunteers are normally contracted for a period of two years. VSO pays travel expenses and offers certain grants and allowances, while the employer provides accommodation and wages at the local rates. As training is an important function of the VSO programme, volunteers are usually required to train a local person to take over from them when they leave.

• **VTOL** ▶ Vertical take-off and landing. Denoting an aircraft, other than a helicopter or airship, that can take off and land vertically. Among fixed-wing aircraft with this facility, the most successful is the Harrier jump jet, which uses swivelling exhaust nozzles to discharge the propellent jet downwards when taking off or landing. Other aircraft may be described as **CTOL** (conventional take-off and landing), **STOL** (short), and **QSTOL** (quiet short).

• **V2** ▶ A long-range rocket with an explosive warhead, projected against England by the Germans in the autumn of 1944. V2s were so named because they were the second *Vergeltungswaffe* (reprisal weapon) devised by the Germans (the buzz bomb or V1 being the first). The V2 weapons were designed by Wernher von Braun, who later developed NASA's Saturn rockets.

> It was very successful, but it fell on the wrong planet. – WERNHER VON BRAUN, about the first V2 to reach London.

• **vulnerable species** ▶ A category of threatened species identified by the International Union for the Conservation of Nature and Natural Resources (IUCN). Vulnerable species include those whose wild populations (1) are decreasing because of continuing destruction of their habitat, hunting, etc.; (2) have decreased but not yet recovered to their former levels; (3) are still abundant but are threatened by adverse factors. Vulnerable species are likely to become endangered species if the factors causing or threatening their decline continue to operate; they include:

gorilla (*Gorilla gorilla*)
grey wolf (*Canis lupus*)
polar bear (*Ursus maritimus*)
European otter (*Lutra lutra lutra*)
cheetah (*Acinonyx jubatus*)
ocelot (*Felis pardalis*)
jaguar (*Panthera onca*)
African elephant (*Loxodonta africana*)
pigmy hippopotamus (*Choeropsis liberiensis*)
Indian python (*Python molurus*).

# W

• **WAAC** ▶ Women's Army Auxiliary Corps. A body of women raised for non-combatant army service in World War I; members of the corps were known colloquially as **Waacs**. In World War II, the name of the corps was changed to the Auxiliary Territorial Service and the girls were called **Ats**. The corps became the WRAC (Women's Royal Army Corps) in 1949.

• **WAAF** ▶ Women's Auxilary Air Force. It was established in 1939, its members being known as **Waafs**, and became the WRAF (Women's Royal Air Force) in 1949. There was an earlier WRAF in World War I.

• **WAC** ▶ Women's Army Corps. The US Army's women's force in World War II. It was equivalent to the British ATS (*see*: WAAC). *See also*: WAVES.

• **Waco siege** ▶ The siege and subsequent mass suicide by fire of 75 members of the Branch Davidian cult, led by David Koresh, in Waco, Texas. Koresh, a clearly demented but apparently persuasive 33-year-old, was born Vernon Wayne Howell – he adopted the name Koresh (Hebrew for Cyrus, the Persian king who protected the Israelites from the Babylonians) when he became leader of this breakaway sect of the Seventh Day Adventist Church in the 1980s.

Koresh established the sect in a 77-acre walled citadel in Waco, known to its adherents as Mount Carmel. Trouble with the outside world began on 28 February 1993 when the US Bureau of Alcohol, Tobacco, and Firearms attempted to serve search warrants on Mount Carmel, following reports that illegal firearms and ammunition were concealed in the compound. The reports were true – the hail of bullets that met the ATF agents killed four of them and wounded 15; in addition, some six cult members died in the battle. In the ensuing 51-day siege of the citadel by the FBI, the water was cut off and tear gas was used in an attempt to make Koresh and his followers leave peacefully. On 19 April, after the FBI had attempted to break in, Koresh apparently gave the order to set fire to the buildings in which his followers were huddled. Amongst those who perished in the biblical conflagration were 24 Britons, some 17 children, and Koresh himself.

> If the Bible is true then I'm Christ. – DAVID KORESH, March 1993.

> Just sit back and wait until you see God. – KORESH's reported instruction when he ordered the fires to be lit.

This incident, like the earlier Jonestown massacre, is a terrible warning to those who may be tempted by charismatic self-styled religious leaders. *See also*: Oklahoma bombing.

• **Wailing Wall** ▶ *See*: Western Wall.

• **Wait and see** ▶ A phrase associated with the Liberal prime minister H. H. Asquith; 'What did Asquith say?' is another way of saying 'Wait and see'. Asquith used the phrase in answer to a question in the House of Commons on 4 April 1910 and took to repeating it subsequently when faced with an awkward question. Eventually the Opposition took it up and chanted it when questions were put to him.

• **Wakey-Wakey!** ▶ The catchphrase of the British bandleader Billy Cotton (1899–1969). *The Billy Cotton Band Show* was an extremely popular radio and TV show first broadcast in 1949; it ran for 20 years. Each show opened with a short chorus from the band followed by a shout of 'Wakey-Wakey!' from the leader. The catchphrase is said to have arisen because the show originally went out early in the morning and on one occasion the musicians looked rather sleepy.

• **waldo** ▶ 1. Any remote-controlled device designed to manipulate objects, after Waldo F. Jones, an inventor in a science-fiction story by Robert Heinlein (1940s). 2. US teenage slang for a stupid person, a fool; equivalent to the British wally.

• **Waldsterben** ▶ (German, forest death) The death of large tracts of forest as a result of pollution. The phenomenon was first observed in Germany in the 1970s; the German word began to be used in English as awareness of the problem grew in the following decade. The depletion of the forests of N Europe, largely as a result of acid rain, continues to cause concern.

## • walk ►

**so dumb he can't walk and chew gum at the same time** A derisive phrase associated with the US politician Gerald Ford, who succeeded Nixon as president in 1974. Although regarded as honest and dependable, Ford was no intellectual and became notorious for his verbal gaffes. According to the US economist J. K. Galbraith, the phrase was first applied to Ford by Lyndon Johnson, who actually said 'fart' rather than 'walk'. *See also*: piss-up.

## • walkabout ►

In the Aboriginal culture of Australia, a long, solitary, and sometimes contemplative journey. The word acquired a new sense in the 1970s when it was applied to Elizabeth II's habit of straying from her planned route to meet ordinary people who had come to see her during her tour of Australia. These royal 'walkabouts' alarmed security men but did much to promote the popularity of the British monarch in Australia. Other celebrities are now also said to go on walkabouts when they depart from an official programme by mixing with crowds.

## • walking bass ►

In jazz, a bass line in boogie-woogie piano playing, consisting of ascending broken octaves. It is also used to describe a pizzicato accompaniment on a double base in regular crotchets moving up step by step in 4/4 time.

## • walking the dog ►

A popular jazz dance of the post-World War II period.

## • Walkman ►

Tradename for a portable cassette tape player (also called a personal stereo or personal hi fi) which is listened to through a small set of headphones. Although widely used as a generic name for any portable cassette player, Walkman actually refers to one of the first models on the market, manufactured by the Japanese firm Sony.

## • Wallace and Gromit ►

The plasticine stars of three short films by the British animator Nick Park (1958–   ) – *A Grand Day Out* (1992), *The Wrong Trousers* (1993), and *A Close Shave* (1995). All three films received major awards, including Oscars for Best Short Animated Film for the last two. Wallace is an inventor of gadgets, which have limited practical use, and Gromit is his long-suffering dog. The appeal of the films lies mainly in the superbly scripted comedy partnership of the two leads and the clever, yet essentially gentle, humour that arises from juxtaposing melodramatic plots with life in a rural backwater. The characters have become familiar faces all over the world, even to those who have not seen the films; their recognizability has been exploited by several advertising campaigns.

Park, a leading animator at the Bristol-based company Aardman Animations, first came to public notice when his plasticine animals starred in the delightful 'Creature Comforts' series of TV advertisements for an electricity company. Founded in 1972 by David Sproxton and Peter Lord, Aardman was also behind the legendary Morph – a minimalist clay man who, after a regular slot in the BBC's *Take Hart* went on to star in his own show – the TV series *Rex the Runt*, and Park's feature-length film *Chicken Run* (2000). The work of Park and Aardman has contributed significantly to the popularization of this type of animation, now termed **claymation**.

## • Wallenberg, Raoul ►

(1912–?47) A Swedish diplomat who was sent by his government to Hungary as a special envoy in 1944 to save the Hungarian Jews from the holocaust. A member of a well-known Swedish banking family, Wallenberg joined a foodstuff firm in 1939, the senior partner of which was a Jewish refugee from Budapest. As a frequent visitor to Budapest on business, he soon had a number of contacts with the Jewish community there. When the Swedish legation in Budapest decided in 1944 to try to protect Hungarian Jews from deportation to Auschwitz, the Ministry of Foreign Affairs sent Wallenberg to the city as a special envoy. At great personal risk, Wallenberg issued thousands of protective Swedish passports to Jews and established a large number of Swedish houses to shelter them. By these means, it is estimated that he saved some 25,000 Jews in addition to the 70,000 lives he helped to save by his various actions on behalf of the inhabitants of Budapest's ghetto.

When the Red Army arrived in Budapest, Wallenberg approached the Soviet command in January 1945 to discuss further relief operations. He was arrested and taken to Moscow. Subsequent intensive inquiries failed to disclose either the reasons for the arrest or the fate of Wallenberg. Although the Russians later took the line that he had died of a heart attack in the 1940s, many in the West refused to accept this without proof, arguing that he could still be alive in a Soviet prison. In 1981, in a largely symbolic gesture, he was made an honorary US citizen.

> Raoul Wallenberg considered his friends to be all those who suffered injustice. Each day he willingly jeopardized his own life so that others might live. In the face of the horror of evil, Raoul Wallenberg stood tall and unflinching.
> – RONALD REAGAN, in a message to the Raoul Wallenberg Commemoration in 1985.

In 1989 the newly liberalized Soviet Union opened its files on Wallenberg in a determined effort to discover his fate. The conclusion reached was that he was shot in the Lubyanka prison in 1947. Subsequently, however, a 10-year investigation into his fate by the Swedish authorities produced (2000) circumstantial evidence that he had been seen alive in Moscow in the 1980s. In January 2001 the Swedish prime minister declared that without unequivocal evidence of his fate Wallenberg should not, even now, be assumed to be dead.

In Israel, Raoul Wallenberg is honoured at Yad Vashem, the Memorial to the Holocaust in Jerusalem, as the most outstanding of the Righteous Gentiles. One of the true heroes of the 20th century, he proved that one man alone can challenge an entire empire of tyranny and evil.

• **wall of death** ▶ A fairground attraction consisting of a huge drum, around the inside of which a stunt motorcyclist rides his machine. The angular momentum enables the motorcycle to ride higher and higher up the inside wall, appearing to defy gravity.

• **Wall of Sound** ▶ The distinctive musical sound created in the mid-1960s by Phil Spector (1940– ), the US record producer. His records used a number of musicians playing identical instruments in unison to create a deep full-bodied sound that gave a monumental quality to simple teenage pop songs (his 'little symphonies for the kiddies' as Spector called them). The Wall of Sound can be heard at its most powerful on The Righteous Brothers' 'You've Lost That Lovin' Feelin', The Ronettes' 'Be My Baby', and Ike and Tina Turner's 'River Deep – Mountain High'.

• **wallpecker** ▶ One of the many German citizens who assisted in the demolition of the Berlin Wall with hammers, chisels, pickaxes, etc., following its opening in November 1989. While most wished simply to express their hatred of the Wall or to gather a personal memento, others had more entrepreneurial intentions; by Christmas 'authentic' pieces of the Wall were being sold at inflated prices through newspaper advertisements and on London markets. The term is a contraction of wallwoodpecker, a literal translation of the German *Mauerspecht*.

• **walls have ears** ▶ A World War II government slogan designed to make people aware of the dangers of idle talk that might provide useful information to spies. *See also*: Keep it dark; Keep it under your hat *at* hat.

• **Wall Street Crash** ▶ The collapse of the New York stock exchange on Black Monday, 28 October 1929, which plunged the world economy into the Great Depression. The Crash came as a reaction to one of the greatest speculative booms in history, an orgy of gambling in shares during which values rose precipitously and never seemed to reach a ceiling. The public's urge to speculate, encouraged by easy credit and the overweening optimism of the business community, was satisfied by a vast increase in the volume of shares available – especially from new investment trusts, the reckless issue of glamour stocks, and the marketing of securities to finance a flood of corporate mergers. Throughout the summer of 1929 share prices and the volume of trading rose inexorably; the underlying economy, however, was already entering a decline, with the indices of industrial production falling and unemployment rising. In the autumn, as this downturn became apparent, confidence in the market drained away and the frightened speculators sought to unload their holdings, causing the market to crash. On Thursday 24 October, panic selling resulted in 12,894,650 shares changing hands at disastrous prices, while hysterical crowds gathered outside the exchange. In the aftermath of the crash banks failed, businesses and factories closed down, and unemployment rose sharply. By 1933 the American GNP was one-third less than it had been in 1929, and one-quarter (13 million people) of the labour force was out of work. The crisis spread to the economies of all the other Western nations and did not end until World War II boosted production and employment.

• **wall-to-wall** ▶ An informal figurative expression to indicate that something is available in abundance. For example, the scene at a funeral may be described as 'wall-to-wall gloom'. The expression derives from its 1950s use to describe fitted carpet leaving no floor space uncarpeted from one wall to another; this is now normal but at that time was considered the height of luxury and comfort.

• **wally** ▶ British slang for a stupid unsophisticated person who can do nothing right; it became extremely popular in the late 1970s. It is thought to have originated in working-class London.

• **Wally blue** ▶ A shade of light blue favoured by Wallis Simpson. It was the colour of her wedding dress when she married the Duke of Windsor (the former Edward VIII) in June 1937. *See also*: Abdication Crisis.

• **Walter Mitty** ▶ *See*: Mitty, Walter.

• **wanker** ▶ Slang for a masturbator. By extension it is used to describe any irritating, incompetent, or unpleasant person, especially one who is excessively self-indulgent.

He would practise things like opening his zippo

lighter with just one hand and throwing his cigarettes up in the air and catching them in his mouth. Strangely this did not make him look like a total wanker – it nearly did, but not quite. – BEN ELTON; *Stark* (1989).

• **wannabee** or **wannabe►** Slang for someone, often a teenager, who clearly aspires to be someone or something other than themselves. This often takes the form of slavishly imitating a film star or pop personality, *e.g.* 'a Britney Spears wannabee'. A corruption of the phrase 'want to be', the word was first heard in America in the 1980s.

• **Wannsee conference►** The conference held in Wannsee, near Berlin, early in 1942, at which the Germans formulated their plan to exterminate all European Jews. The euphemism used at the conference was the Final Solution. Chaired at Hitler's insistence by Reinhard Heydrich, the conference appointed Adolf Eichmann to formulate the logistics of the plan. Thirty copies of the minutes of this ghoulish meeting were circulated but conveniently lost by the end of the war. However, one copy (known as the **Wannsee Protocol**) came to light in 1947 at the German Foreign Office. Described as 'the most shameful document of modern history', it was used in evidence at the Jerusalem and Nuremberg Trials of German war criminals.

• **WAP►** *See:* White Australia Policy.

• **war baby►** A baby born in wartime; especially the illegitimate offspring of a serviceman. *See:* baby boom.

• **warehouse►** A US term for a large public facility that provides impersonal custodial care for persons who are mentally ill, orphaned, poor, aged, etc. The word originated in the early 1970s and is also used as a verb.

• **warehouse party►** A large professionally organized dance party for teenagers held in a warehouse, aircraft hangar, or similar site. Warehouse parties were closely associated with the acid house craze of 1988–89 and became notorious for their wildness, deafening volume, and the open sale of drugs. The venue was usually publicized only by word of mouth to avoid the attentions of the police. *See also:* orbital; rave.

• **Warminster Thing►** The sighting of UFOs on numerous occasions in the region of Warminster, Wiltshire. The frequency of these sightings in the area first attracted attention in the 1960s. The best-authenticated incident occurred on Christmas Day 1964, when an entire company of Welsh Guards was woken by the sound of inexplicable explosions all around them – although no sign of their source could be detected. Shortly afterwards a woman was pinned to the ground by what she described as a 'sonic blast wave', which also damaged houses in the town. These events were so regular and so well-publicized that the phrase 'The Warminster Thing' came to be used to refer to anything unusual. A more prosaic explanation might lie in the proximity of the School of Infantry, where experiments with new weapons are conducted. The first widely publicized crop circles were seen in the vicinity of Warminster in the 1960s. *See also:* flying saucers.

• **warnography►** A type of literature or film that is thought to glorify war and stimulate aggression in the viewer or reader. The word was coined from *war* plus por*nography*; examples would include such magazines as *Power Fire* and the Rambo films in the 1980s.

• **War of the Worlds scare►** *See:* Martian invasion scare.

• **war on terrorism►** The 'war' against international terrorism announced by President George W. Bush in the wake of the terrorist attacks on America on September 11 2001. On 19 September Bush declared that America would use military force to destroy international terrorist networks and any regimes found to be assisting or harbouring them; he also warned that the campaign could take as long as 10 years. Several countries – most notably the UK, Canada, and Australia – offered military assistance while many others pledged operational or intelligence support.

In the days after September 11 suspicion immediately alighted on the al-Qaida terrorist network created and controlled by the Saudi-born millionaire Osama Bin Laden (1957–   ). Bin Laden, already wanted for a series of terror attacks in the 1990s, had established his base in the mountains of Afghanistan where he was believed to have links with the ruling Taliban regime. After the Taliban refused US demands to surrender Bin Laden, America began its war in earnest by launching cruise missiles against three Afghan cities on 7 October 2001. Air strikes continued for another five weeks before Taliban power suddenly crumbled, enabling their old enemies in the Northern Alliance to take control of Kabul (13 November), Kunduz (25 November), and Kandahar (8 December). America then concentrated its fire power on the Tora Bora, a complex of caves in the S Afghan mountains believed to be the chief stronghold of Bin Laden and al-Qaida. The onslaught resulted in the death or capture of many al-Qaida fighters but the fate of Bin Laden himself is unknown; according to some reports he escaped to Pakistan, where he is living under the protection of tribal chieftains.

Despite the failure to kill or capture Bin Laden, America could reasonably claim a high degree of success in its war by the end of 2001; al-Qaida's Afghan operation had been destroyed and the militant Taliban regime deposed at the cost of a handful of US lives. Critics of the US action, however, point to the 3000 or so Afghan civilians who are believed to have been killed (about the same number as those who perished on 11 September) and the intensification of the country's refugee problem; they also argue that support for Islamic terrorism worldwide may well have been increased rather than the reverse. Unmoved by such criticism, the Bush administration has made it clear that further phases of the war against terrorism will follow – most probably and most imminently in Iraq (a country that is accepted to have had no involvement in the events of 11 September).

• **war poets** ► A group of British poets whose best-known work describes their horrific experiences in World War I. During the conflict itself the most revered war poetry was undoubtedly that of Rupert Brooke (1887–1915), whose work presented a romantic picture of sacrifice in a just cause (see at: England). Brooke, who died of blood poisoning en route to the Dardanelles, did not live to see active service or the horrors of the trenches. If he had done so, it seems possible that his work might have developed in a quite different way. The work of Siegfried Sassoon (1886–1967), for example, presents an angry and disillusioned view of the conflict that is remarkable for its bleak realism and sardonic wit. Sassoon's refusal to serve after being seriously wounded in 1917 resulted in his spending the rest of the war in a military hospital. Here he met and befriended Wilfred Owen (1893–1918), whose poignant and evocative poetry was published by Sassoon after its author was killed in action. With its emphasis on the waste and pity of war and the inadequacy of traditional notions of 'honour' and 'sacrifice', Owen's poetry has probably done more to fix later attitudes to the conflict than any other work. Isaac Rosenberg (1890–1918) is also well-known for his devastating descriptions of life and death in the trenches; he, too, was killed in action. Survivors of the war who wrote powerfully of their experiences included Robert Graves (1895–1985), Edmund Blunden (1896–1974), and Ivor Gurney (1890–1937).

• **Warren Commission** ► See: Kennedy assassination.

• **Warsaw Pact** ► The Warsaw Treaty of Friendship, Co-operation, and Mutual Assistance: a treaty signed in 1955 by the Soviet Union, Albania, Bulgaria, Czechoslovakia, East Germany, Hungary, Poland, and Romania. The Pact, organized in response to West Germany's admission to NATO, bound the communist bloc countries in a formal military alliance and created a single unified command based in Moscow. It also gave the Soviet Union the right to station troops on the soil of the other signatories and a pretext to suppress reform movements in these countries on security grounds (see: Brezhnev Doctrine; Hungarian Rising; Prague Spring). Of the communist nations of E Europe only Tito's Yugoslavia declined to join (see: Titoism); Albania withdrew in 1968. Following the collapse of the communist regimes in E Europe in 1989 and East Germany's decision to leave the Pact (1990), the remaining members formally wound up the organization in 1991.

• **Warsaw Uprising** ► 1. The Warsaw Ghetto Uprising. The revolt on 19 April 1943 by the remaining inhabitants of the Warsaw ghetto, into which the Germans had herded some 500,000 Jewish men, women, and children. From 22 July 1942 some 5000 Jews per day were transported from the ghetto to the gas chambers at Treblinka. When news of the fate awaiting them reached the ghetto via escapees from Treblinka, the Warsaw Jews staged an uprising on 18 January 1943. The Germans lost 50 men and withdrew, abandoning the deportations for four months. On 19 April Himmler launched a full-scale attack on the ghetto with tanks and artillery, in honour of Hitler's birthday on the following day. The 1500 Jewish guerrillas, under the command of Mordecai Anielewicz, managed to kill several hundred Germans before their inevitable defeat on 16 May. Many of the guerrillas, including Anielewicz, committed suicide to avoid capture. 2. The attempt by the Polish underground to seize control of Warsaw from the Germans in August–September 1944. Their aim was to capture the city before the arrival of the Red Army, which had crossed the River Vistula in July and was within striking distance of the capital. On 1 August 50,000 Poles of the Home Army, the communist-led People's Army, and a band of armed civilians commanded by General Tadeusz Bor-Komorowski attacked the German forces; within three days they had managed to capture two-thirds of the city. The Germans then went on the offensive and SS detachments proceeded to crush the insurgents with a maximum of brutality. Although the rebels appealed for help, the Soviets refused to allow their airfields to be used by Allied planes; it was 13 September before Stalin relented and the first drops of supplies into the city were made. By this time it was already too late and the last of the Polish fighters were forced to surrender two weeks later. Some 15,000 Polish resistance fighters were killed during the fighting, while over 200,000 civilians were killed by the Germans afterwards in reprisal. The Germans lost an estimated 10,000 dead. Stalin's reluctance to support the uprising is explained largely by his determination that the largely non-communist Home Army should present no political or military threat to postwar communist domination of Poland through the Soviet-sponsored Lublin Committee.

• **Washington Conference** ▸ 1. (November 1921–February 1922) A conference of the major powers dealing with naval and Far Eastern affairs. The UK agreed to parity in battleships with America (five each), while the Japanese agreed to a limit of three. The UK and America also promised not to develop their bases in Hong Kong and in the Philippines. The naval agreement was the only effective measure of disarmament achieved between the wars and the conference also relieved tensions in the Far East, at least in the short term. 2. (22 December 1941–12 January 1942) The first Allied conference (codenamed Arcadia) between Prime Minister Churchill and President Roosevelt. In the discussions of long-term strategy, Churchill secured a US commitment to the defeat of Germany in the Atlantic and European theatres before it concentrated on Japan. A Combined Chiefs of Staff committee was established and various plans implemented to boost US armaments productions. The conference also produced a Joint Declaration, formally announcing an alliance to defeat the Axis Powers, which was signed by 26 countries, including China and the Soviet Union. 3. *See*: Trident.

• **Washkansky transplant** ▸ The first human heart transplant, carried out at Groote Schuur Hospital in Cape Town, South Africa, by Dr Christiaan N. Barnard (1922–2001) and his team on 3 December 1967. Louis Washkansky, a 53-year-old grocer, was given the heart of Denise Darvall, a 25-year-old bank clerk, who had been killed in a road accident. Washkansky died 18 days after the operation – not from heart failure, as Barnard was keen to emphasize, but due to lung failure arising from double pneumonia. The transplant caused considerable controversy at the time but is now a common procedure.

• **WASP** ▸ White Anglo-Saxon Protestant. A US acronym for the ethnic group that still dominates the upper echelons of society in America.

• **Wassermann test** ▸ A blood-serum test for syphilis developed by the German scientist August

von Wassermann (1866–1925) in 1906. Working at the Robert Koch Institute for Infectious Diseases in Berlin, Wassermann, together with the dermatologist Albert Neisser, developed a test for the antibody produced in the blood of persons infected by the syphilis bacterium. For many years the most commonly used test for diagnosing syphilis, it is now one of several indicators of the presence of the disease.

• **waste** ▸ US street slang first heard in the 1950s meaning to kill.

> He prefers not to remember the night in 1978 when 'some English junkie wasted a broad'.
> – *The Independent*, 27 April 1991.

• **wasted** ▸ 1. Slang for exhausted. 2. Intoxicated with drugs or drink. This is an extension of the slang sense of waste. Many words to describe intoxication are equally violent, *e.g.* bombed, smashed, blitzed.

• **-watch** ▸ A suffix that indicates organized or attentive monitoring of the subject specified. It is often used in the titles of TV programmes, newspaper columns, etc.: *Crimewatch* is a BBC programme that appeals to the public for help in defeating crime, while *Newswatch* was a news section of *The Observer*. The first coinage of this kind was **doomwatch**, a vogue term of the early 1970s referring to the expectation of imminent global catastrophe, nuclear or ecological. *See also*: Neighbourhood Watch.

• **watchful waiting** ▸ The phrase used by President Woodrow Wilson in 1913 to describe his policy of non-recognition of the Mexican government of General Huerta. The waiting did not last long as, in 1914, the Americans occupied Vera Cruz. The phrase was previously used by President Jackson in 1836.

• **Watergate** ▸ A complex of flats and offices, etc., beside the river Potomac in Washington, DC, which gave its name to America's gravest political scandal. On 17 June 1972, during President Nixon's campaign for re-election to the presidency, five burglars were apprehended breaking into Democratic Party headquarters in the Watergate. Over the coming months, thanks largely to persistent investigative journalism by Bernstein and Woodward of the *Washington Post* (*see*: Deep Throat), links were established between the burglars and an organization set up to finance Nixon's campaign. Nixon himself denied any knowledge of these matters and was returned to the White House by a landslide. However, the scandal returned with a vengeance in mid-1973, when the burglars gave full statements in order to avoid punitive sentences (*see*: Maximum John) and Congress established formal hearings into the matter. It now emerged that several senior figures – including the White House chief of staff and the for-mer attorney-general – had either consented to or known about the burglary and that there had been a concerted attempt to cover up the facts. The key question now became, What did Nixon himself know, and when? This might have remained unanswerable, had it not been revealed that Nixon was in the habit of tape recording all his discussions with senior staff. After prolonged stalling, Nixon was obliged to release transcripts of the tapes in April 1974. The effect was devastating; not only was the full extent of Nixon's involvement in the cover-up revealed beyond question, but the tapes caught the president and his aides speaking with a coarseness, cynicism, and disregard for the law that reminded many of Chicago gangsters (see: expletive deleted). Matters then moved swiftly to their conclusion. In July the House Judiciary Committee voted in favour of starting impeachment proceedings and in early August Nixon publicly admitted his role in the cover-up. With impeachment now certain, he resigned the presidency on 8 August 1974. Although 25 people would eventually go to gaol as a result of the scandal, Tricky Dicky was not one of them – he was granted an immediate free pardon by his successor, President Ford.

> I let down my friends, I let down my country. I let down our system of government. – RICHARD NIXON, 1977.

• **wave power** ▶ The generation of electricity by means of energy derived from sea waves (see: alternative energy). Various devices have been developed to effect this conversion, the best known being the **nodding duck**, consisting of a string of floats that bob up and down in the waves and turn a generator in so doing. However, the design of wave-power generators and the transmission of the current to the land involve difficult technical problems that have not yet found a practical solution.

• **WAVES** or **Waves** ▶ Women Appointed for Voluntary Emergency Service. The women's section of the US Naval Reserve. See also: Wren.

• **Wavy Navy** ▶ The popular name for the former Royal Naval Volunteer Reserve (RNVR), whose officers wore gold distinction lace made in wavy lines instead of the straight lines worn on the sleeves of regular officers. The RNVR lost its separate existence, after a brilliant wartime record, in December 1957, when it was combined with the Royal Naval Reserve (RNR). See also: Harry Tate's Navy.

• **way** ▶
**And that's the way it is** The catchphrase of the US broadcaster Walter Cronkite (1916–   ),

which he used at the end of each CBS TV Evening News programme between 1962 and 1981.

• **way-out** ▶ Slang for eccentric, or unusual, or extreme – a term of approval first used by the jazz enthusiasts in the 1930s and taken up again by beatniks in the 1950s and hippies a decade later. By the 1970s it had become the type of word that a middle-aged person might use in an attempt to sound with it.

• **weasel words** ▶ Words of convenient ambiguity, or an evasive statement from which the original meaning has been sucked or retracted. Theodore Roosevelt popularized the term by using it in a speech criticizing President Wilson in 1916:

> You can have universal training, or you can have voluntary training, but when you use the word *voluntary* to qualify the word *universal*, you are using a weasel word; it has sucked all the meaning out of *universal*. The two words flatly contradict one another.

Roosevelt was indebted to a story by Stewart Chaplin, 'Stained-Glass Political Platform', which appeared in the *Century Magazine* in June 1900 and contained this sentence:

> Why, weasel words are words that suck the life out of the words next to them, just as a weasel sucks the egg and leaves the shell.

In America a politician who sits on the fence is sometimes called a **weasler**.

• **Weatherman** ▶ A member of the **Weather Underground**, a US revolutionary terrorist group that emerged during the era of protests against the Vietnam War. The youthful militants were responsible for a series of bombings; three of them were accidentally killed in 1970, when their bomb factory exploded in New York City. Another three Weathermen, including leader Kathy Boudin, were arrested in 1982 after two police officers and a security guard were killed during an attempted robbery of a Brinks armoured truck. The group took its name from a line in the Bob Dylan song 'Subterranean Homesick Blues' (1965): 'You don't need a weatherman to know which way the wind blows'.

• **Web, the** ▶ See: Internet.

• **wedges** or **wedgies** ▶ See: platform sole.

• **weed** ▶ 1. Slang for tobacco or a cigarette, often referred to as the 'evil weed' because of its toxic effects. 2. Slang for cannabis, either because it is smoked like tobacco or because it grows like a weed, i.e. prolifically in favourable conditions. See: pot. 3. British schoolchildren's slang from the 1950s and 1960s for a weak, timid, and unsporty child, especially one who cries easily. It is still in use.

• **Wee Frees** ► The ultra-Calvinist minority of the Free Church of Scotland, which refused to go along with the majority when the Free Church joined with the United Presbyterian Church to form the United Free Church in 1900. The Wee Frees remain a powerful influence in certain areas of the Highlands and Islands of Scotland. Their strict observance of the Sabbath prevents Wee Frees from doing any kind of labour on a Sunday (even using scissors). An even stricter breakaway faction is known derisively as the **Wee Wee Frees**.

• **week** ►
   **A week is a long time in politics** A phrase used by Harold Wilson (Labour prime minister 1964–70, 1974–76) to journalists in 1964. It is now generally used to mean something fairly cynical – either that everything may have changed by the end of the week for reasons of political expediency, or that the electorate has a short memory. However, Wilson himself insisted that what he meant was that politics should be seen on a longer time-scale and not be judged by day-to-day issues.

• **weeny-bopper** ► A child, usually 8 to 12 years old, who is an avid fan of pop music and the latest fashions, *i.e.* a teeny-bopper who has yet to reach his or her teens.

• **weepie** ► *See*: tear-jerker.

• **weight-watcher** ► A person who tries to control his or her weight, especially by following a diet. Weight Watchers International Inc. is an organization founded in America in 1964 to promote slimming through dieting: attenders at Weight Watchers clubs are given personal target weights and various incentives to meet them.

• **Weimar Republic** ► The German federal republic established under the Constitution of 1919, which lasted until it was overthrown by Hitler in 1933. So called from the Thuringian town of Weimar, particularly associated with Goethe, in which the constitution was adopted by the National Assembly.

• **weirdo** ► A strange or eccentric person. The term was originally used to mean somebody of unconventional appearance or lifestyle, such as a beatnik or hippie. Until the mid-1960s, the usual British word was **weirdie**, the phrase **bearded weirdie** being especially common.

• **weisenheimer** ► US slang from the 1900s for a know-all. It is formed from the German *weise*, wise, and the suffix *-heimer*, to make it sound like a typical German surname.

• **welfare state** ► The system of universal 'cradle to grave' health-care and social-security provision established by the first postwar Labour government. Its main pillars were the National Insurance Act of 1946 and the establishment of a National Health Service in 1948. Both were based on recommendations in the wartime Beveridge Report (1942). In the 1950s the British welfare state was greatly admired by other countries, but subsequent decades have revealed many doubts and problems, leading to various attempts at reform. The main problem is the combination of escalating costs with the electorate's unwillingness to pay higher taxes.

• **wellie-wanging** ► British slang for a game the object of which is to see who can throw a Wellington boot the farthest. Popular at country fêtes and other fund-raising events in the 1970s, it has since declined in popularity.

• **Welsh Windbag** ► A derisive nickname for Neil Kinnock (1942–   ), the former (1983–92) leader of the Labour Party. His passionate but somewhat orotund rhetoric proved unpersuasive in the era of the sound bite. After failing to lead the Party to victory in either the 1987 or 1992 elections, he resigned as leader and in 1995 became a European Commissioner.

• **Welsh Wizard** ► Nickname of the Welsh Liberal politician David Lloyd George (1863–1945), who was prime minister from 1916 to 1922. It derives from his spellbinding rhetoric, mastery of political surprise, and ability to wrong-foot opponents and rivals. Although initially regarded as a left-wing maverick – he supported the Afrikaners in the Boer Wars and was a proponent of Welsh nationalism – he later showed a talent for intrigue and opportunism that led many to conclude that he had no fixed principles at all. As chancellor of the exchequer (1908–15), he introduced the innovative People's Budget and laid the foundations of the welfare state by bringing in old-age pensions (1908) and national insurance (1911). Despite a previous reputation for pacifism, he went on to become one of Britain's greatest war leaders, directing his small war cabinet with great energy and efficiency. He also took a prominent role at the Paris Peace Conference. However, his intrigues in first gaining the premiership and the various wiles and ruses he used to retain power after the war (*see*: Coupon Election; Honours Scandal; Lloyd George Fund) meant that he ended up mistrusted by all the main parties. After his coalition collapsed in 1922 (*see*: Chanak crisis) he spent the rest of his career in the wilderness. Lloyd George's colourful private life also inspired a good deal of gossip, much of it relating to his long affair with his secretary Frances Stevenson

(1888–1972), whom he married after his first wife died.

> Well, I find that a change of nuisances is as good as a vacation. – LLOYD GEORGE, on being asked how he managed to remain cheerful in the face of political difficulties.

• **Wembley Stadium** ▶ A large stadium built in the NW London suburb of Wembley in the early 1920s as part of the British Empire Exhibition. The Football Association (FA) Cup Final was played here every year from 1923 until 2000, when the stadium closed for redevelopment. It was also used for football internationals, Rugby League Cup Finals, and various other sports, including hockey, Gaelic Football, greyhound meetings, and even American baseball. The 1948 Olympic Games were held here as was the 1966 World Cup. Wembley was also a popular venue for rock concerts and charity galas, such as the Live Aid concert in 1985. Plans for a major redevelopment of the stadium (first announced in 2000) have caused a good deal of controversy.

• **Wendy house** ▶ A child's toy house that is large enough to enter; it is named after the little house constructed around the character Wendy in the play Peter Pan (1904) by J. M. Barrie. The name Wendy was invented by Barrie for this character.

• **wessis** ▶ See: ossis.

• **West Bank** ▶ The region on the west bank of the River Jordan, including Judaea, Samaria, and Jerusalem, which was occupied by Israel after the Six-Day War in June 1967. Formerly part of British Palestine, it was left in Arab hands after partition (1948) and became part of Jordan after the ceasefire of 1949. The Israeli military occupation of the West Bank and the encouragement of Jewish settlements in the area has been a major factor in the Palestinian-Israeli conflict since the late 1960s. Nearly one million Palestinians live in the region, in towns, villages, and refugee camps. Over 60% of the land, however, is owned by Israelis; although more than 150 settlements have been built since 1967 (encouraged by generous state subsidies), the Jewish population remains at around 50,000. In 1993 Israel agreed to remove its troops from parts of the West Bank as part of a peace agreement with the Palestine Liberation Organization (see: PLO). The new Palestinian National Authority assumed control of the Jericho area in 1995, but further Israeli withdrawals were postponed on security grounds. The early 2000s have seen the total breakdown of the peace process and the resumption of full-scale violence in the region. Israel reoccupied much of the West Bank in early 2002. See also: intifada.

• **Western** ▶ A story or film romanticizing America's Wild West in the early years of expansion and settlement. The struggles of the pioneers and the battles between lawmen and outlaws are invested with an almost mythical significance. The genre has a long history in the cinema, extending from Edwin S. Porter's The Great Train Robbery (1903) to the great collaborations of John Wayne and John Ford in the late 1930s and 1940s (Stagecoach, 1939; My Darling Clementine, 1946) and such modern classics as Clint Eastwood's Unforgiven (1993). See also: spaghetti Western.

• **Western Front** ▶ The largely static ground across which Germany and the Allied Powers, principally the UK and France, faced each other during World War I. The front extended from Nieuport on the Belgian coast, south through Ypres, Arras, Soissons, and Rheims to the area around Verdun. Over five million soldiers died in the trenches of the Western Front, which have remained a uniquely powerful symbol of the folly and horror of war. See: Somme, Battle of the.

• **Western Wall** or **Wailing Wall** ▶ The high stone wall that forms a retaining structure along the western side of the **Temple Mount** in Jerusalem. The Temple Mount, traditionally the site upon which Jacob had his dream of angels ascending a ladder to heaven, is the foundation upon which both the biblical Temples (those of Solomon and the Maccabees) were built. The Western Wall, all that remains of these structures, is therefore a holy site for Jews; until Israel achieved statehood in 1948 it was a shrine to which orthodox Jews came to bewail their lack of a national home in the Promised Land (hence the name, Wailing Wall, which is no longer used in Israel).

Unfortunately, according to Muslim tradition, the prophet Mohammed chose the Temple Mount as the place from which to ascend to Paradise in 632 AD. Some 60 years later Umayyad Caliph, Abd al Malik, built the Dome of the Rock, a Muslim mosque to commemorate this event, making it Islam's third most holy shrine (after Mecca and Medina).

Conflict between orthodox Jews and devout Muslims has persisted ever since. A fanatical Jewish sect annually (during the festival of Sukkoth) attempts to lay a cornerstone for a third Jewish Temple, implying that the Muslim shrine will be demolished to make room for it. This provocative gesture, not surprisingly, causes a violent Arab reaction. In 1990, when tensions ran high in the Middle East in the run up to the Gulf War, the Israeli police shot dead some 20 protesting stone-throwing Arabs, causing widespread condemnation. Further violent unrest was sparked by a visit to the Temple

Mount in 2000 by the hardline Israeli politician Ariel Sharon (now prime minister), which many Arabs considered a gross provocation.

• **Westland affair** ► A political crisis that erupted in January 1986 over the future of the Westland helicopter company, causing the resignation of the defence secretary, Michael Heseltine, and the trade secretary, Leon Brittan. Heseltine had backed the sale of Westland to a European consortium, while Brittan and the rest of the cabinet supported the sale to the US company Sikorsky. A confidential letter from a government law officer, critical of Heseltine's role in the sale, was deliberately leaked to the press from the Department of Trade and Industry. It later emerged that this leak had been sanctioned by Brittan and cleared by Margaret Thatcher's press secretary. The assumption, which could not be proven, that Mrs Thatcher herself had authorized the ploy briefly put her premiership in jeopardy.

Journalists referred to the affair as **Westlandgate**, a name coined – like those of other political scandals – by analogy with Watergate.

• **West Lothian question**► An anomaly raised by Scottish devolution; although Scottish MPs at Westminster retain the right to vote on English and Welsh affairs, English and Welsh MPs can no longer vote on matters devolved to the Scottish parliament. During debates on the Scotland Bill in 1977, this point was raised repeatedly by Tam Dalyell, Labour MP for West Lothian, as a fundamental flaw in the proposed legislation; accordingly it was soon dubbed the 'West Lothian question'. It remains unresolved, even though a Scottish parliament was opened in 1999.

> There is a slightly more sophisticated defence of this anomaly than Lord Irvine's notorious observation that 'the thing to do about the West Lothian question is to stop asking it'. It is that since every decision involving public spending in England and Wales indirectly affects the Scottish block grant...Scottish MPs are entitled to vote on them. – *The Independent*, 20 April 2000.

• **wetback** ► US slang for an illegal immigrant from Mexico. Such immigrants usually had to swim the Rio Grande.

• **wets** ► In the 1980s, a derogatory term for the more centrist element in the Conservative party, who shrank from the hard-line policies of Thatcherism and favoured a less confrontational approach. They were seen by their opponents, the **dries** or dyed-in-the-wool Thatcherites, as weak and cowardly.

• **wet sell** ► Salesman's slang for the technique of making a potential client drunk over lunch in order to facilitate a deal and extract the best terms.

• **wham-bam-thank-you-ma'am** ► A phrase used mostly by women to describe a short and perfunctory act of sexual intercourse in which male gratification is the only motive. It was originally used by the US forces during World War II.

• **What's up, Doc?**► The catchphrase used by the cartoon character Bugs Bunny; it was always said to the farmer Elmer Fudd, whose sole purpose in life was to find a way of doing away with Bugs. In 1972 the phrase was used as the title for a film starring Ryan O'Neal and Barbra Streisand.

• **wheel clamp**► *See*: Denver boot.

• **wheeler-dealer**► A businessman or politician who pulls off his deals by smart manoeuvres and elaborate scheming.

• **wheelie**► A stunt on a bicycle or motorcycle in which the front wheel is raised and the rider balances for a short distance on the back wheel. A car driven briefly on two wheels on the same side is also referred to as doing a wheelie.

• **whennies** ► *See*: bubs.

• **Which?** ► *See*: Consumers' Association.

• **whinge** or **winge**► To moan and complain incessantly in a peevish whining voice. The word was widely used in Australia before it began to be heard in the UK in the late 1970s. A **whingeing pom** is the Australian's favourite description of a typical British immigrant who does nothing but complain (*see*: pommy).

• **whiplash hustler**► US term for someone who fakes injury from a car accident in order to claim the insurance money. Whiplash is a very common injury to the neck incurred in relatively mild traffic accidents; it is easy to fake as nothing is actually broken.

• **whistle** ► British rhyming slang, first heard in the 1930s for a suit, from 'whistle and flute'. It was used by the mods (*see*: mods and rockers) in the 1960s and is still heard among working-class Londoners and those media types who ape their speech habits.

• **whistle-blower**► Slang for an informer. It derives from the phrase 'to blow the whistle on', meaning to stop a corrupt practice in the same way as a referee blows his whistle to stop play after a foul in football. A whistle-blower is usually someone in a business or a government office, who exposes a malpractice or a cover-up to the press. Often such a person is asked to leave his or her job.

• **White Australia Policy** ► (WAP) The policy

embodied in the Australian Immigration Restriction Bill (1901), which barred immigrants from non-White countries, especially Japan and China. In the last quarter of the 19th century, fear of the economic and cultural impact of such immigration was a powerful impetus towards federation, which took place in 1900. In the first Commonwealth parliament of 1901, all parties were agreed on the importance of preserving a predominantly European society in Australia. The Immigration Restriction Bill was duly introduced and excluded Asians by the simple device of a dictation test in a European language, which all immigrants were required to pass. The determination to preserve Australia for Whites remained a significant feature of government policy from federation until the 1960s. Although the dictation test for immigrants was abolished in 1958, it was not until the mid-1960s that *The Bulletin*, a national newspaper, dropped the motto 'Australia for the White Man' from its masthead and the measures against Asian immigration were officially relaxed.

• **white-collar** ▸ Denoting non-manual work or workers, usually salaried professionals. The phrase, used in such combinations as 'white-collar union' etc., originated in America in the 1920s. **White-collar crime** generally means financial fraud of some kind. *See:* blue-collar; pink-collar.

• **white goods** ▸ A type of consumer durable that includes refrigerators, deep-freezes, washing machines, dishwashers, etc. They are so called because they have been traditionally finished in white enamel paint. However, they are sometimes now painted in a less stark colour, including various shades of brown, in order to make them harmonize with wooden kitchen fittings. *See also:* brown goods.

• **Whitehall farces** ▸ A series of popular farces produced by Brian Rix (1924– ) at the Whitehall Theatre in London in the 1950s and 1960s. These included *Reluctant Heroes* (1950) by Colin Morris, John Chapman's *Dry Rot* (1954) and *Simple Spymen* (1958), Ray Cooney and Tony Hilton's *One For The Pot* (1961), and Ray Cooney's *Chase Me Comrade* (1964), all of which starred Rix.

• **white knight** ▸ A firm or individual that rescues a company from an unwelcome bid by a **black knight**. A company under attack by a black knight might seek a white knight, whom it considers to be a more suitable owner, and encourage him to make an offer that will prove to be more attractive to the shareholders than that made by the black knight. A **grey knight** in such a takeover battle is a counterbidder whose ultimate intentions are unknown;

his intervention will therefore be unwelcome to the company, the black knight, and the white knight.

• **White Russian** ▸ A counter-revolutionary or *émigré* at the time of the Bolshevik revolution. The most active counter-revolutionaries joined the so-called **White Army** that fought against the Bolshevik Red Army in the Russian Civil War (1917–22; *see:* reds). The term can also mean an inhabitant of Belarus or White Russia (Russian *byely*, white).

• **Whiteside, Sheridan** ▸ The central character, a venomous theatre critic, in *The Man Who Came to Dinner* (1939) by George S. Kaufman and Moss Hart. The play was inspired by a visit by the notoriously outspoken US critic Alexander Woollcott (1887–1943) to the house of Hart's family. Woollcott proved an impossible guest; among his many acid comments during his stay was the observation on Hart's home: 'Just what God would have done if he had the money'. Surprisingly, Woollcott was very amused by the piece – he even toured in the role himself with great success.

• **White trash** ▸ *See:* peckerwood.

• **Whitewater affair** ▸ A scandal surrounding the financial dealings of Bill Clinton (1946– ), subsequently president of the United States (1993–2001), during his governorship of Arkansas in the 1980s. It concerned the role played by the Whitewater Development Corp., a real-estate venture part-owned by Clinton and his wife Hillary, in the collapse of the Madison Guaranty Bank in 1989. The key allegation was that Clinton granted political favours to Madison Guaranty in return for an improper diversion of funds to Whitewater (and thence to his political campaigns). The scandal came to national attention following the suicide of Vincent Foster Jr, a White House counsel, in July 1993. A close friend and associate of the Clintons, he had been attempting to sort out the tangled legacy of Whitewater at the time of his death. Attempts to investigate Foster's suicide led to allegations of a cover-up orchestrated by Mrs Clinton and White House staff. Bowing to political pressure, Clinton appointed a special prosecutor to investigate all these matters in January 1994. Although a number of his former business associates were subsequently convicted on fraud charges, no evidence of misconduct by either the president or his wife emerged. Nor, to the fury of his opponents, was Clinton much damaged by the scandal in the eyes of the electorate. This may be explained by the obscurity of the allegations, the obvious partisanship of the Republican-led investigating committee, and the cynicism of the public. By 1998 the special prosecutor, Kenneth Starr, had found a juicier bone to chew in the unfolding Lewinsky affair. When the final report on Whitewater was published in 2002, the Clintons were formally exonerated on all counts.

• **whizz** or **whiz**▶ Another name for speed.

• **whizz kid**▶ A highly intelligent young person who achieves rapid success.

• **Who Dares Wins**▶ *See*: SAS.

• **whodunit**▶ A colloquial name for a detective story; the expression is probably of US origin.

• **wholefood**▶ Unprocessed food that retains all its natural attributes. For example, wholemeal bread is baked with flour made from the whole grain rather than from white flour, which has not only had the bran extracted but is often bleached. Wholefoods include cereals, grains, pulses, natural fruit juices, and fresh organic vegetables. They first appeared in health food shops in the late 1960s but are now widely available in supermarkets.

• **wicked**▶ Teenage slang for excellent or wonderful. Used widely among young US Blacks in the 1980s, it was quickly picked up by teenagers of all races in the UK.

• **Wickedest Man in the World**▶ *See*: Great Beast 666.

• **wide boy**▶ A flashily dressed young male who lives, often dishonestly, on his wits. *See also*: spiv.

• **widget**▶ Slang for a device or gadget the name of which is temporarily forgotten or unknown. It was used before World War II in America, but was not widely known in the UK until the late 1970s.

• **Widmerpool, Kenneth**▶ The most memorable character in Anthony Powell's 12-volume sequence of novels *A Dance to the Music of Time* (1951–75). Having first met at school, Widmerpool and the novels' narrator, Nick Jenkins, continue to cross paths at frequent intervals in later life – often in the most unlikely settings and contexts. To the amazement of Jenkins and his contemporaries, Widmerpool, the pompous schoolboy they once mocked, becomes an ever more prominent figure in industry, politics, and the military; by the end of his career he is the famous Lord Widmerpool, an all-powerful and slightly sinister *éminence grise* with shadowy intelligence connections. This astonishing rise seems to be the product of will-power and self-belief alone – Widmerpool clearly has no special talent and is completely lacking in either charm or charisma. Not surprisingly, a fair number of real-life candidates have been suggested as the model for this unattractive and faintly ludicrous character. It has been said that every Englishman with a university or a public-school education will have a Widmerpool in his life – an overlooked contemporary who somehow rose to undreamt of prominence and power.

• **Wiesenthal Centre**▶ An organization dedicated to bringing Nazi war criminals to justice, founded by Simon Wiesenthal (1908–   ), a survivor of the Nazi concentration camps. Originally an architect in Poland, Wiesenthal was imprisoned in a Nazi forced labour camp from 1941 to 1943, escaped, and was then recaptured and sent to Mauthausen in 1944. After the liberation of the camp by US forces in May 1945, Wiesenthal discovered that 89 members of his family had perished at the hands of the Nazis, although he was reunited with his wife, whom he had thought dead. After the war he worked with the Americans in collecting evidence against war criminals; in 1947 he and a group of volunteers founded the Documentation Centre on the Fate of the Jews and their Persecutors in Linz, Austria. The centre specialized in aiding Jewish refugees and collecting evidence against Gestapo agents, SS officers, and other perpetrators of the Final Solution. In 1954 the Centre was closed and its files transferred to Israel. Wiesenthal continued to hunt for war criminals with the aid of the Israelis and managed to track down Adolf Eichmann (*see*: Eichmann trial) in Argentina in 1959. This success prompted Wiesenthal to reopen the Jewish Documentation Centre in Vienna in 1961. Wiesenthal has been responsible for the identification of over 1000 other war criminals, notably Karl Silberbauer, the Gestapo officer who had arrested Anne Frank.

• **Wigan**▶ A town in NW England considered the archetypal northern industrial town. As such it was the butt of jokes by many music-hall comedians, often based on the fanciful notion that it had a seaside pier. The joke seems to have been inspired by the jetties on the Leeds–Liverpool Canal, which were used to load coal from rail trucks into barges. According to some, it was invented by George Formby Sr, father of the film entertainer. The 'pier' was immortalized by George Orwell in the title of his account of northern working-class life, *The Road to Wigan Pier* (1937). In 1986 the Wigan Pier Heritage Centre (*see*: heritage industry) was opened on the site of one of the original jetties.

• **Wild Geese**▶ Nickname of a band of White, mainly European, mercenaries who in 1964 joined Congolese government forces in their struggle against the rebels led by Christophe Gbenye. Their exploits were viewed with some sympathy in the UK, as Gbenye's forces were notorious for their atrocities against Europeans, including the massacre of 15 British missionaries and a threat to grill 1500 White hostages alive. The leader of the Wild Geese was the South African Mad Mike Hoare. In 1978 their exploits formed the basis of the film *The Wild Geese*, starring Roger Moore, Richard Burton, and Richard Harris.

• **wilding** ▶ US slang for running about in a wild and violent fashion, usually in a gang. It first came to public attention in 1989, when a young woman was gang-raped and left in a coma in New York's Central Park by Black youths. When questioned, one of the youths apparently said that they had been 'wilding' and the word was immediately picked up by the newspapers. Later reports suggested that he had merely said 'wild thing' with a Black pronunciation; if so, this is an example of a new word entering the language entirely through a misapprehension. The gang's victim recovered to testify against them, and they were convicted.

• **Willy Loman** ▶ See: Loman, Willy.

• **wimp** ▶ **1.** Contemptuous slang for a weak and ineffectual person. It was first heard among US schoolchildren and students in the 1970s. Its derivation is obscure; some suggest it comes from 'whimper', others from Mr Wimpy, a character in the *Popeye* cartoons. **2.** *See*: menu.

• **Wimsey, Lord Peter** ▶ The aristocratic amateur detective in the novels of Dorothy L. Sayers (1893–1957). His character was based on the schoolmaster and travel writer Eric Whelpton (1894–1981), for whom Sayers had an unrequited love at Oxford. In the novels, Wimsey finally falls for, and marries, his fellow-sleuth Harriet Vane, thought by many to represent Sayers herself.

• **wind of change** ▶ A new current of opinion, a markedly reformist or novel trend, especially one considered too strong to resist. A phrase popularized by Harold Macmillan in his speech to the South African Parliament (3 February 1960), with reference to the growing movement for national independence in the African continent:

> The wind of change is blowing through this continent, and, whether we like it or not, this growth of national consciousness is a political fact.

• **Window** ▶ The codename for the metallic chaff dropped during Allied bombing raids over Germany to confuse enemy radar in World War II. It was first used in a series of night raids over Hamburg (24 July–2 August 1943) and proved immediately effective; large areas of the city were destroyed and some 40,000 civilians were killed in firestorms caused by RAF bombs. Window disabled or confused ground and enemy fighter radar by producing spurious traces rendering accurate location and targeting of the bombing force impossible. The Germans later developed their own version of Window and also evolved effective countermeasures.

• **Windows** ▶ A computer operating system introduced in 1983 by Microsoft that has become the industry standard. It enables a user to carry out a variety of tasks by choosing from a series of on-screen menus and icons with a mouse or other pointing device, rather than by complex keyboard commands. The 'windows' themselves are rectangular areas on the screen in which part of a stored file can be displayed; these can be made any size up to that of the screen and can be moved around to suit the user; more than one window can be displayed at a time. The earlier versions of Windows ran on MS-DOS-based computers, but Windows 95 (released in 1995) and its successors have been self-contained operating systems. Windows 98 provides direct Internet access via the Internet Explorer web browser, while Windows 2000 incorporates various refinements including new features for mobile users.

• **wind power** ▶ The generation of electricity by means of energy derived from the wind (*see*: alternative energy). The advantage of wind power is that it uses no fuel and creates no pollution. The disadvantages are that modern **wind farms** (groups of around 100 turbines) take up a great deal of space and usually have to be sited away from the cities, in which the power is needed. In the UK a growing number of wind turbines are now supplying power to the national grid. It is estimated that this renewable energy source could provide some 20% of the UK's electricity requirement if all the available sites were to be utilized.

• **Windscale** ▶ *See*: Sellafield.

• **Windsor** ▶ The official name of the British royal family adopted in 1917, in deference to anti-German sentiment, to replace the existing name of Saxe-Coburg-Gotha, derived from Albert the Prince Consort. It was changed in 1960 to Mountbatten-Windsor for the descendants of Queen Elizabeth II, other than those entitled to the style of Royal Highness or of Prince and Princess. After his abdication on 11 December 1936, King Edward VIII was created Duke of Windsor.

• **windsurfing** ▶ A watersport in which the participant stands up on a narrow moulded board equipped with a mast and sail. The craft, known as a **sailboard**, is steered with a hand-held boom to which the windsurfer also clings for support. The board resembles a surfboard but is propelled by the wind rather than the waves.

• **wine lake** ▶ See: CAP.

• **winkle-pickers** ▶ Shoes with very elongated and pointed toes, affected by some teenagers in the late 1950s. The allusion is to the use of a pin for picking winkles out of their shells.

• **Winnie** ▶ Nickname of Sir Winston Churchill (1874–1965), whose leadership of the UK during World War II established him as one of the great heroes of British history. In the dark days after Dunkirk, Churchill's inspired oratory galvanized morale and helped to create the very determination that it expressed so eloquently. By the end of his life, Churchill had come to seem the very embodiment of British greatness; his humour and eccentricity also meant that he was widely loved. However, it was not always so. Churchill's long, brilliant, and adventurous career contained more than its share of failed causes and reckless misjudgements; indeed, before the crisis of 1940, many were ready to dismiss him as a crank and a has-been.

As a young man Churchill served as a war correspondent in the Boer Wars and was praised for his resourceful escape from captivity. Entering parliament as a Conservative, he later served in both Liberal and Conservative cabinets in a variety of posts, including home secretary (1910–11), first lord of the Admiralty (1911–15), and chancellor of the exchequer (1924–29). During the 1930s he was confined to the backbenches (his 'wilderness years') and became the foremost critic of the government's policy of appeasement (see: Munich). Towards the end of this period it was suggested to Stanley Baldwin, the prime minister, that a post in the government should be offered to Churchill. Baldwin refused to do so saying, with remarkable foresight, that if war came, the nation would need Churchill – a Churchill unsullied by party politics. He was, in fact, recalled to the Admiralty at the outbreak of hostilities in 1939 and became head of the coalition government in 1940 after Chamberlain's resignation. It is in the role of war leader that he is best remembered, not only in the UK but throughout the free world. His defeat in the general election of 1945 caused him and his party considerable surprise; he was, however, returned to office, as head of a Conservative government, from 1951 to 1955. His historical writings won him the Nobel Prize for Literature in 1953.

> The nation had the lion's heart. I had the luck to give the roar. – SIR WINSTON CHURCHILL, on his 80th birthday.

See also: blood, toil, tears and sweat; Few, the; their finest hour at hour; Iron Curtain; We shall never surrender at surrender; V for Victory; etc.

• **Winnie-the-Pooh** ▶ The teddy-bear character created by A. A. Milne in the stories he wrote for his son Christopher Robin. Winnie-the-Pooh's adventures with his friends Piglet and Eeyore became enormously successful after publication in the 1920s and the 'bear of very little brain' was soon established as a perennial children's favourite.

It is said that Milne named the character after a real Canadian black bear called Winnie (after Winnipeg). This Winnie was the mascot of Princess Patricia's Canadian Light Infantry, who brought him to Britain when they came to fight in World War I. Because of quarantine rules, Winnie had to spend some time in London zoo, where Milne apparently saw him. He was not to every reader's taste, however. Dorothy Parker, in her 'Constant Reader' column, reported that:

> ...it is the word 'hummy'...that marks the first place in The House at Pooh Corner at which Tonstant Weader Fwowed up.

• **Winslow, Ronnie** ▶ The young naval cadet at the centre of Terence Rattigan's play The Winslow Boy (1946). The story of the cadet's trial for petty theft was based on the case of the 13-year-old George Archer-Shee, who was expelled from Osborne Naval College on the Isle of Wight in 1908 after being accused of stealing a postal order. The cadet's father engaged the famous barrister Sir Edward Carson to represent his son in suing the Admiralty. The case ended with George Archer-Shee receiving £7000 compensation from the Admiralty. He was killed at Ypres in World War I.

• **Winterhilfe** ▶ (German, winter aid) A Nazi scheme to aid the less fortunate to which all Germans were supposed to contribute under veiled threats of violence or public humiliation. Workers' wages were docked 10% during the winter, industrialists sponsored special charity events, and families were supposed to restrict themselves to 'one-pot-meals' six times a year (an idea dreamed up by Goebbels) and add the savings to their donation. In 1937 about 10 million people received parcels of food and clothing or cash under the scheme.

• **Winter of Discontent** ▶ A reference to Shakespeare (Richard III I, i) used by the popular press to describe the winter of 1978–79, when the Labour government under James Callaghan faced a wave of industrial unrest provoked by the frustration of workers after three years of government-imposed pay restraint. Strikes by dustmen, hospital porters, road-haulage and oil-tanker drivers, and Liverpool grave diggers provoked considerable dissatisfaction among the electorate with Labour's handling of the unions. This discontent effectively lost Labour the 1979 election, which ushered in 18 years of Conservative rule.

• **Winter War ▶** The Russo-Finnish War, fought between 30 November 1939 and 13 March 1940. After the division of Poland between the Soviet Union and Germany in September 1939, the Soviets, fearful of a German attack, sought to consolidate their position in the Baltic with a series of mutual defence pacts with Latvia, Estonia, and Lithuania, which effectively placed them under Soviet military control. Finland boldly resisted Soviet overtures and on 30 November the Soviet Union launched an air attack on Helsinki. The invasion that followed involved a force of nearly one million Soviet troops, which crashed into Finland from the east and southeast and (in an amphibious operation) across the Gulf of Finland. Opposing them were 300,000 Finnish soldiers, the majority reservists, commanded by Marshal Baron Carl Mannerheim, a veteran of three wars. The Finns successfully repulsed the Soviet advances in battles at Kemijarvi, Suomussalmi, and at the Mannerheim Line across the Karelian Isthmus, largely by virtue of their superior mobility, imperviousness to sub-zero temperatures, better organization, and indomitable fighting spirit. The UK and France prepared an expeditionary force to aid the Finns, but neutral Norway and Sweden refused to allow it to pass. By March a massive Soviet assault in the northwest, together with incessant attacks on the Mannerheim Line, effected a breakthrough. In the absence of Allied support, the Finns were forced to sue for peace and formally accepted the Soviet terms on 13 March 1940. The war cost the Soviet Union 200,000 men, 700 planes, and 1600 tanks, against Finnish losses of 25,000. The abysmal performance of the Red Army convinced Hitler that the Soviet Union could easily be defeated by his superior war machine – a mistake that, above any other, cost him the war. The aftermath of the Winter War led to radical reorganization of the Red Army, which would astonish enemies and Allies alike with its performance in the later stages of the war.

• **wire-guided ▶** Describing a type of missile that is guided by electrical signals transmitted through a fine wire connecting it to the control device from which it is launched. The wire, which uncoils during the missile's flight, may be several miles long. *See*: guided missile.

• **wireless ▶** A former name for a radio. When Marconi (1874–1937) sent his first signal across the Atlantic in 1901, the word 'wireless' was widely used to contrast his invention with telegraphy, which depended on undersea cables. At that time it seemed like a miracle that messages could be transmitted without wires. Some members of the older generation still refer to 'the wireless'.

• **Wise forgeries ▶** A series of forgeries of rare Victorian first editions manufactured by Thomas James Wise (1859–1937), a prominent bibliographer and book collector. Wise loved the Romantic and Victorian poets and acquired a valuable collection of the first and early editions of their works. He was a founder member of the Browning and Shelley Societies, and compiled influential bibliographies of works by Browning (1897), Tennyson (1908), and the Brontës (1917). In addition to his legitimate bibliographical researches, however, Wise was also a talented forger. From 1880 he began forging whole editions, single poems, or short prose works by his favourite authors, using type facsimiles from genuine editions and the services of a printer, who remained innocent of his true purposes. The forgeries were entered into his bibliographies, copies were lodged with the British Museum to verify their existence, and others were sold for large sums as rare collectors' items. The operation was eventually exposed in 1934 by John Carter and Graham Pollard in their *Enquiry into the Nature of Certain Nineteenth-century Pamphlets*, a pioneering work of investigation that used the latest scientific techniques accurately to date the forgeries. Wise died shortly afterwards, refusing to acknowledge his guilt.

• **with-it ▶ 1.** Dated slang meaning fashionable, up-to-date. This classic piece of 1960s argot arose from the Black musician's phrase of the 1930s and 1940s 'get with it', which was later taken up by the beatniks. **2.** A colloquialism meaning alert, aware, having all one's faculties intact. It is mainly used in the negative, in such phrases as 'Sorry – I'm not really with-it this morning'.

• **Wizard of Dribble ▶** Nickname of the British footballer Sir Stanley Matthews (1915–2000), whose skill at 'dribbling' the ball was proverbial. Playing at outside right, he represented Stoke City (1931–47; 1961–65), Blackpool (1947–61), and England, for whom he appeared 54 times. Possibly the most famous British footballer of the 20th century, he finally retired at the age of 50, having played 886 first-class matches. In 1965 he became the first British footballer to receive a knighthood.

• **Wizard of Oz ▶** The title character in the popular children's book, *The Wonderful Wizard of Oz*

(1900), by L. Frank Baum (1856–1919), a well-known US journalist. The all-powerful wizard is finally unveiled as an impostor with no magical gifts. A musical comedy of the same name (1901) was a great success, as (eventually) was the 1939 film, which made a star of the young Judy Garland.

• **Wobblies** ► Nickname of the **Industrial Workers of the World** (IWW), a radical US labour movement founded in Chicago on 7 July 1905. It was set up as an alternative to the conservative American Federation of Labor, which excluded the unskilled and craft unions. The movement was plagued from its inception by divisions between Syndicalists, such as William D. ('Big Bill') Haywood, who advocated direct action to establish worker control over the means of production, and those who favoured more conventional political methods. At the height of its popularity, in 1912–17 the movement had over 100,000 members, but violence by activists alienated popular support and gave the government an excuse to arrest and suppress the membership; by the mid-1920s the Wobblies had effectively been hounded out of existence. The radical vision of the IWW lives on in popular folk songs, such as 'Joe Hill', commemorating the murdered IWW organizer; the phrase pie in the sky derives from another song used by the movement. The source of the nickname 'Wobblies' is disputed; according to one version, it derives from the attempts of a Chinese restaurant keeper to pronounce the Ws in IWW.

• **Wolf Cub** ► The original name for a member of the junior branch of the Boy Scouts, now called **Cub Scouts** (age range 8–11 years). The concept was taken from Kipling's *Jungle Books*, in which the infant Mowgli is brought up by wolves.

• **wombles** ► Small furry creatures inhabiting Wimbledon Common in S London who collect and reuse human litter in a variety of ingenious ways. The invention of Elizabeth Beresford, who introduced them in her children's book *The Wombles* (1968), they later featured in an animated television series of the mid-1970s. The popularity of the series even led to the creation of a pop group, who dressed up in furry costumes and mimed to such hits as 'Remember You're a Womble' (1974). In the later 1970s 'womble' became British schoolchildren's slang for an unattractive and unstylish person.

• **Women's Lib**; **Women's Movement** ► *See*: feminism.

• **women's studies** ► Courses of study related to women that were first introduced in US colleges and universities in the 1970s. Prompted by the feminist movement (*see*: feminism), academic departments offered courses on 'Women's Role in Society', 'Women in Literature', etc. Such courses proliferated in the wake of the political correctness movement of the late 1980s and early 1990s.

• **Woodbines** ►
    **Packet of Woodbines** Nickname of the Russian cruiser *Askold*, from its five long thin funnels – Woodbine cigarettes being thin and sold in packets of five. She was taken from the Bolsheviks after the October Revolution of 1917 and used by the Royal Navy against the revolutionaries in the White Sea.

• **Woodbine Willie** ► Nickname of the Revd Geoffrey A. Studdert-Kennedy (1883–1929), one of the best-liked and best-known padres of World War I. His nickname came from the Woodbine cigarettes which he gave to the men in the trenches.

• **Woodstock** ► A US rock music festival, held from 15 to 17 August 1969 on a 600-acre farm near the small town of Woodstock, in the foothills of the Catskill Mountains in upstate New York. The 'Woodstock Music and Art Fair' was the largest and most celebrated of the rock and folk music festivals of the late 1960s and early 1970s. Some half a million young people survived 20-mile traffic tailbacks, inadequate facilities, rain, and copious quantities of mud to hear such musicians as Joan Baez, Jimi Hendrix, The Who, Creedence Clearwater Revival, The Grateful Dead, and Crosby, Stills, Nash & Young, all of whom appeared without payment. The festival, which passed off peacefully and happily despite the huge numbers involved and the amateurish organization, immediately became a symbol of the non-violent anarchist ideals of the hippie movement. A second festival organized on the same site 25 years later proved a far more calculated and commercial operation; it was also marred by violence and crime.

• **Woolton Pie** ► A pie made from miscellaneous leftovers and vegetables that was recommended to the British public during World War II as a means to make the greatest possible use of rationed food. Containing carrots, parsnips, turnips, and potatoes in a white sauce, it was one of the recipes publicized under the aegis of Frederick Marquis, First Earl of Woolton (1883–1964), who was minister of food (1940–43).

• **Woomera** ► The rocket testing range in South Australia; appropriately, the name is an Aborigine word for a spear-throwing stick.

• **Wooster, Bertie** ► The hapless young man-about-town created by P. G. Wodehouse in the story 'The Artistic Career of Corky' (1916) and subsequently the central character in a series of popular comic novels. Constantly in trouble, from which his manservant Jeeves always extricates him, he was based upon the comic actor George Grossmith Jnr (1874–1935). Other traits were inspired by Anthony Bingham Mildmay, Second Baron Mildmay of Flete (1909–50), who was Wodehouse's son-in-law. Actors to play Bertie both on stage and screen include Ian Carmichael, John Alderton, and Hugh Laurie (with Stephen Fry as Jeeves).

• **word blindness** ► *See*: dyslexia.

• **word processor** ► A software package for a computer enabling letters, documents, books, etc., to be created, edited, stored, and printed. Modern word processors enable text to be justified and correctly hyphenated and provide a variety of fonts and typefaces. Many now produce documents of near-print quality. *See*: desktop publishing.

• **workaholic** ► A person who is addicted to work; someone who compulsively works very long hours to the detriment of their family and social life. The term was coined (from 'work' plus 'alc*oholic*' by the US psychologist and Protestant minister W. E. Oates (late 1960s).

• **work ethic** ► A system of values that emphasizes the moral and psychological importance of work and other productive activities. This basic tenet of Protestant Christianity (strongly espoused by the Puritan settlers in America) is also the mainstay of the capitalist economic system. The term was introduced by the German sociologist Max Weber (1900s).

• **work to rule** ► A form of industrial action in which all the regulations relating to a particular form of work are literally and pedantically obeyed, in order to bring about delays in working. It is a form of go-slow.

• **World Bank** ► The International Bank for Reconstruction and Development, established in accordance with agreements reached at the Bretton Woods Conference in July 1944. A specialized agency of the United Nations, it began operations in 1947. Initially the Bank concentrated on providing finance for the reconstruction of war-torn Europe but by 1949 its efforts were increasingly directed to funding aid in the developing countries. Most of its capital is provided by the developed nations, although the Bank also raises money on international capital markets. It operates strictly as a commercial entity, lending at commercial rates of interest to governments, or to private concerns with the government as guarantor, but only to countries capable of servicing and repaying debt. An affiliate

agency, the International Development Agency, was established in 1960 to provide low-interest loans to poorer members. The Bank's headquarters are in Washington, DC.

• **World Cup** ► Association Football's most prestigious competition, held every four years under the auspices of FIFA. National teams compete for the Jules Rimet Trophy, named after the honorary president of FIFA from 1921 to 1954, who first proposed the competition.
Winners:
    1930 Uruguay
    1934 Italy
    1938 Italy
    1950 Uruguay
    1954 West Germany
    1958 Brazil
    1962 Brazil
    1966 England
    1970 Brazil
    1974 West Germany
    1978 Argentina
    1982 Italy
    1986 Argentina
    1990 West Germany
    1994 Brazil
    1998 France

• **World Disarmament Conference** ► An international conference convened in Geneva on 2 February 1932 and attended by all major countries, including America and the Soviet Union (who were not members of the League of Nations). The conference had been planned at a time of considerable optimism in the wake of the Young Plan of August 1929; it was hoped that new talks might revive the spirit of the Locarno Pacts, leading to a relaxation in international tensions and real progress on disarmament. By 1932, however, European affairs had deteriorated to such an extent that negotiations tended to widen rather than narrow the gulfs. The irreconcilable interests of France and Germany proved the most intractable problem. France insisted on a guarantee of security from German invasion, either by an international police force or by the preservation of German military inferiority. Germany demanded equality; eventually the French offered equality after a trial period of four years during which Germany should prove her good intentions. Meanwhile, as negotiations dragged on, the Weimar Republic was disintegrating as the Nazis rose to political dominance. Hitler was appointed chancellor in January 1933; on 14 October Germany withdrew from the Conference and a week later from the League of Nations. The Conference lingered on into 1934 but by then most participants had concluded privately that only by vigorous rearmament could international security be guaranteed.

• **world music** ► A recording industry label that embraces all kinds of ethnic music, but especially those from non-Western traditions; it is also used of rock music that incorporates or imitates ethnic styles. In the later 1980s and 1990s African, South American, and Eastern European sounds in particular became fashionable among followers of pop and rock music. The term seems to have been coined to attract a young sophisticated audience who would probably have been repelled by the associations of 'folk music'.

• **World Service** ► A BBC radio service, first established as the Empire Service in 1932. During World War II, the Empire Service became a universal service in English, broadcasting not only to Dominion and Colonial audiences but also to the British and Commonwealth troops throughout the various theatres of war. It was called variously the Overseas Forces Programme, the General Forces Programme, and the General Overseas Service, before becoming the World Service. During the same period its range was extended to cover North Africa, South America, the Pacific, and North America. Since 1989 the name World Service has been applied to the full range of the BBC's external services and not just to its English-language branch. The World Service in English continues to broadcast 24 hours a day, offering news, drama, music, sport, and comedy; a worldwide television service has also been added.

• **World's Greatest Entertainer** ► The self-bestowed title of the US singer Al Jolson (Asa Yoelson; 1886–1950), who became the first major star of the talkies with the release of *The Jazz Singer* in 1927. Jolson was known for his magnetic stage presence. His most successful song was 'Mammy', which he delivered on one knee while imploring his audiences' sympathy with outstretched hands. He invariably performed in black-face.

> It was easy enough to make Jolson happy at home. You just had to cheer him for breakfast, applaud wildly for lunch, and give him a standing ovation for dinner. – GEORGE BURNS.

*See also*: You ain't heard nothing yet *at* heard.

• **World's Sweetheart** ► Nickname of the US film actress Mary Pickford (Gladys Mary Smith; 1893–1979), one of the great stars of silent films in the 1910s. The wide-eyed heroine of such movies as *Rebecca of Sunnybrook Farm* (1917) proved to be a shrewd business woman. In 1919 she co-founded United Artists Films with Charlie Chaplin, D. W. Griffiths, and Douglas Fairbanks (her husband) and went on to become one of the wealthiest women in the world. When her career was still developing she was more modestly referred to as **America's Sweetheart**; victims of her financial acumen called her the **Attila of Sunnybrook Farm**.

> I can't afford to work for only ten thousand dollars a week. – MARY PICKFORD, to Adolph Zukor.

• **World Trade Center** ► (WTC) A building complex, including two towers each 110 storeys high, that formerly stood in New York's Manhattan district; the famous twin towers were reduced to rubble and ash, with the loss of nearly 3000 lives, in the infamous terrorist attack of September 11 2001. When the building opened in 1974, the 417 m (1368 ft) and 415 m (1362 ft) towers were the tallest in the world; ironically the complex had been designed by Minotu Yamasaki, an architect notoriously afraid of heights. The towers, which housed some 50,000 employees working largely in the financial sector, became a celebrated feature of the New York skyline and a potent symbol of US economic power.

On the morning of September 11 each of the towers was struck by a hijacked 767 airliner laden with passengers and jet fuel. The towers were set alight and collapsed from the top downward. Although a final death toll is still not available, at least 2034 workers and tourists in the WTC are known to have lost their lives, as did 243 New York firefighters. With the addition of other emergency workers, passers by, and the 156 passengers and crew on the aircraft, the death toll is believed to stand at around 2830. *See also*: al-Qaida; war on terrorism.

• **World Trade Organization** ► *See*: GATT.

• **World Wars** ► The wars of 1914–18 (World War I) and of 1939–45 (World War II), in which participation was worldwide.

• **World Wide Web** ► *See*: Internet.

• **wormhole** ► A path through space that has been suggested as a drain down which energy from a black hole passes to a so-called **white hole**.

• **worst-case** ► Indicating something that is or relates to the worst possible combination of circumstances. For example, a **worst-case scenario** is a hypothetical situation in which everything that could go wrong does go wrong (also called a **nightmare scenario**); a **worst-case analysis** is planning that takes such a scenario into account, with the aim of producing an absolutely foolproof scheme, design, etc. The usage originated in military planning, in which it was used especially to refer to the possible outcome of a nuclear exchange.

• **Worth, Patience** ▶ Pseudonym of Mrs J. H. Curran, a US novelist who claimed that her books were 'communicated' to her from beyond the grave. The historical novel *Hope Trueblood* was particularly well received by critics, while *Telka*, set in medieval England, was praised for its authenticity – although Mrs Curran professed to know nothing of the period. The novels were, she claimed, dictated to her while in a trance, the first contact having been made during a séance on 8 July 1913. Patience Worth, as the spirit responsible called herself, explained that she had been born in Dorset in the 17th century and had subsequently emigrated to America, where she died at the hand of an Indian war party. Whatever the truth behind the origin of the novels, literary commentators have never explained how the comparatively unimaginative and unacademic Mrs Curran managed to produce such apparently well-researched works.

• **would** ▶
   **Well, he would, wouldn't he?** *See*: Profumo affair.

• **WPA** ▶ Works Progress Administration. An organization established by the US government in 1934 in an attempt to provide employment for the many artists unable to find work during the Great Depression. 5000 artists worked on various projects, including the decoration of public buildings with enormous murals. The projects were closed down from 1939.

• **Wren** ▶ A member of the Women's Royal Naval Service (WRNS). *See also*: WAAC; WAAF.

• **Wright brothers** ▶ The brothers Wilbur Wright (1867–1912) and Orville Wright (1871–1948) who, at 10.35 a.m. on 17 December 1903, achieved the first controlled and sustained powered flight. It took place at Kitty Hawk, North Carolina, and lasted just 12 seconds, with Orville at the controls. Before the day was ended the brothers had managed a further three flights, the fourth lasting 59 seconds and covering 852 feet. Their 12 hp chain-driven aircraft, *Flyer I*, recorded an air speed of 48 kph (30 mph); it is now preserved at the National Air and Space Museum at the Smithsonian Institute, Washington DC. The Wright brothers are usually credited with being the forerunners of the age of aviation; the first flight by a powered aircraft was, however, made on 9 October 1890 by the Frenchman Clément Ader (1841–1925), who flew 50m (164 feet) in his 20 hp steam driven aircraft *Eole*.

• **wrinklie** or **wrinkly** ▶ British slang for an older person. As used by young people, it is not usually intended to cause offence (although it may well do so). It has been fashionable since the 1970s and is also used in the form of its common variants, **crinkle** or **crumblie** (or **crumbly**). *See also*: dusty.

> Rod Stewart launched his first British tour for five years and proved he's still the liveliest wrinkly rocker around. – *The Sun*, 27 March 1991.

• **wrong sort of snow** ▶ *See*: leaves on the line.

• **WRVS** ▶ Women's Royal Voluntary Service. Set up in 1938 as the Women's Voluntary Service (WVS), primarily to help with air-raid precautions, it became the WRVS in 1949. It does valuable social and welfare work with the aged and infirm and gives help in emergencies. It is particularly noted for its meals on wheels service.

• **Wurlitzer organ** ▶ The spectacular pipe organ, able to imitate a whole orchestra of instruments, that became a feature of the lavish picture theatres built in America and Europe during the early decades of cinema. The instrument characterized 40 years of cinemagoing – first as accompaniment to silent films, later as entertainment before and between talkies. The 'Mighty Wurlitzer' was developed in Elmira, New York, in 1910 by the Wurlitzer family, long established in America as musical-instrument makers and dealers. Although more were produced than any other model of a pipe organ in history, they are now difficult to find. Those that have survived are usually cherished and restored by dedicated enthusiasts.

• **wysiwyg** ▶ Computer jargon for 'What you see is what you get' *i.e.* what you see on the screen is exactly what will appear on the printout. It is pronounced 'wizzy-wig'.

# X

• **X** ► A former category of film classification indicating that in the opinion of the British Board of Film Censors a movie was unsuitable for showing to children. The category was introduced in 1951 to exclude under-16s (the threshold was raised to 18 in 1970) and replaced by the 18 rating in the 1980s. In America the X rating was introduced in 1968 to exclude children under 17. The US X classification is reserved almost entirely for pornography; mainstream or artistic films with a violent or sexual content are usually rated R (Reserved) or NC-17 (No Children under 17). **X-rated** is now used to describe anything considered shocking, *e.g.* 'X-rated language' or 'an X-rated foul'.

• **Xerox** ► Tradename for a type of copier for text, diagrams, etc., manufactured by the Rank-Xerox Corporation. The name, which is often used generically, comes from xerography – a process invented by the US scientist Chester Carlton in 1937. In this, copies are made by producing a photographic pattern of electric charge on a semiconducting surface. Carbon powder sticks to the charged areas of the surface and is then transferred to paper, where it is fixed by heat. The name is from Greek *xeros*, dry. Xerox type copiers, which make copies on plain (*i.e.* untreated) paper, are now to be found in every office.

• **Xi An incident** ► The kidnapping of the Chinese Nationalist (Guomindang) leader Chiang Kai-shek in 1936. The seizure of the commander by two young marshals in Manchuria was a major factor in the forging of an alliance between the rival Nationalist and Communist forces to resist the Japanese invasion. Once the Japanese were defeated, however, the alliance soon broke up.

• **X marks the spot** ► An expression used to identify an exact location. It is derived from hypothetical treasure maps, in which the location of the treasure is marked with a cross. The expression became widely associated with 'spot the ball' competitions in newspapers, in which competitors are required to place a cross where they presume the ball to be in an action shot from a ball game.

# Y

• **yakkety-yak** ▶ Idle chatter or gossip. It is an onomatopoeic extension of US slang 'yak', to chatter. A pop-song of 1958 by the Coasters, written by Leiber and Stoller, had this title.

• **Yalta Conference** ▶ The second Allied summit between Churchill, Roosevelt, and Stalin (the first was the Tehran Conference), held at Yalta in the Crimea, 4–11 February 1945. With regard to Allied military strategy, the ailing Roosevelt achieved his main aim in securing a Soviet commitment to enter the war against Japan three months after the end of the European conflict. The conference was, however, mainly concerned with the shape of the postwar settlement. It was agreed that Germany should be divided into four occupation zones, would have to pay reparations, and that war crimes would be investigated and punished. The precise details of the implementation of these measures were left to later discussions. Agreement was also reached on the use of the veto in the Security Council of the United Nations and on the allocation of three seats on the Council to the Soviet Union. Dominating much of the conference sessions was the issue of the Polish frontier settlement and the composition of the Polish government. Churchill and Roosevelt agreed to the extension of Poland's western border to the Oder and Neisse rivers and the ceding of territory in the east to the Soviet Union. Stalin gave assurances that the Polish government would be reorganized to represent non-communist factions as well as the communist-backed Lublin Committee. He also promised that free democratic elections would be held in Poland and all the countries in E Europe currently under Red Army control. Subsequently, Stalin did not fulfil this commitment to free elections; as a result Churchill and Roosevelt have been accused of allowing E Europe to fall under Soviet control at Yalta. At the time, however, there was no reason to believe that Stalin would betray his promises. Moreover, given the occupation of the region by the Red Army, the West had the option of accepting Soviet assurances, or embarking on a Third World War.

• **Yardbird** ▶ *See*: Bird.

• **yardie** ▶ **1.** Jamaican slang for a Jamaican or sometimes any Caribbean person. **Yard** is the Jamaican name for Jamaica or home, as in the expression 'my own backyard'. **2.** Slang for a member of a secret Jamaican criminal organization operating in the UK and America since the late 1980s.

> Yardies sent gunmen on drugs' quest. – Headline in *The Independent*, 12 February 1991.

• **yarra** ▶ Australian slang for insane. From the name of a mental hospital at Yarra Bend, Victoria.

• **yellow card** ▶ The card displayed by a soccer referee when cautioning a player. On the football field it is used as a highly visible indicator of the reprimand, and in this sense has come to mean any type of public rebuke or warning. In its original soccer context, offences that can incur the yellow card include unsporting behaviour, dissent, persistent infringement of the laws of the game, and entering or leaving the field without the referee's permission. A second yellow card during a game automatically results in a red card, which signals that the player is being sent off.

> Not that Mrs Gorman is unused to reprimand: the Whips' Office has called in the colourful Essex Woman for a wave of the yellow card before: that time it was over her opposition to Maastricht, during which she claimed she was sexually harassed in the Commons chamber by a pair of Europhile MPs. – *The Independent*, 30 November 1993.

• **yellow dog contracts** ▶ A US name for agreements made by employers with employees to prevent the latter from joining labour unions. These contracts became invalid under an Act of 1932. In America a 'yellow dog' is any low or contemptible person (from the fact that many mongrels have yellowish fur).

• **yellow flu** ▶ US slang for the unauthorized absence of students from schools, organized by families as a protest against the busing of children to distant schools to achieve racial balance. The expression comes from the traditional yellow colour of US school buses.

• **Yellow Journalism** ▶ *See*: muckrakers.

• **yellow star** ► *See*: Schandband.

• **yes-man** ► One who always expresses agreement with his superior, irrespective of his private opinions.

• **yeti** ► Tibetan name for the Abominable Snowman.

• **Yezhovshchina** ► (Russian, Yezhof times) The period of the **Great Terror** in the Soviet Union in the late 1930s, when at least 10 million people were executed or deported to labour camps as part of Stalin's purge of supposed dissidents and opponents of the regime. From 1936 to 1938, the chief instigator of this purge was Nikolai Ivanovich Yezhof (1884–1940), head of the people's commissariat of internal affairs, the NKVD. Yezhof was a brutal man of low intelligence and small physical stature (he was barely five feet tall), who was described by a contemporary as a 'bloodthirsty dwarf'. He joined the Communist Party in 1917, became a political commissar in the Red Army, and from 1927 was a member of the party's Central Committee. He became commissar for internal affairs in September 1936. One of his first actions was the purge of the NKVD itself; he then embarked on a purge of the high command of the army and was responsible for preparing the great show trials of the old Bolshevik leaders. Although these purges were orchestrated by Stalin, it was Yezhof whose name became synonymous with the Great Terror in the minds of contemporaries and it was Yezhof who was regarded as the principal agent of the policy. Yezhof himself fell victim to Stalin in December 1938, when he was arrested and replaced as head of the NKVD by Beria. He was probably shot two years later, a convenient scapegoat for the excesses of the Great Terror. However, the exact circumstances of his death are not known. *See also*: Law of December 1; Leningrad purge.

• **Y-front** ► Tradename for men's underwear by Lyle and Scott; from the design of their underpants, which have front seaming, allowing an opening, in the shape of an inverted Y. The name is now used generically for any garment of this type, although the company has taken legal action to prevent others from using it commercially. Despite their obvious convenience, Y-fronts were anathematized by style pundits in the 1980s and 1990s; it was also suggested that their confinement of the testicles could cause, or at least contribute to, infertility. As a result, fashion-conscious young men with parental aspirations have abandoned them in favour of boxer shorts or briefs.

• **Y-gun** ► A Y-shaped gun mounted in ships for firing a pair of depth charges.

• **YHA** ► Youth Hostels Association. An organization that provides cheap accommodation in order to promote the appreciation and understanding of the countryside, especially among students and other young people of limited means. The YHA was inspired by the German *Jugendherbergen*, a national system of cheap hostels started in 1909 by a school teacher, Richard Schirrmann, to provide overnight stays for pupils on school trips. The YHA was established in England and Wales in 1930 and in Scotland and Ireland in the following year. The first 12 hostels were opened for Easter 1931 in N Wales, Yorkshire, and the Mendips; by 1939 the number of hostels had risen to 297 and the Association had a membership of over 80,000. The YHA now has over 350 hostels throughout the UK and a membership of over 250,000. Members also have access to 50,000 similar hostels run by National Associations in 45 other countries throughout the world, which are coordinated by the international YHA. Although youth hostels were formerly associated with a somewhat spartan regime and strictly enforced rules (guests were accommodated in single-sex dormitories and had to arrive under their own power), they have taken steps to reform this image since the 1980s.

• **Yippie** ► US slang for a politically active hippie; the name is derived from the initials of the Youth International Party, an anarchic left-wing group founded by Abbie Hoffman and Jerry Rubin in 1968. The Yippies adopted deliberately provocative tactics to publicize their protest against the Vietnam War and their disgust with US society in general – most notably by putting up a pig as presidential candidate at the Chicago Democratic convention. The authorities were not amused, and when the anti-War protests that accompanied the convention degenerated into violent street battles – largely provoked by brutal policing – Hoffman, Rubin, and five others found themselves on trial for incitement to cause riots. The conviction of the Chicago Seven, as they were styled by their supporters, caused further protests in America and elsewhere. All seven were later acquitted on appeal.

• **yob** ► British slang for an uncivilized youth; a lout, thug. One of the few examples of working-class and underworld back slang (for 'boy') to enter the general vocabulary. It has been widely used since the 1960s.

• **yob culture** ► A subculture of young males characterized by excessive drinking and loutish antisocial behaviour. The term hit the headlines in July 2000, when prime minister Tony Blair promised drastic measures to clamp down on the 'yob culture' in Britain's towns and cities, including on-the-spot fines of £100 for drunken rowdiness. This particular idea was quickly dropped when police chiefs pointed out its impracticality. A more embarrassing setback for Blair followed when his own teenage son, Euan, was arrested for public drunkenness. Nevertheless, the government has since renewed its attack on yob culture with a package of measures including an extension of child curfew orders, bans on drinking in public places, and increased police powers to shut down rowdy pubs and clubs.

• **yogic flying** ▶ A type of bodily levitation supposedly practised by some students of transcendental meditation. During the British 1992 general election campaign the Natural Law Party (an offshoot of the TM movement) recommended its candidates to the electorate on the grounds that only they possessed the 'greater orderliness of brain functioning...and greater command of Natural Law, indicated by improved mind body co-ordination' necessary for unaided flight. Somewhat unadventurously, the voters preferred in every case to return more earthbound candidates. When a session of yogic flying was broadcast on national television, its adherents appeared to be doing little more than bouncing up and down rather inelegantly on their behinds.

• **Yoknapatawpha Country** ▶ A fictitious area of N Mississippi, with the main town of Jefferson at its centre, which is the setting for many of the novels and short stories of the US author William Faulkner (1897–1962). These include *Sartoris* (1929); *Absalom, Absalom!* (1936); *The Hamlet* (1940), the first part of a trilogy dealing with the Snopes family, which he continued in *The Town* (1957) and *The Mansion* (1959); *Go Down, Moses* (1942), a collection of short stories; *Light in August* (1952); and *The Reivers* (1962), his last novel.

• **yomping** ▶ Military slang for trekking across difficult terrain heavily laden with a full army pack. It emerged during the Falklands Conflict of 1982; the derivation is unknown.

• **yordim** or **jordim** ▶ A derogatory term for Israeli citizens who emigrate to another country, generally America, in search of opportunities for advancement. They tend to be regarded as deserters by those who remain. Yordim is Hebrew for 'those who descend'; it is an ironic reversal of olim. *See also*: chozrim.

• **Yorkshire Ripper** ▶ The press nickname for Peter Sutcliffe (1946–    ), a lorry driver from Bradford, Yorkshire, who murdered 13 women and at-

tempted to kill seven others in the period 1975–80. The name arose from similarities to the Jack the Ripper killings of the 1880s. Both killers appeared to have a vendetta against prostitutes and both subjected their victims' bodies to horrific mutilation. Moreover, until Sutcliffe's belated arrest in 1981 it seemed as though the identity of the 20th-century Ripper might remain as much of a mystery as that of his 19th-century predecessor. Sutcliffe's plea of insanity – he claimed to have been acting on the orders of a supernatural voice – was rejected by the jury and he received a life sentence. After three years in prison he was transferred to Broadmoor, a secure hospital for the criminally insane.

• **Young England** ▶ A play intended as a stirring morality tale, which opened at the Victoria Palace in September 1934 and convulsed audiences because of its unintentional comedy. Essentially a wholesome entertainment about young lovers beset by a variety of villains, the plot included a troop of Boy Scouts and Girl Guides, who foil the plans of a devious scoutmaster. The performances quickly degenerated into a riot of audience participation as theatregoers joined in or supplemented the dialogue. The author, Walter Reynolds, an 83-year-old dramatist and proprietor of the Theatre Royal, Leeds, used to sit in a box glaring at the audience as they joined in the Boy Scouts' Song or shouted lewd remarks at younger female characters. It is estimated that 250,000 people saw the play before it finally closed in May 1935 after 278 performances.

> Away we go to camp and all its pleasures,
> A merry mob, a merry mob!
> – Boy Scouts' Song.

• **Young Farmers** ▶ An organization of clubs first established in the 1930s to provide social, educational, and leisure activities for young country people between the ages of 14 and 26. The original aim of the organization was to produce good farmers, good countrymen, and good citizens; however, the clubs are now open to everyone (not only young farmers) and their activities are tailored to suit the interests of the members.

• **young fogey** ▶ British term from the later 1980s for a middle-class young male who espoused the conservative views, manners, and dress of a previous era. Although comfortably off, the young fogies differed from their contemporaries the yuppies by shunning any ostentatious display of affluence and favouring traditional tweeds and corduroys in place of designer clothes. They tended to be quietly and traditionally religious and to deplore most social, cultural, and sartorial developments since around 1920. The novelist A. N. Wilson (1950–    )

was usually considered the personification of a young fogey. The expression is a parody of 'old fogey', a familiar name for a member of the older generation, known for his tediously conservative views.

• **Young Plan**▶ An agreement negotiated at a series of conferences held in The Hague during 1929–30 between the Allied powers and Germany; its purpose was to reduce the level of German reparations imposed by the Versailles Treaty. The plan, which was named after the US banker Owen D. Young (1874–1962), then chairman of the Allied Committee, came into operation on 17 May 1930. German penalties were reduced by 75% with the balance of 89 billion Reichsmarks to be paid in annuities until 1988 into a Bank for International Settlements. Allied control of German finances was removed, German securities taken into Allied hands were returned, responsibility for converting payments into foreign currency was transferred to Germany, the Reparations Commission abolished, and the Allied right to impose sanctions if payments were defaulted ended. Despite its many concessions, the Plan was vehemently attacked by German Nationalists and was no more successful than its predecessor, the Dawes Plan, in settling the issue of the Allied war debt and claims for reparations. In 1931, beset by the political and economic crisis caused by the Great Depression, Germany suspended repayments; after 1935 Hitler blocked any further Allied claims for reparations.

• **Young Turks** ▶ Young up-and-coming men whose energy and ambition are likely to make them succeed. The expression derives from a Turkish revolutionary group of this name that transformed the decadent Turkish Empire into a modern state. It had its origins in a committee formed in Geneva in 1891, which eventually deposed Sultan Abdul Hamid in 1908, and replaced him by his brother as Mohammed V. The Young Turks, led by Enver Pasha (1881–1922), remained the major force in Turkish politics until the end of World War I.

• **Your Country Needs You**▶ *See at*: country.

• **Yo-Yo** ▶ Tradename for a toy consisting of a weighted spool attached to a string: the player holds the string in his or her hand and spins the spool up and down repeatedly. The Yo-Yo craze began in America in the late 1920s, reputedly in Chicago, reaching the UK a few years later. The device was first produced commercially by Louis Marx, who registered the name as a trademark in 1929. The term is now used figuratively of anything that repeatedly rises and falls or fluctuates wildly between

extremes, *e.g.* a 'yo-yo economy'. It also has a slang sense (mainly US), meaning a foolish or insignificant person. The original *yo-yo* was a Filipino weapon consisting of two sticks and a thong: the name is thought to mean 'come come'. The toy itself experienced a resurgence of interest among the young in the late 1990s.

• **Ypres**▶ A town in Flanders, Belgium, which was the scene of bitter fighting during World War I. In mid-October 1914 (*see*: Race for the Sea), the German armies commanded by Erich von Falkenhayn launched a drive to capture the Channel Ports, which resulted in the **First Battle of Ypres** (20 October–18 November). Both sides experienced for the first time the true horrors of modern warfare, as reflected in the massive casualties inflicted by the devastating firepower of the opposing weaponry. In early November the Germans finally achieved a breakthrough but the breach was sealed before they could exploit their opportunity. The grim struggle resulted in 50,000 casualties for the BEF and marked the demise of the old British regular army. In the **Second Battle of Ypres**, 22 April–25 May 1915, the Germans launched an assault to divert Allied reinforcements from the offensives in Artois and Champagne. The Germans used chlorine gas for the first time and achieved some initial successes against the French; however, British and Canadian reserves prevented any major German advance. For the Third Battle of Ypres, *see*: Passchendaele.

• **Y2K** ▶ An abbreviation for 'Year 2000' that was widely used in the run-up to the millennium, especially with regard to the supposedly devastating effects of the millennium bug.

• **yuppie** ▶ A *y*oung *u*rban (or *u*pwardly mobile) *p*rofessional *p*erson. An acronym suffixed with '-ie' on the model of hippie, Yippie, etc., the term was coined in late 1970s America to characterize the rising generation of ambitious career-minded materialists who made no bones about wanting to earn lots and lots of money. Rapidly spreading throughout the English-speaking world, it was the first of a series of lifestyle acronyms that proliferated during the 1980s (*see also*: dinkie; pippy; rumpie; etc.). In the UK, the yuppies were especially associated with the high-water mark of Thatcherism around 1985–87. The archetypal yuppie worked 15-hour days in the City, owned a penthouse flat in Docklands, and sported a mobile phone, a Filofax, and a Porsche, among other designer accessories.

• **yuppie flu**▶ *See*: ME.

# Z

• **Zabern incident** ▶ A military incident in a small garrison town in Alsace in November 1913, which precipitated a political crisis in Germany. The Alsace region had been annexed from France by Germany after the Franco-Prussian War of 1870. In Zabern, repressive action by officers of the local garrison led to popular demonstrations; in response the colonel of the regiment, von Reutner, exceeded his authority in ordering the arrest and detention of a number of townspeople. In Germany, the incident was regarded as indicative of Prussian military arrogance; when Erich von Falkenhayn, the war minister, and the imperial chancellor, Bethmann-Hollwegg, defended the actions of the military authorities, the left and centre parties in the Reichstag raised a storm of protest. On 13 December 1913, the government's actions were condemned by a vote of 293 to 54. The incident is regarded as significant because of the tensions it revealed between the ruling military class and the wider German population; some historians believe that these would have toppled the Hohenzollern regime had it not been for the outbreak of World War I.

• **zap** ▶ **1.** Slang meaning to destroy, to kill violently; from the language of comic-strip cartoons of the 1950s and 1960s in which 'zap' represented the sound of a laser gun. It is often used figuratively, meaning bombard (*e.g.* with witticisms).

> Madcap tube driver Cozmik Wilson cheers up depressed commuters...he zaps them with: 'I am to boldly go where only a man being paid double time would go'. – *Daily Sport*, 5 May 1991.

**2.** Slang meaning to bypass the advertisement breaks in a television programme using a remote-control device (a **zapper**), either by switching to another channel or by operating the fast-forward control on the video. **3.** Slang for power, lifeforce.

> You get curious, especially if you've been past 41 yourself, which reminds you how your legs lose their spring and your reflexes their zap. – *The Independent*, 10 April 1991.

• **Zapata moustache** ▶ A type of bushy moustache that became fashionable in the late 1960s and 1970s, especially among rock musicians. During the hippie era it was sported by the Beatles (especially in their *Sergeant Pepper* days), Frank Zappa, and others. The moustache, which bends around and below the sides of the mouth, imitates that worn by the Mexican revolutionary Emiliano Zapata (1877–1919).

• **Zé Arigó** ▶ Nickname of José Pedro de Freitas, a poor Brazilian peasant who became world famous in the 1950s for his miraculous healing powers; a rough English equivalent would be 'Joe from the sticks'. Without any medical training and using only an old kitchen knife, he is said to have performed intricate eye operations, restored lame patients' ability to walk, and treated thousands of other poor Brazilians for a variety of disorders. He was twice prosecuted as a charlatan but none of his patients would testify against him. Zé Arigó claimed that his remarkable powers originated from his spiritual contact with **Dr Fritz**, a German surgeon who died in World War I. It is said that he never accepted a fee for his work and that he predicted his own death, in a car crash, in 1971.

• **zebra crossing** ▶ *See*: pelican crossing.

• **zeppelin** ▶ A dirigible airship designed by Count Ferdinand von Zeppelin (1838–1917). Zeppelins were used for bombing and reconnaissance during World War I, but with the development of the aeroplane and the tragedy of the Hindenburg airship in 1937, the more cumbersome and unsafe zeppelin was eclipsed. *See also*: Graf Zeppelin.

• **zero hour** ▶ A military term (first used in World War I) for the exact time at which an attack, etc., is to begin. Subsequent operations are often timed in relation to zero hour, *e.g.* zero + 3 means 3 minutes after zero hour.

• **zero option** ▶ President Reagan's proposal in the early 1980s for a deal in which America would reduce to zero its stock of cruise missiles in Europe if the Soviet Union would no longer deploy its medium-range SS-20s. The proposal met a stony reception from the Kremlin, which saw it as a US propaganda stunt rather than a serious contribution to disarmament. Both sides' weapons were eventually withdrawn from Europe under the INF Treaty agreed by Reagan and Gorbachov in 1987. *See also*: Greenham Common; IRBM.

• **zero-sum game** ▶ *See*: game theory.

• **zero tolerance** ▶ A policing policy in which even minor infringements of the most commonly flouted laws are not tolerated. The policy was introduced in the 1990s in certain US cities, especially New York, where it was zealously enforced by Mayor Rudolph Giuliani. Previously there had been a tacit acceptance that in crime-ridden inner cities the police were obliged to turn a blind eye to much minor lawlessness in order to concentrate on homicide and other serious crimes. However, the advocates of zero tolerance argued that a crackdown on *all* visible forms of lawbreaking – including littering, graffiti, and general rowdiness – would not only improve the quality of life but lead to a fall in serious offences. By stressing the importance of the law and the penalties for non-compliance, zero tolerance would (it was argued) deter petty offenders and serious criminals alike. This theory appeared to be confirmed by its successful application in New York, which in the early years of Giuliani's mayoralty went from being perhaps the most dangerous city in America to being one of the safest. Amongst other benefits, the police discovered that many of those arrested for antisocial behaviour turned out, when investigated, to be involved in far more serious forms of crime (few drug dealers, for instance, have scruples about dropping litter).

As a result, the policy was widely imitated in cities around the world. By 2000, however, doubts about the New York record had begun to emerge. Critics of zero tolerance argued that the spectacular drop in homicide rates was attributable to other long-term factors and maintained that the police were using the policy as a charter for harrassing racial minorities. There was also a public outcry in June 2000, when three people were arrested and jailed for smoking on deserted subway stations late at night.

In the UK, zero tolerance policing was pioneered in the Cleveland region of NW England by a flamboyant senior officer named Roy Mallon. However, allegations that Mallon's detectives had abused the laws on criminal evidence (and even offered drugs for information) led to his suspension in 1997. He was subsequently (2000) acquitted of criminal wrongdoing but continues to face disciplinary charges.

• **ZETA** ▶ *See*: nuclear reactor.

• **Ziegfeld Follies** ▶ The spectacular revues first presented by the US theatre producer Florenz Ziegfeld (1867–1932) in 1907. The Follies, modelled on the Folies Bergère shows in Paris, became the last word in lavish entertainment, with a chorus line of beautiful girls, stunning sets, and glamorous costumes. The revues ran continuously until 1932 and then periodically until 1957.

• **zilch** ▶ Nothing. First widely heard in America during the 1960s, it reached the UK a decade later. It seems to be an amalgam of 'zero', 'nil', and the Yiddish *nich*. The US magazine *Ballyhoo* featured a family of comic characters called the Zilches in the 1930s.

• **Zinoviev Letter** ▶ A letter, which purported to be signed by the Soviet politican Grigori Zinoviev (1883–1936), president of the Comintern, calling on the British Communist Party to intensify its revolutionary activities and to subvert the armed forces of the Crown; it was published in the British press on 25 October 1924, four days before a general election. The letter whipped up a 'red scare' and almost certainly increased the Conservatives' majority (although the outcome of the election was already in little doubt). Many Labour leaders held it to be a forgery and its authenticity was denied by the Soviet Union. In December 1966 *The Sunday Times* published an article establishing that the letter was a forgery perpetrated by a group of White Russian *émigrés*, and suggesting that Conservative Central Office knew that it was a fake but decided to use it anyway. These conclusions were endorsed by an official enquiry into the role of British Intelligence in the matter in 1999.

• **Zionism** ▶ The Jewish movement for the establishment of 'national home' in Palestine. The Zionist movement was founded by Dr Theodore Herzl of Vienna in 1895, although it was the Balfour declaration of 1917 that first recognized Zionist aspirations and gave them political teeth. From 1920 to 1948 Palestine was a British mandate, administered under great difficulties arising from the friction between Jews and Arabs. However, the holocaust provided Zionism with an unanswerable case and with strong US support the state of Israel was established in 1948. Zionism has continued to exist as a political force advocating the right of all Jews to live in Israel as Israeli citizens. The conflict between this principle and the rights of the Palestinians has not, however, been resolved. The term Zionism is now often used in a strongly negative sense to mean hardline Israeli nationalism.

• **zip code** ▶ The US system used to differentiate the mail delivery zones based on five- or nine-digit numbers. The name 'zip' is derived from the initial letters of the name of the system, Zone Improvement Plan. The British post code composed of letters and numbers is a similar system.

• **zip fastener** ▶ A type of fastener for clothing, bags, etc., consisting of two parallel strips with interlocking teeth opened or closed with a sliding clip. Although a fastener of this type was patented as early as 1893, the name did not appear until the 1920s, when the US company B. F. Goodrich marketed the 'zipper boot', a type of galosh fastened with a zip. The name – deriving from the verb to zip, *i.e.* to move briskly or hurriedly – was presumably chosen to highlight the quickness of the zip fastener as compared with buttons, etc. There may also be an allusion to the sound made when a zip is opened or closed.

• **Zippergate** ▶ A facetious term, modelled on Watergate, for the Lewinsky affair – because the scandal centred on President Clinton's trouser zipper.

• **zit** ▶ Slang for a spot or a pimple. Originally an Americanism, it had become well established in the UK by the 1980s.

• **Zodiac murders** ▶ A series of murders in California, which captured world headlines in the 1960s; they were subsequently seen as the first murders by a modern serial killer. The murders began in 1968 with the motiveless shooting of two teenagers in a car near Vallejo, California. As the killings continued, the murderer maintained contact with the press in numerous cryptic messages, calling himself 'Zodiac' and explaining that he was acquiring 'slaves in the afterlife'. Panic reached such levels that police officers accompanied school buses (which had been threatened by 'Zodiac'), while the authorities were plagued by letters and calls from hoaxers. The killer (or possibly a hoaxer) even rang a popular television chat show to say he was suffering from a mental illness. The murderer has never been identified. As late as 1974 a message was received to the effect that 'Zodiac' claimed to have murdered 37 people.

• **zoftig** or **zaftig** ▶ US slang for delicious or attractive; it comes through Yiddish from the German *saft*, juice. It is typically used by men of women whom they find sexually desirable.

• **zombie** ▶ A dull-witted unresponsive person, or someone who cannot think or act for themselves. It is generally used as a mild term of abuse, as in 'He sits there like a zombie, never saying a word.' The name refers to the belief, current in the Caribbean (especially Haiti) and parts of Africa, that voodoo magicians have the power to revive corpses and use them as robot-like slaves (known as zombies). There

is speculation that real zombies may have been created from the living by the use of certain drugs. The word is derived from the Kongo *zumbi*, a good-luck fetish; it was also the name of a python god in W Africa.

> And, like a zombie, I found myself going into the shop and saying 'how much is it?' Which is not a question you are entitled to ask when you have not got a bean. – *The Independent*, 20 May 1991.

• **zombie food** ▶ US slang for junk food. It is not certain whether 'zombie' in this case refers to the anticipated results of eating such food, the amount of intelligence required to prepare it (usually only opening the container), or to the kind of person who is willing to eat it. It is perhaps a combination of all three.

• **zonked** ▶ Slang meaning incapacitated by drugs, alcohol, or simple exhaustion. Zonk echoes 'bonk', a bang on the head, which has much the same effect as being zonked by alcohol.

• **zoo daddy** ▶ US slang for a divorced father who has access to his children and typically takes them on a treat outing to the zoo when they visit him. There is a double implication in the term – first that he spoils his children and secondly that he doesn't know what else to do with them. A similar expression is **Disneyland daddy**.

• **zoo television** ▶ A type of television programming consisting of live broadcasts with a fast-moving and largely unstructured format. The movements and reactions of technical crew, etc., are usually visible to the audience. The intention is to create a spontaneous and slightly anarchic atmosphere. The expression originated in America in the early 1990s. In the UK, *Saturday Zoo* was the name of a weekly television programme of this nature hosted by Jonathan Ross. The format and the term were adopted by the Irish rock band U2 for their idiosyncratic stage show of 1992–93.

• **zoot-suit** ▶ An exaggerated style of clothing adopted in the late 1930s by US hep-cats and followers of fashionable swing music. It usually consisted of baggy trousers caught in at the bottom, a long coat resembling a frock coat, a broad-brimmed hat, and a flowing tie, all in vivid colours. An essential article of equipment was a vast key chain.

• **Zorro** ▶ The masked sabre-wielding hero of numerous Hollywood B-movies. The character, who originated in a comic strip in 1919, first appeared on screen in *The Mark of Zorro* (1920), an unlikely combination of swordplay and the Wild West that nevertheless proved enormously successful; Douglas Fairbanks played the hero. Other actors to play the debonair Robin Hood of the West include Robert Livingston, John Carroll, Tyrone Power, Guy Williams, Alain Delon, and George Hamilton. A big-budget remake of *The Mark of Zorro* was released in 1998, starring Antonio Banderas. Zorro's trademark (known as the **mark of Zorro**) is a letter Z cut into the shirt of his opponent.

• **zouk** ► A style of music combining ethnic elements from the French Antilles with Western pop. Characterized by highly energetic rhythms, it was created by Guadeloupean musicians living in Paris and came to the attention of US and British audiences in the late 1980s. The name is thought to derive from a creole word meaning to revel. *See also*: rai; world music.

# Index

Balfour, Arthur Balfour declaration; Balfour's Poodle; Diehards

Bamford, Joseph Cyril JCB

Bannister, R. G. four-minute mile

Bara, Theda vamp

Barbera, Joe Tom and Jerry

Barbie, Klaus Butcher of Lyons

Bardeen, John superconductivity

Bardot, Brigitte Sex Kitten

Barker, Ronnie porridge

Barnard, Christiaan spare-part surgery; Washkansky transplant

Barnes, Kenneth RADA

Barraud, Francis His Master's Voice

Barrett, Lawrence sleaze

Barrie, J. M. Nana; Never Never Land; Peter Pan; Tinker Bell; Wendy house

Barrington, Jonah Lord Haw-Haw

Barrow, Clyde Bonnie and Clyde

Barrow, Eliza Mary Seddon Murder

Barrymore, John Great Profile

Barrymore, Lionel epitaph; Hardy family

Bart, Lionel Fings Ain't Wot They Used T'Be

Baruch, Bernard Cold War

Basov, Nicolai laser

Bates, H. E. Flying Officer X

Baudot, J. M. E. baud

Baum, L. Frank munchkin; Wizard of Oz

Baylis, Lilian Old Vic

Bayly, Doreen reflexology

Bazna, Elyesa Cicero

Beaton, Cecil Shrimp, The

Beatty, David, Earl Beatty; Jutland, Battle of; Queen Elizabeth

Beatty, Warren Kid, The

Beaumont-Dark, Anthony Keep it dark

Beaverbrook, Max, Baron backroom boys; Beaver, the; Empire Free Trade; Press Barons

Bechet, Sidney New Orleans style

Beckett, Samuel Theatre of the Absurd

Bedford, Mary, Duchess of Flying Duchess

Beeching, Richard, Baron Beeching's axe

Begin, Menachem Camp David; Likud

Behan, Brendan famous last words

Belafonte, Harry King of Calypso

Bell, Alexander Graham Ma Bell

Bell, Clive Bloomsbury Group

Bell, Jocelyn LGM

Bell, Vanessa Bloomsbury Group; Omega workshops

Belloc, Hilaire Chesterbelloc

Ben Barka, Mehdi Ben Barka disappearance

Ben Bella, Ahmed FLN

Benchley, Peter Jaws

Benchley, Robert Algonquin Round Table

Benda, Julien trahison des clercs

Ben Gurion, David Jewish Agency

Benioff, Victor Hugo Benioff zone

Benn, Tony Bennery

Bennett, Alan Beyond the Fringe

Bennett, James Gordon deleted by French censor; Gordon Bennett

Bensley, Harry Man in the Iron Mask

Benson, A. C. Land of Hope and Glory

Bentine, Michael Goon Show

Bentley, W. O. Lagonda

Benz, Carl Mercedes

Berg, Alban twelve-tone music

Berg, Moe good field, no hit

Berg, Paul RNA

Bergman, Ingrid Play it again, Sam

Bergson, Henri creative evolution; élan vital

Beria, L. P. Leningrad purge; MGB

Berlin, Irving ritzy

Bernhardt, Sarah Sarah

Bernstein, Carl all the president's men; Deep Throat; Watergate

Bernstein, Edouard revisionism

Bernstein, Morey Murphy, Bridey

Berry, Chuck rhythm-and-blues

Bessie, Alvah Hollywood Ten

Best, Sigismund Payne Venlo incident

Bestall, Alfred Rupert Bear

Bethmann-Hollweg, Theobald von necessity knows no law; Scrap of Paper

Bevan, Aneurin Bevanite; National Health Service; Nye

Beveridge, William Henry Beveridge Report

Bevin, Ernest Bevin Boys; 'Keep Left' group

Beyers, C. R. de Wet Rebellion

Bhaktivedanta, A. C. Hare Krishna

Biberman, Herbert Hollywood Ten

Bidault, Georges Resistance

Biggers, Earl Derr Chan, Charlie

Biggs, Ronald Great Train Robbery

Biko, Steve Biko affair

Billings, John and Evelyn Billings method

Binet, Alfred Binet test

Bingham, Hiram Machu Picchu

Bin Laden, Osama al-Qaida; September 11; war on terrorism

Bird, Kenneth Fougasse

Birdseye, Clarence Birds Eye

Biró, Laszlo Biro

Blackburn, Tony Radio Caroline

Blair, Tony Blairism; Cool Britannia; cronyism; Labour Party; New Labour; sleaze; spin doctor; stakeholder society; Third Way

Blair, Lionel Grosvenor Squares

Blake, George Blake case

Blanc, Giuseppe Giovinezza, La

Blanc, Mel folks

Bloxham, Arnall Bloxham tapes

Blum, Léon Riom trials

Blunt, Anthony double agent; fourth man; Magnificent Five

Blyton, Enid Noddy

Bocchini, Arturo Ovra

Bogart, Humphrey Bogey; Here's looking at you, kid; Marlowe, Philip; Play it again, Sam

Bohr, Niels Maud Committee; quantum theory

Bolt, Robert man for all seasons

Bonano, Joseph Joe Bananas

Bondi, Hermann steady-state theory

Booker, Christopher Private Eye

Boon, Charles Mills & Boon

Boothman, J. N. Schneider Trophy

Borel, Emile game theory

Borglum, Gutzon Rushmore, Mount

Bor-Komorowski, Tadeusz Warsaw Uprising

Bosanquet, B. J. bosey

**Bosustow, Stephen** Mr Magoo

**Botham, Ian** Guy the Gorilla

**Bottomley, Horatio** Bottomley case

**Boudin, Kathy** Weatherman

**Boulez, Pierre** serialism

**Bow, Clara** It Girl

**Bowen, Lord** Clapham

**Bowers, H. R.** Scott of the Antarctic

**Boyer, Charles** come with me to the Casbah

**Brabham, John** Brabham

**Brabazon, Lord Brabazon**

**Bradbury, J. S.** Bradbury

**Brady, Ian** Moors murders

**Bragg, Billy** agitpop

**Braine, John** Lampton, Joe

**Brand, Max** Kildare, Dr

**Brandenberger, Jacques** Cellophane

**Brando, Marlon** Actors' Studio; Method, the

**Brandt, Willy** Ostpolitik

**Brague, Georges** assemblage; cubism

**Bratby, John** kitchen sink

**Brecht, Bertolt** A-effect; Berliner Ensemble; Brechtian; epic theatre; Schweik

**Breton, André** surrealism

**Brezhnev, Leonid** Brezhnev Doctrine; SALT

**Briand, Aristide** Kellogg Pact

**Brianin, Norbert** Amadeus String Quartet

**Brighouse, Harold** Manchester school

**Brittan, Leon** Westland affair

**Britten, Benjamin** Aldeburgh

**Brooke, Rupert** England; Georgian poets; Grantchester; Lost Generation; war poets

**Brooke-Taylor, Tim** Mornington Crescent

**Brown, Arthur Whitten** Alcock and Brown

**Brown, George** Gnomes of Zürich; National Plan; tired and emotional

**Brown, Melanie** Spice Girls

**Brown, Rosemary** musical medium

**Brubeck, Dave** five

**Brunhoff, Jean de** Babar the Elephant

**Bryan, William Jennings** Dayton anti-Darwinist trial

**Buchan, John** Hannay, Richard

**Buchman, Frank** Moral Rearmament; Oxford Group

**Bulganin, Nicolai** B and K

**Buller, Sir Redvers** Relief of Ladysmith; Spion Kop

**Bunton, Emma** Spice Girls

**Burgess, Anthony** clockwork orange; nadsat

**Burgess, Gelett** blurb; bromide

**Burgess, Guy** double agent; Magnificent Five

**Burnham, Edward Levy-Lawson, Viscount** Burnham scale

**Burr, Raymond** Mason, Perry

**Burroughs, Edgar Rice** Tarzan

**Burroughs, William** beat

**Busby, Matt** Munich air crash

**Bush, George** happy; New World Order; point man; read my lips

**Bush, George W.** ABM; chad; Dubya; Star Wars; war on terrorism

**Bushman, Francis X.** Handsomest Man in the World

**Buthelezi, Mangosouthu** Inkatha

**Butler, R. A.** Butler Act; Butskellism; Rab; Rab's Boys; Politics is the art of the possible

**Butler, Robert** ageism

**Butlin, Billy** Butlins

**Butt, Dame Clara** Land of Hope and Glory; muck

**Butts, Alfred M.** Scrabble

# C

**Cagney, James** Public Enemy No. 1; rat

**Caillaux, Joseph** Caillaux affair

**Caine, Michael** people

**Cairncross, John** Magnificent Five

**Calder, Alexander** kinetic art

**Callaghan, James** Labour Party; Lib-Lab; Sunny Jim

**Calley, Lt. William** My Lai

**Calmette, Gaston** Caillaux affair

**Cameron, James** Titanic

**Campbell, Commander** Brains Trust

**Campbell, Donald Malcolm** Bluebird

**Campbell, Malcolm** Bluebird; Daytona Beach

**Campbell-Bannerman, Henry** Liberal Landslide

**Camus, Albert** existentialism

**Canaris, Wilhelm** Abwehr

**Capek, Karel** robot

**Caplin, Alfred G.** Li'l Abner

**Capone, Al** Alcatraz; Lindbergh baby murder; St Valentine's Day Massacre

**Capote, Truman** Holcomb murders

**Cardin, Pierre** Cardin

**Carey, Peter** illywhacker

**Carlton, Chester** Xerox

**Carmichael, Stokely** Black is beautiful; Black Power; Student Nonviolent Coordinating Committee

**Carnap, Rudolph** Vienna circle

**Carnarvon, George Herbert, Earl of** curse of Tutankhamun

**Carnegie, Dale** How to win friends and influence people

**Carnera, Primo** Italian Alp

**Carson, Edward** Ulster Covenant; Ulster Volunteers; Winslow, Ronnie

**Carter, Howard** curse of Tutankhamun

**Carter, Jimmy** Camp David; President Peanuts; SALT

**Carter, Lillian** Miz Lillian

**Cartland, Barbara** Animated Meringue; bright young things; social class

**Caruso, Enrico** Man with the Orchid-Lined Voice

**Casement, Roger** Casement diaries

**Cashin, Bonnie** layered look

**Casson, Hugh** Festival of Britain

**Castro, Fidel** Castroism

**Cavell, Edith** Cavell Memorial

**Cavendish, Henry** Cavendish Laboratory

**Ceauşescu, Nicolae** Securitate

**Cecil, Lord Robert** Peace Ballot

**Chabrol, Claude** New Wave

**Chadwick, James** elementary particle; neutron

**Chain, Ernst** penicillin

**Chamberlain, Houston Stewart** Aryan myth

**Chamberlain, Joseph** clearing house of the world; Tariff Reform

**Chamberlain, Neville** England; Munich; National Governments; peace in our time

**Chamberlain, Richard** Kildare, Dr

**Chambers, Whittaker** Hiss affair

**Chamorro, Violeta de**
Sandinista

**Chandler, Raymond** Marlowe,
Philip

**Chanel, Gabrielle** Chanel

**Chaney, Lon** Man of a Thousand
Faces

**Chang, Min Chuch** Pill, the

**Chaplin, Charlie** silent films;
star; take; Tramp, The

**Chapman, Graham** Monty
Python's Flying Circus

**Charles, Prince** Camillagate;
carbuncular; hydrophonics;
People's Princess; Royal
National Theatre

**Charlesworth, Violet** fall

**Charrière, Henri** Devil's Island

**Charteris, Leslie** Saint, The

**Chatterton, George Edward**
Chad

**Chaudron, Yves** Mona Lisa theft

**Chennault, C. L.** Flying Tigers

**Cheshire, Leonard** Cheshire
Homes

**Chesterton, G. K.** Chesterbelloc;
Father Brown; heroes

**Chevalier, Albert** Old Dutch

**Chevalier, Haakon**
Oppenheimer affair

**Chevalier, Maurice** Mistinguett

**Chiang Kai-shek** generalissimo;
Guomindang; Long March;
Suchow, Battle of; Xi An
incident

**Chichester, Francis** Gipsy Moth
IV

**Chifley, J. B.** light on the hill

**Chisholm, Melanie** Spice Girls

**Chomsky, Noam**
transformational grammar

**Chou En-lai,** Quemoy crisis

**Christian X,** Schandband

**Christie, Agatha** Marple, Miss;
Mousetrap, The; Poirot,
Hercule; Queen of Crime

**Christie, John** Glyndebourne

**Christie, John Reginald**
Christie murders

**Churchill, Caryl** serious money

**Churchill, Sir Winston** Arcadia;
Atlantic Charter; blood, toil,
tears and sweat; Casablanca
Conference; end of the
beginning; famous last words;
Few, the; Former Naval Person;
future; General Strike;
Haldane mission; hour; Iron
curtain; jaw-jaw; King and
Country debate; locust years;
Lusitania; Moscow Conference;
Other Club; peace sign;

Quadrant; riddle; Second
Front; sheep in sheep's
clothing; Sidney Street siege;
siren suit; surrender; Tehran
Conference; terminological
inexactitude; Tonypandy riots;
Trident; Washington
Conference; Winnie; Yalta
Conference

**Clanmorris, John Bingham,
Baron** Smiley, George

**Clapton, Eric** Old Slow Hand

**Clark, Alan** K

**Clark, Sir Kenneth** K

**Clark, Mark** Salerno landing

**Clayton, P. B.** Toc H

**Cleese, John** different; Fawlty
Towers; Monty Python's Flying
Circus; read

**Clemenceau, Georges** Tiger,
the; Versailles Treaty

**Clifton-James, M. E.** Monty's
double

**Clinton, Bill** Lewinsky affair;
Third Way; Whitewater affair;
Zippergate

**Cockerell, Christopher**
hovercraft

**Cocteau, Jean** Six, Les

**Coe, Sebastian** four-minute mile

**Cohen, Harry** enjoy!

**Cohen, Sir John** pile it high, sell
it cheap; supermarket

**Cohn-Bendit, Daniel** Danny the
Red

**Cole, George** 'er indoors; minder

**Cole, Lester** Hollywood Ten

**Cole, William Horace de Vere**
Dreadnought hoax

**Collins, Jackie** s 'n' s

**Collins, John** CND

**Collins, Michael** Free Staters;
Troubles, the

**Compagnoni, Achille** K2

**Compton, Arthur** nuclear
reactor

**Condon, Richard** Manchurian
candidate

**Conlon, Gerard** Guildford Four

**Connolly, Billy** jessie

**Connolly, James** Easter Rising

**Connolly, Maureen** Little Mo

**Connor, William** Cassandra

**Conrad, Joseph** Marlow, Captain

**Conran, Shirley** s 'n' s

**Conway, John** game of life

**Cook, Peter** Beyond the Fringe;
Private Eye; Sex Thimble

**Cook, Robin** ethical foreign
policy

**Coolidge, Calvin** choose

**Cooper, Dame Gladys** famous
last words

**Cooper, L. N.** superconductivity

**Corbett, Harry** Sooty

**Cornwell, J. T.** Cornwell Badge

**Correll, Charles** Amos 'n' Andy

**Coryell, John Russell** Carter,
Nick

**Cosgrave, Liam** Sunningdale
Agreement

**Cosgrave, William T.** Fine Gael;
Irish Free State

**Cotton, Billy** Wakey-Wakey!

**Coué, Emile** Couéism

**Coupland, Douglas** Generation
X

**Courrèges, André** miniskirt

**Courtauld, Samuel** Courtauld
Institute of Art

**Coward, Noël** famous last words;
kitchen sink; Master, the;
Stately Homes of England

**Crabb, Commander Lionel**
Crabb Affair

**Crabbe, Buster** Flash Gordon;
King of the Serials; ray gun

**Crabtree, Shirley** Big Daddy

**Craven, Wes** Krueger, Freddy

**Crawford, Cheryl** Actors' Studio

**Crawford, Marion** Crawfie

**Crawford, Michael** mothers

**Creutzfeldt, H. G.** CJD

**Crichton, Michael** Andromeda
strain

**Crick, Francis** DNA; RNA

**Crippen, Hawley Harvey**
Crippen murder

**Cripps, Sir Stafford** Cripps
mission

**Croker, John** decimal currency

**Cronkite, Walter** go, man, go!;
way

**Crosby, Bing** Old Groaner; One-
Take; road movie

**Crosland, Anthony** Hampstead
set

**Crossman, Richard** 'Keep Left'
group

**Crowley, Aleister** Great Beast
666

**Cruise, Tom** bratpack; Mission
Impossible

**Crumb, Robert** keep on truckin'

**Cryer, Barry** Mornington
Crescent

**Cummings, Homer** Public
Enemy No. 1

**Cummings, W. T.** atheists

**Cunningham, John** Cat's Eyes

**Curcio, Renato** Red Brigades

**Eaton, Cyrus** Pugwash
**Ecclestone, Bernie** sleaze
**Eddington, Arthur** quantum theory; relativity
**Eddy, Nelson** Iron Butterfly
**Eden, Anthony** Anthony Eden; Hoare-Laval pact; Suez crisis
**Edward VII** Alexandra Day; Bertie; Darling Daisy; Edwardian; Entente Cordiale; Queen's birthday
**Edward VIII** Abdication Crisis; Fort Belvedere; Round Table
**Edwards, Ifan al Owen** Urdd Gobaith Cymru
**Edwards, Robert** IVF
**Egas Moniz, António** lobotomy
**Ehn, Karl** Karlmarxhof
**Ehrlich, Paul** magic bullet
**Eichmann, Adolf** Eichmann trial; Final Solution; ODESSA; Wannsee Conference
**Einstein, Albert** E=mc²; fourth dimension; nuclear weapon; quantum theory; relativity
**Eisenhower, Dwight D.** D-Day; Eisenhower Doctrine; Eisenhower jacket; Eisenhower Platz; Ike; Paris summit; U-2
**Eisenstein, Sergei** silent films
**Elder, Mark** Land of Hope and Glory
**Elgar, Edward** Land of Hope and Glory; Malvern Festival
**Eliot, T. S.** free verse; Hell is other people; Macavity; Old Possum; Prufrock, J. Alfred
**Elizabeth II** annus horribilis; Corgi and Bess; husband; Treetops
**Elizabeth the Queen Mother** East End
**Ellington, Duke** Cotton Club; Duke
**Elliott, A. G.** Spitfire
**Elliott, Alonzo** trail
**Ellis, Ruth** Ellis hanging
**Elmhirst, Leonard and Dorothy** Dartington Hall
**Elton, Ben** beautiful game, the; motormouth
**Emery, Dick** awful
**Emin, Tracey** Turner Prize
**Enfield, Harry** loadsamoney
**Englund, Robert** Krueger, Freddy
**Ernst, Max** dadaism
**Estevez, Emilio** bratpack
**Evans, Sir Arthur** Linear B script
**Evans, Edgar** Scott of the Antarctic

**Evans, Edward** Evans of the Broke

# F

**Fabergé, Peter Carl** Fabergé
**Fairbanks, Douglas** famous last words; star
**Fairlie, G. T.** Sapper
**Falk, Oswald Toynbee** Tuesday Club
**Falkender, Marcia Williams, Lady** Lavender list
**Falkenhayn, Erich von** Neuve Chapelle; Verdun
**Fall, Albert B.** Teapot Dome scandal
**Falwell, Jerry** moral majority
**Farrakhan, Louis** Black Muslims
**Farrow, Mia** Peyton Place
**Faulkner, Brian** power sharing
**Faulkner, William** Yoknapatawpha Country
**Fayed, Dodi** People's Princess
**Fayed, Mohammed al** cash for questions; ritzy
**Feisal, King** Arab Union
**Fellini, Federico** dolce vita, la; neorealism;
**Fermi, Enrico** mushroom cloud; nuclear reactor
**Ferrier, Kathleen** famous last words
**Feuchtwanger, Leon** Jew Süss
**Fey, Dietrich** Marienkirche frescoes
**Feynman, Richard** Feynman diagram
**Fielding, Helen** Jones, Bridget
**Fields, Gracie** Our Gracie
**Fisher, Bud** Mutt and Jeff
**Fisher, H. A. L.** Fisher Act
**Fisher, Ham** Joe Palooka
**Fitzgerald, Ella** amateur night
**Fitzgerald, F. Scott** Gatsby; Jazz Age; Lost Generation
**Fitzgerald, Garrett** Fine Gael
**Fitzgerald, William H.** reflexology
**Fitzwater, Marlin** no comment
**Flanagan, Bud** Crazy Gang
**Fleischer, Max** Betty Boop
**Fleming, Alexander** penicillin
**Fleming, Ian** Bond, James; Goldfinger; Martini, shaken not stirred; Mr Big; Oddjob; Q; SMERSH
**Fletcher, Cyril** Nice one, Cyril!
**Flettner, Anton** rotor ship
**Flischer, Max** spinach
**Florey, Howard** penicillin

**Flynn, Errol** Flynn; Objective Burma
**Foch, Marshal Ferdinand** generalissimo; Marne, Battles of the
**Fokker, A. H. G.** Fokker
**Foot, Michael** 'Keep Left' group; Labour Party
**Ford, Gerald** credibility gap; SALT; walk
**Ford, Henry** black; exercise is bunk; Ford's Peace Ship; history is bunk; mass production; Tin Lizzie
**Forester, C. S.** Hornblower, Horatio
**Forlanini, Enrico** hydrofoil
**Formby, George** nice
**Forsyth, Frederick** Jackal, The; ODESSA
**Foster, Norman, Baron** Millennium Bridge
**Foster Jr, Vincent** Whitewater affair
**Foucault, Michel** same-sex
**Fraceschini, Alberto** Red Brigades
**Franco, General Francisco** aperturismo; Burgos government; Caudillo; Falange; generalissimo; Spanish Civil War
**Frank, Anne** Belsen; Frank
**Franklin, Aretha** soul
**Franks, Bobby** Leopold and Loeb murder
**Franks, Lord** Franks Report
**Franzen, Anders** Vasa project
**Franz Ferdinand, Archduke** Sarajevo assassination
**Fraser, Malcolm** life wasn't meant to be easy
**Freitas, José Pedro de** Zé Arigó
**French, Sir John** Neuve Chapelle
**Freud, Sigmund** Freudian slip; reality principle
**Friedman, Milton** Friedmanism
**Friedrich Wilhelm, Crown Prince** Little Willie
**Frisch, Otto** nuclear fission
**Frohman, Carl** Lusitania
**Frost, David** TW3
**Fry, Roger** Bloomsbury Group; Omega workshops
**Fuchs, Klaus** Fuchs spy case; Ottawa spy ring
**Fulbright, James William** Fulbright scholar
**Fuller, R. Buckminster** buckminsterfullerene;

geodesic dome; Spaceship Earth

**Furguson, Arthur** Statue of Liberty sale

**Furnivall, Frederick James** Rat

**Fussell, Paul** dumbing down

# G

**Gable, Clark** King of Hollywood

**Gabo, Naum** constructivism; St Ives group

**Gabor, Dennis** hologram

**Gabor, Zsa-Zsa** macho

**Gaddafi, Muammar** flaky; Senoussi

**Gagarin, Yuri** astronaut; cosmonaut; Mercury Project; space age

**Gaitskell, Hugh** Hampstead set

**Galbraith, J. K.** Affluent Society; Galbraithian

**Gallico, Paul** Rhayader

**Gallup, George** Gallup Poll

**Galsworthy, John** Forsyte Saga; skin game

**Galtieri, Leopoldo** Falklands Conflict

**Galvani, Patrick** supermarket

**Galway, Sir James** Man with the Golden Flute

**Gamelin, Maurice** Riom trials

**Gandhi, Indira** Nehru dynasty

**Gandhi, Mohandas** Amritsar Massacre; Mahâtma; satyagraha

**Gandhi, Rajiv, Sanjay** and **Sonia** Nehru dynasty

**Garbo, Greta** alone

**Garden, Graeme** Mornington Crescent

**Gardner, Erle Stanley** Mason, Perry

**Garland, Judy** Hardy family; Wizard of Oz

**Garnett, David** Bloomsbury Group

**Garson, Greer** Miniver, Mrs

**Gascoigne, Paul** Gazza

**Gaudí, Antonio** Art Nouveau

**Gaumont, Léon** Gaumont

**Gbenye, Christophe** Wild Geese

**Gehrig, Lou** Murderers' Row

**Geiger, Hans** Geiger counter

**Geldof, Bob** band aid; Live Aid

**Geller, Uri** Uri Geller

**Gell-Mann, Murray** quark; strangeness

**Gennep, Arnold van** rite of passage

**George V** Empire

**Georges-Picot, François** Sykes-Picot agreement

**Gerasimov, Gennady** Sinatra doctrine

**Gibbons, Stella** Cold Comfort Farm; nasty

**Gibson, Charles Dana** Gibson Girl

**Gibson, Guy** Dambusters

**Gibson, William** cyberpunk; cyberspace

**Gilbey, James** Squidgygate

**Gillespie, Dizzy** Dizzy

**Gillette, King C.** safety razor

**Gilliam, Terry** Monty Python's Flying Circus

**Ginsberg, Allen** beat

**Gish, Lillian** silent films

**Giuliani, Rudolph** zero tolerance

**Glackens, William James** ash-can school

**Glashow, Sheldon** charm

**Glass, Philip** minimalism

**Glubb, John Bagot** Arab Legion

**Glyn, Elinor** It

**Godard, Jean-Luc** New Wave

**Goddard, Henry** moron

**Goddard, Robert** space age

**Gödel, Kurt** Gödel's proof; Vienna circle

**Godley, Alex** NZEF

**Goebbels, Joseph** guns before butter; Hitlerjunge Quex; Nostradamus; Nuremberg Trials

**Goering, Herman** culture; Gestapo; guns before butter; Nuremberg Trials; Reichstag fire; Van Meegeren forgeries

**Gold, Harry** Rosenberg spy case

**Gold, Jimmy** Crazy Gang

**Gold, Thomas** steady-state theory

**Goldberg, Reuben L.** Rube Goldberg machine

**Goldfine, Bernard** Goldfine affair

**Goldsmith, Sir James** Lavender list; Private Eye; Referendum Party

**Goldstein, Ruby** Jewel of the Ghetto

**Goldwater, Barry** Goldwater caper; heart

**Goldwyn, Samuel** cast of thousands; Goldwynisms; MGM

**Gollancz, Victor** Left Book Club

**Gonchorova, Natalia** Rayonism

**Goodman, Benny** King of Swing

**Goodrich, B. F.** zip fastener

**Gorbachov, Mikhail** glasnost; Gorbymania; khozraschot; perestroika; SALT; Tiananmen Square massacre

**Gore, Al** chad; information superhighway

**Górecki, Henryk** minimalism

**Gormley, Anthony** Angel of the North

**Gosden, Freeman** Amos 'n' Andy

**Gouzenko, Igor** Ottawa spy ring

**Grable, Betty** pin-up

**Graham, Billy** Billy Graham crusades

**Grahame, Kenneth** Rat; Toad

**Grant, Duncan** Bloomsbury Group; Omega workshops

**Graves, Philip** Protocols of the Elders of Zion

**Gray, Harold** leaping lizards!

**Grayson, Kathryn** Hardy family

**Grayson, Larry** Shut that door!

**Graziano, Rocky** somebody up there likes me

**Green, Hughie** clapometer; Opportunity Knocks

**Green, Kensal** heroes

**Greene, Graham** Chips, Mr; Lime, Harry

**Greenglass, David** Rosenberg spy case

**Greenwood, Arthur** England

**Gregoire, Marc** nonstick

**Grenfell, Joyce** Effort, St Swithins!; jolly hockey sticks!

**Grewe, Wilhelm** Hallstein doctrine

**Grey, Anthony** Holt drowning

**Grey, Sir Edward** lamps

**Griffith, Arthur** Free Staters; Sinn Féin

**Griffith, D. W.** silent films; Master, the

**Grivas, Georgios** EOKA

**Groening, Matt** Simpsons, the

**Gromyko, Andrei** Grim Grom

**Gropius, Walter** Bauhaus; International Style

**Guevara, Che** Che

**Guggenheim, Solomon R.** Guggenheim Museum

**Guimard, Hector** Art Nouveau

**Guinness, Sir Alec** Smiley, George

**Guinot, René** cathiodermie

**Gunn, Wilbur** Lagonda

**Gurevich, Mikhail** MiG

**Guth, Alan** inflationary universe

Hoover, William Henry Hoover
Hope, Bob road movie; signature tune
Hopkins, Anthony Lecter, Hannibal
Hore-Belisha, Leslie Belisha beacon
Hornby, Frank Meccano
Horniman, Annie Abbey Theatre; Manchester school
Horta, Victor Art Nouveau
Houghton, Stanley Manchester school
House, R. E. truth drug
Howard, Ebenezer garden city
Howe, Geoffrey sheep in sheep's clothing
Hoyle, Fred steady-state theory
Hu Yaobang Tiananmen Square massacre
Hubbard, L. Ron Scientology
Hubble, Edwin Big Bang; Hubble's Law; redshift
Hughes, Francis Maze prison
Hugh-Jones, Noel Sittang River Disaster
Hulme, T. E. Imagism
Humphries, Barry Archie; ceiling inspector; daks; kangaroo valley; norks
Hunter, Evan Blackboard Jungle
Hurd, Douglas Douglas
Hussein, King Arab Legion; Arab Union
Hussein, Sherif Arab Revolt; McMahon letters
Hussein, Saddam Butcher of Baghdad; Desert Storm; Gulf War; human shield; mother of all battles; safe havens
Huston, John heist
Huxley, Aldous Brave New World; feelie
Huxley, Julian Brains Trust; UNESCO

I

Ibarruri, Dolores pass
Ibsen, Henrik famous last words
Idle, Eric Monty Python's Flying Circus; nudge nudge, wink wink, say no more
Ilyushin, Sergei Ilyushin
Imber, Naftali Hatikvah
Immelmann, Max Immelmann turn
Ingrams, Richard Private Eye
Ionesco, Eugène Theatre of the Absurd

Ironside, William Hannay, Richard
Isaacs, Alick interferon
Isaacs, Rufus Marconi affair
Isherwood, Christopher Norris, Arthur
Issigonis, Sir Alec Mini
Ivanov, Yevgeny Profumo affair
Ivory, James Merchant-Ivory films

J

Jackson, Sir Barry Malvern Festival
Jackson, Michael moonwalk
Jacobs, Joe robbed
Jacques-Dalcroze, Emile eurhythmics
Jagger, Mick Rolling Stones
Jakob, A. M. CJD
James, Henry famous last words; human
Janov, Arthur primal scream
Jansky, Karl radioastronomy
Jason, David plonker
Jeffreys, George Four Square Gospel
Jellicoe, John R. Jutland, Battle of
Jellinek, Mercedes Mercedes
Jenkins, Roy Gang of Four; Hampstead set
Jiang Qing Gang of Four
Joad, C. E. M. Brains Trust
Joffe, Roland Killing Fields
Joffre, Marshal Joseph Marne, Battles of the
John XXIII aggiornamento; Second Vatican Council
John Paul II Our Lady of Fatima
Johns, Jasper pop art
Johns, W. E. Biggles
Johnson, Amy aircraft; Queen of the Air
Johnson, Claudia Lady Bird
Johnson, Hewlett Red Dean
Johnson, Lyndon B. Big Daddy; Goldwater caper; Great Society; Lady Bird; LBJ; SALT; walk
Johnson, Philip International Style
Johnson, Virginia Masters and Johnson
Johnson, W. E. Pussyfoot Johnson
Johst, Hanns culture
Jolson, Al California, here I come; heard; talkies; World's Greatest Entertainer
Jones, Brian Rolling Stones

Jones, Daniel Received Pronunciation
Jones, Davy Monkees
Jones, Jim Jonestown massacre
Jones, Reginald $H_2S$
Jones, Terry Monty Python's Flying Circus
Joplin, Scott ragtime
Jorn, Asger Cobra
Joyce, James Bloom, Leopold; Dedalus, Stephen; famous last words; HCE; quark; stream of consciousness
Joyce, William Lord Haw-Haw
Joynson-Hicks, Sir William Jix
Judge, Jack Tipperary
Junkers, Hugo Junkers bombers

K

Kádár, János Hungarian Rising
Kafka, Franz Kafkaesque
Kagan, Joseph Gannex; Lavender list
Kahn, Herman Doomsday machine
Kalashnikov, Mikhail Kalashnikov
Kamenev, Lev Law of December 1
Kandinsky, Wassily Bauhaus; Blaue Reiter
Kaposi, Moritz Kohn Kaposi's sarcoma
Kapp, Wolfgang Kapp Putsch
Karas, Anton Lime, Harry
Karlin, Miriam everybody out
Karno, Fred Fred Karno's army
Kaufman, George S. Algonquin Round Table; epitaph; Whiteside, Sheridan
Kavanagh, Ted ITMA
Kazan, Elia Actors' Studio
Keating, Tom Keating pictures
Keeler, Christine Cliveden set; Denning report; Profumo affair
Keillor, Garrison Lake Wobegon effect
Kekulé von Stradonitz, August Clapham
Kellogg, Frank B. Kellogg Pact
Kelly, Grace Iceberg
Kelly, Margaret Bluebell girls
Kemal, Mustapha Atatürk
Kemsley, James Berry, Viscount Press Barons
Kendall, Kay Genevieve
Kennedy, Charles Liberal Democrats
Kennedy, Edward Chappaquiddick

**Kennedy, John F.** Berliner; Camelot; Jackie O.; Kennedy assassination; moving; Nassau conference; New Frontier; Oval Office; Peace Corps; Runnymede; Thousand Days

**Kennedy, Joseph P.** going

**Kennelly, Arthur Edwin** Heaviside layer

**Kenny, Elizabeth** Kenny polio treatment

**Kent, Bruce** CND

**Kenyatta, Jomo** KANU; Mau Mau

**Kerans, J. S.** Amethyst, HMS

**Kerensky, Alexander** Kerensky government; October Revolution

**Kerouac, Jack** beat

**Kesselring, Albert** Salerno landing

**Keynes, J. M.** general theory; Keynesianism; Tuesday Club

**Khachaturian, Aram** Onedin Line, The

**Khama, Seretse** Seretse Khama affair

**Khomeini, Ayatollah** fatwa

**Khrushchev, Nikita** B and K; de-Stalinization; Paris summit; Troika Plan; U-2

**Kilbride, Percy** Kettle, Ma and Pa

**King, Billie Jean** Kingledon

**King, Martin Luther** civil rights movement; dream; long hot summer; Montgomery bus boycott; NAACP; Student Nonviolent Coordinating Committee

**Kington, Miles** Franglais

**Kinnock, Neil** Labour Party; loony left; somebody up there likes me; Welsh Windbag

**Kinsey, Alfred C.** Kinsey reports

**Kipling, Rudyard** Akela; east is east and west is west; Just So Stories

**Kirchner, Ernst** Brücke, Die

**Kirchner, Raphaël** Kirchner girls

**Kirov, Sergei Mironovich** Kirov murder; Law of December 1

**Kissinger, Henry** all the president's men; linkage; shuttle diplomacy

**Kitchener, Horatio Herbert, Lord** country; Hampshire, HMS; Kitchener's army; Kitchener wants you

**Klee, Paul** Bauhaus; Blaue Reiter

**Klein, Calvin** heroin chic

**Klein, Melanie** Kleinian

**Kneale, Nigel** Quatermass

**Knight, Eric** Lassie

**Knowles, Cyril** Nice one, Cyril!

**Knox, Teddy** Crazy Gang

**Koch, Ilse** Bitch of Buchenwald; Buchenwald

**Koestler, Arthur** ghost in the machine; holon

**Koffka, Kurt** Gestalt

**Kohl, Helmut** Maastricht Treaty

**Köhler, Wolfgang** Gestalt

**Kondratieff, N. D.** Kondratieff waves

**Korda, Alexander** star

**Koresh, David** Waco siege

**Kraft, Joseph** Grand Design

**Kramer, Josef** Beast of Belsen; Belsen

**Kray, Reginald** and **Ronald** People's Villain

**Kretschmer, Ernst** Kretschmer's types

**Kreuger, Ivar** Kreuger crash

**Krishnamurti, Jiddu** Krishnamurti

**Kroc, Ray A.** McDonald's

**Kroger, Peter** and **Helen** Kroger affair

**Krosigk, Count Schwerin von** Iron Curtain

**Kruger, Bernhard** Operation Bernhard

**Krupp, Bertha** Big Bertha

**Kubrick, Stanley** clockwork orange; Lolita; Strangelove

**Kujau, Konrad** Hitler Diaries

**Kwok, Robert Ho Man** Chinese restaurant syndrome

# L

**Lacedelli, Lino** K2

**La Guardia, Henry** La Guardia

**Laing, R. D.** Laingian

**Lalique, René** Lalique glass

**Lamb, B. J.** Pip, Squeak, and Wilfred

**Lamont, Norman** Black Wednesday

**Lamour, Dorothy** road movie

**Lancaster, Osbert** bypass variegated; Festival Gardens

**Land, Edwin** instant camera; Polaroid

**Landi, Elissa** Empress of Emotion

**Landru, Henri** Bluebeard

**Lane, Allen** Penguin

**Lane, Lupino** Lambeth Walk

**Lang, Fritz** countdown; expressionism; film noir; silent films

**Lang, Jack** tall poppy

**Langsdorff, Commander Hans** Plate, Battle of the River

**Langtry, Lillie** Jersey Lily

**Lansdowne, Marquess of** Lansdowne letter

**Lardner, Ring** Hollywood ten

**Larionov, Mikhail** Rayonism

**Larwood, Harold** body line

**Lasdun, Sir Denys** Royal National Theatre

**Laslett, Peter** University of the Third Age

**Lasseter, Harold Bell** Lasseter's gold reef

**Lauder, Sir Harry** Stop yer tickling, Jock!

**Laval, Pierre** Hoare-Laval pact; Vichy

**Lavaleye, Victor de** V for Victory

**Laver, Rod** Rockhampton Rocket

**Law, A. Bonar** Coupon Election; Unknown Prime Minister

**Lawrence, D. H.** Georgian poets; Lady Chatterley trial; Morel, Paul

**Lawrence, Florence** Biograph Girl

**Lawrence, Stephen** Stephen Lawrence case

**Lawrence, T. E.** Arab Revolt; Boanerges; joy-firing; Lawrence of Arabia; Meek, Private Napoleon Alexander Trotsky

**Lawson, John Howard** Hollywood Ten

**Leader, Harry** music, maestro, please

**Leaf, Munro** Ferdinand the Bull

**Leakey, Louis** Kenyapithecus; Olduvai Gorge

**Lean, David** Lawrence of Arabia

**Lear, William** Learjet

**Leary, Timothy** dropout; turn-on

**Leavis, F. R.** Two Cultures, the

**Leblanc, Maurice** Lupin, Arsène

**Leboyer, Frédérick** Leboyer

**Le Carré, John** cold; Smiley, George

**Leclerc, J.-P.** Leclerc

**Le Corbusier** functionalism; high rise; International Style; Le Corbusier

**Ledbetter, Huddie** Leadbelly

**Lee, Brenda** Little Miss Dynamite

**Lee, Bruce** Lee, Bruce

**Lee, Gypsy Rose** Queen of Burlesque; striptease

**Lee, Jenny** Open University

**Lee, Manfred** Queen, Ellery

**Lee, Peter** Peterlee

**Leigh, Vivien** O'Hara, Scarlett

**Lejeune, C. A.** flashback

**Lenin, V. I.** Bolshevik; Lenin; Leninism; Lenin's Testament; New Economic Policy; Ochrana; October Revolution

**Lennon, John** Apple Corps; Beatles

**Leone, Sergio** spaghetti Western

**Leopold, Nathan** Leopold and Loeb murder

**Levin, Bernard** TW3

**Levy, Yisrael** Irgun Zvai Leumi

**Lewin, Kurt** sensitivity training

**Lewinsky, Monica** Lewinsky affair

**Lewis, C. S.** Inklings; Narnia; Screwtape Letters

**Lewis, Isaac Newton** Lewis gun

**Lewis, Jennie** dagmars

**Lewis, Jerry Lee** fire

**Lewis, Wyndham** Blast; vorticism

**Lewis, Robert** Actors' Studio

**Lewis, Sinclair** Babbitt; Main Street

**Liberman, Evsei** Libermanism

**Liddell, Alvar** Received Pronunciation

**Liebknecht, Karl** Spartacists

**Lilienthal, Otto** aircraft

**Lillie, Beatrice** bob

**Lindbergh, Charles A.** aircraft; Le Bourget; Lindbergh baby murder; Lindbergh jacket; lindy hop; Spirit of St Louis

**Lindemann, Jean** interferon

**Link, Edwin A.** flight simulator

**Linklater, Richard** slacker

**Linley, David, Viscount** Hooray Henry

**Littlewood, Joan** Fings Ain't Wot They Used T'Be; Theatre Workshop

**Livingstone, Ken** Mayor of London; Red Ken

**Llewellyn, Harry** Foxhunter

**Lloyd, Marie** Queen of the Halls

**Lloyd George, David** Chanak crisis; Coupon Election; garden suburb; hang the Kaiser!; heroes; Honours Scandal; Limehouse; Lloyd George Fund; Lloyd George knew my father; Mansion House speech; Marconi affair; People's Budget; Squiffites; Versailles Treaty; Welsh Wizard

**Lloyd Webber, Andrew** beautiful game, the; Evita; rock opera

**Lodge, David** Rummidge

**Loeb, Richard** Leopold and Loeb murder

**Loesser, Frank** Praise the Lord and pass the ammunition

**Loew, Marcus** MGM

**Lofting, Hugh** Doctor Dolittle

**Lollobrigida, Gina** La Lollo

**Long, Huey Pierce** Kingfish

**Longbaugh, Harry** Butch Cassidy and the Sundance Kid

**Longford, Frank Pakenham, Lord** Hampstead set; Holy Fool; Lord Porn

**Longworth, Alice Roosevelt** Alice blue

**Lon Nol,** Khmer Rouge

**Lonsdale, Gordon** Kroger affair; Lonsdale affair

**Lonsdale, Lord** Man in the Iron Mask

**Loos, Anita** Lee, Lorelei

**Lorre, Peter** Moto, Mr

**Loudon, Norman** Shepperton studios

**Louis, Joe** Brown Bomber; hide

**Lovell, Sir Bernard** Jodrell Bank

**Lovelock, James** Gaia hypothesis

**Lovett, Martin** Amadeus String Quartet

**Low, David** blimp

**Lucan, Richard Bingham, Earl of** Lucky

**Lucas, George** special effects

**Luce, Clare Boothe** stuffed shirt

**Luciano, Salvatore** Lucky

**Ludendorff, Erich** Somme, Battle of the; Munich Putsch; Tannenberg

**Lüger, George** Lüger

**Luks, George Benjamin** ash-can school

**Lutyens, Edwin** Cenotaph

**Luxemburg, Rosa** Spartacists

**Lygon, Hugh** Brideshead

**Lynn, Vera** Forces' Sweetheart

**Lysenko, Trofim Denisovich** Lysenkoism

**Lyttleton, Humphrey** Mornington Crescent

**Lytton, Victor Bulwer-Lytton, Earl of** Lytton report

# M

**MacArthur, General Douglas** American Caesar; Corregidor; Korean War; Marines; Old soldiers never die, they simply fade away

**McAuliffe, Anthony C.** Old Crock

**McCarthy, Senator Joseph** McCarthyism; reds under the bed; sleeper

**McCartney, Paul** Beatles

**McCrae, John** Flanders poppies

**McDonald, Hugh C.** Identikit

**Macdonald, Jeanette** Iron Butterfly

**MacDonald, Ramsay** Doctor's mandate; Geneva Protocol; Labour Party; National Governments; National Labour Party; Safety First; Union of Democratic Control

**McEachern, Malcolm** flotsam and jetsam

**McEnroe, John** Superbrat

**Mcferrin, Bobby** happy

**McGough, Roger** Mersey poets

**MacGregor, Ian** Mac the Knife

**Mach, Ernst** Mach number

**McIndoe, Sir Archibald** Guinea Pig Club

**McKenna, Reginald** McKenna duties

**Mackinder, Sir Halford** geopolitics

**Mackintosh, Charles Rennie** Art Nouveau

**Maclaine, Shirley** Kid, The

**Maclean, Donald** double agent; Magnificent Five

**Macleod, Iain** Acol system

**McLuhan, Marshall** global village; McLuhanism

**McMahon, Sir Henry** Ladakh crisis; McMahon letters; McMahon Line

**Macmillan, Harold** good; jaw-jaw; Mac the Knife; Nassau conference; Paris summit; sell the family silver; Supermac; unflappable; wind of change

**MacNeice, Louis** Pylon Poets

**MacNeil, Eoin** Irish National Volunteers

**McNeile, Hermann Cyril** Sapper

**MacPherson, Stewart** Twenty Questions

**Macpherson, Sir William** Stephen Lawrence case

**McVeigh, Timothy** Oklahoma bombing

**Madonna** vogueing

**Maginot, André** Maginot Line

**Magnusson, Magnus** started

**Maherero, Samuel** Herero

**Mahler, Gustav** famous last words

**Maiman, Theodore** laser

**Moore, Dudley** Beyond the Fringe; Sex Thimble

**Moore, Henry** Unit One

**Moore, Roger** Saint, The

**Moran, George 'Bugsy'** St Valentine's Day Massacre

**More, Kenneth** Genevieve

**Morecambe, Eric** short, fat, hairy legs

**Morel, E. D.** Union of Democratic Control

**Morell, André** Quatermass

**Moreno, Jacob** role play

**Morgan, John Pierpont** Man in the Iron Mask

**Morganstern, Oskar** game theory

**Morgenthau, Henry** Morgenthau Plan

**Morley, Eric** Miss World order

**Moro, Aldo** Red Brigades

**Morris, Desmond** naked ape

**Morris, William** MG

**Morrison, Herbert Stanley** Morrison shelter

**Mortimer, John** She who must be obeyed

**Morton, J. B.** Beachcomber

**Morton, 'Jelly Roll'** Jelly Roll; scat

**Mosley, Sir Oswald** Blackshirts; Mitford girls; Mosleyites; New Party; Regulation 18b

**Moss, Stirling** Mille Miglia

**Moulin, Jean** Resistance

**Mountbatten, Louis, Earl** Forgotten Army

**Muggeridge, Malcolm** Saint Mugg

**Muhammed, Wallace Fard** Black Muslims

**Müller, W.** Geiger counter

**Munro, H. H.** Saki

**Murdoch, Rupert** satellite television

**Mussolini, Benito** Bullfrog of the Pontine Marshes; Duce; Fascism; March on Rome; Pact of Steel; Salò, Republic of

## N

**Nabokov, Vladimir** Lolita; nymphet

**Nader, Ralph** consumerism; Naderite

**Nagy, Imre** Hungarian Rising

**Nansen, Fridtjof** Nansen passport

**Nash, Ogden** epitaph

**Nash, Paul** Unit One

**Nasser, Gamal Abdel** Six-Day War; Suez crisis

**Naughton, Charlie** Crazy Gang

**Nehru, Jawaharlal** Nehru dynasty; Nehru jacket

**Neill, A. S.** Summerhill

**Neilson, Donald** Black Panther

**Nenni, Pietro Sandro** Nenni telegram

**Nervo, Jimmy** Crazy Gang

**Nesbit, Evelyn** Girl in the Red Velvet Swing

**Nesmith, Mike** Monkees

**Netanyahu, Binyamin** Likud

**Neurath, Otto** Vienna circle

**Neville, Richard** Oz trial

**Nicholas II** admiral; February Revolution; Mad Monk; October Manifesto

**Nicholson, Ben** St Ives group; Unit One

**Nicholson, Vivien** spend, spend, spend!

**Nickolaev, Leonid** Kirov murder

**Niehan, Dr** Niehan clinic

**Nilus, Serge** Protocols of the Elders of Zion

**Nissel, Sigmund** Amadeus String Quartet

**Nivelle, General Robert Georges** Nivelle offensive; pass; Verdun

**Nixon, Richard M.** cut off at the pass; Deep Throat; expletive deleted; heartbeat; Hiss affair; Houdini of American Politics; Middle America; nixon; Nixon doctrine; one small step for man; SALT; silent majority; Tricky Dicky; Vietnam War; Watergate

**Norgay, Sherpa Tenzing** Everest syndrome

**Norman, Frank** Fings Ain't Wot They Used T'Be

**North, Oliver** Irangate; loose cannon

**Northcliffe, Alfred Harmsworth, Lord** Northcliffe Press; Press Barons; tabloid

**Nunn May, Alan** Nunn May affair; Ottawa spy ring

**Nureyev, Rudolf** Valentino

## O

**Oates, Captain Laurence** epitaph; famous last words; Scott of the Antarctic

**O'Duffy, Eoin** Blue Shirts

**Ogden, C. K.** Basic English

**Ogilvie, Ian** Saint, The

**O'Keefe, Patrick** flowers

**Olds, Ransom Eli** Oldsmobile

**Olivier, Laurence** Larrys; Rice, Archie

**Onassis, Aristotle** Jackie O.

**Onassis, Christina** Thunderthighs

**Onassis, Jacqueline** Jackie O.

**O'Neill, Ryan** Peyton Place

**Oparin, Alexander** primordial soup

**Ophüls, Max** film noir

**Oppenheimer, J. Robert** Manhattan Project; nuclear weapon; Oppenheimer affair

**Orage, A. R.** Guild Socialism

**O'Rahilly, Ronan** Radio Caroline

**Orczy, Baroness Emmuska** Scarlet Pimpernel

**Ornitz, Sam** Hollywood Ten

**Ortega, Daniel** Sandinista

**Orwell, George** Animal Farm; Big Brother; doublethink; equal; International Brigades; legs; newspeak; Nineteen Eighty-Four; Orwellian; Thought Police; Wigan

**Osborne, John** Angry Young Men; kitchen sink; Porter, Jimmy; Rice, Archie

**O'Shea, Tessie** Two-Ton Tessie

**Oswald, Lee Harvey** Kennedy assassination

**O'Toole, Peter** Lawrence of Arabia

**Oveissi, Gholam Ali** Butcher of Tehran

**Ovett, Steve** four-minute mile

**Owen, David** Gang of Four

**Owen, Wilfred** war poets

## P

**Page, Sir Frederick Handley** Handley Page bomber

**Paige, Elaine** Leather Lungs

**Painting, Norman** Archers, The

**Paisley, Ian** Paisleyite; power sharing

**Palin, Michael** Monty Python's Flying Circus

**Pankhurst, Christabel** suffragettes

**Pankhurst, Emmeline** feminism; suffragettes

**Papanicolaou, George N.** Pap test

**Park, Nick** Wallace and Gromit

**Parker, Bonnie** Bonnie and Clyde

**Parker, Charlie** bebop; Bird
**Parker, Dorothy** Algonquin Round Table; chew up the scenery; choose; epitaph
**Parker-Bowles, Camilla** Camillagate; People's Princess
**Parkhurst, Helen** Dalton Plan
**Parkinson, Cyril Northcote** Parkinson's Law
**Parks, Rosa** Montgomery bus boycott
**Parsons, Talcott** functionalism
**Pasolini, Pier Paolo** neorealism
**Patten, Brian** Mersey poets
**Patten, Chris** gobsmacked
**Patton, George Smith** Old Blood 'n' Guts
**Paul VI** aggiornamento; Humanae Vitae; Second Vatican Council
**Pauli, Wolfgang** neutrino; Pauli exclusion principle
**Paulus, Friedrich** Stalingrad
**Pavlov, Ivan Petrovich** Pavlov's dog
**Pavlova, Anna** Happiness is...; pavlova
**Peake, G. F.** Arab Legion
**Peake, Mervyn** Gormenghast
**Pears, Peter** Aldeburgh
**Pearse, Patrick** Easter Rising
**Pearson, Arthur Cyril** St Dunstan's
**Peck, Gregory** gregory
**Pelé** beautiful game; Pelé
**Peniakoff, Vladimir** Popski's Private Army
**Pennebaker, D. A.** fly-on-the-wall
**Penry, Jacques** Photofit
**Penty, A. J.** Guild Socialism
**Percival, Lance** TW3
**Pérez, Manuel Benitéz** Cordobes, El
**Perkins, Carl** go, man, go!
**Perón, Eva** and **Juan** Evita
**Perry, Antoinette** Tony Awards
**Pershing, General John** Lafayette, we are here; Pershing missile
**Perugia, Vincenzo** Mona Lisa theft
**Pétain, Marshal Henri-Philippe** pass; Verdun; Vichy
**Peter, Laurence J.** Peter Principle
**Peters, Arno** Peters' projection
**Pett, Norman** Jane
**Pevsner, Antoine** constructivism
**Philby, Harold ('Kim')** double agent; Kim; Magnificent Five; mole
**Phillips, Arthur** cultural cringe

**Phillips, Leslie** Received Pronunciation
**Phillips, Mark** Fog
**Piaf, Edith** Little Sparrow
**Piaget, Jean** cognitive psychology
**Picasso, Pablo** assemblage; collage; cubism; Guernica
**Piccard, Auguste** and **Jacques** bathyscaph
**Pickford, Mary** America's Boy Friend; silent films; star; World's Sweetheart
**Pickles, Wilfred** Have a Go
**Pilger, John** Pilgerism
**Pilkington, Harry** Pilkington Report
**Pinckney, Callan** callanetics
**Pincus, Gregory** Pill, the
**Piper, John** Festival Gardens
**Pitkin, William B.** forty
**Pius X** modernism
**Pius XII** Immaculate Heart of Mary
**Planck, Max** Planck constant; quantum theory
**Platts-Mills, John** Nenni telegram
**Plomley, Roy** Desert Island Discs
**Plunkett, Roy J.** nonstick
**Polanski, Roman** Manson Family
**Polley, George Gibson** Human Fly
**Pollock, Jackson** action painting
**Pol Pot** Khmer Rouge; Killing Fields
**Porsche, Ferdinand** Beetle; Mouse; Porsche
**Portago, Alfonso ('Fon') de** Mille Miglia
**Porter, Cole** do it; Miss Otis regrets
**Porter, Edwin S.** special effects; stock shot
**Potter, Beatrix** Jemima Puddle-duck; Peter Rabbit; Tailor of Gloucester
**Potter, Stephen** gamesmanship; lifemanship; one-upmanship
**Poujade, Pierre** Poujadists
**Poulenc, Francis** Six, Les
**Pound, Ezra** Blast; free verse; HD; Imagism; Old Possum; vorticism
**Powell, Adam Clayton** Keep the faith, baby!
**Powell, Anthony** Widmerpool, Kenneth
**Powell, Enoch** Powellism
**Powell, Felix** Pack up your troubles in your old kit-bag

**Powell, Sandy** hear
**Powers, Francis Gary** U-2
**Pratchett, Terry** Discworld
**Preminger, Otto** film noir
**Presley, Elvis** Elvis the Pelvis; Graceland
**Priestley, J. B.** admass; Jolly Jack
**Princip, Gavrilo** Sarajevo assassination
**Profumo, John** Cliveden set; Denning report; Profumo affair
**Prokhorov, A. M.** laser
**P'ui, Henry** Manchukuo
**Pulitzer, Joseph** muckrakers; Pulitzer Prizes
**Puzo, Mario** refuse

# Q

**Quant, Mary** miniskirt
**Quayle, Dan** heartbeat
**Quiller-Couch, Arthur** Q
**Quisling, Vidkun** quisling

# R

**Rachman, Peter** Rachmanism
**Raft, George** George Raft
**Raine, A. B.** Pip, Squeak, and Wilfred
**Rákosi, Mátyás** Hungarian Rising
**Rank, J. Arthur** Arthur Rank; Rank Organization
**Rank, Otto** rebirthing
**Rantzen, Esther** Childline
**Rasputin, Gregory** Mad Monk
**Rattigan, Terence** Aunt Edna; kitchen sink; Lawrence of Arabia; Winslow, Ronnie
**Rawlinson, Henry** Somme, Battle of the
**Ray, James Earl** dream
**Ray, Johnnie** Prince of Wails
**Ray, Maud** Maud Committee
**Ray, Satyajit** neorealism
**Raymond, Alex** Jungle Jim
**Read, Herbert** Unit One
**Reagan, Ronald** B-movie; bozo; duck; flaky; Gipper, the; Great Communicator; hide; point man; Reaganomics; SALT; Star Wars; zero option
**Redesdale, Baron** Mitford girls
**Redmond, John** Irish National Volunteers
**Redmond, Phil** Brookside
**Reed, Carol** Lime, Harry
**Reeve, Christopher** Superman
**Reich, Steve** minimalism

Reich, Wilhelm orgasmatron
Reid, Beryl actress
Reis, Arthur Virgilio Alves Reis forgery
Reith, John, Baron BBC; Reith lectures
Rendall, Montague John Nation shall speak peace unto nation
Rensberg, Hans van Ossewa-Brandwag
Reuther, Walter duck
Reye, R. D. Reye's syndrome
Reynard, Paul Riom trials
Reynolds, Albert Downing Street Declaration
Reynolds, Walter Young England
Rhine, J. B. ESP
Rhodes, Cecil famous last words; Rhodes scholars
Ribbentrop, Joachim von Hitler-Stalin pact; Nuremberg Trials
Rice, Tim Evita; rock opera
Rice-Davies, Mandy Profumo affair
Richard, Cliff Britain's Oldest Teenager
Richard(s), Keith Rolling Stones
Richards, Frank Bunter, Billy
Richardson, Carole Guildford Four
Richardson, Dorothy stream of consciousness
Richter, Charles Richter scale
Richthofen, Manfred, Freiherr von dogfight; Red Baron
Ricketts, F. J. Colonel Bogey
Riefenstahl, Leni Nuremberg rallies
Rigg, Diana kinky boots
Riley, Bridget op art
Rintelen, Franz von Rintelen spy ring
Ripley, Robert Leroy believe it or not!
Ritz, César ritzy
Rivera, José Antonio Primo de Falange
Rix, Brian Whitehall farces
Robbe-Grillet, Alain nouveau roman
Roberts, Oral televangelists
Roberts, Tommy Rhys Lloyd George knew my father
Robertson, Morgan Titanic
Robey, George Archibald, certainly not!; Prime Minister of Mirth

Robinson, John South Bank religion
Robinson, W. Heath Heath Robinson
Rockefeller, John D. Rockefeller Foundation
Rockefeller Jr, John D. Rockefeller Center; Rockefeller Foundation
Rockefeller, Margaretta Happy
Rodgers, William Gang of Four
Roe, J. V. Stopes clinic
Roessler, Rudolph Lucy ring
Rogers, Charles ('Buddy') America's Boy Friend
Rogers, Richard high tech
Rogers, Major Robert Rangers
Rogers, Roy King of the Cowboys; Singing Cowboy
Rogers, Will bananas; papers
Röhm, Ernst Freikorps; Night of the Long Knives
Rohmer, Sax Fu Manchu
Rolls, Charles Stewart Rolls-Royce
Rommel, Erwin Afrika Korps; Desert Fox; Tobruk
Rooney, Mickey Hardy family
Roosevelt, Alice choose
Roosevelt, Franklin D. Arcadia; Atlantic Charter; Boss, the; Casablanca Conference; end; Fireside chats; Forgotten Man; Four Freedoms; FDR; good neighbour policy; Happy days are here again; Houdini in the White House; National Recovery Administration; New Deal; Quadrant; Second Front; Tehran Conference; TVA; 22nd Amendment; Trident; Washington Conference; Yalta Conference
Roosevelt, Theodore able and willing to pull his weight; Bull Moose; good to the last drop; Hague Conference; hearts and minds; lunatic fringe; Oval Office; speak softly and carry a big stick; Square Deal; teddy-bear; weasel words
Rorschach, Hermann Rorschach ink-blot test
Rose, Frederick rose is a rose
Rosen, R. D. psychobabble
Rosenberg, Ethel and Julius Ottawa spy ring; Rosenberg spy case
Rosenberg, Harold action painting
Rosenberg, Isaac war poets
Ross, A. S. C. U and Non-U

Ross, Jonathan zoo television
Ross, Leonard Q. Kaplan, Hyman
Rossellini, Roberto neorealism
Rosten, Leo kike
Rothermere, Sydney Harmsworth, Viscount Empire Free Trade; Press Barons
Rothschild, Victor, Baron think-tank
Rowling, J. K. Potter, Harry
Rowntree, Joseph Union of Democratic Control
Royce, Frederick Henry Rolls-Royce
Royden, Agnes Maude Conservative Party at prayer
Rozhdestvenski, Admiral Tsushima
Rubik, Erno Rubik's cube
Rubin, Jerry Yippie
Ruby, Jack Kennedy assassination
Rudd, Steele Dad and Dave
Runyon, Damon doll; famous last words
Rushdie, Salman fatwa
Rushton, Willie Mornington Crescent; Private Eye
Russell, Bertrand CND; Happiness is...; red; Union of Democratic Control
Russell, George William AE
Russell, Morgan synchronism
Ruth, George Herman ('Babe') Babe; Murderers' Row
Rutherford, Ernest Cavendish Laboratory; elementary particle
Ryan, Michael Hungerford massacre
Ryder, Sue, Baroness Cheshire Homes
Ryle, Gilbert ghost in the machine
Ryle, Martin LGM

# S

Sabin, Albert Sabin vaccine
Sacco, Nicola Sacco and Vanzetti
Sachs, Andrew Fawlty Towers
Sackville-West, Vita Orlando
Sadat, Anwar Camp David
Salam, Abdus unified-field theory
Salan, Raoul OAS
Salieri, Paolo arcology
Salk, Jonas Edward Salk vaccine
Salten, Felix Bambi
Samsonov, Alexander Tannenberg

**Sandage, Allan** quasar
**Sanders, George** Falcon, the; famous last words
**Sandino, August Cesar** Sandinista
**Sands, Bobby** Maze prison
**Sandys, Duncan** Civic Trust; Lonrho affair
**Sansom, Odette** Ravensbrück
**Santos, Lucia** Our Lady of Fatima
**Sargent, Malcolm** Flash Harry
**Saroyan, William** famous last words
**Sartre, Jean-Paul** existentialism; Hell is other people
**Sassoon, Siegfried** war poets
**Satie, Erik** Six, Les
**Saunders, Cicely** hospice movement
**Savimbi, Jonas** UNITA
**Sayers, Dorothy L.** Wimsey, Lord Peter
**Scales, Prunella** Fawlty Towers
**Scargill, Arthur** King Arthur
**Scarman, Leslie George, Lord** community policing
**Scharansky, Anatoly** refusenik
**Scheer, Reinhard** Jutland, Battle of
**Schidlof, Peter** Amadeus String Quartet
**Schirrmann, Richard** YHA
**Schleicher, Kurt von** Night of the Long Knives
**Schlesinger Jr, Arthur** Thousand Days
**Schlick, Moritz** Vienna circle
**Schlieffen, Alfred, Count von** Schlieffen Plan
**Schmeling, Max** robbed
**Schneider, Jacques** Schneider Trophy
**Schoenberg, Arnold** serialism; sprechgesang; twelve-tone music
**Schrieffer, J. R.** superconductivity
**Schrödinger, Erwin** Schrödinger's cat; Schrödinger wave equation
**Schultze, Norbert** Lili Marlene
**Schulz, Charles M.** Charlie Brown; Happiness is...; Peanuts
**Schumacher, E. F.** small is beautiful
**Schuschnigg, Kurt von** Anschluss
**Schwarzchild, Karl** black hole
**Schwarzenegger, Arnold** morphing; pump iron

**Schwarzkopf, General H. Norman** Stormin' Norman
**Schweitzer, Albert** Lambaréné
**Scopes, John T.** Dayton anti-Darwinist trial; fundamentalism
**Scott, Adrian** Hollywood Ten
**Scott, Paul** jewel in the crown
**Scott, Sir Peter** Rhayader; Slimbridge
**Scott, Robert Falcon** Discovery; Scott of the Antarctic
**Seaman, Sir Owen** Eeyore
**Searle, Ronald** St Trinian's
**Secombe, Harry** Goon Show
**Seddon, Frederick Henry** Seddon Murder
**Segar, E. C.** goon
**Selassie, Haile** Lion of Judah; Rastafarians
**Selfridge, H. Gordon** customer
**Sellar, Walter Carruthers** 1066 and All That
**Sellers, Peter** Goon Show; Strangelove
**Sennett, Mack** Keystone Comedies
**Senoussi, Idris Al** Senoussi
**Sensburg, Helen** Mary of Arnhem
**Shackleton, Ernest** Endurance
**Shamir, Yitzhak** Likud
**Sharif, Omar** Cairo Fred
**Sharman, Helen** Juno space mission
**Sharon, Ariel** Likud
**Shaw, George Bernard** Assassination is the extreme form of censorship; Malvern Festival; Meek, Private Napoleon Alexander Trotsky; Straker, Henry; Higgins, Professor
**Shawcross, Lord** new morality
**Shearer, Norma** First Lady of the Screen
**Sheeler, Charles** cubist-realism
**Shephard, Alan** astronaut; Mercury Project; splashdown; space age
**Sheppard, Dick** Peace Pledge Union
**Sheridan, Ann** Oomph Girl
**Sherrin, Ned** TW3
**Shinn, Everett** ash-can school
**Shipman, Harold** Shipman murders
**Shipton, Eric** Abominable Snowman
**Shostakovich, Dmitry** Babi Yar
**Shrimpton, Jean** Shrimp, The

**Sickert, Walter** Camden Town Group; London Group
**Sihanouk, Norodim** Ho Chi Minh Trail; Khmer Rouge
**Silverheels, Jay** Lone Ranger
**Sim, Sheila** Mousetrap, The
**Simenon, Georges** Maigret
**Simmonds, William** Ku Klux Klan
**Simon, Sir John** National Liberal Party
**Simpson, O. J.** Simpson trial
**Simpson, Simeon** daks
**Simpson, Wallis** Abdication Crisis; Wally blue
**Sinatra, Frank** Old Blue Eyes; Rat Pack; Sinatra doctrine
**Sirica, John** Maximum John
**Skinner, B. F.** behaviourism; reinforcement therapy
**Skinner, Dennis** Beast of Bolsover
**Slater, Oscar** Oscar Slater case
**Sliwa, Curtis** Guardian Angels
**Sloan, John** ash-can school
**Smith, Sir Cyril** Big Cyril; Nice one, Cyril!
**Smith, Dodie** Cruella De Vil
**Smith, F. E.** Other Club
**Smith, G. J.** Brides in the Bath
**Smith, Herbert** Sopwith Camel
**Smith, Howard W.** Smith Act
**Smith, Ian** UDI
**Smith, John** Labour Party
**Smith, Logan Pearsall** famous last words
**Smith, Ormond G.** Carter, Nick
**Smith, Robert Holbrook** Alcoholics Anonymous
**Smith, Stevie** good; not waving, but drowning
**Smuts, Jan** holistic medicine
**Smythe, Reg** Andy Capp
**Snell, Hannah** Hannah
**Snow, C. P.** corridors of power; Two Cultures, the
**Solzhenitsyn, Alexander** gulag
**Somoza, Anastasio** Sandinista
**Sondheim, Stephen** clowns
**Sonnenfeldt, Helmut** Sonnenfeldt doctrine
**Sopwith, Thomas** Sopwith Camel
**Sorge, Richard** Sorge spy affair
**Soveral, Luis Augusto Pinto de** Blue Monkey
**Spangler, J. Murray** Hoover
**Spector, Phil** Wall of Sound
**Speer, Albert** Nuremberg rallies
**Speight, Johnny** Garnett, Alf

**Spencer, Charles, Earl** People's Princess

**Spencer, Stanley** famous last words

**Spender, John** Never knowingly undersold

**Spender, Stephen** Pylon Poets

**Sperati, Jean de** Sperati forgeries

**Spielberg, Steven** close encounter; ET

**Spock, Dr Benjamin** Spock baby

**Springer, Axel** Springer empire

**Springsteen, Bruce** Boss, the

**Stakhanov, Alexei** Stakhanovite

**Stalin, Joseph** de-Stalinization; Five-Year Plans; generalissimo; Kirov murder; Law of December 1; Man of Steel; Moscow Conference; purges; Second Front; Stalinism; Stalingrad; Tehran Conference; Trotskyism; Uncle Joe; Yalta Conference

**Stallone, Sylvester** Rambo

**Stanislavsky, Konstantin** Method, the

**Stanton, Colonel Charles E.** Lafayette, we are here

**Starr, Kenneth** Lewinsky affair; Whitewater affair

**Starr, Ringo** Beatles; Ringo

**Stauffenberg, Claus, Count von** Stauffenberg Plot

**Stavisky, Serge Alexandre** Stavisky affair

**Steel, David** Lib-Lab

**Steffens, Lincoln** future; muckrakers

**Stein, Gertrude** Lost Generation; rose is a rose

**Steinbeck, John** Dust Bowl

**Steinem, Gloria** fish

**Steiner, Rudolph** Anthroposophical Society

**Stephens, Annie Fitzgerald** O'Hara, Scarlett

**Steptoe, Patrick** IVF

**Stern, Abraham** Stern Gang

**Stevens, R. H.** Venlo incident

**Stevenson, Adlai** atom; brinkmanship

**Stilwell, Joseph** nil carborundum; Vinegar Joe

**Stimson, Henry** Morgenthau Plan

**Stirling, David** Phantom Major; SAS

**Stockwood, Mervyn** South Bank religion

**Stokes, Frederick** Stokes mortar

**Stone, Christopher** disc jockey

**Stone, Lewis** Hardy family

**Stopes, Marie** Stopes clinic

**Strachey, Lytton** Bloomsbury Group; famous last words

**Straffen, John Thomas** Straffen murders

**Strand, Robert** Alcatraz

**Strasberg, Lee** Method, the

**Streisand, Barbra** Nose, The

**Struther, Jan** Miniver, Mrs

**Studdert-Kennedy, Geoffrey A.** Woodbine Willie

**Suffolk and Berkshire, Jack Howard, Earl of** Mad Jack

**Sullivan, Louis** functionalism

**Summer, W. G.** Forgotten Man

**Sutch, David ('Lord')** Radio Caroline

**Sutcliffe, Peter** Yorkshire Ripper

**Sutcliffe, Sonia** Private Eye

**Sutherland, Joan** Stupenda, La

**Suzuki, Shinichi** Suzuki method

**Swaggart, Jimmy** televangelists

**Sykes, Mark** Sykes-Picot agreement

# T

**Taafe, Pat** Arkle

**Tailleferre, Germaine** Six, Les

**Talbot, Gilbert** Toc H

**Tanaka Giichi** Tanaka Memorial

**Tarantino, Quentin** heist

**Tarbell, Ira M.** muckrakers

**Tate, Harry** Harry Tate's Navy

**Tate, Sharon** Manson Family

**Tati, Jacques** Hulot, Monsieur

**Tatlin, Vladimir** constructivism

**Tavener, John** minimalism

**Taylor, Mick** Rolling Stones

**Tebbit, Norman** bike; cricket test; Eurosceptic

**Temple, Shirley** Curly Top; One-Take

**Teresa, Mother** Teresa, Mother

**Thalberg, Irving** MGM

**Thatcher, Margaret** Attila the Hen; Bruges group; Eurosceptic; Falklands Conflict; handbag; Iron Lady; men in grey suits; monetarism; oxygen of publicity; popular capitalism; sense; Thatcherism

**Thaw, Harry K.** Girl in the Red Velvet Swing

**Thom, René** catastrophe theory

**Thomas, Brandon** running

**Thomas, Dylan** famous last words; Llareggub

**Thomas, Lowell** Lawrence of Arabia

**Thompson, Flora** Lark Rise to Candleford

**Thompson, William Hale** Big Bill

**Thomson, George Paget** Maud Committee

**Thomson, James** Honours Scandal

**Thomson, J. J.** elementary particle

**Thomson, Roy Herbert, Baron** press barons

**Thornley, Arnold** Stormont

**Thurber, James** Algonquin Round Table; famous last words

**Thurmond, Strom** Dixiecrats

**Tirtoff, Romain de** Erté

**Tito, Josip Broz** Titoism

**Tizard, Henry** nuclear fission

**Todt, Fritz** Todt Organization

**Tolkein, J. R. R.** gollum; hobbit; Inklings; Lord of the Rings; Middle-earth

**Tolstoy, Leo** famous last words

**Tork, Peter** Monkees

**Tormé, Mel** Velvet Fog

**Tourtel, Mary** Rupert Bear

**Townes, Charles** laser

**Townshend, Charles** Kut, Siege of

**Townshend, Pete** rock opera

**Trachtenberg, Jakow** Trachtenberg System

**Tracy, Spencer** last hurrah

**Train, Jack** Twenty Questions

**Traven, B.** Traven, B.

**Travers, Ben** Aldwych farces

**Travolta, John** medallion man

**Tree, Herbert Beerhohm** RADA

**Trenchard, Hugh, Viscount** RAF

**Trevelyan, Charles** Union of Democratic Control

**Trevor-Roper, Hugh** Hitler Diaries

**Trimble, David** power sharing; Ulster Unionist Party

**Trinder, Tommy** over-paid, over-fed, over-sexed, and over here

**Trollope, Joanna** Aga saga

**Trotsky, Leon** fellow-traveller; Kronstadt mutiny; Trotskyism

**Trueman, Fred** Fiery Fred

**Truffaut, Francois** New Wave

**Truman, Bess** Boss, the

**Truman, Harry S.** buck; Fair Deal; Give 'em Hell Harry; heat; Man on the Wedding Cake; Truman Doctrine

Trumbo, Dalton Hollywood Ten
Truscot, Bruce redbrick
Tschiffley, A. F. Tschiffley's Ride
Tucker, Sophie forty; Last of the Red Hot Mommas
Tukachevsky, Mikhail Kronstadt mutiny
Tunney, Gene Manassa Mauler; robbed
Tuohy, Kevin contact lens
Tupper, Earl Tupperware
Turing, Alan artificial intelligence; Turing machine
Turner, Bradwell Altmark
Turner, Joe rhythm-and-blues
Turner, Lana Hardy family
Tutu, Desmond Desmond
Tynan, Kenneth Holcomb murders
Tyrwhitt, Commodore Reginald Heligoland Bight
Tzara, Tristan dadaism

# U

Updike, John neutrino
Utzon, Jorn Sydney Opera House

# V

Vadim, Roger Sex Kitten
Valfierno, Eduardo de Mona Lisa theft
Van Allen, James Van Allen belts
Vance, Louis Joseph Lone Wolf
van den Bergh, Hendrik Ossewa-Brandwag
Vanderbilt, Alfred Lusitania
van der Lubbe, Marius Reichstag fire
Van Meegeren, Hans Van Meegeren forgeries
Vanzetti, Bartolomeo Sacco and Vanzetti
Varah, Chad Samaritans
Vasarely, Victor op art
Vascancellas, Antonio Marchioness disaster
Vaughan, Harry heat
Vaughan, Sarah amateur night
Vavilov, Nicolai Lysenkoism
Vellus, Pierre University of the Third Age
Ventris, Michael Linear B script
Vian, Philip Altmark
Victoria, Queen famous last words
Visconti, Luchino neorealism
Voigt, Wilhelm Köpenick hoax
von Braun, Wernher Jupiter-C; Saturn rockets; space age; V2

von Neumann, John game theory
von Stroheim, Erich Man You Love to Hate
Vorster, John Ossewa-Brandwag
Vreeland, Diana pizazz

# W

Wade, Virginia Our Ginny
Wadsworth, Edward vorticism
Walker, Johnny Radio Caroline
Wallace, Henry A. Century of the Common Man
Wallas, Graham Great Society
Waller, Thomas 'Fats' Fats
Wallis, Barnes Dambusters; Lancaster bomber; swing-wing
Walton William sprechgesang
Wander, George Ovaltine
Wang Hungwen Gang of Four
Ward, Stephen Profumo affair
Warhol, Andy pop art
Warner, Jack Evenin' all; mind my bike!
Warner, Pelham Francis Plum
Warrell, Charles I-Spy
Warwick, Frances, Countess of Darling Daisy
Washington, Dinah rhythm-and-blues
Washkansky, Louis Washkansky transplant
Wassermann, August von Wassermann test
Waterman, Dennis minder
Watson, James DNA
Watson, J. B. behaviourism
Watson-Watt, Robert radar
Watts, Charlie Rolling Stones
Waugh, Auberon Pilgerism
Waugh, Evelyn Brideshead; Crouchback, Guy; Metroland
Wax, Ruby Jewish American Princess
Wayne, John big C; Duke; man; Western
Webb, Sidney LSE
Weber, Max work ethic
Webern, Anton twelve-tone music
Wegener, Alfred Pangaea
Weigel, Helene Berliner Ensemble
Weinberg, Steven unified-field theory
Weiss, Carl Austin Kingfish
Weiss, Peter Theatre of Fact
Weissmuller, Johnny Jungle Jim; Tarzan
Weisz, Victor Vicky; Supermac

Weizmann, Chaim Jewish Agency
Welch, Robert H. W. John Birch Society
Weldon, Fay egg
Welles, Orson Kane, Citizen; Lime, Harry; Martian invasion scare
Wells, H. G. Kipps; Martian invasion scare
Wertheimer, Max Gestalt
Wesker, Arnold Centre 42; chips with everything
Wessel, Horst Hitlerjunge Quex; Horst Wessel Lied
West, Mae come up and see me some time; grape; Mae West; tall, dark, and handsome
Wheeler, Jimmy aye, aye, that's yer lot
Whelpton, Eric Wimsey, Lord Peter
White, Ed Gemini
White, Sir George Relief of Ladysmith; Spion Kop
White, Stanford Girl in the Red Velvet Swing
Wiesenthal, Simon Wiesenthal Centre
Wigner, Eugene Schrödinger's cat
Wilde, Oscar famous last words
Wilder, Billy film noir
Wilhelm II admiral; hang the Kaiser!; Kaiser Bill; sun
Wilhelmina, Queen IJsselmeer
Wilkinson, Ellen Jarrow march
Willett, William daylight saving
William, Lloyd S. Retreat? Hell, no! We just got here!
Williams, Charles Inklings
Williams, Esther Hardy family
Williams, Harry J. Tipperary
Williams, Shirley Gang of Four
Williams, Spencer Basin Street
Williams, Tennessee off-Broadway
Williams, W. Billy Williams's Cabbage Patch
Williams-Ellis, Sir Clough Portmeirion
Williamson, Henry Tarka
Wilson, A. N. young fogey
Wilson, Charles E. good for General Motors
Wilson, Dooley Play it again, Sam
Wilson, E. A. Scott of the Antarctic